OUR SUNDAY VISITOR'S

# 1997

# CATHOLIC ALMANAC

The Most Complete One-Volume
Source Of Facts And Information
On The Catholic Church

COMPILED AND EDITED BY

## Felician A. Foy, O.F.M.

AND

## Rose M. Avato

Our Sunday Visitor Publishing Division
Our Sunday Visitor, Inc.
Huntington, Indiana 46750

ACKNOWLEDGMENTS: Catholic News Service, for coverage of news and documentary texts; *The Documents of Vatican II*, ed. W. M. Abbott (Herder and Herder, America Press: New York 1966), for quotations of Council documents; *Annuario Pontificio (1996); Statistical Yearbook of the Church (1994); L'Osservatore Romano* (English editions); *The Official Catholic Directory* — Excerpts of statistical data and other material, reprinted with permission of *The Official Catholic Directory*, © 1996 by Reed Reference Publishing, a division of Reed Publishing (USA) Inc. Trademark used under license from Reed Publishing (Nederland) B.V.; *The Papal Encyclicals*, 5 vols., ed. C. Carlen (Pierian Press, Ann Arbor, Mich.); Newsletter of the U.S. Bishops' Committee on the Liturgy; The United States Catholic Mission Assoc. (3029 Fourth St. N.E., Washington, D.C. 20017), for U.S. overseas-mission compilations and statistics; *Catholic Press Directory (1996); Annuaire Directory 1996-1997,* Canadian Conference of Catholic Bishops, for latest available Canadian Catholic statistics; Rev. Thomas J. Reese, S.J., for names of dioceses for which U.S. bishops were ordained; other sources as credited in particular entries.

1997 Catholic Almanac

Published annually by Our Sunday Visitor Publishing Division, Our Sunday Visitor, Inc., 200 Noll Plaza, Huntington, IN 46750
Address queries to the Publisher.
ISBN 0-87973-277-6 (Kivar edition)
ISBN 0-87973-278-4 (cloth edition)
Library of Congress Catalog Card No. 73-641001
International Standard Serial Number (ISSN) 0069-1208

# TABLE OF CONTENTS

# INDEX

Sick Calls, 327
Siena, Papal Visit, 91-2
Sierra Leone, 360, 370
Sign of Cross, 327
Signatura, Apostolic, 147
Signs of the Times, 327
Signum Fidei Medal, 599
Silva Henriquez, Raul, S.D.B., Card., 163, 166, 167
Silvestrini, Achille, Card., 163, 166
Simon, St. (Apostle), 195
Simon, William (Catholics in Presidents' Cabinets), 414
Simonis, Adrianus J., Card., 163, 166, 167
Simony, 327
Sin, 327
    Original, 320
    Punishment, 323
Sin, Jaime L., Card., 163, 166, 167
Singapore, 360, 370
Sins
    against Holy Spirit, 327
    Capital, 301
    Forgiveness, 310
    See also Penance (Sacrament)
    Occasions, 327
    That Cry to Heaven for Vengeance, 327
Sirach, 189
Sister, 327
Sisterhood, 327
Sisters, United States, 506-23
    Statistics, 432-35
    See also Religious, Women
Situation Ethics, 327-28
Sixtus II, St., 256
Sklba, Richard J., Bp., 470
Skylstad, William, Bp., 51, 62, 470
Sladkevicius, Vincentas, Card., 163, 166, 167
    See also Lithuania
Slander, 328
Slattery, Edward J., Bp., 470
Sloth (Acedia), 328
Slovak Byzantine Catholics, 268
Slovak Catholic Federation of America, 581
Slovak Catholic Sokol, 581
Slovakia, 360-61, 371
    See also Czechoslovakia
Slovenia, 57-8, 99-100, 361, 371
    Papal Visit, 57-8, 99-100
Smith, Alfred E. (Catholic History in U.S., Bigotry), 398
Smith, Christopher, Rep., 104, 383
Smith, John M., Bp., 470
Smith, Philip F., O.M.I., Abp., 470
Snyder, John J., Bp., 470
Social Communications Council, 148
    See also Communications
Social Doctrine of the Church, 200-07
Social Health, Index of, 72-3
Social Sciences, Pontifical Academy, 547
Social Service, Sisters of, 522
Social Services, Catholic, U.S., 548-64
    World Statistics, 368
Socially Maladjusted, Facilities for, 558-60
Societies, Catholic, in U.S., 574-81
Societies, Religious, see Religious, Men, Women, in U.S.
Society for the Propagation of the Faith, 581
Society of Our Lady of the Most Holy Trinity, 504
Society of St. Monica, 581
Society of St. Paul, 503
Society of St. Peter the Apostle, 92, 581
Society of St. Vincent de Paul, 548
Society of the Divine Attributes, 581
Sodano, Angelo, Card., 74, 163, 166
SODEPAX (Society for Development and Peace), 285
Soenneker, Henry J., Bp., 491
Soens, Lawrence D., Bp., 470
Solanus, Francis, St., 392

Solemnity of Mary, 249
*Sollicitudo Omnium Ecclesiarum* (Representatives of the Holy See), 168
Solomon (Kings 1 and 2), 188
Solomon Islands, 361, 371
Somalia, 361
Somascan Fathers, 504
Song of Songs (Bible), 189
Sons of Mary Missionary Society, 504
Sophia, Catholic University (Japan),543
Sorcery, 328
Sorin, Edward F., 392
Soroka, Stephen, Bp., 387
Sorrows (Dolors) of the Blessed Virgin Mary, 248
Soteriology, 328
Souls, Holy, see All Souls
South Africa, 52, 54, 102, 361
    Papal Visit, 52, 54
South America
    Cardinals, 167
    Catholic Statistics, 368
    Eastern Rite Jurisdictions, 270
    Episcopal Conferences, 372
    Missionary Bishops, 431
South Carolina, 105, 412, 434, 437, 439, 534, 556, 570
    Ruling on Viable Fetuses, 105
South Dakota, 412, 434, 437, 439, 534, 556, 570
South Korea, 350, 370
    See also Korea
South West Africa, see Namibia
Southern Africa Bishops' Conference, 369, 372
Southern Baptist Convention, 278
Southwell, Robert, St., 256
Sowada, Alphonse, O.S.C., Bp., 470
Spain, 66, 86, 90, 102, 361-62, 371
    Civil War (1936), 119
    Inquisition, 315
    Persecution (1931), 119
Spanish Sahara, see Western Sahara
Spanish-Speaking in U.S., see Hispanics
Species, Sacred, 328
Spellman, Francis J. (U.S. Cardinals), 167, 491
Speltz, George H., Bp., 470
Spence, Francis J., Abp., 387
Speyrer, Jude, Bp., 470
Spiritism, 328
Spiritual Life Institute of America, 581
Spiritual Works of Mercy, 318
Sponsor, see Confirmation
Spoon, 274
Sri Lanka, 362, 371
Stafford, James Francis, Abp., 85, 470-71, 600
Stamps, Vatican, 175-76
Stanislaus, St., 256
"Stand Up for Life," 46-7
State and Church, see Church-State
State Catholic Conferences, 448-49
State of Grace, see Grace
Stational Churches, Days, 328
Stations (Way) of the Cross, 328
Statistical Yearbook of the Church, 177
Statistics, Catholic, 101
    Canada, 337, 382-83
    Countries of World, 333-67
    Men Religious, 505-06
    Seminarians (1989-94), 542
    United States, see Statistics, Catholic, U.S.
    World (Summary), 368
Statistics, Catholic, United States
    Baptisms (Infant and Adult), 438-39
    Brothers, 432-35
    Eastern Rite, 270-71, 435, 439, 533
    Missionary Personnel Abroad, 529
    Percentage in Total Population, 436-37
    Permanent Deacons, 230, 432-35
    Population, 432-35, 436-37
    Press, 582
    Priests, 432-35
    Priests, Newly Ordained, 440

Statistics
    Receptions into Church, 438-39
    Schools and Students, 532-36
    Seminarians, 440, 536
    Seminarians (1989-94), 542
    Sisters, 432-35
    Summary, 440
Statistics Office, Central, 149
Statuary Hall, U.S., Catholics in, 415
Statues, 217
Statutes, 328
Steib, J. (James) Terry, S.V.D., Bp.,471
Stein, Edith, Bl., 252
Steinbock, John T., Bp., 471
Steiner, Kenneth D., Bp., 100-01, 471
Steinfels, Margaret O'Brien, 72
Stephen, St. (Deacon), 256
Stephen, St. (King), 256
Stepinac, Aloysius (Yugoslavia), 367
Steponavicius, Julijonas, Abp., see Lithuania
Sterzinsky, Georg Maximilian, Card., 163, 166, 167
Sticharion, 274
Stickler, Alfons, S.D.B., Card., 163, 166
Stigmata, 328-29
Stigmata, Congregation of Sacred (Stigmatine Fathers and Brothers), 504
Stipend, Mass, 329
Stole, 215
Stole Fee, 329
Stoup, 329
Straling, Phillip F., Bp., 471
Strecker, Ignatius, Abp., 471
Stritch, Samuel (U.S. Card.), 167, 491
Students, Catholic
    United States, 532-35
    University, College, U.S., 536-40
    World (Catholic World Statistics), 368
Suarez Rivera, Adolfo Antonio, Card., 163, 166, 167
Subdeacon, 229
Sudan, 66, 362, 371
Suenens, Leo J., Card. (Death), 600
Suffragan See, 329
Suicide, 329
Suicide, Assisted, 48-50, 88, 92, 93, 95
Sukkoth, 290
Sullivan, James S., Bp., 471
Sullivan, John J., Bp., 471
Sullivan, Joseph M., Bp., 471
Sullivan, Walter F., Bp., 471
Sulpice, Society of Priests of St. (Sulpicians), 504
Sulyk, Stephen, Abp., 105, 471
Sunday, 238
Sunday Mass on Saturday, 219
Supererogation, 329
Supernatural, 329
Supernatural Virtue, 331
Superstition, 329
Support Our Aging Religious, 581
Supremacy, Act of (1533), 116
Supreme Court, U.S.
    Abortion Rulings, 47-8
    Church-State Decisions, 415-20
    Rust v. Sullivan Decision, 48
    Webster Decision, 48
Supreme Court, U.S., Catholics in, 415
Supreme Order of Christ, 596
Suquia Goicoechea, Angel, Card., 164, 166
Suriname, 362
Surplice, 216
Suspension, 329
Sutton, Peter A., O.M.I., Abp., 388
Swaziland, 362
Swearing, 329
Sweden, 362
Swedenborgianism, 329
Swenson, John S., 100
Swiatek, Kazimierz, Card., 164, **166**
Swiss Guards, 175
Switzerland, 362-63, 371
Sword of Loyola Award, 599
Syllabus, 329

## PUBLICATION HISTORY

The 1997 edition of the Catholic Almanac, published by Our Sunday Visitor, Inc., marks the 93rd anniversary of its printing history. It is the 90th edition; no volumes were published in 1930, 1934 and 1935.

The Catholic Almanac originated remotely from St. Antony's Almanac, a 64-page annual with calendar, feature and devotional contents, published by the Franciscans of Holy Name Province from 1904 to 1929. The Franciscan Almanac was the title of the completely revised work published in 1931, 1932 and 1933 by The Franciscan Magazine. A volume of 320 pages, it represented a radical change from previous Almanac editions and inaugurated content development that has continued to the present time.

The current 600-page edition is a one-of-a-kind factual volume of basic and contemporary information on an encyclopedic range of subjects pertaining to the Catholic Church and its activity in the world.

St. Anthony's Guild published the book from 1936 to 1971. Editions from 1940 to 1968 were issued under the title, The National Catholic Almanac; the present title was adopted in 1969. Editions from 1959 to 1971 were produced jointly by St. Anthony's Guild and Doubleday & Co., Inc. Editions from 1972 to the present have been published by Our Sunday Visitor, Inc.

## POLITICAL PLATFORMS

**Democratic Party Platform:** Portions of the Democratic Party's 1996 platform were more or less in accord with policy recommendations of the U.S. Catholic bishops regarding: arms control, welfare reform, family television programming, economic reform, environmental protection, family priorities, immigration and controlling violence. In significant contrast, however, were the issues of abortion — to which the bishops are absolutely opposed — and school choice. Several subjects on which the bishops expressed concern but on which the Democratic Party was silent included euthanasia and the protection of refugees. The platform discussed economics in great detail, while the bishops primarily mentioned the economy in the context of protecting the poor.

**Republican Party Platform:** Items at issue in the Republican Party platform included: tax reduction, call for a constitutional amendment against abortion, equal rights without quotas, gun control, rejection of the "distortion"of civil rights laws that would "cover sexual preference."The bishops were opposed to restrictive proposals affecting immigrants in the areas of education, health care and welfare.

**Statement to Both Parties:** In their statement to both parties, the bishops called for: analysis of every policy and program for their impact on children and families; insistence that policies support families and encourage self-help; adoption of policies that would empower families to stay together.

• On health care: "Our criteria for reform include respect for life, priority concern for the poor, universal health care coverage, pluralism, cost containment and equitable financing.

• On abortion: It is "the fundamental human rights issue of our day because it is the deliberate destruction of a human being before birth."

# SPECIAL REPORTS

## PAPAL VISIT TO UNITED NATIONS AND UNITED STATES

### ITINERARY

**Oct. 4:** 3:00 p.m., Arrival at Newark International Airport, and welcoming ceremony.

5:00 p.m., Evening Prayer at Sacred Heart Cathedral, Newark.

**Oct. 5:** 9:15 a.m., Visit to the United Nations, with addresses to the General Assembly and the U.N. staff.

5:30 p.m., Tour by popemobile inside Giants Stadium, followed by Mass at 6:00 p.m.

**Oct. 6:** Tour inside Aqueduct Racetrack, Queens, N.Y., followed by Mass at 9:30.

5:00 p.m., Tour on grounds of St. Joseph's Seminary, Yonkers, N.Y., followed by Evening Prayer and an address to seminarians.

**Oct. 7:** 9:00 a.m., Tour on Great Lawn of Central Park, N.Y., followed by Mass at 9:30.

12:15 p.m., Arrival at residence of Cardinal John J. O'Connor.

3:30 p.m., Recitation of the Rosary in St. Patrick's Cathedral.

5:00 p.m., Blessing of offices of the Holy See's Permanent Observer Mission to the United Nations.

6:30 p.m., Informal meeting with leadership of other Christian churches and ecclesial communities at Cardinal O'Connor's residence.

7:00 p.m., Dinner with bishops of the region, followed by an informal meeting with leaders of the Jewish community, at the cardinal's residence.

**Oct. 8:** 9:50 a.m., Arrival and informal welcome at Baltimore-Washington International Airport.

10:15 Tour inside Oriole Park at Camden Yards, Baltimore, followed by Mass at 10:45 and recitation of the Angelus.

1:30 p.m., Parade to residence of Cardinal William H. Keeler.

5:00 p.m., Visit to the Basilica of the Assumption and meeting with the leadership of Catholic Relief Services.

5:45 p.m., Visit to the Cathedral of Mary Our Queen.

6:25 p.m., Arrival at St. Mary's Seminary for transfer to Baltimore-Washington International Airport for departure ceremony at 7:30 p.m., and departure for Rome at 8:00 p.m.

### AT SACRED HEART CATHEDRAL

The Pope spoke during Evening Prayer at Newark's Sacred Heart Cathedral after his arrival at the city's international airport and his exchange of greetings with Archbishop Theodore McCarrick and President Bill Clinton.

In the context of "selfless service" as the "model of all ministry in the Church," he addressed remarks to:

• Priests: "Ordination configures you to Christ the servant."

• Seminarians: "Without the virtues of self-discipline, diligent contemplation of the truth, simplicity of life and joyful dedication to others, you will not have the inner strength to combat the culture of death which is threatening the modern world."

• Religious, especially women: "The recognition of the 'genius of women' and of the specifically feminine charisms which women religious bring to the Church's life and mission is a providential sign of our times."

The Holy Father also called attention to the relation of the 1994 archdiocesan synod to "the stirring challenge of the new evangelization."

### THE FABRIC OF RELATIONS AMONG PEOPLES: U.N. Address

The Pope said his visit and words were "meant as a sign of the interest and esteem of the Apostolic See and of the Catholic Church for this institution. They echo the voices of all those who see in the United Nations the hope of a better future for human society." "The Church and the United Nations constantly find wide areas of cooperation on the basis of their common concern for the human family." (No. 1)

"On the threshold of a new millennium, we are witnessing an extraordinary global acceleration of that quest for freedom which is one of the great dynamics of human history. This phenomenon is not limited to any one part of the world nor is it the expression of any single culture.

"The quest for freedom in our time has its basis in those universal rights which human beings enjoy by the very fact of their humanity." (No. 2)

"There are indeed universal human rights rooted in the nature of the person, rights which reflect the objective and inviolable demands of a universal moral law.... There is a moral logic which is built into human life and which makes possible dialogue between individuals and peoples.... The universal moral law written in the human heart is precisely that kind of 'grammar' which is needed if the world is to engage this discussion of its future." (No. 3)

"It is important to remember that World War II was fought because of violations of the rights of nations." (No. 5)

"The Universal Declaration of Human Rights, adopted in 1948, spoke eloquently of the rights of persons; but no similar international agreement has yet adequately addressed the rights of nations." (No. 6)

### Rights of Nations

"The 'rights of nations,' are nothing but human rights fostered at the specific level of community life.... A presupposition of a nation's rights is certainly its right to exist. Therefore, no one — neither a state nor another nation nor an international organization — is ever justified in asserting that an individual nation is not worthy of existence." The "right to exist naturally implies that every nation also enjoys the right to its language and culture.... Every nation therefore has also the right to shape its life according to its own traditions, excluding, of course, every abuse of basic human rights.

"While the 'rights of the nation' express the vital requirements of 'particularity,' it is no less important to emphasize the requirements of universality, expressed through a clear awareness of the duties which nations have vis-a-vis other nations and humanity as a whole. Foremost among these duties is certainly that of living in a spirit of peace, respect and solidarity with other nations. Thus, the exercise of the rights of nations, balanced by the acknowledgment and the practice of duties, promotes a fruitful 'exchange of gifts,' which strengthens the unity of all mankind." (No. 8)

"The world has yet to learn how to live with diversity, as recent events in the Balkans and Central Africa have painfully reminded us.... From bitter experience we know that the fear of 'difference,' especially when it expresses itself in a narrow and exclusive nationalism which denies any rights to 'the other,' can lead to a true nightmare of violence and terror." (No. 9)

"We need to clarify the essential difference between an unhealthy form of nationalism, which teaches contempt for other nations or cultures, and patriotism, which is a proper love of one's country. True patriotism never seeks to advance the well-being of one's nation at the expense of others. Nationalism, particularly in its most radical forms, is the antithesis of true patriotism." (No. 10).

### Freedom and Moral Truth

"Freedom is not simply the absence of tyranny or oppression. Nor is freedom a license to do whatever we like. Freedom has an inner 'logic' which distinguishes it and ennobles it. Freedom is ordered to the truth and is fulfilled in man's quest for truth and in man's living in the truth. Detached from the truth about the human person, freedom deteriorates into license in the lives of individuals; and, in political life, it becomes the caprice of the most powerful and the arrogance of power.... Reference to the truth about the human person ... is, in fact, the guarantor of freedom's future." (No. 12)

"In the light of what has been said, we understand how utilitarianism, the doctrine which defines morality not in terms of what is good but in what is advantageous, threatens the freedom of individuals and nations and obstructs the building of a true culture of freedom. Utilitarianism often has devastating political consequences because it inspires an aggressive nationalism.... No less grave are the results of economic utilitarianism, which drives more powerful countries to manipulate and exploit weaker ones."

"The international economic scene needs an ethic of solidarity, if participation, economic growth and a just distribution of goods are to characterize the future of humanity." (No.13)

### U.N. and Future of Freedom

The need for such an organization as the United Nations is more obvious now than it was at its founding 50 years ago. "The United Nations (now) needs to rise more and more above the cold status of an administrative institution and to become a moral center where all the nations of the world feel at home and develop a shared awareness of being, as it were, a 'family of nations.' "

"The United Nations has the historic, even momentous, task of promoting this qualitative leap in international life, not only by serving as a center of effective mediation for the resolution of conflicts but also by fostering values, attitudes and concrete initiatives of solidarity which prove capable of raising the level of relations between nations from the 'organizational' to a more 'organic' level, from simple 'existence with' others to 'existence for' others, in a fruitful exchange of gifts, primarily for the good of the weaker nations, but even so a harbinger of greater good for everyone." (No. 14)

### Beyond Fear

"In order to ensure that the new millennium now approaching will witness a new flourishing of the human spirit, mediated through an authentic culture of freedom, men and women must learn to conquer fear." (No. 16)

"We must overcome our fear of the future.... The answer to the fear which darkens human existence at the end of the 20th century is the common effort to build the civilization of love, founded on the universal values of peace, solidarity, justice and liberty. And the 'soul' of the civilization of love is the culture of freedom: the freedom of individuals and the freedom of nations, lived in self-giving solidarity and responsibility." (No. 18.)

### ADDRESS TO U.N. STAFF

The Pope spoke briefly to U.N. staff members after his address to the General Assembly. He said in part: "In this climate of international cooperation, your contribution as staff members of the United Nations is indispensable.... You show a special concern for the entire human family. I would assure you that in the work of promoting justice, building peace and ensuring that human dignity and human rights are respected throughout the world, you have the full and complete support of the Catholic Church.... Your dedicated work here at the United Nations is a promising sign that the new millennium will see a reflowering of true humanity in compassion, openness and solidarity between peoples and nations. My prayers are with you and your families."

### ADDRESSES

**Questions for the United States:** "Is present-day America becoming less sensitive, less caring toward the poor, the weak, the stranger, the needy? It must not! Today, as before, the United States is called to be a hospitable society, a welcoming culture. If America were to turn in on itself, would this not be the beginning of the end of what constitutes the very essence of the 'American experience'?"

Pope John Paul posed these questions in his homily at an evening Mass Oct. 5 in Giants Stadium, East Rutherford, N.J. Addressing a rain-soaked throng of 85,000 persons, he spoke about the right to life, vocations to the priesthood and religious life, and the mission of lay persons.

"The question of vocations is vital to the Church," he said. "Everyone has a vocation: parents, teachers, students, workers, professional people, people who are retired. Everyone has something to do for God. We must pray that young people especially will listen to the Lord's call to serve as priests, as religious sisters and brothers, as missionaries at home and in other lands."

He called the right to life "the first of all rights. It

is the foundation of democratic liberties and the keystone of the edifice of civil society."

## Respect for Life

Addressing this subject, the Pope said:

"To a great extent, the story of America has been the story of long and difficult struggles to overcome the prejudices which excluded certain categories of people from a full share in the country's life: first, the struggle against religious intolerance, then the struggle against racial discrimination and in favor of civil rights for everyone.

"Sadly, today a new class of people is being excluded When the unborn child — the 'stranger in the womb' — is declared to be beyond the protection of society, not only are America's deepest traditions radically undermined and endangered, but a moral blight is brought upon society.

"I am also thinking of threats to the elderly, the severely handicapped and all those who do not seem to have any social usefulness. When innocent human beings are declared inconvenient or burdensome, and thus unworthy of legal and societal protection, grievous damage is done to the moral foundations of the democratic community. The right to life is the first of all rights. It is the foundation of democratic liberties and the keystone of the edifice of civil society. Both as Americans and as followers of Christ, American Catholics must be committed to the defense of life in all its stages and in every condition."

## AT AQUEDUCT RACETRACK

**The Progress of Peoples:** This was the theme of the morning Mass at Aqueduct Racetrack where the Holy Father spoke of the family as the "domestic church" and asked a serious question.

"From the viewpoint of the kingdom of God, we must ask a very basic question: Have the people living in this huge metropolis lost sight of the blessings which belong to the poor in spirit? In the midst of the magnificent scientific and technological civilization of which America is proud, ... is there room for the mystery of God? ... Is there room for the revelation of life — the transcendent life which Christ brings us at the price of the cross and through the victory of his resurrection?"

## SEMINARIANS

The Pope addressed students for the priesthood at St. Joseph's Seminary, Yonkers, N.Y., during an Evening Prayer service Oct. 6.

• "If you are to become priests, it will be for the purpose — above all other purposes — of proclaiming the word of God and feeding God's people with the Body and Blood of Christ."

• "If there is one challenge facing the Church and her priests today, it is the challenge of transmitting the Christian message whole and entire, without letting it be emptied of its substance. The Gospel cannot be reduced to mere human wisdom."

• Do not be afraid to confront worldly wisdom "with the certainty of the teachings of Christ ... but, above all, with the love of Christ, with the compassion and the mercy of Christ."

• "You will not become priests to be served by or to lord it over others, but to serve others, especially the poorest of the poor, the materially poor and the spiritually poor."

## AT CENTRAL PARK

**Challenge to Youth:** A great many young people were among the more than 100,000 persons who attended the Pope's Mass Oct. 7 at the Great Lawn of New York's Central Park. He said it was "especially wonderful to see so many" of them there.

He took advantage of their presence to say: "I invite you to reflect on what makes each one of you truly marvelous and unique." He urged them to "visit the needs of the poor, the hungry, the homeless, those who are alone or ill; for example, those suffering from AIDS"; also, "to respect and defend the mystery of life always and everywhere, including the lives of unborn babies, and to give real help and encouragement to mothers in difficult situations."

He also said: "You young people will live most of your lives in the next millennium. You must help the Holy Spirit to shape its social, moral and spiritual character. You must transmit your joy in being adopted sons of God through the creative power of the Holy Spirit. Do this with the help of Mary, Mother of Jesus. Cling to her rosary, and you will never wander far from her side."

## AT BALTIMORE

**Freedom and Truth:** Every generation of Americans needs to know that freedom consists not in doing what we like, but in having the right to do what we ought." So stated the Pope during a Mass in Oriole Park at Camden Yards Stadium in Baltimore. The Mass was concelebrated by more than 200 bishops and 300 priests before a congregation of an estimated 60,000 people.

He called on U.S. Catholics to "guard the truth that is the condition of authentic freedom, the truth that allows freedom to be fulfilled in goodness."

He said "the basic question before a democratic society is, How ought we to live together?" In seeking to answer the question, he urged Americans to recall the role "biblical wisdom" has played in the country's history. "Surely it is important for America that the moral truths which make freedom possible should be passed on to each new generation." Forgetting past wisdom would mean that "tens of millions of Americans could no longer offer the contribution of their deepest convictions to the formation of public policy."

In conclusion, the Pope said: "Catholics of America! Always be guided by the truth — by the truth about God who created and redeemed us, and by the truth about the human person, made in the image and likeness of God and destined for a glorious fulfillment in the kingdom to come. Always be convincing witnesses to the truth. 'Stir into flame the gift of God that has been bestowed upon you in baptism. Light your nation — light of the world — with the power of that flame."

**The Legacy of Religious Freedom:** The final large public event of the Pope's visit to the United States took place Oct. 8 in Baltimore's Cathedral of Mary Our Queen, where he spoke about religious freedom before an assembly of nearly 1,400 invited Christians, Muslims and Jews. He said:

"The source of your commitment to religious freedom is itself a deep religious conviction. Religious tolerance is based on the conviction that God wishes to be adored by people who are free: a conviction which requires us to respect and honor the inner sanctuary of conscience in which each person meets God. The Catholic Church wholly supports this conviction."

"The challenge facing you, dear friends, is to increase people's awareness of the importance for society of religious freedom; to defend that freedom against those who would take religion out of the public domain and establish secularism as America's official faith. And it is vitally necessary for the very

survival of the American experience to transmit to the next generation the precious legacy of religious freedom and the convictions which sustain it."

In conclusion, the Pope said: "The world looks to America in the hope of finding a model of a free and virtuous society. To make this land of freedom a hospitable home for all its people is still a challenge, and increasingly so. It is important to peoples around the world that you citizens of the United States succeed in making American society a more perfect embodiment of its commitment to liberty and justice for all."

# THE CONSECRATED LIFE: Apostolic Exhortation

The apostolic exhortation entitled *Vita Consecrata* was issued by Pope John Paul Mar. 25, 1996, on the theme of the 1994 assembly of the Synod of Bishops.

We are all aware of the treasure which the gift of consecrated life in the variety of its charisms and institutions represents for the ecclesial community. Together, let us thank God for the religious orders and institutes devoted to contemplation or the works of the apostolate, for societies of apostolic life, for secular institutes and for other groups of consecrated persons as well as for all those individuals who, in their inmost hearts, dedicate themselves to God by a special consecration. (2)

## A Gift to the Church

Its universal presence and the evangelical nature of its witness are clear evidence that the consecrated life is not something isolated and marginal, but a reality which affects the whole Church.... The consecrated life is at the very heart of the Church as a decisive element of her mission

The present difficulties which a number of institutes are encountering in some parts of the world must not lead to a questioning of the fact that the profession of the evangelical counsels is an integral part of the Church's life and a much-needed incentive toward greater fidelity to the Gospel. The consecrated life may experience further changes in its historical forms, but there will be no change in the substance of a choice which finds expression in a radical gift of self for love of the Lord Jesus and, in him, of every member of the human family. (3)

## Contemplative Institutes

Institutes completely devoted to contemplation, composed of either women or men, are for the Church a reason for pride and a source of heavenly graces. By their lives and mission, the members of these institutes imitate Christ in his prayer on the mountain, bear witness to God's lordship over history and anticipate the glory which is to come.

In solitude and silence, by listening to the word of God, participating in divine worship, personal asceticism, prayer, mortification and the communion of fraternal love, they direct the whole of their lives and all their activities to the contemplation of God. In this way they offer the ecclesial community a singular testimony of the Church's love for her Lord, and they contribute, with hidden apostolic fruitfulness, to the growth of the people of God. (8)

## Apostolic Religious Life

The West has also known down the centuries a variety of other expressions of religious life in which countless persons, renouncing the world, have consecrated themselves to God through the public profession of the evangelical counsels in accordance with a specific charism and in a stable form of common life, for the sake of carrying out different forms of apostolic service to the people of God. Thus there arose the different families of canons regular, the mendicant orders, the clerics regular and in general the religious congregations of men and women devoted to apostolic and missionary activity and the many different works inspired by Christian charity. (9)

## Secular Institutes

The Holy Spirit, who wondrously fashions the variety of charisms, has given rise in our time to new expressions of consecrated life, which appear as a providential response to the new needs encountered by the Church today as she carries out her mission in the world.

One thinks in the first place of members of secular institutes seeking to live out their consecration to God in the world through the profession of the evangelical counsels in the midst of temporal realities; they wish in this way to be a leaven of wisdom and a witness of grace within cultural, economic and political life. Through their own specific blending of presence in the world and consecration, they seek to make present in society the newness and power of Christ's kingdom, striving to transfigure the world from within by the power of the Beatitudes.... Secular institutes, each in accordance with its specific nature, thus help to ensure that the Church has an effective presence in society. (10)

## Societies of Apostolic Life

Also worthy of special mention are societies of apostolic life or of common life, composed of men or women. These pursue, each in its own particular way, a specific apostolic or missionary end. In many of them an explicit commitment to the evangelical counsels is made through sacred bonds officially recognized by the Church. Even in this case, however, the specific nature of their consecration distinguishes them from religious institutes and secular institutes, The specific identity of this form of life is to be preserved and promoted; in recent centuries it has produced many fruits of holiness and of the apostolate, especially in the field of charity and in the spread of the Gospel in the missions. (11)

## New Expressions

New forms of consecrated life now taking their place alongside the older ones bear witness to the constant attraction which the total gift of self to the Lord, the ideal of the apostolic community and the founding charisms continue to exert, even on the present generation. They also show how the gifts of the Holy Spirit complement one another.

## Duty of the Consecrated Life

It is the duty of the consecrated life to show that the incarnate Son of God is the eschatological (final, ultimate) goal toward which all things tend, the splendor before which every other light pales and the infinite beauty which alone can satisfy the human heart. In the consecrated life, then, it is not only a matter of following Christ with one's whole heart, … for this is required of every disciple — but of living and expressing this by conforming one's whole existence to Christ in an all-encompassing commitment which foreshadows the eschatological perfection to the extent that this is possible in time and in accordance with the different charisms.

By professing the evangelical counsels, consecrated persons not only make Christ the whole meaning of their lives, but strive to reproduce in themselves as far as possible "that form of life which, he as the Son of God, accepted in entering this world." By embracing chastity, they make their own the pure love of Christ and proclaim to the world that he is the only begotten Son who is one with the Father. By imitating Christ's poverty, they profess that he is the Son who receives everything from the Father and gives everything back to the Father in love. By accepting through the sacrifice of their own freedom the mystery of Christ's filial obedience, they profess that he is infinitely beloved and loving, as the one who delights only in the will of the Father, to whom he is perfectly united and on whom he depends for everything. (16)

Cloistered nuns share in Christ's emptying of himself by means of a radical poverty expressed in the renunciation not only of things but also of "space," of contacts, of so many benefits of creation. This particular way of offering up the "body" allows them to enter more fully into the eucharistic mystery. They offer themselves with Jesus for the world's salvation. (59)

## Religious Brothers

According to the traditional doctrine of the Church, the consecrated life by its nature is neither lay nor clerical. For this reason, the "lay consecration" of both men and women constitutes a state which in its profession of the evangelical counsels is complete in itself. Consequently, both for the individual and for the Church it is a value in itself apart from the sacred ministry.

Following the teaching of the Second Vatican Council, the synod expressed great esteem for the kind of consecrated life in which religious brothers provide valuable services of various kinds, inside or outside the community, participating in this way in the mission of proclaiming the Gospel and bearing witness to it with charity in everyday life. Indeed, some of these services can be considered ecclesial ministries, granted by legitimate authority. This requires an appropriate and integral formation: human, spiritual, theological, pastoral and professional.

Institutes which by reason of their founders' design or by legitimate tradition have a character and purpose which do not entail the exercise of holy orders are called *lay institutes.*

For this reason the synod fathers, in order to avoid ambiguity and confusion with the secular state of the lay faithful, proposed the term religious institutes of brothers.

In these religious institutes of brothers nothing prevents certain members from receiving holy orders for the priestly service of the religious community, provided that this is approved by the general chapter (of the institute). However, the Second Vatican Council does not give any explicit encouragement for this, precisely because it wishes institutes of brothers to remain faithful to their vocation and mission. The same holds true with regard to assuming the office of superior, since that office reflects in a special way the nature of the institute itself.

The vocation of brothers in what are known as *clerical* institutes is different since, according to the design of the founder or by reason of legitimate tradition, these institutes presuppose the exercise of holy orders, are governed by clerics and as such are approved by church authority. In these institutes the sacred ministry is constitutive of the charism itself and determines its nature, purpose and spirit. The presence of brothers constitutes a different form of participation in an institute's mission, through services rendered both within the community and in the apostolate in collaboration with those who exercise the priestly ministry. (60)

## Mixed Institutes

Some religious institutes, which in the founder's original design were envisaged as a brotherhood in which all the members, priests and those who were not priests, were considered equal among themselves, have acquired a different form with the passing of time. It is necessary that these institutes, known as *mixed,* evaluate on the basis of a deeper understanding of their founding charism whether it is appropriate and possible to return to their original inspiration.

The synod fathers expressed the hope that in these institutes all the religious would be recognized as having equal rights and obligations, with the exception of those which stem from holy orders.

## New Forms of Evangelical Life

New foundations display new characteristics (as) compared to those of traditional foundations.

The originality of the new communities often consists in the fact that they are composed of mixed groups of men and women, of clerics and lay persons, of married couples and celibates, all of whom pursue a particular style of life. These communities are sometimes inspired by one or other traditional form adapted to the needs of modern society. Their commitment to the evangelical life also takes on different forms, while, as a general rule, they are characterized by an intense aspiration to community life, poverty and prayer. Both clerics and lay persons share in the duties of governing, according to the responsibilities assigned to them, and the apostolate focuses on the demands of the new evangelization.

If on the one hand there is reason to rejoice at the Holy Spirit's action, there is on the other a need for discernment regarding these charisms. A fundamental principle when speaking of the consecrated life is that the specific features of the new communities and their styles of life must be founded on the essential theological and canonical elements proper to the consecrated life. This discernment is necessary at both the local and universal level in order to manifest a common obedience to the one Spirit. (62)

### Consecrated Life Will Continue

The various difficulties stemming from the decline in personnel and apostolates must in no way lead to a loss of confidence in the evangelical vitality of the consecrated life, which will always be present and active in the Church. While individual institutes have no claim to permanence, the consecrated life itself will continue to sustain among the faithful the response of love toward God and neighbor. Thus it is necessary to distinguish the historical destiny of a specific institute or form of consecrated life from the ecclesial mission of the consecrated life as such. The former is affected by changing circumstances; the latter is destined to perdure. (63)

### ADDITIONAL NOTES

In addition to the foregoing excerpts regarding the nature and various forms of consecrated life, the apostolic exhortation deals with a wide range of other subjects of importance for consecrated persons, including: religious garb, formation for consecrated life, community life, authority, relationships between religious superiors and bishops, roles within the local and universal church, cooperation with lay persons, promotion of vocations to consecrated life, ecumenical involvement, engagement in education and service to the poor.

## PAPAL ELECTION: Apostolic Constitution

*Revised regulations for the government of the Church during a vacancy of the Holy See and for the election of a pope were published Feb. 22, 1996, in an apostolic constitution entitled "Universi Dominici Gregis" ("Of the Lord's Whole Flock"). Excerpts are given below.*

### DURING THE VACANCY

• "The College of Cardinals has no power or jurisdiction in matters which pertain to the supreme pontiff during his lifetime or in the exercise of his office."

• "The government of the Church is entrusted to the College of Cardinals solely for the dispatch of ordinary business and of matters which cannot be postponed, and for the preparation of everything necessary for the election of the new pope."

• "The College of Cardinals may make no dispositions whatsoever concerning the rights of the Apostolic See and of the Roman Church."

• "Laws issued by the Roman pontiffs can in no way be corrected or modified, nor can anything be added or subtracted, nor a dispensation be given even from a part of them."

### Preparatory Congregations

"There are two kinds of congregations of cardinals: general, which include the whole college and are held before the beginning of the election, and particular congregations."

A " particular congregation is made up of the cardinal chamberlain of the holy Roman church and three cardinals, one from each order of cardinals (bishop, priest, deacon), chosen by lot from among cardinal electors already in Rome." Each particular congregation holds office for three days. "Particular congregations are to deal only with questions of lesser importance which arise on a daily basis or from time to time."

"General congregations are to be held (ordinarily) in the Apostolic Palace." The presiding officer is the dean of the college or, in his absence, the subdean. Votes are secret. "General congregations preceding the beginning of the election ... are to be held daily."

Cardinals in general congregations make decisions regarding a number of matters, including the following:

"They shall fix the day, hour and manner in which the body of the deceased pope shall be brought to the Vatican basilica in order to be exposed for the homage of the faithful."

"They shall make all necessary arrangements for the funeral rites of the deceased pope, to be celebrated for nine consecutive days, determining when they are to begin in such a way that burial will take place, except for special reasons, between the fourth and sixth day after death."

"They shall arrange for the destruction of the Fisherman's Ring and of the lead seal with which apostolic letters are dispatched."

"They shall set the day and hour of the beginning of the voting process."

### Certain Offices

"At the death of the pope, all the heads of the dicasteries of the Roman Curia — the cardinal secretary of state and the cardinal prefects, the archbishop presidents, together with the members of the dicasteries — cease to exercise their office." Exceptions are made for the chamberlain of the holy Roman church, the major penitentiary, the cardinal vicar for the Diocese of Rome, the cardinal archpriest of the Vatican basilica and the vicar general for Vatican City.

The chamberlain of the holy Roman church has numerous responsibilities, including the following: ascertaining the pope's death, sealing his rooms, notifying various officials of the pontiff's death, safeguarding and administering the goods and temporal rights of the Holy See, determining details related to burial of the pope.

The dean of the College of Cardinals informs all

of the cardinals about the death of the pope and convokes them for the general congregations of the college. He also informs the diplomatic corps about the death of the pope.

## ELECTION OF THE POPE
### The Electors

"The right to elect the Roman pontiff belongs exclusively to the cardinals of the holy Roman church, with the exception of those who have reached their 80th birthday before the day of the Roman pontiff's death or the day when the Apostolic See becomes vacant. The maximum number of cardinal electors must not exceed 120. The right of active election by any other ecclesiastical dignitary or the intervention of any lay power whatsoever is absolutely excluded."

If a vacancy of the Apostolic See should occur while an ecumenical council or an assembly of the Synod of Bishops is in progress, the council or assembly would be automatically suspended.

The electoral conclave must begin 15 to 20 days after the death of the pope. It takes place within the territory of Vatican City. Voting takes place in the Sistine Chapel in the Apostolic Palace. The cardinal electors reside at the Domus Sanctae Marthae; suitable accommodations are provided for necessary service personnel.

At the beginning of the conclave, the electors bind themselves by oath to observe all requirements related to the papal election, as follows:

"We, the cardinal electors present in this election of the supreme pontiff, promise, pledge and swear, as individuals and as a group, to observe faithfully and scrupulously the prescriptions contained in the apostolic constitution of the Supreme Pontiff John Paul II, *Universi Dominici Gregis,* published on Feb. 22, 1996.

"We likewise promise, pledge and swear that whichever of us by divine disposition is elected Roman pontiff will commit himself faithfully to carrying out the *munus Petrinum* of pastor of the universal Church and will not fail to affirm and defend strenuously the spiritual and temporal rights and the liberty of the Holy See.

"In a particular way, we promise and swear to observe with the greatest fidelity and with all persons, clerical or lay, secrecy regarding everything that in any way relates to the election of the Roman pontiff and regarding what occurs in the place of the election, directly or indirectly related to the results of the voting; we promise and swear not to break this secret in any way, either during or after the election of the new pontiff, unless explicit authorization is granted by the same pontiff; and never to lend support or favor to any interference, opposition or other form of intervention, whereby secular authorities of whatever order and degree or any group of people or individuals might wish to intervene in the election of the Roman pontiff."

## Election Procedure

"The forms of election" by acclamation and compromise "are abolished," and "the form of electing the Roman pontiff shall henceforth be by balloting alone."

"I therefore decree that for the valid election of the Roman pontiff two-thirds of the votes are required, calculated on the basis of the total number of electors present."

"Should it be impossible to divide the number of cardinals present into three equal parts, for the validity of the election of the supreme pontiff one additional vote is required."

"Should the election begin on the afternoon of the first day, only one ballot is to be held; then, on the following days, if no one is elected on the first ballot, two ballots shall be held in the morning and two in the afternoon."

"In the event that the cardinal electors find it difficult to agree on the person to be elected, after balloting has been carried out for three days ... without result, voting is to be suspended for a maximum of one day in order to allow for prayer, informal discussion among the voters and a brief spiritual exhortation." Given the same circumstances, this procedure can be repeated three times.

"If the balloting does not result in an election, ... the cardinal electors shall be invited ... to express an opinion about the manner of proceeding. The election will then proceed in accordance with what the absolute majority of the electors decides.

"Nevertheless, there can be no waiving of the requirement that a valid election takes place only by an absolute majority of the votes or else by voting only on the two names which in the ballot immediately preceding have received the greatest number of votes; also in this second case only an absolute majority is required."

"I decree that the dispositions concerning everything that precedes the election of the Roman pontiff and the carrying out of the election itself must be observed in full, even if the vacancy of the Apostolic See should occur as a result of the resignation of the supreme pontiff, in accordance with the provisions of the Code of Canon Law and the Code of Canons of the Eastern Churches."

## The New Pope

After his acceptance (of the canonical election to the papacy) and the designation of his name as pope, "the person elected, if he has already received episcopal ordination, is immediately bishop of the Church of Rome, true pope and head of the college of bishops. He thus acquires and can exercise full and supreme power over the universal Church.

"If the person elected is not already a bishop, he shall immediately be ordained bishop."

After the observance of required formalities, the cardinal electors make an act of homage and obedience to the new pope, who is then introduced to the people, to whom he imparts his blessing "To the City and the World."

"The conclave ends immediately after the new supreme pontiff assents to his election, unless he should determine otherwise."

"After the solemn ceremony of the inauguration of the pontificate and within an appropriate time, the pope will take possession of the Patriarchal Archbasilica of the Lateran."

In accord with longstanding custom, the election of the pope is signalled to the outside world by the white smoke from the burning of the last ballots cast by the cardinals.

# LEBANON SYNOD

*The formulation of pastoral priorities and guidelines was the principal objective of the 119 participants in the Special Assembly for Lebanon of the Synod of Bishops, held Nov. 27 to Dec. 14, 1995, at the Vatican.*

High on the list were unity — in the Church, among Christians and in the nation — and the need to restore to Lebanon its international reputation as a sovereign country in which Christians and Muslims can live in peace.

A message issued at the conclusion of the assembly spotlighted the need for Lebanon's sovereignty while also dealing with ecumenical and interreligious relations, social unity in the multicultural society, education, family life, youth, unemployment, the housing shortage, and emigration of Christians from the country.

The call for church unity was directed toward relations among Catholics of the Roman and five other rites.

One of the synod's efforts was toward "a major and effective relationship of cooperation with Muslim groups," said Cardinal Achille Silvestrini, a co-president of the assembly.

Synod participants presented a number of propositions to Pope John Paul for his consideration in preparing a statement on the accomplishments of the assembly.

The fathers of the synod placed strong emphasis on the part to be played by lay persons in service to church and national union. They said:

"We want our ecclesial and national union to be at the service of everyone, and especially at the service of the most tried — those deprived of hope, freedom, affection, security, or of the goods needed for a decent living for themselves and their families. This service concerns family life as well as cultural, political and economic life. Problems in these sectors are going to be tackled by us together, clergy and laity, in order to find solutions for them.

"However, because of the number of these problems, you lay persons are not only the best placed and most competent; but, above all, you have received from God a special vocation in these areas of secular life in the Church and the grace to take them on ... Shining in faith, hope and charity, you are called by your life and action to work from inside for the sanctification of the world, like the leaven mentioned in the Gospel."

Pope John Paul addressed the synod fathers during the Mass which concluded the assembly Dec. 14. He said in part:

"The synod assemblies that concern the life of the Church in a nation or a continent by their very nature propose to seek the meeting points between men, social groups and nations, and to found them on love.

"This seems to be particularly important for the Near East, and especially for your homeland. We are well aware that Lebanon is a land rich in many religious and cultural traditions. Catholics belonging to various Eastern Churches and the Latin Church live there together with Christians from other churches and communities; with these there are also Muslims. For all of them Lebanon is a 'common task.' All need that special dimension of love that allows men to build together."

## NO ORDINATION OF WOMEN: Church Teaching

*The Congregation for the Doctrine of the Faith issued Nov. 18, 1995, a response to a doubt concerning the teaching and practice of the Church on the ordination of men only to the priesthood. This is the text of the reply.*

Reply to the doubt concerning the teaching in the apostolic letter *Ordinatio Sacerdotalis* ("Priestly Ordination").

*Doubt:* Whether the teaching that the Church has no authority whatsoever to confer priestly ordination on women, which is presented in the apostolic letter *Ordinatio Sacerdotalis,* is to be held definitively, is to be understood as belonging to the deposit of faith.

*Response:* In the affirmative.

This teaching requires definitive assent since, founded on the written word of God and from the beginning constantly preserved and applied in the tradition of the Church, it has been set forth infallibly by the ordinary and universal magisterium (teaching authority of the Church) (cf. Second Vatican Council, Dogmatic Constitution on the Church *Lumen Gentium,* 25, 2). Thus, in the present circumstances, the Roman Pontiff, exercising his proper office of confirming the brethren (cf. Lk. 22:32), has handed on this same teaching by a formal declaration, explicitly stating what is to be held always, everywhere, and by all, as belonging to the deposit of faith.

The Sovereign Pontiff John Paul II, at the audience granted to the undersigned Cardinal Prefect, approved this reply, adopted in the ordinary session of this congregation, and ordered it to be published.

Rome, from the offices of the Congregation for the Doctrine of the Faith, on the Feast of the Apostles Simon and Jude, Oct. 28, 1995.

Joseph Cardinal Ratzinger, prefect; Tarcisio Bertone, archbishop emeritus of Vercelli, secretary.

### Teaching Questioned

Critical questions about the doctrinal status of the Church's teaching were raised in some quarters. The Catholic Theological Society of America, for example, called the teaching into question in a draft paper entitled "Tradition and the Ordination of Women: A Question of Criteria."

After outlining the standard conditions traditionally cited for viewing a church teaching as infallible, the paper said: "None of (the required) conditions is clearly and certainly fulfilled with regard to the teaching that the Church must exclude women from ordination to the priesthood out of fidelity to the revealed will of Christ. And no doctrine should be understood as having been infallibly taught unless this is manifestly the case."

The paper, distributed to some 450 theologians at the society's meeting June 6 to 9, 1996, was placed under study for relevant comment and revisions before the society's next meeting in 1997.

## In Support of the Teaching

Father Avery Dulles addressed the ordination subject at Fordham University Apr. 10, 1996. The title of the lecture was "Gender and Priesthood: Examining the Teaching," from which the following excerpts are given.

*Ordinatio Sacerdotalis* is the culmination of a long series of documents issued under Paul VI and John Paul II since 1975. In these documents the case against women's ordination is made under four principal headings: Bible, tradition, theological reasoning and magisterial authority. These components are not to be taken in isolation but in convergence, since none of them is an independent authority.

**Biblical Argument:** The biblical component in the argument is twofold: first, that Christ did not call women to the apostolic ministry, since he selected only men as members of the Twelve; and second, that the apostles themselves, faithful to the practice of Christ, chose only men for priestly offices, those of bishop, presbyter and their equivalents.

**Tradition:** The argument from tradition is that the Catholic bishops have always observed the norm of conferring sacred orders only on men, and that sects which ordained women to the priesthood or permitted them to perform priestly functions have been denounced as heretical. The Fathers of the early centuries and the theologians of the Middle Ages regarded the question as settled. Since the 16th century, Catholic theologians have regularly characterized the Church's practice as grounded in divine law and have judged the opposed position as heretical or at least verging on heresy.

**Theological Argument:** The theological reasoning is to the effect that the ministerial priest shares in a representative way in the office of Christ as bridegroom of the Church and must therefore be, like Christ, of the male sex. A woman could not suitably represent Christ in this particular capacity.

**Magisterial Teaching:** The teaching of the magisterium, as the fourth component, has likewise been constant. In the early centuries many bishops and a few popes spoke to the question, and over the last 20 years or more explicit statements from the Holy See have made it clear that the hierarchical magisterium is unwavering in holding that the ministerial priesthood cannot be exercised by women.

## Summary

1. In view of the force of the convergent argument and the authority of the papal office, Catholics can and should give the full assent that the Pope has called for.

2. Because the official teaching runs against the prevailing climate of opinion and because plausible objections have been widely publicized, it is inevitable that a significant number of Catholics in a country such as our own will fail to assent.

3. Those who disagree with the approved teaching, while they are entitled to propose their difficulties, should refrain from treating the question as doctrinally undecided and should refrain from strident advocacy. Pressures for doctrinal change at this point would be futile and even detrimental since they would provoke countermeasures on the part of church authorities. The net result would be to divide the Church against itself.

4. The pastoral leadership of the Church, recognizing the complexity of the theological issues and the inevitability of dissenting views, should be patient with Catholics who feel unable to accept the approved position. While asserting the integrity of Catholic doctrine, the bishops should show understanding for dissenters who exhibit good will and avoid disruptive behavior.

Such pastoral consideration, however, should not be taken as a license to contest or call into doubt the tradition of the Church, confirmed as it is by recent pronouncements of exceptional weight.

# AMERICAN SYNOD: Information Wanted

The General Secretariat of the Synod of Bishops issued during the summer of 1996 an Information-seeking document for use in preparing the agenda for the Special Assembly for America of the Synod of Bishops, to be held in the not-too-distant future. The document, called "Lineamenta," deals with the theme of the American Synod, Encounter with the Living Jesus Christ: Way to Conversion, Communion and Solidarity. It seeks input through responses to a set of questions given below under 16 headings.

It is the hope that this *lineamenta* will result in a rich response in every part of the Church in (North and South) America so that the episcopal conferences and the archbishops *sui juris* of the Oriental Churches can have the necessary information to draft their official responses, which will be sent to the General Secretariat. The character and the quantity of the replies will ensure that the synod fathers, gathered in special assembly, will have the material needed for a more in-depth treatment of a topic of great importance for the Church in America.

Therefore, the whole Church in America is invited to participate: diocesan and religious priests, women and men religious, lay men and women, seminaries and faculties of theology, pastoral councils, Catholic movements and groups, parish communities and all church organizations. The more numerous the responses, the more complete and substantial will be the information for those who are responsible to draw up their official reports. This will likewise ensure the complete and substantial character of the ... documents which will be the center of attention and discussion at the Special Assembly of the Synod of Bishops for America.

## QUESTIONS

**Encounter with the Living Christ:** (1) How is the Person of Jesus Christ, the savior and evangelizer, proclaimed and presented to the men and women of the present era so that they might have a true encounter with him in the concrete situations of life? Describe the ways in which the Church can maintain the centrality of the living Jesus Christ in the various manifestations of the Church's life: liturgy, systematic catechesis, formation in the faith, apostolic and charitable activities?

**Conversion in Church and in Society:** (2) List and describe concrete signs of the religious awakening in the local church. On the other hand, what are the most urgent aspects needing conversion within the Church?

**Positive and Negative Elements:** (3) What elements in contemporary society in your area can be considered positive with regard to the Gospel message? What elements of society call for conversion?

**Communion in the Church:** (4) In your area, what are the factors causing significant divisions in the Church with regard to bishops, priests, men and women religious, ecclesial movements, the faithful in general? How can these elements which damage communion be overcome?

**Evaluation:** (5) Evaluate to what measure the teachings of the Second Vatican Council, especially in relation to ecclesial communion, have been faithfully applied in your particular church. In what ways can all the doctrinal and pastoral richness of this council be proposed in response to the Holy Father's invitation to make an "examination of conscience" which "must consider the reception given to the council, this great gift of the Spirit to the Church at the end of the second millennium?"

**Ecumenical and Interreligious Dialogue:** (6) What is being done concretely in the particular churches or at the interdiocesan level to promote ecumenical dialogue, prayer and cooperation in acts of solidarity with our Christian brethren? How are pastoral workers prepared to develop ecumenical activities oriented to building up the unity of the one people of God?

**Interfaith Relations:** (7) Evaluate the relations which your Christian community maintains with other non-Christian religions.

**The Problem of Sects:** (8) Describe briefly the religious situation concerning sects, syncretistic religious movements and other spiritual currents. What are they? What types of activities are they developing? What can the Church do to confirm believers in their faith in light of this situation?

**Evangelization and Culture:** (9) What is the Church doing to evangelize the world of culture (the arts, literature, science, etc.)? How is the Church involved through programs of evangelization in the various fields of education: primary or elementary, secondary or middle school, university, etc.?

**Indigenous Culture:** (10) What are the most significant elements in the cultures of indigenous groups, African-Americans or immigrants — found in the territories of your country or local communities — which deserve to be reconsidered or utilized as "seeds of evangelization?" To what measure do these elements enrich Christian spirituality? To what measure must they be purified of elements which are alien to the Christian faith?

**Popular Piety:** (11) What are the more significant characteristics of popular piety in your area, and to what extent are those aspects taken into consideration in pastoral planning? What place does the Blessed Virgin Mary hold in popular devotion?

**Social Communication:** (12) What is the Church in your area doing at present to promote the proper use of the means of social communication and to make them useful tools at the service of the new evangelization? Describe the Church's presence in the many forms of the so-called modern areopagus.

**Social Solidarity:** (13) What activities are promoted by the Church in your area to offer assistance in solidarity to those most in need, and how do the faithful respond in general to these initiatives? What external collaboration, at the ecclesial or civil level, does the Church receive for this aid of solidarity? Are there programs for forming a consciousness of solidarity in persons or groups having a significant role in society.

**Social Problems:** (14) What use is being made of the Church's social teaching in your area in the new evangelization in light of the diverse situations which demand social action, e.g., human development, migration, the problems of the world of work, etc.? What means are being used to spread an awareness of the Church's social teaching within the Church and beyond the ecclesial dimension?

**Promotion of Human Life:** (15) How does the Church promote respect for human life in all its phases, from conception in the mother's womb to the point of natural death? Give complete examples of the sensitivity of the Christian community in your area concerning this aspect.

**Other Common Themes:** (16) In light of the topic of the special assembly, give any remarks and suggestions on matters common to the whole American continent which, in your opinion, have not been treated sufficiently in the *lineamenta* or not included in the above series of questions.

# WE ARE CHURCH

*Circulation of a referendum for church reforms was announced by a coalition of several activist groups May 22, 1996, at a press conference in Washington. Sponsors of the project, entitled "We Are Church," said they hoped to obtain a million signers of the following document by Pentecost 1997.*

The movement for renewal of the Catholic Church is spreading like the fire of Pentecost across the globe. More than 2.3 million Austrian and German Catholics have signed referenda calling for widespread reforms. Similar initiatives have been undertaken in Italy, France, Belgium and Australia.

In union with our Austrian and German sisters and brothers, and those in other lands, we U.S. Catholics urge support from all sectors of our church for long overdue reforms. We seek genuine dialogue in the whole church on these issues and gradual but steady implementation of the referendum's goals. These changes are necessary for the Gospel message to be heard by the whole people of God as we enter the new millennium.

1. We believe in a loving church where the equality of all the faithful is respected, the gulf between clergy and laity is bridged, and the people of God participate in the process of selecting their bishops and pastors.

2. We believe in a church with equal rights for women, where women are full participants in all

official decision-making and are welcomed in all ministries, including the diaconate and the ministerial priesthood.

3. We believe in a church where priests may choose either a celibate or noncelibate way of life, where the right of a congregation to the Eucharist and pastoral care is more important than a rule of canon law.

4. We believe in a church which affirms:
• the goodness of sexuality;
• the primacy of conscience in deciding issues of sexual morality (for example: birth control);
• the human rights of all persons regardless of sexual orientation;
• the importance and urgency of issues other than sexual morality (for example: peace and nonviolence, social justice, preservation of the environment).
• We believe in a church which:
• affirms people rather than condemns them;
• respects primacy of conscience in all moral decision-making;
• embraces and welcomes those who are divorced and remarried, married priests, theologians and others who exercise freedom of speech.

We sign this with prayerful hope for a new movement of the Spirit in our church.

## Participating Groups

Groups participating in the referendum project include: the Women's Ordination Conference, Catholics Speak Out, Call to Action /Northern Virginia, Catholics for a Free Choice; Chicago Catholic Women; Fellowship of Southern Illinois Laity, Future Church, Green Nation (San Jose, Calif.), Long Island Women's Ordination Conference, Loretto Women's Network, National Coalition of American Nuns, Renewal Coordinating Community, Southeastern Pennsylvania Women's Ordination Conference.

# WILL THE REFERENDUM CREATE NEW POLARIZATION?

*This was the question posed by Bishop Anthony Pilla, president of the National Conference of Catholic Bishops, in a statement issued May 22, several hours after We Are Church announced its signature-solicitation plan.*

The Holy Father and the bishops have the obligation to foster unity among all Catholics. Pope John Paul II has been a model of teaching insistently, but also persuading patiently. In that spirit, I want to reiterate faithfully the teaching of the Church, while also affirming that a spirit of dialogue is appropriate to the Church.

However, for it to be successful, dialogue needs to be honest; and in all honesty I must say that I do not believe this referendum announced today contributes toward creating a spirit of dialogue. Ignored by those sponsoring the referendum are their brother and sister Catholics who do not share their point of view, since this referendum asks only for agreement. Thus, it is hardly an opportunity for all Catholics to enter into dialogue. The text of the referendum also mixes matters on which discussion and debate are possible with others that involve church teaching. It is not even clear that the organizers intend for signers to agree with everything the text proposes.

Because of all these factors, I ask those approached to sign this petition to reflect prayerfully and seriously on the confusion that may be created by a technique so inadequate and inappropriate to deal with these matters. To those Catholics offended by a tactic that implies appealing the teaching of the Church to judgment by media, I ask them to register their disagreement in a way that reflects the love for one another that is the sign that we are Christ's disciples.

In honesty, I also have to say that, with regard to greater participation in the life of the Church by laity, and in particular by women, the Holy See and the bishops favor this goal. It is finding ways to implement it that can be difficult, given past history and the need in the universal Church to be sensitive to both its local and worldwide expressions.

## Teachings Being Challenged

A more painful honesty for those sponsoring the referendum is to admit that they are, in some instances, challenging church teachings. A vague appeal to "reform" is insufficient reason to challenge either church teaching or practice. Seeking the spotlight of the media on issues which are hardly new to the public also is not an appropriate way to foster serious discussion of specifically theological concerns.

The Second Vatican Council, which is the source of reform of the Church in our time, clearly affirmed the centrality of the papal ministry to the Church and the obligation of Catholics to assent to the teaching of the Holy Father even when he is not teaching infallibly. This referendum calls for debate on long-standing teachings which the present Holy Father and his immediate predecessors have addressed and reaffirmed. Fidelity to the council means acceptance of these decisions. Although there is room for discussion and dialogue on matters of discipline, to be a Catholic, by definition, means sharing a common religious heritage and moral vision. It is not something purely subjective, radically private and self-constructed. It is a system of religious teachings and moral imperatives which are to be freely embraced and faithfully handed on to the next generation.

## Inappropriate Mechanism

In response to a request for further dialogue which I was taking to my brother bishops, I recently wrote to a leader of one of the organizations sponsoring this referendum that it would import "into the life of the Church a mechanism which is not appropriate to it and which may have seriously unfortunate consequences. For example, it is not hard to imagine, in a Church as vibrant and diverse as ours in the United States, that your referendum will spark a counter-referendum, leaving some Catholics polarized over certain issues while the majority of Catholics find their witness to the Gospel made less effective by these divisions."

Today the Christian churches and ecclesial communities are seeking to overcome divisions among themselves, acknowledging how centuries of division have impaired our effectiveness in preaching the Gospel. In the spirit of that search for unity, I appeal to the leaders of this referendum not to create new divisions in our own ecclesial family by continued challenges to the teachings and the authority of the Church that has nurtured the faith of us all."

# CATHOLIC COMMON GROUND PROJECT

*Cardinal Joseph L. Bernardin of Chicago drew wide attention with his announcement Aug. 12, 1996, of a new initiative to overcome what is being regarded as a debilitating polarization of Catholics in the United States.*

The name of the initiative is the Catholic Common Ground Project. Its 3,000 page foundational document, "Called To Be Catholic," was developed by the National Pastoral Life Center in consultation with Cardinal Bernardin and other prelates, priests, religious and lay persons. One of the key figures in planning and implementing the statement is Msgr. Philip J. Murnion, a pastoral planning specialist.

The framework document for the project says U.S. Catholicism is being deprived of its vitality and power by "distrust, acrimony and deadlock," and a "dynamic of fear and polarization."

It urges divided Catholics to come together in constructive dialogue, emphasizing their common faith and commitment. It asks them to begin devoting their energies again to the central tasks of building the Church and strengthening its institutions, its mission and its witness to the world.

## Accountability

It says Catholics, whatever their particular interests or agenda, "must be accountable to the Catholic tradition and to the Spirit-filled, living Church that brings to us the revelation of God and Jesus."

It says there can be "legitimate debate, discussion and diversity" about aspects of church teaching and tradition, but "accountability does demand serious engagement with the tradition and its authoritative representatives. It rules out pop scholarship, sound-bite theology, unhistorical assertions and flippant dismissals that have become all too common on both the right and the left of the Church."

Cardinal Bernardin said he planned to convene conferences, beginning with one in 1997, on the Church and U.S. culture, in which representatives of different viewpoints come together in dialogue, trying to understand the others' perspectives rather than to attack them.

Reactions to the Catholic Common Ground Project were mixed. Among those in support were members of the project's advisory committee, including Cardinal Roger M. Mahony, Archbishops Daniel E. Pilarczyk and Rembert G. Weakland, and Bishop James W. Malone. On the critical side were Cardinals Bernard F. Law and James A. Hickey. Bishop Anthony M. Pilla, president of the National Conference of Catholic Bishops, said he would "pray for the success of this effort with hope that its stated purpose and goal of better understanding and reconciliation can be achieved."

## Cardinal Law's View

In a statement issued Aug. 12, Cardinal Law described "Called To Be Catholic" an "unfortunate" choice for a framework statement for the unity initiative.

He said the statement "breathes an ideological bias" and makes "gratuitous assumptions."

"The fundamental flaw in this document is its appeal for 'dialogue' as a path to 'common ground,'" he said. "The Church already has 'common ground.' It is found in sacred Scripture and tradition, and it is mediated to us through the authoritative and binding teaching of the magisterium."

Cardinal Law described the Church's current "pastoral crisis" as the "disconnect" of many Catholics from the Church's faith and practice.

"Dissent from revealed truth or the authoritative teaching of the Church cannot be 'dialogued away,'" he said. "Truth and dissent from truth are not equal partners in ecclesial dialogue."

## Cardinal Hickey's View

Cardinal James A. Hickey commented on the Catholic Common Ground Project in a critical statement released Aug. 13. He said, in part:

"The statement of the National Pastoral Life Center obscures the true 'common ground' for any effort to bring about unity within the Church. That true 'common ground' is found in Scripture and tradition as handed on through the teaching office of the Holy Father and the bishops."

"We cannot achieve church unity by accommodating those who dissent from church teaching — whether on the left or on the right. To compromise the faith of the Church is to forfeit our 'common ground' and to risk deeper polarization."

"Unfortunately, the statement from the National Pastoral Life Center does not give the magisterium its due. To be sure, it recognizes the magisterium as authoritative and deserving of respect. But it also seems to regard magisterial teaching as only one element of a consensus that is to be forged out of contrasting opinions. The statement does not sufficiently acknowledge the truth of authoritative church teaching. While decrying partisanship, the statement tends to reduce authoritative church teaching to a partisan voice in debates on neuralgic issues."

"In several, places, the statement seems to give too much weight to the opinions of Catholics who do not really agree with the magisterium. For example, it speaks of 'the gap between church teachings and the convictions of the faithful.' It even seems to say that church teaching must be 'received,' that is, "accepted," by a majority of Catholics before it can be regarded as authentic."

"The truth of church teaching is not gauged by how many Catholics accept it. On the contrary, church doctrine on faith and morals is deeply rooted in what the Lord has said and done to save us. It is his message we must preach, even when it is distinctly unpopular."

"The statement correctly recognizes that some Catholics today do not really know their faith. But it does not sufficiently acknowledge that poorly catechized Catholics are ill-equipped to form sound convictions about faith and morals. Indeed, they are very vulnerable to cultural influences such as the news media and the entertainment industry which often seek to ridicule and undermine church teaching."

# BEIJING CONFERENCE AND STATEMENT: Vatican Delegation

*Mary Ann Glendon, head of the Holy See's delegation, delivered the following intervention during the final plenary meeting of the Fourth World Conference on Women held Sept. 4 to 15 in Beijing, China. The text of the intervention is given below.*

"When one looks at the great process of women's liberation," one sees that the journey has been a difficult one, with its "share of mistakes," but headed toward a better future for women. These are the words of Pope John Paul II. And he goes on to say, "This journey must go on!" The Holy See delegation joins its voice to his: This great journey must go on!

Women's voyage has been marked by false starts and disappointments as well as by luminous achievements. There have been times, as in the Industrial Revolution, when old forms of oppression were exchanged for new as well as times when intelligence and good will have triumphed.

The (conference) documents before us reflect that complex and uneven history of women's search. They are full of promise but often short on concrete commitment, and in certain respects one could ask if the long-time consequences will really serve the good of women.

## Critical Areas

The delegation of the Holy See has worked hard in a constructive way and in a spirit of good will to make the documents more responsive to women. Certainly the living heart of these documents lies in their sections on the needs of women in poverty, on strategies for development, on literacy and education, on ending violence against women, on a culture of peace and in access to employment, land, capital and technology. My delegation is pleased to note a close correspondence between these points and Catholic social teaching.

My delegation would be remiss in its duty to women, however, if it did not also indicate several critical areas where it strongly disagrees with the text.

My delegation regrets to note in the text an exaggerated individualism in which key relevant provisions of the Universal Declaration of Human Rights are slighted — for example, the obligation to provide "special care and assistance" to motherhood. This selectivity thus marks another stop in the colonization of the broad and rich discourse of universal rights by an impoverished libertarian rights dialect. Surely this international gathering could have done more for women and girls than to leave them alone with their rights!

## Disproportionate Attention

Surely we must do more for the girl child in poor nations than give lip service to providing access to education, health and social service, while carefully avoiding any concrete commitment of new and additional resources to that end.

Surely we can do better than to address the health needs of girls and women by paying disproportionate attention to sexual and reproductive health. Moreover, ambiguous language concerning unqualified control over sexuality and fertility could be interpreted as including societal endorsement of abortion and homosexuality.

A document that respects women's dignity should address the health of the whole woman. A document that respects women's intelligence should devote at least as much attention to literacy as to fertility.

Finally, Madam President, because my delegation is hopeful that out of these documents, which are in some ways at odds with themselves, the good for women will ultimately prevail, it wishes to associate itself with the consensus only on those above-mentioned aspects of the documents that the Holy See considers to be positive and at the service of the real well-being of women.

Unfortunately, the Holy See's participation in the consensus can be only a partial one because of numerous points in the documents which are incompatible with what the Holy See and other countries deem favorable to the true advancement of women. These points are indicated in the reservations which my delegation has annexed to this statement.

My delegation is confident that women themselves will overcome the limitations of, and bring out what is best in, these documents. As John Paul II has so well put it, "The path that lies ahead will be long and difficult; nevertheless, we must have courage to set out on that path and the courage to go on to the end."

I would ask that the text of this statement, the reservations formally indicated below as well as the statement of interpretation of the term *gender*, be included in the report of the conference.

## Reservations and Statements of Interpretation

The Holy See, in conformity with its nature and particular mission, in partial consensus on the documents of the Fourth World Conference on Women, wishes to express its position regarding those documents and make reservations on some of the concepts used in them.

1. The Holy See wishes to reaffirm the dignity and worth of women and the equal rights of men and women, and regrets the failure of the Platform for Action to explicitly reassert this concept.

2. The Holy See, in line with the Universal Declaration of Human Rights, stresses that the family is the basic unit of society and is based on marriage as an equal partnership between husband and wife to which the transmission of life is entrusted. It regrets that in the Platform for Action references were not

made to such a fundamental societal unit without banal qualifying language (cf. Strategic Objective L. 0).

3. The Holy See can only interpret such terms as *women's right to control their sexuality, women's right to control ... their fertility* or *couples and individuals* as referring to the responsible use of sexuality within marriage. At the same time, the Holy See formally condemns all forms of violence against and exploitation of women and girls.

4. The Holy See reaffirms the reservations it expressed at the conclusion of the International Conference on Population and Development, held in Cairo Sept. 5-13, 1994, which are included in the report of that conference, concerning the interpretation given to the terms *reproductive health, sexual health* and *reproductive rights*. In particular, the Holy See reiterates that it does not consider abortion or abortion services to be a dimension of reproductive health or reproductive health services. The Holy See does not endorse any form of legislation which gives legal recognition to abortion.

## No Change in Catholic Position

5. With regard to the terms *family planning* or *widest range of family planning services* and other terms concerning family planning services or regulation of fertility, the Holy See's actions during this conference should in no way be interpreted as changing its well-known position concerning those family planning methods that the Catholic Church considers morally unacceptable or concerning family planning services that do not respect the liberty of spouses, the human dignity or the human rights of those concerned. The Holy See in no way endorses contraception or the use of condoms either as a family planning measure or in HIV/AIDS prevention programs.

6. The Holy See maintains that nothing in the Platform for Action or in other documents' references therein is to be interpreted as requiring any health professional or health facility to perform, cooperate with, refer or arrange for services to which they have objections on the basis of religious belief or moral or ethical conviction.

7. The Holy See interprets all references to the term *forced pregnancy* as a specific instrument of armed conflict, in the context in which that term appears in the Vienna Declaration and Program of Action, Part II, Paragraph 38.

8. The Holy See interprets the term *gender* as described in the statement annexed to these reservations.

9. The Holy See does not associate itself with the consensus on the entire Chapter IV Section C concerning health; it wishes to place a general reservation on the entire section, and it would ask that this general reservation be noted in the chapter. This section devotes a totally unbalanced attention to sexual and reproductive health in comparison to women's other health needs, including means to address maternal mortality and morbidity. Furthermore, the Holy See cannot accept ambiguous terminology concerning unqualified control over sexuality and fertility, particularly as it could be interpreted as a societal endorsement of abortion or homosexuality. The

reservation on this chapter does not, however, indicate any reduction on the Holy See's commitment toward the promotion of the health of women and the girl child.

## Excessive Individualism

10. The Holy See does not join the consensus and expresses a reservation on Paragraph 232(f), with its reference to a text (Paragraph 97) on a right of women to have "control over their sexuality." This ambiguous term could be understood as endorsing sexual relationships outside heterosexual marriage. It asks that this reservation be noted on the paragraph. On the other hand, however, the Holy See wishes to associate itself with the condemnation of violence against women asserted in Paragraph 97, as well as with the importance of mutuality and shared responsibility, respect and free consent in conjugal relations as stated in that paragraph.

The Holy See, with regard to the entire section on human rights, with the exception of quotations from or restatements of already existing human rights instruments, expresses its concern about an excessive individualism in its treatment of human rights. The Holy See further recalls that the mandate of the Fourth World Conference on Women did not include the affirmation of new human rights.

11. With regard to the phrase *women rights are human rights*, the Holy See interprets this phrase to mean that women should have the full enjoyment of all human rights and fundamental freedoms.

12. With regard to all references to international agreements, the Holy See reserves its position in this regard, in particular on any existing international agreement mentioned in the documents, consistent with its manner of acceptance or nonacceptance of them

The Holy See requests that these reservations, together with the annexed statement of interpretation on the term *gender*, be included in the report of the conference.

## Interpretation of the Term "Gender"

In accepting that the word *gender* in this document is to be understood according to ordinary usage in the U.N. context, the Holy See associates itself with the common meaning of that word in languages where it exists.

The term *gender* is understood by the Holy See as grounded in biological sexual identity, male or female. Furthermore, the Platform for Action itself (cf. Paragraph 193(c) clearly uses the term *both genders*.

The Holy See thus excludes dubious interpretations based on world views which assert that sexual identity can be adapted indefinitely to suit new and different purposes.

It also dissociates itself from the biological determinist notion that all the roles and relations of the two sexes are fixed in a single static pattern.

Pope John Paul insists on the distinctiveness and complementarity of women and men. At the same time, he has applauded the assumption of new roles by women, stressed the degree to which cultural conditioning has been an obstacle to women's progress, and exhorted men to assist in "the great process of women's liberation."

In his recent "Letter to Women," (published July 10, 1995), the Pope explained the Church's nuanced view in the following way: "One can also appreciate that the presence of a certain diversity of roles is in no way prejudicial to women, provided that this diversity is not the result of an arbitrary imposition, but is rather an expression of what is specific to being male and female" (No. 11).

# HABITAT II: U.N. Conference on Human Settlements

*The Holy See was represented at the U.N. Conference on Human Settlements by a 14-member delegation led by Archbishop Renato Martino, head of the Vatican's permanent observer mission at the United Nations. The conference, in session from June 3 to 15, 1996, in Istanbul, recognized the right to adequate shelter for every individual and his or her family, and the obligation of nations to provide opportunities for the exercise of this right.*

These were topics of an address to the conference by Msgr. Diarmuid Martin, adjunct head of the Vatican delegation. Vatican reservations and statements of interpretation related to the final document issued by the conference were reported to the plenary assembly June 14 by Archbishop Martino. Following are excerpts from their statements.

## Right to Housing

The Holy See has continuously stressed the equal importance of the two themes of this conference: "Adequate Shelter for All" and "Sustainable Human Settlements." Seen from the point of view of the individuals, families and communities of our world, these two themes cannot be separated. Every child, woman and man needs both the intimacy of the home and the possibility of human enrichment and growth which the community in which they live offers them. Adequate shelter is not simply a roof over one's head. It is a much broader, richer notion which permits all persons to live in dignity and to realize themselves fully, in individual achievement, in their family life at home, at school, at work, in recreation and the enjoyment of creation, in worship, and in working and living together in safety and harmony.

## A Principal Achievement

One of the principal achievements for which this conference will be remembered is the outcome of its negotiations on the right to adequate housing, for all persons and their families. The Universal Declaration of Human Rights recognized this right clearly within the fundamental vocabulary of human rights language. At Istanbul we have taken this right from the textbooks and have given it a new concrete embodiment. Governments have committed themselves to the promotion and protection of this right and to its application. And they have recognized this as a specific obligation. This action of our conference will give new hope and confidence to many people concerning what the United Nations organization can do in its mandate to serve the good of mankind.

Now it is up to the governments of the participating states, to their partners, especially local authorities, and also to all the elements of civil society to make sure that our actions become reality. We must never allow the term "progressive realization," which we use, to hold us back from the obligation to achieve the "full realization" of this right.

The Holy See wishes to play its part, consistent with its own nature and mission, to give concrete realization to this right, and to lead to a broad-based commitment of society in this regard. (Accordingly, the Holy See recognized two significant housing initiatives, one in Chile and the other in Rwanda, with gifts of $50,000 each.).

## RESERVATIONS

1. The Holy See, in conformity with its nature and particular mission, joins the consensus on the documents of the Second United Nations Conference on Human Settlements, Habitat II, and wishes to express the following reservations and statements of interpretation regarding certain concepts in them.

The Holy See reiterates the reservations it expressed at the conclusion of the International Conference on Population and Development, held in Cairo from 5 to 13 September 1994 and which are included in the report of that conference, concerning the interpretation to be given to the terms "reproductive health," "sexual health" and "reproductive rights." In particular, the Holy See reiterates that it does not consider abortions or abortion services to be a dimension of reproductive health or reproductive health services. The Holy See for moral reasons does not endorse any legislation which gives legal recognition to abortion.

With regard to the term "family planning" or other terms concerning family planning services, the Holy See's actions during this conference should in no way be interpreted as changing its well-known position concerning those family planning methods that the Catholic Church considers morally unacceptable or concerning family planning services that do not respect the liberty of spouses, the human dignity or the human rights of those concerned.

2. The Holy See, in line with the Universal Declaration of Human Rights, stresses that the family is the basic unit of society and is based on marriage as an equal partnership between husband and wife, to which the transmission of human life is entrusted. It considers references to "various forms of the family," in par. 18 of the Habitat Agenda, as references to different cultural expressions of the family as described above.

3. The Holy See understands the use of the term "gender" in this document in the light of its statement made at the conclusion of the Fourth World Conference on Women, held at Beijing 4 to 15 September, 1995, and included in the report of that conference.

4. With regard to all references to international agreements, in particular any existing international agreements mentioned in the documents, the Holy See reserves its position in a manner consistent with its acceptance or non-acceptance of these agreements and with any reservations it may have expressed.

5. The Holy See requests that these reservations and statements of interpretation be inserted integrally into the Report of the Conference on Human Settlements (Habitat II).

# THE PARTIAL-BIRTH ABORTION BAN VETO

*The following letter of Apr. 16, 1996, was addressed to President Clinton by eight U.S. cardinals and Bishop Anthony Pilla, president of the National Conference of Catholic Bishops.*

It is with deep sorrow and dismay that we respond to your April 10 veto of the Partial-Birth Abortion Ban Act.

Your veto of this bill is beyond comprehension for those who hold human life sacred. It will ensure the continued use of the most heinous act to kill a tiny infant just seconds from taking his or her first breath outside the womb.

At the veto ceremony you told the American people that you "had no choice but to veto the bill." Mr. President, you and you alone had the choice of whether or not to allow children, almost completely born, to be killed brutally in partial-birth abortions. Members of both houses of Congress made their choice. They said no to partial-birth abortions. American women voters have made their choice. According to a February 1996 poll by Fairbank, Maslin, Maullin & Associates, 78 percent of women voters said no to partial-birth abortions. Your choice was to say yes and to allow this killing more akin to infanticide than abortion to continue.

During the veto ceremony you said you had asked Congress to change H.R. 1833 to allow partial-birth abortions to be done for "serious adverse health consequences" to the mother. You added that, if Congress had included that exception, "everyone in the world will know what we're talking about."

## Specious Definition of Health

On the contrary, Mr. President, not everyone in the world would know that *health,* as the courts define it in the context of abortion, means virtually anything that has to do with a woman's overall "well-being." For example, most people have no idea that, if a woman has an abortion because she is not married, the law considers that an abortion for a "health" reason.

Similarly, if a woman is "too young" or "too old," if she is emotionally upset by pregnancy or if pregnancy interferes with schooling or career, the law considers those situations as "health" reasons for abortion. In other words, as you know and we know, an exception for "health" means abortion on demand.

You say there is a difference between a "health" exception and an exception for "serious adverse health consequences." Mr. President, what is the difference — legally — between a woman's being too young and being seriously too young? What is the

difference — legally — between being emotionally upset and being "seriously" emotionally upset? From your study of this issue, Mr. President, you must know that most partial-birth abortions are done for reasons that are purely elective.

It was instructive that the veto ceremony included no physician able to explain how a woman's physical health is protected by almost fully delivering her living child and then killing that child in the most inhumane manner imaginable before completing the delivery. As a matter of fact, a partial-birth abortion presents a health risk to the woman. Dr. Warren Hern, who wrote the most widely used textbook on how to perform abortions, has said of partial-birth abortions: "I would dispute any statement that this is the safest procedure to use."

Mr. President, all abortions are lethal for unborn children, and many are unsafe for their mothers. This is even more evident in the late-term, partial-birth abortion, in which children are killed cruelly, their mothers placed at risk and the society that condones it brutalized in the process.

## Strenuous Opposition

As Catholic bishops and citizens of the United States, we strenuously oppose and condemn your veto of H.R. 1833, which will allow partial-birth abortions to continue.

In the coming weeks and months, each of us, as well as our bishops' conference, will do all we can to educate people about partial-birth abortions. We will inform them that partial-birth abortions will continue because you chose to veto H.R. 1833.

We will also urge Catholics and other people of good will — including the 65 percent of self-described "pro-choice" voters who oppose partial-birth abortions — to do all that they can to urge Congress to override this shameful veto.

Mr. President, your action on this matter takes our nation to a critical turning point in its treatment of helpless human brings inside and outside the womb. It moves our nation one step further toward acceptance of infanticide. Combined with the two recent federal appeals court decisions seeking to legitimize assisted suicide, it sounds the alarm that public officials are moving our society ever more rapidly to embrace a culture of death.

Writing this response to you in unison is, on our part, virtually unprecedented. It will, we hope, underscore our resolve to be unremitting and unambiguous in our defense of human life.

## STAND UP FOR LIFE

*"Stand Up for Life" is the title of the following statement adopted unanimously by the National Conference of Catholic Bishops in June, 1996. It called for an override of President Clinton's veto of a bill that would have outlawed a late term procedure more like infanticide than abortion.*

Just over a year ago, Pope John Paul II urged Catho-

lics and all persons of good will to stand up for human life. With an unmistakable note of urgency, he spoke of a growing "culture of death." This culture, he warned, claims to advance human freedom but "ends up by becoming the freedom of 'the strong' against the weak, who have no choice but to submit."

Was the Pope unduly pessimistic in assessing our

society at the end of the 20th century? On the contrary, events of the past few months have shown how accurate he was.

Two federal courts ruled this year to exclude seriously ill people from the protection of laws against assisted suicide. Such people, the courts said, have a "right" to receive lethal drugs from their physicians so they can kill themselves. Such rulings devalue the lives of people most in need of compassion and care. We must do all we can to help bring about their reversal.

### Court and President vs. Congress

During this same period, the president of the United States has acted to extend the logic of our Supreme Court's gravely erroneous abortion decisions. He contends that the U.S. Constitution forbids any meaningful legal protection for children who are almost completely born alive and, indeed, that it should forbid such protection. The president is defending partial-birth abortion, a particularly heinous and violent way of killing an infant during the process of birth.

(In the procedure, the fetus is partially delivered, surgical scissors are stabbed into the base of the head and the brain is removed by suction, permitting easier delivery.)

Congress voted to stop this shameful practice. However, because the president vetoed the bill, partial-birth abortion — more truly seen as a form of infanticide — continues in our country. We urge the Congress of the United States to override the president's veto of the Partial-Birth Abortion Act.

### Prayer and Action for Override

Catholic parishes across the country have begun to provide parishioners with information about partial-birth abortion. We will encourage Catholics and other people of good will to urge their senators and representatives to override the president's veto.

On July 11 (1996) churches nationwide will conduct a day of prayer and fasting for life. We will pray that our country rejects partial-birth abortion,

We will pray that the lives of all may be respected, protected and nurtured — including the lives of innocent, unborn children and those now threatened in the final stages of life. It will be our prayer that the culture of death be transformed by a culture of life, by a civilization of love.

We are not unaware of or indifferent to the serious challenges that confront women with difficult pregnancies. Although we can never experience first-hand the hardships and pressures they may face, we hold out our hands and our hearts — with the support of the spiritual, social, medical, legal and financial resources available to us — to help women facing a crisis due to pregnancy.

### Healing Ministry

To those who have had abortions, we say with Pope John Paul: We are "aware of the many factors which may have influenced your decision" and do not doubt that it may have been "painful and even shattering." Without ever condoning abortion, which remains terribly wrong, we encourage women and men who have been involved in abortion not to give up hope. The Church continues to offer her healing ministry, which has helped many thousands of women, men and families to deal with the aftermath of abortion.

We also admire and support the many women who, facing what may seem insurmountable difficulties, nonetheless decide to give their children the one gift no one else can give — the gift of life.

We urge Catholics and others to study and discuss these pressing issues of life and death, and to stand up for life. At the same time, we know that the final outcome of this struggle lies in the hands of an infinitely loving God. As Pope John Paul reminds us: "There is certainly an enormous disparity between the powerful resources available to the forces promoting the 'culture of death' and the means at the disposal of those working for a 'culture of life and love.' But we know that we can rely on the help of God, for whom nothing is impossible" ("The Gospel of Life," 100),

## INCOMPREHENSIBLE INTENTION

*Cardinal Joseph L. Bernardin of Chicago wrote the following letter to President Clinton Apr. 1, 1996, when it was already known that the president intended to veto the Partial-Birth Abortion Ban Act.*

This letter will come as no surprise because of our previous correspondence. I am profoundly saddened by your intention to veto the Partial-Birth Abortion Ban Act. In fact, Mr. President, I find it incomprehensible that you should choose to ignore such an unusual consensus on abortion-related legislation. The bill enjoyed majority support among the American people and among our elected representatives in the House and Senate.

Likewise, I do not find the reasons you have given for your veto to be convincing — medically, legally

or morally — for allowing such an abhorrent procedure as partial-birth abortion to be performed on any member of our human family.

Mr. President, as you have so often noted, we already live in a society plagued by brutality, particularly against children. By your veto, however, I fear that you will send a very disturbing message to the people of this nation, one to which persons of good will must give serious consideration as they cast their ballots in November.

Please reconsider your position. Now is a time for reasoned debate and consensus building. The politics of extremism must be left behind. Let us work together to protect the lives of the vulnerable — most especially the unborn.

## ROE V. WADE; OTHER ABORTION DECISIONS

The key abortion-related decisions were handed down by the U.S. Supreme Court in the case of Roe v. Wade and the companion case of Dole v. Bolton.

The court ruled 7-to-2 Jan. 22, 1973:

(1) During the first three months of pregnancy, a woman's right to privacy is paramount. Accordingly,

she has an unrestricted right to abortion with the consent and cooperation of a physician.

(2) In the second trimester, the principle controlling legislation is the health or welfare of the mother.

(3) In the third trimester, the "state subsequent to viability," the controlling principles of legislation are the State's "interest in the potentiality of human life" and "the preservation of the life or health of the mother."

The decisions legalized abortion nationwide, practically on demand.

In the 23 years subsequent to the Roe v. Wade, Dole v. Bolton decisions, an estimated 40 million legal abortions have been performed in the United States.

## Webster v. Reproductive Health Services

The court upheld, July 3, 1989, 5 to 4, provisions of the Missouri law:

(1) forbidding public employees to perform or assist in abortions

(2) barring the use of public facilities for abortion;

(3) requiring physicians to take steps to determine fetal viability when a woman 20 or more weeks pregnant seeks an abortion.

At issue was an appeal of a lower court ruling in Webster v. Reproductive Health Services, Inc., with respect to the statute, Missouri Senate Committee Substitute for House Bill No. 1596, which was signed into law in June, 1986.

## Rust v. Sullivan:

The U.S. Supreme Court ruled 5-to-4 May 23, 1991 that provisions of Title X (the National Family Planning Program) of the 1970 Public Health Service Act were in accord with the U.S. Constitution. Pertinent regulations forbade family planning clinics from counseling or advising abortion if they received federal funds disbursed under Title X.

The Court observed:

(1) Abortion cannot be equated with family planning. The family planning legislation of 1970 distinguished between abortion and family planning,

and intended to restrict federal funding to planning human life, not destroying it.

(2) The admission of a legal right (in this case, abortion) does not necessarily imply a government duty to promote the right.

(3) The fact that abortion is a legal right does not mean the government and those who do not subscribe to this right have to pay for it.

The Court ruled that the government can establish rules for funding only family planning programs which do not "encourage, promote or advocate abortion."

## Planned Parenthood v. Casey

On June 29, 1992, the court declared constitutional provisions of a 1989 Pennsylvania law regulating the practice of abortion.

Women seeking abortion must receive information about risks, fetal development and alternatives to abortion, and must wait at least 24 hours after receiving such information before having an abortion.

Medical offices must fie detailed, confidential reports about each abortion performed.

Minors must get permission from one parent or a judge before having an abortion.

## Pro-Abortion Executive Orders

Abortion developments in 1993 included President Clinton's executive orders, effective as of Jan. 22, 1994, which reversed:

• regulations prohibiting abortion counseling in federally funded family planning clinics;

• a ban on fetal tissue research;

• restrictions on access to abortion in U.S. military hospitals overseas;

• the "Mexico City Policy" which denied U.S. foreign aid to programs overseas that promoted abortion.

U.S. Supreme Court Associate Justice Antonin Scalia refused Aug. 18, 1994, to set aside a lower court order permitting the federal government to cut off Medicaid funding to Louisiana because of its practice of paying only for abortions deemed necessary to save a mother's life.

# ASSISTED SUICIDE

The 9th U.S. Circuit Court of Appeals moved the nation a giant step toward allowing physician-assisted suicide with its Mar. 6, 1996, ruling that the terminally ill have a constitutional "right to die" when and how they wish with a doctor's help. (The 2nd U.S. Circuit Court of Appeals ruled in the same vein Apr. 2, 1996.)

The court's 8-to-3 decision invalidating a Washington state law against assisted suicide drew sharp criticisms from many religious, medical, legal and pro-life leaders. It was the first time in the United States that a federal appeals court asserted a "constitutionally protected liberty interest in determining the time and manner of one's own death."

"This ruling paves and broadens the road to a complete culture of death," said Cardinal Bernard F. Law, chairman of the bishops' Committee for Pro-Life Activities.

"This is fundamentally incompatible with the physician's role as healer and caregiver," said Dr. Thomas Reardon, chairman of the American Medical Association's Task Force on Quality Care at the End of Life.

The Catholic bishops of Washington urged an immediate appeal to the U.S. Supreme Court for reversal of the decision.

"It does not create 'a right to die,' it creates a right to be killed," they said.

## A THREAT OF UNFORESEEABLE MAGNITUDE

*This statement was issued Mar. 19, 1996, by the Administrative Committee of the National Conference of Catholic Bishops.*

In 1991, the National Conference of Catholic Bishops warned: "To destroy the boundary between healing and killing would mark a radical departure from longstanding legal and medical traditions of our country, posing a threat of unforeseeable magnitude to vulnerable members of our society" (Statement on Euthanasia, Sept. 2, 1991). Many states, including Washington, have heeded such warnings and rejected proposals to allow physicians to prescribe lethal drugs to their patients.

Now, the U.S. Court of Appeals for the 9th Circuit has declared a Washington state law against assisted suicide invalid as applied to the "terminally ill." By doing so, the court's ruling excludes a class of citizens from the protection of laws designed to protect all against deadly harm. The court's opinion rides roughshod over important ethical distinctions, legal precedents and the prevailing judgment of the American Medical Association and medical specialists who treat terminally ill patients. This ruling poses a massive threat to innocent life and to American ideals of equal protection under law. It creates a "right to die" that threatens to sweep away all meaningful limits or restrictions.

While the court speaks of allowing physicians to prescribe lethal drugs for use by "terminally ill, competent adults" who wish to commit suicide, its decision has far broader implications. The decision would lead one to believe that lethal prescriptions could be provided for persons who meet any of several definitions of terminal illness, including persons who are unconscious or comatose. Even persons with serious illnesses or disabilities who would die soon without medical treatment but who can live a long time with treatment — people with diabetes, cancer, kidney disease, high blood pressure and others — would appear to be within the court's understanding of "terminal illness." The court even suggests that third parties may make decisions for death on behalf of incompetent patients. Finding no "principled distinction" between prescribing lethal drugs and administering them, the court sets the stage for physicians to give lethal injections to patients who never asked to be killed.

## Liberty and Responsibility

One cannot help but be concerned for the court's use of past Supreme Court decisions on abortion. Once again, the court focuses on individual liberty rather than on society's responsibility to protect innocent human life. Just as a state's authority to regulate abortion "may vary with the progression of the pregnancy," the court argues, the state's interest in protecting people from assisted suicide varies "at different points along the life cycle as a person's physical or medical condition deteriorates." While young and healthy people who want to commit suicide may be prevented from doing so, the state is not allowed by the Constitution, says this court, to provide the same protection to people further along the "life cycle." This is lethal discrimination against the sick and elderly, who are now branded as having "lives not worth living."

The overwhelming majority of people do not die, as this court would have one believe, in excruciating pain and humiliating circumstances. When a person is truly in the final stages of dying, when disease cannot be reversed, the person may refuse further treatment and receive effective medication to eliminate or control pain. For our part, we will redouble our efforts to provide loving care and support to all those who are terminally and seriously ill and to their families. What Pope John Paul II has called "the way of love and true mercy" — the way of easing suffering, keeping company with dying patients and affirming the dignity of their lives at every stage — is the most complete response to this and other efforts to promote a culture of death.

This decision must be appealed and reversed if the protection of human life and equality under the law are to retain meaning in our constitutional system. In the meantime, we will work with others of good will to prevent the court's dangerous reasoning from influencing other courts and legislatures.

## HITTING ROCK BOTTOM IN CARE FOR LIFE

*Cardinal Roger Mahony of Los Angeles commented as follows on the decision of the 9th U.S. Circuit Court of Appeals.*

We who have been speaking up for and striving to protect each precious human life are still in shock over the incredible decision by an 11-judge *en banc* panel of the U.S. Circuit Court of Appeals for the 9th District in which they held by an 8-to-3 vote that a state of Washington statute banning assisted suicide violated the due process clause of the 14th Amendment "insofar as (it) prohibits physicians from prescribing life-ending medication for use by terminally ill, competent adults who wish to hasten their own deaths."

The 1973 U.S. Supreme Court abortion decisions started us as a nation down the "slippery slope" toward endangering all human life at every stage of development, and the angle and rate of descent on that slippery slope have been increasing over the years as various courts continue to dismantle protections for God's great gift of created human life. In fact, there is no more slope left — we have now

hit rock bottom in our care and concern for the value of human life in this country.

While this decision is appalling on many counts I wish to focus on just two aspects which make the decision so alarming: its reliance upon *Roe vs. Wade* and *Doe vs. Bolton*, the two U.S. Supreme Court decisions legalizing most abortions; and its granting to others, such as family or friends, the authority to end someone's life without their involvement in that decision.

### Commitment to Life Undermined

With respect to our concern about linking this decision with earlier court decisions legalizing abortion, the 9th Circuit Court states:

"The legalization of abortion has not undermined our commitment to life generally; nor, as some have predicted, has it led to widespread infanticide. Similarly, there is no reason to believe that legalizing assisted suicide will lead to the horrific consequences its opponents suggest."

Pardon me? Our commitment as a nation to life

generally has not been undermined since the infamous 1973 abortion decisions? Even the 1973 decisions had some limitations and protections built into them. In the last 33 years, though, the interpretation of the decisions has expanded, and abortion has now become the birth control of choice for many of the 1.3 million unborn children exterminated year after year in their mothers' wombs — the total now well over 43 million.

Our commitment to life has been undermined and it has eroded. We have now created the "culture of death" in our country whereby no human life is safe from being destroyed for a whole host of "reasons." The abortion mentality has had a devastating, negative effect upon our people — and especially upon our young people. The current push among abortionists to legalize late-term abortions is but one more explicit example of this downward erosion. If late-term abortion is not infanticide, then I don't know what is.

And the second aspect of this court decision is even more troubling. This appellate court states without hesitation:

"(A) decision of a duly appointed surrogate decision-maker is for all legal purposes the decision of the patient himself."

Easy translation: Even nonvoluntary euthanasia may now be a constitutional right. That means that a patient, even while comatose, may be killed through euthanasia even though that person has not been consulted, and the person has no role or rights in such a terrible decision

## Consequences To Come

I believe, in sharp contrast to the 9th Circuit Court, that indeed those "horrific consequences" will be swift in coming. It is a very short path from "voluntary" euthanasia to "involuntary" euthanasia. The court seems to believe that we are all safe from inappropriate detrimental actions against us because of their decision. This is foolishness, and the majority know it.

This court decision has placed every single one of us at risk of being killed because others may not value our "quality of life" or the 'contribution" we may or may not make to society. Life in this country just became more scary for all of us.

I have written to Washington State Attorney General Christine Gregoire urging her to appeal this appalling decision to the U.S. Supreme Court, where I am confident that the state's interest in caring for human life will once again be established and the appalling conclusions of this decision will be overturned.

Let us continue our focus upon prayer as the finest way to overcome the anti-life evil that swirls about us — even from some of our courts.

# MISGUIDED JUDICIAL ACTIVISM

*This statement by the bishops of the State of New York was issued one day after the Apr. 2, 1996, assisted suicide decision by the U.S. 2nd Circuit Court of Appeals.*

We are saddened and deeply dismayed by the ill-advised decision of the Federal 2nd Circuit Court of Appeals.... The court has erroneously read into the Constitution an extraordinary and unprecedented "right" to have one person facilitate the killing of another person. This is euthanasia. Such misguided judicial activism severely erodes the value and dignity of human life in our society. It exacerbates what Pope John Paul II has termed the "culture of death."

This case was not about allowing natural death to occur; it was about deliberately and intentionally causing death. The court has attacked and reversed long-standing moral, legal and medical traditions which recognize the significant differences between discontinuing or withholding extraordinary treatment and taking active steps to destroy human life. Unless reversed, the implications will reach far beyond the terminally ill to those who are not so ill — those who are incapacitated, those perceived as burdensome and ultimately to those who do not voluntarily seek death.

We applaud the New York state attorney general for his commitment to appeal this unfortunate opinion. We pledge our continued active support in this case, and we encourage other public officials to become involved in promoting a "culture of life." We pray for a reversal of this decision at the earliest possible instance.

## Reject Euthanasia

The ruling highlights the need for all of us to reach out with care, support and compassion to the sick, the suffering and their caregivers. For our part, Catholic health facilities in New York State will continue to provide pain control, palliative care and support for dying patients, affirming the dignity of their lives at every stage.

We call on Catholics and all persons of good will to reject euthanasia. We urge families to discuss issues surrounding the care of terminally ill loved ones in light of sound moral principles and the demands of human dignity so patients need not feel helpless or abandoned in the face of complex decisions about their future. We urge health-care professionals, legislators and all involved in this debate to seek life-affirming solutions to the problems of terminally ill patients and their families. Let us respect the inherent worth of all human beings, especially those most in need of our love and assistance.

We issue this statement to reaffirm the Church's teaching regarding the sacred dignity of human life and our continuing commitment to protect individual life from conception to natural death. We celebrate life as a precious gift from God, and we profess that the human person is central, the clearest reflection of God among us.

# SAME-SEX MARRIAGES

Same-sex marriages were on bizarre display in San Francisco Mar. 25, 1996, when Mayor Willie L. Brown, Jr., officiated at a ceremony in which nearly 200 gay and lesbian couples were pronounced virtual spouses. As "domestic partners," they either already had or thereby acquired some of the rights traditionally and legally reserved to married couples. The ceremony, however, had no legal effect because California, along with all the other states, does not recognize same-sex marriages.

Such non-recognition was placed at risk in 1993 when the Supreme Court of Hawaii declared that the refusal of the state to grant marriage licenses to three homosexual couples amounted to unconstitutional discrimination against them on the basis of sex.

A year later, the Hawaiian legislature passed a bill defining marriage as intended for man-woman units capable of procreation.

The U.S. House of Representatives passed the Defense of Marriage Act July 12, 1996, defining marriage for federal purposes as a "legal union between one man and one woman." The bill would bar partners in same-sex unions from receiving federal benefits available to marital spouses such as spousal Social Security benefits. The bill does not ban gay marriages or forbid states from permitting them; it says states are not required to recognize same-sex marriages performed in another state. Senate action on the bill was pending at the time of writing.

## BISHOPS' STATEMENT

*The following statement on same-sex unions was issued July 24, 1996, by Bishops Joseph Charron, chairman of the U.S. bishops' Committee on Marriage and Family, and William Skylstad, chairman of the Committee on Domestic Policy.*

The Roman Catholic Church believes that marriage is a faithful, exclusive and lifelong union between one man and one woman joined as husband and wife in an intimate partnership of life and love. This union was established by God with its own proper laws. By reason of its very nature, therefore, marriage exists for the mutual love and support of the spouses and for the procreation and education of children. These two purposes, the unitive and the procreative, are equal and inseparable. The institution of marriage has a very important relationship to the continuation of the human race, to the total development of the human person and to the dignity, stability, peace and prosperity of the family and of society.

Furthermore, we believe the natural institution of marriage has been blessed and elevated by Christ to the dignity of a sacrament. This means that Christian marriage is more than a contract. Because they are married in the Lord, the spouses acquire a special relationship to each other and to society. Their love becomes a living image of the manner in which the Lord personally loves his people and is united with them. Living a Christian, sacramental marriage becomes their fundamental way of attaining salvation.

### Legalization Opposed

Because the marital relationship offers benefits unlike any other to persons, to society and to the Church, we wish to make it clear that the institution of marriage, as the union of one man and one woman, must be preserved, protected and promoted in both private and public realms. At a time when family life is under significant stress, the principled defense of marriage is an urgent necessity for the well-being of children and families, and for the common good of society.

Thus, we oppose attempts to grant the legal status of marriage to a relationship between persons of the same sex. No same-sex union can realize the unique and full potential which the marital relationship expresses. For this reason, our opposition to "same-sex marriage" is not an instance of unjust discrimination or animosity toward homosexual persons. In fact, the Catholic Church teaches emphatically that individuals and society must respect the basic human dignity of all persons, including those with a homosexual orientation. Homosexual persons have a right to and deserve our respect, compassion, understanding and defense against bigotry, attacks and abuse.

We therefore urge Catholics and all our fellow citizens to commit themselves both to upholding the human dignity of every person and to upholding the distinct and irreplaceable community of marriage.

## DOMESTIC PARTNERS

*Related and antecedent to the movement for equating homosexual unions with heterosexual marriage are efforts to provide for unmarried couples benefits which have traditionally and legally been reserved for married couples. These efforts, which jeopardize the status and unique relationship proper to marriage, are the subject of a letter addressed June 7, 1996, by Cardinal Anthony J. Bevilacqua to Mayor Edward Rendel of Philadlphia.*

For many years, we have worked together on issues of common concern, particularly regarding the needs of the poor. Today, however, I must write to express my extreme displeasure with your decision to sign an executive order which will provide so-called "domestic partner" benefits to homosexual municipal employees.

### Destructive Action

This action is destructive to the traditional family, which is rooted in a loving marriage between a man and a woman. At a time when families in our community are increasingly vulnerable, our focus must be on making them stronger. Throughout history, the traditional family has been the very cornerstone of a stable society. Our Catholic teaching calls us to love and respect all human beings — homosexual and heterosexual. Still, this call in faith to love everyone as a brother or a sister does not include endorsing as public policy that which will erode the very fabric of society. God created man and woman as the foundation of the family. To disturb this foundational role of marriage is to weaken society itself.

You have told me this executive order is not about destroying traditional family life, but rather about providing equity for a few. Still, the very language of the executive order proves otherwise. Same-sex unions are equated with "nontraditional families." Further, the executive order indicates a "partner" is entitled to the same health and leave benefits as a "spouse" of an exempt employee. If this bill were truly about equity, an employee caring for an elderly parent or an employee in a similar living arrangement would be included. The exclusion of such employees illustrates the true purpose of this bill as does the language equating homosexual unions with families.

Mayor, you have identified a handful of corporations which have taken this step as justification for your action. Clearly, there is a profound difference between the personnel policies of a private corporation and those of civil government, which normally have the support of the citizenry.

### Executive Order Opposed

As you know, I helped organize citywide opposition to a similar measure which was proposed by the City Council in 1993. Hundreds of thousands of

city residents wrote to the City Council to express their disfavor with the legislation. I appeared before the City Council to express my support for marriage and traditional family life. Joining me at that time were people of many faiths, races and ethnic backgrounds. Today I stand in solidarity with those citizens who are deeply distressed that you would choose to disregard their wishes and summarily sign an executive order which grants so-called "domestic partnership" status to same-sex couples.

I assure you of my continued commitment to protect traditional families and encourage you to do the same. I have already contacted other religious leaders who share my concerns about a "domestic partnership" executive order. I am confident we will once again be joined by hundreds of thousands of citizens of this city who likewise believe in protecting the integrity of the traditional family.

I ask that you rescind your executive order in the interest of the greatest asset our city possesses: the traditional family life of its people.

## PAPAL VISIT TO AFRICA: End of Synod

Pope John Paul, on the 67th foreign trip of his pontificate, visited Africa for the 11th time Sept. 14 to 20, 1995, to celebrate the conclusion of the Special Assembly for Africa and Madagascar of the Synod of Bishops.

The major events of the Pope's visits to Cameroon, South Africa and Kenya were synodal-related meetings in each country with bishops of the entire continent to signal the conclusion of the synod and to focus attention on the twin subjects of evangelization and inculturation. The Pope also covered other

subjects in the light of 64 recommendations which emanated from working sessions of the synod held Apr. 10 to May 8, 1994, at the Vatican. On Sept. 15, he made public an apostolic exhortation bearing the title *Ecclesia in Africa* ("The Church in Africa").

The principal public events were Masses celebrated and homilies delivered in Yaounde, Johannesburg and Nairobi, attended by a total of nearly a million people. The Pope met with the presidents of the three countries — Paul Biya of Cameroon, Nelson Mandela of South Africa and Daniel arap Moi of Kenya.

### THE CHURCH IN AFRICA: Apostolic Exhortation

These excerpts are from the papal document made public Sept. 15, 1995.

**Purpose of the Synodal Assembly:** The Special Assembly for Africa of the Synod of Bishops was convoked so that the whole Church of God on the continent might reflect on its evangelizing mission in the light of the third millennium and prepare an organic pastoral solidarity within the entire African territory and nearby islands. (No. 72)

**Significance of the Assembly:** The celebration of the special assembly showed to the whole world that the local churches of Africa hold a rightful place in the communion of the Church, that they are entitled to preserve and to develop their own traditions, without in any way lessening the primacy of the Chair of Peter. (No. 11)

**Two Centuries of Growth:** The fact that in the course of almost two centuries the number of African Catholics has grown quickly is an outstanding achievement by any standard. In particular, the building up of the Church on the continent is confirmed by facts such as the noteworthy and rapid increase in the number of ecclesiastical circumscriptions; the growth of a native clergy, of seminarians and candidates for institutes of consecrated life; and the steady increase in the network of catechists, whose contribution to the spread of the Gospel among the African peoples is well known. Finally, of fundamental

importance is the high percentage of indigenous bishops who now make up the hierarchy of the continent. (No. 38)

**Problems:** One common situation, without any doubt, is that Africa is full of problems. In almost all our nations there is abject poverty, tragic mismanagement of available scarce resources, political instability and social disorientation. The results stare us in the face: misery, wars, despair. In a world controlled by rich and powerful nations, Africa has practically become an irrelevant appendix, often forgotten and neglected. (No. 40)

All the preparatory documents of the synod, as well as the discussions in the assembly, clearly showed that issues in Africa — such as increasing poverty, urbanization, the international debt, the arms trade, the problem of refugees and displaced persons, demographic concerns and threats to the family, the liberation of women, the spread of AIDS, the survival of the practice of slavery in some places, ethnocentricity and tribal opposition — figure among the fundamental challenges addressed by the synod. (No. 51)

**Need for Evangelization:** The synod recognized the urgency of proclaiming the Good News to the millions of people in Africa who are not yet evangelized. The Church certainly respects and esteems the non-Christian religions professed by very many Africans, for these religions are the living expression of the soul of vast groups of people. However, neither respect and esteem for these religions nor the complexity of the questions raised is an invitation to the Church to withhold from these non-Christians the proclamation of Jesus Christ. On the contrary, the Church holds that these multitudes have the right to know the riches of the mystery of Christ — riches in which we believe that the whole of humanity can find, in unsuspected fullness, everything that it is gropingly searching for concerning God, man and his destiny, life and death, and truth. (No. 47)

**Inculturation:** The synod Fathers stressed the particular importance for evangelization of inculturation, the process by which catechesis takes flesh in the various cultures. Inculturation includes two dimensions: on the one hand, the intimate transformation of authentic cultural values through their integration in Christianity; and, on the other, the insertion of Christianity in the various human cultures. The synod considers inculturation an urgent priority in the life of the particular churches for a firm rooting of the Gospel in Africa. It is a requirement for evangelization, a path toward full evangelization, and one of the greatest challenges for the Church on the continent on the eve of the third millennium. (59)

The challenge of inculturation in Africa consists in ensuring that the followers of Christ will ever more fully assimilate the Gospel message while remaining faithful to all authentic African values. Inculturation of the faith in every area of Christian and human life is an arduous task. (No. 78)

**Agents and Structures of Evangelization:** The Church's task in Africa is immense; in order to face it, everyone's cooperation is essential (the local church, small faith communities, trained lay persons, catechists, the Christian family, youth, priests, religious, deacons. Necessary structures include the parish, apostolic movements and associations, schools, colleges and universities, cultural centers).

It is urgent that the particular churches in Africa have the objective of providing for their own needs as soon as possible, thereby assuring their self-sufficiency.... At the same time, I call on sister churches all over the world to be more generous ... so that, through their structures of assistance, they will be able to offer to poorer dioceses economic assistance dedicated to projects that will generate resources, with a view to increasing the financial self-reliance of the churches. (No. 104)

**Building the Kingdom:** To build the kingdom of God, the Church, as a community of faith, must be an energetic witness to justice and peace. (No. 105)

The Church has both the right and the duty to participate fully in building a just and peaceful society with all the means at her disposal. Here we must mention the Church's apostolate in the areas of education, health care, social awareness and in other programs of assistance. (No. 107)

In the pluralistic societies of our, day, it is especially due to the commitment of Catholics in public life that the Church can exercise a positive influence. Whether they be professionals or teachers, businessmen or civil servants, law enforcement agents or politicians, Catholics are expected to bear witness to goodness, truth, justice and love of God in their daily life. (No. 108)

**Responsibility of Rich Nations:** In the present world order, the African nations are among the most disadvantaged. Rich countries must become clearly aware of their duty to support the efforts of the countries struggling to rise from their poverty and misery. In fact, it is in the interests of the rich counties to choose the path of solidarity, for only in this way can lasting peace and harmony for humanity be ensured. (114)

**Tragedy of War:** The synod incisively described the tragedy of wars which are tearing Africa apart.... This very sad situation, in addition to causes external to Africa, also has internal causes such as tribalism, nepotism, racism, religious intolerance and the thirst for power taken to the extreme by totalitarian regimes which trample with impunity the rights and dignity of the person. Peoples reduced to silence suffer as innocent and resigned victims in all these situations of injustice. (No. 117)

**Refugees:** One of the most bitter fruits of wars and economic hardships is the sad phenomenon of refugees and displaced persons, a phenomenon which has reached tragic dimensions. The ideal solution is the reestablishment of a just peace, reconciliation and economic development. It is, therefore, urgent that national, regional and international organizations should find equitable and long-lasting solutions to the problems of refugees and displaced persons. In the meantime, since the continent continues to suffer from the massive displacement of refugees, I make a pressing appeal that these people be given material help and offered pastoral support wherever they may be, whether in Africa or on other continents. (No. 119)

**Women:** I have repeatedly affirmed the fundamental equality and enriching complementarity that exist between man and woman. The synod applied these principles to the condition of women in Africa. Their rights and duties in building up the family and in taking full part in the development of the Church and society were strongly affirmed. With specific regard to the Church, women should be properly trained so that they can participate at appropriate levels in her apostolic activity.

The Church deplores and condemns, to the extent that they are still found in some African societies, all the customs and practices which deprive women of their rights and the respect due to them. (No. 121)

## PLEA FOR RECONCILIATION

On arrival in Yaounde, Cameroon, Sept. 14, the Pope said: "The future of African populations is close to my heart. I assure them that the Catholic Church respects them in their cultural and religious traditions." He also said that the Church "will not stop asking the world's nations to give concrete help to a continent too often neglected in the course of history."

**Reconciliation:** The Pope urged Africans to end the struggles and conflicts that had caused so much bloodshed: "I hope Africans can rediscover peace and practice reconciliation, so that human rights can be guaranteed for all in justice and dignity, and

so the most needy — especially the sick and the refugees — can receive the assistance they need."

## SOLIDARITY WITH AN EXPLOITED CONTINENT

This was one of the themes of Pope John Paul's address at a synodal-related meeting Sept. 17 in Johannesburg. He said:
"I have wished to hold this celebration phase of the synod on African soil in order to express the solidarity of the universal Church with the particular churches of this continent in the great challenges before you. My presence is meant to reaffirm the universal Church's commitment to this continent."
**Structures of Sin:** "The synod fathers clearly understood that the situation of dehumanization and oppression affecting their peoples presents the ecclesial community with a crisis — in the original sense of a 'judgment'; — and a challenge: the crisis of conversion, holiness and integrity, in order to be a credible witness; the challenge of developing the full potential of the Gospel message of divine adoption in order to free the men and women of our time from sin and the 'structures of sin.'"
The Pope called attention to the fact that Africa "has a long, sad history of exploitation at the hands of others" which "continues in new forms." He cited: "the crushing burden of debts, unjust trading conditions, the dumping of harmful waste and the overly demanding conditions imposed by structural adjustment programs," the international arms trade." He also mentioned problems related to corruption in government.
"Among the evils which drew unanimous condemnation from the synod fathers, one especially has the most serious consequences: ethnic divisions and tensions which sometimes lead to horrendous crimes, as has happened most recently in Rwanda and Burundi. The Church in Africa feels deeply challenged by these divisions, and she feels the pressing responsibility of helping to heal their consequences."

### The African Challenge

"Africa challenges the Church, for it is her universal mission to enlighten, accompany and encourage peoples everywhere along the path of their complete liberation to their salvation in Jesus Christ, the Son of God and Redeemer of man.... When the synod fathers called the Church in Africa to be ever more actively involved in 'the struggle for the defense of

personal dignity, for justice and social peace, for human promotion, liberation and integral human development of all people and of every individual,' they were giving voice to the unbreakable link between evangelization and human advancement. There can be no dichotomy between the commandment to love the Lord God with our whole heart and soul, and the commandment to love our neighbor as ourselves, and therefore to engage in actions on behalf of justice and social transformation."

### Emergence from Apartheid

Pope John Paul hailed South Africa's emergence from apartheid during a public Mass Sept. 17 in Johannesburg. He said:
"Seeing what is happening here, men and women of good will hope that in other parts of this continent and throughout the world violence will give way to dialogue and agreement, and the lives of innocent men, women and children will no longer be in danger."

### AFRICA, CONTINENT OF THE FAMILY

Protection of the family and its central role in education for the faith were themes of Pope John Paul's homily at Mass Sept. 19 in Nairobi. He told a congregation of nearly 500,000 people: "The educational role of the family is never easy, but it is always a sublime and noble human enterprise. Even before parishes and schools, mothers and fathers are the teachers of the Beatitudes."
The Holy Father appealed to the people of all the African nations to seek peace through dialogue, reconciliation and justice. Of Burundi and Rwanda, "swallowed up" by ethnic violence, he said: "Today all of us ... think of the terrible ethnic war still smoldering there."       Forgiveness and reconciliation represent "the only way to scatter the menacing clouds of ethnocentricity hanging over Africa."
The Pope explained how each stage of his visit emphasized "one or another of the guiding themes" of the 1994 special synod for Africa: the evangelization of culture and inculturation, peace and justice in society and the Church, and the agents of evangelization, especially the family.

## POPE JOHN PAUL IN CENTRAL AMERICA

Pope John Paul returned to Central America for a another visit Feb. 5 to 11, 1996, this time to Guatemala, Nicaragua, El Salvador and Venezuela.

### IN GUATEMALA

On arrival Feb. 5, the Pope voiced a recurrent theme for peace, pleading for a stop to the "thunder of war" that had been reverberating around the country for more than 30 years.
Visiting President Alvaro Arzuu, he said peace is gift of God and the fruit of dialogue, a spirit of reconciliation, a serious commitment to holistic devel-

opment along with solidarity reaching all sectors of society and, in a particular way, of respect for the dignity of every person."
**Hope and Faith:** Despite numerous and serious problems, he said it was a time of hope for "spiritual, moral, economic, social and cultural progress for all, in such a way that everyone can live in a climate of freedom, mutual trust, social justice and lasting peace."
During an evening Liturgy of the Word, Feb. 6, the Holy Father urged Guatemalans to be strong in their faith in order to counteract the influence of sects

and help to bring peace to the nation. He pleaded with the people to remain active and united in the Church and thus to stop the flow of Catholics to evangelical sects and Protestant churches.

"Help those who have abandoned the Catholic faith or run the risk of abandoning it so that they can return quickly to the Christian community in which they were born and educated," he urged

During the liturgy, the Pope crowned a gold-ornamented wooden statue of Our Lady of the Assumption, patroness of Guatemala City.

**Catechists Praised and Remembered:** The Pope praised the country's 2,300 catechists and urged them: "Dedicate yourselves in a systematic and profound way to teaching the doctrine of the Gospel, preparing your church communities so that they can correctly celebrate the Eucharist and draw from it the strength to live the new commandment of love."

He paid tribute to the hundreds of catechists who lost their lives during the 35-year-long civil war, saying: "With their blood, they have made the blessed land of Guatemala fruitful forever." The inheritance left "by these heroes of the faith is beautiful, but at the same time binding because it carries with it the urgent task of continuing their evangelization.... It is necessary that the Gospel reach every place and every person."

## IN NICARAGUA

During Mass along the shore of Lake Managua in Nicaragua, the Pope alluded to changes in the country since his visit in 1983, but said he was bringing the same message, "a message of peace and reconciliation, a call to solidarity and brotherhood ... to be authentic builders of a civilization of love."

His earlier visit was marred by demonstrations staged by supporters of the Sandinist government, which was subsequently voted out of office in 1990.

The Pope called on the people to strengthen family and national ties, to promote church unity, and to "reexamine everything that promotes peace, supporting it and pardoning one another.... It is necessary not only that every family but also that the national family of Nicaragua receive from today's liturgy a light for knowing how to behave in this phase of your history."

**Personal Dignity:** The Pope encouraged Nicaraguans to keep the dignity of the person at the center of their policies, working for an equitable distribution of goods and for a political and economic system in which all can participate. "The process of democratization you have begun ... must be accompanied by an authentic revitalization of the traditional moral values of the Nicaraguan people," he said

Before leaving Managua, the Holy Father visited the city's new cathedral and its Sangre de Cristo chapel, where a glass-enclosed crucifix is venerated as a focus of Nicaraguan devotion. He said to people there: "Do not forget the mystery of Christ's death and resurrection when weariness, loneliness or a lack of understanding could dampen your enthusiasm. Do not doubt the fact that you are loved by the Lord, and his love always will proceed and accompany you."

In a final reminder at the airport departure ceremony, following a meeting with President Violeta Chamorro, he repeated his hopes that Nicaraguans would "continue along the path of peace, reconciliation, freedom and justice, building the society you all long for.... Having overcome the civil war and the temptations of totalitarianism, you still must defeat the terrible plagues of poverty and ignorance, seen in the high number of people without work, families living in extreme need and in the children and young people who do not receive an adequate education."

## IN EL SALVADOR

At Mass in San Salvador, the Pope said:

"God places before you two roads from which you must choose the future of your nation: the way of death or the way of life." While civil war and death-squad activity had ended, Salvadorans were still deeply divided, disputes continued and a highly organized crime wave was sweeping the nation, "Evil is still lurking in many hearts.... Sin is the ultimate cause of personal and social disorder, all forms of selfishness and oppression, violence and vengeance."

**Revolution of Love:** He called on people to start a "revolution of love" based on the Sermon on the Mount, saying: "The gift of the Spirit makes it possible to love our enemies, to do good to those who hate us and to pray for those who persecute and slander us."

Pope John Paul said the Church, while devoting renewed attention to the spiritual lives of the nation's Catholics, has to continue its work for peace and justice. Much of the real work, he said, requires religious and moral education. He called the Sermon on the Mount, read earlier at Mass, "a pressing call to follow Jesus Christ in a radical way in order to reach the holiness to which we are called."

At the tomb of Archbishop Oscar Romero, who was "brutally assassinated" in 1980 by a military death squad, the Pope said "many things had changed" since his first visit to the country in 1983, when civil war was still raging. "The face of the country has changed, and so has the pastoral activity of the Church which, as soon as the situation improved, moved to strengthen the life of parishes, church movements and associations."

## IN VENEZUELA

In Venezuela for the last three days of his visit to Central America, the Pope addressed inmates of the Reten di Catia prison, Caracas, Feb. 9.

Speaking from a site several hundred feet away from the infamous institution. He urged them: "Open your hearts, accept the challenge of conversion." He also said prisons must provide "living conditions more consonant with human dignity" and opportunities for re-education so prisoners might return to society as honest and productive citizens.

**Social Conditions:** Against the background of worsening social conditions, the Pope said "one should not forget that the process of material impoverishment often brings about moral and spiritual impoverishment," leading to increasing crime, family disruption and a growing number of street children. Calling attention to the crisis engendered by an absence of values in the fields of ethics, justice, social life, respect for life and the dignity of the human person, he called on leaders in politics, business, labor and cultural affairs to promote social solidarity and "an economy of participation."

In conjunction with the blessing of a new national Shrine of Our Lady of Coromoto Feb. 10, the Holy Father issued a call for a new evangelization for rediscovery of the faith and of ways and means of putting it into practice in any and all circumstances of personal and social life.

At Mass in Caracas on the last day of his visit, the Pope said renewed faith must lead to the renunciation of "the idols of today which are, among others, materialism and selfishness with their corollaries of sensualism, hedonism, violence and corruption."

**Youth:** The last event on the papal agenda was a meeting with young people during which he said: "The Pope believes in you because he has experienced your insatiable thirst for truth, peace and freedom, and because he has seen your generous capacity for service, your will to live and struggle, opening new horizons for the Church and society." He invited them to be "prophets of life" in a country faced with drug trafficking, violence, the neglect of abandoned children, the sick and the aged, and particularly the destructive actions of abortion and euthanasia."

"Christ is the Lord of history," he said in conclusion, and faith in Christ must lead people to transform the history of the societies in which they live.

# POPE JOHN PAUL IN TUNISIA

On a 12-hour visit to Tunis Apr.14, 1996, Pope John Paul: encouraged the small number of Catholics there to be true to the faith and to participate in dialogue and cooperative action with Muslims in cultural life, education, social services and efforts for peace and nonviolence. These and other topics were the substance of his remarks in several addresses during his visit. Several excerpts are given below.

## Purpose of the Visit

*On arrival at the Tunis International Airport, the Pope spoke about the purpose of his visit as he was greeted by the president and other civic officials, the archbishop of Tunis and members of the diplomatic corps.*

The main purpose of my visit is to meet the faithful of the Catholic Church who live in Tunisia.... The Catholics in this country have very different origins, languages and cultures, for they come from many nations. But I know that, faithful to the Gospel, they desire to be loyal partners with their Muslim brothers and sisters. Happy to be accepted in friendship as they are with their faith and religious practices, they would like to contribute to social life as far as their modest means permit. I acknowledge here in particular their concern to participate in development, to be active and ready partners in cultural life, giving priority to educational or health-care tasks among the most underprivileged of their brothers and sisters.

## Image of the Church

*The Pope spoke again about the small Catholic community in the country, during Mass in the Tunis cathedral.*

A little flock, indeed, but, differing in your languages, cultures and origins, you are an eloquent image of the universal Church. By your ties with the North and the South, the East and the West, be the leaven of unity and solidarity here. By putting down roots in this hospitable land, through your fraternal friendship with your companions at work or with your neighbors in the district, in your everyday life and reflections on life's meaning and the world's situation, show the grace you have received of being Jesus Christ's disciples.

## Proclaiming the Kingdom

*Forming communities that manifest Christ was the theme of the Pope's address to bishops of the Re-*

*gional Episcopal Conference of North Africa, which includes, Tunisia, Morocco, Algeria and Libya.*

Today you are writing a new page in this Church's history in a very different context from that with which your Fathers in the faith were familiar, a page of dialogue and collaboration between believers of different religions. This particular ecclesial vocation is also a treasure for the universal Church. I encourage you to share with her whatever you discover of God's work here.

In your (Christian) witness, your relationship with believers in Islam has a special place....

What you witness to in faith will fortify you for an ever deeper and more spiritual relationship with Muslims, leading you to discover and accept and share God's blessings with them.

Where discord and violence are raging, be messengers of the peace that comes from God and of reconciliation, the way that leads to him. No one can kill in the name of God, no one can be willing to kill his brother or sister. Build up fraternal ties that proclaim the coming of God's kingdom, with men and women of good will. Demonstrate your conviction that God is the God of life, that he seeks man's life and not his death. Despite difficulties and misunderstandings, reach out to your brothers and sisters regardless of their origin or religion.... Dialogue is a path toward the kingdom and will certainly bear fruit, even if the times and seasons are known only to the Father.

Your meeting with Muslims must go further than merely sharing life. It must lead to true collaboration. God wants us to bear witness to him through our respect for the values and religious traditions of each person, working together for human progress and development at all levels.

Do not be afraid to be a radiant Church which respects other human and spiritual traditions, but clearly and fearlessly reveals what she is. It is a formidable task for Christians to express what they have become by their baptism.

## Partners in Dialogue

*Muslim-Christian dialogue was the subject of the Pope's remarks in an address to more than 200 political, cultural, and religious leaders at the Presidential Palace in Carthage.*

May I consider once again with you the conditions

necessary if this dialogue is to be fruitful. It is indispensable, first of all, that it be motivated by a true desire to know the other. It is not a question of mere human curiosity. Openness to others is in some way a response to God who allows our differences and who wants us to know one another more deeply. To do this, the discovery of our true place in relation to each other is essential.

The partners in dialogue will be reassured and at ease to the extent that they are firmly rooted in their respective religions. Thus firmly rooted, they will be able to accept their differences and to avoid two contradictory stumbling blocks: syncretism and indifferentism. Each will also be enabled to profit from a critical look at the other's manner of formulating and living his faith.

Faith will also be at the basis of this type of dialogue, which is collaboration in the service of man and which I have already mentioned; for, since we believe in God the Creator, we recognize the dignity of each human person created by him.. We have our origins in God and in him our common destiny. Between these two poles we journey through history, where we must walk together in a spirit of mutual aid, in order to reach the transcendent goal God has established for us."

# POPE JOHN PAUL IN SLOVENIA

Pope John Paul, making his first visit to Slovenia, an island of Balkan prosperity with deep Christian roots, warned that a new emptiness was settling over Eastern Europe in the wake of communism's demise.

While praising Slovenia's social rebuilding efforts as an independent nation, he said there were worrisome signs that Christian beliefs and basic moral values were being written off.

Europe is facing an "hour of truth," he said in a speech May 19 in Maribor, near the Austrian border. The choice is between recognizing human freedom as God-given, or drifting toward the "hedonism and vanity" of a religiously indifferent society.

If he carried a serious message to the tiny Alpine country, the Pope also brought a festive mood. Fifty thousand young people greeted him on his 76th birthday, May 18.

He also met with civil authorities to help smooth out church-state problems, offered special greetings and a $50,000 check for Bosnian refugees in Slovenia, and celebrated Masses and prayer services for the nation's Catholic majority.

## Warm Welcome

Traveling to all three Slovenian dioceses, the Pope was warmly welcomed. He in turn, from the moment of his arrival May 17 in Ljubljana, heaped praise and encouragement on Slovenia for implementing democracy and independence without the bloodshed of its Balkan neighbors.

President Milan Kucan, an ex-communist, thanked the Pope. He said one main reason Slovenia's war with the Yugoslav federal army lasted only 10 days was because the Vatican was so quick to recognize its independence in 1991, setting an example for others.

In his address to more than 200 Slovenian academic and cultural leaders in Maribor, however, the Holy Father examined the less-optimistic side of Eastern Europe's democratic evolution: the ebb of Christian values — a focal issue of his pontificate in recent years.

## Dangerous Currents

He said he was especially concerned about "dangerous currents" of moral skepticism that seemed to overshadow the rediscovery of Christian opportunities. "The walls have collapsed and the iron curtains have fallen, but questions about the meaning of life and the value of freedom are stronger than ever. ..

How could we not see that at the core of this problem lies the question of God?"

People either see themselves as creatures of God bound by certain limits, or they risk elevating themselves to an absolute level that accepts no moral restraints.

The temptation today is not so much basing one's vision of life on pure reason, but of living without any vision whatsoever. This can happen when Christianity is placed on the margins of culture.

"Don't put out the flame of faith in the younger generations," he urged Slovenia's intellectual leaders.

The Pope zeroed in on one worrisome trend in a sermon earlier at the Maribor airport. He asked why Slovenians, with their rich history of local saints, were turning to "the temptation of occult rites or astrology to find hints about their destiny."

Superstition and magic attract many people with simple answers to life's questions, but the saints — including those venerated on a local level — are much more reliable guides.

## Moral Basics

Throughout the visit, the Pope preached moral basics to the nation's 1.7 million Catholics. While the country boasts a 1,250-year history of Christianity, he said, the Gospel is a resource that must be renewed or lost, especially in the changing social situation.

He warned of the influx of individualism and consumerism, and of the illusion of happiness often spread by the mass media. Slovenia, like other Eastern European countries, must not simply imitate extreme forms of Western capitalism, which are "no less dangerous" than communism.

To 50,000 cheering young people outside Postojna May 18, the Pope counseled against taking refuge from problems in sex, drugs or violence. A solid faith is the only real basis for human hope, he said.

On several occasions, the Pope spoke about the more recent fighting in Bosnia and urged church and civil leaders to keep assisting the estimated 18,000 refugees in Slovenia. He said it was part of Slovenia's ancient vocation to serve as a crossroads of peace and bridge between ethnic groups of the surrounding region.

## Risk of Gray Uniformity

The Pope lent moral support to Slovenia's efforts to enter the European Union. But he cautioned against losing the rich national culture that had bound Slovenians together for centuries. There's an increasing risk of disappearing into the "gray uniformity" of an overly homogenized world, he said.

While the Pope concentrated on Slovenia's future, he did not forget its past — including episodes of good and evil.

He highlighted the work of missionaries and church leaders, especially Bishop Anton Marton Slomsek, whose beatification cause had recently moved ahead at the Vatican. The 19th century bishop, a poet and writer, was credited with helping to keep the Slovenian language and culture alive under Austrian rule.

The Pope also recalled priests and other church activists killed, imprisoned or tortured by communist partisans in the 1940s and 1950s. Theirs is a chapter of Slovenian history that cannot be forgotten or canceled, he said.

### The Gospel Needs Heralds

Pope John Paul emphasized the need for new heralds of the Gospel in a homily during Mass May 18, 1996, at a race course in Ljubljana, Slovenia.

As long as the Church is a pilgrim here below, the Gospel is never proclaimed once and for all. Every age needs new heralds and witnesses. It is not enough to recall the heritage of the past, since every generation must make its own choice for Christianity. In view of the risk of separating faith and culture, faith and life, today you are presented with the exalting task of welcoming the Gospel message anew and bringing it to others. The growth of apostolic associations and movements, the multiple forms of charity and assistance to the needy, the laity's cooperation in the Church's life, particularly in catechesis, are precious fruits of the new evangelization. But, dear brothers and sisters, the example of your Christian life is even more necessary. When the Gospel has become your life, it will shine like the light of the world.

### Role of Priests in Slovenia

The Pope spoke to bishops, priests and religious at a prayer service in the Ljubljana cathedral May 17, 1996.

During the trials to which the Slovenian people have been subjected down the ages, the pastors of the Church have not failed to make their presence felt, proclaiming the Gospel of life and defending the dignity and the inalienable rights of every human being. This has happened with even greater courage in recent years, during fascism, Nazism and communism.

The Church in Slovenia, to remain faithful to her own tradition, and especially to the Gospel, is called today to aim at new goals, suitably preparing herself to enter the third millennium of the faith. This requires renewed zeal and indomitable fidelity to Christ and his message of salvation.

The priority task of the new evangelization ... asks priests to be deeply and fully immersed in the mystery of Christ and capable of embodying a new style of pastoral life, marked by a profound union with the pope, the bishops and other priests, and a fruitful cooperation with the lay faithful.

Your people are going through a time of radical change. While they are seeking gradually to free themselves from the negative consequences of the totalitarian ideology by which they have been strongly conditioned, they are striving with every effort to build a more fraternal and democratic society. However, it is still necessary to be particularly alert to preventing the acceptance of another equally dangerous ideology, that of unbridled liberalism, from filling the void left by the previous one. These are years of transition; and your word, together with your example, is indispensable, as was the guidance of Moses who, with firm trust in God, succeeded in leading the Chosen People in the difficult passage from slavery to true freedom.

### Society Needs Saints

This was the theme of the Pope's homily during Mass May 19, 1996, in Maribor.

Man is called to holiness, to be the artisan of a humanity renewed by divine glory. And the believer, through baptism, becomes a witness to that supernatural hope which sustains man's pilgrimage on earth, often marked by trials and suffering. In the Second Vatican Council, the Church affirmed that "all Christians in any state or walk of life are called to the fullness of Christian life and to the perfection of love." By their own holy life, Christians are asked to become light for others on the paths of the world.

Our age seems more a time of amazing scientific and technological discoveries than an era of saints. But, if man is not spiritually fulfilled through interior conformity to Christ, all his achievements remain ultimately insignificant and could even become dangerous. Precisely because people today seek personal fulfillment, there is a greater need of saints. Our time calls for mature persons who, having understood the value of holiness, seek to achieve it in daily life.

Looking at it closely, present-day society reveals a deep need of saints, of people, that is, who, through their closer contact with God, can somehow make his presence felt and mediate his answers.

# POPE JOHN PAUL IN GERMANY

*Germany can be assured of a future free from the horrors and divisions of the past only with the support of Christian values and respect for the lives of all, Pope John Paul said on several occasions during his June 21-23, 1996, trip to Germany. It was the 72nd foreign trip of his pontificate, and his first visit to united Germany.*

Visiting Paderborn and Berlin, he said he came to offer counsel on the spiritual renewal that must parallel the political and economic renewal of the reunited Germany.

He chose Berlin as his platform for announcing a new Assembly of the Synod of Bishops for Europe to discuss the challenges facing the Church on the continent now that democracy and free-market economics have been set up on both sides of the old Iron Curtain.

**Symbolic Setting:** In symbolic Berlin settings, the

Pope remembered the victims of the Nazis and the later division of Germany between democratic West and communist East.

In the stadium Adolf Hitler commissioned for the 1936 Olympic Games, the Pope condemned the evils of Nazism and praised the heroism of priests and other Catholics who resisted Hitler's policies, even at the price of their lives.

He condemned the repressive policies of the former East Germany's communist leaders and their attempts to stamp out religious practices.

## Caution

But he also cautioned Germans that a "radical capitalistic ideology" is not a worthy alternative to the communist ideology that crushed personal dignity and limited individual freedoms.

In Paderborn the Pope met with the Catholic bishops of Germany and leaders of the country's other Christian churches.

The Pope urged the bishops to respond to demands for changes in the Church with openness, but also with a clear and firm affirmation of the teachings of the Church.

Bishops must be servants of the joyful faith of the Church, he said. This service must be offered in dialogue and always with great love, but also with clarity and decisiveness."

**Catholic-Lutheran Relations**: At an evening meeting with Christian leaders and at an ecumenical prayer service in the Paderborn cathedral, the Pope praised progress made over the previous 30 years in relations between Catholics and Lutherans.

The Church recognizes it made mistakes before and during the Reformation, and it has learned from Luther's insistence on the important place of Scripture in the Church and on the need for individual conversion, the Pope said.

But, he added, the Church also insists that Luther allowed his passion to carry him so far beyond his aim of renewing Catholicism that it led to a fracturing of Christianity in the West.

"We have all brought guilt upon ourselves; therefore we are all called upon to repent and allow ourselves to be cleansed by the Lord," the Pope said.

## Two Priests Beatified

The centerpiece of Pope John Paul's trip was the beatification June 23 of two German priests who were victims of Nazi persecution.

Father Bernard Lichtenberg, who used his pulpit in the Berlin cathedral to pray publicly for Jews and other victims of the Nazis, died at age 67 in a cattle car headed for the Dachau concentration camp.

Father Karl Leisner, who was ordained in Dachau by a French bishop also interned there, died at age 30 shortly after the camp was liberated by the Americans. He had tuberculosis and was so weak from his five-year imprisonment that he could not recover.

The Pope told an estimated 90,000 people at Berlin's Olympic Stadium: "Today two beatified martyrs celebrate their triumph precisely in that place where 60 years ago the National Socialist regime tried to celebrate the Olympic Games with the aim of making their inhuman ideology triumph."

In the stadium "the idealism of youth was profaned and men were incited to hatred and enmity instead of peaceful co-existence," he said.

The Pope said the two priests were representatives of the many Catholics who risked their lives to resist the Nazis and help the victims of Nazi brutality.

## All Victims Remembered

At the end of Mass at the stadium, the Pope prayed for "all our brothers and sisters who experienced the concentration camps."

In honoring the memory of all who died in the camps, he said, "we express our gratitude for their enormous sufferings which became the seeds of a better future."

During an afternoon meeting with representatives of Germany's Jewish community, Pope John Paul again spoke of the Catholics who opposed Hitler, but also said "there were nonetheless too few who resisted."

The lives and deaths of the two newly beatified priests, the Pope said, were "an appeal to Christians and Jews to join together in fighting for the dignity of all human beings," and especially "against any form of anti-Semitism, so that a phenomenon like the Holocaust can never occur again."

Ignatz Bubis, chairman of the directorate of Germany's Jewish council, said that, with the beatifications, the Church was "stating its support of humanity and thanking its sons for their steadfastness in times of need, something that could serve as an example for many others."

Bubis asked the Pope to continue encouraging Catholic-Jewish cooperation in fighting anti-Semitism and hate crimes around the world.

Pope John Paul ended his visit to Germany with a walk through the Brandenburg Gate, a monument adopted as a parade staging area and one which the communists blocked as a key part of the Berlin Wall.

German Chancellor Helmut Kohl publicly thanked the Pope for his "major role in overcoming the totalitarian and anti-religious ideology" that split the city, the country and the continent. He said to the Pope: "You never accepted the unnatural division of Europe by the Iron Curtain."

## Culture of Freedom

Before ending his first visit to a united Germany, the Pope encouraged its people to ensure that their freedom will have a future.

"Freedom does not mean the right to do or have anything one wants." Freedom must be based on the truth about the human person, his or her rights and his or her responsibility toward others.

"There can be no freedom without solidarity." Individual freedom without reference to the needs of others becomes a self-serving tyranny.

"The soul of the civilization of love is the culture of freedom: the freedom of individuals and the freedom of nations lived in self-giving solidarity and responsibility," the Holy Father said.

## Unity, Hope, Mission

These were among themes in the papal homily at Mass June 22 in Paderborn.

We are approaching the Great Jubilee of the Year 2000 without fear and discouragement; on the contrary, we have great trust and are united in hope. Because we know that the Lord is ... with us ... and this gives us strength to overcome our little faith and lack of courage, to trust in his word and thus to reach our goal.

Be united in hope and find strength in your common faith! Remember the long history of the Christian faith in this country! Never allow this faith to become weaker and more feeble! On the contrary, advance toward the next millennium with courage and confidence in Jesus Christ.

The Church exists not for herself but for the salvation of the world. Her unity cannot be that of a "closed society." Rather, it must be a missionary communion which bears witness in the world to the great hope which moves us Christians.... It is inherent in the vocation of the Church not to show indifference to the concerns and needs of individuals, but to inspire society with the spirit of the Gospel. The Christian faith strives for the fulfillment of God's will in heaven and on earth. It must therefore be actively present in the fields of politics, the economy and culture; otherwise, it would not be responding to its vocation. The first statement of the dogmatic constitution *Gaudium et Spes* is the guiding principle of this commitment: "The joy and hope, the grief and anguish of the men of our time, especially of those who are poor and afflicted in any way, are the joy and hope, the grief and anguish of the followers of Christ as well."

## Remove Barriers

*Pope John Paul addressed representatives of the Evangelical Church in Germany and the Presidium of the Working Group of the Christian Churches in Germany June 22 in Paderborn.*

The unity we seek demands true agreement on the content of faith itself. In no way will it encroach upon the binding nature of church doctrine; on the other hand, it does not compel us to sacrifice ... the rich diversity that has grown up among Christians in the measure that this diversity remains faithful to the apostolic tradition.

The unity we strive for must grow gradually. We must develop courage and imagination to take whatever steps are possible today, with firm trust in the guidance of the Holy Spirit who leads us and prepares us for whatever step will be possible tomorrow. I am aware that many people are suffering because of the division (between us). Therefore, it is our duty to tear down the barriers and to strive for a greater measure of communion in the firm hope that the Lord is leading us to that blessed day when full unity in faith will be attained and we celebrate together in peace the holy Eucharist of the Lord.

## Role of Bishops

*Pope John Paul addressed members of the German Bishops' Conference June 22 in Paderborn.*

As the Church, we must increasingly fulfill our task of being the moral conscience of society. As Christians, we must once more become the "salt of the earth" and "light of the world." Ecclesial life, which should be exclusively based on the truths of the faith, must remain faithful to Christ and the Gospel message.

The Church can only fulfill her mission if she presents herself as a stronghold of joy in the faith and of trust in the future. The task of self-examination and purification, as called for by the Second Vatican Council, has for many members of the Church unfortunately turned into destructive criticism of institutions and the spread of dissatisfaction fostered by an irritated subjectivism of the "post-modern" culture.

It is precisely the bishops' task to be servants of the joyful faith of the Church. It is a service which requires vigilance and must not dispense with the exercise of authority; and, furthermore, it must not be brought into question, either in public debate or in pastoral discussions. This service must be rendered in dialogue and always with great love, but also with clarity and decisiveness.

## Call to Freedom

*Pope John Paul's last public appearance took place in the evening of June 23 at the Brandenburg Gate near the site where the first section of the Berlin Wall was dismantled in 1989.*

In this place so full of history, I feel urged to address an urgent appeal for freedom to all of you here present, to the German people, to Europe — which is also called to unity in freedom — to all men of good will.

I exhort all Berliners and all Germans, to whom I am grateful for the peaceful revolution of the spirit that led to the opening of the Brandenburg Gate (with the demise of communism): Do not quench the Spirit! Keep this gate open, for you and for all people! Keep it open with the spirit of love, justice and peace! Keep the gate open with the openness of your hearts. There is no freedom without love.

Man is called to freedom. I proclaim to all you who are listening to me: The fullness and perfection of this freedom has a name: Jesus Christ.

He it is who said of himself: "I am the door." In him, man has access to the fullness of freedom and life. It is he who makes man truly free, because he dispels the darkness from people's hearts and reveals the truth. He completes his journey as our brother and he fulfills his solidarity with us by giving his life for us. In that way, he frees us from sin and death. He makes it possible for us to recognize his face in our neighbor, the face of our true brother. He shows us the face of the Father and becomes the bond of love for everyone.

Christ is our Savior. He is our freedom.

---

## THE BRANDENBURG GATE

The Brandenburg Gate is a towering triumphal arch in the center of Berlin, built in the late 18th century. It was used by the Nazis as a staging area for military processions. For nearly 30 years it stood in the center of a no-man's land behind barbed wire, beyond the reach of both East and West Germany. When the Berlin Wall fell in 1989, young people climbed to the top of the gate to wave flags and dance in jubilation.

## PREPARATION FOR THE THIRD MILLENNIUM: Phase II

*Pope John Paul issued an apostolic letter Nov. 10, 1994, in which he called for an appropriate celebration in Jubilee Year 2000 of the beginning of the third millennium of Christianity.*

The letter, entitled *Tertio Millennio Adveniente*, outlined several stages of preparation for the celebration, beginning with an antepreparatory phase from 1994 to 1996 and continuing from 1997 to 1990 with focus on the Holy Trinity. Jesus Christ is the theme of the first year of the preparatory phase, 1997. The Pope wrote as follows:

"The first year, 1997, will be devoted to reflection on Christ, the Word of God made man by the power of the Holy Spirit. The distinctly Christological character of the Jubilee needs to be emphasized, for it will celebrate the Incarnation and coming into the world of the Son of God, the mystery of salvation for all mankind. The general theme proposed ... for this year is: "Jesus Christ, the One Savior of the World, Yesterday, Today and Forever (cf. Heb. 13:8)."

"In order to recognize who Christ truly is, Christians, especially in the course of this year, should turn with renewed interest to the Bible ... to a renewed appreciation of baptism as the basis of Christian living, ... [and should be inspired with] a true longing for holiness, a deep desire for conversion and personal renewal in a context of ever-more intense prayer and of solidarity with one's neighbor, especially the most needy."

### Teaching about Christ

"The first year therefore will be the opportune moment for a renewed appreciation of catechesis in its original meaning as 'the apostles' teaching' (Acts 2:42) about the person of Christ and his mystery of salvation."

"The Blessed Virgin Mary, who will be as it were 'indirectly' present in the whole preparatory phase, will be contemplated in the first year, especially in the mystery of her divine motherhood. It was in her womb that the Word became flesh! The affirmation of the central place of Christ cannot therefore be separated from the recognition of the role played by his most holy Mother. Veneration of her, when properly understood, can in no way take away from the dignity and efficacy of Christ the one Mediator."

### ANTEPREPARATORY PHASE

The introductory phase of preparation for the Jubilee was meant to revive in Christians an awareness of the value and meaning of the Jubilee of the Year 2000 in human history.

"The Jubilee of the Year 2000 is meant to be a great prayer of praise and thanksgiving, especially for the gift of the Incarnation of the Son of God and of the Redemption which he accomplished," the Pope's letter said.

With reference to spiritual preparation for the Jubilee, the Pope wrote:

"The approaching end of the second millennium demands of everyone an examination of conscience.... Christians need to place themselves humbly before the Lord and examine themselves on the responsibility which they have for the evils of our day," including:

•"Religious indifference which causes many people to live as if God did not exist. Related to this is the loss of the transcendent sense of human life and confusion in the ethical sphere, even about the fundamental values of respect for life and the family and other moral obligations."

•"Spiritual life, for many Christians, is passing through a time of uncertainty which affects not only their moral life but also their life of prayer and the theological correctness of their faith. Faith is sometimes disoriented by erroneous theological views, the spread of which is abetted by the crisis of obedience vis-a-vis the magisterium."

•"Lack of discernment, which at times becomes even acquiescence, shown by many Christians concerning the fundamental human rights by totalitarian regimes. And in our own day, the responsibility shared by so many Christians for grave forms of injustice and exclusion. How many Christians really know and put into practice the principles of the Church's social doctrine?"

## 46th INTERNATIONAL EUCHARISTIC CONGRESS

The 46th International Eucharistic Congress, to be held May 25 to June 1, 1997, in Wroclaw, Poland, was expected to be not only a major event in its own right but also one of the key observances related to preparations for the celebration of the beginning of the third millennium of Christianity in Jubilee Year 2000.

Accordingly, it was thought the overall program would be oriented to millennial themes such as the new evangelization and ecumenism as well as concentration on the many aspects of the Eucharist in Catholic doctrine and life. The climactic celebration will be the solemn Mass at the conclusion of the congress.

The eucharistic theme of the congress will find expression in special Masses, exposition of the Blessed Sacrament in churches, processions in the Polish tradition, observances of popular devotion, formal addresses, discussions and workshops on such subjects as theology, religious education, liturgy, pastoral endeavors, social action and any number of other topics.

The first international congress was held in 1881 in Lille, France; it was attended by some 800 persons from about six European countries. Many times that number are expected to take part in this 46th congress, the first of its kind to be celebrated in Poland.

The 41st congress was held in Philadelphia. (See separate entry,)

# LABOR DAY STATEMENT 1996

*These excerpts are from the Labor Day 1996 statement by Bishop William S. Skylstad of Spokane, chairman of the U.S. bishops' Domestic Policy Committee. The statement, released Aug. 23, is entitled "An Economy of Paradoxes: Labor Day Challenges."*

Labor Day 1996 comes in the midst of a national election campaign. Our country is facing a series of economic issues, choices and proposals. It also comes two months before the 10th anniversary of the Catholic bishops' pastoral letter on economic justice. In this Labor Day statement, I wish to share some of the reflections of the Catholic bishops on the continuing challenges of the economic pastoral. Their statement, "A Decade After Economic Justice for All," provides a moral framework for reflection as we celebrate this Labor Day and prepare for Election Day.

Ten years ago, our pastoral letter insisted that the measure of our economy is not only what it produces, but also how it touches human life, whether it protects or undermines the dignity of the human person, and how it promotes the common good. Economic decisions have human consequences and moral content; they help or hurt people, strengthen or weaken family life, advance or diminish the quality of justice in our land.

... The fundamental moral measure of policy choices is how they touch the poor in our midst, especially children and families who struggle against economic, social and moral pressures that leave them poor and powerless.

In the last few weeks, we have seen welfare legislation adopted and signed which cut resources and reallocated responsibilities but failed to provide the decent jobs and protection for vulnerable children, which are at the heart of real welfare reform. The welfare debate was driven more by fiscal and political factors than by the needs of poor families. The nation desperately needs real welfare reform. Sadly, this measure targeted hungry children and legal immigrants instead of the economic and moral forces which leave a fifth of the nation's children in poverty. As the bishops have pointed out, poor children, workers and families may not have the most powerful lobbies, but they have the greatest needs. We welcome a broad debate on economic life, but we cannot support a retreat in the fight against poverty and economic injustice.

## Marketplace and Public Square

It has always been clear that the pursuit of greater economic justice is not carried out primarily in the activities of religious bodies but in the broader marketplace — where investments are made, contracts are negotiated, products are created, workers are hired and policies are set. Owners, investors, consumers and workers are moral agents in economic life, building up or tearing down justice and community.

The search for economic justice is also carried forward in the public square. In this election year, while others are campaigning for office, let us campaign for poor children and vulnerable workers. Let us ask those who seek to lead and represent us how they will govern and vote on key issues of human life, human dignity and economic justice, on wages and work, on poverty and economic growth.

## A Recommitment

Whatever our economic status, political identification or ideological preferences, we are called as Catholics to work for an economy more respectful of human life and human dignity. We may differ on specifics and priorities, but let us recommit ourselves on this Labor Day — whatever our economic, ideological or political positions — to work for a society and economy offering more justice and opportunity, especially for workers and the poor.

In the midst of all the campaign rhetoric and economic debate, it is time to refocus on some traditional values from Catholic teaching — the dignity of work, the living wage, the social contract between employer and employee and the common good. It is time to recall that in our tradition people have a right and duty to work, to decent conditions, and to a fair wage for an honest day's work, to organize and join a union, to start and build a business. These many forms of economic initiative should contribute to a basic measure of economic security for all.. As the pastoral insists, "the economy should serve the person, not the other way around."

These values won't settle the ongoing economic debates, but they can help to shape them. Small business and unions, government and corporations — all have a responsibility to the broader community beyond their own immediate interests. It is time for the leaders of economic and public life to focus on the long-term health of the society instead of just on short-term financial and political gains. By building up the common ground of respect for human dignity and economic fairness, all of us can contribute to a more just and decent society.

In these debates, let us ask what is in it for all of us, not just what is in it for me. The questions should not just be "Am I" better off than I was four years ago, but "Are we" better off — all of us, especially the poor and vulnerable. This concern for others is the essence of the virtue of solidarity which Pope John Paul II called us to in his inspiring visit last fall. He called us to build "a society in which none are so poor that they have nothing to give and none so rich that they have nothing to receive. America will continue to be a land of promise as long as it remains a land of freedom and justice for all."

As we celebrate Labor Day 1996, let us recall these powerful words and the challenges of our economic pastoral of 10 years ago. Let us recommit ourselves to the task of building a more open, more productive and more just economy for all God's children.

The Catholic tradition is complex. It emphasizes rights and responsibilities, promotes charity and insists on justice, advocates personal and social responsibility. In this election year we need to get beyond false choices and ideological polarization in the economic debate. Let us recommit ourslves to the task of building a more open, more productive and more just economy for all God's children.

## AUGUST 1995

### VATICAN

**Music for Harmony** — At the end of a "Music Festival for One World" Aug. 13 at Castel Gandolfo, Pope John Paul said he hoped the festival would continue, "through music, to educate many Europeans about the ideals of peace and solidarity so that, with their artistic contributions they might help build a more free and fraternal world."

**Harmony Sought in Church in China** — Pope John Paul, addressing the bishops of Taiwan Aug. 19, called for new efforts toward church harmony in China. He said existing differences were a source of pain for members of the government-controlled church as well as for those in the underground Church who professed loyalty to the Holy See.

**Refugee Flight an "Eclipse of Mercy"** — The tragic flight of refugees in the Balkans and Central Africa illustrated the "eclipse of mercy" in the international community," according to a front-page commentary in the Aug. 24 edition of *L'Osservatore Romano*. The article said the world seemed to have grown accustomed to watching men, women and children forced to flee their homes. It cited the continuing relocation of more than 180,000 Muslims, Croats and Serbs in ex-Yugoslavia, and the recent expulsion of the about the same number of persons from Zaire. "The entire world community seems to be sliding into a dark chapter of civilization, almost without noticing the horror or the abyss toward which it is moving."

**Glendon Head of Vatican Delegation** — The Vatican announced Aug. 25 that Mary Ann Glendon would head the 21-member Vatican delegation to the United Nations' Fourth World Conference on Women, to be held Sept. 4 to 15 in Beijing. A professor of law at Harvard University since 1986, Mrs. Glendon was the first woman to head a Vatican delegation. Thirteen women and eight men comprised the membership of the delegation; eight members were from the United States.

**Problem of Islamic Fundamentalism** — The Pope told a group of Christian and Muslim experts Aug. 26 that Islamic fundamentalism was a complex phenomenon that is often fueled by the pressure of political and social problems. He said: "One must condemn the intolerance and violence prompted by fundamentalism," but "it is extremely important to look with faith and love upon those people who adopt these attitudes and those who frequently endure them." He urged careful study of Islamic fundamentalism which, he said, was growing in some regions of the world. "An analysis of the political, social and economic situations shows that the phenomenon is not only religious. In many cases, religion is exploited for political ends or to compensate for social and economic problems."

**Married Saints Sought** — A Vatican official said the time was right for seeking out married couples as candidates for sainthood. Msgr. Helmut Moll, writing in *L'Osservatore Romano*, said: "Yes, such couples exist! The majority live hidden lives. Most of them avoid the glare of public opinion." Since that is so, the relevant Vatican congregations rely on local churches to seek and find them.

**Study of Permanent Diaconate** — Archbishop Crescenzio Sepe, secretary of the Congregation for the Clergy, announced that the expanding permanent diaconate would be reviewed because "we don't want this enthusiasm to be a result of some kind of fashion rather than the fruit of a true maturation of the Church's understanding."

According to figures released by the Vatican during the month, there were 20,456 permanent deacons in the world at the end of 1993, three and a half times as many as there were at the end of 1978. More than half of the world's permanent deacons had been ordained in dioceses of the United States.

**Preference for the Poor** — The Pope, at a meeting with about 30 bishops from northern India Aug. 28, said the preference for the poor shown by Catholics of the region was directly in line with the teaching of the Church. He also praised efforts to make sure that the Church's vast network of educational and health institutions effectively serve people with the greatest needs.

**General Audience Topics:**

• As a gift of the Holy Spirit, Christian unity requires of all believers a continual conversion of heart and a commitment to the pursuit of holiness (Aug. 2).

• The Second Vatican Council called for greater appreciation of the spiritual treasures of the Christian East, beginning with the liturgy, the source of Christian life (Aug. 9).

• The Catholic Church and the ecclesial communities stemming from the Reformation have a solid basis for dialogue in the faith they share (Aug. 23).

• Trusting in God, for whom nothing is impossible, Christians must seek to overcome their divisions and move closer to the goal of full communion (Aug. 30).

**Briefs:**

• Pope John Paul visited Sister Ausilia Cortinovis Aug. 23 at Gemelli Hospital. The 61-year-old nun, suffering from cancer, helped care for him after he was shot in 1981.

• Shortly after NATO forces began bombing Bosnian Serb positions in retaliation for the Aug. 28 Serb attack on Sarajevo, the Pope called on 1,000 pilgrims from Bosnia-Herzegovina: "Let us pray together ... so that love and pardon will be victorious so that individuals and peoples can have a safe and dignified future corresponding to their noble, centuries-long traditions and their legitimate aspirations."

• The Holy Father told 15,000 cheering altar boys and girls Aug. 29: "You can't imagine how happy you make the Christians of your parishes and other communities by carrying out service at the altar with dignity, competence and love."

### Contributions of Women to Society

These were the themes of papal addresses on Sundays throughout the month in view of the forthcoming United Nations' Fourth World Conference on Women.

• Art, philosophy, science and literature cannot claim to reflect a given culture so long as the contribution of women in those fields are limited. "It is time close the gap between cultural opportunities open to men and women everywhere" (Aug. 6).

• While thanking the thousands of women who, as doctors and nurses, combine professional skill with compassion, the Pope asked: "How many women, in the Christian community as well as civil society, have been angels of consolation for uncountable numbers of suffering people?" (Aug. 13).

• Women leaders in business and economics should try to bring to their fields "a new breath of humanity and remove the recurring temptation of arid efficiency which stresses only profit" (Aug. 20).

• "Politics, which is aimed at promoting the common good, should take advantage of the complementary gifts of men and women." Increase in the number of women running for office and winning elections "is a process to encourage" (Aug. 27).

On the feast of Mary's Assumption, Aug. 15, the Pope prayed that, through her intercession, women throughout the world, "aware of their own vocation, would generously offer their indispensable contribution in every area of human promotion, especially in the defense of life."

## NATIONAL

**Vietnamese Festival** — More than 50,000 Vietnamese Catholics from the United States, Canada and Europe took part in the 18th Marian Days Festival Aug. 10 to 13 at the motherhouse of the Congregation of the Mother Co-Redemptrix in Carthage, Mo. The festival was inaugurated following resettlement of the religious institute, from Vietnam to Carthage, in 1975; the first one was attended by more than 1,000 persons.

**World War II End Remembered** — The 50th anniversary of the end of World War II was commemorated Aug. 14 at nearly simultaneously celebrated Masses in Washington and Tokyo by Cardinal James A. Hickey and Cardinal Peter Shirayanagi. Cardinal Hickey called the war "a brutal and deadly conflagration" with an estimated death toll of 50 million people. His Japanese counterpart said: "We are one in mind and heart for praying for an end to all war, and for genuine reconciliation and lasting peace."

In a related development, Bishop Daniel P. Reilly, chairman of the Bishops' International Policy Committee, recalled the 50th anniversary of the atomic bombing of Hiroshima Aug. 6, 1945. He said in a statement Aug. 2: "We would like to believe that we have exorcized all the demons of World War II from history, but we know we have not. The physical, psychological and spiritual wounds of 50 years ago persist to this day and, in some cases, continue to fuel new conflicts." Fratricidal wars, widespread disregard for basic human rights and the resurgence of extremism of all kinds "offer ample proof that we retain our individual and collective capacity for violence, inhumanity and ethnic hatred."

*The World Almanac* reported that those killed in the deadliest war in history included: 20 million Soviets, six million Jews, five million Eastern European civilians, 4.5 million Germans, three million Chinese, more that two million Japanese, 1.5 million soldiers from Eastern Europe, 620,000 from the British Empire, 500,000 each from France and Italy, 300,000 from the United States and 200,000 from The Netherlands.

**Concerns of Men and Women Religious** — In a letter released Aug. 14 in anticipation of a joint meeting of men and women religious, Sulpician Father Gerald L. Brown said: "Our member institutes (of the Conference of Major Superiors of Men and the Leadership Conference of Women Religious) appear to need to collaborate more on internal issues of community development and maintenance, and on external issues of ministry and mission. The head of the men's conference wrote: "We have to become ever clearer among ourselves about the urgent need for religious leaders who can work together in our mass society to awaken our world to the transcendent needs of the human person."

**School Enrollment** — Enrollment gains in Catholic schools over the previous two years were the basis of hopes for greater increase in the coming academic year. In 1994-95 the total number of students in elementary and high schools was 2,618,567, an increase of 41,722 over the previous year. Growth trend was high (400 percent) in preschool and kindergarten classes over the past decade. Good marketing of the schools, along with quality of programs, was a factor in increases, according to Sister Catherine McNamee, president of the National Catholic Educational Association.

**Eucharistic Ruling** — In a letter dated June 19 and circulated Aug. 22 by the Catholic News Service in the United States, the Congregation for the Doctrine of the Faith ruled: "Given the centrality of the celebration of the Eucharist in the life of the priest, candidates for the priesthood who are affected by celiac disease or suffer from alcoholism or similar conditions may not be admitted to holy orders." For priests suffering from alcoholism and unable to consume alcohol, the use of must, or unfermented grape juice, ought to be a last resort. "The preferred solution continues to be Communion by intinction (dipping the host in consecrated wine) or in concelebration under the species of bread alone." The letter also said that "permission to use low-gluten altar breads ... may be granted by ordinaries to priests and laypersons affected by celiac disease." Totally gluten-free altar breads cannot be consecrated.

**CHD 25th Anniversary** — The Campaign for Human Development celebrated its 25th anniversary Aug. 25 to 28 at a conference attended by 2,000 people in Chicago. Since its founding the bishops' campaign had raised $250 million and provided funding for more than 3,000 self-help projects. Praise for the campaign's accomplishments was expressed by the Pope, among others. He joined "the Church in the United States in giving thanks for the fruits of justice and solidarity which have taken root in communities throughout the United States ... as a result of the Campaign for Human Development." Grants for the current year — to 232 projects in 45 states, the District of Columbia and Puerto Rico — amounted to $7.6 million.

**Lay Ministry Enrollment** — The number of students in lay ministry programs more than doubled in nine years, from 10,500 in 1986 to 21,800 in 1995, according to a study conducted by the Center for Applied Research in the Apostolate. The number of programs also increased, from 206 to 265. Seventy-one percent of participants in degree programs in 1995 were lay persons; 29 percent were clergy or religious; 97 percent of participants in non-degree programs were lay persons. Most of the students were preparing for ministry in the fields of religious education, the Rite of Christian Initiation of Adults, liturgical planning, youth ministry and evangelization. The study was reported in the *Lay Ministry Formation Directory 1995*.

**Abortion Drug Combination** — Pro-life activists reacted with disgust to a study reported in the Aug. 31 issue of *The New England Journal of Medicine*, that a two-pill combination can induce abortion.

• Helen Alvare, information director of the bishops' Secretariat for Pro-Life Activities: "It just, if possible, reduces even further to pure triviality, apparently, the moral weightiness of these issues."

• Wanda Franz, president of the National Right to Life Committee: "It is a tragedy that pro-abortion advocates want to use women as guinea pigs."

• Michael Ferguson, executive director of the Catholic Campaign for America: "Finding 'simpler,' more 'private' ways to take innocent human life reinforces our modern 'culture of death,' and we all must consider the implications of continuing down this sad and destructive path."

**Meetings:**

• About 2,000 persons participated in the 113th annual convention of the Knights of Columbus Aug. 1 to 3 in Kansas City, Mo. Delegates called Pope John Paul's encyclical letter "Gospel of Life" a direct challenge to the contemporary "culture of death"; urged Congress to pass legislation "to end the barbaric practice" of late-term abortions; were told that pro-life efforts had to focus not only on abortion but also on concern for the poor and weak.

• More than 1,300 Native Americans and Catholic leaders attended the 56th annual Tekakwitha Conference Aug. 2 to 6 in Potsdam, N.Y. Ninety or more Kateri Circles were represented at the conference.

• "Proud To Be Catholic" was the theme of the IX National Cursillo Encounter Aug. 9 to 13 in Denver. Cardinal Bernard F. Law, one of the speakers, refuted what he called "some misconceptions about the Catholic Church," especially regarding the false charge that Catholics and the Church are not biblical.

• Fifty years since its founding after World War II, Pax Christi USA devoted its Aug. 11-to-13 assembly to the theme, "From the Bomb to the Cross: The Journey Continues." The meeting in Portland, Me, was attended by more than 500 persons.

**Briefs:**

• The National Conference of Catholic Bishops established an Office for the Catechism and named Father John Pollard its executive director. The office was created to provide staff assistance to the bishops' Ad Hoc Committee to Oversee the Use of the Catechism.

• Norma McCorvey, the "Jane Roe" in the 1973 Roe v. Wade Supreme Court abortion case, told ABC News Aug. 10: "I think abortion is wrong. I think what I did was wrong. And I just had to take a pro-life decision on choice." She said in one interview, however, that she still supported the right to a first trimester abortion, particularly in cases of fetal deformity.

• About 500 Indian and other Asian Catholics attended a pilgrimage-ending Mass Aug. 12 at the Basilica of the Immaculate Conception in Washington. Their participation was part of an effort to raise funds for a shrine to be erected in the crypt church of the basilica honoring Our Lady of Good Health of Vailankanni.

• Msgr. Arthur S. Thomas of the Diocese of New Ulm was named Air Force Chief of Chaplains.

## Religious Expression in Public Schools

Guidelines on religious expression prepared under the auspices of the U.S. Department of Education were expected to reduce the number of disagreements and law suits in public school districts across the country. A recently drafted statement of principles dealt with the extent to which religious expression and activity are permitted in public schools. The guidelines outlined specific ways in which students may discuss religious beliefs, include them in school work and participate in religious activities on campus, as well as how teachers and administrators should or should not treat religious celebrations and topics. The principles were drafted at the request of President Clinton by attorneys from the White House and the Departments of Education and Justice, working with representatives of various churches and civil rights organizations.

## INTERNATIONAL

**Tension in Northern Ireland** — Violence by Catholics angry over Protestant parades celebrating a 300-year-old battle raised tension in Northern Ireland and concern over progress toward peace. Twelve police officers and 10 Catholics were injured in clashes Aug. 12 when Catholics tried to prevent a march through their area to mark the 17th-century victory of Protestant King William of Orange over Catholic King James II. Catholic youths also firebombed a Protestant building, and violence was reported in several cities. Many Catholics said they felt the parades were needless displays of sectarian superiority that struck at the heart of the peace process. It was the worst violence in a relatively nonviolent year and focused the spotlight on a deadlock in Anglo-Irish attempts to forge a lasting peace from Britain's insistence on disarmament by the Irish Republican Army and the rival Protestant Loyalist guerrillas.

In another development, a new demographic study indicated that Protestant emigration would likely be the main factor in an increasing proportion of Catholics in Northern Ireland. Changing economic conditions, due to improved prospects abroad for the better educated, would encourage more Protestants than Catholics to emigrate, said Cormac O'Grada and Brendan Walsh of University College, Dublin, authors of the study.

**Nuclear Test Protest** — Bishops of 23 Pacific countries signed a joint statement calling on France to stop nuclear testing in their region. The 90 prelates, saying they represented nearly seven million Catholics, described the planned resumption of tests an "intolerable scandal." Using the area as a test site for weapons of mass destruction was "to desecrate that which was created for the nurturing and nourishment of life.... It is an act of theft from the poor of the world and from generations of people yet to come. It wastes funds which should be used to eradicate the poverty afflicting one-fifth of the world's people and engenders a climate of hostility and fear." The bishops said they wanted all nations with nuclear weaponry to stop testing and to take immediate steps to start dismantling weapons of mass destruction.

**Ecumenism in Spain** — Catholic-Protestant relations were called strained in Spain and could "only be described as modest," according to Father Julian Garcia Hernando, director of ecumenism for the Spanish Bishops' Conference. Pedro Tarquis, spokesman for the Federation of Religious Entities of Spain, commented: "The great majority of Spanish evangelicals are opposed to (the Catholic view of) ecumenism. I would say 90 percent are absolutely and viscerally anti-ecumenical." Father Garcia said the evangelical suspicion of Catholic motives was due to several factors: "We have a hard history in respect to the Protestants.... Most of the Spanish Protestants speak hard against Catholics because they are converts." Converts from Catholicism "simply do not have the willingness necessary for an ecumenical dialogue because they come with their own biases against their previous religion."

**Balkan Nationalism** — Cooperation between the Croatian Catholic and Serbian Orthodox churches was blocked by the dominance of "nationalist elements" on both sides, said the former U.N. human rights monitor in former Yugoslavia. He also criticized the "ineffectiveness" of Western policy" and said the Aug. 28 shelling of downtown Sarajevo, in which 37 people died, highlighted the "very nasty politics" being played in the conflict. Tadeusz Mazowiecki, interviewed Aug. 28, said: "It would be wrong to say the churches lack mutual understanding, since their representatives have met and debated. But the practical consequences of these encounters have been impeded by the predominant attitudes of defending only one's believers and talking badly about the other side." He added that the antagonisms between the religious communities was "an accumulation of historical experiences."

**Priests Accused** — Several priests were the subjects of allegations that they had taken part in the previous year's genocide in Rwanda. They included an Italian missionary with 50 years of service in the country and a Rwandan parish priest in Kigali.

**Gay Bashing Condemned** — In response to Zimbabwean President Robert Mugabe's condemnation of homosexuals, the nation's Catholic Justice and Peace Commission said gays should be protected by law from discrimination and that gay bashing could not be justified. "In the eyes of the Church, the physical expression of homosexuality is, and will remain, immoral. However, homosexual people should be treated with compassion and sensitivity, and there should be no discrimination against them."

**Briefs:**
• Nepal's first community church, incorporating Buddhist and Hindu along with Catholic features, was inaugurated Aug. 15 in Katmandu.
• Jerusalem's Latin-rite patriarchate condemned the Aug. 21 bombing of a bus in the residential neighborhood of Ramat Eshkol.
• Children and young women in southern Sudan were being captured and sold as slaves, reported a delegation of Christian Solidarity International on its return to London during the month.
• The strength of devotion to Mary in Poland was evident during the month in attendance by large numbers of people at Mass at various Marian shrines, including 100,000 at Piekary Slaski and 250,000 at Jasna Gora.

## Mexican Incidents

Bishop Raul Vera Lopez was appointed coadjutor to Bishop Samuel Ruiz Garcia of San Cristobal de Las Casas, to carry out pastoral duties more or less neglected, it was alleged, in Bishop Ruiz's preoccupation with social justice and human rights struggles in the State of Chiapas. The appointment was announced Aug. 14.

Other developments included the following.

•The Jesuit director of a human rights center praised a federal panel's call for prosecuting a group of Guerrero state officials implicated in the massacre of farmers by state police, but alleged that the guilt went even higher. Father David Fernandez, head of the Miguel A. Pro Juarez Human Rights Center in Mexico City, said he believed Guerrero Gov. Ruben Figueroa was directly involved and should also be brought to justice. Father Fernandez's comments came after the National Human Rights Commission released a 360-page report Aug. 14, which concluded that 17 unarmed farmworkers were shot to death and 14 others wounded when more than 30 state police opened fire on a vehicle in which they were riding. The incident occurred June 28 near the town of Coyuca de Benitez, 30 miles north of Acapulco.

• Father Fernandez, less than a week after charging that state officials were linked to the massacre of 17 peasant farmers, received two anonymous death threats by telephone during the night of Aug. 17.

• Bishop Luis Gabriel Cuara of Tuxpan disclosed that his priests and pastoral workers had been harassed by police and military intelligence agents in recent months, that they were under tension and felt hampered in their pastoral work among the mostly indigenous people of the diocese. He cited the example of a newly installed parish priest who found himself in trouble because of his preaching "that we are all children of God, that we all have dignity, that we are all brothers, that we all should be respected, and that we should all love one another equally.... Unfortunately, that message was interpreted as subversive and, because it coincided with the uprising in Chiapas, they (local power brokers) began speaking badly of the priest and said he was inciting an uprising, that he was distributing arms to the people."

# SEPTEMBER 1995

## VATICAN

**Meeting with Arafat** — Pope John Paul met Sept. 2 with Palestinian leader Yasser Arafat to discuss peace prospects in the Middle East and hopes for an end-of-the-millennium interfaith celebration in Jerusalem. It was their fourth meeting, and the first since the beginning of Palestinian self-rule in the Gaza Strip and the West Bank town of Jericho. Afterwards, the Vatican said in a statement that "both Palestinians and Israelis can soon enjoy the concrete fruits of peace,"

**Brazilian Bishops, Sects and Ecumenism** — The Pope told bishops of northeastern Brazil Sept. 5 that more had to be done to counteract the influence of religious sects and the "serious damage" such groups were causing the Catholic faithful. He also warned against an overly simplified ecumenical dialogue. "The serious problem of sects is spreading like an oil stain, threatening to cause collapse of the structure of faith in many nations," he said, accusing the sects of taking particular aim at the Catholic Church in an "evil" effort to undermine peoples' faith. He added: "It is clear that their (sects') success can be explained by the lack of religious culture among the people, caused in large part by the loss of religious experience." In 1992, Brazilian Cardinal Lucas Moreira Neves estimated that about 20 million Brazilians had turned to Protestant sects, and that sects had about 60,000 pastors at work in the country.

While noting the value of ecumenical dialogue, he said there was a tendency among some to promote agreement by ignoring basic teachings of the Church: "In the area of inculturation as well as ecumenism, in fact, one can see that ... the search for understanding, welcome or openness toward other religious groups or churches has led to serious mutilations of the Catholic faith and liturgical prayer." Church leaders must never, in the name of ecumenism, modify church teachings, abandon practices of popular piety or weaken centuries of church discipline.

**Soldiers for Peace** — The Holy Father urged several thousands of soldiers from different countries to "make war against war," and to promote ways of peaceful dialogue among armies of the world. He made the remarks Sept. 7 in a talk to participants in the first World Military Games to be held in Rome. "Every soldier," he said, "should always feel in his soul that he is a soldier of peace. The soldier is not, and should not be, a man of war," but someone who, while involved in defense of his country, is persistently promoting ways of cooperation and peace between populations.

**Resignation Accepted** — In a letter released Sept. 14, the Pope accepted the resignation of Cardinal Hans Hermann Groer of Vienna, accused of alleged homosexual acts committed 20 years earlier. The cardinal's ambiguous rebuttal of the allegations was reported to have triggered a crisis of confidence among the Austrian faithful.

**Trip to Africa** — Pope John Paul, on the 67th foreign trip of his pontificate Sept. 14 to 20, visited Cameroon, South Africa and Kenya for special meetings with bishops marking the conclusion of the Special Assembly for Africa of the Synod of Bishops. (See separate entries.)

**Ethics and Atomic Energy** — The International Atomic Energy Agency must not only improve the safety of nuclear power plants, but must also pay greater attention to ethical questions related to the very use of nuclear technology. So stated Msgr. Mario Zenari, Vatican representative to the U.N.-related agency. He praised the work done by the agency to ensure compliance with the 1968 Nuclear Nonproliferation Treaty, and said: "In order to attain the objective of a nuclear-free world, state parties to the NPT have to accept safeguards and cooperate" fully with the inspectors sent by the agency to verify that technology and materials have not been transferred to other countries. Msgr. Zenari spoke on the third day of the International Atomic Energy Agency's meeting Sept. 18 to 25 in Vienna.

**Fund Raising and Awareness** — The seasonal educational and fund-raising campaigns of Catholic agencies raise awareness as well as money, said speakers at a Vatican-sponsored meeting in Rome. The campaigns "have done much to sensitize the community, to stimulate the Christian sharing of goods between North and South and within countries, between members of the same community and also on behalf of the needs of other religious confessions," said Msgr. Ivan Marin. Msgr. Marin, secretary of the Pontifical Council *Cor Unum*, spoke at the opening of a Sept. 25-to-27 meeting to discuss theological and pastoral implications of aid programs.

**Mine Clearance** — In addition to banning the manufacture and use of land mines, industrial nations must increase funding to clear mines from the roads, fields and farms of now-peaceful countries, said Msgr. Mario Zenari in an address Sept. 27. He spoke during an international conference reviewing a 1980 treaty on "conventional weapons which may be deemed to be excessively injurious or to have indiscriminate effects." The weapons include land mines, booby traps and blinding lasers. Msgr. Zenari said: "Thinking of more than 25,000 children, women and men suffering every year as innocent victims of those weapons, governments should realize their moral obligation to take every possible step in order to promote the transformation of swords into plowshares." But attention must also be given to "those mines which are still lying in the territories of many states and which continue to threaten the lives and physical integrity of numerous individuals.... The delegation of the Holy See appeals to all governments, especially those in industrialized countries, to allocate more financial resources" to mine clearance and to assistance for people who have been maimed by the weapons.

**Jesuit Norms** — The Pope formally approved Sept. 27 three changes in norms governing the Jesuit order, providing greater voice for brothers, restricting "ecclesiastical honors" for members of the society, and giving the superior general, in consultation with his council, authority to close houses of the order he thinks should be closed. The norms were enacted by the general congregation of the order earlier in the year.

**Synod for Asia** — Pope John Paul announced the names of 16 members of the pre-synodal council for the special assembly for Asia of the Synod of Bishops. The synod had been proposed in connection with preparations for the celebration of Jubilee Year 2000.

**General Audience Topics:**
• "The Blessed Virgin is the perfect realization of the Church's holiness, and its model" (Sept. 6).
• The mystery of Mary's virginal motherhood and the title *Theotokos* officially attributed to her by the Council of Ephesus in 431 (Sept. 13).
• "One of the main concerns that evangelization must face on this continent (of Africa, just visited), is the work of inculturation" (Sept. 27).

**Briefs:**
• The day before the Sept. 4 beginning of the Fourth World Conference on Women, the Pope urged support for the participation, "without discrimination," of women in church life, including "the teaching of theology; approved forms of liturgical ministry, such as serving at the altar; pastoral and administrative councils; diocesan synods and particular councils; and various church institutions, curias and tribunals.
• During a Sept. 9-to-10 visit to Loreto, the Pope called on 300,000 European youths to reject nationalistic violence and intolerance.
• The Pope seconded Sept. 14 the protest of French bishops against their nation's nuclear tests in the Pacific.
• The social teaching of the Church can help fill "the worrying vacuum of social ethics" seen in many contemporary cultures, said the Pope Sept. 23 at a meeting with representatives of European and Latin American bishops' conferences.
• The Holy Father celebrated a memorial Mass Sept. 28 for his predecessor John Paul I on the 17th anniversary of his death. He also made a special commemoration of Paul VI.

## Beijing Conference on Women

The Vatican, represented by a 21-member delegation, joined the consensus on only part of the documentation produced by the Fourth World Conference on Women Sept. 4 to 15 in Beijing, China, while strongly criticizing sections on women's health and human rights. One hundred and 89 delegations formally adopted a Declaration and Platform for Action at the end of the meeting, but dozens of delegations expressed reservations about them. "Unfortunately, the Holy See's participation in the consensus can only be a partial one because of numerous points in the documents which are incompatible with what the Holy See and other countries deem favorable to the true advancement of women," said Harvard law professor Mary Ann Glendon, head of the Holy See's delegation, at the final plenary meeting. Problems in the health and human rights sections are "very, very serious," and the Vatican "vigorously denounces" their treatment of matters related to sexuality, motherhood and the family, Ms. Glendon said in an interview. (See separate entry, Beijing Statement: Vatican Delegation.)

## NATIONAL

**Labor Day Statement** — The U.S. Catholic Conference's 1995 Labor Day statement declared that most American workers had not reaped the benefits of the recent expansion of the U.S. economy: "Most Americans have seen their income decline or just hold even.... Families must work longer hours with more members of the family in the work force just to keep even." Auxiliary Bishop John H. Ricard of Baltimore was the author of "Renewing the Social Contract, Reclaiming the Dignity of Work and the Rights of Workers." He said many American workers had found that the old ways of doing business no longer existed, and that the employer-employee contract had been replaced by "survival of the fittest." The renewed growth in productivity, accompanied by a decline in wages, had caused "the largest gap between the rich and poor in the industrialized world." The statement urged employers to recognize their responsibility to their workers by providing a living wage, protection against unemployment, a decent work environment and the right to organize and bargain collectively. It also said that society must affirm the social contract between employers and employees by ensuring that everyone who can work has the opportunity to do so.

**Best College Buys** — Twelve Catholic colleges were among the nation's top 100 in terms of value for the money, according to the annual list published by *Money* magazine: Siena College, Loudonville, N.Y. (37th); St. Bonaventure University, Allegany, N.Y. (41st); Creighton University, Omaha, Neb. (51st); Le Moyne College, Syracuse, N.Y. (53rd); St. John's University, New York (65th); Assumption College, Worcester, Mass. (67th); Chestnut Hill College, Phila. Pa. (73rd); St. Vincent College, Latrobe, Pa. (83rd); Thomas More College, Covington, Ky. (91st); Loyola University, New Orleans, La. (92nd); Carroll College, Helena, Mont. (95th); Stonehill College, North Easton, Mass. (98).

**Religious Belief and Practice** — Religious beliefs should not be separated from business practices, said Msgr. Thomas J. Rodi at an annual Red Mass Sept. 8 in Lafayette, La. In his homily, he invited judges, lawyers and others associated with the legal profession to reflect on whether or not their praise of God affects their practice of the law. He observed: "Although we are believers, value our faith and embrace our Judeo-Christian ethics found in sacred Scriptures, there can be a tendency to feel that our public life in business, commerce or the practice of law is somehow separate from religious beliefs."

**No Excuse To Abandon the Poor** — Calls to affirm personal responsibility must not be used as an excuse to abandon the needy, said the bishops of Wisconsin in a statement entitled "Reforming Welfare by Valuing Families" and released Sept. 13. "Nor must the desire to foster responsibility rationalize decisions by the community to deny or withdraw its support from the needy when social and economic conditions prevent a poor person from being self-sufficient." In a six-point set of priorities, the bishops said welfare reform should:
• reduce poverty, especially among children;
• be based on "a culture that values families, marriage and legitimacy";
• make use of the "social capital of communities and neighborhoods";

• emerge from "an economy that values work";

• encourage the working poor;

• "discern differences among individuals and families, and avoid 'one-size-fits-all' approaches."

**Nuns Aid Cubans** — Four U.S. nuns left Miami Sept. 19 to start three months of pastoral work among the more than 10,000 refugees at Guantanamo Bay Naval Base in Cuba. The sister-volunteers were under the sponsorship of the U.S. Catholic Conference for the Pastoral Care of Migrants and Refugees.

**Corporate Responsibility** — Church agencies in the corporate responsibility movement were attempting to develop general principles for operating in the global economy, according to a draft set of "Principles for Global Corporate Responsibility," released Sept. 19. The guidelines called for corporations, wherever they operate, to recognize the stake that all sectors of a community have in economic decisions and to follow recognized principles in such areas as fair employment, safety, advertising, ecology and respect for law. Three agencies involved in the movement were the Interfaith Center on Corporate Responsibility in the United States, the Taskforce on the Churches and Corporate Responsibility in Canada and the Ecumenical Committee for Corporate Responsibility in the United Kingdom.

**Nature of Catholic Universities** — Catholic universities belong in the heart of the Church and therefore must both teach and defend church teachings. So stated Cardinal Anthony J. Bevilacqua Sept. 22 during the 18th annual convention of the Fellowship of Catholic Scholars. He said: "It was from the heart of the Church that the Catholic universities grew, and it is at the heart of the Church that the Catholic universities belong.... The Church is the teacher of truth, and it is her responsibility to teach the truth of Jesus Christ." The Catholic university must be "an institutional witness to Christ and his message," and must have the courage to speak "uncomfortable truths" about such issues as abortion, euthanasia, sexuality, divorce, contraception, homosexuality, family life, virtues and commitment to the common good." He also said: "What a Catholic university should fear is the temptation to remain silent about the word of God." He noted that academic freedom is sometimes mistakenly preferred over truth.

**Statement on Life Issues** — "Faithful for Life," a pastoral statement on abortion, euthanasia and other life-related issues, approved by the U.S. bishops the previous June, was formally released Sept. 28. The 6,000-word document was the bishops' first pastoral statement since 1985 to treat the subjects of abortion and euthanasia at length.

**Briefs:**

• A special Family Rosary campaign resulted in the shipment of more than 2.5 million rosaries worldwide since 1991, reported Family Rosary headquarters in Albany, N.Y.

• Donald McCrabb, executive director of the Catholic Campus Ministry Association, reported Sept. 10 that Catholic and Protestant campus ministry programs across the country were "caught in the poverty cycle" and forced to reduce their activities.

• Honored: Hugh Downs, co-anchor of ABC's 20/20, with the 1995 Gabriel Personal Achievement Award; Franciscan Sister Christina Kraus, founder of the St. Francis Center in Vinton County, Ohio, with the 1995 Lumen Christi Award of the Catholic Church Extension Society.

• Faith, justice and the survival of rural communities and parishes were the principal concerns of those attending the 1995 Heartland Regional meeting in Atchison, Kan.

• Brothers of the Christian Schools, known as the Christian Brothers, celebrated the 150th anniversary of their educational mission in the United States Sept. 16.

• The National Association of the Holy Name Society elected its first black president, Aaron Gilyard of New Orleans, at its 25th anniversary convention Sept. 20 to 24.

## Distorted Version of Scripture

Bishops were warned by the head of their Committee on the Liturgy that a new inclusive-language scriptural translation published Sept. 11 by Oxford University Press was "a distortion of the inspired Word of God.... The editors of this volume have done a great disservice to biblical scholarship and the need for a balanced use of inclusive language."

The text at issue, for example, translated New Testament references to God the Father as "Father-Mother" and changed "son" to "child" or "the human one" when referring to Jesus. *The New Testament and Psalms: An Inclusive Version,* was edited by a panel of U.S. Protestant scholars. Bishop Donald W. Trautman called the text "a most irresponsible translation that offends the doctrine of the Church and revealed truth of the Father, Son and Holy Spirit."

## INTERNATIONAL

**Nuns Killed** — Two European nuns who helped run a vocational school for women in Algeria were shot and killed Sept. 3 in Algiers, presumably by Muslim terrorists. Pope John Paul condemned the slayings as a "hateful assassination" of missionaries who had dedicated 30 years of their lives in service to Algerians. Their deaths brought to 10 the number of religious killed during the previous two years in the North African country, where guerrilla/government violence had taken on the aspect of a civil war. The nuns were French Sister Denise Leclerc and Maltese Sister Jean Littlejohn.

**Sects Worrisome in Russia** — The chairman of the Religious Affairs Committee of the Duma said in an interview published in the weekly *Russkaya Mysl* that the legislature was becoming increasingly worried about the proliferation of sects and cults. Vitaly Savitsky made the statement following the arrest of two satanists on charges of rape and murder. He also said that many of the undesirable groups espoused doctrines "close to the ideology of (Joseph) Goebbels," head of Nazi Germany's propaganda apparatus.

**More Anti-Church Incidents in Mexico** — Foreign-born priests and nuns working in the Diocese of San Cristobal de Las Casas said the government was engaged in a virtual vendetta against them because they were siding with the poor instead of the powerful.

• Diocesan officials called expulsions, revocations

of immigration papers and requests that foreign priests and sisters leave the diocese part of a government 'campaign' against Bishop Samuel Ruiz Garcia and his diocesan team.

• American Father Paul Nadolny was informed in writing Sept. 15 that, because of alleged immigration technicalities, his immigration status had been canceled and he could never re-enter Mexico again, even as a tourist. In addition, there were confirmed reports that the government was seeking the removal of five other priests from the country.

**Catholic Press Congress** — Catholic journalists from many countries attended the 17th World Congress of the International Catholic Union of the Press Sept. 9 to 17 in Graz, Austria. One of the speakers was Barbara Beckwith, editor of the Cincinnati-based *St. Anthony Messenger.* Addressing the congress theme, "Ethics of Peace in a World of Violence," she paraphrased Pope John Paul's advisory," If you want peace, work for justice." She said: "If you want peace, strive for truth."

**Catholic-Lutheran Dialogue** — The International Lutheran-Roman Catholic Commission on Unity opened a new phase of dialogue at a Sept. 10-to-16 meeting in Larkkula, Finland. Much of the meeting was devoted to selecting specific topics for discussion, with focus on "those issues where consensus sufficient for further visible steps toward unity still eludes us," said the commission in a communique. Three main areas were to be addressed:

• "The Apostolicity of the Church," with special emphasis on episcopacy and "possible forms and structures of a universal ministry for Christian unity";

• the Eucharist, where the commission wants to "summarize the results achieved so far regarding a common understanding of the sacrament";

• ethical questions.

**United Nations Praised** — The United Nations remained a "sign of hope" 50 years after its birth, said Archbishop Renato R. Martino, Sept. 18 at an annual prayer service in New York. The Holy See's permanent observer said the U.N. provided a mechanism for the peaceful resolution of conflict and for collaboration on a wide range of issues. U.N. Secretary-General Boutros Boutros-Ghali, one of many diplomats present, called U.N. personnel "servants of the international community." He asked for prayers for U.N. representatives who had died in the service of peace.

**Evangelization by Indigenous Peoples** — Christians are not only called to evangelize indigenous peoples but also to be evangelized by them, said participants in a conference on "Evangelization among the Indigenous Peoples of Asia." The conference was organized by an office of the Federation of Asian Bishops' Conferences. The 45 participants from 10 countries issued a statement in which they recommended:

• compilation of a directory of indigenous clergy, religious and lay leaders, as well as individuals and pastoral centers serving indigenous peoples;

• that concerns of indigenous peoples be made a priority for the Special Assembly for Asia of the Synod of Bishops announced by Pope John Paul;

• that Asian bishops consider the possibility of establishing an Office for the Concerns of Indigenous Peoples.

**Praise for Pope's Commitment, but ...** — The Rev. Konrad Raiser, general secretary of the World Council of Churches, praised the Pope's "irrevocable commitment" to Christian unity, expressed skepticism that his call to discuss the papacy would bear ecumenical fruit, and voiced doubt that there would be closer Catholic-WCC ties in the foreseeable future. He did so in a report presented Sept. 14 to the WCC's Central Committee. He spoke highly of the encyclical letter *Ut Unum Sint,* in which the Pope called for ecumenical dialogue about the role of the papacy. He said: "While we may be inclined to be skeptical about its outcome, it is important that this fundamental question between churches be faced honestly.... The encyclical is very clear in stating that full unity implies and requires communion with the pope, the bishop of Rome.... A sense of realism" indicates that there are too many differences over the issue at present to reach a common understanding. The primary unity sought by the WCC is one of faith, not structural organization, he said.

**Briefs:**

• Israeli Religious Affairs Minister Shimon Shetreet said in a report that some services offered to the Muslim, Christian and Druse communities were inferior to those for Jews and promised to rectify the situation.

• The bishops of Ontario called on Canadian Premier Mike Harris to make sure his proposed budget would not hurt the underprivileged.

• Cardinal Giovanni Saldarini announced that the Shroud of Turin would be displayed publicly in 1998 and the year 2000.

• Cardinal George Basil Hume of Westminster and Bishop Michel Dubost, head of the French Military Ordinariate, joined other leaders who had already called for a ban on the production, stockpiling, export and use of anti-personnel mines.

## Plight of Illegal Immigrants and Refugees

With the release Sept. 5 of his message for World Migration Day 1996, Pope John Paul focused attention on illegal immigrants, refugees and racist or intolerant reactions among local populations.

Archbishop Giovanni Cheli, head of the Pontifical Council for Migrants and Travelers, said that of the world's estimated 125 million people forced to live outside their own countries, only 20 million were officially classified as refugees. In many ways, they were the fortunate ones, because they could qualify for international assistance and U.N. protection. But: "The person forced to leave his country because of hunger is only a 'clandestine immigrant' and, as such, is hunted by the police and destined for forced repatriation." The swelling numbers of these illegal immigrants had already reached about 100,000 million, he said. The largest concentrations were in the United States (about 4.5 million, mostly Mexicans) Western Europe (three million) and industrialized Asian countries like Japan (three million).

Caritas and other Catholic organizations called on the Italian government to take action against the exploitation of women immigrants as prostitutes. It was estimated that prostitution was a criminally dominated $2-billion annual business in the country, and that 60 percent of the 26,000 women involved were immigrants.

# OCTOBER 1995

## VATICAN

**Beatifications** — Pope John Paul started the month Oct. 1 with ceremonies for the beatification of an Italian priest and 109 martyrs, 64 of the French Revolution in the 1790s and 45 of the Spanish Civil War between 1936 and 1939. The Holy Father also beatified Oct. 29 three Swiss women: Sisters Maria Theresia Scherer and Maria Bernarda Butler, founders of religious institutes, and Marguerite Bays, a lay woman.

**Pro-Life Cooperation** — The Pope urged a wide spectrum of pro-life organizations to cooperate closely in efforts to influence public opinion block legislative threats to human life. "It is clear," he said Oct. 3, "that the defense of life is a commitment that concerns not only private morality, but which is also a social and political question." Pro-life actions should be "peaceful, convinced and community based" efforts aimed at affecting local customs, culture and legislation. The Pope spoke at a meeting of the Vatican-sponsored Third World Congress for Pro-Life Movements, attended by representatives of more than 100 organizations.

**Christian Hope** — In a world marked by fear, confusion and conflict, Christians should be witnesses of hope, said the Pope Oct. 11 in follow-up remarks to the address given six days earlier at the United Nations. "Even if sin and the spirit of evil are at work, we have the certainty that the love of God is stronger than human weakness. This allows us to move toward the future without fear."

**American Synod Preparation** — Cardinals and bishops from North and South America appointed by the Pope to plan a Special Assembly for America of the Synod of Bishops met for the first time at the Vatican in the middle of the month. No date for the assembly and no specifics were reported, but one participant indicated there was discussion about challenges to the Church in America, such as evangelization, justice, solidarity among peoples of the continent, and preparations for the millennium celebrations in the year 2000.

**Balkan Peace Plan** — Pope John Paul and bishops of the five states of the former Yugoslavia agreed Oct. 17 on a 10-point plan for "the spiritual and material reconstruction of the peoples of the Balkans." Key points of the program were calls for reconciliation and the rejection of "exacerbated nationalism," according to The Tablet of London.

**Right and Wrong** — The Church provides a service to individuals and to nations when it insists that certain things are right and other are wrong, the Pope said Oct. 18 at a meeting with a group of bishops from Brazil. Rather than toning down its moral teaching to avoid confrontation with contemporary culture, the Church must respond to "the unhealthy confusion which many people feel regarding basic questions of good and evil, of what is correct and what is erroneous." He cited the "very painful" abandonment of faith and morals in Christian countries, and said the Church must continue to insist that freedom is authentic only when it respects the truth about God, human life and behavior necessary for peaceful coexistence.

**Style of Service** — The Second Vatican Council outlined the portrait of a vibrant Church animated by a sense of communion and participation, and always ready to bring its message to the world. So stated the Pope on Mission Sunday, Oct. 22. "The Church of our age should increasingly assume the face of the family, in which no one feels left out," he said. "The exercise of ecclesial authority should be carried out more and more in the style of service" in a "new age of initiative and responsibility" involving lay persons.

The Holy Father paid tribute to men and women missionaries on the "front lines of the Kingdom of God," and urged all other members of the Church to support worldwide evangelization efforts with prayer and financial aid.

**More Missionary Activity Needed** — In a Mission Sunday-related interview in L'Osservatore Romano, Cardinal Jozef Tomko said that missionary activity must go on and be increased even though missionaries and resources are in short supply. We "cannot wait until we have an abundance of personnel.... Our planet has five-and-a-half billion inhabitants, of whom only one-third are Christian, and one billion are Catholic. Two-thirds of humanity, then, does not know or accept Jesus Christ."

**Catholic-Hindu Cooperation** — In a letter to Hindus celebrating a major feast day Oct. 23, Cardinal Francis Arinze called for closer Catholic-Hindu cooperation in promoting religious values, particularly those related to environmental protection. He said: "Hindu dharma (teaching) has always upheld the interconnectedness between all beings and taught that the whole universe, with all 'pranimatre' (living beings) in it, is a single family." Christianity shares this view, while insisting that the human being, created in God's image and likeness, has a particular place and role in creation. Whenever people ignore or are inattentive to their relationship with the created world, the environment and people themselves suffer. The cardinal's letter was released three days before the celebration of the feast of Deepavali, or Diwali, which commemorates the victory of light over darkness and of goodness over evil.

**Agricultural Reform** — Pleading the cause of starving people, Pope John Paul called for reform of global agricultural and marketing practices. He urged food experts Oct. 23 to eliminate what he called "structures of famine" — market mechanisms and social policies that keep less-developed countries in conditions of poverty and dependence. The Pope addressed his comments to participants in the 28th General Conference of the U.N. Food and Agricultural Organization. Other factors affecting the world food situation included unjust criteria in the distribution of resources and production; protectionism and special group interests; the increasing size of the refugee population; administrative corruption, and needy-country spending for arms rather than food.

**Response to Refugee Needs** — With a new climate of suspicion and hostility toward immigrants in mind, the Pope said the Church should increase its efforts to be a "Good Samaritan" to migrants and refugees. "Migration, which once was seen as a factor of economic, social and cultural development for the host nation, is today increasingly felt as a burden, a disturbance and a problem," he said Oct. 27 at a meeting of the Pontifical Council for Migrants and Travelers. He said the host state has a right to react when faced with improper behavior or episodes of intolerance among immigrants, but the overriding Christian response should be to reach out and give special help to these people, who are often without homes, jobs or protection.

**General Audience Topics:**

The Pope was en route to the United States Oct. 4.

• The task facing the United Nations is the creation of an instrument to safeguard and defend the rights of nations, particularly the right to exist (Oct. 11).

• The United States is under challenge to strengthen the truths and values on which the country was founded and without which democracy will not prevail (Oct. 18).

• Through the centuries, the Church's tradition has appreciated ever more profoundly the close sharing of Mary in the redemptive mission of her Son (Oct. 25).

**Briefs:**

• Marjorie Weeke, an American woman with 25 years of Vatican service, was given the honor of Dame of St. Gregory the Great, one of the Church's highest honors.

• The Pope earmarked some of the royalties from his best-seller *Crossing the Threshold of Hope* to help rebuild churches and other places of worship in former Yugoslavia.

• The Vatican Press Office reported that Pope John Paul made 123 personal written or spoken appeals for peace in the Balkans between Jan. 30, 1991, and Oct. 4, 1995.

• The life and ministry of priests was the theme of an Oct. 23-to-28 symposium marking the 30th anniversary of the Second Vatican Council's decree on the subject.

• Cardinal Paul Poupard, marking the 50th anniversary of UNESCO, said Oct. 28 that the organization's emphasis on cultural sharing is crucial in overcoming global trends toward fragmentation and narrow concern for special interests.

### United Nations Visit and Address

The "Fabric of Relations among Peoples" was the theme of Pope John Paul's address before the General Assembly Oct. 5 as the United Nations began celebrations marking the 50th anniversary of its founding. One of the significant points in the papal address was the need for a bill of rights for nations, to complement the bill of universal rights. (See additional entries covering the Pope's visit and address.)

### NATIONAL

**Last Railway Car Chapel** —The last of three railroad cars used as mobile chapels early in the century was expected to go on sale during the month as an item in an Old West museum collection in Montana. Use of the cars was pioneered by Father Francis C. Kelly, founder of the Catholic Church Extension Society in 1905, for service in rural communities without churches.

**Reconciliation Role for Women** — Organizations like the National Council of Catholic Women can help bring reconciliation to a "politically and culturally fragmented" U.S. society and Church, said Margaret O'Brien Steinfels Oct. 2 in a keynote address at the group's 75th anniversary convention in San Francisco. The editor of Commonweal magazine told delegates: "We are confronted in our culture and in our politics by the challenge of maintaining a right relationship between the individual and society, and striking a proper balance between rights and responsibilities." Catholic social teaching, she added, provides guidance in drawing up "an ethic and a theology of accountability" needed to meet that challenge.

**Families against Vengeance** — State-sanctioned vengeance in the form of capital punishment is not the answer to murder, said relatives of victims touring California cities to advocate alternatives to the death penalty. They argued that healing for families of victims will not come from vengeance but by their reconciliation with society and sometimes even with the offender. Members of Murder Victims' Families for Reconciliation spoke at several parishes and schools Oct. 6, near the end of a two-week "Journey of Hope" through the state.

**Suspension of Priest Upheld** — The Pittsburgh Catholic diocesan newspaper reported Oct. 13 that the Supreme Tribunal of the Apostolic Signature had reversed an earlier decision and upheld Bishop Donald W. Wuerl's removal from ministry of a priest accused of sexual abuse of a minor. The decision, dated Sept. 18, was significant because it expanded a bishop's ability to cite "psychic defect" as a basis for such removal.

**Four-Front Plan for Black Men** — Father George Clements, founder of the "One Church One Child" movement, outlined a four-point plan deserving "immediate personal attention" from black men, with emphasis on the homelessness of black children, addiction, men in prison, and the increasing incidence of out-of-wedlock births by teen-agers. Father Clements spoke Oct. 14 at a Summit for Black Catholic Men, held to coincide with the Oct. 16 Million Man March in Washington.

**Health Index Down** — The Index of Social Health, which gauges the nation's performance in addressing key social problems, indicated that social health had dropped to its fourth-lowest level since 1970, when the index was published for the first time. Six of the areas examined — ranging from infant mortality and child abuse to housing and the gap between rich and poor — reached worst-ever levels. "So significant a decline in our society's ability to cope with its social problems may well help to explain the sense of unease felt by so many Americans today," said a report on the index, which was published Oct. 16 by Fordham University's Institute for Innovation in Social Policy.

The years 1993, 1991 and 1900 were three of the four worst years of social performance in the index's history, and the four-year period from 1900-93 was the worst combined four-year period ever.

Among key trends noted in the report were the

worsening of child abuse nearly every year since the mid-70s, and a worsening in levels of children in poverty, average wages and the gap between rich and poor, all despite a lower rate of unemployment. Reaching their worst recorded levels were children in poverty, child abuse, health insurance coverage, average weekly earnings, out-of-pocket health costs for people over age 65, and the gap between rich and poor.

**Archbishop Iakovos Honored** — Greek Orthodox Archbishop Iakovos was honored at a dinner in New York Oct. 21, the day on which it was announced that he had submitted his resignation as the ranking Orthodox prelate of North and South America after 35 years of service. Archbishop Oscar H. Lipscomb, chairman of the bishops' Committee on Ecumenical and Interreligious Affairs, praised his contribution to the cause of Catholic-Greek Orthodox relations, saying, "Our churches are closer together as a result of your witness." In 1959 Archbishop Iakovos became the first Orthodox prelate in centuries to visit a pope when he met with John XXIII, with whom he "prepared the way" for theological dialogue by representatives of their respective churches.

**Mission Sunday Observance** — As parishes observed World Mission Sunday Oct. 22, the national director of the Society for the Propagation of the Faith reported signs of hope and growth in foreign mission churches, while the president of Glenmary Home Missioners said the Church in this country may have lost its missionary spirit because it was failing to spread the Gospel at home. The theme of the observance was "To the Ends of the Earth."

It was also reported that:
• The 1995 mission collection would be divided as follows: 54 percent for pastoral and evangelization programs of poor faith communities in Asia, Africa, parts of Latin America and the Pacific Islands, to be distributed through the Society for the Propagation of the Faith; 37 percent for missionary work in the United States, through the American Board of Catholic Missions; and nine percent for the Catholic Near East Welfare Association.
• In 1994 the American Board of Catholic Missions distributed more than $5.5 million in grants to 75 dioceses, 19 organizations and six religious institutes.

**Response to Child Abuse** — Two bishops' committees recommended a series of steps for parishes to take in response to the problem of child sexual abuse in an Oct. 26 statement entitled "Walk in the Light: A Pastoral Response to Child Sexual Abuse."

**Natural Law** — America needs a restoration of natural law philosophy, said speakers at the 28th National Wanderer Forum in Washington Oct. 27 to 29. "Natural law is simply the story of how things work.... Everything has a nature" that can't be violated without paying the penalty," said one speaker, Charles E. Rice, a professor at the University of Notre Dame law school and president of the Wanderer Forum. The forum was attended by more than 350 priests and lay persons.

**Briefs:**
• Thomas N. Lorsung, director and editor-in-chief

of Catholic News Service, was among new consultants to the Pontifical Council for Social Communications.
• The theme of the annual observance of National Children's Day Oct. 8 was "Mary, the Perfect Woman." The purpose of the observance was to encourage children to participate in the Sunday liturgy in such roles as greeters and readers of Scripture and prayers of the faithful.
• Pentecostal scholars met with representatives of Roman Catholic, Eastern Orthodox and Pentecostal churches Oct. 10 and 11 to discuss issues that unite and divide Christians and to plan a third five-year round of dialogue sessions. Co-sponsors of the dialogue were the Society for Pentecostal Studies and the Faith and Order Commission of the National Council of Churches.
• The Xavier Society for the Blind reported production of three versions (Braille, large print, audio tape) of the *Catechism of the Catholic Church* for the visually impaired.

## Culture of Life
The culture of life — for individuals, families, society, the Church — was the underlying theme of events and addresses of Pope John Paul's visit Oct. 4 to 8 to New Jersey, various sites in New York and Baltimore. Tens and hundreds of thousands of people greeted him along the way as he proclaimed the preeminent values of natural and supernatural life as opposed to a culture of death. (See related entries for selected excerpts from his addresses.)

## INTERNATIONAL
**Wanted: Freedom in Vietnam** — The bishops of Vietnam asked the government for greater freedom for the Church in their country. Specifically, they asked for freedom to assign clergy and religious as needed; to run schools, hospitals, nursing homes and similar facilities; and to publish church bulletins and related material, including the *Catechism of the Catholic Church*. "The Catholic Church in Vietnam wishes..... to make full use of its potential and accordingly contribute to the building of a just, civilized and progressive Vietnam," said the prelates in a report by UCA News, a church news agency based in Thailand.

**Church Growing in Albania** — "One can say that the Albanian church is rising from the ashes," said Archbishop Ivan Dias, Vatican ambassador to the formerly atheistic nation in an interview circulated by the French Catholic newspaper *La Croix*. When communism fell in 1992, there were only 33 native priests and 45 native women religious in the country. Numbers at the time of the interview had increased to 100 priests, many of them missionaries, and more than 200 women religious; government permission had also been received for the establishment of private schools.

**UNICEF Supported** — The president of the Canadian bishops' conference endorsed the United Nations Children's Fund relief programs after some Catholic groups urged the bishops to end their support because of alleged UNICEF family planning policies. Bishop Jean-Guy Hamelin made the statement in a letter to fellow bishops after protestors said the agency participated in promoting abortion and contraception. UNICEF spokeswoman Jacqueline Bradshaw said the agency was not involved in advocating any method of birth control: "Our mandate is to help parents protect their children." The bishop said: "There is no other international organization that can do so much for so many children."

**Shroud's Significance** — The authenticity of the Shroud of Turin as Christ's burial cloth is still open to question despite scientific tests dating its origin to the Middle Ages, said Cardinal Giovanni Saldarini of Turin. Even if it were not the burial cloth, it would still have religious significance as a reminder of the salvation achieved through Jesus' suffering on the cross, he said in an interview in the Oct. 7 edition of the Italian newspaper Avvenire.

**Sex Abuse Reporting** — Cardinal Cahal Daly announced that Irish bishops would report to police all pedophilia cases in which there was reasonable cause to suspect a priest or religious. The bishops were "deeply ashamed that some priests and religious have been abusers of children," said the head of the bishops' conference. The reporting policy was adopted at an Oct. 9-to-11 meeting of the conference.

**Land Mine Control** — A major U.N. conference on land mines ended Oct. 12 without agreement on stricter control of the production and use of the weapons, which were estimated to kill 20,000 civilians a year. Supporters of a ban included the Vatican, Cardinal George Basil Hume of Westminster, U.N. Secretary General Boutros Boutros-Ghali and the International Red Cross. There were about 110 million land mines deployed in 64 countries, according to U.N. estimates.

**Ordination of Deaconesses** — The Canon Law Society of America accepted a report entitled "The Canonical Implications of Ordaining Women to the Permanent Diaconate," in which it said the Church could ordain women and that such ordination "may even be desirable for the United States." The report, adopted at an Oct. 16-to-19 meeting in Montreal, acknowledged disagreement among scholars on interpretation of evidence of ordained deaconesses in the early centuries of the Church. Clear evidence of sacramental ordination appeared to be lacking.

**Burundi Extremists** — Tribal massacres in Burundi were being provoked by extremist political leaders, said Bishop Bernard Bududira, president of the nation's bishops' conference. At a news conference Oct. 23, he said Hutu and Tutsi extremists refused a national dialogue while forming rival armed factions and creating conflict.

**U.N. Is Indispensable** — The United Nations "has become an indispensable instrument of dialogue and solidarity among peoples."

So stated Cardinal Angelo Sodano, Vatican secretary of state, Oct. 24 on the last day of a celebration of the 50th anniversary of the organization. He said: "The Holy See believes that in the current phase of international relations, the action of the U.N. is "irreplaceable for the support of countries in their efforts to strengthen peace, assure social progress and promote liberty."

**Priests Still Banned from Mexico** — The Mexican government expressed no reaction to a three-month campaign to allow the re-entry of several foreign priests ousted from the strife-torn state of Chiapas by immigration authorities. This was so despite the fact that "literally thousands of letters have been sent to the Mexican president" protesting the expulsions of the priests, noted the Department of Social Development and World Peace, U.S. Catholic Conference.

**Trafficking in Children** — Trafficking in children — for adoption, organ transplant and sexual exploitation — was reported to be increasing as world migration made monitoring of abuses more difficult. These relatively new forms of exploitation illustrated the vulnerability of uprooted children, who often suffer the harshest consequences of social and economic instability, said Francois Ruegg of the International Catholic Child Bureau. Speaking Oct. 25 at a meeting of the Pontifical Council for Migrants and Travelers, he said, "the child is always among the first victims of human mobility," in part because migration destabilizes normal monitoring mechanisms, beginning with the protection offered by parents and relatives.

**Briefs:**

• Northern Ireland poet Seamus Heaney, a Catholic, was named winner of the 1995 Nobel Prize for literature.

• The 150th anniversary of Cardinal John Henry Newman's reception into the Catholic Church was observed in ceremonies Oct. 7 and 9 at Littlemore and the Oratory Church in Birmingham, England.

• Count Don Carlo Marullo, functioning as foreign minister, said Oct. 22 that the Knights of Malta was "fully available to cooperate" with the United Nations in "peacemaking and mediative action, in respect of dialogue and understanding among peoples."

• About 3,000 people attended a special Mass marking the provincial opening in Israel of the first synod of the Latin-rite Patriarchate of Jerusalem.

## Diplomats Impressed by Papal Visit

Pope John Paul's appearance at the United Nations Oct. 5 produced a constant stream of favorable comment from U.N. diplomats, reported Archbishop Renato R. Martino at a press conference Oct. 11. He said the diplomats appreciated the support the visit represented. U.S. Ambassador to the U.N. Madeleine Albright called the visit "a real boost."

"The Pope gave a confidence vote to the United Nations, although recognizing its shortcomings," said the Vatican nuncio. He noted that U.N. delegates did not view the appearance merely as a ceremonial event but recognized and responded to the substantive nature of his address, which they found "thought provoking."

Archbishop Martino said the Pope avoided particular issues like those that engaged Vatican delegations to the Cairo and Beijing conferences because he "wished to look at the future" and deal with a "broad spectrum" of ideas. "The fact that he didn't mention them doesn't mean he considers them unimportant, not at all. These problems stay, and we'll keep our accustomed watch."

The papal nuncio said also that a meeting of the Pope with U.N. General Secretary Boutros Boutros-Ghali was more than ceremonial and involved substantive issues on which he could not comment.

# NOVEMBER 1995

## VATICAN

**Sorrow at Rabin's Murder** — Pope John Paul expressed deep sorrow at the assassination of Israeli Prime Minister Yitzhak Rabin and urged that it not derail the peace process in the Middle East. "I profoundly hope that this grave and painful event will not irreparably disturb the search for peace but, on the contrary, may be an additional stimulus" to it, the Holy Father said Nov. 5. Rabin was shot to death the day before as he left a peace rally in Tel Aviv. The Pope called Rabin, winner of the Nobel Peace Prize in 1994, a servant of Israel, a talented statesman and a principal protagonist of Middle East negotiations.

**Public Projects Need Spiritual Dimension** — Any public policy, law or development that claims to be inspired by concern for people must take into account the spiritual and social dimensions of human life, the Pope said Nov. 13 as he welcomed France's new ambassador to the Vatican. "At a time when man risks becoming a slave to the technology which God has allowed him to invent," it is important to reaffirm that "science without conscience is the ruin of souls." He said France is rightly proud of its "humanist tradition" and that the Church shares the humanists' focus on the need to promote the well-being of individuals. But, the Church's position on a variety of issues — including those raised at the September U.N. conference on women in Beijing — is often misunderstood by those who claim to put people first but ignore their spiritual and moral needs.

**Priests Being Readmitted** — Priests who had left active ministry and married in civil ceremonies but were subsequently divorced or widowed were being allowed to return to ministry in many cases, said Archbishop Crescenzio Sepe, secretary of the Congregation for Clergy. "I cannot give a precise figure," he told Catholic News Service Nov. 4. "The important thing to note is that the number of requests for re-admission to the ministry is growing." The phenomenon was not limited to one country or region, but was most obvious in places where the largest number of priests had left in the past. According to statistics published by the Vatican, "defections of diocesan priests" numbered more than 14,000 between 1976 and 1993; more than half of them were from Europe and North America.

**Anniversary of Union of Brest** — In a document marked by strong ecumenical overtones, Pope John Paul celebrated the 400th anniversary of the Ukrainian Church's union with Rome and urged Ukrainian Catholics to help mend relations with Orthodox Christians. The 21-page apostolic letter, entitled "For the Fourth Centenary of the Union of Brest" and released Nov. 16, dealt with a sensitive issue in Catholic-Orthodox relations. The Union of Brest developed from a 1595-96 synod of Orthodox bishops, who proclaimed a union between Rome and the Metropolitan Province of Kiev, thus establishing the Ukrainian rite and the Byzantine rite within the Catholic Church. Orthodox who opposed the Union objected to the very existence of Eastern-rite Catholic Churches. They viewed such churches, with their use of Eastern liturgy and traditions, as a threat to Orthodoxy. Hence, the Pope's concern about fence-mending with the Orthodox. He said some progress toward closer ties with the Orthodox had already been made but noted that there were "forces ready to do almost anything" to impede movement toward unity.

**Clerical Garb** — The Vatican re-emphasized the requirement that priests must wear ecclesiastical garb in accord with norms of their bishops' conference and local custom. Their type of dress should be different from that of laymen and should conform to the "dignity and sacredness" of their ministry. So stated a clarification issued by the Pontifical Council for the Interpretation of Legislative Texts, in response to a query from a Brazilian bishop. The council said the norm on clerical dress is "juridically binding."

**Pastoral Concerns in Sicily** — In Sicily for the third time in as many years, the Pope spoke Nov. 23 about pastoral concerns at a meeting attended by more than 2,000 bishops, priests, religious and lay persons in Palermo. His topics included: "disturbing symptoms" of a loss of Christian heritage; diminishing commitment to the protection of human life and the preservation of family values; "permissiveness regarding abortion and contraception; a declining number of church marriages; signs of agnosticism and practical atheism. He condemned the Mafia and urged Italians to uproot the social causes of organized crime while praising Sicilians struggling to restore morality and legality in a society long dominated by the Mafia. Above all, the Pope cited the need for a new evangelization.

**Criticism Lacking Understanding** — Criticism by theologians and other Catholics of recent papal pronouncements demonstrates a widespread misunderstanding about the Church's teaching authority, the Pope said Nov. 24. Addressing members of the Congregation for the Doctrine of the Faith, he said the dissenting voices threatened to create a "counter-magisterium." Particularly dangerous was the mistaken idea that only those teachings declared infallibly need to be followed. The Holy Father's strongly worded talk reflected the mixed reception several of his key documents had inside the Church. His remarks indicated concern about the level of public opposition expressed in some quarters. "Today we have to acknowledge a widespread misunderstanding of the meaning and role of the Church's magisterium," he said. "This is at the root of the criticisms and challenges which you have observed about some pronouncements, especially the reactions in not a few theological and ecclesial areas to the most recent documents of the pontifical magisterium." This criticism had been directed at such authoritative statements as the two recent encyclicals on human life and moral truths, and his apostolic letter on the all-male priesthood. He said there had also been opposition to the doctrinal congregation's recent reiteration of the ban on Communion for divorced Catholics in invalid second marriages. The Pope called attention to the important distinction between legitimate theological questioning, in which difficulties about certain teachings are presented, and a stance of public opposition by theologians who would propose alternative teachings for the faithful. Theology operates within the Church and its basic doctrines, the Pope said. Theologians cannot ignore this, and they must respect the authority of the magisterium when it clarifies or pronounces on special issues.

**Message to Patriarch** — In a message to the spiritual head of Orthodox Christians, Pope John Paul said he hoped Christians would be closer to full unity by the year 2000. "For our part, we are determined to engage (in dialogue) with all our will.... We need to intensify our efforts in a coherent and harmonious way, so that our dialogue and our relations will lead to full communion of the faith." The Pope made these remarks in an annual message to Orthodox Ecumenical Patriarch Bartholomew I of Constantinople (Istanbul) on the Nov. 30 feast day of St. Andrew, patron of the Orthodox Church.

**General Audience Topics:**
• Under the guidance of the Holy Spirit, the Church has sought to understand more clearly the revealed truth about the Mother of God (Nov. 8).
• Devotion to Mary has inspired a rich treasury of hymns, poetry and art, all celebrating God's great gift of Redemption (Nov. 15).
• The Blessed Virgin invites the Church to meditate constantly on the mystery of Christ; she witnesses to the significance of quiet humility and loving obedience (Nov. 22).
• A proper reading of the figure of Mary in the Gospels provides a model of authentic emancipation for women according to God's plan (Nov. 29).

**Briefs:**
• Pope John Paul marked commemorations of All Saints and All Souls Nov. 1 and 2 with special remembrance of atrocity victims in Bosnia and other parts of the Balkans.
• The Pope celebrated a memorial Mass Nov. 7 for six cardinals and 108 bishops who had died since Nov. 1, 1994.
• The Congregation for the Doctrine of the Faith issued a warning against acceptance of the "heavenly visitations" of Swiss writer Vassula Ryden, saying the alleged revelations contained doctrinal errors and were "merely the result of private meditation."
• The Pope met Nov. 28 with a joint pilgrimage of Catholic and Orthodox bishops from the United States and Canada.

### No Doubt
The Congregation for the Doctrine of the Faith, in reply to a "doubt," declared that "the Church has no authority whatsoever to confer priestly ordination on women." The declaration, dated Oct. 28 and reported in the Nov. 22 English edition of L'Osservatore Romano, sparked a great deal of comment about the extent of its doctrinal authority. (See related article.)

### NATIONAL
**Council Approved** — Final Vatican approval of the statutes of the Council of Major Superiors of Women Religious was announced at a three-day meeting early in the month. The council was formed in 1992 by Vatican decree in response to requests from some U.S. superiors, many of whom were members of the Consortium Perfectae Caritatis. In 1994 the council was invited by the National Conference of Catholic Bishops to join the conference and the Council of Major Superiors of Men and the Leadership Conference for Women Religious — to be part of the Commission on Religious Life and Ministry, formerly called the Tri-Conference Commission on Religious Life and Ministry. The council had 103 member-communities, representing about 12,000 sisters in the United States.

**Political Responsibility** — A year before the 1996 presidential and congressional elections, the Administrative Board, U.S. Catholic Conference, issued a declaration of principles of political responsibility combining discussion of Catholic social teaching with summaries of positions on more than 20 issues of concern. Among subjects covered were: welfare reform, violence, immigration, families and children, environmental justice and euthanasia. The declaration was entitled, "Political Responsibility: Proclaiming the Gospel of Life, Protecting the Least among Us, and Pursuing the Common Good."

**Catholic Health Care** — Cardinal Joseph L. Bernardin called Nov. 6 for a "re-founding" of Catholic health ministry in the contemporary environment of commercialized health care. He said the health care industry was becoming driven by a profit motive and that the integration of health systems threatened the identity of Catholic institutions. Catholic health care must maintain its "ministry of hope," he said, adding that it is centered on belief in God's love and offers hope and reassurance in the face of the chaos and disintegration of illness. "A Sign of Hope" was the title of the cardinal's letter.

**Third Millennium Celebration** — Celebration in the year 2000 of the third millennium of Christianity "present rare opportunities critically important for the future of faith, the Church and civilization," said Father Avery Dulles, S.J., in the McGinley Lecture at Fordham University Nov. 16. Observances could present dangers as well as opportunities. "If celebrated without recognition of the need for repentance and renewal, the festivals could take on a triumphalistic tone that would embarrass Christians and repel adherents of other faiths," he said. Pope John Paul, however, had already taken steps to guard against complacency by calling for "penance as a preparation for the celebration."

**Bishops' Meeting** — About 250 bishops attended the annual meeting of the National Conference of Catholic Bishops and the U.S. Catholic Conference Nov. 13 to 16 in Washington. (See separate article.)

**Eastern Church Developments** — Pope John Paul announced Nov. 18 the formation of the first Syriac-rite diocese in the United States and named Chorbishop Joseph Younan head of the see. Also announced was the appointment of a Miami pastor, Chorbishop Pierre Wadih Tayah, to head the first Maronite-rite diocese in Mexico.

**Proposition 187 Trimmed** — Cardinal Roger M. Mahony of Los Angeles and the presidents of two Catholic health organizations praised a decision by a federal judge that overturned key portions of California's Proposition 187. U.S. District Judge

Mariana Pfaelzer ruled Nov. 20 that the voter-approved initiative prohibiting illegal immigrants from receiving tax-supported benefits was in conflict with federal law. Ruling in a case in which the Catholic Health Association and the California Association of Catholic Hospitals were among the plaintiffs, she said: "The state is powerless to enact its own schemes to regulate immigration or to devise immigration regulations which run parallel to or purport to supplement the federal immigration law." The cardinal said Nov. 17: "Prop 187 was ill-advised and poorly drafted. It attempted to deal with local-level frustrations through punitive measures against innocent people, especially children, the sick and families. It should not have passed and it should not become law." He also said the ruling was correct in highlighting the nation's common constitutional guarantees.

**Contributions to the Vatican** — Contributions to papal charities and diocesan financial aid to the Holy See amounted to $14.8 million in 1994. Among 135 dioceses reporting to date, contributions increased 4.3 percent. It was expected that the 1995 total would exceed $15 million.

**Briefs:**
• Cardinal James A. Hickey, who tendered his resignation as Archbishop of Washington on reaching the age of 75, was asked by Pope John Paul to stay on "until other provision is made."
• More than 100 women from 22 states and the District of Columbia attended a conference of Women for Faith and Family Nov. 3 to 5 in Arlington, Va. The focus of attention was on the world-directed vocation of lay persons, especially women.
• Msgr. Joseph A. Carroll of San Diego called on bishops to support the Catholic scouting movement while calling their attention to the many benefits enjoyed by its 350,000 boy and girl participants.
• Although they have "fundamental differences of content and method," there should be "no irreconcilable conflict between religion and science." So stated a text entitled "Science and the Catholic Church," issued by the Committee on Science and Human Values, National Conference of Catholic Bishops.
• William J. Flynn, chairman of the Mutual of America Life Insurance Co., was named to succeed the late J. Peter Grace as president of the American Association of the Knights of Malta.

## Hispanic Center and Ministry

The Northeast Hispanic Catholic Center got a new lease on life following the adoption of a new structure in 1994, according to director Mario J. Paredes. With a great deal of responsibility in the hands of the seven archbishops of the Northeast, the center's financial situation was improved; membership in the corporation was open to bishops whose dioceses had 500,000 or more Hispanics; and plans provided for an implementing board of diocesan directors of Hispanic ministry and officers of regional associations of Hispanic deacons, catechists and youths.

Cardinal James A, Hickey of Washington, speaking at a dinner Nov. 26 in New York, said Hispanic ministry was facing a "moment of crisis" because of "diminished understanding of its importance" and "discouragement among many who must carry that ministry forward." With the center directly under episcopal authority, he said, bishops can "employ the center more effectively in fulfilling their pastoral responsibility." The current crisis came 50 years after the first national office for ministry to Hispanics was established.

## INTERNATIONAL

**Earmark UNICEF Gifts** — The Vatican mission to the United Nations was reported to be advising Catholic supporters of the U.N. Children's Emergency Fund to designate their gifts for specific programs in line with Catholic moral teaching. The reason for the advisory was concern about pressure on UNICEF to move into programs and activities at odds with its specific mission statement on child welfare. John M. Klink, a volunteer of the Vatican mission, said in an interview Nov. 2 that the Vatican approved "the vast majority" of UNICEF activities and wanted to be able to encourage support for them. "The Holy See is trying to provide a mechanism so the good work of UNICEF can still be supported by Catholic donors."

**Post-Election Calm in Canada** — Canadian bishops appealed for calm, mutual respect and dialogue among those of differing views in the wake of a narrow victory for continuing Canadian unity in the recent Quebec referendum. In Ottawa, the executive committee of the bishops' conference called on all Canadians Nov. 2 "to have open hearts and open minds.... The decision made by the people of Quebec (not to secede from the rest of Canada) was neither easy nor painless.... As a result, the people of Quebec and Canada at this moment are highly charged with profound feelings and conflicting perspectives about their political and social structures." The bishops urged the people of Quebec "to continue, as peacefully as possible, the effects of reflection and imagination needed for the development of Quebec society."

**U.N. Abortion Directives** — The Vatican nuncio to the United Nations protested new directives from the High Commissioner for Refugees to require abortion counseling for women who become pregnant because of rape. Archbishop Renato R. Martino said in a statement Nov. 6: "It would be extremely unfortunate if individuals and humanitarian assistance groups were to be restricted or prevented ... from providing general health care and other necessities to refugee and displaced populations solely because they object on moral, ethical and health-related grounds to the provision of contraceptives and abortion services." He hoped the needs of refugees would come to "take precedence over an ideological preoccupation with a limited concept of reproductive health care." The archbishop made his statement to a committee of the General Assembly reviewing the work of the refugee agency.

**German Churches Sheltering Refugees** — Churches were illegally sheltering asylum-seekers and other refugees who, under tightened federal restrictions, would not be allowed to remain in the country. "Officially, the Catholic Church in Germany cannot support actions which are against the law," said Father Wilhelm Schaetzler, secretary of the bishops' conference. "But the choice to provide protection to refugees is an individual one, and we offer moral support for any of our priests who make this difficult choice." Out of fear of torture, imprisonment or death, refugees were turning to churches instead of the government because they believed their petitions for asylum would be rejected,

**Guatemalan Democracy?** —Despite civilian elections, putting together a true democracy was called a distant reality by Auxiliary Bishop Juan Gerardi Conedera of Guatemala City. "There is a sense of democracy because there are elections, but afterward there is no democracy, neither social nor economic," he said before Nov. 12 elections. Hope of change through civilian rule had waned, despite the proclamation of the birth of democracy and the end of 30 years of military dictatorships in 1985, with the clean election of President Vinicio Cerezo. "What we have here is a formal democracy, not a real democracy," said the bishop, pointing to ongoing violations of human rights and government's inability to consolidate power.

**Divisions in Church in France** — Cardinal Jean-Marie Lustiger said that continuing controversy over the deposition of Bishop Jacques Gaillot had revealed internal divisions among French Catholics and a split between generations. The cardinal spoke openly for the first time on the Bishop Gaillot affair in an interview in the Nov. 14 edition of the Paris daily *Liberation*. Bishop Gaillot was ousted from the Diocese of Evreux in January, 1995, because his disagreements with church positions on priestly celibacy, the ordination of women to the priesthood and sexual morality were disruptive of church unity.

**Critical Stance Won't Change** — "We will continue making critical observations that contribute to resolving the variety of problems facing the country, without regard for the consequences." To do otherwise would be "a dishonor to the memory of our fellow Jesuits who were assassinated six years ago." So stated Father Francisco Ibizate, who was sworn in Nov. 16 as rector of Central American University. At the time of their deaths, the six priests were considered El Salvador's most prominent intellectuals opposed to the civil war which ended in January, 1992.

**Blind Sisters in Albania** — A convent for three blind Sacramentine Sisters, along with two sighted Little Missionaries of Charity, was opened Nov. 1 in Elbasan. Their only ministry is prayer before the Blessed Sacrament. Sacramentine Sisters, with about 60 members, had convents in Albania, Argentina, Brazil, Chile, Kenya, Italy and Spain. The institute was founded by Father Luigi Orione in 1926. The title of their companion institute is the Little Sisters of Charity, also founded by Father Orione.

**Polish Election Results** — The presidential victory of former communist Aleksander Kwasniewski was interpreted as a blow to the Church that could endanger advances in church-state relations made since the 1989 collapse of communist rule. The bishops' conference, which clearly opposed his election, faced stronger opposition in securing church rights under a future constitution, getting government approval of a concordat with the Holy See, and fighting against legalized abortion. It was also opined that the victory might be a window of opportunity for the Church as Kwasniewski attempts to establish his image as a symbol of national stability and unity. With ex-communists in full control of parliament, government and the presidency, the new situation in Poland almost certainly necessitated a change of style and direction by church leaders, as well as an attempt to give the Church a more modern, upbeat image.

**Dayton Accord Called Unjust** — The U.S.-brokered peace accord signed by the presidents of Serbia, Croatia and Bosnia-Herzegovina Nov. 21 in Dayton, Ohio, was called unjust by Cardinal Vinko Puljic of Sarajevo. "This peace might be the prolongation of the war," he said, adding that it jeopardized the idea of a multiethnic, united country. Although the agreement denied that Bosnia would be divided, "there are fears" that this will happen. "Dividing Bosnia means putting into question the very principles of living together of the entire international community." The cardinal criticized the peace accord for giving the Serbs 49 percent of the territory in dispute although they made up only 31 percent of the pre-war population. He said the leaders of Bosnia's three ethnic groups opposed a unified, pluralistic country. "The Serbs dreamed of a greater Serbia; the Croat politicians — not the people — of a greater Croatia; and the Muslims, of an Islamic state." But "each of these three dreams is mistaken."

**Briefs:**

• A report by the Canadian Conference of Catholic Bishops showed that the number of diocesan priests dropped — due to retirement, death, departure from ministry — from 8,973 in 1965 to 6,111 in 1993.

• "We are far away from the social progress our country needs because of corruption," said Bishop Edmundo Luis Flavio Abastoflor Montero at the annual meeting of the Bolivian Bishops' Conference.

• The Vatican renewed its annual pledge of $10,000 for the 1996 budget of the U.N. High Commissioner for Refugees.

• The Ukrainian Catholic Church was becoming stabilized after emerging from 50 years of underground existence and was seeking to help more than 300,000 Ukrainian Catholics in other parts of the former Soviet Union, reported Bishop Basil Losten of Stamford, Conn.

• Britain's Queen Elizabeth II became the first monarch since the Reformation to attend a Roman Catholic service when she took part in Vespers marking the centenary of Westminster Cathedral, London, on Nov. 30.

## Petitions for Change

Leaders of a German movement to reform the Church reported that a petition seeking sweeping changes in church teaching and practices had been signed by 1.4 million Catholics between mid-September and Nov. 12. A similar petition was signed by some 500,000 Austrian Catholics, and other signature campaigns were under way in Switzerland, France, and the region of Italy bordering on Austria. Among other things, the signatories were in favor of the ordination of women to the priesthood, democratically elected bishops, authoritative roles for lay persons and changes regarding sexual morality. (See separate article.)

# DECEMBER 1995

## VATICAN

**Catholic Response to Cultures** — The future of Christianity will depend to a large degree on how well the Catholic Church and other Christian communities respond to the secularization of culture, Pope John Paul said Dec. 2 in a speech at an international meeting on secularism and the future of faith. In some societies, the disregard of religious values in public life has led to "a true desertification of existence.... More than soil ready for sowing, our societies are becoming full of arid spaces awaiting the flood of regenerating water." The Church must learn to propose "the great message of the Gospel in a way which is able to reach the very heart of modern culture in all of its various manifestations."

**Climate for Vocations** — Catholics must not only pray for more vocations to the priesthood, but must also create a climate in which they can be nurtured, said the Pope Dec. 3 as he spoke about the decree on the formation of priests issued by the Second Vatican Council. "The people of God must create a favorable climate for vocations. The response of candidates to the sacred ministry depends a great deal on the ecclesial environment.... Where there are deeply Christian families, lively parishes and groups which transmit the joy of living according to the Gospel, vocations flourish."

**Erroneous Feminism** — "In recent times, some currents of the feminist movement, in attempting to favor the woman's liberation, have tried to make her similar to the male in everything." That is a mistake, said the Pope Dec. 6. While God created women equal in dignity and value to men, he also gave them a different and specific nature. "The woman's identity cannot consist in being a copy of the man."

**Open Debate on Beliefs** — To be truly democratic, a country must allow its citizens to bring their religious convictions to bear on issues being debated publicly, Pope John Paul said Dec. 7 at a conference on religious freedom. Claiming that religious beliefs and related moral convictions should be expressed only in the private sphere, is a "subtle form" of limiting religious freedom.

**For Unity, Against Discrimination** — At a meeting Dec. 13 with bishops from central India, the Pope said the Church must provide an example for society by promoting the dignity and equality of women and refusing to espouse local prejudices about social status. One of the challenges facing Indian Catholics "is the resurgence of that mentality which separates people on social and ethnic grounds. With sadness, we acknowledge that even in the Christian community such problems persist." He called discrimination a violation of the heart of the Gospel message, which calls Christians to love one another.

**Lebanon Synod** — The 19-day special assembly for Lebanon of the Synod of Bishops closed Dec. 14 with a strong call by its participants for national unity, restoration of the country's sovereignty and respect for human rights. The message pledged church assistance in rebuilding a society devastated by 17 years of civil conflict, especially in the fields of education, health care, housing and economic development. Restoration of sovereignty meant "liberating (Lebanese) territory of Israeli occupation by applying the decision of the United Nations" on the southern strip of Lebanon; the bishops also called for the departure of Syrian troops scattered around the country. Reflecting the subjects of many speeches, the message called for greater unity and coordination among the six Catholic rites, saying that church communities "sometimes degrade into simple competing interest groups. The hierarchy planned to develop new permanent structures to enhance cooperation of all the churches, under the authority of the Assembly of Patriarchs and Catholic Bishops of Lebanon.

(See also separate article.)

**Jubilee 2000 Preparations** — Preparations for Holy Year 2000 must be aimed at "reinforcing the faith of the people of God and giving space to expressions of unity," so that belief in Jesus Christ is more evident than the historic divisions among Christians and between Christians and members of other faiths. So stated Cardinal Roger Etchegaray, head of the council in charge of preparations for jubilee celebrations, Dec. 15. "There is a deep desire in every human heart to embrace the Infinite. The desire can be satisfied only if the Infinite goes forth first to meet and embrace the human person. This is the profound meaning which the Church celebrates in the mystery of the incarnation of God. The Infinite toward whom many reach, has a face: that of Jesus of Nazareth."

**Events of 1995** — In an annual end-of-the-year address Dec. 22 to personnel of the Roman Curia, Pope John Paul listed a number of noteworthy events, including: his visit to the United States and address before the General Assembly of the United Nations; the 50th anniversary of the end of World War II; a Bosnian peace agreement; visits to 11 countries, in addition to the U.S; World Youth Day celebrations in the Philippines; publication of major documents — on human life, ecumenism, women, Eastern-rite churches, and the Church in Africa.

**Sex Education** — "Human Sexuality: Truth and Meaning," is the title of a document issued Dec. 21 by the Pontifical Council for the Family. The 65-page text is a critique of contemporary teaching methods; more importantly, it represents an effort to counteract the influence of the sexual revolution dating from the 1960s. The document calls on parents to assume the primary role in the sex education of their children and to be extremely vigilant with respect to school-sponsored and other sex education programs which, it said, often contain inappropriate or immoral material. It said parents should oppose such elements as: the presentation of erotic materials; dramatic or mime representations of genital or erotic questions; the use of sexually explicit images or models; requests to divulge personal or family information; oral or written examinations about genital or erotic questions.

**Record Numbers** — The Pope encountered a record number of people in 1995, well over a million at the Vatican alone. He held 44 general audiences, attended by 536,500 people; had hundreds of personal meetings with individuals or small groups, attended by 185,700. Papal liturgical ceremonies were attended by close to 400,000. Statistics did not include numbers of people encountered in one way or another during parish visits in Rome or trips in Italy and abroad.

**General Audience Topics:**

• God's saving plan, revealed in creation, attributes equal dignity and worth to women and also affirms the uniqueness of the gift of femininity (Dec. 6).

• With great concern for the biblical foundation of Marian doctrine, the Fathers portray Mary as a woman of faith and as the type and exemplar of the Church (Dec. 13).

• "On the night of the Lord's birth, we sense renewed hope for peace for all individuals and peoples afflicted by war" (Dec. 20).

**Briefs:**

• Pope John Paul canonized Bishop Eugene de Mazenod, founder of the Missionary Oblates of Mary Immaculate, Dec. 3.

• With the addition of Mozambique Dec. 14, the number of countries exchanging ambassadors with the Holy See rose to 161.

• The Pope met Dec. 23 with controversial Bishop Jacques Gaillot, whom he admonished to comply with church teachings.

• The Vatican's Internet site was swamped with online traffic over the Christmas holidays. More than 300,000 people from 70 countries logged into the site on the World Wide Web in the 48 hours after its inauguration Dec. 25, reported Vatican spokesman Joaquin Navarro-Valls.

## The Pope's Christmas

The Holy Father celebrated midnight Mass and delivered a reflective homily on the birth of Christ the Lord. He was unable to celebrate Mass in the morning because of a flu attack, but managed to read the customary *Urbi et Orbi* ("To the City and the World") address from his apartment window. He described a "hurt world" of refugees and war victims, recalling the "scattered families" of Bosnia; the refugees of conflict in Rwanda and Burundi; the victims of civil war in Sri Lanka, southern Sudan and Algeria; the population of Iraq still suffering under "long years of embargo"; the plight of Kurds in difficult living conditions and relations with Turkey. "It is in this hurt world that the infant Jesus, in all his love and frailty, appears. He comes to free those caught up in hatred and the slaves of particular interests and divisions."

## NATIONAL

**Challenge to Black High Schools** — The heads of more than 20 predominantly black Catholic high schools across the nation met in Baltimore Dec. 1 to 3 to discuss common challenges and ways and means of coping with them. The meeting was part of an effort by the National Black Catholic Congress to address the needs of the African-American family. "Catholic education has a long tradition of excellence, and we see this as an opportunity to prioritize and build upon that tradition for Catholic schools with significant African-American enrollments," said Hilbert Stanley, executive director of the congress.

**Candlelight Vigil for Runaways** — At a Dec. 7 candlelight vigil in New York, the president of Covenant House said the number of homeless and runaway youths was "growing at an unacceptable rate" and criticized efforts to cut the programs that help them,. "We cannot balance our budgets on the backs of our kids," said Sister Mary Rose McGeady. "We need more and better services, not less. Some cuts never heal." Candlelight vigils similar to the one in New York were held the same evening in other cities where Covenant House operated: Los Angeles, Houston, New Orleans, Washington, Anchorage, Fort Lauderdale, Orlando, Atlantic City and Newark.

**Lay Ministry** — With continuing growth in lay ministry and an interest in it that showed no sign of slacking off, U.S. bishops announced plans to inaugurate a three-year project on "Leadership for Ecclesial Lay Ministry." About 20,000 U.S. Catholics, both nonordained religious and lay persons, were employed at least 20 hours a week in lay ministries in church-related settings, known as "ecclesial lay ministry." A 1992 study by the National Pastoral Life Center found:

• Of the 20,000, 41.5 percent were religious between the ages of 55 and 60. The median age of lay persons was just under 45.

• Eighty-five percent of lay ministers were women.

• Half of the approximately 19,000 parishes employed lay ministers: 35 percent of small parishes; 65 percent of medium-size parishes; 78 percent of large parishes.

• Lay ministries were engaged in education (41 percent), general parish ministry (27 percent), eight percent in music and youth ministry. The remaining 16 percent were in such ministries as liturgy, spirituality, evangelization, social action and ministry with the elderly.

**Moral Renewal of the Medical Profession** — Physicians must work for the "moral renewal" of their profession at a time when "medicine has grown increasingly mechanistic, commercial and soulless," Cardinal Joseph L. Bernardin told the House of Delegates of the American Medical Association Dec. 5. "Failure to ground the profession in a strong set of moral values risks the loss of public respect and confidence.... Society's stake in medical care is too great to sustain the present level of professional autonomy if confidence in the profession declines." Moral crisis is affecting not only medicine but other professions as well. For physicians, it means that "more and more members of the community of medicine no longer agree on the universal moral principles of medicine or on the appropriate means to realize those principles." Doctors, "caught up in a web of economics, politics, business practice and social responsibility" no longer know how to act, he said.

**Liturgical Renewal and the Mass** — Cardinal Godfried Danneels of Malines-Brussel said liturgical renewal should be pursued with attention on the "profound and significant" sacredness of the Mass and without too much emphasis on innovation and relevance. Otherwise, the gathering is trivialized into a human community that is "celebrating itself," he said Dec. 2 at a symposium at the University of Notre Dame. Liturgists must remember that "one cannot simply transform and rearrange the whole thing. And they must realize that "there are levels of compatibility and incompatibility, and there are prayers and practices that are not appropriate" for Christian liturgy. Singling out forms of liturgical manipulation, the cardinal said: "The establishment of all sorts of thematic Sundays and thematic celebrations has little or no future, except in the death of the liturgy as such. Liturgy ought certainly not to serve as a sort of 'warm-up' for another activity, even a church activity."

**Lots of Poverty in the U.S.** — The extent of poverty in the United States was reflected in statistics on its services reported by Catholic Charities USA Dec. 12. In 1994, 7.2 million people received emergency services — 4.9 million adults, 1.8 million children under 18, and 420,000 senior citizens 65 and older. Another 3.9 million people sought social services, bringing the total of people receiving service from Catholic Charities to 11.1 million — up from 10.6 million in 1993. One in four persons needing help were children. Half of those receiving aid were living in poverty and receiving federal and/or state welfare assistance. During 1994, Catholic Charities spent $1.89 billion — 89 percent of it on programs, only one percent on public relations.

**Right to Lobby Endangered** — A proposal that would have restricted the right of nonprofit groups receiving federal funds to lobby with privately raised funds was defeated in both Houses of Congress. Opponents of the Istook Amendment (named for sponsor Republican Ernest Jim Istook of Okla.) called it the "Silence America Amendment," saying it would unfairly prohibit many nonprofit groups from speaking out about problems in their communities. "The Istook proposal would undermine the religious freedom of the nation's faith-based social services and charitable institutions that are obliged by both Scripture and tradition to both serve the poor and vulnerable, and speak up for them," said Jesuit Father Fred Kammer, president of Catholic Charities USA. Proponents of the amendment "have argued that federally funded nonprofits must choose between being service providers or advocacy groups. Religious providers, answering to a higher authority, cannot choose between these roles."

**Web of Life in Appalachia** — Twenty-five bishops of Appalachia issued a new call for the support of what they called the "web of life" in their region. They said Appalachia should become a region of "sustainable communities" with its own permanent social and economic base, instead of an area exploited by outsiders as a source of cheap resources and labor. Their new pastoral message, "At Home in the Web of Life," said the socioeconomic crisis of Appalachia reflected "a larger crisis which now threatens the entire society, including the middle class and indeed the full ecosystem across the entire planet." The crisis is a "conflict between a culture of death and a culture of life" which is a "profoundly moral crisis." The message, released Dec. 15, placed emphasis on the abandonment of people in Appalachia and a pervasive attack on the region's environment. The bishops warned that their area was on its way to becoming a "wasteland" with large-scale unemployment, the death of local business, clearcutting of forests, destructive strip-mining, dump-ing out-of-state garbage and toxic materials, warehousing of prisoners from cities,

**State Must Pay** — The Supreme Court let stand Dec. 4 a ruling that said the State of Colorado cannot refuse to pay for abortions for victims of rape and incest. Without comment, the court declined to hear an appeal of lower court rulings saying that Colorado, in participating in the Medicaid program, had to pay for abortions in cases where poor women seek them after becoming pregnant as a result of rape or incest.

**Briefs:**
• The bishops' Campaign for Human Development reported the award of $750,000 in new economic development grants to 30 low-income groups. The awards brought the agency's total national funding in 1995 to $8.4 million, the highest ever for a single year.
• The 1993 and 1994 collections for the Church in Latin America amounted to $4.3 million. The 1994 funds were distributed as grants to 292 projects in 22 countries.
• Georgetown University announced plans to purchase $1 million in stock in a bank designed to serve low-income and moderate-income neighborhoods in the District of Columbia.
• Law suits against Bishop Donald W. Wuerl for closing or merging three parishes in the Diocese of Pittsburgh were dismissed during the month.

## Leading News Stories of 1995

Catholic editors selected the following 10 leading news stories of 1995: (1) Pope John Paul's visit to the United Nations and the United States, (2) women and the Church, (3) Bosnia, (4) the "Gospel of Life" encyclical letter, (5) the Beijing conference on women, (6) racism in the U.S., (7) budget cuts, (8) welfare reform, (9) religion and public policy, (10) health care.

The leading newsmaker was Pope John II.

## INTERNATIONAL

**Moral Battleground of Economics** — As the world increasingly spins to the tune of dollars, yen and marks, bishops focused attention on economics as a major moral battleground. "Economics has become the new frontier of the Church," said Cardinal Roger Etchegaray at a meeting of politicians, economists, bankers and businessmen. Many experts regarded economics as the main factor in uniting the world in a process of globalization — in which profit-making supercedes political and other concerns in decision-making. Many church leaders, especially those from poor countries, said that globalization was widening the gap between haves and havenots, with wealth and power increasingly concentrated in few hands and countries.

**Reconciliation in Poland** — The bishops urged a "spirit of reconciliation" after the Nov. 19 election of an ex-communist as president but voiced concern that supporters of the country's former communist regime had regained a monopoly of power. "Anxiety is generated by the assumption of all state power by a single channel of ideas that it is impossible for the faithful to accept," the bishops said. They added that the vote of many Poles had been determined by the nation's economic hardships rather than the moral values stressed in pre-election church statements. But, they noted, this vote for a change "does not release anyone from following value systems, especially the fundamental principle of respect for the life of every human being from conception to natural death."

**Secularism Is Poison** — A state does not protect religious freedom by pushing every expression of faith out of the public eye, said speakers at a conference in Rome Dec. 5 to 7.

• The rise of secularism in the United States and Western Europe "is poisoning the environment which religion needs to survive," said Kevin J. Hasson, president of the U.S.-based Becket Fund for Religious Liberty.

• Cardinal Paul Poupard said: "Human dignity is the basis for religious freedom. That means respect for the dignity of the person and for the person's search for truth."

• Mary Ann Glendon, law professor at Harvard University, said the United States has a very religious population but one of the most secular legal codes in the world. Ms. Glendon said she did not attach much significance to the "symbolic cases" involving school prayer or Nativity scenes on public property. The greater threat is a "sort of secularism that frequently masquerades as a form of religious freedom," inviting everyone to shed their religious identity in the name of progress and, while tolerating individual religious belief, shows hostility toward religious institutions. A recurring theme in U.S. Supreme Court decisions is that "religion is a private, individual matter between the individual and God." The more that church-affiliated schools, hospitals and other institutions affirm their religious identity, the less likely it becomes that they and the people they serve can benefit from government assistance generally given to similar institutions. But the worst example are laws and court decisions that "undermine parents' ability to transmit their faith and values to their children.... The school prayer cases are a distraction from the real issue, which is the steady drumbeat of secular proselytizing that characterizes the atmosphere in many public schools."

**Humane Tourism** — Catholics in tourism-related apostolates called for "humane tourism" in the face of child abuse, prostitution and environmental destruction spawned by the industry. Delegates from Asia, Europe and the United States, meeting Dec. 5 to 9 in Pattaya, Thailand, said luxury tourism is a scandal in poor countries. "Tourism has to be humanized and not driven by market forces and solely motivated by profit."

**Crosses in Bavarian Schools** — The Bavarian Parliament closed its 1995 legislative calendar Dec. 13 with passage of a law stating that, "in view of the historical and cultural character of Bavaria ... a cross is to be put up in every classroom." An earlier law said the state had the power to guarantee Bavaria's Christian heritage and assumed — but did not compel — that schools would place crosses or crucifixes in classrooms. It was hoped the new law would resolve months-long controversy over the matter.

**Mutual Forgiveness** — In their first joint decla-

ration, Polish and German bishops asked for mutual forgiveness for past injustices. They also called for church support for European integration, closer ecumenical relations with Orthodox and Protestant churches, and the preservation of ethnic cultures and national traditions within a united Europe. The declaration was signed Dec. 13 by Cardinal Jozef Glemp of Warsaw and Bishop Karl Lehman of Mainz, head of the German bishops' conference.

**Status of Jerusalem** — Amid speculation that Pope John Paul had privately supported Israel's assertion that Jerusalem is its political capital, Archbishop Jean-Louis Tauran restated the Holy See's view that the city is a religious crossroads. He said the Vatican "has no competence" to enter debate over the political status of Jerusalem. On the religious side, however, the assistant secretary of state said Jerusalem must be a "crossroads of peace ... which implies that the three religions (Judaism, Christianity and Islam) should live here in peace with each other.... The most religious part of the city, the Old City, should have international guarantees which allow this part of the city to preserve its uniqueness and sacredness."

**Briefs:**

• Church leaders in India hoisted black flags on Human Rights Day, Dec. 10, to exert pressure on the government to grant equal rights to low-caste Christians and to "remove the blot" on the nation's constitution.

• American Father Richard Timm, a 21-year veteran of missionary work in Bangladesh, was the recipient of a Religious and Peace Award from the International Association for Religious Freedom, for his "contribution toward religious harmony, humanitarian services and peace."

A French priest (Father Robert Besson of the Missionaries of Africa), and a Belgian nun (Immaculate Heart of Mary Sister Christiane) were end-of-the-year missionary casualties, killed Dec. 21 in separate incidents in Zaire.

• Christmas was celebrated in Bethlehem for the first time under the administration of the Palestinian National Authority.

## Doubts about Balkan Accord

The bishops of Bosnia-Herzegovina expressed "serious doubts" that the accord worked out in Dayton, Ohio, would produce lasting peace. The U.S.-mediated agreement contained "several, very strange contradictions" and "pernicious uncertainties," they said. They complained that the agreement:

• established the country's indivisibility but divided Bosnia into two, and allowed for three armies;

• gave half of the territory to Serbs, who comprised only one-third of the population;

• contained no clear mechanism for implementing the safe return of refugees and other displaced people to their homes;

• placed a heavy Croatian Catholic population under minority Serb control in Bosanska Posvina.

"By this agreement," the bishop said, "ethnic cleansing and the principle that might makes right have been confirmed and legalized; the victim and the aggressor have been placed at the same level."

# JANUARY 1996

## VATICAN

**Heroic Witnesses** — Calling them "heroic witnesses of the faith," the Vatican newspaper paid special tribute to the 30 priests, religious and lay missionaries killed during 1995. *L'Osservatore Romano* said they included six Italian nuns who died in Zaire from the Ebola virus as well as 24 missionaries shot, stabbed or strangled to death. Several of the murders occurred during robbery attempts, but most were tied to political or religious conflicts. Twenty-six of the missionaries died in Africa — nine of them in Burundi, the site of ongoing ethnic violence. Two women religious were murdered in India; additional victims were killed in Ecuador and Brazil.

**Rights for Migrants and Host Countries** — Migrants are obliged to obey the laws of any country they enter, but those countries also have an obligation to respect and protect the human rights of anyone who comes to their borders, Pope John Paul said Jan. 6. The fact that people flee their homes because of violence, politics or economics is "one of the most remarkable phenomena of our times, ... which often creates problems for societies. For that reason, I renew my appeal to governments that they always confront immigration with full respect for human rights."

**Priest-Loans Needed** — Assessing a project to better distribute clergy throughout the world, the Pope expressed disappointment at the low level of response by dioceses in making priests available for service around the globe. He said the Church's missionary spirit demands a generosity on the part of all local churches, which must look beyond their own borders. He wanted to appeal to bishops, priests and religious, as well as to each local church community, to cultivate a greater missionary awareness, particularly in the years leading to the next millennium. The Pope made his remarks Jan. 11 at a meeting with members of the Interdicasterial Commission for the Equitable Distribution of Priests.

**State of the World** — In his annual state-of-the-world address Jan. 13 to more than 160 ambassadors accredited to the Holy See, Pope John Paul said the Middle East peace process would be jeopardized if the Jerusalem question were not settled; called for a ban on nuclear testing; appealed to China and some Muslim nations to end discrimination against Christians. He cautiously praised peace efforts in Bosnia as well as in Northern Ireland. He noted that, for the first time, a Palestinian representative was attending the assembly of diplomats, along with the Israeli ambassador. Regarding Jerusalem, he said: "The religious and universal dimension of the Holy City demands a commitment on the part of the whole international community, in order to ensure that the city preserves its uniqueness and retains its living character."

**Redemption** — Christianity is "denatured" if its unique teaching on redemption is ignored, says a study paper released by the International Theological Commission. Only Christianity professes faith in the historical, redemptive life, death and resurrection of the Word of God made man. This distinctiveness from other religions must not be undermined in the name of achieving "harmony between different religious conceptions." The paper warned against some New Age and "human potential" movements that ignore original sin and minimize "the pervasive effects of sin and the incapacity of humanity to redeem itself. Humanity is not redeemed, nor is God fittingly glorified except through God's merciful action in Jesus Christ." .

**No Presumption of Annulment** — Catholic couples have a right to ask for a declaration of marriage annulment but this does not automatically presume a "right to annulment," Pope John Paul said in an address to members of the Roman Rota Jan. 22. The particular circumstances of each case must be weighed carefully by the Church's juridical authorities to determine whether or not the marriage can be declared null and void from its beginning.

**Don't Blame the Poor** — Archbishop Paul J. Cordes, president of the Pontifical Council *Cor Unum,* said Jan. 25 that those who blame poverty on the poor and hungry are dodging their own responsibility for contributing to injustice in the world. Seeing only the faults of others "is a game, a tactic for not looking at one's own life and obligations."

**Volunteers for Vengeance** — The scores of people who volunteered to join a death-penalty firing squad in Utah were motivated by vengeance, not justice, wrote moral theologian Father Gino Concetti in the Jan. 17 edition of *L'Osservatore Romano.* The newspaper condemned the death penalty as against Christian teaching and said the United States was in the grip of a "mad race to capital punishment." Father Concetti's editorial was a response to reports that more than a hundred people in Utah had volunteered to join a firing squad scheduled to execute John A. Taylor, a convicted rapist and murderer, Jan. 26.

**Vatican's E-Mail** — Over the Christmas and New Year holidays, the electronic floodgates opened at "http://www.vatican.va," the Holy See's address on the World Wide Web. More than one million visitors tapped into the site, leaving more than 1,000 messages.

**General Audience Topics:**

• Mary's unique calling and privileges must always be seen as pointing to Christ her Son, while she is also a model of faith and holiness (Jan. 3).

• Mary, who was granted the dignity of being the mother of Jesus, is also the favored daughter of the Father and the temple of the Holy Spirit (Jan. 10).

• "Behold, I stand at the door and knock," the theme for the Week of Prayer for Christian Unity (Jan. 18 to 25) calls all Christians to conversion, spiritual renewal and greater unity (Jan. 17).

• Through her cooperation with Christ in the work of redemption, the Blessed Virgin contributes in a unique way to the triumph over Satan (Jan. 24).

• The Old Testament only points to the mystery of Mary's motherhood, but the New Testament proclaims that the birth of Jesus fulfills the words of the prophet Isaiah (Jan. 31).

**Briefs:**

• While the three Wise Men offered the Infant Jesus material gifts, Christians are called to honor their Redeemer with the gift of their lives, said the Pope on the solemnity of the Epiphany, Jan. 6, as he ordained 14 new bishops.

• A day later, Jan 7, the Pope baptized 20 infants from five countries.

• At the opening of a Syro-Malabar synod Jan. 8, the Pope called on the Indian bishops to restore an atmosphere of communion and trust in their two-million-member, Eastern-rite church

• Vatican Museums reported a record attendance of nearly three million visitors in 1995. The principal attraction was the restored Sistine Chapel.

• A 1995 survey indicated that at least 40 million people throughout the world participate in the Apostleship of Prayer.

### For Children, A Future of Peace

This was the theme of Pope John Paul's message for the World Day of Peace, Jan. 1. He said: "Let us give children a future of peace. This is the confident appeal which I make to men and women of good will, and I invite everyone to help children to grow up in an environment of authentic peace. This is their right, and it is our duty.... I pray that everywhere a harmonious relationship between adults and children will promote a climate of peace and authentic well-being. Sadly, many of the world's children are innocent victims of war. In recent years millions of them have been wounded or killed: a veritable slaughter." The Holy Father also spoke about many other forms of violence suffered by hundreds of thousands of children — in better-off countries as well as in places plagued by poverty and extreme need: child labor, prostitution, military service, drugs, crime, domestic violence, lovelessness.

Near the end of the message, the Pope said: "Peace is a gift of God; but men and women must first accept this gift in order to build a peaceful world. People can do this only if they have a childlike simplicity of heart. This is one of the most profound and paradoxical aspects of the Christian message: To become childlike is more than just a moral requirement but a dimension of the mystery of the Incarnation itself."

### NATIONAL

**Immigrant Impact Misunderstood** — Immigrants have a more positive effect on the economy and unemployment than often portrayed, according to a report published by the Cato Institute and several other research groups. Findings were said to be at odds with claims that tightening immigration laws would solve unemployment problems and lower welfare costs. As Congress prepared for action on restrictive bills — including those that would reduce the number of legal immigrants by one-third, prohibit even legal immigrants from receiving welfare aid, etc. — it was stated that many of the suppositions behind the proposals were based more on rhetoric than statistics. The report was entitled "Immigration: The Demographic and Economic Facts."

**Condom Case** — The U.S. Supreme Court's refusal Jan. 8 to hear an appeal of a Massachusetts case allowing the distribution of condoms in public junior and senior high schools was "an unconscionable dereliction of duty," said the Catholic Action League of Massachusetts. Without comment, the court declined to review a program in which, without requiring parental consent, school nurses are allowed to provide condoms to children upon request and after counseling about their use and sexually transmitted diseases. The refusal was a blow to parental rights, declared C.J Doyle, executive director of the Catholic Action League of Massachusetts.

**Partial-Birth Abortion** — Seventy-one percent of 1,000 registered voters surveyed in a nationwide poll registered support for a bill that would ban partial-birth abortion. The poll was commissioned by the U.S. bishops' Secretariat for Pro-Life Activities. "This strong show of support should not surprise anyone on either side of the debate," said a statement from Helen Alvare, director of planning and information for the secretariat. "Killing a baby who is four-fifths delivered outside of her mother violates every humane instinct Americans possess." In the procedure, an abortion is performed late in pregnancy. The doctor grabs the baby by the feet and pulls the body, up to the head, through the birth canal, then kills it by inserting scissors at the base of the brain. The brain is suctioned out, causing the skull to collapse and allowing easier removal of the head to complete the procedure.

**Religious Leaders and Policy Debates** — Religious leaders have an obligation to engage in public debate over national policies, Cardinal John J. O'Connor said in an address Jan. 16 at the Jewish Theological Seminary in New York. They need to recognize that "popularity cannot be the name of the game" and they must ignore charges that they are trying to impose their views on others. They should contend for their views "with civility" but remain true to their individual values. "If you are ambiguous about your position," he asked, "what are you offering?"

**Corporate Resolution Proxies** — Church organizations in the corporate responsibility movement said they were encountering a major new obstacle because of rulings by the Securities and Exchange Commission. The rulings permit companies to omit resolutions from proxy materials on the grounds that the issues pertain to "ordinary business" appropriate for management decision rather than stockholder vote.

**Anti-Alien Views** — The observance of National Migration Week during the month prompted a number of bishops to take issue with anti-immigration attitudes. One bishop, for example, Cardinal Anthony M. Bevilacqua, said in a Jan. 12 *Philadelphia Inquirer* article that today's immigrants "are no different than those of the past. They may represent an ever larger number of nationalities, but they come seeking what those before them sought, a better life for their families. ... They represent the best of what built our country and what will continue to make it strong." Bishop Andrew J. McDonald of Little Rock said in a pastoral letter that anti-immigrant attitudes stem "from ignorance and selfishness."

**Educational Reform** — This was the subject of "Principles for Educational Reform in the United States," a document issued Jan. 19 by the U.S. bishops. Six general principles were outlined in the document:

• "All persons have an inalienable right to a quality education."

• "Parental rights and responsibilities are primary in education."

• "Students are the central focus of all education."

• "Quality teaching is essential to the learning process."

• "True quality education must address the moral and spiritual needs of students."

• "Government has a responsibility to provide adequate resources for the attainment of a quality education for all children, and these educational policy decisions are best made at the level closest to the teaching and learning situation."

**Caution regarding the Catholic Alliance** — Bishops in two states cautioned Catholics to look beyond the issues on which the Church agrees with the Catholic Alliance, a new offshoot of the Christian Coalition. Bishops Thomas J. O'Brien of Phoenix and the three bishops of Colorado warned that, although church teaching is in line with some of the alliance's positions — on issues like abortion and euthanasia, for instance — there are dramatic differences between the two on other important subjects. "We are concerned by the organizing efforts of many groups, including the Christian Coalition, who seek to mobilize our Catholic people and represent the so-called 'Catholic position' without any word of communication with the bishops' conference or its representatives," said a Jan. 9 statement from the Colorado Catholic Conference.

**Hemlock Society Move** — The January move of the Hemlock Society USA to Colorado Springs alarmed the state's bishops and other Catholic leaders. "For anyone who respects the sacredness of life, it's alarming," said Archbishop J. Francis Stafford of Denver. "If we don't work tirelessly to defend the dignity of the human person from conception to natural death, society will lose its conscience." The Hemlock Society USA, with 40 chapters is the largest organization of its kind in the country. Doug Delaney, director of the Colorado Catholic Conference, called the move unfortunate because the society's main intention is to make it easier for people to end their lives, and that's in opposition to everything we stand." The introduction in 1996 of assisted-suicide bills was expected in Nebraska, Arizona, California, Massachusetts, Maine, New Hampshire and Colorado.

**Briefs:**

• "What makes our faith so beautiful is the diversity of it, embracing all people," Bishop J. Kevin Boland told attendants at a Jan. 7 Mass in Savannah, marking observance of National Migration Week Jan. 7.

• The Interfaith Chapel at the Denver International Airport, the first of its kind in the country designed for use by Catholics, other Christians and Jews, was dedicated Jan. 10.

• Televising executions might work against the death penalty because "the more you bring it close to people, the quicker you've got a chance to abolish it." So stated Sister Helen Prejean, author of *Dead Man Walking*.

• A savage attack on a Waterville, Me., convent by a man with a history of mental illness left two elderly nuns dead and two injured. The dead were Sisters Edna Marie Cardozo and Marie Julien Fortin.

Injured were Sisters Mary Anna DiGiacomo and Patricia Ann Keane.

## March for Life

At least 60,000 people took part in the 23rd annual March for Life Jan. 22 in Washington in a right-to-life demonstration against the U.S. Supreme Court's Roe v. Wade and Doe v. Bolton decisions which legalized abortion in the United States. Similar gatherings and demonstrations were reported in cities across the country. Numerous statements were issued criticizing the practice of abortion and steps taken to preserve it in the country.

• Cardinal Bernard F. Law, chairman of the bishops' Committee for Pro Life Activities: "Only through a combined effort to change laws, change attitudes, and change the dire circumstances which lead some women to consider abortion, will the United States do justice to women and to the unborn children who cannot speak up for themselves.... A year after the Clinton administration began forcing states to fund abortions in violation of their own state laws and constitutions, Congress has yet to address this injustice. Recent appropriations measures have done nothing to prevent taxpayer funding of destructive experiments on living human embryos."

• Bishop Anthony M. Pilla, president of the National Conference of Catholic Bishops: "While abortion may be legal, it is never moral. We, as a caring, faith-filled community, must work to put an end to these deaths (an estimated 1.5 million a year) and to the pains of grief felt by so many. We are called to work toward putting an end to the reasons people choose abortion as their answer."

Meanwhile during the month, the U.S. Supreme Court: (1) let stand a ruling that said states may not refuse to pay for abortions for indigent women who become pregnant as a result of rape or incest; (2) refused to allow Pennsylvania to set reporting requirements for Medicaid-funded abortions that are stricter than federal standards.

On the legislative front in 1995, 171 restrictive bills on abortion were introduced in 44 states and 18 were enacted in 13 states, according to a report made by the National Abortion and Reproductive Rights Action League.

## INTERNATIONAL

**Polish Inauguration Boycotted** — Legal and political considerations were behind the decision of church leaders to boycott the inauguration of the country's new president, a former communist. Bishop Tadeusz Pieronek, secretary general of the bishops' conference, said he and Cardinal Jozef Glemp declined invitations to the Dec. 23 ceremony for President Aleksander Kwasniewski because of:

• a court ruling that Kwasniewski had violated campaign laws;

• former President Lech Walesa's decision not to attend the inaugural;

• allegations that Kwasniewski's ally, Premier Jozef Olesky, had been a KGB agent.

**Anglicans Want To Stay** — More than 1,000 Anglican priests were looking "for an ecclesially acceptable way forward" within the Anglican Communion, said Father John Broadhurst, chairman of the 7,500-member Forward in Faith group of priests and lay persons opposed to the ordination and ministry of women priests. He made the statement Jan. 4 in a report in the *London Daily Telegraph*

**Feminism and Power** — Feminism must go beyond seeking important positions of power and influence currently held by men, said a female member of the Vatican delegation to the U.N. Conference on Women held in Beijing in September, 1995. Feminism must change the way society thinks about issues and how governments and institutions react to problems, said Janne Matlary, a Norwegian political scientist. Women are equal to but different from men and "are privileged in being transmitters of life, which is truly as close as humans ever get to creation." They can bring to politics "specific values that are pro-life in a profound sense." She also asked: "Will women as political leaders be less egotistical than men? If the answer is no, I fail to see why women should replace men as power-holders and decision-makers."

**Religious Influence** — Belief in God and organized religion still have an important influence on society but are changing forms as the 20th century comes to an end, according to a study of religiosity in 13 countries. While traditional religions are losing adherents and influence, new religious movements are developing, and immigration is making many traditionally Catholic countries pluralistic, it said. The study was conducted in the early 1990s by the International Social Survey Program in nine European countries and the United States, Israel, the Philippines and New Zealand.

**Crackdown in China** — Pressure from China's central government was the force behind a recent crackdown on some underground Catholic communities in the Diocese of Baoding in Hebei province, said a Catholic source in northern China. Incidents in 1995 reported by UCA News, a church news agency based in Thailand, included the following:

• In November, a new church built with money raised by a local priest in a village in southern Baoding was demolished by the government, and Bishop James Su Zhemin was summoned to the Public Security Bureau.

• On Dec. 23, eight nuns were arrested; four were detained at the county security bureau office and forced to pay bail, and four were held at a detention center.

• A religious brother, who had been detained previously for more than five years, was re-arrested and fined.

It was also reported that 10 teams of government agents had been assigned to infiltrate and disrupt the underground church in northern China.

**Life Issues in Spain** — In the wake of renewed efforts by Socialists to liberalize Spain's law against abortion, voters were being urged to look carefully at pro-life issues in upcoming elections. "When the time comes to make our decision and cast our vote, ... special attention will have to be paid to the right to life," the bishops said in a voting guide made public Jan. 18. "Parties that include measures favoring abortion, euthanasia and violence in their platforms are in open contradiction with the right to life."

**Indigenous Lands In Danger** — The Brazilian bishops' Indigenous Missionary Council protested President Fernando Henrique Cardoso's decision to review outside claims to traditional indigenous lands. "The Brazilian indigenous peoples had to wait 500 years to get half their land demarcated, and now everything can be annulled with one stroke, said a mid-January statement from the council, which called the act unconstitutional. Cardoso issued a presidential decree Jan. 8 allowing for an administrative review of the boundaries of all indigenous territories that had not completed the demarcation called for under a 1991 presidential decree to protect indigenous lands and cultures. The bishops had repeatedly denounced government delays in completing the process, which often had been accompanied by violent confrontations between the indigenous peoples and land or mineral prospectors or even state militias.

**Middle East Christians Left Out** — The Mideast's small Christian Palestinian community sometimes feels on the fringes of the peace process, a Palestinian Anglican clergyman told some 300 Christians from 30 countries at a conference in Jerusalem. "We have a great heritage, and we have a voice, and it is important that Christians raise their voice to talk about peace and justice," said Canon Naim Ateek of the Anglican cathedral in Jerusalem. "We refuse to be marginalized."

**Briefs:**

• Two North American nuns were stabbed to death during an apparent robbery attempt Jan. 8 near Elmina, Ghana: American Sister Patricia McAleese, 63, and Canadian Sister Claudia Murphy, 65.

• The bishops of Canada praised the government's announcement Jan. 17 of a moratorium on the production and use of anti-personnel mines.

• Haitian President Jean-Bertrand Aristide, a former Salesian priest, married Mildred Trouillot, his legal adviser, Jan. 20 in a ceremony performed by Father Antoine Adrien, Holy Ghost Fathers' provincial for Haiti.

• Forty families affected by Hansen's disease (leprosy) were residents of homes they themselves built through a project organized by Montfort Brothers in Thailand.

## Church Reform Petitions

Reform petitioners in Italy said they hoped to gather 500,000 signatures by May in support of a drive for changes in the Church, with respect to: ordination of women to the priesthood, optional celibacy for Roman-rite priests, lay and clerical participation in the choice of bishops, reception of the Eucharist by divorced and remarried Catholics, freedom of conscience regarding birth control methods, return to active ministry of men who had left the priesthood to marry, and other matters. Petitions for such changes had already yielded 500,000 signatures in Austria, 73,000 in Switzerland and 1.4 million in Germany.

Reactions to the poll-taking were mixed. It was noted that, while some reforms might be order, basic doctrine is not open to negotiation.

# FEBRUARY 1996

## VATICAN

**Threat of Gay Marriage** — State approval of homosexual marriages would legitimize deviant behavior and erode public morality, according to a commentary in the Feb. 3 edition of the Vatican newspaper. By giving civil status to such unions, the state is endorsing an ethical current that goes against universal moral truths. In the name of pluralism, morality is thus reduced to a current of thought. "Every person and every group, according to this view, would have the right to establish a morality which must have a legitimate space in a pluralistic society," wrote moral theologian Father Gino Concetti.

**Latin American Trip** — Pope John Paul returned again to Latin America Feb. 5 to 12 for visits to Guatemala, El Salvador, Nicaragua and Venezuela. (See separate article.)

**Millennium Plans for Jerusalem** — After meeting with church and civil authorities in Jerusalem, Vatican personnel said they were encouraged at the level of cooperation in the holy city as preliminary plans were being made for the year 2000. While no calendar of events had been fixed, committees were discussing the expected influx of pilgrims in the Holy Land, the involvement of the local church, proposed ecumenical ceremonies and a possible visit by Pope John Paul, said Bishop Michael Fitzgerald, secretary of the Pontifical Council for Interreligious Dialogue, Feb. 9.

**Meaning of Religious Freedom** — When the Church calls for respect for religious freedom, it is saying every man and woman has an equal right to search for God, the Pope said Feb. 18 in comment on the Vatican II document on religious freedom. People can fulfill their right and obligation to seek the truth only if they are truly free. Religious liberty must guarantee each person the right to follow his or her conscience, to act on it privately and to worship alone or in a community. "The attitudes of various human communities, states and sometimes even of various believers have not always been marked by respect and tolerance," the Pope said.

**Help for Refugees** — Pope John Paul asked the bishops of Tanzania Feb. 20 to continue assisting the thousands of refugees seeking safety in their country, even though such efforts heavily taxed the resources of their dioceses. "The poorest of the poor among you are the more than 700,000 refugees from Rwanda and Burundi.... Please God, the conditions of peace and security will return to those troubled countries, thus permitting the return of the refugees to their homes and lands." Waves of refugees began flooding into Tanzania in the spring of 1994 when ethnic violence turned Rwanda and Burundi into slaughter grounds. While groups of refugees periodically returned to their homelands, new outbursts of violence sent them and others back over the borders.

**Penance Gives Strength** — By following Christ into the desert during Lent, Christians find the strength they need to resist "the recurring temptations of materialism, power and infidelity," the Pope said during an Ash Wednesday general audience. He urged Catholics to make Lent a time of renewed reflection, prayer and action on behalf of the poor. "Lent, with its austere itinerary, helps all of us to become conscious of the spiritual risks to which our lives are exposed and encourages us, at the same time, to open our eyes to the marvelous prospects of the Christian vocation."

Penance may seem like an outdated religious practice, but the presence of suffering and injustice in the world shows that it is as necessary as ever. It "is a vital theme for every man and woman, and for society itself," the Pope said Feb. 25. "Penance indicates repentance for sins committed and a promise to correct them.... The penitential practice carries not only an individual, but also a communal, obligation. Because sin has a social dimension, it is right that the remedy does as well." But the renewal of the community and reparation for sins must begin with an individual examination of conscience and individual repentance.

**Papal Elections** — Pope John Paul published Feb. 23 an apostolic constitution entitled *Universi Dominici Gregis* ("Of the Lord's Whole Flock"), containing regulations governing papal elections and the conduct of church affairs during the time between the death of a pope and the election of his successor. Two significant changes from previous legislation were the manner of election, only by a two-thirds majority vote of the cardinals, and provision for more comfortable living quarters for the cardinals during the electoral conclave. (See separate article.)

**Attacks Condemned** — The Pope condemned two deadly terrorist attacks in Israel and urged people not to lose hope in the peace process. "I strongly condemn this new, cruel return to violence. Once again I turn to all those who believe in dialogue and ask them not to lose hope." His words came hours after explosions ripped through a crowded commuter bus in Jerusalem and a soldiers' station near the coastal city of Ashkelon Feb. 25. At least 25 persons were killed and dozens injured in the attacks, reportedly carried out by extremist Palestinians.

**Remember Afghanistan** — Pope John Paul asked Christians and the international community not to forget the civil war in Afghanistan, where civilians were under increasing bombardment. He spoke Feb. 25, the day after the pro-Islamic Taliban rebel movement launched another rocket attack on a residential district in Kabul. He suggested that Catholics around the world turn their attention during Lent to "the martyred population" of Afghanistan. He cited reports of numerous civilian casualties in recent weeks and a lack of basic necessities in the capital. "I deeply share in the sufferings of so many innocent people," he said. "I want to encourage everyone to pursue a sincere and persistent dialogue, and I ask the international community not to forget this tragic situation."

**Norms on Relics** — Norms on relics, in effect since 1994 but scarcely noticed, limit their distribution "only for public veneration in a church, oratory or chapel.... No relics from the Apostolic Sacristy will be given to individual faithful for private veneration." Msgr. Piero Marini, papal master of liturgical ceremonies, said the rules govern the Vatican and the Diocese of Rome, but he hoped they would serve "as a model for the elaboration of norms for distributing relics" by religious orders and other dioceses as well. The new rules are not a sign that the Church is moving away from the veneration of relics; rather, their purpose is to restore order and dignity to the practice. The rules do not apply to practices of Eastern-rite churches.

**General Audience Topics:**
• Reflections on his Feb. 5-to-12 pastoral visit to four countries of Latin America (Feb. 14).
• In Lent, we are invited to welcome God's gift of salvation by listening to his word and by prayer, mortification and works of mercy (Feb. 21).

**Briefs:**
• The Pope praised the commitment of Mexico's government and people to economic and political reform, but called for special protection and attention to the poor and indigenous peoples, at a meeting with President Ernesto Sedillo Feb. 1,
• All schools, parochial and public, have a responsibility to teach religious values, with due regard for the religious freedom of students, the Pope said Feb. 4.
• Christians and Muslims must go beyond tolerating one another to loving each other and working together to build a better world. So stated Cardinal Francis Arinze in a letter to Muslims released Feb. 15, five days before the celebration of Id al-Fitr at the end of the fasting period of Ramadan. (See separate entry.)
• The Pope asked the international community, and especially Portugal, to work for a peaceful settlement of years-long tensions in East Timor.

## Dissenting Theologians Criticized

An article in the Feb. 2 edition of *L'Osservatore Romano* denounced a German book of dissenting theological essays, saying its criticism of Pope John Paul's encyclical letter *Veritatis Splendor* was an attack on the foundations of the faith. By portraying the Pope's teaching as one position among many, the theologians were straying from their proper role and setting themselves up as instigators of public dissent. The 1994 letter warned that an attitude of moral relativism had invaded society and even some areas of Catholic theology. The newspaper article said the criticism voiced by the theologians writing in the German volume confirmed the Pope's warning. The title of the book of essays was *Moral Theology Set Aside? A Response to the Encyclical "Veritatis Splendor."*

## NATIONAL

**HMO Concerns** — The head of the Boston archdiocesan health care system warned a gathering of bishops that the rapidly expanding for-profit hospital industry threatened the primary doctor-patient relationship in health care. "I'm very concerned that the entrance of for-profit interests in the acute-care marketplace will inject a shareholder between the patient and the provider," Dr. Michael Collins said in an interview with *The Texas Catholic*, the Dallas diocesan newspaper. "I believe that health care is a good — not a commodity — which cannot be bought and sold." The principal ethical issues Catholic health providers face are to keep ministry — not

business — as their imperative and to keep the interests of the patient as their primary concern.

**Assisted Suicide Condemned** — A bill that would legalize physician-assisted suicide in Alaska "twists pain and suffering into being a reason to die," said the heads of the state's three dioceses. "This bill, H.B. 371, is bad public policy and it is bad morals.... A bias in favor of death will pervade society even more than it does now," they said in a joint pastoral letter issued Feb. 6. "The bill is a wake-up call to all Alaskans that the citizens are being asked to make 'suicide' a right ... as basic a right as life, liberty and the pursuit of happiness." Without life, "our rights are meaningless. Euthanasia and assisted suicide contradict life." The bill, if enacted, would make it legal in Alaska for a physician to prescribe a lethal poison for a terminally ill person who would request it. The bishops' letter was entitled "The Care of the Terminally Ill."

**Syrian-Rite Bishop and Diocese** — The installation of Bishop Joseph Younan as head of the first Syrian-rite diocese in the United States was hailed as a "great moment for the Church, not only the local church, but the universal Church." Archbishop Agostino Cacciavillan, papal nuncio the U.S., said the Feb. 10 installation and enthronement ceremony at St. Anthony's Church in Union City, N.J., was also a "great moment for the Eastern rite." The Eparchy of Our Lady of Deliverance of Newark, an Antiochene-rite diocese, was established in November, 1995, to serve Syrian Catholics in the United States and Canada.

**Covenants** — The Catholic, Episcopal and Lutheran bishops in southwestern Pennsylvania signed a "call into covenant" pledging cooperation among their members. Signers of the agreement Feb. 13 were Bishops Donald W. Wuerl of Pittsburgh, Alden Hathaway of the Episcopal Diocese of Pittsburgh and a representative of the Southwestern Pennsylvania Synod of the Evangelical Lutheran Church in America. In it, they recognized that Christian unity is "the will of our Lord Jesus Christ" and noted the conviction that "mission carried out together can often have a greater impact for the Gospel than parallel undertakings separately employed." The agreement called upon local congregations to pray for one another, share parish events, hold staff meetings for exploring areas of potential cooperation, share unused or underused facilities, mutual action against bigotry and intolerance, cooperation in ministering to the needy.

Earlier, the Catholic and Lutheran bishops of North Carolina renewed a five-year covenant between their churches.

At a meeting Feb. 15 to 17 in Convent Station, N.J., the Roman Catholic-United Methodist Dialogue in the United States asked the United Methodist Church to take up Pope John Paul's invitation to dialogue with him on the subject of papal ministry .

**Boycott More Drugs** — A coalition of pro-life groups expanded its drug boycott related to the French abortion pill RU-486 to include Cardizem, Seldane and Nicoderm. The additions resulted from the merger of U.S. drug manufacturer Marion Merrell Dow and European pharmaceutical makers Hoechst AG of Germany and Roussel Uclaf of France. Signing on to the boycott were Priests for Life, Human Life International, the Pro-Life Action League, Concerned Women for America, the Republican National Coalition for Life and the International Right to Life Federation.

**Identity of Catholic Universities** — The Catholic character of a Catholic university ought to be a pervasive, palpable part of campus life, theologian Monika Hellwig said Feb. 22. She expressed concern that younger Catholic scholars in the sciences, social sciences and humanities lack the necessary formation in the Catholic heritage to contribute effectively to a much-needed dialogue of Catholic theology with culture. A university's Catholic identity should come through clearly not only in its academic program or theology curriculum, but in the whole "shape of life on a Catholic campus." The Georgetown University theologian spoke at the Catholic University of America on the future of Catholic universities in the light of the 1990 papal document *Ex Corde Ecclesiae*.

**Land-Mine Moratorium** — The bishops played a critical role in getting Congress to approve the first moratorium on U.S. military use of anti-personnel land mines. The passage of the moratorium through Congress "was a surprising victory — and unexpected," said John Carr, U.S. Catholic Conference secretary for social development and world peace. "The bishops had an important impact" in the legislative process, said Sen. Patrick Leahy of Vermont who introduced the bill. Contributing to passage were favorable indications from the Holy See, a constant refrain from bishops abroad, the moral issue of civilian and postwar casualties, and an "impassioned appeal" from Leahy.

**Guidelines for Political Activity** — Although certain political activities could endanger their tax-exempt status, Catholic organizations can still get involved in electoral issues without losing their tax exempt status, advised the Office of General Counsel, U.S. Catholic Conference. "Issue-oriented participation in the political process is entirely consistent with the Section 501 (c)(3) regulatory framework, which restricts candidate-oriented activities (by tax exempt organizations), not debate on the values and principles that should guide our public life," said Mark E. Chopko in a memo accompanying a set of guidelines on political activity. Permitted political activities include:

• educating candidates about issues and attempting to change their positions;

• educating voters about issues through unbiased means;

• sponsoring voter registration drives;

• holding "unbiased public forums, debates and lectures in which candidates explain their views to the public.

Also permitted would be political activity by leaders or members of Catholic organizations acting as individuals and not as representatives of tax exempt organizations.

**Briefs:**

• *Vida Nueva*, the Spanish-language publication of the Archdiocese of Los Angeles, was the winner of 14 awards at the National Association of Hispanic Publications' 1996 convention.

• Cardinal John J. O'Connor celebrated an annual Mass in St. Patrick's Cathedral, New York, Feb. 4, marking February as Black History Month; the Mass also commemorated the National Day of Prayer for the African-American Family.

• Archbishop Patrick F. Flores of San Antonio urged Catholics Feb. 12 to become "communicators of hope and workers for peace" by making a pledge against violence during Lent.

• Father (Cmdr.) John M. Gubbins, a chaplain for 13 years, was named command chaplain for U.S. naval forces in England, Scotland, Wales, Belgium and Holland.

• The Christophers presented their Life Achievement award to David Brinkley, veteran television newscaster and commentator, Feb. 29.

## Immigration Obligation

A sense of social obligation to all people as taught in the Gospel should prevail in the nation's approach to immigration, said Cardinal Roger M. Mahony in an address prepared for delivery Feb. 13 at Rockhurst College, Kansas City, Mo. "People must be able to see that the lines of self-interest that connect us to one another — as a nation and as an international community — bring together people from both the center and edge of society." Debate about the matter, particularly as it has developed recently, "cannot be confined to its economic and social consequences," he said. "Barely below the surface, the immigration debate touches on much more fundamental questions about the values which underpin those policies. Because contemporary politics have turned discussion about values to other purposes, "the potency and meaning of those values have been weakened significantly," presenting a formidable challenge to all Americans, particularly in the Catholic Church."

The cardinal used California's passage of Proposition 187 in 1994 as an example that the debate over immigration went beyond a movement to stop illegal immigration. Particularly after opponents of the measure publicized its legal shortcomings, "by election day there were no credible objections to the charge that the initiative would do little, if anything, to significantly curb illegal immigration," he said. Proposition 187 was tied up in court since its passage. District Court Judge Mariana Pfaelzer ruled recently that a number of its provisions are in conflict with federal law.

## INTERNATIONAL

**Health Care Worries** — The president of the Catholic Health Association of Ontario warned a government committee that new provincial legislation would threaten the administration and future of Ontario's church-run hospitals. Ronald Marr said amendments to the Public Hospital Act would give the health minister powers "far beyond the authority needed" and would encroach "upon the corporate integrity of Catholic and other denominational hospitals" in the province. Provisions of proposed legislation would give the health ministry unilateral authority to close or merge hospitals, set doctors' fees, charge seniors and welfare recipients user fees for prescription drugs, and create a form of U.S.-style health care. Worry was also expressed that the law could force denominational hospitals to merge with those not sharing the same missions and values, provide services inconsistent with their respective missions, and force them to stop providing services in accord with their goals.

**Priests in Belarus** — The head of the Church in Belarus had hopes that foreign priests would not be expelled from the former Soviet republic. Cardinal Kazimierz Swiatek of Minsk-Mohilev spoke after 100 Polish priests were threatened with deportation under a new church-state law. He also hoped that future talks with the government would result in permission for 200 foreign nuns to stay in the country. The priest-religious situation became complicated with application of a law requiring visiting priests to have invitations and national government approval to be in the country.

**Church Controls in Vietnam** — Vietnamese officials let stand restrictions on the Church by failing to respond to petitions of the bishops with respect to:
- the bishops' authority to transfer priests and religious from one place to another;
- church administration of its own schools, hospitals, leprosariums, homes for the handicapped and shelters for the aged in dioceses and parishes;
- more favorable conditions for congregations of religious to develop activities and promote vocations;
- resumption of pastoral duties by priests detained in re-education camps;
- the opening of seminaries.

**Asian Solutions** — The Church in Asia faces issues that need responses suitable to the Asian context and beyond approaches worked out in the West, Cardinal Michael Michai Kitbunchu of Bangkok told Southeast Asian lay leaders attending a meeting Feb. 5 to 10 in Thailand. He recalled the turbulent post-World War II decades and the manner in which the Church in Asia was confronted with "issues, problems and often-burning questions" of newly liberated countries. "Historical and cultural situations developing in Asian contexts were and are markedly different and pose diverse challenges which sometimes call for new responses," he said.

**Divorce in Ireland** — The Irish High Court upheld Feb. 7 a November, 1995, referendum that ended the nation's constitutional ban on divorce.

**Underground Priests** — A married man secretly ordained as a bishop in communist-era Czechoslovakia warned that many secretly ordained priests would return to underground ministry unless the Czech bishops eased procedures for incorporating them into normal ministry. About 220 married men were secretly ordained during the communist era.

**Anything Goes Bad** — As national elections drew near, Spanish bishops denounced widespread corruption in the government and appealed for spiritual renewal in what they called an "anything goes" society. Numerous scandals involving public officials "indicate that public and private morality seem to have worsened," said Father Juan Antonio Martinez Camino, secretary of the bishops' doctrinal commission. The bishops' document, entitled "Morality and Democratic Society" and issued Feb. 14, called for measures to curb government corrup-

tion. It made reference to "the suspicion — already proven more than once — that public positions have been utilized as a means of illicit enrichment."

**Pastoral Ministries** — In a 40-page document issued during the month, the bishops of Canada invited "those called to ministry to reflect on our responsibilities to those we serve in our dioceses and in our communities, to our colleagues and to ourselves." So stated Bishop Brendan O'Brien of Pembroke, a member of the committee that wrote "Responsibility in Ministry: A Statement of Commitment." The first part of the document covered responsibilities point by point; the latter part offered exercises for reflection on pastoral commitment.

**Casa Alianza Concerns** — The Latin American branch of Covenant House was engaged in negotiations with the government of Honduras about the jailing of juveniles with adults and the government of Guatemala about the torture and murder of street children.

**Briefs:**
- Msgr. Noel Mullin, the Royal Navy's chief Catholic chaplain, was named Honorary Chaplain to Britain's Queen Elizabeth II; he was the first Catholic in the United Kingdom to receive the title.
- A Mexican evangelical group predicted that within 10 years or so Chiapas would be the first state in Mexico in which the majority of the population would be Protestant.
- Dominican Father Marcel Dubois was thought to be the first Christian named to receive the prestigious Israel Prize, awarded by the Israeli government. A resident of Israel since 1962 and an Israeli citizen since 1973, he taught philosophy at Hebrew University for 20 years and was a long-time participant in Christian-Jewish dialogue.
- Jerusalem's Latin-rite patriarchate condemned the two terrorist attacks which took place in Israel Feb. 25. "We condemn this act because, as always, we say that violence creates violence," said Father Adib Zmoot, chancellor of the patriarchate. "Now in this new era of peace, we hope that everybody can work for peace, so we condemn this act."

## Condom Use

Using condoms may be a necessary but insufficient means for battling AIDS, said a document prepared by the French bishops' Social Commission and released Feb. 12. In the case of adults who cannot abstain from sexual activity and who are in danger of contracting or transmitting AIDS, a condom could be used to avoid risk of infection. Condom use in such circumstances is the less of two evils — but still immoral. In fighting AIDS, the document said, greater stress must be placed on abstinence from sexual relations, fidelity in marriage and educational programs.

Vatican theologian Father Georges Cottier, O.P., interviewed on Vatican Radio Feb. 14, said the use of condoms to prevent AIDS is a legitimate question for theological debate. But the Church cannot accept "propaganda campaigns" that promote condoms as completely effective in preventing disease or that seek to legitimize an immoral view of sexuality.

# MARCH 1996

## VATICAN

**Relation of Values to Economy** — The impact of economies on families and the influence of families on economies were themes of a Mar. 7-to-9 symposium of economists and church personnel sponsored by the Pontifical Council for the Family. Moral and religious values such as honesty, hard work and solidarity are necessary components of a strong economy, the Pope said Mar. 8. He also called attention to various aspects of economies that affect the life and harmony of families. Poverty, underdevelopment, unemployment and low wages, for example, "make the mission God has willed for parents and children very difficult,"

**Isolate Terrorists** — Arab terrorists need to be isolated to prevent them from disrupting the peace process in the Middle East, but in a way that does not hurt the "decent people" in the Holy Land, said Vatican Secretary of State Cardinal Angelo Sodano in an interview published Mar. 12 by the Rome newspaper *La Repubblica*. "At this point, the terrorist groups have to be isolated. How many are there compared to the entire Arab population? Everyone says not many," but the important thing is to avoid "irritating either side with overly repressive measures so the decent people do not pay!" The cardinal spoke as world leaders were preparing to meet in Egypt to devise strategies against a new wave of terrorism in the region.

**Rwanda Killers To Face Justice** — Rwanda cannot be rebuilt without truth and justice, including the punishment of any Catholics who may have been involved in the mass killings that occurred in 1994, Pope John Paul said in a letter to people of the nation. "The Church as such cannot be held responsible for the faults of its members who acted against evangelical law." However, "all members of the Church who sinned during the genocide must have the courage to face the consequences of the acts which they committed against God and against their neighbor." The papal letter, dated Mar. 15, marked the second anniversary of the slaughter that claimed hundreds of thousands of lives and caused many more thousands to flee their homeland. Several priests and women religious were accused of participating in the massacres that set members of the Hutu and Tutsi ethnic groups against each other. The Pope called on all members of the Church in Rwanda "of various ethnic origins" to "turn to God with a sincere heart, to pardon and to reconcile yourselves when it is necessary, in order to reinforce your unity and to work together for the one mission of Christ.... Christians must be witnesses of the truth," and they must dedicate themselves completely to the task of reconciliation and peace."

**Pope Indisposed** — The Pope was indisposed for several days about the middle of the month because of a mild fever associated with an unspecified ailment of the digestive tract.

**Beatifications** — The Holy Father beatified Mar. 17 two Italian bishops who founded missionary orders in the 1800s: Daniel Comboni, of the Comboni missionaries, and Guido Maria Conforti, of the Xaverian missionaries.

**Donations** — In what the Vatican termed symbolic gestures toward victims of war, earthquakes, drought and drug traffic violence, the Pope donated almost $500,000 to emergency relief efforts in 1995, according to figures released Mar. 18 by the Pontifical Council "Cor Unum." Recipients of at least $10,000 each included national Catholic charities in Bangladesh, Benin, Brazil, Indonesia, Pakistan, the Philippines and Togo.

**Muslim Turmoil** — The contemporary turmoil throughout much of the Muslim world stems from an internal struggle between Islamic conservatives and reformers, a conflict with strong political repercussions, said Jesuit Father Samir Khalil Samir, a professor at Rome's Gregorian University and at the University of St. Joseph in Beirut. The conflict could erupt into terrorism, with condemnations and threats against scholars who want to reinterpret the Koran in the light of modern science. "Currently, the struggle we see — which sometimes assumes the form of terrorism — is really a struggle between an open tendency and a conservative tendency in Islam." One factor involved is a major difference with respect to the application of Muslim law in countries with a majority population of Muslims.

**Confession of Mortal Sins** — Catholics must be specific and numerically complete in the confession of mortal sins, the Pope said Mar. 23 in a message to seminarians and newly ordained priests. "Unfortunately today, not a few faithful, availing themselves of the sacrament of penance," do not comply with this requirement. "I hope and pray that the faithful ... would become convinced that the norm which requires a specific and numerical completeness insofar as their honestly examined memory allows them to know — is not an arbitrarily imposed burden, but a means of liberation and serenity." He also commented that confession and reconciliation can never be approached as exercises that are helpful only on a psychological level, because what is at stake is the person's relationship with God and his or her call to holiness. "For this reason, it is clear that the confession must be humble, complete, accompanied by the solid and generous intention to mend one's ways and, finally, by faith that this commitment can be followed."

**Trip to Tuscany** — Pope John Paul traveled to Tuscany Mar. 30 to visit a glass factory in Colle di Val d'Elsa and to celebrate Mass in Siena.

• In an address to management and operating personnel at the glass works, he called for a re-examination of enterprise and employment: "One must rethink industry, considering it not as a place of conflicting interests, but as a community of work aimed at promoting the common good of all its members." Relationships must be reformed in the context of "a new policy of social solidarity." Government action must "aim at stimulating ... the sense of responsibility and willingness to work of the weakest categories of people, assuring at the same time that they have the concrete possibility of expressing their abilities." One must "safeguard the right to work and the right to have work for everyone."

• At Mass in Siena, the Holy Father exhorted sev-

eral thousands of people: "Do not be afraid to welcome Christ in your homes, your offices, your shops,
your factories, your farms and craft centers, your
schools and places of recreation and sport. Do not
be afraid to make room for God, who helped man to
the extent that he wished his Son to share, with Mary
and Joseph, a normal family life and to share with
them their daily toil, necessary for earning their
bread."

**General Audience Topics:**
• "The Bible's message regarding motherhood reveals important and ever-timely aspects" (Mar. 6).
• The example of St. Joseph invites believers to
harmonize their prayer and work (Mar. 20).
• Women of the Old Testament played an active
role in the history of Israel (Mar. 27).

**Briefs:**
• Members of the Society of St. Peter the Apostle
are "godfathers and godmothers" to thousands of
bishops, priests, seminarians and religious in missionary territories whom they support with their
prayers and donations, said the Pope Mar. 9.
• Terrorist attacks in Israel make it important for
Catholics and Jews to renew their commitment to
prayer, mutual understanding and peace in the
Middle East, the Pope told members of B'nai B'rith
Mar. 11.
• The Pope encouraged the bishops of South Korea Mar. 26 to fight against the spread of materialistic attitudes in Asia and to lead efforts for the evangelization of their country.

## Consecrated Life

The Pope issued Mar. 25 a post-synodal apostolic
exhortation entitled *Vita Consecrata*, on a wide range
of subjects related to the nature and forms of consecrated life. In one key paragraph he sought to allay
fears expressed in some quarters about the survival
of consecrated life: "The present difficulties which
a number of institutes are encountering in some parts
of the world must not lead to a questioning of the
fact that the profession of the evangelical counsels
is an integral part of the Church's life and a much-
needed incentive toward greater fidelity to the Gospel. The consecrated life may experience further
changes in its historical forms, but there will be no
change in the substance of a choice which finds expression in a radical gift of self for love of the Lord
Jesus and, in him, of every member of the human
family." (See separate article for excerpts.)

## NATIONAL

**No Assisted Suicide** — In the wake of a federal
court ruling that terminally ill persons have a constitutional right to physician-assisted suicide, the
Catholic Health Association declared Mar. 11 that
its members must "reject participation in any form
of assisted suicide.... The mission, values and philosophy of the Catholic health care ministry" demand that stance. Five days earlier, the 9th U.S. Circuit Court of Appeals invalidated a Washington state
law prohibiting anyone from assisting another person to commit suicide. It ruled that the terminally
ill have a constitutional "right to die" when and how
they wish, with a doctor's help. It was the first time
in the U.S. that a federal appeals court asserted what

the court's majority opinion described as a "constitutionally protected liberty interest in determining
the time and manner of one's own death." The Catholic Health Association's statement said: "The opposition of Catholic providers to assisted suicide is
based upon fundamental values of respect for the
sacredness of life and respect for the integrity of the
medical, nursing and allied health professions. The
Catholic health ministry believes individuals are
stewards of their own lives and that they may not
unduly prolong nor hasten the natural process of
dying." (See separate article.)

**Draconian Cuts** —The president of Covenant
House told a congressional subcommittee Mar. 12
that proposals to cut welfare benefits for unwed
mothers were "draconian" and would lead to more
misery. Sister Mary Rose McGeady, head of the
shelter for runaway and homeless young people,
said that measures being considered in Congress
left her dismayed. "Unless these punitive recommendations are reconsidered, far from encouraging these young people to responsible and productive adulthood, we will simply see more examples
of the kind of frustration, and despair, and broken
lives our Band-Aid welfare system has produced
in the past." Calling proposals "draconian," she
protested that they would systematically cut the
elements that make Covenant House programs for
unwed mothers successful. Sister began her testimony by challenging the assumption that most out-
of-wedlock births occur among women on welfare.
Rather, two-thirds are not on welfare, not living
below the poverty level and not high school drop-
outs. Consequently, freezing welfare for those who
have a second child cannot be viewed as a solution
to the overall problem.

**Must Pay for Abortions** — The U.S. Supreme
Court unanimously rejected Mar. 18 an attempt by
Arkansas officials to deny the use of federal Medicaid funds to pay for abortions in the case of rape and
incest, and sent the case back to a lower court. Similar appeals had already been rejected within the previous three months, in cases from Nebraska, Colorado and Pennsylvania. All of the cases were in reaction to a change in the original 1994 federal Hyde
Amendment. Until that year, the only use of federal
Medicaid money permitted for an abortion was to
save the life of the mother. But in 1994 and 1995
President Clinton and lawmakers broadened the
scope of the Hyde Amendment to include federal
Medicaid payment when the pregnancy resulted from
rape or incest. States refusing compliance with federal requirements would lose all of their federal
Medicaid funding.

**Health Care Ministry** — The need for the Church
to intensify and expand its health care ministry "is
going to be ever greater as public dollars are reduced
in the care of the poor and the elderly, ... So we
need to be present ever more effectively to those at
the outer boundaries of life, providing the kind of
compassionate, loving care that every human being
is entitled to as they move from this life to the next."
So stated Cardinal Bernard F. Law Mar. 20 following a press conference at which he addressed various legal, moral and public policy issues posed by
recent federal appeals court decisions that declared

physician-assisted suicide a constitutional right for the terminally ill.

**Censure** — Bishop Fabian Bruskewitz of Lincoln formally warned Catholic members of groups supporting legal abortion, euthanasia, opposition to Vatican II reforms and other stances of the Church, would be automatically excommunicated if they continued their membership beyond May 15. The penalties would apply to members of Planned Parenthood, the Hemlock Society, Catholics for a Free Choice, Call to Action or its Nebraska chapter, traditionalist groups opposed to church reforms and groups affiliated with Freemasons. "Membership in these organizations or groups is always perilous to the Catholic faith, and most often is totally incompatible with the Catholic faith," said an announcement published in the Mar. 22 edition of the *Southern Nebraska Register*.

The announcement, called "extra-synodal legislation," was dated Mar. 19 and signed by Msgr. Timothy Thorburn, chancellor of the diocese, "by mandate of" Bishop Bruskewitz. It said: If any Catholics "in or of the Diocese of Lincoln who attain or retain membership" in any of the organizations after Apr. 15 are automatically "under interdict and are absolutely forbidden to receive holy Communion.... Contumacious persistence in such membership for one month following the interdict on the part of any such Catholics will by that very fact cause them to be excommunicated." (See separate article.)

**Death Penalty** — Cardinal John J. O'Connor of New York told police officers and others attending Mass at St. Patrick's Cathedral Mar. 24 that he opposed capital punishment but that Catholics "can responsibly be for or against use of the death penalty under certain restricted conditions." His statement was in line with Pope John Paul's comment on the subject in the encyclical letter *Evangelium Vitae*. The relevant restrictions mentioned in the letter, however, are so severe that they would rule out justification for the penalty in all but extreme cases.

**Homosexual "Marriages"** — Archbishop William J. Levada of San Francisco called a mass "gay marriage" ceremony with the exchange of "marriage-like vows" at City Hall Mar. 25 an attack on the sanctity of marriage." Mayor Willie Brown and several members of the governing board of supervisors presided over a ceremony giving 175 homosexual couples official recognition as "domestic partners." With the mock nuptials, San Francisco became the first city in the United States to recognize gay partnerships with a civil ceremony. The city had about 3,000 couples registered as domestic partners over the previous five years. Archbishop Levada said: "A 'ceremony of recognition' of gay and lesbian relationships symbolizes an attempt to redefine the basic human institution of marriage established by nature and creation." (See separate article.)

**Briefs:**

•Winner of the 1996 Templeton Prize for Progress in Religion was William R. Bright, founder and president of Campus Crusade for Christ International.

• Catholic News Service established a permanent site on America Online, providing AOL's five million members access to news and information on the worldwide activities of the Church. The site can be accessed directly by use of the key word CNS.

• The University of Notre Dame announced Mar. 17 that the 1996 Laetare Medal would be awarded to Sister Helen Prejean, author of *Dead Man Walking*.

• More than 21,000 catechists explored "God's Liberating Power" at the annual Religious Education Congress in the Archdiocese of Los Angeles Mar. 22 to 24.

## Physician-Assisted Suicide

The 9th U.S. Circuit Court of Appeals in San Francisco struck down Mar. 6 Washington state's law against physician-assisted suicide, saying that the U.S. Constitution protects an individual's "right to die." In an 8-to-3 decision, the court said the law at issue violated the right of adults who are terminally ill and mentally competent to decide to bring about their deaths with drugs prescribed by their doctors. The majority opinion, written by Justice Stephen Reinhardt, said the preservation of life is a legitimate function of the state but, "when patients are no longer able to pursue life, liberty or happiness and do not wish to pursue life, the state's interest in forcing them to remain alive is less compelling."

Cardinal Bernard F. Law said in a statement issued Mar. 7: "This decision treats the vulnerable elderly the way 'Roe v. Wade' treated unborn children. By constitutionalizing a 'right' to assisted suicide, it threatens the same large-scale assault in their lives as 'Roe' unleashed on the unborn. In so doing, it provides ample evidence that the abortion debate is not about 'when life begins' but about whether or not our society will hold human life to be cheap. This ruling paves and broadens the road to a complete culture of death."

(See separate entry.)

## INTERNATIONAL

**Christian Factor Missing** — The Christian element was missing in the Middle East peace talks between Israel and Syria, a Lebanese academic said at a Christian Zionist conference in Jerusalem. "We are left out," said Professor Walid Phares, a Lebanese professor of political science and secretary general of the World Maronite Union. "We are concerned that Israel will abandon its Christian allies in Lebanon in return for a political agreement with Syria. We appeal to the United States, Europe and Israel to widen the scope of the peace process to include the Christians."

**French Cardinal Honored** — Cardinal Jean-Marie Lustiger was formally received into the French Academy Mar. 14, joining the country's literary elite. Despite France's secular tradition, one seat among "The Immortals," as academy members are known, is usually held for a prominent Catholic. Since its establishment in 1635 by Cardinal Richelieu to "purify the language," members have included 20 cardinals, about 30 bishops and 60 priests.

**Racist Statements in Australia** — The Australian bishops condemned statements against aborigines during the most recent federal election campaigns. Bishop Kevin Manning, chairman of the bishops' Social Justice Council, said it was ill-informed and irresponsible to "assert resentfully in the public forum that aborigines are a privileged group.... There is much more to be gained by encouraging people to be fair and just in their treatment of all Australians."

**Credit Courses in Religion** — The Irish bishops welcomed a government decision to introduce optional religion courses for academic credit into public schools by the year 2001. The decision required repeal of an 1878 law enacted by the British Parliament prohibiting funds to pay for examiners in religion — special teachers who give and correct examinations for academic credit. The law, which remained among Irish statutes, had already been repealed in the United Kingdom.

**Ecumenism in Asia** — The Christian Conference of Asia and the Federation of Asian Bishops' Conferences agreed to form an Asian Ecumenical Committee to implement proposals, share information, cooperate on social issues and provide ecumenical formation. The decision came after an ecumenical consultation held Mar. 12 to 16 in Hong Kong. The 42 participants included representatives from 15 Asian countries and officials from the World Council of Churches and the Pontifical Council for Promoting Christian Unity. A final statement, "Our Pilgrimage of Hope," gave details about their vision and understanding of ecumenism, outlined challenges and barriers to unity, and proposed the creation of the ecumenical committee.

**Catholics Hindered** — Bosnia's Muslim-led government, intent on making Sarajevo a Muslim city, was making it difficult for Catholics to return to the city, said Msgr. Ivo Tomashevic, an assistant to Cardinal Vinko Puljic. He appealed to world leaders to exert pressure on the government to respect minority rights and the pluralism of the city's ethnic and religious population. Discrimination came not from the people but from politicians and political leaders, he said in an interview published in the Mar. 20 edition of the Milan-based Catholic newspaper *Avvenire*.

**Married Priest Problem** — A spokesman for the Czech bishops said Mar. 20 that problems concerning married priests secretly ordained under communist rule might finally be settled following the establishment of an Eastern-rite jurisdiction. The Church had already accepted many clandestine priests whose ordination was originally questioned, said Father Miloslav Fiala. Negotiations were planned with the remainder, who would be asked to choose between joining the Eastern-rite jurisdiction as active priests or exercising other ministerial roles in the Latin rite. The Eastern rite permits married men to become priests, while the Latin rite requires celibacy. Father Fiala said about 250 priests and 16 bishops, many of them married, had been secretly ordained during the communist period but did not have proper documentation or witnesses to confirm the fact of their ordination. Investigations were under way to determine who had, or had not, been validly ordained.

**Acquittal Overturned** — Poland's Appeals Court overturned the acquittal of two communist secret police generals and ordered fresh investigations into their suspected involvement in the 1984 killing of social activist Father Jerzy Popieluszko. In a Mar. 21 ruling, Judge Jan Krosnicki said the county court that cleared the generals had failed to "analyze responsibly" key evidence against them, including courtroom testimony by the priest's convicted kill-

ers. He noted that the written justification for their acquittal had been "one-sided, tendentious and selective," and had violated legal procedure by failing to assess the reliability of particular witnesses. Generals Wladyslaw Ciaston and Zenon Platek, first arrested in 1990, were released in August, 1994, when the court ruled that the charge of "inciting and assisting" Father Popieluszko's kidnapping and murder had not been proved.

**Rights in Burundi** — An international investigation of human rights violations in Burundi was called an important factor in bringing peace and justice to the country, but it was not enough, a Vatican official said during a special meeting in Geneva of a U.N. commission examining the roots of 1994 massacres in the country. Archbishop Giuseppe Bertello said Mar. 27 that the international community's involvement in Burundi must go beyond the condemnation of crimes by providing material support to the people. "This extraordinary session dedicated to Burundi cannot limit itself to the condemnation of serious human rights violations perpetuated for too long in this nation. The international community should help the people of Burundi to create the social fabric of their country and to find their national identity in a community in which the diversity of ethnic, social and political groups will be not only tolerated, but accepted as a richness.... The Catholic Church will continue to seek every possible way to foster a drawing together of communities and, through its organizations, to bring humanitarian aid to refugees and to projects of development for the country."

**Briefs:**
• An association of 29 family life groups reported that it had gathered 1.4 million signatures to a petition asking government leaders to pass laws favoring family life.
• Bishop Felipe Aguirre Franco of Tuxla Gutierrez said in a Lenten message: Mexican "authorities ought to review whether the application of the present economic system, in which the profits are for a few and the cost is for the majority, is moral."
• Lay ministry was reported to be on the increase in at least 20 or more dioceses in the regions of Andalucia, the Basque country and Catalonia,

### Definition of Reproductive Rights

Bishop James T. McHugh of Camden called for more careful definition of such terms as "reproductive rights" in follow-up to the 1994 Cairo Conference on Population and Development. Bishop McHugh represented the Vatican at a meeting of the U.N. Commission on Population and Development Feb. 26 to Mar. 1 at U.N. headquarters. Precision is required, he said, because the concept and meaning of "reproductive rights" were still subject to debate. "The need for precision is evident when actions are encouraged to implement reproductive rights at the local level." The only "reproductive right" that had thus far received clear international standing was "the basic right of couples and individuals to decide freely and responsibly the number, spacing and timing of their children, and to have the information and means to do so." This definition is in accord with Vatican understanding, provided the "means" do not violate Catholic moral teaching, the bishop said.

# APRIL 1996

## VATICAN

**Holy Week Observances** — Pope John Paul celebrated the whole round of liturgical ceremonies during Holy Week, from the Mass of Palm Sunday through the solemnities of the Easter Triduum to the glorious solemn Easter Mass celebrated before thousands of people in St. Peter's Square. He said in a special message: "The Lord of life has risen with power, bringing with him "love, justice, respect, forgiveness and reconciliation. The One who from nothingness had called the world into existence, only he could break the seals of the tomb, only he could become the source of New Life." The Holy Father extended Easter greetings in 56 languages to people throughout the world.

**Letter to Priests** — Ordination is the beginning of a priest's response to his vocation, a response which must be renewed each day and in every task he is called to carry out, Pope John Paul said in a Holy Thursday letter addressed to priests throughout the world. Ordination, he said as he noted the 50th anniversary of his ordination to the priesthood, is just the beginning "of a journey which continues until death.... Our priestly life, like every other form of Christian existence, is a succession of responses to God who calls." Anniversaries are special opportunities to review how well one has responded to God's call and to remember the people who have offered encouragement and support. "We know that we are 'unworthy servants,' but we are grateful to the Lord for having wished to make us his ministers.... As we give thanks, we also ask pardon of God and of our brothers and sisters for our negligence and failures, the results of human weakness." At the same time, "we cannot forget our brothers in the priesthood who have not persevered on the journey undertaken. We entrust them to the Father's love and assure each of them of our prayers."

**Assisted Suicide Decision** — A *L'Osservatore Romano* commentary condemned Apr. 5 the court decision overturning New York state's ban on assisted suicide, saying it reflected a "total eclipse of values" and a disregard for life. "Life and death cannot be reduced to a private matter, nor to a bilateral choice between an individual and the doctor." The article said the decision was a sign of a seemingly unstoppable trend toward legitimizing euthanasia in the United States and in Europe. The writer, Father Gino Concetti, called the decision "dangerous legal reasoning which distorts the role of the state, omitting its duty to protect basic human rights."

**Deadly Economic Wars** — The Pope, warning that "economic wars" are as deadly as those fought with guns, said the Church must keep assailing the global imbalance between rich and poor. Along with pro-life issues, church teaching is increasingly focused on financial questions because they affect the lives of so many millions of people. "Social, economic and financial problems are becoming more important for the destiny of humanity. On one hand, they can provoke economic wars no less deadly and cruel than those fought with weapons and, on the other, they aggravate social injustice in a world that is beset by poverty and underdevelopment in so many

places." He made the remarks in a message to the magazine, *La Civilta Cattolica*.

**Tunisia Visit** — The Pope, on a 12-hour visit to Tunisia Apr. 14, celebrated Mass for the small, mostly foreign Catholic community of 14,000 and met amicably with religious and civil leaders of the Muslim majority. (See separate article.)

**Gay Unions** — The growing acceptance and legal recognition of gay unions is a victory for secular attitudes that make each individual the arbiter of right and wrong. "It is predictable that the phenomenon is destined to spread," wrote Father Gino Concetti after the Dutch Parliament voted Apr. 16 to allow the marriage of homosexuals and to extend to couples in long-term relationships all of the legal benefits of marriage. In his article in the Apr. 18 edition of *L'Osservatore Romano*, the moral theologian said the legalization of such unions is a "subversion of the creative plan of God" and, therefore, an attack on the dignity of the human person, created male and female, to use sexuality for union and procreation within marriage.

**Violence in Lebanon** — Pope John Paul appealed Apr. 21 on behalf of civilian victims for an end to "incredible violence" in southern Lebanon, saying there was no apparent justification for the Israeli shelling which took a toll of more than 130 persons, most of whom were Lebanese civilians. "Once again it has been the civilian population — especially the Lebanese — which has paid the price of the actions of war, for which it is difficult to find acceptable justifications."

**Ruthenian Anniversary** — The 350th anniversary of Ruthenian Catholics' reunion with Rome was an occasion to rejoice over the return of religious freedom in the former Soviet bloc and for Catholics to recommit themselves to work for Christian unity, said the Pope in an apostolic letter released Apr. 22. Marking the anniversary of the Apr. 24, 1646, Union of Uzhorod, he praised the faithfulness and courage of Ruthenian Catholics of old along with their modern descendants living in dioceses in Ukraine, Slovakia and the United States.

**Child Slavery** — Articles in *L'Osservatore Romano* late in the month condemned the sexual exploitation of children as a new form of slavery involving several million young people around the world, and said the lack of a public outcry over the expanding sex-tourism industry was particularly worrisome. Experts at two U.N. conferences in Geneva and Strasbourg, France, said that in Asia more than a million children under the age of 14 were forced to work as prostitutes, and that the sex tourist trade had spread to the former Soviet countries in Eastern Europe. The newspaper articles said it was shameful that modern society cannot protect its children and allows them to be "reduced to the status of slaves or to be sold for sex."

**Models of Integrity** — In a society with a gap between faith and practice, church workers must be models of integrity, the Pope told a group of Colombian bishops Apr. 30. "In the face of the disassociation between faith and life which exists in society, the Church is the first to be called to show —

through the daily witness of bishops, priests, religious and laity — how faith includes a moral content." He also said the weakened moral standards are at the base of "the spread of corruption, injustice and violence which suffocates the very foundations of human coexistence."

**General Audience Topics:**
• During the Easter Triduum, the Church invites us to share sacramentally in Christ's paschal mystery and to be transformed by its saving power (Apr. 3).
• The predominant image of women in the Bible is one of strong individuals who work with and for God (Apr. 10).
• Reflections on his Apr. 14 visit to Tunisia (Apr. 17).
• God is ever faithful to his covenant (Apr. 24).

**Briefs:**
• The Pope met formally with the Chief Rabbi of Rome, Elio Toaff, Apr. 15 to commemorate the 10th anniversary of his historic visit to Rome's synagogue.
• Pope John Paul, marking the 10th anniversary of the Chernobyl, Ukraine, nuclear accident, urged experts to do all in their power to prevent a similar occurrence, and called for continuing aid to survivors of the disaster.
• At a meeting with bishops from the Middle East, the Holy Father said the Church's delicate mission in the region should be based on charity to the poor and unity among the faithful.
• The Pope met with U.S. bishops Apr. 23 for an "informal informational session" on a variety of topics.
• To date, Pope John Paul canonized more than 200 saints and beatified 700 individuals during the 18 years of his pontificate.

## Defending Life

"The denial of life — consolidated and ratified as a culture of death in legal abortion — continues to take root in modern society with the intention of legalizing euthanasia as well," said Pope John Paul in a message to an international conference sponsored by the Pontifical Council for the Family. Modern society is immersed in a contradiction when it promotes human rights "but is not able to apply them in defense of the weakest." Abortion, euthanasia and other attacks on life are contrary to a true ideal of humanism, which must include "support for the human person from conception to natural death.... There is a pressing need to rediscover an authentic anthropology which highlights and values the human dignity of every person and views life as a sacred and fundamental gift."

## NATIONAL

**Prayer for Life** — The Family Rosary launched a worldwide campaign asking families and individuals to pledge to pray the rosary for the pro-life cause during the month of May. "Since Easter is a time for the renewal of life, as we profess our faith and rejoice in the knowledge of our eternal life through Christ, it is the perfect season to announce this special worldwide prayer effort," said Father Leo Polselli, president of the Family Rosary and Family Theater.

**Church Agencies Can't Do It** — A suggestion

made on Capitol Hill that church agencies take up the slack from cuts in federal social service funding is unacceptable to Catholic Charities USA, the organization's president told a congressional committee. "Such a position rests upon a very flawed philosophical foundation," said Jesuit Father Fred Kammer. It also "flies in the face of the magnitude of the cuts that each church would be asked to replace." While churches have a duty of charity and justice, government has a moral duty "to protect human rights and human dignity, and to secure justice for all in the society." That responsibility extends to ensuring living wages and adequate income for those who are unable to work. The U.S. bishops and the staff of Catholic Charities watched "with great dismay" at welfare bills that would reduce the effort required of state governments to help the poor, while ending federal responsibility for the poorest members of society. Services including protection of abused and neglected children, Medicaid benefits, substance abuse programs and basic welfare, all would face funding cuts that would dramatically affect already under-financed programs run by 200 Catholic Charities agencies nationwide, according to Father Kammer. A conservative estimate of the combined impact of welfare program cuts over the next seven years was $504 billion.

**NCEA Convention** — More than 17,000 persons attended sessions of the annual convention of the National Catholic Educational Association Apr. 9 to 12 in Philadelphia. One of the positive reports issued during the convention was an increase of 16,000 students in enrollment for the 1995-96 school year, bringing total elementary and high school enrollment to more than 2.6 million students. Twenty-five percent of students were from minority groups, 17 percent were non-Catholics. It was also reported that less than one-third of the teachers were members of religious institutes; 66 percent were laypersons. Cardinal Joseph L. Bernardin was honored with the NCEA's 1996 John Carroll Award, given annually to a bishop for "outstanding work to promote U.S. Catholic elementary and secondary schools."

**McBrien Book Criticized** — The revised edition of *Catholicism* has "certain shortcomings" as an introductory text on Catholic theology, said a critical review of the book by the Secretariat for Doctrine and Pastoral Practices, National Conference of Catholic Bishops. The critique, made public Apr. 9, said the book has some "inaccurate or at least misleading" statements and at times is not clear enough on what is normative in Catholic tradition. Archbishop Daniel E. Pilarczyk, head of the committee which had criticized the second edition of the book, said the current committee determined that the new edition "had not corrected the ambiguities identified in 1985 and that additional problems had been introduced into the text." Father McBrien, whose status as a priest was not questioned, was critical of the manner in which the bishops conducted and publicized their critique.

**Suit for Charity Care** — The New Jersey Hospital Association sued the state Apr. 15, seeking payment for charity care of uninsured patients by its members. The lawsuit was the latest tactic in a months-long struggle for restoration of state funding for state-mandated charity care valued at several hundred million dollars a year. The suit, filed in Essex County, contended that, since the state makes the hospitals provide the services, it must provide just reimbursement. State funding stopped at the end of the previous December.

**Evangelize by Living Faith** — The "strongest magnate" that African-American Catholics have to draw people to the Church is not spirit-filled music or colorful ethnic clothing. "Sometimes we get sidetracked by experiences or by externals that have a value but are not at the heart of the matter," said Auxiliary Bishop George V. Murry of Chicago Apr. 17 at the National Black Catholic Congress conference in Louisville. "The best way we can evangelize and welcome people into our community is our faith. It is how you and I live on a daily basis. It is the fact that the Lord has made us new and that, as children of the light, we carry that light of the Lord into our world." The Apr. 14-to-18 conference on the theme, "Refounding Parishes: Models for Evangelization," was attended by about 300 African-American Catholics.

**Thousands Become Catholics** — Tens of thousands of persons were baptized or received into full communion with the Church at Easter Vigil ceremonies Apr. 6 in parishes across the country. Later in the month in Orlando, approximately 15,000 Catholics participated in a "Diocesan Day of Rededication and Confirmation in the Faith"Apr. 21. The highlight of the day was reception of the sacrament of confirmation by more than 2,200 people from the 50 parishes of the diocese.

**Bold Proclamation of the Faith** — We Catholics must be bold in proclaiming our faith because "we have something profound and life-giving to say to the world." So stated Bishop Wilton D. Gregory of Belleville at the annual National Conference of Catechetical Leadership Apr. 21 to 25 in Detroit. He told more than 800 participants in the conference: "We have a great and rich heritage that stretches across 20 centuries.... The Gospel is good news. Christ triumphed over sin, death and even cynicism. The Church still enjoys the apostolic mandate ... Our challenge is to know the full heritage and content of our faith.... The new language that we must speak is the language of hope, possibility, reconciliation, trust and charity." The theme of the meeting was "Compelled by Mission — Declaring Our Direction."

**Genetic Testing** — "Genetic testing raises and will continue to raise moral issues for the individual, for the family, for racial or ethnic groups, and for society as a whole," said the bishops' Committee on Science and Human Values in a statement released Apr. 23. The Church supports research "directed toward respect for personal dignity and support of human life," but opposes the use of such research for decisions "not in accord with sound morality." Prenatal testing, for example, is legitimate if it does not involve disproportionate risks to the child or mother, and is done for the sake of early therapy. But, if prenatal diagnosis were conducted with the intention of abortion if genetic problems were found, it would be wrong — "since it presumes to measure the value of a human life only within the parameters

of 'normality' and physical well-being," as Pope John Paul has said. "The Church condemns and will never cease condemning the taking of innocent unborn life, surely the saddest aggression of our violent time," the committee said.

**Assisted Suicide Ruling** — The New York-based 2nd Circuit Court of Appeals ruled Apr. 2 against the constitutionality of two New York laws banning physician-assisted suicide. Gail Quinn, head of the bishops' Secretariat for Pro-Life Activities, said the decision "marks another radical judicial departure from our nation's legal and medical traditions." It shows that "the courts are developing a bias against life." This ruling came one month after the 9th Circuit Court of Appeals in San Francisco said there is a constitutionally protected "right to die." (See separate article.)

**Briefs:**

• Bishop Nicholas C. Dattilo of Harrisburg turned down an award from a local chapter of the American Diabetes Association because of the national group's support for fetal-tissue research that includes the use of tissues from elective abortions.

• The observance of Earth Day Apr. 22 "calls for a renewed appreciation and respect for planet Earth, the common home for all humanity," said Bishop Michael D. Pfeifer of San Angelo in the month's edition of the diocesan newspaper.

• Archbishop Elden F. Curtiss of Omaha banned from church offices and ministries Catholics of the archdiocese who publicly support abortion or euthanasia or publicly dissent from church teaching on the ordination of women to the priesthood,

## Partial-Birth Abortion

President Clinton vetoed Apr. 10 a bill banning partial-birth abortion in all cases except danger of maternal death. He said he would have signed the measure into law if it had included an exception permitting the procedure for the health of the mother. Several weeks before the veto, Helen Alvare, the bishops' pro-life spokeswoman said: "We are deeply offended by the president's decision to support a procedure in which doctors mostly deliver a live human child, then brutally kill that child before completing delivery.... The president's response is disingenuous. It is well known that a 'health' exception is a legal term of art that means any abortion a woman elects to have. Since Roe v. Wade and its companion case Doe v. Bolton, the Supreme Court has defined 'health' in the context of abortions to include all forms of psychological, emotional or social well-being." (See separate article.)

## INTERNATIONAL

**Reconciliation in Rwanda** — About 2,000 exiled Rwandan Hutus gathered at Nairobi's Holy Family Basilica early in the month to pray for reconciliation in their country. Some of those in attendance had been accused of participating in genocide against Tutsis; all of them had fled during the civil war and massacres that began Apr. 6, 1994, after the assassination of Rwandan President Juvenal Habyarimana. Father Roger Tessier, a Canadian priest, urged the congregation: "Let us pray for national reconciliation in Rwanda. Everyone needs to convert their hearts to peace and reconciliation."

**Criticism Defended** — Cardinal Franjo Kuharic of Zagreb defended criticism of Croatia's human rights violations, according to an Apr. 10 report by his archdiocesan press agency. "The good functioning of the state is in the interest of the Church, and it means a state in which human rights will be respected.... We are warning with good intentions. We have never been malicious." The cardinal's remarks were a response to newspaper criticism that churchmen had misrepresented the human rights situation after Croats recaptured Serb-held territory the year before.

**Bishops Won't Keep Quiet** — Political pressure will not keep Colombian bishops from denouncing corruption within the government and the whole country, said Archbishop Pedro Rubiano Saenz, president of the bishops' conference. His statement came after politicians close to President Ernesto Samper Pizano said the Church lacked moral authority because it had received money from drug lords. "We are ready to do an internal purge" if it can be shown that priests have accepted money from drug trafficking, the archbishop said. Even though there had been no proof of the accusations, "we are ready to condemn and publicly punish any church member who could have sold his conscience for drug money." Regarding the accusers, the archbishop said they were "politicians who do not accept Catholic bishops being involved in the daily life of the country."

**Preventive Diplomacy** — Religious leaders help to prevent war by being faithful to "their own common teaching that we are all brothers and sisters in the same human family because we are all children of the one God." So stated Archbishop John P. Foley, president of the Pontifical Council for Social Communications, in an address Apr. 24 at the United Nations. He called attention to the fact that Pope John Paul's address at the U.N. Oct. 5, 1995, held up the ideal of the peoples of the world living as a "family of nations," and said: "If spiritual leaders and religious organizations can effectively inculcate by word and example this lesson of the unity of the human family and of the sanctity of life, most conflicts could be averted, most violence could be avoided, and we could be blessed with one world at peace under God." The theme of the two-day symposium was "Preventive Diplomacy: The Therapeutics of Mediation."

**Role of Catholics in Romania** — A Romanian Orthodox leader said he believed the country's previously outlawed Romanian Catholic Church has a key role to play in the life of the nation. "I think the Greek Catholic Church lies at the very foundation of our national unity, alongside the Orthodox," said Metropolitan Nicolae Courneanu of Banat. "That thought easily tipped the balance when I opted to seek an agreement rather than allow the conflicts between us to drag on." Among the conflicts was the return of former Catholic church properties expropriated by the communists in 1948 and turned over to the Orthodox.

**Debt Relief** — Developing nations should join together in a call for debt relief, said Archbishop Norberto Rivera Carrera of Mexico City. At a press conference Apr. 28, he said that the distribution of wealth in Mexico was "tremendously unfair" and that the nation's external debt was a "bloodletting" that was paralyzing the country. Regarding the indebtedness of other countries like Mexico and a way of dealing with it, he said: "One of the roads that looks most viable is the joining together of the countries because, as long as we are treated in isolation, the fat fish always eats up the little ones. So, it is necessary for countries that have the same problem as Mexico to band together and appear together before the World Bank, before the powerful countries, to let them know how we poor, developing countries cannot pay if there is not growth, if there is not production, if there is not progress. This, I think, has to make the developed countries think that, for their own convenience, they have to help the countries that are on the path to development. Because otherwise, we will all perish in the same shipwreck."

**Wanted: Information on Guatemala** — American and Salvadoran religious in El Salvador demanded that the U.S. government release information about human rights abuses in Guatemala over the previous 40 years, including the 1989 kidnap and rape of a U.S. nun. More than 100 religious protested outside the U.S. Embassy Apr. 30 against what they called U.S. complicity in abuses in Guatemala. Thirty Americans living in El Salvador presented a statement to embassy officials in which they urged the Clinton administration to immediately declassify all information related to the case of Ursuline Sister Dianna Ortiz, who was abducted, tortured and raped, allegedly by members of the Guatemalan security forces.

**Some Stay, Some Leave** — Some missionaries in Liberia were evacuated from danger zones in Liberia, particularly from Monrovia, while others opted to stay in the hope that somehow they might be able to carry on their ministry despite perilous conditions of civil war.

**Briefs:**

• Auxiliary Bishop Gregorio Rosa Chavez of San Salvador was named recipient of a special award from a German state parliament for his efforts to end 12 years of civil war in his country.

• Archbishop Franc Perko of Belgrade said a recent spate of attacks on minority places of worship in the city would not disrupt church life. "These acts were the work of extremist elements only," he said. "They have no real significance for the atmosphere in Belgrade, which is now much better for Catholics."

## They Didn't Do Enough

The bishops of Argentina issued a document late in the month in which they said they had not done enough to stop human rights violations during the country's "dirty war" of the 1970s and early 1980s, in which 4,000 people were killed and 10,000 or more "disappeared." The bishops said in the statement: "We ask forgiveness of God and of our brothers and sisters because our actions were insufficient to prevent the illegal repression that left thousands of dead and disappeared people in the country."

# MAY 1996

## VATICAN

**Ethics** — The Catholic university has a crucial role to play in examining today's complex ethical issues and promoting the overall good of society, Pope John Paul said May 11 at a meeting of international university rectors. "In today's world, the tasks of a Catholic university are urgent and relevant.... Scientific and material progress increasingly raises the question of meaning and purpose, a question which needs to be addressed in order to ensure that development serves the authentic good of individuals and of society as a whole," He also said that men and women need the ethical reflections that church-run universities can offer on new questions raised by an increasingly complicated society.

**Bishop-Priest Relations** — For the good of the whole Church, there is no better way a bishop can spend his time than in teaching, encouraging and listening to his priests, the Pope said at a meeting with Colombian bishops May 11. "Priests are your primary and indispensable collaborators.... You must love them much, and more each day." At the same time, unless lay people are educated to take up their responsibilities as Christians in the world of culture and politics, the strong guidance provided by priests cannot lead to a transformation of society. "The preaching of the Gospel" would be unthinkable without the ministry of suitable priests and without the witness and activity of well-formed lay people, committed to various fields of the apostolate."

**Agca Wants Out** —Fifteen years after he shot and seriously wounded Pope John Paul in St. Peter's Square, Mehmet Ali Agca thought he had served enough time in prison. Claiming a moral metamorphosis, the 38-year-old Turk told Italian TV viewers that he was a new man and considered his attack an "infantile" attempt to make history. "I have atoned for my guilt. I have paid for my mistakes, which I recognize," he said in an interview broadcast May 13, the anniversary of the shooting. The Pope had already forgiven his attacker.

**Rights and Values** —Abortion, euthanasia and other attacks on human life and the family are supported by an attitude that recognizes the rights only of those who are independent and self-sufficient, said speakers May 24 at a Vatican conference on "Law and 'The Gospel of Life,' " Pope John Paul's 1995 encyclical letter. When rights spring from a concept of the individual as autonomous, self-determining and independent — from others, from responsibility and from a set of objective values — anyone who is weak or chooses to be dependent suffers, declared Mary Ann Glendon, one of the principal speakers. The Harvard Law School professor told the conferees that an individualistic, "libertarian" concept of rights and freedoms is gaining ground over a "dignitarian" concept that stresses human dignity and the connections between rights and responsibilities.

**Violence in Colombia** — Pope John Paul told a group of Colombian bishops May 25 that the Church in their country must raise its voice against continuing forms of violence ranging from abortion to drug wars — violence that had for decades sown "grief and terror," blocking social peace and slowing national de-

velopment. He said he was referring to a pattern of social aggression that included persistent fighting between guerrillas and armed forces, the actions of paramilitary groups, the "abominable crime of abortion," slayings linked to drug trafficking, common crime and internal family conflicts. It was time, he said, for the Church to undertake a general mobilization in favor of national reconciliation and justice.

**Hardships To Be Shared** — Measures to boost economic activity in Uruguay must not bring unequal hardships to the poor, said the Pope at a meeting May 28 with President Julio Maria Sanguinetti. When sacrifices are involved in economic activity, they must be shared equally by all sectors of society and must be accompanied by concrete acts of solidarity so that everyone lives in a way consistent with human dignity. He told the president that the Church would continue to support programs of "integral development" whose aim would be not only improving economic standards, but also the life, education, health and spiritual well-being of individuals. "Of particular importance is the theme of defending life, that is to say, the respect which all must give because of the sacred value of human life from its beginning to its end.

**General Audience Topics:**

• As the new "Daughter of Zion," Mary represents all of humanity, called to the marriage banquet which celebrates God's covenant with his people (May 1).

• Mary's being "full of grace" is not due to any human merit, but is wholly the result of God's wonderful work (May 8).

• The Church's reflection has made explicit the profound meaning of the words, "full of grace," spoken by the angel Gabriel to the Virgin of Nazareth (May 15).

• Reflections on his May 17-to-19 visit to Slovenia (May 22).

• Mary's faithful cooperation in the saving work of her Son made it fitting that she should be completely free from sin and should share fully in Christ's grace (May 29).

**Briefs:**

• The Vatican approved the designation of Italian Franciscan Father Francesco Caracciolo (1563 to 1608) as the patron saint of Italian cooks.

• With the Dalai Lama, Pope John Paul had "a spiritual meeting, with prayer and an exchange of thoughts on religious themes," May 20.

• Legislators who personally oppose abortion but follow the pro-abortion consensus of their constituents are modern-day Pontius Pilates, said Archbishop Julian Herranz, president of the Pontifical Council for the Interpretation of Legislative Texts, May 24, at the opening of a conference on law and Pope Paul's encyclical letter, "The Gospel of Life."

• The Pope paid a visit May 31 to the Vatican's newest building, Domus Sanctae Marthae, the guest house for cardinals during conclaves for the election of a pope.

## Visit to Slovenia

Pope John Paul, on arrival at Ljubljana's Brnik Airport at the start of his May 17-to-19 visit to

Slovenia, expressed hope that the nation "will remain faithful to her vocation as the crossroads of peoples and bridge between the Slav, Germanic, Latin and Hungarian worlds," He also said:

"In sharing the efforts you are making to overcome the inevitable difficulties connected with this new phase in your history (since the establishment of independence), the Holy See urges you to seek courageously in your people's staunchest virtues and in their Christian faith the strength to build your future together.

"The celebration of the 1,250th anniversary of our people's conversion to the Christian faith offers you an opportunity to appreciate and to recover the humanizing energy flowing from a people's encounter with Jesus Christ.

"This event is not only an ecclesial fact. It is also a most important stage in the nation's history. The commemoration of the initial evangelization of your ancestors must therefore be an occasion for rediscovering your ancient roots and for opening new horizons for your culture."

(See additional article.)

## NATIONAL

**New Feminism** — As the "old feminism" dies out, women must take care to ensure that the new movement that rises in its place does not make the same mistakes, said Mary Ann Glendon at a national "Women and the Culture of Life" national conference May 2 in Washington. "There is a widespread sense that the old feminism veered off course somewhere along the way." The Harvard law professor said she had seen evidence of increasing alienation among women from the word "feminism. The majority of women (today) decline to identify themselves as feminists. And younger women are even more alienated from the word than older women." Most women characterize the old feminism as having negative attitudes with respect to marriage and motherhood, antagonism toward men and "an inattention to the practical problems of balancing work and family." Although many young women are "profoundly appreciative of the gains made" in the early days of feminism, some "are beginning to count up the casualties of the women's movement, especially with regard to children.... I do believe a new approach to women's issues is emerging." The new Catholic feminism, she opined, would be "inclusive rather than polarizing," with men and women as "partners in the quest for better ways to love and work," and it would be "radical" in the sense of the Second Vatican Council."

**Fast Ended, Information Wanted** — Ursuline Sister Dianna Ortiz ended her vigil and fast in front of the White House May 6, saying that, while information released to date was inadequate, there seemed to be momentum toward resolving questions about her abduction, rape and torture in Guatemala in 1989. At a press conference, she also announced plans to sue the federal government for additional documents, and provided sketches of her assailants and of an American she believed was their superior. The press conference capped an eight-day campaign of civil disobedience in front of the White House in which more than 100 people were arrested. Sister Ortiz said

several thousand pages of documents released voluntarily by the State Department May 4 provided no information about the American she believed supervised the men who kidnapped and tortured her, but they did reveal "a pronounced bias against me, from the very beginning, on the part of the U.S. Embassy in Guatemala." As an example, she quoted from a report by then-Ambassador Thomas Strook in Guatemala, suggesting that, with the help of U.S. priests and nuns and the Guatemalan archbishop, she simulated her abduction as a political strategy timed to coincide with congressional debate on aid to that country.

**$25.5 Million for Retired Religious** — The annual collection to help meet the retirement needs of religious netted $25.53 million in 1995, reported the National Religious Retirement Office. Officials said the collection fell $1.3 million shy of 1994's all-time high of $26.8 million, but noted that many dioceses in the eastern part of the country were hit by a blizzard during the Dec. 9-to-10 weekend of the collection, keeping some people away from church. Sister Janet Roesener, director of the national office, said 75 dioceses registered higher collection totals than in 1994, while several other diocesan coordinators said the snow could be blamed for lower collection levels. In all, 167 dioceses took part in the 1995 collection, termed "Your Chance To Say Thanks." Twenty-six dioceses had their own local fund drives. Catholics continued their generous contributions to the Retirement Fund for Religious, making the collection the most lucrative national collection in U.S. history.

**Immigrants and Refugees** — Public attitudes toward immigrants reflect economic conditions, according to John J. Swenson, executive director of Migration and Refugee Services, U.S. Catholic Conference. "In times of economic uncertainty and lack of confidence, immigrants become a cause of concern and fear" because of their assumed negative influence on the economy and job opportunities for citizens. Swenson made his comments in a newspaper interview in St. Louis during a May 16-to-18 meeting sponsored by MRS to help personnel of diocesan resettlement programs adapt to changes in the U.S. refugee situation. Representatives of 42 dioceses took part in the meeting, which focused on "free case" refugees, or those with no family ties in the U.S. Refugees are a special class of legal immigrants — persons fleeing persecution for political or religious beliefs who cannot be safely repatriated to their countries of origin. According to USCC figures for 1994, there were about 121,000 refugees among approximately 800,000 legal U.S. immigrants. Since 1975, MRS had resettled more than 800,000 refugees in dioceses across the country.

**Sacramental Confession on Tape** — Lawyers for the Archdiocese of Portland, Ore., were in negotiations with the Lane County Sheriff's Department for a settlement they hoped would result in the destruction of a taped recording of a sacramental confession. Jailers secretly tape-recorded an April 22 session in which Conan Hale, a 20-year-old murder suspect, received the sacrament of reconciliation from Father Timothy Mockaitis, pastor of St.

Paul Parish in Eugene. Both were unaware that they were being recorded. Oregon law exempts clergy from being questioned about private conversations, but District Attorney Doug Harcleroad said laws allowing recording of conversations inside jails do not exempt sacramental confessions. Only conversations between a prisoner and his attorney are specifically exempted in the law. Auxiliary Bishop D. Kenneth Steiner asked Harcleroad to destroy the tape and any information prosecutors and investigators obtained from it. "In response to the civil authorities' shocking disregard of our religious practice, I have asked (Harcleroad) to destroy the tape and to guarantee the future integrity of the sacrament for the incarcerated," said the bishop. Harcleroad said May 22 that he had made a mistake in authorizing the taping, but the bishop indicated that the apology was not enough. He said the archdiocese "remains committed to the destruction of the tape and the guarantee that never again will such a violation occur in the state of Oregon." Calling the taping "not a past event but a present sacramental transgression," Bishop Steiner said he had instructed legal counsel to inform a Lane County judge that the archdiocese would formally petition for destruction of the tape.

**Ethics in Managed Health Care** — Catholics who want the Church to continue its hospital ministries must confront the ethical problems associated with managed care, according to Father Dennis A. Brodeur, stewardship vice president for the Sisters of Mary Health Care System in St. Louis. People responsible for Catholic hospital ministries must find ways of working with partners who do not share their values with respect to moral issues and other considerations, he added

**U.S. Catholic Statistics** — The 1996 edition of *The Official Catholic Directory* reported a Catholic population of 60,280,454, about 90,000 more than for the previous year. Catholic hospitals and health care centers assisted more than 61.3 million patients, nearly 10 percent more than the 55.9 million reported for the previous year. Elementary schools enrolled about 20,000 more children than the year before; high school enrollment dropped by about 4,500 while colleges had enrollment gains. Following the trends of recent years, the numbers of priests, brothers, sisters and seminarians declined while the number of deacons increased. A new feature in the 1996 edition is a 72-page unofficial "Catholic Internet Directory," listing World Wide Web or Internet sites and e-mail addresses of thousands of diocesan offices, schools, parishes, publications, online communications services and other entities.

**Briefs:**
• Officials of the Diocese of Cleveland expressed doubt about reports that a woman had been receiving visions and messages from the Blessed Virgin Mary for the past 11 years.
• Bills were introduced in both houses of Congress that would permit states to decide whether to give legal recognition to same-sex marriages performed in other states.
• Moral disgust was the reaction of Cardinals Adam J. Maida of Detroit and Anthony J. Bevilacqua of Philadelphia to Dr. Jack Kevorkian's acquittal of two

more counts of assisted suicide, bringing the total number of his assisted deaths to about 30.
• The ordination of married women to the priesthood in Germany's Old Catholic Church was opposed by its counterpart in the United States and Canada, declared Bishop Anthony M. Rysz of the Polish National Catholic Church in the U.S. and Canada, May 28.
• The United Farm Workers and lettuce products grower Bruce Church, Inc., of California ended years of labor controversy with the signing of an agreement May 29. Cesar Chavez, UFW founder and president, died in 1993.

## Fewer Priests and Seminarians

Diminishing numbers of priests and seminarians were the subjects of reports issued by the Center for Applied Research in the Apostolate.

**Priests:** If U.S. vocations to the priesthood start to rise gradually, the decline in active diocesan priests since the late 1960s could bottom out around 2012 to 2015. While two-thirds of dioceses studied are likely to have fewer priests by 2020, about one-third "are projected to increase or hold steady in active priest population between now and 2020." Figures supplied by 66 dioceses indicated that currently 60 percent of their priests were 55 years of age or older, and 25 percent of those — 15 percent of all the priests — were over 75. Eleven percent of priests in the study were under 40; 29 percent were between 40 and 54; 22 percent were between 55 and 64; 23 percent were between 65 and 74. Just over half of the dioceses reported policies of priest retirement at age 70; 14 percent set retirement at 65 and 27 percent at 75.

**Seminarians:** The number of post-college seminarians dropped nearly five percent in 1995. There were 3,172 candidates for the priesthood in Catholic theology schools in 1995-96, down from 3,328 enrolled in 1994-95. It was the third straight year of decline after a slight rise in 1992-93 figures. Most of the decline occurred among candidates preparing for the priesthood in religious orders; their total dropped from 923 in 1994-95 to 812 in 1995-96. In the same period, the number of candidates for diocesan priesthood in theologates dropped from 2,405 to 2,360.

## INTERNATIONAL

**Church Teachings Questioned** — Latin Americans in and outside the Church were reported to be challenging church teachings on a variety of subjects including abortion and sterilization, said Vatican and Latin American attendants at a May 6-to-10 meeting in Guadalajara, Mexico. At the same time, they warned of the moral damage done by the drug trade, the proliferation of religious sects and exploitative economic policies. A two-page statement issued after the meeting said that behind many of contemporary moral problems is a moral relativism that "leaves no space for the supernatural. This is immediately reflected in the problem of dissent, even among Catholics, especially regarding daily ethical problems." Challenges were being raised against a number of teachings, especially: respect for human life in all its stages, legislation that contradicts moral values, waffling of legislators on abortion, mass sterilization as a means of population control, sterilization of disabled persons, euthanasia, transsexualism and the fate of frozen embryos facing possible future "genocide." Bishop Javier Lozano Barragan, president of the Economic Committee of the Latin American Bishops' Council said: "Our work was much more concentrated on the challenge of secularism, moral relativism and the advance of the sects, especially the New Age movement." He admitted that "some concern was focused around the so-called 'Indian theology,' viewed as a new way of theological reflection based on Marxist ideology." Nevertheless, ":We agreed with Cardinal Ratzinger that the main doctrinal challenge is given to us by the secular humanism that causes Catholics in the region to live and act as if God did not exist."

**Send Food, not Weapons** —The heads of four religious orders which still had members in Liberia pleaded with the international community to send food and medicine rather than weapons to the nation. They launched their appeal May 13 "in the name of human dignity and freedom, which are being attacked hour after hour in Liberia, in the name God, the Father of all, and especially in the name of the poor and oppressed." Despite the presence of a multinational African peacekeeping force and an international mediation effort, fierce street fighting erupted in the latest phase of a six-year-old civil war. Foreign missionaries remaining in the country "have decided to share the destiny of their people because they do not feel they can abandon the service they carry out ... being aware that this service is more important than ever for Liberia," said a statement by the superiors published in *L'Osservatore Romano*.

**Preparation for All-Europe Meeting** — Bishops from Eastern Europe were preparing a common position for the ninth symposium of the Council of European Bishops' Conferences to be held Oct. 23 to 27 in Rome. Cardinal Miroslav Vlk, council president, said he believed the bishops should emphasize to their Western counterparts the need for a balance between "external and spiritual preoccupations." He added that the European Union's two most recent secretaries-general had stressed Europe's "need for a soul." The cardinal said: "The Church is not the only institution that can support this dimension of life, although it has a special duty to bring God close. If it wishes to be a spiritual sign, it must exist in the public sphere, assuming co-responsibility for contemporary society. But it must also find a balance between the external social instincts of the Church in the West and the internal spiritual concerns more characteristic of the East."

**Gay Rights** — A spokesman for the Hungarian bishops deplored a parliamentary vote to give homosexual partners equal rights with married couples. "At a time when more and more young people, here as elsewhere, are living together with no legal commitment, this amendment removes any legal distinction between heterosexual and homosexual partners.... It's clear that neither Christian nor humane principles can allow such a form of equality."

**Woman Was Ordained** — Cardinal Miloslav Vlk said it was true that Ludmila Javorova had been ordained for priestly ministry in the underground Church in Czechoslovakia during the time of communist rule. Vatican spokesman Joaquin Navarro-Valls told Catholic News Service May 21, however: "If a ceremony of ordination of a woman took place, it was and remains invalid."

**Church Taxation in Spain** — Spanish bishops defended the Church's historic dependence on government subsidies as the deadline approached for taxpayer contributions. Such contributions were on the decline as the nation's increasingly secular society began to question why state revenues should be allocated to the Church. The prelates estimated that government subsidy provided for about a half of the Church's annual financial needs.

**Priests and Religious Murdered** — Fourteen of the 18 priests or religious assassinated in Algeria since May, 1944, were French. It was also reported that since October, 1993, 115 non-Algerians and 50,000 Algerians had been killed.

**Excommunication for Kidnapping** — Bishop Reynoso Cervantes of Cuernavaca read a decree excommunicating anyone in the state of Morelos who was or had been involved in kidnappings that terrorize the state. "As a bishop, I could not let this moment pass, and so I found myself obliged to impose the maximum penalty of the Church," he said May 26. A government report estimated that at least 800 kidnappings were reported between 1991 and 1996.

**Briefs:**
• French Bishop Jacques Gaillot, removed from his diocese in January, 1995, refused to accept any one of three chaplaincy offers from Archbishop Joseph Duval, president of the bishops' conference.
• The Southern African Catholic Bishops' Conference welcomed South Africa's new constitution, although it found parts of it unacceptable. The bishops objected to the wording of one of the clauses that would probably lead to the legalization of abortion on demand.
• Several bishops in Ontario reacted cautiously to news that students attending public schools in the province might soon be praying in their classrooms. "It's hard to be against that but, with so many religions represented in schools, where to do we go from agreeing that we all need to pray?" said Auxiliary Bishop Paul Marchand of Ottawa. "Can there be a common prayer everyone can agree with?"

## Seven Trappists Murdered

Seven Trappist monks of the Monastery of Notre Dame d'Atlas in Algeria were brutally murdered May 23 by members of the Armed Islamic Group. The monks, seized and held hostage since Mar. 7, were pawns in the terrorists' game plan to win the release of some of their members held in detention in France. The monks, lamented in death, were praised for their witness to prayer and Christian love among many Muslims who held them in reverence while a few used them to death.

# JUNE 1996

## VATICAN

**Three Saints Canonized** — Pope John Paul canonized three saints June 2: Juan Grande Roman, a member of the Hospitaller Order of St. John of God, who died of bubonic plague in 1600 while caring for plague victims in Seville; Jean-Gabriel Perboyre, a French-born Vincentian priest martyred in 1840 in China; Egidio Maria di San Giuseppe, an Italian Franciscan and alms-beggar who died in 1812 in Naples.

**Prevention of Environmental Disaster** — The Pope, at a meeting sponsored by the European Bureau of the Environment, said June 7 the world needs better cooperation to make sure that accelerated development does not produce environmental catastrophe. "Among all creatures, the human being is the only one responsible for the consequences of his actions, not just for himself but for future generations.... No person or group can make demands on the environment without considering the rest of humanity. No one can appropriate the goods of the earth."

**Reuniting Families in Bosnia** — The Pope urged a peacekeeping agency in Bosnia to give priority to reuniting families who fled their homes during four years of civil war. Resolving property claims and other disputes in Bosnia would be impossible without an attitude of forgiveness among the people. He made the remarks before members of the Commission for the Real Property Claims of Displaced Persons and Refugees in Bosnia-Herzegovina. The commission, with Bosnian Muslim, Croat and Serb representatives, was overseeing the restitution of property in the war zone.

**Wanted: Return of Property** — The Pope appealed June 8 to Czech authorities to work out a plan for the restoration of church property seized by the former communist government. He also said that religious instruction and pastoral activities in state institutions were areas of disagreement in need of settlement. Since 1992, church leaders were in dispute with the government over demands for the return of 3,400 church buildings and 350,000 acres of land expropriated during communist rule.

**No "Official" Pilgrimages** — Confirming an earlier statement, the Vatican said "official" pilgrimages should not be made to the popular Marian site of Medjugorje in Bosnia- Herzegovina. The Vatican position, reflecting the opinion of local bishops in the former Yugoslavian Republic, was outlined in a recent letter by Archbishop Tarcisio Bertone, secretary of the Congregation for the Doctrine of the Faith. He cited a 1991 report by Yugoslavian bishops which said that, after much study, it could not be confirmed that supernatural apparitions were occurring at Medjugorje. "From what was said, it follows that official pilgrimages to Medjugorje, understood as a place of authentic Marian apparitions, should not be organized."

**$1.7 Million Surplus** — The Vatican posted a $1.7 million surplus in 1995, the third straight year in which operating expenses were under budget. Cardinal Edmund C. Szoka, head of the Prefecture for the Economic Affairs of the Holy See said June 19 that the surplus was largely the result of cost-containment at the Vatican and greater contributions from around the world. "With our continuing efforts to restrain expenses and the increasing generosity of all, we have good reason to hope that the Holy See can continue to operate without a deficit." Vatican income in 1995 totaled $194.1 million while expenses amounted to $192.4 million.

## Trip to Germany

Pope John Paul, on the 72nd foreign trip of his pontificate June 21 to 23, visited Paderborn and Berlin. At an ecumenical prayer service, he recalled the terrible loss of life in Nazi concentration camps and said: "It is necessary to educate individuals and communities in a new spirit, the spirit of human rights, of national rights, of international justice and solidarity. This program is not far removed from the one that the Church is proposing for herself in view of the now imminent Year 2000." (See additional entries.)

## NATIONAL

**Religion Is Best Hidden** — In modern society, "religion has become an obscene thing, something best kept hidden," former presidential candidate Alan Keyes told a group of several hundred, mostly young, people at a "Signs of the Times" conference in Washington June 2. Yet, "I can't escape what some would like to forget: that the U.S. as a political and cultural entity is based upon the central idea that human justice is derived not from the human, but from God alone." As such, "American life is based upon moral premises and must have a moral content." Earlier in the year, Keyes came to national attention as a possible Republican contender for the presidency, but ended his campaign after a poor showing in three primaries. The conference was designed to help young Catholics answer how they can live a life of faith in a culture that rejects their principles.

**Father Drinan Criticized** — A bishop and a Catholic newspaper criticized Jesuit Father Robert F. Drinan, a former Congressman, for his support of President Clinton's veto of the Partial-Birth Abortion Act. In an op-ed article in the June 4 edition of *The New York Times,* he said "Congress should sustain the veto" because the Act "would allow federal power to intrude into the practice of medicine in an unprecedented way." Bishop Thomas V. Daily of Brooklyn said Father Drinan erred by focusing "on the political, legal and medical aspects of partial-birth abortion" instead of on the moral issue. "Abortion is a grave moral evil, and it is for that reason the issue must be clearly defined. I invite the author to focus his attention to that stark truth." *The Pilot* of Boston, in an unsigned editorial June 6, called Father Drinan's article "a shocking, schizophrenic and even scandalous reflection on the role of law."

**Burned Churches Fund** — An interfaith effort to respond to the burning since January, 1995, of more than 35 mostly black churches in the South resulted in outcries of outrage across the country and also in the creation of a Burned Churches Fund by the National Council of Churches, with participation by the National Conference of Catholic Bishops, the American Jewish Committee and nine foundations. On June 20 Bishop Anthony M. Pilla announced a $50,000 donation to the fund from the bishops' conference. Members of the National Black Catholic Clergy Caucus called the burnings a "demonic conspiracy" that "must not be tolerated." The caucus labeled the burnings "senseless acts of terrorism toward the black community" and urged the national government and local law enforcement agencies to bring to justice all perpetrators of "these crimes against humanity."

## INTERNATIONAL

**Monks Eulogized** — Seven French Trappist monks murdered May 23 in Algeria came to the country to establish bonds of friendship with the Algerian people and "to give their lives for them," said Cardinal Francis Arinze during their funeral service June 2. "What tragic deaths" they suffered, he said. "What profound suffering! What indescribable pain! How difficult it is to make sense of these events, to understand them! ... They gave all men and women an example of total sacrifice in honor of God and of religion." The monks were knifed to death by Muslim terrorists in reprisal for the refusal of French authorities to release from detention terrorists held in France. The monks were: Father Christian-Marie de Cherge, the prior; Brothers Dochier, Michel Fleury, Paul Favre-Miville; Fathers Celestin Ringeard, Bruno Lemarchand and Christophe Lebreton.

Cardinal Leon-Etienne Duval, retired archbishop of Algiers who died May 30, was buried with the monks.

**Religion Classes Continue** — Lithuania's parliament resisted an attempt by ex-communist deputies to remove religious teaching from the school curriculum. The bill, tabled by members of the ruling Lithuanian Democratic Labor Party, would have overturned a law passed shortly before the nation's 1991 secession from the Soviet Union, requiring all students to choose classes in religion or ethics.

**Others Too Should Admit Fault** — Four weeks after Argentina's bishops published an "examination of conscience" for actions during the Dirty War, Bishop Alfonso Delgado Evers of Posada said others should do the same. The spokesman for the bishops' conference said "there are other sectors of society that must express their own repentance too.... Regarding the political and social situation in which our country lived during the '70s, we still wait for the examination of conscience of other sectors, like union leaders, opinion makers and journalists. What were their attitudes, their positions, their actions and their responsibilities at that time?" He deplored what he called "the disproportion between the pressure placed on the bishops' conference for our statement," and the almost total lack of responsibility attributed to others.

**Separate Relations** — Relations between the Holy See and the State of Israel were not part of the peace process and were independent of it, said Archbishop Andrea Corero Lanza di Montezemolo, Vatican nuncio. "Relations between the Vatican and the State of Israel have undergone a unique process of normalization parallel to the peace process with the Palestinians, not because of it." He spoke at a ceremony June 5 where he was awarded the Interfaith Gold Medallion of the International Council of Christian and Jews,

**Defense of Life** — Speakers at an international conference in Mexico City urged governments to defend life, while acknowledging that it is not always easy to do so. The Vatican-sponsored conference, which drew about 150 church officials, politicians and others from the U.S., Canada and Latin America, examined "The Dignity of the Family and of Life in the Politics and Legislation of America." U.S. Rep. Christopher Smith said June 7: "Abortion is the defining issue of our time. It used to be that the womb was the greatest sanctuary a child could have. Now it has become a tomb — the end of the road on earth — for so many children." He criticized elected officials who are afraid to stand up for their beliefs, and had harsh words for President Clinton and his recent veto of legislation that would ban partial-birth abortions. "For over three years President Clinton has pushed to make abortions available at any time, in every place, at any cost," he said.

**Cardinal Returns** — A spokesman for the Jesuits announced that Father Fernando Cardenal, who was expelled from the society in 1984 for his involvement in Nicaragua's Sandinista government, had been readmitted to the order. During his absence, he remained a priest although he could not exercise his ministry because he lacked the necessary authorization of a bishop or religious superior.

**Priests and the Eucharist** — Priests from all over the world gathered at the Marian shrine at Fatima were encouraged to allow Christ in the Eucharist to "form, re-form and transform" them each day. In addressing more than 1,000 participants in an International Reunion for Priests, Cardinal John J. O'Connor said June 18 that such an intimate bond with Christ is the best way to strengthen them in their priesthood and to offset any "identity crisis" stemming from "a cooling of ardor for the Eucharist."

**China and Hong Kong Religion** — China's Religious Affairs Bureau will not set up any office or implement religious regulations or policy in Hong Kong after its return to Chinese sovereignty in 1997. So stated Ye Xiaowen who led an 11-member delegation from Beijing to Hong Kong June 20 to 29 at the invitation of Buddhists, Catholics, Confucianists, Muslims, Protestants and Taoists. He said: "Hong Kong religions are not required to support the socialist system, but must respect the nation and motherland, not undermine Hong Kong's stability and prosperity, and love the country, Hong Kong and religion." Also, he said the relationship between Hong Kong religious bodies and their counterparts in China should be based on the three principles of nonsubordination, noninterference and mutual respect laid down in the Basic Law. He added that mainlanders should not try to make Hong Kong conform to mainland ideas, nor should Hong Kong people attempt this with mainlanders.

# JULY 1996

## VATICAN

**Risk of Specialized Research** — Pope John Paul said the increasing specialization of academic research risks overemphasis on the work of "solitary geniuses" and the undervaluing of the free exchange of ideas. As a result, personal gain and private interests can easily find their way into fields of research, he told a group of Latin American and European scholars July 4. He said the university has traditionally served the entire society and the common good, but there is greater emphasis now on research in highly technical and complex areas. This changing role of the university has far-reaching consequences in an age when technological progress can affect the lives of so many people. The Pope also said that ethical considerations are sometimes ignored by research that is "too restricted by pragmatic interests." Detaching research topics from wider ethical points of view risks turning them against human beings.

**Buddhist-Christian Relations** — At a meeting with the bishops of Myanmar July 5, the Pope said that "in a special way Myanmar's ancient monastic tradition can form a spiritual bridge of fellowship which will stimulate dialogue between Buddhists and Christians." He also commented that "interreligious dialogue is a delicate but indispensable task of your particular churches. Indeed, as in the rest of Asia, in Myanmar the issue of the encounter of Christianity with ancient local cultures and religions is a pressing one. In this you are guided by a profound esteem for the followers of other religious traditions — the prerequisite for all dialogue. An attitude of respect avoids both a false irenicism rooted in religious indifferentism and a militant fundamentalism which fails to recognize the individual and personal nature of the quest to know the truth and live according to it."

**Burundi Brutality** —The Pope condemned the massacre of hundreds of Tutsis in Burundi and the forced repatriation of thousands of Hutus who fled to Burundi after ethnic warfare broke out in Rwanda. He said the July 20 massacre of more than 300 displaced Tutsis, mostly women and children, in the Bugendana refugee camp and the Burundi government's plan to expel 85,000 Rwandan Hutu refugees "cannot but give rise to horror and firm disapproval." He appealed to the Tutsi-led government of Burundi and the international community to take decisive steps to end the ethnic violence which had flared repeatedly since April, 1994, and had led to the deaths of hundreds of thousands of people. "Burundi continues to sink into an abyss of violence which reaps its victims among the most defenseless people — children, women, elderly people — and which smothers the voice of the more moderate individuals and social forces," he said July 24.

## NATIONAL

**Survival and Union** — The survival of the Ukrainian Catholic Church despite persecution showed the importance of union with the Holy See in achieving Christian unity, according to the leading U.S. Ukrainian Catholic prelate. Archbishop Stephen S. Sulyk of Philadelphia made the comment in an interview with *The Way*, the archdiocesan newspaper. He said: In the 20th century, "our church was brutally liquidated, outlawed and persecuted by the most inhumane methods of the communists' KGB agents. All our bishops were arrested, imprisoned and tortured. None of them denied his faith, not one apostatized, and all but one died the death of a martyr." Such adherence to the faith "could not be achieved without God's special grace and constant support. This is in itself to me the best proof that union with the Apostolic See of Rome, with the successor of St. Peter and the vicar of Christ on earth, is still the best and only proven method to achieve the unity of the Church."

**Viable Fetus Included** — The South Carolina Supreme Court ruled that a state statute protecting children from abuse and endangerment "includes viable fetuses." The 3-to-2 ruling was handed down July 15 on an appeal of a petition overturning the sentencing of a woman for child abuse after her newborn son was found to have in his system traces of crack cocaine that his mother used while she was pregnant.

**Plenty of Postcards** —Postcards urging an override of President Clinton's veto of the Partial-Birth Abortion Ban Act flooded Congress during the month, and organizers of the campaign expected the flood to continue throughout the summer. "We're pushing the 10-million mark" on the number of postcard sets ordered for mailing to members of Congress by Catholic parishioners, said Michael Taylor, director of the National Committee for a Human Life Amendment. The grass-roots Catholic pro-life group was sponsoring the campaign with the bishops' Secretariat for Pro-Life Activities. An official of the House of Representatives said more than 2.4 million postcards had been delivered to House members as of late July, with an unknown number still to be processed.

## INTERNATIONAL

**Concordat Postponement** — Cardinal Jozef Glemp of Warsaw said a vote by parliamentarians to postpone discussion of Poland's concordat with the Holy See reflected their "narrowly defined interests." The government chief of staff defended the vote, saying it furthered church-state separation. "We are not an anti-Church group, and we are not fighting against God. But we want to live in a country in which the state's relations with the Church are clear, and both institutions are separated from each other even if they are cooperating for the good of man. I think the prejudices are on the church side," said Lszek, chief of staff. The 29-article concordat, signed in July, 1993, would give international treaty status to important church rights. The Sejm voted July 3 to postpone formal debate on the concordat until after the adoption of a national constitution.

**The Irish Constitution and God** — An Irish government review group recommended that all references to God be removed the republic's constitution. The Constitution Review Group's 700-page report was published early in the month.

# AUGUST 1996

**Taping Denounced** — The head of the National Conference of Catholic Bishops denounced a judge's decision to let two defense attorneys listen to the recording of a sacramental confession secretly taped in an Oregon jail. "The lack of respect for the sanctity of the sacrament of penance shown in this case is a dangerous precedent which must be reversed," said Bishop Anthony J. Pilla. Judge Jack A. Billings of Oregon's Lane County Circuit Court let Terri Wood and Steven Miller, attorneys for murder suspect Conan Hale, hear the tape on grounds that they were entitled to review all recorded statements of their client in possession of the prosecution. The decision brought to at least six the number of people who reportedly listened to the recording. "This is proof that the existence of the tape is indeed a continuing violation of the religious rights of all Catholics," the bishop said in a statement issued in Washington. "Unless it is destroyed," he added, " there can be no guarantee that other uses of this kind and perhaps even more abusive uses will not be made of the tape."

**American Synod** — The future special assembly of the Synod of Bishops for America must help the region's Catholics to strengthen their bonds with the Church, preach salvation in Christ and aid the poor. So stated an outline for reflection in preparation for the synod, addressed in July to bishops' conferences in the Caribbean, and in North, Central and South America. The 60-page document included 16 questions for reflection regarding: practice of the faith, unity among members of the Church, fidelity to church teaching, evangelization efforts, social problems, the protection of human life and other concerns. Responses to the questions will provide a base for drafting the working document of the synod. The theme of the synod will be "Encounter with the Living Jesus Christ: The Way to Conversion, Communion and Solidarity in America."

**Paul VI Remembered** — Even when contemporary culture seemed to dismiss the importance of faith, Pope Paul VI continued to seek ways of preaching the Gospel to new generations, Pope John Paul said at Mass Aug. 6, the anniversary of the death of his predecessor. "Encountering the Lord, the center of his difficult days as a pastor assailed by the worries of his brothers and sisters, made him see the real meaning of things and sustained him in generous self-giving to Christ for the good of the Christian people.... : He never gave up" in his efforts "to encounter contemporary culture in order to offer everyone the Gospel plan of salvation and liberation from confusion and despair," the Pope said.

**Knights of Columbus** —Knights, at their 114th international convention Aug. 6 to 8 in Chicago, heard praise for the life and work of their founder, Father Michael J. McGivney, and an exhortation to fight contemporary "threats to marriage and family life."

**Youth Ministry Study** — The Center for Applied Research in the Apostolate reported Aug. 7 the findings of its study of youth programs entitled "New Directions in Youth Ministry." The study found that participants in youth programs "strongly value helping others" but "do not place a strong emphasis on community service"; do well in many areas of religious values and practice; tend to attach little importance to Bible reading. Nearly three-fourths said they attended Mass once a week of more often. Study findings were gleaned from survey responses during the spring by more than 6,000 youths participating in youth ministry programs in 37 dioceses across the country. Participants came from more than 600 parishes, selected to represent a wide range of ministry programs and all types of parishes. The study was co-sponsored by the National Federation of Catholic Youth Ministry and the Subcommittee on Youth of the Committee on the Laity, National Conference of Catholic Bishops.

**Hispanic Congress** — "Roots and Wings '96: Creating Pathways of Hope," was the theme of the national Hispanic congress convened Aug. 8 to 11 in Chicago under the sponsorship of the National Catholic Council for Hispanic Ministry. Jesuit Father Marcello Azevedo, in a keynote address on the opening night, said the new millennium brings challenges and opportunities to Hispanic Catholics, whose cultural and religious identity is still evolving and who can best serve as a bridge between old and new.

Speaking about youth in particular, he said they need to feel themselves called "to be the subjects, the protagonists" of efforts to evangelize Hispanics. "In our youth and young adults, we place our solid hope of achieving a dual presence in the United States. First, a presence that stands out for its clarity, for its critical awareness and sense of spiritual discernment.... Hispanic youth and young adult leaders will be creative agents of the Church's future, remaining immersed in the dynamic process of cultural change and firmly rooted in their Hispanic heritage." Father Azevedo was the director of the John XXIII Center for Social Research and Action of the Brazilian Development Institute in Rio de Janeiro.

**Catholic Common Ground Project** — This is the name of an initiative for dialogue to overcome divisions among members of the Church. Its beginning was announced Aug. 12 at a press conference in Chicago by Cardinal Joseph L. Bernardin, who called it an effort to counteract the polarization among U. S. Catholics which threatens the unity of the Church. Collaborating in the dialogue project is a 24-member advisory committee which includes, among others: Cardinal Roger Mahony of Los Angeles, Archbishop Rembert G. Weakland of Milwaukee, Robert P. Casey, former governor of Pennsylvania, and Harvard law professor Mary Ann Glendon. "Called To Be Catholic: Church in a Time of Peril," is the title of a statement issued by Cardinal Bernardin at the press conference.

**Cardinal's Cancer Recurs** — Cardinal Joseph L. Bernardin of Chicago announced Aug. 30 at a press conference that the pancreatic cancer for which he underwent surgery in June, 1995, had recurred in his liver. He said: "I have been told that it is terminal and my life expectancy is one year or less."

# POPE JOHN PAUL II

*(See many related entries under John Paul II in the Index.)*

Cardinal Archbishop Karol Wojtyla of Krakow was elected Bishop of Rome Oct. 16, 1978, on the seventh or eighth ballot cast on the second day of voting at a conclave of 111 cardinals. He chose the name John Paul II and was invested with the pallium, the symbol of his papal office, Oct. 22 in ceremonies attended by more than 250,000 persons in St. Peter's Square.

The 263rd successor of St. Peter as Bishop of Rome and Supreme Pastor of the Universal Church, he is the first non-Italian Pope since Adrian VI (1522-23), the first Polish Pope in the history of the Church, and the youngest at the time of his election since Pius IX (1846-78).

## Early Career

Karol Wojtyla was born May 18, 1920, in Wadowice, Poland.

He began higher studies at the age of 18, with major interests in poetry and theater arts. Forced to suspend university courses because of the outbreak of World War II, he went to work in a stone quarry and a chemical plant, thereby earning the later designation of himself as the "Worker Cardinal."

He started studies for the priesthood in 1942 in the underground seminary of Krakow, whose operations had been banned after the Nazi invasion of Poland.

Ordained to the priesthood Nov. 1, 1946, he was immediately sent to Rome for studies at the Angelicum University, where he earned a doctorate in ethics.

Back home in Poland, he worked as an assistant pastor in a village parish and as a chaplain to university students while continuing studies at the Catholic University of Lublin. He was awarded another doctorate there, in moral theology.

He began writing about this time, and eventually produced more than 100 articles and several books on ethical and other themes. Phenomenology was one of his fields of expertise.

University teaching came next, in 1953, with appointment in 1954 to the position of lecturer and later to the chair of ethics at the Catholic University of Lublin, the most prestigious institute of higher learning in Poland.

## Bishop and Cardinal

He was ordained Auxiliary Bishop of Krakow Sept. 28, 1958, became Vicar Capitular in 1962 after the death of Apostolic Administrator Eugeniusz Baziak, and was appointed Archbishop Jan. 13, 1964. He was the first residential bishop of the see since the death of Cardinal Adam Sapieha in 1951. Between then and 1964 the archdiocese was run by administrators because the communist government refused to permit the appointment and ministry of a residential bishop.

Archbishop Wojtyla attended all sessions of the Second Vatican Council from 1962 to 1965, and was one of the writers of the *Pastoral Constitution on the Church in the Modern World*. He also contributed input to the *Declaration on Religious Freedom* and the *Decree on the Instruments of Social Communication*.

His efforts to put into effect the directives of the council induced him to write a book, *Foundations of Renewal,* in 1972 and to start that same year an archdiocesan synod he saw concluded as Pope during his visit to Poland in 1979.

He was inducted into the College of Cardinals June 26, 1967, as one of the younger members, and subsequently served actively in the Congregation for the Sacraments and Divine Worship, the Congregation for the Clergy, and the Congregation for Catholic Education.

He served as a theological consultant to Pope Paul VI, attended assemblies of the Synod of Bishops as a representative of the Polish Bishops' Conference, and was a member of the Synod's permanent council.

From the beginning of his priestly career, and especially during his episcopate, the Cardinal was vigorous in the defense of human and religious rights, the rights of workers, and rights to religious education.

Close to Cardinal Wyszynski and in company with his fellow bishops, he negotiated the tightrope of Catholic survival in a country under communist control. With them, and as their spokesman at times, he was stalwart in resisting efforts of the regime to impose atheism, materialism and secularism on the people and culture of Poland.

## Active in Rome and Italy

Since the beginning of his pontificate, John Paul has been active as Bishop of Rome, with frequent visits to parishes and institutions of the diocese for the celebration of Mass and participation in other events. During these visits as well as others to places of pilgrimage and historic significance in Italy, he has had more personal contact with the faithful than any other pope. The number of attendants at weekly general audiences at the Vatican and Castel Gandolfo has been unprecedented.

## 72 Foreign Pastoral Trips

At the time of writing (Aug. 14,1996) the Pope had traveled more than 540,000 miles in 72 pastoral trips and visits to more than 115 countries since the start of his pontificate. Homilies and addresses delivered by the Pope on these trips covered a wide variety of doctrinal, pastoral and social subjects.

• 1979, four trips: Dominican Republic and Mexico, Jan 5 to Feb. 1; Poland, June 2 to 10; Ireland and the United States, Sept. 29 to Oct. 7; Turkey, Nov. 28 to 30.

• 1980, four trips: Africa (Zaire, Congo Republic, Kenya, Ghana, Upper Volta, Ivory Coast), May 2 to 12; France, May 30 to June 2; Brazil (13 cities), June 30 to July 12; West Germany, Nov. 15 to 19.

• 1981, one trip: Philippines, Guam and Japan, with stopovers in Pakistan and Alaska, Feb. 16 to 27.

• 1982, seven trips: Africa (Nigeria, Benin, Gabon, Equatorial Guinea), Feb. 12 to 19; Portugal, May 12 to 15; Great Britain, May 28 to June 2; Argentina, June 11 and 12; Switzerland, June 15; San Marino, Aug. 29; Spain, Oct. 31 to Nov. 9.

• 1983, four trips: Central America (Costa Rica, Nicaragua, Panama, El Salvador, Guatemala, Belize, Honduras) and Haiti, Mar. 2 to 10; Poland, June 16 to 23; Lourdes, France, Aug. 14 and 15; Austria, Sept. 10 to 13.

• 1984, four trips: South Korea, Papua New Guinea, Solomon Islands, Thailand, May 2 to 12; Switzerland, June 12 to 17; Canada, Sept. 9 to 20; Spain, Dominican Republic and Puerto Rico, Oct. 10 to 12.
• 1985, four trips: Venezuela, Ecuador, Peru, Trinidad and Tobago, Jan. 26 to Feb. 6; Belgium, The Netherlands and Luxembourg, May 11 to 21; Africa (Togo, Ivory Coast, Cameroon, Central African Republic, Zaire, Kenya and Morocco), Aug. 8 to 19; Liechtenstein, Sept. 8.
• 1986, four trips: India, Feb. 1 to 10; Colombia and Saint Lucia, July 1 to 7; France, Oct. 4 to 7; Oceania (Australia, New Zealand, Bangladesh, Fiji, Singapore and Seychelles), Nov. 18 to Dec. 1.
• 1987, four trips: Uruguay, Chile and Argentina, Mar. 31 to Apr. 12; West Germany, Apr. 30 to May 4; Poland, June 8 to 14; the United States and Canada, Sept. 10 to 19.
• 1988, four trips: Uruguay, Bolivia, Peru and Paraguay, May 7 to 18; Austria, June 23 to 27; Africa (Zimbabwe, Botswana, Lesotho, Swaziland and Mozambique), Sept. 10 to 19; France, Oct. 8 to 11.
• 1989, four trips: Madagascar, Reunion, Zambia and Malawi, Apr. 28 to May 6; Norway, Iceland, Finland, Denmark and Sweden, June 1 to 10; Spain, Aug. 19 to 21; South Korea, Indonesia, East Timor and Mauritius, Oct. 6 to 16.
• 1990, five trips: Africa (Cape Verde, Guinea Bissau, Mali and Burkina Faso), Jan. 25 to Feb. 1; Czechoslovakia, Apr. 21 and 22; Mexico and Curacao, May 6 to 13; Malta, May 25 to 27; Africa (Tanzania, Burundi, Rwanda and Ivory Coast), Sept. 1 to 10.
• 1991, four trips: Portugal, May 10 to 13; Poland, June 1 to 9; Poland and Hungary, Aug. 13 to 20; Brazil, Oct. 12 to 21.
• 1992, three trips: Africa (Senegal, The Gambia, Guinea), Feb. 10 to 26; Africa (Angola, Sao Tome and Principe), June 4 to 10; Dominican Republic, Oct. 10 to 14.
• 1993, five trips: Africa (Benin, Uganda, Sudan), Feb. 2 to 10; Albania, April 25; Spain, June 12 to 17; Jamaica, Mexico, Denver (U.S.), Aug. 9 to 15; Lithuania, Latvia, Estonia, Sept. 4 to 10.
• 1994, one trip: Zagreb, Croatia, Sept. 10 • 1995, six trips: Philippines, Papua New Guinea, Australia, Sri Lanka, Jan. 12 to 21; Czech Republic and Poland, May 20 to 22; Belgium, June 3 and 4; Slovakia, June 30 to July 3; Africa (Cameroon, South Africa, Kenya), Sept. 14 to 20; United Nations and United States, Oct. 4 to 8.
• 1996, four trips (as of Aug. 15): Central America (Guatemala, Nicaragua, El Salvador), Feb. 5 TO 11; Tunisia, Apr. 17; Slovenia, May 17 to 19; Germany, June 21 to 23.

## Encyclical Letters

Encyclicals: Homilies and addresses delivered by the Pope have generally been related in greater or less degree to the key document issued in the first year of his pontificate. That was the encyclical letter, *Redemptor Hominis* ("Redeemer of Man"), a treatise on Christian anthropology dealing with the divine and human aspects of redemption and the mission of the Church to carry on a dialogue of salvation with all peoples. His other encyclical letters

are: *Dives in Misericordia* ("On the Mercy of God") in 1980 and *Laborem Exercens* ("On Human Work") in 1981; *Slavorum Apostoli* in 1985 honoring Sts. Cyril and Methodius, apostles of the Slavic peoples; *Dominum et Vivificantem* ("Lord and Giver of Life") in 1986; *Redemptoris Mater* ("Mother of the Redeemer") in 1987; *Sollicitudo Rei Socialis* ("On Social Concerns") in 1988; *Redemptoris Missio* ("Mission of the Redeemer") and *Centesimus Annus* ("The Hundredth Year") in 1991; *Veritatis Splendor* ("The Splendor of Truth") in 1993; *Evangelium Vitae* ("The Gospel of Life") and *Ut Unum Sint* ("That All May Be One") in 1995.

The Pope's most recent apostolic letters are *Tertio Millennio Adveniente*, Nov. 14, 1994, regarding the jubilee celebration of the third millennium of Christianity; and *Orientale Lumen*, May 2, 1995, on the need for greater understanding and appreciation of the traditions of the Eastern Churches.

The Pope also addressed a letter to women throughout the world July 10, 1995, in anticipation of the Fourth International Conference on Women scheduled to be held in September in Beijing, China.

## Other Writings

The Pope published a lengthy exhortation on the family, *Familiaris Consortio* in 1981.

Writings published in 1984 included two apostolic letters — on suffering, *Salvifici Doloris*, and on Jerusalem; an apostolic exhortation, *Redemptionis Donum*, addressed to and about religious; a "Charter on the Rights of the Family," and an apostolic exhortation, "Reconciliation and Penance in the Ministry of the Church."

In 1986, the Pope issued an apostolic letter on the 1600th anniversary of the conversion of St. Augustine. Two apostolic letters were published in 1988, on the millennium of Christianity in the Ukraine and the present territory of the Soviet Union.

Writings issued in 1989 included *Christifideles Laici*, an apostolic exhortation on the theme of the 1987 assembly of the Synod of Bishops, and an apostolic letter commemorating the 25th anniversary of the Second Vatican Council's *Constitution on the Liturgy*.

In 1990, the Pope issued the first-ever papal statement exclusively on ecology, entitled "Peace with God and All of Creation." *Pastores Dabo Vobis* ("I Will Give You Pastors"), an apostolic exhortation on the formation of priests, was issued in 1992.

*Ordinatio Sacerdotalis*, on the ordination of men only to the priesthood, was issued May 30, 1994.

The most recent apostolic letters of Pope John Paul are *Tertio Millennio Adveniente*, on the coming of the third millennium of Christianity, Nov. 14, 1994; and *Orientale Lumen*, on the need for greater understanding and appreciation of the traditions of Eastern Churches, May 2, 1995.

Also in 1995, the Pope addressed a letter to women throughout the world on July 10 in anticipation of the Fourth International Conference on Women to be held in September, 1995, in Beijing, China.

In 1996 the Pope issued an apostolic exhortation entitled *Vita Consecrata* ("The Consecrated Life") and the apostolic constitution *Universi Dominici Gregis* ("Of the Lord's Whole

Flock") on the election of a pope and the government of the Church during a vacancy of the Apostolic See.

## Various Subjects

**Doctrinal Concerns:** The Holy Father regarded as extremely important a series of talks begun at general audiences in the summer of 1984 on marriage and sexual morality, explaining and firmly supporting traditional doctrine, with emphasis on teaching contained in the encyclical letter, *Humanae Vitae*, by Pope Paul VI.

Clarification of issues involved in liberation theology were published in 1984 and 1986.

Doctrine concerning the nature of the Church and the roles of its members in mission were running subjects of general audience talks in 1993-94. The mystery of the Church and the role of Mary were the principal themes of general audience talks in 1995.

**Canon Law:** The Pope was deeply involved in the work of completing the revision of the Code of Canon Law, which he ordered into effect as of Nov. 27, 1983. He called it, in effect, the final act of the Second Vatican Council. He emphasized its innovative force in an address Jan. 26, 1984, to personnel of the Roman Rota.

He promulgated the Code of Canon Law for the Eastern Churches Apr. 18, 1990.

**Catechism of the Catholic Church:** On publication of the new *Catechism of the Catholic Church*, first in French in 1992, the Pope called it, along with the new Code of Canon Law, one of the most significant events in the line of accomplishments since the Second Vatican Council.

**Causes of Saints:** Pope John Paul has canonized more than 270 saints. (See Canonizations.)

**Synods:** The Holy Father has convoked six general assemblies of the Synod of Bishops and two significant particular assemblies.

With the bishops of The Netherlands at the Vatican in January, 1980, he called for measures to cope with differences among the prelates and polarization among the people, along with action to remedy doctrinal and disciplinary irregularities; later reports indicated that results of the synod were less than satisfactory. Meeting in special assembly with Ukrainian bishops in March, also in 1980, he named a successor to Cardinal Josyf Slipyi as the ranking bishop and turned down demands of some Ukrainians for a patriarchate.

**Holy Year:** The Holy Father proclaimed a Jubilee celebration of the 1950th anniversary of the Redemption from the Solemnity of the Annunciation of the Lord, Mar. 25, 1983, to Easter Sunday, Apr. 22, 1984, and a Marian Year from Pentecost, 1987, to the Solemnity of the Ascension, 1988.

**Cardinals:** In June, 1979, the Pope inducted 14 new cardinals into the Sacred College, raising its membership to 135. A second group was inducted Feb. 3, 1983, at which time the total membership was 138. Twenty-eight new cardinals inducted May 25, 1985, brought membership to 152. Twenty-four were inducted in 1988. By late September, 1990, the total was 144. Twenty-two new cardinals were inducted in 1991, along with a cardinal whose name had been held in secret since 1979. Thirty new cardinals were inducted into the college in 1995. As of Aug. 10, 1996, there were 154 cardinals; 112 of them were eligible to vote in a papal election; 42 others were over the electoral age limit of 80.

**Ecumenism:** Ecumenical and interfaith relations have been high on the list of the Pope's priorities since the beginning of his pontificate. He has had numerous meetings with representatives of other churches and ecclesial bodies; has repeatedly spoken about the quest for unity among Christians and called on Catholics and members of other churches to pray and work together for unity. Two significant events of 1995 were the publication of the encyclical letter, "That All May Be One," May 30 and the meeting of the Pope and Orthodox Patriarch Bartholomew I late in June.

While visiting the headquarters of the World Council of Churches in Geneva June 12, 1984, the Pope said the Church's engagement in the quest for religious unity is irreversible. At the same time, he mentioned two points of extreme significance in Catholic doctrine and practice.

The Church, he said, "entered on the hard ecumenical task, bringing with it a conviction" about the role of the bishop of Rome. "It is convinced that in the ministry of the bishop of Rome it has preserved the visible pole and guarantee of unity in full fidelity to the apostolic tradition and to the faith of the Fathers."

He also reiterated doctrinal opposition to sharing the Eucharist until full unity is achieved. "It is not yet possible for us to celebrate the Eucharist together and communicate at the same table," he said. Nevertheless, he placed emphasis on things Christians have in common.

**World Affairs:** In 1984, the Pope agreed to a new concordat with Italy, regulating church-state relations. He agreed also to the establishment of diplomatic relations with the United States. In July, 1989, following years of negotiations, diplomatic relations were re-established with Poland. Relations have also been established with other Eastern European countries, Mexico and a number of other nations.

One of the more significant diplomatic accomplishments was the 1993 agreement for the establishment of Vatican-Israeli relations at the ambassadorial level; the agreement was implemented in 1994.

For years, the Pope has repeatedly called for peace in the Middle East, the Balkans, beleaguered nations of Africa and other countries, and stressed the need for re-evangelization worldwide, but especially in Europe. Since 1993 he has pleaded constantly for the end of hostilities and mass murder in Bosnia-Herzegovina, Rwanda and other countries.

In 1994 Pope John Paul mounted a strong and sustained campaign against proposals on population control, abortion, contraception, adolescent sexuality and related subjects on the agenda of the third U.N.-sponsored International Conference on Population and Development be held Sept. 5 to 13, 1994, in Cairo. On his travels as well as at the Vatican the Pope has been an outstanding advocate for human rights and dignity, respect for life, peace, nuclear and conventional disarmament, reconciliation among nations, aid and relief for distressed peoples and nations; of people first and things second in all areas of life.

# DATES AND EVENTS IN CHURCH HISTORY_____

## FIRST CENTURY

**c. 33:** First Christian Pentecost; descent of the Holy Spirit upon the disciples; preaching of St. Peter in Jerusalem; conversion, baptism and aggregation of some 3,000 persons to the first Christian community.

St. Stephen, deacon, was stoned to death at Jerusalem; he is venerated as the first Christian martyr.

**c. 34:** St. Paul, formerly Saul the persecutor of Christians, was converted and baptized. After three years of solitude in the desert, he joined the college of the apostles; he made three major missionary journeys and became known as the Apostle to the Gentiles; he was imprisoned twice in Rome and was beheaded there between 64 and 67.

**39:** Cornelius (the Gentile) and his family were baptized by St. Peter; a significant event signalling the mission of the Church to all peoples.

**42:** Persecution of Christians in Palestine broke out during the rule of Herod Agrippa; St. James the Greater, the first apostle to die, was beheaded in 44; St. Peter was imprisoned for a short time; many Christians fled to Antioch, marking the beginning of the dispersion of Christians beyond the confines of Palestine. At Antioch, the followers of Christ were called Christians for the first time.

**49:** Christians at Rome, considered members of a Jewish sect, were adversely affected by a decree of Claudius which forbade Jewish worship there.

**51:** The Council of Jerusalem, in which all the apostles participated under the presidency of St. Peter, decreed that circumcision, dietary regulations, and various other prescriptions of Mosaic Law were not obligatory for Gentile converts to the Christian community. The crucial decree was issued in opposition to Judaizers who contended that observance of the Mosaic Law in its entirety was necessary for salvation.

**64:** Persecution broke out at Rome under Nero, the emperor said to have accused Christians of starting the fire which destroyed half of Rome.

**64 or 67:** Martyrdom of St. Peter at Rome during the Neronian persecution. He established his see and spent his last years there after preaching in and around Jerusalem, establishing a see at Antioch, and presiding at the Council of Jerusalem.

**70:** Destruction of Jerusalem by Titus.

**88-97:** Pontificate of St. Clement I, third successor of St. Peter as bishop of Rome, one of the Apostolic Fathers. The *First Epistle of Clement to the Corinthians,* with which he has been identified, was addressed by the Church of Rome to the Church at Corinth, the scene of irregularities and divisions in the Christian community.

**95:** Domitian persecuted Christians, principally at Rome.

**c. 100:** Death of St. John, apostle and evangelist, marking the end of the Age of the Apostles and the first generation of the Church.

By the end of the century, Antioch, Alexandria and Ephesus in the East and Rome in the West were established centers of Christian population and influence.

## SECOND CENTURY

**c. 107:** St. Ignatius of Antioch was martyred at Rome. He was the first writer to use the expression, "the Catholic Church."

**112:** Emperor Trajan, in a rescript to Pliny the Younger, governor of Bithynia, instructed him not to search out Christians but to punish them if they were publicly denounced and refused to do homage to the Roman gods. This rescript set a pattern for Roman magistrates in dealing with Christians.

**117-38:** Persecution under Hadrian. Many *Acts of Martyrs* date from this period.

**c. 125:** Spread of Gnosticism, a combination of elements of Platonic philosophy and Eastern mystery religions. Its adherents claimed that its secret-knowledge principle provided a deeper insight into Christian doctrine than divine revelation and faith. One gnostic thesis denied the divinity of Christ; others denied the reality of his humanity, calling it mere appearance (Docetism, Phantasiasm).

**c. 144:** Excommunication of Marcion, bishop and heretic, who claimed that there was total opposition and no connection at all between the Old Testament and the New Testament, between the God of the Jews and the God of the Christians; and that the Canon (list of inspired writings) of the Bible consisted only of parts of St. Luke's Gospel and 10 letters of St. Paul. Marcionism was checked at Rome by 200 and was condemned by a council held there about 260, but the heresy persisted for several centuries in the East and had some adherents as late as the Middle Ages.

**c. 155:** St. Polycarp, bishop of Smyrna and disciple of St. John the Evangelist, was martyred.

**c. 156:** Beginning of Montanism, a form of religious extremism. Its principal tenets were the imminent second coming of Christ, denial of the divine nature of the Church and its power to forgive sin, and excessively rigorous morality. The heresy, preached by Montanus of Phrygia and others, was condemned by Pope St. Zephyrinus (199-217).

**161-80:** Reign of Marcus Aurelius. His persecution, launched in the wake of natural disasters, was more violent than those of his predecessors.

**165:** St. Justin, an important early Christian writer, was martyred at Rome.

**c. 180:** St. Irenaeus, bishop of Lyons and one of the great early theologians, wrote *Adversus Haereses.* He stated that the teaching and tradition of the Roman See was the standard for belief.

**196:** Easter Controversy, concerning the day of celebration — a Sunday, according to practice in the West, or the 14th of the month of Nisan (in the Hebrew calendar), no matter what day of the week, according to practice in the East. The controversy was not resolved at this time.

The *Didache,* whose extant form dates from the second century, is an important record of Christian belief, practice and governance in the first century.

Latin was introduced as a liturgical language in the West. Other liturgical languages were Aramaic and Greek.

The Catechetical School of Alexandria, founded about the middle of the century, gained increasing influence on doctrinal study and instruction, and interpretation of the Bible.

## THIRD CENTURY

**202:** Persecution under Septimius Severus, who wanted to establish a simple common religion in the Empire.

**206:** Tertullian, a convert since 197 and the first great ecclesiastical writer in Latin, joined the heretical Montanists; he died in 230.

**215:** Death of Clement of Alexandria, teacher of Origen and a founding father of the School of Alexandria.

**217-35:** St. Hippolytus, the first antipope; he was reconciled to the Church while in prison during persecution in 235.

**232-54:** Origen established the School of Caesarea after being deposed in 231 as head of the School of Alexandria; he died in 254. A scholar and voluminous writer, he was one of the founders of systematic theology and exerted wide influence for many years.

**c. 242:** Manichaeism originated in Persia: a combination of errors based on the assumption that two supreme principles (good and evil) are operative in creation and life, and that the supreme objective of human endeavor is liberation from evil (matter). The heresy denied the humanity of Christ, the sacramental system, the authority of the Church (and state), and endorsed a moral code which threatened the fabric of society. In the 12th and 13th centuries, it took on the features of Albigensianism and Catharism.

**249-51:** Persecution under Decius. Many of those who denied the faith *(lapsi)* sought readmission to the Church at the end of the persecution in 251. Pope St. Cornelius agreed with St. Cyprian that *lapsi* were to be readmitted to the Church after satisfying the requirements of appropriate penance. Antipope Novatian, on the other hand, contended that persons who fell away from the Church under persecution and/or those guilty of serious sin after baptism could not be absolved and readmitted to communion with the Church. The heresy was condemned by a Roman synod in 251.

**250-300:** Neo-Platonism of Plotinus and Porphyry gained followers.

**251:** Novatian, an antipope, was condemned at Rome.

**256:** Pope St. Stephen I upheld the validity of baptism properly administered by heretics, in the Rebaptism Controversy.

**257:** Persecution under Valerian, who attempted to destroy the Church as a social structure.

**258:** St. Cyprian, bishop of Carthage, was martyred.

**c. 260:** St. Lucian founded the School of Antioch, a center of influence on biblical studies.

Pope St. Dionysius condemned Sabellianism, a form of modalism (like Monarchianism and Patripassianism). The heresy contended that the Father, Son and Holy Spirit are not distinct divine persons but are only three different modes of being and self-manifestations of the one God.

St. Paul of Thebes became a hermit.

**261:** Gallienus issued an edict of toleration which ended general persecution for nearly 40 years.

**c. 292:** Diocletian divided the Roman Empire into East and West. The division emphasized political, cultural and other differences between the two parts of the Empire and influenced different developments in the Church in the East and West. The prestige of Rome began to decline.

## FOURTH CENTURY

**303:** Persecution broke out under Diocletian; it was particularly violent in 304.

**305:** St. Anthony of Heracles established a foundation for hermits near the Red Sea in Egypt.

**c. 306:** The first local legislation on clerical celibacy was enacted by a council held at Elvira, Spain; bishops, priests, deacons and other ministers were forbidden to have wives.

**311:** An edict of toleration issued by Galerius at the urging of Constantine and Licinius officially ended persecution in the West; some persecution continued in the East.

**313:** The *Edict of Milan* issued by Constantine and Licinius recognized Christianity as a lawful religion in the Roman Empire.

**314:** A council of Arles condemned Donatism, declaring that baptism properly administered by heretics is valid, in view of the principle that sacraments have their efficacy from Christ, not from the spiritual condition of their human ministers. The heresy was condemned again by a council of Carthage in 411.

**318:** St. Pachomius established the first foundation of the cenobitic (common) life, as compared with the solitary life of hermits in Upper Egypt.

**325:** Ecumenical Council of Nicaea (I). Its principal action was the condemnation of Arianism, the most devastating of the early heresies, which denied the divinity of Christ. The heresy was authored by Arius of Alexandria, a priest. Arians and several kinds of Semi-Arians propagandized their tenets widely, established their own hierarchies and churches, and raised havoc in the Church for several centuries. The council contributed to formulation of the Nicene Creed (Creed of Nicaea-Constantinople); fixed the date for the observance of Easter; passed regulations concerning clerical discipline; adopted the civil divisions of the Empire as the model for the jurisdictional organization of the Church.

**326:** Discovery of the True Cross on which Christ was crucified.

**337:** Baptism and death of Constantine.

**c. 342:** Beginning of a 40-year persecution in Persia.

**343-44:** A council of Sardica reaffirmed doctrine formulated by Nicaea I and declared also that bishops had the right of appeal to the pope as the highest authority in the Church.

**361-63:** Emperor Julian the Apostate waged an unsuccessful campaign against the Church in an attempt to restore paganism as the religion of the Empire.

**c. 365:** Persecution under Valens in the East.

**c. 376:** Beginning of the barbarian invasion in the West.

**379:** Death of St. Basil, the Father of Monasticism in the East. His writings contributed greatly to the development of rules for the life of Religious.

**381:** Ecumenical Council of Constantinople (I). It condemned various brands of Arianism as well as Macedonianism, which denied the divinity of the Holy Spirit; contributed to formulation of the Nicene Creed; approved a canon acknowledging Constantinople as the second see after Rome in honor and dignity.

**382:** The Canon of Sacred Scripture, the official list of the inspired books of the Bible, was contained in the *Decree of Pope St. Damasus* and published by a regional council of Carthage in 397; the Canon was formally defined by the Council of Trent in the 16th century.

**382-c. 406:** St. Jerome translated the Old and New Testaments into Latin; his work is called the Vulgate version of the Bible.

**396:** St. Augustine became bishop of Hippo in North Africa.

## FIFTH CENTURY

**410:** Visigoths sacked Rome.

**430:** St. Augustine, bishop of Hippo for 35 years, died. He was a strong defender of orthodox doctrine against Manichaeism, Donatism and Pelagianism. The depth and range of his writings made him a dominant influence in Christian thought for centuries.

**431:** Ecumenical Council of Ephesus. It condemned Nestorianism, which denied the unity of the divine and human natures in the Person of Christ; defined *Theotokos* (Bearer of God) as the title of Mary, Mother of the Son of God made Man; condemned Pelagianism. The heresy of Pelagianism, proceeding from the assumption that Adam had a natural right to supernatural life, held that man could attain salvation through the efforts of his natural powers and free will; it involved errors concerning the nature of original sin, the meaning of grace and other matters. Related Semi-Pelagianism was condemned by a council of Orange in 529.

**432:** St. Patrick arrived in Ireland. By the time of his death in 461 most of the country had been converted, monasteries founded and the hierarchy established.

**438:** The *Theodosian Code*, a compilation of decrees for the Empire, was issued by Theodosius II; it had great influence on subsequent civil and ecclesiastical law.

**451:** Ecumenical Council of Chalcedon. Its principal action was the condemnation of Monophysitism (also called Eutychianism), which denied the humanity of Christ by holding that he had only one, the divine, nature.

**452:** Pope St. Leo the Great persuaded Attila the Hun to spare Rome.

**455:** Vandals sacked Rome. The decline of imperial Rome dates approximately from this time.

**484:** Patriarch Acacius of Constantinople was excommunicated for signing the *Henoticon,* a document which capitulated to the Monophysite heresy. The excommunication triggered a schism which lasted for 35 years.

**494:** Pope St. Gelasius I declared in a letter to Emperor Anastasius that the pope had power and authority over the emperor in spiritual matters.

**496:** Clovis, King of the Franks, was converted and became the defender of Christianity in the West. The Franks became a Catholic people.

## SIXTH CENTURY

**520 on:** Irish monasteries flourished as centers for spiritual life, missionary training and scholarly activity.

**529:** The Second Council of Orange condemned Semi-Pelagianism.

**c. 529:** St. Benedict founded the Monte Cassino Abbey. Some years before his death in 543 he wrote a monastic rule which exercised tremendous influence on the form and style of religious life. He is called the Father of Monasticism in the West.

**533:** John II became the first pope to change his name. The practice did not become general until the time of Sergius IV (1009).

**533-34:** Emperor Justinian promulgated the *Corpus Juris Civilis* for the Roman world; like the *Theodosian Code,* it influenced subsequent civil and ecclesiastical law.

**c. 545:** Death of Dionysius Exiguus who was the first to date history from the birth of Christ, a practice which resulted in use of the B.C. and A.D. abbreviations. His calculations were at least four years late.

**553:** Ecumenical Council of Constantinople (II). It condemned the *Three Chapters,* Nestorian-tainted writings of Theodore of Mopsuestia, Theodoret of Cyrus and Ibas of Edessa.

**585:** St. Columban founded an influential monastic school at Luxeuil.

**589:** The most important of several councils of Toledo was held. The Visigoths renounced Arianism, and St. Leander began the organization of the Church in Spain.

**590-604:** Pontificate of Pope St. Gregory I the Great. He set the form and style of the papacy which prevailed throughout the Middle Ages; exerted great influence on doctrine and liturgy; was strong in support of monastic discipline and clerical celibacy; authored writings on many subjects. Gregorian Chant is named in his honor.

**596:** Pope St. Gregory I sent St. Augustine of Canterbury and 40 monks to do missionary work in England.

**597:** St. Columba died. He founded an important monastery at Iona, established schools and did notable missionary work in Scotland. By the end of the century, monasteries of nuns were common; Western monasticism was flourishing; monasticism in the East, under the influence of Monophysitism and other factors, was losing its vigor.

## SEVENTH CENTURY

**613:** St. Columban established the influential monastery of Bobbio in northern Italy; he died there in 615.

**622:** The Hegira (flight) of Mohammed from Mecca to Medina signalled the beginning of Islam which, by the end of the century, claimed almost all of the southern Mediterranean area.

**628:** Heraclius, Eastern Emperor, recovered the True Cross from the Persians.

**649:** A Lateran council condemned two erroneous formulas (*Ecthesis* and *Type*) issued by emperors Heraclius and Constans II as means of reconciling Monophysites with the Church.

**664:** Actions of the Synod of Whitby advanced the adoption of Roman usages in England, especially regarding the date for the observance of Easter. (See Easter Controversy.)

**680-81:** Ecumenical Council of Constantinople (III). It condemned Monothelitism, which held that Christ had only one will, the divine; censured Pope Honorius I for a letter to Sergius, bishop of Constantinople, in which he made an ambiguous but not infallible statement about the unity of will and/or operation in Christ.

**692:** Trullan Synod. Eastern-Church discipline on clerical celibacy was settled, permitting marriage before ordination to the diaconate and continuation in marriage afterwards, but prohibiting marriage following the death of the wife thereafter. Anti-Roman canons contributed to East-West alienation.

During the century, the monastic influence of Ireland and England increased in Western Europe; schools and learning declined; regulations regarding clerical celibacy became more strict in the East.

## EIGHTH CENTURY

**711:** Moslems began the conquest of Spain.

**726:** Emperor Leo III, the Isaurian, launched a campaign against the veneration of sacred images and relics; called Iconoclasm (image-breaking), it caused turmoil in the East until about 843.

**731:** Pope Gregory III and a synod at Rome condemned Iconoclasm, with a declaration that the veneration of sacred images was in accord with Catholic tradition.

Venerable Bede issued his *Ecclesiastical History of the English People.*

**732:** Charles Martel defeated the Moslems at Poitiers, halting their advance in the West.

**744:** The Monastery of Fulda was established by St. Sturmi, a disciple of St. Boniface; it was influential in the evangelization of Germany.

**754:** A council of more than 300 Byzantine bishops endorsed Iconoclast errors. This council and its actions were condemned by the Lateran synod of 769.

Stephen II (III) crowned Pepin ruler of the Franks. Pepin twice invaded Italy, in 754 and 756, to defend the pope against the Lombards. His land grants to the papacy, called the Donation of Pepin, were later extended by Charlemagne (773) and formed part of the States of the Church.

**c. 755:** St. Boniface (Winfrid) was martyred. He was called the Apostle of Germany for his missionary work and organization of the hierarchy there.

**781:** Alcuin was chosen by Charlemagne to organize a palace school, which became a center of intellectual leadership.

**787:** Ecumenical Council of Nicaea (II). It condemned Iconoclasm, which held that the use of images was idolatry, and Adoptionism, which claimed that Christ was not the Son of God by nature but only by adoption. This was the last council regarded as ecumenical by Orthodox Churches.

**792:** A council at Ratisbon condemned Adoptionism. The famous *Book of Kells* ("The Great Gospel of Columcille") dates from the early eighth or late seventh century.

## NINTH CENTURY

**800:** Charlemagne was crowned Emperor by Pope Leo III on Christmas Day.

Egbert became king of West Saxons; he unified England and strengthened the See of Canterbury.

**813:** Emperor Leo V, the Armenian, revived Iconoclasm, which persisted until about 843.

**814:** Charlemagne died.

**843:** The Treaty of Verdun split the Frankish kingdom among Charlemagne's three grandsons.

**844:** A Eucharistic controversy involving the writings of St. Paschasius Radbertus, Ratramnus and Rabanus Maurus occasioned the development of terminology regarding the doctrine of the Real Presence.

**846:** Moslems invaded Italy and attacked Rome.

**847-52:** Period of composition of the *False Decretals,* a collection of forged documents attributed to popes from St. Clement (88-97) to Gregory II (714-731). The *Decretals,* which strongly supported the autonomy and rights of bishops, were suspect for a long time before being repudiated entirely about 1628.

**848:** The Council of Mainz condemned Gottschalk for heretical teaching regarding predestination. He was also condemned by the Council of Quierzy in 853.

**857:** Photius displaced Ignatius as patriarch of Constantinople. This marked the beginning of the Photian Schism, a confused state of East-West relations which has not yet been cleared up by historical research. Photius, a man of exceptional ability, died in 891.

**865:** St. Ansgar, apostle of Scandinavia, died.

**869:** St. Cyril died and his brother, St. Methodius (d. 885), was ordained a bishop. The Apostles of the Slavs devised an alphabet and translated the Gospels and liturgy into the Slavonic language.

**869-70:** Ecumenical Council of Constantinople (IV). It issued a second condemnation of Iconoclasm, condemned and deposed Photius as patriarch of Constantinople and restored Ignatius to the patriarchate. This was the last ecumenical council held in the East. It was first called ecumenical by canonists toward the end of the 11th century.

**871-c. 900:** Reign of Alfred the Great, the only English king ever anointed by a pope at Rome.

## TENTH CENTURY

**910:** William, duke of Aquitaine, founded the Benedictine Abbey of Cluny, which became a center of monastic and ecclesiastical reform, especially in France.

**915:** Pope John X played a leading role in the expulsion of Saracens from central and southern Italy.

**955:** St. Olga, of the Russian royal family, was baptized.

**962:** Otto I, the Great, crowned by Pope John XII, revived Charlemagne's kingdom, which became the Holy Roman Empire.

**966:** Mieszko, first of a royal line in Poland, was baptized; he brought Latin Christianity to Poland.

**988:** Conversion and baptism of St. Vladimir and the people of Kiev which subsequently became part of Russia.

**993:** John XV was the first pope to decree the official canonization of a saint — Bishop Ulrich (Uldaric) of Augsburg — for the universal Church.

**997:** St. Stephen became ruler of Hungary. He assisted in organizing the hierarchy and establishing Latin Christianity in that country.

**999-1003:** Pontificate of Sylvester II (Gerbert of Aquitaine), a Benedictine monk and the first French pope.

## ELEVENTH CENTURY

**1009:** Beginning of lasting East-West Schism in the Church, marked by dropping of the name of Pope Sergius IV from the Byzantine diptychs (the listing of persons prayed for during the liturgy). The deletion was made by Patriarch Sergius II of Constantinople.

**1012:** St. Romuald founded the Camaldolese Hermits.

**1025:** The Council of Arras, and other councils later, condemned the Cathari (Neo-Manichaeans, Albigenses).

**1027:** The Council of Elne proclaimed the Truce of God as a means of stemming violence; it involved armistice periods of varying length, which were later extended.

**1038:** St. John Gualbert founded the Vallombrosians.

**1043-59:** Constantinople patriarchate of Michael Cerularius, the key figure in a controversy concerning the primacy of the papacy. His and the Byzantine synod's refusal to acknowledge this primacy in 1054 widened and hardened the East-West Schism in the Church.

**1047:** Pope Clement II died; he was the only pope ever buried in Germany.

**1049-54:** Pontificate of St. Leo IX, who inaugurated a movement of papal, diocesan, monastic and clerical reform.

**1054:** Great East-West Schism, separation of Orthodox Churches from unity with the pope.

**1055:** Condemnation of the Eucharistic doctrine of Berengarius.

**1059:** A Lateran council issued new legislation regarding papal elections; voting power was entrusted to the Roman cardinals.

**1066:** Death of St. Edward the Confessor, king of England from 1042 and restorer of Westminster Abbey.
Defeat, at Hastings, of Harold by William, Duke of Normandy (later William I), who subsequently exerted strong influence on the life-style of the Church in England.

**1073-85:** Pontificate of St. Gregory VII (Hildebrand). A strong pope, he carried forward programs of

clerical and general ecclesiastical reform and struggled against Henry IV and other rulers to end the evils of lay investiture. He introduced the Latin liturgy in Spain and set definite dates for the observance of ember days.

**1077:** Henry IV, excommunicated and suspended from the exercise of imperial powers by Gregory VII, sought absolution from the pope at Canossa. Henry later repudiated this action and in 1084 forced Gregory to leave Rome.

**1079:** The Council of Rome condemned Eucharistic errors (denial of the Real Presence of Christ under the appearances of bread and wine) of Berengarius, who retracted.

**1084:** St. Bruno founded the Carthusians.

**1097-99:** The first of several Crusades undertaken between this time and 1265. Recovery of the Holy Places and gaining free access to them for Christians were the original purposes, but these were diverted to less worthy objectives in various ways. Results included: a Latin Kingdom of Jerusalem, 1099-1187; a military and political misadventure in the form of a Latin Empire of Constantinople, 1204-1261; acquisition, by treaties, of visiting rights for Christians in the Holy Land. East-West economic and cultural relationships increased during the period. In the religious sphere, actions of the Crusaders had the effect of increasing the alienation of the East from the West.

**1098:** St. Robert founded the Cistercians.

## TWELFTH CENTURY

**1108:** Beginnings of the influential Abbey and School of St. Victor in France.

**1115:** St. Bernard established the Abbey of Clairvaux and inaugurated the Cistercian Reform.

**1118:** Christian forces captured Saragossa, Spain; the beginning of the Moslem decline in that country.

**1121:** St. Norbert established the original monastery of the Praemonstratensians near Laon, France.

**1122:** The Concordat of Worms (*Pactum Callixtinum*) was formulated and approved by Pope Callistus II and Emperor Henry V to settle controversy concerning the investiture of prelates. The concordat provided that the emperor could invest prelates with symbols of temporal authority but had no right to invest them with spiritual authority, which came from the Church alone, and that the emperor was not to interfere in papal elections. This was the first concordat in history.

**1123:** Ecumenical Council of the Lateran (I), the first of its kind in the West. It endorsed provisions of the Concordat of Worms concerning the investiture of prelates and approved reform measures in 25 canons.

**1139:** Ecumenical Council of the Lateran (II). It adopted measures against a schism organized by antipope Anacletus and approved 30 canons related to discipline and other matters; one of the canons stated that holy orders is an invalidating impediment to marriage.

**1140:** St. Bernard met Abelard in debate at the Council of Sens. Abelard, whose rationalism in theology was condemned for the first time in 1121, died in 1142 at Cluny.

**1148:** The Synod of Rheims enacted strict disciplinary decrees for communities of women Religious.

**1152:** The Synod of Kells reorganized the Church in Ireland.

**1160:** Gratian, whose *Decretum* became a basic text of canon law, died.

Peter Lombard, compiler of the *Four Books of Sentences,* a standard theology text for nearly 200 years, died.

**1170:** St. Thomas Becket, archbishop of Canterbury, who clashed with Henry II over church-state relations, was murdered in his cathedral.

**1171:** Pope Alexander III reserved the process of canonization of saints to the Holy See.

**1179:** Ecumenical Council of the Lateran (III). It enacted measures against Waldensianism and Albigensianism (see year 242 regarding Manichaeism), approved reform decrees in 27 canons, provided that popes be elected by a two-thirds vote of the cardinals.

**1184:** Waldenses and other heretics were excommunicated by Pope Lucius III.

## THIRTEENTH CENTURY

**1198-1216:** Pontificate of Innocent III, during which the papacy reached its medieval peak of authority, influence and prestige in the Church and in relations with civil rulers.

**1208:** Innocent III called for a crusade, the first in Christendom itself, against the Albigensians; their beliefs and practices threatened the fabric of society in southern France and northern Italy.

**1209:** Verbal approval was given by Innocent III to a rule of life for the Order of Friars Minor, started by St. Francis of Assisi.

**1212:** The Second Order of Franciscans, the Poor Clares, was founded.

**1215:** Ecumenical Council of the Lateran (IV). It ordered annual reception of the sacraments of penance and the Eucharist; defined and made the first official use of the term transubstantiation to explain the change of bread and wine into the body and blood of Christ; adopted additional measures to counteract teachings and practices of the Albigensians and Cathari; approved 70 canons.

**1216:** Formal papal approval was given to a rule of life for the Order of Preachers, started by St. Dominic.

The Portiuncula Indulgence was granted by the Holy See at the request of St. Francis of Assisi.

**1221:** Rule of the Third Order Secular of St. Francis (Secular Franciscan Order) approved verbally by Honorius III.

**1226:** Death of St. Francis of Assisi.

**1231:** Pope Gregory IX authorized establishment of the Papal Inquisition for dealing with heretics. It was a creature of its time, when crimes against faith and heretical doctrines of extremists like the Cathari and Albigenses threatened the good of the Christian community, the welfare of the state and the very fabric of society. The institution, which was responsible for excesses in punishment, was most active in the second half of the century in southern France, Italy and Germany.

**1245:** Ecumenical Council of Lyons (I). It confirmed the deposition of Emperor Frederick II and approved 22 canons.

**1247:** Preliminary approval was given by the Holy See to a Carmelite rule of life.

**1270:** St. Louis IX, king of France, died.

Beginning of papal decline.

**1274:** Ecumenical Council of Lyons (II). It accomplished a temporary reunion of separated Eastern Churches with the Roman Church; issued regulations concerning conclaves for papal elections; approved 31 canons.

Death of St. Thomas Aquinas, Doctor of the Church, of lasting influence.

**1280:** Pope Nicholas III, who made the *Breviary* the official prayer book for clergy of the Roman Church, died.

**1281:** The excommunication of Michael Palaeologus by Pope Martin IV ruptured the union effected with the Eastern Church in 1274.

## FOURTEENTH CENTURY

**1302:** Pope Boniface VIII issued the bull *Unam Sanctam,* concerning the unity of the Church and the temporal power of princes, against the background of a struggle with Philip IV of France; it was the most famous medieval document on the subject.

**1309-77:** For a period of approximately 70 years, seven popes resided at Avignon because of unsettled conditions in Rome and other reasons; see separate entry.

**1311-12:** Ecumenical Council of Vienne. It suppressed the Knights Templar and enacted a number of reform decrees.

**1321:** Dante Alighieri died a year after completing the *Divine Comedy.*

**1324:** Marsilius of Padua completed *Defensor Pacis,* a work condemned by Pope John XXII as heretical because of its denial of papal primacy and the hierarchical structure of the Church, and for other reasons. It was a charter for conciliarism (an ecumenical council is superior to the pope in authority).

**1337-1453:** Period of the Hundred Years' War, a dynastic struggle between France and England.

**1338:** Four years after the death of Pope John XXII, who had opposed Louis IV of Bavaria in a years-long controversy, electoral princes declared at the Diet of Rhense that the emperor did not need papal confirmation of his title and right to rule. Charles IV later (1356) said the same thing in a *Golden Bull,* eliminating papal rights in the election of emperors.

**1347-50:** The Black Death swept across Europe, killing perhaps one-fourth to one-third of the total population; an estimated 40 per cent of the clergy succumbed.

**1374:** Petrarch, poet and humanist, died.

**1377:** Return of the papacy from Avignon to Rome. Beginning of the Western Schism; see separate entry.

## FIFTEENTH CENTURY

**1409:** The Council of Pisa, without canonical authority, tried to end the Western Schism but succeeded only in complicating it by electing a third claimant to the papacy; see Western Schism.

**1414-18:** Ecumenical Council of Constance. It took successful action to end the Western Schism involving rival claimants to the papacy; rejected the teachings of Wycliff; condemned Hus as a heretic. One decree — passed in the earlier stages of the council but later rejected — asserted the superiority of an ecumenical council over the pope (conciliarism).

**1431:** St. Joan of Arc was burned at the stake.

**1431-45:** Ecumenical Council of Florence (also called Basel-Ferrara-Florence). It affirmed the primacy of the pope against the claims of conciliarists that an ecumenical council is superior to the pope. It also formulated and approved decrees of union with several separated Eastern Churches — Greek, Armenian, Jacobite — which failed to gain general or lasting acceptance.

**1438:** The Pragmatic Sanction of Bourges was enacted by Charles VII and the French Parliament to curtail papal authority over the Church in France, in the spirit of conciliarism. It found expression in Gallicanism and had effects lasting at least until the French Revolution.

**1453:** The fall of Constantinople to the Turks.

**c. 1456:** Gutenberg issued the first edition of the Bible printed from movable type, at Mainz, Germany.

**1476:** Pope Sixtus IV approved observance of the feast of the Immaculate Conception on Dec. 8 throughout the Church.

**1478:** Pope Sixtus IV, at the urging of King Ferdinand of Spain, approved establishment of the Spanish Inquisition for dealing with Jewish and Moorish converts accused of heresy. The institution, which was peculiar to Spain and its colonies in America, acquired jurisdiction over other cases as well and fell into disrepute because of its procedures, cruelty and the manner in which it served the Spanish crown, rather than the accused and the good of the Church. Protests by the Holy See failed to curb excesses of the Inquisition, which lingered in Spanish history until early in the 19th century.

**1492:** Columbus discovered the Americas.

**1493:** Pope Alexander VI issued a *Bull of Demarcation* which determined spheres of influence for the Spanish and Portuguese in the Americas.

The Renaissance, a humanistic movement which originated in Italy in the 14th century, spread to France, Germany, the Low Countries and England. A transitional period between the medieval world and the modern secular world, it introduced profound changes which affected literature and the other arts, general culture, politics and religion.

## SIXTEENTH CENTURY

**1512-17:** Ecumenical Council of the Lateran (V). It stated the relation and position of the pope with respect to an ecumenical council; acted to counteract the Pragmatic Sanction of Bourges and exaggerated claims of liberty by the Church in France; condemned erroneous teachings concerning the nature of the human soul; stated doctrine concerning indulgences. The council reflected concern for abuses in the Church and the need for reforms but failed to take decisive action in the years immediately preceding the Reformation.

**1517:** Martin Luther signalled the beginning of the Reformation by posting 95 theses at Wittenberg. Subsequently, he broke completely from doctrinal orthodoxy in discourses and three published works (1519 and 1520); was excommunicated on more than 40 charges of heresy (1521); remained the dominant figure in the Reformation in Germany until his death in 1546.

**1519:** Zwingli triggered the Reformation in Zurich and became its leading proponent there until his death in combat in 1531.

**1524:** Luther's encouragement of German princes in putting down the two-year Peasants' Revolt gained political support for his cause.

**1528:** The Order of Friars Minor Capuchin was approved as an autonomous division of the Franciscan Order; like the Jesuits, the Capuchins became leaders in the Counter-Reformation.

**1530:** The *Augsburg Confession* of Lutheran faith was issued; it was later supplemented by the *Smalcald Articles,* approved in 1537.

**1533:** Henry VIII divorced Catherine of Aragon, married Anne Boleyn, was excommunicated. In 1534 he decreed the Act of Supremacy, making the sovereign the head of the Church in England, under which Sts. John Fisher and Thomas More were executed in 1535. Despite his rejection of papal primacy and actions against monastic life in England, he generally maintained doctrinal orthodoxy until his death in 1547.

**1536:** John Calvin, leader of the Reformation in Switzerland until his death in 1564, issued the first edition of *Institutes of the Christian Religion,* which became the classical text of Reformed (non-Lutheran) theology.

**1540:** The constitutions of the Society of Jesus (Jesuits), founded by St. Ignatius of Loyola, were approved.

**1541:** Start of the 11-year career of St. Francis Xavier as a missionary to the East Indies and Japan.

**1545-63:** Ecumenical Council of Trent. It issued a great number of decrees concerning doctrinal matters opposed by the Reformers, and mobilized the Counter-Reformation. Definitions covered the Canon of the Bible, the rule of faith, the nature of justification, grace, faith, original sin and its effects, the seven sacraments, the sacrificial nature of the Mass, the veneration of saints, use of sacred images, belief in purgatory, the doctrine of indulgences, the jurisdiction of the pope over the whole Church. It initiated many reforms for renewal in the liturgy and general discipline in the Church, the promotion of religious instruction, the education of the clergy through the foundation of seminaries, etc. Trent ranks with Vatican II as the greatest ecumenical council held in the West.

**1549:** The first Anglican *Book of Common Prayer* was issued by Edward VI. Revised editions were published in 1552, 1559 and 1662 and later.

**1553:** Start of the five-year reign of Mary Tudor who tried to counteract actions of Henry VIII against the Roman Church.

**1555:** Enactment of the Peace of Augsburg, an arrangement of religious territorialism rather than toleration, which recognized the existence of Catholicism and Lutheranism in the German Empire and provided that citizens should adopt the religion of their respective rulers.

**1558:** Beginning of the reign (to 1603) of Queen Elizabeth I of England and Ireland, during which the Church of England took on its definitive form.

**1559:** Establishment of the hierarchy of the Church of England, with the consecration of Matthew Parker as archbishop of Canterbury.

**1563:** The first text of the *39 Articles* of the Church of England was issued. Also enacted were a new Act of Supremacy and Oath of Succession to the English throne.

**1570:** Elizabeth I was excommunicated. Penal measures against Catholics subsequently became more severe.

**1571:** Defeat of the Turkish armada at Lepanto staved off the invasion of Eastern Europe.

**1577:** The *Formula of Concord,* the classical statement of Lutheran faith, was issued; it was, generally, a Lutheran counterpart of the canons of the Council of Trent. In 1580, along with other formulas of doctrine, it was included in the *Book of Concord.*

**1582:** The Gregorian Calendar, named for Pope Gregory XIII, was put into effect and was eventually adopted in most countries: England delayed adoption until 1752.

## SEVENTEENTH CENTURY

**1605:** The Gunpowder Plot, an attempt by Catholic fanatics to blow up James I of England and the houses of Parliament, resulted in an anti-Catholic Oath of Allegiance.

**1610:** Death of Matteo Ricci, outstanding Jesuit missionary to China, pioneer in cultural relations between China and Europe.

Founding of the first community of Visitation Nuns by Sts. Francis de Sales and Jane de Chantal.

**1611:** Founding of the Oratorians.

**1613:** Catholics were banned from Scandinavia.

**1625:** Founding of the Congregation of the Mission (Vincentians) by St. Vincent de Paul. He founded the Sisters of Charity in 1633.

**1642:** Death of Galileo, scientist, who was censured by the Congregation of the Holy Office for supporting the Copernican theory of the sun-centered planetary system. The case against him was closed in his favor in 1992.

Founding of the Sulpicians by Jacques Olier.

**1643:** Start of publication of the Bollandist *Acta Sanctorum,* a critical work on lives of the saints.

**1648:** Provisions in the Peace of Westphalia, ending the Thirty Years' War, extended terms of the Peace of Augsburg (1555) to Calvinists and gave equality to Catholics and Protestants in the 300 states of the Holy Roman Empire.

**1649:** Oliver Cromwell invaded Ireland and began a severe persecution of the Church there.

**1653:** Pope Innocent X condemned five propositions of Jansenism, a complex theory which distorted doctrine concerning the relations between divine grace and human freedom. Jansenism was also a rigoristic movement which seriously disturbed the Church in France, the Low Countries and Italy in this and the 18th century.

**1673:** The Test Act in England barred from public office Catholics who would not deny the doctrine of transubstantiation and receive Communion in the Church of England.

**1678:** Many English Catholics suffered death as a consequence of the Popish Plot, a false allegation by Titus Oates that Catholics planned to assassinate Charles II, land a French army in the country, burn London, and turn over the government to the Jesuits.

**1682:** The four Gallican articles, drawn up by Bossuet, asserted political and ecclesiastical immunities of France from papal control. The articles, which rejected the primacy of the pope, were declared null and void by Pope Alexander VIII in 1690.

**1689:** The Toleration Act granted a measure of freedom of worship to other English dissenters but not to Catholics.

## EIGHTEENTH CENTURY

**1704:** Chinese Rites — involving the Christian adaptation of elements of Confucianism, veneration of ancestors and Chinese terminology in religion — were condemned by Clement XI.

**1720:** The Passionists were founded by St. Paul of the Cross.

**1724:** Persecution in China.

**1732:** The Redemptorists were founded by St. Alphonsus Liguori.

**1738:** Freemasonry was condemned by Clement XII and Catholics were forbidden to join, under penalty of excommunication; the prohibition was repeated by Benedict XIV in 1751 and by later popes.

**1760s:** Josephinism, a theory and system of state control of the Church, was initiated in Austria; it remained in force until about 1850.

**1764:** Febronianism, an unorthodox theory and practice regarding the constitution of the Church and relations between Church and state, was condemned for the first of several times. Proposed by an auxiliary bishop of Trier using the pseudonym Justinus Febronius, it had the effects of minimizing the office of the pope and supporting national churches under state control.

**1773:** Clement XIV issued a brief of suppression against the Jesuits, following their expulsion from Portugal in 1759, from France in 1764 and from Spain in 1767. Political intrigue and unsubstantiated accusations were principal factors in these developments. The ban, which crippled the society, contained no condemnation of the Jesuit constitutions, particular Jesuits or Jesuit teaching. The society was restored in 1814.

**1778:** Catholics in England were relieved of some civil disabilities dating back to the time of Henry VIII, by an act which permitted them to acquire, own and inherit property. Additional liberties were restored by the Roman Catholic Relief Act of 1791 and subsequent enactments of Parliament.

**1789:** Religious freedom in the United States was guaranteed under the First Amendment to the Constitution.

Beginning of the French Revolution which resulted in: the secularization of church property and the Civil Constitution of the Clergy in 1790; the persecution of priests, religious and lay persons loyal to papal authority; invasion of the Papal States by

Napoleon in 1796; renewal of persecution from 1797-1799; attempts to dechristianize France and establish a new religion; the occupation of Rome by French troops and the forced removal of Pius VI to France in 1798.

This century is called the age of Enlightenment or Reason because of the predominating rational and scientific approach of its leading philosophers, scientists and writers with respect to religion, ethics and natural law. This approach downgraded the fact and significance of revealed religion. Also characteristic of the Enlightenment were subjectivism, secularism and optimism regarding human perfectibility.

## NINETEENTH CENTURY

**1809:** Pope Pius VII was made a captive by Napoleon and deported to France where he remained in exile until 1814. During this time he refused to cooperate with Napoleon who sought to bring the Church in France under his own control.

The turbulence in church-state relations in France at the beginning of the century recurred in connection with the Bourbon Restoration, the July Revolution, the second and third Republics, the Second Empire and the Dreyfus case.

**1814:** The Society of Jesus, suppressed since 1773, was restored.

**1817:** Reestablishment of the Congregation for the Propagation of the Faith (Propaganda) by Pius VII was an important factor in increasing missionary activity during the century.

• **1820:** Years-long persecution, during which thousands died for the faith, ended in China. Thereafter, communication with the West remained cut off until about 1834. Vigorous missionary work got under way in 1842.

**1822:** The Pontifical Society for the Propagation of the Faith, inaugurated in France by Pauline Jaricot for the support of missionary activity, was established.

**1829:** The Catholic Emancipation Act relieved Catholics in England and Ireland of most of the civil disabilities to which they had been subject from the time of Henry VIII.

**1832:** Gregory XVI, in the encyclical *Mirari vos,* condemned indifferentism, one of the many ideologies at odds with Christian doctrine which were proposed during the century.

**1833:** Start of the Oxford Movement which affected the Church of England and resulted in some notable conversions, including that of John Henry Newman in 1845, to the Catholic Church.

Frederic Ozanam founded the Society of St. Vincent de Paul in France. The society, whose objective was works of charity, became worldwide.

**1848:** The *Communist Manifesto,* a revolutionary document symptomatic of socio-economic crisis, was issued.

**1850:** The hierarchy was reestablished in England and Nicholas Wiseman made the first archbishop of Westminster. He was succeeded in 1865 by Henry Manning, an Oxford convert and proponent of the rights of labor.

**1853:** The Catholic hierarchy was reestablished in Holland.

**1854:** Pius IX proclaimed the dogma of the Immaculate Conception in the bull *Ineffabilis Deus.*

**1858:** The Blessed Virgin Mary appeared to St. Bernadette at Lourdes, France; see separate entry.

**1864:** Pius IX issued the encyclical *Quanta cura* and the *Syllabus of Errors* in condemnation of some 80 propositions derived from the scientific mentality and rationalism of the century. The subjects in question had deep ramifications in many areas of thought and human endeavor; in religion, they explicitly and/or implicitly rejected divine revelation and the supernatural order.

**1867:** The first volume of *Das Kapital* was published. Together with the Communist First International, formed in the same year, it had great influence on the subsequent development of communism and socialism.

**1869:** The Anglican Church was disestablished in Ireland.

**1869-70:** Ecumenical Council of the Vatican (I). It defined papal primacy and infallibility in a dogmatic constitution on the Church; covered natural religion, revelation, faith, and the relations between faith and reason in a dogmatic constitution on the Cathoic faith.

**1870-71:** Victor Emmanuel II of Sardinia, crowned king of Italy after defeating Austrian and papal forces, marched into Rome in 1870 and expropriated the Papal States after a plebiscite in which Catholics, at the order of Pius IX, did not vote. In 1871, Pius IX refused to accept a Law of Guarantees. Confiscation of church property and hindrance of ecclesiastical administration by the regime followed.

**1871:** The German Empire, a confederation of 26 states, was formed. Government policy launched a Kulturkampf whose May Laws of 1873 were designed to annul papal jurisdiction in Prussia and other states and to place the Church under imperial control. Resistance to the enactments and the persecution they legalized forced the government to modify its anti-Church policy by 1887.

**1878:** Beginning of the pontificate of Leo XIII, who was pope until his death in 1903. Leo is best known for the encyclical *Rerum novarum,* which greatly influenced the course of Christian social thought and the labor movement. His other accomplishments included promotion of Scholastic philosophy and the impetus he gave to scriptural studies.

**1881:** The first International Eucharistic Congress was held in Lille, France.

Alexander II of Russia died. His policies of Russification — as well as those of his two predecessors and a successor during the century — caused great suffering to Catholics, Jews and Protestants in Poland, Lithuania, the Ukraine and Bessarabia.

**1882:** Charles Darwin died. His theory of evolution by natural selection, one of several scientific highlights of the century, had extensive repercussions in the faith-and-science controversy.

**1887:** The Catholic University of America was founded in Washington, D.C.

**1893:** The U.S. apostolic delegation was set up in Washington, D.C.

# TWENTIETH CENTURY

**1901:** Restrictive measures in France forced the Jesuits, Benedictines, Carmelites and other religious orders to leave the country. Subsequently, 14,000 schools were suppressed; religious orders and congregations were expelled; the concordat was renounced in 1905; church property was confiscated in 1906. For some years the Holy See, refusing to comply with government demands for the control of bishops' appointments, left some ecclesiastical offices vacant.

**1903-14:** Pontificate of St. Pius X. He initiated the codification of canon law, 1904; removed the ban against participation by Catholics in Italian national elections, 1905; issued decrees calling upon the faithful to receive Holy Communion frequently and daily, and stating that children should begin receiving the Eucharist at the age of seven, 1905 and 1910, respectively; ordered the establishment of the Confraternity of Christian Doctrine in all parishes throughout the world, 1905; condemned Modernism in the decree *Lamentabili* and the encyclical *Pascendi*, 1907.

**1908:** The United States and England, long under the jurisdiction of the Congregation for the Propagation of the Faith as mission territories, were removed from its control and placed under the common law of the Church.

**1910:** Laws of separation were enacted in Portugal, marking a point of departure in church-state relations.

**1911:** The Catholic Foreign Mission Society of America — Maryknoll, the first U.S.-founded society of its type — was established.

**1914:** Start of World War I, which lasted until 1918.

**1914-22:** Pontificate of Benedict XV. Much of his pontificate was devoted to seeking ways and means of minimizing the material and spiritual havoc of World War I. In 1917 he offered his services as a mediator to the belligerent nations, but his pleas for settlement of the conflict went unheeded.

**1917:** The Blessed Virgin Mary appeared to three children at Fatima, Portugal; see separate entry.

A new constitution, embodying repressive laws against the Church, was enacted in Mexico. Its implementation resulted in persecution in the 1920s and 1930s.

Bolsheviks seized power in Russia and set up a communist dictatorship. The event marked the rise of communism in Russian and world affairs. One of its immediate, and lasting, results was persecution of the Church, Jews and other segments of the population.

**1918:** The *Code of Canon Law,* in preparation for more than 10 years, went into effect in the Western Church.

**1919:** Benedict XV stimulated missionary work through the decree *Maximum Illud,* in which he urged the recruiting and training of native clergy in places where the Church was not firmly established.

**1920-22:** Ireland was partitioned by two enactments of the British government which (1) made the six counties of Northern Ireland part of the United Kingdom in 1920 and (2) gave dominion status to the Irish Free State in 1922. The Irish Free State became an independent republic in 1949.

**1922-39:** Pontificate of Pius XI. He subscribed to the Lateran Treaty, 1929, which settled the Roman Question created by the confiscation of the Papal States in 1871; issued the encyclical *Casti connubii,* 1930, an authoritative statement on Christian marriage; resisted the efforts of Benito Mussolini to control Catholic Action and the Church, in the encyclical *Non abbiamo bisogno,* 1931; opposed various fascist policies; issued the encyclicals *Quadragesimo anno,* 1931, developing the social doctrine of Leo XIII's *Rerum novarum,* and *Divini Redemptoris,* 1937, calling for social justice and condemning atheistic communism; condemned anti-Semitism, 1937.

**1926:** The Catholic Relief Act repealed virtually all legal disabilities of Catholics in England.

**1931:** Leftists proclaimed Spain a republic and proceeded to disestablish the Church, confiscate church property, deny salaries to the clergy, expel the Jesuits and ban teaching of the Catholic faith. These actions were preludes to the civil war of 1936-1939.

**1933:** Emergence of Adolf Hitler to power in Germany. By 1935 two of his aims were clear, the elimination of the Jews and control of a single national church. Six million Jews were killed in the Holocaust. The Church was subject to repressive measures, which Pius XI protested futilely in the encyclical *Mit brennender sorge* in 1937.

**1936-39:** Civil war in Spain between the leftist Loyalist and rightist Franco forces. The Loyalists were defeated and one-man, one-party rule was established. Priests, Religious and lay persons fell victims to Loyalist persecution.

**1939-45:** World War II.

**1939-58:** Pontificate of Pius XII. He condemned communism, proclaimed the dogma of the Assumption of Mary in 1950, in various documents and other enactments provided ideological background for many of the accomplishments of the Second Vatican Council. (See Twentieth Century Popes.)

**1940:** Start of a decade of communist conquest in more than 13 countries, resulting in conditions of persecution for a minimum of 60 million Catholics as well as members of other faiths.

Persecution diminished in Mexico because of nonenforcement of anti-religious laws still on record.

**1950:** Pius XII proclaimed the dogma of the Assumption of the Blessed Virgin Mary.

**1957:** The communist regime of China established the Patriotic Association of Chinese Catholics in opposition to the Church in union with the pope.

**1958-63:** Pontificate of John XXIII. His principal accomplishment was the convocation of the Second Vatican Council, the twenty-first ecumenical council in the history of the Church. (See Twentieth Century Popes.)

**1962-65:** Ecumenical Council of the Vatican (II). It formulated and promulgated 16 documents — two dogmatic and two pastoral constitutions, nine decrees and three declarations — reflecting pastoral orientation toward renewal and reform in the Church, and making explicit dimensions of doctrine and Christian life requiring emphasis for the full development of the Church and the better accomplishment of its mission in the contemporary world.

**1963-78:** Pontificate of Paul VI. His main purpose and effort was to give direction and provide guidance for the authentic trends of church renewal set in motion by the Second Vatican Council. (See Twentieth Century Popes.)

**1978:** The thirty-four-day pontificate of John Paul I. (See Twentieth Century Popes.)

Start of the pontificate of John Paul II; see Index.

**1983:** The revised Code of Canon Law, embodying reforms enacted by the Second Vatican Council, went into effect in the Church of Roman Rite.

**1985:** Formal ratification of a Vatican-Italy concordat replacing the Lateran Treaty of 1929.

**1989-91:** Decline and fall of communist influence and control in Middle and Eastern Europe and the Soviet Union.

**1991:** The Code of Canon Law for Eastern Churches went into effect.

**1992:** Approval of the new Catechism of the Catholic Church.

**1994:** Initiation of preparations for celebration of the start of the third Christian millennium in the year 2000.

# ECUMENICAL COUNCILS

An ecumenical council is an assembly of the college of bishops, with and under the presidency of the pope, which has supreme authority over the Church in matters pertaining to faith, morals, worship and discipline.

The Second Vatican Council stated: "The supreme authority with which this college (of bishops) is empowered over the whole Church is exercised in a solemn way through an ecumenical council. A council is never ecumenical unless it is confirmed or at least accepted as such by the successor of Peter. It is the prerogative of the Roman Pontiff to convoke these councils, to preside over them, and to confirm them" (*Dogmatic Constitution on the Church*, No. 22).

## Pope Presides

The pope is the head of an ecumenical council; he presides over it either personally or through legates. Conciliar decrees and other actions have binding force only when confirmed and promulgated by him. If a pope dies during a council, it is suspended until reconvened by another pope. An ecumenical council is not superior to a pope; hence, there is no appeal from a pope to a council.

Collectively, the bishops with the pope represent the whole Church. They do this not as democratic representatives of the faithful in a kind of church parliament, but as the successors of the Apostles with divinely given authority, care and responsibility over the whole Church.

All and only bishops are council participants with deliberative vote. The supreme authority of the Church can invite others and determine the manner of their participation.

Basic legislation concerning ecumenical councils is contained in Canons 337-41 of the Code of Canon Law. Basic doctrinal considerations were stated by the Second Vatican Council in the *Dogmatic Constitution on the Church*.

## Background

Ecumenical councils had their prototype in the Council of Jerusalem in 51, at which the Apostles under the leadership of St. Peter decided that converts to the Christian faith were not obliged to observe all the prescriptions of Old Testament law (Acts 15). As early as the second century, bishops got together in regional meetings, synods or councils to take common action for the doctrinal and pastoral good of their communities of faithful. The expansion of such limited assemblies to ecumenical councils was a logical and historical evolution, given the nature and needs of the Church.

## Emperors Involved

Emperors were active in summoning or convoking the first eight councils, especially the first five and the eighth. Among reasons for intervention of this kind were the facts that the emperors regarded themselves as guardians of the faith; that the settlement of religious controversies, which had repercussions in political and social turmoil, served the cause of peace in the state; and that the emperors had at their disposal ways and means of facilitating gatherings of bishops. Imperial actions, however, did not account for the formally ecumenical nature of the councils.

Some councils were attended by relatively few bishops, and the ecumenical character of several was open to question for a time. However, confirmation and de facto recognition of their actions by popes and subsequent councils established them as ecumenical.

## Role in History

The councils have played a highly significant role in the history of the Church by witnessing to and defining truths of revelation, by shaping forms of worship and discipline, and by promoting measures for the ever-necessary reform and renewal of Catholic life. In general, they have represented attempts of the Church to mobilize itself in times of crisis for self-preservation, self-purification and growth.

The first eight ecumenical councils were held in the East; the other 13, in the West. The majority of separated Eastern Churches — e.g., the Orthodox — recognize the ecumenical character of the first seven councils, which formulated a great deal of basic doctrine. Other separated Eastern Churches acknowledge only the first two or first three ecumenical councils.

## The 21 Councils

The 21 ecumenical councils in the history of the Church are listed below, with indication of their names or titles (taken from the names of the places where they were held); the dates; the reigning and/or approving popes; the emperors who were instrumental in convoking the eight councils in the East; the number of bishops who attended, when available; the number of sessions. Significant actions of the first 20 councils are indicated under appropriate dates in Dates and Events in Church History.

1. **Nicaea I,** 325: St. Sylvester I (Emperor Constantine I); attended by approximately 300 bishops; sessions held between May 20 or June 19 to near the end of August.
2. **Constantinople I,** 381: St. Damasus I (Emperor Theodosius I); attended by approximately 150 bishops; sessions held from May to July.
3. **Ephesus,** 431: St. Celestine I (Emperor Theodosius II); attended by 150 to 200 bishops; five sessions held between June 22 and July 17.
4. **Chalcedon,** 451: St. Leo I (Emperor Marcian); attended by approximately 600 bishops; 17 sessions held between Oct. 8 and Nov. 1.
5. **Constantinople II,** 553: Vigilius (Emperor Justinian I); attended by 165 bishops; eight sessions held between May 5 and June 2.
6. **Constantinople III,** 680-681: St. Agatho, St. Leo II (Emperor Constantine IV); attended by approximately 170 bishops; 16 sessions held between Nov. 7, 680, and Sept. 6, 681.
7. **Nicaea II,** 787: Adrian I (Empress Irene); attended by approximately 300 bishops; eight sessions held between Sept. 24 and Oct. 23.
8. **Constantinople IV,** 869-870: Adrian II (Emperor Basil I); attended by 102 bishops; six sessions held between Oct. 5, 869, and Feb. 28, 870.
9. **Lateran I,** 1123: Callistus II; attended by approximately 300 bishops; sessions held between Mar. 8 and Apr. 6.
10. **Lateran II,** 1139: Innocent II; attended by 900 to 1,000 bishops and abbots; three sessions held in April.
11. **Lateran III,** 1179: Alexander III; attended by at least 300 bishops; three sessions held between Mar. 5 and 19.
12. **Lateran IV,** 1215: Innocent III; sessions held between Nov. 11 and 30.
13. **Lyons I,** 1245: Innocent IV; attended by approximately 150 bishops; three sessions held between June 28 and July 17.
14. **Lyons II,** 1274: Gregory X; attended by approximately 500 bishops; six sessions held between May 7 and July 17.
15. **Vienne,** 1311-1312: Clement V; attended by 132 bishops; three sessions held between Oct. 16, 1311, and May 6, 1312.
16. **Constance,** 1414-1418: Gregory XII, Martin V; attended by nearly 200 bishops, plus other prelates and many experts; 45 sessions held between Nov. 5, 1414, and Apr. 22, 1418.
17. **Florence** (also called Basel-Ferrara-Florence), 1431-1445(?): Eugene IV; attended by many Latin-Rite and Eastern-Rite bishops; preliminary sessions were held at Basel and Ferrara before definitive work was accomplished at Florence.
18. **Lateran V,** 1512-1517: Julius II, Leo X; 12 sessions held between May 3, 1512, and Mar. 6, 1517.
19. **Trent,** 1545-1563: Paul III, Julius III, Pius IV; 25 sessions held between Dec. 13, 1545, and Dec. 4, 1563.
20. **Vatican I,** 1869-1870: Pius IX; attended by approximately 800 bishops and other prelates; four public sessions and 89 general meetings held between Dec. 8, 1869, and Sept. 1, 1870.

## VATICAN II

The Second Vatican Council, which was forecast by Pope John XXIII Jan. 25, 1959, was held in four sessions in St. Peter's Basilica.

Pope John convoked it and opened the first session, which ran from Oct. 11 to Dec. 8, 1962. Following John's death June 3, 1963, Pope Paul VI reconvened the council for the other three sessions which ran from Sept. 29 to Dec. 4, 1963; Sept. 14 to Nov. 21, 1964; Sept. 14 to Dec. 8, 1965.

A total of 2,860 Fathers participated in council proceedings, and attendance at meetings varied between 2,000 and 2,500. For various reasons, including the denial of exit from Communist-dominated countries, 274 Fathers could not attend.

The council formulated and promulgated 16 documents — two dogmatic and two pastoral constitutions, nine decrees and three declarations — all of which reflect its basic pastoral orientation toward renewal and reform in the Church. Given below are the Latin and English titles of the documents and their dates of promulgation.

- *Lumen Gentium* (Dogmatic Constitution on the Church), Nov. 21, 1964.
- *Dei Verbum* (Dogmatic Constitution on Divine Revelation), Nov. 18, 1965.
- *Sacrosanctum Concilium* (Constitution on the Sacred Liturgy), Dec. 4, 1963.
- *Gaudium et Spes* (Pastoral Constitution on the Church in the Modern World), Dec. 7, 1965.
- *Christus Dominus* (Decree on the Bishops' Pastoral Office in the Church), Oct. 28, 1965.
- *Ad Gentes* (Decree on the Church's Missionary Activity), Dec. 7, 1965.
- *Unitatis Redintegratio* (Decree on Ecumenism), Nov. 21, 1964.
- *Orientalium Ecclesiarum* (Decree on Eastern Catholic Churches), Nov. 21, 1964.
- *Presbyterorum Ordinis* (Decree on the Ministry and Life of Priests), Dec. 7, 1965.
- *Optatam Totius* (Decree on Priestly Formation), Oct. 28, 1965.
- *Perfectae Caritatis* (Decree on the Appropriate Renewal of the Religious Life), Oct. 28, 1965.
- *Apostolicam Actuositatem* (Decree on the Apostolate of the Laity), Nov. 18, 1965.
- *Inter Mirifica* (Decree on the Instruments of Social Communication), Dec. 4, 1963.
- *Dignitatis Humanae* (Declaration on Religious Freedom), Dec. 7, 1965.
- *Nostra Aetate* (Declaration on the Relationship of the Church to Non-Christian Religions), Oct. 28, 1965.
- *Gravissimum Educationis* (Declaration on Christian Education), Oct. 28, 1965.

The key documents were the four constitutions, which set the ideological basis for all the others. To date, the documents with the most visible effects are those on the liturgy, the Church, the Church in the world, ecumenism, the renewal of religious life, the life and ministry of priests, the lay apostolate.

The main business of the council was to explore and make explicit dimensions of doctrine and Christian life requiring emphasis for the full development of the Church and the better accomplishment of its mission in the contemporary world.

# THE CHURCH AS COMMUNION

Following are excerpts from a "Letter to the Bishops of the Catholic Church on Some Aspects of the Church Understood as Communion," issued by the Congregation for the Doctrine of the Faith June 15, 1992.

*These excerpts are from the Vatican text circulated by the CNS Documentary Service, Origins, June 25, 1992 (Vol. 22, No. 7). Subheads have been added.*

Some approaches to ecclesiology suffer from a clearly inadequate awareness of the Church as a mystery of communion, especially insofar as they have not sufficiently integrated the concept of communion with the concepts of the people of God and body of Christ, and have not given due importance to the relationship between the Church as communion and the Church as sacrament.

## Invisible and Visible Communion

Ecclesial communion is at the same time both invisible and visible. As an invisible reality, it is the communion of each human being with the Father through Christ in the Holy Spirit, and with the others who are fellow sharers in the divine nature, in the passion of Christ, in the same faith, in the same spirit. In the Church on earth, there is an intimate relationship between this invisible communion and the visible communion in the teaching of the apostles, in the sacraments and in the hierarchical order. . . . (The) link between the invisible and visible elements of ecclesial communion constitutes the Church as the sacrament of salvation.

Ecclesial communion, into which each individual is introduced by faith and by baptism, has its root and center in the holy Eucharist. Indeed, baptism is an incorporation into a body that the risen Lord builds up and keeps alive through the Eucharist, so that this body can truly be called the body of Christ. The Eucharist is the creative force and source of communion among the members of the Church, precisely because it unites each one of them with Christ himself.

## Universal and Particular Churches

The Church of Christ, which we profess in the Creed to be one, holy, catholic and apostolic, is the universal Church, that is, the worldwide community of the disciples of the Lord, which is present and active . . . (in) those entities which are in themselves churches because, although they are particular (churches), the universal Church becomes present in them with all her essential elements. They are therefore constituted after the model of the universal Church, and each of them is a portion of the people of God entrusted to a bishop to be guided by him with the assistance of his clergy.

The universal Church is therefore the body of the churches. . . . Sometimes the idea of a communion of particular churches is presented in such a way as to weaken the concept of the unity of the Church at the visible and institutional level. Thus it is asserted that every particular church is a subject complete in itself, and that the universal Church is the result of a reciprocal recognition on the part of the particular churches. (But) the universal Church cannot be conceived as the sum of the particular churches or as a federation of particular churches.

From the point of view of the Church understood as communion, the universal communion of the faithful and the communion of the churches are not consequences of one another but constitute the same reality from different viewpoints.

## Eucharistic and Episcopal Roots

Unity, or communion between the particular churches in the universal Church, is rooted not only in the same faith and in the common baptism, but above all in the Eucharist and in the episcopate. It is rooted in the Eucharist because the Eucharistic Sacrifice, while always offered in a particular community, is never a celebration of that community alone.

## Supreme Authority of the Church

For each particular church to be fully church, that is, the particular presence of the universal Church with all its essential elements, and hence constituted after the model of the universal Church, there must be present in it, as a proper element, the supreme authority of the Church: the episcopal college together with their head, the Supreme Pontiff, and never apart from him. The primacy of the bishop of Rome and the episcopal college are proper elements of the universal Church that are not derived from the particularity of the churches, but are nevertheless interior to each particular church. Consequently we must see the ministry of the successor of Peter not only as a global service reaching each particular church from outside, as it were, but as belonging already to the essence of each particular church from within. Indeed, the ministry of the primacy involves, in essence, a truly episcopal power which is not only supreme, full and universal but also immediate, over all, whether pastors or faithful. The ministry of the successor of Peter as something interior to each particular church is a necessary expression of that fundamental mutual interiority between universal Church and particular church.

The concept of the Church as communion is complementary to other concepts like those described in the "constitution on the Church" — the people of God, the universal sacrament, the body of Christ. All such concepts represent attempts to clarify and deepen understanding of the manifold mystery of the Church established by Christ for the salvation of all peoples.

# POPES

*Information includes the name of the pope, in many cases his name before becoming pope, his birthplace or country of origin, the date of accession to the papacy, and the date of the end of reign which, in all but a few cases, was the date of death. Double dates indicate date of election and date of solemn beginning of ministry as Pastor of the universal Church.*

*Source: "Annuario Pontificio."*

St. Peter (Simon Bar-Jona): Bethsaida in Galilee; d. c. 64 or 67.

St. Linus: Tuscany; 67-76.

St. Anacletus (Cletus): Rome; 76-88.

St. Clement: Rome; 88-97.

St. Evaristus: Greece; 97-105.

St. Alexander I: Rome; 105-115.

St. Sixtus I: Rome; 115-125.

St. Telesphorus: Greece; 125-136.

St. Hyginus: Greece; 136-140.

St. Pius I: Aquileia; 140-155.

St. Anicetus: Syria; 155-166.

St. Soter: Campania; 166-175.

St. Eleutherius: Nicopolis in Epirus; 175-189.

Up to the time of St. Eleutherius, the years indicated for the beginning and end of pontificates are not absolutely certain. Also, up to the middle of the 11th century, there are some doubts about the exact days and months given in chronological tables.

St. Victor I: Africa; 189-199.

St. Zephyrinus: Rome; 199-217.

St. Callistus I: Rome; 217-222.

St. Urban I: Rome; 222-230.

St. Pontian: Rome; July 21, 230, to Sept. 28, 235.

St. Anterus: Greece; Nov. 21, 235, to Jan. 3, 236.

St. Fabian: Rome; Jan. 10, 236, to Jan. 20, 250.

St. Cornelius: Rome; Mar., 251, to June, 253.

St. Lucius I: Rome; June 25, 253, to Mar. 5, 254.

St. Stephen I: Rome; May 12, 254, to Aug. 2, 257.

St. Sixtus II: Greece; Aug. 30, 257, to Aug. 6, 258.

St. Dionysius: July 22, 259, to Dec. 26, 268.

St. Felix I: Rome; Jan. 5, 269, to Dec. 30, 274.

St. Eutychian: Luni; Jan. 4, 275, to Dec. 7, 283.

St. Caius: Dalmatia; Dec. 17, 283, to Apr. 22, 296.

St. Marcellinus: Rome; June 30, 296, to Oct. 25, 304.

St. Marcellus I: Rome; May 27, 308, or June 26, 308, to Jan. 16, 309.

St. Eusebius: Greece; Apr. 18, 309, to Aug. 17, 309 or 310.

St. Melchiades (Miltiades): Africa; July 2, 311, to Jan. 11, 314.

St. Sylvester I: Rome; Jan. 31, 314, to Dec. 31, 335. (Most of the popes before St. Sylvester I were martyrs.)

St. Marcus: Rome; Jan. 18, 336, to Oct. 7, 336.

St. Julius I: Rome; Feb. 6, 337, to Apr. 12, 352.

Liberius: Rome; May 17, 352, to Sept. 24, 366.

St. Damasus I: Spain; Oct. 1, 366, to Dec. 11, 384.

St. Siricius: Rome; Dec. 15, or 22 or 29, 384, to Nov. 26, 399.

St. Anastasius I: Rome; Nov. 27, 399, to Dec. 19, 401.

St. Innocent I: Albano; Dec. 22, 401, to Mar. 12, 417.

St. Zozimus: Greece; Mar. 18, 417, to Dec. 26, 418.

St. Boniface I: Rome; Dec. 28 or 29, 418, to Sept. 4, 422.

St. Celestine I: Campania; Sept. 10, 422, to July 27, 432.

St. Sixtus III: Rome; July 31, 432, to Aug. 19, 440.

St. Leo I (the Great): Tuscany; Sept. 29, 440, to Nov. 10, 461.

St. Hilary: Sardinia; Nov. 19, 461, to Feb. 29, 468.

St. Simplicius: Tivoli; Mar. 3, 468, to Mar. 10, 483.

St. Felix III (II): Rome; Mar. 13, 483, to Mar. 1, 492.

He should be called Felix II, and his successors of the same name should be numbered accordingly. The discrepancy in the numerical designation of popes named Felix was caused by the erroneous insertion in some lists of the name of St. Felix of Rome, a martyr.

St. Gelasius I: Africa; Mar. 1, 492, to Nov. 21, 496.

Anastasius II: Rome; Nov. 24, 496, to Nov. 19, 498.

St. Symmachus: Sardinia; Nov. 22, 498, to July 19, 514.

St. Hormisdas: Frosinone; July 20, 514, to Aug. 6, 523.

St. John I, Martyr: Tuscany; Aug. 13, 523, to May 18, 526.

St. Felix IV (III): Samnium; July 12, 526, to Sept. 22, 530.

Boniface II: Rome; Sept. 22, 530, to Oct. 17, 532.

John II: Rome; Jan. 2, 533, to May 8, 535.

John II was the first pope to change his name. His given name was Mercury.

St. Agapitus I: Rome; May 13, 535, to Apr. 22, 536.

St. Silverius, Martyr: Campania; June 1 or 8, 536, to Nov. 11, 537 (d. Dec. 2, 537).

St. Silverius was violently deposed in March, 537, and abdicated Nov. 11, 537. His successor, Vigilius, was not recognized as pope by all the Roman clergy until his abdication.

Vigilius: Rome; Mar. 29, 537, to June 7, 555.

Pelagius I: Rome; Apr. 16, 556, to Mar. 4, 561.

John III: Rome; July 17, 561, to July 13, 574.

Benedict I: Rome; June 2, 575, to July 30, 579.

Pelagius II: Rome; Nov. 26, 579, to Feb. 7, 590.

St. Gregory I (the Great): Rome; Sept. 3, 590, to Mar. 12, 604.

Sabinian: Blera in Tuscany; Sept. 13, 604, to Feb. 22, 606.

Boniface III: Rome; Feb. 19, 607, to Nov. 12, 607.

St. Boniface IV: Abruzzi; Aug. 25, 608, to May 8, 615.

St. Deusdedit (Adeodatus I): Rome; Oct. 19, 615, to Nov. 8, 618.

Boniface V: Naples; Dec. 23, 619, to Oct. 25, 625.

Honorius I: Campania; Oct. 27, 625, to Oct. 12, 638.

Severinus: Rome; May 28, 640, to Aug. 2, 640.

John IV: Dalmatia; Dec. 24, 640, to Oct. 12, 642.

Theodore I: Greece; Nov. 24, 642, to May 14, 649.

St. Martin I, Martyr: Todi; July, 649, to Sept. 16, 655 (in exile from June 17, 653).

St. Eugene I: Rome; Aug. 10, 654, to June 2, 657.

St. Eugene I was elected during the exile of St. Martin I, who is believed to have endorsed him as pope.

St. Vitalian: Segni; July 30, 657, to Jan. 27, 672.

Adeodatus II: Rome; Apr. 11, 672, to June 17, 676.

Donus: Rome; Nov. 2, 676, to Apr. 11, 678.

St. Agatho: Sicily; June 27, 678, to Jan. 10, 681.

St. Leo II: Sicily; Aug. 17, 682, to July 3, 683.

St. Benedict II: Rome; June 26, 684, to May 8, 685.

John V: Syria; July 23, 685, to Aug. 2, 686.

Conon: birthplace unknown; Oct. 21, 686, to Sept. 21, 687.

St. Sergius I: Syria; Dec. 15, 687, to Sept. 8, 701.

John VI: Greece; Oct. 30, 701, to Jan. 11, 705.

John VII: Greece; Mar. 1, 705, to Oct. 18, 707.

Sisinnius: Syria; Jan. 15, 708, to Feb. 4, 708.

Constantine: Syria; Mar. 25, 708, to Apr. 9, 715.

St. Gregory II: Rome; May 19, 715, to Feb. 11, 731.

St. Gregory III: Syria; Mar. 18, 731, to Nov., 741.

St. Zachary: Greece; Dec. 10, 741, to Mar. 22, 752.

Stephen II (III): Rome; Mar. 26, 752, to Apr. 26, 757.

After the death of St. Zachary, a Roman priest named Stephen was elected but died (four days later) before his consecration as bishop of Rome, which would have marked the beginning of his pontificate. Another Stephen was elected to succeed Zachary as Stephen II. (The first pope with this name was St. Stephen I, 254-57.) The ordinal III appears in parentheses after the name of Stephen II because the name of the earlier elected but deceased priest was included in some lists. Other Stephens have double numbers.

St. Paul I: Rome; Apr. (May 29), 757, to June 28, 767.

Stephen III (IV): Sicily; Aug. 1 (7), 768, to Jan. 24, 772.

Adrian I: Rome; Feb. 1 (9), 772, to Dec. 25, 795.

St. Leo III: Rome; Dec. 26 (27), 795, to June 12, 816.

Stephen IV (V): Rome; June 22, 816, to Jan. 24, 817.

St. Paschal I: Rome; Jan. 25, 817, to Feb. 11, 824.

Eugene II: Rome; Feb. (May), 824, to Aug., 827.

Valentine: Rome; Aug. 827, to Sept., 827.

Gregory IV: Rome; 827, to Jan., 844.

Sergius II: Rome; Jan., 844 to Jan. 27, 847.

St. Leo IV: Rome; Jan. (Apr. 10), 847, to July 17, 855.

Benedict III: Rome; July (Sept. 29), 855, to Apr. 17, 858.

St. Nicholas I (the Great): Rome; Apr. 24, 858, to Nov. 13, 867.

Adrian II: Rome; Dec. 14, 867, to Dec. 14, 872.

John VIII: Rome; Dec. 14, 872, to Dec. 16, 882.

Marinus I: Gallese; Dec. 16, 882, to May 15, 884.

St. Adrian III: Rome; May 17, 884, to Sept., 885. Cult confirmed June 2, 1891.

Stephen V (VI): Rome; Sept., 885, to Sept. 14, 891.

Formosus: Bishop of Porto; Oct. 6, 891, to Apr. 4, 896.

Boniface VI: Rome; Apr., 896, to Apr., 896.

Stephen VI (VII): Rome; May, 896, to Aug., 897.

Romanus: Gallese; Aug., 897, to Nov., 897.

Theodore II: Rome; Dec., 897, to Dec., 897.

John IX: Tivoli; Jan., 898, to Jan., 900.

Benedict IV: Rome; Jan. (Feb.), 900, to July, 903.

Leo V: Ardea; July, 903, to Sept., 903.

Sergius III: Rome; Jan. 29, 904, to Apr. 14, 911.

Anastasius III: Rome; Apr., 911, to June, 913.

Landus: Sabina; July, 913, to Feb., 914.

John X: Tossignano (Imola); Mar., 914, to May, 928.

Leo VI: Rome; May, 928, to Dec., 928.

Stephen VII (VIII): Rome; Dec., 928, to Feb., 931.

John XI: Rome; Feb. (Mar.), 931, to Dec., 935.

Leo VII: Rome; Jan. 3, 936, to July 13, 939.

Stephen VIII (IX): Rome; July 14, 939, to Oct., 942.

Marinus II: Rome; Oct. 30, 942, to May, 946.

Agapitus II: Rome; May 10, 946, to Dec., 955.

John XII (Octavius): Tusculum; Dec. 16, 955, to May 14, 964 (date of his death).

Leo VIII: Rome; Dec. 4 (6), 963, to Mar. 1, 965.

Benedict V: Rome; May 22, 964, to July 4, 966.

Confusion exists concerning the legitimacy of claims to the pontificate by Leo VIII and Benedict V. John XII was deposed Dec. 4, 963, by a Roman council. If this deposition was invalid, Leo was an antipope. If the deposition of John was valid, Leo was the legitimate pope and Benedict was an antipope.

John XIII: Rome; Oct. 1, 965, to Sept. 6, 972.

Benedict VI: Rome; Jan. 19, 973, to June, 974.

Benedict VII: Rome; Oct. 974, to July 10, 983.

John XIV (Peter Campenora): Pavia; Dec., 983, to Aug. 20, 984.

John XV: Rome; Aug., 985, to Mar. 996.

Gregory V (Bruno of Carinthia): Saxony; May 3, 996, to Feb. 18, 999.

Sylvester II (Gerbert): Auvergne; Apr. 2, 999, to May 12, 1003.

John XVII (Siccone): Rome; June 1003, to Dec., 1003.

John XVIII (Phasianus): Rome; Jan., 1004, to July, 1009.

Sergius IV (Peter): Rome; July 31, 1009, to May 12, 1012.

The custom of changing one's name on election to the papacy is generally considered to date from the time of Sergius IV. Before his time, several popes had changed their names. After his time, this became a regular practice, with few exceptions; e.g., Adrian VI and Marcellus II.

Benedict VIII (Theophylactus): Tusculum; May 18, 1012, to Apr. 9, 1024.

John XIX (Romanus): Tusculum; Apr. (May), 1024, to 1032.

Benedict IX (Theophylactus): Tusculum; 1032, to 1044.

Sylvester III (John): Rome; Jan. 20, 1045, to Feb. 10, 1045.

Sylvester III was an antipope if the forcible removal of Benedict IX in 1044 was not legitimate.

Benedict IX (second time): Apr. 10, 1045, to May 1, 1045.

Gregory VI (John Gratian): Rome; May 5, 1045, to Dec. 20, 1046.

Clement II (Suitger, Lord of Morsleben and Hornburg): Saxony; Dec. 24 (25), 1046, to Oct. 9, 1047.

If the resignation of Benedict IX in 1045 and his removal at the December, 1046, synod were not legitimate, Gregory VI and Clement II were antipopes.

Benedict IX (third time): Nov. 8, 1047, to July 17, 1048 (d. c. 1055).

Damasus II (Poppo): Bavaria; July 17, 1048, to Aug. 9, 1048.

St. Leo IX (Bruno): Alsace; Feb. 12, 1049, to Apr. 19, 1054.

Victor II (Gebhard): Swabia; Apr. 16, 1055, to July 28, 1057.

Stephen IX (X) (Frederick): Lorraine; Aug. 3, 1057, to Mar. 29, 1058.

Nicholas II (Gerard): Burgundy; Jan. 24, 1059, to July 27, 1061.

Alexander II (Anselmo da Baggio): Milan; Oct. 1, 1061, to Apr. 21, 1073.

St. Gregory VII (Hildebrand): Tuscany; Apr. 22 (June 30), 1073, to May 25, 1085.

Bl. Victor III (Dauferius; Desiderius): Benevento; May 24, 1086, to Sept. 16, 1087. Cult confirmed July 23, 1887.

Bl. Urban II (Otto di Lagery): France; Mar. 12, 1088, to July 29, 1099. Cult confirmed July 14, 1881.

Paschal II (Raniero): Ravenna; Aug. 13 (14), 1099, to Jan. 21, 1118.

Gelasius II (Giovanni Caetani): Gaeta; Jan. 24 (Mar. 10), 1118, to Jan. 28, 1119.

Callistus II (Guido of Burgundy): Burgundy; Feb. 2 (9), 1119, to Dec. 13, 1124.

Honorius II (Lamberto): Fiagnano (Imola); Dec. 15 (21), 1124, to Feb. 13, 1130.

Innocent II (Grgorio Papareschi): Rome; Feb. 14 (23), 1130, to Sept. 24, 1143.

Celestine II (Guido): Citta di Castello; Sept. 26 (Oct. 3), 1143, to Mar. 8, 1144.

Lucius II (Gerardo Caccianemici): Bologna: Mar. 12, 1144, to Feb. 15, 1145.

Bl. Eugene III (Bernardo Paganelli di Montemagno): Pisa; Feb. 15 (18), 1145, to July 8, 1153. Cult confirmed Oct. 3, 1872.

Anastasius IV (Corrado): Rome; July 12, 1153, to Dec, 3, 1154.

Adrian IV (Nicholas Breakspear): England; Dec. 4 (5), 1154, to Sept. 1, 1159.

Alexander III (Rolando Bandinelli): Siena; Sept. 7 (20), 1159, to Aug. 30, 1181.

Lucius III (Ubaldo Allucingoli): Lucca; Sept. 1 (6), 1181, to Sept. 25, 1185.

Urban III (Uberto Crivelli): Milan; Nov. 25 (Dec. 1), 1185, to Oct. 20, 1187.

Gregory VIII (Alberto de Morra): Benevento; Oct. 21 (25), 1187, to Dec. 17, 1187.

Clement III (Paolo Scolari): Rome; Dec. 19 (20), 1187, to Mar., 1191.

Celestine III (Giacinto Bobone): Rome; Mar. 30 (Apr. 14), 1191, to Jan. 8, 1198.

Innocent III (Lotario dei Conti di Segni); Anagni; Jan. 8 (Feb. 22), 1198, to July 16, 1216.

Honorius III (Cencio Savelli): Rome; July 18 (24), 1216, to Mar. 18, 1227.

Gregory IX (Ugolino, Count of Segni): Anagni; Mar. 19 (21), 1227, to Aug. 22, 1241.

Celestine IV (Goffredo Castiglioni): Milan; Oct. 25 (28), 1241, to Nov. 10, 1241.

Innocent IV (Sinibaldo Fieschi): Genoa; June 25 (28), 1243, to Dec. 7, 1254.

Alexander IV (Rinaldo, House of Ienne): Ienne (Rome); Dec. 12 (20), 1254, to May 25, 1261.

Urban IV (Jacques Pantaléon): Troyes; Aug. 29 (Sept. 4), 1261, to Oct. 2, 1264.

Clement IV (Guy Foulques or Guido le Gros): France; Feb. 5 (15), 1265, to Nov. 29, 1268.

Bl. Gregory X (Teobaldo Visconti): Piacenza; Sept. 1, 1271 (Mar. 27, 1272), to Jan. 10, 1276. Cult confirmed Sept. 12, 1713.

Bl. Innocent V (Peter of Tarentaise): Savoy; Jan. 21 (Feb. 22), 1276, to June 22, 1276. Cult confirmed Mar. 13, 1898.

Adrian V (Ottobono Fieschi): Genoa: July 11, 1276, to Aug. 18, 1276.

John XXI (Petrus Juliani or Petrus Hispanus): Portugal; Sept. 8 (20), 1276, to May 20, 1277.

There is confusion in the numerical designation of popes named John. The error dates back to the time of John XV.

Nichols III (Giovanni Gaetano Orsini): Rome; Nov. 25 (Dec. 26), 1277, to Aug. 22, 1280.

Martin IV (Simon de Brie): France; Feb. 22 (Mar. 23), 1281, to Mar. 28, 1285.

The names of Marinus I (882-84) and Marinus II (942-46) were construed as Martin. In view of these two pontificates and the earlier reign of St. Martin I (649-55), this pope was called Martin IV.

Honorius IV (Giacomo Savelli): Rome; Apr. 2 (May 20), 1285, to Apr. 3, 1287.

Nicholas IV (Girolamo Masci): Ascoli; Feb. 22, 1288, to Apr. 4, 1292.

St. Celestine V (Pietro del Murrone): Isernia; July 5 (Aug. 29), 1294, to Dec. 13, 1294; d. 1296. Canonized May 5, 1313.

Boniface VIII (Benedetto Caetani): Anagni; Dec. 24, 1294 (Jan. 23, 1295), to Oct. 11, 1303.

Bl. Benedict XI (Niccolo Boccasini): Treviso; Oct. 22 (27), 1303, to July 7, 1304. Cult confirmed Apr. 24, 1736.

Clement V (Bertrand de Got): France; June 5 (Nov. 14), 1305, to Apr. 20, 1314. (First of Avignon popes.)

John XXII (Jacques d'Euse): Cahors; Aug. 7 (Sept. 5), 1316, to Dec. 4, 1334.

Benedict XII (Jacques Fournier): France; Dec. 20, 1334 (Jan. 8, 1335), to Apr. 25, 1342.

Clement VI (Pierre Roger): France; May 7 (19), 1342, to Dec. 6, 1352.

Innocent VI (Etienne Aubert): France; Dec. 18 (30), 1352, to Sept. 12, 1362.

Bl. Urban V (Guillaume de Grimoard): France; Sept. 28 (Nov. 6), 1362, to Dec. 19, 1370. Cult confirmed Mar. 10, 1870.

Gregory XI (Pierre Roger de Beaufort): France; Dec. 30, 1370 (Jan. 5, 1371), to Mar. 26, 1378. (Last of Avignon popes.)

Urban VI (Bartolomeo Prignano): Naples; Apr. 8 (18), 1378, to Oct. 15, 1389.

Boniface IX (Pietro Tomacelli): Naples; Nov. 2 (9), 1389, to Oct. 1, 1404.

Innocent VII (Cosma Migliorati): Sulmona; Oct. 17 (Nov. 11), 1404, to Nov. 6, 1406.

Gregory XII (Angelo Correr): Venice; Nov. 30 (Dec. 19), 1406, to July 4, 1415, when he voluntarily resigned from the papacy to permit the election ofhis successor. He died Oct. 18, 1417. (See The Western Schism.)

Martin V (Oddone Colonna): Rome; Nov. 11 (21), 1417, to Feb. 20, 1431.

Eugene IV (Gabriele Condulmer): Venice; Mar. 3 (11), 1431, to Feb. 23, 1447.

Nicholas V (Tommaso Parentucelli): Sarzana; Mar. 6 (19), 1447, to Mar. 24, 1455.

Callistus III (Alfonso Borgia): Jativa (Valencia); Apr. 8 (20), 1455, to Aug. 6, 1458.

Pius II (Enea Silvio Piccolomini): Siena; Aug. 19 (Sept. 3), 1458, to Aug. 14, 1464.

Paul II (Pietro Barbo): Venice; Aug. 30 (Sept. 16), 1464, to July 26, 1471.

Sixtus IV (Francesco della Rovere): Savona; Aug. 9 (25), 1471, to Aug. 12, 1484.

Innocent VIII (Giovanni Battista Cibo): Genoa; Aug. 29 (Sept. 12), 1484, to July 25, 1492.

Alexander VI (Rodrigo Borgia): Jativa (Valencia); Aug. 11 (26), 1492, to Aug. 18, 1503.

Pius III (Francesco Todeschini-Piccolomini): Siena; Sept. 22 (Oct. 1, 8), 1503, to Oct. 18, 1503.

Julius II (Giuliano della Rovere): Savona; Oct. 31 (Nov. 26), 1503, to Feb. 21, 1513.

Leo X (Giovanni de' Medici): Florence; Mar. 9 (19), 1513, to Dec. 1, 1521.

Adrian VI (Adrian Florensz): Utrecht; Jan. 9 (Aug. 31), 1522, to Sept. 14, 1523.

Clement VII (Giulio de' Medici): Florence; Nov. 19 (26), 1523, to Sept. 25, 1534.

Paul III (Alessandro Farnese): Rome; Oct. 13 (Nov. 3), 1534, to Nov. 10, 1549.

Julius III (Giovanni Maria Ciocchi del Monte): Rome; Feb. 7 (22), 1550, to Mar. 23, 1555.

Marcellus II (Marcello Cervini): Montepulciano; Apr. 9 (10), 1555, to May 1, 1555.

Paul IV (Gian Pietro Carafa): Naples; May 23 (26), 1555, to Aug. 18, 1559.

Pius IV (Giovan Angelo de' Medici): Milan; Dec. 25, 1559 (Jan. 6, 1560), to Dec. 9, 1565.

St. Pius V (Antonio-Michele Ghislieri): Bosco (Alexandria); Jan. 7 (17), 1566, to May 1, 1572. Canonized May 22, 1712.

Gregory XIII (Ugo Buoncompagni): Bologna; May 13 (25), 1572, to Apr. 10, 1585.

Sixtus V (Felice Peretti): Grottammare (Ripatransone); Apr. 24 (May 1), 1585, to Aug. 27, 1590.

Urban VII (Giovanni Battista Castagna): Rome; Sept. 15, 1590, to Sept. 27, 1590.

Gregory XIV (Niccolo Sfondrati): Cremona; Dec. 5 (8), 1590, to Oct. 16, 1591.

Innocent IX (Giovanni Antonio Facchinetti): Bologna; Oct. 29 (Nov. 3), 1591, to Dec. 30, 1591.

Clement VIII (Ippolito Aldobrandini): Florence; Jan. 30 (Feb. 9), 1592, to Mar. 3, 1605.

Leo XI (Alessandro de' Medici): Florence; Apr. 1 (10), 1605, to Apr. 27, 1605.

Paul V (Camillo Borghese): Rome; May 16 (29), 1605, to Jan. 28, 1621.

Gregory XV (Alessandro Ludovisi): Bologna; Feb. 9 (14), 1621, to July 8, 1623.

Urban VIII (Maffeo Barberini): Florence; Aug. 6 (Sept. 29), 1623, to July 29, 1644.

Innocent X (Giovanni Battista Pamfili): Rome; Sept. 15 (Oct. 4), 1644, to Jan. 7, 1655.

Alexander VII (Fabio Chigi): Siena; Apr. 7 (18), 1655, to May 22, 1667.

Clement IX (Giulio Rospigliosi): Pistoia; June 20 (26), 1667, to Dec. 9, 1669.

Clement X (Emilio Altieri): Rome; Apr. 29 (May 11), 1670, to July 22, 1676.

Bl. Innocent XI (Benedetto Odescalchi): Como; Sept. 21 (Oct. 4), 1676, to Aug. 12, 1689. Beatified Oct. 7, 1956.

Alexander VIII (Pietro Ottoboni): Venice; Oct. 6 (16), 1689, to Feb. 1, 1691.

Innocent XII (Antonio Pignatelli): Spinazzola (Venosa); July 12 (15), 1691, to Sept. 27, 1700.

Clement XI (Giovanni Francesco Albani): Urbino; Nov. 23, 30 (Dec. 8), 1700, to Mar. 19, 1721.

Innocent XIII (Michelangelo dei Conti): Rome; May 8 (18), 1721, to Mar. 7, 1724.

Benedict XIII (Pietro Francesco — Vincenzo Maria — Orsini): Gravina (Bari); May 29 (June 4), 1724, to Feb. 21, 1730.

Clement XII (Lorenzo Corsini): Florence; July 12 (16), 1730, to Feb. 6, 1740.

Benedict XIV (Prospero Lambertini): Bologna; Aug. 17 (22), 1740, to May 3, 1758.

Clement XIII (Carlo Rezzonico): Venice; July 6 (16), 1758, to Feb. 2, 1769.

Clement XIV (Giovanni Vincenzo Antonio — Lorenzo — Ganganelli): Rimini; May 19, 28 (June 4), 1769, to Sept. 22, 1774.

Pius VI (Giovanni Angelo Braschi): Cesena; Feb. 15 (22), 1775, to Aug. 29, 1799.

Pius VII (Barnaba — Gregorio — Chiaramonti): Cesena; Mar. 14 (21), 1800, to Aug. 20, 1823.

Leo XII (Annibale della Genga): Genga (Fabriano); Sept. 28 (Oct. 5), 1823, to Feb. 10, 1829.

Pius VIII (Francesco Saverio Castiglioni): Cingoli; Mar. 31 (Apr. 5), 1829, to Nov. 30, 1830.

Gregory XVI (Bartolomeo Alberto — Mauro — Cappellari): Belluno; Feb. 2 (6), 1831, to June 1, 1846.

Pius IX (Giovanni M. Mastai-Ferretti): Senigallia; June 16 (21), 1846, to Feb. 7, 1878.

Leo XIII (Gioacchino Pecci): Carpineto (Anagni); Feb. 20 (Mar. 3), 1878, to July 20, 1903.

St. Pius X (Giuseppe Sarto): Riese (Treviso); Aug. 4 (9), 1903, to Aug. 20, 1914. Canonized May 29, 1954.

Benedit XV (Giacomo della Chiesa): Genoa; Sept. 3 (6), 1914, to Jan. 22, 1922.

Pius XI (Achille Ratti): Desio (Milan); Feb. 6 (12), 1922, to Feb. 10, 1939.

Pius XII (Eugenio Pacelli): Rome; Mar. 2 (12), 1939, to Oct. 9, 1958.

John XXIII (Angelo Giuseppe Roncalli): Sotto il Monte (Bergamo); Oct. 28 (Nov. 4), 1958, to June 3, 1963.

Paul VI (Giovanni Battista Montini): Concessio (Brescia); June 21 (30), 1963, to Aug. 6, 1978.

John Paul I (Albino Luciani): Forno di Canale (Belluno); Aug. 26 (Sept. 3), 1978, to Sept. 28, 1978.

John Paul II (Karol Wojtyla): Wadowice, Poland; Oct. 16 (22), 1978.

## ANTIPOPES

*This list of men who claimed or exercised the papal office in an uncanonical manner includes names, birthplaces and dates of alleged reigns.*
*Source: "Annuario Pontificio."*

St. Hippolytus: Rome; 217-235; was reconciled before his death.

Novatian: Rome; 251.

Felix II: Rome; 355 to Nov. 22, 365.

Ursinus: 366-367.

Eulalius: Dec. 27 or 29, 418, to 419.

Lawrence: 498; 501-505.

Dioscorus: Alexandria; Sept. 22, 530, to Oct. 14, 530.

Theodore: ended alleged reign, 687.

Paschal: ended alleged reign, 687.

Constantine: Nepi; June 28 (July 5), 767, to 769.

Philip: July 31, 768; retired to his monastery on the same day.

John: ended alleged reign, Jan., 844.

Anastasius: Aug., 855, to Sept., 855; d. 880.

Christopher: Rome; July or Sept., 903, to Jan., 904.

Boniface VII: Rome; June, 974, to July, 974; Aug., 984, to July, 985.

John XVI: Rossano; Apr., 997, to Feb., 998.

Gregory: ended alleged reign, 1012.

Benedict X: Rome; Apr. 5, 1058, to Jan. 24, 1059.

Honorius II: Verona; Oct. 28, 1061, to 1072.

Clement III: Parma; June 25, 1080 (Mar. 24, 1084), to Sept. 8, 1100.

Theodoric: ended alleged reign, 1100; d. 1102.

Albert: ended alleged reign, 1102.

Sylvester IV: Rome; Nov. 18, 1105, to 1111.

Gregory VIII: France; Mar. 8, 1118, to 1121.

Celestine II: Rome; ended alleged reign, Dec., 1124.

Anacletus II: Rome; Feb. 14 (23), 1130, to Jan. 25, 1138.

Victor IV: Mar., 1138, to May 29, 1138; submitted to Pope Innocent II.

Victor IV: Montecelio; Sept. 7 (Oct. 4), 1159, to Apr. 20, 1164; he did not recognize his predecessor (Victor IV, above).

Paschal III: Apr. 22 (26), 1164, to Sept. 20, 1168.

Callistus III: Arezzo; Sept., 1168, to Aug. 29, 1178; submitted to Pope Alexander III.

Innocent III: Sezze; Sept. 29, 1179, to 1180.

Nicholas V: Corvaro (Rieti); May 12 (22), 1328, to Aug. 25, 1330; d. Oct. 16, 1333.

*Four antipopes of the Western Schism:*

Clement VII: Sept. 20 (Oct. 31), 1378, to Sept. 16, 1394.

Benedict XIII: Aragon; Sept. 28 (Oct. 11), 1394, to May 23, 1423.

Alexander V: Crete; June 26 (July 7), 1409, to May 3, 1410.

John XXIII: Naples; May 17 (25), 1410, to May 29, 1415. (Date of deposition by Council of Constance which ended the Western Schism; d. Nov. 22, 1419.)

Felix V: Savoy; Nov. 5, 1439 (July 24, 1440), to April 7, 1449; d. 1451.

## AVIGNON PAPCY

Avignon was the residence (1309-77) of a series of French popes (Clement V, John XXII, Benedict XII, Clement VI, Innocent VI, Urban V and Gregory XI). Prominent in the period were power struggles over the mixed interests of Church and state with the rulers of France (Philip IV, John II), Bavaria (Lewis IV), England (Edward III); factionalism of French and Italian churchmen; political as well as ecclesiastical turmoil in Italy, a factor of significance in prolonging the stay of popes in Avignon. Despite some positive achievements, the Avignon papacy was a prologue to the Western Schism which began in 1378.

## WESTERN SCHISM

The Western Schism was a confused state of affairs which divided Christendom into two and then three papal obediences from 1378 to 1417.

It occurred some 50 years after Marsilius theorized that a general (not ecumenical) council of bishops and other persons was superior to a pope and nearly 30 years before the Council of Florence stated definitively that no kind of council had such authority.

It was a period of disaster preceding the even more disastrous period of the Reformation.

Urban VI, following the return of the papal residence to Rome after approximately 70 years at Avignon, was elected pope Apr. 8, 1378, and reigned until his death in 1389. He was succeeded by Boniface IX (1389-1404), Innocent VII (1404-1406) and Gregory XII (1406-1415). These four are considered the legitimate popes of the period.

Some of the cardinals who chose Urban pope, dissatisfied with his conduct of the office, declared that his election was invalid. They proceeded to elect Clement VII, who claimed the papacy from 1378 to 1394. He was succeeded by Benedict XIII.

Prelates seeking to end the state of divided papal loyalties convoked the Council of Pisa (1409) which, without authority, found Gregory XII and Benedict XIII, in absentia, guilty on 30-odd charges of schism and heresy, deposed them, and elected a third claimant to the papacy, Alexander V (1409-1410). He was succeeded by John XXIII (1410-1415).

The schism was ended by the Council of Constance (1414-1418). This council, although originally called into session in an irregular manner, acquired authority after being convoked by Gregory XII in 1415. In its early irregular phase, it deposed John XXIII whose election to the papacy was uncanonical anyway. After being formally convoked, it accepted the abdication of Gregory in 1415 and dismissed the claims of Benedict XIII two years later, thus clearing the way for the election of Martin V on Nov. 11, 1417. The Council of Constance also rejected the theories of John Wycliff and condemned John Hus as a heretic.

# TWENTIETH CENTURY POPES

## LEO XIII

Leo XIII (Gioacchino Vincenzo Pecci) was born May 2, 1810, in Carpineto, Italy. Although all but three years of his life and pontificate were of the 19th century, his influence extended well into the 20th century.

He was educated at the Jesuit college in Viterbo, the Roman College, the Academy of Noble Ecclesiastics, and the University of the Sapienza. He was ordained to the priesthood in 1837.

He served as an apostolic delegate to two States of the Church, Benevento from 1838 to 1841 and Perugia in 1841 and 1842. Ordained titular archbishop of Damietta, he was papal nuncio to Belgium from January, 1843, until May, 1846; in the post, he had controversial relations with the government over education issues and acquired his first significant experience of industrialized society.

He was archbishop of Perugia from 1846 to 1878. He became a cardinal in 1853 and chamberlain of the Roman Curia in 1877. He was elected to the papacy Feb. 20, 1878. He died July 20, 1903.

**Canonizations:** He canonized 18 saints and beatified a group of English martyrs.

**Church Administration:** He established 300 new dioceses and vicariates; restored the hierarchy in Scotland, set up an English, as contrasted with the

Portuguese, hierarchy in India; approved the action of the Congregation for the Propagation of the Faith in reorganizing missions in China.

**Encyclicals:** He issued 86 encyclicals, on subjects ranging from devotional to social. In the former category were *Annum Sacrum,* on the Sacred Heart, in 1899, and 11 letters on Mary and the Rosary.

**Social Questions:** Much of Leo's influence stemmed from social doctrine stated in numerous encyclicals, concerning liberalism, liberty, the divine origin of authority; socialism, in *Quod Apostolici Muneris,* 1878; the Christian concept of the family, in *Arcanum,* 1880; socialism and economic liberalism, relations between capital and labor, in *Rerum Novarum,* 1891. Two of his social encyclicals were against the African slave trade.

**Interfaith Relations:** He was unsuccessful in unity overtures made to Orthodox and Slavic Churches. He declared Anglican orders invalid in the apostolic bull *Apostolicae Curae* Sept. 13, 1896.

**International Relations:** Leo was frustrated in seeking solutions to the Roman Question arising from the seizure of church lands by the Kingdom of Italy in 1870. He also faced anticlerical situations in Belgium and France and in the Kulturkampf policies of Bismarck in Germany.

**Studies:** In the encyclical *Aeterni Patris* of Aug. 4, 1879, he ordered a renewal of philosophical and theological studies in seminaries along scholastic, and especially Thomistic, lines, to counteract influential trends of liberalism and Modernism. He issued guidelines for biblical exegesis in *Providentissimus Deus* Nov. 18, 1893, and established the Pontifical Biblical Commission in 1902.

In other actions affecting scholarship and study, he opened the Vatican Archives to scholars in 1883 and established the Vatican Observatory.

**United States:** He authorized establishment of the apostolic delegation in Washington, D.C., Jan. 24, 1893. He refused to issue a condemnation of the Knights of Labor. With a document entitled *Testem Benevolentiae,* he eased resolution of questions concerning what was called an American heresy in 1899.

## ST. PIUS X

St. Pius X (Giuseppe Melchiorre Sarto) was born in 1835 in Riese, Italy. Educated at the college of Castelfranco and the seminary at Padua, he was ordained to the priesthood Sept. 18, 1858. He served as a curate in Trombolo for nine years before beginning an eight-year pastorate at Salzano. He was chancellor of the Treviso diocese from November, 1875, and bishop of Mantua from 1884 until 1893. He was cardinal-patriarch of Venice from that year until his election to the papacy by the conclave held from July 31 to Aug. 4, 1903.

**Aims:** Pius' principal objectives as pope were "to restore all things in Christ, in order that Christ may be all and in all," and "to teach (and defend) Christian truth and law."

**Canonizations, Encyclicals:** He canonized four saints and issued 16 encyclicals. One of the encyclicals was issued in commemoration of the 50th anniversary of the proclamation of the dogma of the Immaculate Conception of Mary.

**Catechetics:** He introduced a whole new era of religious instruction and formation with the encyclical *Acerbo Nimis* of Apr. 15, 1905, in which he called for vigor in establishing and conducting parochial programs of the Confraternity of Christian Doctrine.

**Catholic Action:** He outlined the role of official Catholic Action in two encyclicals in 1905 and 1906. Favoring organized action by Catholics themselves, he had serious reservations about interconfessional collaboration.

He stoutly maintained claims to papal rights in the anticlerical climate of Italy. He authorized bishops to relax prohibitions against participation by Catholics in some Italian elections.

**Church Administration:** With the motu proprio *Arduum Sane* of Mar. 19, 1904, he inaugurated the work which resulted in the Code of Canon Law; the code was completed in 1917 and went into effect in the following year. He reorganized and strengthened the Roman Curia with the apostolic constitution *Sapienti Consilio* of June 29, 1908.

While promoting the expansion of missionary work, he removed from the jurisdiction of the Congregation for the Propagation of the Faith the Church in the United States, Canada, Newfoundland, England, Ireland, Holland and Luxembourg.

**International Relations:** He ended traditional prerogatives of Catholic governments with respect to papal elections, in 1904. He opposed anti-Church and anticlerical actions in several countries: Bolivia in 1905, because of anti-religious legislation; France in 1906, for its 1901 action in annulling its concordat with the Holy See, and for the 1905 Law of Separation by which it decreed separation of Church and state, ordered the confiscation of church property, and blocked religious education and the activities of religious orders; Portugal in 1911, for the separation of Church and state and repressive measures which resulted in persecution later.

In 1912 he called on the bishops of Brazil to work for the improvement of conditions among Indians.

**Liturgy:** "The Pope of the Eucharist," he strongly recommended the frequent reception of Holy Communion in a decree dated Dec. 20, 1905; in another decree, *Quam Singulari,* of Aug. 8, 1910, he called for the early reception of the sacrament by children. He initiated measures for liturgical reform with new norms for sacred music and the start of work on revision of the *Breviary* for recitation of the Divine Office.

**Modernism:** Pius was a vigorous opponent of "the synthesis of all heresies," which threatened the integrity of doctrine through its influence in philosophy, theology and biblical exegesis. In opposition, he condemned 65 of its propositions as erroneous in the decree *Lamentabili* July 3, 1907; issued the encyclical *Pascendi* in the same vein Sept. 8, 1907; backed both of these with censures; and published the Oath against Modernism in September, 1910, to be taken by all the clergy. Ecclesiastical studies suffered to some extent from these actions, necessary as they were at the time.

Pius followed the lead of Leo XIII in promoting the study of scholastic philosophy. He established the Pontifical Biblical Institute May 7, 1909.

His death, Aug. 20, 1914, was hastened by the outbreak of World War I. He was beatified in 1951 and canonized May 29, 1954. His feast is observed Aug. 21.

## BENEDICT XV

Benedict XV (Giacomo della Chiesa) was born Nov. 21, 1854, in Pegli, Italy.

He was educated at the Royal University of Genoa and Gregorian University in Rome. He was ordained to the priesthood Dec. 21, 1878.

He served in the papal diplomatic corps from 1882 to 1907; as secretary to the nuncio to Spain from 1882 to 1887, as secretary to the papal secretary of state from 1887, and as undersecretary from 1901.

He was ordained archbishop of Bologna Dec. 22, 1907, and spent four years completing a pastoral visitation there. He was made a cardinal just three months before being elected to the papacy Sept. 3, 1914. He died Jan. 22, 1922. Two key efforts of his pontificate were for peace and the relief of human suffering caused by World War I.

**Canonizations:** Benedict canonized three saints; one of them was Joan of Arc.

**Canon Law:** He published the Code of Canon Law, developed by the commission set up by St. Pius X, May 27, 1917; it went into effect the following year.

**Curia:** He made great changes in the personnel of the Curia. He established the Congregation for the Oriental Churches May 1, 1917, and founded the Pontifical Oriental Institute in Rome later in the year.

**Encyclicals:** He issued 12 encyclicals. Peace was the theme of three of them. In another, published two years after the cessation of hostilities, he wrote about child victims of the war. He followed the lead of Leo XIII in *Spiritus Paraclitus*, Sept. 15, 1920, on biblical studies.

**International Relations:** He was largely frustrated on the international level because of the events and attitudes of the war period, but the number of diplomats accredited to the Vatican nearly doubled, from 14 to 26, between the time of his accession to the papacy and his death.

**Peace Efforts:** Benedict's stance in the war was one of absolute impartiality but not of uninterested neutrality. Because he would not take sides, he was suspected by both sides and the seven-point peace plan he offered to all belligerents Aug. 1, 1917, was turned down. The points of the plan were: recognition of the moral force of right; disarmament; acceptance of arbitration in cases of dispute; guarantee of freedom of the seas; renunciation of war indemnities; evacuation and restoration of occupied territories; examination of territorial claims in dispute.

**Relief Efforts:** Benedict assumed personal charge of Vatican relief efforts during the war. He set up an international missing persons bureau for contacts between prisoners and their families, but was forced to close it because of the suspicion of warring nations that it was a front for espionage operations. He persuaded the Swiss government to admit into the country military victims of tuberculosis.

**Roman Question:** Benedict prepared the way for the meetings and negotiations which led to settlement of the question in 1929.

## PIUS XI

Pius XI (Ambrogio Damiano Achille Ratti) was born May 31, 1857, in Desio, Italy.

Educated at seminaries in Seviso and Milan, and at the Lombard College, Gregorian University and Academy of St. Thomas in Rome, he was ordained to the priesthood in 1879.

He taught at the major seminary of Milan from 1882 to 1888. Appointed to the staff of the Ambrosian Library in 1888, he remained there until 1911, acquiring a reputation for publishing works on paleography and serving as director from 1907 to 1911. He then moved to the Vatican Library, of which he was prefect from 1914 to 1918. In 1919, he was named apostolic visitor to Poland in April, nuncio in June, and was made titular archbishop of Lepanto Oct. 28. He was made archbishop of Milan and cardinal June 13, 1921, before being elected to the papacy Feb. 6, 1922. He died Feb. 10, 1939.

**Aim:** The objective of his pontificate, as stated in the encyclical *Ubi Arcano*, Dec. 23, 1922, was to establish the reign and peace of Christ in society.

**Canonizations:** He canonized 34 saints, including the Jesuit Martyrs of North America, and conferred the title of Doctor of the Church on Sts. Peter Canisius, John of the Cross, Robert Bellarmine and Albertus Magnus.

**Eastern Churches:** He called for better understanding of the Eastern Churches in the encyclical *Rerum Orientalium* of Sept. 8, 1928, and developed facilities for the training of Eastern-Rite priests. He inaugurated steps for the codification of Eastern-Church law in 1929. In 1935 he made Syrian Patriarch Tappouni a cardinal.

**Encyclicals:** His first encyclical, *Ubi Arcano*, in addition to stating the aims of his pontificate, blueprinted Catholic Action and called for its development throughout the Church. In *Quas Primas*, Dec. 11, 1925, he established the feast of Christ the King for universal observance. Subjects of some of his other encyclicals were: Christian education, in *Rappresentanti in Terra*, Dec. 31, 1929; Christian marriage, in *Casti Connubii*, Dec. 31, 1930; social conditions and pressure for social change in line with the teaching in *Rerum Novarum*, in *Quadragesimo Anno*, May 15, 1931; atheistic Communism, in *Divini Redemptoris*, Mar. 19, 1937; the priesthood, in *Ad Catholici Sacerdotii*, Dec. 20, 1935.

**Missions:** Following the lead of Benedict XV, Pius called for the training of native clergy in the pattern of their own respective cultures, and promoted missionary developments in various ways. He ordained six native bishops for China in 1926, one for Japan in 1927, and others for regions of Asia, China and India in 1933. He placed the first 40 mission dioceses under native bishops, saw the number of native priests increase from about 2,600 to more than 7,000 and the number of Catholics in missionary areas more than double from nine million.

In the apostolic constitution *Deus Scientiarum Dominus* of May 24, 1931, he ordered the introduction of missiology into theology courses.

**Interfaith Relations:** Pius was negative to the ecumenical movement among Protestants but approved the Malines Conversations, 1921 to 1926, between Anglicans and Catholics.

**International Relations:** Relations with the Mussolini government deteriorated from 1931 on, as indicated in the encyclical *Non Abbiamo Bisogno*, when the regime took steps to curb liberties and activities of the Church; they turned critical in 1938 with the emergence of racist policies. Relations deteriorated also in Germany from 1933 on, resulting finally in condemnation of the Nazis in the encyclical *Mit Brennender Sorge*, March, 1937. Pius sparked a revival of the Church in France by encouraging Catholics to work within the democratic framework of the Republic rather than foment trouble over restoration of a monarchy. Pius was powerless to influence developments related to the civil war which erupted in Spain in July, 1936, sporadic persecution and repression by the Calles regime in Mexico, and systematic persecution of the Church in the Soviet Union. Many of the 10 concordats and two agreements reached with European countries after World War I became casualties of World War II.

**Roman Question:** Pius negotiated for two and one-half years with the Italian government to settle the Roman Question by means of the Lateran Agreement of 1929. The agreement provided independent status for the State of Vatican City; made Catholicism the official religion of Italy, with pastoral and educational freedom and state recognition of Catholic marriages, religious orders and societies; and provided a financial payment to the Vatican for expropriation of the former States of the Church.

## PIUS XII

Pius XII (Eugenio Maria Giovanni Pacelli) was born Mar. 2, 1876, in Rome.

Educated at the Gregorian University and the Lateran University, in Rome, he was ordained to the priesthood Apr. 2, 1899.

He entered the Vatican diplomatic service in 1901, worked on the codification of canon law, and was appointed secretary of the Congregation for Ecclesiastical Affairs in 1914. Three years later he was ordained titular archbishop of Sardis and made apostolic nuncio to Bavaria. He was nuncio to Germany from 1920 to 1929, when he was made a cardinal, and took office as papal secretary of state the following year. His diplomatic negotiations resulted in concordats between the Vatican and Bavaria (1924), Prussia (1929), Baden (1932), Austria and the German Republic (1933). He took part in negotiations which led to settlement of the Roman Question in 1929.

He was elected to the papacy Mar. 2, 1939. He died Oct. 9, 1958, at Castel Gandolfo after the 12th longest pontificate in history.

**Canonizations:** He canonized 34 saints, including Mother Frances X. Cabrini, the first U.S. citizen-Saint.

**Cardinals:** He raised 56 prelates to the rank of cardinal in two consistories held in 1946 and 1953. There were 57 cardinals at the time of his death.

**Church Organization and Missions:** He increased the number of dioceses from 1,696 to 2,048. He established native hierarchies in China (1946), Burma (1955) and parts of Africa, and extended the native structure of the Church in India. He ordained the first black bishop for Africa.

**Communism:** In addition to opposing and condemning Communism on numerous occasions, he decreed in 1949 the penalty of excommunication for all Catholics holding formal and willing allegiance to the Communist Party and its policies. During his reign the Church was persecuted in some 15 countries which fell under communist domination.

**Doctrine and Liturgy:** He proclaimed the dogma of the Assumption of the Blessed Virgin Mary Nov. 1, 1950 (apostolic constitution, *Munificentissimus Deus*).

In various encyclicals and other enactments, he provided background for the *aggiornamento* introduced by his successor, John XXIII: by his formulations of doctrine and practice regarding the Mystical Body of Christ, the liturgy, sacred music and biblical studies; by the revision of the Rites of Holy Week; by initiation of the work which led to the calendar-missal-breviary reform ordered into effect Jan. 1, 1961; by the first of several modifications of the Eucharistic fast; by extending the time of Mass to the evening. He instituted the feasts of Mary, Queen, and of St. Joseph the Worker, and clarified teaching concerning devotion to the Sacred Heart.

His 41 encyclicals and nearly 1,000 public addresses made Pius one of the greatest teaching popes. His concern in all his communications was to deal with specific points at issue and/or to bring Christian principles to bear on contemporary world problems.

**Peace Efforts:** Before the start of World War II, he tried unsuccessfully to get the contending nations — Germany and Poland, France and Italy — to settle their differences peaceably. During the war, he offered his services to mediate the widened conflict, spoke out against the horrors of war and the suffering it caused, mobilized relief work for its victims, proposed a five-point program for peace in Christmas messages from 1939 to 1942, and secured a generally open status for the city of Rome. After the war, he endorsed the principles and intent of the United Nations and continued efforts for peace.

**United States:** Pius appointed more than 200 of the 265 American bishops resident in the U.S. and abroad in 1958, erected 27 dioceses in this country, and raised seven dioceses to archiepiscopal rank.

## JOHN XXIII

John XXIII (Angelo Roncalli) was born Nov. 25, 1881, at Sotte il Monte, Italy.

He was educated at the seminary of the Bergamo diocese and the Pontifical Seminary in Rome, where he was ordained to the priesthood Aug. 10, 1904.

He spent the first nine or 10 years of his priesthood as secretary to the bishop of Bergamo and as an instructor in the seminary there. He served as a medic and chaplain in the Italian army during World War I. Afterwards, he resumed duties in his own diocese until he was called to Rome in 1921 for work with the Society for the Propagation of the Faith.

He began diplomatic service in 1925 as titular archbishop of Areopolis and apostolic visitor to Bulgaria. A succession of offices followed: apostolic delegate to Bulgaria (1931-1935); titular archbishop of Mesembria, apostolic delegate to Turkey and Greece, administrator of the Latin vicariate apostolic of Istanbul (1935-1944); apostolic nuncio to France (1944-1953). On these missions, he was engaged in delicate negotiations involving Roman, Eastern-Rite and Orthodox relations; the needs of people suffering from the consequences of World War II; and unsettling suspicions arising from wartime conditions.

He was made a cardinal Jan. 12, 1953, and three days later was appointed patriarch of Venice, the position he held until his election to the papacy Oct. 28, 1958. He died of stomach cancer June 3, 1963.

John was a strong and vigorous pope whose influence far out-measured both his age and the shortness of his time in the papacy.

**Second Vatican Council:** John announced Jan. 25, 1959, his intention of convoking the 21st ecumenical council in history to renew life in the Church, to reform its structures and institutions, and to explore ways and means of promoting unity among Christians. Through the council, which completed its work two and one-half years after his death, he ushered in a new era in the history of the Church.

**Canon Law:** He established a commission Mar. 28, 1963, for revision of the Code of Canon Law. The revised Code was promulgated in 1983.

**Canonizations:** He canonized 10 saints and beatified Mother Elizabeth Ann Seton, the first native of the U.S. ever so honored. He named St. Lawrence of Brindisi a Doctor of the Church.

**Cardinals:** He created 52 cardinals in five consistories, raising membership of the College of Cardinals above the traditional number of 70; at one time in 1962, the membership was 87. He made the college more international in representation than it had ever been, appointing the first cardinals from the Philippines, Japan and Africa. He ordered episcopal ordination for all cardinals. He relieved the suburban bishops of Rome of ordinary jurisdiction over their dioceses so they might devote all their time to business of the Roman Curia.

**Eastern Rites:** He made all Eastern-Rite patriarchs members of the Congregation for the Oriental Churches.

**Ecumenism:** He assigned to the Second Vatican Council the task of finding ways and means of promoting unity among Christians. He established the Vatican Secretariat for Promoting Christian Unity June 5, 1960. He showed his desire for more cordial relations with the Orthodox by sending personal representatives to visit Patriarch Athenagoras I June 27, 1961; approved a mission of five delegates to the General Assembly of the World Council of Churches which met in New Delhi, India, in November, 1961; removed a number of pejorative references to Jews in the Roman-Rite liturgy for Good Friday.

**Encyclicals:** Of the eight encyclicals he issued, the two outstanding ones were *Mater et Magistra* ("Christianity and Social Progress"), in which he recapitulated, updated and extended the social doctrine stated earlier by Leo XIII and Pius XI; and *Pacem in Terris* ("Peace on Earth"), the first encyclical ever addressed to all men of good will as well as to Catholics, on the natural-law principles of peace.

**Liturgy:** In forwarding liturgical reforms already begun by Pius XII, he ordered a calendar-missal-breviary reform into effect Jan. 1, 1961. He authorized the use of vernacular languages in the administration of the sacraments and approved giving Holy Communion to the sick in afternoon hours. He se-

lected the liturgy as the first topic of major discussion by the Second Vatican Council.

**Missions:** He issued an encyclical on the missionary activity of the Church; established native hierarchies in Indonesia, Vietnam and Korea; and called on North American superiors of religious institutes to have one-tenth of their members assigned to work in Latin America by 1971.

**Peace:** John spoke and used his moral influence for peace in 1961 when tension developed over Berlin, in 1962 during the Algerian revolt from France, and later the same year in the Cuban missile crisis. His efforts were singled out for honor by the Balzan Peace Foundation. In 1963, he was posthumously awarded the U.S. Presidential Medal of Freedom.

## PAUL VI

Paul VI (Giovanni Battista Montini) was born Sept. 26, 1897, at Concesio in northern Italy.

Educated at Brescia, he was ordained to the priesthood May 29, 1920. He pursued additional studies at the Pontifical Academy for Noble Ecclesiastics and the Pontifical Gregorian University. In 1924 he began 30 years of service in the Secretariat of State; as undersecretary from 1937 until 1954, he was closely associated with Pius XII and was heavily engaged in organizing informational and relief services during and after World War II.

He was ordained archbishop of Milan Dec. 12, 1954, and was inducted into the College of Cardinals Dec. 15, 1958. He was elected to the papacy June 21, 1963, two days after the conclave began. He died of a heart attack Aug. 6, 1978.

**Second Vatican Council:** He reconvened the Second Vatican Council after the death of John XXIII, presided over its second, third and fourth sessions, formally promulgated the 16 documents it produced, and devoted the whole of his pontificate to the task of putting them into effect throughout the Church. The main thrust of his pontificate — in a milieu of cultural and other changes in the Church and the world — was toward institutionalization and control of the authentic trends articulated and set in motion by the council.

**Canonizations:** He canonized 84 saints. They included groups of 22 Ugandan martyrs and 40 martyrs of England and Wales, as well as two Americans — Elizabeth Ann Bayley Seton and John Nepomucene Neumann.

**Cardinals:** He created 144 cardinals, and gave the Sacred College a more international complexion than it ever had before. He limited participation in papal elections to 120 cardinals under the age of 80.

**Collegiality:** He established the Synod of Bishops in 1965 and called it into session five times. He stimulated the formation and operation of regional conferences of bishops, and of consultative bodies on other levels.

**Creed and Holy Year:** On June 30, 1968, he issued a Creed of the People of God in conjunction with the celebration of a Year of Faith. He proclaimed and led the observance of a Holy Year from Christmas Eve of 1974 to Christmas Eve of 1975.

**Diplomacy:** He met with many world leaders, including Soviet President Nikolai Podgorny in 1967, Marshal Tito of Yugoslavia in 1971 and President

Nicolas Ceausescu of Romania in 1973. He worked constantly to reduce tension between the Church and the intransigent regimes of Eastern European countries by means of a detente type of policy called Ostpolitik. He agreed to significant revisions of the Vatican's concordat with Spain and initiated efforts to revise the concordat with Italy. More than 40 countries established diplomatic relations with the Vatican during his pontificate.

**Encyclicals:** He issued seven encyclicals, three of which are the best known. In *Populorum Progressio* ("Development of Peoples") he appealed to wealthy countries to take "concrete action" to promote human development and to remedy imbalances between richer and poorer nations; this encyclical, coupled with other documents and related actions, launched the Church into a new depth of involvement as a public advocate for human rights and for humanizing social, political and economic policies. In *Sacerdotalis Caelibatus* ("Priestly Celibacy") he reaffirmed the strict observance of priestly celibacy throughout the Western Church. In *Humanae Vitae* ("Of Human Life") he condemned abortion, sterilization and artificial birth control, in line with traditional teaching and in "defense of life, the gift of God, the glory of the family, the strength of the people."

**Interfaith Relations:** He initiated formal consultation and informal dialogue on international and national levels between Catholics and non-Catholics — Orthodox, Anglicans, Protestants, Jews, Moslems, Buddhists, Hindus, and unbelievers. He and Greek Orthodox Patriarch Athenagoras I of Constantinople nullified in 1965 the mutual excommunications imposed by their respective churches in 1054.

**Liturgy:** He carried out the most extensive liturgical reform in history, involving a new Order of the Mass effective in 1969, a revised church calendar in 1970, revisions and translations into vernacular languages of all sacramental rites and other liturgical texts.

**Ministries:** He authorized the restoration of the permanent diaconate in the Roman Rite and the establishment of new ministries of lay persons.

**Peace:** In 1968, he instituted the annual observance of a World Day of Peace on New Year's Day as a means of addressing a message of peace to all the world's political leaders and the peoples of all nations. The most dramatic of his many appeals for peace and efforts to ease international tensions was his plea for "No more war!" before the United Nations Oct. 4, 1965.

**Pilgrimages:** A "Pilgrim Pope," he made pastoral visits to the Holy Land and India in 1964, the United Nations and New York City in 1965, Portugal and Turkey in 1967, Colombia in 1968, Switzerland and Uganda in 1969, and Asia, Pacific islands and Australia in 1970. While in Manila in 1970, he was stabbed by a Bolivian artist who made an attempt on his life.

**Roman Curia:** He reorganized the central administrative organs of the Church in line with provisions of the apostolic constitution, *Regimini Ecclesiae Universae,* streamlining procedures for more effective service and giving the agencies a more international perspective by drawing officials and consultors from all over the world. He also instituted a number of new commissions and other bodies. Coupled with curial reorganization was a simplification of papal ceremonies.

## JOHN PAUL I

John Paul I (Albino Luciani) was born Oct. 17, 1912, in Forno di Canale (now Canale d'Agordo) in northern Italy.

Educated at the minor seminary in Feltre and the major seminary of the Diocese of Belluno, he was ordained to the priesthood July 7, 1935. He pursued further studies at the Pontifical Gregorian University in Rome and was awarded a doctorate in theology. From 1937 to 1947 he was vice rector of the Belluno seminary, where he taught dogmatic and moral theology, canon law and sacred art. He was appointed vicar general of his diocese in 1947 and served as director of catechetics.

Ordained bishop of Vittorio Veneto Dec. 27, 1958, he attended all sessions of the Second Vatican Council, participated in three assemblies of the Synod of Bishops (1971, 1974 and 1977), and was vice president of the Italian Bishops' Conference from 1972 to 1975.

He was appointed archbishop and patriarch of Venice Dec. 15, 1969, and was inducted into the College of Cardinals Mar. 5, 1973.

He was elected to the papacy Aug. 26, 1978, on the fourth ballot cast by the 111 cardinals participating in the largest and one of the shortest conclaves in history. The quickness of his election was matched by the brevity of his pontificate of 33 days, during which he delivered 19 addresses. He died of a heart attack Sept. 28, 1978.

## JOHN PAUL II
See separate entry.

# PAPAL ENCYCLICALS — BENEDICT XIV (1740) TO JOHN PAUL II

(Source: *The Papal Encyclicals* [5 vols.], Claudia Carlen, I.H.M.; Pieran Press, Ann Arbor, Mich. Used with permission.)

An encyclical letter is a pastoral letter addressed by a pope to the whole Church. In general, it concerns matters of doctrine, morals or discipline, or significant commemorations. Its formal title consists of the first few words of the official text. Some encyclicals, notably *Pacem in terris* by John XXIII, *Ecclesiam Suam* by Paul VI and several by John Paul II, have been addressed to people of good will in general as well as to bishops and the faithful in communion with the Church.

An encyclical epistle resembles an encyclical letter but is addressed only to part of the Church.

The authority of encyclicals was stated by Pius XII in the encyclical *Humani generis* Aug. 12, 1950: "Nor must it be thought that what is contained in encyclical letters does not of itself demand assent, on the pretext that the popes do not exercise in them the supreme power of their teaching authority. Rather, such teachings belong to the ordinary magisterium, of which it is true to say: 'He who hears you, hears me' (Lk. 10:16); for the most part, too, what is expounded and inculcated in encyclical letters already appertains to Catholic doctrine for other reasons."

The Second Vatican Council declared: "Religious submission of will and of mind must be shown in a special way to the authentic teaching authority of the Roman Pontiff, even when he is not speaking *ex cathedra*. That is, it must be shown in such a way that his supreme magisterium is acknowledged with reverence, the judgments made by him are sincerely adhered to, according to his manifest mind and will. His mind and will in the matter may be known chiefly either from the character of the documents (one of which could be an encyclical), from his frequent repetition of the same doctrine, or from his manner of speaking" (*Dogmatic Constitution on the Church*, No. 25).

The following list contains the titles and indicates the subject matter of encyclical letters and epistles. The latter are generally distinguishable by the limited scope of their titles or contents.

## Benedict XIV
### (1740-1758)

**1740:** *Ubi primum* (On the duties of bishops), Dec. 3.
**1741:** *Quanta cura* (Forbidding traffic in alms), June 30.
**1743:** *Nimiam licentiam* (To the bishops of Poland: on validity of marriages), May 18.
**1745:** *Vix pervenit* (To the bishops of Italy: on usury and other dishonest profit), Nov. 1.
**1748:** *Magnae Nobis* (To the bishops of Poland: on marriage impediments and dispensations), June 29.
**1749:** *Peregrinantes* (To all the faithful: proclaiming a Holy Year for 1750), May 5.
*Apostolica Constitutio* (On preparation for the Holy Year), June 26.
**1751:** *A quo primum* (To the bishops of Poland: on Jews and Christians living in the same place), June 14.
**1754:** *Cum Religiosi* (To the bishops of the States of the Church: on catechesis), June 26.
*Quod Provinciale* (To the bishops of Albania: on Christians using Mohammedan names), Aug. 1.
**1755:** *Allatae sunt* (To missionaries of the Orient: on the observance of Oriental rites), July 26.
**1756:** *Ex quo primum* (To bishops of the Greek rite: on the Euchologion), Mar. 1.
*Ex omnibus* (To the bishops of France: on the apostolic constitution, *Unigenitus*), Oct. 16.

## Clement XIII
### (1758-1769)

**1758:** *A quo die* (Unity among Christians), Sept. 13.
**1759:** *Cum primum* (On observing canonical sanctions), Sept. 17.
*Appetente Sacro* (On the spiritual advantages of fasting), Dec. 20.
**1761:** *In Dominico agro* (On instruction in the faith), June 14.
**1766:** *Christianae reipublicae* (On the dangers of anti-Christian writings), Nov. 25.

**1768:** *Summa quae* (To the bishops of Poland: on the Church in Poland), Jan. 6.

## Clement XIV
### (1769-1774)

**1769:** *Decet quam maxime* (To the bishops of Sardinia: on abuses in taxes and benefices), Sept. 21.
*Inscrutabili divinae sapientiae* (To all Christians: proclaiming a universal jubilee), Dec. 12.
*Cum summi* (Proclaiming a universal jubilee), Dec. 12.
**1774:** *Salutis nostra* (To all Christians: proclaiming a universal jubilee), Apr. 30.

## Pius VI
### (1775-1799)

**1775:** *Inscrutabile* (On the problems of the pontificate), Dec. 25.
**1791:** *Charitas* (To the bishops of France: on the civil oath in France), Apr. 13.

## Pius VII
### (1800-1823)

**1800:** *Diu satis* (To the bishops of France: on a return to Gospel principles), May 15.

## Leo XII
### (1823-1829)

**1824:** *Ubi primum* (To all bishops: on Leo XII's assuming the pontificate), May 5.
*Quod hoc ineunte* (Proclaiming a universal jubilee), May 24.
**1825:** *Charitate Christi* (Extending jubilee to the entire Church), Dec. 25.

## Pius VIII
### (1829-1830)

**1829:** *Traditi humilitati* (On Pius VIII's program for the pontificate), May 24.

## Gregory XVI
### (1831-1846)

**1832:** *Summo iugiter studio* (To the bishops of Bavaria: on mixed marriages), May 27.
*Cum primum* (To the bishops of Poland: on civil obedience), June 9.
*Mirari vos* (On liberalism and religious indifferentism), Aug. 15.
**1833:** *Quo graviora* (To the bishops of the Rhineland: on the "pragmatic Constitution"), Oct. 4.
**1834:** *Singulari Nos* (On the errors of Lammenais), June 25.
**1835:** *Commissum divinitus* (To clergy of Switzerland: on Church and State), May 17.
**1840:** *Probe nostis* (On the Propagation of the Faith), Sept. 18.
**1841:** *Quas vestro* (To the bishops of Hungary: on mixed marriages), Apr. 30.
**1844:** *Inter praecipuas* (On biblical societies), May 8.

## Pius IX
### (1846-1878)

**1846:** *Qui pluribus* (On faith and religion), Nov. 9.
**1847:** *Praedecessores Nostros* (On aid for Ireland), Mar. 25.

*Ubi primum* (To religious superiors: on discipline for religious), June 17.

**1849:** *Ubi primum* (On the Immaculate Conception), Feb. 2.

*Nostis et Nobiscum* (To the bishops of Italy: on the Church in the Pontifical States), Dec. 8.

**1851:** *Exultavit cor Nostrum* (On the effects of jubilee), Nov. 21.

**1852:** *Nemo certe ignorat* (To the bishops of Ireland: on the discipline for clergy), Mar. 25.

*Probe noscitis Venerabiles* (To the bishops of Spain: on the discipline for clergy), May 17.

**1853:** *Inter multiplices* (To the bishops of France: pleading for unity of spirit), Mar. 21.

**1854:** *Neminem vestrum* (To clergy and faithful of Constantinople: on the persecution of Armenians), Feb. 2.

*Optime noscitis* (To the bishops of Ireland: on the proposed Catholic university for Ireland), Mar. 20.

*Apostolicae Nostrae caritatis* (Urging prayers for peace), Aug. 1.

**1855:** *Optime noscitis* (To the bishops of Austria: on episcopal meetings), Nov. 5.

**1856:** *Singulari quidem* (To the bishops of Austria: on the Church in Austria), Mar. 17.

**1858:** *Cum nuper* (To the bishops of the Kingdom of the Two Sicilies: on care for clerics), Jan. 20.

*Amantissimi Redemptoris* (On priests and the care of souls), May 3.

**1859:** *Cum sancta mater Ecclesia* (Pleading for public prayer), Apr. 27.

*Qui nuper* (On Pontifical States), June 18.

**1860:** *Nullis certe verbis* (On the need for civil sovereignty), Jan. 19.

**1862:** *Amantissimus* (To bishops of the Oriental rite: on the care of the churches), Apr. 8.

**1863:** *Quanto conficiamur moerore* (To the bishops of Italy: on promotion of false doctrines), Aug. 10.

*Incredibili* (To the bishops of Bogota: on persecution in New Granada), Sept. 17.

**1864:** *Maximae quidem* (To the bishops of Bavaria: on the Church in Bavaria), Aug. 18.

*Quanta cura* (Condemning current errors), Dec. 8.

**1865:** *Meridionali Americae* (To the bishops of South America: on the seminary for native clergy), Sept. 30.

**1867:** *Levate* (On the afflictions of the Church), Oct. 27.

**1870:** *Respicientes* (Protesting the taking of the Pontifical States), Nov. 1.

**1871:** *Ubi Nos* (To all bishops: on Pontifical States), May 15.

*Beneficia Dei* (On the twenty-fifth anniversary of his pontificate), June 4.

*Saepe Venerabiles Fratres* (On thanksgiving for twenty-five years of pontificate), Aug. 5.

**1872:** *Quae in Patriarchatu* (To bishops and people of Chaldea: on the Church in Chaldea), Nov. 16.

**1873:** *Quartus supra* (To bishops and people of the Armenian rite: on the Church in Armenia), Jan. 6.

*Etsi multa* (On the Church in Italy, Germany and Switzerland), Nov. 21.

**1874:** *Vix dum a Nobis* (To the bishops of Austria: on the Church in Austria), Mar. 7.

*Gravibus Ecclesiae* (To all bishops and faithful: proclaiming a jubilee for 1875), Dec. 24.

**1875:** *Quod nunquam* (To the bishops of Prussia: on the Church in Prussia), Feb. 5.

*Graves ac diuturnae* (To the bishops of Switzerland: on the Church in Switzerland), Mar. 23.

## Leo XIII
### (1878-1903)

**1878:** *Inscrutabili Dei consilio* (On the evils of society), Apr. 21.

*Quod Apostolici muneris* (On socialism), Dec. 28.

**1879:** *Aeterni Patris* (On the restoration of Christian philosophy), Aug. 4.

**1880:** *Arcanum* (On Christian marriage), Feb. 10.

*Grande munus* (On Sts. Cyril and Methodius), Sept. 30.

*Sancta Dei civitas* (On mission societies), Dec. 3.

**1881:** *Diuturnum* (On the origin of civil power), June 29.

*Licet multa* (To the bishops of Belgium: on Catholics in Belgium), Aug. 3.

**1882:** *Etsi Nos* (To the bishops of Italy: on conditions in Italy), Feb. 15.

*Auspicato concessum* (On St. Francis of Assisi), Sept. 17.

*Cum multa* (To the bishops of Spain: on conditions in Spain), Dec. 8.

**1883:** *Supremi Apostolatus officio* (On devotion to the Rosary), Sept. 1.

**1884:** *Nobilissima Gallorum gens* (To the bishops of France: on the religious question), Feb. 8.

*Humanum genus* (On Freemasonry), Apr. 20.

*Superiore anno* (On the recitation of the Rosary), Aug. 30.

**1885:** *Immortale Dei* (On the Christian constitution of states), Nov. 1.

*Spectata fides* (To the bishops of England: on Christian education), Nov. 27.

*Quod auctoritate* (Proclamation of extraordinary Jubilee), Dec. 22.

**1886:** *Iampridem* (To the bishops of Prussia: on Catholicism in Germany), Jan. 6.

*Quod multum* (To the bishops of Hungary: on the liberty of the Church), Aug. 22.

*Pergrata* (To the bishops of Portugal: on the Church in Portugal), Sept. 14.

**1887:** *Vi e ben noto* (To the bishops of Italy: on the Rosary and public life), Sept. 20.

*Officio sanctissimo* (To the bishops of Bavaria: on the Church in Bavaria), Dec. 22.

**1888:** *Quod anniversarius* (On his sacerdotal jubilee), Apr. 1.

*In plurimis* (To the bishops of Brazil: on the abolition of slavery), May 5.

*Libertas* (On the nature of human liberty), June 20.

*Saepe Nos* (To the bishops of Ireland: on boycotting in Ireland), June 24.

*Paterna caritas* (To the Patriarch of Cilicia and the archbishops and bishops of the Armenian people: on reunion with Rome), July 25.

*Quam aerumnosa* (To the bishops of America: on Italian immigrants), Dec. 10.

*Etsi cunctas* (To the bishops of Ireland: on the Church in Ireland), Dec. 21.

*Exeunte iam anno* (On the right ordering of Christian life), Dec. 25.

**1889:** *Magni Nobis* (To the bishops of the United

States: on the Catholic University of America), Mar. 7.

*Quamquam pluries* (On devotion to St. Joseph),Aug. 15.

**1890:** *Sapientiae Christianae* (On Christians as citizens), Jan. 10.

*Dall'alto Dell'Apostolico seggio* (To the bishops and people of Italy: on Freemasonry in Italy), Oct. 15.

*Catholicae Ecclesiae* (On slavery in the missions), Nov. 20.

**1891:** *In ipso* (To the bishops of Austria: on episcopal reunions in Austria), Mar. 3.

*Rerum novarum* (On capital and labor), May 15.

*Pastoralis* (To the bishops of Portugal: on religious union), June 25.

*Pastoralis officii* (To the bishops of Germany and Austria: on the morality of dueling), Sept. 12.

*Octobri mense* (On the Rosary), Sept. 22.

**1892:** *Au milieu des sollicitudes* (To the bishops, clergy and faithful of France: on the Church and State in France), Feb. 16.

*Quarto abeunte saeculo* (To the bishops of Spain, Italy, and the two Americas: on the Columbus quadricentennial), July 16.

*Magnae Dei Matris* (On the Rosary), Sept. 8.

*Inimica vis* (To the bishops of Italy: on Freemasonry), Dec. 8.

*Custodi di quella fede* (To the Italian people: on Freemasonry), Dec. 8.

**1893:** *Ad extremas* (On seminaries for native clergy), June 24.

*Constanti Hungarorum* (To the bishops of Hungary: on the Church in Hungary), Sept. 2.

*Laetitiae sanctae* (Commending devotion to the Rosary), Sept. 8.

*Non mediocri* (To the bishops of Spain: on the Spanish College in Rome), Oct. 25.

*Providentissimus Deus* (On the study of Holy Scripture), Nov. 18.

**1894:** *Caritatis* (To the bishops of Poland: on the Church in Poland), Mar. 19.

*Inter graves* (To the bishops of Peru: on the Church in Peru), May 1.

*Litteras a vobis* (To the bishops of Brazil: on the clergy in Brazil), July 2.

*Iucunda semper expectatione* (On the Rosary), Sept. 8.

*Christi nomen* (On the propagation of the Faith and Eastern churches), Dec. 24.

**1895:** *Longinqua* (To the bishops of the United States: on Catholicism in the United States), Jan. 6.

*Permoti Nos* (To the bishops of Belgium: on social conditions in Belgium), July 10.

*Adiutricem* (On the Rosary), Sept. 5.

**1896:** *Insignes* (To the bishops of Hungary: on the Hungarian millennium), May 1.

*Satis cognitum* (On the unity of the Church), June 29.

*Fidentem piumque animum* (On the Rosary), Sept. 20.

**1897:** *Divinum illud munus* (On the Holy Spirit), May 9.

*Militantis Ecclesiae* (To the bishops of Austria, Germany, and Switzerland: on St. Peter Canisius), Aug. 1.

*Augustissimae Virginis Mariae* (On the Confraternity of the Holy Rosary), Sept. 12.

*Affari vos* (To the bishops of Canada: on the Manitoba school question), Dec. 8.

**1898:** *Caritatis studium* (To the bishops of Scotland: on the Church in Scotland), July 25.

*Spesse volte* (To the bishops, priests, and people of Italy: on the suppression of Catholic institutions), Aug. 5.

*Quam religiosa* (To the bishops of Peru: on civil marriage law), Aug. 16.

*Diuturni temporis* (On the Rosary), Sept. 5.

*Quum diuturnum* (To the bishops of Latin America: on Latin American bishops' plenary council), Dec. 25.

**1899:** *Annum Sacrum* (On consecration to the Sacred Heart), May 25.

*Depuis le jour* (To the archbishops, bishops, and clergy of France: on the education of the clergy), Sept. 8.

*Paternae* (To the bishops of Brazil: on the education of the clergy), Sept. 18.

**1900:** *Omnibus compertum* (To the Patriarch and bishops of the Greek-Melkite rite: on unity among the Greek Melkites), July 21.

*Tametsi futura prospicientibus* (On Jesus Christ the Redeemer), Nov. 1.

**1901:** *Graves de communi re* (On Christian democracy), Jan. 18.

*Gravissimas* (To the bishops of Portugal: on religious orders in Portugal), May 16.

*Reputantibus* (To the bishops of Bohemia and Moravia: on the language question in Bohemia), Aug. 20.

*Urbanitatis Veteris* (To the bishops of the Latin church in Greece: on the foundation of a seminary in Athens), Nov. 20.

**1902:** *In amplissimo* (To the bishops of the United States: on the Church in the United States), Apr. 15.

*Quod votis* (To the bishops of Austria: on the proposed Catholic University), Apr. 30.

*Mirae caritatis* (On the Holy Eucharist), May 28.

*Quae ad Nos* (To the bishops of Bohemia and Moravia: on the Church in Bohemia and Moravia), Nov. 22.

*Fin dal principio* (To the bishops of Italy: on the education of the clergy), Dec. 8.

*Dum multa* (To the bishops of Ecuador: on marriage legislation), Dec. 24.

## Saint Pius X
### (1903-1914)

**1903:** *E supremi* (On the restoration of all things in Christ), Oct. 4.

**1904:** *Ad diem illum laetissimum* (On the Immaculate Conception), Feb. 2.

*Iucunda sane* (On Pope Gregory the Great), Mar. 12.

**1905:** *Acerbo nimis* (On teaching Christian doctrine), Apr. 15.

*Il fermo proposito* (To the bishops of Italy: on Catholic Action in Italy), June 11.

**1906:** *Vehementer Nos* (To the bishops, clergy, and people of France: on the French Law of Separation), Feb. 11.

*Tribus circiter* (On the Mariavites or Mystic Priests of Poland), Apr. 5.

*Pieni l'animo* (To the bishops of Italy: on the clergy in Italy), July 28.

*Gravissimo officio munere* (To the bishops of France: on French associations of worship), Aug. 10.

**1907:** *Une fois encore* (To the bishops, clergy, and people of France: on the separation of Church and State), Jan. 6.

*Pascendi dominici gregis* (On the doctrines of the Modernists), Sept. 8.

**1909:** *Communium rerum* (On St. Anselm of Aosta), Apr. 21.

**1910:** *Editae saepe* (On St. Charles Borromeo), May 26.

**1911:** *Iamdudum* (On the Law of Separation in Portugal), May 24.

**1912:** *Lacrimabili statu* (To the bishops of Latin America: on the Indians of South America), June 7.

*Singulari quadam* (To the bishops of Germany: on labor organizations), Sept. 24.

## Benedict XV
### (1914-1922)

**1914:** *Ad beatissimi Apostolorum* (Appeal for peace), Nov. 1.

**1917:** *Humani generis Redemptionem* (On preaching the Word of God), June 15.

**1918:** *Quod iam diu* (On the future peace conference), Dec. 1.

**1919:** *In hac tanta* (To the bishops of Germany: on St. Boniface), May 14.

*Paterno iam diu* (On children of central Europe), Nov. 24.

**1920:** *Pacem, Dei munus pulcherrimum* (On peace and Christian reconciliation), May 23.

*Spiritus Paraclitus* (On St. Jerome), Sept. 15.

*Principi Apostolorum Petro* (On St. Ephrem the Syrian), Oct. 5.

*Annus iam plenus* (On children of central Europe), Dec. 1.

**1921:** *Sacra propediem* (On the Third Order of St. Francis), Jan. 6.

*In praeclara summorum* (To professors and students of fine arts in Catholic institutions of learning: on Dante), Apr. 30.

*Fausto appetente die* (On St. Dominic), June 29.

## Pius XI
### (1922-1939)

**1922:** *Ubi arcano Dei consilio* (On the peace of Christ in the Kingdom of Christ), Dec. 23.

**1923:** *Rerum omnium perturbationem* (On St. Francis de Sales), Jan. 26.

*Studiorum Ducem* (On St. Thomas Aquinas), June 29.

*Ecclesiam Dei* (On St. Josaphat), Nov. 12.

**1924:** *Maximam gravissimamque* (To the bishops, clergy, and people of France: on French diocesan associations), Jan. 18.

**1925:** *Quas primas* (On the feast of Christ the King), Dec. 11.

**1926:** *Rerum Ecclesiae* (On Catholic missions), Feb. 28.

*Rite expiatis* (On St. Francis of Assisi), Apr. 30.

*Iniquis afflictisque* (On the persecution of the Church in Mexico), Nov. 18.

**1928:** *Mortalium animos* (On religious unity), Jan. 6.

*Miserentissimus Redemptor* (On reparation to the Sacred Heart), May 8.

*Rerum Orientalium* (On the promotion of Oriental Studies), Sept. 8.

**1929:** *Mens Nostra* (On the promotion of Spiritual Exercises), Dec. 20.

*Quinquagesimo ante* (On his sacerdotal jubilee), Dec. 23.

*Rappresentanti in terra* (On Christian education), Dec. 31. [Latin text, *Divini illius magistri*, published several months later with minor changes.]

**1930:** *Ad salutem* (On St. Augustine), Apr. 20.

*Casti connubii* (On Christian Marriage), Dec. 31.

**1931:** *Quadragesimo anno* (Commemorating the fortieth anniversary of Leo XIII's *Rerum novarum:* on reconstruction of the soical order), May 15.

*Non abbiamo bisogno* (On Catholic Action in Italy), June 29.

*Nova impendet* (On the economic crisis), Oct. 2.

*Lux veritatis* (On the Council of Ephesus), Dec. 25.

**1932:** *Caritate Christi compulsi* (On the Sacred Heart), May 3.

*Acerba animi* (To the bishops of Mexico: on persecution of the Church in Mexico), Sept. 29.

**1933:** *Dilectissima Nobis* (To the bishops, clergy, and people of Spain: on oppression of the Church in Spain), June 3.

**1935:** *Ad Catholici sacerdotii* (On the Catholic priesthood), Dec. 20.

**1936:** *Vigilanti cura* (To the bishops of the United States: on motion pictures), June 29.

**1937:** *Mit brennender Sorge* (To the bishops of Germany: on the Church and the German Reich), Mar. 14.

*Divini Redemptoris* (On atheistic communism), Mar. 19.

*Nos es muy conocida* (To the bishops of Mexico: on the religious situation in Mexico), Mar. 28

*Ingravescentibus malis* (On the Rosary) Sept. 29.

## Pius XII
### (1939-1958)

**1939:** *Summi Pontificatus* (On the unity of human society), Oct. 20.

*Sertum laetitiae* (To the bishops of the United States: on the 150th anniversary of the establishment of the hierarchy in the United States), Nov. 1.

**1940:** *Saeculo exeunte octavo* (To the bishops of Portugal and its colonies: on the eighth centenary of the independence of Portugal), June 13.

**1943:** *Mystici Corporis Christi* (On the Mystical Body of Christ), June 29.

*Divino afflante Spiritu* (On promoting biblical studies, commemorating the fiftieth anniversary of *Providentissimus Deus*), Sept. 30.

**1944:** *Orientalis Ecclesiae* (On St. Cyril, Patriarch of Alexandria), Apr. 9.

**1945:** *Communium interpretes dolorum* (To the bishops of the world: appealing for prayers for peace during May), Apr. 15.

*Orientales omnes Ecclesias* (On the 350th anniversary of the reunion of the Ruthenian Church with the Apostolic See), Dec. 23.

**1946:** *Quemadmodum* (Pleading for the care of the world's destitute children), Jan. 6.

*Deiparae Virginis Mariae* (To all bishops: on the possibility of defining the Assumption of the Blessed Virgin Mary as a dogma of faith), May 1.

**1947:** *Fulgens radiatur* (On St. Benedict), Mar. 21.

*Mediator Dei* (On the sacred liturgy), Nov. 20.

*Optatissima pax* (Prescribing public prayers for social and world peace), Dec. 18.

**1948:** *Auspicia quaedam* (On public prayers for world peace and solution of the problem of Palestine), May 1.

*In multiplicibus curis* (On prayers for peace in Palestine), Oct. 24.

**1949:** *Redemptoris nostri cruciatus* (On the holy places in Palestine), Apr. 15.

**1950:** *Anni Sacri* (On the program for combatting atheistic propaganda throughout the world), Mar. 12.

*Summi maeroris* (On public prayers for peace), July 19.

*Humani generis* (Concerning some false opinions threatening to undermine the foundations of Catholic doctrine), Aug. 12.

*Mirabile illud* (On the crusade of prayers for peace), Dec. 6.

**1951:** *Evangelii praecones* (On the promotion of Catholic missions), June 2.

*Sempiternus Rex Christus* (On the Council of Chalcedon), Sept. 8.

*Ingruentium malorum* (On reciting the Rosary), Sept. 15.

**1952:** *Orientales Ecclesias* (On the persecuted Eastern Church), Dec. 15.

**1953:** *Doctor Mellifluus* (On St. Bernard of Clairvaux, the last of the fathers), May 24.

*Fulgens corona* (Proclaiming a Marian Year to commemorate the centenary of the definition of the dogma of the Immaculate Conception), Sept. 8.

**1954:** *Sacra virginitas* (On consecrated virginity), Mar. 25.

*Ecclesiae fastos* (To the bishops of Great Britain, Germany, Austria, France, Belgium, and Holland: on St. Boniface), June 5.

*Ad Sinarum gentem* (To the bishops, clergy, and people of China: on the supranationality of the Church), Oct. 7.

*Ad Caeli Reginam* (Proclaiming the Queenship of Mary), Oct. 11.

**1955:** *Musicae sacrae* (On sacred music), Dec. 25

**1956:** *Haurietis aquas* (On devotion to the Sacred Heart), May 15.

*Luctuosissimi eventus* (Urging public prayers for peace and freedom for the people of Hungary), Oct. 28.

*Laetamur admodum* (Renewing exhortation for prayers for peace for Poland, Hungary, and especially for the Middle East), Nov. 1.

*Datis nuperrime* (Lamenting the sorrowful events in Hungary and condemning the ruthless use of force), Nov. 5.

**1957:** *Fidei donum* (On the present condition of the Catholic missions, especially in Africa), Apr. 21.

*Invicti athletae* (On St. Andrew Bobola), May 16.

*Le pelerinage de Lourdes* (Warning against materialism on the centenary of the apparitions at Lourdes), July 2.

*Miranda prorsus* (On the communications field: motion picture, radio, television), Sept. 8.

**1958:** *Ad Apostolorum Principis* (To the bishops of China; on Communism and the Church in China), June 29.

*Meminisse iuvat* (On prayers for persecuted Church), July 14.

## John XXIII
### (1958-1963)

**1959:** *Ad Petri Cathedram* (On truth, unity, and peace, in a spirit of charity), June 29.

*Sacerdotii Nostri primordia* (On St. John Vianney), Aug. 1.

*Grata recordatio* (On the Rosary: prayer for the Church, missions, international and social problems), Sept. 26.

*Princeps Pastorum* (On the missions, native clergy, lay participation), Nov. 28.

**1961:** *Mater et Magistra* (On Christianity and social progress), May 15.

*Aeterna Dei sapientia* (On fifteenth centenary of the death of Pope St. Leo I: the see of Peter as the center of Christian unity), Nov. 11.

**1962:** *Paenitentiam agere* (On the need for the practice of interior and exterior penance), July 1.

**1963:** *Pacem in terris* (On establishing universal peace in truth, justice, charity, and liberty), Apr. 11.

## Paul VI
### (1963-1978)

**1964:** *Ecclesiam Suam* (On the Church), Aug. 6.

**1965:** *Mense maio* (On prayers during May for the preservation of peace), Apr. 29.

*Mysterium Fidei* (On the Holy Eucharist), Sept. 3.

**1966:** *Christi Matri* (On prayers for peace during October), Sept. 15.

**1967:** *Populorum progressio* (On the development of peoples), Mar. 26.

*Sacerdotalis caelibatus* (On the celibacy of the priest), June 24.

**1968:** *Humanae vitae* (On the regulation of birth), July 25.

## John Paul II
### (1978- )

**1979:** *Redemptor hominis* (On redemption and dignity of the human race), Mar. 4

**1980:** *Dives in misericordia* (On the mercy of God), Nov. 30.

**1981:** *Laborem exercens* (On human work), Sept. 14.

**1985:** *Slavorum Apostoli* (Commemorating Sts. Cyril and Methodius, on the eleventh centenary of the death of St. Methodius), June 2.

**1986:** *Dominum et Vivificantem* (On the Holy Spirit in the life of the Church and the world), May 18.

**1987:** *Redemptoris Mater* (On the role of Mary in the mystery of Christ and her active and exemplary presence in the life of the Church), Mar. 25.

*Sollicitudo Rei Socialis* (On social concerns, on the twentieth anniversary of *Populorum progressio*), Dec. 30.

**1991:** *Redemptoris missio* (On the permanent validity of the Church's missionary mandate), Jan. 22.

*Centesimus annus* (Commemorating the centenary

of *Rerum novarum* and addressing the social question in a contemporary perspective), May 1.

**1993:** *Veritatis Splendor* (Regarding fundamental questions on the Church's moral teaching), Aug. 6.

**1995:** *Evangelium Vitae* (On the value and inviolability of human life), Mar. 25.

*Ut Unum Sint* (On commitment to ecumenism), May 25.

# CANONIZATIONS BY LEO XIII AND HIS SUCCESSORS

Canonization (see entry in Glossary) is an infallible declaration by the pope that a person who suffered martyrdom and/or practiced Christian virtue to a heroic degree is in glory with God in heaven and is worthy of public honor by the universal Church and of imitation by the faithful.

Biographies of some of the saints listed below are given elsewhere in the Almanac. See Index.

## Leo XIII
### (1878-1903)

**1881:** Clare of Montefalco (d. 1308); John Baptist de Rossi (1698-1764); Lawrence of Brindisi (d. 1619).

**1883:** Benedict J. Labre (1748-1783).

**1888:** Seven Holy Founders of the Servite Order; Peter Claver (1581-1654); John Berchmans (1599-1621); Alphonsus Rodriguez (1531-1617).

**1897:** Anthony M. Zaccaria (1502-1539); Peter Fourier of Our Lady (1565-1640).

**1900:** John Baptist de La Salle (1651-1719); Rita of Cascia (1381-1457).

## St. Pius X
### (1903-1914)

**1904:** Alexander Sauli (1534-1593); Gerard Majella (1725-1755).

**1909:** Joseph Oriol (1650-1702); Clement M. Hofbauer (1751-1820).

## Benedict XV
### (1914-1922)

**1920:** Gabriel of the Sorrowful Mother (1838-1862); Margaret Mary Alacoque (1647-1690); Joan of Arc (1412-1431).

## Pius XI
### (1922-1939)

**1925:** Therese of Lisieux (1873-1897); Peter Canisius (1521-1597); Mary Magdalen Postel (1756-1846); Mary Magdalen Sophie Barat (1779-1865); John Eudes (1601-1680); John Baptist Vianney (Curé of Ars) (1786-1859).

**1930:** Lucy Filippini (1672-1732); Catherine Tomas (1533-1574); Jesuit North American Martyrs; Robert Bellarmine (1542-1621); Theophilus of Corte (1676-1740).

**1931:** Albert the Great (1206-1280) (equivalent canonization).

**1933:** Andrew Fournet (1752-1834); Bernadette Soubirous (1844-1879).

**1934:** Joan Antida Thouret (1765-1826); Mary Michaeli (1809-1865); Louise de Marillac (1591-1660); Joseph Benedict Cottolengo (1786-1842); Pompilius M. Pirotti, priest (1710-1756); Teresa Margaret Redi (1747-1770); John Bosco (1815-1888); Conrad of Parzham (1818-1894).

**1935:** John Fisher (1469-1535); Thomas More (1478-1535).

**1938:** Andrew Bobola (1592-1657); John Leonardi (c. 1550-1609); Salvatore of Horta (1520-1567).

## Pius XII
### (1939-1958)

**1940:** Gemma Galgani (1878-1903); Mary Euphrasia Pelletier (1796-1868).

**1943:** Margaret of Hungary (d. 1270) (equvalent canonization).

**1946:** Frances Xavier Cabrini (1850-1917).

**1947:** Nicholas of Flue (1417-1487); John of Britto (1647-1693); Bernard Realini (1530-1616); Joseph Cafasso (1811-1860); Michael Garicoits (1797-1863); Jeanne Elizabeth des Ages (1773-1838); Louis Marie Grignon de Montfort (1673-1716); Catherine Laboure (1806-1876).

**1949:** Jeanne de Lestonnac (1556-1640); Maria Josepha Rossello (1811-1880).

**1950:** Emily de Rodat (1787-1852); Anthony Mary Claret (1807-1870); Bartolomea Capitanio (1807-1833); Vincenza Gerosa (1784-1847) Jeanne de Valois (1461-1504); Vincenzo M. Strambi (1745-1824); Maria Goretti (1890-1902); Mariana Paredes of Jesus (1618-1645).

**1951:** Maria Domenica Mazzarello (1837-1881); Emilie de Vialar (1797-1856); Anthony M. Gianelli (1789-1846); Ignatius of Laconi (1701-1781); Francis Xavier Bianchi (1743-1815).

**1954:** Pope Pius X (1835-1914); Dominic Savio (1842-1857); Maria Crocifissa di Rosa (1813-1855); Peter Chanel (1803-1841); Gaspar del Bufalo (1786-1837); Joseph M. Pignatelli (1737-1811).

**1958:** Herman Joseph, O. Praem. (1150-1241) (equivalent canonization).

## John XXIII
### (1958-1963)

**1959:** Joaquina de Vedruna de Mas (1783-1854); Charles of Sezze (1613-1670).

**1960:** Gregory Barbarigo (1625-1697) (equivalent canonization); John de Ribera (1532-1611).

**1961:** Bertilla Boscardin (1888-1922).

**1962:** Martin de Porres (1579-1639); Peter Julian Eymard (1811-1868); Anthony Pucci, priest (1819-1892); Francis Mary of Camporosso (1804-1866).

**1963:** Vincent Pallotti (1795-1850).

## Paul VI
### (1963-1978)

**1964:** Charles Lwanga and Twenty-One Companions, Martyrs of Uganda (d. between 1885-1887).

**1967:** Benilde Romacon (1805-1862).

**1969:** Julia Billiart (1751-1816).

**1970:** Maria Della Dolorato Torres Acosta (1826-1887); Leonard Murialdo (1828-1900); Therese Couderc (1805-1885); John of Avila (1499-1569); Nicholas Tavelic, Deodatus of Aquitaine, Peter of Narbonne and Stephen of Cuneo, martyrs (d. 1391); Forty English and Welsh Martyrs (d. 16th cent.).

**1974:** Teresa of Jesus Jornet Ibars (1843-1897).

**1975:** Vicenta Maria Lopez y Vicuna (1847-1890); Elizabeth Bayley Seton (1774-1821); John Masias (1585-1645); Oliver Plunket (1629-1681); Justin de Jacobis (1800-1860); John Baptist of the Conception (1561-1613).

**1976:** Beatrice da Silva (1424 or 1426-1490); John Ogilvie (1579-1615).

**1977:** Rafaela Maria Porras y Ayllon (1850-1925); John Nepomucene Neumann (1811-1860); Sharbel Makhlouf (1828-1898).

### John Paul II
(1978- )

**1982:** Crispin of Viterbo (1668-1750); Maximilian Kolbe (1894-1941); Marguerite Bourgeoys (1620-1700); Jeanne Delanoue (1666-1736).

**1983:** Leopold Mandic (1866-1942).

**1984:** Paola Frassinetti (1809-1892); 103 Korean Martyrs (d. between 1839-1867); Miguel Febres Cordero (1854-1910).

**1986:** Francis Anthony Fasani (1681-1742); Giuseppe Maria Tomasi (1649-1713).

**1987:** Giuseppe Moscati (d. 1927); Lawrence (Lorenzo) Ruiz and Fifteen Companions, Martyrs of Japan (d. 1630s).

**1988:** Eustochia Calafato (1434-1485); 117 Martyrs of Vietnam (96 Vietnamese, 11 Spanish, 10

French; included 8 bishops, 50 priests, 1 seminarian, 58 lay persons); Roque Gonzalez (1576-1628), Alfonso Rodriguez (1598-1628) and Juan de Castillo (1596-1628), Jesuit martyrs of Paraguay; Rose Philippine Duchesne (1796-1852); Simon de Rojas (1552-1624); Magdalen of Canossa (1774-1835); Maria Rosa Molas y Vollve (d. 1876).

**1989:** Clelia Barbieri (1847-1870); Gaspar Bertoni (1777-1853); Richard Pampuri, religious (1897-1930); Agnes of Bohemia (1211-1282); Albert Chmielowski (1845-1916); Mutien-Marie Wiaux (1841-1917).

**1990:** Marguerite D'Youville (1701-1777).

**1991:** Raphael (Jozef) Kalinowski (1835-1907).

**1992:** Claude La Colombiere (1641-1682); Ezequiel Moreno y Diaz (1848-1905).

**1993:** Marie of St. Ignatius (Claudine Thevenet) (1774-1837); Teresa "de los Andes" (Juana Fernandez Solar) (1900-20); Enrique de Ossó y Cervelló (1840-96).

**1995:** Jan Sarkander (1576-1620), Zdislava of Lemberk (d. 1252); Marek Krizin (1588-1619), Stefan Pongracz (1582-1619), Melichar Grodziecky (1584-1619), martyrs of Kosice; Eugene de Mazenod (1782-1861).

**1996** (as of July 31, 1996): Jean-Gabriel Perboyre, Juan Grande Roman and Bro. Egidio Maria di San Guiseppe.

## BEATIFICATIONS BY POPE JOHN PAUL II, 1979-1996

**1979:** Francis Coll, O.P., Jacques Laval, S.S.Sp. (Apr. 29); Enrique de Ossó y Cervelló (Oct. 14; *canonized June 16, 1993*).

**1980:** Jose de Anchieta, Peter of St. Joseph Betancur, Francois de Montmorency Laval, Kateri Tekakwitha, Marie Guyard of the Incarnation (June 22); Don Luigi Orione, Bartolomea Longo, Maria Anna Sala (Oct. 26).

**1981:** Sixteen Martyrs of Japan (Lorenzo Ruiz and Companions) (Feb 18; *canonized Oct. 18, 1987*); Maria Repetto, Alan de Solminihac, Richard Pampuri, Claudine Thevenet *(canonized 1993)*, Aloysius (Luigi) Scrosoppi (Oct. 4).

**1982:** Peter Donders, C.SS.R., Marie Rose Durocher, Andre Bessette, C.S.C., Maria Angela Astorch, Marie Rivier (May 23); Jeanne Jugan, Salvatore Lilli and 7 Armenian Companions (Oct. 3); Sr. Angela of the Cross (Nov. 5).

**1983:** Maria Gabriella Sagheddu (Jan. 25); Luigi Versiglia, Callisto Caravario (May 15); Ursula Ledochowska (June 20); Raphael (Jozef) Kalinowski *(canonized 1991)*, Bro. Albert (Adam Chmielowski), T.O.R. (June 22); Fra Angelico (equivalent beatification) (July); Giacomo Cusmano, Jeremiah of Valachia, Domingo Iturrate Zubero (Oct. 30); Marie of Jesus Crucified (Marie Baouardy) (Nov. 13).

**1984:** Fr. William Repin and 98 Companions (Martyrs of Angers during French Revolution), Giovanni Mazzucconi (Feb. 19); Marie Leonie Paradis (Sept. 11); Federico Albert, Clemente Marchisio, Isidore of St. Joseph (Isidore de Loor), Rafaela Ybarra de Villalongo (Sept. 30); Jose Manyanet y Vives, Daniel Brottier, C.S.Sp., Sr. Elizabeth of the Trinity (Elizabeth Catez) (Nov. 25).

**1985:** Mercedes of Jesus (Feb. 1); Ana de los Angeles Monteagudo (Feb. 2); Pauline von Mallinckrodt, Catherine Troiano (Apr. 14); Benedict Menni, Peter Friedhofen (June 23); Anwarite Nangapeta (Aug. 15); Virginae Centurione Bracelli (Sept. 22); Diego Luis de San Vitores, S.J., Jose M. Rubio y Peralto, S.J., Francisco Garate, S.J. (Oct. 6); Titus Brandsma, O.Carm. (Nov. 3); Pio Campidelli, C.P., Marie Teresa of Jesus Gerhardinger, Rafqa Ar-Rayes (Nov. 17).

**1986:** Alphonsa Mattathupadathus of the Immaculate Conception, Kuriakose Elias Chavara (Feb. 8); Antoine Chevrier (Oct. 4); Teresa Maria of the Cross Manetti (Oct. 19).

**1987:** Maria Pilar of St. Francis Borgia, Teresa of the Infant Jesus, Maria Angeles of St. Joseph, Cardinal Marcellis Spinola y Maestre, Emmanuel Domingo y Sol (Mar. 29); Teresa of Jesus "de los Andes" (Apr. 3; *canonized Mar. 21, 1993)*; Edith Stein (Teresa Benedicta of the Cross) (May 1); Rupert Meyer, S.J. (May 3); Pierre-Francois Jamet, Cardinal Andrea Carlo Ferrari, Benedetta Cambiogio Frasinello, Louis Moreau (May 10); Carolina Kozka, Michal Kozal (June 10); George Matulaitis (Matulewicz) (June 28); Marcel Callo, Pierino Morosoni, Antonia Mesina (Oct. 4); Blandina Marten, Ulricke Nische, Jules Reche (Bro. Arnold) (Nov. 1); 85 Martyrs (d. between 1584-1689) of England, Scotland and Wales (Nov. 22).

**1988:** John Calabria, Joseph Nascimbeni (Apr. 17); Pietro Bonilli, Kaspar Stanggassinger, Francisco Palau y Quer, Savina Petrilli (Apr. 24), Laura Vicuna (Sept. 3); Joseph Gerard (Sept. 11); Miguel Pro, Giuseppe Benedetto Dusmet, Francisco Faa di

Bruno, Junipero Serra, Frederick Janssoone, Josefa Naval Girke (Sept. 25); Bernardo Maria Silvestrelli, Charles Houben, Honoratus Kozminski (Oct. 16); Niels Stensen (Nicolaus Steno) (Oct. 23); Katharine Drexel, 3 Missionary Martyrs of Ethiopia (Liberato Weiss, Samuel Marzorati, Michele Pio Fasoli) (Nov. 20).

**1989**: Martin of Saint Nicholas, Melchior of St. Augustine, Mary of Jesus of the Good Shepherd, Maria Margaret Caiana, Maria Catherine of St. Augustine (Apr. 23); Victoria Rasoamanarivo (Apr. 30); Bro. Scubilionis (John Bernard Rousseau) (May 2); Elizabeth Renzi, Antonio Lucci (June 17); Niceforo de Jesus y Maria (Vicente Diez Tejerina and 25 Companions (martyred in Spain), Lorenzo Salvia, Gertrude Caterina Comensoli, Francisca Ana Cirer Carbonell (Oct. 1); 7 Martyrs from Thailand (Philip Sipong, Sr. Agnes Phila, Sr. Lucia Khambang, Agatha Phutta, Cecilia Butsi, Bibiana Khampai, Maria Phon), Timothy Giaccardo, Mother Maria of Jesus Deluil-Martiny (Oct. 22); Giuseppe Baldo (Oct. 31).

**1990**: 9 Martyrs of Astoria during Spanish Civil War (De la Salle Brothers Cyrill Bertran, Marciano Jose, Julian Alfredo, Victoriano Pio, Benjamin Julian, Augusto Andres, Benito de Jesus, Aniceto Adolfo; and Passionist priest Innocencio Inmaculada), Mercedes Prat, Manuel Barbal Cosan (Brother Jaime), Philip Rinaldi (Apr. 29); Juan Diego (confirmation of Apr. 9 decree), 3 Child Martyrs (Cristobal, Antonio and Juan), Fr. Jose Maria de Yermo y Porres (May 6); Pierre Giorgio Frassati (May 20); Hanibal Maria Di Francia, Joseph Allamano (Oct. 7); Marthe Aimee LeBouteiller, Louise Therese de Montaignac de Chauvance, Maria Schinina, Elisabeth Vendramini (Nov. 4).

**1991**: Annunciata Cocchetti, Marie Therese Haze, Clara Bosatta (Apr. 21); Jozef Sebastian Pelczar (June 2); Boleslava Lament (June 5); Rafael Chylinski (June 9); Angela Salawa (Aug. 13); Edoardo Giuseppe Rosaz (July 14, Susa, Italy); Pauline of the Heart of Jesus in Agony Visintainer (Oct. 18, Brazil); Adolph Kolping (Oct. 27).

**1992**: Josephine Bakhita, Josemaria Escriva de Balaguer (May 17); Francesco Spinelli (June 21, Caravaggio, Italy); 17 Irish Martyrs, Rafael Arnáiz

Barón, Nazaria Ignacia March Mesa, Léonie Françoise de Sales Aviat, and Maria Josefa Sancho de Guerra (Sept. 27); 122 Martyrs of Spanish Civil War, Narcisa Martillo Morán (Oct. 25); Cristóbal Magellanes and 24 companions, Mexican martyrs, and Maria de Jesús Sacramentado Venegas (Nov. 22).

**1993**: Dina Belanger (Mar. 20); John Duns Scotus (Mar. 20, cult solemnly recognized); Mary Angela Truszkowska, Ludovico of Casoria, Faustina Kowalska, Paula Montal Fornés (Apr. 18); Stanislaus Kazimierczyk (April 18, cult solemnly recognized); Maurice Tornay, Marie-Louise Trichet, Columba Gabriel and Florida Cevoli (May 16); Giuseppe Marello (Sept. 26); Eleven martyrs of Almeria, Spain, during Spanish Civil War (2 bishops, 7 brothers, 1 priest, 1 lay person); Maria Francesca (Anna Maria) Rubatto; Maria Crucified (Elisabetta Maria) Satellico (Oct. 10).

**1994**: Isidore Bakanja, Elizabeth Canori Mora; Dr. Gianna Beretta Molla (Apr. 24); Nicolas Roland, Alberto Hurtado Cruchaga, Maria Rafols, Petra of St. Joseph Perez Florido, Josephine Vannini (Oct. 16); Maddalena Caterina Morano (Nov. 5); Hyacinthe Marie Cormier, Marie Poussepin, Agnes de Jesus Galand, Eugenia Joubert, Claudio Granzotto (Nov. 20).

**1995**: Peter To Rot (Jan. 17); Mother Mary of the Cross MacKillop (Jan. 19); Joseph Vaz (Jan. 21); Rafael Guizar Valencia, Modestino of Jesus and Mary, Genoveva Torres Morales, Grimoaldo of the Purification (Jan. 29); Johann Nepomuk von Tschiderer (Apr. 30); Maria Helena Stollenwerk, Maria Alvarado Cardoza, Giuseppina Bonino, Maria Domenica Brun Barbantini, Agostino Roscelli (May 7); Damien de Veuster (June 4); 109 Martyrs (64 from French Revolution and 45 from Spanish Civil War) and Pietro Casini (Oct. 1); Mary Theresa Scherer, Maria Bernarda Butler and Marguerite Bays (Oct. 29).

**1996** (as of June 30, 1996): Daniel Comboni and Guido Maria Conforti (Mar. 17); Cardinal Alfredo Ildefonso Schuster, Filippo Smaldone and Gennaro Sarnelli (priests) and Candida Maria de Jesus Cipitria y Barriola, Maria Raffaella Cimatti, Maria Antonia Bandres (religious) (May 12); Bernhard Lichtenberg and Karl Leisner (June 23).

## CATHOLIC-ORTHODOX MEETINGS

"To be credible to our faithful, our prayers and concerted efforts must be followed by concrete achievements. Together we must accomplish what we have planned together." So stated the Pope June 29 at a meeting with the delegation sent to Rome by Ecumenical Patriarch Bartholomew I for the feast of Sts. Peter and Paul.

"Each year this exchange of visits between our churches on the feasts of their patron saints, in Rome and at the Phanar (seat of the Orthodox Patriarchate), gives us the opportunity for a fraternal meeting in prayer and dialogue, with a view to intensifying our ecclesial relations and to discerning together the best way to advance toward the re-establishment of full communion.

"With these meetings we wish to follow the path leading to the unity for which the Lord beseeched

the Father. We receive strength from his Spirit for the continual renewal of our enthusiasm.

"These biennial meetings are also an occasion for us to reflect honesrtly and fraternally on the growth of our relations. It is necessary to assess what has been achieved and to consider what remains to be done. We must decide together on the initiatives to be taken in order to continue or to re-start our activity.

"... These conversations must, as far as possible, be the preferred way to adopt a common attitude toward our faithful and thus help to overcome uncontrolled reactions and critical or polemical habits, which deeply marked mentalities in a past now behind us."

By exchanging views, "we can take stock together" of the present state of relations between the Churches.

# HIERARCHY OF THE CATHOLIC CHURCH _____

## ORGANIZATION AND GOVERNMENT

As a structured society, the Catholic Church is organized and governed along lines corresponding mainly to the jurisdictions of the pope and bishops. The pope is the supreme head of the Church. He has primacy of jurisdiction as well as honor over the entire Church.

Bishops, in union with and in subordination to the pope, are the successors of the Apostles for care of the Church and for the continuation of Christ's mission in the world. They serve the people of their own dioceses, or particular churches, with ordinary authority and jurisdiction. They also share, with the pope and each other, in common concern and effort for the general welfare of the whole Church.

Bishops of exceptional status are patriarchs of Eastern Catholic Churches who, subject only to the pope, are heads of the faithful belonging to their rites throughout the world.

Subject to the Holy Father and directly responsible to him for the exercise of their ministry of service to people in various jurisdictions or divisions of the Church throughout the world are: resident archbishops and metropolitans (heads of archdioceses), diocesan bishops, vicars and prefects apostolic (heads of vicariates apostolic and prefectures apostolic), certain abbots and prelates, apostolic administrators. Each of these, within his respective territory and according to the provisions of canon law, has ordinary jurisdiction over pastors (who are responsible for the administration of parishes), priests, Religious and lay persons.

Also subject to the Holy Father are titular archbishops and bishops, religious orders and congregations of pontifical right, pontifical institutes and faculties, papal nuncios and apostolic delegates.

Assisting the pope and acting in his name in the central government and administration of the Church are cardinals and other officials of the Roman Curia.

## THE HIERARCHY

The ministerial hierarchy is the orderly arrangement of the ranks and orders of the clergy to provide for the spiritual care of the faithful, the government of the Church, and the accomplishment of the Church's total mission in the world.

Persons belong to this hierarchy by virtue of ordination and canonical mission.

The term hierarchy is also used to designate an entire body or group of bishops; for example, the hierarchy of the Church, the hierarchy of the United States.

**Hierarchy of Order:** Consists of the pope, bishops, priests and deacons. Their purpose, for which they are ordained to holy orders, is to carry out the sacramental and pastoral ministry of the Church.

**Hierarchy of Jurisdiction:** Consists of the pope and bishops by divine institution, and other church officials by ecclesiastical institution and mandate, who have authority to govern and direct the faithful for spiritual ends.

### The Pope

His Holiness the Pope is the Bishop of Rome, the Vicar of Jesus Christ, the successor of St. Peter, Prince of the Apostles, the Supreme Pontiff who has the primacy of jurisdiction and not merely of honor over the universal Church, the Patriarch of the West, the Primate of Italy, the Archbishop and Metropolitan of the Roman Province, the Sovereign of the State of Vatican City, Servant of the Servants of God.

### Cardinals

(See Index)

### Patriarchs

Patriarch, a term which had its origin in the Eastern Church, is the title of a bishop who, second only to the pope, has the highest rank in the hierarchy of jurisdiction. He is the incumbent of one of the sees listed below. Subject only to the pope, a patriarch of the Eastern Church is the head of the faithful belonging to his rite throughout the world. The patri-archal sees are so called because of their special status and dignity in the history of the Church.

The Council of Nicaea (325) recognized three patriarchs — the bishops of Alexandria and Antioch in the East, and of Rome in the West. The First Council of Constantinople (381) added the bishop of Constantinople to the list of patriarchs and gave him rank second only to that of the pope, the bishop of Rome and patriarch of the West; this action was seconded by the Council of Chalcedon (451) and was given full recognition by the Fourth Lateran Council (1215). The Council of Chalcedon also acknowledged patriarchal rights of the bishop of Jerusalem.

Eastern patriarchs are as follows: one of Alexandria, for the Copts; three of Antioch, one each for the Syrians, Maronites and Greek Melkites (the latter also has the personal title of Greek Melkite patriarch of Alexandria and of Jerusalem). The patriarch of Babylonia, for the Chaldeans, and the patriarch of Sis, or Cilicia, for the Armenians, should be called, more properly, *Katholikos* — that is, a prelate delegated for a universality of causes. These patriarchs are elected by bishops of their churches: they receive approval and the pallium, symbolic of their office, from the pope.

Latin Rite patriarchates were established for Antioch, Jerusalem, Alexandria and Constantinople during the Crusades; afterwards, they became patriarchates in name only. Jerusalem, however, was reconstituted as a patriarchate by Pius IX, in virtue of the bull *Nulla Celebrior* of July 23, 1847. In 1964, the Latin titular patriarchates of Constantinople, Alexandria and Antioch, long a bone of contention in relations with Eastern Churches, were abolished.

As of July 31, 1996, the patriarchs in the Church were:

The Pope, Bishop of Rome, Patriarch of the West; Stephanos II Ghattas, C.M., of Alexandria, for the Copts; Ignace Antoine II Hayek, of Antioch, for the Syrians; Maximos V Hakim, of Antioch, for the Greek Melkites (he also has personal titles of Alexandria and Jerusalem for the Greek Melkites); Cardinal Nasrallah Pierre Sfeir, of Antioch, for the Maronites; Michel Sabbah, of Jerusalem, for the Latin Rite; Raphael I Bidawid, of Babylon, for the Chaldeans; Jean Pierre XVIII Kasparian, of Cilicia, for the Armenians.

The titular patriarchs (in name only) of the Latin Rite were: Cardinal Antonio Ribeiro, of Lisbon; Cardinal Marco Cé of Venice and Archbishop Raul Nicolau Gonsalves of the East Indies (Archbishop of Goa and Damao, India). The patriarchate of the West Indies has been vacant since 1963.

## Major Archbishops

An archbishop with the prerogatives but not the title of a patriarch. As of July 31, 1996, major archbishops were: Cardinal Myroslav Ivan Lubachivsky of the major archbishopric of Lviv of the Ukrainian Catholic Church (Ukraine) and Cardinal Anthony Padiyara of the major archbishopric of Ernakulam-Angamaly of the Syro-Malabar Church (India).

## Archbishops, Metropolitans

**Archbishop:** A bishop with the title of an archdiocese.

**Coadjutor Archbishop:** An assistant archbishop with right of succession.

**Metropolitan:** Archbishop of the principal see, an archdiocese, in an ecclesiastical province consisting of several dioceses. He has the full powers of bishop in his own archdiocese and limited supervisory jurisdiction and influence over the other (suffragan) dioceses in the province. The pallium, conferred by the pope, is the symbol of his status as a metropolitan.

**Titular Archbishop:** Has the title of an archdiocese which formerly existed in fact but now exists in title only. He does not have ordinary jurisdiction over an archdiocese. Examples are archbishops in the Roman Curia, papal nuncios, apostolic delegates.

**Archbishop ad personam:** A title of personal honor and distinction granted to some bishops. They do not have ordinary jurisdiction over an archdiocese.

**Primate:** A title of honor given to the ranking prelate of some countries or regions.

## Bishops

**Diocesan Bishop:** A bishop in charge of a diocese.

**Coadjutor Bishop:** An assistant (auxiliary) bishop to a diocesan bishop, with right of succession to the see.

**Titular Bishops:** A bishop with the title of a diocese which formerly existed in fact but now exists in title only; an assistant (auxiliary) bishop to a diocesan bishop.

**Episcopal Vicar:** An assistant, who may or may not be a bishop, appointed by a residential bishop as his deputy for a certain part of a diocese, a determined type of apostolic work, or the faithful of a certain rite.

**Eparch, Exarch:** Titles of bishops of Eastern churches.

**Nomination of Bishops:** Nominees for episcopal ordination are selected in several ways. Final appointment and/or approval in all cases is subject to decision by the pope.

In the U.S., bishops periodically submit the names of candidates to the archbishop of their province. The names are then considered at a meeting of the bishops of the province, and those receiving a favorable vote are forwarded to the pro-nuncio for transmission to the Holy See. Bishops are free to seek the counsel of priests, religious and lay persons with respect to nominees.

Eastern Catholic churches have their own procedures and synodal regulations for nominating and making final selection of candidates for episcopal ordination. Such selection is subject to approval by the pope.

The Code of Canon Law concedes no rights or privileges to civil authorities with respect to the election, nomination, presentation or designation of candidates for the episcopate.

*Ad Limina Visit*: Diocesan bishops and apostolic vicars are obliged to make an *ad limina* visit ("to the threshold" of the Apostles) every five years to the tombs of Sts. Peter and Paul, have audience with the Holy Father and consult with appropriate Vatican officials. They are required to send a report on conditions in their jurisdiction to the Congregation for Bishops approximately six — and not less than three — months in advance of the scheduled visit.

## Others with Ordinary Jurisdiction

**Ordinary:** One who has the jurisdiction of an office: the pope, diocesan bishops, vicars general, prelates of missionary territories, vicars apostolic prefects apostolic, vicars capitular during the vacancy of a see, superiors general, abbots primate and other major superiors of men Religious.

Some prelates and abbots, with jurisdiction like that of diocesan bishops, are pastors of the people of God in territories (prelatures and abbacies) not under the jurisdiction of diocesan bishops.

**Vicar Apostolic:** Usually a titular bishop who has ordinary jurisdiction over a mission territory.

**Prefect Apostolic:** Has ordinary jurisdiction over a mission territory.

**Apostolic Administrator:** Usually a bishop appointed to administer an ecclesiastical jurisdiction temporarily. Administrators of lesser rank are also appointed for special and more restricted supervisory duties.

**Vicar General:** A bishop's deputy for the administration of a diocese. Such a vicar does not have to be a bishop.

## Prelates Without Jurisdiction

The title of protonotary apostolic was originally given by the fourth century or earlier to clergy who collected accounts of martyrdom and other church documents, or who served the Church with distinction in other ways. Other titles — e.g., domestic prelate, papal chamberlain, prelate of honor — are titles of clergy in service to the pope and the papal household, or of clergy honored for particular reasons. All prelates without jurisdiction are appointed by the pope, have designated ceremonial privileges and the title of Rev. Monsignor.

# SYNOD OF BISHOPS

The Synod of Bishops was chartered by Pope Paul VI Sept. 15, 1965, in a document he issued on his own initiative under the title, *Apostolica Sollicitudo.* Provisions of this *motu proprio* are contained in Canons 342 to 348 of the Code of Canon Law. According to major provisions of the Synod charter:

• The purposes of the Synod are: "to encourage close union and valued assistance between the Sovereign Pontiff and the bishops of the entire world; to insure that direct and real information is provided on questions and situations touching upon the internal action of the Church and its necessary activity in the world of today; to facilitate agreement on essential points of doctrine and on methods of procedure in the life of the Church."

• The Synod is a central ecclesiastical institution, permanent by nature.

• The Synod is directly and immediately subject to the Pope, who has authority to assign its agenda, to call it into session, and to give its members deliberative as well as advisory authority.

• In addition to a limited number of ex officio members and a few heads of male religious institutes, the majority of the members are elected by and representative of national or regional episcopal conferences. The Pope reserved the right to appoint the general secretary, special secretaries and no more than 15 per cent of the total membership.

The Pope is president of the Synod.

The secretary general is Cardinal Jan Schotte, C.I.C.M., of Belgium. Address: Palazzo del Bramante, Via della Concilizione 34, 00193 Rome, Italy.

An advisory council of 15 members (12 elected, three appointed by the pope) provides the secretariat with adequate staff for carrying on liaison with episcopal conferences and for preparing the agenda of synodal assemblies.

## Assemblies

**1. First Assembly:** The first assembly was held from Sept. 29 to Oct. 29, 1967. Its objectives, as stated by Pope Paul VI, were "the preservation and strengthening of the Catholic faith, its integrity, its force, its development, its doctrinal and historical coherence." One result was a recommendation for the establishment of an international commission of theologians to assist the Congregation for the Doctrine of the Faith and to broaden approaches to theological research. Pope Paul set up the commission in 1969.

**2. Pope-Bishop Relations:** The second assembly held Oct. 11 to 28, 1969, was extraordinary in character. It opened the way toward greater participation by bishops with the pope and each other in the governance of the Church. Proceedings were oriented to three main points: (1) the nature and implications of collegiality; (2) the relationship of bishops and their conferences to the pope; (3) the relationships of bishops and their conferences to each other.

**3. Priesthood and Justice:** The ministerial priesthood and justice in the world were the principal topics under discussion at the second ordinary assembly, Sept. 30 to Nov. 6, 1971. In one report, the Synod emphasized the primary and permanent dedication of priests in the Church to the ministry of word, sacrament and pastoral service as a full-time vocation. In another report, the assembly stated: "Action on behalf of justice and participation in the transformation of the world fully appear to us as a constitutive dimension of the preaching of the Gospel; or, in other words, of the Church's mission for the redemption of the human race and its liberation from every oppressive situation."

**4. Evangelization:** The assembly of Sept. 27 to Oct. 26, 1974, produced a general statement on evangelization of the modern world, covering the need for it and its relationship to efforts for total human liberation from personal and social evil. The assembly observed: "The Church does not remain within merely political, social and economic limits (elements which she must certainly take into account) but leads towards freedom under all its forms — liberation from sin, from individual or collective selfishness — and to full communion with God and with men who are like brothers. In this way the Church, in her evangelical way, promotes the true and complete liberation of all men, groups and peoples."

**5. Catechetics:** The fourth ordinary assembly, Sept. 30 to Oct. 29, 1977, focused attention on catechetics, with special reference to children and young people. The participants issued a "Message to the People of God," the first synodal statement issued since inception of the body, and also presented to Pope Paul VI a set of 34 related propositions and a number of suggestions.

**6. Family:** "A Message to Christian Families in the Modern World" and a proposal for a "Charter of Family Rights" were produced by the assembly held Sept. 26 to Oct. 25, 1980. The assembly reaffirmed the indissolubility of marriage and the contents of the encyclical letter *Humanae Vitae* (see separate entry), and urged married couples who find it hard to live up to "the difficult but loving demands" of Christ not to be discouraged but to avail themselves of the aid of divine grace. In response to synodal recommendation, Pope John Paul issued a charter of family rights late in 1983.

**7. Reconciliation:** Penance and reconciliation in the mission of the Church was the theme of the assembly held Sept. 29 to Oct. 29, 1983. Sixty-three propositions related to this theme were formulated on a wide variety of subjects, including: personal sin and so-called systemic or institutional sin; the nature of serious sin; the diminished sense of sin and of the need of redemption, related to decline in the administration and reception of the sacrament of penance; general absolution; individual and social reconciliation; violence and violations of human rights; reconciliation as the basis of peace and justice in society. In a statement issued Oct. 27, the Synod stressed the need of the world to become, increasingly, "a reconciled community of peoples," and said that "the Church, as sacrament of reconciliation to the world, has to be an effective sign of God's mercy."

**8. Vatican II Review:** The second extraordinary

assembly was convened Nov. 24 to Dec. 8, 1985, for the purposes of: (1) recalling the Second Vatican Council; (2) evaluating the implementation of its enactments during the 20 years since its conclusion; (3) seeking ways and means of promoting renewal in the Church in accordance with the spirit and letter of the council. At the conclusion of the assembly the bishops issued two documents. (1) In A Message to the People of God, they noted the need for greater appreciation of the enactments of Vatican II and for greater efforts to put them into effect, so that all members of the Church might discharge their responsibility of proclaiming the good news of salvation. (2) In a Final Report, the first of its kind published by a synodal assembly, the bishops reflected on lights and shadows since Vatican II, stating that negative developments had come from partial and superficial interpretations of conciliar enactments and from incomplete or ineffective implementation thereof. The report also covered a considerable number of subjects discussed during the assembly, including the mystery of the Church, inculturation, the preferential (but not exclusive) option for the poor, and a suggestion for the development of a new universal catechism of the Catholic faith.

**9. Vocation and Mission of the Laity** in the Church and in the World 20 years after the Second Vatican Council: The seventh ordinary assembly, Oct. 1 to 30, 1987, said in a Message to the People of God: "The majority of the Christian laity live out their vocation as followers and disciples of Christ in all spheres of life which we call 'the world': the family, the field of work, the local community and the like. To permeate this day-to-day living with the spirit of Christ has always been the task of the lay faithful; and it should be with still greater force their challenge today. It is in this way that they sanctify the world and collaborate in the realization of the kingdom of God." The assembly produced a set of 54 propositions which were presented to the Pope for consideration in the preparation of a document of his own on the theme of the assembly. He responded with the apostolic exhortation, *Christifideles Laici*, "The Christian Faithful Laity," released by the Vatican Jan. 30, 1989.

**10. Formation of Priests in Circumstances of the Present Day:** The eighth general assembly, Sept. 30 to Oct. 28, 1990, dealt principally with the nature and mission of the priesthood; the identity, multi-faceted formation and spirituality of priests; and, in a Message to the People of God, the need on all levels of the Church for the promotion of vocations to the priesthood. Forty-one proposals were presented to the Pope for his consideration in preparing a document of his own on the theme of the assembly. Pope John Paul issued an apostolic exhortation entitled *Pastores Dabo Vobis* ("I Will Give You Shepherds") Apr. 7, 1992, in response to the Synods' recommendations.

**11. The Consecrated Life and Its Role in the Church and in the World:** The ninth general assembly was held Oct. 2 to 29, 1994. (See the related apostolic exhortation *Vita Consecrata*.)

Recent special assemblies of the Synod of Bishops have been held: for Europe (Nov. 28 to Dec. 14, 1991); for Africa (Apr. 10 to May 8, 1994; see the related apostolic exhortation The Church in Africa); for Lebanon (Nov. 27 to Dec. 14, 1995, Other special assemblies are being planned for the Americas and for Asia.

# ROMAN CURIA

The Roman Curia is the Church's network of central administrative agencies (called dicasteries) serving the Vatican and the local churches, with authority granted by the Pope.

The Curia evolved gradually from advisory assemblies or synods of the Roman clergy with whose assistance the popes directed church affairs during the first 11 centuries. Its original office was the Apostolic Chancery, established in the fourth century to transmit documents. The antecedents of its permanently functioning agencies and offices were special commissions of cardinals and prelates. Its establishment in a form resembling what it is now dates from the second half of the 16th century.

Pope Paul VI initiated a four-year reorganization study in 1963 which resulted in the constitution *Regimini Ecclesiae Universae*. The document was published Aug. 18, 1967, and went into full effect in March, 1968.

Pope John Paul II, in the apostolic constitution *Pastor Bonus*, published June 28, 1988, and effective Mar. 1, 1989, ordered modifications of the Curia based on the broad outline of Paul VI's reorganization.

The Curia (in accordance with Pope John Paul II's reform effective Mar. 1, 1989, and later revisions), consists of the Secretariat of State, nine congregations (governing agencies), three tribunals (judicial agencies), 11 councils (promotional agencies) and three offices (specialized service agencies). All have equal juridical status with authority granted by the Pope.

## SECRETARIAT OF STATE

The Secretariat of State, Palazzo Apostolico Vaticano, Vatican City. Cardinal Angelo Sodano, Secretary of State; Most Rev. Giovanni Battista Re, Deputy for General Affairs; Most Rev. Jean Louis Tauran, Secretary for Relations with States.

The Secretariat of State provides the pope with the closest possible assistance in the care of the universal Church. It consists of two sections:

• The Section for General Affairs assists the Pope in expediting daily business of the Holy See. It coordinates curial operations; prepares drafts of documents entrusted to it by the pope; has supervisory duties over the *Acta Apostolicae Sedis, Annuario Pontificio*, the Vatican Press Office and the Central Statistics Office.

• The Section for Relations with States (formerly the Council for Public Affairs of the Church, a separate body) handles diplomatic and other relations with civil governments. Attached to it is a Council of Cardinals and Bishops.

Background: Evolved gradually from secretarial

offices (dating back to the 15th century) and the Congregation for Extraordinary Ecclesiastical Affairs (dating back to 1793; restructured as the Council for the Public Affairs of the Church by Paul VI in 1967). John Paul II gave it its present form in his June 28, 1988, reform of the Curia.

## CONGREGATIONS

**Congregation for the Doctrine of the Faith:** Piazza del S. Uffizio 11, 00193 Rome, Italy. Cardinal Joseph Ratzinger, prefect; Most Rev. Tarcisio Bertone, S.D.B., secretary.

Has responsibility to safeguard the doctrine of faith and morals. Accordingly, it examines doctrinal questions; promotes studies thereon; evaluates theological opinions and, when necessary and after prior consultation with concerned bishops, reproves those regarded as opposed to principles of the faith; examines books on doctrinal matters and can reprove such works, if the contents so warrant, after giving authors the opportunity to defend themselves. It examines matters pertaining to the Privilege of Faith (Petrine Privilege) in marriage cases, and safeguards the dignity of the sacrament of penance. Attached to the congregation are the Pontifical Biblical Commission and the Theological Commission.

Background: At the beginning of the 13th century, legates of Innocent III were commissioned as the Holy Office of the Inquisition to combat heresy; the same task was entrusted to the Dominican Order by Gregory IX in 1231 and to the Friars Minor by Innocent IV from 1243 to 1254. On July 21, 1542 (apostolic constitution *Licet*), Paul III instituted a permanent congregation of cardinals with supreme and universal competence over matters concerning heretics and those suspected of heresy. Pius IV, St. Pius V and Sixtus V further defined the work of the congregation. St. Pius X changed its name to the Congregation of the Holy Office. Paul VI (motu proprio *Integrae Servandae*, Dec. 7, 1965), began reorganization of the Curia with this body, to which he gave the new title, Congregation for the Doctrine of the Faith. Its orientation is not merely negative, in the condemnation of error, but positive, in the promotion of orthodox doctrine.

**Congregation for the Oriental Churches:** Palazzo del Bramante, Via della Conciliazione 34, 00193 Rome, Italy. Cardinal Achille Silvestrini, prefect; Most Rev. Miroslav Stefan Marusyn, secretary. Members include all patriarchs of the Eastern Catholic Churches and major archbishops.

Has competence in matters concerning the persons and discipline of Eastern Catholic Churches. It has jurisdiction over territories in which the majority of Christians belong to Eastern Churches (i.e., Egypt, the Sinai Peninsula, Eritrea, Northern Ethiopia, Southern Albania, Bulgaria, Cyprus, Greece, Iran, Iraq, Lebanon, Palestine, Syria, Jordan, Turkey, Afghanistan); also, over minority communities of Eastern Church members no matter where they live.

Background: Established by Pius IX Jan. 6, 1862 (apostolic constitution *Romani Pontifices*), and united with the Congregation for the Propagation of the Faith. The congregation was made autonomous by Benedict XV May 1, 1917 (motu proprio *Dei Providentis*), and given wider authority by Pius XI

Mar. 25, 1938 (motu proprio *Sancta Dei Ecclesia*).

**Congregation for Bishops:** Piazza Pio XII 10, 00193 Rome, Italy. Cardinal Bernardin Gantin, prefect; Most Rev. Jorge Maria Mejia, secretary.

Has functions related in one way or another to bishops and the jurisdictions in which they serve. It supervises the Pontifical Commission for Latin America. Attached to the congregation are a central coordinating office for Military Vicars (established Feb. 2, 1985) and an office for coordinating *ad limina* visits (established June 29, 1988).

Background: Established by Sixtus V Jan. 22, 1588 (apostolic constitution *Immensa*); given an extension of powers by St. Pius X June 20, 1908, and Pius XII Aug. 1, 1952 (apostolic constitution *Exsul Familia*); given present title (was known as Consistorial Congregation) by Paul VI (Aug. 1, 1967); competencies redefined by John Paul II, June 28, 1988.

**Congregation for Divine Worship and the Discipline of the Sacraments:** Piazza Pio XII 10, 00193 Rome, Italy. Most Rev. Jorge Arturo Medina Estevez, pro-prefect; Most Rev. Geraldo Majella Agnelo, secretary.

Supervises everything pertaining to the promotion and regulation of the liturgy, primarily the sacraments, without prejudice to the competencies of the Congregation for the Doctrine of the Faith. Attached to the congregation are special commissions treating causes of nullity of sacred ordinations and dispensations from obligations of sacred ordination of deacons and priests.

Background: Originally two separate congregations: the Congregation for Divine Worship (instituted by Paul VI, May 8, 1969) and the Congregation for the Discipline of the Sacraments (established by St. Pius X, June 29, 1908, to replace the Congregation of Rites instituted by Pope Sixtus V in 1588). They were united by Paul VI, July 11, 1975, as the Congregation for the Sacraments and Divine Worship; reestablished as separate congregations by John Paul II in an autograph letter of Apr. 5, 1984, and reunited anew by the same Pope, June 28, 1988 (apostolic constitution *Pastor Bonus*) as the Congregation for Divine Worship and the Discipline of the Sacraments.

**Congregation for the Causes of Saints:** Piazza Pio XII 10, 00193 Rome, Italy. Most Rev. Alberto Bovone, pro-prefect; Most Rev. Edward Nowak, secretary.

Handles matters connected with beatification and canonization causes (in accordance with revised procedures decreed in 1983), and the preservation of relics.

Background: Established by Sixtus V in 1588 as the Congregation of Rites; affected by legislation of Pius XI in 1930; title changed and functions defined by Paul VI, 1969 (apostolic constitution *Sacra Rituum Congregatio*). It was restructured and canonization procedures were revised by John Paul II in 1983 (apostolic constitution *Divinus Perfectionis Magister*).

**Congregation for the Clergy:** Piazza Pio XII 3, 00193 Rome, Italy. Most Rev. Dario Castrillon Hoyos, pro-prefect; Most Rev. Crescenzio Sepe, secretary.

Has three offices with competencies concerning the

life, discipline, rights and duties of the clergy; the preaching of the Word, catechetics, norms for religious education of children and adults; preservation and administration of the temporal goods of the Church. Attached to it are the International Council for Catechetics (established in 1973 by Paul VI) and the Institute "Sacrum Ministerium" for the permanent formation of the clergy (established in line with John Paul II's 1992 apostolic exhortation *Pastores dabo Vobis*).

Background: Established by Pius IV Aug. 2, 1564 (apostolic constitution *Alias Nos*), under the title, Congregation of the Cardinals Interpreters of the Council of Trent; affected by legislation of Gregory XIII and Sixtus V; known as Congregation of the Council until Aug. 15, 1967, when Paul VI renamed it the Congregation for the Clergy and redefined its competency; John Paul II gave it added responsibilities June 28, 1988.

**Congregation for Institutes of Consecrated Life and Societies of Apostolic Life:** Piazza Pio XII 3, 00193 Rome, Italy. Cardinal Eduardo Martinez Somalo, prefect; Most. Rev. Francisco Javier Errazuriz Ossa, secretary.

Has competence over institutes of Religious, secular institutes, societies of the apostolic life and third (secular) orders. With two sections, the congregation has authority in matters related to the establishment, general direction and suppression of the various institutes; general discipline in line with their rules and constitutions; the movement toward renewal and adaptation of institutes in contemporary circumstances; the setting up and encouragement of councils and conferences of major religious superiors for intercommunication and other purposes.

Background: Founded by Sixtus V May 27, 1586, with the title, Congregation for Consultations of Regulars; confirmed by the apostolic constitution *Immensa* Jan. 22, 1588; made part of the Congregation for Consultations of Bishops and other Prelates in 1601; made autonomous by St. Pius X in 1908 as Congregation of Religious; title changed to Congregation for Religious and Secular Institutes by Paul VI in 1967; given present title by John Paul II, June 28, 1988.

**Congregation for Catholic Education (for Seminaries and Institutes of Study):** Piazza Pio XII 3, 00193 Rome, Italy. Cardinal Pio Laghi, prefect; Most Rev. Jose Saraiva Martins, C.M.F., secretary.

Has supervisory competence over institutions and works of Catholic education. It carries on its work through three offices. One office handles matters connected with the direction, discipline and temporal administration of seminaries, and with the education of diocesan clergy, religious and members of secular institutes. A second office oversees Catholic universities, faculties of study and other institutions of higher learning inasmuch as they depend on the authority of the Church; encourages cooperation and mutual assistance among Catholic institutions, and the establishment of Catholic hospices and centers on campuses of non-Catholic institutions. A third office is concerned in various ways with all Catholic schools below the college-university level, with general questions concerning education and studies, and with the cooperation of conferences of bishops

and civil authorities in educational matters. The congregation supervises Pontifical Works for Priestly Vocations.

Background: The title (Congregation of Seminaries and Universities) and functions of the congregation were defined by Benedict XV Nov. 4, 1915; Pius XI, in 1931 and 1932, and Pius XII, in 1941 and 1949, extended its functions; Paul VI changed its title to Congregation for Catholic Education in 1967; given its present title by Pope John Paul II, June 28, 1988. Its work had previously been carried on by two other congregations erected by Sixtus V in 1588 and Leo XII in 1824.

**Congregation for the Evangelization of Peoples:** Piazza di Spagna 48, 00187 Rome, Italy. Cardinal Jozef Tomko, prefect; Most Rev. Giuseppe Uhac, secretary; Most Rev. Charles A. Schleck, C.S.C., adjunct secretary.

Directs and coordinates missionary work throughout the world. Accordingly, it has competence over those matters which concern all the missions established for the spread of Christ's kingdom without prejudice to the competence of other congregations. These include: fostering missionary vocations; assigning missionaries to fields of work; establishing ecclesiastical jurisdictions and proposing candidates to serve them as bishops and in other capacities; encouraging the recruitment and development of indigenous clergy; mobilizing spiritual and financial support for missionary activity.

To promote missionary cooperation, the congregation has a Supreme Council for the Direction of Pontifical Missionary Works composed of the Missionary Union of the Clergy and Religious, the Society for the Propagation of the Faith, the Society of St. Peter the Apostle for Native Clergy, the Society of the Holy Childhood, and the International Center of Missionary Animation.

Background: Originated as a commission of cardinals by St. Pius V and Gregory XII for missions in East and West Indies, Italo-Greeks and for ecclesiastical affairs in Protestant territories of Europe; Clement VIII instituted a Congregation of the Propagation of the Faith in 1599 which ceased to exist after several years. Erected as a stable congregation by Gregory XV June 22, 1622 (apostolic constitution *Inscrutabili Divinae);* its functions were redefined by John Paul II, June 28, 1988.

## Inter-Agency Curia Commissions

In accordance with provisions of the apostolic constitution *Pastor Bonus,* John Paul II established the following interdepartmental permanent commissions to handle matters when more than one agency of the Curia is involved in activities:

• For matters concerning appointments to local Churches and the setting up and alteration of them and their constitution (Mar. 22, 1989). Members include officials of the Secretariat of State and Congregation for Bishops. President, Cardinal Angelo Sodano, Secretary of State.

• For matters concerning members, individually or as a community, of Institutes of Consecrated Life founded or working in mission territories (Mar. 22, 1989). Members include officials of the Congregations for the Evangelization of Peoples and for Institutes of Consecrated Life and Societies of Apostolic Life. President: Cardinal Jozef Tomko, prefect of the Congregation for the Evangelization of Peoples.

• For the formation of candidates for Sacred Orders (Mar. 22, 1989). Members include officials of the Congregations for Catholic Education, for Institutes of Consecrated Life and Societies of Apostolic Life, for Evangelization of Peoples, for Oriental Churches. President: Cardinal Pio Laghi, prefect of the Congregation for Catholic Education.

• For promoting a more equitable distribution of priests throughout the world (July 20, 1991). Members include secretaries of congregations for Evangelization of Peoples, for the Clergy, Catholic Education, for the Institutes of Consecrated Life and Societies of Apostolic Life; and vice-president of Commission for Latin America. Co-Presidents, Cardinal Pio Laghi, prefect of the Congregation for Catholic Education and Most Rev. Dario Castrillon Hoyos, pro-prefect of the Congregation for the Clergy.

• For the Church in Eastern Europe (Jan. 15, 1993), replacing the Pontifical Commission for Russia which was terminated. The commission is concerned with both Latin and Eastern-rite churches in territories of the former Soviet Union and other nations affected by the historical circumstances resulting from atheistic communism. It is responsible for promoting the apostolic mission of the Church and fostering ecumenical dialogue with the Orthodox and other Churches of the Eastern tradition. Members, under presidency of Cardinal Secretary of State, include the secretary and undersecretary of the Section for Relations with States and secretaries of Congregations for the Oriental Churches, for the Clergy, for Institutes of Consecrated Life and Societies of Apostolic Life, secretary of the Pontifical Council for Promoting Christian Unity. President, Cardinal Angelo Sodano.

## TRIBUNALS

**Apostolic Penitentiary:** Piazza della Cancelleria 1, 00186 Rome, Italy. Cardinal William Wakefield Baum, major penitentiary; Msgr. Luigi de Magistris, regent.

Has jurisdiction for the internal forum only (sacramental and non-sacramental). It issues decisions on questions of conscience; grants absolutions, dispensations, commutations, sanations and condonations; has charge of non-doctrinal matters pertaining to indulgences.

Background: Origin dates back to the 12th century; affected by the legislation of many popes; radically reorganized by St. Pius V in 1569; jurisdiction limited to the internal forum by St. Pius X; Benedict XV annexed the Office of Indulgences to it Mar. 25, 1917.

**Apostolic Signatura:** Piazza della Cancelleria 1, 00186 Rome, Italy. Cardinal Gilberto Agustoni, prefect; Most Rev. Zenon Grocholewski, secretary.

The principal concerns of this supreme court of the Church are to resolve questions concerning juridical procedure and to supervise the observance of laws and rights at the highest level. It decides the jurisdictional competence of lower courts and has jurisdiction in cases involving personnel and decisions of the Rota. It is the supreme court of the State of Vatican City.

Background: A permanent office of the Signatura has existed since the time of Eugene IV in the 15th century; affected by the legislation of many popes; reorganized by St. Pius X in 1908 and made the supreme tribunal of the Church.

**Roman Rota:** Piazza della Cancelleria 1, 00186 Rome, Italy. Msgr. Mario Francesco Pompedda, dean.

The ordinary court of appeal for cases appealed to the Holy See. It is best known for its competence and decisions in cases involving the validity of marriage.

Background: Originated in the Apostolic Chancery; affected by the legislation of many popes; reorganized by St. Pius X in 1908; further revised by Pius XI in 1934; new norms approved and promulgated by John Paul II in 1982 and 1987.

## COUNCILS

**Pontifical Council for the Laity:** Piazza S. Calisto 16, 00153 Rome, Italy. Most Rev. James Francis Stafford, president; Most Rev. Stanislaw Rylko, secretary; Prof. Guzman Carriquiry, undersecretary.

Its competence covers the apostolate of the laity and their participation in the life and mission of the Church. Members are mostly lay people from different parts of the world and involved in different apostolates.

Background: Established on an experimental basis by Paul VI Jan. 6, 1967; given permanent status Dec. 10, 1976 (motu proprio *Apostolatus Peragendi*).

**Pontifical Council for Promoting Christian Unity:** Via dell' Erba 1, 00193 Rome, Italy. Cardinal Edward I. Cassidy, president; Cardinal Johannes Willebrands, president emeritus; Most Rev. Pierre Duprey, M. Afr., secretary.

Handles relations with members of other Christian ecclesial communities; deals with the correct interpretation and execution of the principles of ecumenism; initiates or promotes Catholic ecumenical groups and coordinates on national and international levels the efforts of those promoting Christian unity; undertakes dialogue regarding ecumenical questions and activities with churches and ecclesial communities separated from the Apostolic See; sends Catholic observer-representatives to Christian gatherings, and invites to Catholic gatherings observers of other churches; orders into execution conciliar decrees dealing with ecumenical affairs. The Commission for Religious Relations with Jews is attached to the secretariat.

Background: Established by John XXIII June 5, 1960, as a preparatory secretariat of the Second Vatican Council; raised to commission status during the first session of the council in the fall of 1962; status as a secretariat confirmed and functions defined by Paul VI in 1966 and 1967; made a pontifical council by John Paul II, June 28, 1988.

**Pontifical Council for the Family:** Piazza S. Calisto 16, 00153 Rome, Italy. Cardinal Alfonso Lopez Trujillo, president; Most Rev. Francisco Gil Hellin, secretary.

Is concerned with promoting the pastoral care of

families so they may carry out their educative, evangelizing and apostolic mission and make their influence felt in areas such as defense of human life and responsible procreation according to the teachings of the Church. Members, chosen by the Pope, are married couples and men and women from all parts of the world and representing different cultures. They meet in general assembly at least once a year.

Background: Instituted by John Paul II May 9, 1981, replacing the Committee for the Family established by Paul VI Jan. 11, 1973.

**Pontifical Council for Justice and Peace:** Piazza S. Calisto 16, 00153 Rome, Italy. Cardinal Roger Etchegaray, president; Msgr. Diarmuid Martin, secretary.

Its primary competence is to promote justice and peace in the world according to the Gospels and social teaching of the Church.

Background: Instituted by Paul VI Jan. 6, 1967, on an experimental basis; reconstituted and made a permanent commission Dec. 10, 1976; its competence was redefined and it was made a pontifical council June 28, 1988, by John Paul II.

**Pontifical Council "Cor Unum":** Piazza S. Calisto 16, 00153 Rome, Italy. Most Rev. Paul Josef Cordes, president; Rev. Ivan Marin Lopez, secretary.

Its principal aims are to provide informational and coordinating services for Catholic aid and human development organizations and projects on a worldwide scale. Attached to the council are the John Paul II Foundation for the Sahel and "Populorum Progressio."

Background: Instituted by Paul VI July 15, 1971.

**Pontifical Council for Pastoral Care of Migrants and Itinerant Peoples:** Piazza S. Calisto 16, 00153 Rome, Italy. Most Rev. Giovanni Cheli, president; Most Rev. Francesco Gioia, O.F.M. Cap., secretary.

Is concerned with pastoral assistance to migrants, nomads, tourists, sea and air travelers.

Background: Instituted by Paul VI and placed under general supervision of Congregation for Bishops, Mar. 19, 1970; made autonomous as a pontifical council and renamed by John Paul II, June 28, 1988.

**Pontifical Council for Pastoral Assistance to Health Care Workers:** Via della Conciliazione 3, 00193 Rome, Italy. Cardinal Fiorenzo Angelini, president; Very Rev. Jose Luis Redrado Marchite, O.H., secretary.

Its functions are to stimulate and foster the work of formation, study and action carried out by various international Catholic organizations in the health care field.

Background: Established in 1985 as a commission by John Paul II; made a council June 28, 1988.

**Pontifical Council for the Interpretation of Legislative Texts:** Piazza Pio XII 10, 00193 Rome, Italy. Most Rev. Julian Herranz, president; Most Rev. Bruno Bertagna, secretary.

Primary function is the authentic interpretation of the universal laws of the Church.

Background: Established by John Paul II, Jan. 2, 1984, as the Pontifical Commission for the Authentic Interpretation of the Code of Canon Law; name changed and given additional functions June 28, 1988. Its competency was extended in 1991 to include interpretation of Code of Canon Law of Oriental Church which was promulgated in 1990.

**Pontifical Council for Interreligious Dialogue:** Via dell' Erba 1, 00193 Rome, Italy. Cardinal Francis Arinze, president; Most Rev. Michael Louis Fitzgerald, M. Afr., secretary.

Its function is to promote studies and dialogue for the purpose of increasing mutual understanding and respect between Christians and non-Christians. The Commission for Religious Relations with Muslims is attached to the council.

Background: Established by Paul VI May 19, 1964, as the Secretariat for Non-Christians; given present title and functions by John Paul II, June 28, 1988.

**Pontifical Council for Culture:** Piazza S. Calisto 16, 00153 Rome, Italy. Cardinal Paul Poupard, president; Msgr. Franc Rodé, C.M., secretary.

Its functions are to foster the Church's and the Holy See's relations with the world of culture and to establish dialogue with those who do not believe in God or who profess no religion provided these are open to sincere cooperation. It consists of two sections: (1) faith and culture; (2) dialogue with cultures.

Background: Present council with expanded functions was instituted by John Paul II (motu proprio of Mar. 25, 1993) through the merger of the Pontifical Council for Culture (established May 20, 1982, by John Paul II) and the Pontifical Council for Dialogue with Non-Believers (established by Paul VI Apr. 9, 1965, as the secretariat for Non-Believers).

**Pontifical Council for Social Communications:** Palazzo S. Carlo, 00120 Vatican City. Most Rev. John P. Foley, president; Most Rev. Pierfranco Pastore, secretary; Mr. Hans-Peter Rothin, undersecretary; Cardinal Andrzej M. Deskur, president emeritus.

Engaged in matters pertaining to instruments of social communication so that through them the message of salvation and human progress is fostered and carried forward in civil culture and mores.

Background: Instituted on an experimental basis by Pius XII in 1948; reorganized three times in the 1950s; made permanent commission by John XXIII Feb. 22, 1959; established as council and functions restated by John Paul II June 28, 1988.

## OFFICES

**Apostolic Chamber:** Palazzo Apostolico, 00120 Vatican City. Cardinal Eduardo Martinez Somalo, chamberlain of the Holy Roman Church; Most Rev. Ettore Cunial, vice-chamberlain.

Administers the temporal goods and rights of the Holy See between the death of one pope and the election of another, in accordance with special laws.

Background: Originated in the 11th century; reorganized by Pius XI in 1934; functions redefined (especially of camerlengo) by subsequent legislation in 1945, 1962 and 1975.

**Prefecture for the Economic Affairs of the Holy See:** Largo del Colonnato 3, 00193 Rome, Italy. Cardinal Edmund C. Szoka, president; Most Rev. Luigi Sposito, secretary.

A financial office which coordinates and supervises administration of the temporalities of the Holy See.

Background: Established by Paul VI Aug. 15, 1967; functions redefined by John Paul II, June 28, 1988.

**Administration of the Patrimony of the Apostolic See:** Palazzo Apostolico, 00120 Vatican City. Most Rev. Lorenzo Antonetti, pro-president; Most Rev. Claudio Maria Celli, secretary.

Handles the estate of the Apostolic See under the direction of papal delegates acting with ordinary or extraordinary authorization.

Background: Some of its functions date back to 1878; established by Paul VI Aug. 15, 1967.

## Other Curia Agencies

**Prefecture of the Papal Household:** Most Rev. Dino Monduzzi, prefect.

Oversees the papal chapel — which is at the service of the pope in his capacity as spiritual head of the Church — and the pontifical family — which is at the service of the pope as a sovereign. It arranges papal audiences, has charge of preparing non-liturgical elements of papal ceremonies, makes all necessary arrangements for papal visits and trips outside the Vatican, and settles questions of protocol connected with papal audiences and other formalities.

Background: Established by Paul VI Aug. 15, 1967, under the title, Prefecture of the Apostolic Palace; it supplanted the Sacred Congregation for Ceremonies founded by Sixtus V Jan. 22, 1588. The office was updated and reorganized under the present title by Paul VI, Mar. 28, 1968.

**Office for Liturgical Celebrations of the Supreme Pontiff:** Apostolico Vaticano, 00120 Vatican City. Msgr. Piero Marini, Master of Ceremonies.

Prepares everything necessary for liturgical and other sacred celebrations by the Pope or in his name; directs everything in accordance with prescriptions of liturgical law.

Background: Evolved gradually from the early office of Apostolic Master of Ceremonies; affected by legislation of Pope Paul IV in 1563 and Benedict XV in 1917; restructured by Paul VI in 1967; given its present title (formerly known as Prefecture of Pontifical Ceremonies) and constituted as an autonomous agency of the Roman Curia by John Paul II, June 28, 1988.

**Vatican Press Office:** Via della Conciliazione 54, 00193 Rome. Joaquin Navarro-Valls, director.

Established Feb. 29, 1968, to replace service agencies formerly operated by L'Osservatore Romano and an office created for press coverage of the Second Vatican Council. New directives were issued in 1986.

**Vatican Information Service (VIS):** Via della Conciliazione 54, 00193 Rome.

Established Mar. 28, 1990, within the framework but distinct from the Vatican Press Office. Furnishes information, in English, French and Spanish, on pastoral and magisterial activity of the Pope through use of electronic mail and fax.

**Central Statistics Office:** Palazzo Apostolico, 00120 Vatican City.

Established by Paul VI Aug. 15, 1967; attached to the Secretariat of State. Compiles, systematizes and analyzes information on the status and condition of the Church.

## Internationalization

As of June 30, 1996, principal officials of the Roman Curia were from the following countries: Italy (Cards. Angelini, Fagiolo, Felici, Laghi, Noè, Silvestrini, Sodano; Abps. Antonetti, Bertone, Bovone, Celli, Cheli, Cunial, Lajolo, Marchisano, Re, Sepe; Bps. Bertagna, Monduzzi, Pastore, Sposito); France (Cards. Etchegaray, Poupard, Abp. Tauran, Bp. Duprey); United States (Cards. Baum, Szoka, Abps. Foley, Schleck); Spain (Card. Martinez Somalo; Abp. Herranz); Argentina (Card. Pironio, Abp. Mejia); Germany (Card. Ratzinger, Bp. Cordes); Poland (Abps. Grocholewski, Nowak); Australia (Card. Cassidy); Belgium (Card. Schotte); Benin (Card. Gantin); Brazil (Abp. Agnelo); Canada (Card. Gagnon); Chile (Abp. Errazuriz Ossa; Bp. Medina Estevez); Colombia (Card. Lopez Trujillo; Abp. Castrillon Hoyos); Croatia (Abp. Uhac); England (Bp. Fitzgerald); Nigeria (Card. Arinze); Portugal (Abp. Saraiva Martins); Slovakia (Card. Tomko); Switzerland (Card. Agustoni); Ukraine (Abp. Marusyn).

## COMMISSIONS AND COMMITTEES

Listed below are non-curial institutes which assist in the work of the Holy See. Some are attached to curial agencies, as indicated. Other institutes are listed elsewhere in the Almanac; see Index.

**Pontifical Commission for the Cultural Heritage of the Church:** Established by John Paul II, June 28, 1988, as Pontifical Commission for Preserving the Church'Patrimony of Art and History and attached to the Congregation for the Clergy; made autonomous and given present title Mar. 25, 1993. Most Rev. Francesco Marchisano, president.

**Pontifical Commission for Sacred Archeology:** Instituted by Pius IX Jan, 6, 1852. Most Rev. Francesco Marchisano, president.

**Pontifical Biblical Commission:** Instituted by Leo XIII Oct. 30, 1902; completely restructured by Paul VI June 27, 1971; attached to the Congregation for the Doctrine of the Faith. Cardinal Joseph Ratzinger, president.

**Pontifical Commission for Latin America:** Instituted by Pius XII Apr. 19, 1958; attached to the Congregation for Bishops July, 1969; restructured by John Paul II in 1988. Cardinal Bernardin Gantin, president.

**Pontifical Commission for the Revision and Emendation of the Vulgate:** Established in 1984 by John Paul II to replace the Abbey of St. Jerome instituted by Pius XI in 1933. Rev. Jean Mallet, O.S.B., director.

**Pontifical Commission "Ecclesia Dei":** Established by John Paul II, July 2, 1988, to facilitate the return to full ecclesial communion of priests, seminarians and religious who belonged to the fraternity founded by Marcel Lefebvre. Cardinal Angelo Felici, president.

**International Theological Commission:** Instituted by Paul VI Apr. 11, 1969, as an advisory adjunct of no more than 30 theologians to the Congregation for the Doctrine of the Faith; definitive statutes promulgated by John Paul II, Aug. 6, 1982. Cardinal Joseph Ratzinger, president.

**Commission for Religious Relations with Jews:** Instituted by Paul VI, Oct. 22, 1974, to promote and foster relations of a religious nature between Jews and Christians; attached to the Council for Promoting Christian Unity. Cardinal Edward I. Cassidy, president.

**Commission for Religious Relations with Muslims:** Instituted by Paul VI, Oct. 22, 1974, to promote, regulate and interpret relations between Catholics and Muslims; attached to the Council for Interreligious Dialogue. Cardinal Francis Arinze, president.

**Pontifical Committee for International Eucharistic Congresses:** Instituted, 1879, by Pope Leo XIII; established as a pontifical committee with new statutes by John Paul II, Feb. 11, 1986. Cardinal Edouard Gagnon, president.

**Pontifical Committee for Historical Sciences:** Instituted by Pius XII Apr. 7, 1954, as a continuation of a commission dating from 1883. Msgr. Victor Saxer, president.

**Committee for the Grand Jubilee of the Holy Year 2000:** Instituted by John Paul II Nov. 15, 1994. Cardinal Roger Etchegaray, president.

**Vatican II Archives:** Preserves the acts and other documents of the Second Vatican Council.

**Cardinalatial Commission for Sanctuaries of Pompei, Loreto and Bari:** Originated by Leo XIII for Sanctuary of Pompei. Loreto placed under commission in 1965, St. Nicholas of Bari, 1980; under supervision of the Congregation for the Clergy. Cardinal Virgilio Noè, president.

**Disciplinary Commission of the Roman Curia:** Cardinal Vincenzo Fagiolo, president.

**Fabric of St. Peter:** Administration, care and preservation of Vatican Basilica. Cardinal Virgilio Noè, Archpriest of the Patriarchal Vatican Basilica, president.

**Office of Papal Charities:** Distributes alms and aid to those in need in the name of the Pope. Most Rev. Oscar Rizzato, almoner.

**Council of Cardinals for Study of Organizational and Economic Problems of the Holy See:** Council established in 1981 by Pope John Paul II; composed of approximately 15 cardinals from countries throughout the world (present membership includes U.S. Cardinals O'Connor and Mahony).

**Commission for the Protection of the Historical and Artistic Monuments of the Holy See:** Instituted by Pius XI in 1923, reorganized by Paul VI in 1963. Cardinal Virgilio Noè, president.

**Institute for Works of Religion:** Instituted by Pius XII June 27, 1942, to bank and administer funds for works of religion; replaced an earlier administration established by Leo XIII in 1887; reorganized by John Paul II (chirograph of Mar. 1, 1990).

**Labor Office of the Apostolic See (ULSA - Ufficio del Lavoro della Sede Apostolica):** Has competence in regard to those who work for the Apostolic See; charged with settling labor issues. Instituted by John Paul II (*motu proprio* of Jan. 1, 1989); functions reaffirmed and definitive text of statutes approved by John Paul II (motu proprio of Sept. 30, 1994). Cardinal Jan Schotte, president.

# COLLEGE OF CARDINALS

Cardinals are chosen by the pope to serve as his principal assistants and advisers in the central administration of church affairs. Collectively, they form the College of Cardinals. Provisions regarding their selection, rank, roles and prerogatives are detailed in Canons 349 to 359 of the Code of Canon Law.

## History of the College

The College of Cardinals was constituted in its present form and categories of membership in the 12th century. Before that time the pope had a body of advisers selected from among the bishops of dioceses neighboring Rome, priests and deacons of Rome. The college was given definite form in 1150, and in 1179 the selection of cardinals was reserved exclusively to the pope. Sixtus V fixed the number at 70, in 1586. John XXIII set aside this rule when he increased membership at the 1959 and subsequent consistories. The number was subsequently raised to 145 by Paul VI in 1973 and to 152 by John Paul II in 1985. The number of cardinals entitled to participate in papal elections was limited to 120.

In 1567 the title of cardinal was reserved to members of the college; previously it had been used by priests attached to parish churches of Rome and by the leading clergy of other notable churches. The Code of Canon Law promulgated in 1918 decreed that all cardinals must be priests. Previously there had been cardinals who were not priests (e.g., Cardinal Giacomo Antonelli, d. 1876, Secretary of State to Pius IX, was a deacon). John XXIII provided in the motu proprio *Cum Gravissima* Apr. 15, 1962,

that cardinals would henceforth be bishops; this provision is included in the revised Code of Canon Law.

## Age Limits

Pope Paul VI placed age limits on the functions of cardinals in the apostolic letter *Ingravescentem Aetatem,* dated Nov. 21, 1970, and effective as of Jan. 1, 1971. At 80, they cease to be members of curial departments and offices, and become ineligible to take part in papal elections. They retain membership in the College of Cardinals, however, with relevant rights and privileges.

## Three Categories

All cardinals except Eastern patriarchs are aggregated to the clergy of Rome. This aggregation is signified by the assignment to each cardinal, except the patriarchs, of a titular church in Rome.

The three categories of members of the college are cardinal bishops, cardinal priests and cardinal deacons.

**Cardinal bishops** include the six titular bishops of the suburbicarian sees and Eastern patriarchs.

First in rank are the titular bishops of the suburbicarian sees, neighboring Rome: Ostia, Palestrina, Porto-Santa Rufina, Albano, Velletri-Segni, Frascati, Sabina-Poggio Mirteto. The dean of the college holds the title of the See of Ostia as well as his other suburbicarian see. These cardinal bishops are engaged in full-time service in the central administration of church affairs in departments of the Roman Curia.

Full recognition is given in the revised Code of Canon Law to the position of Eastern patriarchs as the heads of sees of apostolic origin with ancient liturgies. They are assigned rank among the cardinals in order of seniority, following the suburbicarian titleholders.

**Cardinal priests,** who were formerly in charge of leading churches in Rome, are bishops whose dioceses are outside Rome.

**Cardinal deacons,** who were formerly chosen according to regional divisions of Rome, are titular bishops assigned to full-time service in the Roman Curia.

The **dean** and **sub-dean** of the college are elected by the cardinal bishops — subject to approval by the pope — from among their number. The dean, or the sub-dean in his absence, presides over the college as the first among equals. Cardinals Bernardin Gantin and Agostino Casaroli were elected dean and sub-dean, respectively, June 4, 1993 (papal approval June 5, 1993).

## Selection and Duties

Cardinals are selected by the pope and are inducted into the college in appropriate ceremonies.

Cardinals under the age of 80: elect the pope when the Holy See becomes vacant (see Index: Papal Election); and are major administrators of church affairs, serving in one or more departments of the Roman Curia. Cardinals in charge of agencies of the Roman Curia and Vatican City are asked to submit their resignation from office to the pope on reaching the age of 75. All cardinals enjoy a number of special rights and privileges. Their title, while symbolic of high honor, does not signify any extension of the powers of holy orders. They are called princes of the Church.

A cardinal in pectore (petto) is one whose selection has been made by the pope but whose name has not been disclosed; he has no title, rights or duties until such disclosure is made, at which time he takes precedence from the time of the secret selection.

# BIOGRAPHIES OF CARDINALS

*Biographies of the cardinals, as of Aug. 8, 1996, are given below in alphabetical order. For historical notes, order of seniority and geographical distribution of cardinals, see separate entries.*

*An asterisk indicates cardinals ineligible to take part in papal elections.*

**Agustoni, Gilberto:** b. July 26, 1922, Schaffhausen, Switzerland; ord. priest Apr. 20, 1946; called to Rome in 1950 to work under Cardinal Ottaviani in the Congregation for the Holy Office; a Prelate Auditor of the Roman Rota, 1970-86; ord. titular archbishop of Caorle, Jan. 6, 1987; secretary of the Congregation for the Clergy, 1986-82; pro-prefect of the Apostolic Signatura, 1992-94; cardinal Nov. 26, 1994; deacon Sts. Urban and Laurence at Prima Porta. Prefect of Supreme Tribunal of Apostolic Signatora (Nov. 26, 1994). Curial membership:

Bishops, Catholic Education (congregations); Interpretation of Legislative Texts (council).

**Angelini,\* Fiorenzo:** b. Aug. 1, 1916, Rome, Italy; ord. priest Feb. 3, 1940; master of pontifical ceremonies, 1947-54; ord. bishop (titular see of Messene) July 29, 1956, and head of Rome Vicariate's section for apostolate to health care workers; archbishop, 1985; president of newly established Curia agency for health care workers; cardinal June 28, 1991, deacon, Holy Spirit (in Sassio). President of Pontifical Council for Pastoral Assistance to Health Care Workers, 1989. Curial membership:

Evangelization of Peoples, Institutes of Consecrated Life and Societies of Apostolic Life (congregations); Family (council); Latin America (commission).

**Aponte Martinez, Luis:** b. Aug. 4, 1922, Lajas, Puerto Rico; ord. priest Apr. 10, 1950; parish priest at Ponce; ord. titular bishop of Lares and auxiliary of Ponce, Oct. 12, 1960; bishop of Ponce, 1963-64; archbishop of San Juan, Nov. 4, 1964; cardinal Mar. 5, 1973; titular church, St. Mary Mother of Providence (in Monte Verde). Archbishop of San Juan.

**Aramburu,\* Juan Carlos:** b. Feb. 11, 1912, Reduccion, Argentina; ord. priest in Rome, Oct. 28, 1934; ord. titular bishop of Platea and auxiliary of Tucuman, Argentina, Dec. 15, 1946; bishop, 1953, and first archbishop, 1957, of Tucuman; titular archbishop of Torri di Bizacena and coadjutor archbishop of Buenos Aires, June 14, 1967; archbishop of Buenos Aires, Apr. 22, 1975 (resigned July 10, 1990); cardinal May 24, 1976; titular church, St. John Baptist of the Florentines. Archbishop emeritus of Buenos Aires.

**Arinze, Francis:** b. Nov. 1, 1932, Eziowelle, Nigeria; ord. priest Nov. 23, 1958; ord. titular bishop of Fissiana and auxiliary of Onitsha, Aug. 29, 1965; archbishop of Onitsha, 1967-84; pro-president of Secretariat for Non-Christians (now the Council for Interreligious Dialogue), 1984; cardinal May 25, 1985; deacon, St. John (della Pigna); transferred to the order of cardinal priests Jan. 29, 1996. President of Council for Interreligious Dialogue, 1985. Curial membership:

Doctrine of the Faith, Oriental Churches, Evangelization of Peoples, Causes of Saints (congregations); Laity, Christian Unity, Culture (councils); International Eucharistic Congresses, Holy Year 2000 (committees).

**Arns, Paulo Evaristo, O.F.M.:** b. Sept. 14, 1921, Forquilhinha, Brazil; ord. priest Nov. 30, 1945; held various teaching posts; director of *Sponsa Christi,* monthly review for religious, and of the Franciscan publication center in Brazil; ord. titular bishop of Respetta and auxiliary of Sao Paulo, July 3, 1966; archbishop of Sao Paulo, Oct. 22, 1970; cardinal Mar. 5, 1973; titular church, St. Anthony of Padua (in Via Tuscolana). Archbishop of Sao Paulo. Curial membership:

Divine Worship and Sacraments (congregation).

**Bafile,\* Corrado:** b. July 4, 1903, L'Aquila, Italy; practiced law in Rome for six years before beginning studies for priesthood; ord. priest Apr. 11, 1936; served in Vatican secretariat of state, 1939-59; ord.

titular archbishop of Antiochia in Pisidia, Mar. 19, 1960; apostolic nuncio to Germany, 1960-75; pro-prefect of Congregation for Causes of Saints, July 18, 1975; cardinal May 24, 1976; deacon, S. Maria (in Portico); transferred to order of cardinal priests, June 22, 1987; prefect of Congregation for Causes of Saints, 1976-80.

**Ballestrero,\* Anastasio Alberto, O.C.D.:** b. Oct. 3, 1913, Genoa, Italy; professed in Order of Discalced Carmelites, 1929; ord. priest June 6, 1936; provincial, 1942-48, and superior general, 1955-67, of Carmelites; author of many books on Christian life; ord. archbishop of Bari, Feb. 2, 1974; archbishop of Turin, Aug. 1, 1977 (resigned Jan. 31, 1989); cardinal June 30, 1979; titular church, S. Maria (sopra Minerva). Archbishop emeritus of Turin.

**Baum, William Wakefield:** b. Nov. 21, 1926, Dallas, Tex.; moved to Kansas City, Mo., at an early age; ord. priest (Kansas City-St. Joseph diocese) May 12, 1951; executive director of U.S. bishops com-mission for ecumenical and interreligious affairs, 1964-69; attended Second Vatican Council as *peritus* (expert adviser); ord. bishop of Springfield-Cape Girardeau, Mo., Apr. 6, 1970; archbishop of Wash-ington, D.C., 1973-80; cardinal May 24, 1976; titu-lar church, Holy Cross (on the Via Flaminia); pre-fect of Congregation for Catholic Education (Semi-naries and Institutes of Study), 1980-90. Major Peni-tentiary, 1990. Curial membership:

Secretariat of State (second section); Doctrine of the Faith, Bishops, Oriental Churches, Causes of Saints, Institutes of Consecrated Life and Societies of Apostolic Life, Evangelization of Peoples (con-gregations); Patrimony of Holy See (office).

**Bernardin, Joseph L.:** b. Apr. 2, 1928, Colum-bia, S.C.; ord. priest (Charleston diocese) Apr. 26, 1952; ord. titular bishop of Lugura and auxiliary bishop of Atlanta, Ga., Apr. 26, 1966; general secre-tary, 1968-72, and president, 1974-77, of NCCB/USCC; archbishop of Cincinnati, 1972-82; arch-bishop of Chicago, July 10, 1982, installed Aug. 25, 1982; cardinal Feb. 2, 1983; titular church, Jesus the Divine Worker. Archbishop of Chicago. Curial membership:

Divine Worship and Sacraments (congregation); Christian Unity (council).

**Bertoli,\* Paolo:** b. Feb.1, 1908, Poggio Garfagnana, Italy; ord. priest Aug. 15, 1930; entered diplomatic service of the Holy See, serving in nunciatures in Yugoslavia, France, Haiti and Swit-zerland; ord. titular archbishop of Nicomedia, May 11, 1952; apostolic delegate to Turkey (1952-53), nuncio to Colombia (1953-59), Lebanon (1959-60), France (1960-69); cardinal Apr. 28, 1969; prefect of Congregation for Causes of Saints, 1969-73; entered order of cardinal bishops as titular bishop of Frascati, June 30, 1979; Chamberlain (Camerlengo) of Holy Roman Church, 1979-85.

**Bevilacqua, Anthony Joseph:** b. June 17, 1923, Brooklyn N.Y.; educ. Cathedral College (Brooklyn, N.Y.), Immaculate Conception Seminary (Hunting-ton, N.Y.), Gregorian Univ. (Rome), Columbia Univ. and St. John's Univ. (New York); ord. priest (Brook-lyn diocese) June 11, 1949; ord. titular bishop of Aquae Albae in Byzacena and auxiliary bishop of Brooklyn, Nov. 24, 1980; bishop of Pittsburgh Oct.

7, 1983, installed Dec. 12, 1983; archbishop of Phila-delphia, Feb. 11, 1988; cardinal June 28, 1991; titu-lar church, Most Holy Redeemer and St. Alphonsus (on Via Merulana). Archbishop of Philadelphia. Curial membership:

Clergy, Causes of Saints (congregations); "Cor Unum," Migrants and Itinerant People (councils).

**Biffi, Giacomo:** b. June 13, 1928, Milan, Italy; ord. priest Dec. 23, 1950; ord. titular bishop of Fidene and auxiliary of Milan, Jan. 11, 1976; archbishop of Bologna, Apr. 19, 1984; cardinal May 25, 1985; titu-lar church, Sts. John the Evangelist and Petronius. Archbishop of Bologna. Curial membership:

Doctrine of the Faith, Divine Worship and Sacra-ments, Clergy, Catholic Education (congregations).

**Canestri, Giovanni:** b. Sept. 30, 1918, Castelspina, Italy; ord. priest Apr. 12, 1941; spiritual director of Rome's seminary, 1959; ord. titular bishop of Tenedo and auxiliary to the cardinal vicar of Rome, July 30, 1961; bishop of Tortona, 1971-75; titular bishop of Monterano (personal title of archbishop) and vice regent of Rome, 1975-84; archbishop of Cagliari, 1984-87; archbishop of Genoa, July 6, 1987 (re-signed Apr. 20, 1995); cardinal June 28, 1988; titu-lar church, St. Andrew of the Valley. Archbishop emeritus of Genoa. Curial membership:

Divine Worship and Sacraments, Causes of Saints, Clergy (congregations); Patrimony of the Holy See (office).

**Caprio,\* Giuseppe:** b. Nov. 15, 1914, Lapio, Italy; ord. priest Dec. 17, 1938; served in diplomatic mis-sions in China (1947-51, when Vatican diplomats were expelled by communists), Belgium (1951-54), and South Vietnam (1954-56); internuncio in China with residence at Taiwan, 1959-67; ord. titular arch-bishop of Apollonia, Dec. 17, 1961; pro-nuncio in India, 1967-69; secretary, 1969-77, and president, 1979-81, of Administration of Patrimony of Holy See; substitute secretary of state, 1977-79; cardinal deacon June 30, 1979; transferred to order of cardi-nal priests, November, 1990; titular church, St. Mary of Victory; president of Prefecture of Economic Af-fairs of the Holy See, 1981-90. Grand Master of Equestrian Order of the Holy Sepulchre, 1988-95.

**Carberry,\* John J.:** b. July 31, 1904, Brooklyn, N.Y.; ord. priest (Brooklyn diocese) July 28, 1929; ord. titular bishop of Elis and coadjutor bishop of Lafayette, Ind., July 25, 1956; bishop of Lafayette, Nov. 20, 1957; bishop of Columbus, Ohio, Jan. 16, 1965; archbishop of St. Louis, Mo., 1968-79; cardi-nal Apr. 28, 1969; titular church, St. John Baptist de Rossi (Via Latina). Archbishop emeritus of St. Louis.

**Carles Gordó, Ricardo Maria:** b. Sept. 24, 1926, Valencia, Spain; ord. priest June 29, 1951; ord. bishop of Tortosa, Aug. 3, 1969; archbishop of Barcelona, Mar. 23, 1990; cardinal Nov. 26, 1994; titular church, St. Mary of Consolation in Tiburtino. Archbishop of Barcelona. Curial membership:

Catholic Education (congregation); Justice and Peace (council).

**Carter,\* Gerald Emmett:** b. Mar. 1, 1912, Montreal, Canada; ord. priest May 22, 1937; founder and president of St. Joseph Teachers' College and co-founder and director of Thomas More Institute for adult education; ord. titular bishop of Altiburo and auxiliary bishop of London, Ont., Feb. 2, 1962;

bishop of London, Ont., 1964-78; vice president, 1971-73, and president, 1975-77, of Canadian Conference of Catholic Bishops; archbishop of Toronto, 1978-90; cardinal June 30, 1979; titular church, St. Mary (in Traspontina). Archbishop emeritus of Toronto.

**Casaroli,\* Agostino:** b. Nov. 24, 1914, Castel San Giovanni, Italy; ord. priest May 27, 1937; entered service of Vatican secretariat of state, 1940; undersecretary, 1961-67, of the Congregation for Extraordinary Ecclesiastical Affairs, and secretary, 1967-79, of its successor the Council for Public Affairs of the Church; ord. titular archbishop of Cartagina, July 16, 1967; chief negotiator for the Vatican with East European communist governments; missions included visits to Hungary, Yugoslavia, Poland, Czechoslovakia, Bulgaria; headed Vatican delegations to several UN conferences and the Helsinki Conference (1975); Pro-Secretary of State and Pro-Prefect of Council for Public Affairs of the Church, Apr. 28, 1979; cardinal June 30, 1979; titular church, the Twelve Apostles; president, 1981-84, of Administration of Patrimony of Holy See and Pontifical Commission for Vatican City; entered order of cardinal bishops (retaining title to church of the Twelve Apostles) as titular bishop of Porto-Santa Rufina, May 25, 1985. Secretary of State, 1979-90. Sub-dean of the college of cardinals, 1993.

**Casoria,\* Giuseppe:** b. Oct. 1, 1908, Acerra, Italy; ord. priest Dec. 21, 1930; jurist; Roman Curia official from 1937; under-secretary, 1959-69, and secretary, 1969-73, of Congregation for Divine Worship and Sacraments; secretary of Congregation for Causes of Saints, 1973-81; ord. titular bishop of Vescovia with personal title of archbishop, Feb. 13, 1972; pro-prefect of Congregation for Divine Worship and Sacraments, 1981-83; cardinal deacon Feb. 2, 1983; transferred to order of cardinal priests Apr. 5, 1993; titular church, St. Joseph on Via Trionfale. Prefect of Congregation for Divine Worship and Sacraments, 1983-84.

**Cassidy, Edward Idris:** b. July 5, 1924, Sydney, Australia; ord. priest July 23, 1949; entered Vatican diplomatic service in 1955; served in nunciatures in India, Ireland, El Salvador and Argentina; ord. titular bishop of Amantia with personal title of archbishop, Nov. 15, 1970; pro-nuncio to Republic of China (Taiwan), 1970-79 and pro-nuncio to Bangladesh and apostolic delegate in Burma, 1973-79; pro-nuncio to Lesotho and apostolic delegate to southern Africa, 1979-84; pro-nuncio to the Netherlands, 1984-88; substitute of the Secretary of State for General Affairs, 1988-89; president of Pontifical Council for Promoting Christian Unity, 1989; cardinal June 28, 1991; deacon, St. Mary (in via Lata). President of Pontifical Council for Promoting Christian Unity. Curial membership:

Secretariat of State (second section); Doctrine of the Faith, Divine Worship and Sacraments, Bishops, Oriental Churches, Evangelization of Peoples (congregations); Interreligious Dialogue, "Cor Unum" (councils); Patrimony of the Holy See (office); Latin America, Holy Year 2000 (commission/committee).

**Castillo Lara, Rosalio Jose, S.D.B.:** b. Sept. 4, 1922, San Casimiro, Venezuela; ord. priest Sept. 4, 1949; ord. titular bishop of Precausa, May 24, 1973;

coadjutor bishop of Trujillo, 1973-76; archbishop May 26, 1982; pro-president of Pontifical Commission for Revision of Code of Canon Law, 1982-84; pro-president of Commission for Authentic Interpretation of Code of Canon Law, 1984-85; cardinal May 25, 1985; deacon, Our Lady of Coromoto (in St. John of God); transferred to order of cardinal priests Jan. 29, 1996. President of the Pontifical Commission for the State of Vatican City, 1990. Curial membership:

Secretariat of State (second section); Bishops, Institutes of Consecrated Life and Societies of Apostolic Life (congregations); Apostolic Signatura (tribunal); Institute for Works of Religion (commission).

**Cé, Marco:** b. July 8, 1925, Izano, Italy; ord. priest Mar. 27, 1948; taught sacred scripture and dogmatic theology at seminary in his home diocese of Crema; rector of seminary, 1957; presided over diocesan liturgical commission, preached youth retreats; ord. titular bishop of Vulturia, May 17, 1970; auxiliary bishop of Bologna, 1970-76; general ecclesiastical assistant of Italian Catholic Action, 1976-78; patriarch of Venice, Dec. 7, 1978; cardinal June 30, 1979; titular church, St. Mark. Patriarch of Venice. Curial membership:

Divine Worship and Sacraments, Oriental Churches (congregations).

**Clancy, Edward Bede:** b. Dec. 13, 1923, Lithgow, New South Wales, Australia; ord. priest July 23, 1949; ord. titular bishop of Ard Carna and auxiliary of Sydney, Jan. 19, 1974; archbishop of Canberra, 1978-83; archbishop of Sydney, Feb. 12, 1983; cardinal June 28, 1988; titular church, Holy Mary of Vallicella. Archbishop of Sydney. Curial membership:

Secretariat of State (second section); Economic Affairs of the Holy See (office).

**Corripio Ahumada, Ernesto:** b. June 29, 1919, Tampico, Mexico; ord. priest Oct. 25, 1942, in Rome, where he remained until almost the end of World War II; taught and held various positions in local seminary of Tampico, 1945-50; ord. titular bishop of Zapara and auxiliary bishop of Tampico, Mar. 19, 1953; bishop of Tampico, 1956-67; archbishop of Antequera, 1967-76; archbishop of Puebla de los Angeles, 1976-77; archbishop of Mexico City and primate of Mexico, July 19, 1977 (resigned 1994); cardinal June 30, 1979; titular church, Mary Immaculate al Tiburtino. Archbishop emeritus of Mexico City. Curial membership:

Clergy (congregation).

**Daly, Cahal Brendan:** b. Oct. 1, 1917, Loughguile, Northern Ireland; ord. priest June 22, 1941; earned advanced degrees in philosophy and theology; 30 years of priestly life dedicated to teaching; attended Second Vatican Council as a theological adviser to members of Irish hierarchy; outspoken critic of violence in Northern Ireland; ord. bishop of Ardagh, July 16, 1967; bishop of Down and Connor, 1982-90; archbishop of Armagh and primate of All Ireland, Nov. 6, 1990; cardinal June 28, 1991; titular church, St. Patrick. Archbishop of Armagh and Primate of All Ireland. Curial membership:

Evangelization of Peoples, Clergy (congregations); Christian Unity (council).

**Danneels, Godfried:** b. June 4, 1933, Kanegem,

Belgium; ord. priest Aug. 17, 1957; professor of liturgy and sacramental theology at Catholic University of Louvain, 1969-77; ord. bishop of Antwerp Dec. 18, 1977; app. archbishop of Mechelen-Brussel, Dec. 19, 1979; installed Jan. 4, 1980; cardinal Feb. 2, 1983; titular church, St. Anastasia. Archbishop of Mechelen-Brussel, military ordinary of Belgium. Curial membership:
Secretariat of State (second section); Doctrine of the Faith, Oriental Churches, Divine Worship and Sacraments, Evangelization of Peoples, Catholic Education (congregations).

**Darmaatmadja, Julius Riyadi, S.J.:** b. Dec. 20, 1934, Muntilan, Mageland, Central Java, Indonesia; entered Society of Jesus in 1957; ord. priest Dec. 18, 1969; ord. archbishop of Semarang, June 29, 1983 (app. archbishop of Jakarta, 1996); cardinal Nov. 26, 1994; titular church, Sacred Heart of Mary. Archbishop of Jakarta (1996), military ordinary of Indonesia (1984). Curial membership:
Evangelization of Peoples (congregation); Interreligious Dialogue (council).

**Deskur, Andrzej Maria:** b. Feb. 29, 1924, Sancygniow, Poland; ord. priest Aug. 20, 1950, in France; assigned to Vatican secretariat of state, 1952; undersecretary and later secretary of Pontifical Commission for Film, Radio and TV (Social Communications), 1954-73; ord. titular bishop of Tene, June 30, 1974; archbishop, 1980; president of Pontifical Commission for Social Communications, 1974-84; cardinal May 25, 1985; deacon, St. Cesario (in Palatio); transferred to order of cardinal priests Jan. 29, 1996. President emeritus of Council for Social Communications. Curial membership:
Divine Worship and Sacraments, Causes of Saints (congregations); Health Care Workers (council); State of Vatican City (commission).

**Dezza,\* Paolo, S.J.:** b. Dec. 13, 1901, Parma, Italy; entered Society of Jesus in 1918; ord. priest, Mar. 25, 1928; made solemn profession as Jesuit, 1935; served as rector of Pontifical Gregorian University; delegated as head of Society of Jesus by John Paul II October, 1981, until the election of the new superior general; cardinal June 28, 1991, with permission to decline episcopal ordination; deacon, St. Ignatius of Loyola (a Campo Marzio).

**do Nascimento, Alexandre:** b. Mar. 1, 1925, Malanje, Angola; ord. priest Dec. 20, 1952, in Rome; professor of dogmatic theology in major seminary of Luanda, Angola; editor of *O Apostolada*, Catholic newspaper; forced into exile in Lisbon, Portugal, 1961-71; returned to Angola, 1971; active with student and refugee groups; professor at Pius XII Institute of Social Sciences; ord. bishop of Malanje, Aug. 31, 1975; archbishop of Lubango and apostolic administrator of Onjiva, 1977-86; held hostage by Angolan guerrillas, Oct. 15 to Nov. 16, 1982; cardinal Feb. 2, 1983; titular church, St. Mark in Agro Laurentino. Archbishop of Luanda, 1986. Curial membership:
Evangelization of Peoples, Catholic Education (congregations).

**Echeverria Ruiz,\* Bernardino, O.F.M.:** b. Nov. 12, 1912, Cotacachi, Ecuador; entered Franciscans 1928; ord. priest July 4, 1937; ord. bishop of Ambato Dec. 4, 1949; archbishop of Guayaquil, 1969-89; apostolic administrator of Ibarra, 1989-95; cardinal Nov. 26, 1994; titular church, Sts. Nereus and Achilleus. Archbishop emeritus of Guayaquil.

**Etchegaray, Roger:** b. Sept. 25, 1922, Espelette, France; ord. priest July 13, 1947; deputy director, 1961-66, and secretary general, 1966-70, of French Episcopal Conference; ord. titular bishop of Gemelle di Numidia and auxiliary of Paris, May 27, 1969; archbishop of Marseilles, 1970-84; prelate of Mission de France, 1975-82; president of French Episcopal Conference, 1979-81; cardinal June 30, 1979; titular church, St. Leo I; president of Council *Cor Unum*, 1984-95. President (1984) of Council for Justice and Peace and (1994) of Central Committee for the Jubilee of the Holy Year 2000. Curial membership:
Oriental Churches, Evangelization of Peoples, Catholic Education (congregations); Apostolic Signatura (tribunal); Laity, Christian Unity, Social Communications, Interreligious Dialogue (councils); Patrimony of the Holy See (office).

**Etsou-Nzabi-Bamungwabi, Frédéric, C.I.C.M.:** b. Dec. 3, 1930, Mazalonga, Zaire; ord. priest July 13, 1958; educ. Catholic Institute of Paris (degree in sociology) and "Lumen Vitae" in Belgium (degree in pastoral theology); ord. titular bishop of Menfessi and coadjutor archbishop of Mbandaka-Bikora, Nov. 7, 1976; archbishop of Mbandaka-Bikora, 1977-1990; archbishop of Kinshasa, July 7, 1990; cardinal June 28, 1991; titular church, St. Lucy (a Piazza d'Armi). Archbishop of Kinshasa. Curial membership:
Evangelization of Peoples (congregation); Family (council).

**Eyt, Pierre:** b. June 4, 1934, Laruns, France; ord. priest June 29, 1961; chaplain of St. Louis of the French in Rome, 1963; taught theology at Catholic Institute in Toulouse, 1967-72; ord. coadjutor archbishop of Bordeaux, Sept. 28, 1986; archbishop of Bordeaux, May 31, 1989; cardinal Nov. 26, 1994; titular church, Most Holy Trinity on Monte Pincio. Archbishop of Bordeaux. Curial membership:
Doctrine of the Faith, Catholic Education (congregations).

**Fagiolo, Vincenzo:** b. Feb. 5, 1918, Segni, Italy; ord. priest Mar. 6, 1943; prelate auditor of Roman Rota, 1967-71; ord. archbishop of Chieti-Vasto, Dec. 19, 1971; resigned see July 15, 1984; secretary of Congregation for Institutes of Consecrated Life and Societies of Apostolic Life, 1984-90; president of the Pontifical Council for the Interpretation of Legislative Texts, 1991-94; cardinal Nov. 26, 1994; deacon, St. Theodore. President of Diciplinary Commission of the Roman Curia, Dec. 29, 1990. Curial membership:
Secretariat of State (second section); Bishops (congregation); Apostolic Signatura (tribunal).

**Falcao, Jose Freire:** b. Oct. 23, 1925, Erere, Brazil; ord. priest June 19, 1949; ord. titular bishop of Vardimissa and coadjutor of Limoeiro do Norte, June 17, 1967; bishop of Limoeiro do Norte, Aug. 19,

---

**Death:** Greek Orthodox Patriarch Parthenios III of Alexandria and all Africa, 76, died July 23, 1996, of a heart attack. He was a president of the World Council of Churches.

1967; archbishop of Teresina, Nov. 25, 1971; archbishop of Brasilia, Feb. 15, 1984; cardinal June 28, 1988; titular church, St. Luke (Via Prenestina). Archbishop of Brasilia. Curial membership:
Health Care Workers (council); Latin America (commission).

**Felici, Angelo:** b. July 26, 1919, Segni, Italy; ord. priest Apr. 4, 1942; in Vatican diplomatic service from 1945; ord. titular bishop of Cesariana, with personal title of archbishop, Sept. 24, 1967; nuncio to Netherlands, 1967-76, Portugal, 1976-79, France, 1979-88; cardinal June 28, 1988; deacon, Sts. Blaise and Charles in Catinari. Prefect of Congregation for Causes of Saints, 1988-95. President of Pontifical Commission "Ecclesia Dei," 1995. Curial membership:
Secretariat of State (second section); Oriental Churches, Bishops, Evangelization of Peoples, Clergy (congregations); Christian Unity (council).

**Fresno Larrain,\* Juan Francisco:** b. July 26, 1914, Santiago, Chile; ord. priest Dec. 18, 1937; ord. bishop of Copiapo, Aug. 15, 1958; archbishop of La Serena, 1967-83; archbishop of Santiago, May 3, 1983 (resigned Mar. 30, 1990); cardinal May 25, 1985; titular church, St. Mary Immaculate of Lourdes (a Boccea). Archbishop emeritus of Santiago.

**Furno, Carlo:** b. Dec. 2, 1921, Bairo Canavese, Italy; ord. priest June 25, 1944; entered diplomatic service of the Holy See in the 1950s; served in Colombia, Ecuador and Jerusalem; worked in Secretariat of State for 11 years and taught at Pontifical Ecclesiastical Academy, 1966-73; ord. titular bishop of Abari with personal title of archbishop, Sept. 16, 1973; nuncio in Peru, 1973-78, Lebanon, 1978-82, Brazil, 1982-92, Italy, 1992-94; cardinal Nov. 26, 1994; deacon, Sacred Heart of Christ the King. Grand Master of the Equestrian Order of the Holy Sepulchre. Curial membership:
Secretariat of State (second section); Oriental Churches, Bishops, Evangelization of Peoples(congregations); Institute for Works of Religion (commission).

**Gagnon, Edouard, P.S.S.:** b. Jan. 15, 1918, Port Daniel, Que., Canada; ord. priest Aug. 15, 1940; ord. bishop of St. Paul in Alberta Mar. 25, 1969 (resigned May 3, 1972); rector of Canadian College in Rome, 1972-77; vice president-secretary of Vatican Committee for the Family, 1973-80; titular archbishop of Giustiniana Prima, July 7, 1983; pro-president of Pontifical Council for the Family, 1983; cardinal May 25, 1985; deacon, St. Elena (fuori Porta Prenestina); transferred to order of cardinal priests Jan. 29, 1996; titular church St. Marcellus; president of Pontifical Council for the Family, 1985-90. President of Pontifical Committee for International Eucharistic Congresses, 1991. Curial membership:
Divine Worship and Sacraments, Causes of Saints (congregations); Apostolic Signatura (tribunal).

**Gantin, Bernardin:** b. May 8, 1922, Toffo, Dahomey (now Benin); ord. priest Jan. 14, 1951; ord. titular bishop of Tipasa di Mauritania and auxiliary bishop of Cotonou, Feb. 3, 1957; archbishop of Cotonou, 1960-71; associate secretary (1971-73) and secretary (1973-75) of Congregation for Evangelization of Peoples; vice-president (1975) and president (1976-84) of Pontifical Commission for

Justice and Peace; cardinal deacon June 27, 1977; transferred to order of priests June 25, 1984; titular church, Sacred Heart of Christ the King; titular bishop of suburbicarian see of Palestrina Sept 29, 1986, when he entered the order of cardinal bishops, and of Ostia June 5, 1993, when he became dean of the college of cardinals. Prefect of Congregation for Bishops, 1984; president of commission for Latin America, 1984; dean of college of cardinals, 1993. Curial membership:
Secretariat of State (second section); Divine Worship and Sacraments, Causes of Saints, Evangelization of Peoples, Oriental Churches, Institutes of Consecrated Life and Societies of Apostolic Life, Catholic Education (congregations); Apostolic Signatura (tribunal); Interpretation of Legislative Texts (council); Pompeii, Loreto and Bari (commission).

**Giordano, Michele:** b. Sept. 26, 1930, S. Arcangelo, Italy; ord. priest July 5, 1953; ord. titular bishop of Lari Castello and auxiliary of Matera, Feb. 5, 1972; archbishop of Matera and Irsina, 1974-87; archbishop of Naples, May 9, 1987; cardinal June 28, 1988; titular church, St. Joachim. Archbishop of Naples. Curial membership:
Secretariat of State (second section); Divine Worship and Sacraments, Clergy (congregations); Health Care Workers (council).

**Glemp, Jozef:** b. Dec. 18, 1929, Inowroclaw, Poland; assigned to forced labor on German farm in Rycerzow during Nazi occupation; ord. priest May 25, 1956; studied in Rome, 1958-64; received degree in Roman and canon law from Pontifical Lateran University; secretary of primatial major seminary at Gniezno on his return to Poland, 1964; spokesman for secretariat of primate of Poland and chaplain of primate for archdiocese of Gniezno, 1967; ord. bishop of Warmia, Apr. 21, 1979; archbishop of Gniezno, 1981-92, with title of archbishop of Warsaw and primate of Poland; cardinal Feb. 2, 1983; titular church, St. Mary in Trastevere. Archbishop of Warsaw (Mar. 25, 1992), primate of Poland, ordinary for Eastern-rite faithful in Poland who do not have ordinaries of their own rites. Curial membership:
Oriental Churches (congregation); Justice and Peace, Culture (councils).

**Gong (Kung) Pin-mei,\* Ignatius:** b. Aug. 2, 1901, P'ou-tong, China; ord. priest May 28, 1930; worked in schools and as a missionary; ord. bishop of Soochow Oct. 7, 1949; bishop of Shanghai July 15, 1950; imprisoned by Chinese communists in 1955 and sentenced to life imprisonment in 1960; paroled in 1985 after 30 years; pardoned and political rights restored Jan. 5, 1988, but was not permitted to function as a bishop; came to the United States in 1988; cardinal June 30, 1979 "in pectore"; name revealed and formally invested at June 28, 1991, public consistory; titular church, St. Sixtus. Bishop of Shanghai and apostolic administrator of Soochow. (Resides in U.S.)

**Gonzalez Martin, Marcelo:** b. Jan. 16, 1918, Villanubla, Spain; ord. priest June 29, 1941; taught theology and sociology at Valladolid diocesan seminary; founded organization for construction of houses for poor; ord. bishop of Astorga, Mar. 5, 1961; titu-

lar archbishop of Case Mediane and coadjutor of
Barcelona, Feb. 21, 1966; archbishop of Barcelona,
1967-71; archbishop of Toledo, 1971-95; cardinal
Mar. 5, 1973; titular church, St. Augustine. Arch-
bishop emeritus of Toledo. Curial membership:
Clergy (congregation).

**Gouyon,\* Paul:** b. Oct. 24, 1910, Bordeaux,
France; ord. priest Mar. 13, 1937; ord. bishop of
Bayonne, Oct. 7, 1957; titular archbishop of
Pessinonte and coadjutor archbishop of Rennes, Sept.
6, 1963; archbishop of Rennes, Sept. 4, 1964 (re-
signed Oct. 15, 1985); cardinal Apr. 28, 1969; titu-
lar church, Nativity of Our Lord Jesus Christ (Via
Gallia). Archbishop emeritus of Rennes.

**Grillmeier,\* Alois, S.J.:** b. Jan. 1, 1910,
Pechbrunn, Germany; entered Society of Jesus, 1929;
ord. priest June 24, 1937; taught fundamental and
dogmatic theology and the history of theology at
various ecclesiastical institutes; author of a number
of books on dogmatic theology and the history of
theology; member of the theological commission of
the Second Vatican Council; cardinal Nov. 26, 1994;
deacon, St. Nicholas in Prison.

**Groër, Hans Hermann, O.S.B.:** b. Oct. 13, 1919,
Vienna, Austria; ord. priest Apr. 12, 1942; ord. arch-
bishop of Vienna, Sept. 14, 1986; cardinal June 28,
1988; titular church, Sts. Joachim and Anne al
Tuscolano. Archbishop emeritus of Vienna (resigned
Sept. 14, 1995). Curial membership:
Oriental Churches, Divine Worship and Sacraments,
Institutes of Consecrated Life and Societies of Apos-
tolic Life, Catholic Education (congregations).

**Gulbinowicz, Henryk Roman:** b. Oct. 17, 1928,
Szukiszki, Poland; ord. priest June 18, 1950; ord.
titular bishop of Acci and apostolic administrator of
Polish territory in Lithuanian archdiocese of Vilnius
(Vilna), Feb. 8, 1970; archbishop of Wroclaw, Po-
land, Jan. 3, 1976; cardinal May 25, 1985; titular
church, Immaculate Conception of Mary (a
Grottarosa). Archbishop of Wroclaw. Curial mem-
bership:
Oriental Churches, Evangelization of Peoples,
Clergy (congregations).

**Hamer,\* Jean Jerome, O.P.:** b. June 1, 1916,
Brussels, Belgium; ord. priest Aug. 3, 1941; taught
dogmatic and fundamental theology and ecclesiology in France and Rome, 1944-62; author of several
works; secretary of Christian Unity Secretariat, 1969-
73; ord. titular bishop of Lorium with personal title
of archbishop June 29, 1973; secretary of Congregation for Doctrine of the Faith, 1973-84; pro-prefect of Congregation for Religious and Secular Institutes, 1984; cardinal deacon May 25, 1985; transferred to order of cardinal priests Jan. 29, 1996; titular
church, St. Saba. Prefect of Congregation for Institutes of Consecrated Life and Societies of Apostolic
Life, 1985-92.

**Hickey, James A.:** b. Oct. 11, 1920, Midland,
Mich.; ord. priest (Saginaw diocese) June 15, 1946;
ord. titular bishop of Taraqua and auxiliary of
Saginaw, Apr. 14, 1967; rector of North American
College, Rome, 1969-74; bishop of Cleveland, 1974-
80; app. archbishop of Washington, D.C., installed
Aug. 5, 1980; cardinal June 28, 1988; titular church,
St. Mary Mother of the Redeemer. Archbishop of
Washington, D.C. Curial membership:

Causes of Saints, Institutes of Consecrated Life and
Societies of Apostolic Life, Catholic Education,
Clergy (congregations); Family (council).

**Hume, George Basil, O.S.B.:** b. Mar. 2, 1923,
Newcastle-upon-Tyne, England; began monastic
studies at Benedictine Abbey of St. Laurence at
Ampleforth, 1941; made solemn perpetual vows as
Benedictine, 1945; ord. priest July 23, 1950; abbot
of Ampleforth, 1963-76; ord. archbishop of
Westminster, Mar. 25, 1976; cardinal May 24, 1976;
titular church, St. Silvestro (in Capite). Archbishop
of Westminster. Curial membership:
Oriental Churches, Divine Worship and Sacraments, Institutes of Consecrated Life and Societies
of Apostolic Life (congregations); Christian Unity,
Health Care Workers (councils).

**Innocenti,\* Antonio:** b. Aug. 23, 1915, Poppi,
Italy; ord. priest July 17, 1938; held curial and diplomatic positions; ord. titular bishop of Eclano with
personal title of archbishop, Feb. 18, 1968; nuncio
to Paraguay, 1967-73; secretary of Congregation for
Causes of Saints, 1973-75; secretary of Congregation for Sacraments and Divine Worship, 1975-80;
nuncio to Spain, 1980-85; cardinal deacon May 25,
1985; transferred to order of cardinal priests Jan.
29, 1996; titular church, St. Marie (in Aquiro); prefect of Congregation for the Clergy, 1986-91; president of Pontifical Commission for Preservation of
Artistic Patrimony of the Church, 1988-91; president of Pontifical Commission "Ecclesia Dei," 1991-
95.

**Javierre Ortas, Antonio Maria, S.D.B.:** b. Feb.
21, 1921, Sietamo, Spain; ord. priest Apr. 24, 1949;
leading European writer on ecumenism; ord. titular
bishop of Meta with personal title of archbishop,
June 29, 1976; Secretary of Congregation for Catholic Education, 1976-88; cardinal June 28, 1988; deacon, St. Mary Liberator (a Monte Testaccio). Librarian and Archivist of the Holy Roman Church, 1988-
92. Prefect of Congregation for Divine Worship and
the Sacraments, 1992-96. Curial membership:
Doctrine of the Faith, Bishops, Catholic Education, Clergy (congregations); Apostolic Signatura
(tribunal); Laity, Christian Unity, Interpretation of
Legislative Texts (councils).

**Jubany Arnau,\* Narciso:** b. Aug. 12, 1913, Santa
Coloma de Farnes, Spain; ord. priest July 30, 1939;
professor of law at Barcelona seminary; served on
ecclesiastical tribunal; ord. titular bishop of Ortosia
and auxiliary of Barcelona, Jan. 22, 1956; bishop of
Gerona, 1964-71; archbishop of Barcelona, Dec. 3,
1971 (retired Mar. 23, 1990); cardinal Mar. 5, 1973;
titular church, San Lorenzo (in Damaso). Archbishop
emeritus of Barcelona.

**Keeler, William Henry:** b. Mar. 4, 1931, San Antonio, Tex.; ord. priest (Harrisburg diocese) July 17,
1955; secretary to Bishop Leech at Vatican II, named
peritus by Pope John XXIII; ord. titular bishop of
Ulcinium and auxiliary bishop of Harrisburg, Sept.
21, 1979; bishop of Harrisburg, Nov. 10, 1983, installed Jan. 4, 1984; archbishop of Baltimore, Apr.
6, 1989; cardinal Nov. 26, 1994; titular church, St.
Mary of the Angels. Archbishop of Baltimore. Curial membership:
Oriental Churches (congregation); Christian Unity
(council).

**Kim, Stephen Sou Hwan:** b. May 8, 1922, Tae Gu, Korea; ord. priest Sept. 15, 1951; ord. bishop of Masan, May 31, 1966; archbishop of Seoul, Apr. 9, 1968; cardinal Apr. 28, 1969; titular church, St. Felix of Cantalice (Centocelle). Archbishop of Seoul, apostolic administrator of Pyeong Yang. Curial membership:

Evangelization of Peoples (congregation).

**Kitbunchu, Michael Michai:** b. Jan. 25, 1929, Samphran, Thailand; ord. priest Dec. 20, 1959, in Rome; rector of metropolitan seminary in Bangkok, 1965-72; ord. archbishop of Bangkok, June 3, 1973; cardinal Feb. 2, 1983, the first from Thailand; titular church, St. Laurence in Panisperna. Archbishop of Bangkok. Curial membership:

Evangelization of Peoples (congregation); Economic Affairs of the Holy See (office).

**Koenig,\* Franz:** b. Aug. 3, 1905, Rabenstein, Lower Austria; ord. priest Oct. 29, 1933; ord. titular bishop of Livias and coadjutor bishop of Sankt Poelten, Aug. 31, 1952; archbishop of Vienna, May 10, 1956 (resigned Sept. 16, 1985); cardinal Dec. 15, 1958; titular church, St. Eusebius; president of Secretariat (now Council) for Dialogue with Non-Believers, 1965-80. Archbishop emeritus of Vienna.

**Koliqi,\* Mikel:** b. Sept. 29, 1902, Shkodrë, Albania; ord. priest May 30, 1931; parish priest of the Shkodrë cathedral and vicar general of the archdiocese 1936-91; imprisoned three times during communist persecution and sentenced to a total of 44 years: 21 years of hard labor and 23 years of internment (six years were commuted because of age) for listening to foreign radio broadcasts and organizing young people; cardinal Nov. 26, 1994; deacon, All Saints on Via Appia Nuova.

**Korec, Jan Chryzostom, S.J.:** b. Jan. 22, 1924, Bosany, Slovakia; entered Society of Jesus in 1939; ord. priest Oct. 1, 1950; ord. bishop secretly Aug. 24, 1951; sentenced to 12 years in prison in 1960 for helping seminarians with their study and ordaining priests; paroled in 1968; appointed bishop of Nitra Feb. 6, 1990; cardinal June 28, 1991; titular church, Sts. Fabian and Venantius (a Villa Forelli). Bishop of Nitra. Curial membership:

Institutes of Consecrated Life and Societies of Apostolic Life (congregation); Culture (council).

**Kuharic, Franjo:** b. Apr. 15, 1919, Pribic, Croatia; ord. priest July 15, 1945; ord. titular bishop of Meta and auxiliary bishop of Zagreb, May 3, 1964; apostolic administrator of archdiocese of Zagreb, 1968-70; archbishop of Zagreb, June 16, 1970; cardinal Feb. 2, 1983; titular church, St. Jerome of the Croats. Archbishop of Zagreb. Curial membership:

Divine Worship and Sacraments, Clergy (congregations).

**Laghi, Pio:** b. May 21, 1922, Castiglione, Italy; ord. priest Apr. 20, 1946; entered diplomatic service of the Holy See in 1952; served in Nicaragua, the U.S. (as secretary of the apostolic delegation, 1954-61) and India; recalled to Rome and served on Council for Public Affairs of the Church; ord. titular archbishop of Mauriana June 22, 1969; apostolic delegate to Jerusalem and Palestine, 1969-74; nuncio to Argentina, 1974-80; apostolic delegate, 1980-84, and first pro-nuncio, 1984-90 to the U.S.; pro-

prefect of Congregation for Catholc Education, 1990-91; cardinal June 28, 1991; deacon, St. Mary Auxiliatrix (in Via Tuscolana). Prefect of Congregation for Catholic Education, 1991. Grand chancellor of Pontifical Gregorian University. Patron of Sovereign Military Order of Malta. Curial membership:

Secretariat of State (second section); Bishops, Oriental Churches, Evangelization of Peoples, Causes of Saints, Institutes of Consecrated Life and Societies of Apostolic Life, Clergy (congregations); Interpretation of Legislative Texts (council).

**Landazuri Ricketts,\* Juan, O.F.M:** b. Dec. 19, 1913, Arequipa, Peru; entered Franciscans, 1933; ord. priest May 16, 1939; ord. titular archbishop of Roina and coadjutor archbishop of Lima, Aug. 24, 1952; archbishop of Lima, May 2, 1955 (resigned Dec. 30, 1989); cardinal Mar. 19, 1962; titular church, St. Mary (in Aracoeli). Archbishop emeritus of Lima.

**Law, Bernard F.:** b. Nov. 4, 1931, Torreon, Mexico, the son of U.S. Air Force colonel; ord. priest (Jackson diocese) May 21, 1961; editor of Natchez-Jackson, Miss., diocesan paper, 1963-68; director of NCCB Committee on Ecumenical and Interreligious Affairs, 1968-71; ord. bishop of Springfield-Cape Girardeau, Mo., Dec. 5, 1973; archbishop of Boston, Jan. 11, 1984; cardinal May 25, 1985; titular church, St. Susanna. Archbishop of Boston. Curial membership:

Oriental Churches; Divine Worship and Sacraments, Institutes of Consecrated Life and Societies of Apostolic Life, Evangelization of Peoples, Catholic Education (congregations); Culture (council).

**Lebrun Moratinos, Jose Ali:** b. Mar. 19, 1919, Puerto Cabello, Venezuela; ord. priest Dec. 19, 1943; ord. titular bishop of Arado and auxiliary bishop of Maracaibo, Sept. 2, 1956; first bishop of Maracay, 1958-62; bishop of Valencia, 1962-72; titular bishop of Voncario (personal title of archbishop) and coadjutor archbishop of Caracas, Sept. 16, 1972; archbishop of Caracas, 1980-95; cardinal Feb. 2, 1983; titular church, St. Pancratius. Archbishop emeritus of Caracas. Curial membership:

Secretariat of State (second section).

**Lopez Rodriguez, Nicolas de Jesus:** b. Oct. 31, 1936, Barranca, Dominican Republic; ord. priest Mar. 18, 1961; sent to Rome for advanced studies at the Angelicum and Gregorian Univ.; served in various diocesan offices after returning to his home diocese of La Vega; ord. first bishop of San Francisco de Macoris Feb. 25, 1978; archbishop of Santo Domingo, Nov. 15, 1981; cardinal June 28, 1991; titular church, St. Pius X (alla Balduina). Archbishop of Santo Domingo and Military Ordinary for Dominican Republic. Curial membership:

Divine Worship and Sacraments, Clergy, Institutes of Consecrated Life and Societies of Apostolic Life (congregations); Social Communications (council); Latin America (commission) .

**Lopez Trujillo, Alfonso:** b. Nov. 8, 1935, Villahermosa, Colombia; ord. priest Nov. 13, 1960, in Rome; returned to Colombia, 1963; taught at major seminary; was pastoral coordinator for 1968 International Eucharistic Congress in Bogota; vicar general of Bogota, 1970-72; ord. titular bishop of

Boseta (with personal title of archbishop), Mar. 25, 1971; auxiliary bishop of Bogota, 1971-72; secretary-general of CELAM, 1972-78; helped organize 1979 Puebla Conference in which Pope John Paul II participated; app. coadjutor archbishop of Medellin, May 22, 1978; archbishop of Medellin, June 2, 1979 (resigned Jan 9, 1991); president of CELAM, 1979-83; cardinal Feb. 2, 1983; titular church, St. Prisca. Archbishop emeritus of Medellin. President of the Pontifical Council for the Family, 1990. Curial membership:
Doctrine of the Faith, Bishops, Evangelization of Peoples (congregations); Latin America, State of Vatican City (commissions).

**Lorscheider, Aloisio, O.F.M.:** b. Oct. 8, 1924, Estrela, Brazil; received in Franciscan Order, Feb. 1, 1942; ord. priest Aug. 22, 1948; professor of theology at the Antonianum, Rome, and director of Franciscan international house of studies; ord. bishop of Santo Angelo, Brazil, May 20, 1962; archbishop of Fortaleza, 1973-95; president of CELAM, 1975-79; cardinal May 24, 1976; titular church, S. Pietro (in Montorio). Archbishop of Aparecida, July 12, 1995. Curial membership:
Institutes of Consecrated Life and Societies of Apostolic Life (congregation).

**Lourdusamy, D. Simon:** b. Feb. 5, 1924, Kalleri, India; ord. priest Dec. 21, 1951; ord. titular bishop of Sozusa and auxiliary of Bangalore, Aug. 22, 1962; titular archbishop of Filippi and coadjutor archbishop of Bangalore, Nov. 9, 1964; archbishop of Bangalore, 1968-71; associate secretary, 1971-73, and secretary, 1973-85, of Congregation for Evangelization of Peoples; cardinal May 25, 1985; deacon, St. Mary of Grace; transferred to the order of cardinal priests Jan. 29, 1996; prefect of Congregation for Oriental Churches, 1985-91. Curial membership:
Evangelization of Peoples, Causes of Saints, (congregations); Apostolic Signatura (tribunal); Interreligious Dialogue, Family, Interpretation of Legislative Texts (councils); International Eucharistic Congresses (commission).

**Lubachivsky,\* Myroslav Ivan:** b. June 24, 1914, Dolyna, Ukraine; ord. priest Sept. 21, 1938; began pastoral work in U.S., 1947; became U.S. citizen, 1952; ord. archbishop of Ukrainian-rite archeparchy of Philadelphia, Nov. 12, 1979; coadjutor archbishop of Lviv of the Ukrainians, Mar. 27, 1980; archbishop of Lviv and major archbishop of Ukrainians, Sept. 7, 1984; cardinal May 25, 1985; titular church, St. Sofia (a Via Boccea). Major Archbishop of Lviv of the Ukrainians.

**Lustiger, Jean-Marie:** b. Sept. 17, 1926, Paris, France, of Polish-Jewish parents who emigrated to France after World War I; taken in by Catholic family in Orleans when his parents were deported during Nazi occupation (his mother died in 1943 at Auschwitz); convert to Catholicism, baptized Aug. 25, 1940; active in Young Christian Students during university days; ord. priest Apr. 17, 1954; ord. bishop of Orleans, Dec. 8, 1979; archbishop of Paris, Jan. 31, 1981; cardinal Feb. 2, 1983; titular church, St. Louis of France. Archbishop of Paris, ordinary for Eastern-Rite faithful in France without ordinaries of their own. Curial membership:
Secretariat of State (second section); Divine Wor-

ship and Sacraments, Bishops, Oriental Churches, Clergy, Institutes of Consecrated Life and Societies of Apostolic Life (congregations); Culture (council).

**Macharski, Franciszek:** b. May 20, 1927, Kracow, Poland; ord. priest Apr. 2, 1950; engaged in pastoral work, 1950-56; continued theological studies in Fribourg, Switzerland, 1956-60; taught pastoral theology at the Faculty of Theology in Kracow; app. rector of archdiocesan seminary at Kracow, 1970; ord. archbishop of Kracow, Jan. 6, 1979, by Pope John Paul II; cardinal June 30, 1979; titular church, St. John at the Latin Gate. Archbishop of Kracow. Curial membership:
Secretariat of State (second section); Bishops, Clergy, Institutes of Consecrated Life and Societies of Apostolic Life, Catholic Education (congregations).

**Mahony, Roger M.:** b. Feb. 27, 1936, Hollywood, Calif.; educ. St. John's Seminary (Camarillo, Calif.), National Catholic School of Social Service (Catholic Univ., Washington D.C.); ord. priest (Fresno diocese) May 1, 1962; ord. titular bishop of Tamascani and auxiliary bishop of Fresno, Mar. 19, 1975; bishop of Stockton, installed Apr. 25, 1980; archbishop of Los Angeles, July 16, 1985, installed Sept. 5, 1985; cardinal June 28, 1991; titular church, Four Crowned Saints. Archbishop of Los Angeles. Curial membership:
Justice and Peace, Social Communications (councils).

**Maida, Adam Joseph:** b. Mar. 18, 1930, East Vandergrift, Pa.; ord. priest (Pittsburgh diocese) May 26, 1956; ord. bishop of Green Bay, Jan. 25, 1984; app. archbishop of Detroit, May 7, 1990, installed June 12, 1990; cardinal Nov. 26, 1994; titular church, Sts. Vitalis, Valeria, Gervase and Protase. Archbishop of Detroit. Curial membership:
Clergy, Catholic Education (congregations); Migrants and Itinerant Peoples (Council).

**Margeot,\* Jean:** b. Feb. 3, 1916, Quatre-Bornes, Mauritius; ord. priest Dec. 17, 1938; ord. bishop of Port Louis, May 4, 1969; cardinal June 28, 1988; titular church, St. Gabriel the Archangel all'Acqua Traversa. Bishop emeritus of Port Louis (resigned Feb. 15, 1993). Curial membership:
Family (council).

**Martinez Somalo, Eduardo:** b. Mar. 31, 1927, Baños de Rio Tobia, Spain; ord. priest Mar. 19, 1950; ord. titular bishop of Tagora with personal title of archbishop, Dec. 13, 1975; in secretariat of state from 1956; substitute (assistant) secretary of state, 1979-88; cardinal June 28, 1988; deacon, Most Holy Name of Jesus; prefect of Congregation for Divine Worship and Sacraments, 1988-92. Prefect of Congregation for Institutes of Consecrated Life and Societies of Apostolic Life, Jan. 21, 1992; Chamberlain (Camerlengo) of the Holy Roman Church, Apr. 5, 1993; Protodeacon 1996. Curial membership:
Secretariat of State (second section); Divine Worship and Sacraments, Bishops, Causes of Saints, Evangelization of Peoples, Clergy, Catholic Education (congregations); Interpretation of Legislative Texts (council); Latin America, Institute for Works of Religion (commissions).

**Martini, Carlo Maria, S.J.:** b. Feb. 15, 1927, Turin, Italy; entered Jesuits Sept. 25, 1944; ord. priest

July 13, 1952; biblical scholar; seminary professor, Chieri, Italy, 1958-61; professor and later rector, 1969-78, of Pontifical Biblical Institute; rector of Pontifical Gregorian University, 1978-79; author of theological, biblical and spiritual works; ord. archbishop of Milan, Jan. 6, 1980, by Pope John Paul II; cardinal Feb. 2, 1983; titular church, St. Cecilia. Archbishop of Milan. Curial membership:

Secretariat of State (second section); Oriental Churches, Divine Worship and Sacraments, Institutes of Consecrated Life and Societies of Apostolic Life, Catholic Education (congregations); Culture (council).

**Mayer,\* Paul Augustin, O.S.B.:** b. May 23, 1911, Altötting, Germany; ord. priest Aug. 25, 1935; rector of St. Anselm's Univ., Rome, 1949-66; secretary of Congregation for Religious and Secular Institutes, 1972-84; ord. titular bishop of Satriano with personal title of archbishop, Feb. 13, 1972; pro-prefect of Congregations for Sacraments and Divine Worship, 1984; cardinal May 25, 1985; deacon, St. Anselm; transferred to order of cardinal priests Jan. 29, 1996. Prefect of Congregation for Divine Worship and Sacraments, 1985-88; president of Pontifical Commission "Ecclesia Dei," 1988-91.

**Meisner, Joachim:** b. Dec. 25, 1933, Breslau, Silesia, Germany (present-day Wroclaw, Poland); ord. priest Dec. 22, 1962; regional director of Caritas; ord. titular bishop of Vina and auxiliary of apostolic administration of Erfurt-Meiningen, E. Germany, May 17, 1975; bishop of Berlin, 1980-88; cardinal Feb. 2, 1983; titular church, St. Prudenziana. Archbishop of Cologne, Dec. 20, 1988. Curial membership:

Divine Worship and Sacraments, bishops, Clergy (congregations); Interreligious Dialogue, Culture (councils); Economic Affairs of Holy See (office).

**Neves, Lucas Moreira, O.P.:** b. Sept. 16, 1925, Sao Joao del Rei, Brazil; ord. priest July 9, 1950; ord. titular bishop of Feradi maggiore and auxiliary of Sao Paulo, Aug. 26, 1967; assigned to Vatican, 1974; vice president of Pontifical Commission for Laity, 1974-79; archbishop Oct. 15, 1979; secretary of Congregation for Bishops, 1979-87; assigned titular see of Vescovia, Jan. 3, 1987; archbishp of Sao Salvador da Bahia, July 9, 1987; cardinal June 28, 1988; titular church, Sts. Boniface and Alexius. Archbishop of Sao Salvador da Bahia. Curial membership:

Secretariat of State (second section); Doctrine of the Faith, Bishops, Institutes of Consecrated Life and Societies of Apostolic Life, Catholic Education (congregations); Family, Culture (councils); Latin America (commission).

**Noè, Virgilio:** b. Mar. 30, 1922, Zelata di Bereguardo, Italy; ord. priest Oct. 1, 1944; master of pontifical ceremonies and undersecretary of Congregation for Sacraments and Divine Worship, 1970-82; ord. titular bishop of Voncario with personal title of archbishop, Mar. 6, 1982; coadjutor Archpriest of St. Peter's Basilica, 1989; vicar general of Vatican City State, Jan. 14, 1991; cardinal June 28, 1991; deacon, St. John Bosco (in Via Tuscolana). Archpriest of St. Peter's Basilica, Vicar General of Vatican City State and President of the Fabric of St. Peter, 1991; president of Commission for Sanctuar-

ies of Pompeii, Loreto and Bari, 1993. Curial membership:

Divine Worship and Sacraments, Causes of Saints (congregations); Holy Year 2000 (committee).

**Obando Bravo, Miguel, S.D.B.:** b. Feb. 2, 1926, La Libertad, Nicaragua; ord. priest Aug. 10, 1958; ord. titular bishop of Puzia di Bizacena and auxiliary of Matagalpa, Mar. 31, 1968; archbishop of Managua, Feb. 16, 1970; cardinal May 25, 1985; titular church, St. John the Evangelist (a Spinaceta). Archbishop of Managua. Curial membership:

Clergy, Institutes of Consecrated Life and Societies of Apostolic Life (congregations); Latin America (commission).

**O'Connor, John J.:** b. Jan. 15, 1920, Philadelphia, Pa.; ord. priest (Philadelphia archdiocese) Dec. 15, 1945; joined U.S. Navy and Marine Corps as a chaplain, 1952; overseas posts included service in South Korea and Vietnam; U.S. Navy chief of chaplains, 1975; retired from Navy June 1, 1979, with rank of rear admiral; ord. titular bishop of Curzola and auxiliary of military vicariate, May 27, 1979; bishop of Scranton, May 6, 1983; archbishop of New York, Jan. 26, 1984; cardinal May 25, 1985; titular church, Sts. John and Paul. Archbishop of New York. Curial membership:

Secretariat of State (second section); Bishops, Oriental Churches, Evangelization of Peoples (congregations); Family, Social Communications, Health Care Workers, Migrants and Itinerant People (councils); Institute for Works of Religion (commission).

**Oddi,\* Silvio:** b. Nov. 14, 1910, Morfasso, Italy; ord. priest May 21, 1933; ord. titular archbishop of Mesembria, Sept. 27, 1953; served in Vatican diplomatic corps, 1953-69; apostolic delegate to Jerusalem, Palestine, Jordan and Cyprus, internuncio to the United Arab Republic, and nuncio to Belgium and Luxembourg; cardinal Apr. 28, 1969; titular church, St. Agatha of the Goths. Pontifical legate for Patriarchal Basilica of St. Francis in Assisi; prefect of Sacred Congregation for the Clergy, 1979-86.

**Ortega y Alamino, Jaime Lucas:** b. Oct. 18, 1936, Jagüey Grande, Cuba; ord. priest Aug. 2, 1964; detained in work camps (UMAP) 1966-67; parish priest; ord. bishop of Pinar del Rio, Jan. 14, 1979; app. archbishop of Havana, Nov. 20, 1981; cardinal Nov. 26, 1994; titular church, Sts. Aquila and Priscilla. Archbishop of Havana. Curial membership:

Clergy (congregation); Health Care Workers (council); Latin America (commission).

**Otunga, Maurice Michael:** b. January, 1923, Chebukwa, Kenya; son of pagan tribal chief; baptized 1935, at age of 12; ord. priest Oct. 3, 1950, at Rome; taught at Kisumu major seminary for three years; attaché in apostolic delegation at Mombasa, 1953-56; ord. titular bishop of Tacape and auxiliary of Kisumu, Feb. 25, 1957; bishop of Kisii, 1960-69; titular archbishop of Bomarzo and coadjutor of Nairobi, Nov. 15, 1969; archbishop of Nairobi, Oct. 24, 1971; cardinal Mar. 5, 1973; titular church, St. Gregory Barbarigo. Archbishop of Nairobi, military ordinary of Kenya, 1981. Curial membership:

Institutes of Consecrated Life and Societies of Apostolic Life, Evangelization of Peoples (congregations),

**Oviedo Cavado, Carlos, O. de M.:** b. Jan. 19, 1927, Santiago, Chile; entered Mercedarian novitiate in 1944 and made solemn profession Mar. 19, 1948; ord. priest Sept. 24, 1949; ord. titular bishop of Benevento and auxiliary bishop of Concepcion, June 7, 1964; archbishop of Antofagasta, 1974-90; archbishop of Santiago, Mar. 30, 1990; cardinal Nov. 26, 1994; titular church, St. Mary della Scala. Archbishop of Santiago. Curial membership:

Catholic Education (congregation); Culture (council).

**Padiyara, Anthony:** b. Feb. 11, 1921, Manimala, India; raised in Syro-Malabar rite family; ord. priest for Latin rite diocese of Coimbatore, Dec. 19, 1945; first bishop of Ootacamund (Latin rite), Oct. 16, 1955; app. archbishop of Changanacherry (Syro-Malabar rite), June 14, 1970, at which time he returned to the Syro-Malabar rite; archbishop of Ernakulam, Apr. 23, 1985; cardinal June 28, 1988; titular church, St. Mary Queen of Peace (Monte Verde). First Major Archbishop of Major Archbishopric of Ernakulam-Angamaly of Syro-Malabar Church (established Dec. 16, 1992); enthroned May 20, 1993. Curial membership:

Oriental Churches (congregation); Interpretation of Legislative Texts (councils).

**Palazzini,\* Pietro:** b. May 19, 1912, Piobbico, Pesaro, Italy; ord. priest Dec. 6, 1934; assistant vice-rector of Pontifical Major Roman Seminary and vice-rector and bursar of Pontifical Roman Seminary for Juridical Studies; professor of moral theology at Lateran University; held various offices in Roman Curia; secretary of Congregation of Council (now Clergy), 1958-73; ord. titular archbishop of Caesarea in Cappadocia, Sept. 21, 1962; author of numerous works on moral theology and law; cardinal Mar. 5, 1973; titular church, St. Jerome. Prefect of Congregation for Causes of Saints, 1980-88.

**Pappalardo, Salvatore:** b. Sept. 23, 1918, Villafranca Sicula, Sicily; ord. priest Apr. 12, 1941; entered diplomatic service of secretariat of state, 1947; ord. titular archbishop of Miletus, Jan. 16, 1966; pro-nuncio in Indonesia, 1966-69; president of Pontifical Ecclesiastical Academy, 1969-70; archbishop of Palermo, Oct. 17, 1970; cardinal Mar. 5, 1973; titular church, St. Mary Odigitria of the Sicilians. Archbishop emeritus of Palermo (resigned April, 1996). Curial membership:

Oriental Churches, Clergy (congregations).

**Paskai, Laszlo, O.F.M.:** b. May 8, 1927, Szeged, Hungary; ord. priest Mar. 3, 1951; ord. titular bishop of Bavagaliana and apostolic administrator of Veszprem, Apr. 5, 1978; bishop of Veszprem Mar. 31, 1979; coadjutor archbishop of Kalocsa, Apr. 5, 1982; archbishop of Esztergom (renamed Esztergom-Budapest, 1993), Mar. 3, 1987; cardinal June 28, 1988; titular church, St. Theresa (al Corso d'Italia). Archbishop of Esztergom-Budapest. Curial membership:

Oriental Churches, Institutes of Consecrated Lfe and Societies of Apostolic Life (congregations); Interpretation of Legislative Texts (council).

**Pham Dinh Tung, Paul Joseph:** b. June 15, 1919, Binh-Hoa, Vietnam; ord. priest June 6, 1949; ord. bishop of Bac Ninh, Aug. 15, 1963; apostolic administrator of Hanoi, June 18, 1990; archbishop of Hanoi, Apr. 23, 1994; cardinal Nov. 26, 1994; titular church, St. Mary Queen of Peace in Ostia mare. Archbishop of Hanoi. Curial membership:

Evangelization of Peoples (congregation); "Cor Unum" (council).

**Pimenta, Simon Ignatius:** b. Mar. 1, 1920, Marol, India; ord. priest Dec. 21, 1949; ord. titular bishop of Bocconia and auxiliary of Bombay, June 29, 1971; coadjutor archbishop of Bombay, Feb. 26, 1977; archbishop of Bombay, Sept. 11, 1978; cardinal June 28, 1988; titular church, Mary, Queen of the World (a Torre Spaccata). Archbishop of Bombay. Curial membership:

Evangelization of Peoples, Catholic Education (congregations); Economic Affairs of the Holy See (office); Interreligious Dialogue (council).

**Piovanelli, Silvano:** b. Feb. 21, 1924, Ronta di Mugello, Italy; ord. priest July 13, 1947; ord. titular bishop of Tubune di Mauretania and auxiliary of Florence, June 24, 1982; archbishop of Florence, Mar. 18, 1983; cardinal May 25, 1985; titular church, St. Mary of Graces (Via Trionfale). Archbishop of Florence. Curial membership:

Justice and Peace (council).

**Pironio, Eduardo:** b. Dec. 3, 1920, Nueve de Julio, Argentina; ord. priest Dec. 5, 1943; taught theology at Pius XII Seminary of Mercedes diocese, 1944-59; vicar general of diocese 1958-60; attended Second Vatican Council as *peritus*; ord. titular bishop of Ceciri, May 31, 1964; apostolic administrator of diocese of Avellaneda, 1967-72; secretary general, 1967-72, and president, 1973-75, of CELAM; bishop of Mar del Plata, 1972-75; titular archbishop of Thiges and pro-prefect of Congregation for Religious and Secular Institutes, Sept. 20, 1975; cardinal deacon May 24, 1976; titular church, Sts. Cosmas and Damian; transferred to order of cardinal priests, June 22, 1987; transferred to cardinal bishops July 11, 1995, suburbicarian see of Sabina-Poggia Mirteto. Prefect of the Congregation for Religious and Secular Institutes, 1976-84. President of Pontifical Council for the Laity, 1984-96. Curial membership:

Secretariat of State (second section); Bishops, Causes of Saints, Catholic Education, Oriental Churches, Evangelization of Peoples (congregations); Interpretation of Legislative Texts (council); Latin America (commission).

**Poggi, Luigi:** b. Nov. 25, 1917, Piacenza, Italy; ord. priest July 28, 1940; studied diplomacy at the Pontifical Ecclesiastical Academy, 1944-46; started to work at Secretariat of State; ord. titular bishop of Forontoniana with personal title of archbishop, May 9, 1965; apostolic delegate for Central Africa, 1965; nuncio in Peru; recalled to Rome, 1973; negotiated with various Eastern bloc governments to improve situation of the Church; named head of Holy See's delegation for permanent contact with government of Poland, 1974; nuncio in Italy, 1986-92; pro-librarian and pro-archivist of the Holy Roman Church, 1992-94; cardinal Nov. 26, 1994; deacon, St. Mary in Domnica. Archivist and librarian of the Holy Roman Church (Nov. 26, 1994). Curial membership:

Secretariat of State (second section); Bishops, Evangelization of Peoples (congregations).

**Poletti,\* Ugo:** b. Apr. 19, 1914, Omegna, Italy;

ord. priest June 29, 1938; served in various diocesan offices at Novara; ord. titular bishop of Medeli and auxiliary of Novaro, Sept. 14, 1958; president of Pontifical Mission Aid Society for Italy, 1964-67; archbishop of Spoleto, 1967-69; titular archbishop of Cittanova, 1969; served as second viceregent of Rome, 1969-72; pro-vicar general of Rome, 1972; cardinal Mar. 5, 1973; titular church, Sts. Ambrose and Charles; vicar general of Rome, 1973-91. Archbishop of Patriarchal Liberian Basilica of St. Mary Major, 1991.

**Poupard, Paul:** b. Aug. 30, 1930, Bouzille, France; ord. priest Dec. 18, 1954; scholar; author of a number of works; ord. titular bishop of Usula and auxiliary of Paris, Apr. 6, 1979; title of archbishop and pro-president of the Secretariat for Non-Believers, 1980; cardinal deacon May 25, 1985; transferred to order of cardinal priests Jan. 29, 1996; titular church, St. Praxedes; president of Pontifical Council for Dialogue with Non-Believers, 1985-93. President of Pontifical Council for Culture, 1988. Curial membership:
Divine Worship and Sacraments, Evangelization of Peoples, Catholic Education (congregations); Interreligious Dialogue (council).

**Primatesta, Raul Francisco:** b. Apr. 14, 1919, Capilla del Senor, Argentina; od. priest Oct. 25, 1942, at Rome; taught at minor and major seminaries of La Plata; contributed to several theology reviews; ord. titular bishop of Tanais and auxiliary of La Plata, Aug. 15, 1957; bishop of San Rafael, 1961-65; archbishop of Cordoba, Feb. 16, 1965; cardinal Mar. 5, 1973; titular church, Blessed Mary Sorrowful Virgin. Archbishop of Cordoba, Argentina. Curial membership:
Clergy (congregation).

**Puljic, Vinko:** b. Sept. 8, 1945, Prijecani, Bosnia-Herzegovina; ord. priest June 29, 1970; spiritual director of minor seminary of Zadar, 1978-87; parish priest; app. vice-rector of Sarajevo major seminary, 1990; ord. archbishop of Vrhbosna (Sarajevo), Jan. 6, 1991, in Rome; cardinal Nov. 26, 1994; titular church, St. Clare in Vigna Clara. Archbishop of Sarajevo. Curial membership:
Evangelization of Peoples (congregation); Interreligious Dialogue (council).

**Quarracino, Antonio:** b. Aug. 8, 1923, Pollica, Italy; moved to Argentina when he was a child; ord. priest Dec. 22, 1945; ord. bishop of Nueve de Julio Apr. 8, 1962; bishop of Avellaneda, 1968-85; archbishop of La Plata, 1985-90; archbishop of Buenos Aires, July 10, 1990; cardinal June 28, 1991; titular church, St. Mary of Health (a Primavalle). Archbishop of Buenos Aires, ordinary for Eastern-rite faithful in Argentina without ordinaries of their proper rite. Curial membership:
Bishops (congregation); Christian Unity, Health Care Workers (councils); Latin America (commission).

**Ratzinger, Joseph:** b. Apr. 16, 1927, Marktl am Inn, Germany; ord. priest June 29, 1951; professor of dogmatic theology at University of Regensburg, 1969-77; member of International Theological Commission, 1969-80; ord. archbishop of Munich-Freising, May 28, 1977 (resigned Feb. 15, 1982); cardinal June 27, 1977; titular church, St. Mary of Consolation (in Tiburtina); transferred to order of

cardinal bishops as titular bishop of suburbicarian see of Velletri-Segni, Apr. 5, 1993. Prefect of Congregation for Doctrine of the Faith, 1981; president of Biblical and Theological Commissions. Curial membership:
Secretariat of State (second section); Bishops, Divine Worship and Sacraments, Oriental Churches, Evangelization of Peoples, Catholic Education (congregations); Christian Unity, Culture (councils); Latin America (commission).

**Razafindratandra, Armand Gaétan:** b. Aug. 7, 1925, Ambohimalaza, Madagascar; ord. priest July 27, 1954; ord. bishop of Mahajanga, July 2, 1978; app. archbishop of Antananarivo, Feb. 3, 1994, installed May 15, 1994; cardinal Nov. 26, 1994; titular church, Sts. Sylvester and Martin ai Monti. Archbishop of Antananarivo and apostolic administrator of Miarinarivo. Curial membership:
Evangelization of Peoples (congregation); Laity (council).

**Ribeiro, Antonio:** b. May 21, 1928, Gandarela de Basto, Portugal; ord. priest July 5, 1953; professor of fundamental theology at major seminary at Braga; ord. titular bishop of Tigillava and auxiliary of Braga, Sept. 17, 1967; patriarch of Lisbon, May 10, 1971; cardinal Mar. 5, 1973; titular church, St. Anthony of Padua (in Via Merulana). Patriarch of Lisbon, military ordinary for Portugal. Curial membership:
Clergy, Catholic Education (congregations); Culture (council).

**Righi-Lambertini,\* Egano:** b. Feb. 22, 1906, Casalecchio di Reno, Italy; ord. priest May 25, 1929; entered service of secretariat of state, 1939; served in diplomatic missions in France (1949-54), Costa Rica (1955), England (1955-57); first apostolic delegate to Korea, 1957-60; ord. titular archbishop of Doclea, Oct. 28, 1960; apostolic nuncio in Lebanon, 1960-63, Chile, 1963-67, Italy, 1967-69; France, 1969-79; while nuncio in France he also served as special envoy at the Council of Europe, 1974-79; cardinal deacon June 30, 1979; transferred to order of cardinal priests, Nov. 26, 1990; titular church, Saint Mary (in Via).

**Rossi,\* Opilio:** b. May 14, 1910, New York, N.Y.; holds Italian citizenship; ord. priest for diocese of Piacenza (now Piacenza-Bobbio), Italy, Mar. 11, 1933; served in nunciatures in Belgium, The Netherlands, and Germany, 1938-53; ord. titula archbishop of Ancyra, Dec. 27, 1953; nuncio in Ecuador, 1953-59, Chile, 1959-61, Austria 1961-76; cardinal deacon May 24, 1976; transferred to order of cardinal priests, June 22, 1987; titular church, St. Lawrence (in Lucina); president of Pontifical Committee for International Eucharistic Congresses, 1983-90; president of Commission for the Sanctuaries of Pompeii, Loreto and Bari, 1984-93.

**Rugambwa,\* Laurean:** b. July 12, 1912, Bukongo, Tanzania; ord. priest Dec. 12, 1943; ord. titular bishop of Febiano and vicar apostolic of Lower Kagera, Feb. 10, 1952; bishop of Rutabo, 1953-60 (diocese was restructured as Bukoba); cardinal Mar. 28, 1960; titular church, St. Francis of Assisi (a Ripa Grande); bishop of Bukoba, 1960-68. Archbishop of Dar-es-Salaam, 1968-92. Archbishop emeritus of Dar-es-Salaam.

**Ruini, Camillo:** b. Feb. 19, 1931, Sassuolo, Italy;

ord. priest Dec. 8, 1954; taught at seminaries in central Italy; ord. titular bishop of Nepte and auxiliary bishop of Reggio Emilia and Guastella, June 29, 1983; secretary general of Italian Bishops' Conference, 1986-91; archbishop Jan. 17, 1991 and pro-vicar general of the Pope for the Rome diocese; pro-Archpriest of Patriarchal Lateran Archbasilica; cardinal June 28, 1991; titular church, St. Agnes outside the Wall. Vicar General of the Pope for the Diocese of Rome and Archpriest of Patriarchal Lateran Basilica, July 1, 1991; Grand Chancellor of Pontifical Lateran University; President of the *Peregrinatio ad Petri Sedem*, 1992-96. Curial membership:

Bishops (congregation); Holy Year 2000 (committee).

**Sabattani,\* Aurelio:** b. Oct. 18, 1912, Casal Fiumanese, Italy; ord. priest July 26, 1935; jurist; served in various assignments in his native diocese of Imola and as judge and later an official of the regional ecclesiastical tribunal of Bologna; called to Rome in 1955 as prelate auditor of the Roman Rota; ord. titular archbishop of Justinian Prima, July 25, 1965; prelate of Loreto, 1965-71; secretary of Supreme Tribunal of Apostolic Signatura and consultor of Secretariat of State, 1971; pro-prefect of Apostolic Signatura, 1982-83; cardinal deacon Feb. 2, 1983; transferred to order of cardinal priests Apr. 5, 1993; titular church, St. Apollinaris; prefect of Apostolic Signatura, 1983-88; archpriest of Patriarchal Vatican Basilica and president of the Fabric of St. Peter, 1983-91; former vicar general of the Pope for Vatican City.

**Saldarini, Giovanni:** b. Dec. 11, 1924, Cantu, Italy; ord. priest May 31, 1947; respected scripture scholar; taught scripture at Milan archdiocesan seminary, 1952-67; ord. titular bishop of Guadiaba and auxiliary bishop of Milan, Dec. 7, 1984; archbishop of Turin Jan. 31, 1989; cardinal June 28, 1991; titular church, Sacred Heart of Jesus (a Castro Pretorio). Archbishop of Turin. Curial membership:

Divine Worship and Sacraments, Bishops, Evangelization of Peoples, Clergy (congregations); Laity (council).

**Sales, Eugenio de Araujo:** b. Nov. 8, 1920, Acari, Brazil; ord. priest Nov. 21, 1943; ord. titular bishop of Tibica and auxiliary bishop of Natal, Aug. 15, 1954; archbishop of Sao Salvador, 1968-71; cardinal Apr. 28, 1969; titular church, St. Gregory VII. Archbishop of Rio de Janeiro (1971), ordinary for Eastern Rite Catholics in Brazil without ordinaries of their own rites. Curial membership:

Secretariat of State (second section); Oriental Churches, Divine Worship and Sacraments, Clergy, Evangelization of Peoples (congregations); Social Communications (council).

**Sanchez, Jose T.:** b. Mar. 17, 1920, Pandan, Philippines; ord. priest May 12, 1946; ord. titular bishop of Lesvi and coadjutor bishop of Lucena, May 12, 1968; bishop of Lucena, 1976-82; archbishop of Nueva Segovia Jan. 12, 1982 (resigned Mar. 22, 1986); sec-

retary of Congregation for Evangelization of Peoples, 1985-91; cardinal June 28, 1991; deacon, St. Pius V (a Villa Carpegna); president of Commission for Preservation of Artistic and Historic Patrimony of the Holy See, 1991-93. Prefect of Congregation for the Clergy, 1991-96. Curial membership:

Secretariat of State (second section); Bishops, Evangelization of Peoples, Catholic Education (congregations); Interpretation of Legislative Texts (council); International Eucharistic Congresses (committee), Latin America, Sanctuaries of Pompeii, Loreto and Bari (commissions).

**Sandoval Iñiguez, Juan:** b. Mar. 28, 1933, Yahualica, Mexico; ord. priest Oct. 27, 1957; ord. coadjutor bishop of Ciudad Juárez, Apr. 30, 1988; bishop of Ciudad Juarez, July 11, 1992; app. archbishop of Guadalajara, Apr. 21, 1994; cardinal Nov. 26, 1994; titular church, Our Lady of Guadalupe and St. Philip the Martyr on Via Aurelia. Archbishop of Guadalajara. Curial membership:

Institutes of Consecrated Life and Societies of Apostolic Life, Catholic Education (congregations); Latin America (commission).

**Santos, Alexandre Jose Maria dos, O.F.M.:** b. Mar. 18, 1924, Zavala, Mozambique; ord. priest July 25, 1953; first Mozambican black priest; ord. archbishop of Maputo, Mar. 9, 1975; cardinal June 28, 1988; titular church, St. Frumentius (ai Prati Fiscali). Archbishop of Maputo. Curial membership:

Evangelization of Peoples (congregation); Culture (council).

**Schotte, Jan Pieter, C.I.C.M.:** b. Apr. 29, 1928, Beveren-Leie, Belgium; entered Congregation of the Immaculate Heart of Mary (Scheut Missionaries) in 1946; ord. priest Aug. 3, 1952; taught canon law at Louvain and was rector of community's seminary in Washington, D.C.; general secretary of Congregation of the Immaculate Heart of Mary in Rome, 1967-72; secretary (1980) and vice-president (1983) of the Pontifical Commission of Justice and Peace; ord. titular bishop of Silli, Jan. 6, 1984; promoted to titular archbishop, Apr. 24, 1985; cardinal Nov. 26, 1994; deacon St. Julian of the Flemings. Secretary general of the Synod of Bishops since 1985; president of the Labor Office of the Holy See, 1989. Curial membership:

Bishops, Evangelization of Peoples (congregations); Latin America (commission).

**Schwery, Henri:** b. June 14, 1932, Saint-Leonard, Switzerland; ord. priest July 7, 1957; director of minor seminary and later rector of the College in Sion; ord. bishop of Sion, Sept. 17, 1977; cardinal June 28, 1991; titular church, Protomartyrs (a via Aurelia Antica). Bishop emeritus of Sion (retired Apr. 1, 1995). Curial membership:

Divine Worship and Sacraments, Clergy (congregations); Social Communications (council).

**Sensi,\* Giuseppe Maria:** b. May 27, 1907, Cosenza, Italy; ord. priest Dec. 21, 1929; entered Vatican diplomatic service; served in nunciatures in

---

**Death:** Retired Bishop Adriano Mandarino Hypolito, 78, of Nova Iguacu, Brazil, died Aug. 12, 1996, of a heart attack in a hospital near Rio de Janeiro. A Franciscan, he was bishop of Nova Iguacu, a slum outside Rio de Janeiro, for 28 years. He was the target of persecution by the military dictatorship of Brazil for criticizing the oppression of the poor. In 1976, he was kidnapped by members of the Brazilian Anti-Communist Alliance.. He was beaten, forced to disrobe, and abandoned on a lonely road in a Rio suburb.

Hungary, Switzerland, Belgium and Czechoslovakia, 1934-49; ord. titular archbishop of Sardes, July 24, 1955; apostolic nuncio to Costa Rica, 1955; apostolic delegate to Jerusalem, 1956-62; nuncio to Ireland, 1962-67, and Portugal, 1967-76; cardinal deacon May 24, 1976; transferred to order of cardinal priests, June 22, 1987; titular church, Queen of Apostles.

**Sfeir, Nasrallah Pierre:** b. May 15, 1920, Reyfoun, in Maronite diocese of Sarba, Lebanon; ord. priest May 7, 1950; secretary of Maronite patriarchate, 1956-61; taught Arabic literature and philosphy at Marist Fathers College, Jounieh, 1951-61; ord. titular bishop of Tarsus for the Maronites, July 16, 1961; elected Patriarch of Antioch for Maronites, Apr. 19, 1986, granted ecclesial communion by John Paul II May 7, 1986; cardinal Nov. 26, 1994. Patriarch of Antioch for Maronites. Curial membership:
Oriental Churches (congregation); Health Care Workers, Interpretation of Liturgical Texts (councils).

**Shirayanagi, Peter Seiichi:** b. June 17, 1928, Hachioji City, Japan; ord. priest Dec. 21, 1954; ord. titular bishop of Atenia and auxiliary bishop of Tokyo, May 8, 1966; titular archbishop of Castro and coadjutor archbishop of Tokyo, Nov. 15, 1969; succeeded to see, Feb. 21, 1970; cardinal Nov. 26, 1994; titular church, St. Emerentiana in Tor Fiorenza. Archbishop of Tokyo. Curial membership:
Family, Interreligious Dialogue (councils).

**Silva Henriquez,\* Raul, S.D.B.:** b. Sept. 27, 1907, Talca, Chile; ord. priest July 3, 1938; ord. bishop of Valparaiso, Nov. 29, 1959; archbishop of Santiago de Chile, 1961-83; cardinal Mar. 19, 1962; titular church, St. Bernard (alle Terme). Archbishop emeritus of Santiago de Chile.

**Silvestrini, Achille:** b. Oct. 25, 1923, Brisighella, Italy; ord. priest July 13, 1946; official in Secretariat of State from 1953; ord. titular bishop of Novaliciana with personal title of archbishop, May 2, 1979; undersecretary, 1973-79, and secretary, 1979-88, of the Council for Public Affairs of the Church (now the second section of the Secretariat of State); cardinal June 28, 1988; deacon, St. Benedict Outside St. Paul's Gate; prefect of Apostolic Signatura, 1988-91. Prefect of Congregation for Oriental Churches, 1991; Grand Chancellor of Pontifical Oriental Institute. Curial membership:
Secretariat of State (second section); Doctrine of the Faith, Bishops, Causes of Saints, Evangelization of Peoples, Catholic Education (congregations); Christian Unity, Interpretation of Legislative Texts, Interreligious Dialogue (councils).

**Simonis, Adrianus J.:** b. Nov. 26, 1931, Lisse, Netherlands; ord. priest June 15, 1957; ord. bishop of Rotterdam, Mar. 20, 1971; coadjutor archbishop of Utrecht, June 27, 1983; archbishop of Utrecht, Dec. 3, 1983; cardinal May 25, 1985; titular church, St. Clement. Archbishop of Utrecht. Curial membership:
Institutes of Consecrated Life and Societies of Apostolic Life, Catholic Education (congregations); Christian Unity (council).

**Sin, Jaime L.:** b. Aug. 31, 1928, New Washington, Philippines; ord. priest Apr. 3, 1954; diocesan missionary in Capiz, 1954-57; app. first rector of the St. Pius X Seminary, Roxas City, 1957; ord. titular bishop of Obba and auxiliary bishop of Jaro, Mar. 18, 1967; apostolic administrator of archdiocese of Jaro, June 20, 1970; titular archbishop of Massa Lubrense and coadjutor archbishop of Jaro, Jan. 15, 1972; archbishop of Jaro, 1972-74; archbishop of Manila, Jan. 21, 1974; cardinal May 24, 1976; titular church, S. Maria (ai Monti). Archbishop of Manila. Curial membership:
Divine Worship and Sacraments, Clergy, Institutes of Consecrated Life and Societies of Apostolic Life (congregations); Social Communications (council).

**Sladkevicius, Vincentas, M.I.C.:** b. Aug. 20, 1920, Zasliai, Lithuania; ord. priest Mar. 25, 1944; ord. titular bishop of Abora and auxiliary of Kaisiadorys, Dec. 25, 1957, but was not permitted to exercise his office; under house arrest 1959-82; apostolic administrator of Kaisiadorys, 1982-89; cardinal June 28, 1988; titular church, Holy Spirit (alla Ferratella). Archbishop of Kaunas (Mar. 10, 1989; resigned May 4, 1996). Curial membership:
Catholic Education (congregation).

**Sodano, Angelo:** b. Nov. 23, 1927, Isola d'Asti, Italy; ord. priest Sept. 23, 1950; entered diplomatic service of the Holy See in 1959; served in Ecuador and Uruguay; ord. titular archbishop of Nova di Cesare, Jan. 15, 1978; nuncio to Chile, 1978-88; secretary of the Council for Relations with States, 1988-90; pro-Secretary of State, 1990 (Dec. 1)-1991; cardinal June 28, 1991; titular church, S. Maria Nuova; transferred to order of cardinal bishops, Jan 10, 1994, as titular bishop of suburbicarian see of Albano (while retaining title to S. Maria Nuova). Secretary of State, June 29, 1991. Curial membership:
Doctrine of the Faith, Bishops, Oriental Churches (congregations); Institute for Works of Religion (commission).

**Sterzinsky, Georg Maximilian:** b. Feb. 9, 1936, Warlack, Germany; ord. priest June 29, 1960; vicar general to the apostolic administrator of Erfurt-Meiningen, 1981-89; ord. bishop of Berlin, Sept. 9, 1989; cardinal June 28, 1991; titular church, St. Joseph (all'Aurelio). Archbishop of Berlin (June 27, 1994). Curial membership:
Catholic Education (congregation); Migrants and Itinerant People (council).

**Stickler,\* Alfons, S.D.B.:** b. Aug. 23, 1910, Neunkirchen, Austria; ord. priest Mar. 27, 1937; director of the Vatican Library, 1971; ord. titular bishop of Bolsena, Nov. 1, 1983, with personal title of archbishop; Pro-Librarian and Pro-Archivist, 1984; cardinal May 25, 1985; deacon, St. George (in Velabro); transferred to order of cardinal priests Jan. 29, 1996. Librarian and Archivist of the Holy Roman Church, 1985-88.

**Suarez Rivera, Adolfo Antonio:** b. Jan. 9, 1927, San Cristobal, Mexico; ord. priest Mar. 8, 1952; ord. bishop of Tepic, Aug. 15, 1971; bishop of Tlalnepantla, May 8, 1980; app. archbishop of Monterrey, Nov. 8, 1983; cardinal Nov. 26, 1994; titular church, Our Lady of Guadalupe on Monte Mario. Archbishop of Monterrey. Curial membership:
Clergy (congregation); Latin America (commission).

**Suquia Goicoechea, Angel:** b. Oct. 2, 1916, Zaldivia, Spain; ord. priest July 7, 1940; ord. bishop of Almeria, July 16, 1966; bishop of Malaga, 1969-73; archbishop of Santiago de Compostela, 1973-83; archbishop of Madrid, Apr. 12, 1983; cardinal May 25, 1985; titular church, Great Mother of God. Archbishop emeritus of Madrid (retired July 28, 1994). Curial membership: Secretariat of State (second section); Oriental Churches, Bishops (congregations).

**Swiatek,\* Kazimierz:** b. Oct. 21, 1914, Walga, in apostolic administration of Estonia; ord. priest (of Pinsk, Belarus, clergy) Apr. 8, 1939; arrested by KGB Apr. 21, 1941, and imprisoned on death row until June 22, when he escaped during confusion of German invasion and returned to his parish; arrested again by KGB and imprisoned in Minsk until 1945; sentenced to 10 years of hard labor in concentration camps; released June 16, 1954; resumed pastoral work in cathedral parish in Pinsk; ord. archbishop of Minsk-Mohilev, Belarus, May 21, 1991, and also appointed apostolic administrator of Pinsk; cardinal Nov. 26, 1994; titular church, St. Gerard Majella. Archbishop of Minsk-Mohilev; apostolic administrator of Pinsk.

**Szoka, Edmund C.:** b. Sept. 14, 1927, Grand Rapids, Mich.; educ. Sacred Heart Seminary (Detroit, Mich.), St. John's Provincial Seminary (Plymouth, Mich.), Lateran Univ. (Rome); ord. priest (Marquette diocese), June 5, 1954; ord. first bishop of Gaylord, Mich., July 20, 1971; archbishop of Detroit, 1981-90; cardinal June 28, 1988; titular church, Sts. Andrew and Gregory (al Monte Celio). President of Prefecture for Economic Affairs of the Holy See, 1990. Curial membership: Secretariat of State (second section); Causes of Saints, Bishops, Evangelization of Peoples, Clergy, Institutes of Consecrated Life and Societies of Apostolic Life (congregations).

**Taofinu'u, Pio, S.M.:** b. Dec. 9, 1923, Falealupo, W. Samoa; ord. priest Dec. 8, 1954; joined Society of Mary, 1955; ord. bishop of Apia (Samoa and Tokelau), May 29, 1968, the first Polynesian bishop; cardinal Mar. 5, 1973; titular church, St. Humphrey. Archbishop of Samoa-Apia and Tokelau, Sept. 10, 1982 (title of see changed to Samoa-Apia, June 26, 1992).

**Thiandoum, Hyacinthe:** b. Feb. 2, 1921, Popoguine, Senegal; ord. priest Apr. 18, 1949; studied at Gregorian University, Rome, 1951-53; returned to Senegal, 1953; ord. archbishop of Dakar, May 20, 1962; cardinal May 24, 1976; titular church, S. Maria (del Popolo). Archbishop of Dakar. Curial membership: Clergy, Institutes of Consecrated Life and Societies of Apostolic Life, Evangelization of Peoples (congregations); Social Communications (council).

**Todea,\* Alexandru:** b. June 5, 1912, Teleac, Romania; ord. priest in the Byzantine Romanian rite Mar. 25, 1939; ord. bishop secretly (titular see of Cesarololi), Nov. 19, 1950, by Archbishop Gerald P. O'Hara, Vatican representative to Romania; arrested, 1951, and sentenced to life imprisonment; granted amnesty in 1964; archbishop of Fagaras and Alba Julia, 1990-94; cardinal June 28, 1991; titular church, St. Athanasius. Archbishop emeritus of Fagaras and Alba Julia of the Romanians.

**Tomko, Jozef:** b. Mar. 11, 1924, Udavske, Slovakia; ord. priest Mar. 12, 1949; ord. titular archbishop of Doclea, Sept, 15, 1979; secretary-general of the Synod of Bishops, 1979-85; cardinal deacon May 25, 1985; transferred to order of cardinal priests Jan. 29, 1996; titular church, St. Sabina. Prefect of the Congregation for the Evangelization of Peoples, 1985; Grand Chancellor of Pontifical Urban University. Curial membership: Secretariat of State (second section); Doctrine of the Faith, Divine Worship and Sacraments, Bishops, Clergy, Institutes of Consecrated Life and Societies of Apostolic Life, Catholic Education (congregations); Christian Unity, Interreligious Dialogue, Culture, Interpretation of Legislative Texts (councils); Latin America, State of Vatican City (commissions).

**Tonino,\* Ersilio:** b. July 20, 1914, Centovera di San Giorgio Piacentino, Italy; ord. priest Apr. 18, 1937; vice-rector and later rector of the Piacenza seminary; taught Italian, Latin and Greek; editor of diocesan weekly; ord. bishop of Macerata-Tolentino, June 2, 1969; archbishop of Ravenna-Cervia, Nov. 22, 1975 (retired Oct. 27, 1990); cardinal Nov. 26, 1994; titular church, Most Holy Redeemer in Val Melaina. Archbishop emeritus of Ravenna-Cervia.

**Tumi, Christian Wiyghan:** b. Oct. 15, 1930, Kikaikelaki, Cameroon; ord. priest Apr. 17, 1966; ord. bishop of Yagoua, Jan. 6, 1980; coadjutor archbishop of Garoua, Nov. 19, 1982; archbishop of Garoua, 1984-91; cardinal June 28, 1988; titular church, Martyrs of Uganda (a Pggio Ameno). Archbishop of Douala, Aug. 31, 1991. Curial membership: Evangelization of Peoples, Catholic Education (congregations); Interreligious Dialogue, Culture (councils).

**Turcotte, Jean-Claude:** b. June 26, 1936, Montreal, Canada; ord. priest May 24, 1959; ord. titular bishop of Suas and auxiliary of Montreal, June 29, 1982; archbishop of Montreal, Mar. 17, 1990; cardinal Nov. 26, 1994; titular church, Our Lady of the Blessed Sacrament and the Holy Canadian Martyrs. Archbishop of Montreal. Curial membership: Causes of Saints (congregation); Social Communications (council).

**Tzadua, Paulos:** b. Aug. 25, 1921, Addifini, Ethiopia; ord. priest Mar. 12, 1944; ord. titular bishop of Abila di Palestina and auxiliary of Addis Ababa, May 20, 1973; archbishop of Addis Ababa, Feb. 24, 1977; cardinal May 25, 1985; titular church, Most Holy Name of Mary (a Via Latina). Archbishop of Addis Ababa. Curial membership: Oriental Churches (congregation); Interpretation of Legislative Texts (council).

**Ursi,\* Corrado:** b. July 26, 1908, Andria, Italy; ord. priest July 25, 1931; vice-rector and later rector of the Pontifical Regional Seminary of Molfetta, 1931-51; ord. bishop of Nardo, Sept. 30, 1951; archbishop of Acerenza, Nov. 30, 1961; archbishop of Naples, May 23, 1966 (resigned May 9, 1987); cardinal June 26, 1967; titular church, St. Callistus. Archbishop emeritus of Naples.

**Vachon,\* Louis-Albert:** b. Feb. 4, 1912, Saint-Frederic-de-Beauce, Que., Canada; ord. priest June 11, 1938; ord. titular bishop of Mesarfelta and auxiliary of Quebec, May 14, 1977; archbishop of Quebec, Mar. 20, 1981 (resigned Mar. 17, 1990); cardinal May 25, 1985; titular church, St. Paul of the Cross (a Corviale). Archbishop emeritus of Quebec.

**Vargas Alzamora, Augusto, S.J.:** b. Nov. 9, 1922, Lima, Peru; entered Society of Jesus Mar. 9, 1940; ord. priest July 15, 1955; ord. titular bishop of Cissi, Aug. 15, 1978; vicar apostolic of Jaen in Peru (or San Francisco Javier), 1978-85; archbishop of Lima, De. 30, 1989; made passionate appeals against violence of the *Sendero Luminoso*; cardinal Nov. 26, 1994; titular see, St. Robert Bellarmine. Archbishop of Lima. Curial membership:

Institutes of Consecrated Life and Societies of Apostolic Life (congregation); Latin America (commission).

**Vidal, Ricardo J.:** b. Feb. 6, 1931, Mogpoc, Philippines; ord. priest Mar. 17, 1956; ord. titular bishop of Claterna and coadjutor of Melalos, Nov. 30, 1971; archbishop of Lipa, 1973-81; coadjutor archbishop of Cebu, Apr. 13, 1981; archbishop of Cebu, Aug. 24, 1982; cardinal May 25, 1985; titular church, Sts. Peter and Paul (in Via Ostiensi). Archbishop of Cebu. Curial membership:

Evangelization of Peoples, Catholic Education (congregations); Health Care Workers (council).

**Vlk, Miloslav:** b. May 17, 1932, Lisnice, Czech Republic; during communist persecution when theological studies were impossible he studied archival science at Charles University and worked in various archives in Bohemia; ord. priest June 23, 1968, during "Prague Spring"; sent to isolated parishes in Bohemian Forest by State authorities in 1971; state authorization to exercise his priestly ministry was cancelled in 1978; from then until 1986 he worked as a window-washer in Prague, carrying out his priestly ministry secretly among small groups. In 1989, he was permitted to exercise his priestly ministry for a "trial" year; the situation changed with the "velvet revolution"; ord. bishop of Ceske Budejovice, May 31, 1990; archbishop of Prague, Mar. 27, 1991; cardinal Nov. 26, 1994; titular church, Holy Cross in Jerusalem. Archbishop of Prague, President of the Council of European Episcopal Conferences, 1993- . Curial membership:

Oriental Churches (congregation); Social Communications (council).

**Wamala, Emmanuel:** b. Dec. 15, 1926, Kamaggwa, Uganda; ord. priest Dec. 21, 1957; ord. bishop of Kiyinda-Mityana, Nov. 22, 1981; coadjutor archbishop of Kampala, June 21, 1988; archbishop of Kampala, Feb. 8, 1990; cardinal Nov. 26, 1994; titular church, St. Hugh. Archbishop of Kampala. Curial membership:

Evangelization of Peoples (congregation); "Cor Unum" (council).

**Wetter, Friedrich:** b. Feb. 20, 1928, Landau, Germany; ord. priest Oct. 10, 1953; ord. bishop of Speyer, June 29, 1968; archbishop of Munich and Freising, Oct. 28, 1982; cardinal May 25, 1985; titular church, St. Stephen (al Monte Celio). Archbishop of Munich and Freising. Curial membership:

Evangelization of Peoples, Catholic Education (congregations).

**Willebrands,\* Johannes:** b. Sept. 4, 1909, Bovenkarspel, The Netherlands; ord. priest May 26, 1934; ord. titular bishop of Mauriana, June 28, 1964;

secretary of Secretariat for Christian Unity, 1960-69; cardinal Apr. 28, 1969; titular church, St. Sebastian (alle Catacombe); archbishop of Utrecht, 1975-83; president of Council for Christian Unity, 1969-89. President emeritus of the Council for Promoting Christian Unity; Camerlengo of the College of Cardinals, 1988.

**Williams, Thomas Stafford:** b. Mar. 20, 1930, Wellington, New Zealand; ord. priest Dec. 20, 1959, in Rome; studied in Ireland after ordination, receiving degree in social sciences; served in various pastoral assignments on his return to New Zealand; missionary in Western Samoa to 1976; ord. archbishop of Wellington, New Zealand, Dec. 20, 1979; cardinal Feb. 2, 1983; titular church, Jesus the Divine Teacher (at Pineda Sacchetti). Archbishop of Wellington; Military Ordinary for New Zealand (1995). Curial membership:

Evangelization of Peoples (congregation).

**Winning, Thomas Joseph:** b. June 3, 1925, Wishaw, Scotland; ord. priest Dec. 18, 1948; spiritual director of the Pontifical Scots College in Rome, 1961-66; returned to Scotland, 1966; served as parish priest, episcopal vicar for marriage in Motherwell diocese and first president and officialis (1970-72) of the newly established Scottish National Tribunal, Glasgow; ord. titular bishop of Lugmad and auxiliary of Glasgow Nov. 30, 1971; archbishop of Glasgow, Apr. 23, 1974; cardinal Nov. 26, 1994; titular church, St. Andrew delle Fratte. Archbishop of Glasgow. Curial membership:

Christian Unity, Family (councils).

**Wu Cheng-Chung, John Baptist:** b. Mar. 26, 1925, Shui-Tsai, mainland Chia; ord. priest (for Hsinchu, Taiwan, diocese) July 6, 1952; ord. bishop of Hong Kong, July 25, 1975; cardinal June 28, 1988; titular church, Blessed Virgin Mary of Mount Carmel (a Mostacciano). Bishop of Hong Kong. Curial membership:

Evangelization of Peoples (congregation); Interreligious Dialogue, Culture, Social Communications (councils).

**Yago,\* Bernard:** b. July, 1916, Pass, Ivory Coast (now Côte d'Ivoire); ord. priest May 1, 1947; ord. archbishop of Abidjan, May 8, 1960, by Pope John XXIII in St. Peter's Basilica, becoming the first native member of the hierarchy of Côte d'Ivoire; cardinal Feb. 2, 1983; titular church, St. Chrysogonus. Archbishop emeritus of Abidjan (resigned Dec. 19, 1994).

**Zoungrana, Paul, M. Afr.:** b. Sept 3, 1917, Ouagadougou, Upper Volta (now Burkina Faso); ord. priest May 2, 1942; ord. archbishop of Ouagadougou at St. Peter's Basilica by John XXIII, May 8, 1960; cardinal Feb. 22, 1965; titular church, St. Camillus de Lellis. Archbishop emeritus of Ouagadougou (resigned June, 1995). Curial membership:

Institutes of Consecrated Life and Societies of Apostolic Life (congregation); Health Care Workers (council).

## CATEGORIES OF CARDINALS
*(As of Aug. 8, 1996.)*

Information below includes categories of cardinals and dates of consistories at which they were created. Seniority or precedence usually depends on order of elevation.

Four of these 154 cardinals were named by John XXIII (consistories of Dec. 15, 1958, Mar. 28, 1960, and Mar. 19, 1962); 32 by Paul VI (consistories of Feb. 22, 1965, June 26, 1967, Apr. 28, 1969, Mar. 5, 1973, May 24, 1976, and June 27, 1977); 118 by John Paul II (consistories of June 30, 1979, Feb. 2, 1983, May 25, 1985, June 28, 1988, June 28, 1991, Nov. 26, 1994).

## Order of Bishops

Titular Bishops of Suburbicarian Sees: Paolo Bertoli (Apr. 28, 1969); Bernardin Gantin, dean (June 27, 1977); Joseph Ratzinger (June 27, 1977) Agostino Casaroli, sub-dean (June 30, 1979); Angelo Sodano (June 28, 1991), Eduardo Pironio (May 24, 1976).

Eastern Rite Patriarch: Nasrallah Pierre Sfeir (Nov. 26, 1994).

## Order of Priests

**1958** (Dec. 15): Franz Koenig.
**1960** (Mar. 28): Laurean Rugambwa.
**1962** (Mar. 19): Juan Landazuri Ricketts, O.F.M., Raul Silva Henriquez, S.D.B.
**1965** (Feb. 22): Paul Zoungrana.
**1967** (June 26): Corrado Ursi.
**1969** (Apr. 28): Silvio Oddi, Paul Gouyon, John J. Carberry, Stephan Sou Hwan Kim, Eugenio de Araujo Sales, Johannes Willebrands.
**1973** (Mar. 5): Antonio Ribeiro, Pietro Palazzini, Luis Aponte Martinez, Raul Francisco Primatesta, Salvatore Pappalardo, Marcelo Gonzalez Martin, Ugo Poletti, Maurice Otunga, Paulo Evaristo Arns, Narciso Jubany Arnau, Pio Taofinu'u.
**1976** (May 24): Opilio Rossi, Giuseppe Maria Sensi, Juan Carlos Aramburu, Corrado Bafile, Hyacinthe Thiandoum, Jaime L. Sin, William W. Baum, Aloisio Lorscheider, George Basil Hume, O.S.B.
**1979** (June 30): Giuseppe Caprio, Marco Cé, Egano Righi-Lambertini, Ernesto Corripio Ahumada, Roger Etchegaray, Anastasio Alberto Ballestrero, O.C.D., Gerald Emmett Carter, Franziszek Macharski, Ignatius Gong (Kung) Pin-mei.
**1983** (Feb. 2): Bernard Yago, Aurelio Sabattani, Franjo Kuharic, Giuseppe Casoria, Jose Ali Lebrun Moratinos, Joseph L. Bernardin, Michael Michai Kitbunchu, Alexandre do Nascimento, Alfonso Lopez Trujillo, Godfried Danneels, Thomas Stafford Williams, Carlo Maria Martini, Jean-Marie Lustiger, Jozef Glemp, Joachim Meisner.
**1985** (May 25): Juan Francisco Fresno Larrain, Miguel Obando Bravo, Angel Suquia Goicoechea, Ricardo Vidal, Henryk Roman Gulbinowicz, Paulus Tzadua, Myroslav Ivan Lubachivsky, Louis-Albert Vachon, Friedrich Wetter, Silvano Piovanelli, Adrianus J. Simonis, Bernard F. Law, John J. O'Connor, Giacomo Biffi, Simon D. Lourdusamy, Francis A. Arinze, Antonio Innocenti, Paul Augustin Mayer, Jean Jerome Hamer, Jozef Tomko, Andrzej Maria Deskur, Paul Poupard, Rosalio Jose Castillo Lara, Edouard Gagnon, Alfons Stickler, S.D.B.
**1988** (June 28): Anthony Padiyara, Jose Freire Falcao, Michele Giordano, Alexandre Jose Maria dos Santos, O.F.M., Giovanni Canestri, Simon Ignatius

Pimenta, Edward Bede Clancy, Lucas Moreira Neves, O.P., James Aloysius Hickey, Edmund C. Szoka, Laszlo Paskai, O.F.M., Christian Wiyghan Tumi, Hans Hermann Groër, O.S.B., Vincentas Sladkevicius, Jean Margeot, John Baptist Wu Cheng-Chung.
**1991** (June 28): Alexandru Todea, Frédéric Etsou-Nzabi-Bamungwabi, Nicolas de Jesus Lopez Rodriguez, Antonio Quarracino, Roger Mahony, Anthony J. Bevilacqua, Giovanni Saldarini, Cahal Brendan Daly, Camillo Ruini, Jan Chryzostom Korec, Henri Schwery, Georg Sterzinsky.
**1994** (Nov. 26): Miloslav Vlk, Peter Seiichi Shirayanagi, Carlos Oviedo Cavada, Thomas Joseph Winning, Adolfo Antonio Suarez Rivera, Jaime Lucas Ortega y Alamino, Julius Riyadi Darmaatmadja, Pierre Eyt, Emmanuel Wamala, William Henry Keeler, Augusto Vargas Alzamora, Jean-Claude Turcotte, Ricardo Maria Carles Gordó, Adam Joseph Maida, Vinko Puljic, Armand Gaétan Razafindratandra, Paul Joseph Pham Dinh Tung, Juan Sandoval Iñiguez, Bernardino Echeverria Ruiz, Kazimierz Swiatek, Ersilio Tonino.

## Order of Deacons

**1988** (June 28): Eduardo Martinez Somalo, Achille Silvestrini, Angelo Felici, Antonio Maria Javierre Ortas, S.D.B.
**1991** (June 28): Pio Laghi, Edward I. Cassidy, Jose T. Sanchez, Virgilio Noè, Fiorenzo Angelini, Paolo Dezza, S.J.
**1994** (Nov. 26): Luigi Poggi, Vincenzo Fagiolo, Carlo Furno, Jan Pieter Schotte, Gilberto Agustoni, Mikel Koliqi, Alois Grillmeier.

## DISTRIBUTION OF CARDINALS
*As of Aug. 8, 1996, there were 154 cardinals from more than 50 countries or areas. Listed below are areas, countries, number and last names.*

### Europe — 81
Italy (35): Angelini, Bafile, Ballestrero, Bertoli, Biffi, Canestri, Caprio, Casaroli, Casoria, Cé, Dezza, Fagiolo, Felici, Forno, Giordano, Innocenti, Laghi, Martini, Noè, Oddi, Palazzini, Pappalardo, Piovanelli, Poggi, Poletti, Righi-Lambertini, Rossi, Ruini, Sabattani, Saldarini, Silvestrini, Sensi, Sodano, Tonino, Ursi.
Spain (6): Carles Gordó, Gonzalez Martin, Javierre Ortas, Jubany Arnau, Martinez Somalo, Suquia Goicoechea.
Germany (6): Grillmeier, Mayer, Meisner, Ratzinger, Sterzinsky, Wetter.
France (5): Etchegaray, Eyt, Gouyon, Lustiger, Poupard.
Poland (4): Deskur, Glemp, Gulbinowicz, Macharski.
Belgium (3): Danneels, Hamer, Schotte.
Austria (3): Groer, Koenig, Stickler.
Netherlands (2): Simonis, Willebrands.
Slovakia (2): Korec, Tomko.
Switzerland (2): Agustoni, Schwery.
One from each of the following countries: Albania, Koloqi; Belarus, Swiatek; Bosnia-Herzegovina, Puljic; Croatia, Kuharic; Czech Republic, Vlk; England, Hume; Hungary, Paskai; Ireland, Daly;

Lithuania, Sladkevicius; Portugal, Ribeiro; Romania, Todea; Scotland, Winning; Ukraine, Lubachivsky.

## Asia — 14

India (3): Lourdusamy, Padiyara, Pimenta.

Philippines (3): Sanchez, Sin, Vidal.

One from each of the following countries: China, Gong (Kung) Pin-mei (exiled); Hong Kong, Wu Cheng-Chung; Indonesia, Darmaatmadja; Japan, Shirayangi; Korea, Kim; Lebanon, Sfeir; Thailand, Kitbunchu; Vietnam, Pham Dinh Tung.

## Oceania — 4

Australia (2): Cassidy, Clancy. One each from: New Zealand, Williams; Pacific Islands (Samoa), Taofinu'u.

## Africa — 15

One from each of the following countries: Angola, do Nascimento; Benin, Gantin; Burkina Faso, Zoungrana; Cameroon, Tumi; Ethiopia, Tzadua; Ivory Coast, Yago; Kenya, Otunga; Madagascar, Razafindratandra; Mauritius, Margeot; Mozambique, Santos; Nigeria, Arinze; Senegal, Thiandoum; Tanzania, Rugambwa; Uganda, Wamala; Zaire, Etsou-Nzabi-Bamungwabi.

## North America — 19

United States (11): Baum, Bernardin, Bevilacqua, Carberry, Hickey, Keeler, Law, Mahony, Maida, O'Connor, Szoka.

Canada (4): Carter, Gagnon, Turcotte, Vachon.

Mexico (3): Corripio Ahumada, Sandoval Iñiguez, Suarez Rivera.

Puerto Rico (1): Aponte Martinez.

## Central and South America — 21

Brazil (5): Arns, Falcao, Lorscheider, Neves, Sales.

Argentina (4): Aramburu, Pironio, Primatesta, Quarrachino.

Chile (3): Fresno Larrain, Oviedo Cavada, Silva Henriquez.

Peru (2): Landazuri Ricketts, Vargas Alzamora.

Venezuela (2): Castillo Lara, Lebrun Moratinos.

One from each of the following countries: Colombia, Lopez Trujillo; Cuba, Ortega y Alamino; Dominican Republic, Lopez Rodriquez; Ecuador, Echeverria Ruiz; Nicaragua, Obando Bravo.

## INELIGIBLE TO VOTE

As of Aug. 8, 1996, 42 of the 154 cardinals were ineligible to take part in a papal election in line with the apostolic letter *Ingravescentem Aetatem* effective Jan. 1, 1971, which limited the functions of cardinals after completion of their 80th year.

Cardinals affected were: Angelini, Aramburu, Bafile, Ballestrero, Bertoli, Caprio, Carberry, Carter, Casaroli, Casoria, Dezza, Echeverria Ruiz, Fresno Larrain, Gong Pin-Mei, Gouyon, Grillmeier, Hamer, Innocenti, Jubany Arnau, Koenig, Koloqi, Landazuri Ricketts, Lubachivsky, Margeot, Mayer, Oddi, Palazzini, Poletti, Righi-Lambertini, Rossi, Rugambwa, Sabattani, Sensi, Silva Henriquez, S.D.B., Stickler, S.D.B., Swiatek, Todea, Tonino, Ursi, Vachon, Yago, Willebrands.

Cardinal Angel Suguia Goicoichea will become ineligible to vote after Oct. 2, 1996.

Cardinals completing their 80th year in 1997: Paul Zoungrana (Sept 3); Cahal Brendan Daly (Oct. 1); Luigi Poggi (Nov. 25).

## CARDINALS OF U.S.

As of Aug. 8, 1996, U.S. cardinals according to years of elevation (for biographies, see Index under individual name).

**1969:** John J. Carberry (archbishop emeritus of St. Louis); **1976:** William W. Baum (major penitentiary); **1983:** Joseph L. Bernardin (archbishop of Chicago); **1985:** Bernard F. Law (archbishop of Boston), John J. O'Connor (archbishop of New York); **1988:** James A. Hickey (archbishop of Washington), Edmund C. Szoka (president of Prefecture for Economic Affairs of the Holy See); **1991:** Roger M. Mahony (archbishop of Los Angeles), Anthony J. Bevilacqua (archbishop of Philadelphia); **1994:** William H. Keeler (archbishop of Baltimore), Adam J. Maida (archbishop of Detroit).

[Myroslav Lubachivsky, major archbishop of Lviv of the Ukrainians (Ukraine), was made a cardinal in 1985. He is a U.S. citizen and was metropolitan of the Philadelphia Ukrainian Rite Archeparchy, 1979-81.]

**U.S. cardinals of the past,** according to year of elevation. (For biographical data, see Index: Bishops, U.S., of the Past.)

1875: John McCloskey; 1886: James Gibbons; 1911: John Farley, William O'Connell; 1921: Dennis Dougherty; 1924: Patrick Hayes, George Mundelein; 1946: John Glennon, Edward Mooney, Francis Spellman, Samuel Stritch; 1953: James F. McIntyre; 1958: John O'Hara, C.S.C., Richard Cushing; 1959: Albert Meyer, Aloysius Muench; 1961: Joseph Ritter; 1965: Lawrence J. Shehan; 1967: Francis Brennan, John P. Cody, Patrick A. O'Boyle, John J. Krol; 1969: John J. Wright, Terence J. Cooke, John F. Dearden; 1973: Humbertus S. Medeiros, Timothy Manning.

Prelates who became cardinals after returning to their native countries: John Lefebvre de Chevrus, first bishop of Boston (1808-23) and apostolic administrator of New York (1810-15), elevated to cardinalate, 1836, in France. Ignatius Persico, O.F.M. Cap., bishop of Savannah (1870-72), elevated to cardinalate, 1893, in Italy. Diomede Falconio, O.F.M., ord. priest Buffalo, N.Y.; missionary in U.S.; apostolic delegate to the U.S. (1902-11), elevated to cardinalate, 1911, in Italy.

---

## ORDINATION REJECTED

The ordination of women in Germany's Old Catholic Church was opposed by its counterpart in the United States and Canada. In a May 28, 1996, letter to churches with which it was engaged in dialogue, Bishop Anthony M. Rysz of the Polish National Catholic Church of the U.S. and Canada, said the German church "had broken full communion with our church."

# REPRESENTATIVES OF THE HOLY SEE

Representatives of the Holy See and their functions were the subject of a document entitled *Sollicitudo Omnium Ecclesiarum* which Pope Paul VI issued on his own initiative under the date of June 24, 1969.

## Delegates and Nuncios

Papal representatives "receive from the Roman Pontiff the charge of representing him in a fixed way in the various nations or regions of the world.

"When their legation is only to local churches, they are known as apostolic delegates. When to this legation, of a religious and ecclesial nature, there is added diplomatic legation to states and governments, they receive the title of nuncio, pro-nuncio, and internuncio."

An apostolic nuncio has the diplomatic rank of ambassador extraordinary and plenipotentiary. Traditionally, because the diplomatic service of the Holy See has the longest uninterrupted history in the world, a nuncio has precedence among diplomats in the country to which he is accredited and serves as dean of the diplomatic corps on state occasions. Since 1965 pro-nuncios, also of ambassadorial rank, have been assigned to countries in which this prerogative is not recognized. In recent years, the Vatican started to phase out the title of pro-nuncio. The title of nuncio (with an asterisk denoting he is not dean of the diplomatic corps) has been given to the majority of appointments of ambassadorial rank. See also: Other Representatives.

## Service and Liaison

Representatives, while carrying out their general and special duties, are bound to respect the autonomy of local churches and bishops. Their service and liaison responsibilities include the following:

• Nomination of Bishops: To play a key role in compiling, with the advice of ecclesiastics and lay persons, and submitting lists of names of likely candidates to the Holy See with their own recommendations.

• Bishops: To aid and counsel local bishops without interfering in the affairs of their jurisdictions.

• Episcopal Conferences: To maintain close relations with them and to assist them in every possible way. (Papal representatives do not belong to these conferences.)

• Religious Communities of Pontifical Rank: To advise and assist major superiors for the purpose of promoting and consolidating conferences of men and women religious and to coordinate their apostolic activities.

• Church-State Relations: The thrust in this area is toward the development of sound relations with civil governments and collaboration in work for peace and the total good of the whole human family.

The mission of a papal representative begins with appointment and assignment by the pope and continues until termination of his mandate. He acts "under the guidance and according to the instructions of the cardinal secretary of state to whom he is directly responsible for the execution of the mandate entrusted to him by the Supreme Pontiff." Normally representatives are required to retire at the age of 75.

## NUNCIOS AND DELEGATES

(Sources: *Annuario Pontificio, L'Osservatore Romano, Acta Apostolicae Sedis*, Catholic News Service.)

Data, as of July 31, 1996: country, rank of legation (corresponding to rank of legate unless otherwise noted), name of legate (archbishop unless otherwise noted) as available. An asterisk indicates a nuncio who is not presently dean of the diplomatic corps.

Delegate for Papal Representatives: Archbishop Francesco Monterisi, titular Archbishop of Alba Marittima. The post was established in 1973 to coordinate papal diplomatic efforts throughout the world. The office entails responsibility for "following more closely through timely visits the activities of papal representatives . . . and encouraging their rapport with the central offices" of the Secretariat of State.

**Albania:** Tirana, Nunciature; Ivan Dias*.

**Algeria:** Algiers, Nunciature; Antonio Sozzo*. (He is also Nuncio* to Tunisia.)

**Andorra:** Nunciature; Lajos Kada (Also nuncio to Spain).

**Angola:** Luanda, Apostolic Delegation; Aldo Cavalli (also Nuncio* to Sao Tome and Principe).

**Antigua and Barbuda:** Nunciature; Eugenio Sbarbaro, Pro-Nuncio (resides in Port of Spain, Trinidad).

**Antilles:** Apostolic Delegation; Eugenio Sbarbaro (resides in Port of Spain, Trinidad).

**Arabian Peninsula:** Apostolic Delegation; Pablo Puente (also nuncio in Kuwait and Lebanon; resides in Lebanon).

**Argentina:** Buenos Aires, Nunciature; Ubaldo Calabresi.

**Armenia:** Nunciature; Jean-Paul Gobel* (resides in Tbilisi, Georgia). (Diplomatic relations established May 23, 1992.)

**Australia:** Canberra, Nunciature; Franco Brambilla, Pro-Nuncio.

**Austria:** Vienna, Nunciature; Donato Squicciarini.

**Azerbaijan:** Nunciature; Jean-Paul Gobel* (resides in Tbilisi, Georgia). (Diplomatic relations established May 23, 1992.)

**Bahamas:** Nunciature; Eugenio Sbarbaro, Pro-Nuncio (resides in Port of Spain, Trinidad).

**Bangladesh:** Dhaka, Nunciature; vacant.

**Barbados:** Nunciature; Eugenio Sbarbaro, Pro-Nuncio (resides in Port of Spain, Trinidad).

**Belarus:** Nunciature; Dominik Hrusovsky*.

**Belgium:** Brussels, Nunciature; Giovanni Moretti (also Nuncio to Luxembourg and European Community).

**Belize:** Nunciature; Eugenio Sbarbaro, Pro-Nuncio (resides in Port of Spain, Trinidad).

**Benin** (formerly Dahomey): Nunciature; Andre Dupuy* (resides in Accra, Ghana).

**Bolivia:** La Paz, Nunciature; Pino Passigato.

**Bosnia and Herzegovina:** Nunciature; Francesco Monterisi*. (He is also delegate for Papal Representatives; resides in Vatican City.)

**Botswana:** See South Africa.

**Brazil:** Brasilia, Nunciature; Alfio Rapisarda.

**Brunei:** See Malaysia and Brunei.

**Bulgaria:** Sofia, Nunciature (reestablished, 1990); Blasco Francisco Collaco*.

**Burkina Faso:** Ouagadougou, Nunciature; Luigi Ventura*(resides in Abidjan, Côte d'Ivoire).

**Burma:** See Myanmar.

**Burundi:** Bujumbura, Nunciature; Emil Paul Tscherrig*.

**Cambodia:** Nunciature; Luigi Bressan* (resides in Bangkok, Thailand). Diplomatic relations established March, 1994.

**Cameroon:** Yaounde, Nunciature; Felix del Blanco Prieto* (also Nuncio to Equatorial Guinea).

**Canada:** Ottawa, Nunciature; Carlo Curis*.

**Cape Verde, Republic of:** Nunciature; Antonio Maria Veglio* (resides in Dakar, Senegal).

**Central African Republic:** Bangui, Nunciature; Diego Causero* (also Nuncio* to Chad).

**Chad:** Nunciature; Diego Causero* (resides in Bangui, Central African Republic).

**Chile:** Santiago, Nunciature; Piero Biggio.

**China:** Taipei (Taiwan), Nunciature; vacant.

**Colombia:** Bogota, Nunciature; Paolo Romeo.

**Comoros:** See Madagascar.

**Congo:** Brazzaville, Nunciature; vacant (also pro-nuncio to Gabon).

**Costa Rica:** San Jose, Nunciature; Giacinto Berloco.

**Côte d'Ivoire** (Ivory Coast): Abidjan, Nunciature; Luigi Ventura (also nuncio* to Niger and Burkina Faso).

**Croatia:** Zagreb, Nunciature; Giulio Einaudi.

**Cuba:** Havana, Nunciature; Benjamin Stella*.

**Cyprus:** Nicosia, Nunciature; Andrea Cordero Lanza di Montezemolo, Pro-Nuncio.

**Czech Republic:** Prague, Nunciature; Giovanni Coppa.

**Denmark:** Copenhagen, Nunciature; Giovanni Ceirano* (also Nuncio* to Finland, Iceland, Norway and Sweden).

**Djibouti:** Apostolic Delegation; Silvano Tomasi (resides in Addis Ababa, Ethiopia).

**Dominica:** Nunciature; Eugenio Sbarbaro, Pro-Nuncio (resides in Port-of-Spain, Trinidad).

**Dominican Republic:** Santo Domingo, Nunciature; Francois Bacque (also serves as Apostolic Delegate to Puerto Rico).

**Ecuador:** Quito, Nunciature; Francesco Canalini.

**Egypt:** Cairo, Nunciature; Paolo Giglio*.

**El Salvador:** San Salvador, Nunciature; Manuel Monteiro de Castro.

**Equatorial Guinea:** Santa Isabel, Nunciature; Felix del Blanco Prieto* (resides in Yaounde, Cameroon).

**Eritrea:** Nunciature: Silvano Tomasi* (resides in Ethiopia). Diplomatic relations established July 15, 1995.

**Estonia:** Nunciature; Justo Mullor Garcia* (resides in Vilna, Lithuania).

**Ethiopia:** Addis Ababa, Nunciature; Silvano Tomasi* (also nuncio* to Eritrea and apostolic delegate to Djibouti).

**Fiji:** Nunciature; Thomas A. White, Pro-Nuncio.

**Finland:** Helsinki, Nunciature; Giovanni Ceirano* (resides in Denmark).

**France:** Paris, Nunciature; Lorenzo Antonetti.

**Gabon:** Libreville, Nunciature; vacant (resides in Congo).

**Gambia:** Nunciature; Antonio Lucibello* (resides in Freetown, Sierra Leone).

**Georgia:** Tbilisi, Nunciature; Jean-Paul Gobel* (also nuncio* to Armenia and Azerbaijan). (Diplomatic relations established May 23, 1992.)

**Germany:** Bonn, Nunciature; Giovanni Lajolo.

**Ghana:** Accra, Nunciature; Andre Dupuy* (also Nuncio to Benin and Togo).

**Great Britain:** London, Nunciature; Luigi Barbarito* (also papal representative to Gibraltar).

**Greece:** Athens, Nunciature; Paul Fouad Tabet*.

**Grenada:** Nunciature; Eugenio Sbarbaro, Pro-Nuncio (resides in Port of Spain, Trinidad).

**Guatemala:** Guatemala City, Nunciature; Giovanni Battista Morandini.

**Guinea:** Conakry, Nunciature; Antonio Lucibello*(resides in Freetown, Sierra Leone).

**Guinea-Bissau:** Nunciature; Antonio Maria Veglio* (resides at Dakar, Senegal).

**Haiti:** Port-au-Prince, Nunciature.

**Honduras:** Tegucigalpa, Nunciature; Luigi Conti.

**Hungary:** Budapest, Nunciature; Angelo Acerbi (also nuncio* to Moldava).

**Iceland:** Nunciature; Giovanni Ceirano* (resides in Denmark).

**India:** New Delhi, Nunciature; Giorgio Zur, Pro-Nuncio (also Pro-Nuncio to Nepal).

**Indonesia:** Jakarta, Nunciature; Pietro Sambi, Pro-Nuncio.

**Iran:** Teheran, Nunciature; Romeo Panciroli M.C.C.I.*

**Iraq:** Baghdad, Nunciature; Giuseppe Lazzarotto* (also nuncio to Jordan).

**Ireland:** Dublin, Nunciature; Luciano Storero.

**Israel:** Nunciature; Andrea Cordero Lanza de Montezemolo*. Diplomatic relations established June 15, 1994.

**Italy:** Rome, Nunciature; Francesco Colasuonno.

**Ivory Coast:** See Côte d'Ivoire.

**Jamaica:** Nunciature; Eugenio Sbarbaro, Pro-Nuncio (resides in Port of Spain, Trinidad).

**Japan:** Tokyo, Nunciature; William A. Carew, Pro-Nuncio.

**Jerusalem and Palestine:** Apostolic Delegation; Andrea Cordero Lanza di Montezemolo (also Nuncio to Israel).

**Jordan:** Nunciature; Giuseppe Lazzarotto* (also nuncio to Iraq). Diplomatic relations established 1994.

**Kazakhstan:** Almaty, Nunciature; Marian Oles * (also nuncio* to Kyrgyzstan and Uzbekistan).

**Kenya:** Nairobi, Nunciature; Giovanni Tonucci*.

**Kiribati:** Nunciature; Thomas A. White*. Diplomatic relations established 1995.

**Korea:** Seoul, Nunciature; Giovanni Bulaitis, Pro-Nuncio (also nuncio* to Mongolia).

**Kuwait:** Al Kuwait, Nunciature; Pablo Puente* (resides in Lebanon).

**Kyrgyzstan:** Nunciature; Marian Oles* (resides in Kazakhstan).

**Laos:** Apostolic Delegation; Luigi Bressan, (resides in Bangkok, Thailand).

**Latvia:** Nunciature; Justo Mullor Garcia* (resides in Vilna, Lithuania).

**Lebanon:** Beirut, Nunciature; Pablo Puente (also nuncio* to Kuwait and apostolic delegate to Arabian Peninsula).

**Lesotho:** Maseru, Nunciature; Ambrose De Paoli, Pro-Nuncio (resides in Pretoria, S. Africa).

**Liberia:** Monrovia, Nunciature; Antonio Lucibello* (resides in Freetown, Sierra Leone).

**Libya:** Apostolic Delegation; Jose Sebastian Laboa (resides in Malta).

**Liechtenstein:** Nunciature; Karl-Josef Rauber (resides in Bern, Switzerland).

**Lithuania:** Vilnius, Nunciature; Justo Mullor Garcia (also nuncio* to Estonia and Latvia.).

**Luxembourg:** Nunciature; Giovanni Moretti (resides in Brussels, Belgium).

**Macedonia:** Nunciature; Edmond Farhat* (also nuncio to Slovenia). Diplomatic relations established Dec. 21, 1994.

**Madagascar:** Antananarivo, Nunciature; Adriano Bernardini* (also Nuncio* to Seychelles, Pro-Nuncio to Mauritius and Apostolic Delegate to Comoros and Reunion).

**Malawi:** Lilongwe, Nunciature; Giuseppe Leanza, Pro-Nuncio (resides in Zambia).

**Malaysia and Brunei:** Apostolic Delegation; Luigi Bressan (resides in Bangkok, Thailand).

**Mali:** Nunciature; Antonio Maria Veglio* (resides in Dakar, Senegal).

**Malta:** La Valletta, Nunciature; Jose Sebastian Laboa (also apostolic delgate to Libya).

**Marshall Islands:** Nunciature; Patrick Coveney* (resides in New Zealand).

**Mauritania:** Nouakchott, Apostolic Delegation; Antonio Maria Veglio (resides in Dakar, Senegal).

**Mauritius:** Port Louis, Nunciature; Adriano Bernardini* (resides in Antananarivo, Madagascar).

**Mexico:** Mexico City, Nunciature; Girolamo Prigione* (diplomatic relations established 1992).

**Micronesia, Federated States of:** Nunciature; Thomas A. White*. Diplomatic relations established in 1994.

**Moldava:** Nunciature; Angelo Acerbi* (resides in Budapest, Hungary). (Diplomatic relations established May 23, 1992.)

**Mongolia:** Nunciature; Giovanni Bulaitis* (resides in Seoul, Korea).

**Morocco:** Rabat, Nunciature; Domenico De Luca*.

**Mozambique:** Maputo, nunciature; Peter Stephan Zurbriggen.* Diplomatic relations established 1995.

**Myanmar** (formerly Burma): Apostolic Delegation; Luigi Bressan (resides in Bangkok, Thailand).

**Namibia:** Nunciature; Ambrose De Paoli*. Diplomatic relations established September, 1995.

**Nauru:** Nunciature; Thomas A. White*.

**Nepal:** Nunciature; Giorgio Zur, Pro-Nuncio (resides in New Delhi, India).

**Netherlands:** The Hague, Nunciature; Henri Lemaitre*.

**New Zealand:** Wellington, Nunciature; Patrick Coveney*. (He is also Nuncio* to Marshall Islands, and Western Samoa; Apostolic Delegate to Pacific Islands).

**Nicaragua:** Managua, Nunciature; Luigi Travaglino.

**Niger:** Niamey, Nunciature; Luigi Ventura* (resides in Abidjan, Côte d'Ivoire).

**Nigeria:** Lagos, Nunciature; Carlo M. Vigano, Pro-Nuncio.

**Norway:** Nunciature; Giovanni Ceirano* (resides in Denmark).

**Pacific Islands:** Apostolic Delegation; Patrick Coveney (resides in New Zealand).

**Pakistan:** Islamabad, Nunciature; Renzo Fratini*.

**Panama:** Panama, Nunciature; Bruno Musaro.

**Papua New Guinea:** Port Moresby; Nunciature; Ramiro Moliner Ingles* (also Nuncio* to Solomon Islands).

**Paraguay:** Asuncion, Nunciature; Lorenzo Baldisseri.

**Peru:** Lima, Nunciature; Fortunato Baldelli.

**Philippines:** Manila, Nunciature; Gian Vincenzo Moreni.

**Poland:** Warsaw; Nunciature; Jozef Kowalczyk.

**Portugal:** Lisbon, Nunciature; Edoardo Rovida.

**Puerto Rico:** See Dominican Republic.

**Reunion:** See Madagascar.

**Romania:** Bucharest, Nunciature. Janusz Bolenek, S.V.D.*

**Rwanda:** Kigali, Nunciature. Julius Janusz.

**Saint Lucia:** Nunciature; Eugenio Sbarbaro, Pro-Nuncio (resides in Port of Spain, Trinidad).

**Saint Vincent and the Grenadines:** Nunciature; Eugenio Sbarbaro, Pro-Nuncio (resides in Port of Spain, Trinidad).

**San Marino:** Nunciature; Francesco Colasuonno.

**Sao Tome and Principe:** Nunciature; Aldo Cavalli* (also apostolic delegate to Angola, where he resides).

**Senegal:** Dakar, Nunciature; Antonio Maria Veglio* (also Pro-Nuncio to Cape Verde, Guinea-Bissau and Mali; Apostolic Delegate to Mauritania.)

**Seychelles Islands:** Nunciature; Adriano Bernardini* (resides in Antananrivo, Madagascar).

**Sierra Leone:** Freetown, Nunciature (1996); Antonio Lucibello* (also Nuncio* to Gambia, Guinea and Liberia).

**Singapore:** Nunciature; Luigi Bressan* (He is also nuncio* to Cambodia and Thailand and apostolic delegate to Laos, Malaysia and Brunei, and Myanmar.)

**Slovakia:** Nunciature; Luigi Dossena.

**Slovenia:** Ljubljana, Nunciature; Edmond Farhat (also nuncio to Macedonia).

**Solomon Islands:** Nunciature; Ramiro Moliner Ingles* (resides in Port Moresby, Papua New Guinea).

**Somalia:** Apostolic Delegation (est. 1992); Erwin Josef Ender (resides in Sudan).

**South Africa:** Pretoria, Nunciature; Ambrose De Paoli*. (He is also nuncio* to Namibia and apostolic delegate to Botswana.)

**Spain:** Madrid, Nunciature; Lajos Kada.

**Sri Lanka:** Colombo, Nunciature; Osvaldo Padilla*

**Sudan:** Khartoum, Nunciature; Erwin Josef Ender, Pro-Nuncio (also Apostolic Delegate to Somalia).

**Suriname:** Nunciature; Eugenio Sbarbaro * (resides in Trinidad).

**Swaziland:** Nunciature; Ambrose De Paoli* (resides in Pretoria, South Africa).

**Sweden:** Nunciature; Giovanni Ceirano* (resides in Denmark).

**Switzerland:** Bern, Nunciature; Karl-Josef Rauber (also nuncio to Liechtenstein).

**Syria:** (Syrian Arab Republic): Damascus, Nunciature; Pier Giacomo De Nicola*.

**Tajikistan:** Diplomatic relations established June 15, 1996.

**Tanzania:** Dar-es-Salaam, Nunciature; Francisco-Javier Lozano*.

**Thailand:** Bangkok, Nunciature; Luigi Bressan* (also Nuncio* to Cambodia and Singapore and Apostolic Delegate to Laos, Malaysia, Brunei, Myanmar).

**Togo:** Lome, Nunciature; Andre Dupuy* (resides in Accra, Ghana).

**Tonga:** Nunciature; Patrick Coveney* (resides in New Zealand).

**Trinidad and Tobago:** Port of Spain, Trinidad, Nunciature; Eugenio Sbarbaro, Pro-Nuncio (also Pro-Nuncio to Antigua and Barbuda, Bahamas, Barbados, Belize, Dominica, Grenada, Jamaica, Saint Lucia, Saint Vincent and the Grenadines, Suriname and Apostolic Delegate to Antilles).

**Tunisia:** Tunis, Nunciature; Antonio Sozzo* (resides in Algiers, Algeria).

**Turkey:** Ankara, Nunciature; Pierre Luigi Celata*.

**Turkmenistan:** Diplomatic relations established July 10, 1996.

**Ukraine:** Kiev, Nunciature; Antonio Franco*.

**Uganda:** Kampala, Nunciature; Luiz Robles Diaz, Pro-Nuncio.

**United States of America:** Washington, D.C., Nunciature; Agostino Cacciavillan, Pro-Nuncio.

**Uruguay:** Montevideo, Nunciature; Francesco De Nittis.

**Uzbekistan:** Nunciature. Marian Oles* (resides in Kazakhstan).

**Vanuatu:** Nunciature; Thomas A. White*.

**Venezuela:** Caracas, Nunciature; Oriano Quilici.

**Vietnam:** Apostolic Delegation.

**Western Samoa:** Nunciature; Patrick Coveney* (resides in New Zealand).

**Yugoslavia:** Belgrade, Nunciature; Santos Abril y Castello.

**Zaire:** Kinshasa-Gombe, Nunciature; Faustino Sainz Muñoz*.

**Zambia:** Lusaka, Nunciature; Giuseppe Leanza, Pro-Nuncio (also Pro-Nuncio to Malawi).

**Zimbabwe:** Harare, Nunciature; Peter Paul Prabhu*.

**Russia (Federation of):** Moscow; John Bukovsky, S.V.D., Apostolic Nuncio; appointed Representative of the Holy See to Russian Federation, Dec, 20, 1994.

**European Community:** Brussels, Belgium, Nunciature; Giovanni Moretti, Nuncio.

### Pro-Nuncio to U.S.

The representative of the Pope to the Church in the United States is Archbishop Agostino Cacciavillan. Archbishop Cacciavillan was born Aug. 14, 1926, in Novale, Italy. Ordained to the priesthood June 26, 1949, he entered the Vatican diplomatic service in 1959. He was ordained archbishop (titular see of Amiternum) Feb. 28, 1976, and served as pro-nuncio to Kenya and apostolic delegate to the Seychelles (1976-81) and pro-nuncio to India and Nepal (1981-90). He was appointed pro-nuncio to the United States and permanent observer to the Organization of American States, June 13, 1990. He succeeded Archbishop Pio Laghi who served as first pro-nuncio from 1984-90 (see Index, U.S.-Vatican Relations).

The U.S. Apostolic Nunciature is located at 3339 Massachusetts Ave. N.W., Washington, D.C. 20008.

From 1893 to 1984, papal representatives to the Church in the U.S. were apostolic delegates (all archbishops): Francesco Satolli (1893-96), Sebastiano Martinelli, O.S.A. (1896-1902), Diomede Falconio, O.F.M. (1902-11), Giovanni Bonzano (1911-22), Pietro Fumasoni-Biondi (1922-33), Amleto Cicognani (1933-58), Egidio Vagnozzi (1958-67), Luigi Raimondi (1967-73), Jean Jadot (1973-80), Pio Laghi (apostolic delegate, 1980-84; first pro-nuncio, 1984-90).

## OTHER REPRESENTATIVES

(Sources: *Annuario Pontificio;* Catholic News Service.)

The Holy See has representatives to or is a regular member of a number of quasi-governmental and international organizations. Most Rev. Ernesto Gallina was appointed delegate to International Governmental Organizations Jan. 12, 1991.

**Governmental Organizations:** United Nations (Abp. Renato Raffaele Martino, permanent observer); UN Office in Geneva and Specialized Institutes (Abp. Giuseppe Bertello, permanent observer); International Atomic Energy Agency (Msgr. Mario Zenari, permanent representative); UN Office at Vienna and UN Organization for Industrial Development (Msgr. Mario Zenari, permanent observer); UN Food and Agriculture Organization (Abp. Alois Wagner, permanent observer); UN Educational, Scientific and Cultural Organization (Msgr. Lorenzo Frana, permanent observer);

Council of Europe (Msgr. Michael Courtney, special representative with function of permanent observer); Council for Cultural Cooperation of the Council of Europe (Msgr. Celestino Migliore, delegate); Organization of American States (Abp. Agostino Cacciavillan, permanent observer, with personal title of Apostolic Nuncio); Organization for Security and Cooperation in Europe (Mario Zenari, permanent representative); International Institute for the Unification of Private Law (Prof. Tommaso Mauro, delegate); International Committee of Military Medicine and Pharmacy (Adolphe Vander Perre, delegate), World Organization of Tourism (Msgr. Piero Monni, permanent observer).

Universal Postal Union; International Telecommunications Union; International Council on Grain; World Organization of Intellectual Property; International Organization of Telecommunication via Satellite (Intelsat); European Conference of Postal and Telecommunication Administration (CEPT); European Organization of Telecommunication via Satellite (EUTELSAT). International Institute for the Unification of Private Law (UNIDROIT)

**Non-Governmental Organizations:** International Committee of Historical Sciences (Msgr. Victor Saxer); International Committee of Paleography; International Committee of the History of Art; International Committee of Anthropological and Ethnological Sciences;

International Committee for the Neutrality of Medicine; International Center of Study for the Preservation and Restoration of Cultural Goods; International Council of Monuments and Sites (Msgr. Lorenzo

Frana, delegate); International Alliance on Tourism; World Association of Jurists (Abp. Agostino Cacciavillan, delegate); International Commission of the Civil State; International Astronomical Union; International Institute of Administrative Sciences; International Technical Committee for Prevention and Extinction of Fires; World Medical Association; International Archives Council.

## DIPLOMATS TO THE HOLY SEE

(Sources: *Annuario Pontificio, L'Osservatore Romano*).

Listed below are countries maintaining diplomatic relations with the Holy See, dates of establishment (in some cases) and names of Ambassadors (as of July 31, 1996). Leaders (.....) indicate the post was vacant.

The dean of the diplomatic corps at the Vatican is Ambassador Joseph Amichia, representative of Côte d'Ivoire (Ivory Coast) from 1971. He became dean in 1983.

**Albania** (1991): Willy Gjon Kamsi.
**Algeria** (1972): .....
**Andorra:** Diplomatic relations established in June, 1995.
**Antigua and Barbuda** (1986): .....
**Argentina:** Francisco Eduardo Trusso.
**Armenia** (1992): Armen Sarkissian.
**Australia** (1973): Michael C. Tate.
**Austria:** Christoph Cornaro.
**Azerbaijan** (1992): .....
**Bahamas** (1979): .....
**Bangladesh** (1972): Anwar Hashim.
**Barbados** (1979): .....
**Belarus** (1992): .....
**Belgium** (1835): Juan Cassiers.
**Belize** (1983): Mrs. Ursula Helen Barrow.
**Benin** (formerly Dahomey) (1971): Edmond Cakpo-Tozo.
**Bolivia:** Armando Loaiza Mariaca.
**Bosnia and Herzegovina** (1992): .....
**Brazil:** Francisco Thompson-Flores.
**Bulgaria** (1990): Kiril Kirilov Maritchkov.
**Burkina Faso** (1973): Frederic Assomption Korsaga.
**Burundi** (1963): Albert Mbonerane.
**Cambodia** (1994): .....
**Cameroon** (1966): Jean Melaga.
**Canada** (1969): Leonard H. Legault.
**Cape Verde** (1976): Alfredo Goncalves Teixeira.
**Central African Republic** (1975): .....
**Chad** (1988): .....
**Chile:** Javier Luis Egaña Baraona.
**China, Republic of** (Taiwan) (1966): Edward Wu Tsu-Yu.
**Colombia:** Julio César Turbay Ayala.
**Congo** (1977): Alphonse Niangoula.
**Costa Rica:** .....
**Côte d'Ivoire** (Ivory Coast) (1971): Joseph Amichia.
**Croatia** (1992): Ive Livljanic.
**Cuba:** Hermes Herrera Hernandez.
**Cyprus** (1973): Andros A. Nicolaides.
**Czech Republic** (1929-50, reestablished, 1990, with Czech and Slovak Federative Republic; reaffirmed, 1993): Frantisek X. Halas.
**Denmark** (1982): Jan Marcussen.

**Dominica** (1981): .....
**Dominican Republic:** .....
**Ecuador:** Marcelo Santos Vera.
**Egypt** (1966): Ismail Azmy Elkattan.
**El Salvador:** Roberto Jose Siman Jacir.
**Equatorial Guinea** (1981): .....
**Eritrea:** Established diplomatic relations in July, 1995.
**Estonia** (1991): Tiit Matsulevits.
**Ethiopia** (1969): .....
**Fiji** (1978): Epeli Nailaitikau.
**Finland** (1966): Henry Söderholm.
**France:** Jean-Louis Lucet.
**Gabon** (1967): Eugene Milingout Mangaka.
**Gambia, The** (1978): .....
**Georgia** (1992): .....
**Germany:** Hans Joachim Hallier.
**Ghana** (1976): .....
**Great Britain** (1982): Miss Maureen Elisabeth MacGlashan.
**Greece** (1980): Nikolaos Kalantzianos.
**Grenada** (1979): .....
**Guatemala:** Maurice Rodriguez Wever.
**Guinea** (1986): Lamine Bolivogui.
**Guinea-Bissau** (1986): .....
**Haiti:** .....
**Honduras:** Alejandro Emilio Valladares Lanza.
**Hungary** (1990): Jozef Bratinka.
**Iceland** (1976): .....
**India:** Kizhakke Pisharath Balakrishnan.
**Indonesia** (1965): Radin Suharjono.
**Iran** (1966): Mohammad Masjed Jame'i.
**Iraq** (1966): Wissam Chawkat Al-Zahawi.
**Ireland:** Gearoid P. O'Broin.
**Israel** (1994): Shmuel Hadas.
**Italy:** Bruno Bottai.
**Ivory Coast:** See Côte d'Ivoire.
**Jamaica** (1979): Peter Carlisle Black.
**Japan** (1966): Tadao Johannes Araki.
**Jordan** (1994): Sherif Fawaz Shref.
**Kazakhstan** (1992): .....
**Kenya** (1965) Steven Loyatum.
**Kiribati:** Diplomatic relations established April, 1995.
**Korea** (1966): Heungsoo Kim.
**Kuwait** (1969): Tarek Razzouqi.
**Kyrgyzstan** (1992): .....
**Latvia** (1991): Mrs. Aija Odina.
**Lebanon** (1966): Youssef Arsanios.
**Lesotho** (1967): Miss Lebohang Nts'Inyi.
**Liberia** (1966): .....
**Liechtenstein** (1985): Nikolaus de Liechtenstein.
**Lithuania:** Kazys Lozoraitis.
**Luxembourg** (1955): Jean Wagner.
**Macedonia** (1994): Dimitar Mircev.
**Madagascar** (1967): .....
**Malawi** (1966): Geoffrey Gachuku Chipungu.
**Mali** (1979): Mrs. Madina Ty-Tall.
**Malta** (1965): Alexander Cachia Zammit.
**Marshall Islands** (1993): .....
**Mauritius: Bobooran Mahadoo.**
**Mexico** (personal representative, 1990; diplomatic relations, 1992): Guillermo Jimenez Morales.
**Micronesia, Federated States** (1994): .....
**Moldava** (1992): .....
**Monaco:** Cesar Charles Solamito.
**Mongolia** (1992): Shirchinjavya Yumjav.

**Morocco:** .....
**Mozambique:** Diplomatic relations established December, 1995.
**Namibia:** Diplomatic relations established September, 1995.
**Nauru** (1992): .....
**Nepal** (1983): .....
**Netherlands** (1967): Reynier Flaes.
**New Zealand** (1973): Wilbur Dovey.
**Nicaragua: Filadelfo Chamorro Coronel.**
**Niger** (1971): .....
**Nigeria** (1976): Yaro Yusuf Mamman.
**Norway** (1982): Jan G. Jolle.
**Order of Malta** (see Index): Christophe de Kallay.
**Pakistan** (1965): Zia Ispahani.
**Panama:** Maria Teresa Viggiano de De Obarrio.
**Papua New Guinea** (1977): .....
**Paraguay:** Luis Angel Casati Ferro.
**Peru:** Augusto Antoniolo Vasquez.
**Philippines** (1951): Mrs. Henrietta Tambunting de Villa.
**Poland** (1989): Stefan Frankiewicz.
**Portugal:** Antonio d'Oliveira Pinto da Franco.
**Romania** (1920; broken off, 948; reestablished, 1990): Gheorghe Gheorghiu.
**Rwanda** (1964): Denis Polisi.
**Saint Lucia** (1984): Desmond Arthur McNamara.
**Saint Vincent and the Grenadines** (1990): .....
**San Marino** (1986): Giovanni Galassi.
**Sao Tome and Principe** (1984): .....
**Senegal** (1966): Henri Antoine Turpin.
**Sierra Leone:** Diplomatic relations established July 1996.
**Seychelles** (1984): .....
**Singapore** (1981): Mrs. Mary Seet-Cheng.
**Slovakia** (1993; when it became independent republic): Dr. Anton Neuwirth.
**Slovenia** (1992): Stefan Falez.
**Solomon Islands** (1984): .....
**South Africa** (1994): .....
**Spain:** Pedro Lopez Aguirrenbengoa.
**Sri Lanka** (1975): Bernard Anton Bandara Goonetilleke.

**Sudan** (1972): Nureldin Satti.
**Suriname** (1994): Evert G. Azimullah.
**Swaziland** (1992): Mpumelelo Joseph Ndumiso Hlophe.
**Sweden** (1982): Anders Thunberg.
**Switzerland** (1992): Francois Pictet, Ambassador with special mission to Holy See.
**Syria** (Arab Republic) (1966): .....
**Tajikistan:** Diplomatic relations established June 15, 1996.
**Tanzania** (1968): .....
**Thailand** (1969): Don Pramudwinai.
**Togo** (1981): ......
**Tonga** (1994): .....
**Trinidad and Tobago** (1978): Lingsten Lloyd Cumberbatch.
**Tunisia** (1972): Ismail Lejri.
**Turkey** (1966): Semih Belen.
**Turkmenistan:** Diplomatic relations established July 10, 1996.
**Uganda** (1966): Mrs. Freda Lule Blick.
**Ukraine** (1992): .....
**United States** (1984): Raymond L. Flynn.
**Uruguay:** Jorge Silva Cencio.
**Uzbekistan** (1992): .....
**Vanuatu** (1994): .....
**Venezuela:** Alberto J. Vollmer Herrera.
**Western Samoa** (1994): .....
**Yugoslavia:** Dojcilo Maslovaric.
**Zaire** (1963): Atembina-te-Bombo.
**Zambia** (1965): Love Mtesa.
**Zimbabwe** (1980): Kotsho Lloyd Dube.

## Special Representatives

**Russia (Federation of)** (1989): Viatcheslav Vassilievitch Kostikov, Ambassador Extraordinary and Plenipotentiary.
**United Nations** (Center of Information of UN at the Holy See): Dr. Nadia Younes, director.
**United Nations High Commission for Refugees:** Fazlul Karim, delegate.
**Organization for the Liberation of Palestine:** Afif E. Safieh, director.

## U.S. – HOLY SEE RELATIONS

The United States and the Holy See announced Jan. 10, 1984, the establishment of full diplomatic relations, thus ending a gap of 117 years in their relations. The announcement followed action by the Congress in November, 1983, to end a prohibition on diplomatic relations enacted in 1867.

William A. Wilson, President Reagan's personal representative to the Holy See from 1981, was confirmed as the U.S. ambassador by the Senate, Mar. 7, 1984. He presented his credentials to Pope John Paul II, Apr. 9, 1984, and served until May 1986, when he resigned.

He was succeeded by Frank Shakespeare, 1986-89, and Thomas P. Melady, 1989-93. Raymond L. Flynn, Mayor of Boston, was appointed by President Bill Clinton and confirmed by the Senate in July, 1993.

Archbishop (now Cardinal) Pio Laghi, apostolic delegate to the U.S. since 1980, was named first pro-nuncio by the Pope on Mar. 26, 1984. He served

until 1990, when he was named prefect of the Congregation for Catholic Education. Archbishop Agostino Cacciavillan was appointed pro-nuncio June 13, 1990.

### Nature of Relations

The nature of relations was described in nearly identical statements by John Hughes, a State Department spokesman, and the Vatican.

Hughes said: "The United States of America and the Holy See, in the desire to further promote the existing mutual friendly relations, have decided by common agreement to establish diplomatic relations between them at the level of embassy on the part of the United States of America, and nunciature on the part of the Holy See, as of today, Jan. 10, 1984."

The Vatican statement said: "The Holy See and the United States of America, desiring to develop the mutual friendly relations already existing, have decided by common accord to establish diplomatic relations at the level of apostolic nunciature on the side of the Holy See and of embassy on the side of the United States beginning today, Jan. 10, 1984."

The establishment of relations was criticized as a violation of the separation-of-church-and-state principle by spokesmen for the National Council of Churches, the National Association of Evangelicals, the Baptist Joint Committee on Public Affairs, Seventh Day Adventists, Americans United for Separation of Church and State, and the American Jewish Congress.

## Legal Challenge Dismissed

U.S. District Judge John P. Fullam, ruling May 7, 1985, in Philadelphia, dismissed a legal challenge to U.S.–Holy See relations brought by Americans United for Separation of Church and State. He stated that Americans United and its allies in the challenge lacked legal standing to sue, and that the courts did not have jurisdiction to intervene in foreign policy decisions of the executive branch of the U.S. government. Parties to the suit brought by Americans United were the National Association of Laity, the National Coalition of American Nuns and several Protestant church organizations.

Bishop James W. Malone, president of the U.S. Catholic Conference, said in a statement: "This matter has been discussed at length for many years. It is not a religious issue but a public policy question which, happily, has now been settled in this context."

Russell Shaw, a conference spokesman, said the decision to send an ambassador to the Holy See was not a church-state issue and "confers no special privilege or status on the Church."

## Earlier Relations

Official relations for trade and diplomatic purposes were maintained by the United States and the Papal States while the latter had the character of and acted like other sovereign powers in the international community.

Consular relations developed in the wake of an announcement, made by the papal nuncio in Paris to the American mission there Dec. 15, 1784, that the Papal States had agreed to open several Mediterranean ports to U.S. shipping.

U.S. consular representation in the Papal States began with the appointment of John B. Sartori, a native of Rome, in June, 1797. Sartori's successors as consuls were: Felix Cicognani, also a Roman, and Americans George W. Greene, Nicholas Browne, William C. Sanders, Daniel LeRoy, Horatio V. Glentworth, W.J. Stillman, Edwin C. Cushman, David M. Armstrong.

Consular officials of the Papal States who served in the U.S. were: Count Ferdinand Lucchesi, 1826 to 1829, who resided in Washington; John B. Sartori, 1829 to 1841, who resided in Trenton, N.J.; Daniel J. Desmond, 1841 to 1850, who resided in Philadelphia; Louis B. Binsse, 1850 to 1895, who resided in New York.

U.S. recognition of the consul of the Papal States did not cease when the states were absorbed into the Kingdom of Italy in 1871, despite pressure from Baron Blanc, the Italian minister. Binsse held the title until his death Mar. 28, 1895. No one was appointed to succeed him.

## Diplomatic Relations

The U.S. Senate approved a recommendation, made by President James K. Polk in December, 1847, for the establishment of a diplomatic post in the Papal States. Jacob L. Martin, the first charge d'affaires, arrived in Rome Aug. 2, 1848, and presented his credentials to Pius IX Aug. 19. Martin, who died within a month, was succeeded by Lewis Cass, Jr. Cass became minister resident in 1854 and served in that capacity until his retirement in 1858.

John P. Stockton, who later became a U.S. Senator from New Jersey, was minister resident from 1858 to 1861. Rufus King was named to succeed him but, instead, accepted a commission as a brigadier general in the Army. Alexander W. Randall of Wisconsin took the appointment. He was succeeded in August, 1862, by Richard M. Blatchford who served until the following year. King was again nominated minister resident and served in that capacity until 1867 when the ministry was ended because of objections from some quarters in the U.S. and failure to appropriate funds for its continuation. J. C. Hooker, a secretary, remained in the Papal States until the end of March, 1868, closing the ministry and performing functions of courtesy.

# VATICAN CITY

The State of Vatican City (Stato della Citta del Vaticano) is the territorial seat of the papacy. The smallest sovereign state in the world, it is situated within the city of Rome, embraces an area of 108.7 acres, and includes within its limits the Vatican Palace, museums, art galleries, gardens, libraries, radio station, post office, bank, astronomical observatory, offices, apartments, service facilities, St. Peter's Basilica, and neighboring buildings between the Basilica and Viale Vaticano. The extraterritorial rights of Vatican City extend to more than 10 buildings in Rome, including the major basilicas and office buildings of various congregations of the Roman Curia, and to the papal villas at **Castel Gandolfo** 15 miles southeast of the City of Rome. Castel Gandolfo is the summer residence of the Holy Father.

The government of Vatican City is in the hands of the reigning pope, who has full executive, legislative and judicial power. The administration of affairs, however, is handled by the Pontifical Commission for the State of Vatican City. The legal system is based on Canon Law; in cases where this code does not obtain, the laws of the City of Rome apply. The City is an absolutely neutral state and enjoys all the rights and privileges of a sovereign power. The citizens of Vatican City, and they alone, owe allegiance to the pope as a temporal head of state.

Cardinals of the Roman Curia residing outside Vatican City enjoy the privileges of extraterritoriality.

The normal population is approximately 1,000. While the greater percentage is made up of priests and religious, there are several hundred lay persons living in Vatican City. They are housed in their own apartments in the City and are engaged in secretarial, domestic, trade and service occupations. About 3,400 lay persons are employed by the Vatican.

Services of honor and order are performed by the Swiss Guards, who have been charged with responsibility for the personal safety of popes since 1506. Additional police and ceremonial functions are under the supervision of a special office. These functions were formerly handled by the Papal Gendarmes, the Palatine Guard of Honor, and the Guard of Honor of the Pope (Pontifical Noble Guard) which Pope Paul VI disbanded Sept. 14, 1970.

The **Basilica of St. Peter,** built between 1506 and 1626, is the largest church in Christendom (with the exception of the Basilica of Our Lady Queen of Peace in Ivory Coast) and the site of most papal ceremonies. The pope's own patriarchal basilica, however, is **St. John Lateran,** whose origins date back to 324.

**St. Ann's,** staffed by Augustinian Fathers, is the parish church of Vatican City. Its pastor is appointed by the pope following the recommendation of the prior general of the Augustinians and the archpriest of the Vatican Basilica.

Pastoral care in Vatican City State, which is separate from the diocese of Rome, is entrusted to the archpriest of St. Peter's Basilica, who is also vicar general for Vatican City and the papal villas at Castel Gandolf (chirograph of Pope John Paul II, Jan. 14, 1991). Cardinal Virgilio Noè was appointed to the posts, July 1, 1991.

The **Vatican Library** (00120 Vatican City; Rev. Leonard E. Boyle, O.P., prefect) has among its holdings 150,000 manuscripts, about 1,000,000 printed books, and 7,500 incunabula. The **Vatican Secret Archives** (00120 Vatican City; Rev. Josef Metzler, O.M.I., prefect), opened to scholars by Leo XIII in 1881, contain central church documents dating back to the time of Innocent III (1198-1216). Cardinal Luigi Poggi is librarian and archivist of the Holy Roman Church.

The independent temporal power of the pope, which is limited to the confines of Vatican City and small areas outside, was for many centuries more extensive than it is now. As late as the nineteenth century, the pope ruled 16,000 square miles of Papal States across the middle of Italy, with a population of over 3,000,000. In 1870 forces of the Kingdom of Italy occupied these lands which, with the exception of the small areas surrounding the Vatican and Lateran in Rome and the Villas of Castel Gandolfo, became part of the Kingdom by the Italian law of May 13, 1871.

The **Roman Question,** occasioned by this seizure and the voluntary confinement of the pope to the Vatican, was settled by ratification of the Lateran Agreement June 7, 1929, by the Italian government and Vatican City. The agreement recognized Catholicism as the religion of Italy and provided, among other things, a financial indemnity to the Vatican in return for the former Papal States; it became Article 7 of the Italian Constitution Mar. 26, 1947.

The Lateran Agreement was superseded by a new concordat given final approval by the Italian Chamber of Deputies Mar. 20 and formally ratified June 3, 1985.

## Papal Flag

The papal flag consists of two equal vertical stripes of yellow and white, charged with the insignia of the papacy on the white stripe — a triple crown or tiara over two crossed keys, one of gold and one of silver, tied with a red cord and two tassels. The divisions of the crown represent the teaching, sanctifying and ruling offices of the pope. The keys symbolize his jurisdictional authority.

The papal flag is a national flag inasmuch as it is the standard of the Supreme Pontiff as the sovereign of the state of Vatican City. It is also universally accepted by the faithful as a symbol of the supreme spiritual authority of the Holy Father.

## Vatican Radio

The declared purpose of Vatican Radio Station HVJ is "that the voice of the Supreme Pastor may be heard throughout the world by means of the ether waves, for the glory of Christ and the salvation of souls." Designed by Guglielmo Marconi, the inventor of radio, and supervised by him until his death, the station was inaugurated by Pope Pius XI in 1931. The original purpose has been extended to a wide variety of programming.

Vatican Radio operates on international wave lengths, transmits programs in 37 languages, and serves as a channel of communication between the Vatican, church officials and listeners in general in many parts of the world. The station broadcasts about 400 hours a week throughout the world. The daily English-language program for North America is broadcast on 6095, 7305, 9605 kilohertz.

The staff of 415 broadcasters and technicians includes 30 Jesuits. Studios and offices are at Palazzo Pio, Piazza Pia, 3, 00193 Rome. The transmitters are situated at Santa Maria di Galeria, a short distance north of Rome.

## 1996 Vatican Stamps and Coins

The Vatican Philatelic and Numismatic Office (00120 Vatican City) scheduled the following issues of stamps and coins for 1996. Issue dates are given where available.

700th Anniversary of Marco Polo's return from China; issued March 15, 1996, in four values.

400th Anniversary of the Treaty of Brest-Litovsk and 350th Anniversary of the Treaty of Uzhorod; issued March 15, 1996, in two values.

Centenary of the Olympic Games, Athens-Atlanta 1896-1996; issued May 7, 1996, in five values.

Europe 1996 "Famous Women"; issued May 7, 1996, in two values (feature Gianna Beretta Molla and Edith Stein).

50th Anniversary of His Holiness John Paul II's priestly ordination.

3rd Centenary of the birth of St. Alphonsus Liguori and 7th Centenary of the death of St. Celestine V.

The Journeys of His Holiness John Paul II (1995).

Towards the Holy Year 2000.

Christian Solemnity of Christmas.

**Postal Stationery:** Aerogramme

**Postcards**

**Coins:** Series for seventeenth year (1995) of the Pontificate of John Paul II; issued Feb. 6, 1996, in seven values. Subject: Encyclical Letter *Evangelium Vitae.*

Celebrative 500 Lire Silver Coin.

Diptych of 10,000 Lire Silver Coins. Subject: Towards the Holy Year 2,000 (Baptism in the River Jordan - Jesus the teacher).

Commemorative 500 Lire Silver Coin.

## Papal Audiences

General audiences are scheduled weekly, on Wednesday.

In Vatican City, they are held in the Audience Hall on the south side of St. Peter's Basilica or, weather permitting, in St. Peter's Square. The hall, which was opened in 1971, has a seating capacity of 6,800 and a total capacity of 12,000.

Audiences have been held during the summer at Castel Gandolfo when the pope is there on a working vacation.

General audiences last from about 60 to 90 minutes, during which the pope gives a talk and his blessing. A résumé of the talk, which is usually in Italian, is given in several languages.

Arrangements for papal audiences are handled by an office of the Prefecture of the Apostolic Household.

American visitors can obtain passes for general audiences by applying to the Bishops' Office for United States Visitors to the Vatican, Casa Santa Maria, Via dell'Umilita, 30, 00187 Rome. Private and group audiences are reserved for dignitaries of various categories and for special occasions.

## Publications

**Acta Apostolicae Sedis,** 00120 Vatican City: The only "official commentary" of the Holy See, was established in 1908 for the publication of activities of the Holy See, laws, decrees and acts of congregations and tribunals of the Roman Curia. The first edition was published in January, 1909.

St. Pius X made *AAS* an official organ in 1908. Laws promulgated for the Church ordinarily take effect three months after the date of their publication in this commentary.

The publication, mostly in Latin, is printed by the Vatican Press.

The immediate predecessor of this organ was *Acta Sanctae Sedis,* founded in 1865 and given official status by the Congregation for the Propagation of the Faith in 1904.

**Annuario Pontificio,** 00120 Vatican City: The yearbook of the Holy See. It is edited by the Central Statistics Office of the Church and is printed in Italian, with some portions in other languages, by the Vatican Press. It covers the worldwide organization of the Church, lists members of the hierarchy, and includes a wide range of statistical information.

The publication of a statistical yearbook of the Holy See dates back to 1716, when a volume called *Notizie* appeared. Publication under the present title began in 1860, was suspended in 1870, and resumed again in 1872 under the title *Catholic Hierarchy.* This volume was printed privately at first, but has been issued by the Vatican Press since 1885. The title *Annuario Pontificio* was restored in 1912, and the yearbook was called an "official publication" until 1924.

**L'Osservatore Romano,** Via del Pellegrino, 00120 Vatican City: The daily newspaper of the Holy See. It began publication July 1, 1861, as an independent enterprise under the ownership and direction of four Catholic laymen headed by Marcantonio Pacelli, vice minister of the interior under Pope Pius IX and a grandfather of the late Pius XII. Leo XIII bought the publication in 1890, making it the "pope's" own newspaper.

The only official material in *L'Osservatore Romano* is that which appears under the heading, "Nostre Informazioni." This includes notices of appointments by the Holy See, the texts of papal encyclicals and addresses by the Holy Father and others, various types of documents, accounts of decisions and rulings of administrative bodies, and similar items. Additional material includes news and comment on developments in the Church and the world. Italian is the language most used.

The editorial board is directed by Prof. Mario Agnes. A staff of about 15 reporters covers Rome news sources. A corps of correspondents provides foreign coverage.

A weekly roundup edition in English was inaugurated in 1968 (Rev. Robert J. Dempsey, on leave from Chicago archdiocese, is editor). Other weekly editions are printed in French (1949), Italian (1950), Spanish (1969), Portuguese (1970) and German (1971). The Polish edition (1980) is published monthly. *L'Osservatore della Domenica* is published weekly as a supplement to the Sunday issue of the daily edition.

**Vatican Television Center (Centro Televisivo Vaticano, CTV),** Palazzo Belvedere, 00120 Vatican City: Instituted by John Paul II Oct. 23, 1983, with the rescript, *Ex Audentia.* Dr. Emilio Rossi is president of the administrative council.

**Vatican Press,** 00120 Vatican City: The official printing plant of the Vatican. The Vatican press was conceived by Marcellus II and Pius IV but was actually founded by Sixtus V on Apr. 27, 1587, to print the Vulgate and the writings of the Fathers of the Church and other authors. A Polyglot Press was established in 1626 by the Congregation for the Propagation of the Faith to serve the needs of the Oriental Church. St. Pius X merged both presses under the title Vatican Polyglot Press. It was renamed Vatican Press July 1, 1991, by John Paul II following restructuring. The plant has facilities for the printing of a wide variety of material in about 30 languages.

**Vatican Publishing House (Libreria Editrice Vaticano),** Piazza S. Pietro, 00120 Vatican City: Formerly an office of the Vatican Press to assist in the circulation of the liturgical and juridical publications of the Apostolic See, the congregations and later the *Acta Apostolicae Sedis.* In 1926, with the expansion of publishing activities and following the promulgation of the 1917 Code, the office was made an independent entity. An administrative council and editorial commission were instituted in 1983; in 1988 *Pastor Bonus* listed it among institutes joined to the Holy See; new statutes were approved by the Secretariat of State July 1, 1991.

**Activities of the Holy See:** An annual documentary volume covering the activities of the pope and of the congregations, commissions, tribunals and offices of the Roman Curia.

**Statistical Yearbook of the Church:** Issued by the Central Statistics Office of the Church, it contains principal data concerning the presence and work of the Church in the world. The first issue was published in 1972 under the title *Collection of Statistical Tables, 1969*. It is printed in corresponding columns of Italian and Latin. Some of the introductory material is printed in other languages.

## TRADITIONAL RELIGIONS

"Pastoral Attention to Traditional Religions" is the title of a letter sent by the Pontifical Council for Interreligious Dialogue to the presidents of episcopal conferences in the Americas, Asia and Oceania.

*The following excerpts are from the text circulated in the Jan. 26, 1994, English edition of "L'Osservatore Romano."*

### Nature of Traditional Religions

By Traditional Religions we mean those religions which, unlike the world religions that have spread into many countries and cultures, have remained in their original socio-cultural environment. The word "traditional" does not refer to something static or unchangeable, but rather denotes this localized matrix.

There is no agreement on a single name to be used when referring to these religions. Some names (e.g., paganism, fetishism) convey a negative meaning and, in addition, do not really describe the contents of these religions. Nowadays, even a term such as animism is no longer commonly acceptable. Whereas in Africa these religions are ordinarily referred to as "African Traditional Religions," in Asia they are called "Tribal Religions and Folk Religions," in America "Native Religions and Afro-American Religions," and in Oceania "Indigenous Religions."

### Elements

Traditional Religions generally have a clear belief in One God, in a Supreme Being who goes by such names as Great Spirit, Creator, the Great One, the Mighty Spirit, the Divine, the Transcendent, the One Who Lives Above, Heaven, etc.

There is also a belief in other beings which are above mankind but are less than the Supreme Being. They may be called spirits, and some experts on the Traditional Religions sometimes call them "deities" or "gods," with a small "d" or "g." Deceased adult relatives, i.e., ancestors are also objects of belief.

Cult or worship in Traditional Religions is directed generally to the spirits and the ancestors, and sometimes to God. It takes the form of prayer especially in the family, worship at shrines and communal sacrifices. Fear of the evil spirits or ancestors motivates many acts of worship.

The moral code is regarded as that which has been handed down by past generations and sanctioned by the spirits and the ancestors, and occasionally by God. Traditional Religions do not generally lay claim to revealed books. Nor are they articulated in theoretical statements of a theological or philosophical nature. The riches of their contents and their many values, are more often found in their celebrations, stories and proverbs, and conveyed through attitudes, customs and codes of conduct. It is rare that a Traditional Religion traces itself back to a founder.

### Major Values

In many traditional societies there is a strong sense of the sacred. Religion permeates life to such an extent that it is often difficult to distinguish between strictly religious elements and local custom. Authority is not seen as something secular but is regarded as a sacred trust. People of Traditional Religions show great attention to the earth. They respect life and celebrate its important stages: birth, entrance into adulthood, marriage, death. There is a strong sense of family, which includes love of children, respect for the elders, a community link with the ancestors. Symbolism is important for interpreting the invisible world and the human being's relationship with it. There is an obvious love of ritual.

Traditional Religions also have their negative elements. Examples can be given: inadequate ideas about God, superstition, fear of the spirits, objectionable moral practices, the rejection of twins (in some places), even occasional human sacrifice.

### Pastoral Concern

Traditional Religions constitute the religious context in which a good number of people live or have lived.

Many recent converts to Christianity come from a background of Traditional Religions. This is true not only in those churches where the Gospel has been preached only within the last century or so, but also in some countries where the Church has been established for many centuries. Many of these converts live in cultures and contexts influenced by these religions (e.g., in Latin America, Haiti, Cuba, Jamaica, North America, Australia).

The herald of the Gospel should pay great attention to the Traditional Religions and the cultures which go along with them. Christianity should aim at influencing the whole of life and producing integrated persons, rather than have people live parallel lives, at different levels. The encounter of Gospel and culture, including its religious element, will involve a careful sifting out, a discernment, which is not always easy.

## MEETING OF THEOLOGIANS

The seventh general assembly of the Conference of Catholic Theological Institutions discussed how local "claims to identity" affect their work, during an Aug. 1-to-6, 1996, meeting in Sherbrooke, Canada. Most of the speakers focused their remarks on the role of theology and the Church in affirming the rights and dignity of native peoples or ethnic and cultural minorities whose identity claims have been ignored by dominant cultures.

Well over 100 theologians attended the meeting of the prestigious conference, whose central concern seemed related to a kind of activist theology.

# DOCTRINE OF THE CATHOLIC CHURCH _____

*Following are excerpts from the first two chapters of the "Dogmatic Constitution on the Church" promulgated by the Second Vatican Council. They describe the relation of the Catholic Church to the Kingdom of God, the nature and foundation of the Church, the People of God, the necessity of membership and participation in the Church for salvation. Additional subjects in the constitution are treated in other Almanac entries.*

## I. MYSTERY OF THE CHURCH

By her relationship with Christ, the Church is a kind of sacrament or sign of intimate union with God, and of the unity of all mankind (No. 1).

He (the eternal Father) planned to assemble in the holy Church all those who would believe in Christ. Already from the beginning of the world the foreshadowing of the Church took place. She was prepared for in a remarkable way throughout the history of the people of Israel and by means of the Old Covenant. Established in the present era of time, the Church was made manifest by the outpouring of the Spirit. At the end of time she will achieve her glorious fulfillment. Then all just men from the time of Adam, "from Abel, the just one, to the last of the elect," will be gathered together with the Father in the universal Church (No. 2).

When the work which the Father had given the Son to do on earth (cf. Jn. 17:4) was accomplished, the Holy Spirit was sent on the day of Pentecost in order that he might forever sanctify the Church, and thus all believers would have access to the Father through Christ in the one Spirit (cf. Eph. 2:18).

The Spirit dwells in the Church and in the hearts of the faithful as in a temple (cf. 1 Cor. 3:16; 6:19). The Spirit guides the Church into the fullness of truth (cf. Jn. 16:13) and gives her a unity of fellowship and service. He furnishes and directs her with various gifts, both hierarchical and charismatic, and adorns her with the fruits of His grace (cf. Eph. 4:11-12; 1 Cor. 12:4; Gal. 5:22). By the power of the Gospel he makes the Church grow, perpetually renews her, and leads her to perfect union with her Spouse (No. 4).

## Foundation of the Church

The mystery of the holy Church is manifest in her very foundation, for the Lord Jesus inaugurated her by preaching the Good News, that is, the coming of God's Kingdom, which, for centuries, had been promised in the Scriptures. In Christ's word, in his works, and in his presence this Kingdom reveals itself to men.

The miracles of Jesus also confirm that the Kingdom has already arrived on earth.

Before all things, however, the Kingdom is clearly visible in the very Person of Christ, Son of God and Son of Man.

When Jesus rose up again after suffering death on the cross for mankind, he manifested that he had been appointed Lord, Messiah, and Priest forever (cf. Acts 2:36; Heb. 5:6; 7:17-21), and he poured out on his disciples the Spirit promised by the Father (cf. Acts 2:33). The Church, consequently, equipped with the gifts of her Founder and faithfully guarding his precepts receives the mission to proclaim and to establish among all peoples the Kingdom of Christ and of God. She becomes on earth the initial budding forth of that Kingdom. While she slowly grows, the Church strains toward the consummation of the Kingdom and, with all her strength, hopes and desires to be united in glory with her King (No. 5).

## Figures of the Church

In the Old Testament the revelation of the Kingdom had often been conveyed by figures of speech. In the same way the inner nature of the Church was now to be made known to us through various images.

The Church is a sheepfold a flock a tract of land to be cultivated, the field of God his choice vineyard the true vine is Christ the edifice of God the house of God the holy temple (whose members are) living stones this holy city a bride our Mother the spotless spouse of the spotless Lamb an exile (No. 6).

In the human nature which he united to himself, the Son of God redeemed man and transformed him into a new creation (cf Gal. 6:15; 2 Cor. 5:17) by overcoming death through his own death and resurrection. By communicating his Spirit to his brothers, called together from all peoples, Christ made them mystically into his own body.

In that body, the life of Christ is poured into the believers, who, through the sacraments, are united in a hidden and real way to Christ who suffered and was glorified. Through baptism we are formed in the likeness of Christ.

Truly partaking of the body of the Lord in the breaking of the eucharistic bread, we are taken up into communion with him and with one another (No. 7).

## One Body in Christ

As all the members of the human body, though they are many, form one body, so also are the faithful in Christ (cf. 1 Cor. 12:12). Also, in the building up of Christ's body there is a flourishing variety of members and functions. There is only one Spirit who distributes his different gifts for the welfare of the Church (cf. 1 Cor. 12:1-11). Among these gifts stands out the grace given to the apostles. To their authority, the Spirit himself subjected even those who were endowed with charisms (cf. 1 Cor. 14).

The head of this body is Christ (No. 7).

## Mystical Body of Christ

Christ, the one Mediator, established and ceaselessly sustains here on earth his holy Church, the community of faith, hope, and charity, as a visible structure. Through her he communicates truth and grace to all. But the society furnished with hierarchical agencies and the Mystical Body of Christ are not to be considered as two realities, nor are the visible assembly and the spiritual community, nor the earthly Church and the Church enriched with heavenly things. Rather they form one interlocked reality which is comprised of a divine and a human element. For this reason this reality is compared to the mystery of the incarnate Word. Just as the assumed nature inseparably united to the divine Word serves him as a living instrument of salvation, so, in a similar way, does the communal structure of the Church serve Christ's Spirit, who vivifies it by way of building up the body (cf. Eph. 4:16).

This is the unique Church of Christ which in the Creed we avow as one, holy, catholic, and apostolic. After his Resurrection our Savior handed her over to Peter to be shepherded (Jn. 21:17), commissioning him and the other apostles to propagate and govern her (cf. Mt. 28:18, ff.). Her he erected for all ages as "the pillar and mainstay of the truth" (1 Tm. 3:15). This Church, constituted and organized in the world as a society, subsists in the Catholic Church, which is governed by the successor of Peter and by the bishops in union with that successor, although many elements of sanctification and of truth can be found outside of her visible structure. These elements, however, as gifts properly belonging to the Church of Christ, possess an inner dynamism toward Catholic unity.

The Church, embracing sinners in her bosom, is at the same time holy and always in need of being purified, and incessantly pursues the path of penance and renewal.

The Church, "like a pilgrim in a foreign land, presses forward " announcing the cross and death of the Lord until he comes (cf. 1 Cor. 11:26) (No. 8).

## II. THE PEOPLE OF GOD

At all times and among every people, God has given welcome to whosoever fears him and does what is right (cf. Acts 10:35). It has pleased God, however, to make men holy and save them not merely as individuals without any mutual bonds, but by making them into a single people, a people which acknowledges him in truth and serves him in holiness. He therefore chose the race of Israel as a people unto himself. With it he set up a covenant. Step by step he taught this people by manifesting in its history both himself and the decree of his will, and by making it holy unto himself. All these things, however, were done by way of preparation and as a figure of that new and perfect covenant which was to be ratified in Christ.

Christ instituted this New Covenant, that is to say, the New Testament, in his blood (cf. 1 Cor. 11:25), by calling together a people made up of Jew and Gentile, making them one, not according to the flesh but in the Spirit.

This was to be the new People of God reborn through the Word of the living God (cf. 1 Pt. 1:23) from water and the Holy Spirit (cf. Jn. 3:5-6) "a chosen race, a royal priesthood, a holy nation, a purchased people. You who in times past were not a people, but are now the People of God" (1 Pt. 2:9-10).

That messianic people has for its head Christ. Its law is the new commandment to love as Christ loved us (cf. Jn. 13:34). Its goal is the Kingdom of God, which has been begun by God himself on earth, and which is to be further extended until it is brought to perfection by him at the end of time.

This messianic people, although it does not actually include all men, and may more than once look like a small flock, is nonetheless a lasting and sure seed of unity, hope, and salvation for the whole human race. Established by Christ as a fellowship of life, charity, and truth, it is also used by him as an instrument for the redemption of all, and is sent forth into the whole world as the light of the world and the salt of the earth (cf. Mt. 5:13-16).

Israel according to the flesh was already called the Church of God (Neh. 13:1; cf. Nm. 20:4; Dt. 23:1, ff.). Likewise the new Israel is also called the Church of Christ (cf. Mt. 16:18). For he has bought it for himself with his blood (cf. Acts 20:28), has filled it with his Spirit, and provided it with those means which befit it as a visible and social unity. God has gathered together as one all those who in faith look upon Jesus as the author of salvation and the source of unity and peace, and has established them as the Church, that for each and all she may be the visible sacrament of this saving unity (No. 9).

## Priesthood

The baptized, by regeneration and the anointing of the Holy Spirit, are consecrated into a holy priesthood.

[All members of the Church participate in the priesthood of Christ, through the common priesthood of the faithful. See Priesthood of the Laity.]

Though they differ from one another in essence and not only in degree, the common priesthood of the faithful and the ministerial or hierarchical priesthood are nonetheless interrelated. Each of them in its own special way is a participation in the one priesthood of Christ (No. 10).

It is through the sacraments and the exercise of the virtues that the sacred nature and organic structure of the priestly community is brought into operation (No. 11). (See Role of the Sacraments.)

## Prophetic Office

The holy People of God shares also in Christ's prophetic office. It spreads abroad a living witness to him, especially by means of a life of faith and charity and by offering to God a sacrifice of praise. The body of the faithful as a whole, anointed as they are by the Holy One (cf. Jn. 2:20, 27), cannot err in matters of belief. Thanks to a supernatural sense of faith which characterizes the People as a whole, it m+anifests this unerring quality when, "from the bishops down to the last member of the laity," it shows universal agreement in matters of faith and morals.

God's People accepts not the word of men but the very Word of God (cf. 1 Thes. 2:13). It clings without fail to the faith once delivered to the saints (cf. Jude 3), penetrates it more deeply by accurate insights, and applies it more thoroughly to life. All this it does under the lead of a sacred teaching authority to which it loyally defers.

It is not only through the sacraments and Church ministries that the same Holy Spirit sanctifies and leads the People of God. He distributes special graces among the faithful of every rank. By these gifts he makes them fit and ready to undertake the various tasks or offices advantageous for the renewal and upbuilding of the Church. These charismatic gifts are to be received with thanksgiving and consolation, for they are exceedingly suitable and useful for the needs of the Church.

Judgment as to their genuineness and proper use

belongs to those who preside over the Church, and to whose special competence it belongs to test all things and hold fast to that which is good (cf. 1 Thes. 5:12; 19-21) (No. 12).

## All Are Called

All men are called to belong to the new People of God. Wherefore this People, while remaining one and unique, is to be spread throughout the whole world and must exist in all ages, so that the purpose of God's will may be fulfilled. In thebeginning God made human nature one. After his children were scattered, he decreed that they should at length be united again (cf. Jn. 11:52). It was for this reason that God sent his Son that he might be Teacher, King, and Priest of all, the Head of the new and universal People of the sons of God. For this God finally sent his Son's Spirit as Lord and Lifegiver. He it is who, on behalf of the whole Church and each and every one of those who believe, is the principle of their coming together and remaining together in the teaching of the apostles and in fellowship, in the breaking of bread and in prayers (cf. Acts 2:42) (No. 13).

## One People of God

It follows that among all the nations of earth there is but one People of God, which takes its citizens from every race, making them citizens of a Kingdom which is of a heavenly and not an earthly nature. For all the faithful scattered throughout the world are in communion with each other in the Holy Spirit. the Church or People of God foster(s) and take(s) to herself, insofar as they are good, the ability, resources and customs of each people. Taking them to herself, she purifies, strengthens, and ennobles them This characteristic of universality which adorns the People of God is a gift from the Lord himself. By reason of it, the Catholic Church strives energetically and constantly to bring all humanity with all its riches back to Christ its Head in the unity of his Spirit.

In virtue of this catholicity each individual part of the Church contributes through its special gifts to the good of the other parts and of the whole Church. Thus through the common sharing of gifts the whole and each of the parts receive increase.

All men are called to be part of this catholic unity of the People of God. And there belong to it or are related to it in various ways, the Catholic faithful as well as all who believe in Christ, and indeed the whole of mankind. For all men are called to salvation by the grace of God (No. 13).

## The Catholic Church

This sacred Synod turns its attention first to the Catholic faithful. Basing itself upon sacred Scripture and tradition, it teaches that the Church is necessary for salvation. For Christ, made present to us in his Body, which is the Church, is the one Mediator and the unique Way of salvation. In explicit terms he himself affirmed the necessity of faith and baptism (cf. Mk. 16:16; Jn. 3:5) and thereby affirmed also the necessity of the Church, for through baptism as through a door men enter the Church. Whosoever, therefore, knowing that the Catholic Church was made necessary by God through Jesus Christ,

would refuse to enter her or to remain in her could not be saved.

They are fully incorporated into the society of the Church who, possessing the Spirit of Christ, accept her entire system and all the means of salvation given to her, and through union with her visible structure are joined to Christ, whorules her through the Supreme Pontiff and the bishops. This joining is effected by the bonds of professed faith, of the sacraments, of ecclesiastical government, and of communion. He is not saved, however, who, though he is part of the body of the Church, does not persevere in charity. He remains indeed in the bosom of the Church, but only in a "bodily" manner and not "in his heart."

Catechumens who, moved by the Holy Spirit, seek with explicit intention to be incorporated into the Church, are by that very intention joined to her. Mother Church already embraces them as her own (No. 14).

## Other Christians, The Unbaptized

The Church recognizes that in many ways she is linked with those who, being baptized, are honored with the name of Christian, though they do not profess the faith in its entirety or do not preserve unity of communion with the successor of Peter.

We can say that in some real way they are joined with us in the Holy Spirit, for to them also he gives his gifts and graces, and is thereby operative among them with his sanctifying power (No. 15).

Finally, those who have not yet received the Gospel are related in various ways to the People of God. In the first place there is the people to whom the covenants and the promises were given and from whom Christ was born according to the flesh (cf. Rom. 9:4-5). On account of their fathers, this people remains most dear to God, for God does not repent of the gifts he makes nor of the calls he issues (cf. Rom. 11:28-29).

But the plan of salvation also includes those who acknowledge the Creator. In the first place among these are the Moslems. Nor is God himself far distant from those who in shadows and images seek the unknown God.

Those also can attain to everlasting salvation who through no fault of their own do not know the Gospel of Christ or his Church, yet sincerely seek God and, moved by grace, strive by their deeds to do his will as it is known to them through the dictates of conscience. Nor does divine Providence deny the help necessary for salvation to those who, without blame on their part, have not yet arrived at an explicit knowledge of God, but who strive to live a good life, thanks to his grace. Whatever goodness or truth is found among them is looked upon by the Church as a preparation for the Gospel. She regards such qualities as given by him who enlightens all men so that they may finally have life. (No. 16).

## Oratory of St. Joseph

This oratory in Montreal is the world's largest pilgrimage site devoted to St. Joseph. The main church, at the top of 300 steps, is visited by about two million people a year. Its 56-bell carillon was originally designed for the Eiffel Tower.

# THE POPE, TEACHING AUTHORITY, COLLEGIALITY

The Roman Pontiff — the successor of St. Peter as the Vicar of Christ and head of the Church on earth — has full and supreme authority over the universal Church in matters pertaining to faith and morals (teaching authority), discipline and government (jurisdictional authority).

The primacy of the pope is real and supreme power. It is not merely a prerogative of honor — that is, of his being regarded as the first among equals. Neither does primacy imply that the pope is just the presiding officer of the collective body of bishops. The pope is the head of the Church.

Catholic belief in the primacy of the pope was stated in detail in the dogmatic constitution on the Church, *Pastor Aeternus*, approved in 1870 by the fourth session of the First Vatican Council. Some elaboration of the doctrine was made in the *Dogmatic Constitution on the Church* which was approved and promulgated by the Second Vatican Council Nov. 21, 1964. The entire body of teaching on the subject is based on Scripture and tradition and the centuries-long experience of the Church.

## Infallibility

*The essential points of doctrine concerning infallibility in the Church and the infallibility of the pope were stated by the Second Vatican Council in the "Dogmatic Constitution on the Church," as follows:*

"This infallibility with which the divine Redeemer willed his Church to be endowed in defining a doctrine of faith and morals extends as far as extends the deposit of divine revelation, which must be religiously guarded and faithfully expounded. This is the infallibility which the Roman Pontiff, the head of the college of bishops, enjoys in virtue of his office, when, as the supreme shepherd and teacher of all the faithful who confirms his brethren in their faith (cf. Lk. 22:32), he proclaims by a definitive act some doctrine of faith or morals. Therefore his definitions, of themselves, and not from the consent of the Church, are justly styled irreformable, for they are pronounced with the assistance of the Holy Spirit, an assistance promised to him in blessed Peter. Therefore they need no approval of others, nor do they allow an appeal to any other judgment. For then the Roman Pontiff is not pronouncing judgment as a private person. Rather, as the supreme teacher of the universal Church, as one in whom the charism of the infallibility of the Church herself is individually present, he is expounding or defending a doctrine of Catholic faith.

"The infallibility promised to the Church resides also in the body of bishops when that body exercises supreme teaching authority with the successor of Peter. To the resultant definitions the assent of the Church can never be wanting, on account of the activity of that same Holy Spirit, whereby the whole flock of Christ is preserved and progresses in unity of faith.

"But when either the Roman Pontiff or the body of bishops together with him defines a judgment, they pronounce it in accord with revelation itself. All are obliged to maintain and be ruled by this revelation, which, as written or preserved by tradition, is trans-mitted in its entirety through the legitimate succession of bishops and especially through the care of the Roman Pontiff himself.

"Under the guiding light of the Spirit of truth, revelation is thus religiously preserved and faithfully expounded in the Church. The Roman Pontiff and the bishops, in view of their office and of the importance of the matter, strive painstakingly and by appropriate means to inquire properly into that revelation and to give apt expression to its contents. But they do not allow that there could be any new public revelation pertaining to the divine deposit of faith" (No. 25).

## Authentic Teaching

The pope rarely speaks *ex cathedra* — that is, "from the chair" of St. Peter, for the purpose of making an infallible pronouncement. More often and in various ways he states authentic teaching in line with Scripture, tradition, the living experience of the Church, and the whole analogy of faith. Of such teaching, the Second Vatican Council said in its *Dogmatic Constitution on the Church* (No. 25):

"Religious submission of will and of mind must be shown in a special way to the authentic teaching authority of the Roman Pontiff, even when he is not speaking *ex cathedra*. That is, it must be shown in such a way that his supreme magisterium is acknowledged with reverence, the judgments made by him are sincerely adhered to, according to his manifest mind and will. His mind and will in the matter may be known chiefly either from the character of the documents, from his frequent repetition of the same doctrine, or from his manner of speaking."

With respect to bishops, the constitution states: "They are authentic teachers, that is, teachers endowed with the authority of Christ, who preach to the people committed to them the faith they must believe and put into practice. By the light of the Holy Spirit, they make that faith clear, bringing forth from the treasury of revelation new things and old (cf. Mt. 13:52), making faith bear fruit and vigilantly warding off any errors which threaten their flock (cf. 2 Tm. 4:1-4).

"Bishops, teaching in communion with the Roman Pontiff, are to be respected by all as witnesses to divine and Catholic truth. In matters of faith and morals, the bishops speak in the name of Christ and the faithful are to accept their teaching and adhere to it with a religious assent of soul."

## Magisterium — Teaching Authority

Responsibility for teaching doctrine and judging orthodoxy belongs to the official teaching authority of the Church.

This authority is personalized in the pope, the successor of St. Peter as head of the Church, and in the bishops together and in union with the pope, as it was originally committed to Peter and to the whole college of apostles under his leadership. They are the official teachers of the Church.

Others have auxiliary relationships with the magisterium: theologians, in the study and clarification of doctrine; teachers — priests, religious, lay persons — who cooperate with the pope and bishops in spreading knowledge of religious truth; the faithful, who by their sense of faith and personal witness contribute to the development of doctrine and the establishment of its relevance to life in the Church and the world.

The magisterium, Pope Paul VI noted in an address at a general audience Jan. 11, 1967, "is a subordinate and faithful echo and secure interpreter of the divine word." It does not reveal new truths, "nor is it superior to sacred Scripture." Its competence extends to the limits of divine revelation manifested inScripture and tradition and the living experience of the Church, with respect to matters of faith and morals and related subjects. Official teaching in these areas is infallible when it is formally defined, for belief and acceptance by all members of the Church, by the pope, acting in the capacity of supreme shepherd of the flock of Christ; also, when doctrine is proposed and taught with moral unanimity of bishops with the pope in a solemn collegial manner, as in an ecumenical council, and/or in the ordinary course of events. Even when not infallibly defined, official teaching in the areas of faith and morals is authoritative and requires religious assent.

The teachings of the magisterium have been documented in creeds, formulas of faith, decrees and enactments of ecumenical and particular councils, various kinds of doctrinal statements, encyclical letters and other teaching instruments. They have also been incorporated into the liturgy, with the result that the law of prayer is said to be a law of belief.

## Collegiality

The bishops of the Church, in union with the pope, have supreme teaching and pastoral authority over the whole Church in addition to the authority of office they have for their own dioceses.

This collegial authority is exercised in a solemn manner in an ecumenical council and can be exercised in other ways as well, "provided that the head of the college calls them to collegiate action, or at least so approves or freely accepts the united action of the dispersed bishops that it is made a true collegiate act."

This doctrine is grounded on the fact that: "Just as, by the Lord's will, St. Peter and the other apostles constituted one apostolic college, so in a similar way the Roman Pontiff as the successor of Peter, and the bishops as the successors of the apostles are joined together."

Doctrine on collegiality was stated by the Second Vatican Council in the Dogmatic Constitution on the Church (Nos. 22 and 23).

# REVELATION

*Following are excerpts from the "Dogmatic Constitution on Divine Revelation" promulgated by the Second Vatican Council. They describe the nature and process of divine revelation, inspiration and interpretation of Scripture, the Old and New Testaments, and the role of Scripture in the life of the Church.*

## I. REVELATION ITSELF

God chose to reveal himself and to make known to us the hidden purpose of his will (cf. Eph. 1:9) by which through Christ, the Word made flesh, man has access to the Father in the Holy Spirit and comes to share in the divine nature (cf. Eph. 2:18; 2 Pt. 1:4). Through this revelation, therefore, the invisible God (cf. Col. 1:15; 1 Tm. 1:17) speaks to men as friends (cf. Ex. 33:11; Jn. 15:14-15) and lives among them (cf. Bar. 3:38) so that he may invite and take them into fellowship with himself. This plan of revelation is realized by deeds and words having an inner unity: the deeds wrought by God in the history of salvation manifest and confirm the teaching and realities signified by the words, while the words proclaim the deeds and clarify the mystery contained in them. By this revelation then, the deepest truth about God and the salvation of man is made clear to us in Christ, who is the Mediator and at the same time the fullness of all revelation (No. 2).

God from the start manifested himself to our first parents. Then after their fall his promise of redemption aroused in them the hope of being saved (cf. Gn. 3:15), and from that time on he ceaselessly kept the human race in his care, in order to give eternal life to those who perseveringly do good in search of salvation (cf. Rom. 2:6-7). He called Abraham in order to make of him a great nation (cf. Gn. 12:2).

Through the patriarchs, and after them through Moses and the prophets, he taught this nation to acknowledge himself as the one living and true God and to wait for the Savior promised by him. In this manner he prepared the way for the Gospel down through the centuries (No. 3).

## Revelation in Christ

Then, after speaking in many places and varied ways through the prophets, God "last of all in these days has spoken to us by his Son" (Heb. 1:1-2). Jesus perfected revelation by fulfilling it through his whole work of making himself present and manifesting himself: through his words and deeds, his signs and wonders, but especially through his death and glorious resurrection from the dead and final sending of the Spirit of truth. Moreover, he confirmed with divine testimony what revelation proclaimed: that God is with us to free us from the darkness of sin and death, and to raise us up to life eternal.

The Christian dispensation, therefore, as the new and definitive covenant, will never pass away, and we now await no further new public revelation before the glorious manifestation of our Lord Jesus Christ (cf. 1 Tm. 6:14; Ti. 2:13) (No. 4).

## II. TRANSMISSION OF REVELATION

God has seen to it that what he had revealed for the salvation of all nations would abide perpetually in its full integrity and be handed on to all generations. Therefore Christ the Lord, in whom the full revelation of the supreme God is brought to completion (cf. 2 Cor. 1:20; 3:16; 4:6), commissioned the apostles to prach to all men that Gospel which is the source of all saving truth and moral teaching, and thus to impart to them divine gifts. This Gospel had been promised in former times through the prophets, and Christ himself fulfilled it and promulgated it with his own lips. This commission was faithfully fulfilled by the apostles who, by their oral preaching, by example, and by ordinances, handed on what they had received from Christ or what they had learned through the prompting of the Holy Spirit. The commission was fulfilled, too, by those apostles and apostolic men who under the inspiration of the same Holy Spirit committed the message of salvation to writing (No. 7).

## Tradition

But in order to keep the Gospel forever whole and alive within the Church, the apostles left bishops as their successors, "handing over their own teaching role" to them. This sacred tradition, therefore, and sacred Scripture of both the Old and the New Testament are like a mirror in which the pilgrim Church on earth looks at God (No. 7).

The apostolic preaching, which is expressed in a special way in the inspired books, was to be preserved by a continuous succession of preachers until the end of time. Therefore the apostles, handing on what they themselves had received, warn the faithful to hold fast to the traditions which they have learned. Now what was handed on by the apostles includes everything which contributes to the holiness of life, and the increase in faith of the People of God; and so the Church, in her teaching, life, and worship, perpetuates and hands on to all generations all that she herself is, all that she believes (No. 8).

## Development of Doctrine

This tradition which comes from the apostles develops in the Church with the help of the Holy Spirit. For there is a growth in the understanding of the realities and the words which have been handed down. This happens through the contemplation and study made by believers through the intimate understanding of spiritual things they experience, and through the preaching of those who have received through episcopal succession the sure gift of truth. For, as the centuries succeed one another, the Church constantly moves forward toward the fullness of divine truth until the words of God reach their complete fulfillment in her.

The words of the holy Fathers witness to the living presence of this tradition, whose wealth is poured into the practice and life of the believing and praying Church. Through the same tradition the Church's full canon of the sacred books is known, and the sacred writings themselves are more profoundly understood and unceasingly made active in her; and the Holy Spirit, through whom the living voiceof the Gospel resounds in the Church, and through her, in the world, leads unto all truth those who believe and makes the word of Christ dwell abundantly in them (cf. Col. 3:16) (No. 8).

## Tradition and Scripture

Hence there exist a close connection and communication between sacred tradition and sacred Scripture. For both of them, flowing from the same divine wellspring, in a certain way merge into a unity and tend toward the same end. For sacred Scripture is the word of God inasmuch as it is consigned to writing under the inspiration of the divine Spirit. To the successors of the apostles, sacred tradition hands on in its full purity God's word, which was entrusted to the apostles by Christ the Lord and the Holy Spirit. Thus, led by the light of the Spirit of truth, these successors can in their preaching preserve this word of God faithfully, explain it, and make it more widely known. Consequently, it is not from sacred Scripture alone that the Church draws her certainty about every thing which has been revealed. Therefore both sacred tradition and sacred Scripture are to be accepted and venerated with the same sense of devotion and reverence (No. 9).

Sacred tradition and sacred Scripture form one sacred deposit of the word of God, which is committed to the Church (No. 10).

## Teaching Authority of Church

The task of authentically interpreting the word of God, whether written or handed on, has been entrusted exclusively to the living teaching office of the Church, whose authority is exercised in the name of Jesus Christ. This teaching office is not above the word of God, but serves it, teaching only what has been handed on  it draws from this one deposit of faith everything which it presents for belief as divinely revealed.

It is clear, therefore, that sacred tradition, sacred Scripture, and the teaching authority of the Church are so linked and joined together that one cannot stand without the others, and that all together and each in its own way under the action of the one Holy Spirit contribute effectively to the salvation of souls (No. 10).

## III. INSPIRATION, INTERPRETATION

Those revealed realities contained and presented in sacred Scripture have been committed to writing under the inspiration of the Holy Spirit. Holy Mother Church, relying on the belief of the apostls, holds that the books of both the Old and New Testament in their entirety, with all their parts, are sacred and canonical because, having been written under the inspiration of the Holy Spirit (cf. Jn. 20:31; 2 Tm. 3:16; 2 Pt. 1:19-21; 3:15-16) they have God as their author and have been handed on as such to the Church herself. In composing the sacred books, God chose men and, while employed by him, they made use of their powers and abilities, so that, with him acting in them and through them, they, as true authors, consigned to writing everything and only those things which he wanted (No. 11).

## Inerrancy

Therefore, since everything asserted by the inspired authors or sacred writers must be held to be asserted by the Holy Spirit, it follows that the books of Scripture must be acknowledged as teaching firmly, faithfully, and without error that truth which God wanted put into the sacred writings for the sake of our salvation. Therefore "all Scripture is inspired by God and useful for teaching, for reproving, for correcting, for instruction in justice; that the man of God may be perfect, equipped for every good work" (2 Tm. 3:16-17) (No. 11).

## Literary Forms

However, since God speaks in sacred Scripture through men in human fashion, the interpreter of sacred Scripture, in order to see clearly what God wanted to communicate to us, should carefully investigate what meaning the sacred writers really intended, and what God wanted to mainfest by means of their words.

The interpreter must investigate what meaning the sacred writer intended to express and actually expressed in particular circumstances as he used contemporary literary forms in accordance with the situation of his own time and culture. For the correct understanding of what the sacred author wanted to assert, due attention must be paid to the customary and characteristic styles of perceiving, speaking, and narrating which prevailed at the time of the sacred writer, and to the customs men normally followed at that period in their everyday dealings with one another (No. 12).

## Analogy of Faith

No less serious attention must be given to the content and unity of the whole of Scripture, if the meaning of the sacred texts is to be correctly brought to light. The living tradition of the whole Church must be taken into account along with the harmony whic exists between elements of the faith. All of what has been said about the way of interpreting Scripture is subject finally to the judgment of the Church, which carries out the divine commission and ministry of guarding and interpreting the word of God (No. 12).

## IV. THE OLD TESTAMENT

In carefully planning and preparing the salvation of the whole human race, the God of supreme love, by a special dispensation, chose for himself a people to whom he might entrust his promises. First he entered into a covenant with Abraham (cf. Gn. 15:18) and, through Moses, with the people of Israel (cf. Ex. 24:8). To this people which he had acquired for himself, he so manifested himself through words and deeds as the one true and living God that Israel came to know by experience the ways of God with men. The plan of salvation, foretold by the sacred authors, recounted and explained by them, is found as the true word of God in the books of the Old Testament: these books, therefore, written under divine inspiration, remain permanently valuable (No. 14).

## Principal Purpose

The principal purpose to which the plan of the Old Covenant was directed was to prepare for the coming both of Christ, the universal Redeemer, and of the messianic Kingdom. Now the books of the Old Testament, in accordance with the state of mankind before the time of salvation established by Christ, reveal to all men the knowledge of God and of man and the ways in which God deals with men. These books show us true divine pedagogy (No. 15).

The books of the Old Testament with all their parts, caught up into the proclamation of the Gospel, acquire and show forth their full meaning in the New Testament (cf. Mt. 5:17; Lk. 24:27; Rom. 16:25-26; 2 Cor. 3:14-16) and in turn shed light on it and explain it (No. 16).

## V. THE NEW TESTAMENT

The word of God is set forth and shows its power in a most excellent way in the writings of the New Testament. For when the fullness of time arrived (cf. Gal. 4:4), the Word was made flesh and dwelt among us in the fullness of grace and truth (cf. Jn. 12:32). This mystery had not been manifested to other generations as it was now revealed to his holy apostles and prophets in the Holy Spirit (cf. Eph. 3:4-6), so that they might preach the Gospel, stir up faith in Jesus, Christ and Lord, and gather the Church together. To these realities, the writings of the New Testament stand as a perpetual and divine witness (No. 17).

## The Gospels and Other Writings

The Gospels have a special preeminence for they are the principal witness of the life and teaching of the incarnate Word, our Savior.

The Church has always and everywhere held and continues to hold that the four Gospels are of apostolic origin. For what the apostles preached afterwards they themselves and apostolic men, under the inspiration of the divine Spirit, handed on to us in writing: the foundation of faith, namely, the fourfold Gospel, according to Matthew, Mark, Luke, and John (No. 18).

The four Gospels, whose historical character the Church unhesitatingly asserts, faithfully hand on what Jesus Christ, while living among men, really did and taught for their eternal salvation until the day he was taken up into heaven (see Acts 1:1-2). Indeed, after the ascension of the Lord the apostles handed on to their hearers what he had said and done. The sacred authors wrote the four Gospels, selecting some things from the many which had been handed on by word of mouth or in writing, reducing some of them to a synthesis, explicating some things in view of the situation of their churches, and preserving the form of proclamation but always in such fashion that they told us the honest truth about Jesus. For their intention in writing was that we might know "the truth" concerning those matters about which we have been instructed (cf. Lk. 1:2-4) (No. 19).

Besides the four Gospels, the canon of the New Testament also contains the Epistles of St. Paul and other apostolic writings, composed under the inspiration of the Holy Spirit. In these writings those matters which concern Christ the Lord are confirmed, his true teaching is more and more fully stated, the saving power of the divine work of Christ is preached, the story is told of the beginnings of the Church and her marvelous growth, and her glorious fulfillment is foretold (No. 20).

## VI. SCRIPTURE IN CHURCH LIFE

The Church has always venerated the divine Scriptures just as she venerates the body of the Lord. She has always regarded the Scriptures together with sacred tradition as the supreme rule of faith, and will ever do so. For, inspired by God and committed once and for all to writing, they impart the word of God himself without change, and make the voice of the Holy Spirit resound in the words of the prophets and apostles. Therefore, like the Christian religion itself, all the preaching of the Church must be nourished and ruled by sacred Scripture (No. 21).

Easy access to sacred Scripture should be provided for all the Christian faithful. That is why the Church from the very beginning accepted as her own that very ancient Greek translation of the Old Testament which is named after seventy men (the Septuagint); and she has always given a place of honor to other translaions, Eastern and Latin, especially the one known as the Vulgate. But since the word of God should be available at all times, the Church with maternal concern sees to it that suitable and correct translations are made into different languages, especially from the original texts of the sacred books. And if, given the opportunity and the approval of Church authority, these translations are produced in cooperation with the separated brethren as well, all Christians will be able to use them (No. 22).

## Biblical Studies, Theology

The constitution encouraged the development and progress of biblical studies "under the watchful care of the sacred teaching office of the Church."

It noted also: "Sacred theology rests on the written word of God, together with sacred tradition, as its primary and perpetual foundation," and that "the study of the sacred page is, as it were, the soul of sacred theology" (Nos. 23, 24).

(See separate article, Interpretation of the Bible.)

# THE BIBLE

The Canon of the Bible is the Church's official list of sacred writings. These works, written by men under the inspiration of the Holy Spirit, contain divine revelation and, in conjunction with the tradition and teaching authority of the Church, constitute the rule of Catholic faith. The Canon was fixed and determined by the tradition and teaching authority of the Church.

## The Catholic Canon

The Old Testament Canon of 46 books is as follows.

• **The Pentateuch,** the first five books: Genesis (Gn.), Exodus (Ex.), Leviticus (Lv.), Numbers (Nm.), Deuteronomy (Dt.).

• **Historical Books:** Joshua (Jos.), Judges (Jgs.), Ruth (Ru.) 1 and 2 Samuel (Sm.), 1 and 2 Kings (Kgs.), 1 and 2 Chronicles (Chr.), Ezra (Ezr.), Nehemiah (Neh.), Tobit (Tb.), Judith (Jdt.), Esther (Est.), 1 and 2 Maccabees (Mc.).

• **Wisdom Books:** Job (Jb.), Psalms (Ps.), Proverbs (Prv.), Ecclesiastes (Eccl.), Song of Songs (Song), Wisdom (Wis.), Sirach (Sir.).

• **The Prophets:** Isaiah (Is.), Jeremiah (Jer.), Lamentations (Lam.), Baruch (Bar.), Ezechiel (Ez.), Daniel (Dn.), Hosea (Hos.), Joel (Jl.), Amos (Am.), Obadiah (Ob.), Jonah (Jon.), Micah (Mi.), Nahum (Na.), Habakkuk (Hb.), Zehaniah (Zep.), Haggai (Hg.), Zechariah (Zec.) Malachi (Mal.).

The New Testament Canon of 27 books is as follows.

• **The Gospels** of Matthew (Mt.), Mark (Mk.), Luke (Lk.), John (Jn.)

• **The Acts of the Apostles** (Acts).

• **The Pauline Letters** — Romans (Rom.), 1 and 2 Corinthians (Cor.), Galatians (Gal.), Ephesians (Eph.), Philippians (Phil.), Colossians (Col.), 1 and 2 Thessalonians (Thes.) 1 and 2 Timothy (Tm.), Titus (Ti.), Philemon (Phlm.), Hebrews (Heb.).

• **The Catholic Letters** — James (Jas.), 1 and 2 Peter (Pt.), 1, 2 and 3 John (Jn.), Jude (Jude).

• **Revelation** (Rv.).

## Developments

The Canon of the Old Testament was firm by the fifth century despite some questioning by scholars. It was stated by a council held at Rome in 382, by African councils held in Hippo in 393 and in Carthage in 397 and 419, and by Innocent I in 405.

All of the New Testament books were generally known and most of them were acknowledged as inspired by the end of the second century. The Muratorian Fragment, dating from about 200, listed most of the books recognized as canonical in later decrees. Prior to the end of the fourth century, however, there was controversy over the inspired character of several works — the Letter to the Hebrews, James, Jude, 2 Peter, 2 and 3 John and Revelation. Controversy ended in the fourth century and these books, along with those about which there was no dispute, were enumerated in the canon stated by the councils of Hippo and Carthage and affirmed by Innocent I in 405.

The Canon of the Bible was solemnly defined by the Council of Trent in the dogmatic decree *De Canonicis Scripturis*, Apr. 8, 1546.

## Hebrew and Other Canons

The Hebrew Canon of sacred writings was fixed by tradition and the consensus of rabbis, probably by about 100 A.D. by the Synod or Council of Jamnia and certainly by the end of the second or early in the third century. It consists of the following works in three categories.

• **The Law** (Torah), the five books of Moses: Genesis, Exodus, Leviticus, Numbers, Deuteronomy.

• **The Prophets:** former prophets — Joshua, Judges, 1 and 2 Samuel, 1 and 2 Kings; latter prophets — Isaiah, Jeremiah, Ezekiel, and 12 minor prophets (Hosea, Joel, Amos, Obadiah, Jonah, Micah, Nahum, Habakkuk, Zephaniah, Haggai, Zechariah, Malachi).

• **The Writings:** 1 and 2 Chronicles, Ezra, Nehemiah, Job, Psalms, Proverbs, Ecclesiastes, Song of Songs, Ruth, Esther, Daniel.

This Canon, embodying the tradition and practice of the Palestine community, did not include a number of works contained in the Alexandrian version o sacred writings translated into Greek between 250 and 100 B.C. and in use by Greek-speaking Jews of the Dispersion (outside Palestine). The rejected works, called apocrypha and not regarded as sacred, are: Tobit, Judith, Wisdom, Sirach, Baruch, 1 and 2 Maccabees, the last six chapters of Esther and three passages of Daniel (3:24-90; 13; 14). These books have also been rejected from the Protestant Canon, although they are included in bibles under the heading, Apocrypha.

The aforementioned books are held to be inspired and sacred by the Catholic Church. In Catholic usage, they are called deuterocanonical because they were under discussion for some time before questions about their canonicity were settled. Books regarded as canonical with little or no debate were called protocanonical. The status of both categories of books is the same in the Catholic Bible.

The Protestant Canon of the Old Testament is the same as the Hebrew.

The Old Testament Canon of some separated Eastern churches differs from the Catholic Canon.

Christians are in agreement on the Canon of the New Testament.

## Languages

Hebrew, Aramaic and Greek were the original languages of the Bible. Most of the Old Testament books were written in Hebrew. Portions of Daniel, Ezra, Jeremiah, Esther, and probably the books of Tobit and Judith were written in Aramaic. The Book of Wisdom, 2 Maccabees and all the books of the New Testament were written in Greek.

## Manuscripts and Versions

The original writings of the inspired authors have been lost. The Bible has been transmitted through ancient copies called manuscripts and through translations or versions.

Authoritative Greek manuscripts include the Sinaitic and Vatican manuscripts of the fourth century and the Alexandrine of the fifth century A.D. The Septuagint and Vulgate translations are in a class by themselves.

The Septuagint version, a Greek translation of the Old Testament for Greek-speaking Jews, was begun about 250 and completed about 100 B.C. The work of several Jewish translators at Alexandria, it differed from the Hebrew Bible in the arrangement of books and included several, later called deuterocanonical, which were not acknowledged as sacred by the community in Palestine.

The Vulgate was a Latin version of the Old and New Testaments produced from the original languages by St. Jerome from about 383 to 404. It became the most widely used Latin text for centuries and was regarded as basic long before the Council of Trent designated it as authentic and suitable for use in public reading, controversy, preaching and teaching. Because of its authoritative character, it became the basis for many translations into other languages. A critical revision was completed by a pontifical commission in 1977.

Hebrew and Aramaic manuscripts of great antiquity and value have figured more significantly than before in recent scriptural work by Catholic scholars, especially since their use was strongly encouraged, if not mandated, in 1943 by Pius XII in the encyclical *Divino Afflante Spiritu.*

The English translation of the Bible in general use among Catholics until well into the 20th century was the *Douay-Rheims,* so called because of the places where it was prepared and published, the New Testament at Rheims in 1582 and the Old Testament at Douay in 1609. The translation was made from the Vulgate text. As revised and issued by Bishop Richard Challoner in 1749 and 1750, it became the standard Catholic English version for about 200 years.

A revision of the Challoner New Testament, made on the basis of the Vulgate text by scholars of the Catholic Biblical Association of America, was published in 1941 in the United States under the sponsorship of the Episcopal Committee of the Confraternity of Christian Doctrine.

## New American Bible

A new translation of the entire Bible, the first ever made directly into English from the original languages under Catholic auspices, was projected in 1944 and completed in the fall of 1970 with publication of the *New American Bible.* The Episcopal Committee of the Confraternity of Christian Doctrine sponsored the NAB. The translators were members of the Catholic Biblical Association of America and scholars of other faiths. The typical edition was produced by St. Anthony Guild Press, Paterson, N.J.

*The Jerusalem Bible,* published by Doubleday & Co., Inc., is an English translation of a French version based on the original languages.

Biblical translations approved for liturgical use by the National Conference of Catholic Bishops and the Holy See are the *New American Bible (1970 edition),* the *Revised Standard Version-Catholic Edition,* and the *Jerusalem Bible* (1966).

The Protestant counterpart of the *Douay-Rheims Bible* was the *King James Bible,* called the *Authorized Version* in England. Originally published in 1611 and in general use for more than three centuries, its several revisions include the *Revised Standard Version* and the *New Revised Standard Version.*

## Biblical Federation

In November, 1966, Pope Paul VI commissioned the Secretariat for Promoting Christian Unity to start work for the widest possible distribution of the Bible and to coordinate endeavors toward the production of Catholic-Protestant Bibles in all languages.

The World Catholic Federation for the Biblical Apostolate, established in 1969, sponsors a program designed to create greater awareness among Catholics of the Bible and its use in everyday life.

The U. S. Center for the Catholic Biblical Apostolate is related to the Secretariat for Pastoral Research and Practices, National Conference of Catholic Bishops, 3211 Fourth St. N.E., Washington, DC 20017.

## APOCRYPHA

In Catholic usage, Apocrypha are books which have some resemblance to the canonical books in subject matter and title but which have not been recognized as canonical by the Church. They are characterized by a false claim to divine authority; extravagant accounts of events and miracles alleged to be supplemental revelation; material favoring heresy (especially in "New Testament" apocrypha); minimal, if any, historical value. Among examples of this type of literature itemized by J. McKenzie, S.J., in *Dictionary of the Bible* are: the Books of Adam and Eve, Martyrdom of Isaiah, Testament of the Patriarchs, Assumption of Moses, Sibylline Oracles; Gospel of James, Gospel of Thomas, Arabic Gospel of the Infancy, History of Joseph the Carpenter; Acts of John, Acts of Paul, Acts of Peter, Acts of Andrew, and numerous epistles.

Books of this type are called pseudepigrapha by Protestants.

In Protestant usage, some books of the Catholic Bible (deuterocanonical) are called apocrypha because their inspired character is rejected.

## DEAD SEA SCROLLS

The Qumran Scrolls, popularly called the Dead Sea Scrolls, are a collection of manuscripts, all but one of them in Hebrew, found since 1947 in caves in the Desert of Juda west of the Dead Sea.

Among the findings were a complete text of Isaiah dating from the second century, B.C., more or less extensive fragments of other Old Testament texts (including the deuterocanonical Tobit), and a commentary on Habakkuk. Until the discovery of these materials, the oldest known Hebrew manuscripts were from the 10th century, A.D.

Also found were messianic and apocalyptic texts, and other writings describing the beliefs and practices of the Essenes, a rigoristic Jewish sect.

The scrolls, dating from about the first century before and after Christ, are important sources of information about Hebrew literature, Jewish history during the period between the Old and New Testaments, and the history of Old Testament texts. They established the fact that the Hebrew text of the Old Testament was fixed before the beginning of the Christian era and have had definite effects in recent critical studies and translations of the Old Testament. Together with other scrolls found at Masada, they are still the subject of intensive study.

# BOOKS OF THE BIBLE

## OLD TESTAMENT
(Dates are before Christ)

### Pentateuch

The Pentateuch is the collective title of the first five books of the Bible. Substantially, they identify the Israelites as Yahweh's Chosen People, cover their history from Egypt to the threshold of the Promised Land, contain the Mosaic Law and Covenant, and disclose the promise of salvation to come. Principal themes concern the divine promise of salvation, Yahweh's fidelity and the Covenant. Work on the composition of the Pentateuch was completed in the sixth century.

**Genesis:** The book of origins, according to its title in the Septuagint. In two parts, covers: religious prehistory, including accounts of the origin of the world and man, the original state of innocence and the fall, the promise of salvation, patriarchs before and after the Deluge, the Tower of Babel narrative, genealogies (first 11 chapters); the Covenant with Abraham and patriarchal history from Abraham to Joseph (balance of the 50 chapters). Significant are the themes of Yahweh's universal sovereignty and mercy.

**Exodus:** Named with the Greek word for departure, is a religious epic which describes the oppression of the 12 tribes in Egypt and their departure, liberation or passover therefrom under the leadership of Moses; Yahweh's establishment of the Covenant with them, making them his Chosen People, through the mediation of Moses at Mt. Sinai; instructions concerning the tabernacle, the sanctuary and Ark of the Covenant; the institution of the priesthood. The book is significant because of its theology of liberation and redemption. In Christian interpretation, the Exodus is a figure of baptism.

**Leviticus:** Mainly legislative in theme and purpose, contains laws regarding sacrifices, ceremonies of ordination and the priesthood of Aaron, legal purity, the holiness code, atonement, the redemption of offerings and other subjects. Summarily, Levitical laws provided directives for all aspects of religious observance and for the manner in which the Israelites were to conduct themselves with respect to Yahweh and each other. Leviticus was the liturgical handbook of the priesthood.

**Numbers:** Taking its name from censuses recounted at the beginning and near the end, is a continuation of Exodus. It combines narrative of the Israelites' desert pilgrimage from Sinai to the border of Canaan with laws related to and expansive of those in Leviticus.

**Deuteronomy:** The concluding book of the Pentateuch, recapitulates, in the form of a testament of Moses, the Law and much of the desert history of the Israelites; enjoins fidelity to the Law as the key to good or bad fortune for the people; gives an account of the commissioning of Joshua as the successor of Moses. Notable themes concern the election of Israel by Yahweh, observance of the Law, prohibitions against the worship of foreign gods, worship of and confidence in Yahweh, the power of Yahweh in nature. The Deuteronomic Code or motif, embodying all of these elements, was the norm for interpreting Israelite history.

### Joshua, Judges, Ruth

**Joshua:** Records the fulfillment of Yahweh's promise to the Israelites in their conquest, occupation and division of Canaan under the leadership of Joshua. It also contains an account of the return of Transjordanian Israelites and of a renewal of the Covenant. It was redacted in final form probably in the sixth century or later.

**Judges:** Records the actions of charismatic leaders, called judges, of the tribes of Israel between the death of Joshua and the time of Samuel, and a crisis of idolatry among the people. The basic themes are sin and punishment, repentance and deliverance; its purpose was in line with the Deuteronomic motif, that the fortunes of the Israelites were related to their observance or non-observance of the Law and the Covenant. It was redacted in final form probably in the sixth century.

**Ruth:** Named for the Gentile (Moabite) woman who, through marriage with Boaz, became an Israelite and an ancestress of David (her son, Obed, became his grandfather). Themes are filial piety, faith and trust in Yahweh, the universality of messianic salvation. Dates ranging from c. 950 to the seventh century have been assigned to the origin of the book, whose author is unknown.

## Historical Books

These books, while they contain a great deal of factual material, are unique in their preoccupation with presenting and interpreting it, in the Deuteronomic manner, in primary relation to the Covenant on which the nation of Israel was founded and in accordance with which community and personal life were judged.

The books are: Samuel 1 and 2, from the end of Judges (c. 1020) to the end of David's reign (c. 961); Kings 1 and 2, from the last days of David to the start of the Babylonian Exile and the destruction of the Temple (587); Chronicles 1 and 2, from the reign of Saul (c. 1020-1000) to the return of the people from the Exile (538); Ezra and Nehemiah, covering the reorganization of the Jewish community after the Exile (458-397); Maccabees 1 and 2, recounting the struggle against attempted suppression of Judaism (168-142).

Three of the books listed below — Tobit, Judith and Esther — are categorized as religious novels.

**Samuel 1 and 2:** A single work in concept and contents, containing episodic history of the last two Judges, Eli and Samuel, the establishment and rule of the monarchy under Saul and David, and the political consequences of David's rule. The royal messianic dynasty of David was the subject of Nathan's oracle in 2 Sm. 7. The books were edited in final form probably late in the seventh century or during the Exile.

**Kings 1 and 2:** Cover the last days of David and the career of Solomon, including the building of the Temple and the history of the kingdom during his reign; stories of the prphets Elijah and Elisha; the history of the divided kingdom to the fall of Israel in the North (721) and the fall of Judah in the South (587), the destruction of Jerusalem and the Temple. They reflect the Deuteronomic motif in attributing the downfall of the people to corruption of belief and practice in public and private life. They were completed probably in the sixth century.

**Chronicles 1 and 2:** A collection of historical traditions interpreted in such a way as to present an ideal picture of one people governed by divine law and united in one Temple worship of the one true God. Contents include genealogical tables from Adam to David, the careers of David and Solomon, coverage of the kingdom of Judah to the Exile, and the decree of Cyrus permitting the return of the people and rebuilding of Jerusalem. Both are related to and were written about 400 by the same author, the Chronicler, who composed Ezra and Nehemiah.

**Ezra and Nehemiah:** A running account of the return of the people to their homeland after the Exile and of practical efforts, under the leadership of Ezra and Nehemiah, to restore and reorganize the religious and political community on the basis of Israelite traditions, divine worship and observance of the Law. Events of great significance were the building of the second Temple, the building of a wall around Jerusalem and the proclamation of the Law by Ezra. This restored community was the start of Judaism. Both are related to and were written about 400 by the same author, the Chronicler, who composed Chronicles 1 and 2.

**Tobit:** Written in the literary form of a novel and having greater resemblance to wisdom than to historical literature, narrates the personal history of Tobit, a devout and charitable Jew in exile, and persons connected with him, viz., his son Tobiah, his kinsman Raguel and Raguel's daughter Sarah. Its purpose was to teach people how to be good Jews. One of its principal themes is patience under trial, with trust in divine Providence which is symbolized by the presence and action of the angel Raphael. It was written about 200.

**Judith:** Recounts, in the literary form of a historical novel or romance, the preservation of the Israelites from conquest and ruin through the action of Judith. The essential themes are trust in God for deliverance from danger and emphasis on observance of the Law. It was written probably during the Maccabean period.

**Esther:** Relates, in the literary form of a historical novel or romance, the manner in which Jews in Persia were saved from annihilation through the central role played by Esther, the Jewish wife of Ahasuerus; a fact commemorated by the Jewish feast of Purim. Like Judith, it has trust in divine Providence as its theme and indicates that God's saving will is sometimes realized by persons acting in unlikely ways. It may have been written near the end of the fourth century.

**Maccabees 1 and 2:** While related to some extent because of common subject matter, are quite different from each other.

The first book recounts the background and events of the 40-year (175-135) struggle for religious and political freedom led by Judas Maccabeus and his brothers against the Hellenist Seleucid kings and some Hellenophiles among the Jews. Victory was symbolized by the rededication of the Temple. Against the background of opposition between Jews and Gentiles, the author equated the survival of belief in the one true God with survival of the Jewish people, thus identifying religion with patriotism. It was written probably near the year 100.

The second book supplements the first to some extent, covering and giving a theological interpretation to events from 180 to 162. It explains the feast of the Dedication of the Temple, a key event in the survival of Judaism which is commemorated in the feast of Hanukkah; stresses the primacy of God's action in the struggle for survival; and indicates belief in an afterlife and the resurrection of the body. It was completed probably about 124.

## Wisdom Books

With the exceptions of Psalms and the Song of Songs, the titles listed under this heading are called wisdom books because their purpose was to formulate the fruits of human experience in the context of meditation on sacred Scripture and to present them as an aid toward understanding the problems of life. Hebrew wisdom literature was distinctive from pagan literature of the same type, but it had limitations; these were overcome in the New Testament, which added the dimensions of the New Covenant to those of the Old. Solomon was regarded as the archtype of the wise man.

**Job:** A dramatic, didactic poem consisting mainly of several dialogues between Job and his friends concerning the mystery involved in the coexistence of the just God, evil and the suffering of the just. It describes an innocent man's experience of suffering and conveys the truth that faith in and submission to God rather than complete understanding, which is impossible, make the experience bearable; also, that the justice of God cannot be defended by affirming that it is realized in this world. Of unknown authorship, it was composed between the seventh and fifth centuries.

**Psalms:** A collection of 150 religious songs or lyrics reflecting Israelite belief and piety dating from the time of the monarchy to the post-Exilic period, a span of well over 500 years. The psalms, which are a compendium of Old Testament theology, were used in the temple liturgy and for other occasions. They were of several types suitable for the king, hymns, lamentations, expressions of confidence and thanksgiving, prophecy, historical meditation and reflection, and the statement of wisdom. About one-half of them are attributed to David; many were composed by unknown authors.

**Proverbs:** The oldest book of the wisdom type in the Bible, consisting of collections of sayings attributed to Solomon and other persons regarding a wide variety of subjects including wisdom and its nature, rules of conduct, duties with respect to one's neighbor, the conduct of daily affairs. It reveals many details of Hebrew life. Its nucleus dates from the period before the Exile. The extant form of the book dates probably from the end of the fifth century.

**Ecclesiastes:** A treatise about many subjects whose unifying theme is the vanity of strictly human efforts and accomplishments with respect to the achievement of lasting happiness; the only things which are not vain are fear of the Lord and observance of his commandments. The pessimistic tone of the book is due to the absence of a concept of afterlife. It was written by an unknown author probably in the third century.

**Song of Songs:** A collection of love lyrics reflecting various themes, including the love of God for Israel and the celebration of ideal love and fidelity between man and woman. It was written by an unknown author after the Exile.

**Wisdom:** Deals with many subjects including the reward of justice; praise of wisdom, a gift of Yahweh proceeding from belief in him and the practice of his Law; the part played by him in the history of his people, especially in their liberation from Egypt; the folly and shame of idolatry. Its contents are taken from the whole sacred literature of he Jews and represent a distillation of its wisdom based on the law, beliefs and traditions of Israel. The last of the Old Testament books, it was written in the early part of the first century before Christ by a member of the Jewish community at Alexandria.

**Sirach:** Resembling Proverbs, is a collection of sayings handed on by a grandfather to his grandson. It contains a variety of moral instruction and eulogies of patriarchs and other figures in Israelite history. Its moral maxims apply to individuals, the family and community, relations with God, friendship, education, wealth, the Law, divine worship. Its theme is that true wisdom consists in the Law. (It was formerly called Ecclesiasticus, the Church Book, because of its extensive use by the Church for moral instruction.) It was written in Hebrew between 200 and 175, during a period of strong hellenistic influence, and was translated into Greek after 132.

## The Prophets

These books and the prophecies they contain "express judgments of the people's moral conduct, on the basis of the Mosaic alliance between God and Israel. They teach sublime truths and lofty morals. They contain exhortations, threats, announcements of punishment, promises of deliverance. In the affairs of men, their prime concern is the interests of God, especially in what pertains to the Chosen People through whom the Messiah is to come; hence their denunciations of idolatry and of that externalism in worship which exclude the interior spirit of religion. They are concerned also with the universal nature of the moral law, with personal responsibility, with the person and office of the Messiah, and with the conduct of foreign nations" (*The Holy Bible*, Prophetic Books, CCD Edition, 1961; Preface). There are four major (Isaiah, Jeremiah, Ezekiel, Daniel) and 12 minor prophets (distinguished by the length of books), Lamentations and Baruch. Earlier prophets, mentioned in historical books, include Samuel, Gad, Nathan, Elijah and Elisha.

Before the Exile, prophets were the intermediaries through whom God communicated revelation to the people. Afterwards, prophecy lapsed and the written word of the Law served this purpose.

**Isaiah:** Named for the greatest of the prophets whose career spanned the reigns of three Hebrew kings from 742 to the beginning of the seventh century, in a period of moral breakdown in Judah and threats of invasion by foreign enemies. It is an anthology of poems and oracles credited to him and a number of followers deeply influenced by him. Of special importance are the prophecies concerning Immanuel (6 to 12), including the prophecy of the virgin birth (7:14). Chapters 40 to 55, called Deutero-Isaiah, are attributed to an anonymous poet toward the end of the Exile; this portion contains the Songs of the Servant. The concluding part of the book (56-66) contains oracles by later disciples. One of many themes in Isaiah concerned the saving mission of the remnant of Israel in the divine plan of salvation.

**Jeremiah:** Combines history, biography and prophecy in a setting of crisis caused by internal and external factors, viz., idolatry and general infidelity to the Law among the Israelites and external threats from the Assyrians, Egyptians and Babylonians. Jeremiah prophesied the promise of a new covenant as well as the destruction of Jerusalem and the Temple. His career began in 626 and ended some years after the beginning of the Exile. The book, the longest in the Bible, was edited in final form after the Exile.

**Lamentations:** A collection of five laments or elegies over the fall of Jerusalem and the fate of the people in Exile, written by an unknown eyewitness. They convey the message that Yahweh struck the people because of their sins and reflect confidence in his love and power to restore his converted people.

**Baruch:** Against the background of the already begun Exile, it consists of an introduction and several parts: an exile's prayer of confession and petition for forgiveness and the restoration of Israel; a poem praising wisdom and the Law of Moses; a lament in which Jerusalem, personified, bewails the fate of her people and consoles them with the hope of blessings to come; and a polemic against idolatry. Although ascribed to Baruch, Jeremiah's secretary, it was written by several authors probably in the second century.

**Ezekiel:** Named for the priest-prophet who prophesied in Babylon from 593 to 571, during the first phase of the Exile. To prepare his fellow early exiles for the impending fall of Jerusalem, he reproached the Israelites for past sins and predicted woes to come upon them. After the destruction of the city, the burden of his message was hope and promise of restoration. Ezekiel had great influence on the religion of Israel after the Exile.

**Daniel:** The protagonist is a young Jew, taken early to Babylon where he lived until about 538, who figured in a series of edifying stories which originated in Israelite tradition. The stories, whose characters are not purely legendary but rest on historical tradition, recount the trials and triumphs of Daniel and his three companions, and other episodes including those concerning Susanna, Bel, and the Dragon. The book is more apocalyptic than prophetic: it envisions Israel in glory to come and conveys the message that men of faith can resist temptation and overcome adversity. It states the prophetic themes of right conduct, divine control of men and events, and the final triumph of the kingdom. It was written by an unknown author in the 160's to give moral support to Jews during the persecutions of the Maccabean period.

**Hosea:** Consists of a prophetic parallel between Hosea's marriage and Yahweh's relations with his people. As the prophet was married to a faithless wife whom he would not give up, Yahweh was bound in Covenant with an idolatrous and unjust Israel whom he would not desert but would chastise for purification. Hosea belonged to the Northern Kingdom of Israel and began his career about the middle of the eighth century. He inaugurated the tradition of describing Yahweh's relation to Israel in terms of marriage.

**Joel:** Is apocalyptic and eschatological regarding divine judgment, the Day of the Lord, which is symbolized by a ravaging invasion of locusts, the judgment of the nations in the Valley of Josaphat and the outpouring of the Spirit in the messianic era to come. Its message is that God will vindicate and save Israel, in view of the prayer and repentance of the people, and will punish their enemies. It was composed about 400.

**Amos:** Consists of an indictment against foreign enemies of Israel; a strong denunciation of the people of Israel, whose infidelity, idolatry and injustice made them subject to divine judgment and punishment; and a messianic oracle regarding Israel's restoration. Amos prophesied in the Northern Kingdom of Israel, at Bethel, in the first half of the eighth century; chronologically, he was the first of the canonical prophets.

**Obadiah:** A 21-verse prophecy, the shortest and one of the sternest in the Bible, against the Edomites, invaders of southern Judah and enemies of those returning from the Exile to their homeland. It was probably composed in the fifth century.

**Jonah:** A parable of divine mercy with the theme that Yahweh wills the salvation of all, not just a few, men who respond to his call. Its protagonist is a disobedient prophet; forced by circumstances beyond his control to preach penance among Gentiles, he is highly successful in his mission but baffled by the divine concern for those who do not belong to the Chosen People. It was written after the Exile, probably in the fifth century.

**Micah:** Attacks the injustice and corruption of priests, false prophets, officials and people; announces judgment and punishment to come; foretells the restoration of Israel; refers to the saving remnant of Israel. Micah was a contemporary of Isaiah.

**Nahum:** Concerns the destruction of Nineveh in 612 and the overthrow of the Assyrian Empire by the Babylonians.

**Habakkuk:** Dating from about 605-597, concerns sufferings to be inflicted by oppressors on the people of Judah because of their infidelity to the Lord. It also sounds a note of confidence in the Lord, the Savior, and declares that the just will not perish.

**Zephaniah:** Exercising his ministry in the second half of the seventh century, during a time of widespread idolatry, superstition and religious degradation, he prophesied impending judgment and punishment for Jerusalem and its people. He prophesied too that a holy remnant of the people (*anawim*, mentioned also by Amos) would be spared. Zephaniah was a forerunner of Jeremiah.

**Haggai:** One of the first prophets after the Exile, Haggai in 520 encouraged the returning exiles to reestablish their community and to complete the second Temple (dedicated in 515), for which he envisioned greater glory, in a messianic sense, than that enjoyed by the original Temple of Solomon.

**Zechariah:** A contemporary of Haggai, he prophesied in the same vein. A second part of the book, called Deutero-Zechariah and composed by one or more unknown authors, relates a vision of the coming of the Prince of Peace, the Messiah of the Poor.

**Malachi:** Written by an anonymous author, presents a picture of life in the post-Exilic community between 516 and the initiation of reforms by Ezra and Nehemiah about 432. Blame for the troubles of the community is placed mainly on priests for failure to carry out ritual worship and to instruct the people in the proper manner; other factors were religious indifference and the influence of doubters who were scandalized at the prosperity of the wicked. The vision of a universal sacrifice to be offered to

Yahweh (1:11) is interpreted in Catholic theology as a prophecy of the sacrifice of the Mass. Malachi was the last of the minor prophets.

## OLD TESTAMENT DATES

**c. 1800 — c. 1600:** Period of the patriarchs (Abraham, Isaac, Jacob).

**c. 1600:** Israelites in Egypt.

**c. 1250:** Exodus of Israelites from Egypt.

**c. 1210:** Entrance of Israelites into Canaan.

**c. 1210 — c. 1020:** Period of the Judges.

**c. 1020 — c. 1000:** Reign of Saul, first king.

**c. 1000 — c. 961:** Reign of David.

**c. 961 — 922:** Reign of Solomon. Temple built during his reign.

**922:** Division of the Kingdom into Israel (North) and Judah (South).

**721:** Conquest of Israel by Assyrians.

**587-538:** Conquest of Judah by Babylonians. Babylonian Captivity and Exile. Destruction of Jerusalem and the Temple, 587. Captivity ended with the return of exiles, following the decree of Cyrus permitting the rebuilding of Jerusalem.

**515:** Dedication of the Second Temple.

**458-397:** Restoration and reform of the Jewish religious and political community; building of the Jerusalem wall, 439. Leaders in the movement were Ezra and Nehemiah.

**168-142:** Period of the Maccabees; war against Syrians.

**142:** Independence granted to Jews by Demetrius II of Syria.

**135-37:** Period of the Hasmonean dynasty.

**63:** Beginning of Roman rule.

**37-4:** Period of Herod the Great.

## NEW TESTAMENT BOOKS

### Gospels

The term Gospel is derived from the Anglo-Saxon *god-spell* and the Greek *euangelion*, meaning good news, good tidings. In Christian use, it means the good news of salvation proclaimed by Christ and the Church, and handed on in written form in the Gospels of Matthew, Mark, Luke and John.

The initial proclamation of the coming of the kingdom of God was made by Jesus in and through his Person, teachings and actions, and especially through his Passion, death and resurrection. This proclamation became the center of Christian faith and the core of the oral Gospel tradition with which the Church spread the good news by apostolic preaching for some 30 years before it was committed to writing by the Evangelists.

### Nature of the Gospels

The historical truth of the Gospels was the subject of an instruction issued by the Pontifical Commission for Biblical Studies Apr. 21, 1964.

• The sacred writers selected from the material at their disposal (the oral Gospel tradition, some written collections of sayings and deeds of Jesus, eyewitness accounts) those things which were particularly suitable to the various conditions (liturgical, catechetical, missionary) of the faithful and the aims they had in mind, and they narrated these things in such a way as to correspond with those circumstances and their aims.

• The life and teaching of Jesus were not simply reported in a biographical manner for the purpose of preserving their memory but were "preached" so as to offer the Church the basis of doctrine concerning faith and morals.

• In their works, the Evangelists presented the true sayings of Jesus and the events of his life in the light of the better understanding they had following their enlightenment by the Holy Spirit. They did not transform Christ into a "mythical" Person, nor did they distort his teaching. Passion narratives are the core of all the Gospels, covering the suffering, death and resurrection of Jesus as central events in bringing about and establishing the New Covenant. Leading up to them are accounts of the mission of John the Baptizer and the ministry of Jesus, especially in Galilee and finally in Jerusalem before the Passion. The infancy of Jesus is covered by Luke and Matthew with narratives inspired in part by appropriate Old Testament citations.

Matthew, Mark and Luke, while different in various respects, have so many similarities that they are called Synoptic; their relationships are the subject of the Synoptic Problem.

**Matthew:** Written probably between 80 and 100 for Jewish Christians with clear reference to Jewish background and identification of Jesus as the divine Messiah, the fulfillment of the Old Testament. Distinctive are the use of Old Testament citations regarding the Person, activity and teaching of Jesus, and the presentation of doctrine in sermons and discourses.

**Mark:** The first of the Gospels, dating from about 70. Written for Gentile Christians, it is noted for the realism and wealth of concrete details with which it reveals Jesus as Son of God and Savior more by his actions and miracles than by his discourses. Theologically, it is less refined than the other Gospels.

**Luke:** Written about 75 for Gentile Christians. It is noted for the universality of its address, the insight it provides into the Christian way of life, the place it gives to women, the manner in which it emphasizes Jesus' friendship with sinners and compassion for the suffering.

**John:** Edited and arranged in final form probably between 90 and 100, is the most sublime and theological of the Gospels, and is different from the Synoptics in plan and treatment. Combining accounts of signs with longer discourses and reflections, it progressively reveals the Person and mission of Jesus — as Word, Way, Truth, Life, Light — in line with the purpose, "to help you believe that Jesus is the Messiah, the Son of God, so that through this faith you may have life in his name" (Jn. 20:31). There are questions about the authorship but no doubt about the Johannine authority and tradition behind the Gospel.

### Acts of the Apostles

**Acts of the Apostles:** Written by Luke about 75 as a supplement to his Gospel. It describes the origin and spread of Christian communities through the action of the Holy Spirit from the resurrection of Christ to the time when Paul was placed in custody in Rome in the early 60s.

## Letters (Epistles)

These letters, many of which antedated the Gospels, were written in response to existential needs of the early Christian communities for doctrinal and moral instruction, disciplinary action, practical advice, and exhortation to true Christian living.

## Pauline Letters

These letters, which comprise approximately one-fourth of the New Testament, are primary and monumental sources of the development of Christian theology. Several of them may not have had Paul as their actual author, but evidence of the Pauline tradition behind them is strong. The letters to the Colossians, Philippians, Ephesians and Philemon have been called the "Captivity Letters" because of a tradition that they were written while Paul was under house arrest or another form of detention.

**Romans:** Written about 57 probably from Corinth on the central significance of Christ and faith in him for salvation, and the relationship of Christianity to Judaism; the condition of mankind without Christ; justification and the Christian life; duties of Christians.

**Corinthians 1:** Written near the beginning of 57 from Ephesus to counteract factionalism and disorders, it covers community dissensions, moral irregularities, marriage and celibacy, conduct at religious gatherings, the Eucharist, spiritual gifts (charisms) and their function in the Church, charity, the resurrection of the body.

**Corinthians 2:** Written later in the same year as 1 Cor., concerning Paul's defense of his apostolic ministry, and an appeal for a collection to aid poor Christians in Jerusalem.

**Galatians:** Written probably between 54 and 55 to counteract Judaizing opinions and efforts to undermine his authority, it asserts the divine origin of Paul's authority and doctrine, states that justification is not through Mosaic Law but through faith in Christ, insists on the practice of evangelical virtues, especially charity.

**Ephesians:** Written probably between 61 and 63, mainly on the Church as the Mystical Body of Christ.

**Philippians:** Written between 56 and 57 or 61 and 63 to warn the Philippians against enemies of their faith, to urge them to be faithful to their vocation and unity of belief, and to thank them for their kindness to him while he was being held in detention.

**Colossians:** Written probably while he was under house arrest in Rome from 61 to 63, to counteract the influence of self-appointed teachers who were watering down doctrine concerning Christ. It includes two highly important Christological passages, a warning against false teachers, and an instruction on the ideal Christian life.

**Thessalonians 1 and 2:** Written within a short time of each other probably in 51 from Corinth, mainly on doctrine concerning the Parousia, the second coming of Christ.

**Timothy 1 and 2, Titus:** Written between 65 and 67, or perhaps in the 70's, giving pastoral counsels to Timothy and Titus who were in charge of churches in Ephesus and Crete, respectively. 1 Tm. emphasizes pastoral responsibility for preserving unity of doctrine; 2 Tm. describes Paul's imprisonment in Rome.

**Philemon:** A private letter written between 61 and 63 to a wealthy Colossian concerning a slave, Onesimus, who had escaped from him; Paul appealed for kind treatment of the man.

**Hebrews:** Dating from sometime between 70 and 96, a complex theological treatise on Christology, the priesthood and sacrifice of Christ, the New Covenant, and the pattern for Christian living. Critical opinion is divided as to whether it was addressed to Judaeo or Gentile Christians.

## Catholic Letters, Revelation

These seven letters have been called "catholic" because it was thought for some time, not altogether correctly, that they were not addressed to particular communities.

**James:** Written sometime before 62 in the spirit of Hebrew wisdom literature and the moralism of Tobit. An exhortation to practical Christian living, it is also noteworthy for the doctrine it states on good works and its citation regarding anointing of the sick.

**Peter 1 and 2:** The first letter may have been written between 64 and 67 or between 90 and 95; the second may date from 100 to 125. Addressed to Christians in Asia Minor, both are exhortations to perseverance in the life of faith despite trials and difficulties arising from pagan influences, isolation from other Christians and false teaching.

**John 1:** Written sometime in the 90s and addressed to Asian churches, its message is that God is made known to us in the Son and that fellowship with the Father is attained by living in the light, justice and love of the Son.

**John 2:** Written sometime in the 90s and addressed to a church in Asia, it commends the people for standing firm in the faith and urges them to perseverance.

**John 3:** Written sometime in the 90s, it appears to represent an effort to settle a jurisdictional dispute in one of the churches.

**Jude:** Written probably about 80, it is a brief treatise against erroneous teachings and practices opposed to law, authority and true Christian freedom.

**Revelation:** Written in the 90s along the lines of Johannine thought, it is a symbolic and apocalyptic treatment of things to come and of the struggle between the Church and evil combined with warning but hope and assurance to the Church regarding the coming of the Lord in glory.

## BASILICA IN NEWARK

With prayerful pageantry Mar. 29, 1996, the Archdiocese of Newark marked the designation of its Cathedral of the Sacred Heart as a minor basilica. An example of French Gothic architecture, it covers 40,000 square feet, can accommodate 3,000 people and has 232-feet-high twin towers which are taller than those of Notre Dame in Paris or Westminster Abbey in London. The title of basilica is reserved for churches of exceptional importance for various reasons.

# INTERPRETATION OF THE BIBLE

According to the *Constitution on Revelation* issued by the Second Vatican Council, "the interpreter of Sacred Scripture, in order to see clearly what God wanted to communicate to us, should carefully investigate what meaning the sacred writers really intended, and what God wanted to manifest by means of their words" (No. 12).

## Hermeneutics, Exegesis

This careful investigation proceeds in accordance with the rules of hermeneutics, the normative science of biblical interpetation and explanation. Hermeneutics in practice is called exegesis.

The principles of hermeneutics are derived from various disciplines and many factors which have to be considered in explaining the Bible and its parts. These include: the original languages and languages of translation of the sacred texts, through philology and linguistics; the quality of texts, through textual criticism; literary forms and genres, through literary and form criticism; cultural, historical, geographical and other conditions which influenced the writers, through related studies; facts and truths of salvation history; the truths and analogy of faith.

Distinctive to biblical hermeneutics, which differs in important respects from literary interpretation in general, is the premise that the Bible, though written by human authors, is the work of divine inspiration in which God reveals his plan for the salvation of men through historical events and persons, and especially through the Person and mission of Christ.

## Textual, Form Criticism

Textual criticism is the study of biblical texts, which have been transmitted in copies several times removed from the original manuscripts, for the purpose of establishing the real state of the original texts. This purpose is served by comparison of existing copies; by application to the texts of the disciplines of philology and linguistics; by examination of related works of antiquity; by study of biblical citations in works of the Fathers of the Church and other authors; and by other means of literary study.

Since about 1920, the sayings of Christ have been a particular object of New Testament study, the purpose being to analyze the forms of expression used by the Evangelists in order to ascertain the words actually spoken by him.

## Literary Criticism

Literary criticism aims to determine the origin and kinds of literary composition, called forms or genres, employed by the inspired authors. Such determinations are necessary for decision regarding the nature and purpose and, consequently, the meaning of biblical passages. Underlying these studies is the principle that the manner of writing was conditioned by the intention of the authors, the meaning they wanted to convey, and the then-contemporary literary style, mode or medium best adapted to carry their message — e.g., true history, quasi-historical narrative, poems, prayers, hymns, psalms, aphorisms, allegories, discourses. Understanding these media is necessary for the valid interpretation of their message.

## Literal Sense

The key to all valid interpretation is the literal sense of biblical passages. Regarding this matter and the relevance to it of the studies and procedures described above, Pius XII wrote the following in the encyclical *Divino Afflante Spiritu*.

"What the literal sense of a passage is, is not always as obvious in the speeches and writings of ancient authors of the East as it is in the works of our own time. For what they wished to express is not to be determined by the rules of grammar and philology alone nor solely by the context; the interpreter must, as it were, go back wholly in spirit to those remote centuries of the East and with the aid of history, archeology, ethnology, and other sciences accurately determine what modes of writing, so to speak, the authors of that ancient period would be likely to use and in fact did use. In explaining the Sacred Scripture and in demonstrating and proving its immunity from all error (the Catholic interpreter) should make a prudent use of this means, determine to what extent the manner of expression or literary mode adopted by the sacred writer may lead to a correct and genuine interpretation; and let him be convinced that this part of his office cannot be neglected without serious detriment to Catholic exegesis."

The literal sense of the Bible is the meaning in the mind of and intended by the inspired writer of a book or passage of the Bible. This is determined by the application to texts of the rules of hermeneutics. It is not to be confused with word-for-word literalism.

## Typical Sense

The typical sense is the meaning which a passage has not only in itself but also in reference to something else of which it is a type or foreshadowing. A clear example is the account of the Exodus of the Israelites: in its literal sense, it narrates the liberation of the Israelites from death and oppression in Egypt; in its typical sense, it foreshadowed the liberation of men from sin through the redemptive death and resurrection of Christ. The typical sense of this and other passages emerged in the working out of God's plan of salvation history. It did not have to be in the mind of the author of the original passage.

## Accommodated Senses

Accommodated, allegorical and consequent senses are figurative and adaptive meanings given to books and passages of the Bible for moral and other purposes. Such interpretations involve the danger of stretching the literal sense beyond proper proportions. Hermeneutical principles require that interpretations like these respect the integrity of the literal sense of the passages in question.

In the Catholic view, the final word on questions of biblical interpretation belongs to the teaching authority of the Church. In other views, generally derived from basic principles stated by Martin Luther, John Calvin and other reformers, the primacy belongs to individual judgment acting in response to the inner testimony of the Holy Spirit, the edifying nature of biblical subject matter, the sublimity and simplicity of the message of salvation, the intensity with which Christ is proclaimed.

## Biblical Studies

The first center for biblical studies, in some strict sense of the term, was the School of Alexandria, founded in the latter half of the second century. It was noted for allegorical exegesis. Literal interpretation was a hallmark of the School of Antioch.

St. Jerome, who produced the Vulgate, and St. Augustine, author of numerous commentaries, were the most important figures in biblical studies during the patristic period. By the time of the latter's death, the Old and New Testament canons had been stabilized. For some centuries afterwards, there was little or no progress in scriptural studies, although commentaries were written, collections were made of scriptural excerpts from the writings of the Fathers of the Church, and the systematic reading of Scripture became established as a feature of monastic life.

Advances were made in the 12th and 13th centuries with the introduction of new principles and methods of scriptural analysis stemming from renewed interest in Hebraic studies and the application of dialectics.

By the time of the Reformation, the Bible had become the first book set in movable type, and more than 100 vernacular editions were in use throughout Europe.

## The Council of Trent

In the wake of the Reformation, the Council of Trent formally defined the Canon of the Bible; it also reasserted the authoritative role of tradition and the teaching authority of the Church as well as Scripture with respect to the rule of faith. In the heated atmosphere of the 16th and 17th centuries, the Bible was turned into a polemical weapon; Protestants used it to defend their doctrines, and Catholics countered with citations in support of the dogmas of the Church. One result of this state of affairs was a lack of substantial progress in biblical studies during the period.

Rationalists from the 18th century on and later Modernists denied the reality of the supernatural and doctrine concerning inspiration of the Bible, which they generally regarded as a strictly human production expressive of the religious sense and experience of mankind. In their hands, the tools of positive critical research became weapons for biblical subversion. The defensive Catholic reaction to ther work had the temporary effect of alienating scholars of the Church from solid advances in archeology, philology, history, textual and literary criticism.

## Catholic Developments

Major influences in bringing about a change in Catholic attitude toward use of these disciplines in biblical studies were two papal encyclicals and two institutes of special study, the Ecole Biblique, founded in Jerusalem in 1890, and the Pontifical Biblical Institute established in Rome in 1909. The encyclical *Providentissimus Deus*, issued by Leo XIII in 1893, marked an important breakthrough; in addition to defending the concept of divine inspiration and the formal inspiration of the Scriptures, it encouraged the study of allied and ancillary sciences and techniques for a more fruitful understanding of the sacred writings. The encyclical *Divino Afflante Spiritu*, 50 years later, gave encouragement for the use of various forms of criticism as tools of biblical research. A significant addition to documents on the subject is "The Interpretation of the Bible," published by the Pontifical Biblical Commission in November, 1993. It presents an overview of approaches to the Bible and probes the question: "Which hermeneutical theory best enables a proper grasp of the profound reality of which Scripture speaks and its meaningful expression for people today?"

The documents encouraged the work of scholars and stimulated wide communication of the fruits of their study.

Great changes in the climate and direction of biblical studies have occurred in recent years. One of them has been an increase in cooperative effort among Catholic, Protestant, Orthodox and Jewish scholars. Their common investigation of the Dead Sea Scrolls is well known. Also productive has been the collaboration of Catholics and Protestants in turning out various editions of the Bible.

The development and results of biblical studies in this century have directly and significantly affected all phases of the contemporary renewal movement in the Church. Their influence on theology, liturgy, catechetics, and preaching indicate the importance of their function in the life of the Church.

# APOSTLES AND EVANGELISTS

The Apostles were the men selected, trained and commissioned by Christ to preach the Gospel, to baptize, to establish, direct and care for his Church as servants of God and stewards of his mysteries. They were the first bishops of the Church.

St. Matthew's Gospel lists the Apostles in this order: Peter, Andrew, James the Greater, John, Philip, Bartholomew, Thomas, Matthew, James the Less, Jude, Simon and Judas Iscariot. Matthias was elected to fill the place of Judas. Paul became an Apostle by a special call from Christ. Barnabas was called an Apostle.

Two of the Evangelists, John and Matthew, were Apostles. The other two, Luke and Mark, were closely associated with the apostolic college.

**Andrew:** Born in Bethsaida, brother of Peter, disciple of John the Baptist, a fisherman, the first Apostle called; according to legend, preached the Gospel in northern Greece, Epirus and Scythia, and was martyred at Patras about 70; in art, is represented with an x-shaped cross, called St. Andrew's Cross; is honored as the patron of Russia and Scotland; Nov. 30.

**Barnabas:** Originally called Joseph but named Barnabas by the Apostles, among whom he is ranked because of his collaboration with Paul; a Jew of the Diaspora, born in Cyprus; a cousin of Mark and member of the Christian community at Jerusalem, influenced the Apostles to accept Paul, with whom he became a pioneer missionary outside Palestine and Syria, to Antioch, Cyprus and southern Asia Minor; legend says he was martyred in Cyprus during the Neronian persecution; June 11.

**Bartholomew (Nathaniel):** A friend of Philip; according to various traditions, preached the Gospel in Ethiopia, India, Persia and Armenia, where he was martyred by being flayed and beheaded; in art, is depicted holding a knife, an instrument of his death; Aug. 24 (Roman Rite), Aug. 25 (Byzantine Rite).

**James the Greater:** A Galilean, son of Zebedee, brother of John (with whom he was called a "Son of Thunder"), a fisherman; with Peter and John, witnessed the raising of Jairus' daughter to life, the transfiguration, the agony of Jesus in the Garden of Gethsemani; first of the Apostles to die, by the sword in 44 during the rule of Herod Agrippa; there is doubt about a journey legend says he made to Spain and also about the authenticity of relics said to be his at Santiago de Compostela; in art, is depicted carrying a pilgrim's bell; July 25 (Roman Rite), Apr. 30 (Byzantine Rite).

**James the Less:** Son of Alphaeus, called "Less" because he was younger in age or shorter in stature than James the Greater; one of the Catholic Epistles bears his name; was stoned to death in 62 or thrown from the top of the temple in Jerusalem and clubbed to death in 66; in art, is depicted with a club or heavy staff; May 3 (Roman Rite), Oct. 9 (Byzantine Rite).

**John:** A Galilean, son of Zebedee, brother of James the Greater (with whom he was called a "Son of Thunder"), a fisherman, probably a disciple of John the Baptist, one of the Evangelists, called the "Beloved Disciple"; with Peter and James the Greater, witnessed the raising of Jairus' daughter to life, the transfiguration, the agony of Jesus in the Garden of Gethsemani; Mary was commended to his special care by Christ; the fourth Gospel, three Catholic Epistles and Revelation bear his name; according to various accounts, lived at Ephesus in Asia Minor for some time and died a natural death about 100; in art, is represented by an eagle, symbolic of the sublimity of the contents of his Gospel; Dec. 27 (Roman Rite), May 8 (Byzantine Rite).

**Jude Thaddeus:** One of the Catholic Epistles, the shortest, bears his name; various traditions say he preached the Gospel in Mesopotamia, Persia and elsewhere, and was martyred; in art, is depicted with a halberd, the instrument of his death; Oct. 28 (Roman Rite), June 19 (Byzantine Rite).

**Luke:** A Greek convert to the Christian community, called "our most dear physician" by Paul, of whom he was a missionary companion; author of the third Gospel and Acts of the Apostles; the place — Achaia, Bithynia, Egypt — and circumstances of his death are not certain; in art, is depicted as a man, a writer, or an ox (because his Gospel starts at the scene of temple sacrifice); Oct. 18.

**Mark:** A cousin of Barnabas and member of the first Christian community at Jerusalem; a missionary companion of Paul and Barnabas, then of Peter; author of the Gospel which bears his name; according to legend, founded the Church at Alexandria, was bishop there and was martyred in the streets of the city; in art, is depicted with his Gospel and a winged lion, symbolic of the voice of John the Bap-

tist crying in the wilderness, at the beginning of his Gospel; Apr. 25.

**Matthew:** A Galilean, called Levi by Luke and John and the son of Alphaeus by Mark, a tax collector, one of the Evangelists; according to various accounts, preached the Gospel in Judea, Ethiopia, Persia and Parthia, and was martyred; in art, is depicted with a spear, the instrument of his death, and as a winged man in his role as Evangelist; Sept. 21 (Roman Rite), Nov. 16 (Byzantine Rite).

**Matthias:** A disciple of Jesus whom the faithful 11 Apostles chose to replace Judas before the Resurrection; uncertain traditions report that he preached the Gospel in Palestine, Cappadocia or Ethiopia; in art, is represented with a cross and a halberd, the instruments of his death as a martyr; May 14 (Roman Rite), Aug. 9 (Byzantine Rite).

**Paul:** Born at Tarsus, of the tribe of Benjamin, a Roman citizen; participated in the persecution of Christians until the time of his miraculous conversion on the way to Damascus; called by Christ, who revealed himself to him in a special way; became the Apostle of the Gentiles, among whom he did most of his preaching in the course of three major missionary journeys through areas north of Palestine, Cyprus, Asia Minor and Greece; 14 epistles bear his name; two years of imprisonment at Rome, following initial arrest in Jerusalem and confinement at Caesarea, ended with martyrdom, by beheading, outside the walls of the city in 64 or 67 during the Neronian persecution; in art, is depicted in various ways with St. Peter, with a sword, in the scene of his conversion; June 29 (with St. Peter), Jan. 25 (Conversion).

**Peter:** Simon, son of Jona, born in Bethsaida, brother of Andrew, a fisherman; called Cephas or Peter by Christ who made him the chief of the Apostles and head of the Church as his vicar; named first in the listings of Apostles in the Synoptic Gospels and the Acts of the Apostles; with James the Greater and John, witnessed the raising of Jairus' daughter to life, the transfiguration, the agony of Jesus in the Garden of Gethsemani; was the first to preach the Gospel in and around Jerusalem and was the leader of the first Christian community there; established a local church in Antioch; presided over the Council of Jerusalem in 51; wrote two Catholic Epistles to the Christians in Asia Minor; established his see in Rome where he spent his last years and was martyred by crucifixion in 64 or 65 during the Neronian persecution; in art, is depicted carrying two keys, symbolic of his primacy in the Church; June 29 (with St. Paul), Feb. 22 (Chair of Peter).

**Philip:** Born in Bethsaida; according to legend, preached the Gospel in Phrygia where he suffered martyrdom by crucifixion; May 3 (Roman Rite), Nov. 14 (Byzantine Rite).

**Simon:** Called the Cananean or the Zealot; according to legend, preached in various places in the Middle East and suffered martyrdom by being sawed in two; in art, is depicted with a saw, the instrument of his death, or a book, symbolic of his zeal for the Law; Oct. 28 (Roman Rite), May 10 (Byzantine Rite).

**Thomas (Didymus):** Notable for his initial incredulity regarding the Resurrection and his subsequent forthright confession of the divinity of Christ risen from the dead; according to legend, preached the Gospel in places from the Caspian Sea to the Persian Gulf and eventually reached India where he was martyred near Madras; Thomas Christians trace their origin to him; in art, is depicted kneeling before the risen Christ, or with a carpenter's rule and square; feast, July 3 (Roman Rite), Oct. 6 (Byzantine Rite).

### Judas

The Gospels record only a few facts about Judas, the Apostle who betrayed Christ.

The only non-Galilean among the Apostles, he was from Carioth, a town in southern Judah. He was keeper of the purse in the apostolic band. He was called a petty thief by John. He voiced dismay at the waste of money, which he said might have been spent for the poor, in connection with the anointing incident at Bethany. He took the initiative in arranging the betrayal of Christ. Afterwards, he confessed that he had betrayed an innocent man and cast into the Temple the money he had received for that action. Of his death, Matthew says that he hanged himself; the Acts of the Apostles states that he swelled up and burst open; both reports deal more with the meaning than the manner of his death — the misery of the death of a sinner.

The consensus of speculation over the reason why Judas acted as he did in betraying Christ focuses on disillusionment and unwillingness to accept the concept of a suffering Messiah and personal suffering of his own as an Apostle.

# APOSTOLIC FATHERS, FATHERS, DOCTORS OF THE CHURCH

The writers listed below were outstanding and authoritative witnesses to authentic Christian belief and practice, and played significant roles in giving them expression.

## Apostolic Fathers

The Apostolic Fathers were Christian writers of the first and second centuries whose writings echo genuine apostolic teaching. Chief in importance are: St. Clement (d.c. 97), bishop of Rome and third successor of St. Peter in the papacy; St. Ignatius (50-c. 107), bishop of Antioch and second successor of St. Peter in that see, reputed to be a disciple of St. John; St. Polycarp (69-155), bishop of Smyrna and a disciple of St. John. The authors of the *Didache* and the *Epistle of Barnabas* are also numbered among the Apostolic Fathers.

Other early ecclesiastical writers included: St. Justin, martyr (100-165), of Asia Minor and Rome, a layman and apologist; St. Irenaeus (130-202), bishop of Lyons, who opposed Gnosticism; and St. Cyprian (210-258), bishop of Carthage, who opposed Novatianism.

## Fathers and Doctors

The Fathers of the Church were theologians and writers of the first eight centuries who were outstanding for sanctity and learning. They were such authoritative witnesses to the belief and teaching of the Church that their unanimous acceptance of doctrines as divinely revealed has been regarded as evidence that such doctrines were so received by the Church in line with apostolic tradition and Sacred Scripture. Their unanimous rejection of doctrines branded them as heretical. Their writings, however, were not necessarily free of error in all respects.

The greatest of these Fathers were: Sts. Ambrose, Augustine, Jerome and Gregory the Great in the West; Sts. John Chrysostom, Basil the Great, Gregory of Nazianzen and Athanasius in the East.

The Doctors of the Church were ecclesiastical writers of eminent learning and sanctity who have been given this title because of the great advantage the Church has derived from their work. Their writings, however, were not necessarily free of error in all respects.

**Albert the Great, St.** (c. 1200-1280): Born in Swabia, Germany; Dominican; bishop of Regensburg (1260-1262); wrote extensively on logic, natural sciences, ethics, metaphysics, Scripture, systematic theology; contributed to development of Scholasticism; teacher of St. Thomas Aquinas; canonized and proclaimed doctor, 1931; named patron of natural scientists, 1941; called Doctor Universalis, Doctor Expertus; Nov. 15.

**Alphonsus Liguori, St.** (1696-1787): Born near Naples, Italy; bishop of Saint Agatha of the Goths (1762-1775); founder of the Redemptorists; in addition to his principal work, *Theologiae Moralis*, wrote on prayer, the spiritual life and doctrinal subjects in response to controversy; canonized, 1839; proclaimed doctor, 1871; named patron of confessors and moralists, 1950; Aug. 1.

**Ambrose, St.** (c. 340-397): Born in Trier, Germany; bishop of Milan (374-397); one of the strongest opponents of Arianism in the West; his homilies and other writings — on faith, the Holy Spirit, the Incarnation, the sacraments and other subjects — were pastoral and practical; influenced the development of a liturgy at Milan which was named for him; Father and Doctor of the Church; Dec. 7.

**Anselm, St.** (1033-1109): Born in Aosta, Piedmont, Italy; Benedictine; archbishop of Canterbury (1093-1109); in addition to his principal work, *Cur Deus Homo*, on the atonement and reconciliation of man with God through Christ, wrote about the existence and attributes of God and defended the Filioque explanation of the procession of the Holy Spirit from the Father and the Son; proclaimed doctor, 1720; called Father of Scholasticism; Apr. 21.

**Anthony of Padua, St.** (1195-1231): Born in Lisbon, Portugal; first theologian of the Franciscan Order; preacher; canonized, 1232; proclaimed doctor, 1946; called Evangelical Doctor; June 13.

**Athanasius, St.** (c. 297-373): Born in Alexandria, Egypt; bishop of Alexandria (328-373); participant in the Council of Nicaea I while still a deacon; dominant opponent of Arians whose errors regarding Christ he refuted in *Apology against the Arians, Discourses against the Arians* and other works; Father and Doctor of the Church; called Father of Orthodoxy; May 2.

**Augustine, St.** (354-430): Born in Tagaste, North Africa; bishop of Hippo (395-430) after conversion from Manichaeism; works include the autobiographical and mystical *Confessions, City of God*, treatises on the Trinity, grace, passages of the Bible and doctrines called into question and denied by Manichaeans, Pelagians and Donatists; had strong and lasting influence on Christian theology and philosophy; Father and Doctor of the Church; called Doctor of Grace; Aug. 28.

**Basil the Great, St.** (c. 329-379): Born in Caesarea, Cappadocia, Asia Minor; bishop of Caesarea (370-379); wrote three books *Contra Eunomium* in refutation of Arian errors, a treatise onthe Holy Spirit, many homilies and several rules for monastic life, on which he had lasting influence; Father and Doctor of the Church; called Father of Monasticism in the East; Jan. 2.

**Bede the Venerable, St.** (c. 673-735): Born in Northumberland, England; Benedictine; in addition to his principal work, *Ecclesiastical History of the English Nation* (covering the period 597-731), wrote scriptural commentaries; regarded as probably the most learned man in Western Europe of his time; called Father of English History; May 25.

**Bernard of Clairvaux, St.** (c. 1090-1153): Born near Dijon, France; abbot; monastic reformer, called the second founder of the Cistercian Order; mystical theologian with great influence on devotional life; opponent of the rationalism brought forward by Abelard and others; canonized, 1174; proclaimed doctor, 1830; called Mellifluous Doctor because of his eloquence; Aug. 20.

**Bonaventure, St.** (c. 1217-1274): Born near Viterbo, Italy; Franciscan; bishop of Albano (1273-1274); cardinal; wrote *Itinerarium Mentis in Deum, De Reductione Artium ad Theologiam, Breviloquium*, scriptural commentaries, additional mystical works affecting devotional life and a life of St. Francis of Assisi; canonized, 1482; proclaimed doctor, 1588; called Seraphic Doctor; July 15.

**Catherine of Siena, St.** (c. 1347-1380): Born in Siena, Italy; member of the Third Order of St. Dominic; mystic; authored a long series of letters, mainly concerning spiritual instruction and encouragement, to associates, and *Dialogue*, a spiritual testament in four treatises; was active in support of a crusade against the Turks and efforts to end war between papal forces and the Florentine allies; had great influence in inducing Gregory XI to return himself and the Curia to Rome in 1377, to end the Avignon period of the papacy; canonized, 1461; proclaimed the second woman doctor, Oct. 4, 1970; Apr. 29.

**Cyril of Alexandria, St.** (c. 376-444): Born in Egypt; bishop of Alexandria (412-444); wrote treatises on the Trinity, the Incarnation and other subjects, mostly in refutation of Nestorian errors; made key contributions to the development of Christology; presided at the Council of Ephesus, 431; proclaimed doctor, 1882; June 27.

**Cyril of Jerusalem, St.** (c. 315-386): Bishop of Jerusalem from 350; vigorous opponent of Arianism; principal work, *Catecheses*, a pre-baptismal explanation of the creed of Jerusalem; proclaimed doctor, 1882; Mar. 18.

**Ephraem, St.** (c. 306-373): Born in Nisibis, Mesopotamia; counteracted the spread of Gnostic and Arian errors with poems and hymns of his own composition; wrote also on the Eucharist and Mary; proclaimed doctor, 1920; called Deacon of Edessa and Harp of the Holy Spirit; June 9.

**Francis de Sales, St.** (1567-1622): Born in Savoy; bishop of Geneva (1602-1622); spiritual writer with strong influence on devotional life through treatises such as *Introduction to a Devout Life*, and *The Love of God;* canonized, 1665; proclaimed doctor, 1877; patron of Catholic writers and the Catholic press; Jan. 24.

**Gregory Nazianzen, St.** (c. 330-c. 390): Born in Arianzus, Cappadocia, Asia Minor; bishop of Constantinople (381-390); vigorous opponent of Arianism; in addition to five theological discourses on the Nicene Creed and the Trinity for which he is best known, wrote letters and poetry; Father and Doctor of the Church; called the Christian Demosthenes because of his eloquence and, in the Eastern Church, The Theologian; Jan. 2.

**Gregory I, the Great, St.** (c. 540-604): Born in Rome; pope (590-604): wrote many scriptural commentaries, a compendium of theology in the *Book of Morals* based on Job, *Dialogues* concerning lives of saints, the immortality of the soul, death, purgatory, heaven and hell, and 14 books of letters; enforced papal supremacy and established the position of the pope vis-a-vis the emperor; worked for clerical and monastic reform and the observance of clerical celibacy; Father and Doctor of the Church; Sept. 3.

**Hilary of Poitiers, St.** (c. 315-368): Born in Poitiers, France; bishop of Poitiers (c. 353-368); wrote *De Synodis*, with the Arian controversy in mind, and *De Trinitate*, the first lengthy study of the doctrine in Latin; introduced Eastern theology to the West; contributed to the development of hymnology; proclaimed doctor, 1851; called the Athanasius of the West because of his vigorous defense of the divinity of Christ against Arians; Jan. 13.

**Isidore of Seville, St.** (c. 560-636): Born in Cartagena, Spain; bishop of Seville (c. 600-636); in addition to his principal work, *Etymologiae*, an encyclopedia of the knowledge of his day, wrote on theological and historical subjects; regarded as the most learned man of his time; proclaimed doctor, 1722; Apr. 4.

**Jerome, St.** (c. 343-420): Born in Stridon, Dalmatia; translated the Old Testament from Hebrew into Latin and revised the existing Latin translation of the New Testament to produce the Vulgate version of the Bible; wrote scriptural commentaries and treatises on matters of controversy; regarded as Father and Doctor of the Church from the eighth century; called Father of Biblical Science; Sept. 30.

**John Chrysostom, St.** (c. 347-407): Born in Antioch, Asia Minor; archbishop of Constantinople (398-407); wrote homilies, scriptural commentaries and letters of wide influence in addition to a classical treatise on the priesthood; proclaimed doctor by the Council of Chalcedon, 451; called the greatest of the Greek Fathers; named patron of preachers, 1909; called Golden-Mouthed because of his eloquence; Sept. 13.

**John Damascene, St.** (c. 675-c. 749): Born in

Damascus, Syria; monk; wrote Fountain of Wisdom, a three-part work including a history of heresies and an exposition of the Christian faith, three Discourses against the Iconoclasts, homilies on Mary, biblical commentaries and treatises on moral subjects; proclaimed doctor, 1890; called Golden Speaker because of his eloquence; Dec. 4.

**John of the Cross, St.** (1542-1591): Born in Old Castile, Spain; Carmelite; founder of Discalced Carmelites; one of the greatest mystical theologians, wrote *The Ascent of Mt. Carmel — The Dark Night, The Spiritual Canticle, The Living Flame of Love*; canonized, 1726; proclaimed doctor, 1926; called Doctor of Mystical Theology; Dec. 14.

**Lawrence of Brindisi, St.** (1559-1619): Born in Brindisi, Italy; Franciscan (Capuchin); vigorous preacher of strong influence in the post-Reformation period; 15 tomes of collected works include scriptural commentaries, sermons, homilies and doctrinal writings; canonized, 1881; proclaimed doctor, 1959; July 21.

**Leo I, the Great, St.** (c. 400-461): Born in Tuscany, Italy; pope (440-461); wrote the *Tome of Leo*, to explain doctrine concerning the two natures and one Person of Christ, against the background of the Nestorian and Monophysite heresies; other works included sermons, letters and writings against the errors of Manichaeism and Pelagianism; was instrumental in dissuading Attila from sacking Rome in 452; proclaimed doctor, 1574; Nov. 10.

**Peter Canisius, St.** (1521-1597): Born in Nijmegen, Holland; Jesuit; wrote popular expositions of the Catholic faith in several catechisms which were widely circulated in 20 editions in his lifetime alone; was one of the moving figures in the Counter-Reformation period, especially in southern and western Germany; canonized and proclaimed doctor, 1925; Dec. 21.

**Peter Chrysologus, St.** (c. 400-450): Born in Imola, Italy; served as archbishop of Ravenna (c. 433-450); his sermons and writings, many of which

were designed to counteract Monophysitism, were pastoral and practical; proclaimed doctor, 1729; July 30.

**Peter Damian, St.** (1007-1072): Born in Ravenna, Italy; Benedictine; cardinal; his writings and sermons, any of which concerned ecclesiastical and clerical reform, were pastoral and practical; proclaimed doctor, 1828; Feb. 21.

**Robert Bellarmine, St.** (1542-1621): Born in Tuscany, Italy; Jesuit; archbishop of Capua (1602-1605); wrote *Controversies*, a three-volume exposition of doctrine under attack during and after the Reformation, two catechisms and the spiritual work, *The Art of Dying Well*; was an authority on ecclesiology and Church-state relations; canonized, 1930; proclaimed doctor, 1931; Sept. 17.

**Teresa of Jesus (Avila), St.** (1515-1582): Born in Avila, Spain; entered the Carmelite Order, 1535; in the early 1560s, initiated a primitive Carmelite, discalced-Alcantarine reform which greatly influenced men and women religious, especially in Spain; wrote extensively on spiritual and mystical subjects; principal works included her *Autobiography, Way of Perfection, The Interior Castle, Meditations on the Canticle, The Foundations, Visitation of the Discalced Nuns*; canonized, 1622; proclaimed first woman doctor, Sept. 27, 1970; Oct. 15.

**Thomas Aquinas, St.** (1225-1274): Born near Naples, Italy; Dominican; teacher and writer on virtually the whole range of philosophy and theology; principal works were *Summa contra Gentiles*, a manual and systematic defense of Christian doctrine, and *Summa Theologiae*, a new (at that time) exposition of theology on philosophical principles; canonized, 1323; proclaimed doctor, 1567; called Doctor Communis, Doctor Angelicus, the Great Synthesizer because of the way in which he related faith and reason, theology and philosophy (especially that of Aristotle), and systematized the presentation of Christian doctrine; named patron of Catholic schools and education, 1880; Jan. 28.

# CREEDS

Creeds are formal and official statements of Christian doctrine. As summaries of the principal truths of faith, they are standards of orthodoxy and are useful for instructional purposes, for actual profession of the faith and for expression of the faith in the liturgy.

The classical creeds are the Apostles' Creed and the Creed of Nicaea-Constantinople. Two others are the Athanasian Creed and the Creed of Pius IV.

## Apostles' Creed

**Text:** I believe in God, the Father almighty, Creator of heaven and earth.

And in Jesus Christ, his only Son, our Lord; who was conceived by the Holy Spirit, born of the Virgin Mary, suffered under Pontius Pilate, was crucified, died, and was buried. He descended into hell; the third day he arose again from the dead; he ascended into heaven, sits at the right hand of God, the Father almighty; from thence he shall come to judge the living and the dead.

I believe in the Holy Spirit, the holy Catholic

Church, the communion of saints, the forgiveness of sins, the resurrection of the body, and life everlasting. Amen.

**Background:** The Apostles' Creed reflects the teaching of the Apostles but is not of apostolic origin. It probably originated in the second century as a rudimentary formula of faith professed by catechumens before the reception of baptism. Baptismal creeds in fourth-century use at Rome and elsewhere in the West closely resembled the present text, which was quoted in a handbook of Christian doctrine written between 710 and 724. This text was in wide use throughout the West by the ninth century. The Apostles' Creed is common to all Christian confessional churches in the West, but is not used in Eastern Churches.

## Nicene Creed

The following translation of the Latin text of the creed was prepared by the International Committee on English in the Liturgy.

**Text:** We believe in one God, the Father, the Almighty, maker of heaven and earth, of all that is seen and unseen.

We believe in one Lord, Jesus Christ, the only Son of God, eternally begotten of the Father, God from God, Light from Light, true God from true God, begotten, not made, one in Being with the Father. Through him all things were made. For us men and for our salvation he came down from heaven: by the power of the Holy Spirit he was born of the Virgin Mary, and became man. For our sake he was crucified under Pontius Pilate; he suffered, died, and was buried. On the third day he rose again in fulfillment of the Scriptures; he ascended into heaven and is seated at the right hand of the Father. He will come again in glory to judge the living and the dead, and his kingdom will have no end.

We believe in the Holy Spirit, the Lord, the giver of life, who proceeds from the Father and the Son. With the Father and the Son he is worshiped and glorified. He has spoken through the prophets.

We believe in one holy catholic and apostolic Church. We acknowledge one baptism for the forgiveness of sins. We look for the resurrection of the dead, and the life of the world to come. Amen.

**Background:** The Nicene Creed (Creed of Nicaea-Constantinople) consists of elements of doctrine contained in an early baptismal creed of Jerusalem and enactments of the Council of Nicaea (325) and the Council of Constantinople (381). Its strong trinitarian content reflects the doctrinal errors, especially of Arianism, it served to counteract. Theologically, it is much more sophisticated than the Apostles' Creed. Since late in the fifth century, the Nicene Creed has been the only creed in liturgical use in the Eastern Churches. The Western Church adopted it for liturgical use by the end of the eighth century.

### The Athanasian Creed

The Athanasian Creed, which has a unique structure, is a two-part summary of doctrine concerning the Trinity and the Incarnation-Redemption bracketed at the beginning and end with the statement that belief in the cited truths is necessary for salvation; it also contains a number of anathemas or condemnatory clauses regarding doctrinal errors. Although attributed to St. Athanasius, it was probably written after his death, between 381 and 428, and may have been authored by St. Ambrose. It is not accepted in the East; in the West, it formerly had place in the Roman-Rite Liturgy of the Hours and in the liturgy for the Solemnity of the Holy Trinity.

### Creed of Pius IV

The Creed of Pius IV, also called the Profession of Faith of the Council of Trent, was promulgated in the bull *Injunctum Nobis*, Nov. 13, 1564. It is a summary of doctrine defined by the council concerning: Scripture and tradition, original sin and justification, the Mass and sacraments, veneration of the saints, indulgences, the primacy of the See of Rome. It was slightly modified in 1887 to include doctrinal formulations of the First Vatican Council.

## MORAL OBLIGATIONS

The basic norm of Christian morality is life in Christ. This involves, among other things, the observance of the Ten Commandments, their fulfillment in the twofold law of love of God and neighbor, the implications of the Sermon on the Mount and the whole New Testament, and membership in the Church established by Christ.

### THE TEN COMMANDMENTS

The Ten Commandments, the Decalogue, were given by God through Moses to his Chosen People for the guidance of their moral conduct in accord with the demands of the Covenant he established with them as a divine gift.

In the traditional Catholic enumeration and according to Dt. 5:6-21, the Commandments are:

1. "I, the Lord, am your God You shall not have other gods besides me. You shall not carve idols."
2. "You shall not take the name of the Lord, your God, in vain."
3. "Take care to keep holy the Sabbath day."
4. "Honor your father and your mother."
5. "You shall not kill."
6. "You shall not commit adultery."
7. "You shall not steal."
8. "You shall not bear dishonest witness against your neighbor."
9. "You shall not covet your neighbor's wife."
10. "You shall not desire your neighbor's house or field, nor his male or female slave, nor his ox or ass,

nor anything that belongs to him (summarily, his goods).

Another version of the Commandments, substantially the same, is given in Ex. 20:1-17.

The traditional enumeration of the Commandments in Protestant usage differs from the above. Thus: two commandments are made of the first, as above; the third and fourth are equivalent to the second and third, as above, and so on; and the 10th includes the ninth and 10th, as above.

### Love of God and Neighbor

The first three of the commandments deal directly with man's relations with God, viz.: acknowledgment of one true God and the rejection of false gods and idols; honor due to God and his name; observance of the Sabbath as the Lord's day.

The rest cover interpersonal relationships, viz.: the obedience due to parents and, logically, to other persons in authority, and the obligations of parents to children and of persons in authority to those under their care; respect for life and physical integrity; fidelity in marriage, and chastity; justice and rights; truth; internal respect for faithfulness in marriage, chastity, and the goods of others.

### Perfection in Christian Life

The moral obligations of the Ten Commandments are complemented by others flowing from the twofold law of love, the whole substance and pattern of Christ's teaching, and everything implied in full and active membership and participation in the community of salvation formed by Christ in his Church. Some of these matters are covered in other sections of the Almanac under appropriate headings.

## Precepts of the Church

The purpose of the precepts of the Church, according to the *Catechism of the Catholic Church,* is "to guarantee to the faithful the indispensable minimum in the spirit of prayer and moral effort, in the growth and love of God and neighbor" (No. 2041).

1. Attendance at Mass on Sundays and holy days of obligation. (Observance of Sundays and holy days of obligation involves refraining from work that hinders the worship due to God.)
2. Confession of sins at least once a year.
3. Reception of the Eucharist at least during the Easter season (in the U.S., from the first Sunday of Lent to Trinity Sunday).
4. Keep holy the holy days of obligation.
5. Observance of specified days of fasting and abstinence.

There is also an obligation to provide for the material needs of the Church.

# SOCIAL DOCTRINE

Since the end of the last century, Catholic social doctrine has been formulated in a progressive manner in a number of authoritative documents.

Outstanding examples are the encyclicals: *Rerum Novarum* ("On Capital and Labor") issued by Leo XIII in 1891; *Quadragesimo Anno* ("On Reconstruction of the Social Order") by Pius XI in 1931; *Mater et Magistra* ("Christianity and Social Progress") and *Pacem in Terris* ("Peace on Earth"), by John XXIII in 1961 and 1963, respectively; *Populorum Progressio* ("Development of Peoples"), by Paul VI in 1967; *Laborem Exercens* ("On Human Work"), *Sollicitudo Rei Socialis* ("On Social Concerns") and *Centesimus Annus* ("The 100th Year") by John Paul II in 1981, 1987 and 1991, respectively. Pius XII, among other accomplishments of ideological importance in the social field, made a distinctive contribution with his formulation of a plan for world peace and order in Christmas messages from 1939 to 1941, and in other documents.

Of particular significance are the "Pastoral Constitution on the Church in the Modern World" (*Gaudium et Spes*) issued by the Second Vatican Council and Pope John Paul's encyclical letter, *Centesimus Annus* ("The 100th Year").

These documents represent the most serious attempts in modern times to systematize the social implications of divine revelation as well as the socially relevant writings of the Fathers and Doctors of the Church. Their contents are theological penetrations into social life, with particular reference to human rights, the needs of the poor and those in underdeveloped countries, and humane conditions of life, freedom, justice and peace. In some respects, they read like juridical documents; essentially, however, they are Gospel-oriented and pastoral in intention.

Following are brief descriptions of the nature of social teaching, the contents of the pastoral constitution, and extensive excerpts from *Centesimus Annus.*

## Nature of the Doctrine

Pope John XXIII, writing in *Christianity and Social Progress,* made the following statement about the nature and scope of the doctrine stated in the encyclicals in particular and related writings in general.

"What the Catholic Church teaches and declares regarding the social life and relationships of men is beyond question for all time valid.

"The cardinal point of this teaching is that individual men are necessarily the foundation, cause, and end of all social institutions insofar as they are social by nature, and raised to an order of existence that transcends and subdues nature.

"Beginning with this very basic principle whereby the dignity of the human person is affirmed and defended, Holy Church — especially during the last century and with the assistance of learned priests and laymen, specialists in the field — has arrived at clear social teachings whereby the mutual relationships of men are ordered. Taking general norms into account, these principles are in accord with the nature of things and the changed conditions of man's social life, or with the special genius of our day. Moreover, these norms can be approved by all."

## THE CHURCH IN THE WORLD

Even more Gospel-oriented and pastoral in a distinctive way is the *Pastoral Constitution on the Church in the Modern World* promulgated by the Second Vatican Council in 1965.

Its purpose is to search out the signs of God's presence and meaning in and through the events of this time in human history. Accordingly, it deals with the situation of men in present circumstances of profound change, challenge and crisis on all levels of life.

The first part of the constitution develops the theme of the Church and man's calling, and focuses attention on the dignity of the human person, the problem of atheism, the community of mankind, man's activity throughout the world, and the serving and saving role of the Church in the world. This portion of the document, it has been said, represents the first presentation by the Church in an official text of an organized Christian view of man and society.

The second part of the document considers several problems of special urgency: fostering the nobility of marriage and the family (see Marriage Doctrine), the proper development of culture, socio-economic life, the life of the political community, the fostering of peace, and the promotion of a community of nations.

In conclusion, the constitution calls for action to implement doctrine regarding the role and work of the Church for the total good of mankind.

# CENTESIMUS ANNUS: ENCYCLICAL LETTER

*Centesimus Annus* ("The 100th Year"), the title of Pope John Paul's ninth encyclical letter, commemorated the 100th anniversary of Pope Leo XIII's encyclical *Rerum Novarum* ("On Capital and Labor"). Dated May 1, 1991, it was made public the following day. Its publication was one of the principal events of the year dedicated to commemoration and study of the social teaching of the Church.

*Following are excerpts (in quotations) from the text circulated by the CNS Documentary Service, Origins, May 16, 1991 (Vol. 21,No. 1). Subheads have been added. Quotations indicated by single quotation marks are from other encyclicals, documents of the Second Vatican Council and other authoritative sources.*

## INTRODUCTION

3. "The present encyclical seeks to show the fruitfulness of the principles enunciated by Leo XIII, which belong to the Church's doctrinal patrimony and as such involve the exercise of her teaching authority. But pastoral solicitude also prompts me to propose an analysis of some events of recent history. Such an analysis is not meant to pass definitive judgments, since this does not fall per se within the magisterium's specific domain."

## CHAPTER 1

### Characteristics of Rerum Novarum

5. "The 'new things' to which the Pope devoted his attention were anything but positive. The first paragraph of the encyclical describes in strong terms the 'new things' *(rerum novarum)* which gave it its name: 'That the spirit of revolutionary change which has long been disturbing the nations of the world should have passed beyond the sphere of politics and made its influence felt in the related sphere of practical economics is not surprising. Progress in industry, the development of new trades, the changing relationship between employers and workers, the enormous wealth of a few as opposed to the poverty of the many, the increasing self-reliance of the workers and their closer association with each other, as well as a notable decline in morality: All these elements have led to the conflict now taking place.'"

"The Pope and the Church with him were confronted, as was the civil community, by a society which was torn by a conflict all the more harsh and inhumane because it knew no rule or regulation. It was the conflict between capital and labor or — as the encyclical puts it — the worker question."

### Conditions for Justice

"What was essential to the encyclical was precisely its proclamation of the fundamental conditions for justice in the economic and social situation of the time."

"To teach and to spread her social doctrine pertains to the Church's evangelizing mission and is an essential part of the Christian message, since this doctrine points out the direct consequences of that message in the life of society and situates daily work and struggles for justice in the context of bearing witness to Christ the Savior. This doctrine is likewise a source of unity and peace in dealing with the conflicts which inevitably arise in social and economic life."

"We need to repeat that there can be no genuine solution of the 'social question' apart from the Gospel, and that the 'new things' can find in the Gospel the context for their correct understanding and the proper moral perspective for judgment on them."

### Fundamental Rights

6. "Pope Leo XIII affirmed the fundamental rights of workers. Indeed, the key to reading the encyclical is the dignity of the worker as such and, for the same reason, the dignity of work."

7. to 9. The encyclical stated the important principle of the right to "private property," duly qualified by the "complementary" principle of "the universal destination of the earth's goods" for the good of all.

Also affirmed were the natural right to form private associations, the right to the limitation of working hours, the right to legitimate rest, and the right of children and women to be treated differently with regard to the type and duration of work, the right to a just wage (which should be sufficient to enable a worker to support himself, his wife and his children), and the right to religious freedom.

11. "Pope Leo's encyclical is an encyclical on the poor and on the terrible conditions to which the new and often violent process of industrialization had reduced great multitudes of people."

### The Guiding Principle

"The main thread and in a certain sense the guiding principle of Pope Leo's encyclical and of all of the Church's social doctrine is a correct view of the human person and of his unique value, inasmuch as 'man is the only creature on earth which God willed for itself.' God has imprinted his own image and likeness on man, conferring upon him an incomparable dignity, as the encyclical frequently insists. In effect, beyond the rights which man acquires by his own work, there exist rights which do not correspond to any work he performs but which flow from his essential dignity as a person."

## CHAPTER 2

### Toward the 'New Things' of Today

12. "Pope Leo foresaw the negative consequences — political, social and economic — of the social order proposed by 'socialism.'"

13. He defined the nature of the socialism of his day as "the suppression of private property," and said "its fundamental error is anthropological in nature." It "considers the individual person simply as an element, a molecule within the social organism, so that the good of the individual is completely subordinated to the functioning of the socio-economic organism. Man is thus reduced to a series of social relationships."

However, "according to *Rerum Novarum* and the whole social doctrine of the Church, the social nature of man is not completely fulfilled in the state, but is realized in various intermediary groups, beginning with the family and including economic, social, political and cultural groups which stem from human nature itself and have their own autonomy, always with a view to the common good."

## Atheism's Mistaken Concept

"The first cause of the mistaken concept of the nature of the person is atheism. The denial of God deprives the person of his foundation and consequently leads to a reorganization of the social order without reference to the person's dignity and responsibility."

14. Consequences of socialism, atheism and related errors are class struggle, militarism, war, subjection of people to the state, and a whole range of political, social and economic evils.

## CHAPTER 3

### The Year 1989

22. *Centesimus Annus* notes that "unexpected and promising" events of recent years have produced notable changes in countries in Eastern and Central Europe, as also in nations of Latin America, Asia and Africa. Contributing to these developments was the Church's commitment to human rights. Coupled with the developments was hope for progressive change and for the solution of problems through the exercise of dialogue and negotiation.

23. Among factors involved in the fall of oppressive regimes were the violation of workers' rights (called decisive), peaceful protest through dialogue and negotiation as opposed to Marxist violence, and witness to the truth about conditions, etc.

24. Another factor was the inefficiency of the (Marxist) economic system. The inefficiency was not so much technological as a consequence of violations of human rights to private initiative, ownership of property and economic freedom. A related factor was the failure of oppressive regimes to realize the importance of culture for the understanding of people.

### Spiritual Void

The true cause of the fall of oppressive regimes was the spiritual void brought about by atheism; because of this void, people were cast adrift without any sense of direction. Another cause was the witness of the faithful to truth.

25. to 27. Events of 1989, which had effects not only in Eastern and Central Europe but also in Third World and other countries, were an example of the success achievable by a willingness to negotiate and of the success of the Gospel spirit to stand for moral principles, come what may.

### Need for Reconciliation and Rebuilding

28. "The radical reordering of economic systems, hitherto collectivized, entails problems and sacrifices. It is right that in the present difficulties the formerly communist countries should be aided by the united effort of other nations. Obviously they themselves must be the primary agents of their own development, but they must also be given a reason-

able opportunity to accomplish this goal, something that cannot happen without the help of other countries." Such help, however, should not lead to neglect of the Third World or abandonment of the poor. Special effort must be made to mobilize resources necessary for development in the Third World.

29. "Development must not be understood solely in economic terms, but in a way that is fully human. The apex of development is the exercise of the right and duty to seek God, to know him and to live in accordance with that knowledge."

## CHAPTER 4

### Private Property and the Universal Destination of Material Goods

30. "In *Rerum Novarum*, Leo XIII strongly affirmed the natural character of the right to private property. This right, which is fundamental for the autonomy and development of the person, has always been defended by the Church up to our own day. At the same time, the Church teaches that the possession of material goods is not an absolute right and that its limits are inscribed in its very nature as a human right.

"While the Pope proclaimed the right to private ownership, he affirmed with equal clarity that the 'use' of goods, while marked by freedom, is subordinated to their original common destination" for the common good.

"Of its nature, private property has a social function which is based on the law of the common purpose of goods."

### Origin of Material Goods

31. "The question can be raised concerning the origin of the material goods which sustain human life, satisfy people's needs and are an object of their rights.

"The original source of all that is good is the very act of God, who created both the earth and man, and who gave the earth to man so that he might have dominion over it by his work and enjoy its fruits (Gn. 1:28). God gave the earth to the whole human race for the sustenance of all its members, without excluding or favoring anyone. This is the foundation of the universal destination of the earth's goods. The earth, by reason of its fruitfulness and its capacity to satisfy human needs, is God's first gift for the sustenance of human life. But the earth does not yield its fruits without a particular human response to God's gift, that is to say, without work. It is through work that man, using his intelligence and exercising his freedom, succeeds in dominating the earth and making it a fitting home. In this way, he makes part of the earth his own, precisely the part which he has acquired through work; this is the origin of individual property. Obviously, he also has the responsibility not to hinder others from having their own part of God's gift; indeed, he must cooperate with others so that together all can dominate the earth."

### Work and the Land

"In history, these two factors — work and the land — are to be found at the beginning of every human society. However, they do not always stand in the same relationship to each other. At one time the natural fruitfulness of the earth appeared to be, and was in fact, the primary factor of wealth, while work was, as it were, the help and support for this fruitfulness. In our time, the role of human work is becoming increasingly important as the productive factor both of non-material and of material wealth. Moreover, it is becoming clearer how a person's work is naturally interrelated with the work of others. More than ever, work is work with others and work for others: it is a matter of doing something for someone else. Work becomes ever more fruitful and productive to the extent that people become more knowledgeabl of the productive potentialities of the earth and more profoundly cognizant of the needs of those for whom their work is done."

### Ownership of Know-How

32. "In our time, in particular, there exists another form of ownership which is becoming no less important than land: the possession of know-how, technology and skill. The wealth of the industrialized nations is based much more on this kind of ownership than on natural resources."

"Today the decisive factor (in production) is increasingly man himself, that is, his knowledge, especially his scientific knowledge, his capacity for interrelated and compact organization, as well as his ability to perceive the needs of others and to satisfy them."

### The Free Market

34. "It would appear that, on the level of individual nations and of international relations, the free market is the most efficient instrument for utilizing resources and effectively responding to needs." But this is true only for those needs which are "solvent," insofar as they are endowed with purchasing power, and for those resources which are "marketable," insofar as they are capable of obtaining a satisfactory price. But there are many human needs which find no place on the market. It is a strict duty of justice and truth not to allow fundamental human needs to remain unsatisfied, and not allow those burdened by such needs to perish. It is also necessary to help these needy people to acquire expertise, to enter the circle of exchange, and to develop their skills in order to make the best use of their capacities and resources. Even prior to the logic of a fair exchange of goods and the forms of justice appropriate to it, there exists something which is due to man because he is man, by reason of his lofty dignity. Inseparable from that required "something" is the possibility to survive and, at the same time, to make "an active contribution to the common good of humanity."

35. "Trade unions and other workers' organizations defend workers' rights and protect their interests as persons, while fulfilling a vital cultural role, so as to enable workers to participate more fully and honorably in the life of their nation and to assist them along the path of development."

### A Society of Free Work

"In this sense, it is right to speak of a struggle against an economic system, if the latter is understood as a method of upholding the absolute predominance of capital, the possession of the means of production and of the land, in contrast to the free and personal nature of human work. In the struggle against such a system, what is being proposed as an alternative is not the socialist system, which in fact turns out to be state capitalism, but rather a society of free work, of enterprise and of participation. Such a society is not directed against the market, but demands that the market be appropriately controlled by the forces of society and by the state, so as to guarantee that the basic needs of the whole of society are satisfied."

### Legitimacy of Profit

"The church acknowledges the legitimate role of profit as an indication that a business is functioning well. When a firm makes a profit, this means that productive factors have been properly employed and corresponding human needs have been duly satisfied. But profitability is not the only indicator of a firm's condition. It is possible for the financial accounts to be in order, and yet for the people — who make up the firm's most valuable asset — to be humiliated and their dignity offended. Besides being morally inadmissible, this will eventually have negative repercussions on the firm's economic efficiency. In fact, the purpose of a business firm is not simply to make a profit, but is to be found in its very existence as a community of persons who in various ways are endeavoring to satisfy their basic needs, and who form a particular group at the service of the whole of society. Profit is a regulator of the life of a business, but it is not the only one; other human and moral factors must also be considered which, in the long term, are at least equally important for the life of a business."

### Stronger Nations Must Help

"It is unacceptable to say that the defeat of so-called 'real socialism' leaves capitalism as the only model of economic organization. It is necessary to break down the barriers and monopolies which leave so many countries on the margins of development, and to provide all individuals and nations with the basic conditions which will enable them to share in development. This goal calls for programmed and responsible efforts on the part of the entire international community. Stronger nations must offer weaker ones opportunities for taking their place in international life, and the latter must learn how to use these opportunities by making the necessary efforts and sacrifices, and by ensuring political and economic stability, the certainty of better prospects for the future, the improvement of workers' skills, and the training of competent business leaders who are conscious of their responsibilities."

### Third World Debt

"At present, the positive efforts which have been made along these lines are being affected by the still largely unsolved problem of the foreign debt of the poorer countries. The principle that debts must be paid is certainly just. However, it is not right to demand or expect payment when the effect would be the imposition of political choices leading to hunger and despair for entire peoples. It cannot be expected that the debts which have been contracted should be paid at the price of unbearable sacrifices. In such cases it is necessary to find — as in fact is partly happening — ways to lighten, defer or even cancel the debt, compatible with the fundamental right of peoples to subsistence and progress."

## Consumerism

36. "A given culture reveals its overall understanding of life through the choices it makes in production and consumption. It is here that the phenomenon of consumerism arises. In singling out new needs and new means to meet them, one must be guided by a comprehensive picture of man which respects all the dimensions of his being and which subordinates his material and instinctive dimensions to his interior and spiritual ones. If, on the contrary, a direct appeal is made to his instincts — while ignoring in various ways the reality of the person as intelligent and free —then consumer attitudes and lifestyles can be created which are objectively improper and often damaging to his physical and spiritual health. Of itself, an economic system does not possess criteria for correctly distinguishing new and higher forms of satisfying human needs from artificial new needs which hinder the formation of a mature personality. Thus, a great deal of educational and cultural work is urgently needed, including the education of consumers in the responsible use of their power of choice, the formation of a strong sense of responsibility among producers and among people in the mass media in particular, as well as the necessary intervention by public authorities."

"It is not wrong to want to live better; what is wrong is a style of life which is presumed to be better when it is directed toward 'having' rather than 'being,' and which wants to have more, not in order to be more but in order to spend life in enjoyment as an end in itself."

## Ecological Considerations

37. "Equally worrying is the ecological question which accompanies the problem of consumerism and which is closely connected to it."

38. "In additon to the irrational destruction of the natural environment. we must also mention the more serious destruction of the human environment. Not only has God given the earth to man, who must use it with respect for the original good purpose for which it was given to him, but man too is God's gift to man. He must therefore respect the natural and moral structure with which he has been endowed. In this context, mention should be made of the serious problems of modern urbanization, of the need for urban planning which is concerned with how people are to live, and of the attention which should be given to a 'social ecology' of work.

"Man receives from God his essential dignity and with it the capacity to transcend every social order so as to move toward truth and goodness. But he is also conditioned by the social structure in which he lives, by the education he has received and by his environment. These elements can either help or hinder his living in accordance with the truth. The decisions which create a human environment can give rise to specific structures of sin which impede the full realization of those who are in any way oppressed by them. To destroy such structures and replace them with more authentic forms of living in community is a task which demands courage and patience."

## The Family and Human Ecology

39. "The first and fundamental structure for 'human ecology' is the family, in which man receives his first formative ideas about truth and goodness, and learns what it means to love and to be loved, and thus what it actually means to be a person. Here we mean the family founded on marriage, in which the mutual gift of self by husband and wife creates an environment in which children can be born and develop their potentialities, become aware of their dignity and prepare to face their unique and individual destiny." "It is necessary to go back to seeing the family as the sanctuary of life. The family is indeed sacred: it is the place in which life — the gift of God — can be properly welcomed and protected against the many attacks to which it is exposed, and can develop in accordance with what constitutes authentic human growth. In the face of the so-called culture of death, the family is the heart of the culture of life."

## Abortion

"Human ingenuity seems to be directed more toward limiting, suppressing or destroying the sources of life — including recourse to abortion, which unfortunately is so widespread in the world — than toward defending and opening up the possibilities of life. The encyclical *Sollicitudo Rei Socialis* denounced systematic anti-childbearing campaigns which, on the basis of a distorted view of the demographic problem and in a climate of 'absolute lack of respect for the freedom of choice of the parties involved,' often subject them 'to intolerable pressures in order to force them to submit to this new form of oppression.' These policies are extending their field of action by the use of new techniques, to the point of poisoning the lives of millions of defenseless human beings, as if in a form of 'chemical warfare.'"

## Economic Freedom Not Autonomous

"These criticisms are directed not so much against an economic system as against an ethical and cultural system. The economy in fact is only one aspect and one dimension of the whole of human activity. If economic life is absolutized, if the production and consumption of goods become the center of social life and society's only value, not subject to any other value, the reason is to be found not so much in the economic system itself as in the fact that the entire socio-cultural system, by ignoring the ethical and religious dimension, has been weakened, and ends by limiting itself to the production of goods and services alone.

"All of this can be summed up by repeating once more that economic freedom is only one element of human freedom. When it becomes autonomous, when man is seen more as a producer or consumer of goods than as a subject who produces and consumes in order to live, then economic freedom loses its necessary relationship to the human person and ends up by alienating and oppressing him."

41. "Obedience to the truth about God and man is the first condition of freedom, making it possible for a person to order his needs and desires and to choose the means of satisfying them according to a correct scale of values, so that the ownership of things may become an occasion of growth for him."

## Capitalism

42. "Can it perhaps be said that, after the failure of communism, capitalism is the victorious social system, and that capitalism should be the goal of the countries now making efforts to rebuild their economy and society? Is this the model which ought to be proposed to the countries of the Third World which are searching for the path to true economic and civil progress?

"The answer is obviously complex. If by capitalism is meant an economic system which recognizes the fundamental and positive role of business, the market, private property and the resulting responsibility for the means of production, as well as free human creativity in the economic sector, then the answer is certainly in the affirmative, even though it would perhaps be more appropriate to speak of a *business economy, market economy* or simply *free economy.* But if by capitalism is meant a system in which freedom in the economic sector is not circumscribed within a strong juridical framework which places it at the service of human freedom in its totality, and which sees it as a particular aspect of that freedom, the core of which is ethical and religious, then the reply is certainly negative."

## Marginalization Remains

"The Marxist solution has failed, but the realities of marginalization and exploitation remain in the world, especially the Third World, as does the reality of human alienation, especially in the more advanced countries. Against these phenomena the Church strongly raises her voice. Vast multitudes are still living in conditions of great material and moral poverty. The collapse of the communist system in so many countries certainly removes an obstacle to facing these problems in an appropriate and realistic way, but it is not enough to bring about their solution. Indeed, there is a risk that a radical capitalistic ideology could spread which refuses even to consider these problems, in the a priori belief that any attempt to solve them is doomed to failure, and which blindly entrusts their solution to the free development of market forces."

## Orientation of Church Teaching

43. "The Church has no models to present; models that are real and truly effective can only arise within the framework of different historical situations, through the efforts of all those who responsibly confront concrete problems in all their social, economic, political and cultural aspects, as these interact with one another. For such a task the church offers her social teaching as an indispensable and ideal orientation, a teaching which, as already mentioned, recognizes the positive value of the market and of enterprise, but which at the same time points out that these need to be oriented toward the common good. This teaching also recognizes the legitimacy of workers' efforts to obtain full respect for their dignity and to gain broader areas of participation in the life of industrial enterprises so that, while cooperating with others and under the direction of others, they can in a certain sense 'work for themselves' through the exercise of their intelligence and freedom.

"The integral development of the human person through work does not impede but rather promotes the greater productivity and efficiency of work itself, even though it may weaken consolidated power structures. A business cannot be considered only as a 'society of capital goods'; it is also a 'society of persons' in which people participate in different ways and with specific responsibilities, whether they supply the necessary capital for the company's activities or take part in such activities through their labor. To achieve these goals there is still need for a broad associated workers' movement, directed toward the liberation and promotion of the whole person."

## Private Property and Work

"In the light of today's 'new things,' we have reread the relationship between individual or private property and the universal destination of material wealth. Man fulfills himself by using his intelligence and freedom. In so doing he utilizes the things of this world as objects and instruments and makes them his own. The foundation of the right to private initiative and ownership is to be found in this activity. By means of his work man commits himself, not only for his own sake but also for others and with others. Each person collaborates in the work of others and for their good. Man works in order to provide for the needs of his family, his community, his nation and ultimately all humanity. Moreover, he collaborates in the work of his fellow employees, as well as in the work of suppliers and in the customers' use of goods, in a progressively expanding chain of solidarity. Ownership of the means of production, whether in industry or agriculture, is just and legitimate if it serves useful work. It becomes illegitimate, however, when it is not utilized or when it serves to impede the work of others, in an effort to gain a profit which is not the result of the overall expansion of work and the wealth of society, but rather is the result of curbing them or of illicit exploitation, speculation or the breaking of solidarity among working people. Ownership of this kind has no justification, and represents an abuse in the sight of God and man.

"The obligation to earn one's bread by the sweat of one's brow also presumes the right to do so. A society in which this right is systematically denied, in which economic policies do not allow workers to reach satisfactory levels of employment, cannot be justified from an ethical point of view, nor can that society attain social peace. Just as the person fully realizes himself in the free gift of self, so too ownership morally justifies itself in the creation, at the proper time and in the proper way, of opportunities for work and human growth for all."

## CHAPTER 5

### State and Culture

44. "Pope Leo XIII was aware of the need for a sound theory of the state in order to ensure the normal development of man's spiritual and temporal activities, both of which are indispensable. For this reason, in one passage of *Rerum Novarum* he presents the organization of society according to the three powers — legislative, executive and judicial — something which at the time represented a novelty in church teaching. Such an ordering reflects a realistic vision of man's social nature, which calls for legislation capable of protecting the freedom of all. To that end, it is preferable that each power be balanced by other powers and by other spheres of responsibility which keep it within proper bounds. This is the principle of the 'rule of law,' in which the law is sovereign, and not the arbitrary will of individuals."

46. "The Church values the democratic system inasmuch as it ensures the participation of citizens in making political choices, guarantees to the governed the possibility both of electing and holding accountable those who govern them, and of replacing them through peaceful means when appropriate. Thus, she cannot encourage the formation of narrow ruling groups which usurp the power of the state for individual interests or for ideological ends."

### Authentic Democracy

"Authentic democracy is possible only in a state ruled by law, and on the basis of a correct conception of the human person. It requires that the necessary conditions be present for the advancement both of the individual through education and formation in true ideals, and of the 'subjectivity' of society through the creation of structures of participation and shared responsibility. Nowadays there is a tendency to claim that agnosticism and skeptical relativism are the philosophy and the basic attitude which correspond to democratic forms of political life. Those who are convinced that they know the truth and firmly adhere to it are considered unreliable from a democratic point of view, since they do not accept that truth is determined by the majority, or that it is subject to variation according to different political trends. It must be observed in this regard that if there is no ultimate truth to guide and direct political activity, then ideas and convictions can easily be manipulated for reasons of power. As history demonstrates, a democracy without values easily turns into open or thinly disguised totalitarianism.

"Nor does the Church close her eyes to the danger of fanaticism or fundamentalism among those who, in the name of an ideology which purports to be scientific or religious, claim the right to impose on others their own concept of what is true and good. Christian truth is not of this kind. Since it is not an ideology, the Christian faith does not presume to imprison changing socio-political realities in a rigid schema, and it recognizes that human life is realized in history in conditions that are diverse and imperfect. Furthermore, in constantly reaffirming the transcendent dignity of the person, the Church's method is always that of respect for freedom.

"But freedom attains its full development only by accepting the truth. In a world without truth, freedom loses its foundation and man is exposed to the violence of passion and to manipulation, both open and hidden. The Christian upholds freedom and serves it."

### Rights To Be Recognized

47. "Following the collapse of communist totalitarianism and of many other totalitarian and 'national security' regimes, today we are witnessing a predominance, not without signs of opposition, of the democratic ideal, together with lively attention to and concern for human rights. But for this very reason it is necessary for peoples in the process of reforming their systems to give democracy an authenic and solid foundation through the explicit recognition of those rights. Among the most important of these rights, mention must be made of the right to life, an integral part of which is the right of the child to develop in the mother's womb from the moment of conception; the right to live in a united family and in a moral environment conducive to the growth of the child's personality; the right to develop one's intelligence and freedom in seeking and knowing the truth; the right to share in the work which makes wise use of the earth's material resources, and to derive from that work the means to support oneself and one's dependents; and the right freely to establish a family, to have and to rear children through the responsible exercise of one's sexuality. In a certain sense, the source and synthesis of these rights is religious freedom, understood as the right to live in the truth of one's faith and in conformity with one's transcendent dignity as a person."

### Violations of Rights

"Even in countries with democratic forms of government, these rights are not always fully respected. Here we are referring not only to the scandal of abortion, but also to different aspects of a crisis within democracies themselves, which seem at times to have lost the ability to make decisions aimed at the common good. Certain demands which arise within society are sometimes not examined in accordance with criteria of justice and morality, but rather on the basis of the electoral or financial power of the groups promoting them. With time, such distortions of political conduct create distrust and apathy, with a subsequent decline in the political participation and civic spirit of the general population, which feels abused and disillusioned. As a result, there is a growing inability to situate particular interests within the framework of a coherent vision of the common good. The latter is not simply the sum total of particular interests; rather, it involves an assessment and integration of those interests on the basis of a balanced hierarchy of values; ultimately, it demands a correct understanding of the dignity and the rights of the person.

"The Church respects the legitimate autonomy of the democratic order and is not entitled to express preferences for this or that institutional or constitutional solution. Her contribution to the political order is precisely her vision of the dignity of the person revealed in all its fullness in the mystery of the Incarnate Word."

## The State and the Economic Sector

48. "These general observations also apply to the role of the state in the economic sector. Economic activity, especially the activity of a market economy, cannot be conducted in an institutional, juridical or political vacuum. On the contrary, it presupposes sure guarantees of individual freedom and private property, as well as a stable currency and efficient public services. Hence the principal task of the state is to guarante this security, so that those who work and produce can enjoy the fruits of their labors and thus feel encouraged to work efficiently and honestly. The absence of stability, together with the corruption of public officials and the spread of improper sources of growing rich and of easy profits deriving from illegal or purely speculative activities, constitutes one of the chief obstacles to development and to the economic order."

## State Oversight

"Another task of the state is that of overseeing and directing the exercise of human rights in the economic sector. However, primary responsibility in this area belongs not to the state but to individuals and to the various groups and associations which make up society. The state could not directly ensure the right to work for all its citizens unless it controlled every aspect of economic life and restricted the free initiative of individuals. This does not mean, however, that the state has no competence in this domain, as was claimed by those who argued against any rules in the economic sphere. Rather, the state has a duty to sustain business activities by creating conditions which will ensure job opportunities, by stimulating those activities where they are lacking or by supporting them in moments of crisis.

"The state has the further right to intervene when particular monopolies create delays or obstacles to development. In addition to the tasks of harmonizing and guiding development, in exceptional circumstances the state can also exercise a substitute function, when social sectors or business systems are too weak or are just getting under way, and are not equal to the task at hand. Such supplementary interventions, which are justified by urgent reasons touching the common good, must be as brief as possible, so as to avoid removing permanently from society and business systems the functions which are properly theirs, and so as to avoid enlarging excessively the sphere of state intervention to the detriment of both economic and civil freedom."

## The Welfare State

"In recent years the range of such intervention has vastly expanded, to the point of creating a new type of state, the so-called 'welfare state.' This has happened in some countries in order to respond better to many needs and demands, by remedying forms of poverty and deprivation unworthy of the human person."

However, excesses and abuses, especially in recent years, have provoked very harsh criticisms of the welfare state, dubbed the 'social assistance state.' Malfunctions and defects in the social assistance state are the result of an inadequate understanding of the tasks proper to the state. Here again the principle of subsidiarity must be respected; a community of a higher order should not interfere in the internal life of a community of a lower order, depriving the latter of its functions, but rather should support it in case of need and help to coordinate its activity wit the activities of the rest of society, always with a view to the common good.

"By intervening directly and depriving society of its responsibility, the social assistance state leads to a loss of human energies and an inordinate increase of public agencies, which are dominated more by bureaucratic ways of thinking than by concern for serving their clients, and which are accompanied by an enormous increase in spending. In fact, it would appear that needs are best understood and satisfied by people who are closest to them and who act as neighbors to those in need."

## Church Concern for the Needy

49. "Faithful to the mission received from Christ her founder, the Church has always been present and active among the needy, offering them material assistance in ways that neither humiliate nor reduce them to mere objects of assistance, but which help them to escape their precarious situation by promoting their dignity as persons. With heartfelt gratitude to God, it must be pointed out that active charity has never ceased to be practiced in the Church; indeed, today it is showing a manifold and gratifying increase. In this regard, special mention must be made of volunteer work, which the Church favors and promotes by urging everyone to cooperate in supporting and encouraging its undertakings.

"In order to overcome today's widespread individualistic mentality, what is required is a concrete commitment to solidarity and charity, beginning in the family with the mutual support of husband and wife and the care which the different generations give to one another. It is urgent to promote not only family policies, but also those social policies which have the family as their principal object."

52. "Another name for peace is development. Just as there is a collective responsibility for avoiding war, so too there is a collective responsibility for promoting development. Just as within individual societies it is possible and right to organize a solid economy which will direct the functioning of the market to the common good, so too there is a similar need for adequate interventions on the international level."

## CHAPTER 6

### Man Is the Way of the Church

54. "Today, the Church's social doctrine focuses especially on man as he is involved in a complex network of relationships within modern societies. The human sciences and philosophy are helpful for interpreting man's central place within society and for enabling him to understand himself better as a 'social being.' However, man's true identity is only fully revealed to him through faith, and it is precisely from faith that the Church's social teaching begins. While drawing upon all the contributions made by the sciences and philosophy, her social teaching is aimed at helping man on the path of salvation."

"Given in Rome, at St. Peter's, on May 1, the memorial of St. Joseph the Worker, in the year 1991, the 13th of my pontificate."

# PEACE STATEMENT BY U.S. BISHOPS

Over a period of nearly 80 years, the bishops of the United States have issued a great number of socio-economic statements reflecting papal documents in a U.S. context.

One such statement, entitled "Economic Justice for All: Social Teaching and the U.S. Economy," was issued in November, 1986. Its contents are related in various ways with the subsequently issued enclyclical letter, *Centesimus Annus.*

## THE HARVEST OF JUSTICE IS SOWN IN PEACE

The National Conference of Cathoic Bishops, at a meeting Nov. 17, 1993, issued a statement entitled "The Harvest of Justice Is Sown in Peace," marking the 10th anniversary of their earlier pastoral letter, "The Challenge of Peace: God's Promise and Our Response."

*The following coverage of the statement, with excerpts, is based on the text circulated by the CNS Documentary Service, Origins, Dec. 9, 1993 (Vol. 23, No. 26).*

"The challenge of peace today is different, but no less urgent" than in 1983, and the threat of global nuclear war "may seem more remote than at any time in the nuclear age." Questions of peace and war, however, cannot be addressed "without acknowledging that the nuclear question remains of vital political and moral significance."

The statement outlines an agenda for action to guide future advocacy efforts of the bishops' national conference. It also urges that the cause of peace be reflected constantly in liturgical prayers of petition, preaching and Catholic education at all levels.

Confronting the temptation to isolationism in U.S. foreign policy is among "the major challenges peacemakers face in this new era."

Factors in a vision for peace include a commitment to the universal common good and recognition of the imperative of human solidarity.

Nonviolent revolutions in some countries "challenge us to find ways to take into full account the power of organized, active nonviolence."

With respect to just war criteria, the statement says that "important work needs to be done in refining, clarifying and applying the just war tradition to the choices facing our decision-makers in this still violent and dangerous world."

Subjects of concern include humanitarian intervention, deterrence, conscientious objection and the development of peoples.

### Presumption against Force

"Our conference's approach, as outlined in 'The Challenge of Peace,' can be summarized in this way:

"1) In situations of conflict our constant commitment ought to be, as far as possible, to strive for justice through nonviolent means.

"2) But when sustained attempts at nonviolent action fail to protect the innocent against fundamental injustice, then legitimate political authorities are permitted as a last resort to employ limited force to rescue the innocent and establish justice."

### Lethal Force

"Whether lethal force may be used is governed by the following criteria:

• "Just cause: Force may be used only to correct a grave, public evil, i.e., aggression or massive violation of the basic rights of whole populations.

• "Comparative justice: While there may be rights and wrongs on all sides of a conflict, to override the presumption against the use of force, the injustice suffered by one party must significantly outweigh that suffered by the other.

• "Legitimate authority: Only duly constituted public authorities may use deadly force or wage war.

• "Right intention: Force may be used only in a truly just cause and solely for that purpose.

• "Probability of Success: Arms may not be used in a futile cause or in a case where disproportionate measures are required to achieve success.

• "Proportionality: The overall destruction expected from the use of force must be outweighed by the good to be achieved.

• "Last Resort: Force may be used only after all peaceful alternatives have been seriously tried and exhausted.

"These criteria (of just war), taken as a whole, must be satisfied in order to override the strong presumption against the use of force."

### Just War

"The just war tradition seeks also to curb the violence of war through restraint on armed combat between the contending parties by imposing the following moral standards for the conduct of armed conflict:

• "Noncombatant Immunity: Civilians may not be the object of direct attack, and military personnel must take due care to avoid and miimize indirect harm to civilians.

• "Proportionality: In the conduct of hostilities, efforts must be made to attain military objectives with no more force than is militarily necessary and to avoid disproportionate collateral damage to civilian life and property.

• "Right Intention: Even in the midst of conflict, the aim of political and military leaders must be peace with justice so that acts of vengeance and indiscriminate violence, whether by individuals, military units or governments, are forbidden."

### Structures for Justice and Peace

Quoting an address given by Pope John Paul in August, 1993, in Denver, the statement said:

" 'The international community ought to establish more effective structures for maintaining and promoting justice and peace. This implies that a concept of strategic interest should evolve which is based on the full development of peoples — out of poverty and toward a more dignified existence, out of injustice and exploitation toward fuller respect for the human person and the defense of universal rights.'

"As we consider a new vision of the international community, five areas deserve special attention: 1) strengthening global institutions; (2) securing human rights; (3) promoting human development; (4) restraining nationalism and eliminating religious violence; and (5) building cooperative security."

## Humanitarian Intervention

"Pope John Paul, citing the 'conscience of humanity and international humanitarian law,' has been outspoken in urging that 'humanitarian intervention be obligatory where the survival of populations and entire ethnic groups is seriously compromised. This is a duty for nations and the international community.' He elaborated on this right and duty of humanitarian intervention in his 1993 annual address

to the diplomatic corps (accredited to the Holy See): " 'Once the possibilities afforded by diplomatic negotiations and the procedures provided for by international agreements and organizations have been put into effect, and that (sic) nevertheless, populations are succumbing to the attacks of an unjust aggressor, states no longer have a 'right to indifference.' It seems clear that their duty is to disarm this aggressor if all other means have proved ineffective. The principles of the sovereignty of states and of noninterference in their internal affairs — which retain all their value — cannot constitute a screen behind which torture and murder may be carried out.'"

## A STATEMENT ON IMMIGRATION

*This is the text of a statement entitled "This Is My Commandment: Love One Another as I Have Loved You," issued June 21, 1996, by Bishop Anthony M. Pilla, president of the National Conference of Catholic Bishops, with the concurrence of the U.S. bishops during their national meeting in Portland, Ore.*

"When an alien resides with you in your land, do not molest him. You shall treat an alien who resides with you no differently than the natives born among you; have the same love for him as for yourself; for you too were once aliens in the land of Egypt. I, the Lord, am your God." (Lv. 19: 33-34)

The Catholic bishops of the United States take seriously the responsibility entrusted to them as pastors and teachers to speak on behalf of those who cannot speak for themselves. We have spoken frequently in recent times of our concerns about the treatment of immigrants and refugees in the United States. Regrettably, since our last statement just a year ago, the public debate has become even more acrimonious, and Congress is now considering the final form of restrictive legislation that runs counter both to Christian teaching and the proud tradition of this nation of immigrants.

The Church has long acknowledged the right and the responsibility of nations to regulate their borders for the promotion of the common good. For that reason, it is appropriate for the United States to engage in a debate about its immigration and refugee policies. Unfortunately, though, that debate has taken on a punitive tone which seems to seek to diminish the basic human dignity of the foreign-born.

In particular, I express grave concern and dismay at provisions of the legislation which target the most vulnerable among us — children, the sick and the needy — in an impractical effort to cure our nation's social and economic ills. Health care and education are among the most basic of human rights to which all have a moral claim, yet this legislation seeks to restrict severely or flatly deny these rights to those who were not born in this country. Indeed, there is a disregard for human life in this legislation which is inconsistent with the Gospel and which I find morally objectionable.

Refugees and asylum seekers, those fleeing persecution and possible death in search of safe haven in the United States, risk the real possibility of being returned immediately to their oppressors as a consequence of this legislation. As emphasized by the bishops in a statement last year, these people "have a

special moral standing and thus require special consideration."

The health and well-being of immigrants who gain entry into the United States are similarly threatened by this legislation. All of us at some point may be affected by hunger, poor health, housing needs, family crises and aging. This legislation is so overreaching and restrictive that it would make it almost impossible for legal taxpaying immigrants to seek assistance when confronted with these vicissitudes of life. The undocumented are put even more at risk. They may be faced with deportation simply for seeking food and medical care for themselves and their children. By denying these most basic needs merely on the basis of where a person was born is to place the health and well-being of the entire community at risk.

Furthermore, undocumented children could be denied access to education in a misguided effort to hold them accountable for the actions of their parents. Consequently, immigrant youths face the possibility of being left illiterate and idle, turned out on the streets to be tempted by crime and delinquency - - or to become their victims. Teachers will be forced to become de facto agents of the Immigration and Naturalization Service. Surely, the common good cannot be served by such measures.

Finally, at a time when great emphasis is being placed on the renewal of the American family, this legislation would effectively prevent the reunification of immigrant families by mandating financial tests which would be impossible for most sponsors to meet. I believe this to be contradictory and counterproductive. Immigrants, like the native-born, draw srength from their families in times of need and, as we said in our statement last year: "Family reunification remains the appropriate basis for just immigration policy."

The principles of human dignity and human solidarity, which the Church has long taught, should be factors in shaping the goals of public policy, including immigration. Pope John Paul II has forcefully spoken on the need for solidarity:

"Solidarity is undoubtedly a Christian virtue.... One's neighbor is then not only a human being with his or her own rights and a fundamental equality with everyone else, but becomes the living image of God the Father, redeemed by the blood of Jesus Christ and placed under the permanent action of the Holy Spirit.

# LITURGY

The nature and purpose of the liturgy, along with norms for its revision, were the subject matter of the *Constitution on the Sacred Liturgy* promulgated by the Second Vatican Council. The principles and guidelines stated in this document, the first issued by the Council, are summarized here and/or are incorporated in other Almanac entries on liturgical subjects.

## Nature and Purpose of Liturgy

The paragraphs under this and the following subhead are quoted directly from the "Constitution on the Sacred Liturgy."

"It is through the liturgy, especially the divine Eucharistic Sacrifice, that 'the work of our redemption is exercised.' The liturgy is thus the outstanding means by which the faithful can express in their lives, and manifest to others, the mystery of Christ and the real nature of the true Church " (No. 2).

"The liturgy is considered as an exercise of the priestly office of Jesus Christ. In the liturgy the sanctification of man is manifested by signs perceptible to the senses, and is effected in a way which is proper to each of these signs; in the liturgy full public worship is performed by the Mystical Body of Jesus Christ, that is, by the Head and his members.

"From this it follows that every liturgical celebration, because it is an action of Christ the priest and of his Body the Church, is a sacred action surpassing all others. No other action of the Church can match its claim to efficacy, nor equal the degree of it" (No. 7).

"The liturgy is the summit toward which the activity of the Church is directed; at the same time it is the fountain from which all her power flows. For the goal of apostolic works is that all who are made sons of God by faith and baptism should come together to praise God i the midst of his Church, to take part in her sacrifice, and to eat the Lord's Supper.

" From the liturgy, therefore, and especially from the Eucharist, as from a fountain, grace is channeled into us; and the sanctification of men in Christ and the glorification of God, to which all other activities of the Church are directed as toward their goal, are most powerfully achieved" (No. 10).

## Full Participation

"Mother Church earnestly desires that all the faithful be led to that full, conscious, and active participation in liturgical celebrations which is demanded by the very nature of the liturgy. Such participation by the Christian people as 'a chosen race, a royal priesthood, a holy nation, a purchased people' (1 Pt. 2:9; cf. 2:4-5), is their right and duty by reason of their baptism.

"In the restoration and promotion of the sacred liturgy, this full and active participation by all the people is the aim to be considered before all else; for it is the primary and indispensable source from which the faithful are to derive the true Christian spirit " (No. 14).

"In order that the Christian people may more securely derive an abundance of graces from the sacred liturgy, holy Mother Church desires to undertake with great care a general restoration of the liturgy itself. For the liturgy is made up of unchangeable elements divinely instituted, and elements subject to change. The latter not only may but ought to be changed with the passing of time if features have by chance crept in which are less harmonious with the intimate nature of the liturgy, or if existing elements have grown less functional.

"In this restoration, both texts and rites should be drawn up so that they express more clearly the holy things which they signify. Christian people, as far as possible, should be able to understand them with ease and to take part in them fully, actively, and as befits a community " (No. 21).

## Norms

Norms regarding the reforms concern the greater use of Scripture; emphasis on the importance of the sermon or homily on biblical and liturgical subjects; use of vernacular languages for prayers of the Mass and for administration of the sacraments; provision for adaptation of rites to cultural patterns.

Approval for reforms of various kinds — in liturgical texts, rites, etc. — depends on the Holy See, regional conferences of bishops and individual bishops, according to provisions of law. No priest has authority to initiate reforms on his own. Reforms may not be introduced just for the sake of innovation, and any that are introduced in the light of present-day circumstances should embody sound tradition.

To assure the desired effect of liturgical reforms, training and instruction are necessary for the clergy, religious and the laity. The functions of diocesan and regiona commissions for liturgy, music and art are to set standards and provide leadership for instruction and practical programs in their respective fields.

Most of the constitution's provisions regarding liturgical reforms have to do with the Roman Rite. The document clearly respects the equal dignity of all rites, leaving to the Eastern Churches control over their ancient liturgies.

(For coverage of the Mystery of the Eucharist, see The Mass; Other Sacraments, see separate entries.)

## Sacramentals

Sacramentals, instituted by the Church, "are sacred signs which bear a resemblance to the sacraments: they signify effects, particularly of a spiritual kind, which are obtained through the Church's intercession. By them men are disposed to receive the chief effect of the sacraments, and various occasions in life are rendered holy" (No. 60).

"Thus, for well-disposed members of the faithful, the liturgy of the sacraments and sacramentals sanctifies almost every event in their lives; they are given access to the stream of divine grace which flows from the paschal mystery of the passion, death, and resurrection of Christ, the fountain from which all sacraments and sacramentals draw their power. There is hardly any proper use of material things which cannot thus be directed toward the sanctification of men and the praise of God" (No. 61).

Some common sacramentals are priestly blessings, blessed palm, candles, holy water, medals, scapulars, prayers and ceremonies of the Roman Ritual.

## Liturgy of the Hours

The Liturgy of the Hours (Divine Office) is the public prayer of the Church for praising God and sanctifying the day. Its daily celebration is required as a sacred obligation by men in holy orders and by men and women religious who have professed solemn vows. Its celebration by others is highly commended and is to be encouraged in the community of the faithful.

"By tradition going back to early Christian times, the Divine Office is arranged so that the whole course of the day and night is made holy by the praises of God. Therefore, when this wonderful song of praise is worthily rendered by priests and others who are deputed for this purpose by Church ordinance, or by the faithful praying together with the priest in an approved form, then it is truly the voice of the bride addressing her bridegroom; it is the very prayer which Christ himself, together with his Body, addresses to the Father" (No. 84).

"Hence all who perform this service are not only fulfilling a duty of the Church, but also are sharing in the greatest honor accorded to Christ's spouse, for by offering these praises to God they are standing before God's throne in the name of the Church their Mother" (No. 85).

The Liturgy of the Hours, revised since 1965, was the subject of Pop Paul VI's apostolic constitution *Laudis Canticum*, dated Nov. 1, 1970. The master Latin text was published in 1971; its four volumes have been published in authorized English translation since May, 1975.

One-volume, partial editions of the Liturgy of the Hours containing Morning and Evening Prayer and other elements, have been published in approved English translation.

The revised Liturgy of the Hours consists of:
• Office of Readings, for reflection on the word of God. The principal parts are three psalms, biblical and non-biblical readings.
• Morning and Evening Prayer, called the "hinges" of the Liturgy of the Hours. The principal parts are a hymn, two psalms, an Old or New Testament canticle, a brief biblical reading, Zechariah's canticle (the *Benedictus*, morning) or Mary's canticle (the *Magnificat*, evening), responsories, intercessions and a concluding prayer.
• Daytime Prayer. The principal parts are a hymn, three psalms, a brief biblical reading and one of three concluding prayers corresponding to the time at which the prayer is offered (midmorning, midday, midafternoon).
• Night Prayer: The principal parts are one or two psalms, a brief biblical reading, Simeon's canticle (*Nunc Dimittis*), a concluding prayer and an antiphon in honor of Mary.

In the revised Liturgy of the Hours, the hours are shorter than they had been, with greater textual variety, meditation aids, and provision for intervals of silence and meditation. The psalms are distributed over a four-week period instead of a week; some psalms, entirely or in part, are not included. Additional canticles from the Old and New Testaments are assigned for Morning and Evening Prayer. Additional scriptural texts have been added and variously arranged for greater internal unity, correspondence to readings at Mass, and relevance to events and themes of salvation history. Readings include some of the best material from the Fathers of the Church and other authors, and improved selections on the lives of the saints.

The book used for recitation of the Office is the **Breviary.**

For coverage of the **Liturgical Year,** see Church Calendar.

## Sacred Music

"The musical tradition of the universal Church is a treasure of immeasurable value, greater even than that of any other art. The main reason for this preeminence is that, as sacred melody united to words, it forms a necessary or integral part of the solemn liturgy.

" Sacred music increases in holiness to the degree that it is intimately linked with liturgical action, winningly expresses prayerfulness, promotes solidarity, and enriches sacred rites with heightened solemnity. The Church indeed approves of all forms of true art, and admits them into divine worship when they show appropriate qualities" (No. 112).

The constitution decreed:
• Vernacular languages for the people's parts of the liturgy, as well as Latin, may be used.
• Participation in sacred song by the whole body of the faithful, and not just by choirs, is to be encouraged and brought about.
• Provisions should be made for proper musical training for clergy, religious and lay persons.
• While Gregorian Chant has a unique dignity and relationship to the Latin liturgy, other kinds of music are acceptable.
• Native musical traditions should be used, especially in mission areas.
• Various instruments compatible with the dignity of worship may be used.

**Gregorian Chant:** A form and style of chant called Gregorin was the basis and most highly regarded standard of liturgical music for centuries. It originated probably during the formative period of the Roman liturgy and developed in conjunction with Gallican and other forms of chant. Gregory the Great's connection with it is not clear, although it is known that he had great concern for and interest in church music. The earliest extant written versions of Gregorian Chant date from the ninth century. A thousand years later, the Benedictines of Solesmes, France, initiated a revival of chant which gave impetus to the modern liturgical movement.

## Sacred Art and Furnishings

"Very rightly the fine arts are considered to rank among the noblest expressions of human genius. This judgment applies especially to religious art and to its highest achievement, which is sacred art. By their very nature both of the latter are related to God's boundless beauty, for this is the reality which these human efforts are trying to express in some way. To the extent that these works aim exclusively at turning men's thoughts to God persuasively and devoutly, they are dedicated to God and to the cause of his greater honor and glory" (No. 122).

The objective of sacred art is "that all things set

apart for use in divine worship should be truly worthy, becoming, and beautiful, signs and symbols of heavenly realities. The Church has always reserved to herself the right to pass judgment upon the arts, deciding which of the works of artists are in accordance with faith, piety, and cherished traditional laws, and thereby suited to sacred purposes.

" Sacred furnishings should worthily and beautifully serve the dignity of worship " (No. 122).

According to the constitution:

• Contemporary art, as well as that of the past, shall "be given free scope in the Church, provided that it adorns the sacred buildings and holy rites with due honor and reverence " (No. 123).

• Noble beauty, not sumptuous display, should be sought in art, sacred vestments and ornaments.

• "Let bishops carefully exclude from the house of God and from other sacred places those works of artists which are repugnant to faith, morals, and Christian piety, and which offend true religious sense either by their distortion of forms or by lack of artistic worth, by mediocrity or by pretense.

• "When churches are to be built, let great care be taken that they be suitable for the celebration of liturgical services and for the active participation of the faithful" (No. 124).

• "The practice of placing sacred images in churches so that they may be venerated by the faithful is to be firmly maintained. Nevertheless, their number should be moderate and their relative location should reflect right order. Otherwise they may create confusion among the Christian people and promote a faulty sense of devotion" (No. 125).

• Artists should be trained and inspired in the spirit and for the purposes of the liturgy.

• The norms of sacred art should be revised. "These laws refer especially to the worthy and well-planned construction of sacred buildings, the shape and construction of altars, the nobility, location, and security of the Eucharistic tabernacle, the suitability and dignity of the baptistery, the proper use of sacred images, embellishments, and vestments " (No. 128).

## RITES

Rites are the forms and ceremonial observances of liturgical worship coupled with the total expression of the theological, spiritual and disciplinary hages of particular churches of the East and the West.

Different rites have evolved in the course of church history, giving to liturgical worship and church life in general forms and usages peculiar and proper to the nature of worship and the culture of the faithful in various circumstances of time and place. Thus, there has been development since apostolic times in the prayers and ceremonies of the Mass, in the celebration of the sacraments, sacramentals and the Liturgy of the Hours, and in observances of the liturgical calendar. The principal sources of rites in present use were practices within the patriarchates of Rome (for the West) and Antioch, Alexandria and Constantinople (for the East). Rites are identified as Eastern or Western on the basis of their geographical area of origin in the Roman Empire.

### Eastern and Roman

Eastern rites are proper to Eastern Catholic Churches (see separate entry). The principal rites are Byzantine, Alexandrian, Antiochene, Armenian and Chaldean.

The Latin or Roman rite prevails in the Western Church. It was derived from Roman practices and the use of Latin from the third century onward, and has been the rite in general use in the West since the eighth century. Other rites in limited use in the Western Church have been the Ambrosian (in the Archdiocese of Milan), the Mozarabic (in the Archdiocese of Toledo), the Lyonnais, the Braga, and rites peculiar to some religious orders like the Dominicans, Carmelites and Carthusians.

The purpose of the revision of rites in progress since the Second Vatican Council is to renew them, not to eliminate the rites of particular churches or to reduce all rites to uniformity. The Council reaffirmed the equal dignity and preservation of rites as follows.

"It is the mind of the Catholic Church that each individual church or rite retain its traditions whole and entire, while adjusting its way of life to various needs of time and place. Such individual churches, whether of the East or the West, although they differ somewhat among themselves in what are called rites (that is, in liturgy, ecclesiastical discipline and spiritual heritage), are, nevertheless, equally entrusted to the pastoral guidance of the Roman Pontiff, the divinely appointed successor of St. Peter in supreme government over the universal Church. They are, consequently, of equal dignity, so that none of them is superior to the others by reason of rite."

### Determination of Rite

Determination of a person's rite is regulated by church law. Through baptism, a child becomes a member of the rite of his or her parents. If the parents are of different rites, the child's rite is decided by mutual consent of the parents; if there is lack of mutual consent, the child is baptized in the rite of the father. A candidate for baptism over the age of 14 can choose to be baptized in any approved rite. Catholics baptized in one rite may receive the sacraments in any of the approved ritual churches; they may transfer to another rite only with the permission of the Holy See and in accordance with other provisions of the Code of Canon Law.

# MASS, EUCHARISTIC SACRIFICE AND BANQUET

## Declarations of Vatican II

The Second Vatican Council made the following declarations among others with respect to the Mass. "At the Last Supper, on the night when he was betrayed, our Savior instituted the Eucharistic Sacrifice of his Body and Blood. He did this in order to perpetuate the Sacrifice of the Cross throughout the centuries until he should come again, and so to entrust to his beloved spouse, the Church, a memorial of his death and resurrection: a sacrament of love, a sign of unity, a bond of charity, a paschal banquet in which Christ is consumed, the mind is filled with grace, and a pledge of future glory is given to us" (*Constitution on the Sacred Liturgy,* No. 47).

"... As often as the Sacrifice of the Cross in which 'Christ, our Passover, has been sacrificed' (1 Cor. 5:7) is celebrated on an altar, the work of our redemption is carried on. At the same time, in the sacrament of the Eucharistic bread the unity of all believers who form one body in Christ (cf. 1 Cor. 10:17) is both expressed and brought about. All men are called to this union with Christ ..." (*Dogmatic Constitution on the Church,* No. 3).

"... The ministerial priest, by the sacred power he enjoys, molds and rules the priestly people. Acting in the person of Christ, he brings about the Eucharistic Sacrifice, and offers it to God in the name of all the people. For their part, the faithful join in the offering of the Eucharist by virtue of their royal priesthood ..." (*Ibid.,* No. 10).

## Declarations of Trent

Among its decrees on the Holy Eucharist, the Council of Trent stated the following points of doctrine on the Mass.

1. There is in the Catholic Church a true sacrifice, the Mass instituted by Jesus Christ. It is the sacrifice of his Body and Blood, Soul and Divinity, himself, under the appearances of bread and wine.

2. This Sacrifice is identical with the Sacrifice of the Cross, inasmuch as Christ is the Priest and Victim in both. A difference lies in the manner of offering, which was bloody upon the Cross and is bloodless on the altar.

3. The Mass is a propitiatory Sacrifice, atoning for the sins of the living and dead for whom it is offered.

4. The efficacy of the Mass is derived from the Sacrifice of the Cross, whose superabundant merits it applies to men.

5. Although the Mass is offered to God alone, it may be celebrated in honor and memory of the saints.

6. Christ instituted the Mass at the Last Supper.

7. Christ ordained the Apostles priests, giving them power and the command to consecrate his Body and Blood to perpetuate and renew the Sacrifice.

## ORDER OF MASS

The Mass consists of two principal divisions called the **Liturgy of the Word,** which features the proclamation of the Word of God, and the **Eucharistic Liturgy,** which focuses on the central act of sacrifice in the Consecration and on the Eucharistic Banquet in Holy Communion. (Formerly, these divisions were called, respectively, the **Mass of the Catechumens** and the **Mass of the Faithful.**) In addition to these principal divisions, there are ancillary introductory and concluding rites.

The following description covers the Mass as celebrated with participation by the people. This Order of the Mass was approved by Pope Paul VI in the apostolic constitution *Missale Romanum* dated Apr. 3, 1969, and promulgated in a decree issued Apr. 6, 1969, by the Congregation for Divine Worship. The assigned effective date was Nov. 30, 1969.

## Introductory Rites

**Entrance:** The introductory rites begin with the singing or recitation of an entrance song consisting of one or more scriptural verses stating the theme of the mystery, season or feast commemorated in the Mass.

**Greeting:** The priest and people make the Sign of the Cross together. The priest then greets them in one of several alternative ways and they reply in a corresponding manner.

**Introductory Remarks:** At this point, the priest or another of the ministers may introduce the theme of the Mass.

**Penitential Rite:** The priest and people together acknowledge their sins as a preliminary step toward worthy celebration of the sacred mysteries.

This rite includes a brief examination of conscience, a general confession of sin and plea for divine mercy in one of several ways, and a prayer for forgiveness by the priest.

**Glory to God:** A doxology, a hymn of praise to God, sung or said on festive occasions.

**Opening Prayer:** A prayer of petition offered by the priest on behalf of the worshipping community.

## I. Liturgy of the Word

**Readings:** The featured elements of this liturgy are readings of passages from the Bible. If three readings are in order, the first is usually from the Old Testament, the second from the New Testament (Letters, Acts, Revelation), and the third from one of the Gospels; the final reading is always a selection from a Gospel. The first reading(s) is (are) concluded with the formula, "The Word of the Lord" (effective Feb. 28, 1993; optional before that date), to which the people respond, "Thanks be to God." The Gospel reading is concluded with the formula, "The Gospel of the Lord," (effective as above), to which the people respond, "Praise to you, Lord Jesus Christ." Between the readings, psalm verses are sung or recited. A Gospel acclamation is either sung or omitted.

**Homily:** An explanation, pertinent to the mystery being celebrated and the special needs of the listeners, of some point in either the readings from sacred Scripture or in another text from the Ordinary or Proper parts of the Mass; it is a proclamation of the Good News for a response of faith.

**Creed:** The Nicene profession of faith, by priest and people, on certain occasions.

**Prayer of the Faithful:** Litany-type prayers of petition, with participation by the people. Called general intercessions, they concern needs of the Church, the salvation of the world, public authorities, persons in need, the local community.

## II. Eucharistic Liturgy

**Presentation and Preparation of Gifts:** Presentation to the priest of the gifts of bread and wine, principally, by participating members of the congregation. Preparation of the gifts consists of the prayers and ceremonies with which the priest offers bread and wine as the elements of the sacrifice to take place during the Eucharistic Prayer and of the Lord's Supper to be shared in Holy Communion.

**Washing of Hands:** After offering the bread and

wine, the priest cleanses his fingers with water in a brief ceremony of purification.

**Pray, Brothers and Sisters:** Prayer that the sacrifice to take place will be acceptable to God. The first part of the prayer is said by the priest; the second, by the people.

**Prayer over the Gifts:** A prayer of petition offered by the priest on behalf of the worshipping community.

## Eucharistic Prayer

**Preface:** A hymn of praise, introducing the Eucharistic Prayer or Canon, sung or said by the priest following responses by the people. The Order of the Mass contains a variety of prefaces, for use on different occasions.

**Holy, Holy, Holy; Blessed is He:** Divine praises sung or said by the priest and people.

**Eucharistic Prayer** (Canon): Its central portion is the Consecration, when the essential act of sacrificial offering takes place with the changing of bread and wine into the Body and Blood of Christ. The various parts of the prayer, which are said by the celebrant only, commemorate principal mysteries of salvation history and include petitions for the Church, the living and dead, and remembrances of saints.

**Doxology:** A formula of divine praise sung or said by the priest while he holds aloft the chalice containing the consecrated wine in one hand and the paten containing the consecrated host in the other.

## Communion Rite

**Lord's Prayer:** Sung or said by the priest and people.

**Prayer for Deliverance** from evil: Called an **embolism** because it is a development of the final petition of the Lord's Prayer; said by the priest. It concludes with a memorial of the return of the Lord to which the people respond, "For the kingdom, the power, and the glory are yours, now and forever."

**Prayer for Peace:** Said by the priest, with corresponding responses by the people. The priest can, in accord with local custom, bid the people to exchange a greeting of peace with each other.

**Lamb of God** (*Agnus Dei):* A prayer for divine mercy sung or said while the priest breaks the consecrated host and places a piece of it into the consecrated wine in the chalice.

**Communion:** The priest, after saying a preparatory prayer, administers Holy Communion to himself and then to the people, thus completing the sacrifice-banquet of the Mass. (This completion is realized even if the celebrant alone receives the Eucharist.) On giving the Eucharist to each person under both species separately, the priest or eucharistic minister says, "The Body of Christ," "The Blood of Christ." The customary response is "Amen." If the Eucharist is given by intinction (in which the host is dipped into the consecrated wine), the priest says, "The Body and Blood of Christ."

**Communion Song:** Scriptural verses or a suitable hymn sung or said during the distribution of Holy Communion. After Holy Communion is received, some moments may be spent in silent meditation or in the chanting of a psalm or hymn of praise.

**Prayer after Communion:** A prayer of petition offered by the priest on behalf of the worshipping community.

## Concluding Rite

**Announcements:** Brief announcements to the people are in order at this time.

**Dismissal:** Consists of a final greeting by the priest, a blessing, and a formula of dismissal. This rite is omitted if another liturgical action immediately follows the Mass; e.g., a procession, the blessing of the body during a funeral rite.

Some parts of the Mass are changeable with the liturgical season or feast, and are called the **proper** of the Mass. Other parts are said to be **common** because they always remain the same.

## Additional Mass Notes

Catholics are seriously obliged to attend Mass in a worthy manner on Sundays and holy days of obligation. Failure to do so without a proportionately serious reason is gravely wrong.

It is the custom for priests to celebrate Mass daily whenever possible. To satisfy the needs of the faithful on Sundays and holy days of obligation, they are authorized to say Mass twice (**bination**) or even three times (**trination**). Bination is also permissible on weekdays to satisfy the needs of the faithful. On Christmas every priest may say three Masses.

The **fruits of the Mass,** which in itself is of infinite value, are: **general,** for all the faithful; **special (ministerial),** for the intentions or persons specifically intended by the celebrant; **most special (personal),** for the celebrant himself. On Sundays and certain other days pastors are obliged to offer Mass for their parishioners, or to have another priest do so. If a priest accepts a stipend or offering for a Mass, he is obliged in justice to apply the Mass for the intention of the donor. Mass may be applied for the living and the dead, or for any good intention.

Mass can be celebrated in several ways: e.g., with people present, without their presence (privately), with two or more priests as co-celebrants (concelebration), with greater or less solemnity.

Some of the various types of Masses are: **for the dead** (Funeral Mass or Mass of Christian Burial, Mass for the Dead — formerly called Requiem Mass); **ritual,** in connection with celebration of the sacraments, religious profession, etc.; **nuptial,** for married couples, with or after the wedding ceremony; **votive,** to honor a Person of the Trinity, a saint, or for some special intention.

## Places, Altars for Mass

The ordinary place for celebrating the Eucharist is a church or other sacred place, at a fixed or movable altar.

The altar is a table at which the Eucharistic Sacrifice is celebrated.

A fixed altar is attached to the floor of the church. It should be of stone, preferably, and should be consecrated. The Code of Canon Law orders observance of the custom of placing under a fixed altar relics of martyrs or other saints.

A movable altar can be made of any solid and suitable material, and should be blessed or consecrated.

Outside of a sacred place, Mass may be celebrated

in an appropriate place at a suitable table covered with a linen cloth and corporal. An altar stone containing the relics of saints, which was formerly prescribed, is not required by regulations in effect since the promulgation Apr. 6, 1969, of *Institutio Generalis Missalis Romani.*

## LITURGICAL VESTMENTS

In the early years of the Church, vestments worn by the ministers at liturgical functions were the same as the garments in ordinary popular use. They became distinctive when their form was not altered to correspond with later variations in popular style. Liturgical vestments are symbolic of the sacred ministry and add appropriate decorum to divine worship.

### Mass Vestments

**Alb:** A body-length tunic of white fabric; a vestment common to all ministers of divine worship.

**Amice:** A rectangular piece of white cloth worn about the neck, tucked into the collar and falling over the shoulders; prescribed for use when the alb does not completely cover the ordinary clothing at the neck.

**Chasuble:** Originally, a large mantle or cloak covering the body, it is the outer vestment of a priest celebrating Mass or carrying out other sacred actions connected with the Mass.

**Cincture:** A cord which serves the purpose of a belt, holding the alb close to the body.

**Dalmatic:** The outer vestment worn by a deacon in place of a chasuble.

**Stole:** A long, band-like vestment worn by a priest about the neck and falling to about the knees. A deacon wears a stole over the left shoulder, crossed and fastened at his right side.

The material, form and ornamentation of the aforementioned and other vestments are subject to variation and adaptation, according to norms and decisions of the Holy See and concerned conferences of bishops. The overriding norm is that they should be appropriate for use in divine worship. The customary ornamented vestments are the chasuble, dalmatic and stole.

The minimal vestments required for a priest celebrating Mass are the alb, stole and chasuble.

**Chasuble-Alb:** A vestment combining the features of the chasuble and alb; for use with a stole by concelebrants and, by way of exception, by celebrants in certain circumstances.

### Liturgical Colors

The colors of outer vestments vary with liturgical seasons, feasts and other circumstances. The colors and their use are:

**Green:** For the season of Ordinary Time; symbolic of hope and the vitality of the life of faith.

**Violet (Purple):** For Advent and Lent; may also be used in Masses for the dead; symbolic of penance. (See below, Violet for Advent.)

**Red:** For the Sunday of the Passion, Good Friday, Pentecost; feasts of the Passion of Our Lord, the Apostles and Evangelists, martyrs; symbolic of the supreme sacrifice of life for the love of God.

**Rose:** May be used in place of purple on the Third Sunday of Advent (formerly called Gaudete Sunday) and the Fourth Sunday of Lent (formerly called Laetare Sunday); symbolic of anticipatory joy during a time of penance.

**White:** For the seasons of Christmas and Easter; feasts and commemorations of Our Lord, except those of the Passion; feasts and commemorations of the Blessed Virgin Mary, angels, saints who are not martyrs, All Saints (Nov. 1), St. John the Baptist (June 24), St. John the Evangelist (Dec. 27), the Chair of St. Peter (Feb. 22), the Conversion of St. Paul (Jan. 25). White, symbolic of purity and integrity of the life of faith, may generally be substituted for other colors, and can be used for funeral and other Masses for the dead.

Options are provided regarding the color of vestments used in offices and Masses for the dead. The newsletter of the U.S. Bishops' Committee on the Liturgy, in line with No. 308 of the General Instruction of the Roman Missal, announced in July, 1970: "In the dioceses of the United States, white vestments may be used, in addition to violet (purple) and black, in offices and Masses for the dead."

On more solemn occasions, better than ordinary vestments may be used, even though their color (e.g., gold) does not match the requirements of the day.

**Violet for Advent:** Violet is the official liturgical color for the season of Advent, according to the September, 1988, edition of the newsletter of the U.S. Bishops' Committee on the Liturgy. Blue was being proposed in order to distinguish between the Advent season and the specifically penitential season of Lent. The newsletter said, however, that "the same effect can be achieved by following the official color sequence of the Church, which requires the use of violet for Advent and Lent, while taking advantage of the varying shades which exist for violet. Light blue vestments are not authorized for use in the United States."

Considerable freedom is permitted in the choice of colors of vestments worn for votive Masses.

### Other Vestments

**Cappa Magna:** Flowing vestment with a train, worn by bishops and cardinals.

**Cassock:** A non-liturgical, full-length, close-fitting robe for use by priests and other clerics under liturgical vestments and in ordinary use; usually black for priests, purple for bishops and other prelates, red for cardinals, white for the pope. In place of a cassock, priests belonging to religious institutes wear the habit proper to their institute.

**Cope:** A mantle-like vestment open in front and fastened across the chest; worn by sacred ministers in processions and other ceremonies, as prescribed by appropriate directives.

**Habit:** The ordinary (non-liturgical) garb of members of religious institutes, analogous to the cassock of diocesan priests; the form of habits varies from institute to institute.

**Humeral Veil:** A rectangular vestment worn about the shoulders by a deacon or priest in Eucharistic processions and for other prescribed liturgical ceremonies.

**Mitre:** A headdress worn at some liturgical functions by bishops, abbots and, in certain cases, other ecclesiastics.

**Pallium:** A circular band of white wool about two inches wide, with front and back pendants, marked with six crosses, worn about the neck. It is a symbol of the fullness of the episcopal office. Pope Paul VI, in a document issued July 20, 1978, on his own initiative and entitled Inter *Eximia Episcopalis*, restricted its use to the pope and archbishops of metropolitan sees. In 1984, Pope John Paul II decreed that the pallium would ordinarily be conferred by the pope on the solemnity of Sts. Peter and Paul, June 29. The pallium is made from the wool of lambs blessed by the pope on the feast of St. Agnes (Jan. 21).

**Rochet:** A knee-length, white linen-lace garment of prelates worn under outer vestments.

**Surplice:** a loose, flowing vestment of white fabric with wide sleeves. For some functions, it is interchangeable with an alb.

**Zucchetto:** A skullcap worn by bishops and other prelates.

## SACRED VESSELS, LINENS

### Vessels

**Paten and Chalice:** The principal sacred vessels required for the celebration of Mass are the paten (plate) and chalice (cup) in which bread and wine, respectively, are offered, consecrated and consumed. Both should be made of solid and noble material which is not easily breakable or corruptible. Gold coating is required of the interior parts of sacred vessels subject to rust. The cup of a chalice should be made of non-absorbent material.

Vessels for containing consecrated hosts (see below) can be made of material other than solid and noble metal — e.g., ivory, more durable woods — provided the substitute material is locally regarded as noble or rather precious and is suitable for sacred use.

Sacred vessels should be blessed, according to prescribed requirements.

Vessels, in addition to the paten, for containing consecrated hosts are:

**Ciborium:** Used to hold hosts for distribution to the faithful and for reservation in the tabernacle.

**Luna, Lunula, Lunette:** A small receptacle which holds the sacred host in an upright position in the monstrance.

**Monstrance, Ostensorium:** A portable receptacle so made that the sacred host, when enclosed therein, may be clearly seen, as at Benediction or during extended exposition of the Blessed Sacrament.

**Pyx:** A watch-shaped vessel used in carrying the Eucharist to the sick.

### Linens

**Altar Cloth:** A white cloth, usually of linen, covering the table of an altar. One cloth is sufficient. Three were used according to former requirements.

**Burse:** A square, stiff flat case, open at one end, in which the folded corporal can be placed; the outside is covered with material of the same kind and color as the outer vestments of the celebrant.

**Corporal:** A square piece of white linen spread on the altar cloth, on which rest the vessels holding the Sacred Species — the consecrated host(s) and wine — during the Eucharistic Liturgy. The corporal is similarly used whenever the Blessed Sacrament is removed from the tabernacle; e.g., during Benediction the vessel containing the Blessed Sacrament rests on a corporal.

**Finger Towel:** A white rectangular napkin used by the priest to dry his fingers after cleansing them following the offering of gifts at Mass.

**Pall:** A square piece of stiff material, usually covered with linen, which can be used to cover the chalice at Mass.

**Purificator:** A white rectangular napkin used for cleansing sacred vessels after the reception of Communion at Mass.

**Veil:** The chalice intended for use at Mass can be covered with a veil made of the same material as the outer vestments of the celebrant.

## THE CHURCH BUILDING

A church is a building set aside and dedicated for purposes of divine worship, the place of assembly for a worshipping community.

A Catholic church is the ordinary place in which the faithful assemble for participation in the Eucharistic Liturgy and other forms of divine worship.

In the early years of Christianity, the first places of assembly for the Eucharistic Liturgy were private homes (Acts 2:46; Rom. 16:5; 1 Cor. 16:5; Col. 4:15) and, sometimes, catacombs. Church building began in the latter half of the second century during lulls in persecution and became widespread after enactment of the Edict of Milan in 313, when it finally became possible for the Church to emerge completely from the underground. The oldest and basic norms regarding church buildings date from about that time.

The essential principle underlying all norms for church building was reformulated by the Second Vatican Council, as follows: "When churches are to be built, let great care be taken that they be suitable for the celebration of liturgical services and for the active paticipation of the faithful" (*Constitution on the Sacred Liturgy*, No. 124).

This principle was subsequently elaborated in detail by the Congregation for Divine Worship in a document entitled *Institutio Generalis Missalis Romani*, which was approved by Paul VI Apr. 3 and promulgated by a decree of the congregation dated Apr. 6, 1969. Coverage of the following items reflects the norms stated in Chapter V of this document.

### Main Features

**Sanctuary:** The part of the church where the altar of sacrifice is located, the place where the ministers of the liturgy lead the people in prayer, proclaim the word of God and celebrate the Eucharist. It is set off from the body of the church by a distinctive structural feature — e.g., elevation above the main floor — or by ornamentation. (The traditional communion rail, removed in recent years in many churches, served this purpose of demarcation.) The customary location of the sanctuary is at the front of the church; it may, however, be centrally located.

**Altar:** The main altar of sacrifice and table of the Lord is the focal feature of the sanctuary and entire church. It stands by itself, so that the ministers can move about it freely, and is so situated that they face the people during the liturgical action. In addition to this main altar, there may also be others; in new churches, these are ideally situated in side chapels or alcoves removed to some degree from the body of the church.

**Adornment of the Altar:** The altar table is covered with a suitable linen cloth. Required candelabra and a cross are placed upon or near the altar in plain sight of the people and are so arranged that they do not obscure their view of the liturgical action.

**Seats of the Ministers:** The seats of the ministers should be so arranged that they are part of the seating arrangement of the worshiping congregation and suitably placed for the performance of ministerial functions. The seat of the celebrant or chief concelebrant should be in a presiding position.

**Ambo, Pulpit, Lectern:** The stand at which scriptural lessons and psalm responses are read, the word of God preached, and the prayer of the faithful offered. It is so placed that the ministers can be easily seen and heard by the people.

**Places for the People:** Seats and kneeling benches (pews) and other accommodations for the people are so arranged that they can participate in the most appropriate way in the liturgical action and have freedom of movement for the reception of Holy Communion. Reserved seats are out of order.

**Place for the Choir:** Where it is located depends on the most suitable arrangement for maintaining the unity of the choir with the congregation and for providing its members maximum opportunity for carrying out their proper function and participating fully in the Mass.

**Tabernacle:** The best place for reserving the Blessed Sacrament is in a chapel suitable for the private devotion of the people. If this is not possible, reservation should be at a side altar or other appropriately adorned place. In either case, the Blessed Sacrament should be kept in a tabernacle, i.e., a safe-like, secure receptacle.

**Statues:** Images of the Lord, the Blessed Virgin Mary and the saints are legitimately proposed for the veneration of the faithful in churches. Their number and arrangement, however, shoul be ordered in such a way that they do not distract the people from the central celebration of the Eucharistic Liturgy.

There should be only one statue of one and the same saint in a church.

**General Adornment and Arrangement of Churches:** Churches should be so adorned and fitted out that they serve the direct requirements of divine worship and the needs and reasonable convenience of the people.

## Other Items

**Ambry:** A box containing the holy oils, attached to the wall of the sanctuary in some churches.

**Baptistery:** The place for administering baptism. Some churches have baptisteries adjoining or near the entrance, a position symbolizing the fact that persons are initiated in the Church and incorporated in Christ through this sacrament. Contemporary liturgical practice favors placement of the baptistery near the sanctuary and altar, or the use of a portable font in the same position, to emphasize the relationship of baptism to the Eucharist, the celebration in sacrifice and banquet of the death and resurrection of Christ.

**Candles:** Used more for symbolical than illuminative purposes, they represent Christ, the light and life of grace, at liturgical functions. They are made of beeswax. (See Index: Paschal Candle.)

**Confessional, Reconciliation Room:** A booth-like structure for the hearing of confessions, with separate compartments for the priest and penitents and a grating or screen between them. The use of confessionals became general in the Roman Rite after the Council of Trent. Since the Second Vatican Council, there has been a trend in the U.S. to replace or supplement confessionals with small reconciliation rooms so arranged that priest and penitent can converse face-to-face.

**Crucifix:** A cross bearing the figure of the body of Christ, representative of the Sacrifice of the Cross.

**Cruets:** Vessels containing the wine and water used at Mass. They are placed on a credence table in the sanctuary.

**Holy Water Fonts:** Receptacles containing holy water, usually at church entrances, for the use of the faithful.

**Sanctuary Lamp:** A lamp which is kept burning continuously before a tabernacle in which the Blessed Sacrament is reserved, as a sign of the Real Presence of Christ.

# LITURGICAL DEVELOPMENTS

The principal developments covered in this article are enactments of the Holy See and actions related to their implementation in the United States.

## Modern Movement

Origins of the modern movement for renewal in the liturgy date back to the 19th century. The key contributing factor was a revival of liturgical and scriptural studies. Of special significance was the work of the Benedictine monks of Solesmes, France, who aroused great interest in the liturgy through the restoration of Gregorian Chant. St. Pius X approved their work in a motu proprio of 1903 and gave additional encouragement to liturgical study and development.

St. Pius X did more than any other single pope to promote early first Communion and the practice of frequent Communion, started the research behind a revised breviary, and appointed a group to investigate possible revisions in the Mass.

The movement attracted some attention in the 1920s and 30s but made little progress.

Significant pioneering developments in the U.S. during the 20s, however, were the establishment of the Liturgical Press, the beginning of publication of *Orate Fratres* (now *Worship*), and the inauguration of the League of the Divine Office by the Benedictines at St. John's Abbey, Collegeville, Minn. Later events of influence were the establishment of the Pius X School of Liturgical Music at Manhattanville College of the Sacred Heart and the organization of a summer school of liturgical music at Mary Manse College by the Gregorian Institute of America. The turning point toward real renewal was reached during and after World War II.

Pius XII gave it impetus and direction, principally through the background teaching in his encyclicals on the *Mystical Body* (1943), *Sacred Liturgy* (1947), and *On Sacred Music* (1955), and by means of specific measures affecting the liturgy itself. His work was continued during the pontificates of his successors. The Second Vatican Council, in virtue of its *Constitution on the Sacred Liturgy*, inaugurated changes of the greatest significance.

### Before and After Vatican II

The most significant liturgical changes made in the years immediately preceding the Second Vatican Council were the following:

(1) Revision of the Rites of Holy Week, for universal observance from 1956.

(2) Modification of the Eucharistic fast and permission for afternoon and evening Mass, in effect from 1953 and extended in 1957.

(3) The Dialogue Mass, introduced in 1958.

(4) Use of popular languages in administration of the sacraments.

(5) Calendar-missal-breviary reform, in effect from Jan. 1, 1961.

(6) Seven-step administration of baptism for adults, approved in 1962.

The *Constitution on the Sacred Liturgy* approved (2,174 to 4) and promulgated by the Second Vatican Council Dec. 4, 1963, marked the beginning of a profound renewal in the Church's corporate worship. Implementation of some of its measures was ordered by Paul VI Jan. 25, 1964, in the motu proprio Sacram Liturgiam. On Feb. 29, a special commission, the Consilium for Implementing the Constitution on the Sacred Liturgy, was formed to supervise the execution of the entire program of liturgical reform. Implementation of the program on local and regional levels was left to bishops acting through their own liturgical commissions and in concert with their fellow bishops in national conferences.

Liturgical reform in the United States has been carried out under the direction of the Liturgy Committee, National Conference of Catholic Bishops. Its secretariat, established early in 1965, is located at 3211 Fourth St. N.E., Washington, D.C. 20017.

### Stages of Development

Liturgical development after the Second Vatican Council proceeded in several stages. It started with the formulation of guidelines and directives, and with the translation into vernacular languages of virtually unchanged Latin ritual texts. Then came structural changes in the Mass, the sacraments, the calendar, the Divine Office and other phases of the liturgy. These revisions were just about completed with the publication of a new order for the sacrament of penance in February, 1974. A continuing phase of development, in progress from the beginning, involves efforts to deepen the liturgical sense of the faithful, to increase their participation in worship and to relate it to full Christian life.

### Texts and Translations

The master texts of all documents on liturgical reform are in Latin. Effective dates of their implementation have depended on the completion and approval of appropriate translations into vernacular languages. English translations were made by the International Committee for English in the Liturgy.

The principal features of liturgical changes and the effective dates of their introduction in the United States are covered below under topical headings. (For expanded coverage of various items, especially the sacraments, see additional entries.)

### The Mass

A new Order of the Mass, supplanting the one authorized by the Council of Trent in the 16th century, was introduced in the U.S. Mar. 22, 1970. It had been approved by Paul VI in the apostolic constitution *Missale Romanum*, dated Apr. 3, 1969.

Preliminary and related to it were the following developments.

**Mass in English:** Introduced Nov. 29, 1964. In the same year, Psalm 42 was eliminated from the prayers at the foot of the altar.

**Incidental Changes:** The last Gospel (prologue of John) and vernacular prayers following Mass were eliminated Mar. 7, 1965. At the same time, provision was made for the celebrant to say aloud some prayers formerly said silently.

**Rubrics:** An instruction entitled *Tres Abhinc Annos*, dated May 4 and effective June 29, 1967, simplified directives for the celebration of Mass, approved the practice of saying the canon aloud, altered the Communion and dismissal rites, permitted purple instead of black vestments in Masses for the dead, discontinued wearing of the maniple, and approved in principle the use of vernacular languages for the canon, ordination rites, and lessons of the Divine Office when read in choir.

**Eucharistic Prayers (Canons):** The traditional Roman Canon in English was introduced Oct. 22, 1967. Three additional Eucharistic prayers, authorized May 23, 1968, were approved for use in English the following Aug. 15.

The customary Roman Canon, which dates at least from the beginning of the fifth century and has remained substantially unchanged since the seventh century, is the first in the order of listing of the Eucharistic prayers. It can be used at any time, but is the one of choice for most Sundays, some special feasts like Easter and Pentecost, and for feasts of the Apostles and other saints who are commemorated in the canon. Any preface can be used with it.

The second Eucharistic prayer, the shortest and simplest of all, is best suited for use on weekdays and various special circumstances. It has a preface of its own, but others may be used with it. This canon bears a close resemblance to the one framed by St. Hippolytus about 215.

The third Eucharistic prayer is suitable for use on Sundays and feasts as an alternative to the Roman Canon. It can be used with any preface and has a special formula for remembrance of the dead.

The fourth Eucharistic prayer, the most sophisticated of them all, presents a broad synthesis of salvation history. Based on the Eastern tradition of Antioch, it is best suited for use at Masses attended by persons versed in Sacred Scripture. It has an unchangeable preface.

Five additional Eucharistic prayers — three for Masses with children and two for Masses of reconciliation — were approved in 1974 and 1975, respectively, by the Congregation for the Sacraments and Divine Worship.

Use of the Eucharistic Prayer for Various Needs and Occasions, based on the Latin version of the Swiss Eucharistic Prayer, was approved by the U.S. bishops in 1994, confirmed by the appropriate Vatican congregations May 9, 1995, and ratified for use begining Oct. 1,1995.

**Lectionary:** A new compilation of scriptural readings and psalm responsories for Mass was published in 1969. The *Lectionary* contains a three-year cycle of readings for Sundays and solemn feasts, a two-year weekday cycle, and a one-year cycle for the feasts of saints, in addition to readings for a variety of votive Masses, ritual Masses and Masses for various needs. There are also responsorial psalms to follow the first readings and gospel or alleluia versicles.

A second edition of the *Lectionary*, substantially the same as the first, was published in 1981. New features included an expanded introduction, extensive scriptural references and additional readings for a number of solemnities and feasts.

**Sacramentary (Missal):** The Vatican Polyglot Press began distribution in June, 1970, of the Latin text of a new *Roman Missal*, the first revision published in 400 years. The English translation was authorized for optional use beginning July 1, 1974; the mandatory date for use was Dec. 1, 1974.

The Sacramentary is the celebrant's Mass book of entrance songs, prayers, prefaces and Eucharistic prayers, including special common sets of texts for various commemorations and intentions — dedication of churches, Mary, the apostles, martyrs, doctors of the Church, virgins, holy men and women, the dead, other categories of holy persons, administration of certain sacraments, special intentions.

**Study of the Mass:** The Bishops' Committee on the Liturgy, following approval by the National Conference of Catholic ishops in May, 1979, began a study of the function and position of some elements of the Mass, including the Gloria, the sign of peace, the penitential rite and the readings. Several phases of the study have been completed, and work is still under way toward completion of the project.

**Mass for Special Groups:** Reasons and norms for the celebration of Mass at special gatherings of the faithful were the subject of an instruction issued May 15, 1969. Two years earlier, the U.S. Bishops' Liturgy Committee went on record in support of the celebration of Mass in private homes under appropriate conditions.

**Sunday Mass on Saturday:** The Congregation for the Clergy, under date of Jan. 10, 1970, granted the request that the faithful, where bishops consider it pastorally necessary or useful, may satisfy the precept of participating in Mass in the late afternoon or evening hours of Saturdays and the days before holy days of obligation. This provision is stated in Canon 1248 of the Code of Canon Law.

**Bination and Trination:** Canon 905 of the Code of Canon Law provides that local ordinaries may permit priests to celebrate Mass twice a day (bination), for a just cause; in cases of pastoral need, they may permit priests to celebrate Mass three times a day (trination) on Sundays and holy days of obligation.

**Mass in Latin:** According to notices issued by the Congregation for Divine Worship June 1, 1971, and Oct. 28, 1974: (1) Bishops may permit the celebration of Mass in Latin for mixed-language groups. (2) Bishops may permit the celebration of one or two Masses in Latin on weekdays or Sundays in any church, irrespective of mixed-language groups involved (1971). (3) Priests may celebrate Mass in Latin when people are not present. (4) The approved revised Order of the Mass is to be used in Latin as well as vernacular languages. (5) By way of exception, bishops may permit older and handicapped priests to use the Council of Trent's Order of the Mass in private celebration of the holy Sacrifice. (See Permission for Tridentine Mass.)

**Mass Obligation Waived:** The Congregation for Bishops approved July 4, 1992, a resolution of the U.S. bishops to waive the Mass attendance obligation for the holy days of Mary, the Mother of God (Jan. 1), the Assumption of Mary (Aug. 15) and All Saints (Nov. 1) when these solemnities fall on Saturday or Monday.

**Inter-Ritual Concelebration:** The Apostolic Delegation (now Nunciature) in Washington, D.C., announced in June, 1971, that it had received authorization to permit priests of Roman and Eastern rites to celebrate Mass together in the rite of the host church. It was understood that the inter-ritual concelebrations would always be "a manifestation of the unity of the Church and of communion among particular churches."

**Ordo of the Sung Mass:** In a decree dated June 24 and made public Aug. 24, 1972, the Congregation for Divine Worship issued a new *Ordo of the Sung Mass* — containing Gregorian chants in Latin — to replace the *Graduale Romanum*.

**Mass for Children:** Late in 1973, the Congregation for Divine Worship issued special guidelines for children's Masses, providing accommodations to the mentality and spiritual growth of pre-adolescents while retaining the principal parts and structures of the Mass. The *Directory for Masses with Children* was approved by Paul VI Oct. 22 and was dated Nov. 1, 1973. Three Eucharistic prayers for Masses with children were approved by the congregation in 1974; English versions were approved June 5, 1975. Their use, authorized originally for a limited period of experimentation, was extended indefinitely Dec. 15, 1980.

**Lectionary for Children:** A lectionary for Masses with children, with an announced publication date of Sept., 1993, was authorized for use by choice beginning Nov. 28, 1993.

## Sacraments

The general use of English in administration of the sacraments was approved for the U.S. Sept. 14,

1964. Structural changes of the rites were subsequently made and introduced in the U.S. as follows.

**Pastoral Care of the Sick:** Revised rites, covering also administration of the Eucharist to sick persons, were approved Nov. 30, 1972, and published Jan. 18, 1973. The effective date for use of the provisional English prayer formula was Dec. 1, 1974. The mandatory effective date for use of the ritual, *Pastoral Care of the Sick in English,* was Nov. 27, 1983.

**Baptism:** New rites for the baptism of infants, approved Mar. 19, 1969, were introduced June 1, 1970.

**Rite of Christian Initiation of Adults:** Revised rites were issued Jan. 6, 1972, for the Christian initiation of adults — affecting preparation for and reception of baptism, the Eucharist and confirmation; also, for the reception of already baptized adults into full communion with the Church. These rites, which were introduced in the U.S. on the completion of English translation, nullified a seven-step baptismal process approved in 1962. On Mar. 8, 1988, the National Conference of Catholic Bishops was notified that the Congregation for Divine Worship had approved the final English translation of the Rite of Christian Initiation of Adults. The mandatory date for putting the rite into effect was Sept. 1, 1988.

**Confirmation:** Revised rites, issued Aug. 15, 1971, became mandatory in the U.S. Jan. 1, 1973. The use of a stole by persons being confirmed should be avoided, according to an item in the December, 1984, edition of the *Newsletter of the Bishops' Committee on the Liturgy.* The item said: "The distinction between the universal priesthood of all the baptized and the ministerial priesthood of the ordained is blurred when the distinctive garb (the stole) of ordained ministers is used in this manner."

A decree regarding the proper age for confirmation, approved by the U.S. bishops in June, 1993, was ratified by the Congregation for Bishops Feb. 8, 1994. The decree reads: "In accord with prescriptions of canon 891, the National Conference of Catholic Bishops hereby decrees that the sacrament of confirmation in the Latin rite shall be conferred between the age of discretion, which is about the age of seven, and 18 years of age, within the limits determined by the diocesan bishop and with regard for the legitimate exceptions given in canon 891, namely, when there is danger of death or where, in the judgment of the minister, grave cause urges otherwise." The decree became effective July 1, 1994, and continues in effect until July 1, 1999.

**Special Ministers of the Eucharist:** The designation of lay men and women to serve as special ministers of the Eucharist was authorized by Paul VI in an "Instruction on Facilitating Communion in Particular Circumstances" (*Immensae Caritatis*), dated Jan. 29 and published by the Congregation for Divine Worship Mar. 29, 1973. Provisions concerning them are contained in Canons 230 and 910 of the Code of Canon Law.

Qualified lay persons may serve as special ministers for specific occasions or for extended periods in the absence of a sufficient number of priests and deacons to provide reasonable and appropriate service in the distribution of Holy Communion, during Mass and outside of Mass (to the sick and shut-ins).

Appointments of ministers are made by priests with the approval of the appropriate bishop.

The Newsletter of the U.S. Bishops' Committee on the Liturgy stated in its February, 1988, edition: "When ordinary ministers (bishops, priests, deacons) are present during a Eucharistic celebration, whether they are participating in it or not, and are not prevented from doing so, they are to assist in the distribution of Communion. Accordingly, if the ordinary ministers are in sufficient number, special ministers of the Eucharist are not allowed to distribute Communion at that Eucharistic celebration." Pope John Paul approved this decision and ordered it published June 15, 1987.

**Holy Orders:** Revised ordination rites for deacons, priests and bishops, validated by prior experimental use, were approved in 1970. The sacrament of holy orders underwent further revision in 1972 with the elimination of the Church-instituted orders of porter, reader, exorcist, acolyte and subdeacon, and of the tonsure ceremony symbolic of entrance into the clerical state. The former minor orders of reader and acolyte were changed from orders to ministries.

**Matrimony:** A revised rite for the celebration of marriage was promulgated by the Congregation for Divine Worship and the Discipline of the Sacraments Mar. 19, 1969, and went into effect June 1, 1970. A second typical edition of the order of celebration, with revisions in accord with provisions of the Code of Canon Law promulgated in 1983, was approved and published in 1990 (*Notitiae*, Vol. 26, No.6). The date for implementation was reported to be dependent on the completion of required translations and appropriate formalities.

**Penance:** Ritual revision of the sacraments was completed with the approval by Paul VI Dec. 2, 1973, of new directives for the sacrament of penance or reconciliation. The U.S. Bishops' Committee on the Liturgy set Feb. 27, 1977, as the mandatory date for use of the new rite. The committee also declared that it could be used from Mar. 7, 1976, after adequate preparation of priests and people. Earlier, authorization was given by the Holy See in 1968 for the omission of any reference to excommunication or other censures in the formula of absolution unless there was some indication that a censure had actually been incurred by a penitent.

## Additional Developments

**Music:** An instruction on Music in the Liturgy, dated Mar. 5 and effective May 14, 1967, encouraged congregational singing during liturgical celebrations and attempted to clarify the role of choirs and trained singers. More significantly, the instruction indicated that a major development under way in the liturgy was a gradual erasure of the distinctive lines traditionally drawn between the sung liturgy and the spoken liturgy, between what had been called the high Mass and the low Mass.

In the same year, the U.S. Bishops' Liturgy Committee approved the use of contemporary music, as well as guitars and other suitable instruments, in the liturgy. The Holy See authorized in 1968 the use of musical instruments other than the organ in liturgical services, "provided they are played in a manner suitable to worship."

**Calendar:** A revised liturgical calendar approved by Paul VI Feb. 14 and made public May 9, 1969, went into effect in the U.S. in 1972. Since that time, memorials and feasts of beatified persons and saints have been added.

**Communion in Hand:** Since 1969, the Holy See has approved the practice of in-hand reception of the Eucharist in regions and countries where it had the approval of the appropriate episcopal conferences. The first grant of approval was to Belgium, in May, 1969. Approval was granted the United States in June, 1977.

**Liturgy of the Hours:** The background, contents, scope and purposes of the revised Divine Office, called the Liturgy of the Hours, were described by Paul VI in the apostolic constitution *Laudis Canticum*, dated Nov. 1, 1970. A provisional English version, incorporating basic features of the master Latin text, was published in 1971. The four complete volumes of the Hours in English have been published since May, 1975. One-volume, partial editions have also been published in approved form. Nov. 27, 1977, was set by the Congregation for Divine Worship and the National Conference of Catholic Bishops as the effective date for exclusive use in liturgical worship of the translation of the Latin text of the Liturgy of the Hours approved by the International Committee on English in the Liturgy.

**Holy Week:** The English version of revised Holy Week rites went into effect in 1971. They introduced concelebration of Mass, placed new emphasis on commemorating the institution of the priesthood on Holy Thursday and modified Good Friday prayers for other Christians, Jews and other non-Christians.

In another action, the Congregation for Divine Worship released Feb. 20, 1988, a "Circular Letter concerning the Preparation and Celebration of the Easter Feasts." It called the feasts the "summit of the whole liturgical year," and criticized practices which dilute or change appropriate norms for their celebration. Singled out for blame for the abuse or ignorance of norms was the "inadequate formation given to the clergy and the faithful regarding the paschal mystery as the center of the liturgical year and of Christian life." The document set out the appropriate norms for the Lenten season, Holy Week, the Easter Triduum, Easter and the weeks following. It was particularly insistent on the proper celebration of the Easter Vigil, to take place after nightfall on Saturday and before dawn on Sunday.

**Oils:** The Congregation for Divine Worship issued a directive in 1971 permitting the use of other oils — from plants, seeds or coconuts — instead of the traditional olive oil in administering some of the sacraments. The directive also provided that oils could be blessed at other times than at the usual Mass of Chrism on Holy Thursday, and authorized bishops' conferences to permit priests to bless oils in cases of necessity.

**Dancing and Worship:** Dancing and worship was the subject of an essay which appeared in a 1975 edition of *Notitiae* (11, pp. 202-205), the official journal of the Congregation for the Sacraments and Divine Worship. The article was called a "qualified and authoritative sketch," and should be considered "an authoritative point of reference for every discussion of the matter."

The principal points of the essay were:
• "The dance has never been made an integral part of the official worship of the Latin Church."
• "If the proposal of the religious dance in the West is really to be made welcome, care will have to be taken that in its regard a place be found outside of the liturgy, in assembly areas which are not strictly liturgical. Moreover, the priests must always be excluded from the dance."

**Mass for Deceased Non-Catholic Christians:** The Congregation for the Doctrine of the Faith released a decree June 11, 1976, authorizing the celebration of public Mass for deceased non-Catholic Christians under certain conditions: "(1) The public celebration of the Masses must be explicitly requested by the relatives, friends, or subjects of the deceased person for a genuine religious motive. (2) In the Ordinary's judgment, there must be no scandal for the faithful."

**Environment and Art in Catholic Worship:** A booklet with this title was issued by the U.S. Bishops' Committee on the Liturgy in March, 1978.

**Doxology:** The bishops' committee called attention in August, 1978, to the directive that the Doxology concluding the Eucharistic Prayer is said or sung by the celebrant (concelebrants) alone, to which the people respond, "Amen."

**Churches, Altars, Chalices:** The Newsletter of the U.S. Bishops' Committee on the Liturgy reported in November, 1978, that the Congregation for Divine Worship had given provisional approval of a new English translation for the rite of dedicating churches and altars, and of a new form for the blessing of chalices.

**Eucharistic Worship:** This was the subject of two documents issued in 1980. *Dominicae Coenae* was a letter addressed by Pope John Paul to bishops throughout the world in connection with the celebration of Holy Thursday; it was dated Feb. 24 and released Mar.18. It was more doctrinal in content than the "Instruction on Certain Norms concerning Worship of the Eucharistic Mystery" (*Inaestimabile Donum*, "The Priceless Gift"), which was approved by the Pope Apr. 17 and published by the Congregation for the Sacraments and Divine Worship May 23. Its stated purpose was to reaffirm and clarify teaching on liturgical renewal contained in enactments of the Second Vatican Council and in several related implementing documents.

**Tridentine Mass:** The celebration of Mass according to the 1962 typical (master) edition of the Roman Missal — the so-called Tridentine Mass — was authorized by Pope John Paul under certain conditions. So stated a letter from the Congregation for Divine Worship, dated Oct. 3, 1984. The letter said the Pope wished to be responsive to priests and faithful who remained attached to the so-called Tridentine rite. The principal condition for the celebration was: "There must be unequivocal, even public, evidence that the priest and people petitioning have no ties with those who impugn the lawfulness and doctrinal soundness of the Roman Missal promulgated in 1970 by Pope Paul VI." (This, in particular, with reference to the followers of dissident Archbishop Marcel Lefebvre.)

Six guidelines for celebration of the Tridentine Mass were contained in the letter regarding its "wide and generous" use, for two purposes: to win back Lefebvre followers and to clear up misunderstandings about liberal permission for use of the Tridentine rite. The letter, from the Pontifical Commission Ecclesia Dei, said in part:

• The Tridentine Mass can be celebrated in a parish church, so long as it provides a pastoral service and is harmoniously integrated into the parish liturgical schedule.

• When requested, the Mass should be offered on a regular Sunday and holyday basis, "at a central location, at a convenient time" for a trial period of several months, with "adjustment" later if needed.

• Celebrants of the Mass should make it clear that they acknowledge the validity of the postconciliar liturgy.

• Although the commission has the authority to grant use of the Tridentine rite to all groups that request it, the commission "would much prefer that such faculties be granted by the Ordinary himself so that ecclesial communion can be strengthened."

• While the new Lectionary in the vernacular can be used in the Tridentine Mass, as suggested by the Second Vatican Council, it should not be "imposed on congregations that decidedly wish to maintain the former liturgical tradition in its integrity."

• Older and retired priests who have asked permission to celebrate Mass according to the Tridentine rite should be given the chance to do so for groups that request it.

**Spanish:** In accord with decrees of the Congregation for Divine Worship, Spanish was approved as a liturgical language in the U.S. (Jan. 19, 1985). The *texto unico* of the Ordinary of the Mass became mandatory in the U.S. Dec. 3, 1989. Spanish translations of Proper-of-the-Mass texts proper to U.S. diocess were approved Mar. 12, 1990. An approved Spanish version of the Rite for the Christian Initiation of Adults was published in 1991.

The Institute of Hispanic Liturgy opened its national office June 1, 1995, on the campus of the Catholic University of America in Washington.

**Funeral Rites:** A revised Order of Christian Funerals became mandatory in the U.S. Nov. 2, 1989.

**Popular Piety and Liturgy:** The relation of popular piety to the liturgy was the subject of remarks by Pope John Paul at a meeting with a group of Italian bishops Apr. 24, 1986. He said, in part:

"An authentic liturgical ministry will never be able to neglect the riches of popular piety, the values proper to the culture of a people, so that such riches might be illuminated, purified and introduced into the liturgy as an offering of the people."

**Extended Eucharistic Exposition:** In response to queries, the Secretariat of the U.S. Bishops' Committee on the Liturgy issued an advisory stating that liturgical law permits and encourages in parish churches:

• a. exposition of the Blessed Sacrament for an extended period of time once a year, with consent of the local Ordinary and only if suitable numbers of the faithful are expected to be present;

• b. exposition ordered by the local Ordinary, for a grave and general necessity, for a more extended period of supplication when the faithful assemble in large numbers.

With regard to perpetual exposition, this form is generally permitted only in the case of those religious communities of men or women who have the general practice of perpetual Eucharistic adoration or adoration over extended periods of time.

The Secretariat's advisory appeared in the June-July, 1986, edition of the Newsletter of the Bishops' Committee on the Liturgy.

**Native American Languages:** The Newsletter of the U.S. Bishops' Committee on the Liturgy reported in December, 1986, and May, 1987, respectively, that the Congregation for Divine Worship had authorized Mass translations in Navajo and Choctaw. Lakota was approved as a liturgical language in 1989.

**Communion Guidelines:** The U.S. Bishops' Committee on the Liturgy, in the December, 1986, Newsletter, reported that advisories were to be included in missalettes noting that: (1) The Eucharist is to be received by Catholics only, except in certain specific cases. (2) To receive Communion worthily, a person must be in the state of grace (i.e., free of serious sin) and observe the eucharistic fast (see separate entry).

**Unauthorized Eucharistic Prayers:** The May, 1987, Newsletter of the U.S. Bishops' Committee on the Liturgy restated the standing prohibition against the use of any Eucharistic Prayers other than those contained in the Sacramentary. Specifically, the article referred to the 25 unauthorized prayers in a volume entitled *Spoken Visions.*

**Homilist:** According to the Pontifical Commission for the Authentic Interpretation of Canon Law, the diocesan bishop cannot dispense from the requirement of Canon 767, par. 1, that the homily in the liturgy be reserved to a priest or deacon. Pope John Paul approved this decision and ordered it published June 20, 1987.

**Concerts in Churches:** In a letter released Dec. 5, 1987, the Congregation for Divine Worship declared that churches might be used on a limited basis for concerts of sacred or religious music but not for concerts featuring secular music.

**Blessings:** A revised *Book of Blessings* was ordered into use beginning Dec. 3, 1989.

**Litany of the Blessed Virgin Mary:** "Queen of Families," a new invocation was reported by the U.S.bishops in 1996, for insertion between "Queen of the Rosary" and "Queen of Peace."

**Inclusive Language:** "Criteria for the Evaluation of Inclusive Language Translations of Scriptural Texts Proposed for Liturgical Use" was issued by the U.S. bishops in November, 1990. The criteria distinguish between non-use of vertical inclusiveness in references to God and use of horizontal, gender-inclusive terms (he/she, man/woman and the like) where appropriate in references to persons.

---

**Theology Network:** A working group of Catholic theologians from five continents formed a new international network of Catholic theological societies at a meeting Aug. 2 to 5, 1996, in Sherbrooke, Quebec, Canada, named "Network: Catholic Theology."

# SACRAMENTS

The sacraments are actions of Christ and his Church (itself a kind of sacrament) which signify grace, cause it in the act of signifying it, and confer it upon persons properly disposed to receive it. They perpetuate the redemptive activity of Christ, making it present and effective. They infallibly communicate the fruit of that activity — namely grace — to responsive persons with faith. Sacramental actions consist of the union of sensible signs (matter of the sacraments) with the words of the minister (form of the sacraments).

Christ himself instituted the seven sacraments of the New Law by determining their essence and the efficacy of their signs to produce the grace they signify.

Christ is the principal priest or minister of every sacrament; human agents — an ordained priest, baptized persons contracting marriage with each other, any person conferring emergency baptism in a proper manner — are secondary ministers. Sacraments have efficacy from Christ, not from the personal dispositions of their human ministers.

Each sacrament confers sanctifying grace for the special purpose of the sacrament; this is, accordingly, called sacramental grace. It involves a right to actual graces corresponding to the purposes of the respective sacraments.

Baptism, confirmation and the Eucharist are sacraments of initiation; penance (reconciliation) and anointing of the sick, sacraments of healing; order and matrimony, sacraments for service.

While sacraments infallibly produce the grace they signify, recipients benefit from them in proportion to their personal dispositions. One of these is the intention to receive sacraments as sacred signs of God's saving and grace-giving action. The state of grace is also necessary for fruitful reception of the Holy Eucharist, confirmation, matrimony, holy orders and anointing of the sick. Baptism is the sacrament in which grace is given in the first instance and original sin is remitted. Penance is the secondary sacrament of reconciliation, in which persons guilty of serious sin after baptism are reconciled with God and the Chuch, and in which persons already in the state of grace are strengthened in that state.

## Role of Sacraments

The Second Vatican Council prefaced a description of the role of the sacraments with the following statement concerning participation by all the faithful in the priesthood of Christ and the exercise of that priesthood by receiving the sacraments (*Dogmatic Constitution on the Church*, Nos. 10 and 11).

"The baptized by regeneration and the anointing of the Holy Spirit are consecrated into a spiritual house and a holy priesthood. Thus through all those works befitting Christian men they can offer spiritual sacrifice and proclaim the power of him who has called them out of darkness into his marvelous light (cf. 1 Pt. 2:4-10)."

"Though they differ from one another in essence and not only in degree, the common priesthood of the faithful and the ministerial or hierarchical priesthood (of those ordained to holy orders) are nonetheless interrelated. Each of them in its own special way is a participation in the one priesthood of Christ.

The ministerial priest, by the sacred power he enjoys, molds and rules the priestly people. Act-ing in the Person of Christ, he brings about the Eucharistic Sacrifice, and offers it to God in the name of all the people. For their part, the faithful join in the offering of the Eucharist by virtue of their royal priesthood. They likewise exercise that priesthood by receiving the sacraments, by prayer and thanksgiving, by the witness of a holy life, and by self-denial and active charity."

"It is through the sacraments and the exercise of the virtues that the sacred nature and organic structure of the priestly community is brought into operation."

**Baptism:** "Incorporated into the Church through baptism, the faithful are consecrated to the exercise of the cult of the Christian religion. Reborn as sons of God, they must confess before men the faith which they have received from God through the Church."

**Confirmation:** "Bound more intimately to the Church by the sacrament of confirmation, they are endowed by the Holy Spirit with special strength. Hence they are more strictly obliged to spread and defend the faith both by word and by deed as true witnesses of Christ."

**Eucharist:** "Taking part in the Eucharistic Sacrifice, which is the fount and apex of the whole Christian life, they offer the divine Victim to God, and offer themselves along with It. Thus, both by the act of oblation and through holy Communion, all perform their proper part in this liturgical service, not, indeed. all in the same way but each in that way which is appropriate to himself. Strengthened anew at the holy table by the Body of Christ, they manifest in a practical way that unity of God's People which is suitably signified and wondrously brought about by this most awesome sacrament."

**Penance:** "Those who approach the sacrament of penance obtain pardon from the mercy of God for offenses committed against him. They are at the same time reconciled with the Church, which they have wounded by their sins, and which by charity, example, and prayer seeks their conversion."

**Anointing of the Sick:** "By the sacred anointing of the sick and the prayer of her priests, the whole Church commends those who are ill to the suffering and glorified Lord, asking that he may lighten their uffering and save them (cf. Jas. 5:14-16). She exhorts them, moreover, to contribute to the welfare of the whole People of God by associating themselves freely with the passion and death of Christ (cf. Rom. 8:17; Col. 1:24; 2 Tm. 2:11-12; 1 Pt. 4:13)."

**Order:** "Those of the faithful who are consecrated by holy orders are appointed to feed the Church in Christ's name with the Word and the grace of God."

**Matrimony:** "Christian spouses, in virtue of the sacrament of matrimony, signify and partake of the mystery of that unity and fruitful love which exists between Christ and his Church (cf. Eph. 5:32). The spouses thereby help each other to attain to holiness in their married life and by the rearing and education of their children. And so, in their state and way of life, they have their own special gift among the People of God (cf. 1 Cor. 7:7).

"For from the wedlock of Christians there comes the family, in which new citizens of human society are born. By the grace of the Holy Spirit received in baptism these are made children of God, thus perpetuating the People of God through the centuries. The family is, so to speak, the domestic Church. In it parents should, by their word and example, be the first preachers of the faith to their children. They should encourage them in the vocation which is proper to each of them, fostering with special care any religious vocation."

"Fortified by so many and such powerful means of salvation, all the faithful, whatever their condition or state, are called by the Lord, each in his own way, to that perfect holiness whereby the Father himself is perfect."

## Baptism

Baptism is the sacrament of spiritual regeneration by which a person is incorporated in Christ and made a member of his Mystical Body, given grace, and cleansed of original sin. Actual sins and the punishment due for them are remitted also if the person baptized was guilty of such sins (e.g., in the case of a person baptized after reaching the age of reason). The theological virtues of faith, hope and charity are given with grace. The sacrament confers a character on the soul and can be received only once.

The matter is the pouring of water. The form is: "I baptize you in the name of the Father and of the Son and of the Holy Spirit."

The minister of solemn baptism is a bishop, priest or deacon, but in case of emergency anyone, including a non-Catholic, can validly baptize. The minister pours water on the forehead of the person being baptized and says the words of the form while the water is flowing. The water used in solemn baptism is blessed during the rite.

Baptism is conferred in the Roman Rite by immersion or infusion (pouring of water), depending on the directive of the appropriate conference of bishops, according to the Code of Canon Law. The Church recognizes as valid baptisms properly performed by non-Catholic ministers. The baptism of infants has always been considered valid and the general practice of infant baptism was well established by the fifth century. Baptism is conferred conditionally when there is doubt about the validity of a previous baptism.

Baptism is necessary for salvation. If a person cannot receive the baptism of water described above, this can be supplied by baptism of blood (martyrdom suffered for the Catholic faith or some Christian virtue) or by baptism of desire (perfect contrition joined with atleast the implicit intention of doing whatever God wills that people should do for salvation).

A sponsor is required for the person being baptized. (See Godparents, below).

A person must be validly baptized before he or she can receive any of the other sacraments.

**Christian Initiation of Infants:** Infants should be solemnly baptized as soon after birth as conveniently possible. In danger of death, anyone may baptize an infant. If the child survives, the ceremonies of solemn baptism should be supplied.

The sacrament is ordinarily conferred by a priest or deacon of the parents' parish.

Catholics 16 years of age and over who have received the sacraments of confirmation and the Eucharist and are practicing their faith are eligible to be sponsors or godparents. Only one is required. Two, one of each sex, are permitted. A non-Catholic Christian cannot be a godparent for a Catholic child, but may serve as a witness to the baptism. A Catholic may not be a godparent for a child baptized in a non-Catholic religion, but may be a witness.

"Because of the close communion between the Catholic Church and the Eastern Orthodox churches," states the *1993 Directory on Ecumenism*, "it is permissible for a just cause for an Eastern faithful to act as godparent together with a Catholic godparent at the baptism of a Catholic infant or adult, so long as there is provision for the Catholic education of the person being baptized and it is clear that the godparent is a suitable one.

"A Catholic is not forbidden to stand as godparent in an Eastern Orthodox Church if he/she is so invited. In this case, the duty of providing for the Christian education binds in the first place the godparent who belongs to the church in which the child is baptized."

The role of godparents in baptismal ceremonies is secondary to the role of the parents. They serve as representatives of the community of faith and with the parents request baptism for the child and perform other ritual functions. Their function after baptism is to serve as proxies for the parents if the parents should be unable or fail to provide for the religious training of the child.

At baptism every child should be given a name with Christian significance, usually the name of a saint, to symbolize newness of life in Christ.

**Christian Initiation of Adults:** According to the *Ordo Initiationis Christianae Adultorum* ("Rite of the Christian Initiation of Adults") issued by the Congregation for Divine Worship under date of Jan. 6, 1972, and put into effect in revised form Sept. 1, 1988, adults are prepared for baptism and reception into the Church in several stages:

• An initial period of inquiry, instruction and evangelization.

• The catechumenate, a period of at least a year of formal instruction and progressive formation in and familiarity with Christian life. It starts with a statement of purpose and includes a rite of election.

• Immediate preparation, called a period of purification and enlightenment, from the beginning of Lent to reception of the sacraments of initiation — baptism, confirmation, Holy Eucharist — during ceremonies of the Easter Vigil. The period is marked by scrutinies, formal giving of the creed and the Lord's Prayer, the choice of a Christian name, and a final statement of intention.

• A mystagogic phase whose objective is greater familiarity with Christian life in the Church through observances of the Easter season and association with the community of the faithful, and through extended formation for about a year.

National Statutes for the Catechumenate were approved by the National Conference of Catholic Bishops Nov. 11, 1986, and were subsequently ratified by the Vatican.

The priest who baptizes a catechumen can also administer thesacrament of confirmation.

A sponsor is required for the person being baptized.

The *Ordo* also provides a simple rite of initiation for adults in danger of death and for cases in which all stages of the initiation process are not necessary, and guidelines for: (1) the preparation of adults for the sacraments of confirmation and Holy Eucharist in cases where they have been baptized but have not received further formation in the Christian life; (2) for the formation and initiation of children of catechetical age.

The Church recognizes the right of anyone over the age of seven to request baptism and to receive the sacrament after completing a course of instruction and giving evidence of good will. Practically, in the case of minors in a non-Catholic family or environment, the Church accepts them when other circumstances favor their ability to practice the faith — e.g., well-disposed family situation, the presence of another or several Catholics in the family. Those who are not in such favorable circumstances are prudently advised to defer reception of the sacrament until they attain the maturity necessary for independent practice of the faith.

**Reception of Baptized Christians:** Procedure for the reception of already baptized Christians into full communion with the Catholic Church is distinguished from the catechumenate, since they have received some Christian formation. Instruction and formation are provided as necessary, however; and conditional baptism is administered if there is a reasonable doubt about the validity of the person's previous baptism.

In the rite of reception, the person is invited to join the community of the Church in professing the Nicene Creed and is asked to state: "I believe and profess all that the holy Catholic Church believes, teaches, and proclaims as revealed by God." The priest places his hand on the head of the person, states the formula of admission to full communion, confirms (in the absence of a bishop), gives a sign of peace, and administers Holy Communion during a Eucharistic Liturgy.

## Confirmation

Confirmation is the sacrament by which a baptized person, through anointing with chrism and the imposition of hands, is endowed with the fullness of baptismal grace; is united more intimately to the Church; is enriched with the special power of the Holy Spirit; is committed to be an authentic witness to Christ in word and action. The sacrament confers a character on the soul and can be received only once.

According to the apostolic constitution *Divinae Consortium Naturae* dated Aug. 15, 1971, in conjunction with the *Ordo Confirmationis* ("Rite of Confirmation"): "The sacrament of confirmation is conferred through the anointing with chrism on the forehead, which is done by the imposition of the hand (matter of the sacrament), and through the words: 'N , receive the seal of the Holy Spirit, the Gift of the Father' " (form of the sacrament). On May 5, 1975, bishops' conferences in English-speaking countries were informed by the Congregation for Divine Worship that Pope Paul had approved this English version of the form of the sacrament: "Be sealed with the gift of the Holy Spirit."

The ordinary minister of confirmation in the Roman Rite is a bishop. Priests may be delegated for the purpose. A pastor can confirm a parishioner in danger of death, and a priest can confirm in ceremonies of Christian initiation nd at the reception of a baptized Christian into union with the Church.

Ideally, the sacrament is conferred during the Eucharistic Liturgy. Elements of the rite include renewal of the promises of baptism, which confirmation ratifies and completes, and the laying on of hands by the confirming bishop and priests participating in the ceremony.

"The entire rite," according to the *Ordo*; "has a twofold meaning. The laying of hands upon the candidates, done by the bishop and the concelebrating priests, expresses the biblical gesture by which the gift of the Holy Spirit is invoked . The anointing with chrism and the accompanying words clearly signify the effect of the Holy Spirit. Signed with the perfumed oil by the bishop's hand, the baptized person receives the indelible character, the seal of the Lord, together with the Spirit who is given and who conforms the person more perfectly to Christ and gives him the grace of spreading the Lord's presence among men."

A sponsor is required for the person being confirmed. Eligible is any Catholic 16 years of age or older who has received the sacraments of confirmation and the Eucharist and is practicing the faith. The baptismal sponsor, preferably, can also be the sponsor for confirmation. Parents may present their children for confirmation but cannot be sponsors.

In the Roman Rite, it has been customary for children to receive confirmation within a reasonable time after first Communion and confession. There is a trend, however, to defer confirmation until later when its significance for mature Christian living becomes more evident. In the Eastern Rites, confirmation is administered at the same time as baptism.

## Eucharist

The Holy Eucharist is a sacrifice (see The Mass) and the sacrament in which Christ is present and is received under the appearances of bread and wine.

The matter is bread of wheat, unleavened in the Roman Rite and leavened in the Eastern Rites, and wine of grape. The form consists of the words of consecration said by the priest at Mass: "This is my body . This is the cup of my blood" (according to the traditional usage of the Roman Rite).

Only a priest can consecrate bread and wine so they become the body and blood of Christ. After consecration, however, the Eucharist can be administered by deacons and, for various reasons, by religious and lay persons.

Priests celebrating Mass receive the Eucharist under the species of bread and wine. In the Roman Rite, others receive under the species of bread only, i.e., the consecrated host, or in some circumstances they may receive under the species of both bread and wine. In Eastern-Rite practice, the faithful generally receive a piece of consecrated leavened bread which has been dipped into consecrated wine (i.e., by intinction).

Conditions for receiving the Eucharist, commonly called Holy Communion, are the state of grace, the right intention and observance of the Eucharistic fast.

The faithful of Roman Rite are required by a precept of the Church to receive the Eucharist at least once a year, ordinarily during the Easter time. (See Eucharistic Fast, Mass, Transubstantiation, Viaticum.)

First Communion and Confession: Children are to be prepared for and given opportunity for receiving both sacraments (Eucharist and reconciliation, or peance) on reaching the age of discretion, at which time they become subject to general norms concerning confession and Communion. This, together with a stated preference for first confession before first Communion, was the central theme of a document entitled *Sanctus Pontifex* and published May 24, 1973, by the Congregation for the Discipline of the Sacraments and the Congregation for the Clergy, with the approval of Pope Paul VI.

What the document prescribed was the observance of practices ordered by St. Pius X in the decree *Quam Singulari* of Aug. 8, 1910. Its purpose was to counteract pastoral and catechetical experiments virtually denying children the opportunity of receiving both sacraments at the same time. Termination of such experiments was ordered by the end of the 1972-73 school year.

At the time the document was issued, two- or three-year experiments of this kind — routinely deferring reception of the sacrament of penance until after the first reception of Holy Communion — were in effect in more than half of the dioceses of the U.S. They have remained in effect in many places, despite the advisory from the Vatican.

One reason stated in support of such experiments is the view that children are not capable of serious sin at the age of seven or eight, when Communion is generally received for the first time, and therefore prior reception of the sacrament of penance is not necessary. Another reason is the purpose of making the distinctive nature of the two sacraments clearer to children.

The Vatican view reflected convictions that the principle and practice of devotional reception of penance are as valid for children as they are for adults, and that sound catechetical programs can avoid misconceptions about the two sacraments.

A second letter on the same subject and in the same vein was released May 19, 1977, by the aforementioned congregations. It was issued in response to the question:

" 'Whether it is allowed after the declaration of May 24, 1973, to continue to have, as a general rule, the reception of first Communion precede the reception of the sacrament of penance in those parishes in which this practice developed in the past few years.'

"The Sacred Congregations for the Sacraments and Divine Worship and for the Clergy, with the approval of the Supreme Pontiff, reply: Negative, and according to the mind of the declaration.

"The mind of the declaration is that one year after the promulgation of the same declaration, all experiments of receiving first Communion without the sacrament of penance should cease so that the discipline of the Church might be restored, in the spirit of the decree, *Quam Singulari*."

The two letters from the Vatican congregations have not produced uniformity of practice in this country. Simultaneous preparation for both sacraments is provided in some dioceses where a child has the option of receiving either sacrament first, with the counsel of parents, priests and teachers. Programs in other dioceses are geared first to reception of Communion and later to reception of the sacrament of reconciliation.

Commentators on the letters note that: they are disciplinary rather than doctrinal in content; they are subject to pastoral interpretation by bishops; they cannot be interpreted to mean that a person who is not guilty of serious sin must be required to receive the sacrament of penance before (even first) Communion.

Canon 914 of the Code of Canon Law states that sacramental confession should precede first Communion.

**Holy Communion under the Forms of Bread and Wine** (by separate taking of the consecrated bread and wine or by intinction, the reception of the host dipped in the wine): Such reception is permitted under conditions stated in instructions issued by the Congregation for Divine Worship (May 25, 1967; June 29, 1970), the *General Instruction on the Roman Missal* (No. 242), and direcives of bishops' conferences and individual bishops.

Accordingly, Communion can be administered in this way to: persons being baptized, received into communion with the Church, confirmed, receiving anointing of the sick; couples at their wedding or jubilee; religious at profession or renewal of profession; lay persons receiving an ecclesiastical assignment (e.g., lay missionaries); participants at concelebrated Masses, retreats, pastoral commission meetings, daily Masses and, in the U.S., Masses on Sundays and holy days of obligation.

A communicant has the option of receiving the Eucharist under the form of bread alone or under the forms of bread and wine.

**Holy Communion More Than Once a Day:** A person who has already received the Eucharist may receive it (only) once again on the same day only during a Eucharistic celebration in which the person participates. A person in danger of death who has already received the Eucharist once or twice is urged to receive Communion again as Viaticum. Pope John Paul approved this decision, in accord with Canon 917, and ordered it published July 11, 1984.

Holy Communion and Eucharistic Devotion outside of Mass: These were the subjects of an instruction *De Sacra Communione et de Cultu Mysterii Eucharistici extra Missam* dated June 21 and made public Oct. 18, 1973, by the Congregation for Divine Worship.

Holy Communion can be given outside of Mass to persons unable for a reasonable cause to receive it during Mass on a given day. The ceremonial rite is modeled on the structure of the Mass, consisting of a penitential act, a scriptural reading, the Lord's

Prayer, a sign or gesture of peace, giving of the Eucharist, prayer and final blessing. Viaticum and Communion to the sick can be given by extraordinary ministers (authorized lay persons) with appropriate rites.

Forms of devotion outside of Mass are exposition of the Blessed Sacrament (by men or women religious, especially, or lay persons in the absence of a priest; but only a priest can give the blessing), processions and congresses with appropriate rites.

**Intercommunion:** Church policy on intercommunion was stated in an "Instruction on the Admission of Other Christians to the Eucharist," dated June 1 and made public July 8, 1972, against the background of the *Decree on Ecumenism* approved by the Second Vatican Council, and the *Directory on Ecumenism* issued by the Secretariat for Promoting Christian Unity in 1967, 1970 and 1993.

Basic principles related to intercommunion are:

• "There is an indissoluble link between the mystery of the Church and the mystery of the Eucharist, or between ecclesial and Eucharistic communion; the celebration of the Eucharist of itself signifies the fullness of profession of faith and ecclesial communion" (1972 Instruction).

• "Eucharistic communion practiced by those who are not in full ecclesial communion with each other cannot be the expression of that full unity which the Eucharist of its nature signifies and which in this case does not exist; for this reason such communion cannot be regarded as a means to be used to lead to full ecclesial communion" (1972 Instruction).

• The question of reciprocity "arises only with those churches which have preserved the substance of the Eucharist, the sacrament of orders and apostolic succession" (1967 Directory).

• "A Catholic cannot ask for the Eucharist except from a minister who has been validly ordained" (1967 Directory).

The policy distinguishes between separated Eastern Christians and other Christians.

With Separated Eastern Christians (e.g., Orthodox): These may be given the Eucharist (as well as penance and anointing of the sick) at their request. Catholics may receive these same sacraments from priests of separated Eastern churches if they experience genuine spiritual necessity, seek spiritual benefit, and access to a Catholic priest is morally or physically impossible. This policy (of reciprocity) derives from the facts that the separated Eastern churches have apostolic succession through their bishops, valid priests, and sacramental beliefs and practices in accord with those of the Catholic Church.

With Other Christians (e.g., members of Reformation-related churches, others): Admission to the Eucharist in the Catholic Church, according to the D*irectory on Ecumenism,* "is confined to particular cases of those Christians who have a faith in the sacrament in conformity with that of the Church, who experience a serious spiritual need for the Eucharistic sustenance, who for a prolonged period are unable to have recourse to a minister of their own community and who ask for the sacrament of their own accord; all this provided that they have proper dispositions and lead lives worthy of a Christian." The spiritual need is defined as "a need for an increase in spiritual life and a need for a deeper involvement in the mystery of the Church and its unity."

Circumstances under which Communion may be given to other properly disposed Christians are danger of death, imprisonment, persecution, grave spiritual necessity coupled with no chance of recourse to a minister of their own community.

Catholics cannot ask for the Eucharist from ministers of other Christian churches who have not been validly ordained to the priesthood.

## Penance

Penance is the sacrament by which sins committed after baptism are forgiven and a person is reconciled with God and the Church.

Individual and integral confession and absolution are the only ordinary means for the forgiveness of serious sin and for reconciliation with God and the Church.

(Other than ordinary means are perfect contrition and general absolution without prior confession, both of which require the intention of subsequent confession and absolution.)

A revised ritual for the sacrament — *Ordo Paenitentiae*, published by the Congregation of Divine Worship Feb. 7, 1974, and made mandatory in the U.S. from the first Sunday of Lent, 1977 —reiterates standard doctrine concerning the sacrament; emphasizes the social (communal and ecclesial) aspects of sin and conversion, with due regard for personal aspects and individual reception of the sacrament; prescribes three forms for celebration of the sacrament; and presents models for community penitential services.

The basic elements of the sacrament are sorrow for sin because of a supernatural motive, confession (of previously unconfessed mortal or grave sins, required; of venial sins also, but not of necessity), and reparation (by means of prayer or other act enjoined by the confessor), all of which comprise the matter of the sacrament; and absolution, which is the form of the sacrament.

The traditional words of absolution — "I absolve you from your sins in the name of the Father, and of the Son, and of the Holy Spirit" — remain unchanged at the conclusion of a petition in the new rite that God may grant pardon and peace through the ministry of the Church.

The minister of the sacrament is an authorized priest — i.e., one who, besides having the power of orders to forgive sins, also has faculties of jurisdiction granted by an eclesiastical superior and/or by canon law.

The sacrament can be celebrated in three ways.

• For individuals: The traditional manner remains acceptable but is enriched with additional elements including: reception of the penitent and making of the Sign of the Cross; an exhortation by the confessor to trust in God; a reading from Scripture; confession of sins; manifestation of repentance; petition for God's forgiveness through the ministry of the Church and the absolution of the priest; praise of God's mercy, and dismissal in peace. Some of these elements are optional.

• For several penitents, in the course of a community celebration including a Liturgy of the Word of God and prayers, individual confession and absolution, and an act of thanksgiving.

• For several penitents, in the course of a community celebration, with general confession and general absolution. In extraordinary cases, reconciliation may be attained by general absolution without prior individual confession as, for example, under these circumstances: (1) danger of death, when there is neither time nor priests available for hearing confessions; (2) grave necessity of a number of penitents who, because of a shortage of confessors, would be deprived of sacramental grace or Communion for a lengthy period of time through no fault of their own. Persons receiving general absolution are obliged to be properly disposed and resolved to make an individual confession of the grave sins from which they have been absolved; this confession should be made as soon as the opportunity to confess presents itself and before any second reception of general absolution.

Norms regarding general absolution, issued by the Congregation for the Doctrine of the Faith in 1972, are not intended to provide a basis for convoking large gatherings of the faithful for the purpose of imparting general absolution, in the absence of extraordinary circumstances. Judgment about circumstances that warrant general absolution belongs principally to the bishop of the place, with due regard for related decisions of appropriate episcopal conferences.

Communal celebrations of the sacrament are not held in connection with Mass.

The place of individual confession, as determined by episcopal conferences in accordance with given norms, can be the traditional confessional or another appropriate setting.

A precept of the Church obliges the faithful guilty of grave sin to confess at least once a year.

The Church favors more frequent reception of the sacrament not only for the reconciliation of persons guilty of serious sins but also for reasons of devotion. Devotional confession — in which venial sins or previously forgiven sins are confessed — serves the purpose of confirming persons in penance and conversion.

**Penitential Celebrations**: Communal penitential celebrations are designed to emphasize the social dimensions of Christian life — the community aspects and significance of penance and reconciliation.

Elements of such celebrations are community prayer, hymns and songs, scriptural and other readings, examination of conscience, general confession and expression of sorrow for sin, acts of penance and reconciliation, and a form of non-sacramental absolution resembling the one in the penitential rite of the Mass.

If the sacrament is celebrated during the service, there must be individual confession and absolution of sin.

(See Absolution, Confession, Confessional, Confessor, Contrition, Faculties, Forgiveness of Sin, Power of the Keys, Seal of Confession, Sin.)

### Anointing of the Sick

This sacrament, promulgated by St. James the Apostle (Jas. 5:13-15), can be administered to the faithful after reaching the age of reason who begin to be in danger because of illness or old age. By the anointing with blessed oil and the prayer of a priest, the sacrament confers on the person comforting grace; the remission of venial sins and inculpably unconfessed mortal sins, together with at least some of the temporal punishment due for sins; and, sometimes, results in an improved state of health.

The matter of this sacrament is the anointing with blessed oil (of the sick — olive oil, or vegetable oil if necessary) of the forehead and hands; in cases of necessity, a single anointing of another portion of the body suffices. The form is: "Through this holy anointing and his most loving mercy, may the Lord assist you by the grace of the Holy Spirit so that, when you have been freed from your sins, he may save you and in his goodness raise you up."

Anointing of the sick, formerly called extreme unction, may be received more than once, e.g., in new or continuing stages of serious illness. Ideally, the sacrament should be administered while the recipient is conscious and in conjunction with the sacraments of penance and the Eucharist. It should be administered in cases of doubt as to whether the person has reached the age of reason, is dangerously ill or dead.

The sacrament can be administered during a communal celebration in some circumstances, as in a home for the aged.

### Matrimony

Coverage of the sacrament of matrimony is given in the articles: Marriage Doctrine, *Humanae Vitae*, Marriage Laws, Pastoral Ministry for Divorced and Remarried.

### Order

Order is the sacrament by which the mission given by Christ to the Apostles continues to be exercised in the Church until the end of time; it is the sacrament of apostolic mission. It has three grades: episcopacy, priesthood and diaconate. The sacrament confers a character on the soul and can be received only once. The minister of the sacrament is a bishop.

Order, like matrimony but in a different way, is a social sacrament. As the Second Vatican Council declared in the *Dogmatic Constitution on the Church:*

"For the nurturing and constant growth of the People of God, Christ the Lord instituted in his Church a variety of ministries, which work for the good of the whole body. For those ministers who are endowed with sacred power are servants of their brethren, so that all who are of the People of God, and therefore enjoy a true Christian dignity, can work toward a common goal freely and in an orderly way, and arrive at salvation" (No. 18).

**Bishop:** The fullness of the priesthood belongs to those who have reeived the order of bishop. Bishops, in hierarchical union with the pope and their fellow bishops, are the successors of the Apostles as pastors of the Church: they have individual responsibility for the care of the local churches they serve and collegial responsibility for the care of the universal Church (see Collegiality). In the ordination or consecration of bishops, the essential form is the imposition of hands by the consecrator(s) and the assigned prayer in the preface of the rite of ordination.

"With their helpers, the priests and deacons, bishops have taken up the service of the community presiding in place of God over the flock whose shepherds they are, as teachers of doctrine, priests of sacred worship, and officers of good order" (No. 20).

**Priests:** A priest is an ordained minister with the power to celebrate Mass, administer the sacraments, preach and teach the word of God, impart blessings, and perform additional pastoral functions, according to the mandate of his ecclesiastical superior.

Concerning priests, the Second Vatican Council stated in the *Dogmatic Constitution on the Church* (No. 28):

"The divinely established ecclesiastical ministry is exercised on different levels by those who from antiquity have been called bishops, priests, and deacons. Although priests do not possess the highest degree of the priesthood, and although they are dependent on the bishops in the exercise of their power, they are nevertheless united with the bishops in sacerdotal dignity. By the power of the sacrament of orders, and in the image of Christ the eternal High Priest (Hb. 5:1-10; 7:24; 9:11-28), they are consecrated to preach the Gospel, shepherd the faithful, and celebrate divine worship as true priests of the New Testament.

"Priests, prudent cooperators with the episcopal order as well as its aides and instruments, are called to serve the People of God. They constitute one priesthood with their bishop, although that priesthood is comprised of different functions."

In the ordination of a priest of Roman Rite, the essential matter is the imposition of hands on the heads of those being ordained by the ordaining bishop. The essential form is the accompanying prayer in the preface of the ordination ceremony. Other elements in the rite are the presentation of the implements of sacrifice — the chalice containing the wine and the paten containing a host — with accompanying prayers.

**Deacon:** There are two kinds of deacons: those who receive the order and remain in it permanently, and those who receive the order while advancing to priesthood. The following quotation — from Vatican II's *Dogmatic Constitution on the Church* (No. 29) —describes the nature and role of the diaconate, with emphasis on the permanent diaconate.

"At a lower level of the hierarchy are deacons, upon whom hands are imposed 'not unto the priesthood, but unto a ministry of service.' For strengthened by sacramental grace, in communion with the bishop and his group of priests, they serve the People of God in the ministry of the liturgy, of the word, and of charity. It is the duty of the deacon, to the extent that he has been authorized by competent authority, to administer baptism solemnly, to be custodian and dispenser of the Eucharist, to assist at and bless marriages in the name of the Church, to bring Viaticum to the dying, to read the sacred Scripture to the faithful, to instruct and exhort the people, to preside at the worship and prayer of the faithful, to administer sacramentals, and to officiate at funeral and burial services. (Deacons are) dedicated to duties of charity and administration."

"The diaconate can in the future be restored as a proper and permanent rank of the hierarchy. It pertains to the competent territorial bodies of bishops, of one kind or another, to decide, with the approval of the Supreme Pontiff, whether and where it is opportune for such deacons to be appointed for the care of souls. With the consent o the Roman Pontiff, this diaconate will be able to be conferred upon men of more mature age, even upon those living in the married state. It may also be conferred upon suitable young men. For them, however, the law of celibacy must remain intact" (No. 29).

The Apostles ordained the first seven deacons (Acts 6:1-6): Stephen, Philip, Prochorus, Nicanor, Timon, Parmenas, Nicholas.

**Former Orders, Ministries:** With the revision of the sacrament of order which began in 1971, the orders of subdeacon, acolyte, exorcist, lector and porter were abolished because they and their respective functions had fallen into disuse or did not require ordination. The Holy See started revision of the sacrament of order in 1971. In virtue of an indult of Oct. 5 of that year, the bishops of the United States were permitted to discontinue ordaining porters and exorcists. Another indult, dated three days later, permitted the use of revised rites for ordaining acolytes and lectors.

To complete the revision, Pope Paul VI abolished Sept. 14, 1972, the orders of porter, exorcist and subdeacon; decreed that laymen, as well as candidates for the diaconate and priesthood, can be installed (rather than ordained) in the ministries (rather than orders) of acolyte and lector; reconfirmed the suppression of tonsure and its replacement with a service of dedication to God and the Church; and stated that a man enters the clerical state on ordination to the diaconate.

The abolished orders were:

• Subdeacon, with specific duties in liturgical worship, especially at Mass. The order, whose first extant mention dates from about the middle of the third century, was regarded as minor until the 13th century; afterwards, it was called a major order in the West but not in the East.

• Acolyte, to serve in minor capacities in liturgical worship; a function now performed by Mass servers.

• Exorcist, to perform services of exorcism for expelling evil spirits; a function which came to be reserved to specially delegated priests.

• Lector, to read scriptural and other passages during liturgical worship; a function now generally performed by lay persons.

• Porter, to guard the entrance to an assembly of Christians and to ward off undesirables who tried to gain admittance; an order of early origin and utility but of present insignificance.

## PERMANENT DIACONATE

Restoration of the permanent diaconate in the Roman rite — making it possible for men to become deacons permanently, without going on to the priesthood — was promulgated by Pope Paul VI June 18, 1967, in a document entitled *Sacrum Diaconatus Ordinem* ("Sacred Order of the Diaconate").

The Pope's action implemented the desire expressed by the Second Vatican Council for reestablishment of the diaconate as an independent order in its own right not only to supply ministers for carrying on the work of the Church but also to complete the hierarchical structure of the Church of Roman rite.

Permanent deacons have been traditional in the Eastern Church. The Western Church, however, since the fourth or fifth century, generally followed the practice of conferring the diaconate only as a sacred order preliminary to the priesthood, and of restricting the ministry of deacons to liturgical functions.

The Pope's document, issued on his own initiative, provided:

• Qualified unmarried men 25 years of age or older may be ordained permanent deacons. They cannot marry after ordination.

• Qualified married men 35 years of age or older may be ordained permanent deacons. The consent of the wife of a prospective deacon is required. A married deacon cannot remarry after the death of his wife.

• Preparation for the diaconate includes a course of study and formation over a period of at least three years.

• Candidates who are not Religious must be affiliated with a diocese. Reestablishment of the permanent diaconate among Religious is reserved to the Holy See.

• Deacons will practice their ministry under the direction of a bishop and with the priests with whom they will be associated. (For functions, see also the description of deacon, under Holy Orders.)

Restoration of the permanent diaconate in the United States was approved by the Holy See in October, 1968. Shortly afterwards the U.S. bishops established a committee for the permanent diaconate, which is chaired by Bishop Edward U. Kmiec of Nashville. The committee operates through secretariat, with offices at 3211 Fourth St. N. E., Washington, D.C. 20017. Samuel M. Taub, permanent deacon, is executive director.

### Status and Functions

According to a study conducted under the auspices of the National Conference of Cathoic Bishops and released in summary form in December, 1995, there were more than 11,000 permanent deacons in the United States, the highest total for any single country. Their ages ranged from the 30s to 86; the median age was almost 60. Sixty percent reported professional or managerial careers. Three percent were never married. About half of the 20 percent with minority backgrounds were "Hispanic Latino"; four percent were African American; less than one percent were of Asian descent; of the one percent of other nationalities, most were Native Americans.

Training programs of spiritual, theological and pastoral formation are based on guidelines emanating from the National Conference of Catholic Bishops.

Deacons have various functions, depending on the nature of their assignments. Liturgically, they can officiate at baptisms, weddings, wake services and funerals, can preach and distribute Holy Communion. Some are engaged in religious education work. All are intended to carry out works of charity and pastoral service of one kind or another.

The majority of permanent deacons, 92 per cent of whom are married, continue in their secular work. Their ministry of service is developing in three dimensions: of liturgy, of the word, and of charity. Depending on the individual deacon's abilities and preference, he is assigned by his bishop to either a parochial ministry or to another field of service. Deacons are active in a variety of ministries including those to prison inmates and their families, the sick in hospitals, nursing homes and homes for the aged, alienated youth, the elderly and the poor, and in various areas of legal service to the indigent, of education and campus ministry. The possibilities for diaconal ministry are under realistic assessment in a number of dioceses.

**National Association of Diaconate Directors:** Membership organization of directors, vicars and other staff personnel of diaconate programs. Established in 1977 to promote effective communication and facilitate the exchange of information and resources of members; to develop professional expertise and promote research, training and self evaluation; to foster accountability and seek ways to promote means of implementing solutions to problems. NAPDD is governed by an executive board of elected officers. President for the 1995-96 term: Rev. Msgr. Theodore Kraus of Oakland, CA. Executive Director, Deacon John Pistone. Office, 1337 W. Ohio St., Chicago, IL 60622.

# MARRIAGE DOCTRINE

The following excerpts, stating key points of doctrine on marriage, are from the *Pastoral Constitution on the Church in the Modern World* (Nos. 48 to 51) promulgated by the Second Vatican Council.

### Conjugal Covenant

The intimate partnership of married life and love has been established by the Creator and qualified by his laws. It is rooted in the conjugal covenant of irrevocable personal consent.

God himself is the author of matrimony, endowed as it is with various benefits and purposes. All of these have a very decisive bearing on the continuation of the human race, on the personal development and eternal destiny of the individual members of a family, and on the dignity, stability, peace, and prosperity of the family itself and of human society as a whole. By their very nature, the institution of matrimony itself and conjugal love are ordained for the procreation and education of children, and find in them their ultimate crown.

Thus a man and a woman render mutual help and service to each other through an intimate union of their persons and of their actions. Through this union they experience the meaning of their oneness and attain to it with growing perfection day by day. As a mutual gift of two persons, this intimate union, as well as the good of the children, imposes total fidelity on the spouses and argues for an unbreakable oneness between them (No. 48).

## Sacrament of Matrimony

Christ the Lord abundantly blessed this many-faceted love. The Savior of men and the Spouse of the Church comes into the lives of married Christians through the sacrament of matrimony. He abides with them thereafter so tha, just as he loved the Church and handed himself over on her behalf, the spouses may love each other with perpetual fidelity through mutual self-bestowal.

Graced with the dignity and office of fatherhood and motherhood, parents will energetically acquit themselves of a duty which devolves primarily on them; namely, education, and especially religious education.

The Christian family, which springs from marriage as a reflection of the loving covenant uniting Christ with the Church, and as a participation in that covenant, will manifest to all men the Savior's living presence in the world, and the genuine nature of the Church (No. 48).

## Conjugal Love

The biblical Word of God several times urges the betrothed and the married to nourish and develop their wedlock by pure conjugal love and undivided affection.

This love is an eminently human one since it is directed from one person to another through an affection of the will. It involves the good of the whole person. Therefore it can enrich the expressions of body and mind with a unique dignity, ennobling these expressions as special ingredients and signs of the friendship distinctive of marriage. This love the Lord has judged worthy of special gifts, healing, perfecting, and exalting gifts of grace and of charity.

Such love, merging the human with the divine, leads the spouses to a free and mutual gift of themselves, a gift proving itself by gentle affection and by deed. Such love pervades the whole of their lives. Indeed, by its generous activity it grows better and grows greater. Therefore it far excels mere erotic inclination, which, selfishly pursued, soon enough fades wretchedly away.

This love is uniquely expressed and perfected through the marital act. The actions within marriage by which the couple are united intimately and chastely are noble and worthy ones. Expressed in a manner which is truly human, these actions signify and promote that mutual self-giving by which spouses enrich each other with a joyful and a thankful will.

Sealed by mutual faithfulness and hallowed above all by Christ's sacrament, this love remains steadfastly true in body and in mind, in bright days or dark. It will never be profaned by adultery or divorce. Firmly established by the Lord, the unity of marriage will radiate from the equal personal dignity of wife and husband, a dignity acknowledged by mutual and total love.

The steady fulfillment of the duties of this Christian vocation demands notable virtue. For this reason, strengthened by grace for holiness of life, the couple will painstakingly cultivate and pray for constancy of love, largeheartedness, and the spirit of sacrifice (No. 49).

## Fruitfulness of Marriage

Marriage and conjugal love are by their nature ordained toward the begetting and educating of children. Chilren are really the supreme gift of marriage and contribute very substantially to the welfare of their parents. God himself wished to share with man a certain special participation in his own creative work. Thus he blessed male and female, saying: "Increase and multiply" (Gn. 1:28).

Hence, while not making the other purposes of matrimony of less account, the true practice of conjugal love, and the whole meaning of the family life which results from it, have this aim: that the couple be ready with stout hearts to cooperate with the love of the Creator and the Savior, who through them will enlarge and enrich his own family day by day.

Parents should regard as their proper mission the task of transmitting human life and educating those to whom it has been transmitted. They should realize that they are thereby cooperators with the love of God the Creator, and are, so to speak, the interpreters of that love. Thus they will fulfill their task with human and Christian responsibility (No. 50).

## Norms of Judgment

They will thoughtfully take into account both their own welfare and that of their children, those already born and those who may be foreseen. For this accounting they will reckon with both the material and the spiritual conditions of the times as well as of their state in life. Finally, they will consult the interests of the family group, of temporal society, and of the Church herself.

The parents themselves should ultimately make this judgment in the sight of God. But in their manner of acting, spouses should be aware that they cannot proceed arbitrarily. They must always be governed according to a conscience dutifully conformed to the divine law itself, and should be submissive toward the Church's teaching office, which authentically interprets that law in the light of the Gospel. That divine law reveals and protects the integral meaning of conjugal love, and impels it toward a truly human fulfillment.

Marriage, to be sure, is not instituted solely for procreation. Rather, its very nature as an unbreakable compact between persons, and the welfare of the children, both demand that the mutual love of the spouses, too, be embodied in a rightly ordered manner, that it grow and ripen. Therefore, marriage persists as a whole manner and communion of life, and maintains its value and indissolubility, even when offspring are lacking — despite, rather often, the very intense desire of the couple (No. 50).

## Love and Life

This Council realizes that certain modern conditions often keep couples from arranging their married lives harmoniously, and that they find themselves in circumstances where at least temporarily the size of their families should not be increased. As a result, the faithful exercise of love and the full intimacy of their lives are hard to maintain. But where the intimacy of married life is broken off, it is not rare for its faithfulness to be imperiled and its quality of fruitfulness ruined. For then the upbringing of the children and the courage to accept new ones are both endangered.

To these problems there are those who presume to offer dishonorable solutions. Indeed, they do not recoil from the taking of life. But the Church issues the reminder that a true contradiction cannot exist between the divine laws pertaining to the transmission of life and those pertaining to the fostering of authentic conjugal love.

### Church Teaching

For God, the Lord of Life, has conferred on men the surpassing ministry of safeguarding life — a ministry which must be fulfilled in a manner which is worthy of men. Therefore from the moment of its conception life must be guarded with the greatest care, while abortion and infanticide are unspeakable crimes. The sexual characteristics of man and the human faculty of reproduction wonderfully exceed the dispositions of lower forms of life. Hence the acts themselves which are proper to conjugal love and which are exercised in accord with genuine human dignity must be honored with great reverence (No. 51).

Therefore when there is question of harmonizing conjugal love with the responsible transmission of life, the moral aspect of any procedure does not depend solely on the sincere intentions or on an evaluation of motives. It must be determined by objective standards. These, based on the nature of the human person and his acts, preserve the full sense of mutual self-giving and human procreation in the context of true love. Such a goal cannot be achieved unless the virtue of conjugal chastity is sincerely practiced. Relying on these principles, sons of the Church may not undertake methods of regulating procreation which are found blameworthy by the teaching authority of the Church in its unfolding of the divine law.

Everyone should be persuaded that human life and the task of transmitting it are not realities bound up with this world alone. Hence they cannot be measured or perceived only in terms of it, but always have a bearing on the eternal destiny of men (No. 51).

# HUMANAE VITAE

Marriage doctrine and morality were the subjects of the encyclical letter "Of Human Life," issued by Pope Paul VI, July 29, 1968. Following are a number of key excerpts from the document which was framed in the pattern of traditional teaching and statements by the Second Vatican Council.

Each and every marriage act ("quilibet matrimonii usus") must remain open to the transmission of life (No. 11).

Indeed, by its intimate structure, the conjugal act, while most closely uniting husband and wife, capacitates them for the generation of new lives according to laws inscribed in the very being of man and of woman. By safeguarding both these essential aspects, the unitive and the procreative, the conjugal act preserves in its fullnes the sense of true mutual love and its ordination toward man's most high calling to parenthood (No. 12).

It is, in fact, justly observed that a conjugal act imposed upon one's partner without regard for his or her condition and lawful desires is not a true act of love, and therefore denies an exigency of right moral order in the relationships between husband and wife. Hence, one who reflects well must also recognize that a reciprocal act of love which jeopardizes the responsibility to transmit life — which God the Creator, according to particular laws, inserted therein — is in contradiction with the design constitutive of marriage and with the will of the Author of life. To use this divine gift, destroying, even if only partially, its meaning and its purpose, is to contradict the nature both of man and of woman and of their most intimate relationship, and therefore it is to contradict also the plan of God and his will (No. 13).

### Forbidden Actions

The direct interruption of the generative process already begun, and, above all, directly willed and procured abortion, even if for therapeutic reasons, are to be absolutely excluded as licit means of regulating birth.

Equally to be excluded  is direct sterilization, whether perpetual or temporary, whether of the man or of the woman. Similarly excluded is every action which, either in anticipation of the conjugal act, or in its accomplishment, or in the development of its natural consequences, proposes, whether as an end or as a means, to render procreation impossible.

To justify conjugal acts made intentionally infecund, one cannot invoke as valid reasons the lesser evil, or the fact that such acts would constitute a whole together with the fecund acts already performed or to follow later and hence would share in one and the same moral goodness. In truth, if it is sometimes licit to tolerate a lesser evil in order to avoid a greater evil or to promote a greater good, it is not licit, even for the gravest reasons, to do evil so that good may follow therefrom; that is, to make into the object of a positive act of the will something which is intrinsically disorder, and hence unworthy of the human person, even when the intention is to safeguard or promote individual, family or social well-being.

Consequently, it is an error to think that a conjugal act which is deliberately made infecund, and so is intrinsically dishonest, could be made honest and right by the ensemble of a fecund conjugal life (No. 14).

If, then, there are serious motives to space out births, which derive from the physical or psychological conditions of husband and wife, or from external conditions, the Church teaches that it is then licit to take into account the natural rhythms immanent in the generative functions, for the use of marriage in the infecund periods only, and in this way to regulate birth without offending earlier stated principles (No. 16).

## Pastoral Concerns

We do not at all intend to hide the sometimes serious difficulties inherent in the life of Christian married persons; for them, as for everyone else, "the gate is narrow and the way is hard that leads to life." But the hope of that life must illuminate their way, as with courage they strive to live with wisdom, justice and piety in this present time, knowing that the figure of this world passes away.

Let married couples then, face up to the efforts needed, supported by the faith and hope which "do not disappoint because God's love has been poured into our hearts through the Holy Spirit, who has been given to us." Let them implore divine assistance by persevering prayer; above all, let them draw from the source of grace and charity in the Eucharist. And, if sin should still keep its hold over them, let them not be discouraged but rather have recourse with humble perseverance to the mercy of God, which is poured forth in the sacrament of penance (No. 25).

# MARRIAGE LAWS

The Catholic Church claims jurisdiction over its members in matters pertaining to marriage. which is a sacrament. Church legislation on the subject is stated principally in 111 canons of the Code of Canon Law.

Marriage laws of the Church provide juridical norms in support of the marriage covenant. In 10 chapters, the revised Code covers: pastoral directives for preparing men and women for marriage; impediments in general and in particular; matrimonial consent; form for the celebration of marriage; mixed marriages; secret celebration of marriage; effects of marriage; separation of spouses, and convalidation of marriage.

Catholics are bound by all marriage laws of the Church. Non-Catholics, whether baptized or not, are not considered bound by these ecclesiastical laws except in cases of marriage with a Catholic. Certain natural laws, in the Catholic view, bind all men and women, irrespective of their religious beliefs; accordingly, marriage is prohibited before the time of puberty, without knowledge and free mutual consent, in the case of an already existing valid marriage bond, in the case of antecedent and perpetual impotence.

## Formalities

These include, in addition to arrangements for the time and place of the marriage ceremony, doctrinal and moral instruction concerning marriage and the recording of data which verifies in documentary form the eligibility and freedom of the persons to marry. Records of this kind, which are confidential, are preserved in the archives of the church where the marriage takes place.

Premarital instructions re the subject matter of Pre-Cana Conferences.

## Marital Consent

Matrimonial consent can be invalidated by an essential defect, substantial error, the strong influence of force and fear, the presence of a condition or intention against the nature of marriage.

## Form of Marriage

A Catholic is required, for validity and lawfulness, to contract marriage — with another Catholic or with a non-Catholic — in the presence of a competent priest or deacon and two witnesses.

There are two exceptions to this law. A Roman Rite Catholic (since Mar. 25, 1967) or an Eastern Rite Catholic (since Nov. 21, 1964) can contract marriage validly in the presence of a priest of a separated Eastern Rite Church, provided other requirements of law are complied with. With permission of the competent Roman-Rite or Eastern-Rite bishop, this form of marriage is lawful, as well as valid. (See Eastern Rite Laws, below.)

With these two exceptions, and aside from cases covered by special permission, the Church does not regard as valid any marriages involving Catholics which take place before non-Catholic ministers of religion or civil officials.

(An excommunication formerly in force against Catholics who celebrated marriage before a non-Catholic minister was abrogated in a decree issued by the Sacred Congregation for the Doctrine of the Faith on Mar. 18, 1966.)

The ordinary place of marriage is the parish of either Catholic party or of the Catholic party in case of a mixed marriage.

Church law regarding the form of marriage does not affect non-Catholics in marriages among themselves. The Church recognizes as valid the marriages of non-Catholics before ministers of religion and civil officials, unless they are rendered null and void on other grounds.

The canonical form is not to be observed in the case of a marriage between a non-Catholic and a baptized Catholic who has left the Church by a formal act.

## Impediments

**Diriment Impediments** to marriage are factors which render a marriage invalid.

• age, which obtains before completion of the 14th year for a woman and the 16th year for a man;

• impotency, if it is anteceent to the marriage and permanent (this differs from sterility, which is not an impediment);

• the bond of an existing valid marriage;

• disparity of worship, which obtains when one party is a Catholic and the other party is unbaptized;

• sacred orders;

• religious profession of the perpetual vow of chastity;

• abduction, which impedes the freedom of the person abducted;

• crime, variously involving elements of adultery, promise or attempt to marry, conspiracy to murder a husband or wife;

• blood relationship in the direct line (father-daughter, mother-son, etc.) and to the fourth degree inclusive of the collateral line (brother-sister, first cousins);

• affinity, or relationship resulting from a valid marriage, in any degree of the direct line;

• public honesty, arising from an invalid marriage or from public or notorious concubinage; it renders either party incapable of marrying blood relatives of the other in the first degree of the direct line.

• legal relationship arising from adoption; it renders either party incapable of marrying relatives of the other in the direct line or in the second degree of the collateral line.

**Dispensations from Impediments**: Persons hindered by impediments cannot marry unless they are dispensed therefrom in view of reasons recognized in canon law. Local bishops can dispense from the impediments most often encountered (e.g., disparity of worship) as well as others.

Decision regarding some dispensations is reserved to the Holy See.

## Separation

A valid and consummated marriage of baptized persons cannot be dissolved by any human authority or any cause other than the death of one of the persons.

In other circumstances:

• 1. A valid but unconsummated marriage of baptized persons, or of a baptized and an unbaptized person, can be dissolved:

a. by the solemn religious profession of one of the persons, made with permission of the pope. In such a case, the bond is dissolved at the time of profession, and the other person is free to marry again.

b. by dispensation from the pope, requested for a grave reason by one or both of the persons. If the dispensation is granted, both persons are free to marry again.

Dispensations in these cases are granted for reasons connected with the spiritual welfare of the concerned persons.

• 2. A legitimate marriage, even consummated, of unbaptized persons can be dissolved in favor of one of them who subsequently receives the sacrament of baptism. This is the Pauline Privilege, so called because it was promulgated by St. Paul (1 Cor. 7:12-15) as a means of protecting the faith of converts. Requisites for granting the privilege are:

a. marriage prior to the baptism of either person;

b. reception of baptism by one person;

c. refusal of the unbaptized person to live in peace with the baptized person and without interfering with his or her freedom to practice the Christian faith. The privilege does not apply if the unbaptized person agrees to these conditions.

• 3. A legitimate and consummated marriage of a baptized and an unbaptized person can be dissolved by the pope in virtue of the Privilege of Faith, also called the Petrine Privilege.

## Civil Divorce

Because of the unity and the indissolubility of marriage, the Church denies that civil divorce can break the bond of a valid marriage, whether the marriage involves two Catholics, a Catholic and a non-Catholic, or non-Catholics with each other.

In view of serious circumstances of marital distress, the Church permits an innocent and aggrieved party, whether wife or husband, to seek and obtain a civil divorce for the purpose of acquiring title and right to the civil effects of divorce, such as separate habitation and maintenance, and the custody of children. Permission for this kind of action should be obtained from proper church authority. The divorce, if obtained, does not break the bond of a valid marriage.

Under other circumstances — as would obtain if a marriage was invalid (see Annulment, below) — civil divorce is permitted for civil effects and as a civil ratification of the fact that the marriage bond really does not exist.

## Annulment

This is a decision by a competent church authority — e.g., a bishop, a diocesan marriage tribunal, the Roman Rota — that an apparently valid marriage was actually invalid from the beginning because of the unknown or concealed existence, from the beginning, of a diriment impediment, an essential defect in consent, radical incapability for marriage, or a condition placed by one or both of the parties against the very nature of marriage.

## Eastern Rite Laws

Marriage laws of the Eastern Church differ in several respects from the legislation of the Roman Rite. The regulations in effect since May 2, 1949, were contained in the motu proprio *Crebre Allatae* issued by Pius XII the previous February.

According to both the Roman Code of Canon Law and the Oriental Code, marriages between Roman Rite Catholics and Eastern Rite Catholics ordinarily take place in the rite of the groom and have canonical effects in that rite.

Regarding the form for the celebration of marriages between Eastern Catholics and baptized Eastern non-Catholics, the Second Vatican Council declared:

"By way of preventing invalid marriages between Eastern Catholics and baptized Eastern non-Catholics, and in the interests of the permanence and sanctity of marriage and of domestic harmony, this sacred Synod decrees that the canonical 'form' for the celebration of such marriages obliges only for lawfulness. For their validity, the presence of a sacred minister suffices, as long as the other requirements of law are honored" (*Decree on Eastern Catholic Churches*, No. 18).

Marriages taking place in this manner are lawful, as well as valid, with permission of a competent Eastern Rite bishop.

## The Rota

The Roman Rota is the ordinary court of appeal for marriage, and some other cases, which are appealed to the Holy See from lower church courts. Appeals are made to the Rota if decisions by diocesan and archdiocesan courts fail to settle the matter in dispute. Pope John Paul, at annual meetings with Rota personnel, speaks about the importance of the court's actions in providing norms of practice for other tribunals.

# MIXED MARRIAGES

"Mixed Marriages" *(Matrimonia Mixta)* was the subject of: (1) a letter issued under this title by Pope Paul VI Mar. 31, 1970, and (2) a statement, *Implementation of the Apostolic Letter on Mixed Marriages,* approved by the National Conference of Catholic Bishops Nov. 16, 1970.

One of the key points in the bishops' statement referred to the need for mutual pastoral care by ministers of different faiths for the sacredness of marriage and for appropriate preparation and continuing support of parties to a mixed marriage.

Pastoral experience, which the Catholic Church shares with other religious bodies, confirms the fact that marriages of persons of different beliefs involve special problems related to the continuing religious practice of the concerned persons and to the religious education and formation of their children.

Pastoral measures to minimize these problems include instruction of a non-Catholic party in essentials of the Catholic faith for purposes of understanding. Desirably, some instruction should also be given the Catholic party regarding his or her partner's beliefs.

## Requirements

The Catolic party to a mixed marriage is required to declare his (her) intention of continuing practice of the Catholic faith and to promise to do all in his (her) power to share his (her) faith with children born of the marriage by having them baptized and raised as Catholics. No declarations or promises are required of the non-Catholic party, but he (she) must be informed of the declaration and promise made by the Catholic.

Notice of the Catholic's declaration and promise is an essential part of the application made to a bishop for (1) permission to marry a baptized non-Catholic, or (2) a dispensation to marry an unbaptized non-Catholic.

A mixed marriage can take place with a Nuptial Mass. (The bishops' statement added this caution: "To the extent that Eucharistic sharing is not permitted by the general discipline of the Church, this is to be considered when plans are being made to have the mixed marriage at Mass or not.")

The ordinary minister at a mixed marriage is an authorized priest or deacon, and the ordinary place is the parish church of the Catholic party. A non-Catholic minister may not only attend the marriage ceremony but may also address, pray with and bless the couple.

For appropriate pastoral reasons, a bishop can grant a dispensation from the Catholic form of marriage and can permit the marriage to take place in a non-Catholic church with a non-Catholic minister as the officiating minister. A priest may not only attend such a ceremony but may also address, pray with and bless the couple.

"It is not permitted," however, the bishops' statement declared, "to have two religious services or to have a single service in which both the Catholic marriage ritual and a non-Catholic marriage ritual are celebrated jointly or successively."

# PASTORAL MINISTRY FOR DIVORCED AND REMARRIED

Ministry to divorced and remarried Catholics is a difficult field of pastoral endeavor, situated as it is in circumstances tantamount to the horns of a dilemma.

## At Issue

On the one side is firm church teaching on the permanence of marriage and norms against reception of the Eucharist and full participation in the life of the Church by Catholics in irregular unions.

On the other side are men and women with broken unions followed by second and perhaps happier attempts at marriage which the Church does not recognize as valid and which may not be capable of being validated because of the existence of an earlier marriage bond.

Factors involved in these circumstances are those of the Church, upholding its doctrine and practice regarding the permanence of marriage, and those of many men and women in irregular second marriages who desire full participation in the life of the Church.

Sacramental participation is not possible forthose whose first marriage was valid, although there is no bar to their attendance at Mass, to sharing in other activities of the Church, or to their efforts to have children baptized and raised in the Catholic faith.

An exception to this rule is the condition of a divorced and remarried couple living in a brother-sister relationship.

There is no ban against sacramental participation by separated or divorced persons who have not attempted a second marriage, provided the usual conditions for reception of the sacraments are in order.

Unverified estimates of the number of U.S. Catholics who are divorced and remarried vary be tween six and eight million.

## Tribunal Action

What can the Church do for them and with them in pastoral ministry, is an old question charged with new urgency because of the rising number of divorced and remarried Catholics.

One way to help is through the agency of marriage tribunals charged with responsibility for investigating and settling questions concerning the validity or invalidity of a prior marriage. There are reasons in canon law justifying the Church in declaring a particular marriage null and void from the beginning, despite the short- or long-term existence of an apparently valid union.

Decrees of nullity (annulments) are not new in the history of the Church. If such a decree is issued, a man or woman is free to validate a second marriage and live in complete union with the Church.

The 1994 *Statistical Yearbook of the Church,* reported that in 1994 U.S. tribunals issued 54,463 annulments (in ordinary and documentary processes). The canonical reasons were: invalid consent

(38,699), impotence (6), other impediments (3,163), defect of form (12,595). Worldwide, 72,744 decrees or declarations of nullity were issued in 1994.

## Reasons behind Decrees

Pastoral experience reveals that some married persons, a short or long time after contracting an apparently valid marriage, exhibit signs that point back to the existence, at the time of marriage, of latent and serious personal deficiencies which made them incapable of valid consent and sacramental commitment.

Such deficiencies might include gross immaturity and those affecting in a serious way the capacity to love, to have a true interpersonal and conjugal relationship, to fulfill marital obligations, to accept the faith aspect of marriage.

Psychological and behavioral factors like these have been given greater attention by tribunals in recent years and have provided grounds for numerous decrees of nullity.

Decisions of this type do not indicate any softening of the Church's attitude regarding the permanence of marriage. They affirm, rather, that some persons who have married were really not capable of doing so.

Serious deficiencies in the capacity for real interpersonal relationship in marriage were the reasons behind a landmark decree of nullity issued in 1973 by the Roman Rota, the Vatican high court of appeals in marriage cases. Pope John Paul referred to such deficiencies — the "grave lack of discretionary judgment," incapability of assuming "essential matrimonial rights and obligations," for example — in an address Jan. 26, 1984, to personnel of the Rota.

The tribunal way to a decree of nullity regarding a previous marriage, however, is not open to many persons in second marriages — because grounds are either lacking or, if present, cannot be verified in tribunal process.

## Unacceptable Solutions

One unacceptable solution of the problem, called "good conscience procedure," involves administration of the sacraments of penance and the Eucharist to divorced and remarried Catholics unable to obtain a decree of nullity for a first marriage who are living in a subsequent marriage "in good faith."

This procedure, despite the fact that it has no standing or recognition in church law, is being advocated and practiced by some priests and remarried Catholics.

This issue was addressed by the Congregation for the Doctrine of the Faith in a letter to bishops dated Oct. 14, 1994, and published with the approval of Pope John Paul. The letter said in part:

"Pastoral solutions in this area have been suggested according to which ... divorced-and-remarried members of the faithful could approach holy Communion in specific cases when they considered themselves authoritzed according to a judgment of conscience to do so. This would be the case, for example, when they had been abandoned completely unjustly although they sincerely tried to save the previous marriage; or when they are convinced of the nullity of their previous marriage although (they are) unable to demonstrate it in the external forum; or when they have gone through a long period of reflection and penance; or also when for morally valid reasons they cannot satisfy the obligation to separate.

"In some places it has also been proposed that, in order objectively to examine their actual situation, the divorced-and-remarried would have to consult a prudent and experienced priest. This priest, however, would have to respect their eventual decision in conscience to approach holy Communion, without this implying an official authorization.

"In these and similar cases, it would be a matter of a tolerant and benevolent pastoral solution in order to do justice to the different situations of the divorced-and-remarried.

"Even if analogous solutions have been proposed by a few fathers of the Church and in some measure were practiced, nevertheless these never attained the consensus of the fathers and in no way came to constitute the common doctrine of the Church nor to determine her discipline. It falls to the universal magisterium, in fidelity to sacred Scripture and tradition, to teach and to interpret authentically the deposit of faith."

## Conditions for Receiving Communion

Practically speaking,"when for serious reasons — for example, for the children's upbringing — a man and a woman cannot satisfy the obligation to separate," they may be admitted to Communion if "they take on themselves the duty to live in complete continence, that is, by abstinence from the acts proper to married couples. In such a case they may receive holy Communion as long as they respect the obligation to avoid giving scandal."

The teaching of the Church on this subject "does not mean that the Church does not take to heart the situation of those faithful who, moreover, are not excluded from ecclesial communion. She is concerned to accompany them pastorally and invite them to share in the life of the Church in the measure that is compatible with the dispositions of divine law, from which the Church has no power to dispense. On the other hand, it is necessary to instruct these faithful so that they do not think their participation in the life of the Church is reduced exclusively to the question of the reception of the Eucharist. The faithful are to be helped to deepen their understanding of the value of sharing in the sacrifice of Christ in the Mass, or spiritual communion, of prayer, of meditation on the word of God, and of works of charity and justice."

## MARRIAGE ENCOUNTER

Marriage Encounter brings couples together for a weekend program of events directed by a team of several couples and a priest, for the purpose of developing their abilities to communicate with each other in their life together as husband and wife. This purpose is served by direction in techniques given by the team and by private dialogue of each couple. The address of National Marriage Encounter is 4704 Jamerson Pl., Orlando, FL 32807. The national office of Worldwide Marriage Encounter is located at 1908 E. Highland Ave., Suite A, San Bernardino, CA 92404.

# THE CHURCH CALENDAR

The calendar of the Roman Church consists of an arrangement throughout the year of a series of liturgical seasons, commemorations of divine mysteries and commemorations of saints for purposes of worship.

The key to the calendar is the central celebration of the Easter Triduum, commemorating the supreme saving act of Jesus in his death and resurrection to which all other observances and acts of worship are related.

The purposes of this calendar were outlined in the *Constitution on the Sacred Liturgy* (Nos. 102-105) promulgated by the Second Vatican Council.

Within the cycle of a year ... (the Church) unfolds the whole mystery of Christ, not only from his incarnation and birth until his ascension, but also as reflected in the day of Pentecost, and the expectation of a blessed, hoped-for return of the Lord.

Recalling thus the mysteries of redemption, the Church opens to the faithful the riches of her Lord's powers and merits, so that these are in some way made present at all times, and the faithful are enabled to lay hold of them and become filled with saving grace (No. 102).

In celebrating this annual cycle of Christ's mysteries, holy Church honors with special love the Blessed Mary, Mother of God (No. 103).

The Church has also included in the annual cycle days devoted to the memory of the martyrs and the other saints (who) sing God's perfect praise in heaven and offer prayers for us. By celebrating the passage of these saints from earth to heaven the Church proclaims the paschal mystery as achieved in the saints who have suffered and been glorified with Christ; she proposes them to the faithful as examples who draw all to the Father through Christ, and through their merits she pleads for God's favors (No. 104).

In the various seasons of the year and according to her traditional discipline, the Church completes the formation of the faithful by means of pious practices for soul and body, by instruction, prayer, and works of penance and mercy (No. 105).

## THE ROMAN CALENDAR

Norms for a revised calendar for the Western Church as decreed by the Second Vatican Council were approved by Paul VI in the *motu proprio Mysterii Paschalis* dated Feb. 14, 1969. The revised calendar was promulgated a month later by a decree of the Congregation for Divine Worship and went into effect Jan. 1, 1970, with provisional modifications. Full implementation of all its parts was delayed in 1970 and 1971, pending the completion of work on related liturgical texts. The U.S. bishops ordered the calendar into effect for 1972.

### The Seasons

**Advent:** The liturgical year begins with the first Sunday of Advent, which introduces a season of four weeks or slightly less duration with the theme of expectation of the coming of Christ. During the first two weeks, the final coming of Christ as Lord and Judge at the end of the world is the focus of attention. From Dec. 17 to 24, the emphasis shifts to anticipation of the celebration of his Nativity on the solemnity of Christmas.

Advent has four Sundays. Since the 10th century, the first Sunday has marked the beginning of the liturgical year in the Western Church. In the Middle Ages, a kind of pre-Christmas fast was in vogue during the season.

**Christmas Season:** The Christmas season begins with the vigil of Christmas and lasts until the Sunday after January 6, inclusive.

The period between the end of the Christmas season and the beginning of Lent belongs to the Ordinary Time of the year. Of variable length, the pre-Lenten phase of this season includes what were formerly called the Sundays after Epiphany and the suppressed Sundays of Septuagesima, Sexagesima and Quinquagesima.

**Lent:** The penitential season of Lent begins on Ash Wednesday, which occurs between Feb. 4 and Mar. 11, depending on the date of Easter, and lasts until the Mass of the Lord's Supper (Holy Thursday). It has six Sundays. The sixth Sunday marks the beginning of Holy Week and is known as Passion (formerly called Palm) Sunday.

The origin of Lenten observances dates back to the fourth century or earlier.

**Easter Triduum:** The Easter Triduum begins with evening Mass of the Lord's Supper and ends with Evening Prayer on Easter Sunday.

**Easter Season:** The Easter season whose theme is resurrection from sin to the life of grace, lasts for 50 days, from Easter to Pentecost. Easter, the first Sunday after the full moon following the vernal equinox, occurs between Mar. 22 and Apr. 25. The terminal phase of the Easter season, between the solemnities of the Ascension of the Lord and Pentecost, stresses anticipation of the coming and action of the Holy Spirit.

**Ordinary Time:** The season of Ordinary Time begins on Monday (or Tuesday if the feast of the Baptism of the Lord is celebrated on that Monday) after the Sunday following January 6 and continues until the day before Ash Wednesday, inclusive. It begins again on the Monday after Pentecost and ends on the Saturday before the first Sunday of Advent. It consists of 33 or 34 weeks. The last Sunday is celebrated as the Solemnity of Christ the King. The overall purpose of the season is to elaborate the themes of salvation history.

The various liturgical seasons are characterized in part by the scriptural readings and Mass prayers assigned to each of them. During Advent, for example, the readings are messianic; during the Easter season, from the Acts of the Apostles, chronicling the Resurrection and the original proclamation of Christ by the Apostles, and from the Gospel of John; during Lent, baptismal and penitential passages. Mass prayers reflect the meaning and purpose of the various seasons.

### Commemorations of Saints

The commemorations of saints are celebrated concurrently with the liturgical seasons and feasts of our Lord. Their purpose is to illustrate the paschal mysteries as reflected in the lives of saints, to honor them as heroes of holiness, and to appeal for their intercession.

In line with revised regulations, some former feasts were either abolished or relegated to observance in particular places by local option for one of two reasons: (1) lack of sufficient historical evidence for observance of the feasts; (2) lack of universal significance.

The commemoration of a saint, as a general rule, is observed on the day of death (*dies natalis,* day of birth to glory with God in heaven). Exceptions to this rule include the feasts of St. John the Baptist, who is honored on the day of his birth; Sts. Basil the Great and Gregory Nazianzen, and the brother Saints, Cyril and Methodius, who are commemorated in joint feasts. Application of this general rule in the revised calendar resulted in date changes of some observances.

## Sundays and Other Holy Days

Sunday is the original Christian feast day and holy day of obligation because of the unusually significant events of salvation history which took place and are commemorated on the first day of the week — viz., the Resurrection of Christ, the key event of his life and the fundamental fact of Christianity; and the descent of the Holy Spirit upon the Apostles on Pentecost, the birthday of the Church. The transfer of observance of the Lord's Day from the Sabbath to Sunday was made in apostolic times. The Mass and Liturgy of the Hours (Divine Office) of each Sunday reflect the themes and set the tones of the various liturgical seasons.

Holy days of obligation are special occasions on which Catholics who have reached the age of reason are seriously obliged, as on Sundays, to assist at Mass: they are also to refrain from work and involvement with business which impede participation in divine worship and the enjoyment of appropriate rest and relaxation.

The holy days of obligation observed in the United States are: Christmas, the Nativity of Jesus, Dec. 25; Solemnity of Mary the Mother of God, Jan. 1; Ascension of the Lord; Assumption of Blessed Mary the Virgin, Aug. 15; All Saints' Day, Nov. 1; Immaculate Conception of Blessed Mary the Virgin, Dec. 8.

The precept to attend Mass is abrogated in the U.S. whenever the Solemnity of Mary, the Assumption, or All Saints falls on a Saturday or Monday (1991 decree of U.S. bishops; approved by Holy See July 4, 1992, and effective Jan. 1, 1993).

In addition to these, there are four other holy days of obligation prescribed in the general law of the Church which are not so observed in the U.S.: Epiphany, Jan. 6; St. Joseph, Mar. 19; Corpus Christi; Sts. Peter and Paul, June 29. The solemnities of Epiphany and Corpus Christi are transferred to a Sunday in countries where they are not observed as holy days of obligation.

## Solemnities, Feasts, Memorials

**Categories of observances** according to dignity and manner of observance are: solemnities, principal days in the calendar (observance begins with Evening Prayer I of the preceding day; some have their own vigil Mass); feasts (celebrated within the limits of the natural day); obligatory memorials (celebrated throughout the Church); optional memorials (observable by choice).

**Fixed observances** are those which are regularly celebrated on the same calendar day each year.

**Movable observances** are those which are not observed on the same calendar day each year. Examples of these are Easter (the first Sunday after the first full moon following the vernal equinox), Ascension (40 days after Easter), Pentecost (50 days after Easter), Trinity Sunday (first after Pentecost), Christ the King (last Sunday of the liturgical year).

## Weekdays, Days of Prayer

**Weekdays** are those on which no proper feast or vigil is celebrated in the Mass or Liturgy of the Hours (Divine Office). On such days, the Mass may be that of the preceding Sunday, which expresses the liturgical spirit of the season, an optional memorial, a votive Mass, or a Mass for the dead. Weekdays of Advent and Lent are in a special category of their own.

**Days of Prayer:** Dioceses, at times to be designated by local bishops, should observe "days or periods of prayer for the fruits of the earth, prayer for human rights and equality, prayer for world justice and peace, and penitential observance outside of Lent." So stated the *Instruction on Particular Calendars* (No. 331) issued by the Congregation for the Sacraments and Divine Worship June 24, 1970.

These days are contemporary equivalents of what were formerly called ember and rogation days.

Ember days originated at Rome about the fifth century, probably as Christian replacements for seasonal festivals of agrarian cults. They were observances of penance, thanksgiving, and petition for divine blessing on the various seasons; they also were occasions of special prayer for clergy to be ordained. These days were observed four times a year.

Rogation days originated in France about the fifth century. They were penitential in character and also occasions of prayer for a bountiful harvest and protection against evil.

## Days and Times of Penance

Fridays throughout the year and the season of Lent are penitential times.

• Abstinence: Catholics in the United States, from the age of 14 throughout life, are obliged to abstain from meat on Ash Wednesday, the Fridays of Lent and Good Friday. The law forbids the use of meat, but not of eggs, the products of milk or condiments made of animal fat. Permissible are soup flavored with meat, meat gravy and sauces. The obligation to abstain from meat is not in force on days celebrated as solemnities (e.g., Christmas, Sacred Heart).

• Fasting: Catholics in the United States, from the day after their 18th birthday to the day after their 59th birthday, are also obliged to fast on Ash Wednesday and Good Friday. The law allows only one full meal a day, but does not prohibit the taking of some food in the morning and evening, observing — as far as quantity and quality are concerned — approved local custom. The order of meals is optional; i.e., the full meal may be taken in the evening instead of at midday. Also: (1) The combined quantity of food taken at the two lighter meals should not exceed the quantity taken at the full meal. (2) The drinking of ordinary liquids does not break the fast.

• Obligation: There is a general obligation to do penance for sins committed and for the remission of punishment due because of sin. Substantial observance of fasting and abstinence, prescribed for the community of the Church, is a matter of serious obligation; it allows, however, for alternate ways of doing penance (e.g., works of charity, prayer and prayer-related practices, almsgiving).

## Readings at Mass

The texts of scriptural readings for Mass on Sundays, holy days and some other days are indicated under the respective dates in the 1997 calendar pages which follow. The second (B) cycle is prescribed for Sunday Masses in the 1997 liturgical year (Dec. 1, 1996, to Nov. 29, 1997). The third (C) cycle is prescribed for the 1998 liturgical year which begins with the first Sunday of Advent, Nov. 30, 1997.

Weekday cycles of readings are the first and second, respectively, for liturgical years 1997 and 1998.

## Monthly Prayer Intentions

Intentions chosen and recommended by Pope John Paul II to the prayers of the faithful and circulated by the Apostleship of Prayer are given for each month of the calendar. He has expressed his desire that all Catholics make these intentions their own "in the certainty of being united with the Holy Father and praying according to his intentions and desires." These intentions represent the worldwide needs of the Church as seen through the eyes of the Holy Father.

## Celebrations in U.S. Particular Calendar

The General Norms for the Liturgical Year and the Calendar, issued in 1969 and published along with the General Roman Calendar for the Universal Church, noted that the calendar consists of the General Roman Calendar used by the entire Church and of particular calendars used in particular churches (nations or dioceses) or in families of religious. Particular calendars must be drawn up by appropriate episcopal conferences and approved by the Apostolic See.

The particular calendar for the U.S. contains the following celebrations. **January:** 4, Elizabeth Ann Seton; 5, John Neumann; 6, Bl. Andre Bessette. **March:** 3, Bl. Katharine Drexel. **May:** 15, Isidore the Farmer. **July:** 1, Bl. Junipero Serra; 4, Independence Day; 14, Bl. Kateri Tekakwitha. **August:** 18, Jane Frances de Chantal. **September:** 9, Peter Claver. **October:** 6, Bl. Marie-Rose Durocher; 19, Isaac Jogues and John de Brebeuf and Companions; 20, Paul of the Cross. **November:** 13, Frances Xavier Cabrini; 18, Rose Philippine Duchesne; 23, Bl. Miguel Agustín Pro; Fourth Thursday, Thanksgiving Day. **December:** 9, Bl. Juan Diego; 12, Our Lady of Guadalupe.

## TABLE OF MOVABLE FEASTS

| Year | Ash Wednesday | Easter | Ascension | Pentecost | Weeks of Ordinary Time | | | | First Sunday of Advent |
|------|---------------|--------|-----------|-----------|------------|------|-----------|--------|------------------------|
| | | | | | Before Lent | | After Pent. | | |
| | | | | | Wk. | Ends | Wk. | Begins | |
| 1997 | Feb. 12 | Mar. 30 | May 8 | May 18 | 5 | Feb. 11 | 7 | May 19 | Nov. 30 |
| 1998 | Feb. 25 | Apr. 12 | May 21 | May 31 | 7 | Feb. 24 | 9 | June 1 | Nov. 29 |
| 1999 | Feb. 17 | Apr. 4 | May 13 | May 23 | 6 | Feb. 16 | 8 | May 24 | Nov. 28 |
| 2000 | Mar. 8 | Apr. 23 | June 1 | June 11 | 9 | Mar. 7 | 10 | June 12 | Dec. 3 |
| 2001 | Feb. 28 | Apr. 15 | May 24 | June 3 | 8 | Feb. 27 | 9 | June 4 | Dec. 2 |
| 2002 | Feb. 13 | Mar. 31 | May 9 | May 19 | 5 | Feb. 12 | 7 | May 20 | Dec. 1 |
| 2003 | Mar. 5 | Apr. 20 | May 29 | June 8 | 8 | Mar. 4 | 10 | June 9 | Nov. 30 |
| 2004 | Feb. 25 | Apr. 11 | May 20 | May 30 | 7 | Feb. 24 | 9 | May 31 | Nov. 28 |
| 2005 | Feb. 9 | Mar. 27 | May 5 | May 15 | 5 | Feb. 8 | 7 | May 16 | Nov. 27 |
| 2006 | Mar. 1 | Apr. 16 | May 25 | June 4 | 8 | Feb. 28 | 9 | June 5 | Dec. 3 |
| 2007 | Feb. 21 | Apr. 8 | May 17 | May 27 | 7 | Feb. 20 | 8 | May 28 | Dec. 2 |
| 2008 | Feb. 6 | Mar. 23 | May 1 | May 11 | 4 | Feb. 5 | 6 | May 12 | Nov. 30 |
| 2009 | Feb. 25 | Apr. 12 | May 21 | May 31 | 7 | Feb. 24 | 9 | June 1 | Nov. 29 |
| 2010 | Feb. 17 | Apr. 4 | May 13 | May 23 | 6 | Feb. 16 | 8 | May 24 | Nov. 28 |
| 2011 | Mar. 9 | Apr. 24 | June 2 | June 12 | 9 | Mar. 8 | 11 | June 13 | Nov. 27 |
| 2012 | Feb. 22 | Apr. 8 | May 17 | May 27 | 7 | Feb. 21 | 8 | May 28 | Dec. 2 |
| 2013 | Feb. 13 | Mar. 31 | May 9 | May 19 | 5 | Feb. 12 | 7 | May 20 | Dec. 1 |
| 2014 | Mar. 5 | Apr. 20 | May 29 | June 8 | 8 | Mar. 4 | 10 | June 9 | Nov. 30 |
| 2015 | Feb. 18 | Apr. 5 | May 14 | May 24 | 6 | Feb. 17 | 8 | May 25 | Nov. 29 |
| 2016 | Feb. 10 | Mar. 27 | May 5 | May 15 | 5 | Feb. 9 | 7 | May 16 | Nov. 27 |
| 2017 | Mar. 1 | Apr. 16 | May 25 | June 4 | 8 | Feb. 28 | 9 | June 5 | Dec. 3 |
| 2018 | Feb. 14 | Apr. 1 | May 10 | May 20 | 6 | Feb. 13 | 7 | May 21 | Dec. 2 |
| 2019 | Mar. 6 | Apr. 21 | May 30 | June 9 | 8 | Mar. 5 | 10 | June 10 | Dec. 1 |
| 2020 | Feb. 26 | Apr. 12 | May 21 | May 31 | 7 | Feb. 25 | 9 | June 1 | Nov. 30 |

## JANUARY 1997

*Prayer Intentions. Christians: That Catholics and Christians of different confessions may collaborate effectively to bring out what united them (General). Renewed appreciation of Baptism: That baptized people may be a testimony with their lives to the proclamation of universal salvation in Jesus Christ (Mission).*

**1—Wed. Solemnity of Mary, Mother of God. Holy day of obligation.** (Nm. 6:22-27; Gal. 4:4-7; Lk. 2:16-21.)

2—Thurs. Sts. Basil the Great and Gregory Nazianzen, bishops-doctors; memorial.

3—Fri. Weekday.

4—Sat. St. ElizabethAnn Seton; memorial (in U.S.).

**5—Sun. Epiphany of the Lord (U.S.); solemnity.** (Is. 60:1-6; Eph. 3:2-3a, 5-6; Mt. 2:1-12.) [St. John Neumann, bishop; memorial in U.S.]

6—Mon. Weekday. Bl. Andre Bessette, religious; optional memorial (in U.S.).

7—Tues. Weekday. St. Raymond of Penyafort; optional memorial.

8—Wed. Weekday.

9—Thurs. Weekday.

10—Fri. Weekday.

11—Sat. Weekday.

**12—Sun. The Baptism of the Lord; feast.** (Is. 55:1-11 or Is. 42:1-4, 6-7; 1 Jn. 5:1-9 or Acts 10:34-38; Mk. 1:7-11.)

13—Mon. Weekday. St. Hilary, bishop-doctor; optional memorial. (First Week in Ordinary Time.)

14—Tues. Weekday.

15—Wed. Weekday.

16—Thurs. Weekday

17—Fri. St. Anthony, abbot; memorial.

18—Sat. Weekday. BVM on Saturday; optional memorial.

**19—Second Sunday in Ordinary Time.** (1 Sm. 3:3b-10, 19; 1 Cor. 6:13c-15a, 17-20; Jn. 1:35-42.)

20—Mon. Weekday. St. Fabian, pope-martyr, or St. Sebastian, martyr; optional memorials.

21—Tues. St. Agnes, virgin-martyr; memorial.

22—Wed. Weekday. St. Vincent, deacon-martyr; optional memorial.

23—Thurs. Weekday.

24—Fri. St. Francis de Sales, bishop-doctor; memorial.

25—Sat. Conversion of St. Paul; feast.

**26—Third Sunday in Ordinary Time.** (Jon. 3:1-5, 10; 1 Cor. 7:29-31; Mk. 1:14-20.) [Sts. Timothy and Titus, bishops; memorial.]

27—Mon. Weekday. St. Angela Merici, virgin; optional memorial.

28—Tues. St. Thomas Aquinas, priest-doctor; memorial.

29—Wed. Weekday.

30—Thurs. Weekday.

31—Fri. St. John Bosco, priest; memorial.

*Scheduled Events: World Day of Peace, Jan. 1; National Migration Week, Jan. 6 to 12; Martin Luther King Day observed, Jan. 13; National Vocation Awareness Week, Jan 12-18; Week of Prayer for Christian Unity, Jan. 18 to 25; National Prayer Vigil for Life, Jan. 21-22; March for Life, Jan. 22, anniversary of Roe v. Wade, the pro-abortion decision of the U.S. Supreme Court; Catholic Schools Week, Jan. 27 to Feb. 2.*

## FEBRUARY 1997

*Prayer Intentions. Attention for the sick: That in every Christian community attention toward the suffering may turn into practical gestures of charitable solidarity (General). Union with Christ in suffering: That the sick and the elderly may know how to unite their sufferings to those of Christ and offer them for the universal Church (Mission).*

1—Sat. Weekday. BVM on Saturday; optional memorial.

**2—Sun. Presentation of the Lord; feast.** (Mal. 3:1-4; Heb. 2:14-18; Lk. 2:22-40 or 2:22-32.)

3—Mon. Weekday. St. Blase, bishop-martyr, or St. Ansgar, bishop; optional memorials. (Fourth Week in Ordinary Time)

4—Tues. Weekday.

5—Wed. St. Agatha, virgin-martyr; memorial.

6—Thurs. Sts. Paul Miki and Companions, martyrs; memorial.

7—Fri. Weekday.

8—Sat. Weekday. St. Jerome Emiliani or BVM on Saturday; optional memorials.

**9—Fifth Sunday in Ordinary Time.** (Jb. 7:1-4, 6-7; 1 Cor. 9:16-19, 22-23; Mk. 1:29-39.)

10—Mon. St. Scholastica, virgin; memorial.

11—Tues. Weekday. Our Lady of Lourdes; optional memorial.

12—Wed. Ash Wednesday. Beginning of Lent. *Fast and abstinence.* Ashes are blessed on this day and imposed on the forehead of the faithful to remind them of their obligation to do penance for sin and to seek spiritual renewal by means of prayer, fasting, good works, and by bearing with patience and for God's purposes the trials and difficulties of everyday life.

13—Thurs. Weekday of Lent.

14—Fri. Weekday of Lent. *Abstinence.* [Sts. Cyril, monk, and Methodius, bishop; memorial.]

15—Sat. Weekday of Lent.

**16—First Sunday of Lent.** (Gn. 9:8-15; 1 Pt. 3:18-22; Mk. 1:12-15.)

17—Mon. Weekday of Lent. [Seven Holy Founders of the Servite Order; optional memorial.]

18—Tues. Weekday of Lent.

19—Wed. Weekday of Lent.

20—Thurs. Weekday of Lent.

21—Fri. Weekday of Lent. *Abstinence.* [St. Peter Damien, bishop-doctor; optional memorial.]

22—Sat. Chair of Peter, apostle; feast. [Weekday of Lent]

**23—Second Sunday of Lent.** (Gn. 22:1-2, 9a, 10-13, 15-18; Rom. 8:31b-34; Mk. 9:2-10.) [St. Polycarp, bishop-martyr; memorial.]

24—Mon. Weekday of Lent.

25—Tues. Weekday of Lent.

26—Wed. Weekday of Lent.

27—Thurs. Weekday of Lent.

28—Fri. Weekday of Lent. *Abstinence.*

*The blessing of candles for use during the year takes place on the feast of the Presentation, also called Candlemas Day, according to longstanding custom.*

*The blessing of throats on the optional memorial of St. Blase Feb. 3 is in accord with the legend that a boy in danger of choking to death was saved through his intercession. The blessing is given with the prayer: "Through the intercession of St. Blase, bishop and martyr, may God deliver you from every disease of the throat and from every other illness."*

*Scheduled Events: Catholic Press Month; National Day of Prayer for the African-American Family, Feb. 2; World Day of the Sick, Feb. 11; Presidents Day, Feb. 17.*

## MARCH 1997

*Prayer Intentions. Just North-South relationship: That both the rich countries and the poor countries, in a spirit of responsible agreement, may work together for development and peace (General). Missionary engagement: That the 175th anniversary of the foundation of the Society for the Propagation of the Faith may stimulate Christian communities to fuller collaboration with the missions (Mission).*

1—Sat. Weekday of Lent.
2—**Third Sunday of Lent.** (Ex. 20:1-17; 1 Cor. 1:22-25; Jn. 2:13-25.)
3—Mon. Weekday of Lent. [Bl. Katherine Drexel, virgin; optional memorial (in U.S.).]
4—Tues. Weekday of Lent. [St. Casimir; memorial.]
5—Wed. Weekday of Lent.
6—Thurs. Weekday of Lent.
7—Fri. Weekday of Lent. *Abstinence.* [Sts. Perpetua and Felicity, martyrs; memorial.]
8—Sat. Weekday of Lent. [St. John of God; op. mem.]
9—**Fourth Sunday of Lent.** (2 Chr. 36:14-16, 19-23; Eph. 2: 4-10; Jn. 3: 14-21.) [St. Frances of Rome; op. mem.]
10—Mon. Weekday of Lent.
11—Tues. Weekday of Lent.
12—Wed. Weekday of Lent.
13—Thurs. Weekday of Lent.
14—Fri. Weekday of Lent. *Abstinence.*
15—Sat. Weekday of Lent.
16—**Fifth Sunday of Lent.** (Jer. 31:31-34; Heb. 5:7-9; Jn. 12: 20-33.)
17—Mon. Weekday of Lent. [St. Patrick, bishop; optional memorial.]
18—Tues. Weekday of Lent. [St. Cyril of Jerusalem, bishop-doctor; optional memorial.]
19—Wed. St. Joseph, solemnity.
20—Thurs. Weekday of Lent.
21—Fri. Weekday of Lent. *Abstinence.*
22—Sat. Weekday of Lent.
23—**Passion (Palm) Sunday.** (Procession—Mk. 11:1-10, or Jn. 12:12-16. Mass—Is. 50:4-7; Phil. 2:6-11; Mk. 14: 1 to 15:47, or 15:1-39.) [St. Turibius de Mogrovejo, bishop; optional memorial.]
24—Monday of Holy Week
25—Tuesday of Holy Week. (Annunciation of the Lord transferred to April 7.)
26—Wednesday of Holy Week.
27—Holy Thursday. The Easter Triduum begins with evening Mass of the Supper of the Lord.
28—Good Friday. *Fast and abstinence.*
29—Holy Saturday.
30—**Easter Sunday; solemnity.** (Acts 10:34a, 37-43; Col. 3:1-4 or 1 Cor. 5:6b-8; Jn. 20:1-9 or Mk. 16:1-7 or (evening Mass) Lk. 24:13-35.
31—Easter Monday; solemnity.

*Support for the needy, care for others in straitened circumstances, is an expression of the virtue of charity or love of neighbor. Such witness is powerful, not only for the relief of the unfortunate but also as a convincing sign of faith in practice. The kind of sign that made people say, as noted in the Acts of the Apostles, "See how these Christians love one another." And those of other faiths besides. Giving support to persons in need, as an expression of love for God, is an authentic and purifying penitential practice.*
*Scheduled Events: Meetings of the U.S. bishops' National Advisory Committee and Administrative Board, Mar. 14 to 16 and 18 to 20.*

## APRIL 1997

*Prayer Intentions. Eucharist and Christian liberty: That participation in the Eucharist may awaken in the faithful the sense of true Christian freedom according to the message of the 46th International Eucharistic Congress (General). The Christian community of Hong Kong: That the Christian community of Hong Kong may continue bearing witness to faith and unity to proclamation and dialogue with the entire Chinese people (Mission).*

1—Easter Tuesday; solemnity.
2—Easter Wednesday; solemnity. [St. Francis of Paola, hermit; optional memorial.]
3—Easter Thursday; solemnity.
4—Easter Friday; solemnity. [St. Isidore of Seville, bishop-doctor; optional memorial.]
5—Easter Saturday; solemnity. [St. Vincent Ferrer, priest; optional memorial.]
6—**Second Sunday of Easter; solemnity.** (Acts 4:32-35; 1 Jn. 5:1-6; Jn. 20:19-31.)
7—Mon. The Annunciation of the Lord; solemnity (transferred from March 25). [St. John Baptist de la Salle, priest; memorial.]
8—Tues. Easter Weekday.
9—Wed. Easter Weekday.
10—Thurs. Easter Weekday.
11—Fri. St. Stanislaus, bishop-martyr; memorial.
12—Sat. Easter Weekday.
13—**Third Sunday of Easter.** (Acts 3:13-15, 17-19; 1 Jn. 2:1-5a; Lk. 24: 35-48.) [St. Martin I, pope-martyr; optional memorial.]
14—Mon. Easter Weekday.
15—Tues. Easter Weekday.
16—Wed. Easter Weekday.
17—Thurs. Easter Weekday.
18—Fri. Easter Weekday.
19—Sat. Easter Weekday.
20—**Fourth Sunday of Easter.** (Acts 4:8-12; 1 Jn. 3:1-2; Jn. 10:11-18.)
21—Mon. Easter Weekday. St. Anselm, bishop-doctor; optional memorial.
22—Tues. Easter Weekday.
23—Wed. Easter Weekday. St. George, martyr or St. Adalbert, bishop-martyr; optional memorials.
24—Thurs. Easter Weekday. St. Fidelis of Sigmaringen, priest-martyr; optional memorial.
25—Fri. St. Mark, evangelist; feast.
26—Sat. Easter Weekday.
27—**Fifth Sunday of Easter.** (Acts 9:26-31; 1 Jn. 3:18-24; Jn. 15:1-8.)
28—Mon. Easter Weekday. St. Peter Chanel, priest-martyr; optional memorial.
29—Tues. St. Catherine of Siena, virgin-doctor; memorial.
30—Wed. Easter Weekday. St. Pius V, pope; optional memorial.

*The Sacred Triduum, from Holy Thursday to the Vigil of Easter, and the week-long celebration of Easter comprise the most solemn and deeply mysterious period in the liturgical year.*
*Scheduled Events: Convention of the National Catholic Educational Association, Apr. 1 to 4; Beginning of Passover, Apr. 22; World Day of Prayer for Vocations to the Priesthood and Religious Life, Apr. 27.*

## MAY 1997

*Prayer Intentions. Mary, model of faith: That Mary's faith may be an encouragement for all those who seek to know and accomplish God's will (General). Promotion of women: For the integral promotion of women in accordance with the model of Mary, Mother of Jesus and Mother of the Church (Mission).*

1—Thurs. Easter Weekday. St. Joseph the Worker; optional memorial.

2—Fri. St. Athanasius, bishop-doctor; memorial.

3—Sat. Sts. Philip and James, apostles; feast.

**4—Sixth Sunday of Easter.** (Acts 10:25-26, 34-35, 44-48; 1 Jn. 4:7-10; Jn. 15:9-17.)

5—Mon. Easter Weekday.

6—Tues. Easter Weekday.

7—Wed. Easter Weekday.

**8—Thurs. The Ascension of the Lord; solemnity. Holyday of Obligation.** (Acts 1:1-11; Eph 4:1-13 or 4:1-7, 11-13, or Eph. 1:17-23; Mk 16:15-20.)

9—Fri. Easter Weekday.

10—Sat. Easter Weekday.

**11—Seventh Sunday of Easter.** (Acts 1:15-17, 20a, 20c-26; 1 Jn. 4:11-16; Jn. 17:11b-19.)

12—Easter Weekday. Sts. Nereus and Achilleus, martyrs, or St. Pancras, martyr; optional memorials.

13—Tues. Easter Weekday.

14—Wed. St. Matthias, apostle; feast.

15—Thurs. Easter Weekday. St. Isidore the Farmer; optional memorial (in U.S.).

16—Fri. Easter Weekday.

17—Sat. Easter Weekday.

**18—Pentecost Sunday; solemnity.** (Acts 2:1-11; 1 Cor. 12:3b-7, 12-13; Jn. 20:19-23.) [St. John I, pope-martyr; optional memorial.]

19—Mon. Weekday. (Seventh Week in Ordinary Time.)

20—Tues. Weekday. St. Bernardine of Siena, priest; optional memorial.

21—Wed. Weekday.

22—Thurs. Weekday.

23—Fri. Weekday.

24—Sat. Weekday. BVM on Saturday; optional memorial.

**25—Sun. The Holy Trinity; solemnity.** (Dt. 4:32-34, 39-40; Rom. 8:14-17; Mt. 28:16-20.) [St. Bede the Venerable, priest-doctor, or St. Gregory VII, pope, or St. Mary Magdalene de Pazzi, virgin; optional memorials.]

26—Mon. St. Philip Neri, priest; memorial. (Eighth Week in Ordinary Time.)

27—Tues. Weekday. St. Augustine of Canterbury, bishop; optional memorial.

28—Wed. Weekday.

29—Thurs. Weekday.

30—Fri. Weekday.

31—Sat. Visitation of Blessed Mary the Virgin; feast.

*Solemnities of the Easter Season, Ascension of the Lord, May 8 and Pentecost, May 18. Visitation of the Blessed Virgin Mary, May 31, recalls Mary's readiness to help Elizabeth and the prophetic Magnificat canticle.*

*Scheduled Events: National Day of prayer, May 1; Mother's Day, May 11; 46th International Eucharistic Congress, Wroclaw, Poland, May 25-June 1; Memorial Day, May 26 (observed).*

## JUNE 1997

*Prayer Intentions. Christians, living images of Christ: That Christians, as living images of Christ who welcomes and forgives, may be the promoters of reconciliation and evangelic joy (General). Peaceful development in Africa: That the peoples of Africa, welcoming the Pope's and bishops' voices, may resume with increased zeal the way of faith and of peaceful development (Mission).*

**1—Sun. The Body and Blood of Christ (Corpus Christi) (in U.S.); solemnity.** (Ex. 24:3-8; Heb. 9:11-15; Mk. 14:12-16, 22-26.) [St. Justin, martyr; memorial.]

2—Mon. Weekday. Sts. Marcellinus and Peter, martyrs; optional memorial. (Ninth Week in Ordinary Time.)

3—Tues. Sts. Charles Lwanga and Companions, martyrs; memorial.

4—Wed. Weekday.

5—Thurs. St. Boniface, bishop-martyr; memorial.

6—Fri. The Sacred Heart of Jesus. [St. Norbert, bishop; optional memorial.]

7—Sat. Weekday. Immaculate Heart of Mary or BVM on Saturday; optional memorials.

**8—Tenth Sunday in Ordinary Time.** (Gn. 3:9-15; 2 Cor. 4:13 to 5:1; Mk. 3:20-35.)

9—Mon. Weekday. St. Ephraem, deacon-doctor, optional memorial.

10—Tues. Weekday.

11—Wed. St. Barnabas, apostle; memorial.

12—Thurs. Weekday.

13—Fri. St. Anthony of Padua, priest-doctor; memorial.

14—Sat. Weekday. BVM on Saturday; optional memorial.

**15—Eleventh Sunday in Ordinary Time.** (Ez. 17:22-24; 2 Cor. 5:6-10; Mk. 4:26-34.)

16—Mon. Weekday.

17—Tues. Weekday.

18—Wed. Weekday.

19—Thurs. Weekday. St. Romuald, abbot; optional memorial.

20—Fri. Weekday.

21—Sat. St. Aloysius Gonzaga, religious; memorial.

**22—Twelfth Sunday in Ordinary Time.** (Jb. 38:1,8-11; 2 Cor. 5:14-17; Mk 4:35-41.) [St. Paulinus of Nola, bishop, or Sts. John Fisher, bishop-martyr, and Thomas More, martyr; optional memorials.]

23—Mon. Weekday.

24—Tues. Birth of St. John the Baptist; solemnity.

25—Wed. Weekday.

26—Thurs. Weekday.

27—Fri. Weekday. St. Cyril of Alexandria, bishop-doctor; optional memorial.

28—Sat. St. Irenaeus, bishop-martyr; memorial.

**29—Sun. Sts. Peter and Paul, apostles; solemnity.** (Acts 12:1-11; 2 Tm. 4:6-8, 17-18; Mt. 16:13-19.)

30—Mon. Weekday. First Martyrs of the Roman Church; optional memorial. (Thirteenth Week in Ordinary Time.)

*Feasts: Corpus Christi, June 1 (in U.S.); Sacred Heart, June 6; St. Anthony of Padua, June 13; Birth of St. John the Baptist, June 24; Sts. Peter and Paul, June 29.*

*Scheduled Events: General Meeting of the National Conference of Catholic Bishops; Father's Day, June 15.*

## JULY 1997

*Prayer Intentions. A civilization of love and life: That the Church may promote the "civilization of love and life" in a world afflicted by the culture of violence and death (General). Cultures and religions in Asia and Christianity: That the people of Asia may be open to Christ's light and love and discover in the Gospel the fullness of the values which are in their cultures and religions (Mission).*

1—Tues. Weekday. Bl. Junipero Serra, priest; optional memorial (in U.S.).

2—Wed. Weekday.

3—Thurs. St. Thomas, apostle; feast.

4—Fri. Independence Day, proper Mass in U.S. Weekday. St. Elizabeth of Portugal, optional memorial.

5—Sat. Weekday. St. Anthony Zaccaria, priest, or BVM on Saturday; optional memorials.

6—**Fourteenth Sunday in Ordinary Time.** (Ez. 2:2-5; 2 Cor. 12:7-10; Mk. 6:1-6.) [St. Maria Goretti, virgin-martyr; optional memorial.]

7—Mon. Weekday.

8—Tues. Weekday.

9—Wed. Weekday.

10—Thurs. Weekday.

11—Fri. St. Benedict, abbot; memorial.

12—Sat. Weekday. BVM on Saturday; optional memorial.

13—**Fifteenth Sunday in Ordinary Time.** (Am. 7:12-15; Eph. 1:3-14; Mk. 6:7-13.) [St. Henry; optional memorial.]

14—Mon. Bl. Kateri Tekakwitha, virgin; memorial (in U.S.). Weekday. St. Camillus de Lellis, priest; optional memorial.

15—Tues. St. Bonaventure, bishop-doctor; memorial.

16—Wed. Weekday. Our Lady of Mt. Carmel; optional memorial.

17—Thurs. Weekday.

18—Fri. Weekday.

19—Sat. Weekday. BVM on Saturday; optional memorial.

20—**Sixteenth Sunday in Ordinary Time.** (Jer. 23:1-6; Eph. 2:13-18; Mk. 6:30-34.)

21— Mon. Weekday. St. Lawrence of Brindisi, priest-doctor; optional memorial.

22—Tues. St. Mary Magdalene; memorial.

23—Wed. Weekday. St. Bridget of Sweden, religious; optional memorial.

24—Thurs. Weekday.

25—Fri. St. James, apostle; feast.

26—Sat. Sts. Joachim and Anne, parents of Blessed Mary the Virgin; memorial.

27—**Seventeenth Sunday of the Year.** (2 Kgs. 4:42-44; Eph. 4:1-6; Jn. 6:1-15.)

28—Mon. Weekday.

29—Tues. St. Martha; memorial.

30—Wed. Weekday. St. Peter Chrysologus, bishop-doctor; optional memorial.

31—Thurs. St. Ignatius of Loyola, priest; memorial.

*Feasts: Blessed Junipero Serra, whose optional memorial may be observed July 1, founder of California missions; St. Thomas, apostle, pioneer evangelizer of India, July 3; St. Benedict, July 11, founder of monasticism in Western Europe, patron saint of Europe; St. Bonaventure, July 15, called the second founder of the Franciscan Order; St. Ignatius of Loyola, July 31, founder of the Society of Jesus.*
*Scheduled Event: Independence Day, July 4.*

## AUGUST 1997

*Prayer Intentions. Variety of charisms: That the Church, in its diversity of charisms and gifts, may increasingly manifest communion in the Spirit (General). Jesus Christ, the only Savior of the world: That preparation for the third millennium may revive in the Church ardor for the proclamation of Jesus Christ, the only Savior of man (Mission).*

1—Fri. St. Alphonsus Liguori, bishop-doctor; memorial.

2—Sat. Weekday. St. Eusebius of Vercelli, bishop, or St. Peter Julian Eymard, or BVM on Saturday; optional memorials.

3—**Eighteenth Sunday in Ordinary Time.** (Ex. 16:2-4, 12-15; Eph. 4:17, 20-24; Jn. 6:24-35.)

4—Mon. St. John Vianney, priest; memorial.

5—Tues. Weekday. Dedication of St. Mary Major Basilica in Rome; optional memorial.

6—Wed. Transfiguration of the Lord; feast.

7—Thurs. Weekday. Sts. Sixtus II, pope, and Companions, martyrs, or St. Cajetan, priest; optional memorials.

8—Fri. St. Dominic, priest; memorial.

9—Sat. Weekday. BVM on Saturday; optional memorial.

10—**Nineteenth Sunday in Ordinary Time.** (1 Kgs. 19:4-8; Eph. 4:30 to 5:2; Jn. 6: 41-51.) [St. Lawrence, deacon-martyr; feast.]

11—Mon. St. Clare, virgin; memorial.

12—Tues. Weekday.

13—Wed. Weekday. Sts. Pontian, pope, and Hippolytus, priest, martyrs; optional memorial.

14—Thurs. St. Maximilian Kolbe, priest-martyr; memorial.

15—**Fri. Assumption of Blessed Mary the Virgin; solemnity. Holy day of obligation.** (Rv. 11:19a and 12:1-6a, 10ab; 1 Cor. 15:20-26; Lk. 1:39-56.)

16—Sat. Weekday. St. Stephen of Hungary, or BVM on Saturday; optional memorials.

17—**Twentieth Sunday in Ordinary Time.** (Prv. 9:1-6; Eph. 5:15-20; Jn. 6:51-58.)

18—Mon. St. Jane Frances de Chantal, virgin; optional memorial (in U.S.).

19—Tues. Weekday. St. John Eudes, priest; op. mem.

20—Wed. St. Bernard of Clairvaux, abbot-doctor; memorial.

21—Thurs. St. Pius X, pope; memorial.

22—Fri. Queenship of Mary; memorial.

23—Sat. Weekday. St. Rose of Lima, virgin, or BVM on Saturday; optional memorials.

24—**Twenty-First Sunday in Ordinary Time.** (Jos. 24:1-2a, 15-17, 18b; Eph. 5:21-32; Jn. 6:60-69.) [St. Bartholomew, apostle; feast.]

25—Mon. Weekday. St. Louis, or St. Joseph Calasanz, priest; optional memorials.

26—Tues. Weekday.

27—Wed. St. Monica; memorial.

28—Thurs. St. Augustine, bishop-doctor; memorial.

29—Fri. Martyrdom of St. John the Baptist; memorial.

30—Sat. Weekday. BVM on Saturday; optional memorial.

31—**Twenty-Second Sunday in Ordinary Time.** (Dt. 4:1-2, 6-8; Jas. 1:17-18, 21b-22, 27; Mk. 7:1-8, 14-15, 21-23.)

*Feasts: Assumption of Mary, Aug. 15; St. Bernard, Aug. 20, leader of monasticism; St. Augustine, Aug. 28, Father and Doctor of the Church.*

## SEPTEMBER 1997

*Prayer Intentions. Teachers and educators: That educators and teachers may bear witness credibly so that young people may discover the meaning and the beauty of a life lived as a gift for others (General). Youth and new evangelization: That welcoming the Holy Father's invitation, young Christians may become true and active protagonists of the new evangelization (Mission).*

1—Mon. Labor Day, proper Mass in U.S. Weekday.
2—Tues. Weekday.
3—Wed. St. Gregory the Great, pope-doctor; memorial.
4—Thurs. Weekday.
5—Fri. Weekday.
6—Sat. Weekday. BVM on Saturday; optional memorial.
**7—Twenty-Third Sunday in Ordinary Time.** (Is 35:4-7a; Jas. 2:1-5; Mk. 7:31-37.)
8—Mon. Birth of Mary; feast.
9—Tues. St. Peter Claver, priest; memorial (in U.S.). Weekday.
10—Wed. Weekday.
11—Thurs. Weekday.
12—Fri. Weekday.
13—Sat. St. John Chrysostom, bishop-doctor; memorial.
**14—Sun. The Holy Cross; feast.** (Nm. 21:4-9; Phil. 2:6-11; Jn. 3:13-17.)
15—Mon. Our Lady of Sorrows; memorial. (Twenty-Fourth Week in Ordinary Time.)
16—Tues. Sts. Cornelius, pope, and Cyprian, bishop, martyrs; memorial.
17—Wed. Weekday. St. Robert Bellarmine, bishop-doctor; optional memorial.
18—Thurs. Weekday.
19—Fri. Weekday. St. Januarius, bishop-martyr; optional memorial.
20—Sat. Sts. Andrew Kim Taegon, priest, Paul Chong Hasang, lay apostle, and Companions, martyrs of Korea; memorial.
**21—Twenty-Fifth Sunday in Ordinary Time.** (Wis. 2:12, 17-20; Jas. 3:16 to 4:3; Mk. 9:30-37.) [St. Matthew, apostle-evangelist; feast.]
22—Mon. Weekday.
23—Tues. Weekday.
24—Wed. Weekday.
25—Thurs. Weekday.
26—Fri. Weekday. Sts. Cosmas and Damian, martyrs; optional memorial.
27—Sat. St. Vincent de Paul, priest; memorial.
**28—Twenty-Sixth Sunday in Ordinary Time.** (Nm. 11:25-29; Jas. 5:1-6; Mk 9:38-43, 45, 47-48.) [St. Wenceslaus, martyr, or Sts. Lawrence Ruiz and Companions, martyrs; optional memorial.]
29—Mon. Sts. Michael, Gabriel and Raphael, archangels; feast.
30—Tues. St. Jerome, priest-doctor; memorial.

*The celebration of Labor Day pinpoints the dignity of work by Christians in collaborating with the Father in making good things, with the Son in the ministering of redemption to and with others, in sharing the gifts of the Holy Spirit for the transformation of the world.*

*The Labor Day theme, the dignity of work, was the subject of Pope John Paul's encyclical, "Laborem Exercens."*

## OCTOBER 1997

*Prayer Intentions. The love of God for humanity: That the experience of the Spirit of Christ may lead Christians to bear witness to the Father's love for humankind with greater conviction and coherence (General). The Church in Japan: For the Church in Japan, that the memory of the testimony of the first martyrs may act as an incentive for its missionary dynamism (Mission).*

1—Wed. St. Therese of the Child Jesus, virgin; memorial.
2—Thurs. Guardian Angels; memorial.
3—Fri. Weekday.
4—Sat. St. Francis of Assisi; memorial.
**5—Twenty-Seventh Sunday in Ordinary Time.** (Gn. 2:18-24; Heb. 2:9-11; Mk 10:2-16.)
6—Mon. Weekday. Bl. Marie-Rose Durocher, virgin; optional memorial (in U.S.). St. Bruno, priest; optional memorial.
7—Tues. Our Lady of the Rosary; memorial.
8—Wed. Weekday.
9—Thurs. Weekday. Sts. Denis, bishop, and Companions, martyrs, or St. John Leonardi, priest; optional memorials.
10—Fri. Weekday.
11—Sat. Weekday. BVM on Saturday; optional memorial.
**12—Twenty-Eighth Sunday in Ordinary Time.** (Wis. 7:7-11; Heb. 4:12-13; Mk. 10:17-30.)
13—Mon. Weekday.
14—Tues. Weekday. St. Callistus I, pope-martyr optional memorial.
15—Wed. St. Teresa of Jesus (Avila), virgin-doctor; memorial.
16—Thurs. Weekday. St. Hedwig, religious, or St. Margaret Mary Alacoque, virgin; optional memorials.
17—Fri. St. Ignatius of Antioch, bishop-martyr; memorial.
18—Sat. St. Luke, evangelist; feast.
**19—Twenty-Ninth Sunday in Ordinary Time.** (Is. 53:10-11; Heb. 4:14-16; Mk. 10:35-45.) [Sts. Isaac Jogues, John de Brebeuf, priests, and Companions, martyrs; memorial in U.S.; St. Paul of the Cross (general calendar); optional memorial.]
20—Mon. St. Paul of the Cross (in U.S.); optional memorial.
21—Tues. Weekday.
22—Wed. Weekday.
23—Thurs. Weekday. St. John of Capistrano, priest; optional memorial.
24—Fri. Weekday. St. Anthony Mary Claret, bishop; optional memorial.
25—Sat. Weekday. BVM on Saturday; op. mem.
**26—Thirtieth Sunday in Ordinary Time.** (Jer. 31:7-9; Heb. 5:1-6; Mk. 10:46-52.)
27—Mon. Weekday.
28—Tues. Sts. Simon and Jude, apostles; feast.
29—Wed. Weekday.
30—Thurs. Weekday.
31—Fri. Weekday.

*Feasts: St. Therese of the Child Jesus, Oct. 1; Guardian Angels, Oct. 2; St. Francis of Assisi, Oct. 4; Our Lady of the Rosary, Oct. 7; St. Teresa of Jesus (Avila), doctor of the Church, mystic, Oct. 15; St. Luke, one of the evangelists, Oct. 18; Sts. Isaac Jogues and Companions, North American martyrs, Oct. 19.*

*October is the Month of the Rosary.*

## NOVEMBER 1997

*Prayer Intentions. Disunited families: For broken families and for spouses that have lost their reciprocal trust, that they may rediscover through faith and Christian charity their right path (General). Consecrated life: That, answering to the synodal call, the institutes of consecrated life may rediscover and profoundly live the peculiar dimensions of their own charism (Mission).*

**1—Sat. All Saints; solemnity. Holy day of obligation.** (Rv. 7:2-4, 9-14; 1 Jn. 3:1-3; Mt. 5:1-12a.) The obligation to attend Mass is abrogated in the U.S.

**2—Sun. Commemoration of All the Faithful Departed (All Souls' Day).**

3—Mon. Weekday. St. Martin de Porres, religious, optional memorial. (Thirty-First Week in Ordinary Time.)

4—Tues. St. Charles Borromeo, bishop; memorial.

5—Wed. Weekday.

6—Thurs. Weekday.

7—Fri. Weekday.

8—Sat. Weekday. BVM on Saturday; op. mem.

**9—Sun. Dedication of St. John Lateran Basilica in Rome (Archbasilica of Most Holy Savior); feast.** (Ez. 47:1-2, 8-9, 12; 1 Cor. 3:9c-11, 16-17; Jn. 2:13-22; or any readings from the Common of the Dedication of a Church.)

10—Mon. St. Leo the Great, pope-doctor; memorial. (Thirty-Second Week in Ordinary Time.)

11—Tues. St. Martin of Tours, bishop; memorial.

12—Wed. St. Josaphat, bishop-martyr; memorial.

13—Thurs. St. Frances Xavier Cabrini, virgin; memorial (in U.S.).

14—Fri. Weekday.

15—Sat. Weekday. St. Albert the Great, bishop-doctor, or BVM on Saturday; optional memorials.

**16—Thirty-Third Sunday in Ordinary Time.** (Dn. 12:1-3; Heb. 10:11-14, 18; Mk. 13:24-32.) [St. Margaret of Scotland, or St. Gertrude, virgin; optional memorials.]

17—Mon. St. Elizabeth of Hungary, religious; memorial.

18—Tues. Weekday. Dedication of Basilicas of Sts. Peter and Paul or (in U.S.) St. Rose Philippine Duchesne, virgin; optional memorials.

19—Wed. Weekday.

20—Thurs. Weekday.

21—Fri. Presentation of Blessed Mary the Virgin; memorial.

22—Sat. St. Cecilia, virgin-martyr; memorial.

**23—Christ the King; solemnity.** (Dn. 7:13-14; Rv. 1:5-8; Jn. 18:33b-37.) [Bl. Miguel Agustin Pro, priest-martyr, optional memorial in U.S.; St. Clement I, pope-martyr, or St. Columban, abbot; optional memorials.]

24—Mon. St. Andrew Dung-Lac, priest, and Companions, martyrs; memorial. (Thirty-Fourth [Last] Week in Ordinary Time.)

25—Tues. Weekday.

26—Wed. Weekday.

27—Thurs. Thanksgiving Day (in U.S.); proper Mass. Weekday.

28—Fri. Weekday.

29—Sat. Weekday. BVM on Saturday; optional memorial. [Last day of 1997 liturgical year.]

**30—First Sunday of Advent.** [Start of 1998 liturgical year.] (Jer. 33:14-16; 1 Thes. 3:12 to 4:2; Lk. 21:25-28, 34-36.) [St. Andrew, apostle; feast.]

*Feasts: All Saints, Nov. 1, and All Souls, Nov. 2.*

## DECEMBER 1997

*Prayer Intentions. Abandoned children: For the "street children" and all abandoned, rejected, ill-treated children who are victims of violence (General). Missionary spirit in Latin America: That voluntary missionary service may also develop among the lay people of Latin America (Mission).*

1—Mon. Advent Weekday.

2—Tues. Advent Weekday.

3—Wed. St. Francis Xavier, priest; memorial.

4—Thurs. Advent Weekday. St. John Damascene, priest-doctor; optional memorial.

5—Fri. Advent Weekday.

6—Sat. Advent Weekday. St. Nicholas, bishop; optional memorial.

**7—Second Sunday of Advent.** (Bar. 5:1-9; Phil. 1:4-6, 8-11; Lk. 3:1-6.) [St. Ambrose, bishop-doctor; memorial.]

**8—Mon. Immaculate Conception of Blessed Mary the Virgin; solemnity; Holy Day of Obligation.** (Gn. 3:9-15, 20; Eph. 1:3-6, 11-12; Lk. 1:26-38.)

9—Tues. Advent Weekday. Bl. Juan Diego; optional memorial (in U.S.).

10—Wed. Advent Weekday.

11—Thurs. Advent Weekday. St. Damasus I, pope; optional memorial.

12—Fri. Our Lady of Guadalupe; feast (in U.S.).

13—Sat. St. Lucy, virgin-martyr; memorial.

**14—Third Sunday of Advent.** (Zep. 3:14-18a; Phil. 4:4-7; Lk. 3:10-18.) [St. John of the Cross, priest-doctor; memorial.]

15—Mon. Advent Weekday.

16—Tues. Advent Weekday.

17—Wed. Advent Weekday.

18—Thurs. Advent Weekday.

19—Fri. Advent Weekday.

20—Sat. Advent Weekday.

**21—Fourth Sunday of Advent.** (Mi. 5:1-4a; Heb. 10:5-10; Lk. 1:39-45.) [St. Peter Canisius, priest-doctor; optional memorial.]

22—Mon. Advent Weekday.

23—Tues. Advent Weekday. [St. John of Kanty, priest; optional memorial.]

24—Wed. Advent Weekday.

**25—Thurs. Christmas. Birth of the Lord; solemnity. Holy day of obligation.** (Vigil — Is. 62:1-5; Acts 13:16-17, 22-25; Mt. 1:1-25. Midnight — Is. 9:1-6; Ti. 2:11-14; Lk. 2:1-14. At Dawn — Is. 62:11-12; Ti. 3:4-7; Lk. 2:15-20. During the Day — Is. 52:7-10; Heb. 1:1-6; Jn. 1:1-18.)

26—Fri. St. Stephen, first martyr; feast.

27—Sat. St. John, apostle-evangelist; feast.

**28—Sun. The Holy Family; feast.** (1 Sm 1:20-22, 24-28, or Sir. 3:2-6, 12-14; 1 Jn. 3:1-2, 21-24 or Col. 3: 12-17 or Col. 3:12-21; Lk. 2:41-52.) [Holy Innocents, martyrs; feast.]

29—Mon. Fifth Day in the Octave of Christmas. St. Thomas Becket, bishop-martyr; optional memorial.

30—Tues. Sixth Day in the Octave of Christmas.

31—Wed. Seventh Day in the Octave of Christmas. St. Sylvester I, pope; optional memorial.

*Feasts: St. Francis Xavier, Dec. 3, patron of missions and missionaries; Immaculate Conception, Dec. 8; Our Lady of Guadalupe, Dec. 12, patroness of the Americas; Birth of the Lord, Dec. 25.*

# HOLY DAYS AND OTHER OBSERVANCES

The following list includes the six holy days of obligation observed in the United States and additional observances of devotional and historical significance. The dignity or rank of observances is indicated by the terms: **solemnity** (highest in rank); **feast; memorial** (for universal observance); **optional memorial** (for celebration by choice).

**All Saints,** Nov. 1, holy day of obligation, solemnity. Commemorates all the blessed in heaven, and is intended particularly to honor the blessed who have no special feasts. The background of the feast dates to the fourth century when groups of martyrs, and later other saints, were honored on a common day in various places. In 609 or 610, the Pantheon, a pagan temple at Rome, was consecrated as a Christian church for the honor of Our Lady and the martyrs (later all saints). In 835, Gregory IV fixed Nov. 1 as the date of observance.

**All Souls,** Commemoration of the Faithful Departed, Nov. 2. The dead were prayed for from the earliest days of Christianity. By the sixth century it was customary in Benedictine monasteries to hold a commemoration of deceased members of the order at Pentecost. A common commemoration of all the faithful departed on the day after All Saints was instituted in 998 by St. Odilo, of the Abbey of Cluny, and an observance of this kind was accepted in Rome in the 14th century.

**Annunciation of the Lord** (formerly, Annunciation of the Blessed Virgin Mary), Mar. 25, solemnity. A feast of the Incarnation which commemorates the announcement by the Archangel Gabriel to the Virgin Mary that she was to become the Mother of Christ (Lk. 1:26-38), and the miraculous conception of Christ by her. The feast was instituted about 430 in the East. The Roman observance dates from the seventh century, when celebration was said to be universal.

**Ascension of the Lord,** movable observance held 40 days after Easter, holy day of obligation, solemnity. Commemorates the Ascension of Christ into heaven 40 days after his Resurrection from the dead (Mk. 16:19; Lk. 24:51; Acts 1:2). The feast recalls the completion of Christ's mission on earth for the salvation of all people and his entry into heaven with glorified human nature. The Ascension is a pledge of the final glorification of all who achieve salvation. Documentary evidence of the feast dates from early in the fifth century, but it was observed long before that time in connection with Pentecost and Easter.

**Ash Wednesday,** movable observance, six and one-half weeks before Easter. It was set as the first day of Lent by Pope St. Gregory the Great (590-604) with the extension of an earlier and shorter penitential season to a total period including 40 weekdays of fasting before Easter. It is a day of fast and abstinence. Ashes, symbolic of penance, are blessed and distributed among the faithful during the day. They are used to mark the forehead with the Sign of the Cross, with the reminder: "Remember you are dust, and to dust you will return," or: "Turn away from sin and be faithful to the Gospel."

**Assumption,** Aug. 15, holy day of obligation, solemnity. Commemorates the taking into heaven of Mary, soul and body, at the end of her life on earth, a truth of faith that was proclaimed a dogma by Pius XII on Nov. 1, 1950. One of the oldest and most solemn feasts of Mary, it has a history dating back to at least the seventh century when its celebration was already established at Jerusalem and Rome.

**Baptism of the Lord,** movable, usually celebrated on the Sunday after January 6, feast. Recalls the baptism of Christ by John the Baptist (Mk. 1:9-11), an event associated with the liturgy of the Epiphany. This baptism was the occasion for Christ's manifestation of himself at the beginning of his public life.

**Birth of Mary,** Sept. 8, feast. This is a very old feast which originated in the East and found place in the Roman liturgy in the seventh century.

**Candlemas Day,** Feb. 2. See Presentation of the Lord.

**Chair of Peter,** Feb. 22, feast. The feast, which has been in the Roman calendar since 336, is a liturgical expression of belief in the episcopacy and hierarchy of the Church.

**Christmas, Birth of Our Lord Jesus Christ,** Dec. 25, holy day of obligation, solemnity. Commemorates the birth of Christ (Lk. 2:1-20). This event was originally commemorated in the East on the feast of Epiphany or Theophany. The Christmas feast itself originated in the West; by 354 it was certainly kept on Dec. 25. This date may have been set for the observance to offset pagan ceremonies held at about the same time to commemorate the birth of the sun at the winter solstice. There are texts for three Christmas Masses — at midnight, dawn and during the day.

**Christ the King,** movable, celebrated on the last Sunday of the liturgical year, solemnity. Commemorates the royal prerogatives of Christ and is equivalent to a declaration of his rights to the homage, service and fidelity of all people in all phases of individual and social life. Pius XI instituted the feast Dec. 11, 1925.

**Conversion of St. Paul,** Jan. 25, feast. An observance mentioned in some calendars from the 8th and 9th centuries. Pope Innocent III (1198-1216) ordered its observance with great solemnity.

**Corpus Christi** (The Body and Blood of Christ), movable, celebrated on the Thursday (or Sunday, as in the U.S.) following Trinity Sunday, solemnity. Commemorates the institution of the Holy Eucharist (Mt. 26:26-28). The feast originated at Liege in 1246 and was extended throughout the Church in the West by Urban IV in 1264. St. Thomas Aquinas composed the Liturgy of the Hours for the feast.

**Cross, The Holy,** Sept. 14, feast. Commemorates the finding of the cross on which Christ was crucified, in 326 through the efforts of St. Helena, mother of Constantine; the consecration of the Basilica of the Holy Sepulchre nearly 10 years later: and the recovery in 628 or 629 by Emperor Heraclius of a major portion of the cross which had been removed by the Persians from its place of veneration at Jerusalem. The feast originated in Jerusalem and spread through the East before being adopted in the West. General adoption followed the building at Rome of the Basilica of the Holy Cross "in Jerusalem," so called because it was the place of enshrinement of a major portion of the cross of crucifixion.

**Dedication of St. John Lateran,** Nov. 9, feast. Commemorates the first public consecration of a church, that of the Basilica of the Most Holy Savior by Pope St. Sylvester about 324. The church, as well as the Lateran Palace, was the gift of Emperor Constantine. Since the 12th century it has been known as St. John Lateran, in honor of John the Baptist after whom the adjoining baptistery was named. It was rebuilt by Innocent X (1644-55), reconsecrated by Benedict XIII in 1726, and enlarged by Leo XIII (1878-1903). This basilica is regarded as the church of highest dignity in Rome and throughout the Roman Rite.

**Dedication of St. Mary Major,** Aug. 5, optional memorial. Commemorates the rebuilding and dedication by Pope Sixtus III (432-40) of a church in honor of Blessed Mary the Virgin. This is the Basilica of St. Mary Major on the Esquiline Hill in Rome. An earlier building was erected during the pontificate of Liberius (352-66); according to legend, it was located on a site covered by a miraculous fall of snow seen by a nobleman favored with a vision of Mary.

**Easter,** movable celebration held on the first Sunday after the full moon following the vernal equinox (between Mar. 22 and Apr. 25), solemnity with an octave. Commemorates the Resurrection of Christ from the dead (Mk. 16:1-7). The observance of this mystery, kept since the first days of the Church, extends throughout the Easter season which lasts until the feast of Pentecost, a period of 50 days. Every Sunday in the year is regarded as a "little" Easter. The date of Easter determines the dates of movable feasts, such as Ascension and Pentecost, and the number of weeks before Lent and after Pentecost.

**Easter Vigil,** called by St. Augustine the "Mother of All Vigils," the night before Easter. Ceremonies are all related to the Resurrection and renewal-in-grace theme of Easter: blessing of the new fire, procession with the Easter Candle, singing of the Easter Proclamation (Exsultet), Liturgy of the Word with at least three Old Testament readings, the Litany of Saints, blessing of water, baptism of converts and infants, renewal of baptismal promises, Liturgy of the Eucharist. The vigil ceremonies are held after nightfall on Saturday.

**Epiphany of the Lord,** Jan. 6 or (in the U.S.) a Sunday between Jan. 2 and 8, solemnity. Commemorates the manifestations of the divinity of Christ. It is one of the oldest Christian feasts, with an Eastern origin traceable to the beginning of the third century and antedating the Western feast of Christmas. Originally, it commemorated the manifestations of Christ's divinity — or Theophany — in his birth, the homage of the Magi, and baptism by John the Baptist. Later, the first two of these commemorations were transferred to Christmas when the Eastern Church adopted that feast between 380 and 430. The central feature of the Eastern observance now is the manifestation or declaration of Christ's divinity in his baptism and at the beginning of his public life. The Epiphany was adopted by the Western Church during the same period in which the Eastern

Church accepted Christmas. In the Roman Rite, commemoration is made in the Mass of the homage of the wise men from the East (Mt. 2:1-12).

**Good Friday,** the Friday before Easter, the second day of the Easter Triduum. Liturgical elements of the observance are commemoration of the Passion and Death of Christ in the reading of the Passion (according to John), special prayers for the Church and people of all ranks, the veneration of the Cross, and a Communion service. The celebration takes place in the afternoon, preferably at 3:00 p.m.

**Guardian Angels,** Oct. 2, memorial. Commemorates the angels who protect people from spiritual and physical dangers and assist them in doing good. A feast in their honor celebrated in Spain in the 16th century was placed in the Roman calendar in 1615 and Oct. 2 was set as the date of observance. Earlier, guardian angels were honored liturgically in conjunction with the feast of St. Michael.

**Holy Family,** movable observance on the Sunday after Christmas, feast. Commemorates the Holy Family of Jesus, Mary and Joseph as the model of domestic society, holiness and virtue. The devotional background of the feast was very strong in the 17th century. In the 18th century, in prayers composed for a special Mass, a Canadian bishop likened the Christian family to the Holy Family. Leo XIII consecrated families to the Holy Family. In 1921, Benedict XV extended the Divine Office and Mass of the feast to the whole Church.

**Holy Innocents,** Dec. 28, feast. Commemorates the infants who suffered death at the hands of Herod's soldiers seeking to kill the child Jesus (Mt. 2:13-18). A feast in their honor has been observed since the fifth century.

**Holy Saturday,** the day before Easter. The Sacrifice of the Mass is not celebrated, and Holy Communion may be given only as Viaticum. If possible the Easter fast should be observed until the Easter Vigil.

**Holy Thursday,** the Thursday before Easter. Commemorates the institution of the sacraments of the Eucharist and holy orders, and the washing of the feet of the Apostles by Jesus at the Last Supper. The Mass of the Lord's Supper in the evening marks the beginning of the Easter Triduum. Following the Mass, there is a procession of the Blessed Sacrament to a place of reposition for adoration by the faithful. Usually at an earlier Mass of Chrism, bishops bless oils (of catechumens, chrism, the sick) for use during the year. (For pastoral reasons, diocesan bishops may permit additional Masses, but these should not overshadow the principal Mass of the Lord's Supper.)

**Immaculate Conception,** Dec. 8, holy day of obligation, solemnity. Commemorates the fact that Mary, in view of her calling to be the Mother of Christ and in virtue of his merits, was preserved from the first moment of her conception from original sin and was filled with grace from the very beginning of her life. She was the only person so preserved from original sin. The present form of the feast dates from Dec. 8, 1854, when Pius IX defined the dogma of the Immaculate Conception An earlier feast of the Conception, which testified to long-existing belief in this truth, was observed in the East by the eighth century, in Ireland in the ninth, and subsequently in European countries. In 1846, Mary was proclaimed patroness of the U.S. under this title.

**Immaculate Heart of Mary,** Saturday following the second Sunday after Pentecost, optional memorial. On May 4, 1944, Pius XII ordered this feast observed throughout the Church in order to obtain Mary's intercession for "peace among nations, freedom for the Church, the conversion of sinners, the love of purity and the practice of virtue." Two years earlier, he consecrated the entire human race to Mary under this title. Devotion to Mary under the title of her Most Pure Heart originated during the Middle Ages. It was given great impetus in the 17th century by the preaching of St. John Eudes, who was the first to celebrate a Mass and Divine Office of Mary under this title. A feast, celebrated in various places and on different dates, was authorized in 1799.

**Joachim and Ann,** July 26, memorial. Commemorates the parents of Mary. A joint feast, celebrated Sept. 9, originated in the East near the end of the sixth century. Devotion to Ann, introduced in the eighth century at Rome, became widespread in Europe in the 14th century; her feast was extended throughout the Latin Church in 1584. A feast of Joachim was introduced in the West in the 15th century.

**John the Baptist, Birth,** June 24, solemnity. The precursor of Christ, whose cousin he was, was commemorated universally in the liturgy by the fourth century. He is the only saint, except the Blessed Virgin Mary, whose birthday is observed as a feast. Another feast, on Aug. 29, commemorates his passion and death at the order of Herod (Mk. 6:14-29).

**Joseph,** Mar. 19, solemnity. Joseph is honored as the husband of the Blessed Virgin Mary, the patron and protector of the universal Church and workman. Devotion to him already existed in the eighth century in the East, and in the 11th in the West. Various feasts were celebrated before the 15th century when Mar. 19 was fixed for his commemoration; this feast was extended to the whole Church in 1621 by Gregory XV. In 1955, Pius XII instituted the feast of St. Joseph the Workman for observance May 1; this feast, which may be celebrated by local option, supplanted the Solemnity or Patronage of St. Joseph formerly observed on the third Wednesday after Easter. St. Joseph was proclaimed protector and patron of the universal Church in 1870 by Pius IX.

**Michael, Gabriel and Raphael, Archangels,** Sept. 29, feast. A feast bearing the title of Dedication of St. Michael the Archangel formerly commemorated on this date the consecration in 530 of a church near Rome in honor of Michael, the first angel given a liturgical feast. For a while, this feast was combined with a commemoration of the Guardian Angels. The separate feasts of Gabriel (Mar. 24) and Raphael (Oct. 24) were suppressed by the calendar in effect since 1970 and this joint feast of the three archangels was instituted.

**Octave of Christmas,** Jan. 1. See Solemnity of Mary, Mother of God.

**Our Lady of Guadalupe,** Dec. 12, feast (in the U.S.). Commemorates under this title the appearances of the Blessed Virgin Mary in 1531 to an Indian, Juan Diego, on Tepeyac hill outside Mexico City (see Apparitions of the Blessed Virgin Mary). The celebration, observed as a memorial in the U.S., was raised to the rank of feast at the request of the National Conference of Catholic Bishops. Approval was granted in a decree dated Jan. 8, 1988.

**Our Lady of Sorrows,** Sept. 15, memorial. Recalls the sorrows experienced by Mary in her association with Christ: the prophecy of Simeon (Lk. 2:34-35), the flight into Egypt (Mt. 2:13-21), the three-day separation from Jesus (Lk. 2:41-50), and four incidents connected with the Passion: her meeting with Christ on the way to Calvary, the crucifixion, the removal of Christ's body from the cross, and his burial (Mt. 27:31-61; Mk. 15:20-47; Lk. 23:26-56; Jn. 19:17-42). A Mass and Divine Office of the feast were celebrated by the Servites, especially, in the 17th century, and in 1814 Pius VII extended the observance to the whole Church.

**Our Lady of the Rosary,** Oct. 7, memorial. Commemorates the Virgin Mary through recall of the mysteries of the Rosary which recapitulate events in her life and the life of Christ. The feast was instituted in 1573 to commemorate a Christian victory over invading Mohammedan forces at Lepanto in 1571, and was extended throughout the Church by Clement XI in 1716.

**Passion Sunday** (formerly called **Palm Sunday**), the Sunday before Easter. Marks the start of Holy Week by recalling the triumphal entry of Christ into Jerusalem at the beginning of the last week of his life (Mt. 21:1-9). A procession and other ceremonies commemorating this event were held in Jerusalem from very early Christian times and were adopted in Rome by the ninth century, when the blessing of palm for the occasion was introduced. Full liturgical observance includes the blessing of palm and a procession before the principal Mass of the day. The Passion, by Matthew, Mark or Luke, is read during the Mass.

**Pentecost,** also called **Whitsunday,** movable celebration held 50 days after Easter, solemnity. Commemorates the descent of the Holy Spirit upon the Apostles, the preaching of Peter and the other Apostles to Jews in Jerusalem, the baptism and aggregation of some 3,000 persons to the Christian community (Acts 2:1-41). It is regarded as the birthday of the Catholic Church. The original observance of the feast antedated the earliest extant documentary evidence from the third century.

**Peter and Paul,** June 29, solemnity. Commemorates the martyrdoms of Peter by crucifixion and Paul by beheading during the Neronian persecution. This joint commemoration of the chief Apostles dates at least from 258 at Rome.

**Presentation of the Lord** (formerly called Purification of the Blessed Virgin Mary, also Candlemas), Feb. 2, feast. Commemorates the presentation of Jesus in the Temple — according to prescriptions of Mosaic Law (Lv. 12:2-8; Ex. 13:2; Lk. 2:22-32) — and the purification of Mary 40 days after his birth. In the East, where the feast antedated fourth century testimony regarding its existence, it was observed primarily as a feast of Our Lord; in the West, where it was adopted later, it was regarded more as a feast of Mary until the calendar in effect since 1970. Its date was set for Feb. 2 after the celebration of Christmas was fixed for Dec. 25, late in the fourth century. The blessing of candles, probably in commemoration of Christ who was the Light to enlighten the Gentiles, became common about the 11th century and gave the feast the secondary name of Candlemas.

**Queenship of Mary,** Aug. 22, memorial. Commemorates the high dignity of Mary as Queen of heaven, angels and men. Universal observance of the memorial was ordered by Pius XII in the encyclical *Ad Caeli Reginam,* Oct. 11, 1954, near the close of a Marian Year observed in connection with the centenary of the proclamation of the dogma of the Immaculate Conception and four years after the proclamation of the dogma of the Assumption. The original date of the memorial was May 31.

**Resurrection.** See Easter.

**Sacred Heart of Jesus,** movable observance held on the Friday after the second Sunday after Pentecost (Corpus Christi, in the U.S.), solemnity. The object of the devotion is the divine Person of Christ, whose heart is the symbol of his love for all people — for whom he accomplished the work of Redemption. The Mass and Office now used on the feast were prescribed by Pius XI in 1929. Devotion to the Sacred Heart was introduced into the liturgy in the 17th century through the efforts of St. John Eudes who composed an Office and Mass for the feast. It was furthered as the result of the revelations of St. Margaret Mary Alacoque after 1675 and by the work of St. Claude La Colombiere, S.J. In 1765, Clement XIII approved a Mass and Office for the feast, and in 1856 Pius IX extended the observance throughout the Roman Rite.

**Solemnity of Mary, Mother of God,** Jan. 1, holy day of obligation, solemnity. The calendar in effect since 1970, in accord with Eastern tradition, reinstated the Marian character of this commemoration on the octave day of Christmas. The former feast of the Circumcision, dating at least from the first half of the sixth century, marked the initiation of Jesus (Lk. 2:21) in Judaism and by analogy focused attention on the initiation of persons in the Christian religion and their incorporation in Christ through baptism. The feast of the Solemnity supplants the former feast of the Maternity of Mary observed on Oct. 11.

**Transfiguration of the Lord,** Aug. 6, feast. Commemorates the revelation of his divinity by Christ to Peter, James and John on Mt. Tabor (Mt. 17:1-9). The feast, which is very old, was extended throughout the universal Church in 1457 by Callistus III.

**Trinity, The Holy,** movable observance held on the Sunday after Pentecost, solemnity. Commemorates the most sublime mystery of the Christian faith, i.e., that there are Three Divine Persons — Father, Son and Holy Spirit — in one God (Mt. 28:18-20). A votive Mass of the Most Holy Trinity dates from the seventh century; an Office was composed in the 10th century; in 1334, John XXII extended the feast to the universal Church.

**Visitation,** May 31, feast. Commemorates Mary's visit to her cousin Elizabeth after the Annunciation and before the birth of John the Baptist, the precursor of Christ (Lk. 1:39-47). The feast had a medieval origin and was observed in the Franciscan Order before being extended throughout the Church by Urban VI in 1389. It is one of the feasts of the Incarnation and is notable for its recall of the Magnificat, one of the few New Testament canticles, which acknowledges the unique gifts of God to Mary because of her role in the redemptive work of Christ. The canticle is recited at Evening Prayer in the Liturgy of the Hours.

# SAINTS

Biographical sketches of additional saints and blessed are under other Almanac titles. See Index, under name of saint. For Beatification and Canonization procedures, see those entries in the Glossary.

An asterisk with a feast date indicates that the saint is listed in the General Roman Calendar or the proper calendar for U.S. dioceses. For rank of observances, see listing in calendar for current year on preceding pages.

**Adalbert** (956-997): Born in Bohemia; bishop of Prague; Benedictine; missionary in Poland, Prussia and Hungary; martyred by Prussians near Danzig; Apr. 23*.

**Adjutor** (d. 1131): Norman knight; fought in First Crusade; monk-recluse after his return; Apr. 30.

**Agatha** (d. c. 250): Sicilian virgin-martyr; her intercession credited in Sicily with stilling eruptions of Mt. Etna; patron of nurses; Feb. 5*.

**Agnes** (d. c. 304): Roman virgin-martyr; martyred at age of 10 or 12; patron of young girls; Jan. 21*.

**Aloysius Gonzaga** (1568-1591): Italian Jesuit; died while nursing plague-stricken; canonized 1726; patron of youth; June 21*.

**Amand** (d. c. 676): Apostle of Belgium; b. France; established monasteries throughout Belgium; Feb. 6.

**Andre Bessette, Bl.** (Bro. Andre) (1845-1937): Canadian Holy Cross Brother; prime mover in building of St. Joseph's Oratory, Montreal; beatified May 23, 1982; Jan. 6* (U.S.).

**Andre Grasset de Saint Sauveur, Bl.** (1758-1792): Canadian priest; martyred in France, Sept. 2, 1792, during the Revolution; one of a group called the Martyrs of Paris who were beatified in 1926; Sept. 2.

**Andrew Bobola** (1592-1657): Polish Jesuit; joined Jesuits at Vilna; worked for return of Orthodox to union with Rome; martyred; canonized 1938; May 16.

**Andrew Corsini** (1302-1373): Italian Carmelite; bishop of Fiesoli; mediator between quarrelsome Italian states; canonized 1629; Feb. 4.

**Andrew Dung-Lac and Companions** (d. 18th-19th c.): Martyrs of Vietnam. Total of 117 included 96 Vietnamese, 11 Spanish and 10 French missionaries (8 bishops; 50 priests, including Andrew Dung-Lac; 1 seminarian, 58 lay persons). Canonized June 19, 1988; inscribed in General Roman Calendar, 1989, as a memorial. Nov. 24*.

**Andrew Fournet** (1752-1834): French priest; co-founder with St. Jeanne Elizabeth Bichier des Anges of the Daughters of the Holy Cross of St. Andrew; canonized 1933; May 13.

**Andrew Kim, Paul Chong and Companions** (d. between 1839-1867): Korean martyrs (103) killed in persecutions of 1839, 1846, 1866, and 1867; among them were Andrew Kim, the first Korean priest, and Paul Chong, lay apostle; canonized May

6, 1984, during Pope John Paul II's visit to Korea; entered into General Roman Calendar, 1985, as a memorial. Sept. 20*.

**Angela Merici** (1474-1540): Italian secular Franciscan; foundress of Company of St. Ursula, 1535, the first teaching order of women Religious in the Church; canonized 1807; Jan. 27*.

**Angelico, Bl.** (Fra Angelico; John of Faesulis) (1387-1455): Dominican; Florentine painter of early Renaissance; proclaimed blessed by John Paul II, Feb. 3, 1982; patron of artists; Feb. 18.

**Anne Mary Javouhey, Bl.** (1779-1851): French virgin; foundress of Institute of St. Joseph of Cluny, 1812; beatified 1950; July 15.

**Ansgar** (801-865): Benedictine monk; b. near Amiens; archbishop of Hamburg; missionary in Denmark, Sweden, Norway and northern Germany; apostle of Scandinavia; Feb. 3.*

**Anthony** (c. 251-c. 354): Abbot; Egyptian hermit; patriarch of all monks; established communities for hermits which became models for monastic life, especially in the East; friend and supporter of St. Athanasius in the latter's struggle with the Arians; Jan. 17*.

**Anthony Claret** (1807-1870): Spanish bishop; founder of Missionary Sons of the Immaculate Heart of Mary (Claretians), 1849; archbishop of Santiago, Cuba, 1851-57; canonized 1950; Oct. 24*.

**Anthony Gianelli** (1789-1846): Italian bishop; founded the Daughters of Our Lady of the Garden, 1829; bishop of Bobbio, 1838; canonized 1951; June 7.

**Anthony Zaccaria** (1502-1539): Italian priest; founder of Barnabites (Clerks Regular of St. Paul), 1530; canonized 1897; July 5*.

**Apollonia** (d. 249): Deaconess of Alexandria; martyred during persecution of Decius; her patronage of dentists and those suffering from toothaches probably rests on tradition that her teeth were broken by her persecutors; Feb. 9.

**Augustine of Canterbury** (d. 604 or 605): Italian missionary; apostle of the English; sent by Pope Gregory I with 40 monks to evangelize England; arrived there 597; first archbishop of Canterbury; May 27*.

**Bartolomea Capitania** (1807-1833): Italian foundress with Vincenza Gerosa of the Sisters of Charity of Lovere; canonized 1950; July 26.

**Beatrice da Silva Meneses** (1424-1490): Foundress, b. Portugal; founded Congregation of the Immaculate Conception, 1484,in Spain; canonized 1976; Sept. 1.

**Benedict Joseph Labre** (1748-1783): French layman; pilgrim-beggar; noted for his piety and love of prayer before the Blessed Sacrament; canonized 1883; Apr. 16.

**Benedict of Nursia** (c. 480-547): Abbot; founder of monasticism in Western Europe; established monastery at Monte Cassino; proclaimed patron of Europe by Paul VI in 1964; July 11*.

**Benedict the Black (il Moro)** (1526-1589): Sicilian Franciscan; born a slave; joined Franciscans as lay brother; appointed guardian and novice master; canonized 1807; Apr. 3.

**Bernadette Soubirous** (1844-1879): French peasant girl favored with series of visions of Blessed Virgin Mary at Lourdes (see Lourdes Apparitions);

joined Institute of Sisters of Notre Dame at Nevers, 1866; canonized 1933; Apr. 16.

**Bernard of Montjoux (or Menthon)** (d. 1081): Augustinian canon; probably born in Italy; founded Alpine hospices near the two passes named for him; patron of mountaineers; May 28.

**Bernardine of Feltre, Bl.** (1439-1494): Italian Franciscan preacher; a founder of *montes pietatis;* Sept. 28.

**Bernardine of Siena** (1380-1444): Italian Franciscan; noted preacher and missioner; spread of devotion to Holy Name is attributed to him; represented in art holding to his breast the monogram IHS; canonized 1450; May 20*.

**Blase** (d. c. 316): Armenian bishop; martyr; the blessing of throats on his feast day derives from tradition that he miraculously saved the life of a boy who had half-swallowed a fish bone; Feb. 3*.

**Boniface (Winfrid)** (d. 754): English Benedictine; bishop; martyr; apostle of Germany; established monastery at Fulda which became center of missionary work in Germany; archbishop of Mainz; martyred near Dukkum in Holland; June 5*.

**Brendan** (c. 489-583): Irish abbot; founded monasteries; his patronage of sailors probably rests on a legend that he made a seven-year voyage in search of a fabled paradise; called Brendan the Navigator; May 16.

**Bridget (Brigid)** (c. 450-525): Irish nun; founded religious community at Kildare, the first in Ireland; patron, with Sts. Patrick and Columba, of Ireland; Feb. 1.

**Bridget (Birgitta)** (c. 1303-1373): Swedish mystic; widow; foundress of Order of Our Savior (Brigittines); canonized 1391; patroness of Sweden; July 23*.

**Bruno** (1030-1101): German monk; founded Carthusians, 1084, in France; Oct. 6*.

**Cabrini, Mother:** See Frances Xavier Cabrini.

**Cajetan (Gaetano) of Thiene** (1480-1547): Italian lawyer; religious reformer; a founder of Oratory of Divine Love, forerunner of the Theatines; canonized 1671; Aug. 7*.

**Callistus I** (d. 222): Pope, 217-222; martyr; condemned Sabellianism and other heresies; advocated a policy of mercy toward repentant sinners; Oct. 14*.

**Camillus de Lellis** (1550-1614): Italian priest; founder of Camillians (Ministers of the Sick); canonized 1746; patron of the sick and of nurses; July 14*.

**Casimir** (1458-1484): Polish prince; grand duke of Lithuania; noted for his piety; buried at cathedral in Vilna, Lithuania; canonized 1521; patron of Poland and Lithuania; Mar. 4*.

**Cassian of Tangier** (d. 298): Roman martyr; an official court stenographer who declared himself a Christian; patron of stenographers; Dec. 3.

**Catherine Laboure** (1806-1876): French Religious; favored with series of visions soon after she joined Sisters of Charity of St. Vincent de Paul in Paris in 1830; first Miraculous Medal (see Index) struck in 1832 in accord with one of the visions; canonized 1947; Nov. 28.

**Catherine of Bologna** (1413-1463): Italian Poor Clare; mystic, writer, artist canonized 1712; patron of artists; May 9.

Cecilia (2nd-3rd century): Roman virgin-martyr; traditional patroness of musicians; Nov. 22.*

Charles Borromeo (1538-1584): Italian cardinal; nephew of Pope Pius IV; cardinal bishop of Milan; influential figure in Church reform in Italy; promoted education of clergy; canonized 1610; Nov. 4*.

Charles Lwanga and Companions (d. between 1885 and 1887): Twenty-two Martyrs of Uganda, many of them pages of King Mwanga of Uganda, who were put to death because they denounced his corrupt lifestyle; canonized 1964; first martyrs of black Africa; June 3.*

Charles of Sezze (1616-1670): Italian Franciscan lay brother who served in humble capacities; canonized 1959; Jan. 6.

Christopher (3rd cent.): Early Christian martyr inscribed in Roman calendar about 1550; feast relegated to particular calendars because of legendary nature of accounts of his life; traditional patron of travelers; July 25.

Clare (1194-1253): Foundress of Poor Clares; b. at Assisi; was joined in religious life by her sisters, Agnes and Beatrice, and eventually her widowed mother Ortolana; canonized 1255; patroness of television; Aug. 11.*

Claude La Colombiere (1641-1682): French Jesuit; spiritual director of St. Margaret Mary Alacoque; instrumental in spreading devotion to the Sacred Heart; beatified, 1929; canonized May 31, 1992; Feb. 15.

Clement Hofbauer (1751-1820): Redemptorist priest, missionary; born in Moravia; helped spread Redemptorists north of the Alps; canonized 1909; Mar. 15.

Clement I (d. c. 100): Pope, 88-97; third successor of St. Peter; wrote important letter to Church in Corinth settling disputes there; venerated as a martyr; Nov. 23*.

Columba (521-597): Irish monk; founded monasteries in Ireland; missionary in Scotland; established monastery at Iona which became the center for conversion of Picts, Scots, and Northern English; Scotland's most famous saint; patron saint of Ireland (with Sts. Patrick and Brigid); June 9.

Columban (545-615): Irish monk; scholar; founded monasteries in England and Brittany (famous abbey of Luxeuil), forced into exile because of his criticism of Frankish court; spent last years in northern Italy where he founded abbey at Bobbio; Nov. 23*.

Conrad of Parzham (1818-1894): Bavarian Capuchin lay brother; served as porter at the Marian shrine of Altotting in Upper Bavaria for 40 years; canonized 1934; Apr. 21.

Contardo Ferrini, Bl. (1859-1902): Italian secular Franciscan; model of the Catholic professor; beatified 1947; patron of universities; Oct. 20.

Cornelius (d. 253): Pope, 251-253; promoted a policy of mercy with respect to readmission of repentant Christians who had fallen away during the persecution of Decius (lapsi); banished from Rome during persecution of Gallus; regarded as a martyr; Sept. 16 (with Cyprian)*.

Cosmas and Damian (d. c. 303): Arabian twin brothers, physicians; martyred during Diocletian persecution; patrons of physicians; Sept. 26*.

Crispin and Crispinian (3rd cent.): Early Chris-

tian martyrs; said to have met their deaths in Gaul; patrons of shoemakers, a trade they pursued; Oct. 25.

Crispin of Viterbo (1668-1750): Capuchin brother; canonized June 20, 1982; May 21.

Cyprian (d. 258): Early ecclesiastical writer; b. Africa; bishop of Carthage, 249-258; supported Pope St. Cornelius concerning the readmission of Christians who had apostasized in time of persecution; erred in his teaching that baptism administered by heretics and schismatics was invalid; wrote De Unitate; Sept. 16 (with St. Cornelius)*.

Cyril and Methodius (9th century): Greek missionaries, bothers; venerated as apostles of the Slavs; Cyril (d. 869) and Methodius (d. 885) began their missionary work in Moravia in 863; developed a Slavonic alphabet; used the vernacular in the liturgy, a practice that was eventually approved; declared patrons of Europe with St. Benedict, Dec. 31, 1980; Feb. 14*.

Damasus I (d. 384): Pope, 366-384; opposed Arians and Apollinarians; commissioned St. Jerome to work on Bible translation; developed Roman liturgy; Dec. 11*.

Damian: See Cosmas and Damian.

David (5th or 6th cent.): Nothing for certain known of his life; said to have founded monastery at Menevia; patron saint of Wales; Mar. 1.

Denis and Companions (d. 3rd cent.): Denis, bishop of Paris, and two companions identified by early writers as Rusticus, a priest, and Eleutherius, a deacon; martyred near Paris; Denis is popularly regarded as the apostle and a patron saint of France; Oct. 9*.

Dismas (1st cent.): Name given to repentant thief (Good Thief) to whom Jesus promised salvation (Lk. 23:40-43); regarded as patron of prisoners; Mar. 25 (observed on second Sunday of October in U.S. prison chapels).

Dominic (Dominic de Guzman) (1170-1221): Spanish priest; founded the Order of Preachers (Dominicans), 1215, in France; preached against the Albigensian heresy; a contemporary of St. Francis of Assisi; canonized 1234; Aug. 8*.

Dominic Savio (1842-1857): Italian youth; pupil of St. John Bosco; died before his 15th birthday; canonized 1954; patron of choir boys; May 6.

Duns Scotus, John (d. 1308): Scottish Franciscan; theologian; advanced theological arguments for doctrine of the Immaculate Conception; proclaimed blessed; cult solemnly confirmed by John Paul II, Mar. 20, 1993; Nov. 8.

Dunstan (c. 910-988): English monk; archbishop of Canterbury; initiated reforms in religious life; counselor to several kings; considered one of greatest Anglo-Saxon saints; patron of goldsmiths, locksmiths, jewelers (trades in which he is said to have excelled); May 19.

Dymphna (dates unknown): Nothing certain known of her life; according to legend, she was an Irish maiden murdered by her heathen father at Gheel near Antwerp, Belgium, where she had fled to escape his advances; her relics were discovered there in the 13th century; since that time cures of mental illness and epilepsy have been attributed to her intercession; patron of those suffering from mental illness; May 15.

**Edith Stein, Bl.** (1891-1942): German Carmelite (Teresa Benedicta of the Cross); born of Jewish parents; author and lecturer; baptized in Catholic Church, 1922; arrested with her sister Rosa in 1942 and put to death at Auschwitz; beatified 1987, by Pope John Paul II during his visit to West Germany. Aug. 10.

**Edmund Campion** (1540-1581): English Jesuit; convert 1573; martyred at Tyburn; canonized 1970, one of the Forty English and Welsh Martyrs; Dec. 1.

**Edward the Confessor** (d. 1066): King of England, 1042-66; canonized 1161; Oct. 13.

**Eligius** (c. 590-660): Bishop; born in Gaul; founded monasteries and convents; bishop of Noyon and Tournai; famous worker in gold and silver; Dec. 1.

**Elizabeth Ann Seton** (1774-1821): American foundress; convert, 1805; founded Sisters of Charity in the U.S.; beatified 1963; canonized Sept. 14, 1975; the first American-born saint; Jan. 4 (U.S.)*.

**Elizabeth of Hungary** (1207-1231): Became secular Franciscan after death of her husband in 1227; devoted life to poor and destitute; a patron of the Secular Franciscan Order; canonized 1235; Nov. 17*.

**Elizabeth of Portugal** (1271-1336): Queen of Portugal; b. Spain; retired to Poor Clare convent as a secular Franciscan after the death of her husband; canonized 1626; July 4*.

**Emily de Rodat** (1787-1852): French foundress of the Congregation of the Holy Family of Villefranche; canonized 1950; Sept. 19.

**Emily de Vialar** (1797-1856): French foundress of the Sisters of St. Joseph of the Apparition; canonized 1951; June 17.

**Erasmus (Elmo)** (d. 303): Life surrounded by legend; martyred during Diocletian persecution; patron of sailors; June 2.

**Ethelbert** (552-616): King of Kent, England; baptized by St. Augustine of Canterbury, 597; issued legal code; furthered spread of Christianity; Feb. 26.

**Euphrasia Pelletier** (1796-1868): French Religious; founded Sisters of the Good Shepherd at Angers, 1829; canonized 1940; Apr. 24.

**Eusebius of Vercelli** (283-370): Italian bishop; exiled from his see (Vercelli) for a time because of his opposition to Arianism; considered a martyr because of sufferings he endured; Aug. 2*.

**Fabian** (d. 250): Pope, 236-250; martyred under Decius; Jan. 20*.

**Felicity:** See Perpetua and Felicity.

**Ferdinand III** (1198-1252): King of Castile and Leon; waged successful crusade against Mohammedans in Spain; founded university at Salamanca; canonized 1671; May 30.

**Fiacre (Fiachra)** (d. c. 670): Irish hermit; patron of gardeners; Aug. 30.

**Fidelis of Sigmaringen** (Mark Rey) (1577-1622): German Capuchin; lawyer before he joined the Capuchins; missionary to Swiss Protestants; stabbed to death by peasants who were told he was agent of Austrian emperor; Apr. 24*.

**Frances of Rome** (1384-1440): Italian model for housewives and widows; happily married for 40 years; after death of her husband in 1436 joined community of Benedictine Oblates she had founded; canonized 1608; patron of motorists; Mar. 9*.

**Frances Xavier Cabrini** (Mother Cabrini) (1850-1917): American foundress; b. Italy; founded the Missionary Sisters of the Sacred Heart, 1877; settled in the U.S. 1889; became an American citizen at Seattle 1909; worked among Italian immigrants; canonized 1946, the first American citizen so honored; Nov. 13 (U.S.)*.

**Francis Borgia** (1510-1572): Spanish Jesuit; joined Jesuits after death of his wife in 1546; became general of the Order, 1565; Oct. 10.

**Francis Caracciolo** (1563-1608): Italian priest; founder with Father Augustine Adorno of the Clerks Regular Minor (Adorno Fathers); canonized 1807; June 4.

**Francis Fasani** (1681-1742): Italian Conventual Franciscan; model of priestly ministry, especially in service to poor and imprisoned; canonized 1986; Nov. 27.

**Francis of Assisi** (Giovanni di Bernardone) (1181/82-1226): Founder of the Franciscans, 1209; received stigmata 1224; canonized 1228; one of best known and best loved saints; patron of Italy, Catholic Action and ecologists; Oct. 4*.

**Francis of Paola** (1416-1507): Italian hermit: founder of Minim Friars; Apr. 2*.

**Francis Xavier** (1506-1552): Spanish Jesuit; missionary to Far East; canonized 1602; patron of foreign missions; considered one of greatest Christian missionaries; Dec. 3*.

**Francis Xavier Bianchi** (1743-1815): Italian Barnabite; acclaimed apostle of Naples because of his work there among the poor and abandoned; canonized 1951; Jan. 31.

**Gabriel of the Sorrowful Mother** (Francis Possenti) (1838-1862): Italian Passionist; died while a scholastic; canonized 1920; Feb. 27.

**Gaspar (Caspar) del Bufalo** (1786-1836): Italian priest; founded Missionaries of the Precious Blood, 1815; canonized 1954; Jan. 2.

**Gemma Galgani** (1878-1903): Italian laywoman; visionary; subject of extraordinary religious experiences; canonized 1940; Apr. 11.

**Genesius** (d. c. 300): Roman actor; according to legend, was converted while performing a burlesque of Christian baptism and was subsequently martyred; patron of actors; Aug. 25.

**Genevieve** (422-500): French nun; a patroness and protectress of Paris; events of her life not authenticated; Jan. 3.

**George** (d. c. 300): Martyr, probably during Diocletian persecution in Palestine; all other incidents of his life, including story of the dragon, are legendary; patron of England; Apr. 23*.

**Gerard Majella** (1725-1755): Italian Redemptorist lay brother; noted for supernatural occurrences in his life including bilocation and reading of consciences; canonized 1904; patron of mothers; Oct. 16.

**Gertrude** (1256-1302): German mystic; writer; helped spread devotion to the Sacred Heart; Nov. 16*.

**Gregory VII (Hildebrand)** (1020?-1085): Pope, 1075-1085; Benedictine monk; adviser to several popes; as pope, strengthened interior life of Church and fought against lay investiture; driven from Rome by Henry IV; died in exile; canonized 1584; May 25.*

**Gregory Barbarigo** (1626-1697): Italian cardinal; noted for his efforts to bring about reunion of separated Christians; canonized 1960; June 18.

**Gregory of Nyssa** (c. 335-395): Bishop; theologian; younger brother of St. Basil the Great; Mar. 9.

**Gregory Thaumaturgus** (c. 213-268): Bishop of Neocaesarea; missionary, famed as wonder worker; Nov. 17.

**Gregory the Illuminator** (257-332): Martyr; bishop; apostle and patron saint of Armenia; helped free Armenia from the Persians; Sept. 30.

**Hedwig** (1174-1243): Moravian noblewoman; married duke of Silesia, head of Polish royal family; fostered religious life in country; canonized 1266; Oct. 16*.

**Helena** (250-330): Empress; mother of Constantine the Great; associated with discovery of the True Cross; Aug. 18.

**Henry** (972-1024): Bavarian emperor; cooperated with Benedictine abbeys in restoration of ecclesiastical and social discipline; canonized 1146; July 13*.

**Herman Joseph** (1150-1241): German Premonstratensian; his visions were the subjects of artists; writer; cult approved, 1958; Apr. 7.

**Hippolytus** (d. c. 236): Roman priest; opposed Pope St. Callistus I in his teaching about the readmission to the Church of repentant Christians who had apostasized during time of persecution; elected antipope; exiled to Sardinia; reconciled before his martyrdom; important ecclesiastical writer; Aug. 13* (with Pontian).

**Hubert** (d. 727): Bishop; his patronage of hunters is based on legend that he was converted while hunting; Nov. 3.

**Hugh of Cluny (the Great)** (1024-1109): Abbot of Benedictine foundation at Cluny; supported popes in efforts to reform ecclesiastical abuses; canonized 1120; Apr. 29.

**Ignatius of Antioch** (d. c. 107): Early ecclesiastical writer; martyr; bishop of Antioch in Syria for 40 years; Oct. 17*.

**Ignatius of Laconi** (1701-1781): Italian Capuchin lay brother whose 60 years of religious life were spent in Franciscan simplicity; canonized 1951; May 11.

**Ignatius of Loyola** (1491-1556): Spanish soldier; renounced military career after recovering from wounds received at siege of Pampeluna (Pamplona) in 1521; founded Society of Jesus (Jesuits), 1534, at Paris; wrote *The Book of Spiritual Exercises;* canonized 1622; July 31*.

**Irenaeus of Lyons** (130-202): Early ecclesiastical writer; opposed Gnosticism; bishop of Lyons; traditionally regarded as a martyr; June 28*.

**Isidore the Farmer** (d. 1170): Spanish layman; farmer; canonized 1622; patron of farmers; May 15 (U.S.)*.

**Jane Frances de Chantal** (1572-1641): French widow; foundress, under guidance of St. Francis de Sales, of Order of the Visitation; canonized 1767; Dec. 12* (General Roman Calendar); Aug. 18* (U.S.).

**Januarius (Gennaro)** (d. 304): Bishop of Benevento; martyred during Diocletian persecution; fame rests on liquefaction of some of his blood preserved in a phial at Naples, an unexplained phenom-

enon which has occurred regularly several times each year for over 400 years; Sept. 19*.

**Jeanne Delanoue** (1666-1736): French foundress of Sisters of St. Anne of Providence, 1704; canonized 1982; Aug. 16.

**Jeanne (Joan) de Lestonnac** (1556-1640): French foundress; widowed in 1597; founded the Religious of Notre Dame 1607; canonized 1947; Feb. 2.

**Jeanne de Valois (Jeanne of France)** (1464-1505): French foundress; deformed daughter of King Louis XI; was married in 1476 to Duke Louis of Orleans who had the marriage annulled when he ascended the throne as Louis XII; Jeanne retired to life of prayer; founded contemplative Annonciades of Bourges, 1504; canonized 1950; Feb. 5.

**Jeanne Elizabeth Bichier des Anges** (1773-1838): French Religious; co-founder with St. Andrew Fournet of Daughters of the Cross of St. Andrew, 1807; canonized 1947; Aug. 26.

**Jeanne Jugan, Bl.** (1792-1879): French Religious; foundress of Little Sisters of the Poor; beatified Oct. 3, 1982; Aug. 30.

**Jerome Emiliani** (1481-1537): Venetian priest; founded Somascan Fathers, 1532, for care of orphans; canonized 1767; patron of orphans and abandoned children; Feb. 8*.

**Joan Antida Thouret** (1765-1826): French Religious; founded, 1799, congregation now known as Sisters of Charity of St. Joan Antida; canonized 1934; Aug. 24.

**Joan of Arc** (1412-1431): French heroine, called The Maid of Orleans, La Pucelle; led French army in 1429 against English invaders besieging Orleans; captured by Burgundians the following year; turned over to ecclesiastical court on charge of heresy, found guilty and burned at the stake; her innocence was declared in 1456; canonized 1920; patroness of France; May 30.

**Joaquina de Vedruna de Mas** (1783-1854): Spanish foundress; widowed in 1816; after providing for her children, founded the Carmelite Sisters of Charity; canonized 1959; Aug. 28.

**John I** (d. 526): Pope, 523-526; martyr; May 18*.

**John Baptist de la Salle** (1651-1719): French priest; founder of Brothers of the Christian Schools, 1680; canonized 1900; patron of teachers; Apr. 7*.

**John Berchmans** (1599-1621): Belgian Jesuit scholastic; patron of Mass servers; canonized 1888; Aug. 13.

**John (Don) Bosco** (1815-1888): Italian priest; founded Salesians, 1859, for education of boys; co-founder of Daughters of Mary Help of Christians for education of girls; canonized 1934; Jan. 31*.

**John Capistran** (1386-1456): Italian Franciscan; preacher; papal diplomat; canonized 1690; declared patron of military chaplains, Feb. 10, 1984. Oct. 23*.

**John de Ribera** (1532-1611): Spanish bishop and statesman; archbishop of Valencia, 1568-1611, and viceroy of that province; canonized 1960; Jan. 6.

**John Eudes** (1601-1680): French priest; founder of Sisters of Our Lady of Charity of Refuge, 1642, and Congregation of Jesus-Mary (Eudists), 1643; canonized 1925; Aug. 19*.

**John Fisher** (1469-1535): English prelate; theologian; martyr; bishop of Rochester, cardinal; refused to recognize validity of Henry VIII's marriage to

Anne Boleyn; upheld supremacy of the pope; beheaded for refusing to acknowledge Henry as head of the Church; canonized 1935; June 22 (with St. Thomas More)*.

**John Francis Regis** (1597-1640): French Jesuit priest; preached missions among poor and unlettered; canonized 1737; patron of social workers, particularly medical social workers, because of his concern for poor and needy and sick in hospitals; July 2.

**John Gualbert** (d. 1073): Italian priest; founder of Benedictine congregation of Vallombrosians, 1039; canonized 1193; July 12.

**John Kanty (Cantius)** (1395-1473): Polish theologian; canonized 1767; Dec. 23*.

**John Leonardi** (1550-1609): Italian priest; worked among prisoners and the sick; founded Clerics Regular of the Mother of God; canonized 1938; Oct. 9*.

**John Nepomucene** (1345-1393): Bohemian priest; regarded as a martyr; canonized 1729; patron of Czechoslovakia; May 16.

**John Nepomucene Neumann** (1811-1860): American prelate; b. Bohemia; ordained in New York 1836; missionary among Germans near Niagara Falls before joining Redemptorists, 1840; bishop of Philadelphia, 1852; first bishop in U.S. to prescribe Forty Hours devotion in his diocese; beatified 1963; canonized June 19, 1977; Jan. 5 (U.S.)*.

**John of Avila** (1499-1569): Spanish priest; preacher; ascetical writer; spiritual adviser of St. Teresa of Jesus (Avila); canonized 1970; May 10.

**John of Britto** (1647-1693): Portuguese Jesuit; missionary in India where he was martyred; canonized 1947; Feb. 4.

**John of God** (1495-1550): Portuguese founder; his work among the sick poor led to foundation of Brothers Hospitallers of St. John of God, 1540, in Spain; canonized 1690; patron of sick, nurses, hospitals; Mar. 8*.

**John of Matha** (1160-1213): French priest; founder of the Order of Most Holy Trinity, whose original purpose was the ransom of prisoners from the Moslems; Feb. 8.

**John Ogilvie** (1579-1615): Scottish Jesuit; martyr; canonized 1976, the first canonized Scottish saint since 1250 (Margaret of Scotland); Mar. 10.

**John Vianney (Cure of Ars)** (1786-1859): French parish priest; noted confessor, spent 16 to 18 hours a day in confessional; canonized 1925; patron of parish priests; Aug. 4*.

**Josaphat Kuncevyc** (1584-1623): Basilian monk; b. Poland; archbishop of Polotsk, Lithuania; worked for reunion of separated Eastern Christians with Rome; martyred by mob of schismatics; canonized 1867; Nov. 12*.

**Joseph Benedict Cottolengo** (1786-1842): Italian priest; established Little Houses of Divine Providence (Piccolo Casa) for care of orphans and the sick; canonized 1934; Apr. 30.

**Joseph Cafasso** (1811-1860): Italian priest; renowned confessor; promoted devotion to Blessed Sacrament; canonized 1947; June 23.

**Joseph Calasanz** (1556-1648): Spanish priest; founder of Piarists (Order of Pious Schools); canonized 1767; Aug. 25*.

**Joseph of Cupertino** (1603-1663): Italian

Franciscan; noted for remarkable incidents of levitation; canonized 1767; Sept. 18.

**Joseph Pignatelli** (1737-1811): Spanish Jesuit; left Spain when Jesuits were banished in 1767; worked for revival of the Order; named first superior when Jesuits were reestablished in Kingdom of Naples, 1804; canonized 1954; Nov. 28.

**Juan Diego, Bl.** (16th cent.): Mexican Indian, convert; indigenous name according to tradition *Cuauhtlatohuac* ("The eagle who speaks"); favored with apparitions of Our Lady (see Index: Our Lady of Guadalupe) on Tepeyac hill; beatified, 1990; Dec. 9* (U.S.).

**Julia Billiart** (1751-1816): French foundress; founded Sisters of Notre Dame de Namur, 1804; canonized 1969; Apr. 8.

**Justin de Jacobis** (1800-1860): Italian Vincentian; bishop; missionary in Ethiopia; canonized 1975; July 31.

**Justin Martyr** (100-165): Early ecclesiastical writer; *Apologies for the Christian Religion, Dialog with the Jew Tryphon;* martyred at Rome; June 1*.

**Kateri Tekakwitha, Bl.** (1656-1680): "Lily of the Mohawks." Indian maiden born at Ossernenon (Auriesville), N.Y.; baptized Christian, Easter, 1676, by Jesuit missionary Father Jacques de Lambertville; lived life devoted to prayer, penitential practices and care of sick and aged in Christian village of Caughnawaga near Montreal where her relics are now enshrined; beatified June 22, 1980; July 14* (in U.S.).

**Katharine Drexel, Bl.** (1858-1955): Philadelphia-born heiress; devoted wealth to founding schools and missions for Indians and Blacks; foundress of Sisters of Blessed Sacrament for Indians and Colored People, 1891; beatified 1988; Mar. 3* (U.S.).

**Ladislaus** (1040-1095): King of Hungary; supported Pope Gregory VII against Henry IV; canonized 1192; June 27.

**Lawrence** (d. 258): Widely venerated martyr who suffered death, according to a long-standing but unverifiable legend, by fire on a gridiron; Aug. 10*.

**Lawrence (Lorenzo) Ruiz and Companions** (d. 1630s): Martyred in or near the city of Nagasaki, Japan; Lawrence Ruiz, first Filipino saint, and 15 companions (nine Japanese, four Spaniards, one Italian and one Frenchman); canonized 1987; Sept. 28*.

**Leonard Murialdo** (1828-1900): Italian priest; educator; founder of Pious Society of St. Joseph of Turin, 1873; canonized 1970; Mar. 30.

**Leonard of Port Maurice** (1676-1751): Italian Franciscan; ascetical writer; preached missions throughout Italy; canonized 1867; patron of parish missions; Nov. 26.

**Leopold Mandic** (1866-1942): Croatian-born Franciscan priest, noted confessor; spent most of his priestly life in Padua, Italy; canonized, 1983, July 30.

**Louis IX** (1215-1270): King of France, 1226-1270; participated in Sixth Crusade; patron of Secular Franciscan Order; canonized 1297; Aug. 25*.

**Louis de Montfort** (1673-1716): French priest; founder of Sisters of Divine Wisdom, 1703, and Missionaries of Company of Mary, 1715; wrote *True Devotion to the Blessed Virgin;* canonized 1947; Apr. 28.

**Louis Zepherin Moreau, Bl.** (d. 1901): Canadian bishop; headed St. Hyacinthe, Que., diocese, 1876-1901; beatified 1987; May 24.

**Louise de Marillac** (1591-1660): French foundress, with St. Vincent de Paul, of the Sisters of Charity; canonized 1934; Mar. 15.

**Lucy** (d. 304): Sicilian maiden; martyred during Diocletian persecution; one of most widely venerated early virgin-martyrs; patron of Syracuse, Sicily; invoked by those suffering from eye diseases; Dec. 13*.

**Lucy Filippini** (1672-1732): Italian educator, helped improve status of women through education; considered a founder of the Religious Teachers Filippini, 1692; canonized 1930; Mar. 25.

**Madeleine Sophie Barat** (1779-1865): French foundress of the Society of the Sacred Heart of Jesus; canonized 1925; May 25.

**Malachy** (1095-1148): Irish bishop; instrumental in establishing first Cistercian house in Ireland, 1142; canonized 1190; Nov. 3 (See Index: Prophecies of St. Malachy).

**Marcellinus and Peter** (d.c. 304): Early Roman martyrs; June 2*.

**Margaret Clitherow** (1556-1586): English martyr; convert shortly after her marriage; one of Forty Martyrs of England and Wales; canonized 1970; Mar. 25.

**Margaret Mary Alacoque** (1647-1690): French Religious; spread devotion to Sacred Heart in accordance with revelations made to her in 1675 (see Sacred Heart); canonized 1920; Oct. 16*.

**Margaret of Cortona** (1247-1297): Secular Franciscan; reformed her life in 1273 following the violent death of her lover; canonized 1728; May 16.

**Margaret of Hungary** (1242-1270): Contemplative; daughter of King Bela IV of Hungary; lived a life of self-imposed penances; canonized 1943; Jan. 18.

**Margaret of Scotland** (1050-1093): Queen of Scotland; noted for solicitude for the poor and promotion of justice; canonized 1250; Nov. 16*.

**Maria Goretti** (1890-1902): Italian virgin-martyr; a model of purity; canonized 1950; July 6*.

**Mariana Paredes of Jesus** (1618-1645): South American recluse; Lily of Quito; canonized, 1950; May 28.

**Marie-Leonie Paradis, Bl.** (1840-1912): Canadian Religious; founded Little Sisters of the Holy Family, 1880; beatified 1984; May 4.

**Marie-Rose Durocher, Bl.** (1811-1849): Canadian Religious; foundress of Sisters of Holy Names of Jesus and Mary; beatified 1982; Oct. 6* (in U.S.).

**Martha** (1st cent.): Sister of Lazarus and Mary of Bethany; Gospel accounts record her concern for homely details; patron of cooks; July 29*.

**Martin I** (d. 655): Pope, 649-55; banished from Rome by emperor in 653 because of his condemnation of Monothelites; considered a martyr; Apr. 13*.

**Martin of Tours** (316-397): Bishop of Tours; opposed Arianism and Priscillianism; pioneer of Western monasticism, before St. Benedict; Nov. 11*.

**Mary Domenica Mazzarello** (1837-1881): Italian foundress, with St. John Bosco, of the Daughters of Mary Help of Christians, 1872; canonized 1951; May 14.

**Mary Josepha Rossello** (1811-1881): Italian-born foundress of the Daughters of Our Lady of Mercy; canonized 1949; Dec. 7.

**Mary Magdalen Postel** (1756-1846): French foundress of the Sisters of Christian Schools of Mercy, 1807; canonized 1925; July 16.

**Mary Magdalene** (1st cent.): Gospels record her as devoted follower of Christ to whom he appeared after the Resurrection; her identification with Mary of Bethany (sister of Martha and Lazarus) and the woman sinner (Lk 7:36-50) has been questioned; July 22*.

**Mary Magdalene dei Pazzi** (1566-1607): Italian Carmelite nun; recipient of mystical experiences; canonized 1669; May 25*.

**Mary Michaela Desmaisières** (1809-1865): Spanish-born foundress of the Institute of the Handmaids of the Blessed Sacrament, 1848; canonized 1934; Aug. 24.

**Maximilian Kolbe** (1894-1941): Polish Conventual Franciscan; prisoner at Auschwitz who heroically offered his life in place of a fellow prisoner; beatified 1971, canonized 1982; Aug. 14*.

**Methodius:** See Index.

**Miguel Febres Cordero** (1854-1910): Ecuadorean Christian Brother; educator; canonized 1984; Feb. 9.

**Miguel Pro, Bl.** (1891-1927): Mexican Jesuit; joined Jesuits, 1911; forced to flee because of religious persecution; ordained in Belgium, 1925; returned to Mexico, 1926, to minister to people despite government prohibition; unjustly accused of assassination plot against president; arrested and executed; beatified 1988. Nov. 23* (U.S.).

**Monica** (332-387): Mother of St. Augustine; model of a patient mother; her feast is observed in the Roman calendar the day before her son's; Aug. 27*.

**Nereus and Achilleus** (d. c. 100): Early Christian martyrs; soldiers who, according to legend, were baptized by St. Peter; May 12*.

**Nicholas of Flue** (1417-1487): Swiss layman; at the age of 50, with the consent of his wife and 10 children, he retreated from the world to live as a hermit; called Brother Claus by the Swiss; canonized 1947; Mar. 21.

**Nicholas of Myra** (4th cent.): Bishop of Myra in Asia Minor; one of most popular saints in both East and West; most of the incidents of his life are based on legend; patron of Russia; Dec. 6*.

**Nicholas of Tolentino** (1245-1305): Italian hermit; famed preacher; canonized 1446; Sept. 10.

**Nicholas Tavelic and Companions** (Deodatus of Aquitaine, Peter of Narbonne, Stephen of Cuneo) (d. 1391): Franciscan missionaries; martyred by Moslems in the Holy Land: canonized 1970; Nov. 14.

**Norbert** (1080-1134): German bishop; founded Canons Regular of Premontre (Premonstratensians, Norbertines), 1120; promoted reform of the clergy, devotion to Blessed Sacrament; canonized 1582; June 6*.

**Odilia** (d. c. 720): Benedictine abbess; according to legend she was born blind, abandoned by her family and adopted by a convent of nuns where her sight was miraculously restored; patroness of blind; Dec. 13.

**Oliver Plunket** (1629-1681): Irish martyr; theologian; archbishop of Armagh and primate of Ireland; beatified 1920; canonized, 1975; July 1.

**Pancras** (d. c. 304): Roman martyr; May 12*.

**Paola Frassinetti** (1809-1882): Italian Religious; foundress, 1834, of Sisters of St. Dorothy; canonized 1984; June 11.

**Paschal Baylon** (1540-1592): Spanish Franciscan lay brother; spent life as door-keeper in various Franciscan friaries; defended doctrine of Real Presence in Blessed Sacrament; canonized 1690; patron of all Eucharistic confraternities and congresses, 1897; May 17.

**Patrick** (389-461): Famous missionary of Ireland; began missionary work in Ireland about 432; organized the Church there and established it on a lasting foundation; patron of Ireland, with Sts. Bridget and Columba; Mar. 17*.

**Paul Miki and Companions** (d. 1597): Martyrs of Japan; Paul Miki, Jesuit, and twenty-five other priests and laymen were martyred at Nagasaki; canonized 1862, the first canonized martyrs of the Far East; Feb. 6*.

**Paul of the Cross** (1694-1775): Italian Religious; founder of the Passionists; canonized 1867; Oct 19* (Oct. 20, U.S.*).

**Paulinus of Nola** (d. 451): Bishop of Nola (Spain); writer; June 22*.

**Peregrine** (1260-1347): Italian Servite; invoked against cancer (he was miraculously cured of cancer of the foot after a vision); canonized 1726; May 1.

**Perpetua and Felicity** (d. 203): Martyrs; Perpetua was a young married woman; Felicity was a slave girl; Mar. 7*.

**Peter Chanel** (1803-1841): French Marist; missionary to Oceania, where he was martyred; canonized 1954; Apr. 28*.

**Peter Fourier** (1565-1640): French priest; cofounder with Alice LeClercq (Mother Teresa of Jesus) of the Augustinian Canonesses of Our Lady, 1598; canonized 1897; Dec. 9.

**Peter Gonzalez** (1190-1246): Spanish Dominican; worked among sailors; court chaplain and confessor of King St. Ferdinand of Castile; patron of sailors; Apr. 14.

**Peter Julian Eymard** (1811-1868): French priest; founder of the Congregation of the Blessed Sacrament (men), 1856, and Servants of the Blessed Sacrament (women), 1864; dedicated to Eucharistic apostolate; canonized 1962; Aug. 2*.

**Peter Nolasco** (c. 1189-1258): Born in Langueduc area of present-day France; founded the Mercedarians (Order of Our Lady of Mercy), 1218, in Spain; canonized 1628; Jan. 31.

**Peter of Alcantara** (1499-1562): Spanish Franciscan; mystic; initiated Franciscan reform; confessor of St. Teresa of Jesus (Avila); canonized 1669; Oct. 22 (in U.S.).

**Philip Benizi** (1233-1285): Italian Servite; noted preacher, peacemaker; canonized 1671; Aug. 23.

**Philip Neri** (1515-1595): Italian Religious; founded Congregation of the Oratory; considered a second apostle of Rome because of his mission activity there; canonized 1622; May 26*.

**Philip of Jesus** (1517-157): Mexican Franciscan; martyred at Nagasaki, Japan; canonized 1862; patron of Mexico City; Feb. 6*.

**Pius V** (1504-1572): Pope, 1566-1572; enforced decrees of Council of Trent; organized expedition against Turks resulting in victory at Lepanto; canonized 1712; Apr. 30*.

**Polycarp** (2nd cent.): Bishop of Smyrna; ecclesiastical writer; martyr; Feb. 23*.

**Pontian** (d. c. 235): Pope, 230-235; exiled to Sardinia by the emperor; regarded as a martyr; Aug. 13 (with Hippolytus)*.

**Rafaela Maria Porras y Ayllon** (1850-1925): Spanish Religious; founded the Handmaids of the Sacred Heart, 1877; canonized 1977; Jan. 6.

**Raymond Nonnatus** (d. 1240): Spanish Mercedarian; cardinal; devoted his life to ransoming captives from the Moors; Aug. 31.

**Raymond of Penyafort** (1175-1275): Spanish Dominican; confessor of Gregory IX; systematized and codified canon law, in effect until 1917; master general of Dominicans, 1238; canonized 1601; Jan. 7*.

**Rita of Cascia** (1381-1457): Widow; cloistered Augustinian Religious of Umbria; invoked in impossible and desperate cases; May 22.

**Robert Southwell** (1561-1595): English Jesuit; poet; martyred at Tyburn; canonized 1970, one of the Forty English and Welsh Martyrs; Feb. 21.

**Roch** (1350-1379): French layman; pilgrim; devoted life to care of plague-stricken; widely venerated; invoked against pestilence; Aug. 17.

**Romuald** (951-1027): Italian monk; founded Camaldolese Benedictines; June 19*.

**Rose of Lima** (1586-1617): Peruvian Dominican tertiary; first native-born saint of the New World; canonized 1671; Aug. 23*.

**Scholastica** (d. c. 559): Sister of St. Benedict; regarded as first nun of the Benedictine Order; Feb. 10*.

**Sebastian** (3rd cent.): Roman martyr; traditionally pictured as a handsome youth with arrows; martyred; patron of athletes, archers; Jan. 20*.

**Seven Holy Founders of the Servants of Mary** (Buonfiglio Monaldo, Alexis Falconieri, Benedict dell'Antello, Bartholomew Amidei, Ricovero Uguccione, Gerardino Sostegni, John Buonagiunta Monetti): Florentine youths who founded Servites, 1233, in obedience to a vision; canonized 1888; Feb. 17*.

**Sharbel Makhlouf** (1828-1898): Lebanese Maronite monk-hermit; canonized 1977; Dec. 24.

**Sixtus II and Companions** (d. 258): Sixtus, pope 257-258, and four deacons, martyrs; Aug. 7*.

**Stanislaus** (1030-1079): Polish bishop; martyr; canonized 1253; Apr. 11*.

**Stephen** (d. c. 33): First Christian martyr; chosen by the Apostles as the first of the seven deacons; stoned to death; Dec. 26*.

**Stephen** (975-1038): King; apostle of Hungary; welded Magyars into national unity; canonized 1083; Aug. 16*.

**Sylvester I** (d. 335): Pope 314-335; first ecumenical council held at Nicaea during his pontificate; Dec. 31*.

**Tarcisius** (d. 3rd cent.): Early martyr; according to tradition, was martyred while carrying the Blessed Sacrament to some Christians in prison; patron of first communicants; Aug. 15.

**Teresa Margaret Redi** (1747-1770): Italian

Carmelite; lived life of prayer and austere penance; canonized 1934; Mar. 11.

**Teresa of Jesus Jornet Ibars** (1843-1897): Spanish Religious; founded the Little Sisters of the Abandoned Aged, 1873; canonized 1974; Aug. 26.

**Therese Couderc** (1805-1885): French Religious; foundress of the Religious of Our Lady of the Retreat in the Cenacle, 1827; canonized 1970; Sept. 26.

**Therese of Lisieux** (1873-1897): French Carmelite nun; b. Therese Martin; allowed to enter Carmel at 15, died nine years later of tuberculosis; her "little way" of spiritual perfection became widely known through her spiritual autobiography; despite her obscure life, became one of the most popular saints; canonized 1925; patron of foreign missions; Oct. 1*.

**Thomas Becket** (1118-1170): English martyr; archbishop of Canterbury; chancellor under Henry II; murdered for upholding rights of the Church; canonized 1173; Dec. 29*.

**Thomas More** (1478-1535): English martyr; statesman, chancellor under Henry VIII; author of *Utopia;* opposed Henry's divorce, refused to renounce authority of the papacy; beheaded; canonized 1935; June 22 (with St. John Fisher)*.

**Thorlac** (1133-1193): Icelandic bishop; instituted reforms; although his cult was never officially approved, he was declared patron of Iceland, Jan. 14, 1984; Dec. 23.

**Timothy** (d. c. 97): Bishop of Ephesus; disciple and companion of St. Paul; martyr; Jan. 26*.

**Titus** (d. c. 96): Bishop; companion of St. Paul; recipient of one of Paul's epistles; Jan. 26*.

**Titus Brandsma, Bl.** (1881-1942): Dutch Carmelite priest; professor, scholar, journalist; denounced Nazi persecution of Jews; arrested by Na-zis, Jan. 19, 1942; executed by lethal injection at Dachau, July 26, 1942; beatified 1985; July 26.

**Valentine** (d. 269): Priest, physician; martyred at Rome; legendary patron of lovers; Feb. 14.

**Vicenta Maria Lopez y Vicuna** (1847-1896): Spanish foundress of the Daughters of Mary Immaculate for domestic service; canonized 1975; Dec. 26.

**Vincent** (d. 304): Spanish deacon; martyr; Jan. 22.*

**Vincent de Paul** (1581?-1660): French priest; founder of Congregation of the Mission (Vincentians, Lazarists) and co-founder of Sisters of Charity; declared patron of all charitable organizations and works by Leo XIII; canonized 1737; Sept. 27*.

**Vincent Ferrer** (1350-1418): Spanish Dominican; famed preacher; Apr. 5*.

**Vincent Pallotti** (1795-1850): Italian priest; founded Society of the Catholic Apostolate (Pallottines), 1835; Jan. 22.

**Vincent Strambi** (1745-1824): Italian Passionist; bishop; reformer; canonized 1950; Sept. 25.

**Vincenza Gerosa** (1784-1847): Italian co-foundress of the Sisters of Charity of Lovere; canonized 1950; June 28.

**Vitus** (d.c. 300): Martyr; died in Lucania, southern Italy; regarded as protector of epileptics and those suffering from St. Vitus Dance (chorea); June 15.

**Walburga** (d. 779): English-born Benedictine Religious; belonged to group of nuns who established convents in Germany at the invitation of St. Boniface; abbess of Heidenheim; Feb. 25.

**Wenceslaus** (d. 935): Duke of Bohemia; martyr; patron of Bohemia; Sept. 28*.

**Zita** (1218-1278): Italian maid; noted for charity to poor; patron of domestics; Apr. 27.

# SAINTS—PATRONS AND INTERCESSORS

A patron is a saint who is venerated as a special intercessor before God. Most patrons have been so designated as the result of popular devotion and long-standing custom. In many cases, the fact of existing patronal devotion is clear despite historical obscurity regarding its origin. The Church has made official designation of relatively few patrons; in such cases, the dates of designation are given in parentheses in the list below. The theological background of the patronage of saints includes the dogmas of the Mystical Body of Christ and the Communion of Saints.

Listed below are patron saints of occupations and professions, and saints whose intercession is sought for special needs.

Accountants: Matthew.
Actors: Genesius.
Advertisers: Bernardine of Siena (May 20, 1960).
Alpinists: Bernard of Montjoux (or Menthon) (Aug. 20, 1923).
Altar servers: John Berchmans.
Anesthetists: Rene Goupil.
Animals: Francis of Assisi.
Archers: Sebastian.
Architects: Thomas, Apostle.
Art: Catherine of Bologna.
Artists: Luke, Catherine of Bologna, Bl. Angelico (Feb. 21, 1984).
Astronomers: Dominic.
Athletes: Sebastian.

Authors: Francis de Sales.
Aviators: Our Lady of Loreto (1920), Therese of Lisieux, Joseph of Cupertino.
Bakers: Elizabeth of Hungary, Nicholas.
Bankers: Matthew.
Barbers: Cosmas and Damian, Louis.
Barren women: Anthony of Padua, Felicity.
Basket-makers: Anthony, Abbot.
Beggars: Martin of Tours.
Blacksmiths: Dunstan.
Blind: Odilia, Raphael.
Blood banks: Januarius.
Bodily ills: Our Lady of Lourdes.
Bookbinders: Peter Celestine.

Bookkeepers: Matthew.
Booksellers: John of God.
Boy Scouts: George.
Brewers: Augustine of Hippo, Luke, Nicholas of Myra.
Bricklayers: Stephen.
Brides: Nicholas of Myra.
Brushmakers: Anthony, Abbot.
Builders: Vincent Ferrer.
Butchers: Anthony (Abbot), Luke.
Cabdrivers: Fiacre.
Cabinetmakers: Anne.
Cancer patients: Peregrine.
Canonists: Raymond of Peñafort.
Carpenters: Joseph.
Catechists: Viator, Charles Borromeo, Robert Bellarmine.

Catholic Action: Francis of Assisi (1916).

Chandlers: Ambrose, Bernard of Clairvaux.

Charitable societies: Vincent de Paul (May 12, 1885).

Children: Nicholas of Myra.

Children of Mary: Agnes, Maria Goretti.

Choirboys: Dominic Savio (June 8, 1956), Holy Innocents.

Church: Joseph (Dec. 8, 1870).

Clerics: Gabriel of the Sorrowful Mother.

Communications personnel: Bernardine.

Confessors: Alphonsus Liguori (Apr. 26, 1950), John Nepomucene.

Convulsive children: Scholastica.

Cooks: Lawrence, Martha.

Coopers: Nicholas of Myra.

Coppersmiths: Maurus.

Dairy workers: Brigid.

Deaf: Francis de Sales.

Dentists: Apollonia.

Desperate situations: Gregory of Neocaesarea, Jude Thaddeus, Rita of Cascia.

Dietitians (in hospitals): Martha.

Dyers: Maurice, Lydia.

Dying: Joseph.

Ecologists: Francis of Assisi (Nov. 29, 1979).

Editors: John Bosco.

Emigrants: Frances Xavier Cabrini (Sept. 8, 1950).

Engineers: Ferdinand III.

Epilepsy, Motor Diseases: Vitus, Willibrord.

Eucharistic congresses and societies: Paschal Baylon (Nov. 28, 1897).

Expectant mothers: Raymond Nonnatus, Gerard Majella.

Eye diseases: Lucy.

Falsely accused: Raymond Nonnatus.

Farmers: George, Isidore.

Farriers: John the Baptist.

Firemen: Florian.

Fire prevention: Catherine of Siena.

First communicants: Tarcisius.

Fishermen: Andrew.

Florists: Therese of Lisieux.

Forest workers: John Gualbert.

Foundlings: Holy Innocents.

Fullers: Anastasius the Fuller, James the Less.

Funeral directors: Joseph of Arimathea, Dismas.

Gardeners: Adelard, Tryphon, Fiacre, Phocas.

Glassworkers: Luke.

Goldsmiths: Dunstan, Anastasius.

Gravediggers: Anthony, Abbot.

Greetings: Valentine.

Grocers: Michael.

Hairdressers: Martin de Porres.

Happy meetings: Raphael.

Hatters: Severus of Ravenna, James the Less.

Headache sufferers: Teresa of Jesus (Avila).

Heart patients: John of God.

Hospital administrators: Basil the Great, Frances X. Cabrini.

Hospitals: Camillus de Lellis and John of God (June 22, 1886), Jude Thaddeus.

Housewives: Anne.

Hunters: Hubert, Eustachius.

Infantrymen: Maurice.

Innkeepers: Amand, Martha.

Invalids: Roch.

Jewelers: Eligius, Dunstan.

Journalists: Francis de Sales (Apr. 26, 1923).

Jurists: John Capistran.

Laborers: Isidore, James, John Bosco.

Lawyers: Ivo (Yves Helory), Genesius, Thomas More.

Learning: Ambrose.

Librarians: Jerome.

Lighthouse keepers: Venerius (Mar. 10, 1961).

Locksmiths: Dunstan.

Maids: Zita.

Marble workers: Clement I.

Mariners: Michael, Nicholas of Tolentino.

Medical record librarians: Raymond of Peñafort.

Medical social workers: John Regis.

Medical technicians: Albert the Great.

Mentally ill: Dymphna.

Merchants: Francis of Assisi, Nicholas of Myra.

Messengers: Gabriel.

Metal workers: Eligius.

Military chaplains: John Capistran (Feb. 10, 1984).

Millers: Arnulph, Victor.

Missions, Foreign: Francis Xavier (Mar. 25, 1904), Therese of Lisieux (Dec. 14, 1927).

Missions, Black: Peter Claver (1896, Leo XIII), Benedict the Black.

Missions, Parish: Leonard of Port Maurice (Mar. 17, 1923).

Mothers: Monica.

Motorcyclists: Our Lady of Grace.

Motorists: Christopher, Frances of Rome.

Mountaineers: Bernard of Montjoux (or Menthon).

Musicians: Gregory the Great, Cecilia, Dunstan.

Notaries: Luke, Mark.

Nurses: Camillus de Lellis and John of God (1930, Pius XI), Agatha, Raphael.

Nursing and nursing service: Elizabeth of Hungary, Catherine of Siena.

Orators: John Chrysostom (July 8, 1908).

Organ builders: Cecilia.

Orphans: Jerome Emiliani.

Painters: Luke.

Paratroopers: Michael.

Pawnbrokers: Nicholas.

Pharmacists: Cosmas and Damian, James the Greater.

Pharmacists (in hospitals): Gemma Galgani.

Philosophers: Justin.

Physicians: Pantaleon, Cosmas and Damian, Luke, Raphael.

Pilgrims: James the Greater.

Plasterers: Bartholomew.

Poets: David, Cecilia.

Poison sufferers: Benedict.

Policemen: Michael.

Poor: Lawrence, Anthony of Padua.

Poor souls: Nicholas of Tolentino.

Porters: Christopher.

Possessed: Bruno, Denis.

Postal employees: Gabriel.

Priests: Jean-Baptiste Vianney (Apr. 23, 1929).

Printers: John of God, Augustine of Hippo, Genesius.

Prisoners: Dismas, Joseph Cafasso.

Protector of crops: Ansovinus.

Public relations: Bernardine of Siena (May 20, 1960).

Public relations (of hospitals): Paul, Apostle.

Radiologists: Michael (Jan. 15, 1941).

Radio workers: Gabriel.

Retreats: Ignatius Loyola (July 25, 1922).

Rheumatism: James the Greater.

Saddlers: Crispin and Crispinian.

Sailors: Cuthbert, Brendan, Eulalia, Christopher, Peter Gonzalez, Erasmus, Nicholas.

Scholars: Brigid.

Schools, Catholic: Thomas Aquinas (Aug. 4, 1880), Joseph Calasanz (Aug. 13, 1948).

Scientists: Albert (Aug. 13, 1948).

Sculptors: Four Crowned Martyrs.

Seamen: Francis of Paola.

Searchers of lost articles: Anthony of Padua.

Secretaries: Genesius.

Secular Franciscans: Louis of France, Elizabeth of Hungary.
Seminarians: Charles Borromeo.
Servants: Martha, Zita.
Shoemakers: Crispin and Crispinian.
Sick: Michael, John of God and Camillus de Lellis (June 22, 1886).
Silversmiths: Andronicus.
Singers: Gregory, Cecilia.
Skaters: Lidwina.
Skiers: Bernard of Montjoux (or Menthon).
Social workers: Louise de Marillac (Feb. 12, 1960).
Soldiers: Hadrian, George, Ignatius, Sebastian, Martin of Tours, Joan of Arc.
Speleologists: Benedict.
Stenographers: Genesius, Cassian.
Stonecutters: Clement.
Stonemasons: Stephen.
Students: Thomas Aquinas.
Surgeons: Cosmas and Damian, Luke.
Swordsmiths: Maurice.
Tailors: Homobonus.
Tanners: Crispin and Crispinian, Simon.
Tax collectors: Matthew.
Teachers: Gregory the Great, John Baptist de la Salle (May 15, 1950).
Telecommunications workers: Gabriel (Jan. 12, 1951).
Television: Clare of Assisi (Feb. 14, 1958).
Television workers: Gabriel.
Theologians: Augustine, Alphonsus Liguori.
Throat ailments: Blase.
Travelers: Anthony of Padua, Nicholas of Myra, Christopher, Raphael.
Travel hostesses: Bona (Mar. 2, 1962).
Universities: Blessed Contardo Ferrini.
Vocations: Alphonsus.
Watchmen: Peter of Alcantara.
Weavers: Paul the Hermit, Anastasius the Fuller, Anastasia.
Wine merchants: Amand.
Women in labor: Anne.
Workingmen: Joseph.
Writers: Francis de Sales (Apr. 26, 1923), Lucy.
Yachtsmen: Adjutor.
Young girls: Agnes.
Youth: Aloysius Gonzaga (1729, Benedict XIII; 1926, Pius XI), John Berchmans, Gabriel of the Sorrowful Mother.

## Patron Saints of Places

Albania: Our Lady of Good Counsel.
Alsace: Odilia.
Americas: Our Lady of Guadalupe, Rose of Lima.
Angola: Immaculate Heart of Mary (Nov. 21, 1984).
Argentina: Our Lady of Lujan.
Armenia: Gregory Illuminator.
Asia Minor: John, Evangelist.
Australia: Our Lady Help of Christians.
Belgium: Joseph.
Bohemia: Wenceslaus, Ludmilla.
Bolivia: Our Lady of Copacabana "Virgen de la Candelaria."
Borneo: Francis Xavier.
Brazil: Nossa Senhora de Aparecida, Immaculate Conception, Peter of Alcantara.
Canada: Joseph, Anne.
Chile: James the Greater, Our Lady of Mt. Carmel.
China: Joseph.
Colombia: Peter Claver, Louis Bertran.
Corsica: Immaculate Conception.
Cuba: Our Lady of Charity.
Czechoslovakia: Wenceslaus, John Nepomucene, Procopius.
Denmark: Ansgar, Canute.
Dominican Republic: Our Lady of High Grace, Dominic.
East Indies: Thomas, Apostle.
Ecuador: Sacred Heart.
El Salvador: Our Lady of Peace (Oct. 10, 1966).
England: George.
Equatorial Guinea: Immaculate Conception (May 25, 1986).
Europe: Benedict (1964), Cyril and Methodius, co-patrons (Dec. 31, 1980).
Finland: Henry.
France: Our Lady of the Assumption, Joan of Arc, Therese (May 3, 1944).
Germany: Boniface, Michael.
Gibraltar: Blessed Virgin Mary under title, "Our Lady of Europe" (May 31, 1979).
Greece: Nicholas, Andrew.
Holland: Willibrord.
Hungary: Blessed Virgin, "Great Lady of Hungary," Stephen, King.
Iceland: Thorlac (Jan. 14, 1984).
India: Our Lady of Assumption.
Ireland: Patrick, Brigid and Columba.
Italy: Francis of Assisi, Catherine of Siena.
Japan: Peter Baptist.
Korea: Joseph and Mary, Mother of the Church.

Lesotho: Immaculate Heart of Mary.
Lithuania: Casimir, Bl. Cunegunda.
Luxembourg: Willibrord.
Malta: Paul, Our Lady of the Assumption.
Mexico: Our Lady of Guadalupe.
Monaco: Devota.
Moravia: Cyril and Methodius.
New Zealand: Our Lady Help of Christians.
Norway: Olaf.
Papua New Guinea (including northern Solomon Islands): Michael the Archangel (May 31, 1979).
Paraguay: Our Lady of Assumption (July 13, 1951).
Peru: Joseph (Mar. 19, 1957).
Philippines: Sacred Heart of Mary.
Poland: Casimir, Bl. Cunegunda, Stanislaus of Cracow, Our Lady of Czestochowa.
Portugal: Immaculate Conception, Francis Borgia, Anthony of Padua, Vincent of Saragossa, George.
Russia: Andrew, Nicholas of Myra, Therese of Lisieux.
Scandinavia: Ansgar.
Scotland: Andrew, Columba.
Silesia: Hedwig.
Slovakia: Our Lady of Sorrows.
South Africa: Our Lady of Assumption (Mar. 15, 1952).
South America: Rose of Lima.
Solomon Islands: BVM, under title Most Holy Name of Mary (Sept. 4, 1991).
Spain: James the Greater, Teresa.
Sri Lanka (Ceylon): Lawrence.
Sweden: Bridget, Eric.
Tanzania: Immaculate Conception (Dec. 8, 1964).
United States: Immaculate Conception (1846).
Uruguay: Blessed Virgin Mary under title "La Virgen de los Treinte y Tres" (Nov. 21, 1963).
Venezuela: Our Lady of Coromoto.
Wales: David.
West Indies: Gertrude.

## Emblems, Portrayals of Saints

Agatha: Tongs, veil.
Agnes: Lamb.
Ambrose: Bees, dove, ox, pen.
Andrew: Transverse cross.
Anne, Mother of the Blessed Virgin: Door.
Anthony, Abbot: Bell, hog.
Anthony of Padua: Infant Jesus, bread, book, lily.

Augustine of Hippo: Dove, child, shell, pen.

Barnabas: Stones, ax, lance.

Bartholomew: Knife, flayed and holding his skin.

Benedict: Broken cup, raven, bell, crosier, bush.

Bernard of Clairvaux: Pen, bees, instruments of the Passion.

Bernardine of Siena: Tablet or sun inscribed with IHS.

Blase: Wax, taper, iron comb.

Bonaventure: Communion, ciborium, cardinal's hat.

Boniface: Oak, ax, book, fox, scourge, fountain, raven, sword.

Bridget of Sweden: Book, pilgrim's staff.

Bridget of Kildare: Cross, flame over her head, candle.

Catherine of Ricci: Ring, crown, crucifix.

Catherine of Siena: Stigmata, cross, ring, lily.

Cecilia: Organ.

Charles Borromeo: Communion, coat of arms with word Humilitas.

Christopher: Giant, torrent, tree, Child Jesus on his shoulders.

Clare of Assisi: Monstrance.

Cosmas and Damian: A phial, box of ointment.

Cyril of Alexandria: Blessed Virgin holding the Child Jesus, pen.

Cyril of Jerusalem: Purse, book.

Dominic: Rosary, star.

Edmund the Martyr: Arrow, sword.

Elizabeth of Hungary: Alms, flowers, bread, the poor, a pitcher.

Francis of Assisi: Wolf, birds, fish, skull, the Stigmata.

Francis Xavier: Crucifix, bell, vessel.

Genevieve: Bread, keys, herd, candle.

George: Dragon.

Gertrude: Crown, taper, lily.

Gervase and Protase: Scourge, club, sword.

Gregory I (the Great): Tiara, crosier, dove.

Helena: Cross.

Hilary: Stick, pen, child.

Ignatius of Loyola: Communion, chasuble, book, apparition of Our Lord.

Isidore: Bees, pen.

James the Greater: Pilgrim's staff, shell, key, sword.

James the Less: Square rule, halberd, club.

Jerome: Lion.

John Berchmans: Rule of St. Ignatius, cross, rosary.

John Chrysostom: Bees, dove, pen.

John of God: Alms, a heart, crown of thorns.

John the Baptist: Lamb, head on platter, skin of an animal.

John the Evangelist: Eagle, chalice, kettle, armor.

Josaphat Kuncevyc: Chalice, crown, winged deacon.

Joseph, Spouse of the Blessed Virgin: Infant Jesus, lily, rod, plane, carpenter's square.

Jude: Sword, square rule, club.

Justin Martyr: Ax, sword.

Lawrence: Cross, book of the Gospels, gridiron.

Leander of Seville: A pen.

Liborius: Pebbles, peacock.

Longinus: In arms at foot of the cross.

Louis IX of France: Crown of thorns, nails.

Lucy: Cord, eyes on a dish.

Luke: Ox, book, brush, palette.

Mark: Lion, book.

Martha: Holy water sprinkler, dragon.

Mary Magdalene: Alabaster box of ointment.

Matilda: Purse, alms.

Matthew: Winged man, purse, lance.

Matthias: Lance.

Maurus: Scales, spade, crutch.

Meinrad: Two ravens.

Michael: Scales, banner, sword, dragon.

Monica: Girdle, tears.

Nicholas: Three purses or balls, anchor or boat, child.

Patrick: Cross, harp, serpent, baptismal font, demons, shamrock.

Paul: Sword, book or scroll.

Peter: Keys, boat, cock.

Philip, Apostle: Column.

Philip Neri: Altar, chasuble, vial.

Rita of Cascia: Rose, crucifix, thorn.

Roch: Angel, dog, bread.

Rose of Lima: Crown of thorns, anchor, city.

Sebastian: Arrows, crown.

Simon Stock: Scapular.

Teresa of Jesus (Avila): Heart, arrow, book.

Therese of Lisieux: Roses entwining a crucifix.

Thomas, Apostle: Lance, ax.

Thomas Aquinas: Chalice, monstrance, dove, ox, person trampled under foot.

Vincent (Deacon): Gridiron, boat.

Vincent de Paul: Children.

Vincent Ferrer: Pulpit, cardinal's hat, trumpet, captives.

# ROLE OF MARY IN THE MYSTERY OF CHRIST AND THE CHURCH

*The following excerpts are from Chapter VIII of the Second Vatican Council's Constitution on the Church.*

## I. Preface

Wishing in his supreme goodness and wisdom to effect the redemption of the world, "when the fullness of time came, God sent his Son, born of a woman, ... that we might receive the adoption of sons" (Gal. 4:4-5). "For us men, and for our salvation, came down from heaven, and was incarnate by the Holy Spirit from the Virgin Mary." This divine mystery of salvation is revealed to us and continued in the Church, which the Lord established as his own body. In this Church, adhering to Christ the head and having communion with all his saints, the faithful must also venerate the memory "above all of the glorious and perpetual Virgin Mary. Mother of our God and Lord Jesus Christ." (52)

At the message of the angel, the Virgin Mary received the Word of God in her heart and in her body, and gave Life to the world. Hence, she is acknowledged and honored as being truly the Mother of God and Mother of the Redeemer. Redeemed in an especially sublime manner by reason of the merits of her Son, and united to him by a close and indissoluble tie, she is endowed with the supreme office and dignity of being the Mother of the Son of God. As a result, she is also the favorite daughter of the Father and the temple of the Holy Spirit. Because of this gift of sublime grace, she far surpasses all other creatures, both in heaven and on earth.

At the same time, however, because she belongs to the offspring of Adam, she is one with all human beings in their need for salvation. Indeed, she is "clearly the Mother of the members of Christ ... since she cooperated out of love so that there might be born in the Church the faithful, who are members of Christ their head. Therefore, she is also hailed as a pre-eminent and altogether singular member of the Church, and as the Church's model and excellent exemplar in faith and charity. Taught by the Holy Spirit, the Catholic Church honors her with filial affection and piety as a most beloved Mother. (53)

This sacred synod intends to describe with diligence the role of the Blessed Virgin in the mystery of the Incarnate Word and the Mystical Body. It also wishes to describe the duties of redeemed mankind toward the Mother of God, who is the Mother of Christ and Mother of men, particularly of the faithful.

The synod does not, however, have it in mind to give a complete doctrine on Mary, nor does it wish to decide those questions which have not yet been fully illuminated by the work of theologians. (54)

## II. The Role of the Blessed Virgin in the Economy of Salvation

The Father of mercies willed that the consent of the predestined Mother should precede the Incarnation so that, just as a woman contributed to death, so also a woman should contribute to life. This contrast was verified in outstanding fashion by the Mother of Jesus. She gave to the world that very Life which renews all things, and she was enriched by God with gifts befitting such a role.

It is no wonder, then, that the usage prevailed among the holy Fathers whereby they called the Mother of God entirely holy and free from all stain of sin, fashioned by the Holy Spirit into a kind of new substance and new creature. Adorned from the first instant of her conception with the splendors of an entirely unique holiness, the Virgin of Nazareth is, on God's command, greeted by an angel messenger as "full of grace" (cf. Lk. 1:28). To the heavenly messenger she replies: "Behold the handmaid of the Lord; be it done to me according to thy word" (Lk. 1:38).

By thus consenting to the divine utterance, Mary, a daughter of Adam, became the Mother of Jesus. Embracing God's saving will with a full heart and impeded by no sin, she devoted herself totally as a handmaid of the Lord to the person and work of her Son. In subordination to him and along with him, by the grace of almighty God she served the mystery of redemption.

Rightly, therefore, the holy Fathers see her as used by God not merely in a passive way but as cooperating in the work of human salvation through free faith and obedience. (56)

This union of the Mother with the Son in the work of salvation was manifested from the time of Christ's virginal conception up to his death. It is shown first of all when Mary, arising in haste to go to visit Elizabeth, was greeted by her as blessed because of her belief in the promise of salvation, while the precursor leaped for joy in the womb of his mother (cf. Lk. 1:41-45). This association was shown also at the birth of our Lord, who did not diminish his Mother's virginal integrity but sanctified it, when the Mother of God joyfully showed her first-born Son to the shepherds and the Magi.

When she presented him to the Lord in the temple, making the offering of the poor, she heard Simeon foretelling at the same time that her Son would be a sign of contradiction and that a sword would pierce the Mother's soul, that out of many hearts thoughts might be revealed (cf. Lk. 2:34-35). When the Child Jesus was lost and they had sought him sorrowing, his parents found him in the temple, taken up with things which were his Father's business. They did not understand the reply of the Son. But his Mother, to be sure, kept all these things to be pondered over in her heart (cf. Lk. 2:41-51). (57)

In the public life of Jesus, Mary made significant appearances. This was so even at the very beginning, when she was moved with pity at the marriage feast of Cana, and her intercession brought about the beginning of the miracles by Jesus the Messiah (Cf. Jn. 2:1-11). In the course of her Son's preaching, she received his praise when, in extolling a kingdom beyond the calculations and bonds of flesh and blood, he declared blessed (cf. Mk. 3:35 par.; Lk. 11:27-28) those who heard and kept the word of the Lord as she was faithfully doing (cf. Lk. 2:19, 51).

Thus, the Blessed Virgin advanced in her pilgrimage of faith and loyally persevered in her union with her Son unto the cross. There she stood, in keeping with the divine plan (cf. Jn. 19:25), suffering grievously with her only-begotten Son. There she united herself with a maternal heart to his sacrifice, and lovingly consented to the immolation of this Victim whom she herself had brought forth. Finally, the same Christ Jesus dying on the cross gave her as a mother to his disciple. This he did when he said: "Woman, behold your son" (Jn. 19:26-27). (58)

But since it pleased God not to manifest solemnly the mystery of the salvation of the human race until he poured forth the Spirit promised by Christ, we see the apostles before the day of Pentecost "continuing with one mind in prayer with the women and Mary, the Mother of Jesus, and with his brethren" (Acts 1:14). We see Mary prayerfully imploring the gift of the Spirit, who had already overshadowed her in the Annunciation.

Finally, preserved free from all guilt of original sin, the Immaculate Virgin was taken up body and soul into heavenly glory upon the completion of her earthly sojourn. She was exalted by the Lord as Queen of all, in order that she might be the more thoroughly conformed to her Son, the Lord of lords (cf. Rev. 19:16) and the conqueror of sin and death. (59)

## III. The Blessed Virgin and the Church

We have but one Mediator, as we know from the words of the apostle: "For there is one God, and one Mediator between God and men, himself man, Christ Jesus, who gave himself as a ransom for all" (1 Tim. 2:5-6). The maternal duty of Mary toward men in no way obscures or diminishes this unique mediation of Christ, but rather shows its power. For all the saving influences of the Blessed Virgin on men originate, not from some inner necessity, but from the divine pleasure. They flow forth from the superabundance of the merits of Christ, rest on his mediation, depend entirely on it, and draw all their power from it. In no way do they impede the immediate union of the faithful with Christ. Rather, they foster this union. (60)

In an utterly singular way, she (Mary) cooperated by her obedience, faith, hope and burning charity in the Savior's work of restoring supernatural life to souls. For this reason she is a mother to us in the order of grace. (61)

This maternity of Mary in the order of grace began with the consent which she gave in faith at the Annunciation and which she sustained without wavering beneath the cross. This maternity will last without interruption until the eternal fulfillment of all the elect. For, taken up to heaven, she did not lay aside this saving role, but by her manifold acts of intercession continues to win for us gifts of eternal salvation.

By her maternal charity, Mary cares for the brethren of her Son who still journey on earth surrounded by dangers and difficulties until they are led to their happy fatherland. Therefore, the Blessed Virgin is invoked by the Church under the titles of Advocate, Auxiliatrix, Adjutrix and Mediatrix. These, however, are to be so understood that they neither take away nor add anything to the dignity and efficacy of Christ the one Mediator.

For no creature could ever be classed with the Incarnate Word and Redeemer. But, just as the priesthood of Christ is shared in various ways both by sacred ministers and by the faithful; and as the one goodness of God is in reality communicated diversely to his creatures: so also the unique mediation of the Redeemer does not exclude but rather gives rise among creatures to a manifold cooperation which is but a sharing in this unique source. The Church does not hesitate to profess this subordinate role of Mary. She experiences it continuously and commends it to the hearts of the faithful so that, encouraged by this maternal help, they may more closely adhere to the Mediator and Redeemer. (62)

Through the gift and role of divine maternity, Mary is united with her Son, the Redeemer, and with his singular graces and offices. By these, the Blessed Virgin is also intimately united with the Church. As St. Ambrose taught, the Mother of God is a model of the Church in the matter of faith, hope and charity, and perfect union with Christ. For in the mystery of the Church, herself rightly called Mother and Virgin, the Blessed Virgin stands out in eminent and singular fashion as exemplar of both virginity and motherhood. (63)

In the most holy Virgin, the Church has already reached that perfection whereby she exists without spot or wrinkle (cf. Eph. 5:27). Yet, the followers of Christ still strive to increase in holiness by conquering sin. And so they raise their eyes to Mary who shines forth to the whole community of the elect as a model of the virtues. Devotedly meditating on her and contemplating her in the light of the Word made man, the Church with reverence enters more intimately into the supreme mystery of the Incarnation and becomes ever increasingly like her Spouse.

The Church in her apostolic work looks to her who brought forth Christ, conceived by the Holy Spirit and born of the Virgin, so that through the Church Christ may be born and grow in the hearts of the faithful also. The Virgin Mary in her own life lived as an example of that maternal love by which all should be fittingly animated who cooperate in the apostolic mission of the Church on behalf of the rebirth of men. (65)

## IV. Devotion to the Blessed Virgin in the Church

Mary was involved in the mystery of Christ. As the most holy Mother of God she was, after her Son, exalted by divine grace above all angels and men. Hence, the Church appropriately honors her with special reverence. Indeed, from most ancient times the Blessed Virgin has been venerated under the title of "God-bearer." In all perils and needs, the faithful; have fled prayerfully to her protection. Especially after the Council of Ephesus the cult of the people of God toward Mary wonderfully increased in veneration and love, in invocation and imitation, according to her own prophetic words: "All generations shall call me blessed; because he who is mighty has done great things for me" (Lk. 1:48).

As it has always existed in the Church, this cult (of Mary) is altogether special, Still, it differs essentially from the cult of adoration which is offered to the Incarnate Word, as well as to the Father and the Holy Spirit. Yet, devotion to Mary is most favorable to this supreme cult. The Church has endorsed many forms of piety toward the Mother of God, provided that they were within the limits of sound and orthodox doctrine. These forms have varied according to the circumstances of time and place, and have reflected the diversity of native characteristics and temperament among the faithful. While honoring Christ's Mother, these devotions cause her Son to be rightly known, loved and glorified, and all his commands observed. Through him all things have their beginning (cf. Col. 1: 15-16) and in him "it has pleased (the eternal Father) that … all his fullness should dwell" (Col. 1:19). (66)

This most holy synod deliberately teaches this Catholic doctrine. At the same time, it admonishes all the sons of the Church that the cult, especially the liturgical cult, of the Blessed Virgin, be generously fostered. It charges that practices and exercises of devotion toward her be treasured as recommended by the teaching authority of the Church in the course of centuries.

This synod earnestly exhorts theologians and preachers of the divine word that, in treating of the unique dignity of the Mother of God, they carefully and equally avoid the falsity of exaggeration on the one hand and the excess of narrow-mindedness on the other.

Let the faithful remember, moreover, that true devotion consists neither in fruitless and passing emotion, nor in a certain vain credulity. Rather, it proceeds from the true faith, by which we are led to know the excellence of the Mother of God, and are moved to a filial love toward our Mother and to the imitation of her virtues. (67)

# MOTHER OF THE REDEEMER

*Mater Redemptoris*, Pope John Paul's sixth encyclical letter, is a "reflection on the role of Mary in the mystery of Christ and on her active and exemplary presence in the life of the Church. The letter was published Mar. 25, 1987.

Central to consideration of Mary is the fact that she is the Mother of God (*Theotokos*), since by the power of the Holy Spirit she conceived in her virginal womb and brought into the world Jesus Christ, the Son of God, who is of one being with the Father and the Holy Spirit.

Mary was preserved from original sin in view of her calling to be the Mother of Jesus. She was gifted in grace beyond measure. She fulfilled her role in a unique pilgrimage of faith. She is the Mother of the Church and the spiritual mother of all people.

*The following excerpts from the encyclical are from the English text provided by the Vatican and circulated by the CNS Documentary Service, Origins, Apr. 9, 1987 (Vol. 16, No. 43). Subheads have been added. Quotations are from pertinent documents of the Second Vatican Council.*

## MARY'S PRESENCE IN THE CHURCH

Mary, through the same faith which made her blessed, especially from the moment of the Annunciation, is present in the Church's mission, present in the Church's work of introducing into the world the kingdom of her Son.

This presence of Mary finds as many different expressions in our day just as it did throughout the Church's history. It also has a wide field of action: through the faith and piety of individual believers; through the traditions of Christian families or "domestic churches," of parish and missionary communities, religious institutes and dioceses; through the radiance and attraction of the great shrines where not only individuals or local groups, but sometimes whole nations and societies, even whole continents, seek to meet the Mother of the Lord, the one who is blessed because she believed, is the first among believers, and therefore became the Mother of Emmanuel.

This is the message of the land of Palestine, the spiritual homeland of all Christians, because it was the homeland of the Savior of the world and of his Mother. This is the message of the many churches in Rome and throughout the world which have been raised up in the course of the centuries by the faith of Christians. This is the message of centers like Guadalupe, Lourdes, Fatima and others situated in the various countries. Among them, how could I fail to mention the one in my own native land, Jasna Gora? One could perhaps speak of a specific "geography" of faith and Marian devotion which includes all of these special places of pilgrimage where the people of God seek to meet the Mother of God in order to find, within the radius of the maternal presence of her "who believed," a strengthening of their own faith.

## MARY AND ECUMENISM

"In all of Christ's disciples the Spirit arouses the desire to be peacefully united, in the manner determined by Christ, as one flock under one shepherd." The journey of the Church, especially in our own time, is marked by the sign of ecumenism: Christians are seeking ways to restore that unity which Christ implored from the Father for his disciples on the day before his passion.

Christians must deepen in themselves and each of their communities that "obedience of faith" of which Mary is the first and brightest example.

Christians know that their unity will be truly rediscovered only if it is based on the unity of their faith. They must resolve considerable discrepancies of doctrine concerning the mystery and ministry of the Church, and sometimes also concerning the role of Mary in the work of salvation.

Mary, who is still the model of this pilgrimage, is to lead them to the unity which is willed by their one Lord, and which is so much desired by those who are attentively listening to what "the Spirit is saying to the churches" today.

## A Hopeful Sign

Meanwhile, it is a hopeful sign that these churches and ecclesial communities are finding agreement with the Catholic Church on fundamental points of Christian belief, including matters relating to the Virgin Mary. For they recognize her as the Mother of the Lord and hold that this forms part of our faith in Christ, true God and true man. They look to her who at the foot of the cross accepted as her son the Beloved Disciple (John), the one who in his turn accepted her as his Mother.

On the other hand, I wish to emphasize how profoundly the Catholic Church, the Orthodox Church and the ancient churches of the East feel united by love and praise of the *Theotokos*. Not only "basic dogmas of the Christian faith concerning the Trinity and God's Word made flesh of the Virgin Mary were defined in ecumenical councils held in the East," but also in their liturgical worship "the Eastern Christians pay high tribute, in very beautiful hymns, to Mary ever-Virgin ... God's most holy Mother."

The churches which profess the doctrine of Ephesus proclaim the Virgin as "true Mother of God" since "our Lord Jesus Christ, born of the Father before time began according to his divinity, in the last days he himself, for our sake and for our salvation, was begotten of Mary the Virgin Mother of God according to his humanity." The Greek Fathers and the Byzantine tradition, contemplating the Virgin in the light of the Word made flesh, have sought to penetrate the depth of that bond which unites Mary, as the Mother of God, to Christ and the Church. The Virgin is a permanent presence in the whole reality of the salvific mystery.

## MARIAN MEDIATION

The Church knows and teaches with St. Paul that there is only one mediator: "For there is one God, and there is one mediator between God and men, the man Christ Jesus, who gave himself as a ransom for all" (1 Tm. 2:5-6). "The maternal role of Mary toward people in no way obscures or diminishes the unique mediation of Christ, but rather shows its power." It is mediation in Christ.

The Church knows and teaches that "all the saving influences of the Blessed Virgin on mankind originate ... from the divine pleasure. They flow forth from the superabundance of the merits of Christ, rest on his mediation, depend entirely on it and draw all their power from it. In no way do they impede the immediate union of the faithful with Christ. Rather, they foster this union." This saving influence is sustained by the Holy Spirit, who, just as he overshadowed the Virgin Mary when he began in her the divine motherhood, in a similar way constantly sustains her solicitude for the brothers and sisters of her Son.

### Mediation and Motherhood

In effect, Mary's mediation is intimately linked with her motherhood. It possesses a specifically maternal character, which distinguishes it from the mediation of the other creatures who in various and always subordinate ways share in the one mediation of Christ, although her own mediation is also a shared mediation. In fact, while it is true that "no creature could ever be classed with the Incarnate Word and Redeemer," at the same time "the unique mediation of the Redeemer does not exclude but rather gives rise among creatures a manifold cooperation which is but a sharing in this unique source." And thus "the one goodness of God is in reality communicated diversely to his creatures."

### Subordinate Mediation

The teaching of the Second Vatican Council presents the truth of Mary's mediation as "a sharing in the one unique source that is the mediation of Christ himself." Thus we read: "The Church does not hesitate to profess this subordinate role of Mary. She experiences it continuously and commends it to the hearts of the faithful so that, encouraged by this maternal help, they may more closely adhere to the Mediator and Redeemer."

This role is at the same time special and extraordinary. It flows from her divine motherhood and can be understood and lived in faith only on the basis of the full truth of this motherhood. Since by virtue of

divine election Mary is the earthly Mother of the Father's consubstantial Son and his "generous companion" in the work of redemption, "she is a Mother to us in the order of grace." This role constitutes a real dimension of her presence in the saving mystery of Christ and the Church.

Mary is honored in the Church "with special reverence. Indeed, from most ancient times the Blessed Virgin Mary has been venerated under the title of 'God-bearer.' In all perils and needs, the faithful have fled prayerfully to her protection." This cult is altogether special; it bears in itself and expresses the profound link which exists between the Mother of Christ and the Church. As Virgin and Mother, Mary remains for the Church a "permanent model." It can therefore be said that, especially under this aspect, namely, as a model or rather as a "figure," Mary, present in the mystery of Christ, remains constantly present also in the mystery of the Church. For the Church too is "called mother and virgin," and these names have a profound biblical and theological justification.

### MARY AND WOMEN

This Marian dimension of Christian life takes on special importance in relation to women and their status. In fact, femininity has a unique relationship with the Mother of the Redeemer, a subject which can be studied in greater depth elsewhere. Here I simply wish to note that the figure of Mary of Nazareth sheds light on womanhood as such by the very fact that God, in the sublime event of the incarnation of his Son, entrusted himself to the ministry, the free and active ministry, of a woman.

It can thus be said that women, by looking to Mary, find in her the secret of living their femininity with dignity and of achieving their own true advancement. In the light of Mary, the Church sees in the face of women the reflection of a beauty which mirrors the loftiest sentiments of which the human heart is capable: the self-offering totality of love; the strength that is capable of bearing the greatest sorrows; limitless fidelity and tireless devotion to work; the ability to combine penetrating intuition with words of support and encouragement.

## APPARITIONS OF THE BLESSED VIRGIN MARY

*Only seven of the best known apparitions of the Blessed Virgin Mary are described briefly below.*

The sites of the following apparitions have become shrines and centers of pilgrimage. Miracles of the moral and physical orders have been reported as occurring at these places and/or in connection with related practices of prayer and penance.

**Banneux,** near Liege, Belgium: Mary appeared eight times between Jan. 15 and Mar. 2, 1933, to an 11-year-old peasant girl, Mariette Beco, in a garden behind the family cottage in Banneux, near Liege. She called herself the Virgin of the Poor, and has since been venerated as Our Lady of the Poor, the Sick, and the Indifferent. A small chapel was built by a spring near the site of the apparitions and was blessed Aug. 15, 1933. Approval of devotion to Our

Lady of Banneux was given in 1949 by Bishop Louis J. Kerkhofs of Liege, and a statue of that title was solemnly crowned in 1956.

**Beauraing,** Belgium: Mary appeared 33 times between Nov. 29, 1932, and Jan. 3, 1933, to five children in the garden of a convent school in Beauraing. A chapel, which became a pilgrimage center, was erected on the spot. Reserved approval of devotion to Our Lady of Beauraing was given Feb. 2, 1943, and final approbation July 2, 1949, by Bishop Charue of Namur (d. 1977).

**Fatima,** Portugal: Mary appeared six times between May 13 and Oct. 13, 1917, to three children (Lucia dos Santos, 10, who is now a Carmelite nun; Francisco Marto, 9, who died in 1919; and his sister Jacinta, 7, who died in 1920) in a field called Cova da Iria near Fatima, north of Lisbon. She recommended frequent recitation of the Rosary; urged works of mortification for the conversion of sinners; called for devotion to herself under the title of her Immaculate Heart; asked that the people of Russia be consecrated to her under this title, and that the faithful make a Communion of reparation on the first Saturday of each month.

The apparitions were declared worthy of belief in October, 1930, after a seven-year canonical investigation, and devotion to Our Lady of Fatima was authorized under the title of Our Lady of the Rosary. In October, 1942, Pius XII consecrated the world to Mary under the title of her Immaculate Heart. Ten years later, in the first apostolic letter addressed directly to the peoples of Russia, he consecrated them in a special manner to Mary.

Fatima, with its sanctuary and basilica, ranks with Lourdes as the greatest of modern Marian shrines. (See First Saturday Devotion.)

**Guadalupe,** Mexico: Mary appeared four times in 1531 to an Indian, Juan Diego (declared Blessed in 1990), on Tepeyac hill outside of Mexico City, and instructed him to tell Bishop Zumarraga of her wish that a church be built there. The bishop complied with the request about two years later after being convinced of the genuineness of the apparition by the evidence of a miraculously painted life-size figure of the Virgin on the mantle of the Indian. The mantle bearing the picture has been preserved and is enshrined in the Basilica of Our Lady of Guadalupe, which has a long history as a center of devotion and pilgrimage in Mexico. The shrine church, originally dedicated in 1709 and subsequently enlarged, has the title of basilica.

Benedict XIV, in a decree issued in 1754, authorized a Mass and Office under the title of Our Lady of Guadalupe for celebration on Dec. 12, and named Mary the patroness of New Spain. Our Lady of Guadalupe was designated patroness of Latin America by St. Pius X in 1910 and patroness of the Americas by Pius XII in 1945.

**La Salette,** France: Mary appeared as a sorrowing and weeping figure Sept. 19, 1846, to two peasant children, Melanie Matthieu, 15, and Maximin Giraud, 11, at La Salette in southern France. The message she confided to them, regarding the necessity of penance, was communicated to Pius IX in 1851 and has since been known as the "secret" of La Salette. Bishop de Bruillard of Grenoble declared in 1851 that the apparition was credible, and devotion to Mary under the title of Our Lady of La Salette was authorized. The devotion has been confirmed by popes since the time of Pius IX, and a Mass and office with this title were authorized in 1942. The shrine church was given the title of minor basilica in 1879.

**Lourdes,** France: Mary, identifying herself as the Immaculate Conception, appeared 18 times between Feb. 11 and July 16, 1858, to 14-year-old Bernadette Soubirous (canonized in 1933) at the grotto of Massabielle near Lourdes in southern France. Her message concerned the necessity of prayer and penance for the conversion of peoples. Mary's request that a chapel be built at the grotto and spring was fulfilled in 1862 after four years of rigid examination established the credibility of the apparitions. Devotion under the title of Our Lady of Lourdes was authorized later, and a Feb. 11 feast commemorating the apparitions was instituted by Leo XIII. St. Pius X extended this feast throughout the Church in 1907.

The Church of Notre Dame was made a basilica in 1870, and the Church of the Rosary was built later. The underground Church of St. Pius X, with a capacity of 20,000 persons, was consecrated Mar. 25, 1958. Plans were announced in 1994 for renovation and reconstruction of the Lourdes sanctuary.

**Our Lady of the Miraculous Medal,** France: Mary appeared three times in 1830 to Catherine Laboure (canonized in 1947) in the chapel of the motherhouse of the Daughters of Charity of St. Vincent de Paul, Rue de Bac, Paris. She commissioned Catherine to have made the medal of the Immaculate Conception, now known as the Miraculous Medal, and to spread devotion to her under this title. In 1832, the medal was struck according to the model revealed to Catherine.

# CRITERIA OF APPARITIONS

These were the subjects of a series of articles published early in 1990 in *La Civilta Cattolica,* the influential Jesuit periodical. Father Giandomenico Mucci, the author, said the articles were not specifically written with Medjugorje in mind, but that many of the criteria could be applied to that case.

Discernment is necessary because of the "great dangers" to spiritual life posed by the "enthusiastic, acritical and naive acceptance of such phenomena," he said. He cited an estimate that three-fourths of private "revelations" are illusory.

Among the traditional criteria of an apparition's authenticity, he cited the following.

• While God can choose anyone, even public sinners, for visions or apparitions, they should show spiritual progress afterward. The purpose of such revelations, after all, is to help the person grow in grace.

• To aid in discernment, visionaries need spiritual directors, "a species that cannot be improvised and which today is painfully missing."

• Spiritual directors should never push seers to ask questions about people during apparitions. This is mere "childishness."

• The apparitions should "never produce any sentiment of contempt toward anyone."

• Authentic texts of the revelation must be procured, without corrections or amendments.

• "Predictions that do not come true or are continually postponed do not speak in favor of their divine origin."

• Revelations are suspect when they aim to settle theological or other disputes.

• "In giving visions and revelations, the Lord does not intend to do archeological or historical work in front of the seer."

Father Mucci was skeptical about Medjugorje. (See separate article.)

# EASTERN CATHOLIC CHURCHES

The Second Vatican Council, in its *Decree on Eastern Catholic Churches*, stated the following points regarding Eastern heritage, patriarchs, sacraments and worship.

**Venerable Churches:** The Catholic Church holds in high esteem the institutions of the Eastern Churches, their liturgical rites, ecclesiastical traditions, and Christian way of life. For, distinguished as they are by their venerable antiquity, they are bright with that tradition which was handed down from the Apostles through the Fathers, and which forms part of the divinely revealed and undivided heritage of the universal Church (No. 1).

That Church, Holy and Catholic, which is the Mystical Body of Christ, is made up of the faithful who are organically united in the Holy Spirit through the same faith, the same sacraments, and the same government and who, combining into various groups held together by a hierarchy, form separate Churches or rites. It is the mind of the Catholic Church that each individual Church or rite retain its traditions whole and entire, while adjusting its way of life to the various needs of time and place (No. 2).

Such individual Churches, whether of the East or of the West, although they differ somewhat among themselves in what are called rites (that is, in liturgy, ecclesiastical discipline, and spiritual heritage) are, nevertheless, equally entrusted to the pastoral guidance of the Roman Pontiff, the divinely appointed successor of St. Peter in supreme government over the universal Church. They are consequently of equal dignity, so that none of them is superior to the others by reason of rite (No. 3).

**Eastern Heritage:** Each and every Catholic, as also the baptized of every non-Catholic Church or community who enters into the fullness of Catholic communion, should everywhere retain his proper rite, cherish it, and observe it to the best of his ability (No. 4).

The Churches of the East, as much as those of the West, fully enjoy the right, and are in duty bound, to rule themselves. Each should do so according to its proper and individual procedures (No. 5).

All Eastern rite members should know and be convinced that they can and should always preserve their lawful liturgical rites and their established way of life, and that these should not be altered except by way of an appropriate and organic development (No. 6)

**Patriarchs:** The institution of the patriarchate has existed in the Church from the earliest times and was recognized by the first ecumenical Synods.

By the name Eastern Patriarch is meant the bishop who has jurisdiction over all bishops (including metropolitans), clergy, and people of his own territory or rite, in accordance with the norms of law and without prejudice to the primacy of the Roman Pontiff (No. 7).

Though some of the patriarchates of the Eastern Churches are of later origin than others, all are equal in patriarchal dignity. Still the honorary and lawfully established order of precedence among them is to be preserved (No. 8).

In keeping with the most ancient tradition of the Church, the Patriarchs of the Eastern Churches are to be accorded exceptional respect, since each presides over his patriarchate as father and head.

This sacred Synod, therefore, decrees that their rights and privileges should be re-established in accord with the ancient traditions of each Church and the decrees of the ecumenical Synods.

The rights and privileges in question are those which flourished when East and West were in union, though they should be somewhat adapted to modern conditions.

The Patriarchs with their synods constitute the superior authority for all affairs of the patriarchate, including the right to establish new eparchies and to nominate bishops of their rite within the territorial bounds of the patriarchate, without prejudice to the inalienable right of the Roman Pontiff to intervene in individual cases (No. 9).

What has been said of Patriarchs applies as well, under the norm of law, to major archbishops, who preside over the whole of some individual Church or rite (No. 10).

**Sacraments:** This sacred Ecumenical Synod endorses and lauds the ancient discipline of the sacraments existing in the Eastern Churches, as also the practices connected with their celebration and administration (No. 12).

With respect to the minister of holy chrism (confirmation), let that practice be fully restored which existed among Easterners in most ancient times. Priests, therefore, can validly confer this sacrament, provided they use chrism blessed by a Patriarch or bishop (No. 13).

In conjunction with baptism or otherwise, all Eastern-Rite priests can confer this sacrament validly on all the faithful of any rite, including the Latin; licitly, however, only if the regulations of both common and particular law are observed. Priests of the Latin rite, to the extent of the faculties they enjoy for administering this sacrament, can confer it also on the faithful of Eastern Churches, without prejudice to rite. They do so licitly if the regulations of both common and particular law are observed (No. 14).

The faithful are bound on Sundays and feast days to attend the divine liturgy or, according to the regulations or custom of their own rite, the celebration of the Divine Praises. That the faithful may be able to satisfy their obligation more easily, it is decreed that this obligation can be fulfilled from the Vespers of the vigil to the end of the Sunday or the feast day (No. 15).

Because of the everyday intermingling of the communicants of diverse Eastern Churches in the same Eastern region or territory, the faculty for hearing confession, duly and unrestrictedly granted by his proper bishop to a priest of any rite, is applicable to the entire territory of the grantor, also to the places and the faithful belonging to any other rite in the same territory, unless an Ordinary of the place explicitly decides otherwise with respect to the places pertaining to his rite (No. 16).

This sacred Synod ardently desires that where it has fallen into disuse the office of the permanent diaconate be restored. The legislative authority of each individual church should decide about the subdiaconate and the minor orders (No. 17).

By way of preventing invalid marriages between Eastern Catholics and baptized Eastern non-Catholics, and in the interests of the permanence and sanctity of marriage and of domestic harmony, this sacred Synod decrees that the canonical 'form' for the celebration of such marriages obliges only for lawfulness. For their validity, the presence of a sacred minister suffices, as long as the other requirements of law are honored (No. 18).

**Worship:** Henceforth, it will be the exclusive right of an ecumenical Synod or the Apostolic See to establish, transfer, or suppress feast days common to all the Eastern Churches. To establish, transfer, or suppress feast days for any of the individual Churches is within the competence not only of the Apostolic See but also of a patriarchal or archiepiscopal synod, provided due consideration is given to the entire region and to other individual Churches (No. 19).

Until such time as all Christians desirably concur on a fixed day for the celebration of Easter, and with a view meantime to promoting unity among the Christians of a given area or nation, it is left to the Patriarchs or supreme authorities of a place to reach a unanimous agreement, after ascertaining the views of all concerned, on a single Sunday for the observance of Easter (No. 20).

With respect to rules concerning sacred seasons, individual faithful dwelling outside the area or territory of their own rite may conform completely to the established custom of the place where they live. When members of a family belong to different rites, they are all permitted to observe sacred seasons according to the rules of any one of these rites (No. 21).

From ancient times the Divine Praises have been held in high esteem among all Eastern Churches. Eastern clerics and religious should celebrate these Praises as the laws and customs of their own traditions require. To the extent they can, the faithful too should follow the example of their forebears by assisting devoutly at the Divine Praises (No. 22).

## Restoration of Ancient Practices

An "Instruction for the Application of the Liturgical Prescriptions of the Code of Canons of the Eastern Churches" was published in Italian by the Congregation for Eastern-Rite Churches in January, 1996. Msgr. Alan Detscher, executive director of the U.S. bishops' Secretariat for the Liturgy, said it was the first instruction on liturgical renewal of the Eastern Catholic Churches since the Second Vatican Council (1962-65).

# RITES, JURISDICTIONS AND FAITHFUL OF EASTERN CHURCHES

## Introduction

The Catholic Church originated in Palestine, whence it spread to other regions of the world where certain places became key centers of Christian life with great influence on the local churches in their respective areas. Such centers were Jerusalem, Alexandria, Antioch and Constantinople in the East, and Rome in the West. The eastern Mother Churches, with rites bearing their names, were Alexandrian, Antiochene, Armenian, Byzantine and Chaldean. The usages of these churches expressed the one faith in different ways in theology, liturgy, hierarchy and governance, tradition and culture. Hence, the different rites.

The main lines of Eastern Church patriarchal organization and usages were drawn before the Roman Empire became two empires, East (Byzantine) and West (Roman), in 292. Eastern Church members, originally within the boundaries of the Eastern Empire, eventually spread to other parts of the world where they have continued to maintain their distinctive religious identity and heritage on a par with the faithful of Roman (Latin) rite.

Most of the Eastern Churches now in communion with the Holy See were at some time in the past separated from it because of developments and events connected with the Schism of 1054.

## Statistics

(Principal source: *Annuario Pontificio, 1996.*)

These statistics are for Eastern-rite jurisdictions only, and do not include Eastern-rite Catholics under the jurisdiction of Roman-rite bishops. Some of the figures reported are only approximate. Some of the jurisdictions listed were long inactive because of government suppression.

## Alexandrian

Called the Liturgy of St. Mark, the Alexandrian Rite was modified by the Copts and Melkites, and contains elements of the Byzantine Rite of St. Basil and the liturgies of Sts. Mark, Cyril and Gregory of Nazianzen. The liturgy is substantially that of the Coptic Church, which is divided into two branches — the Coptic or Egyptian, and the Ethiopian or Abyssinian. The churches of this rite are:

COPTIC: Jurisdictions (located in Egypt): patriarchate of Alexandria, five dioceses; 192,044. Copts resumed communion with Rome about 1741; situated in Egypt, the Near East; liturgical languages are Coptic, Arabic.

ETHIOPIAN: Jurisdictions (located in Ethiopia and Eritrea): one metropolitan, five dioceses; 138,731. Ethiopians resumed communion with Rome in 1846; situated in Ethiopia, Eritrea, Jerusalem, Somalia; liturgical language is Geez.

## Antiochene

This is the source of more derived rites than any of the other parent rites. Its origin can be traced to the Eighth Book of the *Apostolic Constitutions* and to the Liturgy of St. James of Jerusalem, which ultimately spread throughout the whole patriarchate and displaced older forms based on the *Apostolic Constitutions*. The churches of this rite are:

MALANKAR: Jurisdictions (located in India): one metropolitan, two dioceses; 314,476. Malankarese resumed communion with Rome in 1930; situated in India, North America; liturgical languages are Syriac, Malayalam.

MARONITE: Jurisdictions (located in Lebanon, Cyprus, Egypt, Syria, U.S., Argentina, Brazil, Australia, Canada, Mexico): patriarchate of Antioch, 22 archdioceses and dioceses, one patriarchal vicariate; 2,998,006. Where no special jurisdictions exist, they are under jurisdiction of local Roman-rite bishops. United to the Holy See since the time of their founder, St. Maron; have no counterparts among the separated Eastern Christians: situated throughout the world: liturgical languages are Syriac, Arabic.

SYRIAN: Jurisdictions (located in Lebanon, Iraq, Egypt, Syria and the United States (for Canada and the U.S.): patriarchate of Antioch, two metropolitans, seven archdioceses and dioceses, three patriarchal vicariates; 108,665. Syrians resumed communion with Rome in 1781; situated in Asia, Africa, the Americas, Australia; liturgical languages are Syriac, Arabic.

## Armenian

Substantially, although using a different language, this is the Greek Liturgy of St. Basil; it is considered an older form of the Byzantine Rite, and incorporates some modifications from the Antiochene Rite. The church of this rite is:

ARMENIAN, exclusively: Jurisdictions (located in Lebanon, Iran, Iraq, Egypt, Syria, Turkey, Ukraine, France, Greece, Romania, Armenia (for Eastern Europe), Argentina (eparchy and exarchate for Latin America, including Mexico), and the United States (for Canada and the U.S.): patriarchate of Cilicia, 10 archdioceses and dioceses, two patriarchal exarchates, two apostolic exarchates, three ordinariates; 302,150. Armenians resumed communion with Rome during the time of the Crusades; situated in the Near East, Europe, Africa, the Americas, Australasia: liturgical language is Classical Armenian.

## Byzantine

Based on the Rite of St. James of Jerusalem and the churches of Antioch, and reformed by Sts. Basil and John Chrysostom, the Byzantine Rite is proper to the Church of Constantinople. (The city was called Byzantium before Constantine changed its name; the modern name is Istanbul.) It is now used by the majority of Eastern Catholics and by the Eastern Orthodox Church (which is not in union with Rome). It is, after the Roman, the most widely used rite. The churches of this rite are:

ALBANIAN: Jurisdiction (located in Albania): one apostolic administration. Albanians resumed communion with Rome about 1628; situated in Albania; liturgical language is Albanian.

BELARUSSIAN (formerly Byelorussian, also known as White Russian): Belarussians resumed communion with Rome in the 17th century; situated in Europe, the Americas, Australia; liturgical language is Old Slavonic.

BULGARIAN: Jurisdiction (located in Bulgaria): one apostolic exarchate; 20,000. Bulgarians resumed communion with Rome about 1861; situated in Bulgaria; liturgical language is Old Slavonic.

EPARCHY OF KRIZEVCI: Jurisdiction (located in Croatia): one diocese; 48,970. Resumed communion with Rome in 1611; situated in Croatia, the Americas; liturgical language is Old Slavonic.

GREEK: Jurisdictions (located in Greece and Turkey): two exarchates; 2,350. Greeks resumed communion with Rome in 1829; situated in Greece, Asia Minor, Europe; liturgical language is Greek.

HUNGARIAN: Jurisdictions (located in Hungary): one diocese and one exarchate: 278,750. Descendants of Ruthenians who resumed communion with Rome in 1646; situated in Hungary, the rest of Europe, the Americas; liturgical languages are Greek, Hungarian, English.

ITALO-ALBANIAN: Jurisdictions (located in Italy): two dioceses, one abbacy; 61,608. Italo-Albanians were never separated from Rome; situated in Italy, Sicily, the Americas; liturgical languages are Greek, Italo-Albanian.

MELKITE (GREEK MELKITE): Jurisdictions (located in Syria, Lebanon, Jordan, Israel, U.S., Brazil, Venezuela, Canada, Australia, Mexico): patriarchate of Antioch (with patriarchal vicariates in Egypt, Sudan, Jerusalem, Iraq and Kuwait), 19 archdioceses and dioceses, one exarchate; 1,111,975. Melkites resumed communion with Rome during the time of the Crusades, but definitive reunion did not take place until early in the 18th century; situated in the Middle East, Asia, Africa, Europe, the Americas, Australia; liturgical languages are Greek, Arabic, English, Portuguese, Spanish.

ROMANIAN: Jurisdictions (located in Romania and U.S.): one metropolitan, five dioceses; 1,544,400. Romanians resumed communion with Rome in 1697; situated in Romania, the rest of Europe, the Americas; liturgical language is Modern Romanian.

RUSSIAN: Jurisdictions (located in Russia and China): two exarchates. Russians resumed communion with Rome about 1905; situated in Europe, the Americas, Australia, China; liturgical language is Old Slavonic.

RUTHENIAN, or CARPATHO-RUSSIAN (Rusin): Jurisdictions (located in Ukraine and the U.S.): one metropolitan, four dioceses; 421,122. Ruthenians resumed communion with Rome in the Union of Brest-Litovsk, 1596, and the Union of Uzhorod, Apr. 24, 1646; situated in Europe, the Americas, Australia; liturgical languages are Old Slavonic, English.

SLOVAK: Jurisdictions (located in Slovakia and Canada): two dioceses; 233,533.

UKRAINIAN, or GALICIAN RUTHENIAN: Jurisdictions (located in Ukraine, Poland, the U.S., Canada, England, Australia, Germany, France, Brazil, Argentina): major archbishopric of Lviv, two metropolitans, 16 dioceses, three apostolic exarchates; 5,081,365. Ukrainians resumed communion with Rome about 1595; situated in Europe, the Americas, Australasia; liturgical languages are Old Slavonic and Ukrainian.

## Chaldean

This rite, listed as separate and distinct by the Congregation for the Oriental Churches, was derived from the Antiochene Rite. The churches of this rite are:

CHALDEAN: Jurisdictions (located in Iraq, Iran, Lebanon, Egypt, Syria, Turkey, U.S.): patriarchate of Babylonia, 19 archdioceses and dioceses; 316,396. There is a patriarchal exarch for Jerusalem. Chaldeans, descendants of the Nestorians, resumed communion with Rome in 1692; situated throughout the Middle East, in Europe, Africa, the Americas; liturgical languages are Syriac, Arabic.

SYRO-MALABAR: Jurisdictions (located in India): major archbishopric of Ernakulam-Angamaly (1993), three metropolitans, 17 dioceses; 3,206,503. Descended from the St. Thomas Christians of India; liturgical languages are Syriac and Malayalam.

## EASTERN JURISDICTIONS

For centuries Eastern Churches were identifiable with a limited number of nationality and language groups in certain countries of the Middle East, Eastern Europe, Asia and Africa. The persecution of religion in the former Soviet Union since 1917 and in communist-controlled countries for more than 40 years following World War II — in addition to decimating and destroying the Church in those places — resulted in the emigration of many Eastern-Rite Catholics from their homelands. This forced emigration, together with voluntary emigration, has led to the spread of Eastern Churches to many other countries.

### Europe

(Bishop Krikor Ghabroyan, of the Armenian Eparchy of Sainte-Croix-de-Paris, France, is apostolic visitator for Armenian Catholics in Western Europe who do not have their own bishop. Bishop Youssef Ibrahim Sarraf of Cairo of the Chaldeans is apostolic visitator for Chaldeans in Europe. Bishop Joseph Khoury, an official of the Congregation for the Oriental Churches, is apostolic visitator for Maronites in Western and Northern Europe.)

ALBANIA: Byzantine Rite, apostolic administration.

AUSTRIA: Byzantine Rite, ordinariate.

BULGARIA: Byzantine Rite (Bulgarians), apostolic exarchate.

CROATIA: Byzantine Rite, eparchy.

FRANCE: Byzantine Rite (Ukrainians), apostolic exarchate.

Armenian Rite, eparchy (1986).

Ordinariate for all other Eastern-Rite Catholics.

GERMANY: Byzantine Rite (Ukrainians), apostolic exarchate.

GREAT BRITAIN: Byzantine Rite (Ukrainians), apostolic exarchate.

GREECE: Byzantine Rite, apostolic exarchate.

Armenian Rite, ordinariate.

HUNGARY: Byzantine Rite (Hungarians), eparchy, apostolic exarchate.

ITALY: Byzantine Rite (Italo-Albanians), two eparchies, one abbacy.

POLAND: Byzantine Rite (Ukrainian), eparchy.

Ordinariate for all other Eastern-Rite Catholics.

ROMANIA: Byzantine Rite (Romanians), metropolitan, four eparchies.

Armenian Rite, ordinariate.

RUSSIA: Byzantine Rite (Russians), apostolic exarchate (for Byzantine-rite Catholics in Moscow).

SLOVAKIA: Byzantine Rite (Slovakians and other Byzantine-Rite Catholics), eparchy.

UKRAINE: Armenian Rite, archeparchy.

Byzantine Rite (Ruthenians), eparchy; (Ukrainians), major archbishopric, five eparchies.

### Asia

ARMENIA: Armenian Rite, ordinariate (for Armenians of Eastern Europe).

CHINA: Byzantine Rite (Russians), apostolic exarchate.

CYPRUS: Antiochene Rite (Maronites), archeparchy.

INDIA: Antiochene Rite (Malankarese), metropolitan see, two eparchies.

Chaldean Rite (Syro-Malabarese), major archbishopric (1993), three metropolitan sees (1995), 17 eparchies.

IRAN: Chaldean Rite (Chaldeans), two metropolitan sees, one archeparchy, one eparchy.

Armenian Rite, eparchy.

IRAQ: Antiochene Rite (Syrians), two archeparchies.

Byzantine Rite (Greek-Melkites), patriarchal exarchate.

Chaldean Rite (Chaldeans), patriarchate, two metropolitan sees, eight archeparchies and eparchies.

Armenian Rite, archeparchy.

ISRAEL (includes Jerusalem): Antiochene Rite (Syrians), patriarchal exarchate; (Maronites), patriarchal exarchate.

Byzantine Rite (Greek-Melkites), archeparchy, patriarchal exarchate.

Chaldean Rite (Chaldeans), patriarchal exarchate.

Armenian Rite, patriarchal exarchate.

JORDAN: Byzantine Rite (Greek-Melkites), archeparchy.

KUWAIT: Byzantine Rite (Greek-Melkites), patriarchal exarchate.

LEBANON: Antiochene Rite (Maronites), patriarchate, ten archeparchies and eparchies; (Syrians), patriarchate, patriarchal exarchate.

Byzantine Rite (Greek-Melkites), two metropolitan and five archeparchal sees.

Chaldean Rite (Chaldeans), eparchy.

Armenian Rite, patriarchate, eparchy.

SYRIA: Antiochene Rite (Maronites), two archeparchies, one eparchy; (Syrians), two metropolitan and two archeparchal sees.

Byzantine Rite (Greek-Melkites), patriarchate, four metropolitan sees, one archeparchy.

Chaldean Rite (Chaldeans), eparchy.

Armenian Rite, archeparchy, eparchy, patriarchal exarchate.

TURKEY (Europe and Asia): Antiochene Rite (Syrians), patriarchal exarchate.

Byzantine Rite (Greeks), apostolic exarchate.

Chaldean Rite (Chaldeans), one archeparchy.

Armenian Rite, archeparchy.

### Oceania

AUSTRALIA: Byzantine Rite (Ukrainians), eparchy; (Greek-Melkites), eparchy (1987).

Antiochene Rite (Maronites), eparchy.

### Africa

EGYPT: Alexandrian Rite (Copts), patriarchate, five eparchies.

Antiochene Rite (Maronites), eparchy; (Syrians), eparchy.

Byzantine Rite (Greek-Melkites), patriarchal exarchate.

Chaldean Rite (Chaldeans), eparchy.

Armenian Rite, eparchy.

ERITREA: Alexandrian Rite (Ethiopians), three eparchies.

ETHIOPIA: Alexandrian Rite (Ethiopians), metropolitan see, one eparchy.

SUDAN: Byzantine Rite (Greek-Melkites), patriarchal vicariate.

## North America

CANADA: Byzantine Rite (Ukrainians), one metropolitan, four eparchies; (Slovaks), eparchy; (Greek-Melkites), eparchy.

Armenian Rite, apostolic exarchate for Canada and the U.S. (New York is see city).

Antiochene Rite (Maronites), eparchy.

UNITED STATES: Antiochene Rite (Maronites), two eparchies; (Syrians), eparchy (1995).

Byzantine Rite (Ukrainians), one metropolitan see, three eparchies; (Ruthenians), one metropolitan see, three eparchies; (Greek-Melkites), eparchy; (Romanians), eparchy; (Belarussians), apostolic visitator.

Armenian Rite, apostolic exarchate for Canada and U.S. (New York is see city).

Chaldean Rite, eparchy.

Other Eastern-Rite Catholics are under the jurisdiction of local Roman-Rite bishops. (See Eastern-Rite Catholics in the United States.)

MEXICO: Byzantine Rite (Greek-Melkites), eparchy.

Antiochene Rite (Maronites), eparchy (1995).

## South America

Armenian-Rite Catholics in Latin America (including Mexico and excluding Argentina) are under the jurisdiction of an apostolic exarchate (see city, Buenos Aires, Argentina).

ARGENTINA: Byzantine Rite (Ukrainians), eparchy.

Antiochene Rite (Maronites), eparchy.

Armenian Rite, eparchy.

Ordinariate for all other Eastern-Rite Catholics.

BRAZIL: Antiochene Rite (Maronites), eparchy.

Byzantine Rite (Greek-Melkites), eparchy; (Ukrainians), eparchy.

Ordinariate for all other Eastern-Rite Catholics.

VENEZUELA: Byzantine Rite (Greek-Melkites) apostolic exarchate.

## SYNODS, ASSEMBLIES

These assemblies are collegial bodies which have pastoral authority over members of the Eastern Catholic Churches. (Canons 102-113, 152-153, 322 of Oriental Code of Canon Law.)

**Patriarchal Synods:** Synod of the Catholic Coptic Church: Stephanos II Ghattas, C.M., patriarch of Alexandria of the Copts.

Synod of the Greek-Melkite Catholic Church: Maximos V Hakim, patriarch of Antioch of the Greek Catholics-Melkites.

Synod of the Syrian Catholic Church: Ignace Antoine II Hayek, patriarch of Antioch of the Syrians.

Synod of the Maronite Church: Cardinal Nasrallah Pierre Sfeir, patriarch of Antioch of the Maronites.

Synod of the Chaldean Church: Raphael I Bidawid, patriarch of Babylonia of the Chaldeans.

Synod of the Armenian Catholic Church: Jean Pierre XVIII Kasparian, patriarch of Cilicia of the Armenians.

**Major Archiepiscopal Synods:** The Synod of the Ukrainian Catholic Church (raised to major archiepiscopal status Dec. 23, 1963): Cardinal Myroslav Ivan Lubachivsky, major archbishop of Lviv of the Ukrainians, president.

The Synod of the Syro-Malabar Church (raised to major archiepiscopal status, Jan. 29, 1993): Cardinal Anthony Padiyara, major archbishop of Ernakulam-Angamaly of the Syro-Malabars.

**Councils, Assemblies, Conferences:** Council of Ethiopian Churches: Cardinal Paul Tzadua, president.

Council of Romanian Churches: Abp. Lucian Muresan of Fagaras and Alba Julia, president.

Council of Ruthenian Churches, U.S.A.: Abp. Judson Michael Procyk of Pittsburgh of the Byzantines, president.

Council of Syro-Malankarese Churches: Abp. Cyril Baselios Malacharuvil, O.I.C., of Trivandrum of the Syro-Malankarese, president.

Assembly of the Catholic Hierarchy of Egypt (Dec. 5, 1983): Stephanos II Ghattas, C.M., patriarch of Alexandria of the Copts, president.

Assembly of Catholic Patriarchs and Bishops of Lebanon: Cardinal Nasrallah Pierre Sfeir, patriarch of Antioch of the Maronites, president.

Assembly of Ordinaries of the Syrian Arab Republic: Maximos V Hakim, patriarch of Antioch of the Greek Catholics-Melkites, president.

Assembly of Catholic Ordinaries of the Holy Land (Jan. 27, 1992): Michel Sabbah, patriarch of Jerusalem of the Latins, president.

Interritual Union of the Bishops of Iraq: Raphael I Bidawid, patriarch of Babylonia of the Chaldeans, president.

Iranian Episcopal Conference (Aug. 11, 1977): Most Rev. Vartan Tekeyan, bishop of Ispahan of the Armenians, president.

Episcopal Conference of Turkey (Nov. 30, 1987): Most Rev. Louis A. Pelatre, A.A., vicar apotolic of Istanbul, president.

## EASTERN CATHOLIC CHURCHES IN U.S.

(Statistics, from the *1996 Annuario Pontificio* unless noted otherwise, are membership figures reported by Eastern-Rite jurisdictions. Additional Eastern-Rite Catholics are included in statistics for Roman-Rite dioceses.)

### Byzantine Tradition

**Ukrainians:** There were 132,636 reported in four jurisdictions in the U.S.: the metropolitan see of Philadelphia (1924, metropolitan 1958) and the suffragan sees of Stamford, Conn. (1956), St. Nicholas of Chicago (1961) and St. Josaphat in Parma (1983).

**Ruthenians:** There were 189,407 reported in four jurisdictions in the U.S.: the metropolitan see of Pittsburgh (est. 1924 at Pittsburgh; metropolitan and transferred to Munhall, 1969; transferred to Pittsburgh, 1977) and the suffragan sees of Passaic, N.J. (1963), Parma, Ohio (1969) and Van Nuys, Calif. (1981). Hungarian and Croatian Byzantine Catholics in the U.S. are also under the jurisdiction of Ruthenian-Rite bishops.

**Melkites (Greek Catholics-Melkites):** There were 27,000 reported under the jurisdiction of the Melkite eparchy of Newton, Mass. (established as an exarchate, 1965; eparchy, 1976).

**Romanians:** There were 5,300 reported in 15 Romanian Catholic Byzantine Rite parishes in the U.S., under the jurisdiction of the Romanian eparchy of St. George Martyr, Canton, Ohio (established as an exarchate, 1982; eparchy, 1987).

**Belarussians:** Have one parish in the U.S. — Christ the Redeemer, Chicago, Ill.

**Russians:** Have parishes in California (St. Andrew, El Segundo, and Our Lady of Fatima Center, San Francisco); New York (St. Michael's Chapel of St. Patrick's Old Cathedral). They are under the jurisdiction of local Roman-Rite bishops.

### Alexandrian Tradition

**Copts:** Have a Catholic Chapel — Resurrection, in Brooklyn, N.Y.

### Antiochene Tradition

**Maronites:** There were 55,000 reported in two jurisdictions in the U.S.: the eparchy of St. Maron, Brooklyn (established at Detroit as an exarchate, 1966; eparchy, 1972; transferred to Brooklyn, 1977) and the eparchy of Our Lady of Lebanon of Los Angeles (established Mar. 1, 1994).

**Syrians:** The eparchy of Our Lady of the Deliverance of Newark (see city, Newark, N.J.) was established in 1995 for Syrian-rite Catholics of the U.S. and Canada.

**Malankarese:** Have a mission in Chicago.

### Armenian Tradition

An apostolic exarchate for Canada and the United States (see city, New York) was established July 3, 1981; 36,800 in both countries.

### Chaldean Tradition

**Chaldeans:** There were 60,000 reported under the jurisdiction of the eparchy of St. Thomas Apostle of Detroit (established as an exarchate, 1982; eparchy, 1986).

**Syro-Malabarese (Malabar):** Have mission churches in Chicago and several other cities. Estimated 200,000 faithful with 50 priests.

### Eastern Catholic Associates

Eastern Catholic Associates is the association of all Eastern Catholic bishops and their equivalents in law in the United States, representing the Armenian, Chaldean, Maronite, Melkite, Syriac, Romanian, Ruthenian and Ukrainian churches. The Syro-Malabar and Russian churches are also represented even though they do not have bishops in the U.S. President: Melkite Auxiliary Bishop Nicholas J. Samra of Newton, Mass.

The association meets at the same time as the National Conference of Catholic Bishops in the fall of each year.

### SYRO-MALABAR SYNOD

Pope John Paul, in remarks at the opening Jan. 8, 1996, of a synod of Syro-Malabar bishops, urged the prelates to restore an atmosphere of communion and trust in their two-million-member church. The disputes at issue were about liturgy and tradition, with one faction favoring the restoration of ancient customs and practices, and the other seeking to streamline the liturgy and to align it more closely with the Latin rite. Also at issue were differences regarding the pastoral care of Syro-Malabar migrants and missionary activity of the Syro-Malabar Church and seminaries.

The Pope said that "conflicts must be banned, since no good can come except from love." He added that he would "continue to walk each step with you, not in order to deny you your just autonomy, but to fulfill to the utmost the ministry which Christ entrusted to Peter: to strengthen the brethren and confirm them in faith and communion."

Synodal sessions continued in India, with reports due to be referred to the Holy Father for his consideration in responding to recommendations by the bishops.

### BREST, UZHOROD ANNIVERSARIES

With apostolic letters issued Nov. 16, 1995, and Apr. 16, 1996, commemorating the Union of Brest in 1595-96 and the Union of Uzhorod in 1646, respectively, Pope John Paul marked the restoration of communion between the Roman Catholic Church and Byzantine-rite Christians in Ukraine and the Transcarpathian region. The letters focused attention on the long-standing sensitive issue of the coexistence of Catholic and Orthodox Eastern Churches, and called on Eastern Catholics to work toward better relations with their Orthodox counterparts.

Ceremonies marking the anniversaries were held May 19,1996, at the Marian shrine of Zarvanycia, Ukraine. Cardinal Edward I. Cassidy, president of the Pontifical Council for Promoting Christian Unity, attended the ceremonies as the papal envoy and spoke in the name of the Holy Father.

"We cannot but meditate on the long years of suffering and oppression endured (under communist rule) by the two communities in full communion with the Successor of Peter, who are heirs of those responsible for the Union of Brest and the Union of Uzhorod. As communities, you have been called upon to carry your own cross, to endure your own passion, to appear in the eyes of many to have died. Yet, in all that time, you never lost hope, you preserved your faith, and in 'the end you returned to a new life, to a resurrection....

"Let us 'embrace one another, let us call brothers even those who hate us, let us forgive everything for the sake of the Resurrection,' It is with sentiments such as these that Pope John Paul has wished, in his apostolic letter of 12 November, 1995, in preparation for these present celebrations, to encourage the Ukrainian Greek Catholic Church to reflect and deepen its understanding 'of the proper role which it is called on to play today in the ecumenical movement.'"

## BYZANTINE DIVINE LITURGY

The Divine Liturgy in all rites is based on the consecration of bread and wine by the narration-reactualization of the actions of Christ at the Last Supper. Aside from this fundamental usage, there are differences between the Roman (Latin) Rite ad Eastern Rites, and among the Eastern Rites themselves. Following is a general description of the Byzantine Divine Liturgy which is in widest use in the Eastern-Rite Churches.

In the Byzantine, as in all Eastern Rites, the bread and wine are prepared at the start of the Liturgy. The priest does this in a little niche or at a table in the sanctuary. Taking a round loaf of leavened bread stamped with religious symbols, he cuts out a square host and other particles while reciting verses expressing the symbolism of the action. When the bread and wine are ready, he says a prayer of offering and incenses the oblations, the altar, the icons and the people.

**Liturgy of the Catechumens:** At the altar a litany for all classes of people is sung by the priest. The congregation answers, "Lord, have mercy."

The Little Entrance comes next. In procession, the priest leaves the sanctuary carrying the Book of the Gospels, and then returns. He sings prayers especially selected for the day and the feast. These are followed by the solemn singing of the prayer, "Holy God, Holy Mighty One, Holy Immortal One."

The Epistle follows. The Gospel is sung or read by the priest facing the people at the middle door of the sanctuary.

An interruption after the Liturgy of the Catechumens, formerly an instructional period for those learning the faith, is clearly marked. Catechumens, if present, are dismissed with a prayer. Following this are a prayer and litany for the faithful.

**Great Entrance:** The Great Entrance or solemn Offertory Procession then takes place. The priest first says a long silent prayer for himself, in preparation for the great act to come. Again he incenses the oblations, the altar, the icons and people. He goes to the table on the gospel side for the veil-covered paten and chalice. When he arrives back at the sanctuary door, he announces the intention of the Mass in the prayer: "May the Lord God remember all of you in his kingdom, now and forever."

After another litany, the congregation recites the Nicene Creed.

**Consecration:** The most solemn portion of the sacrifice is introduced by the preface, which is very much like the preface of the Roman Rite. At the beginning of the last phrase, the priest raises his voice to introduce the singing of the Sanctus. During the singing he reads the introduction to the words of consecration.

The words of consecration are sung aloud, and the people sing "Amen" to both consecrations. As the priest raises the Sacred Species in solemn offering, he sings: "Thine of Thine Own we offer unto Thee in behalf of all and for all."

A prayer to the Holy Spirit is followed by the commemorations, in which special mention is made of the all-holy, most blessed and glorious Lady, the Mother of God and ever-Virgin Mary. The dead are remembered and then the living.

**Holy Communion:** A final litany for spiritual gifts precedes the Our Father. The Sacred Body and Blood are elevated with the words, "Holy Things for the Holy." The Host is then broken and commingled with the Precious Blood. The priest recites preparatory prayers for Holy Communion, consumes the Sacred Species, and distributes Holy Communion to the people under the forms of both bread and wine. During this time a communion verse is sung by the choir or congregation.

The Liturgy closes quickly after this. The consecrated Species of bread and wine are removed to the side table to be consumed later by the priest. A prayer of thanksgiving is recited, a prayer for all the people is said in front of the icon of Christ, a blessing is invoked upon all, and the people are dismissed.

## BYZANTINE CALENDAR

The Byzantine-Rite calendar has many distinctive features of its own, although it shares common elements with the Roman-Rite calendar — e.g., general purpose, commemoration of the mysteries of faith and of the saints, identical dates for some feasts. Among the distinctive things are the following.

The liturgical year begins on Sept. 1, the **Day of Indiction,** in contrast with the Latin or Roman start on the First Sunday of Advent late in November or early in December. The Advent season begins on Dec. 10.

### Cycles of the Year

As in the Roman usage, the dating of feasts follows the Gregorian Calendar. Formerly, until well into this century, the Julian Calendar was used. (The Julian Calendar, which is now about 13 days late, is still used by some Eastern-Rite Churches.)

The year has several cycles, which include proper seasons, the feasts of saints, and series of New Testament readings. All of these elements of worship are contained in liturgical books of the rite.

The ecclesiastical calendar, called the **Menologion,** explains the nature of feasts, other observances and matters pertaining to the liturgy for each day of the year. In some cases, its contents include the lives of saints and the history and meaning of feasts.

The Divine Liturgy (Mass) and Divine Office for the proper of the saints, fixed feasts, and the Christmas season are contained in the **Menaion.** The **Triodion** covers the pre-Lenten season of preparation for Easter; Lent begins two days before the Ash Wednesday observance of the Roman Rite. The **Pentecostarion** contains the liturgical services from Easter to the Sunday of All Saints, the first after Pentecost. The **Evangelion** and **Apostolos** are books in which the Gospels, and Acts of the Apostles and the Epistles, respectively, are arranged according to the order of their reading in the Divine Liturgy and Divine Office throughout the year.

The cyclic progression of liturgical music throughout the year, in successive and repetitive periods of eight weeks, is governed by the **Oktoechos,** the Book of Eight Tones.

### Sunday Names

Many Sundays are named after the subject of the Gospel read in the Mass of the day or after the name of a feast falling on the day — e.g., Sunday of the Publican and Pharisee, of the Prodigal Son, of the Samaritan Woman, of St. Thomas the Apostle, of the Fore-Fathers (Old Testament Patriarchs). Other Sundays are named in the same manner as in the

Roman calendar e.g., numbered Sundays of Lent and after Pentecost.

## Holy Days

The calendar lists about 28 holy days. Many of the major holy days coincide with those of the Roman calendar, but the feast of the Immaculate Conception is observed on Dec. 9 instead of Dec. 8, and the feast of All Saints falls on the Sunday after Pentecost rather than on Nov. 1. Instead of a single All Souls' Day, there are five All Souls' Saturdays.

According to regulations in effect in the Byzantine-Rite (Ruthenian) Archeparchy of Pittsburgh and its suffragan sees of Passaic, Parma and Van Nuys, holy days are obligatory, solemn and simple, and attendance at the Divine Liturgy is required on five obligatory days — the feasts of the Epiphany, the Ascension, Sts. Peter and Paul, the Assumption of the Blessed Virgin Mary, and Christmas. Although attendance at the liturgy is not obligatory on 15 solemn and seven simple holy days, it is recommended.

In the Byzantine-Rite (Ukrainian) Archeparchy of Philadelphia and its suffragan sees of St. Josaphat in Parma, St. Nicholas (Chicago) and Stamford, the obligatory feasts are the Circumcision, Epiphany, Annunciation, Easter, Ascension, Pentecost, Dormition (Assumption of Mary), Immaculate Conception and Christmas.

## Lent

The first day of Lent — the Monday before Ash Wednesday of the Roman Rite — and Good Friday are days of strict abstinence for persons in the age bracket of obligation. No meat, eggs, or dairy products may be eaten on these days.

All persons over the age of 14 must abstain from meat on Fridays during Lent, Holy Saturday, and the vigils of the feasts of Christmas and Epiphany; abstinence is urged, but is not obligatory, on Wednesdays of Lent. The abstinence obligation is not in force on certain "free" or "privileged" Fridays.

## Synaxis

An observance without a counterpart in the Roman calendar is the synaxis. This is a commemoration, on the day following a feast, of persons involved with the occasion for the feast — e.g., Sept. 9, the day following the feast of the Nativity of the Blessed Virgin Mary, is the Synaxis of Joachim and Anna, her parents.

## Holy Week

In the Byzantine Rite, Lent is liturgically concluded with the Saturday of Lazarus, the day before Palm Sunday, which commemorates the raising of Lazarus from the dead.

On the following Monday, Tuesday and Wednesday, the Liturgy of the Presanctified is prescribed.

On Holy Thursday, the Liturgy of St. Basil the Great is celebrated together with Vespers.

The Divine Liturgy is not celebrated on Good Friday.

On Holy Saturday, the Liturgy of St. Basil the Great is celebrated along with Vespers.

## BYZANTINE FEATURES

**Art:** Named for the empire in which it developed, Byzantine art is a unique blend of imperial Roman and classic Hellenic culture with Christian inspiration. The art of the Greek Middle Ages, it reached a peak of development in the 10th or 11th century. Characteristic of its products, particularly in mosaic and painting, are majesty, dignity, refinement and grace. Its sacred paintings, called icons, are reverenced highly in all Eastern Rites.

**Church Building:** The classical model of Byzantine church architecture is the Church of the Holy Wisdom (Hagia Sophia), built in Constantinople in the first half of the sixth century and still standing. The square structure, extended in some cases in the form of a cross, is topped by a distinctive onion-shaped dome and surmounted by a triple-bar cross. The altar is at the eastern end of building, where the wall bellies out to form an apse. The altar and sanctuary are separated from the body of the church by a fixed or movable screen, the iconostas, to which icons or sacred pictures are attached (see below).

**Clergy:** The Byzantine Rite has married as well as celibate priests. In places other than the U.S., where married candidates have not been accepted for ordination since about 1929, men already married can be ordained to the diaconate and priesthood and can continue in marriage after ordination. Celibate deacons and priests cannot marry after ordination; neither can a married priest remarry after the death of his wife. Bishops must be unmarried.

**Iconostas:** A large screen decorated with sacred pictures or icons which separates the sanctuary from the nave of a church; its equivalent in the Roman Rite, for thus separating the sanctuary from the nave, is an altar rail.

An iconostas has three doors through which the sacred ministers enter the sanctuary during the Divine Liturgy: smaller (north and south) Deacons' Doors and a large central Royal Door.

The Deacons' Doors usually feature the icons of Sts. Gabriel and Michael; the Royal Door, the icons of the Evangelists — Matthew, Mark, Luke and John. To the right and left of the Royal Door are the icons of Christ the Teacher and of the Blessed Virgin Mary with the Infant Jesus. To the extreme right and left are the icons of the patron of the church and St. John the Baptist (or St. Nicholas of Myra).

Immediately above the Royal Door is a picture of the Last Supper. To the right are six icons depicting the major feasts of Christ, and to the left are six icons portraying the major feasts of the Blessed Virgin Mary. Above the picture of the Last Supper is a large icon of Christ the King.

Some icon screens also have pictures of the 12 Apostles and the major Old Testament prophets surmounted by a crucifixion scene.

**Liturgical Language:** In line with Eastern tradition, Byzantine practice has favored the use of the language of the people in the liturgy. Two great advocates of the practice were Sts. Cyril and Methodius, apostles of the Slavs, who devised the Cyrillic alphabet and pioneered the adoption of Slavonic in the liturgy.

**Sacraments:** Baptism is administered by immersion, and confirmation (Chrismation) is conferred at the same time. The Eucharist is administered by intinction, i.e., by giving the communicant a piece of consecrated leavened bread which has been dipped into the consecrated wine. When giving absolution in the sacrament of penance, the priest holds his stole over the head of the penitent. Distinctive marriage ceremonies include the crowning of the bride and groom. Ceremonies for anointing the sick closely resemble those of the Roman Rite. Holy orders are conferred by a bishop.

**Sign of the Cross:** The sign of the cross in conjunction with a deep bow expresses reverence for the presence of Christ in the Blessed Sacrament. (See also entry in Glossary.)

## VESTMENTS, APPURTENANCES

**Sticharion:** A long white garment of linen or silk with wide sleeves and decorated with embroidery; formerly the vestment for clerics in minor orders, acolytes, lectors, chanters, and subdeacons; symbolic of purity.

**Epitrachelion:** A stole with ends sewn together, having a loop through which the head is passed; its several crosses symbolize priestly duties.

**Zone:** A narrow clasped belt made of the same material as the epitrachelion; symbolic of the wisdom of the priest, his strength against enemies of the Church and his willingness to perform holy duties.

**Epimanikia:** Ornamental cuffs; the right cuff symbolizing strength, the left, patience and good will.

**Phelonion:** An ample cape, long in the back and sides and cut away in front; symbolic of the higher gifts of the Holy Spirit.

**Antimension:** A silk or linen cloth laid on the altar for the Liturgy; it may be decorated with a picture of the burial of Christ and the instruments of his passion; the relics of martyrs are sewn into the front border.

**Eileton:** A linen cloth which corresponds to the Roman-Rite corporal.

**Poterion:** A chalice or cup which holds the wine and Precious Blood.

**Diskos:** A shallow plate, which may be elevated on a small stand, corresponding to the Roman-Rite paten.

**Asteriskos:** Made of two curved bands of gold or silver which cross each other to form a double arch; a star depends from the junction, which forms a cross; it is placed over the diskos holding the consecrated bread and is covered with a veil.

**Veils:** Three are used, one to cover the poterion, the second to cover the diskos, and the third to cover both.

**Spoon:** Used in administering Holy Communion by intinction; consecrated leavened bread is dipped into consecrated wine and spooned onto the tongue of the communicant.

**Lance:** A metal knife used for cutting up the bread to be consecrated during the Liturgy.

# SEPARATED EASTERN CHURCHES

## ORTHODOX

Orthodox Churches are churches of Eastern rites which were in communion with the Holy See until the Schism of 1054. Although they withdrew from communion at that time, they retained, and still retain, essential features of the Mother Churches from which they derived: matters of faith and morals, valid orders and sacraments, liturgy, patriarchal jurisdiction and general discipline. Along with the lack of communion with the Holy See, the Orthodox Churches recognize only the first seven ecumenical councils.

Like their Catholic counterparts, Orthodox Churches are organized in jurisdictions under patriarchs. The patriarchs are the heads of approximately 15 autocephalic and several other autonomous jurisdictions organized along lines of nationality and/or language.

The Ecumenical Patriarch of Constantinople (Istanbul) has the primacy of honor among his equal patriarchs but his actual jurisdiction is limited to his own patriarchate. As the spiritual head of worldwide Orthodoxy, he keeps the book of the Holy Canons of the Autocephalous Churches, in which recognized Orthodox Churches are registered, and has the right to call Pan-Orthodox assemblies.

Top-level relations between the Churches have improved in recent years through the efforts of Ecumenical Patriarch Athenagoras I, John XXIII, Paul VI and Patriarch Dimitrios I. Pope Paul met with Athenagoras three times before the latter's death in 1972. The most significant action of both spiritual leaders was their mutual nullification of excommunications imposed by the two Churches on each other in 1054. Development of better relations with the Orthodox has been a priority of John Paul II since the beginning of his pontificate. Both he and Orthodox Ecumenical Patriarch Bartholomew have made known their commitment to better relations, despite contentions between Eastern Catholic and Orthodox Churches over charges of proselytism and rival property claims in places liberated from anti-religious communist control in the recent past.

The largest Orthodox body in the western hemisphere is the Greek Orthodox Archdiocese of North and South America consisting of the Archdiocese of New York, nine dioceses in the U.S., and one diocese each in Canada and South America; it has an estimated membership of 1.9 million. The second largest is the Orthodox Church in America, with more than one million members; it was given independent status by the Patriarchate of Moscow May 18, 1970, against the will of Athenagoras I who refused to register it in the book of the Holy Canons of Autocephalous Churches. An additional 650,000 or more Orthodox belong to smaller national and language jurisdictions.

Heads of orthodox jurisdictions in this hemisphere hold membership in the Standing Conference of Canonical Orthodox Bishops in the Americas.

### Jurisdictions

The principal jurisdictions of the Greek, Russian and other Orthodox Churches are as follows.

**Greek:** Patriarchate of Constantinople, with jurisdiction in Turkey, Crete, the Dodecanese, Western Europe, the Americas, Australia.

Patriarchate of Alexandria, with jurisdiction in Egypt and the rest of Africa; there is also a native African Orthodox Church in Kenya and Uganda.

Patriarchate of Antioch (Melkites or Syrian Orthodox), with jurisdiction in Syria, Lebanon, Iraq, Australasia, the Americas; Syrian or Arabic, in place of Greek, is the liturgical language.

Patriarchate of Jerusalem, with jurisdiction in Israel and Jordan.

Churches of Greece, Cyprus and Sinai are autocephalic but maintain relations with their fellow Orthodox.

**Russian:** Patriarchate of Moscow with jurisdiction centered in the former Soviet Union.

**Other:** Patriarchate of Serbia, with jurisdiction in Yugoslavia, Western Europe, the Americas, Australasia.

Patriarchates of Rumania and Bulgaria.

Katholikate of Georgia, the Soviet Union.

Belarussians and Ukrainian Byzantines.

Churches of Albania, China, Czechoslovakia, Estonia, Finland, Hungary, Japan, Latvia, Lithuania, Poland.

Other minor communities in various places; e.g., Korea, the U.S., Carpatho-Russia.

The Division of Archives and Statistics of the Eastern Orthodox World Foundation reported a 1970 estimate of more than 200 million Orthodox Church members throughout the world. Other sources estimate the total to be approximately 125 million.

### Conference of Orthodox Bishops

The Standing Conference of Canonical Orthodox Bishops in the Americas was established in 1960 to achieve cooperation among the various Orthodox jurisdictions in the Americas. Ecumenical office: 8-10 East 79th St., New York, N.Y. 10021.

Member churches of the conference are the: Albanian Orthodox Diocese of America (Ecumenical Patriarchate), American Carpatho-Russian Orthodox Greek Catholic Diocese in the U.S.A. (Ecumenical Patriarchate), Antiochian Orthodox Christian Archdiocese of North America, Bulgarian Eastern Orthodox Church, Greek Orthodox Archdiocese of North and South America (Ecumenical Patriarchate), Orthodox Church in America, Romanian Orthodox Archdiocese in America and Canada, Serbian Orthodox Church in the United States of America and Canada, Ukrainian Orthodox Church in the United States (Ecumenical Patriarchate), Ukrainian Orthodox Church of Canada (Ecumenical Patriarchate).

### ANCIENT CHURCHES OF THE EAST

Ancient Churches of the East, which are distinct from Orthodox Churches, were the subject of an article by Gerard Daucourt published in the Feb. 16, 1987, English edition of *L'Osservatore Romano*. Following is an excerpt.

By Ancient Churches of the East one means: the Assyrian Oriental Church (formerly called Nestorian), the Armenian Church, the Coptic Church, the Ethiopian Church, the Syrian Church (sometimes called Syro-Jacobite) and the Syrian Church of India.

After the Council of Ephesus (431), the Assyrian Oriental Church did not maintain communion with the rest of the Christian world. For reasons as much and perhaps more political than doctrinal, it did not accept the Council's teaching (that Mary is not the Mother of God, in opposition to the opinion of Nestorius; see Nestorianism. For this reason, the Assyrian Oriental Church came to be called Nestorian.) It is well known that in the 16th century a great segment of the faithful of this Church entered into communion with the See of Rome and constitutes today, among the Oriental Catholic Churches, the Chaldean Patriarchate.

The Patriarch of the Assyrian Oriental Church, His Holiness Mar Denkha IV, in the course of his visit to the Holy Father and to the Church of Rome of 7 to 9 November, 1984, requested that people stop using the term "Nestorian" to designate his Church and expressed the desire that a declaration made jointly by the Pope of Rome and himself may one day serve to express the common faith of the two Churches in Jesus Christ, Son of God incarnate, born of the Virgin Mary. The labours of Catholic historians and theologians have, moreover, already contributed to showing that such a declaration would be possible.

The other Ancient Churches of the East for a long time have been designated by the term "Monophysite Churches" (see Monophysitism). It is regrettable to find this name still employed sometimes in certain publications, since already in 1951, in the encyclical *Sempiternus Rex*, on the occasion of the 15th centenary of the Council of Chalcedon, Pius XII declared with regard to the Christians of these Churches: "They depart from the right way only in terminology, when they expound the doctrine of the Incarnation of the Lord. This may be deduced from their liturgical and theological books."

In this same encyclical, Pius XII expressed the view that the separation at the doctrinal level came about "above all, through a certain ambiguity of terminology that occurred at the beginning."

Since then, two important declarations have been arrived at in line with the ecumenical stance taken by the Church at the Second Vatican Council and the labors of the theologians (particularly in the framework of the Foundation "Pro Oriente" of Vienna). One was signed by Pope Paul VI and Coptic Patriarch Shenouda III on 10 May, 1973, and the other by Pope John Paul II and the Syrian Patriarch Ignace Zakka I Iwas, on 23 June, 1984. In both of these texts, the hierarchies of the respective Churches confess one and the same faith in the mystery of the Word Incarnate. After such declarations, it is no longer possible to speak in general terms of the "Monophysite" Churches.

The Armenian Church has communicants in the Soviet Unon, the Middle and Far East, the Americas. The Coptic Church has communicants in the Middle East, the Americas, India.

Members of the Assyrian Oriental Church are scattered throughout the world.

It is estimated that there are approximately 10 million or more members of these other Eastern Churches throughout the world. For various reasons, a more accurate determination is not possible.

# EASTERN ECUMENISM

The Second Vatican Council, in the *Decree on Eastern Catholic Churches,* pointed out the special role they have to play "in promoting the unity of all Christians. " The document also stated in part as follows.

The Eastern Churches in communion with the Apostolic See of Rome have a special role to play in promoting the unity of all Christians, particularly Easterners, according to the principles of this sacred Synod's *Decree on Ecumenism* first of all by prayer, then by the example of their lives, by religious fidelity to ancient Eastern traditions, by greater mutual knowledge, by collaboration, and by a brotherly regard for objects and attitudes (No. 24).

If any separated Eastern Christian should, under the guidance of grace of the Holy Spirit, join himself to Catholic unity, no more should be required of him than what a simple profession of the Catholic faith demands. A valid priesthood is preserved among Eastern clerics. Hence, upon joining themselves to the unity of the Catholic Church, Eastern clerics are permitted to exercise the orders they possess, in accordance with the regulations established by the competent authority (No. 25).

Divine Law forbids any common worship (*communicatio in sacris*) which would damage the unity of the Church, or involve formal acceptance of falsehood or the danger of deviation in the faith, of scandal, or of indifferentism. At the same time, pastoral experience clearly shows that with respect to our Eastern brethren there should and can be taken into consideration various circumstances affecting individuals, wherein the unity of the Church is not jeopardized nor are intolerable risks involved, but in which salvation itself and the spiritual profit of souls are urgently at issue.

Hence, in view of special circumstances of time, place, and personage, the Catholic Church has often adopted and now adopts a milder policy, offering to all the means of salvation and an example of charity among Christians through participation in the sacraments and in other sacred functions and objects. With these considerations in mind, and "lest because of the harshness of our judgment we prove an obstacle to those seeking salvation," and in order to promote closer union with the Eastern Churches separated from us, this sacred Synod lays down the following policy:

In view of the principles recalled above, Eastern Christians who are separated in good faith from the Catholic Church, if they ask of their own accord and have the right dispositions, may be granted the sacraments of penance, the Eucharist, and the anointing of the sick. Furthermore, Catholics may ask for these same sacraments from those non-Catholic ministers whose Churches possess valid sacraments, as often as necessity or a genuine spiritual benefit recommends such a course of action, and when access to a Catholic priest is physically or morally impossible (Nos. 26, 27).

Again, in view of these very same principles, Catholics may for a just cause join with their separated Eastern brethren in sacred functions, things, and places (No. 28). Bishops decide when and if to follow this lenient policy.

## Recent Documents

Three recent documents of importance with respect to relations between Catholic and separated Eastern Churches are the apostolic letter, *Orientale Lumen*, issued May 5, 1995; the encyclical letter, *Ut Unum Sint*, issued May 30, 1995; and the Christological Declaration signed Nov. 11, 1994, by Pope John Paul and His Holiness Mar Dinkha IV, Catholicos-Patriarch of the Assyrian Church of the East.

Excerpts from the first two documents were given under their proper titles in the 1996 edition of the Almanac. The text of the Christological Document follows.

# CHRISTOLOGICAL DECLARATION

Following is the text of the "Common Christological Declaration" between the Catholic Church and the Assyrian Church of the East, signed Nov. 11, 1994, by Pope John Paul II and His Holiness Mar Dinkha IV, Catholicos-Patriarch of the Assyrian Church of the East.

The declaration acknowledges that, despite past differences, both churches profess the same faith in the real union of divine and human natures in the divine Person of Christ. Backgrounding the declaration was the Assyrian Church's adherence to the teaching of Nestorius who, in the fifth century, denied the real unity of divine and human natures in the single divine Person of Christ.

*The text was published in the Nov. 16, 1994, English edition of "L'Osservatore Romano."*

As heirs and guardians of the faith received from the Apostles as formulated by our common Fathers in the Nicene Creed, we confess one Lord Jesus Christ, the only Son of God, begotten of the Father from all eternity who, in the fullness of time, came down from heaven and became man for our salvation. The Word of God, second Person of the Holy Trinity, became incarnate by the power of the Holy Spirit in assuming from the Virgin Mary a body animated by a rational soul, with which he was indissolubly united from the moment of conception.

## Unity of Two Natures in One Person

Therefore our Lord Jesus Christ is true God and true man, perfect in his divinity and perfect in his humanity, consubstantial with the Father and consubstantial with us in all things but sin. His divinity and his humanity are united in one person, without confusion or change, without division or separation. In him has been preserved the difference of the natures of divinity and humanity, with all their properties, faculties and operations. But far from constituting "one and another," the dignity and humanity are united in the person of the same and unique Son of God and Lord Jesus Christ, who is the object of a single adoration.

Christ therefore is not an "ordinary man" whom God adopted in order to reside in him and inspire him, as in the righteous ones and the prophets. But the same God the Word, begotten of his Father before all worlds without beginning according to his divinity, was born of a mother without a father in the last times according to his humanity. The humanity to which the Blessed Virgin Mary gave birth always was that of the Son of God himself. That is the reason the Assyrian Church of the East is praying the Virgin Mary as "the Mother of Christ our God and Savior." In the light of this same faith the Catholic tradition addresses the Virgin Mary as "the Mother of God" and also as "the Mother of Christ." We both recognize the legitimacy and rightness of these expressions of the same faith and we both respect the preference of each Church in her liturgical life and piety.

## Confession of the Same Faith

This is the unique faith that we profess in the mystery of Christ. The controversies of the past led to anathemas, bearing on persons and on formulas. The Lord's Spirit permits us to understand better today that the divisions brought about in this way were due in large part to misunderstandings.

Whatever our Christological divergences have been, we experience ourselves united today in the confession of the same faith in the Son of God who became man so that we might become children of God by his grace. We wish from now on to witness together to this faith in the One who is the Way, the Truth and the Life, proclaiming it in appropriate ways to our contemporaries, so that the world may believe in the Gospel of salvation.

The mystery of the Incarnation which we profess in common is not an abstract and isolated truth. It refers to the Son of God sent to save us. The economy of salvation, which has its origin in the mystery of communion of the Holy Trinity — Father, Son and Holy Spirit — is brought to its fulfillment through the sharing in this communion, by grace, within the one, holy, catholic and apostolic church, which is the People of God, the Body of Christ and the Temple of the Spirit.

## The Sacraments

Believers become members of this Body through the sacrament of Baptism, through which, by water and the working of the Holy Spirit, they are born again as new creatures. They are confirmed by the seal of the Holy Spirit who bestows the sacrament of anointing. Their communion with God and among themselves is brought to full realization by the celebration of the unique offering of Christ in the sacrament of the Eucharist. This communion is restored for the sinful members of the Church when they are reconciled with God and with one another through the sacrament of Forgiveness. The sacrament of Ordination to the ministerial priesthood in the apostolic succession assures the authenticity of the faith, the sacraments and the communion in each local Church.

## Sister Churches but not Full Communion

Living by this faith and these sacraments, it follows as a consequence that the particular Catholic Churches and the particular Assyrian Churches can recognize each other as sister Churches. To be full and entire, communion presupposes the unanimity concerning the content of the faith, the sacraments and the constitution of the Church. Since this unanimity for which we aim has not yet been attained, we cannot unfortunately celebrate together the Eucharist which is the sign of the ecclesial communion already fully restored.

Nevertheless, the deep spiritual communion in the faith and the mutual trust already existing between our Churches entitles us from now on to consider witnessing together to the gospel message and co-operating in particular pastoral situations, including especially the areas of catechesis and the formation of future priests.

## Commitment to Unity Efforts

In thanking God for having made us rediscover what already unites us in the faith and the sacraments, we pledge ourselves to do everything possible to dispel the obstacles of the past which still prevent the attainment of full communion between our Churches, so that we can better respond to the Lord's call for the unity of his own, a unity which has of course to be expressed visibly. To overcome these obstacles, we now establish a Mixed Committee for theological dialogue between the Catholic Church and the Assyrian Church of the East.

Given at Saint Peter's on 11 November 1994.

---

## COMMON DECLARATION OF POPE AND PATRIARCH

On June 29, 1995, Pope John Paul and Ecumenical Orthodox Patriarch Bartholomew I signed a common declaration at their last meeting.

"Our meeting has followed other important events which have seen our Churches declare their desire to relegate the excommunications of the past to oblivion and to set out on the way to reestablishing full communion.

"Our new-found brotherhood in the name of the Lord has led us to frank discussion, a dialogue that seeks understanding and unity. This dialogue — through the Joint International (Catholic-Orthodox) Commission — has proved fruitful and has made substantial progress.

"A common sacramental conception of the Church has emerged, sustained and passed on in time by the apostolic succession. In our Churches, the apostolic succession is fundamental to the sanctification and unity of the People of God. Considering that in every local Church the mystery of divine love is realized and that this is how the Church of Christ shows forth its active presence in each one of them, the Joint Commission has been able to declare that our Churches recognize one another as Sister Churches, responsible together for safeguarding the one Church of God, in fidelity to the divine plan, and in an altogether special way with regard to unity."

## MEN, DOCTRINES, CHURCHES OF THE REFORMATION

Some of the leading figures, doctrines and churches of the Reformation are covered below. A companion article covers Major Protestant Churches in the United States.

**John Wycliff** (c. 1320-1384): English priest and scholar who advanced one of the leading Reformation ideas nearly 200 years before Martin Luther — that the Bible alone is the sufficient rule of faith — but had only an indirect influence on the 16th century Reformers. Supporting belief in an inward and practical religion, he denied the divinely commissioned authority of the pope and bishops of the Church; he also denied the Real Presence of Christ in the Holy Eucharist, and wrote against the sacrament of penance and the doctrine of indulgences. Nearly 20 of his propositions were condemned by Gregory XI in 1377; his writings were proscribed more extensively by the Council of Constance in 1415. His influence was strongest in Bohemia and Central Europe.

**John Hus** (c. 1369-1415): A Bohemian priest and preacher of reform who authored 30 propositions condemned by the Council of Constance. Excommunicated in 1411 or 1412, he was burned at the stake in 1415. His principal errors concerned the nature of the Church and the origin of papal authority. He spread some of the ideas of Wycliff but did not subscribe to his views regarding faith alone as the condition for justification and salvation, the sole sufficiency of Scripture as the rule of faith, the Real Presence of Christ in the Eucharist, and the sacramental system. In 1457 some of his followers founded the Church of the Brotherhood which later became known as the United Brethren or Moravian Church and is considered the earliest independent Protestant body.

**Martin Luther** (1483-1546): An Augustinian friar, priest and doctor of theology, the key figure in the Reformation. In 1517, as a special indulgence was being preached in Germany, and in view of needed reforms within the Church, he published at Wittenberg 95 theses concerning matters of Catholic belief and practice. Leo X condemned 41 statements from Luther's writings in 1520. Luther, refusing to recant, was excommunicated the following year. His teachings strongly influenced subsequent Lutheran theology; its statements of faith are found in the Book of Concord (1580).

Luther's doctrine included the following: The sin of Adam, which corrupted human nature radically (but not substantially), has affected every aspect of man's being. Justification, understood as the forgiveness of sins and the state of righteousness, is by grace for Christ's sake through faith. Faith involves not merely intellectual assent but an act of confidence by the will. Good works are indispensable necessary concomitants of faith, but do not merit salvation. Of the sacraments, Luther retained baptism, penance and the Holy Communion as effective vehicles of the grace of the Holy Spirit; he held that in the Holy Communion the consecrated bread and wine are the Body and Blood of Christ. The rule of faith is the divine revelation in the Sacred Scriptures. He rejected purgatory, indulgences and the invocation of the saints, and held that prayers for the dead have no efficacy. Lutheran tenets not in agreement with Catholic doctrine were condemned by the Council of Trent.

**Anabaptism:** Originated in Saxony in the first quarter of the 16th century and spread rapidly through southern Germany. Its doctrine included several key Lutheran tenets but was not regarded with favor by Luther, Calvin or Zwingli. Anabaptists believed that baptism is for adults only and that infant baptism is invalid. Their doctrine of the Inner Light, concerning the direct influence of the Holy Spirit on the believer, implied rejection of Catholic doctrine concerning the sacraments and the nature of the Church. Eighteen articles of faith were formulated in 1632 in Holland. Mennonites are Anabaptists.

**Ulrich Zwingli** (1484-1531): A priest who triggered the Reformation in Switzerland with a series of New Testament lectures in 1519, later disputations and by other actions. He held the Gospel to be the only basis of truth; rejected the Mass (which he suppressed in 1525 at Zurich), penance and other sacraments; denied papal primacy and doctrine concerning purgatory and the invocation of saints; rejected celibacy, monasticism and many traditional practices of piety. His symbolic view of the Eucharist, which was at odds with Catholic doctrine, caused an irreconcilable controversy with Luther and his followers. Zwingli was killed in a battle between the forces of Protestant and Catholic cantons in Switzerland.

**John Calvin** (1509-1564): French leader of the Reformation in Switzerland, whose key tenet was absolute predestination of some persons to heaven and others to hell. He rejected Catholic doctrine in 1533 after becoming convinced of a personal mission to reform the Church. In 1536 he published the first edition of *Institutes of the Christian Religion,* a systematic exposition of his doctrine which became the classic textbook of Reformed — as distinguished from Lutheran — theology. To Luther's principal theses — regarding Scripture as the sole rule of faith, the radical corruption of human nature, and justification by faith alone — he added absolute predestination, certitude of salvation for the elect, and the incapability of the elect to lose grace. His Eucharistic theory, which failed to mediate the Zwingli-Luther controversy, was at odds with Catholic doctrine. From 1555 until his death Calvin was the virtual dictator of Geneva, the capital of the non-Lutheran Reformation in Europe.

**Arminianism:** A modification of the rigid predestinationism of Calvin, set forth by Jacob Arminius (1560-1609) and formally stated in the *Remonstrance* of 1610. Arminianism influenced some Calvinist bodies.

**Unitarianism:** A 16th century doctrine which rejected the Trinity and the divinity of Christ in favor of a uni-personal God. It claimed scriptural support for a long time but became generally rationalistic with respect to "revealed" doctrine as well as in ethics and its world-view. One of its principal early proponents was Faustus Socinus (1539-1604), a leader of the Polish Brethren.

A variety of communions developed in England in the Reformation and post-Reformation periods.

**Puritans:** Extremists who sought church reform along Calvinist lines in severe simplicity. (Use of the term was generally discontinued after 1660.)

**Presbyterians:** Basically Calvinistic, called Presbyterian because church polity centers around assemblies of presbyters or elders. John Knox (c. 1513-1572) established the church in Scotland.

**Congregationalists:** Evangelical in spirit and seeking a return to forms of the primitive church, they uphold individual freedom in religious matters, do not require the acceptance of a creed as a condition for communion, and regard each congregation as autonomous. Robert Browne influenced the beginnings of Congregationalism.

**Quakers:** Their key belief is in internal divine illumination, the inner light of the living Christ, as the only source of truth and inspiration. George Fox (1624-1691) was one of their leaders in England. Called the Society of Friends, the Quakers are noted for their pacifism.

**Baptists:** So called because of their doctrine concerning baptism. They reject infant baptism and consider only baptism by immersion as valid. Leaders in the formation of the church were John Smyth (d. 1612) in England and Roger Williams (d. 1683) in America.

**Methodists:** A group who broke away from the Anglican Communion under the leadership of John Wesley (1703-1791), although some Anglican beliefs were retained. Doctrines include the witness of the Spirit to the individual and personal assurance of salvation. Wesleyan Methodists do not subscribe to some of the more rigid Calvinistic tenets held by other Methodists.

**Universalism:** A product of 18th-century liberal Protestantism in England. The doctrine is not Trinitarian and includes a tenet that all men will ultimately be saved.

## ANGLICAN COMMUNION

This communion, which regards itself as the same apostolic Church as that which was established by early Christians in England, derived not from Reformation influences but from the renunciation of papal jurisdiction by Henry VIII (1491-1547). His Act of Supremacy in 1534 called Christ's Church an assembly of local churches subject to the prince, who was vested with fullness of authority and jurisdiction. In spite of Henry's denial of papal authority, this Act did not reject substantially other principal articles of faith. Notable changes, proposed and adopted for the reformation of the church, took place in the subsequent reigns of James VI and Elizabeth, with respect to such matters as Scripture as the rule of faith, the sacraments, the nature of the Mass, and the constitution of the hierarchy. There are 27 provinces in the Anglican Communion. (See Episcopal Church, Anglican Orders, Anglican-Catholic Final Report.)

# MAJOR PROTESTANT CHURCHES IN THE UNITED STATES

There are more than 250 Protestant church bodies in the United States.

The majority of U.S. Protestants belong to the following denominations: Baptist, Methodist, Lutheran, Presbyterian, Protestant Episcopal, the United Church of Christ, the Christian Church (Disciples of Christ), Evangelicals.

See Ecumenical Dialogues, Reports and related entries for coverage of relations between the Catholic Church and other Christian churches.

## Baptist Churches

Baptist churches, comprising the largest of all American Protestant denominations, were first established by John Smyth near the beginning of the 17th century in England. The first Baptist church in America was founded at Providence by Roger Williams in 1639.

Largest of the nearly 30 Baptist bodies in the U.S. are:

The Southern Baptist Convention, 901 Commerce St., Suite 750, Nashville, Tenn. 37203, with 15.5 million members.

The National Baptist Convention, U.S.A., Inc., 915 Spain St., Baton Rouge, La. 70802, with 8 million members;

The National Baptist Convention of America, Inc., 1320 Pierre Ave., Shreveport, La. 71103, with 4.5 million members.

The American Baptist Churches in the U.S.A., P.O. Box 851, Valley Forge, Pa. 19482, with 1.5 million members.

The total number of U.S. Baptists is more than 29 million. The world total is 33 million.

Proper to Baptists is their doctrine on baptism. Called an "ordinance" rather than a sacrament, baptism by immersion is a sign that one has experienced and decided in favor of the salvation offered by Christ. It is administered only to persons who are able to make a responsible decision. Baptism is not administered to infants.

Baptists do not have a formal creed but generally subscribe to two professions of faith formulated in 1689 and 1832 and are in general agreement with classical Protestant theology regarding Scripture as the sole rule of faith, original sin, justification through faith in Christ, and the nature of the Church. Their local churches are autonomous.

Worship services differ in form from one congregation to another. Usual elements are the reading of Scripture, a sermon, hymns, vocal and silent prayer. The Lord's Supper, called an "ordinance," is celebrated at various times.

## Christian Church (Disciples of Christ)

*(Courtesy of Cathy Hinkle, Office of Communication.)*

The Christian Church (Disciples of Christ) originated early in the 1800's from two movements against rigid denominationalism led by Presbyterians Thomas and Alexander Campbell in western Pennsylvania and Barton W. Stone in Kentucky. The two movements developed separately for about 25 years before being merged in 1832.

The church, which identifies itself with the Protestant mainstream, has nearly one million members in almost 4,000 congregations in the U.S. and Canada. The greatest concentration of members in the U.S. is located roughly along the old frontier line, in an arc sweeping from Ohio and Kentucky through the Midwest and down into Oklahoma and Texas.

The general offices of the church are located at 130 E. Washington St., Indianapolis, Ind. 46204.

The church's persistent concern for Christian unity is based on a conviction expressed in a basic document, *Declaration and Address,* dating from its founding. The document states: "The church of Christ upon earth is essentially, intentionally and constitutionally one."

The Disciples have no official doctrine or dogma. Their worship practices vary widely from more common informal services to what could almost be described as "high church" services. Membership is granted after a simple statement of belief in Jesus Christ and baptism by immersion; most congregations admit un-immersed transfers from other denominations. The Lord's Supper or Eucharist, generally called Communion, is always open to Christians of all persuasions. Lay men and women routinely preside over the Lord's Supper, which is celebrated each Sunday; they often preach and perform other pastoral functions as well. Distinction between ordained and non-ordained members is blurred somewhat because of the Disciples' emphasis on all members of the church as ministers.

The Christian Church is oriented to congregational government, and has a unique structure in which three sections of polity (general, regional and congregational) operate as equals rather than in a pyramid of authority. At the national or international level, it is governed by a general assembly which has voting representation direct from congregations and regions as well as all ordained and licensed clergy.

## Episcopal Church

*(Courtesy of The Episcopal Church Center, Office of News and Information.)*

The Episcopal Church, which includes 119 dioceses in the United States, Central and South America, and elsewhere overseas, regards itself as part of the same apostolic church which was established by early Christians in England. Established in this country during the colonial period, it became independent of the jurisdiction of the Church of England when a new constitution and Prayer Book were adopted at a general convention held in 1789. It has approximately 2.5 million members worldwide.

Offices of the presiding bishop and the executive council are located at 815 Second Ave., New York, N.Y. 10017.

The presiding bishop is chief pastor and primate; he is elected by the House of Bishops and confirmed by the House of Deputies for a term of nine years.

The Episcopal Church, which is a part of the Anglican Communion, regards the Archbishop of Canterbury as the "First among Equals," though not under his authority.

The Anglican Communion, worldwide, has 70 million members in 31 self-governing churches.

Official statements of belief and practice are found in the Book of Common Prayer. Scripture has primary importance with respect to the rule of faith, and authority is also attached to tradition.

An episcopal system of church government prevails, but presbyters, deacons and lay persons also have an active voice in church affairs. The levels of government are the general convention, and executive council, dioceses, and local parishes. At the parish level, the congregation has the right to select its own rector, with the consent of the bishop.

Liturgical worship is according to the Book of Common Prayer as adopted in 1979, but details of ceremonial practice vary from one congregation to another.

## Lutheran Churches

The origin of Lutheranism is generally traced to Oct. 31, 1517, when Martin Luther — Augustinian friar, priest, doctor of theology — tacked "95 Theses" to the door of the castle church in Wittenberg, Germany. This call to debate on the subject of indulgences and related concerns has come to symbolize the beginning of the Reformation. Luther and his supporters intended to reform the Church they knew. Though Lutheranism has come to be visible in separate denominations and national churches, at its heart it professes itself to be a confessional movement within the one, holy, catholic and apostolic Church.

The world's 60 million Lutherans form the third largest grouping of Christians, after Roman Catholics and Orthodox. About 55 million of them belong to church bodies which make up the Lutheran World Federation, headquartered in Geneva.

There are about 8.5 million Lutherans in the United States, making them the fourth largest Christian grouping, after Roman Catholics, Baptists and Methodists. Although there are nearly 20 U.S. Lutheran church bodies, all but 100,000 Lutherans belong to either the Evangelical Lutheran Church in America (with 5.2 million members and headquarters at 8765 W. Higgins Rd., Chicago, Ill. 60631), The Lutheran Church-Missouri Synod (with 2.61 million members and headquarters at 1333 S. Kirkwood Rd., St. Louis, Mo. 63122), or the Wisconsin Evangelical Lutheran Synod (with 420,000 members and headquarters at 2929 N. Mayfair Rd., Milwaukee, Wis. 53222).

The Evangelical Lutheran Church in America and the Lutheran Church-Missouri Synod carry out some work together through inter-Lutheran agencies such as Lutheran World Relief and Lutheran Immigration and Refugee Services; both agencies have offices at 390 Park Ave. South, New York, N.Y. 10010.

The statements of faith which have shaped the confessional life of Lutheranism are found in the *Book of Concord.* This 1580 collection includes the three ancient ecumenical creeds (Apostles', Nicene and Athanasian), Luther's *Large and Small Catechisms* (1529), the *Augsburg Confession* (1530) and the *Apology* in defense of it (1531), the *Smalcald Articles* (including the "Treatise on the Power and Primacy of the Pope") (1537), and the *Formula of Concord* (1577).

The central Lutheran doctrinal proposition is that Christians "receive forgiveness of sins and become righteous before God by grace, for Christ's sake." Baptism and the Lord's Supper (Holy Communion, the Eucharist) are universally celebrated among Lutherans as sacramental means of grace. Lutherans also treasure the Word proclaimed in the reading of the Scriptures, preaching and absolution.

Generally in Lutheranism, the bishop, or a pastor (presbyter/priest) authorized by the bishop, is the minister of ordination. Much of Lutheranism continues what it understands as the historic succession of bishops (though without considering the historic episcopate essential for the church). All of Lutheranism is concerned to preserve apostolic succession in life and doctrine.

Lutheran jurisdictions corresponding to dioceses are called districts or synods in North America. There are more than 100 of them; each of them is headed by a bishop or president.

## Methodist Churches

*(Courtesy of Joe Hale, General Secretary of the World Methodist Council.)*

John Wesley (1703-1791), an Anglican clergyman, was the founder of Methodism. In 1738, following a period of missionary work in America and strongly influenced by the Moravians, he experienced a new conversion to Christ and shortly thereafter became a leader in a religious awakening in England. By the end of the 18th century, Methodism was strongly rooted also in America.

The United Methodist Church, formed in 1968 by a merger of the Methodist Church and the Evangelical United Brethren Church, is the second largest Protestant denomination in the U.S., with more than nine million members; its principal agencies are located in New York, Evanston, Ill., Nashville, Tenn., Washington, D.C., Dayton, O., and Lake Junaluska, N.C. (World Methodist Council, P.O. Box 518. 28745). The second largest body, with just under two million communicants, is the African Methodist Episcopal Church. Four other major churches in the U.S. are the African Methodist Episcopal Zion, Christian Methodist Episcopal, Free Methodist Church and the Wesleyan Church. The total Methodist membership in the U.S. is about 15.5 million.

Worldwide, there are more than 71 autonomous Methodist/Wesleyan churches in 107 countries, with a membership of more than 29 million. All of them participate in the World Methodist Council, which gives global unity to the witness of Methodist communicants.

Methodism, although it has a base in Calvinistic theology, rejects absolute predestination and maintains that Christ offers grace freely to all men, not just to a select elite. Wesley's distinctive doctrine was the "witness of the Spirit" to the individual soul and personal assurance of salvation. He also emphasized the central themes of conversion and holiness. Methodists are in general agreement with classical Protestant theology regarding Scripture as the sole rule of faith, original sin, justification through faith in Christ, the nature of the Church, and the sacraments of baptism and the Lord's Supper. Church polity is structured along episcopal lines in America,

with ministers being appointed to local churches by a bishop; churches stemming from British Methodism do not have bishops but vest appointive powers within an appropriate conference. Congregations are free to choose various forms of worship services; typical elements are readings from Scripture, sermons, hymns and prayers.

## Presbyterian Churches

Presbyterians are so called because of their tradition of governing the church through a system of representative bodies composed of elders (presbyters).

Presbyterianism is a part of the Reformed Family of Churches that grew out of the theological work of John Calvin following the Lutheran Reformation, to which it is heavily indebted. Countries in which it acquired early strength and influence were Switzerland, France, Holland, Scotland and England.

Presbyterianism spread widely in this country in the latter part of the 18th century and afterwards. Presently, it has approximately 3.0 million communicants in nine bodies.

The two largest Presbyterian bodies in the country — the United Presbyterian Church in the U.S.A. and the Presbyterian Church in the United States — were reunited in June, 1983, to form the Presbyterian Church (U.S.A.), with a membership of 2.7 million. Its national offices are located at 100 Witherspoon St., Louisville, Ky. 40202.

These churches, now merged, are closely allied with the Reformed Church in America, the United Church of Christ, the Cumberland Presbyterian Churches and the Associate Reformed Presbyterian Church.

In Presbyterian doctrine, baptism and the Lord's Supper, viewed as seals of the covenant of grace, are regarded as sacraments. Baptism, which is not necessary for salvation, is conferred on infants and adults The Lord's Supper is celebrated as a covenant of the Sacrifice of Christ. In both sacraments, a doctrine of the real presence of Christ is considered the central theological principle.

The Church is twofold, being invisible and also visible; it consists of all of the elect and all those Christians who are united in Christ as their immediate head.

Presbyterians are in general agreement with classical Protestant theology regarding Scripture as the sole rule of faith and practice, salvation by grace, and justification through faith in Christ.

Presbyterian congregations are governed by a session composed of elders elected by the communicant membership. On higher levels there are presbyteries, synods and a general assembly with various degrees of authority over local bodies; all such representative bodies are composed of elected elders and ministers in approximately equal numbers. The church annually elects a moderator who presides at the General Assembly and travels throughout the church to speak to and hear from the members.

Worship services, simple and dignified, include sermons, prayer, reading of the Scriptures and hymns. The Lord's Supper is celebrated at intervals. Doctrinal developments of the past several years included approval in May, 1967, by the General Assembly of the United Presbyterian Church of a contemporary confession of faith to supplement the historic Westminster Confession. A statement entitled "The Declaration of Faith" was approved in 1977 by the Presbyterian Church in the U.S. for teaching and liturgical use.

The reunited church adopted "A Brief Statement of Reformed Faith" in 1991 regarding urgent concerns of the church.

## United Church of Christ

*(Courtesy of Darrell J. Ludwig/UCC Yearbook Office.)*

The 1,501,310-member (in 1994) United Church of Christ was formed in 1957 by a union of the Congregational Christian and the Evangelical and Reformed Churches. The former was originally established by the Pilgrims and the Puritans of the Massachusetts Bay Colony, while the latter was founded in Pennsylvania in the early 1700s by settlers from Central Europe. The denomination had 6,362 congregations throughout the United States in 1988.

It considers itself "a united and uniting church" and keeps itself open to all ecumenical options.

Its headquarters are located at 700 Prospect, Cleveland, Ohio 44115.

Its statement of faith recognizes Jesus Christ as "our crucified and risen Lord (who) shared our common lot, conquering sin and death and reconciling the world to himself." It believes in the life after death, and the fact that God "judges men and nations by his righteous will declared through prophets and apostles."

The United Church further believes that Christ calls its members to share in his baptism "and eat at his table, to join him in his passion and victory." Each local church is free to adopt its own methods of worship and to formulate its own covenants and confessions of faith. Some celebrate communion weekly; others, monthly or on another periodical basis. Like other Calvinistic bodies, it believes that Christ is spiritually present in the sacrament.

The United Church is governed along congregational lines, and each local church is autonomous. However, the actions of its biennial General Synod are taken with great seriousness by congregations. Between synods, a 44-member executive council oversees the work of the church.

## Evangelicalism

Evangelicalism, dating from 1735 in England (the Evangelical Revival) and after 1740 in the United States (the Great Awakening), has had and continues to have widespread influence in Protestant churches. It has been estimated that about 45 millon American Protestants — communicants of both large denominations and small bodies — are evangelicals.

The Bible is their rule of faith and religious practice. Being born again in a life-changing experience through faith in Christ is the promise of salvation. Missionary work for the spread of the Gospel is a normal and necessary activity.

Additional matters of belief and practice are generally of a conservative character. Fundamentalists, numbering perhaps 4.5 million, comprise an extreme right-wing subculture of evangelicalism. They are distinguished mainly by militant biblicism, belief in the absolute inerrancy of the Bible and emphasis on the Second Coming of Christ. Fundamentalism developed early in the 20th century in reaction against liberal theology and secularizing trends in mainstream and other Protestant denominations.

The Holiness or Perfectionist wing of evangelicalism evolved from Methodist efforts to preserve, against a contrary trend, the personal-piety and inner-religion concepts of John Wesley. There are at least 30 Holiness bodies in the U.S.

Pentecostals, probably the most demonstrative of evangelicals, are noted for speaking in tongues and the stress they place on healing, prophecy and personal testimony to the practice and power of evangelical faith.

## Assemblies of God

Assemblies (Churches) of God form the largest body (more than 2 million members) in the Pentecostal Movement which developed from (1) the Holiness Revival in the Methodist Church after the Civil War and (2) the Apostolic Faith Movement at the beginning of the 20th century. Members share with other Pentecostals belief in the religious experience of conversion and in the baptism by the Holy Spirit that sanctifies. Distinctive to them is the emphasis they place on the charismatic gifts of the apostolic church, healing and speaking in tongues, which are signs of the "second blessing" of the Holy Spirit.

The Assemblies are strongly fundamentalist in theology; are loosely organized in various districts, with democratic procedures; are vigorously evangelistic. There is considerable freedom in expressions of the Spirit, sermons and hymns. The moral code is rigid.

---

## RETROUVAILLE

Retrouvaille is a ministry to hurting marriages, consisting of a weekend experience with follow-up sessions designed to provide husbands and wives with ways and means of healing and reconciliation. Emphasis is on communication between husband and wife, enabling them to rediscover each other and to examine their lives in a new and positive way.

Retrouvaille is not a retreat, is not a sensitivity group, does not include group dynamics or group discussions. The program is conducted under the direction of trained couples and priests. Programs are usually offered under the auspices of diocesan family life agencies. International Coordinating Team: Roger and Pat Bate, 231 Ballantrae, Houston, TX 77015.

The modern ecumenical movement, which started about 1910 among Protestants and led to formation of the World Council of Churches in 1948, developed outside the mainstream of Catholic interest for many years. It has now become for Catholics as well one of the great religious facts of our time.

The magna charta of ecumenism for Catholics is a complex of several documents which include, in the first place, the *Decree on Ecumenism* promulgated by the Second Vatican Council Nov. 21, 1964. Other enactments underlying and expanding this decree are the *Dogmatic Constitution on the Church*, the *Decree on Eastern Catholic Churches*, the *Pastoral Constitution on the Church in the Modern World and the encyclical letter Ut Unum Sint.*

## VATICAN II DECREE

*The following excerpts from the "Decree on Ecumenism" cover the broad theological background and principles and indicate the thrust of the Church's commitment to ecumenism, under the subheads: Elements Common to Christians, Unity Lacking, What the Movement Involves, Primary Duty of Catholics.*

Men who believe in Christ and have been properly baptized are brought into a certain, though imperfect, communion with the Catholic Church. Undoubtedly, the differences that exist in varying degrees between them and the Catholic Church — whether in doctrine and sometimes in discipline, or concerning the structure of the Church — do indeed create many and sometimes serious obstacles to full ecclesiastical communion. These the ecumenical movement is striving to overcome (No. 3).

### Elements Common to Christians

Moreover some, even very many, of the most significant elements or endowments which together go to build up and give life to the Church herself can exist outside the visible boundaries of the Catholic Church: the written word of God; the life of grace; faith, hope, and charity, along with other interior gifts of the Holy Spirit and visible elements. All of these, which come from Christ and lead back to Him, belong by right to the one Church of Christ (No. 3).

[In a later passage, the decree singled out a number of elements which the Catholic Church and other churches have in common but not in complete agreement: confession of Christ as Lord and God and as mediator between God and man; belief in the Trinity; reverence for Scripture as the revealed word of God; baptism and the Lord's Supper Christian life and worship; faith in action; concern with moral questions.]

The brethren divided from us also carry out many of the sacred actions of the Christian religion. Undoubtedly, in ways that vary according to the condition of each church or community, these actions can truly engender a life of grace, and can be rightly described as capable of providing access to the community of salvation.

It follows that these separated Churches and Communities, though we believe they suffer from defects already mentioned, have by no means been deprived of significance and importance in the mystery of salvation. For the Spirit of Christ has not refrained from using them as means of salvation which derive their efficacy from the very fullness of grace and truth entrusted to the Catholic Church (No. 3).

### Unity Lacking

Nevertheless, our separated brethren, whether considered as individuals or as Communities and Churches, are not blessed with that unity which Jesus Christ wished to bestow on all those whom he has regenerated and vivified into one body and newness of life — that unity which the holy Scriptures and the revered tradition of the Church proclaim. For it is through Christ's Catholic Church alone, which is the all-embracing means of salvation, that the fullness of the means of salvation can be obtained. It was to the apostolic college alone, of which Peter is the head, that we believe our Lord entrusted all the blessings of the New Covenant, in order to establish on earth the one Body of Christ into which all those should be fully incorporated who already belong in any way to God's People (No. 3).

### What the Movement Involves

Today, in many parts of the world, under the inspiring grace of the Holy Spirit, multiple efforts are being expended through prayer, word, and action to attain that fullness of unity which Jesus Christ desires. This sacred Synod, therefore, exhorts all the Catholic faithful to recognize the signs of the times and to participate skillfully in the work of ecumenism.

The "ecumenical movement" means those activities and enterprises which, according to various needs of the Church and opportune occasions, are started and organized for the fostering of unity among Christians. These are:

• First, every effort to eliminate words, judgments, and actions which do not respond to the condition of separated brethren with truth and fairness and so make mutual relations between them more difficult.

• Then, "dialogue" between competent experts from different Churches and Communities [scholarly ecumenism].

• In addition, these Communions cooperate more closely in whatever projects a Christian conscience demands for the common good [social ecumenism].

• They also come together for common prayer, where this is permitted [spiritual ecumenism].

• Finally, all are led to examine their own faithfulness to Christ's will for the Church and, wherever necessary, undertake with vigor the task of renewal and reform.

It is evident that the work of preparing and reconciling those individuals who wish for full Catholic communion is of its nature distinct from ecumenical action. But there is no opposition between the two, since both proceed from the wondrous providence of God (No. 4).

### Primary Duty of Catholics

In ecumenical work, Catholics must assuredly be concerned for their separated brethren, praying for them, keeping them informed about the Church, making the first approaches toward them. But their primary duty is to make an honest and careful appraisal of whatever needs to be renewed and achieved in the Catholic household itself, in order that its life may bear witness more loyally and luminously to the teachings and ordinances which have been handed down from Christ through the Apostles.

Every Catholic must aim at Christian perfection (cf. Jas. 1:4; Rom. 12:1-2) and, each according to his station, play his part so that the Church may daily be more purified and renewed, against the day when Christ will present her to himself in all her glory, without spot or wrinkle (cf. Eph. 5:27).

Catholics must joyfully acknowledge and esteem the truly Christian endowments from our common heritage which are to be found among our separated brethren.

Nor should we forget that whatever is wrought by the grace of the Holy Spirit in the hearts of our separated brethren can contribute to our own edification. Whatever is truly Christian never conflicts with the genuine interests of the faith; indeed, it can always result in a more ample realization of the very mystery of Christ and the Church (No. 4).

## Participation in Worship

Norms concerning participation by Catholics in the worship of other Christian Churches were sketched in this conciliar decree and elaborated in a number of other documents such as: the *Decree on Eastern Catholic Churches*, promulgated by the Second Vatican Council in 1964; *Interim Guidelines for Prayer in Common*, issued June 18, 1965, by the U.S. Bishops' Committee for Ecumenical and Inter-religious Affairs; a *Directory on Ecumenism*, published in 1967, 1970 and 1993 by the Pontifical Council for Promoting Christian Unity; additional communications from the U.S. Bishops' Committee, and numerous sets of guidelines issued locally by and for dioceses throughout the U.S.

The norms encourage common prayer services for Christian unity and other intentions. Beyond that, they draw a distinction between separated churches of the Reformation tradition and of the Anglican Communion, and separated Eastern churches, in view of doctrine and practice the Catholic Church has in common wit the separated Eastern churches concerning the apostolic succession of bishops, holy orders, liturgy and other credal matters.

Full participation by Catholics in official Protestant liturgies is prohibited, because it implies profession of the faith expressed in the liturgy. Intercommunion by Catholics at Protestant liturgies is prohibited. Under certain conditions, Protestants may be given Holy Communion in the Catholic Church (see Intercommunion). A Catholic may stand as a witness, but not as a sponsor, in baptism, and as a witness in the marriage of separated Christians. Similarly, a Protestant may stand as a witness, but not as a sponsor, in a Catholic baptism, and as a witness in the marriage of Catholics.

## Separated Eastern Churches

The principal norms regarding liturgical participation with separated Eastern Christians are included under Eastern Ecumenism.

# DIRECTORY ON ECUMENISM

A new *Directory for the Application of the Principles and Norms of Ecumenism* was approved by Pope John Paul Mar. 25, 1993, and published early in June. The Pontifical Council for Promoting Christian Unity said on release of the document that revision of Directories issued in 1967 and 1970 was necessary in view of subsequent developments. These included promulgation of the *Code of Canon Law* for the Latin Church in 1983 and of the *Code of Canons of the Eastern Churches* in 1990; publication of the Catechism of the Catholic Church in 1992; additional documents and the results of theological dialogues.

*The following excerpts are from the text published in the June 16, 1993, English edition of L'Osservatore Romano.*

## Address and Purpose

"The Directory is addressed to the pastors of the Catholic Church, but it also concerns all the faithful, who are called to pray and work for the unity of Christians, under the direction of their bishops."

"At the same time, it is hoped that the Directory will also be useful to members of churches and ecclesial communities that are not in full communion with the Catholic Church."

"The new edition of the Directory is meant to be an instrument at the service of the whole Church, and especially of those who are directly engaged in ecumenical activity in the Catholic Church. The Directory intends to motivate, enlighten and guide this activity, and in some particular cases also to give binding directives in accordance with the proper competence of the Pontifical Council for Promoting Christian Unity."

## Outline

Principles and norms of the document are covered in five chapters.

"**I. The Search for Christian Unity.** The ecumenical commitment of the Catholic Church based on the doctrinal principles of the Second Vatican Council.

"**II. Organization in the Catholic Church at the Service of Christian Unity.** Persons and structures involved in promoting ecumenism at all levels, and the norms that direct their activity.

"**III. Ecumenical Formation in the Catholic Church.** Categories of people to be formed, those responsible for formation; the aims and methods of formation; its doctrinal and practical aspects.

"**IV. Communion in Life and Spiritual Activity among the Baptized.** The communion that exists with other Christians on the basis of the sacramental bond of baptism, and the norms for sharing in prayer and other spiritual activities, including, in particular cases, sacramental sharing.

"**V. Ecumenical Cooperation, Dialogue and Common Witness.** Principles, different forms and norms for cooperation between Christians with a view to dialogue and common witness in the world."

# ECUMENICAL AGENCIES

## Pontifical Council

The top-level agency for Catholic ecumenical efforts is the Pontifical Council for Promoting Christian Unity (formerly the Secretariat for Promoting Christian Unity), which originated in 1960 as a preparatory commission for the Second Vatican Council. Its purposes are to provide guidance and, where necessary, coordination for ecumenical endeavor by Catholics, and to establish and maintain relations with representatives of other Christian Churches for ecumenical dialogue and action.

The council, under the direction of Cardinal Edward I. Cassidy (successor to Cardinal Johannes Willebrands), has established firm working relations with representative agencies of other churches and the World Council of Churches. It has joined in dialogue with Orthodox Churches, the Anglican Communion, the Lutheran World Federation, the World Alliance of Reformed Churches, the World Methodist Council and other religious bodies. In the past several years, staff members and representatives of the council have been involved in one way or another in nearly every significant ecumenical enterprise and meeting held throughout the world.

While the council and its counterparts in other churches have focused primary attention on theological and other related problems of Christian unity, they have also begun, and in increasing measure, to emphasize the responsibilities of the churches for greater unity of witness and effort in areas of humanitarian need.

## Bishops' Committee

The U.S. Bishops' Committee for Ecumenical and Interreligious Affairs was established by the American hierarchy in 1964. Its purposes are to maintain relationships with other Christian churches and other religious communities at the national level, to advise and assist dioceses in developing and applying ecumenical policies, and to maintain liaison with corresponding Vatican offices — the Councils for Christian Unity and for Interreligious Dialogue.

This standing committee of the National Conference of Catholic Bishops is chaired by Bishop Alexander J. Brunett of Helena. Operationally, the committee is assisted by a secretariat with the Rev. John F. Hotchkin, director; Dr. Eugene J. Fisher, executive secretary for Catholic-Jewish Relations; Dr. John Borelli, Jr., executive secretary for Interreligious Relations and Bro. Jeffrey Gros, Associate Director.

The committee co-sponsors several national consultations with other churches and confessional families. These bring together Catholic representatives and their counterparts from the Episcopal Church, the Lutheran Church, the Polish National Catholic Church, the United Methodist Church, the Orthodox Churches, the Oriental Orthodox Churches, the Alliance of Reformed Churches (North American area), the Interfaith Witness Department of the Home Mission Board of the Southern Baptist Convention. (See Ecumenical Dialogues.)

The committee relates with the National Council of Churches of Christ, through membership in the Faith and Order Commission and through observer relationship with the Commission on Regional and Local Ecumenism, and has sponsored a joint study committee investigating the possibility of Roman Catholic membership in that body.

Advisory and other services are provided by the committee to ecumenical commissions and agencies in dioceses throughout the country.

Through its Section for Catholic-Jewish Relations, the committee is in contact with several national Jewish agencies and bodies. Issues of mutual interest and shared concern are reviewed for the purpose of furthering deeper understanding between the Catholic and Jewish communities.

Through its Section for Interreligious Relations, the committee promotes activity in wider areas of dialogue with other religions, notably, with Muslims, Buddhists and Hindus.

Offices of the committee are located at 3211 Fourth St. N.E., Washington, D.C. 20017.

## World Council

The World Council of Churches is a fellowship of churches which acknowledge "Jesus Christ as Lord and Savior." It is a permanent organization providing constituent members — 330 churches with some 450 million communicants in 100 countries — with opportunities for meeting, consultation and cooperative action with respect to doctrine, worship, practice, social mission, evangelism and missionary work, and other matters of mutual concern.

The WCC was formally established Aug. 23, 1948, in Amsterdam with ratification of a constitution by 147 communions. This action merged two previously existing movements — Life and Work (social mission), Faith and Order (doctrine) — which had initiated practical steps toward founding a fellowship of Christian churches at meetings held in Oxford, Edinburgh and Utrecht in 1937 and 1938. A third movement for cooperative missionary work, which originated about 1910 and, remotely, led to formation of the WCC, was incorporated into the council in 1971 under the title of the International Missionary Council (now the Commission for World Mission and Evangelism).

Additional general assemblies of the council have been held since the charter meeting of 1948: in Evanston, Ill. (1954), New Delhi, India (1961), Uppsala, Sweden (1968), Nairobi, Kenya (1975), Vancouver, British Columbia, Canada (1983) and Canberra, Australia (1991). The 1998 general assembly is scheduled to be held in Harare, Zimbabwe.

The council continues the work of the International Missionary Council, the Commission on Faith and Order, and the Commission on Church and Society. The work of the council is carried out through four program units: unity and renewal; mission, education and witness; justice, peace and creation; sharing and service.

Liaison between the council and the Vatican has been maintained since 1966 through a joint working group. Roman Catholic membership in the WCC is a question officially on the agenda of this body. The Joint Commission on Society, Development and Peace (SODEPAX) was an agency of the council and the Pontifical Commission for Justice and Peace from 1968 to Dec. 31, 1980, after which another working group was formed. Roman Catholics serve individually as full members of the Commission on Faith and Order and in various capacities on other program committees of the council.

WCC headquarters are located in Geneva, Switzerland. The United States Conference for the World Council of Churches at 475 Riverside Drive, Room 915, New York, N.Y. 10115, provides liaison between the U.S. churches and Geneva, a communications office for secular and church media relations, and a publications office. The WCC also maintains fraternal relations with regional, national and local councils of churches throughout the world.

The Rev. Konrad Raiser, a Lutheran from Germany, was elected general secretary, Aug. 24, 1992.

## National Council of Churches

The National Council of the Churches of Christ in the U.S.A., the largest ecumenical body in the United States, is an organization of 33 Protestant, Orthodox and Anglican church bodies with an aggregate membership of about 50 million.

The NCC, established by the churches in 1950, was structured through the merger of 12 separate cooperative agencies. Presently, the NCC carries on work in behalf of member churches in overseas ministries, Christian education, domestic social action, communications, disaster relief, refugee assistance, rehabilitation and development, biblical translation, international affairs, theological dialogue, interfaith activities, worship and evangelism, and other areas.

Policies of the NCC are determined by a general board of approximately 270 members appointed by the constituent churches. The board meets once a year.

NCC presidents: Bishop Melvin Talbert (1996-97), Bishop Craig B. Anderson (1988-99). General secretary: The Rev. Joan Brown Campbell.

NCC headquarters are located at 475 Riverside Drive, New York, N.Y. 10115.

## Consultation on Church Union

*(Courtesy of Rev. David W.A. Taylor, General Secretary.)*

The Consultation on Church Union, officially begun in 1962, is a venture of American churches seeking a united church "truly catholic, truly evangelical, and truly reformed." The churches engaged in this process, representing 25 million Christians, are the African Methodist Episcopal Church, the African Methodist Episcopal Zion Church, the Christian Church (Disciples of Christ), the Christian Methodist Episcopal Church, the Episcopal Church, the Presbyterian Church (U.S.A); the United Church of Christ, the United Methodist Church and the International Council of Community Churches.

At a plenary assembly of COCU in December, 1988, a plan of church unity was unanimously approved for submission to member churches for their action. The plan is contained in a 102-page document entitled "Churches in Covenant Communion: The Church of Christ Uniting." It proposes the formation of a covenant communion of the churches which, while remaining institutionally autonomous, would embrace together eight elements of ecclesial communion: claiming unity in faith, commitment to seek unity with wholeness, mutual recognition of members in one baptism, mutual recognition of each other as churches, mutual recognition and reconciliation of ordained ministries, celebrating the Eucharist together, engaging together in Christ's mission, and the formation together of covenanting councils at each level (national, regional, and local).

Vivian U. Robinson, Ph.D., a lay member of the Christian Methodist Episcopal Church, was elected president in 1988. The Rev. David W.A. Taylor is General Secretary. Offices are located at 151 Wall St., Princeton, N.J. 08540.

## Graymoor Institute

The Graymoor Ecumenical and Interreligious Institute is a forum where issues that confront the Christian Churches are addressed, the spiritual dimensions of ecumenism are fostered, and information, documentation and developments within the ecumenical movement are published through *Ecumenical Trends*, a monthly journal. Director: The Rev. Elias D. Mallon, S.A. Address: 475 Riverside Dr., Rm. 1960, New York, N.Y. 10115.

# U.S. ECUMENICAL DIALOGUES

Representatives of the Bishops' Committee for Ecumenical and Interreligious Affairs, National Conference of Catholic Bishops, have met in dialogue with representatives of other churches since the 1960s, for discussion of a wide variety of subjects related to the quest for unity among Christians. Following is a list of dialogue groups and the years in which dialogue began.

Anglican-Roman Catholic Consultation, 1965;

Eastern Orthodox Consultation (Theologians), 1965; Eastern Orthodox and Roman Catholic Bishops, Joint Committee, 1981; Lutheran Consultation, 1965; Oriental Orthodox Consultation (with Armenian, Coptic, Ethiopian, Indian Malabar and Syrian Orthodox Churches), 1978; Polish National-Catholic Consultation, 1984; Presbyterian/Reformed Consultation, 1965; Southern Baptist Conversations, 1969; United Methodist Consultation, 1966.

# ECUMENICAL REPORTS

*(Source: Rev. John F. Hotchkin, Secretariat of the Bishops' Committee for Ecumenical and Interreligious Affairs, National Conference of Catholic Bishops.)*

## Common Declarations of Popes, Other Prelates

The following ecumenical statements, issued by

several popes and prelates of other Christian churches, carry the authority given them by their signators.

**Paul VI and Orthodox Ecumenical Patriarch Athenagoras I,** First Common Declaration, Dec. 7, 1965: They hoped the differences between the churches would be overcome with the help of the Holy Spirit, and that their "full communion of faith, brotherly concord and sacramental life" would be restored.

**Paul VI and Anglican Archbishop Michael Ramsey** of Canterbury, Mar. 24, 1966: They stated their intention "to inaugurate between the Roman Catholic Church and the Anglican Communion a serious dialogue which, founded on the Gospels and on the ancient common traditions, may lead to that unity in truth for which Christ prayed."

**Paul VI and Patriarch Athenagoras I,** Second Common Declaration, Oct. 27, 1967: They wished "to emphasize their conviction that the restoration of full communion (between the churches) is to be found within the framework of the renewal of the Church and of Christians in fidelity to the traditions of the Fathers and to the inspirations of the Holy Spirit who remains always with the Church."

**Paul VI and Vasken I,** Orthodox Catholicos-Patriarch of All Armenians, May 12, 1970: They called for closer collaboration "in all domains of Christian life. .. . This collaboration must be based on the mutual recognition of the common Christian faith and the sacramental life, on the mutual respect of persons and their churches."

**Paul VI and Mar Ignatius Jacob III,** Syrian Orthodox Patriarch of Antioch, Oct. 27, 1971: They declared themselves to be "in agreement that there is no difference in the faith they profess concerning the mystery of the Word of God made flesh and become really man, even if over the centuries difficulties have arisen out of the different theological expressions by which this faith was expressed."

**Paul VI and Shenouda III,** Coptic Orthodox Pope of Alexandria, May 10, 1973: Their common declaration recalls the common elements of the Catholic and Coptic Orthodox faith in the Trinity, the divinity and humanity of Christ, the seven sacraments, the Virgin Mary, the Church founded upon the Apostles, and the Second Coming of Christ. It recognizes that the two churches "are not able to give more perfect witness to this new life in Christ because of existing divisions which have behind them centuries of difficult history" dating back to the year 451 A.D. In spite of these difficulties, they expressed "determination and confidence in the Lord to achieve the fullness and perfection of that unity which is his gift."

**Paul VI and Anglican Archbishop Donald Coggan** of Canterbury, Apr. 29, 1977: They stated many points on which Anglicans and Roman Catholics hold the faith in common and called for greater cooperation between Anglicans and Roman Catholics.

**John Paul II and Orthodox Ecumenical Patriarch Dimitrios I,** First Common Declaration, Nov. 30, 1979: "Purification of the collective memory of our churches is an important fruit of the dialogue of charity and an indispensable condition of future progress." They announced the establishment of the Catholic-Orthodox Theological Commission.

**John Paul II and Anglican Archbishop Robert Runcie** of Canterbury, May 29, 1982: They agreed to establish a new Anglican-Roman Catholic commission with the task of continuing work already begun toward the eventual resolution of doctrinal differences.

**John Paul II and Ignatius Zakka I,** Syrian Orthodox Patriarch of Antioch, June 23, 1984: They recalled and solemnly reaffirmed the common profession of faith made by their predecessors, Paul VI and Mar Ignatius Jacob III, in 1971. They said: "The confusions and the schisms that occurred between the churches, they realize today, in no way affect or touch the substance of their faith, since these arose only because of differences in terminology and culture, and in the various formulae adopted by different theological schools to express the same matter. Accordingly, we find today no real basis for the sad divisions which arose between us concerning the doctrine of the Incarnation." On the pastoral level, they declared: "It is not rare for our faithful to find access to a priest of their own church materially or morally impossible. Anxious to meet their needs and with their spiritual benefit in mind, we authorize them in such cases to ask for the sacraments of penance, Eucharist and anointing of the sick from lawful priests of either of our two sister churches, when they need them."

**John Paul II and Orthodox Ecumenical Patriarch Dimitrios I,** Second Common Declaration, Dec. 7, 1987: Dialogue conducted since 1979 indicated that the churches can already profess together as common faith about the mystery of the Church and the connection between faith and the sacraments. They also stated that, "when unity of faith is assured, a certain diversity of expressions does not create obstacles to unity, but enriches the life of the Church and the understanding, always imperfect, of the revealed mystery.

**John Paul II and Anglican Archbishop Robert Runcie** of Canterbury, Oct. 2, 1989: They said: "We solemnly re-commit ourselves and those we represent to the restoration of visible unity and full ecclesial communion in the confidence that to seek anything less would be to betray our Lord's intention for the unity of his people."

**John Paul II and His Holiness Mar Dinkha IV, Catholicos-Patriarch of the Assyrian Church of the East,** Nov. 11, 1994: They acknowledged that, despite past differences, both churches profess the same faith in the real union of divine and human natures in the divine Person of Christ.

## INTERNATIONAL BILATERAL COMMISSIONS

**Anglican-Roman Catholic International Commission,** sponsored by the Pontifical Council for Promoting Christian Unity and the Lambeth Conference, from 1970 to 1981; succeeded by a **Second Anglican-Roman Catholic International Commission,** called into being by the Common Declaration of Pope John Paul and the Archbishop of Canterbury in 1982.

**The International Theological Colloquium between Baptists and Catholics,** established in 1984 by the Pontifical Council for Promoting Christian Unity and the Commission for Faith and Interchurch Cooperation of the Baptist World Alliance.

**The Disciples of Christ-Roman Catholic Dialogue,** organized by the Council of Christian Unity of the Christian Church (Disciples of Christ) and the U.S. Bishops' Committee for Ecumenical and

InterreligiousAffairs, along with participation by the Disciples' Ecumenical Consultative Council and the Unity Council; since 1977.

**The Evangelical-Roman Catholic Dialogue on Mission,** organized by Evangelicals and the Pontifical Council for Promoting Christian Unity; from 1977.

**The Joint Lutheran-Roman Catholic Study Commission,** established by the Pontifical Council for Promoting Christian Unity and the Lutheran World Federation; from 1967.

**The International Catholic-Orthodox Theologi-**

**cal Commission,** established by the Holy See and 14 autocephalous Orthodox Churches, began its work at a first session held at Patmos/Rhodes in 1980. Subsequent sessions have been held at Munich (1982), Crete (1984), Bari (1987), Valamo (1988) and Freising (1990).

**Pentecostal-Roman Catholic Conversations,** since 1966.

**The Reformed-Roman Catholic Conversations,** inaugurated in 1970 by the Pontifical Council for Promoting Christian Unity and the World Alliance of Reformed Churches.

# INTERFAITH STATEMENTS

The ecumenical statements listed below, and others like them, reflect the views of participants in the dialogues which produced them. They have not been formally accepted by the respective churches as formulations of doctrine or points of departure for practical changes in discipline. (For other titles, see U.S. Ecumenical Dialogues, Ecumenical Reports.)

• The "Windsor Statement" on Eucharistic doctrine, published Dec. 31, 1971, by the Anglican-Roman Catholic International Commission of theologians. (For text, see pages 132-33 of the 1973 *Catholic Almanac.*)

• The "Canterbury Statement" on ministry and ordination, published Dec. 13, 1973, by the same commission. (For excerpts, see pages 127-30 of the 1975 *Catholic Almanac.*)

• "Papal Primacy / Converging Viewpoints," published Mar. 4, 1974, by the dialogue group sanctioned by the U.S.A. National Convention of the World Lutheran Federation and the U.S. Bishops' Committee for Ecumenical and Interreligious Affairs. (For excerpts, see pages 130-31 of the 1975 *Catholic Almanac.*)

• An "Agreed Statement on the Purpose of the Church," published Oct. 31, 1975, by the Anglican-Roman Catholic Consultation in the U.S.

• "Christian Unity and Women's Ordination," published Nov. 7, 1975, by the same consultation, in which it was said that the ordination of women (approved in principle by the Anglican Communion but not by the Catholic Church) would "introduce a new element" in dialogue but would not mean the end of consultation nor the abandonment of its declared goal of full communion and organic unity.

• "Holiness and Spirituality of the Ordained Ministry," issued early in 1976 by theologians of the Catholic Church and the United Methodist Church; the first statement resulting from dialogue begun in 1966.

• "Mixed Marriages," published in the spring of 1976 by the Anglican-Roman Catholic Consultation in the U.S.

• "Bishops and Presbyters," published in July, 1976, by the Orthodox-Roman Catholic Consultation in the U.S. on the following points of common understanding: (1) Ordination in apostolic succession is required for pastoral office in the Church. (2) Presiding at the Eucharistic Celebration is a task belonging to those ordained to pastoral service. (3) The offices of bishop and presbyter are different realizations of the sacrament of order. (4) Those ordained

are claimed permanently for the service of the Church.

• "The Principle of Economy," published by the body named above at the same time, concerning God's plan and activities in human history for salvation.

• "Venice Statement" on authority in the Church, published Jan. 20, 1977, by the Anglican-Roman Catholic International Commission of theologians. (For text, see pages 145-50 of the 1978 *Catholic Almanac.*)

• "Response to the Venice Statement," issued Jan. 4, 1978, by the Anglican-Roman Catholic Consultation in the U.S.A., citing additional questions.

• "An Ecumenical Approach to Marriage," published in January, 1978, by representatives of the Catholic Church, the Lutheran World Federation and the World Alliance of Reformed Churches.

• "Teaching Authority and Infallibility in the Church," released in October, 1978, by the Catholic-Lutheran dialogue group in the U.S.

• "The Eucharist," reported early in 1979, in which the Roman Catholic-Lutheran Commission indicated developing convergence of views.

• "The Holy Spirit," issued Feb. 12, 1979, by the International Catholic-Methodist Commission.

• A statement on "Ministry in the Church," published in March, 1981, by the International Roman Catholic-Lutheran Joint Commission, regarding possible mutual recognition of ministries.

• The Final Report of the Anglican-Roman Catholic International Commission, 1982, on the results of 12 years of dialogue. (See separate entry.)

• "Justification by Faith," issued Sept. 30, 1983, by the U.S. Lutheran-Roman Catholic dialogue group, claiming a "fundamental consensus on the Gospel."

• "Images of God: Reflections on Christian Anthropology," released Dec. 22, 1983, by the Anglican-Roman Catholic Dialogue in the United States.

• "The Journeying Together in Christ — The Report of the Polish National Catholic-Roman Catholic Dialogue (1984-89)."

• "Salvation and the Church," issued Jan. 22, 1987, by the Second Anglican-Roman Catholic International Commission.

• "Faith, Sacraments and the Unity of the Church," issued by the Mixed International Commission for Theological Dialogue between the Catholic Church and the Orthodox Churches in June, 1987.

• "The Presence of Christ in Church and World" (developed in dialogue between 1970 and 1977) and "Toward a Common Understanding of the Church" (developed between 1984 and 1990), by the Re-formed-Roman Catholic Conversations, under the auspices of the Pontifical Council for Promoting Christian Unity and the World Alliance of Reformed Churches.

# ANGLICAN-ROMAN CATHOLIC FINAL REPORT

The Anglican-Roman Catholic International Commission issued a Final Report in 1982 on 12 years of dialogue on major issues of concern, especially the Eucharist and ordained ministry.

In 1988 the Lambeth Conference called parts of the report on these two subjects "consonant in substance with the faith of Anglicans." In 1991 the Congregation for the Doctrine of the Faith and the Pontifical Council for Promoting Christian Unity called the Report a significant milestone not only in relations between the Catholic Church and the Anglican Communion but in the ecumenical movement as a whole. They said, however, that it was not yet possible to state that substantial agreement had been reached on all the questions studied by the commission, and that important differences still remained with respect to essential matters of Catholic doctrine regarding the Eucharist, ordination and other subjects. Clarifications were asked for.

The Anglican-Roman Catholic Commission II responded in 1994, saying that its members were in agreement regarding:

• the substantial and sacramental presence of Christ in the Eucharist;
• the propitiatory nature of the Eucharistic Sacrifice, which can also be applied to the deceased;
• institution of the sacrament of order from Christ;
• the character of priestly ordination, implying configuration to the priesthood of Christ.

The clarifications have been under study at the Vatican since the summer of 1994, according to a letter addressed to the Catholic and Anglican co-chairmen of the commission by Cardinal Edward I. Cassidy, president of the Pontifical Council for Interreligious Dialogue. Questions still remained to be answered about a number of subjects, including the Eucharist, authority in the Church, infallibility and Marian doctrine.

## THE QUESTION OF AUTHORITY

Authority is a key subject of interest and concern in the quest for unity among churches. Cases in point are the official Catholic-Orthodox and Catholic-Anglican dialogues.

On the eve of the annual Week of Prayer for Christian Unity in January, 1996, Pope John Paul told a general audience that there is substantial agreement between Catholics and Orthodox on most of the es-sential matters of faith and church life, including the sacraments. But, the key historical obstacle is the primacy of the bishop of Rome. That is why, in his 1995 encyclical letter *Ut Unum Sint* he "encouraged everyone to research, obviously together, the forms under which this ministry — that is, the bishop of Rome's ministry of unity — could perform a service of love recognized by both" Catholics and Orthodox.

Since 1994, the Anglican-Roman Catholic International Commission has been examining:

• the relationship of "the exercise of authority in the church to Scripture and tradition";
• ways in which the exercise of authority serves members' commitment to Christ;
• how authority promotes "the communion in faithfulness of all the churches."

Authority and unity within the Anglican Communion have been compromised by the ordination of women to the priesthood, according to an article written by an official of the Pontifical Council for Promoting Christian Unity.

Father Timothy Galligan said in an article published in January, 1996: "The question of the interrelationship of communion, authority and disagreement in the (Anglican) church has become a matter of considerable controversy among some Anglicans as the ordination of women becomes part of the life of Anglican communities in many parts of the world."

Not only are some Anglicans arguing about the authority the church has to ordain women, but also about the relationship among Anglican bishops who disagree on the issue and between bishops and Anglicans who disagree.

Women have been ordained priests in 15 Anglican provinces, about half of the world total.

In an effort to cope with the situation, the Church of England has appointed special bishops for parishes and clergy who do not accept women priests nor the bishops who ordained them.

"Such solutions," said Father Galligan, highlight the reality of diminished communion, with some clergy and lay people no longer prepared to accept the sacramental ministry of their diocesan bishop and some of his clergy.... That one fundamental expression of full ecclesial communion, namely a universally accepted ministry, is absent."

# JUDAISM

Judaism is the religion of the Hebrew Bible and of contemporary Jews. Divinely revealed and with a patriarchal background (Abraham, Isaac, Jacob), it originated with the Mosaic Covenant, was identified with the Israelites, and achieved distinctive form and character as the religion of the Torah (Law, "The Teaching") from this Covenant and reforms initi-ated by Ezra and Nehemiah after the Babylonian Exile.

Judaism does not have a formal creed but its principal points of belief are clear. Basic is belief in one transcendent God who reveals himself through the Torah, the prophets, the life of his people and events of history. The fatherhood of God involves the brotherhood of all humanity. Religious faith and practice are equated with just living according to God's Law. Moral conviction and practice are regarded as more important than precise doctrinal formulation and profession. Formal worship, whose principal act was sacrifice from the Exodus times to 70 A.D., is by prayer, reading and meditating upon the sacred writings, and observance of the Sabbath and festivals.

Judaism has messianic expectations of the complete fulfillment of the Covenant, the coming of God's kingdom, the ingathering of his people, and final judgment and retribution for all. Views differ regarding the manner in which these expectations will be realized — through a person, the community of God's people, an evolution of historical events, an eschatological act of God himself. Individual salvation expectations also differ, depending on views about the nature of immortality, punishment and reward, and related matters.

## Sacred Books

The sacred books are the 24 books of the Masoretic Hebrew Text of The Law, the Prophets and the Writings (see The Bible). Together, they contain the basic instruction or norms for just living. In some contexts, the term Law or Torah refers only to the Pentateuch (Genesis, Exodus, Leviticus, Numbers, Deuteronomy); in others, it denotes all the sacred books and/or the whole complex of written and oral tradition.

Also of great authority are two Talmuds which were composed in Palestine and Babylon in the fourth and fifth centuries A.D., respectively. They consist of the Mishna, a compilation of oral laws, and the Gemara, a collection of rabbinical commentary on the Mishna. Midrash are collections of scriptural comments and moral counsels.

Priests were the principal religious leaders during the period of sacrificial and temple worship. Rabbis were originally teachers; today they share with cantors the function of leaders of prayer. The synagogue is the place of community worship. The family and home are focal points of many aspects of Jewish worship and practice.

Of the various categories of Jews, Orthodox are the most conservative in adherence to strict religious traditions. Others — Reformed, Conservative, Reconstructionist — are liberal in comparison with the Orthodox. They favor greater or less modification of religious practices in accommodation to contemporary culture and living conditions.

Principal events in Jewish life include the circum-cision of males, according to prescriptions of the Covenant; the bar and bat mitzvah which marks the coming-of-age of boys and girls in Judaism at the age of 13; marriage; and observance of the Sabbath and festivals.

Observances of the Sabbath and festivals begin at sundown of the previous calendar day and continue until the following sundown.

**Sabbath:** Saturday, the weekly day of rest prescribed in the Decalogue.

**Sukkoth** (Tabernacles): A seven-to-nine-day festival in the month of Tishri (Sept.-Oct.), marked by some Jews with Covenant-renewal and reading of The Law. It originated as an agricultural feast at the end of the harvest and got its name from the temporary shelters used by workers in the fields.

**Hanukkah** (The Festival of Lights, the Feast of Consecration and of the Maccabees): Commemorates the dedication of the new altar in the Temple at Jerusalem by Judas Maccabeus in 165 B.C. The eight-day festival, during which candles in an eight-branch candelabra are lighted in succession, one each day, occurs near the winter solstice, close to Christmas time.

**Pesach** (Passover): A seven-day festival commemorating the liberation of the Israelites from Egypt. The narrative of the Exodus, the Haggadah, is read at ceremonial Seder meals on the first and second days of the festival, which begins on the 14th day of Nisan (Mar.-Apr.).

**Shavuoth, Pentecost** (Feast of Weeks): Observed 50 days after Passover, commemorating the anniversary of the revelation of the Law to Moses.

**Purim:** A joyous festival observed on the 14th day of Adar (Feb.-Mar.), commemorating the rescue of the Israelites from massacre by the Persians through the intervention of Esther. The festival is preceded by a day of fasting. A gift- and alms-giving custom became associated with it in medieval times.

**Rosh Hashana** (Feast of Trumpets, New Year): Observed on the first day of Tishri (Sept.-Oct.), the festival focuses attention on the ways of life and the ways of death. It is second in importance only to the most solemn observance of Yom Kippur, which is celebrated 10 days later.

**Yom Kippur** (Day of Atonement): The highest holy day, observed with strict fasting. It occurs 10 days after Rosh Hashana.

**Yom HaShoah** (Holocaust Memorial Day): Observed in the week after Passover; increasingly observed with joint Christian-Jewish services of remembrance.

# CATHOLIC-JEWISH RELATIONS

The Second Vatican Council, in addition to the Decree on Ecumenism concerning the movement for unity among Christians, stated the mind of the Church on a similar matter in a Declaration on the Relationship of the Church to Non-Christian Religions. This document, as the following excerpts indicate, backgrounds the reasons and directions of the Church's regard for the Jews. (Other portions of the document refer to Hindus, Buddhists and Muslims.)

## Spiritual Bond

As this sacred Synod searches into the mystery of he Church, it recalls the spiritual bond linking the people of the New Covenant with Abraham's stock.

For the Church of Christ acknowledges that, according to the mystery of God's saving design, the beginnings of her faith and her election are already found among the patriarchs, Moses, and the prophets. She professes that all who believe in Christ, Abraham's sons according to faith (cf. Gal. 3:7), are included in the same patriarch's call, and likewise that the salvation of the Church was mystically foreshadowed by the Chosen People's exodus from the land of bondage.

The Church, therefore, cannot forget that she received the revelation of the Old Testament through the people with whom God in his inexpressible mercy deigned to establish the Ancient Covenant. Nor can she forget that she draws sustenance from the root of that good olive tree onto which have been grafted the wild olive branches of the Gentiles (cf. Rom. 11:17-24). Indeed, the Church believes that by his cross Christ, our Peace, reconciled Jew and Gentile, making them both one in himself (cf. Eph. 2:14-16).

The Jews still remain most dear to God because of their fathers, for he does not repent of the gifts he makes nor of the calls he issues (cf. Rom. 11:28-29). In company with the prophets and the same Apostle (Paul), the Church awaits that day, known to God alone, on which all peoples will address the Lord in a single voice and "serve him with one accord" (Zeph. 3:9; cf. Is. 66:23; Ps. 65:4; Rom. 11:11-32).

Since the spiritual patrimony common to Christians and Jews is thus so great, this sacred Synod wishes to foster and recommend that mutual understanding and respect which is the fruit above all of biblical and theological studies, and of brotherly dialogues.

## No Anti-Semitism

True, authorities of the Jews and those who followed their lead pressed for the death of Christ (cf. Jn. 19:6); still, what happened in his passion cannot be blamed upon all the Jews then living, without distinction, nor upon the Jews of today. Although the Church is the new People of God, the Jews should not be presented as repudiated or cursed by God, as if such views followed from the holy Scriptures. All should take pains, then, lest in catechetical instruction and in the preaching of God's Word they teach anything out of harmony with the truth of the Gospel and the spirit of Christ.

The Church repudiates all persecutions against any person. Moreover, mindful of her common patrimony with the Jews, and motivated by the Gospel's spiritual love and by no political considerations, she deplores the hatred, persecutions, and displays of anti-Semitism directed against the Jews at any time and from any source (No. 4).

The Church rejects, as foreign to the mind of Christ, any discrimination against men or harassment of them because of their race, color, condition of life, or religion (No. 5).

## Bishops' Secretariat

The American hierarchy's first move toward implementation of the Vatican II *Declaration on the Relationship of the Church to Non-Christian Religions (Nostra Aetate)* was to establish, in 1965, a Subcommission for Catholic-Jewish Relations in the framework of its Commission for Ecumenical and Interreligious Affairs. Its moderator is Cardinal William H. Keeler of Baltimore. The Secretariat for Ecumenical and Interreligious Relations is located at 3211 Fourth St. N.E., Washington, D.C. 20017. Its Catholic-Jewish efforts are directed by Dr. Eugene J. Fisher.

According to the key norm of a set of guidelines issued by the secretariat Mar. 16, 1967, and updated Apr. 9, 1985: "The general aim of all Catholic-Jewish meetings (and relations) is to increase our understanding both of Judaism and the Catholic faith, to eliminate sources of tension and misunderstanding, to initiate dialogue or conversations on different levels, to multiply intergroup meetings between Catholics and Jews, and to promote cooperative social action."

## Vatican Guidelines

In a document issued Jan. 3, 1975, the Vatican Commission for Religious Relations with the Jews offered a number of suggestions and guidelines for implementing the Christian-Jewish portion of the Second Vatican Council's *Declaration on Relations with Non-Christian Religions.*

Among "suggestions from experience" were those concerning dialogue, liturgical links between Christian and Jewish worship, the interpretation of biblical texts, teaching and education for the purpose of increasing mutual understanding, and joint social action.

## Notes on Preaching and Catechesis

On June 24, 1985, the Vatican Commission for Religious Relations with the Jews promulgated its "Notes on the Correct Way to Present Jews and Judaism in Preaching and Catechesis in the Roman Catholic Church," with the intent of providing "a helpful frame of reference for those who are called upon in the course of their teaching assignments to speak about Jews and Judaism and who wish to do so in keeping with the current teaching of the Church in this area."

The document states emphatically that, since the relationship between the Church and the Jewish people is one "founded on the design of the God of the Covenant," Judaism does not occupy "an occasional and marginal place in catechesis," but an "essential" one that "should be organically integrated" throughout the curriculum on all levels of Catholic education.

The Notes discuss the relationship between the Hebrew Scriptures and the New Testament, focusing especially on typology, which is called "the sign of a problem unresolved." Underlined is the "eschatological dimension," that "the people of God of the Old and the New Testament are tending toward a like end in the future: the coming or return of the Messiah." Jewish witness to God's Kingdom, the Notes declare, challenges Christians to "accept our responsibility to prepare the world for the coming of the Messiah by working together for social justice and reconciliation."

The Notes emphasize the Jewishness of Jesus' teaching, correct misunderstandings concerning the portrayal of Jews in the New Testament and describe the Jewish origins of Christian liturgy. One section addresses the "spiritual fecundity" of Judaism to the present, its continuing "witness — often heroic — of its fidelity to the one God," and mandates the development of Holocaust curricula and a positive approach in Catholic education to the "religious attachment which finds its roots in biblical tradition" between the Jewish people and the Land of Israel, affirming the "existence of the State of Israel" on the basis of "the common principles of international law."

## Papal Statements

*(Courtesy of Dr. Eugene Fisher, associate director of the Bishops' Committee for Ecumenical and Interreligious Affairs.)*

Pope John Paul, in a remarkable series of addresses beginning in 1979, has sought to promote and give shape to the development of dialogue between Catholics and Jews.

In a homily delivered June 7, 1979, at Auschwitz, which he called the "Golgotha of the Modern World," he prayed movingly for "the memory of the people whose sons and daughters were intended for total extermination."

In a key address delivered Nov. 17, 1980, to the Jewish community in Mainz, the Pope articulated his vision of the three "dimensions" of the dialogue: (1) "the meeting between the people of God of the Old Covenant and the people of the New Covenant"; (2) the encounter of "mutual esteem between today's Christian churches and today's people of the Covenant concluded with Moses"; (3) the "holy duty" of witnessing to the one God in the world and "jointly to work for peace and justice."

On Mar. 22, 1984, at an audience with members of the Anti-Defamation League of B'nai B'rith, the Pope commented on "the mysterious spiritual link which brings us close together, in Abraham and through Abraham, in God who chose Israel and brought forth the Church from Israel." He urged joint social action on "the great task of promoting justice and peace."

In receiving a delegation of the American Jewish Committee Feb. 14, 1985, the Holy Father confirmed that *Nostra Aetate* "remains always for us a teaching which is necessary to accept not merely as something fitting, but much more as an expression of the faith, as an inspiration of the Holy Spirit, as a word of the divine wisdom."

During his historic visit to the Great Synagogue in Rome Apr. 13, 1986, the Holy Father affirmed that God's covenant with the Jewish people is "irrevocable," and stated: "The Jewish religion is not 'extrinsic' to us, but in a certain way is 'intrinsic' to our own religion. With Judaism, therefore, we have a relationship which we do not have with any other religion."

Meeting with the Jewish community in Sydney, Australia, Nov. 26, 1986, the Holy Father termed the 20th century "the century of the Shoah" (Holocaust) and called "sinful" any "acts of discrimination or persecution against Jews."

On June 14, 1987, meeting with the Jewish community of Warsaw, the Pope called the Jewish witness to the Shoah (Holocaust) a "saving warning before all of humanity" which reveals "your particular vocation, showing you (Jews) to be still the heirs of that election to which God is faithful."

A collection of Pope John Paul's addresses, *On Jews and Judaism* 1979-1986, prepared by the NCCB

Secretariat was sent to the Pope Aug. 12, 1987. In a response of Aug. 17, the Pope reiterated his Warsaw statement and added: "Before the vivid memory of the extermination (Shoah), it is not permissible for anyone to pass by with indifference. The sufferings endured by the Jews are also for the Catholic Church a motive of sincere sorrow, especially when one thinks of the indifference and sometimes resentment which have divided Jews and Christians."

In 1995, an updated edition of the collection of papal texts entitled *Spiritual Pilgrimage* won the National Jewish Book Award and became the third best-selling "Jewish" book, according to the *Jewish Book News*.

Meeting with Jewish leaders Sept. 11, 1987, in Miami, the Pope praised the efforts in theological dialogue and educational reform implemented in the U.S. since the Second Vatican Council; affirmed the existence of the State of Israel "according to international law," and urged "common educational programs on the Holocaust so that never again will such a horror be possible. Never again!"

In an apostolic letter on the 50th anniversary of World War II (Aug. 27, 1989), the Pope stressed the uniqueness of the Jewish sufferings of the Shoah, "which will forever remain a shame for humanity."

On Aug. 14, 1991, during a visit to his home town of Wadowice, Poland, the Pope recalled with sadness the deaths of his Jewish classmates at the hands of the Nazis during World War II: "In the school of Wadowice there were Jewish believers who are no longer with us. There is no longer a synagogue near the school. It is true that your people (the Jews) were on the front lines. The Polish Pope has a special relationship to that period because, together with you, we lived through all that in our Fatherland."

On Apr. 7, 1994, the eve of *Yom HaShoah*, the Jewish day of prayer commemorating the victims of the Holocaust, Pope John Paul II hosted a memorial concert at the Vatican. It was, he noted, a moment of "common meditation and shared prayer," as the *Kaddish*, the prayer for the dead, and the *Kol Nidre*, the prayer for forgiveness and atonement, were recited.

In April, 1996, Pope John Paul hosted Elio Toaff, chief rabbi of Rome, to mark the 10th anniversary of his visit to the Synagogue of Rome. During their meeting, the Pope said: "Our meeting today, in addition to recalling a significant event, arose from the desire we both have to give shape to a future with characteristics different from those of the past.... Our meeting is a sign of hope for a world that anxiously seeks authentic values of human brotherhood.... We intend to give them an example, and our fraternal bond is even more real because it is rooted in a common spiritual heritage that is extraordinarily rich and deep."

## International Liaison Committee

The International Catholic-Jewish Liaison Committee was formed in 1971 and is the official link between the Commission for Religious Relations with the Jewish People and the International Jewish Committee for Interreligious Consultations. The committee meets every 18 months to examine matters of common interest.

Topics under discussion have included: mission and witness (Venice, 1977), religious education (Madrid, 1978), religious liberty and pluralism (Regensburg, 1979), religious commitment (London, 1981), the sanctity of human life in an age of violence (Milan, 1982), youth and faith (Amsterdam, 1984), the Vatican Notes on Preaching and Catechesis (Rome, 1985), the Holocaust (Prague, 1990), education and social action (Baltimore, Md., 1992), family and ecology (Jerusalem, 1994).

Pope John Paul, addressing in Rome a celebration of *Nostra Aetate* (the Second Vatican Council's "Declaration on the Relationship of the Church to Non-Christian Religions") by the Liaison Committee, stated: "What you are celebrating is nothing other than the divine mercy which is guiding Christians and Jews to mutual awareness, respect, cooperation and solidarity. The universal openness of *Nostra Aetate* is anchored in and takes its orientation from a high sense of the absolute singularity of God's choice of a particular people. The Church is fully aware that Sacred Scripture bears witness that the Jewish people, this community of faith and custodian of a tradition thousands of years old, is an intimate part of the mystery of revelation and of salvation."

### Family Rights and Obligations

The Liaison Committee, at its May, 1994, meeting in Jerusalem, issued its first joint statement, on the family — in anticipation of the UN Cairo Conference subsequently held in September.

The statement affirmed that "the rights and obligations of the family do not come from the State but exist prior to the State and ultimately have their source in God the Creator. The family is far more than a legal, social or economic unit. For both Jews and Christians, it is a stable community of love and solidarity based on God's covenant."

### Holocaust Anniversary

Statements commemorating the 50th anniversary of the liberation of the Auschwitz-Birkenau death camp, Jan. 27, 1995, were issued by Pope John Paul and the bishops' conferences of Germany and Poland.

An American statement was issued by Archbishop Oscar H. Lipscomb, speaking for the U.S. Bishops' Committee for Ecumenical and Interreligious Affairs. He noted that it was "fitting that the first major anniversary of the year" marking the end of World War II be that of the liberation of Auschwitz, "the name of which has come to symbolize in our collective memory the worst evils of which humanity has shown itself capable."

### Vatican-Israel Accord

On Dec. 30, 1993, a year of dramatic developments in the Middle East was capped by the signing in Jerusalem of a "Fundamental Agreement" between representatives of the Holy See and the State of Israel. The agreement acknowledged in its preamble that the signers were "aware of the unique nature of the relationship between the Catholic Church and the Jewish people, and of the historic process of reconciliation and growth in mutual understanding and friendship between Catholics and Jews." Archbishop William H. Keeler, president of the National Conference of Catholic Bishops, welcomed the accord together with the Israeli Ambassador to the United States at a ceremony at the NCCB headquarters in Washington. Noting that at that time of the year Catholics and Jews, each in their own ways, "celebrate God's light shining in the darkness," Cardinal Keeler prayed "that this agreement will be seen as a beacon along the path to lasting peace in the land that all believers call holy." Dioceses throughout the country similarly joined with representatives of local Jewish communities to welcome the diplomatic exchange and discuss its very positive implications for ongoing Jewish-Catholic relations.

### U.S. Dialogue

The National Workshop on Christian-Jewish Relations, begun in 1973 by the NCCB Secretariat, draws more than 1,000 participants from around the world. Recent workshops have been held in Baltimore (1986), Minneapolis (1987), Charleston, S.C (1989), Chicago (1990), Pittsburgh (1992), Tulsa (1994) and Stamford (1996).

In October, 1987, the Bishops' Committee for Ecumenical and Interreligious Affairs began a series of twice-yearly consultations with representatives of the Synagogue Council of America. Topics of discussion have included education, human rights, respect for life, the Middle East. The consultation has issued three joint statements: "On Moral Values in Public Education" (1990), "On Stemming the Proliferation of Pornography" (1993) and "On Dealing with Holocaust Revisionism" (1994).

Ongoing relationships are maintained by the NCCB Secretariat with such Jewish agencies as the American Jewish Committee, the Anti-Defamation League of B'nai B'rith, the Union of American Hebrew Congregations, the American Jewish Congress and the National Jewish Community Relations Council.

In June, 1988, the Bishops' Committee for Ecumenical and Interreligious Affairs published in Spanish and English *Criteria for the Evaluation of Dramatizations of the Passion,* providing for the first time Catholic guidelines for passion plays.

In January, 1989, the Bishops' Committee for the Liturgy issued guidelines for the homiletic presentation of Judaism under the title, "God's mercy Endures Forever."

# ISLAM

*(Courtesy of Dr. John Borelli, executive secretary for Interreligious Relations, NCCB.)*

Islam, meaning grateful surrender (to God), originated with Muhammad and the revelation he is believed to have received. Muslims acknowledge that this revelation, recorded in the Quran, is from the one God and do not view Islam as a new religion. They profess that Muhammad was the last in a long series of prophets, most of whom are named in the Hebrew Bible and the New Testament, beginning with Adam and continuing through Noah, Abraham, Moses, Jesus and down to Muhammad.

Muslims believe in the one God, Allah in Arabic, and cognate with the Hebrew Elohim and the ancient Aramaic Elah. According to the Quran, God is one and transcendent, Creator and Sustainer of the universe, all-merciful and all-compassionate Ruler and Judge. God possesses numerous other titles, known collectively as the 99 names of God. The profession of faith states: "There is no god but the God and Muhammad is the messenger of God."

The essential duties of Muslims are to: witness the faith by daily recitation of the profession of faith; worship five times a day facing in the direction of the holy city of Mecca; give alms; fast daily from dawn to dusk during the month of Ramadan; make a pilgrimage to Mecca once if possible.

Muslims believe in final judgment, heaven and hell. Morality and following divinely revealed moral norms are extremely important to Muslims. Some dietary regulations are in effect. On Fridays, the noon prayer is a congregational (juma) prayer which should be said in a mosque. The general themes of prayer are adoration and thanksgiving. Muslims do not have an ordained ministry.

The basis of Islamic belief is the Quran, the created word of God revealed to Muhammad through the angel Gabriel over a period of 23 years. The contents of this sacred book are complemented by the Sunna, a collection of sacred traditions from the life of the prophet Muhammad, and reinforced by Ijma, the consensus of Islamic scholars of Islamic Law (Shariah) which guarantees them against errors in matters of belief and practice.

## Conciliar Statement

The attitude of the Church toward Islam was stated as follows in the Second Vatican Council's *Declaration on the Relation of the Church to Non-Christian Religions* (No. 3).

"The Church has a high regard for the Muslims. They worship God, who is one, living and subsistent, merciful and almighty, the Creator of heaven and earth, who has also spoken to men. They strive to submit themselves without reserve to the hidden decrees of God, just as Abraham submitted himself to God's plan, to whose faith Muslims eagerly link their own. Although not acknowledging him as God, they venerate Jesus as a prophet, his virgin Mother they also honor, and even at times devoutly invoke. Further, they await the day of judgment and the reward of God following the resurrection of the dead, For this reason, they highly esteem an upright life and worship God, especially by way of prayer, alms-deeds and fasting.

"Over the centuries many quarrels and dissensions have arisen between Christians and Muslims. The sacred Council now pleads with all to forget the past, and urges that a sincere effort be made to achieve mutual understanding; for the benefit of all men, let them together preserve and promote peace, liberty, social justice and moral values."

## Dialogue

Pope John Paul has met with Muslim leaders and delegations both in Rome and during his trips abroad.

He has addressed large gatherings of Muslims in Morocco, Indonesia, Mali and elsewhere. The Pontifical Council for Interreligious Dialogue has held formal dialogues with Islamic organizations from time to time. In the U.S., the bishops' Secretariat for Ecumenical and Interreligious Affairs has held consultations on relations with Muslims and several special dialogues with Muslims related to international issues. Dialogue with participation of Catholics and Muslims from several U.S. cities was initiated in October, 1991. These continue, and in 1996 a dialogue between representatives of the ministry of W.D. Mohammed and the National Conference of Catholic Bishops began.

In 1995, the American Muslim Council presented its Mahmoud Abu-Saud Award for Excellence to Cardinal William H. Keeler for his leadership in promoting Christian-Muslim relations during his term as president of the National Conference of Catholic Bishops/United States Catholic Conference.

## Id al-Fitr Messages

"The believer's commitment to promoting a healthy environment derives from his faith in God the Creator; he must think and act accordingly." So stated Cardinal Francis Arinze, president of the Pontifical Council for Interreligious Dialogue in a message to Muslims on the feast of Id al-Fitr, marking the end of Ramadan, the month of fasting commemorating the giving of the Quran to Muhammad. As reported in the Mar. 1, 1995, English edition of *L'Osservatore Romano*, he also said:

"I am happy to greet you on behalf of the members of the Catholic Church as the month of Ramadan draws to a close. A time of fasting, prayer and sharing, this practice allows persons to develop their relationship with God, the Creator of humanity, and with their fellow humans, his creatures.

"Indeed, the person who fasts is making his effort for God. By this gesture, the believer proclaims the nobility of the Most High, humiliates himself before him, and asks forgiveness for his sins. It is a time of purification that brings man closer to God, who alone is the Holy One.

"By striving in this way to be closer to God, man also brings himself closer to his brothers and sisters, and becomes more compassionate toward them."

"Fasting teaches us the proper use of material goods. This is a topic which concerns us all, firstly as inhabitants of the same planet, and above all as believers in 'one God, Maker of all things visible and invisible,' to whom all that exists 'in heaven and on earth' belongs.'"

"We observe that unfortunately we do not always faithfully fulfill the role to which the Creator has appointed us. It happens that we do not use the earth's resources according to God's plan, with due measure and wisdom."

"The safeguarding of the environment and natural resources concerns the entire human community: individuals, associations, states, international organizations, both governmental and non-governmental. Could we not work together for the good of future generations, so as to keep the earth clean, the air pure, the water drinkable, and to save the riches of the earth? Would it not be appropriate or even necessary to arouse the awareness of the public and especially of political leaders? An education in ecological responsibility and in the respect for life in the family, at school, by the media, would be a precious aid to the youth of all religions, by bringing them matter for thought and motives for action at the same time as developing their ecological awareness. A new solidarity would likewise foster peace between nations, for many ethical values linked to respect for the environment are extremely important for the development of a peaceful society."

Beyond tolerance was the theme of Cardinal Arinze's 1996 letter on the occasion of Id al-Fitr: "Our relations as believers, Christians and Muslims, should go beyond mere tolerance, understood as simply putting up with the other. A brother is not just to be tolerated; he is to be loved. For us as Christians and Muslims to reach beyond tolerance to reconciliation and love, there is still a long way to go. As we prepare for the future, we cannot afford to forget the past or neglect the present."

The cardinal quoted an address to young Muslims delivered by Pope John Paul Aug. 19, 1985, at Casablanca:

"'Christians and Muslims, in general we have badly understood each other, and sometimes, in the past, we have opposed and even exhausted each other in polemics and in wars.' We cannot forget the past; we must both own it and go beyond it. The time has come to free our memories of the negative consequences of the past, however painful they may be, and look resolutely toward the future. The one who has given offense must repent and ask for pardon. We need mutual pardon. Without true reconciliation we cannot commit ourselves together on behalf of our fellow believers and for the good of the whole world. Muslims and Christians can become, in today's world, examples of reconciliation for the good of the whole world. Muslims and Christians can become, in today's world, examples of reconciliation and instruments of peace."

# OTHER RELIGIONS

*(Courtesy of Dr. John Borelli.)*

Hinduism and Buddhism — along with Confucianism, Taoism, Shinto, Native American Traditions and other religions — unlike Judaism, Christianity and Islam, are called non-Abrahamic because in them Abraham is not shared as a father in faith.

Common elements among Judaism, Christianity and Islam are more extensive than each has with any other religion. All three are scriptural religions, with Christian scripture making reference to Jewish scripture and Islamic scripture making references to the earlier two. The life of the religious community of each religion is defined through the content and use of its scripture. More common elements among the three religions can be discovered through the study of religious law, liturgy, spirituality and theology.

Two of the principal non-Abrahamic religions are Hinduism and Buddhism.

In its *Declaration on the Relation of the Church to Non-Christian Religions,* the Second Vatican Council stated: "In Hinduism men explore the divine mystery and express it both in the limitless riches of myth and the accurately defined insights of philosophy. They seek release from the trials of the present life by ascetical practices, profound meditation and recourse to God in confidence and love." (2)

Catholics, especially in India, have sought good relations with Hindus and have engaged in numerous dialogues and conferences. In papal visits to India, Paul VI in 1964 and John Paul II in 1986 addressed words of respect for Indian, particularly Hindu, religious leaders. Pope John Paul said to Hindus in 1986: "Your overwhelming sense of the primacy of religion and of the greatness of the Supreme Being has been a powerful witness against a materialistic and atheistic view of life."

In 1995, the Pontifical Council for Interreligious Dialogue began sending a general message to Hindus on the occasion of Diwali, a feast memorating the victory of light over darkness.

"Buddhism in its multiple forms acknowledges the radical insufficiency of this shifting world. It teaches a path by which men, in a devout and confident spirit, can either reach a state of absolute freedom or attain supreme enlightenment by their own efforts or by higher assistance." So stated the Second Vatican Council in its *Declaration on the Relation of the Church to Non-Christian Religions.*

Numerous delegations of Buddhists and leading monks have been received by the popes. At the 1986 World Day of Prayer for Peace at Assisi, the Dalai Lama, principal teacher of the Gelugpa lineage, was placed immediately to the Holy Father's left. Numerous dialogues and good relations between Catholics and Buddhists exist in many countries.

In 1995, the Pontifical Council for Interreligious Dialogue organized a Buddhist-Christian colloquium hosted by the Fo Kuang Shan Buddhist order in Taiwan. Also in 1995, the council began sending a message to Buddhists on the feast of Vesakh, the celebration of Gautama Buddha's life.

In 1996, Cardinal Arinze, in a letter to "Dear Buddhist Friends," wrote: "The pluralistic society in which we live demands more than mere tolerance. Tolerance is usually thought of as putting up with the other or, at best, as a code of public conduct. Yet, this resigned, lukewarm attitude does not create the right atmosphere for true harmonious coexistence. The spirit of our religions challenges us to go beyond this. We are commanded, in fact, to love our neighbors as ourselves." The cardinal wrote in the same vein to Muslims on the occasion of their 1996 celebration of Id al-Fitr.

Formal dialogues in the Archdioceses of Los Angeles, San Francisco, Chicago and the Diocese of Honolulu are held from time to time. The Monastic Interreligious Dialogue, a consortium of Catholic monastics, has enjoyed rich exchanges with Buddhist monastics since 1981. In 1989, the bishops' Secretariat for Ecumenical and Interreligious Affairs convened its first national consultation on relations with Buddhists; a second consultation was held in 1990.

# GLOSSARY

## A

**Abbacy:** A non-diocesan territory whose people are under the pastoral care of an abbot acting in general in the manner of a bishop.

**Abbess:** The female superior of a monastic community of nuns; e.g., Benedictines, Poor Clares, some others. Elected by members of the community, an abbess has general authority over her community but no sacramental jurisdiction.

**Abbey:** See Monastery.

**Abbot:** The male superior of a monastic community of men religious; e.g., Benedictines, Cistercians, some others. Elected by members of the community, an abbot has ordinary jurisdiction and general authority over his community. Eastern-Rite equivalents of an abbot are a *hegumen* and an *archimandrite*. A regular abbot is the head of an abbey or monastery. An abbot general or archabbot is the head of a congregation consisting of several monasteries. An abbot primate is the head of the modern Benedictine Confederation.

**Ablution:** A term derived from Latin, meaning washing or cleansing, and referring to the cleansing of the hands of a priest celebrating Mass, after the offering of gifts; and to the cleansing of the chalice with water and wine after Communion.

**Abortion:** Abortion is not only "the ejection of an immature fetus" from the womb, but is "also the killing of the same fetus in whatever way at whatever time from the moment of conception it may be procured." (This clarification of Canon 1398, reported in the Dec. 5, 1988, edition of *L'Osservatore Romano,* was issued by the Pontifical Council for the Interpretation of Legislative Texts — in view of scientific developments regarding ways and means of procuring abortion.) Accidental expulsion, as in cases of miscarriage, is without moral fault. Direct abortion, in which a fetus is intentionally removed from the womb, constitutes a direct attack on an innocent human being, a violation of the Fifth Commandment. A person who procures a completed abortion is automatically excommunicated (Canon 1398 of the Code of Canon Law); also excommunicated are all persons involved in a deliberate and successful effort to bring about an abortion. Direct abortion is not justifiable for any reason, e.g.: therapeutic, for the physical and/or psychological welfare of the mother; preventive, to avoid the birth of a defective or unwanted child; social, in the interests of family and/or community. Indirect abortion, which occurs when a fetus is expelled during medical or other treatment of the mother for a reason other than procuring expulsion, is permissible under the principle of double effect for a proportionately serious reason; e.g., when a medical or surgical procedure is necessary to save the life of the mother.

**Absolution, Sacramental:** The act by which bishops and priests, acting as agents of Christ and ministers of the Church, grant forgiveness of sins in the sacrament of penance. The essential formula of absolution is: "I absolve you from your sins; in the name of the Father, and of the Son, and of the Holy Spirit. Amen." The power to absolve is given with ordination to the priesthood and episcopate. Priests exercise this power in virtue of authorization (faculties) granted by a bishop, a religious superior or

canon law. Authorization can be limited or restricted regarding certain sins and penalties or censures. In cases of necessity, and also in cases of the absence of their own confessors, Eastern- and Latin-rite Catholics may ask for and receive sacramental absolution from an Eastern- or Latin-rite priest; so may Polish National Catholics, according to a Vatican decision issued in May, 1993. Any priest can absolve a person in danger of death; in the absence of a priest with the usual faculties, this includes a laicized priest or a priest under censure. (See additional entry under Sacraments.)

**Adoration:** The highest act and purpose of religious worship, which is directed in love and reverence to God alone in acknowledgment of his infinite perfection and goodness, and of his total dominion over creatures. Adoration, which is also called *latria,* consists of internal and external elements, private and social prayer, liturgical acts and ceremonies, and especially sacrifice.

**Adultery:** Marital infidelity. Sexual intercourse between a married person and another to whom one is not married, a violation of the obligations of the marital covenant, chastity and justice; any sin of impurity (thought, desire, word, action) involving a married person who is not one's husband or wife has the nature of adultery.

**Adventists:** Members of several Christian sects whose doctrines are dominated by belief in a more or less imminent second advent or coming of Christ upon earth for a glorious 1,000-year reign of righteousness. This reign, following victory by the forces of good over evil in a final Battle of Armageddon, will begin with the resurrection of the chosen and will end with the resurrection of all others and the annihilation of the wicked. Thereafter, the just will live forever in a renewed heaven and earth. A sleep of the soul takes place between the time of death and the day of judgment. There is no hell. The Bible, in fundamentalist interpretation, is regarded as the only rule of faith and practice. About six sects have developed in the course of the Adventist movement which originated with William Miller (1782-1849) in the United States. Miller, on the basis of calculations made from the Book of Daniel, predicted that the second advent of Christ would occur between 1843 and 1844. After the prophecy went unfulfilled, divisions occurred in the movement and the Seventh Day Adventists, whose actual formation dates from 1860, emerged as the largest single body. The observance of Saturday instead of Sunday as the Lord's Day dates from 1844.

**Advent Wreath:** A wreath of laurel, spruce, or similar foliage with four candles which are lighted successively in the weeks of Advent to symbolize the approaching celebration of the birth of Christ, the Light of the World, at Christmas. The wreath originated among German Protestants.

**Agape:** A Greek word, meaning love, love feast, designating the meal of fellowship eaten at some gatherings of early Christians. Although held in some places in connection with the Mass, the agape was not part of the Mass, nor was it of universal institution and observance. It was infrequently observed by the fifth century and disappeared altogether between the sixth and eighth centuries.

**Age of Reason:** (1) The time of life when one begins to distinguish between right and wrong, to understand an obligation and take on moral responsibility; seven years of age is the presumption in church law. (2) Historically, the 18th century period of Enlightenment in England and France, the age of the Encyclopedists and Deists. According to a basic thesis of the Enlightenment, human experience and reason are the only sources of certain knowledge of truth; consequently, faith and revelation are discounted as valid sources of knowledge, and the reality of supernatural truth is called into doubt and/or denied.

**Aggiornamento:** An Italian word having the general meaning of bringing up to date, renewal, revitalization, descriptive of the processes of spiritual renewal and institutional reform and change in the Church; fostered by the Second Vatican Council.

**Agnosticism:** A theory which holds that a person cannot have certain knowledge of immaterial reality, especially the existence of God and things pertaining to him. Immanuel Kant, one of the philosophical fathers of agnosticism, stood for the position that God, as well as the human soul, is unknowable on speculative grounds; nevertheless, he found practical imperatives for acknowledging God's existence, a view shared by many agnostics. The First Vatican Council declared that the existence of God and some of his attributes can be known with certainty by human reason, even without divine revelation. The word agnosticism was first used, in the sense given here, by T. H. Huxley in 1869.

**Agnus Dei:** A Latin phrase, meaning Lamb of God. (1) A title given to Christ, the Lamb (victim) of the Sacrifice of the New Law (on Calvary and in Mass). (2) A prayer said at Mass before the reception of Holy Communion. (3) A sacramental. It is a round paschal-candle fragment blessed by the pope. On one side it bears the impression of a lamb, symbolic of Christ. On the reverse side, there may be any one of a number of impressions; e.g., the figure of a saint, the name and coat of arms of the reigning pope. The *agnus dei* may have originated at Rome in the fifth century. The first definite mention of it dates from about 820.

**Akathist Hymn:** The most profound and famous expression of Marian devotion in churches of the Byzantine rite. It consists of 24 sections, 12 of which relate to the Gospel of the Infancy and 12 to the mysteries of the Incarnation and the virginal motherhood of Mary. In liturgical usage, it is sung in part in Byzantine churches on the first four Saturdays of Lent and in toto on the fifth Saturday; it is also recited in private devotion. It is of unknown origin prior to 626, when its popularity increased as a hymn of thanksgiving after the successful defense and liberation of Constantinople, which had been under siege by Persians and Avars. Akathist means "without sitting," indicating that the hymn is recited or sung while standing. Pope John Paul, in a decree dated May 25, 1991, granted a plenary indulgence to the faithful of any rite who recite the hymn in a church or oratory, as a family, in a religious community or in a pious association — in conjunction with the usual conditions of freedom from attachment to sin, reception of the sacraments of penance and the Eucharist, and prayers for the intention of the Pope (e.g., an Our Father, the Apostles' Creed and an aspiration). A partial indulgence can be gained for recitation of the hymn in other circumstances.

**Alleluia:** An exclamation of joy derived from Hebrew, "All hail to him who is, praise God," with various use in the liturgy and other expressions of worship.

**Allocution:** A formal type of papal address, as distinguished from an ordinary sermon or statement of views.

**Alms:** An act, gift or service of compassion, motivated by love of God and neighbor, for the help of persons in need; an obligation of charity, which is measurable by the ability of one person to give assistance and by the degree of another's need. Almsgiving, along with prayer and fasting, is regarded as a work of penance as well as an exercise of charity. (See Mercy, Works of.)

**Alpha and Omega:** The first and last letters of the Greek alphabet, used to symbolize the eternity of God (Rv. 1:8) and the divinity and eternity of Christ, the beginning and end of all things (Rv. 21:6; 22:13). Use of the letters as a monogram of Christ originated in the fourth century or earlier.

**Amen:** A Hebrew word meaning truly, it is true. In the Gospels, Christ used the word to add a note of authority to his statements. In other New Testament writings, as in Hebrew usage, it was the concluding word to doxologies. As the concluding word of prayers, it expresses assent to and acceptance of God's will.

**Anamnesis:** A prayer recalling the saving mysteries of the death and resurrection of Jesus, following the consecration at Mass in the Latin rite.

**Anaphora:** A Greek term for the Canon or Eucharistic Prayer of the Mass.

**Anathema:** A Greek word with the root meaning of cursed or separated and the adapted meaning of excommunication, used in church documents, especially the canons of ecumenical councils, for the condemnation of heretical doctrines and of practices opposed to proper discipline.

**Anchorite:** A kind of hermit living in complete isolation and devoting himself exclusively to exercises of religion and severe penance according to a rule and way of life of his own devising. In early Christian times, anchorites were the forerunners of the monastic life. The closest contemporary approach to the life of an anchorite is that of Carthusian and Camaldolese hermits.

**Angels:** Purely spiritual beings with intelligence and free will whose name indicates their mission as servants and messengers of God. They were created before the creation of the visible universe. Good angels enjoy the perfect good of the beatific vision. They can intercede for persons. The doctrine of guardian angels, although not explicitly defined as a matter of faith, is rooted in long-standing tradition. No authoritative declaration has ever been issued regarding choirs or various categories of angels: seraphim, cherubim, thrones, dominations, principalities, powers, virtues, archangels and angels. Archangels commemorated in the liturgy are: Michael, leader of the angelic host and protector of the synagogue; Raphael, guide of Tobiah and healer of his father; Gabriel, angel of the Incarnation. Fallen angels, the chief of whom is called the Devil or Satan, rejected the love of God and were therefore banished from heaven to hell. They can tempt persons to commit sin.

**Angelus:** A devotion which commemorates the Incarnation of Christ. It consists of three versicles, three Hail Marys and a special prayer, and recalls the announcement to Mary by the Archangel Gabriel that she was chosen to be the Mother of Christ, her acceptance of the divine will, and the Incarnation (Lk. 1:26-38). The Angelus is recited in the morning, at noon and in the evening. The practice of reciting the Hail Mary in honor of the Incarnation was introduced by the Franciscans in 1263. The *Regina Caeli,* commemorating the joy of Mary at Christ's Resurrection, replaces the Angelus during the Easter season.

**Anger (Wrath):** Passionate displeasure arising from some kind of offense suffered at the hands of another person, frustration or other cause, combined with a tendency to strike back at the cause of the displeasure; a violation of the Fifth Commandment and one of the capital sins if the displeasure is out of proportion to the cause and/ or if the retaliation is unjust.

**Anglican Orders:** Holy orders conferred according to the rite of the Anglican Church, which Leo XIII declared null and void in the bull *Apostolicae Curae,* Sept. 13, 1896. The orders were declared null because they were conferred according to a rite that was substantially defective in form and intent, and because of a break in apostolic succession that occurred when Matthew Parker became head of the Anglican hierarchy in 1559. In making his declaration, Pope Leo cited earlier arguments against validity made by Julius III in 1553 and 1554 and by Paul IV in 1555. He also noted related directives requiring absolute ordination, according to the Catholic ritual, of convert ministers who had been ordained according to the Anglican Ordinal.

**Anglican Use Parishes:** In line with Vatican-approved developments since 1980, several Anglican use parishes have been established in the United States with the right to continue using some elements of Anglican usage in their liturgical celebrations. A Vatican document dated Mar. 31, 1981, said: "In June, 1980, the Holy See, through the Congregation for the Doctrine of the Faith, agreed to the request presented by the bishops of the United States of America in behalf of some clergy and laity formerly or actually belonging to the Episcopal (Anglican) Church for full communion with the Catholic Church. The Holy See's response to the initiative of these Episcopalians includes the possibility of a 'pastoral provision' which will provide, for those who desire it, a common identity reflecting certain elements of their own heritage."

**Animals:** Creatures of God, they are entrusted to human stewardship for appropriate care, use for human needs, as pets, for reasonable experimentation for the good of people. They should not be subject to cruel treatment.

**Antichrist:** The "deceitful one," the "antichrist" (2 Jn. 7), adversary of Christ and the kingdom of God, especially in the end time before the Second Coming of Christ. The term is also used in reference to anti-Christian persons and forces in the world.

**Antiphon:** (1) A short verse or text, generally from Scripture, recited in the Liturgy of the Hours before and after psalms and canticles. (2) Any verse sung or recited by one part of a choir or congregation in response to the other part, as in antiphonal or alternate chanting.

**Apologetics:** The science and art of developing and presenting the case for the reasonableness of the Christian faith, by a wide variety of means including facts of experience, history, science, philosophy. The constant objective of apologetics, as well as of the total process of pre-evangelization, is preparation for response to God in faith; its ways and means, however, are subject to change in accordance with the various needs of people and different sets of circumstances.

**Apostasy:** (1) The total and obstinate repudiation of the Christian faith. An apostate automatically incurs a penalty of excommunication. (2) Apostasy from orders is the unlawful withdrawal from or rejection of the obligations of the clerical state by a man who has received major orders. An apostate from orders is subject to a canonical penalty. (3) Apostasy from the religious life occurs when a Religious with perpetual vows unlawfully leaves the community with the intention of not returning, or actually remains outside the community without permission. An apostate from religious life is subject to a canonical penalty.

**Apostolate:** The ministry or work of an apostle. In Catholic usage, the word is an umbrella-like term covering all kinds and areas of work and endeavor for the service of God and the Church and the good of people. Thus, the apostolate of bishops is to carry on the mission of the Apostles as pastors of the People of God: of priests, to preach the word of God and to carry out the sacramental and pastoral ministry for which they are ordained; of religious, to follow and do the work of Christ in conformity with the evangelical counsels and their rule of life; of lay persons, as individuals and/or in groups, to give witness to Christ and build up the kingdom of God through practice of their faith, professional competence and the performance of good works in the concrete circumstances of daily life. Apostolic works are not limited to those done within the Church or by specifically Catholic groups, although some apostolates are officially assigned to certain persons or groups and are under the direction of church authorities. Apostolate derives from the commitment and obligation of baptism, confirmation, holy orders, matrimony, the duties of one's state in life, etc.

**Apostolic Succession:** Bishops of the Church, who form a collective body or college, are successors to the Apostles by ordination and divine right; as such they carry on the mission entrusted by Christ to the Apostles as guardians and teachers of the deposit of faith, principal pastors and spiritual authorities of the faithful. The doctrine of apostolic succession is based on New Testament evidence and the constant teaching of the Church, reflected as early as the end of the first century in a letter of Pope St. Clement to the Corinthians. A significant facet of the doctrine is the role of the pope as the successor of St. Peter, the vicar of Christ and head of the college of bishops. The doctrine of apostolic succession means more than continuity of apostolic faith and doctrine; its basic requisite is ordination by the laying on of hands in apostolic succession.

**Archdiocese**: An ecclesiastical jurisdiction headed by an archbishop. An archdiocese is usually a metropolitan see, i.e., the principal one of a group of dioceses comprising a province; the other dioceses in the province are suffragan sees.

**Archives**: Documentary records, and the place where they are kept, of the spiritual and temporal government and affairs of the Church, a diocese, church agencies like the departments of the Roman Curia, bodies like religious institutes, and individual parishes. The collection, cataloguing, preserving, and use of these records are governed by norms stated in canon law and particular regulations. The strictest secrecy is always in effect for confidential records concerning matters of conscience, and documents of this kind are destroyed as soon as circumstances permit.

**Ark of the Covenant**: The sacred chest of the Israelites in which were placed and carried the tablets of stone inscribed with the Ten Commandments, the basic moral precepts of the Old Covenant (Ex. 25: 10-22; 37:1-9). The Ark was also a symbol of God's presence. The Ark was probably destroyed with the Temple in 586 B.C.

**Asceticism**: The practice of self-discipline. In the spiritual life, asceticism — by personal prayer, meditation, self-denial, works of mortification, and outgoing interpersonal works — is motivated by love of God and contributes to growth in holiness.

**Ashes**: Religious significance has been associated with their use as symbolic of penance since Old Testament times. Thus, ashes of palm blessed on the previous Sunday of the Passion are placed on the foreheads of the faithful on Ash Wednesday to remind them to do works of penance, especially during the season of Lent, and that they are dust and unto dust will return. Ashes are a sacramental.

**Aspergillum**: A vessel or device used for sprinkling holy water. The ordinary type is a metallic rod with a bulbous tip which absorbs the water and discharges it at the motion of the user's hand.

**Aspersory**: A portable metallic vessel, similar to a pail, for carrying holy water.

**Aspiration (Ejaculation)**: Short exclamatory prayer; e.g., My Jesus, mercy.

**Atheism**: Denial of the existence of God, finding expression in a system of thought (speculative atheism) or a manner of acting (practical atheism) as though there were no God. The Second Vatican Council, in its *Pastoral Constitution on the Church in the Modern World* (Nos. 19 to 21), noted that a profession of atheism may represent an explicit denial of God, the rejection of a wrong notion of God, an affirmation of man rather than of God, an extreme protest against evil. It said that such a profession might result from acceptance of such propositions as: there is no absolute truth; man can assert nothing, absolutely nothing, about God; everything can be explained by scientific reasoning alone; the whole question of God is devoid of meaning. The constitution also cited two opinions of influence in

atheistic thought. One of them regards recognition of dependence on God as incompatible with human freedom and independence. The other views belief in God and religion as a kind of opiate which sedates man on earth, reconciling him to the acceptance of suffering, injustice, shortcomings, etc., because of hope for greater things after death, and thereby hindering him from seeking and working for improvement and change for the better here and now. All of these views, in one way or another, have been involved in the No-God and Death-of-God schools of thought in recent and remote history.

**Atonement**: The redemptive activity of Christ, who reconciled man with God through his Incarnation and entire life, and especially by his suffering and Resurrection. The word also applies to prayer and good works by which persons join themselves with and take part in Christ's work of reconciliation and reparation for sin.

**Attributes of God**: Perfections of God. God possesses — and is — all the perfections of being, without limitation. Because he is infinite, all of these perfections are one, perfectly united in him. Because of the limited power of human intelligence, divine perfections — such as omnipotence, truth, love, etc. — are viewed separately, as distinct characteristics, even though they are not actually distinct in God.

**Avarice (Covetousness)**: A disorderly and unreasonable attachment to and desire for material things; called a capital sin because it involves preoccupation with material things to the neglect of spiritual goods and obligations of justice and charity.

**Ave Maria**: See Hail Mary.

## B

**Baldachino**: A canopy over an altar.

**Base Ecclesial Communities**: The concept and operational model of basic Christian communities — comunidades de base — envision relatively small communities of the faithful integrated for religious and secular life, with maximum potential for liturgical and sacramental participation, pastoral ministry, apostolic activity, and for personal and social development. Communities of this type originated mainly in Latin America; thousands of them are now contributing to the vitality of parishes and dioceses in many countries throughout the world.

Pope Paul VI, in *Evangelii Nuntiandi*, stated: The name "Ecclesial Communities" can be given only to those "that appear and develop within the Church, having solidarity with her life, being nourished by her teaching and united with her pastors." The name should not be attributed to those "that come together in a spirit of bitter criticism of the Church" and radically oppose the Church. Only the genuine base ecclesial communities "will be a place of evangelization for the benefit of the bigger communities, especially the individual churches and will be a hope for the universal Church to the extent that they constantly grow in missionary consciousness, fervor, commitment and zeal."

**Beatification**: A preliminary step toward canonization of a saint. It begins with an investigation of the candidate's life, writings and heroic practice of virtue, and, except in the case of martyrs, the certification of one miracle worked by God through his or her intercession. If the findings of the investigation so indicate, the pope decrees that the Servant of God may be called *Blessed* and may be honored locally or in a limited way in the liturgy. Additional procedures lead to canonization. (See separate entry).

**Beatific Vision:** The intuitive, immediate and direct vision and experience of God enjoyed in the light of glory by all the blessed in heaven. The vision is a supernatural mystery.

**Beatitude:** A literary form of the Old and New Testaments in which blessings are promised to persons for various reasons. Beatitudes are mentioned 26 times in the Psalms, and in other books of the Old Testament. The best known Beatitudes — identifying blessedness with participation in the kingdom of God and his righteousness, and descriptive of the qualities of Christian perfection — are those recounted in Mt. 5:3-12 and Lk. 6:20-23. The Beatitudes are of central importance in the teaching of Jesus.

**Benedictus:** The canticle or hymn of Zechariah at the circumcision of St. John the Baptist (Lk. 1:68-79). It is an expression of praise and thanks to God for sending John as a precursor of the Messiah. The *Benedictus* is recited in the Liturgy of the Hours as part of the Morning Prayer.

**Biglietto:** A papal document of notification of appointment to the cardinalate.

**Biretta:** A stiff, square hat with three ridges on top worn by clerics in church and on other occasions.

**Blasphemy:** Any internal or external expression of hatred, reproach, insult, defiance or contempt with respect to God and the use of his name, principally, and to the Church, saints and sacred things, secondarily; a serious sin, directly opposed to the second commandment.

**Blasphemy against the Spirit:** Deliberate refusal to accept divine mercy, rejection of forgiveness of sins and of the promise of salvation. The sin that is unforgivable because a person refuses to seek or accept forgiveness.

**Blessing:** Invocation of God's favor, by official ministers of the Church or by private individuals. Blessings are recounted in the Old and New Testaments, and are common in the Christian tradition. Many types of blessings are listed in the *Book of Blessings of the Roman Ritual.* Private blessings, as well as those of an official kind, are efficacious. Blessings are imparted with the Sign of the Cross and appropriate prayer.

**Boat:** A small vessel used to hold incense which is to be placed in the censer.

**Brief, Apostolic:** A papal letter, less formal than a bull, signed for the pope by a secretary and impressed with the seal of the Fisherman's Ring. Simple apostolic letters of this kind are issued for beatifications and with respect to other matters.

**Bull, Apostolic:** Apostolic letter, a solemn form of papal document, beginning with the name and title of the pope (e.g., John Paul II, Servant of the Servants of God), dealing with an important subject, sealed with a bulla or red-ink imprint of the device on the bulla. Bulls are issued to confer the titles of bishops and cardinals, to promulgate canonizations, to proclaim Holy Years and for other purposes. A collection of bulls is called a *bullarium.*

**Burial, Ecclesiastical:** Interment with ecclesiastical rites, a right of the Christian faithful. The Church recommends burial of the bodies of the dead, but cremation is permissible if it does not involve reasons against church teaching. Ecclesiastical burial is in order for catechumens; for unbaptized children whose parents intended to have them baptized before death; and even, in the absence of their own ministers, for baptized non-Catholics unless it would be considered against their will.

## C

**Calumny (Slander):** Harming the name and good reputation of a person by lies; a violation of obligations of justice and truth. Restitution is due for calumny.

**Calvary:** A knoll about 15 feet high just outside the western wall of Jerusalem where Christ was crucified, so called from the Latin *calvaria* (skull) which described its shape.

**Canon:** A Greek word meaning rule, norm, standard, measure. (1) The word designates the Canon of Sacred Scripture, which is the list of books recognized by the Church as inspired by the Holy Spirit. (2) The term also designates the canons (Eucharistic Prayers, anaphoras) of the Mass, the core of the eucharistic liturgy. (3) Certain dignitaries of the Church have the title of Canon, and some religious are known as Canons.

**Canonization:** An infallible declaration by the pope that a person, who died as a martyr and/or practiced Christian virtue to a heroic degree, is now in heaven and is worthy of honor and imitation by all the faithful. Such a declaration is preceded by the process of beatification and another detailed investigation concerning the person's reputation for holiness, writings, and (except in the case of martyrs) a miracle ascribed to his or her intercession after death. The pope can dispense from some of the formalities ordinarily required in canonization procedures (equivalent canonization), as Pope John XXIII did in the canonization of St. Gregory Barbarigo on May 26, 1960. A saint is worthy of honor in liturgical worship throughout the universal Church. From its earliest years the Church has venerated saints. Public official honor always required the approval of the bishop of the place. Martyrs were the first to be honored. St. Martin of Tours, who died in 397, was an early non-martyr venerated as a saint. The earliest canonization by a pope with positive documentation was that of St. Ulrich (Uldaric) of Augsburg by John XV in 993. Alexander III reserved the process of canonization to the Holy See in 1171. In 1588 Sixtus V established the Sacred Congregation of Rites for the principal purpose of handling causes for beatification and canonization: this function is now the work of the Congregation for the Causes of Saints. The official listing of saints and blessed is contained in the *Roman Martyrology* (being revised and updated) and related decrees issued after its last publication. Butler's unofficial *Lives of the Saints* (1956) contains 2,565 entries. The Church regards all persons in heaven as saints, not just those who have been officially canonized. (See Beatification, Saints, Canonizations by Leo XIII and His Successors.)

**Canon Law:** The Code of Canon Law enacted and promulgated by ecclesiastical authority for the orderly and pastoral administration and government of the Church. A revised Code for the Latin rite, effective Nov. 27, 1983, consists of 1,752 canons in seven books under the titles of general norms, the people of God, the teaching mission of the Church, the sanctifying mission of the Church, temporal goods of the Church, penal law and procedural law. The antecedent of this Code was promulgated in 1917 and became effective in 1918; it consisted of 2,414 canons in five books covering general rules, ecclesiastical persons, sacred things, trials, crimes and punishments. There is a separate Code of the Canons of Eastern Churches, in effect since Oct. 1, 1991.

**Canticle:** A scriptural chant or prayer differing from the psalms. Three of the canticles prescribed for use in the Liturgy of the Hours are: the *Magnificat*, the Canticle of Mary (Lk. 1:46-55); the *Benedictus*, the Canticle of Zechariah (Lk. 1:68-79); and the *Nunc Dimittis*, the Canticle of Simeon (Lk. 2:29-32).

**Capital Punishment:** Punishment for crime by means of the death penalty. The political community, which has authority to provide for the common good, has the right to defend itself and its members against unjust aggression and may in extreme cases punish with the death penalty persons found guilty before the law of serious crimes against individuals and a just social order. Such punishment is essentially vindictive. Its value as a crime deterrent is a matter of perennial debate. The prudential judgment as to whether or not there should be capital punishment belongs to the civic community. The U.S. Supreme Court, in a series of decisions dating from June 29, 1972, ruled against the constitutionality of statutes on capital punishment except in specific cases and with appropriate consideration, with respect to sentence, of mitigating circumstances of the crime. Capital punishment was the subject of a statement issued Mar. 1, 1978, by the Committee on Social Development and World Peace, U.S. Catholic Conference. The statement said, in part: "The use of the death penalty involves deep moral and religious questions as well as political and legal issues. In 1974, out of a commitment to the value and dignity of human life, the Catholic bishops of the United States declared their opposition to capital punishment. We continue to support this position, in the belief that a return to the use of the death penalty can only lead to the further erosion of respect for life in our society." Additional statements against capital punishment have been issued by Pope John Paul II, numerous bishops and other sources. Pope John Paul, in his encyclical letter "The Gospel of Life," wrote: "There is a growing tendency, both in the Church and in civil society, to demand that it (capital punishment) be applied in a very limited way or even that it be abolished completely. The nature and extent of the punishment must be carefully evaluated and decided upon, and ought not go to the extreme of executing the offender except in cases of absolute necessity; in other words, when it would not be possible otherwise to defend society. Today such cases are rare if not practically nonexistent." Quoting the Catechism of the Catholic Church, the Pope wrote: " 'If bloodless means are sufficient to defend human lives against an aggressor and to protect public order and the safety of persons, public authority must limit itself to such means, because they better correspond to the concrete conditions of the common good and are more in conformity to the dignity of the human person.' "

**Capital Sins:** Sins which give rise to other sins: pride, avarice, lust, wrath (anger), gluttony, envy, sloth.

**Cardinal Virtues:** The four principal moral virtues are prudence, justice, temperance and fortitude.

**Catacombs:** Underground Christian cemeteries in various cities of the Roman Empire and Italy, especially in the vicinity of Rome; the burial sites of many martyrs and other Christians.

**Catechesis:** The whole complex of church efforts to make disciples of Christ, involving doctrinal instruction and spiritual formation through practice of the faith.

**Catechism:** A systematic presentation of the fundamentals of Catholic doctrine regarding faith and morals. Sources are Sacred Scripture, tradition, the magisterium (teaching authority of the Church), the writings of Fathers and Doctors of the Church, liturgy. The new Catechism of the Catholic Church, published Oct. 11, 1992, consists of four principal sections: the profession of faith, (the Creed), the sacraments of faith, the life of faith (the Commandments) and the prayer of the believer (the Lord's Prayer). The 16th century Council of Trent mandated publication of the Roman Catechism. Catechisms such as these two are useful sources for other catechisms serving particular needs of the faithful and persons seeking admission to the Catholic Church.

**Catechumen:** A person preparing in a program (catechumenate) of instruction and spiritual formation for baptism and reception into the Church. The Church has a special relationship with catechumens. It invites them to lead the life of the Gospel, introduces them to the celebration of the sacred rites, and grants them various prerogatives that are proper to the faithful (one of which is the right to ecclesiastical burial). (See Rite of Christian Initiation of Adults, under Baptism.)

**Cathedra:** A Greek word for chair, designating the chair or seat of a bishop in the principal church of his diocese, which is therefore called a cathedral (see separate entry).

**Cathedraticum:** The tax paid to a bishop by all churches and benefices subject to him for the support of episcopal administration and for works of charity.

**Catholic:** A Greek word, meaning universal, first used in the title Catholic Church in a letter written by St. Ignatius of Antioch about 107 to the Christians of Smyrna.

**Celebret:** A Latin word, meaning Let him celebrate, the name of a letter of recommendation issued by a bishop or other superior stating that a priest is in good standing and therefore eligible to celebrate Mass or perform other priestly functions.

**Celibacy:** The unmarried state of life, required in the Roman Church of candidates for holy orders and of men already ordained to holy orders, for the practice of perfect chastity and total dedication to the service of people in the ministry of the Church. Celibacy is enjoined as a condition for ordination by church discipline and law, not by dogmatic necessity. In the Roman Church, a consensus in favor of celibacy developed in the early centuries while the clergy included both celibates and men who had been married once. The first local legislation on the subject was enacted by a local council held in Elvira, Spain, about 306; it forbade bishops, priests, deacons and other ministers to have wives. Similar enactments were passed by other local councils from that time on, and by the 12th century particular laws regarded marriage by clerics in major orders to be not only unlawful but also null and void. The latter view was translated by the Second Lateran Council in 1139 into what seems to be the first written universal law making holy orders an invalidating impediment to marriage. In 1563 the Council of Trent ruled definitely on the matter and established the discipline in force in the Roman Church. Some exceptions to this discipline have been made in recent years. A number of married Protestant and Episcopalian (Anglican) clergymen who became converts and were subsequently ordained to the priesthood have been permitted to continue in marriage. Married men over the age of 35 can be ordained to the permanent diaconate. Eastern Church discipline on celibacy differs from that of the Roman Church. In line with legislation enacted by the Synod of Trullo in 692 and still in force, candidates for holy orders may marry before becoming deacons and may continue in marriage thereafter, but marriage after ordination is forbidden. Bishops of Eastern Catholic Churches in the U.S., however, do not ordain married candidates for the priesthood. Bishops of Eastern Catholic Churches are unmarried.

**Cenacle:** The upper room in Jerusalem where Christ ate the Las Supper with his Apostles.

**Censer:** A metal vessel with a perforated cover and suspended by chains, in which incense is burned. It is used at some Masses, Benediction of the Blessed Sacrament and other liturgical functions.

**Censorship of Books:** An exercise of vigilance by the Church for safeguarding authentic religious teaching. Pertinent legislation in a decree issued by the Congregation for the Doctrine of the Faith Apr. 9, 1975, is embodied in the Code of Canon Law (Book III, Title IV). The legislation deals with requirements for pre-publication review and clearance of various types of writings on religious subjects. Permission to publish works of a religious character, together with the apparatus of reviewing them beforehand, falls under the authority of the bishop of the place where the writer lives or where the works are published. Clearance for publication is usually indicated by the terms *Nihil obstat* (Nothing stands in the way) issued by the censor and *Imprimatur* (Let it be printed) authorized by the bishop. The clearing of works for publication does not necessarily imply approval of an author's viewpoint or his manner of handling a subject.

**Censures:** Sanctions imposed by the Church on baptized Roman Catholics 18 years of age or older for committing certain serious offenses and for being or remaining obstinate therein: (1) excommunication (exclusion from the community of the faithful, barring a person from sacramental and other participation in the goods and offices of the community of the Church), (2) suspension (prohibition of a cleric to exercise orders) and (3) interdict (deprivation of the sacraments and liturgical activities). The intended purposes of censures are to correct and punish offenders; to deter persons from committing sins which, more seriously and openly than others, threaten the common good of the Church and its members; and to provide for the making of reparation for harm done to the community of the Church. Censures may be incurred automatically (*ipso facto*) on the commission of certain offenses for which fixed penalties have been laid down in church law (*latae sententiae*); or they may be inflicted by sentence of a judge (*ferendae sententiae*). Automatic excommunication is incurred for the offenses of abortion, apostasy, heresy and schism. Obstinacy in crime — also called contumacy, disregard of a penalty, defiance of church authority — is presumed by law in the commission of offenses for which automatic censures are decreed. The presence and degree of contumacy in other cases, for which judicial sentence is required, is subject to determination by a judge. Absolution can be obtained from any censure, provided the person repents and desists from obstinacy. Absolution may be reserved to the pope, the bishop of a place, or the major superior of an exempt clerical religious institute. In danger of death, any priest can absolve from all censures; in other cases, faculties to absolve from reserved censures can be exercised by competent authorities or given to other priests. The penal law of the Church is contained in Book VI of the Code of Canon Law.

**Ceremonies, Master of:** One who directs the proceedings of a rite or ceremony during the function.

**Chamberlain (Camerlengo):** (1) the Chamberlain of the Holy Roman Church is a cardinal with special responsibilities, especially during the time between the death of one pope and the election of his successor; among other things, he safeguards and administers the goods and revenues of the Holy See and heads particular congregations of cardinals for special purposes. (2) the Chamberlain of the College of Cardinals has charge of the property and revenues of the College and keeps the record of business transacted in consistories. (3) the Chamberlain of the Roman Clergy is the president of the secular clergy of Rome.

**Chancellor:** Notary of a diocese, who draws up written documents in the government of the diocese; takes care of, arranges and indexes diocesan archives, records of dispensations and ecclesiastical trials.

**Chancery:** (1) A branch of church administration that handles written documents used in the government of a diocese. (2) The administrative office of a diocese, a bishop's office.

**Chapel:** A building or part of another building used for divine worship; a portion of a church set aside for the celebration of Mass or for some special devotion.

**Chaplain:** A priest — or, in some instances, a properly qualified religious or lay person — serving the pastoral needs of particular groups of people and institutions, such as hospitals, schools, correctional facilities, religious communities, the armed forces, etc.

**Chaplet:** A term, meaning little crown, applied to a rosary or, more commonly, to a small string of beads used for devotional purposes; e.g., the Infant of Prague chaplet.

**Chapter:** A general meeting of delegates of religious orders for elections and the handling of other important affairs of their communities.

**Charismatic Renewal:** A movement which originated with a handful of Duquesne University students and faculty members in the 1966-67 academic year and spread from there to Notre Dame, Michigan State University, the University of Michigan, other campuses and cities throughout the U.S., and to well over 100 other countries. Scriptural keys to the renewal are: Christ's promise to send the Holy Spirit upon the Apostles; the description, in the Acts of the Apostles, of the effects of the coming of the Holy Spirit upon the Apostles on Pentecost; St. Paul's explanation, in the Letter to the Romans and I Corinthians, of the charismatic gifts (for the good of the Church and persons) the Holy Spirit would bestow on Christians; New Testament evidence concerning the effects of charismatic gifts in and through the early Church. The personal key to the renewal is baptism in the Holy Spirit. This is not a new sacrament but the personally experienced actualization of grace already sacramentally received, principally in baptism and confirmation. The experience of baptism in the Holy Spirit is often accompanied by the reception of one or more charismatic gifts. A characteristic form of the renewal is the weekly prayer meeting, a gathering which includes periods of spontaneous prayer, singing, sharing of experience and testimony, fellowship and teaching. The International Catholic Charismatic Renewal Office is located at Palazzo della Cancelleria, 00120 Vatican City. The mailing address of the U.S. National Service Committee is P.O. Box 628, Locust Grove, VA 22508.

**Charisms:** Gifts or graces given by God to persons for the good of others and the Church. Examples are special gifts for apostolic work, prophecy, healing, discernment of spirits, the life of evangelical poverty, here-and-now witness to faith in various circumstances of life. The Second Vatican Council made the following statement about charisms in the *Dogmatic Constitution on the Church* (No. 12): "It is not only through the sacraments and Church ministries that the same Holy Spirit sanctifies and leads the People of God and enriches it with virtues. Allotting his gifts 'to everyone according as he will' (1 Cor. 12:11), he distributes special graces among the faithful of every rank. By these gifts he makes them fit and ready to undertake the various tasks or offices advantageous for the renewal and upbuilding of the Church, according to the words of the Apostle: 'The manifestation of the Spirit is given to everyone for profit' (1 Cor. 12:7). These charismatic gifts, whether they be the most outstanding or the more simple and widely diffused, are to be received with thanksgiving and consolation, for they are exceedingly suitable and useful for the needs of the Church. Still, extraordinary gifts are not to be rashly sought after, nor are the fruits of apostolic labor to be presumptuously expected from them. In any case, judgment as to their genuineness and proper use belongs to those who preside over the Church, and to whose special competence it belongs, not indeed to extinguish the Spirit, but to test all things and hold fast to that which is good" (cf. 1 Thes. 5:12; 19-21).

**Charity:** Love of God above all things for his own sake, and love of one's neighbor as oneself because and as an expression of one's love for God; the greatest of the three theological virtues. The term is sometimes also used to designate sanctifying grace.

**Chastity:** Properly ordered behavior with respect to sex. In marriage, the exercise of the procreative power is integrated with the norms and purposes of marriage. Outside of marriage, the rule is self-denial of the voluntary exercise and enjoyment of the procreative faculty in thought, word or action. The vow of chastity, which reinforces the virtue of chastity with the virtue of religion, is one of the three vows professed publicly by members of institutes of consecrated life.

**Chirograph or Autograph Letter:** A letter written by a pope himself, in his own handwriting.

**Christ:** The title of Jesus, derived from the Greek translation *Christos* of the Hebrew term *Messiah*, meaning the Anointed of God, the Savior and Deliverer of his people. Christian use of the title is a confession of belief that Jesus is the Savior.

**Christianity:** The sum total of things related to belief in Christ — the Christian religion, Christian churches, Christians themselves, society based on and expressive of Christian beliefs, culture reflecting Christian values.

**Christians:** The name first applied about the year 43 to followers of Christ at Antioch, the capital of Syria. It was used by the pagans as a contemptuous term. The word applies to persons who profess belief in the divinity and teachings of Christ and who give witness to him in life.

**Christian Science:** A religious doctrine consisting of Mary Baker Eddy's interpretation and formulation of the actions and teachings of Christ. Its basic tenets reflect Mrs. Eddy's ideas regarding the reality of spirit and its control and domination of what is not spirit. The basic statement of the doctrine is contained in *Science and Health, with Key to the Scriptures,* which she first published in 1875, nine years after being saved from death and healed on reading the New Testament. Mary Baker Eddy (1821-1910) established the church in 1879, and in 1892 founded at Boston the First Church of Christ, Scientist, of which all other Christian Science churches are branches. The individual churches are self-governing and self-supporting under the general supervision of a board of directors. Services consist of readings of portions of Scripture and *Science and Health.* One of the church's publications, *The Christian Science Monitor,* has a worldwide reputation as a journal of news and opinion.

**Church:** (1) See several entries under Church, Catholic. The universal Church is the Church spread throughout the world. The particular Church is the Church in a particular locality; e.g., a diocese. The Church embraces all of its members — on earth, in heaven, in purgatory. (2) In general, any religious body. (3) A building set aside and dedicated for divine worship.

**Circumcision:** A ceremonial practice symbolic of

initiation and participation in the covenant between God and Abraham.

**Circumincession:** The indwelling of each divine Person of the Holy Trinity in the others.

**Clergy:** Men ordained to holy orders and commissioned for sacred ministries and assigned to pastoral and other duties for the service of the people and the Church. (1) Diocesan or secular clergy are committed to pastoral ministry in parishes and in other capacities in a particular church (diocese) under the direction of their bishop, to whom they are bound by a promise of obedience. (2) Regular clergy belong to religious institutes (orders, congregations, societies — institutes of consecrated life) and are so called because they observe the rule (*regula,* in Latin) of their respective institutes. They are committed to the ways of life and apostolates of their institutes. In ordinary pastoral ministry, they are under the direction of local bishops as well as their own superiors.

**Clericalism:** A term generally used in a derogatory sense to mean action, influence and interference by the Church and the clergy in matters with which they allegedly should not be concerned. Anticlericalism is a reaction of antipathy, hostility, distrust and opposition to the Church and clergy arising from real and/or alleged faults of the clergy, overextension of the role of the laity, or for other reasons.

**Cloister:** Part of a monastery, convent or other house of religious reserved for use by members of the institute. Houses of contemplative Religious have a strict enclosure.

**Code:** A digest of rules or regulations, such as the Code of Canon Law.

**Collegiality:** A term in use especially since the Second Vatican Council to describe the authority exercised by the College of Bishops. The bishops of the Church, in union with and subordinate to the pope — who has full, supreme and universal power over the Church which he can always exercise independently — have supreme teaching and pastoral authority over the whole Church. In addition to their proper authority of office for the good of the faithful in their respective dioceses or other jurisdictions, the bishops have authority to act for the good of the universal Church. This collegial authority is exercised in a solemn manner in an ecumenical council and can also be exercised in other ways sanctioned by the pope. Doctrine on collegiality was set forth by the Second Vatican Council in the *Dogmatic Constitution on the Church.* (See separate entry.) By extension, the concept of collegiality is applied to other forms of participation and co-responsibility by members of a community.

**Commissariat of the Holy Land:** A special jurisdiction within the Order of Friars Minor, whose main purposes are the collecting of alms for support of the Holy Places in Palestine and staffing of the Holy Places and missions in the Middle East with priests and brothers. There are about 70 such commissariats in more than 30 countries. One of them has headquarters at Mt. St. Sepulchre, Washington, D.C. Franciscans have had custody of the Holy Places since 1342.

**Communion of Saints:** "The communion of all the faithful of Christ, those who are pilgrims on earth, the dead who are being purified, and the blessed in heaven, all together forming one Church; in this communion, the merciful love of God and his saints is always (attentive) to our prayers" (Paul VI, Creed of the People of God).

**Communism:** The substantive principles of modern communism, a theory and system of economics and social organization, were stated about the middle of the 19th century by Karl Marx, author of *The Communist Manifesto* and, with Friedrich Engels, *Das Kapital.* The elements of communist ideology include: radical materialism; dialectical determinism; the inevitability of class struggle and conflict, which is to be furthered for the ultimate establishment of a worldwide, classless society; common ownership of productive and other goods; the subordination of all persons and institutions to the dictatorship of the collectivity; denial of the rights, dignity and liberty of persons; militant atheism and hostility to religion, utilitarian morality. Communism in theory and practice has been the subject of many papal documents and statements. Pius IX condemned it in 1846. Leo XIII dealt with it at length in the encyclical letters *Quod Apostolici Muneris* in 1878 and *Rerum Novarum* in 1891. Pius XI wrote on the same subject in the encyclicals *Quadragesimo Anno* in 1931 and *Divini Redemptoris* in 1937. These writings have been updated and developed in new directions by Pius XII, John XXIII, Paul VI and John Paul II.

**Concelebration:** The liturgical act in which several priests, led by one member of the group, offer Mass together, all consecrating the bread and wine. Concelebration has always been common in churches of Eastern Rite. In the Roman Rite, it was long restricted, taking place only at the ordination of bishops and the ordination of priests. The *Constitution on the Sacred Liturgy* issued by the Second Vatican Council set new norms for concelebration, which is now relatively common in the Roman Rite.

**Concordance, Biblical:** An alphabetical verbal index enabling a user knowing one or more words of a scriptural passage to locate the entire text.

**Concordat:** A church-state treaty with the force of law concerning matters of mutual concern — e.g., rights of the Church, arrangement of ecclesiastical jurisdictions, marriage laws, education. Approximately 150 agreements of this kind have been negotiated since the Concordat of Worms in 1122.

**Concupiscence:** Any tendency of the sensitive appetite. The term is most frequently used in reference to desires and tendencies for sinful sense pleasure.

**Confession:** Sacramental confession is the act by which a person tells or confesses his sins to a priest who is authorized to give absolution in the sacrament of penance.

**Confessor:** A priest who administers the sacrament of penance. The title of confessor, formerly given to a category of male saints, was suppressed with publication of the calendar reform of 1969.

**Confraternity:** An association whose members practice a particular form of religious devotion and/ or are engaged in some kind of apostolic work.

**Conscience:** Practical judgment concerning the moral goodness or sinfulness of an action (thought, word, desire). In the Catholic view, this judgment is made by reference of the action, its attendant circumstances and the intentions of the person to the requirements of moral law as expressed in the Ten Commandments, the summary law of love for God and neighbor, the life and teaching of Christ, and the authoritative teaching and practice of the Church with respect to the total demands of divine Revelation. A person is obliged: (1) to obey a certain and correct conscience; (2) to obey a certain conscience even if it is inculpably erroneous; (3) not to obey, but to correct, a conscience known to be erroneous or lax; (4) to rectify a scrupulous conscience by following the advice of a confessor and by other measures; (5) to resolve doubts of conscience before acting. It is legitimate to act for solid and probable reasons when a question of moral responsibility admits of argument (see Probabilism).

**Conscience, Examination of:** Self-examination to determine one's spiritual state before God, regarding one's sins and faults. It is recommended as a regular practice and is practically necessary in preparing for the sacrament of penance. The *particular examen* is a regular examination to assist in overcoming specific faults and imperfections.

**Consistory:** An assembly of cardinals presided over by the pope.

**Constitution:** (1) An apostolic or papal constitution is a document in which a pope enacts and promulgates law. (2) A formal and solemn document issued by an ecumenical council on a doctrinal or pastoral subject, with binding force in the whole Church; e.g., the four constitutions issued by the Second Vatican Council on the Church, liturgy, Revelation, and the Church in the modern world. (3) The constitutions of institutes of consecrated life and societies of apostolic life spell out details of and norms drawn from the various rules for the guidance and direction of the life and work of their members.

**Consubstantiation:** A theory which holds that the Body and Blood of Christ coexist with the substance of bread and wine in the Holy Eucharist. This theory, also called *impanation,* is incompatible with the doctrine of transubstantiation.

**Contraception:** Anything done by positive interference to prevent sexual intercourse from resulting in conception. Direct contraception is against the order of nature. Indirect contraception — as a secondary effect of medical treatment or other action having a necessary, good, non-contraceptive purpose — is permissible under the principle of the double effect. The practice of periodic continence is not contraception because it does not involve positive interference with the order of nature. (See *Humanae Vitae,* other entries.)

**Contrition:** Sorrow for sin coupled with a purpose of amendment. Contrition arising from a supernatural motive is necessary for the forgiveness of sin. (1) Perfect contrition is total sorrow for and renunciation of attachment to sin, arising from the motive of pure love of God. Perfect contrition, which implies the intention of doing all God wants done for the forgiveness of sin (including confession in a reasonable period of time), is sufficient for the forgiveness of serious sin and the remission of all temporal punishment due for sin. (The intention to receive the sacrament of penance is implicit — even if unrealized, as in the case of some persons — in perfect contrition.) (2) Imperfect contrition or attrition is sorrow arising from a quasi-selfish supernatural motive; e.g., the fear of losing heaven, suffering the pains of hell, etc. Imperfect contrition is sufficient for the forgiveness of serious sin when joined with absolution in confession, and sufficient for the forgiveness of venial sin even outside of confession.

**Contumely:** Personal insult, reviling a person in his presence by accusation of moral faults, by refusal of recognition or due respect; a violation of obligations of justice and charity.

**Council, Plenary:** A council held for the particular churches belonging to the same episcopal conference. Such a council can be convoked to take action related to the pastoral activity and mission of the Church in the territory. The membership of such councils is fixed by canon law; their decrees, when approved by the Holy See, are binding in the territory (see Index, Plenary Councils of Baltimore).

**Councils, Provincial:** Meetings of the bishops of a province. The metropolitan, or ranking archbishop, of an ecclesiastical province convenes and presides over such councils in a manner prescribed by canon law to take action related to the life and mission of the Church in the province. Acts and decrees must be approved by the Holy See before being promulgated.

**Counsels, Evangelical:** Gospel counsels of perfection, especially voluntary poverty, perfect chastity and obedience, which were recommended by Christ to those who would devote themselves exclusively and completely to the immediate service of God. Religious (members of institutes of consecrated life) bind themselves by public vows to observe these counsels in a life of total consecration to God and service to people through various kinds of apostolic works.

**Counter-Reformation:** The period of approximately 100 years following the Council of Trent, which witnessed a reform within the Church to stimulate genuine Catholic life and to counteract effects of the Reformation.

**Covenant:** A bond of relationship between parties pledged to each other. God-initiated covenants in the Old Testament included those with Noah, Abraham, Moses, Levi, David. The Mosaic (Sinai) covenant made Israel God's Chosen People on terms of fidelity to true faith, true worship, and righteous conduct according to the Decalogue. The New Testament covenant, prefigured in the Old Testament, is the bond people have with God through Christ. All people are called to be parties to this perfect and everlasting covenant, which was mediated and ratified by Christ. The marriage covenant seals the closest possible relationship between a man and a woman.

**Creation:** The production by God of something out of nothing. The biblical account of creation is contained in the first two chapters of Genesis.

**Creator:** God, the supreme, self-existing Being, the absolute and infinite First Cause of all things.

**Creature:** Everything in the realm of being is a creature, except God.

**Cremation:** The reduction of a human corpse to

ashes by means of fire. Cremation is not in line with Catholic tradition and practice, even though it is not opposed to any article of faith. The Congregation for the Doctrine of the Faith, under date of May 8, 1963, circulated among bishops an instruction which upheld the traditional practices of Christian burial but modified anti-cremation legislation. Cremation may be permitted for serious reasons, of a private as well as public nature, provided it does not involve any contempt of the Church or of religion, or any attempt to deny, question, or belittle the doctrine of the resurrection of the body. The person may receive the last rites and be given ecclesiastical burial. A priest may say prayers for the deceased at the crematorium, but full liturgical ceremonies may not take place there. The U.S. bishops petitioned the Vatican in 1996 for permission to celebrate Christian burial with the ashes present in the church. The remains must be treated with respect and be given appropriate burial. The principal reason behind the earlier prohibition against cremation was the fact that, historically, the practice had represented an attempt to deny the doctrine of the resurrection of the body. (See Burial, Ecclesiastical).

**Crib:** A devotional representation of the birth of Jesus. The custom of erecting cribs is generally attributed to St. Francis of Assisi who in 1223 obtained from Pope Honorius III permission to use a crib and figures of the Christ Child, Mary, St. Joseph, and others, to represent the mystery of the Nativity.

**Crosier:** The bishop's staff, symbolic of his pastoral office, responsibility and authority; used at liturgical functions.

**Crypt:** An underground or partly underground chamber; e.g., the lower part of a church used for worship and/or burial.

**Cura Animarum:** A Latin phrase, meaning care of souls, designating the pastoral ministry and responsibility of bishops and priests.

**Curia:** The personnel and offices through which (1) the pope administers the affairs of the universal Church, the Roman Curia (see separate entry), or (2) a bishop the affairs of a diocese, diocesan curia. The principal officials of a diocesan curia are the vicar general of the diocese, the chancellor, officials of the diocesan tribunal or court, examiners, consultors, auditors, notaries.

**Custos:** A religious superior who presides over a number of convents collectively called a custody. In some institutes of consecrated life a custos may be the deputy of a higher superior.

## D

**Deaconess:** A woman officially appointed and charged by the Church to carry out service-like functions. Phoebe apparently was one (Rom. 16:1-2); a second probable reference to the office is in 1 Tm. 3:11. The office — for assistance at the baptism of women, for pastoral service to women and for works of charity — had considerable development in the third and also in the fourth century when the actual term came into use (in place of such designations as diacona, vidua, virgo canonica). Its importance declined subsequently with the substitution of infusion in place of immersion as the common method of baptism in the West, and with the increase of the practice of infant baptism. There is no record of the ministry of deaconess in the West after the beginning of the 11th century. The office continued, however, for a longer time in the East. The Vatican's Theological Commission, in a paper prepared in 1971, noted that there had been in the past a form of diaconal ordination for women. With a rite and purpose distinctive to women, it differed essentially from the ordination of deacons, which had sacramental effects. Several Christian churches have had revivals of the office of deaconess since the 1830s. There is a contemporary movement in support of such a revival among some Catholics.

**Dean:** (1) A priest with supervisory responsibility over a section of a diocese known as a deanery. The post-Vatican II counterpart of a dean is an episcopal vicar. (2) The senior or ranking member of a group.

**Dean of the College of Cardinals:** See Index.

**Decision:** A judgment or pronouncement on a cause or suit, given by a church tribunal or official with judicial authority. A decision has the force of law for concerned parties.

**Declaration:** (1) An ecclesiastical document which presents an interpretation of an existing law. (2) A position paper on a specific subject; e.g., the three declarations issued by the Second Vatican Council on religious freedom, non-Christian religions, and Christian education.

**Decree:** An edict or ordinance issued by a pope and/or by an ecumenical council, with binding force in the whole Church; by a department of the Roman Curia, with binding force for concerned parties; by a territorial body of bishops, with binding force for persons in the area; by individual bishops, with binding force for concerned parties until revocation or the death of the bishop. The nine decrees issued by the Second Vatican Council were combinations of doctrinal and pastoral statements with executive orders for action and movement toward renewal and reform in the Church.

**Dedication of a Church:** The ceremony whereby a church is solemnly set apart for the worship of God. The custom of dedicating churches had an antecedent in Old Testament ceremonies for the dedication of the Temple, as in the times of Solomon and the Maccabees. The earliest extant record of the dedication of a Christian church dates from early in the fourth century, when it was done simply by the celebration of Mass. Other ceremonies developed later. A church can be dedicated by a simple blessing or a solemn consecration. The rite of consecration is generally performed by a bishop.

**Deism:** A system of natural religion which acknowledges the existence of God but regards him as so transcendent and remote from man and the universe that divine revelation and the supernatural order of things are irrelevant and unacceptable. It developed from rationalistic principles in England in the 17th and 18th centuries, and had Voltaire, Rousseau and the Encyclopedists among its advocates in France.

**Despair:** Abandonment of hope for salvation arising from the conviction that God will not provide the necessary means for attaining it, that following God's way of life for salvation is impossible, or that one's sins are unforgivable; a serious sin against the

Holy Spirit and the theological virtues of hope and faith, involving distrust in the mercy and goodness of God and a denial of the truths that God wills the salvation of all persons and provides sufficient grace for it. Real despair is distinguished from unreasonable fear with respect to the difficulties of attaining salvation, from morbid anxiety over the demands of divine justice, and from feelings of despair.

**Detraction:** Revelation of true but hidden faults of a person without sufficient and justifying reason; a violation of requirements of justice and charity, involving the obligation to make restitution when this is possible without doing more harm to the good name of the offended party. In some cases, e.g., to prevent evil, secret faults may and should e disclosed.

**Devil:** (1) Lucifer, Satan, chief of the fallen angels who sinned and were banished from heaven. Still possessing angelic powers, he can cause such diabolical phenomena as possession and obsession, and can tempt men to sin. (2) Any fallen angel.

**Devotion:** (1) Religious fervor, piety; dedication. (2) The consolation experienced at times during prayer; a reverent manner of praying.

**Devotions:** Pious practices of members of the Church include not only participation in various acts of the liturgy but also in other acts of worship generally called popular or private devotions. Concerning these, the Second Vatican Council said in the *Constitution on the Sacred Liturgy* (No. 13): "Popular devotions of the Christian people are warmly commended, provided they accord with the laws and norms of the Church. Such is especially the case with devotions called for by the Apostolic See. Devotions proper to the individual churches also have a special dignity. These devotions should be so drawn up that they harmonize with the liturgical seasons, accord with the sacred liturgy, are in some fashion derived from it, and lead the people to it, since the liturgy by its very nature far surpasses any of them." Devotions of a liturgical type are Exposition of the Blessed Sacrament, recitation of Evening Prayer and Night Prayer of the Liturgy of the Hours. Examples of paraliturgical devotion are a Bible Service or Vigil, and the Angelus, Rosary and Stations of the Cross, which have a strong scriptural basis.

**Diocese:** A particular church, a fully organized ecclesiastical jurisdiction under the pastoral direction of a bishop as local Ordinary.

**Discalced:** Of Latin derivation and meaning without shoes, the word is applied to religious orders or congregations whose members go barefoot or wear sandals.

**Disciple:** A term used sometimes in reference to the Apostles but more often to a larger number of followers (70 or 72) of Christ mentioned in Lk. 10:1.

**Disciplina Arcani:** A Latin phrase, meaning discipline of the secret and referring to a practice of the early Church, especially during the Roman persecutions, to: (1) conceal Christian truths from those who, it was feared, would misinterpret, ridicule and profane the teachings, and persecute Christians for believing them; (2) instruct catechumens in a gradual manner, withholding the teaching of certain doctrines until the catechumens proved themselves of good faith and sufficient understanding.

**Dispensation:** The relaxation of a law in a particular case. Laws made for the common good sometimes work undue hardship in particular cases. In such cases, where sufficient reasons are present, dispensations may be granted by proper authorities. Bishops, religious superiors and others may dispense from certain laws; the pope can dispense from all ecclesiastical laws. No one has authority to dispense from obligations of the divine law.

**Divination:** Attempting to foretell future or hidden things by means of things like dreams, necromancy, spiritism, examination of entrails, astrology, augury, omens, palmistry, drawing straws, dice, cards, etc. Practices like these attribute to creatural things a power which belongs to God alone and are violations of the First Commandment.

**Divine Praises:** Fourteen praises recited or sung at Benediction of the Blessed Sacrament in reparation for sins of sacrilege, blasphemy and profanity. Some of these praises date from the end of the 18th century: Blessed be God. / Blessed be his holy Name. / Blessed be Jesus Christ, true God and true Man. / Blessed be the Name of Jesus. / Blessed be his most Sacred Heart. / Blessed be his most Precious Blood. / Blessed be Jesus in the most holy Sacrament of the Altar. / Blessed be the Holy Spirit, the Paraclete. / Blessed be the great Mother of God, Mary most holy. / Blessed be her holy and Immaculate Conception. / Blessed be her glorious Assumption. / Blessed be the name of Mary, Virgin and Mother. / Blessed be St. Joseph, her most chaste Spouse. / Blessed be God in his Angels and in his Saints.

**Double Effect Principle:** Actions sometimes have two effects closely related to each other, one good and the other bad, and a difficult moral question can arise: Is it permissible to place an action from which two such results follow? It is permissible to place the action, if: the action is good in itself and is directly productive of the good effect; the circumstances are good; the intention of the person is good; the reason for placing the action is proportionately serious to the seriousness of the indirect bad effect. For example: Is it morally permissible for a pregnant woman to undergo medical or surgical treatment for a pathological condition if the indirect and secondary effect of the treatment will be the loss of the child? The reply is affirmative, for these reasons: The action, i.e., the treatment, is good in itself, cannot be deferred until a later time without very serious consequences, and is ordered directly to the cure of critically grave pathology. By means of the treatment, the woman intends to save her life, which she has a right to do. The loss of the child is not directly sought as a means for the cure of the mother but results indirectly and in a secondary manner from the placing of the action, i.e., the treatment, which is good in itself. The double effect principle does not support the principle that the end justifies the means.

**Doxology:** (1) The lesser doxology, or ascription of glory to the Trinity, is the Glory be to the Father. The first part dates back to the third or fourth century, and came from the form of baptism. The concluding words, As it was in the beginning, etc., are of later origin. (2) The greater doxology, Glory to God in the highest, begins with the words of angelic praise at the birth of Christ recounted in the Infancy

Narrative (Lk. 2:14). It is often recited at Mass. Of early Eastern origin, it is found in the *Apostolic Constitutions* in a form much like the present. (3) The formula of praise at the end of the Eucharistic Prayer at Mass, sung or said by the celebrant while he holds aloft the paten containing the consecrated host in one hand and the chalice containing the consecrated wine in the other.

**Dulia:** A Greek term meaning the veneration or homage, different in nature and degree from that given to God, paid to the saints. It includes honoring the saints and seeking their intercession with God.

**Duty:** A moral obligation deriving from the binding force of law, the exigencies of one's state in life, and other sources.

# E

**Easter Controversy:** A three-phase controversy over the time for the celebration of Easter. Some early Christians in the Near East, called Quartodecimans, favored the observance of Easter on the 14th day of Nisan, the spring month of the Hebrew calendar, whenever it occurred. Against this practice, Pope St. Victor I, about 190, ordered a Sunday observance of the feast. The Council of Nicaea, in line with usages of the Church at Rome and Alexandria, decreed in 325 that Easter should be observed on the Sunday following the first full moon of spring. Uniformity of practice in the West was not achieved until several centuries later, when the British Isles, in delayed compliance with measures enacted by the Synod of Whitby in 664, accepted the Roman date of observance. Unrelated to the controversy is the fact that some Eastern Christians, in accordance with traditional calendar practices, celebrate Easter at a different time than the Roman and Eastern Churches.

**Easter Duty, Season:** The serious obligation binding Catholics of Roman Rite, to receive the Eucharist during the Easter season (in the U.S., from the first Sunday of Lent to and including Trinity Sunday).

**Easter Water:** Holy water blessed with special ceremonies and distributed on the Easter Vigil; used during Easter Week for blessing the faithful and homes.

**Ecclesiology:** Study of the nature, constitution, members, mission, functions, etc., of the Church.

**Ecology:** The natural environment of the total range of creation — mineral, vegetable, animal, human — entrusted to people for respect, care and appropriate use as well as conservation and development for the good of present and future generations.

**Ecstasy:** An extraordinary state of mystical experience in which a person is so absorbed in God that the activity of the exterior senses is suspended.

**Ecumenism:** The movement of Christians and their churches toward the unity willed by Christ. The Second Vatican Council called the movement "those activities and enterprises which, according to various needs of the Church and opportune occasions, are started and organized for the fostering of unity among Christians" (*Decree on Ecumenism,* No. 4). Spiritual ecumenism, i.e., mutual prayer for unity, is the heart of the movement. The movement also involves scholarly and pew-level efforts for the development of mutual understanding and better interfaith relations in general, and collaboration by the churches and their members in the social area. (See Index for other entries.)

**Elevation:** The raising of the host after consecration at Mass for adoration by the faithful. The custom was introduced in the Diocese of Paris about the close of the 12th century to offset an erroneous teaching of the time which held that transubstantiation of the bread did not take place until after the consecration of the wine in the chalice. The elevation of the chalice following the consecration of the wine was introduced in the 15th century.

**End Justifies the Means:** An unacceptable ethical principle which states that evil means may be used to produce good effects.

**Envy:** Sadness over another's good fortune because it is considered a loss to oneself or a detraction from one's own excellence; one of the seven capital sins, a violation of the obligations of charity.

**Epiclesis:** An invocation of the Holy Spirit, to bless the offerings consecrated at Mass; before the consecration in the Latin rite, after the consecration in Eastern usage.

**Epikeia:** A Greek word meaning reasonableness and designating a moral theory and practice, a mild interpretation of the mind of a legislator who is prudently considered not to wish positive law to bind in certain circumstances. Use of the principle is justified in practice when the lawgiver himself cannot be appealed to and when it can be prudently assumed that in particular cases, e.g., because of special hardship, he would not wish the law to be applied in a strict manner. Epikeia may not be applied with respect to acts that are intrinsically wrong or those covered by laws which automatically make them invalid.

**Episcopate:** (1) The office, dignity and sacramental powers bestowed upon a bishop at his ordination. (2) The body of bishops collectively.

**Equivocation:** (1) The use of words, phrases, or gestures having more than one meaning in order to conceal information which a questioner has no strict right to know. It is permissible to equivocate (have a broad mental reservation) in some circumstances. (2) A lie, i.e., a statement of untruth. Lying is intrinsically wrong. A lie told in joking, evident as such, is not wrong.

**Eschatology:** Doctrine concerning the 1st things: death, judgment, heaven and hell, and the final state of perfection of the people and kingdom of God at the end of time.

**Eternity:** The interminable, perfect possession of life in its totality without beginning or end; an attribute of God, who has no past or future but always is. Man's existence has a beginning but no end and is, accordingly, called immortal.

**Ethics:** Moral philosophy, the science of the morality of human acts deriving from natural law, the natural end of man, and the powers of human reason. It includes all the spheres of human activity — personal, social, economic, political, etc. Ethics is distinct from but can be related to moral theology, whose primary principles are drawn from divine revelation.

**Eucharistic Congresses**: Public demonstrations of faith in the Holy Eucharist. Combining liturgical services, other public ceremonies, subsidiary meetings, different kinds of instructional and inspirational elements, they are unified by central themes and serve to increase understanding of and devotion to Christ in the Eucharist, and to relate this liturgy of worship and witness to life. The first international congress developed from a proposal by Marie Marthe Tamisier of Touraine, organizing efforts of Msgr. Louis Gaston de Segur, and backing by industrialist Philibert Vrau. It was held with the approval of Pope Leo XIII at the University of Lille, France, and was attended by some 800 persons from France, Belgium, Holland, England, Spain and Switzerland. International congresses are organized by the Pontifical Committee for International Eucharistic Congresses. Participants include clergy, religious and lay persons from many countries, and representatives of national and international Catholic organizations. Forty-five international congresses were held from 1881 to 1993: Lille (1881), Avignon (1882), Liege (1883), Freiburg (1885), Toulouse (1886), Paris (1888), Antwerp (1890), Jerusalem (1893), Rheims (1894), Paray-le-Monial (1897), Brussels (1898), Lourdes (1899), Angers (1901), Namur (1902), Angouleme (1904), Rome (1905), Tournai (1906), Metz (1907), London (1908), Cologne (1909), Montreal (1910), Madrid (1911), Vienna (1912), Malta (1913), Lourdes (1914), Rome (1922), Amsterdam (1924), Chicago (1926), Sydney (1928), Carthage (1930), Dublin (1932), Buenos Aires (1934), Manila (1937), Budapest (1938), Barcelona (1952), Rio de Janeiro (1955), Munich, Germany (1960), Bombay, India (1964), Bogota, Colombia (1968), Melbourne, Australia (1973), Philadelphia (1976), Lourdes (1981), Nairobi, Kenya (1985), Seoul, South Korea (1989), Seville, Spain (1993). The 46th Congress is to be held in 1997 in Wroclaw, Poland.

**Eugenics**: The science of heredity and environment for the physical and mental improvement of offspring. Extreme eugenics is untenable in practice because it advocates immoral means, such as compulsory breeding of the select, sterilization of persons said to be unfit, abortion, and unacceptable methods of birth regulation.

**Euthanasia**: Mercy killing, the direct causing of death for the purpose of ending human suffering. Euthanasia is murder and is totally illicit, for the natural law forbids the direct taking of one's own life or that of an innocent person. The use of drugs to relieve suffering in serious cases, even when this results in a shortening of life as an indirect and secondary effect, is permissible under conditions of the double effect principle. It is also permissible for a seriously ill person to refuse to follow — or for other responsible persons to refuse to permit — extraordinary medical procedures even though the refusal might entail shortening of life.

**Evangelization**: Proclamation of the Gospel, the Good News of salvation in and through Christ, among those who have not yet known or received it; and efforts for the progressive development of the life of faith among those who have already received the Gospel and all that it entails. Evangelization is the primary mission of the Church, in which all members of the Church are called to participate.

**Evolution**: Scientific theory concerning the development of the physical universe from unorganized matter (inorganic evolution) and, especially, the development of existing forms of vegetable, animal and human life from earlier and more primitive organisms (organic evolution). Various ideas about evolution were advanced for some centuries before scientific evidence in support of the main-line theory of organic evolution, which has several formulations, was discovered and verified in the second half of the 19th century and afterwards. This evidence — from the findings of comparative anatomy and other sciences — confirmed evolution within species and cleared the way to further investigation of questions regarding the processes of its accomplishment. While a number of such questions remain open with respect to human evolution, a point of doctrine not open to question is the immediate creation of the human soul by God. For some time, theologians regarded the theory with hostility, considering it to be in opposition to the account of creation in the early chapters of Genesis and subversive of belief in such doctrines as creation, the early state of man in grace, and the fall of man from grace. This state of affairs and the tension it generated led to considerable controversy regarding an alleged conflict between religion and science. Gradually, however, the tension was diminished with the development of biblical studies from the latter part of the 19th century onwards, with clarification of the distinctive features of religious truth and scientific truth, and with the refinement of evolutionary concepts. So far as the Genesis account of creation is concerned, the Catholic view is that the writer(s) did not write as a scientist but as the communicator of religious truth in a manner adapted to the understanding of the people of his time. He used anthropomorphic language, the figure of days and other literary devices to state the salvation truths of creation, the fall of man from grace, and the promise of redemption. It was beyond the competency and purpose of the writer(s) to describe creation and related events in a scientific manner.

**Excommunication**: A penalty or censure by which a baptized Roman Catholic is excluded from the communion of the faithful, for committing and remaining obstinate in certain serious offenses specified in canon law; e.g. heresy, schism, apostasy, abortion. As by baptism a person is made a member of the Church in which there is a communication of spiritual goods, so by excommunication he is deprived of the same spiritual goods until he repents and receives absolution. Even though excommunicated, a person is still responsible for fulfillment of the normal obligations of a Catholic. (See Censures).

**Existentialism**: A philosophy with radical concern for the problems of individual existence and identity viewed in particular here-and-now patterns of thought which presuppose irrationality and absurdity in human life and the whole universe. It is preoccupied with questions about freedom, moral decision and responsibility against a background of denial of objective truth and universal norms of conduct; is characterized by prevailing anguish, dread, fear, pessimism, despair; is generally atheistic, although its modern originator, Soren Kierkegaard (d. 1855), and Gabriel Marcel (d. 1973) attempted to give it a Christian orientation. Pius XII called it "the new erroneous philosophy which, opposing itself to idealism, immanentism and pragmatism, has assumed the name of existentialism, since it concerns itself only with the existence of individual things and neglects all consideration of their immutable essences" (Encyclical *Humani Generis*, Aug. 12, 1950).

**Exorcism:** (1) Driving out evil spirits; a rite in which evil spirits are charged and commanded on the authority of God and with the prayer of the Church to depart from a person or to cease causing harm to a person suffering from diabolical possession or obsession. The sacramental is officially administered by a priest delegated for the purpose by the bishop of the place. Elements of the rite include the Litany of Saints; recitation of the Our Father, one or more creeds, and other prayers; specific prayers of exorcism; the reading of Gospel passages and use of the Sign of the Cross. (2) Exorcisms which do not imply the conditions of either diabolical possession or obsession form part of the ceremony of baptism and are also included in formulas for various blessings; e.g., of water.

**Exposition of the Blessed Sacrament:** "In churches where the Eucharist is regularly reserved, it is recommended that solemn exposition of the Blessed Sacrament for an extended period of time should take place once a year, even though the period is not strictly continuous. Shorter expositions of the Eucharist (Benediction) are to be arranged in such a way that the blessing with the Eucharist is preceded by a reasonable time for readings of the word of God, songs, prayers and a period for silent prayer." So stated Vatican directives issued in 1973.

## F

**Faculties:** Grants of jurisdiction or authority by the law of the Church or superiors (pope, bishop, religious superior) for exercise of the powers of holy orders; e.g., priests are given faculties to hear confessions, officiate at weddings; bishops are given faculties to grant dispensations, etc.

**Faith:** In religion, faith has several aspects. Catholic doctrine calls faith the assent of the mind to truths revealed by God, the assent being made with the help of grace and by command of the will on account of the authority and trustworthiness of God revealing. The term faith also refers to the truths that are believed (content of faith) and to the way in which a person, in response to Christ, gives witness to and expresses belief in daily life (living faith). All of these elements, and more, are included in the following statement: " 'The obedience of faith' (Rom. 16:26; 1:5; 2 Cor. 10:5-6) must be given to God who reveals, an obedience by which man entrusts his whole self freely to God, offering 'the full submission of intellect and will to God who reveals' (First Vatican Council, *Dogmatic Constitution on the Catholic Faith,* Chap. 3), and freely assenting to the truth revealed by him. If this faith is to be shown, the grace of God and the interior help of the Holy Spirit must precede and assist,

moving the heart and turning it to God, opening the eyes of the mind, and giving 'joy and ease to everyone in assenting to the truth and believing it' " (Second Council of Orange, Canon 7) (Second Vatican Council, *Constitution on Revelation,* No. 5). Faith is necessary for salvation.

**Faith, Rule of:** The norm or standard of religious belief. The Catholic doctrine is that belief must be professed in the divinely revealed truths in the Bible and tradition as interpreted and proposed by the infallible teaching authority of the Church.

**Fast, Eucharistic:** Abstinence from food and drink, except water and medicine, is required for one hour before the reception of the Eucharist. Persons who are advanced in age or suffer from infirmity or illness, together with those who care for them, can receive Holy Communion even if they have not abstained from food and drink for an hour. A priest celebrating two or three Masses on the same day can eat and drink something before the second or third Mass without regard for the hour limit.

**Father:** A title of priests, who are regarded as spiritual fathers because they are the ordinary ministers of baptism, by which persons are born to supernatural life, and because of their pastoral service to people.

**Fear:** A mental state caused by the apprehension of present or future danger. Grave fear does not necessarily remove moral responsibility for an act, but may lessen it.

**First Friday:** A devotion consisting of the reception of Holy Communion on the first Friday of nine consecutive months in honor of the Sacred Heart of Jesus and in reparation for sin. (See Sacred Heart, Promises.)

**First Saturday:** A devotion tracing its origin to the apparitions of the Blessed Virgin Mary at Fatima in 1917. Those practicing the devotion go to confession and, on the first Saturday of five consecutive months, receive Holy Communion, recite five decades of the Rosary, and meditate on the mysteries for 15 minutes.

**Fisherman's Ring:** A signet ring engraved with the image of St. Peter fishing from a boat, and encircled with the name of the reigning pope. It is not worn by the pope. It is used to seal briefs, and is destroyed after each pope's death.

**Forgiveness of Sin:** Catholics believe that sins are forgiven by God through the mediation of Christ in view of the repentance of the sinner and by means of the sacrament of penance. (See Penance, Contrition).

**Fortitude:** Courage to face dangers or hardships for the sake of what is good; one of the four cardinal virtues and one of the seven gifts of the Holy Spirit.

**Fortune Telling:** Attempting to predict the future or the occult by means of cards, palm reading, etc.; a form of divination, prohibited by the First Commandment.

**Forty Hours Devotion:** A Eucharistic observance consisting of solemn exposition of the Blessed Sacrament coupled with special Masses and forms of prayer, for the purposes of making reparation for sin and praying for God's blessings of grace and peace. The devotion was instituted in 1534 in Milan. St. John Neumann of Philadelphia was the first bishop in the U.S. to prescribe its observance in his diocese. For many years in this country, the observance was held annually on a rotating basis in all parishes of a diocese. Simplified and abbreviated Eucharistic observances have taken the place of the devotion in some places.

**Forum**: The sphere in which ecclesiastical authority or jurisdiction is exercised. (1) External: Authority is exercised in the external forum to deal with matters affecting the public welfare of the Church and its members. Those who have such authority because of their office (e.g., diocesan bishops) are called ordinaries. (2) Internal: Authority is exercised in the internal forum to deal with matters affecting the private spiritual good of individuals. The sacramental forum is the sphere in which the sacrament of penance is administered; other exercises of jurisdiction in the internal forum take place in the nonsacramental forum.

**Franciscan Crown**: A seven-decade rosary used to commemorate the seven Joys of the Blessed Virgin: the Annunciation, the Visitation, the Nativity of Our Lord, the Adoration of the Magi, the Finding of the Child Jesus in the Temple, the Apparition of the Risen Christ to his Mother, the Assumption and Coronation of the Blessed Virgin. Introduced in 1422, the Crown originally consisted only of seven Our Fathers and 70 Hail Marys. Two Hail Marys were added to complete the number 72 (thought to be the number of years of Mary's life), and one Our Father, Hail Mary and Glory be to the Father are said for the intention of the pope.

**Freedom, Religious**: The Second Vatican Council declared that the right to religious freedom in civil society "means that all men are to be immune from coercion on the part of individuals or of social groups and of any human power, in such wise that in matters religious no one is to be forced to act in a manner contrary to his own beliefs. Nor is anyone to be restrained from acting in accordance with his own beliefs, whether privately or publicly, whether alone or in association with others, within due limits" of requirements for the common good. The foundation of this right in civil society is the "very dignity of the human person" (*Declaration on Religious Freedom*, No. 2). The conciliar statement did not deal with the subject of freedom within the Church. It noted the responsibility of the faithful "carefully to attend to the sacred and certain doctrine of the Church" (No. 14).

**Freemasons**: A fraternal order which originated in London in 1717 with the formation of the first Grand Lodge of Freemasons. From England, the order spread to Europe and elsewhere. Its principles and basic rituals embody a naturalistic religion, active participation in which is incompatible with Christian faith and practice. Grand Orient Freemasonry, developed in Latin countries, is atheistic, irreligious and anticlerical. In some places, Freemasonry has been regarded as subversive of the state; in Catholic quarters, it has been considered hostile to the Church and its doctrine. In the United States, Freemasonry has been widely regarded as a fraternal and philanthropic order. For serious doctrinal and pastoral reasons, Catholics were forbidden to join the Freemasons under penalty of excommunication,

according to church law before 1983. Eight different popes in 17 different pronouncements, and at least six different local councils, condemned Freemasonry. The first condemnation was made by Clement XII in 1738. Eastern Orthodox and many Protestant bodies have also opposed the order. In the U.S., there was some easing of the ban against Masonic membership by Catholics in view of a letter written in 1974 by Cardinal Franjo Seper, prefect of the Congregation for the Doctrine of the Faith. The letter was interpreted to mean that Catholics might join Masonic lodges which were not anti-Catholic. This was called erroneous in a declaration issued by the Doctrinal Congregation Feb. 17, 1981. The prohibition against Masonic membership was restated in a declaration issued by the Doctrinal Congregation Nov. 26, 1983, with the approval of Pope John Paul II, as follows. "The Church's negative position on Masonic associations remains unaltered, since their principles have always been regarded as irreconcilable with the Church's doctrine. Hence, joining them remains prohibited by the Church. Catholics enrolled in Masonic associations are involved in serious sin and may not approach Holy Communion. Local ecclesiastical authorities do not have the faculty to pronounce a judgment on the nature of Masonic associations which might include a diminution of the above-mentioned judgment." This latest declaration, like the revised Code of Canon Law, does not include a penalty of excommunication for Catholics who join the Masons. Local bishops are not authorized to grant dispensations from the prohibition. The foregoing strictures against Masonic membership by Catholics were reiterated in a report by the Committee for Pastoral Research and Practice, National Conference of Catholic Bishops, released through Catholic News Service June 7, 1985.

**Free Will**: The faculty or capability of making a reasonable choice among several alternatives. Freedom of will underlies the possibility and fact of moral responsibility.

**Friar**: Term applied to members of mendicant orders to distinguish them from members of monastic orders. (See Mendicants.)

**Fruits of the Holy Spirit**: Charity, joy, peace, patience, kindness, goodness, generosity, gentleness, faithfulness, modesty, self-control, chastity.

# G

**Gambling**: The backing of an issue with a sum of money or other valuables, which is permissible if the object is honest, if the two parties have the free disposal of their stakes without prejudice to the rights of others, if the terms are thoroughly understood by both parties, and if the outcome is not known beforehand. Gambling often falls into disrepute and may be forbidden by civil law, as well as by divine law, because of cheating, fraud and other accompanying evils.

**Gehenna**: Greek form of a Jewish name, *Gehinnom*, for a valley near Jerusalem, the site of Moloch worship; used as a synonym for hell.

**Genuflection**: Bending of the knee, a natural sign of adoration or reverence, as when persons genuflect with the right knee in passing before the tabernacle to acknowledge the Eucharistic presence of Christ.

**Gethsemani:** A Hebrew word meaning oil press, designating the place on the Mount of Olives where Christ prayed and suffered in agony the night before he died.

**Gifts of the Holy Spirit:** Supernatural habits disposing a person to respond promptly to the inspiration of grace; promised by Christ and communicated through the Holy Spirit, especially in the sacrament of confirmation. They are: wisdom, understanding, counsel, fortitude, knowledge, piety, fear of the Lord.

**Gluttony:** An unreasonable appetite for food and drink; one of the seven capital sins.

**God:** The infinitely perfect Supreme Being, uncaused and absolutely self-sufficient, eternal, the Creator and final end of all things. The one God subsists in three equal Persons, the Father and the Son and the Holy Spirit. God, although transcendent and distinct from the universe, is present and active in the world in realization of his plan for the salvation of human beings, principally through Revelation, the operations of the Holy Spirit, the life and ministry of Christ, and the continuation of Christ's ministry in the Church. The existence of God is an article of faith, clearly communicated in divine Revelation. Even without this Revelation, however, the Church teaches, in a declaration by the First Vatican Council, that human beings can acquire certain knowledge of the existence of God and some of his attributes. This can be done on the bases of principles of reason and reflection on human experience. Non-revealed arguments or demonstrations for the existence of God have been developed from the principle of causality; the contingency of human beings and the universe; the existence of design, change and movement in the universe; human awareness of moral responsibility; widespread human testimony to the existence of God.

**Grace:** A free gift of God to persons (and angels), grace is a created sharing or participation in the life of God. It is given to persons through the merits of Christ and is communicated by the Holy Spirit. It is necessary for salvation. The principal means of grace are the sacraments (especially the Eucharist), prayer and good works. (1) Sanctifying or habitual grace makes persons holy and pleasing to God, adopted children of God, members of Christ, temples of the Holy Spirit, heirs of heaven capable of supernaturally meritorious acts. With grace, God gives persons the supernatural virtues and gifts of the Holy Spirit. The sacraments of baptism and penance were instituted to give grace to those who do not have it; the other sacraments, to increase it in those already in the state of grace. The means for growth in holiness, or the increase of grace, are prayer, the sacraments, and good works. Sanctifying grace is lost by the commission of serious sin. Each sacrament confers sanctifying grace for the special purpose of the sacrament; in this context, grace is called sacramental grace. (2) Actual grace is a supernatural help of God which enlightens and strengthens a person to do good and to avoid evil. It is not a permanent quality, like sanctifying grace. It is necessary for the performance of supernatural acts. It can be resisted and refused. Persons in the state of serious sin are given actual grace to lead them to repentance.

**Grace at Meals:** Prayers said before meals, asking a blessing of God, and after meals, giving thanks to God. In addition to traditional prayers for these purposes, many variations suitable for different occasions are possible, at personal option.

# H

**Habit:** (1) A disposition to do things easily, given with grace (and therefore supernatural) and/or acquired by repetition of similar acts. (2) The garb worn by Religious.

**Hagiography:** Writings or documents about saints and other holy persons.

**Hail Mary:** A prayer addressed to the Blessed Virgin Mary; also called the *Ave Maria* (Latin equivalent of Hail Mary) and the Angelic Salutation. In three parts, it consists of the words addressed to Mary by the Archangel Gabriel on the occasion of the Annunciation, in the Infancy Narrative (Hail full of grace, the Lord is with you, blessed are you among women.); the words addressed to Mary by her cousin Elizabeth on the occasion of the Visitation (Blessed is the fruit of your womb.); a concluding petition (Holy Mary, Mother of God, pray for us sinners now and at the hour of our death. Amen.). The first two salutations were joined in Eastern Rite formulas by the sixth century, and were similarly used at Rome in the seventh century. Insertion of the name of Jesus at the conclusion of the salutations was probably made by Urban IV about 1262. The present form of the petition was incorporated into the breviary in 1514.

**Heaven:** The state of those who, having achieved salvation, are in glory with God and enjoy the beatific vision. The phrase, kingdom of heaven, refers to the order or kingdom of God, grace, salvation.

**Hell:** The state of persons who die in mortal sin, in a condition of self-alienation from God which will last forever.

**Heresy:** The obstinate post-baptismal denial or doubt by a Catholic of any truth which must be believed as a matter of divine and Catholic faith (Canon 751, of the Code of Canon Law). Formal heresy involves deliberate resistance to the authority of God who communicates revelation through Scripture and tradition and the teaching authority of the Church. Heretics automatically incur the penalty of excommunication (Canon 1364 of the Code of Canon Law). Heresies have been significant not only as disruptions of unity of faith but also as occasions for the clarification and development of doctrine. Heresies from the beginning of the Church to the 13th century are described in Dates and Events in Church History.

**Hermit:** See Anchorite.

**Heroic Act of Charity:** The completely unselfish offering to God of one's good works and merits for the benefit of the souls in purgatory rather than for oneself. Thus a person may offer to God for the souls in purgatory all the good works he performs during life, all the indulgences he gains, and all the prayers and indulgences that will be offered for him after his death. The act is revocable at will, and is not a vow. Its actual ratification depends on the will of God.

**Heterodoxy:** False doctrine teaching or belief; a departure from truth.

**Holy See:** (1) The diocese of the pope, Rome. (2) The pope himself and/or the various officials and bodies of the Church's central administration at Vatican City — the Roman Curia — which act in the name and by authority of the pope.

**Holy Spirit:** God the Holy Spirit, third Person of the Holy Trinity, who proceeds from the Father and the Son and with whom he is equal in every respect; inspirer of the prophets and writers of sacred Scripture; promised by Christ to the Apostles as their advocate and strengthener; appeared in the form of a dove at the baptism of Christ and as tongues of fire at his descent upon the Apostles; soul of the Church and guarantor, by his abiding presence and action, of truth in doctrine; communicator of grace to human beings, for which reason he is called the sanctifier.

**Holy Water:** Water blessed by the Church and used as a sacramental, a practice which originated in apostolic times.

**Holy Year:** A year during which the pope grants the plenary Jubilee Indulgence to the faithful who fulfill certain conditions. For those who make a pilgrimage to Rome during the year, the conditions are reception of the sacraments of penance and the Eucharist, visits and prayer for the intention of the pope in the basilicas of St. Peter, St. John Lateran, St. Paul and St. Mary Major. For those who do not make a pilgrimage to Rome, the conditions are reception of the sacraments and prayer for the pope during a visit or community celebration in a church designated by the bishop of the locality. Holy Year observances have biblical counterparts in the Years of Jubilee observed at 50-year intervals by the pre-exilic Israelites — when debts were pardoned and slaves freed (Lv. 25:25-54) — and in sabbatical years observed from the end of the Exile to 70 A.D. — in which debts to fellow Jews were remitted. The practice of Christians from early times to go on pilgrimage to the Holy Land, the shrines of martyrs and the tombs of the Apostles in Rome influenced the institution of Holy Years. There was also a prevailing belief among the people that every 100th year was a year of "Great Pardon." Accordingly, even before Boniface VIII formally proclaimed the first Holy Year Feb. 22, 1300, scores of thousands of pilgrims were already on the way to or in Rome. Medieval popes embodied in the observance of Holy Years the practice of good works (reception of the sacraments of penance and the Eucharist, pilgrimages and/or visits to the tombs of the Apostles, and related actions) and spiritual benefits (particularly, special indulgences for the souls in purgatory). These and related practices, with suitable changes for celebrations in local churches, remain staple features of Holy Year observances. The first three Holy Years were observed in 1300, 1350 and 1390. Subsequent ones were celebrated at 25-year intervals except in 1800 and 1850 when, respectively, the French invasion of Italy and political turmoil made observance impossible. Pope Paul II (1464-1471) set the 25-year timetable. In 1500, Pope Alexander VI prescribed the start and finish ceremonies — the opening and closing of the Holy Doors in the major basilicas on suc-

cessive Christmas Eves. All but a few of the earlier Holy Years were classified as ordinary. Several — like those of 1933 and 1983-84 to commemorate the 1900th and 1950th anniversaries of the death and resurrection of Christ — were in the extraordinary category.

**Homosexuality:** The condition of a person whose sexual orientation is toward persons of the same rather than the opposite sex. The condition, is not sinful in itself. Homosexual acts are seriously sinful in themselves; subjective responsibility for such acts, however, may be conditioned and diminished by compulsion and related factors.

**Hope:** The theological virtue by which a person firmly trusts in God for the means and attainment salvation.

**Hosanna:** A Hebrew word, meaning O Lord, save, we pray.

**Host, The Sacred:** The bread under whose appearances Christ is and remains present in a unique manner after the consecration which takes place during Mass. (See Transubstantiation.)

**Humanism:** A world view centered on man. Types of humanism which exclude the supernatural are related to secularism.

**Humility:** A virtue which induces a person to evaluate himself or herself at his or her true worth, to recognize his or her dependence on God, and to give glory to God for the good he or she has and can do.

**Hyperdulia:** The special veneration accorded the Blessed Virgin Mary because of her unique role in the mystery of Redemption, her exceptional gifts of grace from God, and her pre-eminence among the saints. Hyperdulia is not adoration; only God is adored.

**Hypnosis:** A mental state resembling sleep, induced by suggestion, in which the subject does the bidding of the hypnotist. Hypnotism is permissible under certain conditions: the existence of a serious reason, e.g., for anesthetic or therapeutic purposes, and the competence and integrity of the hypnotist. Hypnotism may not be practiced for the sake of amusement. Experiments indicate that, contrary to popular opinion, hypnotized subjects may be induced to perform immoral acts which, normally, they would not do.

**Hypostatic Union:** The union of the human and divine natures in the one divine Person of Christ.

# I

**Icons:** Byzantine-style paintings or representations of Christ, the Blessed Virgin and other saints, venerated in the Eastern Churches where they take the place of statues.

**Idolatry:** Worship of any but the true God; a violation of the First Commandment.

**IHS:** In Greek, the first three letters of the name of Jesus — Iota, Eta, Sigma.

**Immortality:** The survival and continuing existence of the human soul after death.

**Impurity:** Unlawful indulgence in sexual pleasure. (See Chastity.)

**Incardination:** The affiliation of a priest to his diocese. Every secular priest must belong to a certain diocese. Similarly, every priest of a religious community must belong to some jurisdiction of his community; this affiliation, however, is not called incardination.

**Incarnation:** (1) The coming-into-flesh or taking of human nature by the Second Person of the Trinity. He became human as the Son of Mary, being miraculously conceived by the power of the Holy Spirit, without ceasing to be divine. His divine Person hypostatically unites his divine and human natures. (2) The supernatural mystery coextensive with Christ from the moment of his human conception and continuing through his life on earth; his sufferings and death; his resurrection from the dead and ascension to glory with the Father; his sending, with the Father, of the Holy Spirit upon the Apostles and the Church; and his unending mediation with the Father for the salvation of human beings.

**Incense:** A granulated substance which, when burnt, emits an aromatic smoke. It symbolizes the zeal with which the faithful should be consumed, the good odor of Christian virtue, the ascent of prayer to God.

**Incest:** Sexual intercourse with relatives by blood or marriage; a sin of impurity and also a grave violation of the natural reverence due to relatives. Other sins of impurity desire, etc.) concerning relatives have the nature of incest.

**Inculturation:** This was one of the subjects of an address delivered by Pope John Paul II Feb. 15, 1982, at a meeting in Lagos with the bishops of Nigeria. "An important aspect of your own evangelizing role is the whole dimension of the inculturation of the Gospel into the lives of your people. The Church truly respects the culture of each people. In offering the Gospel message, the Church does not intend to destroy or to abolish what is good and beautiful. In fact, she recognizes many cultural values and, through the power of the Gospel, purifies and takes into Christian worship certain elements of a people's customs. The Church comes to bring Christ; she does not come to bring the culture of another race. Evangelization aims at penetrating and elevating culture by the power of the Gospel.... It is through the Providence of God that the divine message is made incarnate and is communicated through the culture of each people. It is forever true that the path of culture is the path of man, and it is on this path that man encounters the one who embodies the values of all cultures and fully reveals the man of each culture to himself. The Gospel of Christ, the Incarnate Word, finds its home along the path of culture, and from this path it continues to offer its message of salvation and eternal life."

**Index of Prohibited Books:** A list of books which Catholics were formerly forbidden to read, possess or sell, under penalty of excommunication. The books were banned by the Holy See after publication because their treatment of matters of faith and morals and related subjects were judged to be erroneous or serious occasions of doctrinal error. Some books were listed in the Index by name; others were covered under general norms. The Congregation for the Doctrine of the Faith declared June 14, 1966, that the Index and its related penalties of excommunication no longer had the force of law in the Church. Persons are still obliged, however, to take normal precautions against occasions of doctrinal error.

**Indifferentism:** A theory that any one religion is as true and good — or false — as any other religion, and that it makes no difference, objectively, what religion one professes, if any. The theory is completely subjective, finding its justification entirely in personal choice without reference to or respect for objective validity. It is also self-contradictory, since it regards as equally acceptable — or unacceptable — the beliefs of all religions, which in fact are not only not all the same but are in some cases opposed to each other.

**Indulgence:** According to *The Doctrine and Practice of Indulgences,* an apostolic constitution issued by Paul VI Jan. 1, 1967, an indulgence is the remission before God of the temporal punishment due for sins already forgiven as far as their guilt is concerned, which a follower of Christ — with the proper dispositions and under certain determined conditions — acquires through the intervention of the Church. The Church grants indulgences in accordance with doctrine concerning the superabundant merits of Christ and the saints, the Power of the Keys, and the sharing of spiritual goods in the communion of saints. An indulgence is partial or plenary, depending on whether it does away with either part or all of the temporal punishment due for sin. Both types of indulgences can always be applied to the dead by way of suffrage; the actual disposition of indulgences applied to the dead rests with God. (1) Partial indulgence: Properly disposed faithful who perform an action to which a partial indulgence is attached obtain, in addition to the remission of temporal punishment acquired by the action itself, an equal remission of punishment through the intervention of the Church. (This grant was formerly designated in terms of days and years.) The proper dispositions for gaining a partial indulgence are sorrow for sin and freedom from serious sin, performance of the required good work, and the intention (which can be general or immediate) to gain the indulgence. In addition to customary prayer and other good works to which partial indulgences are attached, there are general grants of partial indulgences to the faithful who: (a) with some kind of prayer, raise their minds to God with humble confidence while carrying out their duties and bearing the difficulties of everyday life; (b) motivated by the spirit of faith and compassion, give of themselves or their goods for the service of persons in need; (c) in a spirit of penance, spontaneously refrain from the enjoyment of things which are lawful and pleasing to them. (2) Plenary indulgence: To gain a plenary indulgence, it is necessary for a person to be free of all attachment to sin, to perform the work to which the indulgence is attached, and to fulfill the three conditions of sacramental confession, Eucharistic Communion, and prayer for the intention of the pope. The three conditions may be fulfilled several days before or after the performance of the prescribed work, but it is fitting that Communion be received and prayers for the intentions of the pope be offered on the same day the work is performed. The condition of praying for the pope's intention is fully satisfied by praying one Our Father and one Hail Mary, and sometimes the Creed, but persons are free to choose other prayers. Four of the several devotional practices for which a plenary indulgence is granted are: (a) adoration of the Blessed Sacrament for at least one-half hour; (b) devout reading of sacred Scripture for at least one-half hour; (c) the Way of the Cross; (d) recitation of the Rosary in a church, public oratory or private chapel, or in a family group, a religious community or pious association. Only one plenary indulgence can be gained in a single day. The Apostolic Penitentiary issued a decree Dec. 14, 1985, granting diocesan bishops the right to impart — three times a year on solemn feasts of their choice — the papal blessing with a plenary indulgence to those who cannot be physically present but who follow the sacred rites at which the blessing is imparted by radio or television transmission. In July, 1986, publication was announced of a new and simplified *Enchiridion Indulgentiarum,* in accord with provisions of the revised Code of Canon Law.

**Indult:** A favor or privilege granted by competent ecclesiastical authority, giving permission to do something not allowed by the common law of the Church.

**Infant Jesus of Prague:** An 18-inch-high wooden statue of the Child Jesus which has figured in a form of devotion to the Holy Childhood and Kingship of Christ since the 17th century. Of uncertain origin, the statue was presented by Princess Polixena to the Carmelites of Our Lady of Victory Church, Prague, in 1628.

**Infused Virtues:** The theological virtues of faith, hope, and charity; principles or capabilities of supernatural action, they are given with sanctifying grace by God rather than acquired by repeated acts of a person. They can be increased by practice; they are lost by contrary acts. Natural-acquired moral virtues, like the cardinal virtues of prudence, justice, temperance, and fortitude, can be considered infused in a person whose state of grace gives them supernatural orientation.

**Inquisition:** A tribunal for dealing with heretics, authorized by Gregory IX in 1231 to search them out, hear and judge them, sentence them to various forms of punishment, and in some cases to hand them over to civil authorities for punishment. The Inquisition was a creature of its time when crimes against faith, which threatened the good of the Christian community, were regarded also as crimes against the state, and when heretical doctrines of such extremists as the Cathari and Albigensians threatened the very fabric of society. The institution, which was responsible for many excesses, was most active in the second half of the 13th century.

**Inquisition, Spanish:** An institution peculiar to Spain and the colonies in Spanish America. In 1478, at the urging of King Ferdinand, Pope Sixtus IV approved the establishment of the Inquisition for trying charges of heresy brought against Jewish (Marranos) and Moorish (Moriscos) converts. It acquired jurisdiction over other cases as well, however, and fell into disrepute because of irregularities in its functions, cruelty in its sentences, and the manner in which it served the interests of the Spanish crown more than the accused persons and the good of the Church. Protests by the Holy See failed to curb excesses of the Inquisition, which lingered in Spanish history until early in the 19th century.

**I N R I:** The first letters of words in the Latin inscription atop the cross on which Christ was crucified: (I)esus (N)azaraenus, (R)ex (I)udaeorum — Jesus of Nazareth, King of the Jews.

**Insemination, Artificial:** The implanting of human semen by some means other than consummation of natural marital intercourse. In view of the principle that procreation should result only from marital intercourse, donor insemination is not permissible.

**In Sin:** The condition of a person called spiritually dead because he or she does not possess sanctifying grace, the principle of supernatural life, action and merit. Such grace can be regained through repentance.

**Instruction:** A document containing doctrinal explanations, directive norms, rules, recommendations, admonitions, issued by the pope, a department of the Roman Curia or other competent authority in the Church. To the extent that they so prescribe, instructions have the force of law.

**Intercommunion, Eucharistic Sharing:** The common celebration and reception of the Eucharist by members of different Christian churches; a pivotal issue in ecumenical theory and practice. Catholic participation and intercommunion in the Eucharistic liturgy of another church without a valid priesthood and with a variant Eucharistic belief is out of order. Under certain conditions, other Christians may receive the Eucharist in the Catholic Church. (See additional Intercommunion entry). Intercommunion is acceptable to some Protestant churches and unacceptable to others.

**Interdict:** A censure imposed on persons for certain violations of church law. Interdicted persons may not take part in certain liturgical services, administer or receive certain sacraments.

**Intinction:** A method of administering Holy Communion under the dual appearances of bread and wine, in which the consecrated host is dipped in the consecrated wine before being given to the communicant. The administering of Holy Communion in this manner, which has been traditional in Eastern-Rite liturgies, was authorized in the Roman Rite for various occasions by the *Constitution on the Sacred Liturgy* promulgated by the Second Vatican Council.

**Irenicism:** Peace-seeking, conciliation, as opposed to polemics; an important element in ecumenism, provided it furthers pursuit of the Christian unity willed by Christ without degenerating into a peace-at-any-price disregard for religious truth.

**Irregularity:** A permanent impediment to the lawful reception or exercise of holy orders. The Church instituted irregularities — which include apostasy, heresy, homicide, attempted suicide — out of reverence for the dignity of the sacraments.

**Itinerarium:** Prayers for a spiritually profitable journey.

**J**

**Jansenism:** Opinions developed and proposed by Cornelius Jansenius (1585-1638). He held that: human nature was radically and intrinsically corrupted by original sin; some men are predestined to heaven and others to hell; Christ died only for those predestined to heaven; for those who are predestined, the operations of grace are irresistible. Jansenism also advocated an extremely rigorous code of morals and asceticism. The errors were proscribed by Urban VIII in 1642, by Innocent X in 1653, by Clement XI in 1713, and by other popes. Despite these condemnations, the rigoristic spirit of Jansenism lingered for a long time afterwards, particularly in France.

**Jehovah's Witnesses:** The Witnesses, together with the Watchtower and Bible Tract Society, trace their beginnings to a Bible class organized by Charles Taze Russell in 1872 at Allegheny, Pa. They take their name from a passage in Isaiah (43:12): " 'You are my witnesses,' says Jehovah." They are generally fundamentalist and revivalist with respect to the Bible, and believe that Christ is God's Son but is inferior to God. They place great emphasis on the Battle of Armageddon (as a decisive confrontation of good and evil) that is depicted vividly in Revelation, believing that God will then destroy the existing system of things and that, with the establishment of Jehovah's Kingdom, a small band of 144,000 spiritual sons of God will go to heaven, rule with Christ, and share in some way their happiness with some others. Each Witness is considered by the society to be an ordained minister charged with the duty of spreading the message of Jehovah, which is accomplished through publications, house-to-house visitations, and other methods. The Witnesses refuse to salute the flag of any nation, regarding this as a form of idolatry, or to sanction blood transfusions even for the saving of life. There are approximately one million Witnesses in more than 22,000 congregations in some 80 countries. The freedom and activities of Witnesses are restricted in some places.

**Jesus:** The name of Jesus, meaning "God saves," expressing the identity and mission of the second Person of the Trinity become man; derived from the Aramaic and Hebrew *Yeshua* and *Joshua,* meaning *Yahweh* is salvation.

**Jesus Prayer:** A prayer of Eastern origin, dating back to the fifth century: "Lord Jesus Christ, Son of God, have mercy on me (a sinner)."

**Judgment:** (1) Last or final judgment: Final judgment by Christ, at the end of the world and the general resurrection. (2) Particular judgment: The judgment that takes place immediately after a person's death, followed by entrance into heaven, hell or purgatory.

**Jurisdiction:** Right, power, authority to rule. Jurisdiction in the Church is of divine institution; has pastoral service for its purpose; includes legislative, judicial and executive authority; can be exercised only by persons with the power of orders. (1) Ordinary jurisdiction is attached to ecclesiastical offices by law; the officeholders, called Ordinaries, have authority over those who are subject to them. (2) Delegated jurisdiction is that which is granted to persons rather than attached to offices. Its extent depends on the terms of the delegation.

**Justice:** One of the four cardinal virtues by which a person gives to others what is due to them as a matter of right. (See Cardinal Virtues.)

**Justification:** The act by which God makes a person just, and the consequent change in the spiritual status of a person, from sin to grace; the remission of sin and the infusion of sanctifying grace through the merits of Christ and the action of the Holy Spirit.

## K

**Kerygma:** Proclaiming the word of God, in the manner of the Apostles, as here and now effective for salvation. This method of preaching or instruction, centered on Christ and geared to the facts and themes of salvation history, is designed to dispose people to faith in Christ and or to intensify the experience and practice of that faith in those who have it.

**Keys, Power of the:** Spiritual authority and jurisdiction in the Church, symbolized by the keys of the kingdom of heaven. Christ promised the keys to St. Peter, as head-to-be of the Church (Mt. 16:19), and commissioned him with full pastoral responsibility to feed his lambs and sheep (Jn. 21:15-17), The pope, as the successor of St. Peter, has this power in a primary and supreme manner. The bishops of the Church also have the power, in union with and subordinate to the pope. Priests share in it through holy orders and the delegation of authority. Examples of the application of the Power of the Keys are the exercise of teaching and pastoral authority by the pope and bishops, the absolving of sins in the sacrament of penance, the granting of indulgences, the imposing of spiritual penalties on persons who commit certain serious sins.

## L

**Laicization:** The process by which a man ordained to holy orders is relieved of the obligations of orders and the ministry and is returned to the status of a lay person.

**Languages of the Church:** The first language in church use, for divine worship and the conduct of ecclesiastical affairs, was Aramaic, the language of the first Christians in and around Jerusalem. As the Church spread westward, Greek was adopted and prevailed until the third century when it was supplanted by Latin for official use in the West. According to traditions established very early in churches of the Eastern Rites, many different languages were adopted for use in divine worship and for the conduct of ecclesiastical affairs. The practice was, and still is, to use the vernacular or a language closely related to the common tongue of the people. In the Western Church, Latin prevailed as the general official language until the promulgation on Dec. 4, 1963, of the *Constitution on the Sacred Liturgy* by the second session of the Second Vatican Council. Since that time, vernacular languages have come into use in the Mass, administration of the sacraments, and the Liturgy of the Hours. The change was introduced in order to make the prayers and ceremonies of divine worship more informative and meaningful to all. Latin, however, remains the official language for documents of the Holy See, administrative and procedural matters.

**Law:** An ordinance or rule governing the activity of things. (1) Natural law: Moral norms corresponding to man's nature by which he orders his conduct toward God, neighbor, society and himself. This law, which is rooted in human nature, is of divine origin, can be known by the use of reason, and binds all persons having the use of reason. The Ten Commandments are declarations and amplifications of natural law. The primary precepts of natural law, to do good and to avoid evil, are universally recognized, despite differences with respect to understanding and application resulting from different philosophies of good and evil. (2) Divine positive law: That which has been revealed by God. Among its essentials are the twin precepts of love of God and love of neighbor, and the Ten Commandments. (3) Ecclesiastical law: That which is established by the Church for the spiritual welfare of the faithful and the orderly conduct of ecclesiastical affairs. (See Canon Law.) (4) Civil law: That which is established by a socio-political community for the common good.

**Liberalism:** A multiphased trend of thought and movement favoring liberty, independence and progress in moral, intellectual, religious, social, economic and political life. Traceable to the Renaissance, it developed through the Enlightenment, the rationalism of the 19th century, and modernist- and existentialist-related theories of the 20th century. Evaluations of various kinds of liberalism depend on the validity of their underlying principles. Extremist positions — regarding subjectivism, libertinarianism, naturalist denials of the supernatural, and the alienation of individuals and society from God and the Church were condemned by Gregory XVI in the 1830s, Pius IX in 1864, Leo XIII in 1899, and St. Pius X in 1907. There is, however, nothing objectionable about forms of liberalism patterned according to sound principles of Christian doctrine.

**Liberation Theology:** Deals with the relevance of Christian faith and salvation — and, therefore, of the mission of the Church — to efforts for the promotion of human rights, social justice and human development. It originated in the religious, social, political and economic environment of Latin America, with its contemporary need for a theory and corresponding action by the Church, in the pattern of its overall mission, for human rights and integral personal and social development. Some versions of liberation theology are at variance with the body of church teaching because of their ideological concept of Christ as liberator, and also because they play down the primary spiritual nature and mission of the Church. Instructions from the Congregation for the Doctrine of the Faith — "On Certain Aspects of the Theology of Liberation" (Sept. 3, 1984) and "On Christian Freedom and Liberation" (Apr. 5, 1986) — contain warnings against translating sociology into theology and advocating violence in social activism.

**Life in Outer Space:** Whether rational life exists on other bodies in the universe besides earth, is a question for scientific investigation to settle. The possibility can be granted, without prejudice to the body of revealed truth.

**Limbo:** The limbo of the fathers was the state of rest and natural happiness after death enjoyed by the just of pre-Christian times until they were admitted to heaven following the Ascension of Christ. Belief in this matter is implied in the Apostles' Creed.

**Litany:** A prayer in the form of responsive petition; e.g., St. Joseph, pray for us, etc. Examples are the litanies of Loreto (Litany of the Blessed Mother), the Holy Name, All Saints, the Sacred Heart, the Precious Blood, St. Joseph, Litany for the Dying.

**Loreto, House of:** A Marian shrine in Loreto, Italy, consisting of the home of the Holy Family which, according to an old tradition, was transported in a miraculous manner from Nazareth to Dalmatia and finally to Loreto between 1291 and 1294. Investigations conducted shortly after the appearance of the structure in Loreto revealed that its dimensions matched those of the house of the Holy Family missing from its place of enshrinement in a basilica at Nazareth. Among the many popes who regarded it with high honor was John XXIII, who went there on pilgrimage Oct. 4, 1962. The house of the Holy Family is enshrined in the Basilica of Our Lady.

**Lust:** A disorderly desire for sexual pleasure; one of the seven capital sins.

# M

**Magi:** In the Infancy Narrative of St. Matthew's Gospel (2:1-12), three wise men from the East whose visit and homage to the Child Jesus at Bethlehem indicated Christ's manifestation of himself to non-Jewish people. The narrative teaches the universality of salvation. The traditional names of the Magi are Caspar, Melchior and Balthasar.

**Magnificat:** The canticle or hymn of the Virgin Mary on the occasion of her visitation to her cousin Elizabeth (Lk. 1:46-55). It is an expression of praise, thanksgiving and acknowledgment of the great blessings given by God to Mary, the Mother of the Second Person of the Blessed Trinity made Man. The Magnificat is recited in the Liturgy of the Hours as part of the Evening Prayer.

**Martyr:** A Greek word, meaning witness, denoting one who voluntarily suffered death for the faith or some Christian virtue.

**Martyrology:** A catalogue of martyrs and other saints, arranged according to the calendar. The *Roman Martyrology* contains the official list of saints venerated by the Church. Additions to the list are made in beatification and canonization decrees of the Congregation for the Causes of Saints.

**Mass for the People:** On Sundays and certain feasts throughout the year pastors are required to offer Mass for the faithful entrusted to their care. If they cannot offer the Mass on these days, they must do so at a later date or provide that another priest offer the Mass.

**Materialism:** Theory which holds that matter is the only reality, and everything in existence is merely a manifestation of matter; there is no such thing as spirit, and the supernatural does not exist. Materialism is incompatible with Christian doctrine.

**Meditation:** Mental, as distinguished from vocal, prayer, in which thought, affections, and resolutions of the will predominate. There is a meditative element to all forms of prayer, which always involves the raising of the heart and mind to God.

**Mendicants:** A term derived from Latin and meaning beggars, applied to members of religious orders without property rights; the members, accordingly, worked or begged for their support. The original mendicants were Franciscans and Dominicans in the early 13th century; later, the Carmelites, Augustinians, Servites and others were given the mendicant title and privileges, with respect to exemption from episcopal jurisdiction and wide faculties for preaching and administering the sacrament of penance. The practice of begging is limited at the present time, although it is still allowed with the permission of competent superiors and bishops. Mendicants are supported by free will offerings and income received for spiritual services and other work.

**Mercy, Divine:** The love and goodness of God, manifested particularly in a time of need.

**Mercy, Works of :** Works of corporal or spiritual assistance, motivated by love of God and neighbor, to persons in need. (1) Corporal works: feeding the hungry, giving drink to the thirsty, clothing the naked, visiting the imprisoned, sheltering the homeless, visiting the sick, burying the dead. (2) Spiritual works: counseling the doubtful, instructing the ignorant, admonishing sinners, comforting the afflicted, forgiving offenses, bearing wrongs patiently, praying for the living and the dead.

**Merit:** In religion, the right to a supernatural reward for good works freely done for a supernatural motive by a person in the state of and with the assistance of grace. The right to such reward is from God, who binds himself to give it. Accordingly, good works, as described above, are meritorious for salvation.

**Metempsychosis:** Theory of the passage or migration of the human soul after death from one body to another for the purpose of purification from guilt. The theory denies the unity of the soul and human personality, and the doctrine of individual moral responsibility.

**Millennium:** A thousand-year reign of Christ and the just upon earth before the end of the world. This belief of the Millenarians, Chiliasts, and some sects of modern times is based on an erroneous interpretation of Rv. 20.

**Miracles:** Observable events or effects in the physical or moral order of things, with reference to salvation, which cannot be explained by the ordinary operation of laws of nature and which, therefore, are attributed to the direct action of God. They make known, in an unusual way, the concern and intervention of God in human affairs for the salvation of men. The most striking examples are the miracles worked by Christ. Numbering about 35, they included his own Resurrection; the raising of three persons to life (Lazarus, the daughter of Jairus, the son of the widow of Naim); the healing of blind, leprous and other persons; nature miracles; and prophecies, or miracles of the intellectual order. The foregoing notion of miracles, which is based on the concept of a fixed order of nature, was not known by the writers of Sacred Scripture. In the Old Testament, particularly, they called some things miraculous which, according to the definition in contemporary use, may or may not have been miracles. Essentially, however, the occurrences so designated were regarded as exceptional manifestations of God's care and concern for the salvation of his people. The miracles of Christ were miracles in the full sense of the term. The Church believes it is reasonable to accept miracles as manifestations of divine power for purposes of salvation. God, who created the laws of nature, is their master; hence, without disturbing

the ordinary course of things, he can — and has in the course of history before and after Christ — occasionally set aside these laws and has also produced effects beyond their power of operation. The Church does not regard as miraculous just anything which does not admit of easy explanation; on the contrary, miracles are acknowledged only when the events have a bearing on the order of grace and every possible natural explanation has been tried and found wanting. (The transubstantiation — i.e., the conversion of the whole substance of bread and wine, their sensible appearances alone remaining, into the Body and Blood of Christ in the act of Consecration at Mass — is not an observable event. Traditionally, however, it has been called a miracle.)

**Missal:** A liturgical book of Roman Rite also called the *Sacramentary,* containing the celebrant's prayers of the Mass, along with general instructions and ceremonial directives. The Latin text of the new *Roman Missal,* replacing the one authorized by the Council of Trent in the 16th century, was published by the Vatican Polyglot Press in 1970. Its use in English was made mandatory in the U.S. from Dec. 1, 1974. Readings and scriptural responsories formerly in the missal are contained in the *Lectionary.*

**Missiology:** Study of the missionary nature, constitution and activity of the Church in all aspects: theological reasons for missionary activity, laws and instructions of the Holy See, history of the missions, social and cultural background, methods, norms for carrying on missionary work.

**Mission:** (1) Strictly, it means being sent to perform a certain work, such as the mission of Christ to redeem mankind, the mission of the Apostles and the Church and its members to perpetuate the prophetic, priestly and royal mission of Christ. (2) A place where: the Gospel has not been proclaimed; the Church has not been firmly established; the Church, although established, is weak. (3) An ecclesiastical territory with the simplest kind of canonical organization, under the jurisdiction of the Congregation for the Evangelization of Peoples. (4) A church or chapel without a resident priest. (5) A special course of sermons and spiritual exercises conducted in parishes for the purpose of renewing and deepening the spiritual life of the faithful and for the conversion of lapsed Catholics.

**Modernism:** The "synthesis of all heresies," which appeared near the beginning of the 20th century. It undermines the objective validity of religious beliefs and practices which, it contends, are products of the subconscious developed by mankind under the stimulus of a religious sense. It holds that the existence of a personal God cannot be demonstrated, the Bible is not inspired, Christ is not divine, nor did he establish the Church or institute the sacraments. A special danger lies in modernism, which is still influential, because it uses Catholic terms with perverted meanings. St. Pius X condemned 65 propositions of modernism in 1907 in the decree *Lamentabili* and issued the encyclical *Pascendi* to explain and analyze its errors.

**Monastery:** The dwelling place, as well as the community thereof, of monks belonging to the Benedictine and Benedictine-related orders like the Cistercians and Carthusians; also, the Augustinians and Canons Regular. Distinctive of monasteries are: their separation from the world; the enclosure or cloister; the permanence or stability f attachment characteristic of their members; autonomous government in accordance with a monastic rule, like that of St. Benedict in the West or of St. Basil in the East; the special dedication of its members to the community celebration of the liturgy as well as to work that is suitable to the surrounding area and the needs of its people. Monastic superiors of men have such titles as abbot and prior; of women, abbess and prioress. In most essentials, an abbey is the same as a monastery.

**Monk:** A member of a monastic order — e.g., the Benedictines, the Benedictine-related Cistercians and Carthusians, and the Basilians, who bind themselves by religious profession to stable attachment to a monastery, the contemplative life and the work of their community. In popular use, the title is wrongly applied to many men religious who really are not monks.

**Monotheism:** Belief in and worship of one God.

**Morality:** Conformity or difformity of behavior to standards of right conduct. (See Moral Obligations, Commandments of God, Precepts of the Church, Conscience, Law.)

**Mormons:** Members of the Church of Jesus Christ of Latter-Day Saints. The church was established by Joseph Smith (1805-1844) at Fayette, N.Y., three years after he said he had received from an angel golden tablets containing the *Book of the Prophet Mormon.* This book, the Bible, *Doctrine and Covenants,* and *The Pearl of Great Price,* are the basic doctrinal texts of the church. Characteristic of the Mormons are strong belief in the revelations of their leaders, among whom was Brigham Young; a strong community of religious-secular concern; a dual secular and spiritual priesthood, and vigorous missionary activity. The headquarters of the church are located at Salt Lake City, Utah, where the Mormons first settled in 1847.

**Mortification:** Acts of self-discipline, including prayer, hardship, austerities and penances undertaken for the sake of progress in virtue.

**Motu Proprio:** A Latin phrase designating a document issued by a pope on his own initiative. Documents of this kind often concern administrative matters.

**Mystagogy:** Experience of the mystery of Christ, especially through participation in the liturgy and the sacraments.

**Mysteries of Faith:** Supernatural truths whose existence cannot be known without revelation by God and whose intrinsic truth, while not contrary to reason, can never be wholly understood even after revelation. These mysteries are above reason, not against reason. Among them are the divine mysteries of the Trinity, Incarnation and Eucharist. Some mysteries — e.g., concerning God's attributes — can be known by reason without revelation, although they cannot be fully understood.

## N

**Necromancy:** Supposed communication with the dead; a form of divination.

**Non-Expedit:** A Latin expression. It is not expedient (fitting, proper), used to state a prohibition or refusal of permission.

**Novena:** A term designating public or private devotional practices over a period of nine consecutive days; or, by extension, over a period of nine weeks, in which one day a week is set aside for the devotions.

**Novice:** A man or woman preparing, in a formal period of trial and formation called a novitiate, for membership in an institute of consecrated life. The novitiate lasts a minimum of 12 and a maximum of 24 months; at its conclusion, the novice professes temporary promises or vows of poverty, chastity and obedience. Norms require that certain periods of time be spent in the house of novitiate; periods of apostolic work are also required, to acquaint the novice with the apostolate(s) of the institute. A novice is not bound by the obligations of the professed members of the institute, is free to leave at any time, and may be discharged at the discretion of competent superiors. The superior of a novice is a master of novices or director of formation.

**Nun:** (1) Strictly, a member of a religious order of women with solemn vows (moniales). (2) In general, all women religious, even those in simple vows who are more properly called sisters.

**Nunc Dimittis:** The canticle or hymn of Simeon at the sight of Jesus at the Temple on the occasion of his presentation (Lk. 2:29-32). It is an expression of joy and thanksgiving for the blessing of having lived to see the Messiah. It is prescribed for use in the Night Prayer of the Liturgy of the Hours.

## O

**Oath:** Calling upon God to witness the truth of a statement. Violating an oath, e.g., by perjury in court, or taking an oath without sufficient reason, is a violation of the honor due to God.

**Obedience:** Submission to one in authority. General obligations of obedience fall under the Fourth Commandment. The vow of obedience professed by religious is one of the evangelical counsels.

**Obsession, Diabolical:** The extraordinary state of one who is seriously molested by evil spirits in an external manner. Obsession is more than just temptation.

**Occultism:** Practices involving ceremonies, rituals, chants, incantations, other cult-related activities intended to affect the course of nature, the lives of practitioners and others, through esoteric powers of magic, diabolical or other forces; one of many forms of superstition.

**Octave:** A period of eight days given over to the celebration of a major feast such as Easter.

**Oils, Holy:** The oils blessed by a bishop at the Chrism Mass on Holy Thursday or another suitable day, or by a priest under certain conditions. (1) The oil of catechumens (olive or vegetable oil), used at baptism; also, poured with chrism into the baptismal water blessed in Easter Vigil ceremonies. (2) Oil of the sick (olive or vegetable oil) used in anointing the sick. (3) Chrism (olive or vegetable oil mixed with balm), which is ordinarily consecrated by a bishop, for use at baptism, in confirmation, at the ordination of a priest and bishop, in the dedication of churches and altars.

**Old Catholics:** Several churches, including: (1) The Church of Utrecht, which severed relations with Rome in 1724; (2) The Polish National Catholic Church in the U.S., which had its origin near the end of the 19th century; (3) German, Austrian and Swiss Old Catholics, who broke away from union with Rome following the First Vatican Council in 1870 because they objected to the dogma of papal infallibility. The formation of the Old Catholic communion of Germans, Austrians and Swiss began in 1870 at a public meeting held in Nuremberg under the leadership of A. Dollinger. Four years later episcopal succession was established with the ordination o an Old Catholic German bishop by a prelate of the Church of Utrecht. In line with the "Declaration of Utrecht" of 1889, they accept the first seven ecumenical councils and doctrine formulated before 1054, but reject communion with the pope and a number of other Catholic doctrines and practices. They have a valid priesthood and valid sacraments. *The Oxford Dictionary of the Christian Church* notes that they have recognized Anglican ordinations since 1925, that they have had full communion with the Church of England since 1932, and that their bishops, using their own formula, have taken part in the ordination of Anglican bishops. This communion does not recognize the "Old Catholic" status of several smaller ecclesial bodies calling themselves such. In turn, connection with it is disavowed by the Old Roman Catholic Church headquartered in Chicago, which contends that it has abandoned the traditions of the Church of Utrecht. The United States is the only English-speaking country with Old Catholic communities.

**Opus Dei:** Opus Dei was founded in 1928 in Madrid by Msgr. Josemaria Escriva (beatified in 1992) with the aim of spreading throughout all sectors of society a profound awareness of the universal call to holiness and apostolate (of Christian witness and action) in the ordinary circumstances of life, and, more specifically, through one's professional work. On Nov. 28, 1982, Pope John Paul II established Opus Dei as a personal prelature with the full title, Prelature of the Holy Cross and Opus Dei. The 1996 edition of *Annuario Pontificio* reported that the prelature had 1,572 priests (44 newly ordained) and 365 major seminarians. Also, there were 78,517 lay persons — men and women, married and single, of every class and social condition — of about 80 nationalities. In the United States, members of Opus Dei, along with cooperators and friends, conduct apostolic works corporately in major cities in the East and Midwest, Texas and on the West Coast. Elsewhere, corporate works include universities, vocational institutes, training schools for farmers and numerous other apostolic initiatives. An information office is located at 524 North Ave., Suite 200, New Rochelle, NY 10901.

**Oratory:** A chapel.

**Ordinariate:** An ecclesiastical jurisdiction for special purposes and people. Examples are military ordinariates for armed services personnel (in accord with provisions of the apostolic constitution *Spirituali militum curae,* Apr. 21, 1986) and Eastern-Rite ordinariates in places where Eastern-Rite dioceses do not exist.

**Ordination:** The consecration of sacred ministers for divine worship and the service of people in things pertaining to God. The power of ordination comes from Christ and the Church, and must be conferred by a minister capable of communicating it.

**Organ Transplants:** The transplanting of organs from one person to another is permissible provided it is done with the consent of the concerned parties and does not result in the death or essential mutilation of the donor. Advances in methods and technology have increased the range of transplant possibilities in recent years.

**Original Sin:** The sin of Adam (Gn. 2:8—3:24), personal to him and passed on to all persons as a state of privation of grace. Despite this privation and the related wounding of human nature and weakening of natural powers, original sin leaves unchanged all that man himself is by nature. The scriptural basis of the doctrine was stated especially by St. Paul in 1 Cor. 15:21ff., and Romans 5:12-21. Original sin is remitted by baptism and incorporation in Christ, through whom grace is given to persons. Pope John Paul, while describing original sin during a general audience Oct. 1, 1986, called it "the absence of sanctifying grace in nature which has been diverted from its supernatural end."

**O Salutaris Hostia:** The first three Latin words, O Saving Victim, of a Benediction hymn.

**Ostpolitik:** Policy adopted by Pope Paul VI in an attempt to improve the situation of Eastern European Catholics through diplomatic negotiations with their governments.

**Oxford Movement:** A movement in the Church of England from 1833 to about 1845 which had for its objective a threefold defense of the church as a divine institution, the apostolic succession of its bishops, and the Book of Common Prayer as the rule of faith. The movement took its name from Oxford University and involved a number of intellectuals who authored a series of influential *Tracts for Our Times.* Some of its leading figures — e.g., F. W. Faber, John Henry Newman and Henry Edward Manning — became converts to the Catholic Church. In the Church of England, the movement affected the liturgy, historical and theological scholarship, the status of the ministry, and other areas of ecclesiastical life.

**P**

**Paganism:** A term referring to non-revealed religions, i.e., religions other than Christianity, Judaism and Mohammedanism.

**Palms:** Blessed palms are a sacramental. They are blessed and distributed on the Sunday of the Passion in commemoration of the triumphant entrance of Christ into Jerusalem. Ashes of the burnt palms are used on Ash Wednesday.

**Pange Lingua:** First Latin words, Sing, my tongue, of a hymn in honor of the Holy Eucharist, used particularly on Holy Thursday and in Eucharistic processions.

**Pantheism:** Theory that all things are part of God, divine, in the sense that God realizes himself as the ultimate reality of matter or spirit through being and/or becoming all things that have been, are, and will be. The theory leads to hopeless confusion of the Creator and the created realm of being, identifies evil with good, and involves many inherent contradictions.

**Papal Election:** The Pope is elected by the College of Cardinals during a secret conclave which begins no sooner than 15 days and no later than 20 days after the death of his predecessor. Cardinals under the age of 80, totaling no more than 120, are eligible to take part in the election by secret ballot. Election is by a two-thirds vote of participating cardinals. If the number voting cannot be divided by three, one additional vote is required. New legislation regarding papal elections and church government during a vacancy of the Holy See was promulgated by Pope John Paul Feb. 23, 1996, in the apostolic constitution *Universi Dominici Gregis* ("Shepherd of the Lord's Whole Flock"). (For excerpts, see separate article.)

**Paraclete:** A title of the Holy Spirit meaning, in Greek, Advocate, Consoler.

**Parental Duties:** All duties related to the obligation of parents to provide for the welfare of their children. These obligations fall under the Fourth Commandment.

**Parish:** A community of the faithful served by a pastor charged with responsibility for providing them with full pastoral service. Most parishes are territorial, embracing all of the faithful in a certain area of a diocese: some are personal or national, for certain classes of people, without strict regard for their places of residence.

**Parousia:** The coming, or saving presence, of Christ which will mark the completion of salvation history and the coming to perfection of God's kingdom at the end of the world.

**Paschal Candle:** A large candle, symbolic of the risen Christ, blessed and lighted on the Easter Vigil and placed at the altar until Pentecost. It is ornamented with five large grains of incense, representing the wounds of Christ, inserted in the form of a cross; the Greek letters Alpha and Omega, symbolizing Christ the beginning and end of all things, at the top and bottom of the shaft of the cross; and the figures of the current year of salvation in the quadrants formed by the cross.

**Paschal Precept:** Church law requiring reception of the Eucharist in the Easter season (see separate entry) unless, for a just cause, once-a-year reception takes place at another time.

**Passion of Christ:** Sufferings of Christ, recorded in the four Gospels.

**Pastor:** An ordained minister charged with responsibility for the doctrinal, sacramental and related service of people committed to his care; e.g., a bishop for the people in his diocese, a priest for the people of his parish.

**Pater Noster:** The initial Latin words, Our Father, of the Lord's Prayer.

**Peace, Sign of:** A gesture of greeting — e.g., a handshake — exchanged by the ministers and participants at Mass.

**Pectoral Cross:** A cross worn on a chain about the neck and over the breast by bishops and abbots as a mark of their office.

**Penance or Penitence:** (1) The spiritual change or conversion of mind and heart by which a person turns away from sin, and all that it implies, toward God, through a personal renewal under the influence of the Holy Spirit. In the apostolic constitution *Paenitemini,* Pope Paul VI called it "a religious, personal act which has as its aim love and surrender to God." Penance involves sorrow and contrition for sin, together with other internal and external acts of atonement. It serves the purposes of reestablishing in one's life the order of God's love and commandments, and of making satisfaction to God for in. A divine precept states the necessity of penance for salvation: "Unless you do penance, you shall all likewise perish" (Lk. 13:3) "Be converted and believe in the Gospel" (Mk. 1:15). In the penitential discipline of the Church, the various works of penance have been classified under the headings of prayer (interior), fasting and almsgiving (exterior). The Church has established minimum requirements for the common and social observance of the divine precept by Catholics — e.g., by requiring them to fast and/or abstain on certain days of the year. These observances, however, do not exhaust all the demands of the divine precept, whose fulfillment is a matter of personal responsibility; nor do they have any real value unless they proceed from the internal spirit and purpose of penance. Related to works of penance for sins actually committed are works of mortification. The purpose of the latter is to develop — through prayer, fasting, renunciations and similar actions—self-control and detachment from things which could otherwise become occasions of sin. (2) Penance is a virtue disposing a person to turn to God in sorrow for sin and to carry out works of amendment and atonement. (3) The sacrament of penance and sacramental penance.

**Perjury:** Taking a false oath, lying under oath, a violation of the honor due to God.

**Persecution, Religious:** A campaign waged against a church or other religious body by persons and governments intent on its destruction. The best known campaigns of this type against the Christian Church were the Roman persecutions which occurred intermittently from about 54 to the promulgation of the Edict of Milan in 313, The most extensive persecutions took place during the reigns of Nero, the first major Roman persecutor, Domitian, Trajan, Marcus Aurelius, and Diocletian. Besides the Roman persecutions, the Catholic Church has been subject to many others, including those of the 20th century in Communist-controlled countries.

**Personal Prelature:** A special-purpose jurisdiction — for particular pastoral and missionary work, etc. — consisting of secular priests and deacons and open to lay persons willing to dedicate themselves to its apostolic works. The prelate in charge is an Ordinary, with the authority of office; he can establish a national or international seminary, incardinate its students and promote them to holy orders under the title of service to the prelature. The prelature is constituted and governed according to statutes laid down by the Holy See. Statutes define its relationship and mode of operation with the bishops of territories in which members live and work. Opus Dei is a personal prelature.

**Peter's Pence:** A collection made each year among

Catholics for the maintenance of the pope and his works of charity. It was originally a tax of a penny on each house, and was collected on St. Peter's day, whence the name. It originated in England in the eighth century.

**Petition:** One of the four purposes of prayer. In prayers of petition, persons ask of God the blessings they and others need.

**Pharisees:** Influential class among the Jews, referred to in the Gospels, noted for their self-righteousness, legalism, strict interpretation of the Law, acceptance of the traditions of the elders as well as the Law of Moses, and beliefs regarding angels and spirits, the resurrection of the dead and judgment. Most of them were laymen, and they were closely allied with the Scribes; their opposite numbers were the Sadducees. The Pharisaic and rabbinical traditions had a lasting influence on Judaism following the destruction of Jerusalem in 70 A.D.

**Pious Fund:** Property and money originally accumulated by the Jesuits to finance their missionary work in Lower California. When the Jesuits were expelled from the territory in 1767, the fund was appropriated by the Spanish Crown and used to support Dominican and Franciscan missionary work in Upper and Lower California. In 1842 the Mexican government took over administration of the fund, incorporated most of the revenue into the national treasury, and agreed to pay the Church interest of six per cent a year on the capital so incorporated. From 1848 to 1967 the fund was the subject of lengthy negotiations between the U.S. and Mexican governments because of the latter's failure to make payments as agreed. A lump-sum settlement was made in 1967 with payment by Mexico to the U.S. government of more than $700,000, to be turned over to the Archdiocese of San Francisco.

**Polytheism:** Belief in and worship of many gods or divinities, especially prevalent in pre-Christian religions.

**Poor Box:** Alms-box; found in churches from the earliest days of Christianity.

**Pope Joan:** Alleged name of a woman falsely said to have been pope from 855-858, the years of the reign of Benedict III. The myth was not heard of before the 13th century.

**Portiuncula:** (1) Meaning little portion (of land), the Portiuncula was the chapel of Our Lady of the Angels near Assisi, Italy, which the Benedictines gave to St. Francis early in the 13th century. He repaired the chapel and made it the first church of the Franciscan Order. It is now enshrined in the Basilica of St. Mary of the Angels in Assisi. (2) The plenary Portiuncula Indulgence, or Pardon of Assisi, was authorized by Honorius III. Originally, it could be gained for the souls in purgatory only in the chapel of Our Lady of the Angels; by later concessions, it could be gained also in other Franciscan and parish churches. The Portiuncula Indulgence (applicable also to the souls in purgatory) can ordinarily be gained from noon of Aug. 1 to midnight of Aug. 2. The conditions are, in addition to freedom from attachment to sin: reception of the sacraments of penance and the Eucharist on or near the day and a half; a visit to a parish church within the day and a half, during which the Our Father, the Creed and another prayer are offered for the intentions of the pope.

**Possession, Diabolical:** The extraordinary state of a person who is tormented from within by evil spirits who exercise strong influence over his powers of mind and body.

**Postulant:** One of several names used to designate a candidate for membership in a religious institute during the period before novitiate.

**Poverty:** (1) The quality or state of being poor, in actual destitution and need, or being poor in spirit. In the latter sense, poverty means the state of mind and disposition of persons who regard material things in proper perspective as gifts of God for the support of life and its reasonable enrichment, and for the service of others in need. It means freedom from unreasonable attachment to material things as ends in themselves, even though they may be possessed in small or large measure. (2) One of the evangelical counsels professed as a public vow by members of an institute of consecrated life. It involves the voluntary renunciation of rights of ownership and of independent use and disposal of material goods; or, the right of independent use and disposal, but not of the radical right of ownership. Religious institutes provide their members with necessary and useful goods and services from common resources. The manner in which goods are received and/or handled by religious is determined by poverty of spirit and the rule and constitutions of their institute.

**Pragmatism:** Theory that the truth of ideas, concepts and values depends on their utility or capacity to serve a useful purpose rather than on their conformity with objective standards; also called utilitarianism.

**Prayer:** The raising of the mind and heart to God in adoration, thanksgiving, reparation and petition. Prayer, which is always mental because it involves thought and love of God, may be vocal, meditative, private and personal, social, and official. The official prayer of the Church as a worshipping community is called the liturgy.

**Precepts:** Commands or orders given to individuals or communities in particular cases; they establish law for concerned parties. Preceptive documents are issued by the pope, departments of the Roman Curia and other competent authority in the Church.

**Presence of God:** A devotional practice of increasing one's awareness of the presence and action of God in daily life.

**Presumption:** A sin against hope, by which a person striving for salvation (1) either relies too much on his own capabilities or (2) expects God to do things which he cannot do, in keeping with his divine attributes, or does not will to do, according to his divine plan. Presumption is the opposite of despair.

**Preternatural Gifts:** Exceptional gifts, beyond the exigencies and powers of human nature, enjoyed by Adam in the state of original justice: immunity from suffering and death, superior knowledge, integrity or perfect control of the passions. These gifts were lost as the result of original sin; their loss, however, implied no impairment of the integrity of human nature.

**Pride**: Unreasonable self-esteem; one of the seven capital sins.

**Prie-Dieu**: A French phrase, meaning pray God, designating a kneeler or bench suitable for kneeling while at prayer.

**Priesthood**: (1) The common priesthood of the non-ordained faithful. In virtue of baptism and confirmation, the faithful are a priestly people who participate in the priesthood of Christ through acts of worship, witness to the faith in daily life, and efforts to foster the growth of God's kingdom. (2) The ordained priesthood, in virtue of the sacrament of order, of bishops, priests and deacons, for service to the common priesthood.

**Primary Option**: The life-choice of a person for or against God which shapes the basic orientation of moral conduct. A primary option for God does not preclude the possibility of serious sin.

**Prior**: A superior or an assistant to an abbot in a monastery.

**Privilege**: A favor, an exemption from the obligation of a law. Privileges of various kinds, with respect to ecclesiastical laws, are granted by the pope, departments of the Roman Curia and other competent authority in the Church.

**Probabilism**: A moral system for use in cases of conscience which involve the obligation of doubtful laws. There is a general principle that a doubtful law does not bind. Probabilism, therefore, teaches that it is permissible to follow an opinion favoring liberty, provided the opinion is certainly and solidly probable. Probabilism may not be invoked when there is question of: a certain law or the certain obligation of a law; the certain right of another party; the validity of an action; something which is necessary for salvation.

**Pro-Cathedral**: A church used as a cathedral.

**Promoter of the Faith**: An official of the Congregation for the Causes of Saints, whose role in beatification and canonization procedures is to establish beyond reasonable doubt the validity of evidence regarding the holiness of prospective saints and miracles attributed to their intercession.

**Prophecies of St. Malachy**: These so-called prophecies, listing the designations of 102 popes and 10 antipopes, bear the name they have because they have been falsely attributed to St. Malachy, bishop of Armagh, who died in 1148. Actually, they are forgeries by an unknown author and came to light only in the last decade of the 16th century. The first 75 prophecies cover the 65 popes and 10 antipopes from Celestine II (1143-1144) to Gregory XIV (1590-91), and are exact with respect to names, coats of arms, birthplaces, and other identifying characteristics. This portion of the work, far from being prophetic, is the result of historical knowledge or hindsight. The 37 designations following that of Gregory are vague, fanciful, and subject to wide interpretation. According to the prophecies, John Paul II, from the Labor of the Sun, will have only two successors before the end of the world.

**Prophecy**: (1) The communication of divine revelation by inspired intermediaries, called prophets, between God and his people. Old Testament prophecy was unique in its origin and because of its ethical and religious content, which included disclosure of the saving will of Yahweh for the people, moral censures and warnings of divine punishment because of sin and violations of the Law and Covenant, in the form of promises, admonitions, reproaches and threats. Although Moses and other earlier figures are called prophets, the period of prophecy is generally dated from the early years of the monarchy to about 100 years after the Babylonian Exile. From that time on the written Law and its interpreters supplanted the prophets as guides of the people. Old Testament prophets are cited in the New Testament, with awareness that God spoke through them and that some of their oracles were fulfilled in Christ. John the Baptist is the outstanding prophetic figure in the New Testament. Christ never claimed the title of prophet for himself, although some people thought he was one. There were prophets in the early Church, and St. Paul mentioned the charism of prophecy in 1 Cor. 14:1-5. Prophecy disappeared after New Testament times. Revelation is classified as the prophetic book of the New Testament. (2) In contemporary non-scriptural usage, the term is applied to the witness given by persons to the relevance of their beliefs in everyday life and action.

**Province**: (1) A territory comprising one archdiocese called the metropolitan see and one or more dioceses called suffragan sees. The head of the archdiocese, an archbishop, has metropolitan rights and responsibilities over the province. (2) A division of a religious order under the jurisdiction of a provincial superior.

**Prudence**: Practical wisdom and judgment regarding the choice and use of the best ways and means of doing good; one of the four cardinal virtues.

**Punishment Due for Sin**: The punishment which is a consequence of sin. It is of two kinds: (1) Eternal punishment is the punishment of hell, to which one becomes subject by the commission of mortal sin. Such punishment is remitted when mortal sin is forgiven. (2) Temporal punishment is a consequence of venial sin and/or forgiven mortal sin; it is not everlasting and may be remitted in this life by means of penance. Temporal punishment unremitted during this life is remitted by suffering in purgatory.

**Purgatory**: The state or condition of those who have died in the state of grace but with some attachment to sin, and are purified for a time before they are admitted to the glory and happiness of heaven. In this state and period of passive suffering, they are purified of unrepented venial sins, satisfy the demands of divine justice for temporal punishment due for sins, and are thus converted to a state of worthiness of the beatific vision.

# R

**Racism**: A theory which holds that any one or several of the different races of the human family are inherently superior or inferior to any one or several of the others. The teaching denies the essential unity of the human race, the equality and dignity of all persons because of their common possession of the same human nature, and the participation of all in the divine plan of redemption. It is radically opposed to the virtue of justice and the precept of love of neighbor. Differences of superiority and inferiority which do exist are the result of accidental factors operating in a wide variety of circumstances, and are in no way due to essential defects in any one or several of the branches of the one human race. The theory of racism, together with practices related to it, is incompatible with Christian doctrine.

**Rash Judgment:** Attributing faults to another without sufficient reason; a violation of the obligations of justice and charity.

**Rationalism:** A theory which makes the mind the measure and arbiter of all things, including religious truth. A product of the Enlightenment, it rejects the supernatural, divine revelation, and authoritative teaching by any church.

**Recollection:** Meditation, attitude of concentration or awareness of spiritual matters and things pertaining to salvation and the accomplishment of God's will.

**Relativism:** Theory which holds that all truth, including religious truth, is relative, i.e., not absolute, certain or unchanging; a product of agnosticism, indifferentism, and an unwarranted extension of the notion of truth in positive science. Relativism is based on the tenet that certain knowledge of any and all truth is impossible. Therefore, no religion, philosophy or science can be said to possess the real truth; consequently, all religions, philosophies and sciences may be considered to have as much or as little of truth as any of the others.

**Relics:** The physical remains and effects of saints, which are considered worthy of veneration inasmuch as they are representative of persons in glory with God. Catholic doctrine proscribes the view that relics are not worthy of veneration. In line with norms laid down by the Council of Trent and subsequent enactments, discipline concerning relics is subject to control by the Congregations for the Causes of Saints and for Divine Worship and the Discipline of the Sacraments.

**Religion:** The adoration and service of God as expressed in divine worship and in daily life. Religion is concerned with all of the relations existing between God and human beings, and between humans themselves because of the central significance of God. Objectively considered, religion consists of a body of truth which is believed, a code of morality for the guidance of conduct, and a form of divine worship. Subjectively, it is a person's total response, theoretically and practically, to the demands of faith; it is living faith, personal engagement, self-commitment to God. Thus, by creed, code and cult, a person orders and directs his or her life in reference to God and, through what the love and service of God implies, to all people and all things.

**Reliquary:** A vessel for the preservation and exposition of a relic; sometimes made like a small monstrance.

**Reparation:** The making of amends to God for sin committed; one of the four ends of prayer and the purpose of penance.

**Rescript:** A written reply by an ecclesiastical superior regarding a question or request; its provisions bind concerned parties only. Papal dispensations are issued in the form of rescripts.

**Reserved Case:** A sin or censure, absolution from which is reserved to religious superiors, bishops, the pope, or confessors having special faculties. Reservations are made because of the serious nature and social effects of certain sins and censures.

**Restitution:** An act of reparation for an injury done to another. The injury may be caused by taking and/or retaining what belongs to another or by damaging either the property or reputation of another. The intention of making restitution, usually in kind, is required as a condition for the forgiveness of sins of injustice, even though actual restitution is not possible.

**Ring:** In the Church a ring is worn as part of the insignia of bishops, abbots, et al.; by sisters to denote their consecration to God and the Church. The wedding ring symbolizes the love and union of husband and wife.

**Ritual:** A book of prayers and ceremonie used in the administration of the sacraments and other ceremonial functions. In the Roman Rite, the standard book of this kind is the Roman Ritual.

**Rogito:** The official notarial act or document testifying to the burial of a pope.

**Rosary:** A form of mental and vocal prayer centered on mysteries or events in the lives of Jesus and Mary. Its essential elements are meditation on the mysteries and the recitation of a number of decades of Hail Marys, each beginning with the Lord's Prayer. Introductory prayers may include the Apostles' Creed, an initial Our Father, three Hail Marys and a Glory be to the Father; each decade is customarily concluded with a Glory to the Father; at the end, it is customary to say the Hail, Holy Queen and a prayer from the liturgy for the feast of the Blessed Virgin Mary of the Rosary. The Mysteries of the Rosary, which are the subject of meditation, are: (1) Joyful — the Annunciation to Mary that she was to be the Mother of Christ, her visit to Elizabeth, the birth of Jesus, the presentation of Jesus in the Temple, the finding of Jesus in the Temple. (2) Sorrowful — Christ's agony in the Garden of Gethsemani, scourging at the pillar, crowning with thorns, carrying of the Cross to Calvary, and crucifixion. (3) Glorious — the Resurrection and Ascension of Christ, the descent of the Holy Spirit upon the Apostles, Mary's Assumption into heaven and her crowning as Queen of angels and men. The complete Rosary, called the Dominican Rosary, consists of 15 decades. In customary practice, only five decades are usually said at one time. Rosary beads are used to aid in counting the prayers without distraction. The Rosary originated through the coalescence of popular devotions to Jesus and Mary from the 12th century onward. Its present form dates from about the 15th century. Carthusians contributed greatly toward its development; Dominicans have been its greatest promoters.

## S

**Sabbath:** The seventh day of the week, observed by Jews and Sabbatarians as the day for rest and religious observance.

**Sacramentary:** One of the first liturgical books, containing the celebrant's part of the Mass and rites for administration of the sacraments. The earliest book of this kind, the Leonine Sacramentary, dates from the middle or end of the sixth century. The *Sacramentary* in current use is the same as the *Roman Missal*.

**Sacrarium**: A basin with a drain leading directly into the ground; standard equipment of a sacristy.

**Sacred Heart, Enthronement**: An acknowledgment of the sovereignty of Jesus Christ over the Christian family, expressed by the installation of an image or picture of the Sacred Heart in a place of honor in the home, accompanied by an act of consecration.

**Sacred Heart, Promises**: Twelve promises to persons having devotion to the Sacred Heart of Jesus, which were communicated by Christ to St. Margaret Mary Alacoque in a private revelation in 1675: (1) I will give them all the graces necessary in their state in life. (2) I will establish peace in their homes. (3) I will comfort them in all their afflictions. (4) I will be their secure refuge during life and, above all, in death. (5) I will bestow abundant blessing upon all their undertakings. (6) Sinners shall find in my Heart the source and the infinite ocean of mercy. (7) By devotion to my Heart tepid souls shall grow fervent. (8) Fervent souls shall quickly mount to high perfection. (9) I will bless every place where a picture of my Heart shall be set up and honored. (10) I will give to priests the gift of touching the most hardened hearts. (11) Those who promote this devotion shall have their names written in my Heart, never to be blotted out. (12) I will grant the grace of final penitence to those who communicate (receive Holy Communion) on the first Friday of nine consecutive months.

**Sacrilege**: Violation of and irreverence toward a person, place or thing that is sacred because of public dedication to God; a sin against the virtue of religion. Personal sacrilege is violence of some kind against a cleric or religious, or a violation of chastity with a cleric or religious. Local sacrilege is the desecration of sacred places. Real sacrilege is irreverence with respect to sacred things, such as the sacraments and sacred vessels.

**Sacristy**: A utility room where vestments, church furnishings and sacred vessels are kept and where the clergy vest for sacred functions.

**Sadducees**: The predominantly priestly party among the Jews in the time of Christ, noted for extreme conservatism, acceptance only of the Law of Moses, and rejection of the traditions of the elders. Their opposite numbers were the Pharisees.

**Saints, Cult of**: The veneration, called dulia, of holy persons who have died and are in glory with God in heaven; it includes honoring them and petitioning them for their intercession with God. Liturgical veneration is given only to saints officially recognized by the Church; private veneration may be given to anyone thought to be in heaven. The veneration of saints is essentially different from the adoration given to God alone; by its very nature, however, it terminates in the worship of God. According to the Second Vatican Council's *Dogmatic Constitution on the Church* (No. 50): "It is supremely fitting that we love those friends and fellow heirs of Jesus Christ, who are also our brothers and extraordinary benefactors, that we render due thanks to God for them and 'suppliantly invoke them and have recourse to their prayers, their power and help in obtaining benefits from God through his Son, Jesus Christ, our Lord, who is our sole Redeemer and Sav-

ior.' For by its very nature every genuine testimony of love which we show to those in heaven tends toward and terminates in Christ, who is the 'crown of all saints.' Through him it tends toward and terminates in God, who is wonderful in his saints and is magnified in them."

**Salvation**: The liberation of persons from sin and its effects, reconciliation with God in and through Christ, the attainment of union with God forever in the glory of heaven as the supreme purpose of life and as the God-given reward for fulfillment of his will on earth. Salvation-in-process begins and continues in this life through union with Christ in faith professed and in action; its final term is union with God and the whole community of the saved in the ultimate perfection of God's kingdom. The Church teaches that: God wills the salvation of all men; men are saved in and through Christ; membership in the Church established by Christ, known and understood as the community of salvation, is necessary for salvation; men with this knowledge and understanding who deliberately reject this Church, cannot be saved. The Catholic Church is the Church founded by Christ. (See below, Salvation outside the Church.)

**Salvation History**: The facts and the record of God's relations with human beings, in the past, present and future, for the purpose of leading them to live in accordance with his will for the eventual attainment after death of salvation, or everlasting happiness with him in heaven. The essentials of salvation history are: God's love for all human beings and will for their salvation; his intervention and action in the world to express this love and bring about their salvation; the revelation he made of himself and the covenant he established with the Israelites in the Old Testament; the perfecting of this revelation and the new covenant of grace through Christ in the New Testament; the continuing action-for-salvation carried on in and through the Church; the communication of saving grace to people through the merits of Christ and the operations of the Holy Spirit in the here-and-now circumstances of daily life and with the cooperation of people themselves.

**Salvation outside the Church**: The Second Vatican Council covered this subject summarily in the following manner: "Those also can attain to everlasting salvation who through no fault of their own do not know the Gospel of Christ or his Church, yet sincerely seek God and, moved by grace, strive by their deeds to do his will as it is known to them through the dictates of conscience. Nor does divine Providence deny the help necessary for salvation to those who, without blame on their part, have not yet arrived at an explicit knowledge of God, but who strive to live a good life, thanks to his grace. Whatever good or truth is found among them is looked upon by the Church as a preparation for the Gospel. She regards such qualities as given by him who enlightens all men so that they may finally have life" *(Dogmatic Constitution on the Church,* No. 16).

**Satanism**: Worship of the devil, a blasphemous inversion of the order of worship which is due to God alone.

**Scandal**: Conduct which is the occasion of sin to another person.

**Scapular**: (1) A part of the habit of some religious

orders like the Benedictines and Dominicans; a nearly shoulder-wide strip of cloth worn over the tunic and reaching almost to the feet in front and behind. Originally a kind of apron, it came to symbolize the cross and yoke of Christ. (2) Scapulars worn by lay persons as a sign of association with religious orders and for devotional purposes are an adaptation of monastic scapulars. Approved by the Church as sacramentals, they consist of two small squares of woolen cloth joined by strings and are worn about the neck. They are given for wearing in a ceremony of investiture or enrollment. There are nearly 20 scapulars for devotional use: the five principal ones are generally understood to include those of Our Lady of Mt. Carmel (the brown Carmelite Scapular), the Holy Trinity, Our Lady of the Seven Dolors, the Passion, the Immaculate Conception.

**Scapular Medal:** A medallion with a representation of the Sacred Heart on one side and of the Blessed Virgin Mary on the other. Authorized by St. Pius X in 1910, it may be worn or carried in place of a scapular by persons already invested with a scapular.

**Scapular Promise:** According to a legend of the Carmelite Order, the Blessed Virgin Mary appeared to St. Simon Stock in 1251 at Cambridge, England, and declared that wearers of the brown Carmelite Scapular would be the beneficiaries of her special intercession. The scapular tradition has never been the subject of official decision by the Church. Essentially, it expresses belief in the intercession of Mary and the efficacy of sacramentals in the context of truly Christian life.

**Schism:** Derived from a Greek word meaning separation, the term designates formal and obstinate refusal by a baptized Catholic, called a *schismatic,* to be in communion with the pope and the Church. The canonical penalty is excommunication. One of the most disastrous schisms in history resulted in the definitive separation of the Church in the East from union with Rome about 1054.

**Scholasticism:** The term usually applied to the Catholic theology and philosophy which developed in the Middle Ages.

**Scribes:** Hebrew intellectuals noted for their knowledge of the Law of Moses, influential from the time of the Exile to about 70 A.D. Many of them were Pharisees. They were the antecedents of rabbis and their traditions, as well as those o the Pharisees, had a lasting influence on Judaism following the destruction of Jerusalem in 70 A.D.

**Scruple:** A morbid, unreasonable fear and anxiety that one's actions are sinful when they are not, or more seriously sinful than they actually are. Compulsive scrupulosity is quite different from the transient scrupulosity of persons of tender or highly sensitive conscience, or of persons with faulty moral judgment.

**Seal of Confession:** The obligation of secrecy which must be observed regarding knowledge of things learned in connection with the confession of sin in the sacrament of penance. The seal covers matters whose revelation would make the sacrament burdensome. Confessors are prohibited, under penalty of excommunication, from making any direct revelation of confessional matter; this prohibition holds, outside of confession, even with respect to the person who made the confession unless the person releases the priest from the obligation. Persons other than confessors are obliged to maintain secrecy, but not under penalty of excommunication. General, non-specific discussion of confessional matter does not violate the seal.

**Secularism:** A school of thought, a spirit and manner of action which ignores and/or repudiates the validity or influence of supernatural religion with respect to individual and social life. In describing secularism in their annual statement in 1947, the bishops of the United States said in part: "There are many men — and their number is daily increasing — who in practice live their lives without recognizing that this is God's world. For the most part they do not deny God. On formal occasions they may even mention his name. Not all of them would subscribe to the statement that all moral values derive from merely human conventions. But they fail to bring an awareness of their responsibility to God into their thought and action as individuals and members of society. This, in essence, is what we mean by secularism."

**See:** Another name for diocese or archdiocese.

**Seminary:** A house of study and formation for men, called seminarians, preparing for the priesthood. Traditional seminaries date from the Council of Trent in the middle of the 16th century; before that time, candidates for the priesthood were variously trained in monastic schools, universities under church auspices, and in less formal ways. At the present time, seminaries are undergoing considerable change for the improvement of academic and formation programs and procedures.

**Sermon on the Mount:** A compilation of sayings of Our Lord in the form of an extended discourse in Matthew's Gospel (5:1 to 7:27) and, in a shorter discourse, in Luke (6:17-49). The passage in Matthew, called the "Constitution of the New Law," summarizes the living spirit of believers in Christ and members of the kingdom of God. Beginning with the Beatitudes and including the Lord's Prayer, it covers the perfect justice of the New Law, the fulfillment of the Old Law in the New Law of Christ, and the integrity of internal attitude and external conduct with respect to love of God and neighbor, justice, chastity, truth, trust and confidence in God.

**Seven Last Words of Christ:** Words of Christ on the Cross. (1) "Father, forgive them; for they do not know what they are doing." (2) To the penitent thief: "I assure you: today you will be with me in Paradise." (3) To Mary and his Apostle John: "Woman, there is your son There is your mother." (4) "My God, my God, why have you forsaken me?" (5) "I am thirsty." (6) "Now it is finished." (7) "Father, into your hands I commend my spirit."

**Shrine, Crowned:** A shrine approved by the Holy See as a place of pilgrimage. The approval permits public devotion at the shrine and implies that at least one miracle has resulted from devotion at the shrine. Among the best known crowned shrines are those of the Virgin Mary at Lourdes and Fatima. Shrines with statues crowned by Pope John Paul in 1985 in South America were those of Our Lady of Coromoto, patroness of Venezuela, in Caracas, and Our Lady of Carmen of Paucartambo in Cuzco, Peru.

**Shroud of Turin:** A strip of brownish linen cloth, 14 feet, three inches in length and three feet, seven inches in width, bearing the front and back imprint of a human body. A tradition dating from the seventh century, which has not been verified beyond doubt, claims that the shroud is the fine linen in which the body of Christ was wrapped for burial. The early history of the shroud is obscure. It was enshrined at Lirey, France, in 1354 and was transferred in 1578 to Turin, Italy, where it has been kept in the cathedral down to the present time. Scientific investigation, which began in 1898, seems to indicate that the markings on the shroud are those of a human body. The shroud, for the first time since 1933, was placed on public view from Aug. 27 to Oct. 8, 1978, and was seen by an estimated 3.3 million people. Scientists conducted intensive studies of it thereafter, finally determining that the material of the shroud dated from between 1260 and 1390. The shroud, which had been the possession of the House of Savoy, was willed to Pope John Paul II in 1983.

**Sick Calls:** When a person is confined at home by illness or other cause and is unable to go to church for reception of the sacraments, a parish priest should be informed and arrangements made for him to visit the person at home. Such visitations are common in pastoral practice, both for special needs and for providing persons with regular opportunities for receiving the sacraments. If a priest cannot make the visitation, arrangements can be made for a deacon or Eucharistic minister to bring Holy Communion to the homebound or bedridden person.

**Sign of the Cross:** A sign, ceremonial gesture or movement in the form of a cross by which a person confesses faith in the Holy Trinity and Christ, and intercedes for the blessing of himself or herself, other persons and things. In Roman-Rite practice, a person making the sign touches the fingers of the right hand to forehead, below the breast, left shoulder and right shoulder while saying: "In the name of the Father, and of the Son, and of the Holy Spirit." The sign is also made with the thumb on the forehead, the lips, and the breast. For the blessing of persons and objects, a large sign of the cross is made by movement of the right hand. In Eastern-Rite practice, the sign is made with the thumb and first two fingers of the right hand joined together and touching the forehead, below the breast, the right shoulder and the left shoulder; the formula generally used is the doxology, "O Holy God, O Holy Strong One, O Immortal One." The Eastern manner of making the sign was general until the first half of the 13th century; by the 17th century, Western practice involved the whole right hand and the reversal of direction from shoulder to shoulder.

**Signs of the Times:** Contemporary events, trends and features in culture and society, the needs and aspirations of people, all the factors that form the context in and through which the Church has to carry on its saving mission. The Second Vatican Council spoke on numerous occasions about these signs and the relationship between them and a kind of manifestation of God's will, positive or negative, and about subjecting them to judgment and action corresponding to the demands of divine revelation through Scripture, Christ, and the experience, tradition and teaching authority of the Church.

**Simony:** The deliberate intention and act of selling and/or buying spiritual goods or material things so connected with the spiritual that they cannot be separated therefrom; a violation of the virtue of religion, and a sacrilege, because it wrongfully puts a material price on spiritual things, which cannot be either sold or bought. In church law, actual sale or purchase is subject to censure in some cases. The term is derived from the name of Simon Magus, who attempted to buy from Sts. Peter and John the power to confirm people in the Holy Spirit (Acts 8:4-24).

**Sin:** (1) Actual sin is the free and deliberate violation of God's law by thought, word or action. (a) Mortal sin — involving serious matter, sufficient reflection and full consent — results in the loss of sanctifying grace and alienation from God, and renders a person incapable of performing meritorious supernatural acts and subject to everlasting punishment. (b) Venial sin — involving less serious matter, reflection and consent — does not have such serious consequences. (2) Original sin is the sin of Adam, with consequences for all human beings. (See separate entry.)

**Sins against the Holy Spirit:** Despair of salvation, presumption of God's mercy, impugning the known truths of faith, envy at another's spiritual good, obstinacy in sin, final impenitence. Those guilty of such sins stubbornly resist the influence of grace and, as long as they do so, cannot be forgiven.

**Sins, Occasions of:** Circumstances (persons, places, things, etc.) which easily lead to sin. There is an obligation to avoid voluntary proximate occasions of sin, and to take precautions against the dangers of unavoidable occasions.

**Sins That Cry to Heaven for Vengeance:** Willful murder, sins against nature, oppression of the poor, widows and orphans, defrauding laborers of their wages.

**Sister:** Any woman religious, in popular speech; strictly, the title applies only to women religious belonging to institutes whose members never professed solemn vows. Most of the institutes whose members are properly called Sisters were established during and since the 19th century. Women religious with solemn vows, or belonging to institutes whose members formerly professed solemn vows, are properly called nuns.

**Sisterhood:** A generic term referring to the whole institution of the life of women religious in the Church, or to a particular institute of women religious.

**Situation Ethics:** A subjective, individualistic ethical theory which denies the binding force of ethical principles as universal laws and preceptive norms of moral conduct, and proposes that morality is determined only by situational conditions and considerations and the intention of the person. In an instruction issued on the subject in May, 1956, the Congregation for the Holy Office (now the Congregation for the Doctrine of the Faith) said: "It ignores the principles of objective ethics. This 'New Morality,' it is claimed, is not only the equal of objective morality, but is superior to it. The authors who follow this system state that the ultimate determining norm for activity is not the objective order as determined by the natural law and known with certainty from this law. It is instead some internal judgment and illumination of the mind of every individual by which the mind comes to know what is to be done in a concrete situation. This ultimate decision of man is, therefore, not the application of the objective law to a particular case after the particular circumstances of a 'situation' have been considered and weighed according to the rules of prudence, as the more important authors of objective ethics teach; but it is, according to them, immediate, internal illumination and judgment. With regard to its objective truth and correctness, this judgment, at least in many things, is not ultimately measured, is not to be measured or is not measurable by any objective norm found outside man and independent of his subjective persuasion, but it is fully sufficient in itself. Much that is stated in this system of 'Situation Ethics' is contrary to the truth of reality and to the dictate of sound reason. It gives evidence of relativism and modernism, and deviates far from the Catholic teaching handed down through the ages."

**Slander:** Attributing to a person faults which he or she does not have; a violation of the obligations of justice and charity, for which restitution is due.

**Sloth (Acedia):** One of the seven capital sins; spiritual laziness, involving distaste and disgust for spiritual things; spiritual boredom, which saps the vigor of spiritual life. Physical laziness is a counterpart of spiritual sloth.

**Sorcery:** A kind of black magic in which evil is invoked by means of diabolical intervention; a violation of the virtue of religion.

**Soteriology:** The division of theology which treats of the mission and work of Christ as Redeemer.

**Species, Sacred:** The appearances of bread and wine (color, taste, smell, etc.) which remain after the substance has been changed at the Consecration of the Mass into the Body and Blood of Christ. (See Transubstantiation.)

**Spiritism:** Attempts to communicate with spirits and departed souls by means of seances, table tapping, ouija boards, and other methods; a violation of the virtue of religion. Spiritualistic practices are noted for fakery.

**Stational Churches, Days:** Churches, especially in Rome, where the clergy and lay people were accustomed to gather with their bishop on certain days for the celebration of the liturgy. The 25 early titular or parish churches of Rome, plus other churches, each had their turn as the site of divine worship in practices which may have started in the third century. The observances were rather well developed toward the latter part of the fourth century, and by the fifth they included a Mass concelebrated by the pope and attendant priests. On some occasions, the stational liturgy was preceded by a procession from another church called a collecta. There were 42 Roman stational churches in the eighth century, and 89 stational services were scheduled annually in connection with the liturgical seasons. Stational observances fell into disuse toward the end of the Middle Ages. Some revival was begun by John XXIII in 1959 and continued by Paul VI and John Paul II.

**Stations (Way) of the Cross:** A form of devotion commemorating the Passion and death of Christ, consisting of a series of meditations (stations): (1) his condemnation to death, (2) taking up of the cross, (3) the first fall on the way to Calvary, (4) meeting his Mother, (5) being assisted by Simon of Cyrene and (6) by the woman Veronica who wiped his face, (7) the second fall, (8) meeting the women of Jerusalem, (9) the third fall, (10) being stripped and (11) nailed to the cross, (12) his death, (13) the removal of his body from the cross and (14) his burial. Depictions of these scenes are mounted in most churches, chapels and in some other places, beneath small crosses. A person making the Way of the Cross passes before these stations, or stopping points, pausing at each for meditation. If the stations are made by a group of people, only the leader has to pass from station to station. A plenary indulgence is granted to the faithful who make the stations, under the usual conditions: freedom from all attachment to sin, reception of the sacraments of penance and the Eucharist, and prayers for the intentions of the pope. Those who are impeded from making the stations in the usual manner can gain the same indulgence if, along with the aforementioned conditions, they spend at least a half hour in spiritual reading and meditation on the passion and death of Christ. The stations originated remotely from the practice of Holy Land pilgrims who visited the actual scenes of incidents in the Passion of Christ. Representations elsewhere of at least some of these scenes were known as early as the fifth century. Later, the stations evolved in connection with and as a consequence of strong devotion to the Passion in the 12th and 13th centuries. Franciscans, who were given custody of the Holy Places in 1342, promoted the devotion widely; one of them, St. Leonard of Port Maurice, became known as the greatest preacher of the Way of the Cross in the 18th century. The general features of the devotion were fixed by Clement XII in 1731. On Good Friday, 1991, Pope John Paul made the stations in a manner different from the usual way, using stations based entirely on Gospel texts: (1) Jesus in the Garden of Olives, (2) Jesus is betrayed by Judas and arrested, (3) Jesus is condemned by the Sanhedrin, (4) Jesus is denied by Peter, (5) Jesus is condemned by Pilate, (6) Jesus is scourged and crowned with thorns, (7) Jesus is made to carry his cross, (8) Simon of Cyrene helps Jesus carry his cross, (9) Jesus meets the women of Jerusalem, (10) Jesus is crucified, (11) Jesus promises the Kingdom to the repentant thief, (12) On the cross Jesus speaks to his mother and his beloved disciple John, (13) Jesus dies on the cross, (14) Jesus is laid in the tomb.

**Statutes:** Virtually the same as decrees (see separate entry), they almost always designate laws of a particular council or synod rather than pontifical laws.

**Stigmata:** Marks of the wounds suffered by Christ in his crucifixion, in hands and feet by nails, and side by the piercing of a lance. Some persons, called stigmatists, have been reported as recipients or sufferers of marks like these. The Church, however, has never issued any infallible declaration about their possession by anyone, even in the case of St. Francis of Assisi whose stigmata seem to be the best substantiated and may be commemorated in the Roman-

Rite liturgy. Ninety percent of some 300 reputed stigmatists have been women. Judgment regarding the presence, significance, and manner of causation of stigmata would depend, among other things, on irrefutable experimental evidence.

**Stipend, Mass**: An offering given to a priest for applying the fruits of the Mass according to the intention of the donor. The offering is a contribution to the support of the priest. The disposition of the fruits of the sacrifice, in line with doctrine concerning the Mass in particular and prayer in general, is subject to the will of God. In the early Christian centuries, when Mass was not offered for the intentions of particular persons, the participants made offerings of bread and wine for the sacrifice and their own Holy Communion, and of other things useful for the support of the clergy and the poor. Some offerings may have been made as early as the fourth century for the celebration of Mass for particular intentions, and there are indications of the existence of this practice from the sixth century when private Masses began to be offered. The earliest certain proof of stipend practice, however, dates from the eighth century. By the 11th century, along with private Mass, it was established custom. Mass offerings and intentions were the subjects of a decree approved by John Paul II and made public Mar. 22, 1991. (1) Normally, no more than one offering should be accepted for a Mass; the Mass should be offered in accord with the donor's intention; the priest who accepts the offering should celebrate the Mass himself or have another priest do so. (2) Several Mass intentions, for which offerings have been made, can be combined for a "collective" application of a single Mass only if the previous and explicit consent of the donors is obtained. Such Masses are an exception to the general rule.

**Stole Fee**: An offering given on certain occasions; e.g., at a baptism, wedding, funeral, for the support of the clergy who administer the sacraments and perform other sacred rites.

**Stoup**: A vessel used to contain holy water.

**Suffragan See**: Any diocese, except the archdiocese, within a province.

**Suicide**: The taking of one's own life; a violation of God's dominion over human life. Ecclesiastical burial is denied to persons while in full possession of their faculties; it is permitted in cases of doubt.

**Supererogation**: Actions which go beyond the obligations of duty and the requirements enjoined by God's law as necessary for salvation. Examples of these works are the profession and observance of the evangelical counsels of poverty, chastity, and obedience, and efforts to practice charity to the highest degree.

**Supernatural**: Above the natural; that which exceeds and is not due or owed to the essence, exigencies, requirements, powers and merits of created nature. While human beings have no claim on supernatural things and do not need them in order to exist and act on a natural level, they do need them in order to exist and act in the higher order or economy of grace established by God for their salvation. God has freely given them certain things which are beyond the powers and rights of their human nature. Examples of the supernatural are: grace, a kind of participation by human beings in the divine life, by which they become capable of performing acts meritorious for salvation; divine revelation by which God manifests himself to them and makes known truth that is inaccessible to human reason alone; faith, by which they believe divine truth because of the authority of God who reveals it through Sacred Scripture and tradition and the teaching of his Church.

**Superstition**: A violation of the virtue of religion, by which God is worshipped in an unworthy manner or creatures are given honor which belongs to God alone. False, vain, or futile worship involves elements which are incompatible with the honor and respect due to God, such as error, deception, and bizarre practices. Examples are: false and exaggerated devotions, chain prayers and allegedly unfailing prayers, the mixing of unbecoming practices in worship. The second kind of superstition attributes to persons and things powers and honor which belong to God alone. Examples are: idolatry, divination, magic, spiritism, necromancy.

**Suspension**: A censure by which a cleric is forbidden to exercise some or all of his powers of orders and jurisdiction, or to accept the financial support of his benefices.

**Swearing**: Taking an oath; calling upon God to witness the truth of a statement; a legitimate thing to do for serious reasons and under proper circumstances, as in a court of law. To swear without sufficient reason is to dishonor God's name; to swear falsely in a court of law is perjury.

**Swedenborgianism**: A doctrine developed in and from the writings of Emmanuel Swedenborg (1688-1772), who claimed that during a number of visions he had in 1745 Christ taught him the spiritual sense of Sacred Scripture and commissioned him to communicate it to others. He held that, just as Christianity succeeded Judaism, so his teaching supplemented Christianity. He rejected belief in the Trinity, original sin, the Resurrection, and all the sacraments except baptism and the Eucharist. His followers are members of the Church of the New Jerusalem or of the New Church.

**Syllabus, The**: (1) When not qualified, the term refers to the list of 80 errors accompanying Pope Pius IX's encyclical *Quanta Cura*, issued in 1864. (2) The *Syllabus* of St. Pius X in the decree *Lamentabili*, issued by the Holy Office July 4, 1907, condemning 65 heretical propositions of modernism. This schedule of errors was followed shortly by that pope's encyclical *Pascendi*, the principal ecclesiastical document against modernism, issued Sept. 8, 1907.

**Synod, Diocesan**: Meeting of representative persons of a diocese — priests, religious, lay persons — with the bishop, called by him for the purpose of considering and taking action on matters affecting the life and mission of the Church in the diocese. Persons taking part in a synod have consultative status; the bishop alone is the legislator, with power to authorize synodal decrees. According to canon law, every diocese should have a synod every 10 years.

# T

**Te Deum**: The opening Latin words, Thee, God, of a hymn of praise and thanksgiving prescribed for use in the Office of Readings of the Liturgy of the Hours on many Sundays, solemnities and feasts.

**Temperance:** Moderation, one of the four cardinal virtues.

**Temptation:** Any enticement to sin, from any source: the strivings of one's own faculties, the action of the devil, other persons, circumstances of life, etc. Temptation itself is not sin. Temptation can be avoided and overcome with the use of prudence and the help of grace.

**Thanksgiving:** An expression of gratitude to God for his goodness and the blessings he grants; one of the four ends of prayer.

**Theism:** A philosophy which admits the existence of God and the possibility of divine revelation; it is generally monotheistic and acknowledges God as transcendent and also active in the world. Because it is a philosophy rather than a system of theology derived from revelation, it does not include specifically Christian doctrines, like those concerning the Trinity, the Incarnation and Redemption.

**Theological Virtues:** The virtues which have God for their direct object: faith, or belief in God's infallible teaching; hope, or confidence in divine assistance; charity, or love of God. They are given to a person with grace in the first instance, through baptism and incorporation in Christ.

**Theology:** Knowledge of God and religion, deriving from and based on the data of divine Revelation, organized and systematized according to some kind of scientific method. It involves systematic study and presentation of the truths of divine Revelation in Sacred Scripture, tradition, and the teaching of the Church. The Second Vatican Council made the following declaration about theology and its relation to divine Revelation: "Sacred theology rests on the written word of God, together with sacred tradition, as its primary and perpetual foundation. By scrutinizing in the light of faith all truth stored up in the mystery of Christ, theology is most powerfully strengthened and constantly rejuvenated by that word. For the sacred Scriptures contain the word of God and, since they are inspired, really are the word of God; and so the study of the sacred page is, as it were, the soul of sacred theology" (*Constitution on Revelation*, No. 24). Theology has been divided under various subject headings. Some of the major fields have been: dogma (systematic theology), moral, pastoral, ascetics (the practice of virtue and means of attaining holiness and perfection), mysticism (higher states of religious experience). Other subject headings include ecumenism (Christian unity, interfaith relations), ecclesiology (the nature and constitution of the Church), Mariology (doctrine concerning the Blessed Virgin Mary), the sacraments, etc.

**Tithing:** Contribution of a portion of one's income, originally one-tenth, for purposes of religion and charity. The practice is mentioned 46 times in the Bible. In early Christian times, tithing was adopted in continuance of Old Testament practices of the Jewish people, and the earliest positive church legislation on the subject was enacted in 567. Catholics are bound in conscience to contribute to the support of their church, but the manner in which they do so is not fixed by law. Tithing, which amounts to a pledged contribution of a portion of one's income, has aroused new attention in recent years in the United States.

**Titular Sees:** Dioceses where the Church once flourished but which now exist only in name or title. Bishops without a territorial or residential diocese of their own; e.g., auxiliary bishops, are given titular sees. There are more than 2,000 titular sees; 16 of them are in the United States.

**Transfinalization, Transignification:** Terms coined to express the sign value of consecrated bread and wine with respect to the presence and action of Christ in the Eucharistic sacrifice and the spiritually vivifying purpose of the Eucharistic banquet in Holy Communion. The theory behind the terms has strong undertones of existential and "sign" philosophy, and has been criticized for its openness to interpretation at variance with the doctrine of transubstantiation and the abiding presence of Christ under the appearances of bread and wine after the sacrifice of the Mass and Communion have been completed. The terms, if used as substitutes for transubstantiation, are unacceptable; if they presuppose transubstantiation, they are acceptable as clarifications of its meaning.

**Transubstantiation:** "The way Christ is made present in this sacrament (Holy Eucharist) is none other than by the change of the whole substance of the bread into his Body, and of the whole substance of the wine into his Blood (in the Consecration at Mass) this unique and wonderful change the Catholic Church rightly calls transubstantiation" (encyclical *Mysterium Fidei* of Paul VI, Sept. 3, 1965). The first official use of the term was made by the Fourth Council of the Lateran in 1215. Authoritative teaching on the subject was issued by the Council of Trent.

**Treasury of Merit:** The superabundant merits of Christ and the saints from which the Church draws to confer spiritual benefits, such as indulgences.

**Triduum:** A three-day series of public or private devotions.

## U-Z

**Usury:** Excessive interest charged for the loan and use of money; a violation of justice.

**Veronica:** A word resulting from the combination of a Latin word for true, *vera*, and a Greek word for image, *eikon*, designating a likeness of the face of Christ or the name of a woman said to have given him a cloth on which he caused an imprint of his face to appear. The veneration at Rome of a likeness depicted on cloth dates from about the end of the 10th century; it figured in a popular devotion during the Middle Ages, and in the Holy Face devotion practiced since the 19th century. A faint, indiscernible likeness said to be of this kind is preserved in St. Peter's Basilica. The origin of the likeness is uncertain, and the identity of the woman is unknown. Before the 14th century, there were no known artistic representations of an incident concerning a woman who wiped the face of Christ with a piece of cloth while he was carrying the Cross to Calvary.

**Viaticum:** Holy Communion given to those in danger of death. The word, derived from Latin, means provision for a journey through death to life hereafter.

**Vicar General**: A priest or bishop appointed by the bishop of a diocese to serve as his deputy, with ordinary executive power, in the administration of the diocese.

**Virginity**: Observance of perpetual sexual abstinence. The state of virginity, which is embraced for the love of God by religious with a public vow or by others with a private vow, was singled out for high praise by Christ (Mt. 19:10-12) and has always been so regarded by the Church. In the encyclical *Sacra Virginitas*, Pius XII stated: "Holy virginity and that perfect chastity which is consecrated to the service of God is without doubt among the most perfect treasures which the founder of the Church has left in heritage to the society which he established." Paul VI approved in 1970 a rite in which women can consecrate their virginity "to Christ and their brethren" without becoming members of a religious institute. The *Ordo Consecrationis Virginum*, a revision of a rite promulgated by Clement VII in 1596, is traceable to the Roman liturgy of about 500.

**Virtue**: A habit or established capability for performing good actions. Virtues are *natural* (acquired and increased by repeating good acts) and/or *supernatural* (given with grace by God).

**Vocation**: A call to a way of life. Generally, the term applies to the common call of all persons, from God, to holiness and salvation. Specifically, it refers to particular states of life, each called a vocation, in which response is made to this universal call; viz., marriage, the religious life and/or priesthood, the single state freely chosen or accepted for the accomplishment of God's will. The term also applies to the various occupations in which persons make a living. The Church supports the freedom of each individual in choosing a particular vocation, and reserves the right to pass on the acceptability of candidates for the priesthood and religious life. Signs or indicators of particular vocations are many, including a person's talents and interests, circumstances and obligations, invitations of grace and willingness to respond thereto.

**Vow**: A promise made to God with sufficient knowledge and freedom, which has as its object a moral good that is possible and better than its voluntary omission. A person who professes a vow binds himself or herself by the virtue of religion to fulfill the promise. The best known examples of vows are those of poverty, chastity and obedience professed by religious (see Evangelical Counsels, individual entries). Public vows are made before a competent person, acting as an agent of the Church, who accepts the profession in the name of the Church, thereby giving public recognition to the person's dedication and consecration to God and divine worship. Vows of this kind are either solemn, rendering all contrary acts invalid as well as unlawful; or simple, rendering contrary acts unlawful. Solemn vows are for life; simple vows are for a definite period of time or for life. Vows professed without public recognition by the Church are called private vows. The Church, which has authority to accept and give public recognition to vows, also has authority to dispense persons from their obligations for serious reasons.

**Week of Prayer for Christian Unity**: Eight days of prayer, from Jan. 18 to 25, for the union of all persons in the Church established by Christ. On the initiative of Father Paul James Francis Wattson, S.A., of Graymoor, N.Y., it originated in 1908 as the Chair of Unity Octave. In recent years, its observance on an interfaith basis has increased greatly.

**Witness, Christian**: Practical testimony or evidence given by Christians of their faith in all circumstances of life — by prayer and general conduct, through good example and good works, etc.; being and acting in accordance with Christian belief; actual practice of the Christian faith.

---

## BAPTISM, EUCHARIST, MINISTRY

"Baptism, Eucharist and Ministry," produced under the auspices of the Faith and Order Commission of the World Council of Churches and approved by more than 100 Christian theologians at a meeting held in Lima, Peru, in January, 1982. The Lima Document (also referred to as BEM) is an attempt to state what divided Christians can say in common about baptism, the Eucharist and ministry. It was called a significant development in the ecumenical movement by the Secretariat for Promoting Christian Unity and the Congregation for the Doctrine of the Faith; their response was reported by the NC Documentary Service, Origins, Nov. 19, 1987 (Vol. 17, No. 23).

However, the Vatican agencies declared, it "does not offer a fully systematic treatment of baptism, Eucharist or ministry." Deficiencies have to do with, among other things, the notion of sacrament and the treatment of apostolic tradition and decisive authority in the church.

---

## CALL FOR CHANGES

Archbishop John R. Quinn called for major reform of the Roman Curia, new ways of selecting bishops and a new ecumenical council in an address June 29, 1996, at Oxford University. The quest for church unity requires changes in the style of governance in the Church, the recently retired head of the Archdiocese of San Francisco said in a speech marking the 100th anniversary of Oxford's Campion Hall.

He took the cue for his address from Pope John Pauls's own request, in his 1995 encyclical letter on Christian unity, for leaders and theologians of the Christian churches to help the Pope "find a way of exercising the (papal) primacy which, while in no way renouncing what is essential to its mission, is nonetheless open to a new situation."

Archbishop Quinn said he was arguing that one of the chief obstacles to Christian unity is "the way issues are dealt with by the Curia," which is a matter of real concern.

## HISPANICS ON MISSION

To create a new style of leadership and pathways of hope, especially among the young, Hispanic Catholic leaders at their national congress were sent in mission back to the 42 states from which they came to transform society where they live and work.

"Everyone must see us as servants," Archbishop Patrick F. Flores of San Antonio said at the closing of the congress, held at Loyola University, Chicago.

"We only learn this from the No. 1 Leader — Jesus Christ," he stressed, cautioning his listeners against the temptation of feeling too important.

### Roots and Wings

The Aug. 8-to-11 congress was convened under the theme "Roots and Wings '96: Creating Pathways of Hope," and drew between 800 and 1,000 people. It was organized by the National Catholic Council for Hispanic Ministry, an umbrella organization based in Los Angeles for 52 Hispanic groups involved in ministry at national and regional levels.

Among the conferees were at least 12 bishops and 45 priests and deacons.

The congress showcased 16 projects which had proven effective for leadership development, especially among youths.

"Hispanics are a young population, and what we are doing to reach young people is minimal," said Father Mario Vizcaino, vice president of the National, Catholic Council for Hispanic Ministry. He pointed out that, of the 30 million Hispanics in the United States, more than 15 million were under 30 years of age.

"If we count the people we are in touch with and multiply this figure by 100, we do not reach two percent of the population," he said.

Another speaker, Sister Gloria Urrabazo, said that her work in campus ministry in San Antonio had made her aware of the need for Hispanic pastoral workers at universities.

"Campus ministry is the connecting link with the young adults who are away from home and will become (just) a Social Security number at the university," she said. "We need men and women who can serve as models and are willing to work for little money."'

She also challenged the bishops present to contribute to the cause.

Some 50 youth leaders from across the nation attended a special youth track, which ended with the creation of a national network to try to better meet their needs.

### Leadership Initiative

Leaders of the National Catholic Council for Hispanic Ministry also presented the first stage of a leadership initiative that is training Catholic leaders as it develops a curriculum for leadership training of Hispanic Catholics.

"We are trying to develop a concept of Christian leadership which is not simply based in technical and professional competence," said Father Allan Figuero Deck, executive secretary of the national council.

At various times during the congress and at a press conference on immigration issues, bishops deplored the current anti-immigrant sentiment in the nation.

"Our language seems appreciated only when it comes to fostering new markets and avarice, but not to build bridges," said Auxiliary Bishop Gabino Zavala of Los Angeles, referring to English-only legislation.

"Unfortunately, our presence is being questioned, and we must defend it," said Bishop Ricardo Ramirez of Las Cruces, N.M.

"The Church has an important role to play among Hispanics because the roots of our culture are imbued (with) Catholic values. But the Church is not only its ministers," he added. "The majority of the faithful live and work in the areas of education, politics, finance.... It is there that we must have our leaders."

Looking at Hispanic ministry over the previous 50 years, he pointed out that it was directed to the poor and newly arrived.

"Now there is a new reality; the children of the immigrants and refugees are in the colleges and universities," Bishop Ramirez said. Soon there will be a Hispanic as mayor of Chicago, or as president of a university. But, what type of leaders will Hispanics be and with which values," he asked.

"What will be the impact of Hispanic leaders in the culture of the United States?" asked Coadjutor Bishop Roberto O. Gonzalez of Corpus Christi."

It was to respond to this new reality that the national Hispanic ministry council set the theme of leadership for the congress, not as something abstract but specifically applied to Catholic youths and young adults, who live and work in the midst of a dominant Euro-U.S. culture and are interacting with it."

## TEKAKWITHA CONFERENCE

Catholicism and Native American religious practices share many traditions because of their basis in faith in God the Creator, said Archbishop Michael J. Sheehan of Santa Fe in a homily during the 57th annual Tekakwitha Conference.

More than 1,500 people from throughout North America attended the Aug. 7-to-11 conference of Native American Catholics at the University of New Mexico in Albuquerque.

Archbishop Sheehan said: "It is the same Creator God who has breathed into all our ancestors, mine and yours, a love for the Great Spirit and for reli-

gious beliefs and for the desire to express this in ritual and symbol. God revealed many things in natural ways years before he sent his Son. But then God sent his Son Jesus to reveal many more teachings which we could never know otherwise. ...The Church affirms your culture, your language and your religious traditions. For the most part, these are all compatible with Christian teaching."

The conference has a board of 12 directors, most of whom are Indians. Moderator: Bishop Donald Pellotte. Address: Tekakwitha Conference National Center, P.O. Box 6768, Great Falls, MT 59406.

# THE CHURCH IN COUNTRIES THROUGHOUT THE WORLD

(Principal sources for statistics: *Statistical Yearbook of the Church, 1994* (the most recent edition); *Annuario Pontificio, 1996*. Figures are as of Dec. 31, 1994, except for cardinals (as of August 8, 1996) and others which are indicated. For 1996 developments, see Index entries for individual countries.)

An asterisk indicates that the country has full diplomatic relations with the Holy See (see Index: Diplomats to the Holy See).

Abbreviations (in order in which they appear): archd. — archdiocese; dioc. — diocese; ap. ex. — apostolic exarchate; prel. — prelature; abb. — abbacy; v.a. — vicariate apostolic; p.a. — prefecture apostolic; a.a. — apostolic administration; mil. ord. — military ordinariate; card. — cardinal; abp. — archbishops; bp. — bishops (diocesan and titular); priests (dioc. — diocesan or secular priests; rel. — those belonging to religious orders); p.d. — permanent deacons; sem. — major seminarians, diocesan and religious; bros. — brothers; srs. — sisters; bap. — baptisms; Caths. — Catholic population; tot. pop. — total population; (AD), apostolic delegate (see Index: Papal Representatives).

## Afghanistan

Republic in south-central Asia (in transition); capital, Kabul. Christianity antedated Muslim conquest in the seventh century but was overcome by it. All inhabitants are subject to the law of Islam. Christian missionaries are prohibited.

Population, 18,880,000.

## Albania*

*Archd., 2; dioc., 3; abb., 1; a.a. 1; card., 1; abp., 2; bp., 2; parishes, 91; priests, 84 (31 dioc., 53 rel.); sem., 23; bros., 9; srs., 174; bap., 2,970; Caths., 525,000 (15%); tot. pop., 3,410,000.*

Republic in the Balkans, bordering the Adriatic Sea; capital, Tirana. Christianity was introduced in apostolic times. The northern part of the country remained faithful to Rome while the south broke from unity following the schism of 1054. A large percentage of the population was forcibly Islamized following the invasion (15th century) and long centuries of occupation by the Ottoman Turks. Many Catholics fled to southern Italy, Sicily and Greece. In 1945, at the time of the communist takeover, an estimated 68 per cent of the population was Muslim; 19 per cent, Orthodox and 13 per cent, Roman Catholic. The Catholic Church prevailed in the north. During 45 years of communist dictatorship, the Church fell victim, as did all religions, to systematic persecution: non-Albanian missionaries were expelled; death, prison sentences and other repressive measures were enacted against church personnel and laity; Catholic schools and churches were closed and used for other purposes, and lines of communication with the Holy See were cut off. In 1967, the government, declaring it had eliminated all religion in the country, proclaimed itself the first atheist state in the world. The right to practice religion was restored in late 1990. In March, 1991, a delegation from the Vatican was allowed to go to Albania; later in the year diplomatic relations were established with the Holy See at the request of the Albanian prime minister. Pope John Paul II made a historic one-day visit to the country April 25, 1993, during which he ordained four bishops appointed by him in December, 1992, to fill long-vacant sees. Restoration of the Church is a slow and difficult process. The first Albanian cardinal was named in November, 1994.

## Algeria*

*Archd., 1; dioc., 3; abp., 1; bp., 4; parishes, 45; priests, 118 (48 dioc., 70 rel.); p.d., 2; sem., 3; bros., 17; srs., 228; bap., 12; Caths., 23,000 (.08%); tot. pop., 27,320,000.*

Republic in northwest Africa: capital, Algiers. Christianity, introduced at an early date, succumbed to Vandal devastation in the fifth century and Muslim conquest in 709, but survived for centuries in small communities into the 12th century. Missionary work was unsuccessful except in service to traders, military personnel and captives along the coast. Church organization was established after the French gained control of the territory in the 1830s. A large number of Catholics were among the estimated million Europeans who left the country after it secured independence from France July 5, 1962. Sunni-Muslim is the state religion. Seven Trappist monks were among the latest victims of Muslim terrorist violence in May, 1996. (See News Events.)

## Andorra*

*Parishes, 7; priests, 18 (12 dioc., 6 rel.); srs., 13; bap., 388; Caths., 55,000 (91.6%); tot. pop., 60,000.*

Parliamentary state in the Pyrenees; capital, Andorra la Vella. From 1278-1993, it was a co-principality under the rule of the French head of state and the bishop of Urgel, Spain. Christianity was introduced at an early date. Catholicism is the state religion. Ecclesiastical jurisdiction is under the Spanish Diocese of Urgel.

## Angola

*Archd., 3; dioc., 12; card., 1; abp., 4; bp., 13; parishes, 249; priests, 412 (153 dioc., 259 rel.); sem., 698; bros., 90; srs., 1,289; catechists, 17,109; bap., 117,721; Caths., 6,460,000 (60.5%); tot. pop., 10,670,000. (AD)*

Republic in southwest Africa; capital, Luanda. Evangelization by Catholic missionaries, from Portugal, dating from 1491, reached high points in the 17th and 18th centuries. Independence from Portugal in 1975 and the long civil war which followed (peace accord signed in 1991) left the Church with a heavy loss of personnel through the departure of about half of the foreign missionaries and the persecution and martyrdom experienced by the Church during the war. Renewed fighting following elections in late 1992 brought repeated appeals for peace from the nation's bishops and religious in 1993 and 1994. Despite another peace accord signed by the rebels and the government in late 1994, conditions remained unsettled. The first Angolan cardinal (Alexandre do Nascimento) was named in 1983.

## Anguilla

*Parish, 1; priests, 1 (rel); catechists, 2; bap., 4; Caths., 200; tot. pop., 7,000. (AD)*

Self-governing British island territory in the Caribbean; capital, The Valley. Under ecclesiastical jurisdiction of St. John's-Basseterre diocese, Antigua.

### Antigua and Barbuda*
*Dioc., 1; bp., 1; parishes, 2; priests, 10 (4 dioc., 6 rel.); sem., 2; bros., 5; srs., 8; catechists, 51; bap., 82; Caths., 7,000 (10.9%); tot. pop., 64,000.*

Independent (1981) Caribbean island nation; capital, St. John's, Antigua.

### Arabian Peninsula
Christianity, introduced in various parts of the peninsula in early Christian centuries, succumbed to Islam in the seventh century. The native population is entirely Muslim. The only Christians are foreign workers mainly from the Philippines, India and Korea. Most of the peninsula is under the ecclesiastical jurisdiction of the Vicariate Apostolic of Arabia with its seat in Abu Dhabi, United Arab Emirates. See individual countries: Bahrain, Oman, Qatar, Saudi Arabia, United Arab Emirates and Yemen.

### Argentina*
*Archd., 13; dioc., 49; prel., 3; ap. ex., 1 (for Armenians of Latin America); ord., 1; mil. ord.; card., 4; abp., 18; bp., 83; parishes, 2,466; priests, 5,904 (3,459 dioc., 2,445 rel.); p.d., 328; sem., 2,015; bros., 904; srs., 11,388; bap., 545,980; Caths., 31,011,000 (90.7%); tot. pop., 34,180,000*

Republic in southeast South America, bordering on the Atlantic; capital, Buenos Aires. Priests were with the Magellan exploration party and the first Mass in the country was celebrated Apr. 1, 1519. Missionary work began in the 1530s, diocesan organization in the late 1540s, and effective evangelization about 1570. Independence from Spain was proclaimed in 1816. Since its establishment in the country, the Church has been influenced by Spanish cultural and institutional forces, antagonistic liberalism, government interference and opposition; the latter reached a climax during the last five years of the first presidency of Juan Peron (1946-1955). Widespread human rights violations including the disappearance of thousands of people marked the period of military rule from 1976 to December, 1983, when an elected civilian government took over.

### Armenia*
*Ord., 1 (for Catholic Armenians of Eastern Europe, with seat in Armenia); a.a., 1 (for Latin-rite Catholics, with seat in Georgia); parishes, 15; priests, 17 (rel.); sem., 5; srs., 12; bap., 333; Caths., 100,000 (2.8%); tot. pop., 3,550,000.*

Republic in Asia Minor; capital Yerevan. Part of the USSR from 1920 until it declared its sovereignty in September, 1991. Ancient Armenia, which also included territory annexed by Turkey in 1920, was Christianized in the fourth century. Diplomatic relations were established with the Holy See May 23, 1992.

### Aruba
*Parishes, 8; priests, 13 (9 dioc., 4 rel.); bros., 5; srs., 8; catechists, 16; bap., 620; Caths., 53,000; tot. pop., 67,000. (AD)*

Autonomous island member of The Netherlands in West Indies. Under ecclesiastical jurisdiction of Willemstad, Curacao, in Netherlands Antilles.

### Australia*
*Archd., 7; dioc., 24; mil. ord., 1; card., 2; abp., 11; bp., 48; parishes, 1,428; priests, 3,543 (2,150 dioc., 1,393 rel.); p.d., 40; sem., 294; bros., 1,385; srs., 9,056; bap., 75,867; Caths., 5,043,000 (28.2%); tot. pop. 17,840,000.*

Commonwealth; island continent southeast of Asia; capital, Canberra. The first Catholics in the country were Irish under penal sentence, 1795-1804; the first public Mass was celebrated May 15, 1803. Official organization of the Church dates from 1820. The country was officially removed from mission status in March, 1976.

### Austria*
*Archd., 2; dioc., 7; abb., 1; ord., 1; mil. ord.; card., 3; abp., 3; bp., 17; parishes, 3,095; priests, 4,945 (2,995 dioc., 1,950 rel.); p.d., 315; sem., 480; bros., 439; srs., 7,332; bap., 75,039; Caths., 6,286,000 (78.2%); tot. pop., 8,030,000.*

Republic in central Europe; capital, Vienna. Christianity was introduced by the end of the third century, strengthened considerably by conversion of the Bavarians from about 600, and firmly established in the second half of the eighth century. Catholicism survived and grew stronger as the principal religion in the country in the post-Reformation period, but suffered from Josephinism in the 18th century. Although liberated from much government harassment in the aftermath of the Revolution of 1848, the Church came under pressure again some 20 years later in the Kulturkampf. During this time the Church became involved with a developing social movement. The Church faced strong opposition from Socialists after World War I and suffered persecution from 1938 to 1945 during the Nazi regime. Some Church-state matters are regulated by a concordat originally concluded in 1934. (See Index)

### Azerbaijan*
Independent republic (1991) bordering Iran and Turkey; formerly part of the USSR; capital, Baku. Islam is the prevailing religion. There is a small Catholic community of Polish and Armenian origin near the capital. Latin-rite Catholics are under the apostolic administration of the Caucasus (seat in Georgia) established in December, 1993.

Tot. pop., 7,470,000.

### Azores
North Atlantic island group 750 miles west of Portugal, of which it is part. Christianity was introduced in the second quarter of the 15th century. The diocese of Angra was established in 1534. Statistics are included in Portugal.

### Bahamas*
*Dioc., 1; bp., 1; parishes, 27; priests, 30 (14 dioc., 16 rel.); p.d., 9; sem., 2; bros., 2; srs., 37; catechists, 69; bap., 1,328; Caths., 45,000 (16.8%); tot. pop., 267,000.*

Independent (July 10, 1973) island group consisting of some 700 (30 inhabited) small islands southeast of Florida and north of Cuba; capital, Nassau. On Oct. 12, 1492, Columbus landed on one of these islands, where the first Mass was celebrated in the New World. Organization of the Catholic Church in the Bahamas dates from about the middle of the 19th century.

## Bahrain
*Parish, 1; priests, 3 (dioc.); srs., 7; bap., 238; Caths., 30,000; tot. pop., 550,000. (AD)*
Island state in Persian Gulf; capital, Manama. Population is Muslim; Catholics are foreign workers. Under ecclesiastical jurisdiction of Arabia vicariate apostolic.

## Balearic Islands
Spanish province consisting of an island group in the western Mediterranean. Statistics are included in those for Spain.

## Bangladesh*
*Archd., 1; dioc., 5; abp., 2; bp., 5; parishes, 70; priests, 225 (97 dioc., 128 rel.); sem., 69; bros., 69; srs., 957; catechists, 1,111; bap., 6,478; Caths., 225,000 (.19%); tot. pop. 117,790,000.*
Formerly the eastern portion of Pakistan. Officially constituted as a separate nation Dec. 16, 1971; capital, Dhaka. Islam, the principal religion, was declared the state religion in 1988; freedom of religion is granted. There were Jesuit, Dominican and Augustinian missionaries in the area in the 16th century. A vicariate apostolic (of Bengali) was established in 1834; the hierarchy was erected in 1950.

## Barbados*
*Dioc., 1; bp., 2; parishes, 6; priests, 12 (5 dioc., 7 rel.); p.d., 1; bros., 1; srs., 15; bap., 152; Caths., 11,000 (4%); tot. pop., 275,000.*
Parliamentary democracy (independent since 1966), easternmost of the Caribbean islands; capital, Bridgetown. About 70 per cent of the people are Anglicans.

## Belarus*
*Archd., 1; dioc., 2; card., 1; bp., 1; parishes, 301; priests, 210 (91 dioc., 119 rel.); p.d., 1; sem., 188; bros., 10; srs., 267; bap., 8,822; Caths., 1,245,000 (12%); tot. pop., 10,350,000.*
Independent republic (1991) in eastern Europe; former Soviet republic (Byelorussia); capital, Minsk. Slow but steady recovery of the Church was reported after years of repression in the Soviet Union.

## Belgium*
*Archd., 1; dioc., 7; mil ord.; card., 3; bp., 24; parishes, 3,967; priests, 9,404 (5,870 dioc., 3,534 rel.); p.d., 470; sem., 346; bros., 1,586; srs., 19,714; bap., 90,083; Caths., 8,437,000 (83.7%); tot. pop., 10,080,000.*
Constitutional monarchy in northwestern Europe; capital, Brussels. Christianity was introduced about the first quarter of the fourth century and major evangelization was completed about 730. During the rest of the medieval period the Church had firm diocesan and parochial organization, generally vigorous monastic life, and influential monastic and cathe-dral schools. Lutherans and Calvinists made some gains during the Reformation period but there was a strong Catholic restoration in the first half of the 17th century, when the country was under Spanish rule. Jansenism disturbed the Church from about 1640 into the 18th century. Josephinism, imposed by an Austrian regime, hampered the Church late in the same century. Repressive and persecutory measures were enforced during the Napoleonic conquest. Freedom came with separation of Church and state in the wake of the Revolution of 1830, which ended the reign of William I. Thereafter, the Church encountered serious problems with philosophical liberalism and political socialism. Catholics have long been engaged in strong educational, social and political movements. Except for one five-year period (1880-84), Belgium has had diplomatic relations with the Holy See since 1835.

## Belize*
*Dioc., 1; bp., 1; parishes, 13; priests, 43 (14 dioc., 29 rel.); p.d., 1; sem., 6; bros., 6; srs., 74; bap., 3,170; Caths., 122,000 (58%); tot. pop., 210,000.*
Formerly British Honduras. Independent (Sept. 21, 1981) republic on east coast of Central America; capital, Belmopan. Its history has points in common with Guatemala, where evangelization began in the 16th century.

## Benin*
*Archd., 1; dioc., 8; card., 1; abp., 2; bp., 8; parishes, 139; priests, 323 (209 dioc., 114 rel.); p.d., 1; sem., 253; bros., 40; srs., 548; catechists, 6,744; bap., 47,869; Caths., 1,167,000 (21.8%); tot. pop., 5,340,000.*
Formerly Dahomey. Democratic republic in west Africa, bordering on the Atlantic; capital, Porto Novo. Missionary work was very limited from the 16th to the 18th centuries. Effective evangelization dates from 1861. The hierarchy was established in 1955. The majority of Christians are Catholics.

## Bermuda
*Dioc., 1; bp., 1; parishes, 6; priests, 8 (1 dioc., 7 rel.); srs., 5; catechists, 115; bap., 81; Caths., 10,000 (16%); tot. pop., 60,000. (AD)*
British dependency, consisting of 360 islands (20 of them inhabited) nearly 600 miles east of Cape Hatteras; capital, Hamilton. Catholics were not permitted until about 1800. Occasional pastoral care was provided the few Catholics there by visiting priests during the 19th century. Early in the 1900s priests from Halifax began serving the area. A prefecture apostolic was set up in 1953. The first bishop assumed jurisdiction in 1956 when it was made a vicariate apostolic; diocese established, 1967.

## Bhutan
*Parish, 1; catechist, 1; bap., 33; Caths., 1,000; tot. pop., 1,6100,000.*
Kingdom in the Himalayas, northeast of India; capital, Thimphu. Buddhist is the state religion. Jesuits (1963) and Salesians (1965) were invited to country to direct schools. Salesians were expelled in February, 1982, on disputed charges of proselytism. The only Catholic missionary allowed to stay in the coun-

try was Canadian Jesuit Father William Mackey who served Catholics there from 1963 until his death in 1995. Ecclesiastical jurisdiction is under the Darjeeling diocese, India.

## Bolivia*

*Archd., 4; dioc., 6; prel., 2; v.a., 5; mil. ord.; abp., 7; bp., 30; parishes, 516; priests, 1,068 (360 dioc., 708 rel.); p.d., 43; sem., 539; bros., 209; srs., 2,089; catechists, 1,573; bap., 219,551; Caths., 6,484,000 (89.5%); tot. pop., 7,240,000.*

Republic in central South America; capital, Sucre; seat of government, La Paz. Catholicism, the official religion, was introduced in the 1530s and the first bishopric was established in 1552. Effective evangelization among the Indians, slow to start, reached high points in the middle of the 18th and the beginning of the 19th centuries and was resumed about 1840. Independence from Spain was proclaimed in 1825, at the end of a campaign that started in 1809. Church-state relations are regulated by a 1951 concordat with the Holy See. In recent years, human rights violations in conditions of political, economic and social turmoil have occasioned strong protests by members of the hierarchy and other people of the Church.

## Bosnia and Herzegovina*

*Archd., 1; dioc., 3; card., 1; bp., 3; parishes, 284; priests, 607 (250 dioc., 357 rel.); p.d., 3; sem., 153; bros., 12; srs., 364; bap., 4,056; Caths., 786,000 (22.2%); tot. pop., 3,530,000.*

Independent republic (1992) in southeastern Europe; formerly part of Yugoslavia; capital Sarajevo. (See also News Events.)

## Botswana

*Dioc., 1; bp., 1; parishes, 25; priests, 50 (6 dioc., 44 rel.); p.d., 1; sem., 10; bros., 5; srs., 51; catechists, 157; bap., 1,681; Caths., 53,000 (3.6%); tot. pop., 1,440,000. (AD)*

Republic (independent since 1966) in southern Africa; capital, Gaborone. The first Catholic mission was opened in 1928 near Gaborone; earlier attempts at evangelization dating from 1879 were unsuccessful.

## Brazil*

*Archd., 37; dioc., 201; prel., 13; abb., 2; ord., 1; mil. ord.; card., 5; abp., 45; bp., 308; parishes, 7,966; priests, 15,308 (7,645 dioc., 7,663 rel.); p.d., 699; sem., 6,772; bros., 2,181; srs., 36,028; bap., 2,272,842; Caths., 133,680,000 (86.9%); tot. pop., 153,740,000.*

Federal republic in northeast South America; capital, Brasilia. One of several priests with the discovery party celebrated the first Mass in the country Apr. 26, 1500. Evangelization began some years later and the first diocese was erected in 1551. During the colonial period, which lasted until 1822, evangelization made some notable progress — especially in the Amazon region between 1680 and 1750 — but was seriously hindered by government policy and the attitude of colonists regarding Amazon Indians the missionaries tried to protect from exploitation and slavery. The Jesuits were suppressed in

1782 and other missionaries expelled as well. Liberal anti-Church influence grew in strength. The government gave minimal support but exercised maximum control over the Church. After the proclamation of independence from Portugal in 1822 and throughout the regency, government control was tightened and the Church suffered greatly from dissident actions of ecclesiastical brotherhoods, Masonic anticlericalism and general decline in religious life. Church and state were separated by the constitution of 1891, proclaimed two years after the end of the empire. The Church carried into the 20th century a load of inherited liabilities and problems amid increasingly difficult political, economic and social conditions affecting the majority of the population. A number of bishops, priests, religious and lay persons have been active in movements for social and religious reform.

## Brunei Darussalam

*Parishes, 3; priests, 2 (1 dioc., 1 rel); srs., 4; Caths., 8,000; tot. pop., 280,000.*

Independent state (1984) on the northern coast of Borneo; capital, Bandar Seri Begawan. Islam is the official religion; other religions are allowed with some restrictions. Most of the Catholics are technicians and skilled workers from other countries who are not permanent residents; under ecclesiastical jurisdiction of Miri diocese, Malaysia.

## Bulgaria*

*Dioc., 2; ap. ex., 1; abp., 2; bp., 4; parishes, 74; priests, 73 (16 dioc., 57 rel.); sem., 26; bros., 8; srs., 77; bap., 628; Caths., 86,000 (1%) tot. pop., 8,440,000.*

Republic in southeastern Europe on the eastern part of the Balkan peninsula; capital, Sofia. Most of the population is Orthodox. Christianity was introduced before 343 but disappeared with the migration of Slavs into the territory. The baptism of Boris I about 865 ushered in a new period of Christianity which soon became involved in switches of loyalty between Constantinople and Rome. Through it all the Byzantine, and later Orthodox, element remained stronger and survived under the rule of Ottoman Turks into the 19th century. The Byzantines are products of a reunion movement of the 19th century. In 1947 the constitution of the new republic decreed the separation of Church and state. Catholic schools and institutions were abolished and foreign religious banished in 1948. A year later the apostolic delegate was expelled. Ivan Romanoff, vicar general of Plovdiv, died in prison in 1952. Bishop Eugene Bossilkoff, imprisoned in 1948, was sentenced to death in 1952; his fate remained unknown until 1975 when the Bulgarian government informed the Vatican that he had died in prison shortly after being sentenced. Roman and Bulgarian Rite vicars apostolic were permitted to attend the Second Vatican Council from 1962 to 1965. All church activity was under surveillance and/or control by the government, which professed to be atheistic. Pastoral and related activities were strictly limited. There was some improvement in Bulgarian-Vatican relations in 1975, following a visit of Bulgarian President Todor Zhivkov to Pope Paul VI June 19 and talks between

Vatican and Bulgarian representatives at the Helsinki Conference in late July. In 1979, the Sofia-Plovdiv vicariate apostolic was raised to a diocese and a bishop was appointed for the vacant see of Nicopoli. Diplomatic relations with the Holy See were established in 1990.

## Burkina Faso*
Archd., 1; dioc., 8; card., 1; bp., 10; parishes, 112; priests, 454 (307 dioc., 147 rel.); sem., 358; bros., 139; srs., 852; catechists, 7,883; bap., 54,905; Caths., 1,034,000 (10%); tot. pop., 9,890,000.

Republic inland in western Africa; capital, Ouagadougou; formerly, Upper Volta. White Fathers (now known as Missionaries of Africa) started the first missions in 1900 and 1901. White Sisters began work in 1911. A minor and a major seminary were established in 1926 and 1942, respectively. The first native bishop in modern times from West Africa was ordained in 1956 and the first cardinal created in 1965. The hierarchy was established in 1955.

## Burma
(See Myanmar)

## Burundi*
Archd., 1; dioc., 6; abp., 3; bp., 8; parishes, 115; priests, 342 (260 dioc., 82 rel.); sem., 289; bros., 136; srs., 826; catechists, 4,730; bap., 103,596; Caths., 3,554,000 (58%); tot. pop., 6,130,000.

Republic since 1966, near the equator in east-central Africa; capital, Bujumbura. The first permanent Catholic mission station was established late in the 19th century. Large numbers of persons were received into the Church following the ordination of the first Burundi priests in 1925. The first native bishop was appointed in 1959. In 1972-73, the country was torn by tribal warfare between the Tutsis, the ruling minority, and the Hutus. Since 1979, approximately 100 Catholic missionaries have been expelled. In 1986, seminaries were nationalized. A gradual resumption of church activity since 1987 has been hampered by continuing ethnic violence which exploded in 1996. (See News Events.)

## Cambodia*
V.a., 1; p.a., 2; bp., 1; parishes, 14; priests, 21 (9 dioc., 12 rel.); sem., 7; bros., 2; srs., 33; catechists, 25; baptisms, 71; Caths., 20,000 (.2%); tot. pop., 9,570,000.

Republic in southeast Asia, bordering on the Gulf of Siam, Thailand, Laos and Vietnam; capital Phnom Penh. Evangelization dating from the second half of the 16th century had limited results, more among Vietnamese than Khmers. Thousands of Catholics of Vietnamese origin were forced to flee in 1970 because of Khmer hostility. The status of the Church remained uncertain following the Khmer Rouge takeover in April, 1975, the Vietnamese invasion in 1979 and the long civil war which followed. Foreign missionaries were expelled, local clergy and religious were sent to work the land and a general persecution followed. Religious freedom was reestablished in 1990. Diplomatic relations with the Holy See were established in March, 1994. Buddhism is the state religion.

## Cameroon*
Archd., 5; dioc., 17; card., 1; abp., 6; bp., 19; parishes, 552; priests, 1,035 (565 dioc., 470 rel.); p.d., 22; sem., 862; bros., 179; srs., 1,449; catechists, 13,520; bap., 82,893; Caths., 3,789,000 (29.4%); tot. pop., 12,870,000.

Republic in west Africa, bordering on the Gulf of Guinea; capital, Yaounde. Effective evangelization began in 1890, although Catholics had been in the country long before that time. In the 40-year period from 1920 to 1960, the number of Catholics increased from 60,000 to 700,000. The first native priests were ordained in 1935. Twenty years later the first native bishops were ordained and the hierarchy established. The first Cameroonian cardinal (Christian Wiyghan Tumi) was named in 1988. (See Index for 1995 papal visit.)

## Canada*
Archd., 19; dioc., 53; abb., 1; ap. ex., 1; mil. ord.; card., 4 (1 heads archiepiscopal see; 1 is Curia official; 2 are retired); abp., 26 (18 archdiocesan, 1 coadjutor, 1 heads eparchy with personal title of archbishop; 6 retired); bp., 94 (49 diocesan, 1 heads military ordinariate; 17 auxiliary; 1 bishop for Hungarian Emigrants; 26 retired); abbots, 2 (1 retired); parishes, 5,706; priests, 10,192 (6,067 dioc., 4,125 rel.); p.d., 761; sem., 592; bros., 2,755; srs., 27,233; lay assistants, 1,784; bap., 177,252; Caths., 12,600,000 (44%); tot. pop., 28,435,000. (Principal sources: 1996-1997 Directory of the Canadian Conference of Catholic Bishops; Statistical Yearbook of the Church; 1996 Annuario Pontificio.)

Independent federation comprising the northern half of North America; capital, Ottawa. (See Index.)

## Canary Islands
Two Spanish provinces, consisting of seven islands, off the northwest coast of Africa. Evangelization began about 1400. Almost all of the one million inhabitants are Catholic. Statistics are included in those for Spain.

## Cape Verde*
Dioc., 1; bp., 1; parishes, 31; priests, 49 (13 dioc., 36 rel.); sem., 5; bros., 7; srs., 109; catechists, 2,226; bap., 9,813; Caths., 378,000 (95.9%); tot. pop., 394,000.

Independent (July 5, 1975) island group in the Atlantic 300 miles west of Senegal; formerly a Portuguese overseas province; capital, Praia, San Tiago Island. Evangelization began some years before the establishment of a diocese in 1532.

## Cayman Islands
Parish, 1; priests, 1 (dioc.); srs., 2; catechists, 6; bap., 62; Caths. 4,000; tot. pop., 28,000. (AD)

British dependency in Caribbean; capital, Georgetown on Grand Cayman. Under ecclesiastical jurisdiction of Kingston archdiocese, Jamaica.

## Central African Republic*
Archd., 1; dioc., 6; abp., 2; bp., 7; parishes, 110; priests, 270 (99 dioc., 171 rel.); p.d., 1; sem., 124; bros., 53; srs., 326; catechists, 3,903; bap., 27,034; Caths., 612,000 (18.9%); tot. pop., 3,230,000.

Former French colony (independent since 1960) in central Africa; capital, Bangui. Effective evangelization dates from 1894. The region was organized as a mission territory in 1909. The first native priest was ordained in 1938. The hierarchy was organized in 1955.

## Ceuta

Spanish possession (city) on the northern tip of Africa, south of Gibraltar. Statistics are included in those for Spain.

## Chad*

*Archd., 1; dioc., 4; abp., 1; bp., 6; parishes, 93; priests, 191 (68 dioc., 123 rel.); sem., 83; bros., 36; srs., 289; catechists, 6,765; bap., 13,042; Caths., 411,000 (6.6%); tot. pop., 6,210,000.*

Republic (independent since 1960) in north-central Africa; former French possession; capital, N'Djamena. Evangelization began in 1929, leading to firm organization in 1947 and establishment of the hierarchy in 1955.

## Chile*

*Archd., 5; dioc., 17; prel., 2; v.a., 2; mil. ord.; card., 3; abp., 10; bp., 32; parishes, 919; priests, 2,310 (1,071 dioc., 1,239 rel.); p.d., 349; sem., 761; bros., 411; srs., 6,865; catechists, 1,370; bap., 185,850; Caths., 11,162,000 (79.8%); tot. pop., 13,990,000.*

Republic on the southwestern coast of South America; capital, Santiago. Priests were with the Spanish conquistadores on their entrance into the territory early in the 16th century. The first parish was established in 1547 and the first bishopric in 1561. Overall organization of the Church took place later in the century. By 1650 most of the peaceful Indians in the central and northern areas were evangelized. Missionary work was more difficult in the southern region. Church activity was hampered during the campaign for independence, 1810 to 1818, and through the first years of the new government, to 1830. Later gains were made, into this century, but hindering factors were shortages of native clergy and religious and attempts by the government to control church administration through the patronage system in force while the country was under Spanish control. Separation of Church and state was decreed in the constitution of 1925. Church-state relations were strained during the regime of Marxist president Salvator Allende Gossens (1970-73). Conditions remained unsettled under the military government which assumed control after the coup. The Chilean bishops issued numerous statements strongly critical of human rights abuses by the military dictatorship which remained in power until 1990 when an elected president took office.

## China

*Archd., 20; dioc., 92; p.a., 29. No Catholic statistics are available. In 1949 there were between 3,500,000-4,000,000 Catholics, about .7 per cent of the total population. Tot. pop. 1,174,444,000.*

People's republic in eastern part of Asia (mainland China under communist control since 1949); capital, Peking (Beijing). Christianity was introduced by Nestorians who had some influence on part of the area from 635 to 845 and again from the 11th cen-

tury until 1368. John of Monte Corvino started a Franciscan mission in 1294; he was ordained an archbishop about 1307. Missionary activity involving more priests increased for a while thereafter but the Franciscan mission ended in 1368. The Jesuit Matteo Ricci initiated a remarkable period of activity in the 1580s. By 1700 the number of Catholics was reported to be 300,000. The Chinese Rites controversy, concerning the adaptation of rituals and other matters to Chinese traditions and practices, ran throughout the 17th century, ending in a negative decision by mission authorities in Rome. Bl. Francis de Capillas, the protomartyr of China, was killed in 1648. Persecution, a feature of Chinese history as recurrent as changes in dynasties, occurred several times in the 18th century and resulted in the departure of most missionaries from the country. The Chinese door swung open again in the 1840s and progress in evangelization increased with an extension of legal and social tolerance. At the turn of the 20th century, however, the Boxer Rebellion took one or the other kind of toll among an estimated 30,000 victims. Missionary work in the 1900s reached a new high in every respect. The hierarchy was instituted by Pope Pius XII, April 11, 1946 (Apostolic Constitution *Quotidie Nos*). Then followed the disaster of persecution initiated by communists, before and especially after they established the republic in 1949. The government began a savage persecution as soon as it came into power. Among its results were the expulsion of over 5,000 foreign missionaries, 510 of whom were American priests, brothers and nuns; the arrest, imprisonment and harassment of all members of the native religious, clergy and hierarchy; the forced closing of 3,932 schools, 216 hospitals, 781 dispensaries, 254 orphanages, 29 printing presses and 55 periodicals; denial of the free exercise of religion to all the faithful; the detention of hundreds of priests, religious and lay persons in jail and their employment in slave labor; the proscription of the Legion of Mary and other Catholic Action groups for "counter-revolutionary activities" and "crimes against the new China"; complete outlawing of missionary work and pastoral activity. The government formally established a Patriotic Association of Chinese Catholics, independent of the Holy See, in July, 1957. Relatively few priests and lay persons joined the organization, which was condemned by Pius XII in 1958. The government formed the nucleus of what it hoped might become the hierarchy of a schismatic Chinese church in 1958 by "electing" 26 bishops and having them consecrated validly but illicitly between Apr. 13, 1958, and Nov. 15, 1959, without the permission or approval of the Holy See. Additional bishops were subsequently ordained. Activity of the Patriotic Association and official policy of the government are in direct opposition to any connection between the (Underground) Church in China and the Vatican. Growth of the underground Church has been reported for several years despite government actions to the contrary. (See News Events.)

## Colombia*

*Archd., 12; dioc., 40; prel., 2; v.a., 8; p.a., 5; mil. ord., card., 1; abp., 15; bp., 74; parishes, 3,094; priests, 6,800 (4,678 dioc., 2,122 rel.); p.d., 111;*

sem., 4,285; bros., 790; srs., 18,151; catechists, 3,757; bap., 797,653; Caths., 31,727,000 (91.9%); tot. pop., 34,520,000.

Republic in northwest South America, with Atlantic and Pacific borders; capital, Bogota. Evangelization began in 1508. The first two dioceses were established in 1534. Vigorous development of the Church was reported by the middle of the 17th century despite obstacles posed by the multiplicity of Indian languages, government interference through patronage rights and otherwise, rivalry among religious orders and the small number of native priests among the predominantly Spanish clergy. Some persecution, including the confiscation of property, followed in the wake of the proclamation of independence from Spain in 1819. The Church was affected in many ways by the political and civil unrest of the nation through the 19th century and into the 20th. Various aspects of Church-state relations are regulated by a concordat with the Vatican signed July 12, 1973, and ratified July 2, 1975. Guerrilla warfare aimed at Marxist-oriented radical social reform and redistribution of land, along with violence related to drug traffic, has plagued the country since the 1960s, posing problems for the Church which backed reforms but rejected actions of radical groups.

## Comoros
A.a., 1; parishes, 2; priests, 2 (rel.); bro., 1; srs., 7; catechists, 6; bap., 11; Caths.,6,000; tot. pop., 630,000. (AD)

Consists of main islands of Grande Comore, Anjouan and Moheli in Indian Ocean off southeast coast of Africa; capital, Moroni, Grande Comore Island. Former French territory; independent (July 6, 1975). The majority of the population is Muslim. An apostolic administration was established in 1975.

## Congo*
Archd., 1; dioc., 5; abp., 1; bp., 5; parishes, 96; priests, 246 (155 dioc., 91 rel.); sem., 187; bros., 57; srs.,264; catechists, 2,850; bap.,44,900; Caths., 1,111,000 (44%); tot. pop., 2,520,000.

Republic (independent since 1960) in west central Africa; former French possession; capital, Brazzaville. Small-scale missionary work with little effect preceded modern evangelization dating from the 1880s. The work of the Church has been affected by political instability, Communist influence, tribalism and hostility to foreigners. The hierarchy was established in 1955.

## Cook Islands
Dioc., 1; bp., 1; parishes, 14; priests, 9 (4 dioc., 5 rel.); bros., 4; srs., 7; bap., 99; Caths., 3,000; tot. pop., 18,000.

Self-governing territory of New Zealand, an archipelago of small islands in Oceania. Evangelization by Protestant missionaries started in 1821, resulting in a predominantly Protestant population. The first Catholic missionary work began in 1894. The hierarchy was established in 1966.

## Costa Rica*
Archd., 1; dioc., 5; v.a., 1; abp., 2; bp., 7; parishes, 227; priests, 664 (428 dioc., 236 rel.); sem.,

279; bros., 45; srs., 911; bap., 81,917; Caths., 2,774,000 (90.3%); tot. pop., 3,070,000.

Republic in Central America; capital, San Jose. Evangelization began about 1520 and proceeded by degrees to real development and organization of the Church in the 17th and 18th centuries. The republic became independent in 1838. Twelve years later church jurisdiction also became independent with the establishment of a bishopric in the present capital.

## Côte d'Ivoire (Ivory Coast)*
Archd., 4; dioc., 10; card., 1; abp., 4; bp., 11; parishes, 215; priests, 603 (313 dioc., 290 rel.); p.d., 2; sem., 429; bros., 190; srs., 711; catechists, 11,353; bap., 45,999; Caths., 1,837,000 (13.4%); tot. pop., 13,700,000.

Republic in western Africa; capital, Abidjan (de facto); Yamoussouka (official). The Holy Ghost Fathers began systematic evangelization in 1895. The first native priests from the area were ordained in 1934. The hierarchy was set up in 1955; the first native cardinal (Bernard Yago) was named in 1983. Three ecclesiastical provinces were established in 1995.

## Croatia*
Archd., 4; dioc., 7; card., 1; abp., 7; bp., 16; parishes, 1,562; priests, 2,208 (1,425 dioc., 783 rel.); sem., 470; bros., 92; srs., 3,805; bap., 58,634; Caths., 3,750,000 (83%); tot. pop., 4,500,000.

Independent (1991) republic in southeastern Europe; capital Zagreb; formerly a constituent republic of Yugoslavia. (See Yugoslavia for earlier history and events following communist takeover.) Christianity was introduced in the seventh century. Activity of the Church since 1992 has been adversely affected by civil war. Pope John Paul II visited the country Sept. 10 to 11, 1994.

## Cuba*
Archd., 2; dioc. (1996), 8; card., 1; abp., 2; bp., 10; parishes, 247; priests, 234 (121 dioc., 113 rel.); p.d., 31; sem., 60; bros., 24; srs., 411; bap., 78,752; Caths. 4,545,000 (41.5%); tot. pop., 10,960,000.

Republic under Communist dictatorship, south of Florida; capital, Havana. Effective evangelization began about 1514, leading eventually to the predominance of Catholicism on the island. Native vocations to the priesthood and religious life were unusually numerous in the 18th century but declined in the 19th. The island became independent of Spain in 1902 following the Spanish-American War. Fidel Castro took control of the government Jan. 1, 1959. In 1961, after Cuba was officially declared a socialist state, the University of Villanueva was closed, 350 Catholic schools were nationalized and 136 priests expelled. A greater number of foreign priests and religious had already left the country. Freedom of worship and religious instruction are limited to church premises and no social action is permitted the Church, which survives under surveillance. A new constitution approved in 1976 guaranteed freedom of conscience but restricts its exercise. Appeals by the bishops for dialogue with the government to improve church-state relations have had little, if any, effect. Despite some recent surfacing and increase of church activity, the Church is still operating in a limited manner.

## Cyprus*

*Archd., 1 (Maronite); abp., 1; parishes, 13; priests, 18 (6 dioc., 12 rel.); bros., 5; srs., 40; bap., 91; Caths., 11,000 (1.5%); tot. pop., 730,000.*

Republic in the eastern Mediterranean; capital, Nicosia. Christianity was preached on the island in apostolic times and has a continuous history from the fourth century. Latin and Eastern rites were established but the latter prevailed and became Orthodox after the schism of 1054. Roman and Orthodox Christians have suffered under many governments, particularly during the period of Turkish dominion from late in the 16th to late in the 19th centuries, and from differences between the 80 per cent Greek majority and the Turkish minority. About 80 per cent of the population are Orthodox. Catholics are under the jurisdiction of the archdiocese of Cyprus (of the Maronites).

## Czech Republic*

*Archd., 2; dioc. (1996), 6; ap. ex. (1996), 1; card., 1; abp., 1; bp., 10; parishes, 3,107; priests, 1,845 (1,279 dioc., 566 rel.); p.d., 106; sem., 375; bros., 127; srs., 2,312; bap., 36,561; Caths., 4,088,511 (39.6%); tot. pop., 10,307,296. (Population figures are from 1996 Annuario Pontificio.)*

Independent state (Jan. 1, 1993); formerly part of Czechoslovakia; capital, Prague. The martyrdom of Prince Wenceslaus in 929 triggered the spread of Christianity. Prague has had a continuous history as a diocese since 973. A parish system was organized about the 13th century in Bohemia and Moravia, the land of the Czechs. Mendicant orders strengthened relations with the Latin rite in the 13th century. In the next century the teachings of John Hus in Bohemia brought trouble to the Church in the forms of schism and heresy, and initiated a series of religious wars which continued for decades following his death at the stake in 1415. Church property was confiscated, monastic communities were scattered and even murdered, ecclesiastical organization was shattered, and so many of the faithful joined the Bohemian Brethren that Catholics became a minority. The Reformation, with the way prepared by the Hussites and cleared by other factors, affected the Church seriously. A Counter Reformation got under way in the 1560s and led to a gradual restoration through the thickets of Josephinism, the Enlightenment, liberalism and troubled politics. In 1920, two years after the establishment of the Republic of Czechoslovakia, the schismatic Czechoslovak Church was proclaimed at Prague, resulting in numerous defections from the Catholic Church in the Czech region. In Ruthenia, 112,000 became Russian Orthodox between 1918 and 1930. (For the situation of the Church during the long years of communist domination, see Czechoslovakia, below.)

## Czechoslovakia

*The Czech and Slovak Federal Republic, formed in 1918, was dissolved Jan. 1, 1993, and became two independent states. (See separate entries in this section for Czech Republic and Slovakia for early history of the Church and statistics.) Information below covers the situation of the Church during the long period of communist domination.*

Vigorous persecution of the Church began in Slovakia before the end of World War II when Communists mounted a 1944 offensive against bishops, priests and religious. In 1945, church schools were nationalized, youth organizations were disbanded, the Catholic press was curtailed, the training of students for the priesthood was seriously impeded. Msgr. Josef Tiso, president of the Slovak Republic, was tried for "treason" in December, 1946, and was executed the following April. Between 1945 and 1949 approximately 10 percent of the Slovak population spent some time in jail or a concentration camp. Persecution began later in the Czech part of the country, following the accession of the Gottwald regime to power early in 1948. Hospitals, schools and property were nationalized and Catholic organizations were liquidated. A puppet organization was formed in 1949 to infiltrate the Church and implement an unsuccessful plan for establishing a schismatic church. In the same year Archbishop Josef Beran of Prague was placed under house arrest. (He left the country in 1965, was made a cardinal, and died in 1969 in Rome.) A number of theatrical trials of bishops and priests were staged in 1950. All houses of religious were taken over between March, 1950, and the end of 1951. Pressure was applied on the clergy and faithful of the Eastern Rite in Slovakia to join the Orthodox Church. Diplomatic relations with the Holy See were terminated in 1950. About 3,000 priests were deprived of liberty in 1951 and attempts were made to force "peace priests" on the people. In 1958 it was reported that 450 to 500 priests were in jail; an undisclosed number of religious and Byzantine-Rite priests had been deported; two bishops released from prison in 1956 were under house arrest; one bishop was imprisoned at Leopoldov and two at the Mirov reformatory. In Bohemia, Moravia and Silesia, five of six dioceses were without ruling bishops; one archbishop and two bishops were active but subject to "supervision"; most of the clergy refused to join the "peace priests." In 1962 only three bishops were permitted to attend the first session of the Second Vatican Council. From January to October, 1968, church-state relations improved to some extent under the Dubcek regime: a number of bishops were reinstated; some 3,000 priests were engaged in the pastoral ministry, although 1,500 were still barred from priestly work; the "peace priests" organization was disbanded; the Eastern-Rite Church, with 147 parishes, was reestablished. In 1969, an end was ordered to rehabilitation trials for priests and religious, but no wholesale restoration of priests and religious to their proper ways of life and work was in prospect. In 1972, the government ordered the removal of nuns from visible but limited apostolates to farms and mental hospitals where they would be out of sight. In 1973, the government allowed the ordination of four bishops — one in the Czech region and three in the Slovak region. Reports from Slovakia late in the same year stated that authorities there had placed severe restrictions on the education of seminarians and the functioning of priests. Government restrictions continued to hamper the work of priests and nuns. Signatories of the human rights declaration called Charter 77 were particular objects of government repression and retribution. In December, 1983, the Czechoslovakian foreign minister met with the Pope at Vatican City; it was the first meeting of a high Czech official with a pope since the country came under communist rule. In 1984, two Vatican officials visited Czechoslovakia. Despite the communication breakthrough, there was no indication of any change of policy toward the Church in the country. In 1988, three new bishops were ordained in Czechoslovakia, the first since 1973. Three more episcopal appointments were made in 1989. The communist government fell in late 1989. In 1990: bishops were appointed to fill vacant sees; announcement was made of the reestablishment of diplomatic relations between the Holy See and Czechoslovakia after 40 years, and Pope John Paul II paid a historic visit to the country. (See Czech Republic; Slovakia.)

## Denmark*
*Dioc., 1; bp., 2; parishes, 50; priests, 93 (39 dioc., 54 rel.); p.d., 1; sem., 2; bros., 4; srs., 320; bap., 661; Caths., 32,000 (.6%); tot. pop., 5,200,000.*

Includes the Faroe Islands and Greenland. Constitutional monarchy in northwestern Europe, north of Germany; capital, Copenhagen. Christianity was introduced in the ninth century and the first diocese for the area was established in 831. Intensive evangelization and full-scale organization of the Church occurred from the second half of the 10th century and ushered in a period of great development and influence in the 12th and 13th centuries. Decline followed, resulting in almost total loss to the Church during the Reformation when Lutheranism became the national religion. Catholics were considered foreigners until religious freedom was legally assured in 1849. Modern development of the Church dates from the second half of the 19th century. About 95 per cent of the population are Evangelical Lutherans.

## Djibouti
*Dioc., 1; bp., 1; parishes, 5; priests, 6 (1 dioc., 5 rel.); bros., 6; srs., 18; bap., 27; Caths., 8,000 (1.4%); tot. pop., 570,000. (AD)*

Formerly French Territory of Afars and Issas. Independent (1977) republic in east Africa, on the Gulf of Aden; capital, Djibouti. Christianity in the area, formerly part of Ethiopia, antedated but was overcome by the Arab invasion of 1200. Modern evangelization, begun in the latter part of the 19th century, had meager results. The hierarchy was established in 1955.

## Dominica*
*Dioc., 1; bp., 1; parishes, 17; priests, 37 (5 dioc., 32 rel.); bros., 5; srs., 31; catechists, 390; bap., 1,054; Caths., 57,000 (79%); tot. pop., 72,000.*

Independent (Nov. 3, 1978) state in Caribbean; capital, Roseau. Evangelization began in 1642.

## Dominican Republic*
*Archd., 2; dioc., 7; mil. ord.; card., 1; abp., 3; bp., 11; parishes, 330; priests, 642 (260 dioc., 382 rel.); p.d., 157; sem., 551; bros., 60; srs., 1,523; bap., 106,924; Caths., 7,098,000 (91.3%); tot. pop., 7,770,000.*

Caribbean republic on the eastern two-thirds of the island of Hispaniola, bordering on Haiti; capital, Santo Domingo. Evangelization began shortly after discovery by Columbus in 1492 and church organization, the first in America, was established by 1510. Catholicism is the state religion.

## Ecuador*
*Archd., 4; dioc., 10; prel., 1; v.a., 7; p.a., 1; mil. ord.; card., 1; abp., 5; bp., 30; parishes, 1,041; priests, 1,719 (903 dioc., 816 rel.); p.d., 37; sem., 741; bros., 389; srs., 4,419; catechists, 3,171; bap., 251,194; Caths., 10,488,000 (93.4%); tot. pop., 11,220,000.*

Republic on the west coast of South America, includes Gallapogos Islands; capital, Quito. Evangelization began in the 1530s. The first diocese was established in 1545. A synod, one of the first in the Americas, was held in 1570 or 1594. Multiphased missionary work, spreading from the coastal and mountain regions into the Amazon, made the Church highly influential during the colonial period. The Church was practically enslaved by the constitution enacted in 1824, two years after Ecuador, as part of Colombia, gained independence from Spain. Some change for the better took place later in the century, but from 1891 until the 1930s the Church labored under serious liabilities imposed by liberal governments. The concordat of 1866 was violated; foreign missionaries were barred from the country for some time; the property of religious orders was confiscated; education was taken over by the state; traditional state support was refused; legal standing was denied; attempts to control church offices were made through insistence on rights of patronage. A period of harmony and independence for the Church began after agreement was reached on Church-state relations in 1937.

## Egypt*
*Patriarchates, 2 (Alexandria for the Copts and for the Melkites); dioc., 9; v.a., 1; patriarch, 1; abp., 1; bp., 13; parishes, 225; priests, 378 (214 dioc., 164 rel.); p.d., 4; sem., 158; bros., 73; srs., 1,439; bap., 2,686; Caths., 213,000 (.36%); tot. pop., 58,330,000.*

Arab Republic in northeastern Africa, bordering on the Mediterranean; capital, Cairo. Alexandria was the influential hub of a Christian community established by the end of the second century; it became a patriarchate and the center of the Coptic Church, and had great influence on the spread of Christianity in various parts of Africa. Monasticism developed from desert communities of hermits in the third and fourth centuries. Arianism was first preached in Egypt in the 320s. In the fifth century, the Coptic church went Monophysite through failure to accept doctrine formulated by the Council of Chalcedon in 451 with respect to the two natures of Christ. The country was thoroughly Arabized after 640 and was under the rule of Ottoman Turks from 1517 to 1798. English influence was strong during the 19th century. A monarchy established in 1922 lasted about 30 years, ending with the proclamation of a republic in 1953-54. By that time Egypt had become the leader of pan-Arabism against Israel. It waged two unsuccessful wars against Israel in 1948-49 and 1967. Between 1958 and 1961 it was allied with

Syria and Yemen, in the United Arab Republic. In 1979, following negotiations initiated by Pres. Anwar el-Sadat in 1977, Egypt and Israel signed a peace agreement. Islam, the religion of some 90 percent of the population, is the state religion.

## El Salvador*

*Archd., 1; dioc., 7; mil. ord.; abp., 1; bp., 11; parishes, 269; priests, 525 (337 dioc., 188 rel.); p.d., 2; sem., 323; bros., 119; srs., 1,209; bap., 93,948; Cath., 5,278,000 (93.6%); tot. pop., 5,640,000.*

Republic in Central America; capital, San Salvador. Evangelization affecting the whole territory followed Spanish occupation in the 1520s. The country was administered by the captaincy general of Guatemala until 1821 when independence from Spain was declared and it was annexed to Mexico. El Salvador joined the Central American Federation in 1825, decreed its own independence in 1841 and became a republic formally in 1856. Church efforts in recent years to achieve social justice have resulted in persecution of the Church. Archbishop Oscar Romero of San Salvador, peace advocate and outspoken champion of human rights, was murdered Mar. 24, 1980, while celebrating Mass. Six Jesuits were assassinated Nov. 16, 1989, at Central American University in El Salvador.

## England*

*Archd., 4; dioc., 15; ap. ex., 1; mil. ord. (Great Britain); card., 1; abp., 3; bp., 37; parishes, 2,316; priests, 5,122 (3,521 dioc., 1,601 rel.); newly ordained priests, 65; p.d., 318; sem., 287; bros., 513; srs., 7,982; bap., 72,679; Caths., 4,035,000 (8.2%); tot. pop., 48,675,000. (1996 Annuario Pontificio.)*

Center of the United Kingdom of Great Britain (England, Scotland, Wales) and Northern Ireland, off the northwestern coast of Europe; capital, London. The arrival of St. Augustine of Canterbury and a band of monks in 597 marked the beginning of evangelization. Real organization of the Church took place some years after the Synod of Whitby, held in 663. Heavy losses were sustained in the wake of the Danish invasion in the 780s, but recovery starting from the time of Alfred the Great and dating especially from the middle of the 10th century led to Christianization of the whole country and close Church-state relations. The Norman Conquest of 1066 opened the Church in England to European influence. The 13th century was climactic, but decline had already set in by 1300 when the country had an all-time high of 17,000 religious. In the 14th century, John Wycliff presaged the Protestant Reformation. Henry VIII, failing in 1529 to gain annulment of his marriage to Catherine of Aragon, refused to acknowledge papal authority over the Church in England, had himself proclaimed its head, suppressed all houses of religious, and persecuted persons — Sts. Thomas More and John Fisher, among others — for not subscribing to the Oath of Supremacy and Act of Succession. He held the line on other-than-papal doctrine, however, until his death in 1547. Doctrinal aberrations were introduced during the reign of Edward VI (1547-53), through the Order of Communion, two books of Common Prayer, and the Articles of the Established Church. Mary Tudor's attempted Catholic restoration (1553-58) was a disaster, resulting in the deaths of more than 300 Protestants. Elizabeth (1558-1603) firmed up the Established Church with formation of a hierarchy, legal enactments and multi-phased persecution. One hundred and 11 priests and 62 lay persons were among the casualties of persecution during the underground Catholic revival which followed the return to England of missionary priests from France and The Lowlands. Several periods of comparative toleration ensued after Elizabeth's death. The first of several apostolic vicariates was established in 1685; this form of church government was maintained until the restoration of the hierarchy and diocesan organization in 1850. The revolution of 1688 and subsequent developments to about 1781 subjected Catholics to a wide variety of penal laws and disabilities in religious, civic and social life. The situation began to improve in 1791, and from 1801 Parliament frequently considered proposals for the repeal of penal laws against Catholics. The Act of Emancipation restored citizenship rights to Catholics in 1829. Restrictions remained in force for some time afterwards, however, on public religious worship and activity. The hierarchy was restored in 1850. Since then the Catholic Church, existing side by side with the Established Churches of England and Scotland, has followed a general pattern of growth and development.

## Equatorial Guinea*

*Archd., 1; dioc., 2; abp., 1; bp., 2; parishes, 49; priests, 99 (49 dioc., 50 rel.); p.d. 1; sem., 50; bros., 35; srs., 202; catechists, 1,943; bap., 15,611; Caths., 363,000 (93%); tot. pop., 390,000.*

Republic on the west coast of Africa, consisting of Rio Muni on the mainland and the islands of Bioko (formerly Fernando Po) and Annobon in the Gulf of Guinea: capital, Malabo (Santa Isabel). Evangelization began in 1841. The country became independent of Spain in 1968. The Church was severely repressed during the 11-year rule of Pres. Macias (Masie) Nguema. Developments since his overthrow (August, 1979) indicated some measure of improvement. An ecclesiastical province was established in October, 1982.

## Eritrea*

*Dioc., 3; bp., 4; parishes, 145; priests, 288 (67 dioc., 221 rel); p.d., 5; sem., 121; bros., 37; srs., 388; bap., 3,205; Caths., 114,000 (3%); tot. pop., 3,470,000.*

Independent state (May 24, 1993) in northeast Africa; formerly a province of Ethiopia. Christianity was introduced in the fourth century. Population is evenly divided between Christians and Muslims. Catholics form a small minority; most of the population is Orthodox Christian or Muslim.

## Estonia*

*A.a., 1; abp., 1 (nuncio is apostolic administrator); parishes, 4; priests, 5 (2 dioc., 3 rel); sem., 4; srs., 9; bap., 90; Caths., 5,000; tot. pop., 1,600,000.*

Independent (1991) Baltic republic; capital, Tallinn. (Forcibly absorbed by the U.S.S.R. in 1940; it regained independence in 1991.) Catholicism was introduced in the 11th and 12th centuries. Jurisdiction over the area was made directly subject to the Holy

See in 1215. Lutheran penetration was general in the Reformation period and Russian Orthodox influence was strong from early in the 18h century until 1917 when independence was attained. The first of several apostolic administrators was appointed in 1924. The small Catholic community was hard hit during the 1940-91 Soviet occupation (not recognized by the Holy See or the United States).

## Ethiopia*
*Archd., 1; dioc., 1; v.a., 5; p.a., 1; card., 1; abp., 1; bp., 4; parishes, 164; priests, 343 (132 dioc., 211 rel.); p.d., 1; sem., 257; bros., 61; srs., 709; bap., 19,725; Caths., 334,000 (.64%); tot. pop., 51,430,000.*

People's republic in northeast Africa; capital, Addis Ababa. The country was evangelized by missionaries from Egypt in the fourth century and had a bishop by about 340. Following the lead of its parent body, the Egyptian (Coptic) Church, the Church in the area succumbed to the Monophysite heresy in the sixth century. Catholic influence was negligible for centuries. An ordinariate for the Ethiopian Rite was established in Eritrea in 1930. An apostolic delegation was set up in Addis Ababa in 1937 and several jurisdictions were organized, some under the Congregation for the Oriental Churches and others under the Congregation for the Evangelization of Peoples. The first Ethiopian cardinal (Abp. Paulos Tzadua of Addis Ababa) was named in 1985.

## Falkland Islands
*P.a., 1; parish, 1; priests, 2 (rel.); bap., 6; Caths., 550; tot. pop., 4,100. (1996 Annuario Pontificio.)*

British colony off the southern tip of South America; capital, Port Stanley. The islands are called Islas Malvinas by Argentina which also claims sovereignty.

## Faroe Islands
*Parish, 1; p.d., 1; srs., 8; bap., 2; Caths., 100; tot. pop., 48,000.*

Self-governing island group in North Atlantic; Danish possession. Under ecclesiastical jurisdiction of Copenhagen diocese.

## Fiji*
*Archd., 1; abp., 1; parishes, 34; priests, 98 (28 dioc., 70 rel.); sem., 65; bros., 62; srs., 172; bap., 1,972; Caths., 77,000 (9.8%); tot. pop., 787,000.*

Independent island group (100 inhabited) in the southwest Pacific; capital, Suva. Marist missionaries began work in 1844 after Methodism had been firmly established. A prefecture apostolic was organized in 1863. The hierarchy was established in 1966.

## Finland*
*Dioc., 1; bp., 1; parishes, 7; priests, 21 (5 dioc., 16 rel.); p.d., 2; sem., 1; srs., 38; bap., 163; Caths., 6,000 (.1%); tot. pop., 5,090,000.*

Republic in northern Europe; capital, Helsinki. Swedes evangelized the country in the 12th century. The Reformation swept the country, resulting in the prohibition of Catholicism in 1595, general reorganization of ecclesiastical life and affairs, and dominance of the Evangelical Lutheran Church. Catholics were given religious liberty in 1781 but missionaries and conversions were forbidden by law. The first Finnish priest since the Reformation was ordained in 1903 in Paris. A vicariate apostolic for Finland was erected in 1920 (made a diocese in 1955). A law on religious liberty, enacted in 1923, banned the foundation of monasteries.

## France*
*Archd., 19; dioc., 75; prel., 1; ap. ex., 1; ord., 1; mil. ord.; card., 5; abp., 25; bp., 151; parishes, 33,342; priests, 29,503 (22,860 dioc., 6,643 rel.); p.d., 1,018; sem., 1,601; bros., 4,168; srs., 58,293; bap., 424,561; Caths., 47,683,000 (82.6%); tot. pop., 57,750,000.*

Republic in western Europe; capital, Paris. Christianity was known around Lyons by the middle of the second century. By 250 there were 30 bishoprics. The hierarchy reached a fair degree of organization by the end of the fourth century. Vandals and Franks subsequently invaded the territory and caused barbarian turmoil and doctrinal problems because of their Arianism. The Frankish nation was converted following the baptism of Clovis about 496. Christianization was complete by some time in the seventh century. From then on the Church, its leaders and people, figured in virtually every important development — religious, cultural, political and social — through the periods of the Carolingians, feudalism, the Middle Ages and monarchies to the end of the 18th century. The great University of Paris became one of the intellectual centers of the 13th century. Churchmen and secular rulers were involved with developments surrounding the Avignon residence of the popes and curia from 1309 until near the end of the 14th century and with the disastrous Western Schism that followed. Strong currents of Gallicanism and conciliarism ran through ecclesiastical and secular circles in France; the former was an ideology and movement to restrict papal control of the Church in the country, the latter sought to make the pope subservient to a general council. Calvinism invaded the country about the middle of the 16th century and won a strong body of converts. Jansenism with its rigorous spirit and other aberrations appeared in the next century, to be followed by the highly influential Enlightenment. The Revolution which started in 1789 and was succeeded by the Napoleonic period completely changed the status of the Church, taking a toll of numbers by persecution and defection and disenfranchising the Church in practically every way. Throughout the 19th century the Church was caught up in the whirl of imperial and republican developments and made the victim of official hostility, popular indifference and liberal opposition. In this century, the Church has struggled with problems involving the heritage of the Revolution and its aftermath, the alienation of intellectuals, liberalism, the estrangement of the working classes because of the Church's former identification with the ruling class, and the massive needs of contemporary society.

## French Guiana
*Dioc., 1; bp., 1; parishes, 26; priests, 29 (7 dioc., 22 rel.); p.d., 4; bros., 2; srs., 86; bap., 1,823; Caths., 115,000 (82%); tot. pop., 140,000. (AD)*

French overseas department on the northeast coast of South America; capital, Cayenne. Catholicism was introduced in the 17th century. The Cayenne diocese was established in 1956.

## French Polynesia

*Archd., 1; dioc., 1; abp., 1; bp., 2; parishes, 85; priests, 34 (15 dioc., 19 rel.); p.d., 14; sem., 13; bros., 48; srs., 68; bap., 1,553; Caths., 83,000 (39%); tot. pop., 210,000. (AD)*

French overseas territory in the southern Pacific, including Tahiti and the Marquesas Islands; capital, Papeete. The first phase of evangelization in the Marquesas Islands, begun in 1838, resulted in 216 baptisms in 10 years. A vicariate was organized in 1848 but real progress was not made until after the baptism of native rulers in 1853. Persecution caused missionaries to leave the islands several times. By the 1960s, more than 95 per cent of the population was Catholic. Isolated attempts to evangelize Tahiti were made in the 17th and 18th centuries. Two Picpus Fathers began missionary work in 1831. A vicariate was organized in 1848. By 1908, despite the hindrances of Protestant opposition, disease and other factors, the Church had firm roots.

## Gabon*

*Archd., 1; dioc., 3; abp., 1; bp., 3; parishes, 75; priests, 89 (25 dioc., 64 rel.); p.d., 1; sem., 51; bros., 25; srs., 156; catechists, 1,236; bap., 8,770; Caths., 668,000 (52%); tot. pop., 1,280,000.*

Republic on the west coast of central Africa; capital Libreville. Sporadic missionary effort took place before 1881 when effective evangelization began. The hierarchy was established in 1955.

## The Gambia*

*Dioc., 1; bp., 1; parishes, 13; priests, 26 (8 dioc., 18 rel.); sem., 14; bros., 12; srs., 54; bap., 1,357; Caths., 25,000 (2%); tot. pop., 1,080,000.*

Republic (1970) on the northwest coast of Africa, capital, Banjul. Christianity was introduced by Portuguese explorers in the 15th century; effective evangelization began in 1822. The country was under the jurisdiction of a vicariate apostolic until 1931. The hierarchy was established in 1957.

## Georgia*

*A.a., 1; parishes, 28; priests, 10 (2 dioc., 8 rel); sem., 1; srs., 13; Caths., 100,000 (1.8%); tot. pop., 5,450,000*

Independent (1991) state in the Caucasus; former Soviet republic; capital, Tbilisi. Christianity came to the area under Roman influence and, according to tradition, was spread through the efforts of St. Nino (or Christiana), a maiden who was brought as a captive to the country and is venerated as its apostle. The apostolic administration of the Caucusus (with seat in Georgia) was established in December, 1993, for Latin-rite Catholics of Armenia, Azerbaijan and Georgia.

## Germany*

*Archd., 7; dioc., 20; ap. ex., 1; mil. ord.; card., 6; abp., 8; bp., 91; parishes, 12,379; priests, 21,132 (16,224 dioc., 4,908 rel.); p.d., 1,755; sem., 1,919;*

*bros., 2,132; srs., 45,796; bap., 274,952; Caths., 28,323,000 (34.8%); tot. pop., 81,410,000.*

Country in northern Europe; capital, Berlin; seat of government, Bonn. From 1949-90 it was partitioned into the Communist German Democratic Republic in the East (capital, East Berlin) and the German Federal Republic in the West (capital, Bonn). Christianity was introduced in the third century, if not earlier. Trier, which became a center for missionary activity, had a bishop by 400. Visigoth invaders introduced Arianism in the fifth century but were converted in the seventh century by the East Franks, Celtic and other missionaries. St. Boniface, the apostle of Germany, established real ecclesiastical organization in the eighth century. The Church had great influence during the Carolingian period. Bishops from that time onward began to act in dual roles as pastors and rulers, a state of affairs which led inevitably to confusion and conflict in Church-state relations and perplexing problems of investiture. The Church developed strength and vitality through the Middle Ages but succumbed to abuses which antedated and prepared the ground for the Reformation. Luther's actions from 1517 made Germany a confessional battleground. Religious strife continued until conclusion of the Peace of Westphalia at the end of the Thirty Years' War in 1648. Nearly a century earlier the Peace of Augsburg (1555) had been designed, without success, to assure a degree of tranquillity by recognizing the legitimacy of different religious confessions in different states, depending on the decisions of princes. The implicit principle that princes should control the churches emerged in practice into the absolutism and Josephinism of subsequent years. St. Peter Canisius and his fellow Jesuits spearheaded a Counter Reformation in the second half of the 16th century. Before the end of the century, however, 70 per cent of the population of north and central Germany were Lutheran. Calvinism also had established a strong presence. The Church gained internal strength in a defensive position. Through much of the 19th century, however, its influence was eclipsed by Protestant intellectuals and other influences. It suffered some impoverishment also as a result of shifting boundaries and the secularization of property shortly after 1800. It came under direct attack in the Kulturkampf of the 1870s but helped to generate the opposition which resulted in a dampening of the campaign of Bismarck against it. Despite action by Catholics on the social front and other developments, discrimination against the Church spilled over into the 20th century and lasted beyond World War I. Catholics in politics struggled with others to pull the country through numerous postwar crises. The dissolution of the Center Party, agreed to by the bishops in 1933 without awareness of the ultimate consequences, contributed negatively to the rise of Hitler to supreme power. Church officials protested the Nazi anti-Church and anti-Semitic actions, but to no avail. After World War II Christian leadership had much to do with the recovery of Western Germany. East Germany, gone Communist under Russian auspices, initiated a program of control and repression of the Church in 1948 and 1949. With no prospect of success for measures designed to split bishops, priests, religious and lay persons, the regime concentrated most of its attention on mind control, especially of the younger generation, by the elimination of religious schools, curtailment of freedom for religious instruction and formation, severe restriction of the religious press, and the substitution from the mid-50s of youth initiation and Communist ceremonies for the rites of baptism, confirmation, marriage, and funerals. Bishops were generally forbidden to travel outside the Republic. The number of priests decreased, partly because of reduced seminary enrollments ordered by the East German government. In 1973, the Vatican appointed three apostolic administrators and one auxiliary (all titular bishops) for the areas of three West German dioceses located in East Germany. The official reunification of Germany took place Oct. 3, 1990. The separate episcopal conferences for East and West Germany were merged to form one conference in November, 1990. In July, 1994, ecclesiastical jurisdictions in eastern Germany were reorganized. (See Index for 1996 papal visit.)

## Ghana*

*Archd., 3; dioc., 12; abp., 3; bp., 13; parishes, 263; priests, 776 (615 dioc., 161 rel.); p.d., 1; sem., 401; bros., 177; srs., 695; catechists, 4,136; bap., 38,525; Caths., 1,997,000 (11.8%); tot. pop., 16,940,000.*

Republic on the western coast of Africa, bordering on the Gulf of Guinea; capital, Accra. Priests visited the country in 1482, 11 years after discovery by the Portuguese, but missionary effort — hindered by the slave trade and other factors — was slight until 1880 when systematic evangelization began. A prefecture apostolic was set up in 1879. The hierarchy was established in 1950. Five new dioceses were established in 1995.

## Gibraltar

*Dioc., 1; bp., 1; parishes, 5; priests, 11 (dioc.); sem., 3; srs., 6; bap., 245; Caths., 23,000; tot. pop., 26,000.*

British dependency on the tip of the Spanish Peninsula on the Mediterranean. Evangelization took place after the Moors were driven out near the end of the 15th century. The Church was hindered by the British who acquired the colony in 1713. Most of the Catholics were, and are, Spanish and Italian immigrants and their descendants. A vicariate apostolic was organized in 1817. The diocese was erected in 1910.

## Greece*

*Archd., 4; dioc., 4; v.a., 1; ap. ex., 1; ord., 1; abp., 6; bp., 2; parishes, 65; priests, 95 (48 dioc., 47 rel.); sem., 5; bros., 38; srs., 136; bap., 652; Caths., 61,000 (.6%); tot. pop., 10,438,000.*

Republic in southeastern Europe on the Balkan Peninsula; capital, Athens. St. Paul preached the Gospel at Athens and Corinth on his second missionary journey and visited the country again on his third tour. Other Apostles may have passed through also. Two bishops from Greece attended the First Council of Nicaea. After the division of the Roman Empire, the Church remained Eastern in rite and later broke ties with Rome as a result of the schism of

1054. A Latin-Rite jurisdiction was set up during the period of the Latin Empire of Constantinople, 1204-1261, but crumbled afterwards. Unity efforts of the Council of Florence had poor results. The country now has Greek Catholic and Latin jurisdictions. The Greek Orthodox Church is predominant.

## Greenland (Kalaallit Nunaat)

*Parish, 1; priests, 2 (rel.); srs., 2; Caths., 100; tot. pop., 62,000.*

Danish island province northeast of North America; granted self rule in 1979; capital, Nuuk (Godthaab). Catholicism was introduced about 1000. The first diocese was established in 1124 and a line of bishops dated from then until 1537. The first known churches in the western hemisphere, dating from about the 11th century, were on Greenland; the remains of 19 have been unearthed. The departure of Scandinavians and spread of the Reformation reduced the Church to nothing. The Moravian Brethren evangelized the Eskimos from the 1720s to 1901. By 1930 the Danish Church — Evangelical Lutheran — was in full possession. Since 1930, priests have been in Greenland, which is part of the Copenhagen diocese.

## Grenada*

*Dioc., 1; bp., 1; parishes, 20; priests, 23 (7 dioc., 16 rel.); p.d., 3; sem., 1; bros., 3; srs., 35; catechists, 125; bap., 857; Caths., 53,000; tot. pop., 91,000.*

Independent island state in the West Indies; capital, St. George's.

## Guadeloupe

*Dioc., 1; bp., 2; parishes, 43; priests, 64 (46 dioc., 18 rel.); p.d., 3; sem., 5; bros., 2; srs., 255; catechists, 2,675; bap., 3,908; Caths., 380,000 (93%); tot. pop., 408,000 (AD).*

French overseas department in the Leeward Islands of the West Indies; capital, Basse-Terre. Catholicism was introduced in the islands in the 16th century.

## Guam

*Archd., 1; archbp., 1; parishes, 25; priests, 40 (26 dioc., 14 rel.); p.d., 7; sem., 5; bros., 5; srs., 130; bap., 2,563; Caths., 122,000; tot. pop., 142,000.*

Outlying area of U.S. in the southwest Pacific; capital, Agana. The first Mass was offered in the Mariana Islands in 1521. The islands were evangelized by the Jesuits, from 1668, and other missionaries. The first native Micronesian bishop was ordained in 1970. The Agana diocese, which had been a suffragan of San Francisco, was made a metropolitan see in 1984.

## Guatemala*

*Archd. (1996), 2; dioc., 8; prel., 1; v.a., 2; abp., 2; bp., 18; parishes, 390; priests, 835 (295 dioc., 540 rel.); p.d., 6; sem., 562; bros., 444; srs., 1,576; catechists, 2,310; bap., 325,723; Caths. 8,788,000 (85%); tot. pop. 10,320,000.*

Republic in Central America; capital, Guatemala City. Evangelization dates from the beginning of Spanish occupation in 1524. The first diocese, for all Central American territories administered by the captaincy general of Guatemala, was established in 1534. The country became independent in 1839, following annexation to Mexico in 1821, secession in 1823 and membership in the Central American Federation from 1825. In 1870, a government installed by a liberal revolution repudiated the concordat of 1853 and took active measures against the Church. Separation of Church and state was decreed; religious orders were suppressed and their property seized; priests and religious were exiled; schools were secularized. Full freedom was subsequently granted. In recent years, the bishops have repeatedly condemned political violence and social injustice which have created a crisis in the country. (See Index for 1996 papal visit.)

## Guinea*

*Archd., 1; dioc., 2; abp., 1; bp., 2; parishes, 35; priests, 67 (49 dioc., 18 rel.); sem., 30; bros., 12; srs., 77; bap., 3,054; Caths., 126,000 (2%); tot. pop., 6,500,000.*

Republic on the west coast of Africa; capital, Conakry. Occasional missionary work followed exploration by the Portuguese about the middle of the 15th century; organized effort dates from 1877. The hierarchy was established in 1955. Following independence from France in 1958, Catholic schools were nationalized, youth organizations banned and missionaries restricted. Foreign missionaries were expelled in 1967. Archbishop Tchidimbo of Conakry, sentenced to life imprisonment in 1971 on a charge of conspiring to overthrow the government, was released in August, 1979; he resigned his see. Private schools, suppressed by the government for more than 20 years, were again authorized in 1984.

## Guinea-Bissau*

*Dioc., 1; bp., 1; parishes, 28; priests, 68 (10 dioc., 58 rel.); p.d., 1; sem., 14; bros., 28; srs., 134; bap., 556; Caths., 81,000 (7.7%); tot. pop., 1,050,000.*

Formerly Portuguese Guinea. Independent state on the west coast of Africa; capital, Bissau. Catholicism was introduced in the second half of the 15th century but limited missionary work, hampered by the slave trade, had meager results. Missionary work in this century dates from 1933. A prefecture apostolic was established in 1955 (made a diocese in 1977).

## Guyana

*Dioc., 1; bp., 1; parishes, 30; priests, 37 (6 dioc., 31 rel.); sem., 1; bros., 2; srs., 40; catechists, 569; bap., 1,390; Caths., 87,000 (10.6%); tot. pop., 820,000.*

Republic on the northern coast of South America; capital, Georgetown. In 1899 the Catholic Church and other churches were given equal status with the Church of England and the Church of Scotland, which had sole rights up to that time. Most of the Catholics are Portuguese. The Georgetown diocese was established in 1956, 10 years before Guyana became independent of England. The first native bishop was appointed in 1971. Schools were nationalized in 1976. Increased government interference was reported in 1980-81.

## Haiti*

*Archd., 2; dioc., 7; abp., 2; bp., 9; parishes, 236; priests, 535 (320 dioc., 215 rel.); p.d., 1; sem., 223;*

*bros., 293; srs., 1,003; bap., 202,354; Caths., 6,133,000 (87.1%); tot. pop., 7,040,000.*

Caribbean republic on the western third of Hispaniola adjacent to the Dominican Republic; capital, Port-au-Prince. Evangelization followed discovery by Columbus in 1492. Capuchins and Jesuits did most of the missionary work in the 18th century. From 1804, when independence was declared, until 1860, the country was in schism. Relations were regularized by a concordat concluded in 1860, when an archdiocese and four dioceses were established. Factors hindering the development of the Church have been a shortage of native clergy, inadequate religious instruction and the prevalence of voodoo. Political upheavals in the 1960s had serious effects on the Church. In 1984, a new concordat was concluded replacing the one in effect since 1860. In October, 1994, Jean Bertrand Aristide, the democratically elected president, returned to his country after more than three years in exile.

## Honduras*

*Archd., 1; dioc., 6; abp., 1; bp., 7; parishes, 143; priests, 311 (120 dioc., 191 rel.); pd., 2; sem., 105; bros., 25; srs., 512; catechists, 655; bap., 61,137; Caths., 5,295,000 (91.7%); tot. pop., 5,770,000.*

Republic in Central America; capital, Tegucigalpa. Evangelization preceded establishment of the first diocese in the 16th century. Under Spanish rule and after independence from 1823, the Church held a favored position until 1880 when equal legal status was given to all religions. Harassment of priests and nuns working among peasants and Salvadoran refugees was reported in recent years.

## Hong Kong

*Dioc., 1; card., 1; bp., 1; parishes, 62; priests, 334 (77 dioc., 262 rel.); sem., 25; bros., 64; srs., 599; bap., 3,911; Caths., 257,000 (4.2%); tot. pop., 6,060,000.*

British crown colony at the mouth of the Canton River, adjacent to the southeast Chinese province of Kwangtung. Most of the territory, leased from China, is scheduled for return in 1997. A prefecture apostolic was established in 1841. Members of the Pontifical Institute for Foreign Missions began work there in 1858. The Hong Kong diocese was erected in 1946.

## Hungary*

*Archd., 4; dioc., 9; abb., 1; ap. ex., 1; mil. ord.; card., 1; abp., 4; bp., 20; parishes, 2,069; priests, 2,755 (2,134 dioc., 621 rel.); p.d., 26; sem., 474; bros., 139; srs., 2,086; bap., 68,481; Caths., 6,628,000 (64.6%); tot. pop., 10,260,000.*

Republic in east central Europe; capital, Budapest. The early origins of Christianity in the country, whose territory was subject to a great deal of change, is not known. Magyars accepted Christianity about the end of the 10th century. St. Stephen I (d. 1038) promoted its spread and helped to organize some of its historical dioceses. Bishops early became influential in politics as well as in the Church. For centuries the country served as a buffer for the Christian West against barbarians from the East, notably the Mongols in the 13th century. Religious orders, whose foundations started from the 1130s, provided the most effective missionaries, pastors and teachers. Outstanding for years were the Franciscans and Dominicans; the Jesuits were noted for their work in the Counter-Reformation from the second half of the 16th century onwards. Hussites and Waldensians prepared the way for the Reformation which struck at almost the same time as the Turks. The Reformation made considerable progress after 1526, resulting in the conversion of large numbers to Lutheranism and Calvinism by the end of the century. Most of them or their descendants returned to the Church later, but many Magyars remained staunch Calvinists. Turks repressed the churches, Protestant as well as Catholic, during a reign of 150 years but they managed to survive. Domination of the Church was one of the objectives of government policy during the reigns of Maria Theresa and Joseph II in the second half of the 18th century; their Josephinism affected Church-state relations until the first World War. More than 100,000 Eastern-Rite schismatics were reunited with Rome about the turn of the 18th century. Secularization increased in the second half of the 19th century, which also witnessed the birth of many new Catholic organizations and movements to influence life in the nation and the Church. Catholics were involved in the social chaos and anti-religious atmosphere of the years following World War I, struggling with their compatriots for religious as well as political survival. After World War II Communist strength, which had manifested itself with less intensity earlier in the century, was great long before it forced the legally elected president out of office in 1947 and imposed a Soviet type of constitution on the country in 1949. The campaign against the Church started with the disbanding of Catholic organizations in 1946. In 1948, "Caritas," the Catholic charitable organization, was taken over and all Catholic schools, colleges and institutions were suppressed. Interference in church administration and attempts to split the bishops preceded the arrest of Cardinal Mindszenty on Dec. 26, 1948, and his sentence to life imprisonment in 1949. (He was free for a few days during the unsuccessful uprising of 1956. He then took up residence at the U.S. Embassy in Budapest where he remained until September, 1971, when he was permitted to leave the country. He died in 1975 in Vienna.) In 1950, religious orders and congregations were suppressed and 10,000 religious were interned. At least 30 priests and monks were assassinated, jailed or deported. About 4,000 priests and religious were confined in jail or concentration camps. The government sponsored a national "Progressive Catholic" church and captive organizations for priests and "Catholic Action," which attracted only a small minority. Signs were clear in 1965 and 1966 that a 1964 agreement with the Holy See regarding episcopal appointments had settled nothing. Six bishops were appointed by the Holy See and some other posts were filled, but none of the prelates were free from government surveillance and harassment. Four new bishops were appointed by the Holy See in January and ordained in Budapest in February, 1969; three elderly prelates resigned their sees. Shortly thereafter, peace priests complained that the "too Roman" new bish-

ops would not deal with them. Talks between Vatican and Hungarian representatives in the 1970s resulted in the appointment of diocesan bishops to fill long-vacant sees. On Feb. 9, 1990, an accord was signed between the Holy See and Hungary reestablishing diplomatic relations. Pope John Paul II reorganized the ecclesiastical structure of the country in May, 1993.

## Iceland*

*Dioc., 1; bp., 1; parishes, 4; priests, 10 (6 dioc., 4 rel.); sem., 1; srs., 48; bap., 46; Caths., 3,000; tot. pop., 270,000.*

Island republic between Norway and Greenland; capital, Reykjavik. Irish hermits were there in the eighth century. Missionaries subsequently evangelized the island and Christianity was officially accepted about 1000. The first bishop was ordained in 1056. The Black Death had dire effects and spiritual decline set in during the 15th century. Lutheranism was introduced from Denmark between 1537 and 1552 and made the official religion. Some Catholic missionary work was done in the 19th century. Religious freedom was granted to the few Catholics in 1874. A vicariate was erected in 1929 (made a diocese in 1968).

## India*

*Patriarchate, 1 (titular of East Indies); major archbishopric (Syro-Malabar), 1; archd. (1996), 23; dioc. (1996), 106; card., 3; patr., 1; abp., 23; bp., 126; parishes, 7,091; priests, 16,317 (9,460 dioc., 6,857 rel.); p.d., 23; sem., 9,414; bros., 2,793; srs., 72,778; catechists, 32,638; bap., 348,602; Caths., 15,722,000 (1.7%); tot. pop. 918,570,000.*

Republic on the subcontinent of south central Asia; capital, New Delhi. Long-standing tradition credits the Apostle Thomas with the introduction of Christianity in the Kerala area. Evangelization followed the establishment of Portuguese posts and the conquest of Goa in 1510. Jesuits, Franciscans, Dominicans, Augustinians and members of other religious orders figured in the early missionary history. An archdiocese for Goa, with two suffragan sees, was set up in 1558. Five provincial councils were held between 1567 and 1606. The number of Catholics in 1572 was estimated to be 280,000. This figure rose to 800,000 in 1700 and declined to 500,000 in 1800. Missionaries had some difficulties with the British East India Co. which exercised virtual government control from 1757 to 1858. They also had trouble because of a conflict that developed between policies of the Portuguese government, which pressed its rights of patronage in episcopal and clerical appointments, and the Congregation for the Propagation of the Faith, which sought greater freedom of action in the same appointments. This struggle eventuated in the schism of Goa between 1838 and 1857. In 1886, when the number of Catholics was estimated to be one million, the hierarchy for India and Ceylon was restored. Jesuits contributed greatly to the development of Catholic education from the second half of the 19th century. A large percentage of the Catholic population is located around Goa and Kerala and farther south. The country is predominantly Hindu. So-called anti-conversion laws in effect in several states have had a restrictive effect on pastoral ministry and social service.

## Indonesia*

*Archd., 8; dioc., 26; mil. ord.; card., 1; abp., 8; bps., 35; parishes, 991; priests, 2,515 (763 dioc., 1,752 rel.); p.d., 17; sem., 2,504; bros., 1,089; srs., 6,498; catechists, 23,631; bap., 181,124; Caths., 5,194,000 (2.7%); tot. pop., 192,220,000.*

*Eastern Timor (former Portuguese Timor annexed by Indonesia in 1976): Dioc., 1; bp., 1; parishes, 30; priests, 85 (32 dioc., 53 rel.); sem., 125; bros., 29; srs., 207; catechists, 1,618; Caths., 709,000 (83%); tot. pop., 853,000. (International Fides Service.)*

Republic southeast of Asia, consisting of some 3,000 islands including Kalimantan (most of Borneo), Sulawesi (Celebes), Java, the Lesser Sundas, Moluccas, Sumatra, Timor and West Irian (Irian Jaya, western part of New Guinea); capital, Jakarta. Evangelization by the Portuguese began about 1511. St. Francis Xavier, greatest of the modern missionaries, spent some 14 months in the area. Christianity was strongly rooted in some parts of the islands by 1600. Islam's rise to dominance began at this time. The Dutch East Indies Co., which gained effective control in the 17th century, banned evangelization by Catholic missionaries for some time but Dutch secular and religious priests managed to resume the work. A vicariate of Batavia for all the Dutch East Indies was set up in 1841. About 90 per cent of the population is Muslim. The hierarchy was established in 1961.

## Iran*

*Archd., 4; dioc., 2; abp., 4; bp., 1; parishes, 19; priests, 17 (10 dioc., 7 rel.); sem., 1; bro., 1; srs., 31; bap., 103; Caths., 14,000 (.02%); tot. pop., 64,625,000.*

Islamic republic (Persia until 1935) in southwestern Asia, between the Caspian Sea and the Persian Gulf; capital, Teheran. Some of the earliest Christian communities were established in this area outside the (then) Roman Empire. They suffered persecution in the fourth century and were then cut off from the outside world. Nestorianism was generally professed in the late fifth century. Islam became dominant after 640. Some later missionary work was attempted but without success. Religious liberty was granted in 1834, but Catholics were the victims of a massacre in 1918. Islam is the religion of perhaps 98 per cent of the population. In 1964 the country had approximately 120,000 Orthodox Oriental Christians (not in union with Rome). Catholics belong to the Latin, Armenian and Chaldean rites.

## Iraq*

*Patriarchate, 1; archd., 9; dioc., 5; patriarch, 1; abp., 11; bp., 3; parishes, 92; priests, 130 (105 dioc., 25 rel.); p.d., 6; sem., 47; bros., 8; srs., 328; bap., 4,542; Caths., 652,000 (3.2%); tot. pop., 19,920,000.*

Republic in southwestern Asia, between Iran and Saudi Arabia; capital, Baghdad. Some of the earliest Christian communities were established in the area, whose history resembles that of Iran. Catho-

lics belong to the Armenian, Chaldean, Latin and Syrian rites; Chaldeans are most numerous. Islam is the religion of some 90 per cent of the population.

## Ireland*

*Archd., 4; dioc., 22; card., 1; abp., 5; bp., 42; parishes, 1,358; priests, 6,025 (3,621 dioc., 2,404 rel.); p.d., 1; sem., 657; bros., 1,187; srs., 10,406; bap., 59,789 (preceding figures include Northern Ireland); Catholics in Ireland were about 95% of the estimated total population of 3,550,000.*

Republic in the British Isles; capital, Dublin. St. Patrick, who is venerated as the apostle of Ireland, evangelized parts of the island for some years after the middle of the fifth century. Conversion of the island was not accomplished, however, until the seventh century or later. Celtic monks were the principal missionaries. The Church was organized along monastic lines at first, but a movement developed in the 11th century for the establishment of jurisdiction along episcopal lines. By that time many Roman usages had been adopted. The Church gathered strength during the period from the Norman Conquest of England to the reign of Henry VIII despite a wide variety of rivalries, wars, and other disturbances. Henry introduced an age of repression of the faith which continued for many years under several of his successors. The Irish suffered from proscription of the Catholic faith, economic and social disabilities, subjection to absentee landlords and a plantation system designed to keep them from owning property, and actual persecution which took an uncertain toll of lives up until about 1714. Some penal laws remained in force until emancipation in 1829. Nearly 100 years later Ireland was divided by two enactments which made Northern Ireland, consisting of six counties, part of the United Kingdom (1920) and gave dominion status to the Irish Free State, made up of the other 26 counties (1922). This state (Eire, in Gaelic) was proclaimed the Republic of Ireland in 1949. The Catholic Church predominates but religious freedom is guaranteed for all.

## Northern Ireland

*Tot. pop., 1,610,000; Catholics comprise more than one third. (Other statistics are included in Ireland).*

Part of the United Kingdom, it consists of six of the nine counties of Ulster in the northeast corner of Ireland; capital, Belfast. History is given under Ireland. (See Index for recent events.)

## Israel*

*Patriarchates, 2 (Jerusalem for Latins; patriarchal vicariate for Greek-Melkites); archd. (1996), 2; patriarch, 1; abp., 3; bp., 2; parishes, 82; priests, 427 (107 dioc., 320 rel.); p.d., 4; sem., 127; bros., 254; srs., 1,024; bap., 938; Caths., 89,000; tot. pop., 5,380,000.*

Parliamentary democracy in the Middle East, at the eastern end of the Mediterranean; capitals, Jerusalem and Tel Aviv (diplomatic). Israel was the birthplace of Christianity, the site of the first Christian communities. Some persecution was suffered in the early Christian era and again during the several hundred years of Roman control. Muslims conquered the territory in the seventh century and, except for the period of the Kingdom of Jerusalem established by Crusaders, remained in control most of the time up until World War I. The Church survived in the area, sometimes just barely, but it did not prosper greatly or show any notable increase in numbers. The British took over the protectorate of the area after World War I. Partition into Israel for the Jews and Palestine for the Arabs was approved by the United Nations in 1947. War broke out a year later with the proclamation of the Republic of Israel. The Isaelis won the war and 50 percent more territory than they had originally been ceded. War broke out again for six days in June, 1967, and in October, 1973, resulting in a Middle East crisis. Judaism is the faith professed by about 85 percent of the inhabitants; approximately one-third of them are considered observants. Most of the Arab minority are Muslims. Israeli-Palestinian relations took a turn for the better in 1994 as Palestinians gained a measure of freedom. Israeli-Holy See relations improved in 1994 with the implementation of full diplomatic relations.

## Italy*

*Patriarchate, 1; archd. 58 (37 are metropolitan sees); dioc., 158; prel., 3; abb., 7; mil. ord.; card., 35; abp., 156; bps., 275 (hierarchy includes 220 residential, 30 coadjutors or auxiliaries, 90 in Curia offices, remainder in other offices or retired); parishes, 25,892; priests, 56,708 (37,228 dioc., 19,480 rel.); p.d., 1,539; sem., 6,357; bros., 4,731; srs., 119,625; bap., 489,441; Caths., 55,609,000 (97.2%); tot. pop., 57,190,000.*

Republic in southern Europe; capital, Rome. A Christian community was formed early at Rome, probably by the middle of the first century. St. Peter established his see there. He and St. Paul suffered death for the faith there in the 60s. The early Christians were persecuted at various times there, as in other parts of the empire, but the Church developed in numbers and influence, gradually spreading out from towns and cities in the center and south to rural areas and the north. Organization, in the process of formation in the second century, developed greatly between the fifth and eighth centuries. By the latter date the Church had already come to grips with serious problems, including doctrinal and disciplinary disputes that threatened the unity of faith, barbarian invasions, and the need for the pope and bishops to take over civil responsibilities because of imperial default. The Church has been at the center of life on the peninsula throughout the centuries. It emerged from underground in 313, with the Edict of Milan, and rose to a position of prestige and lasting influence. It educated and converted the barbarians, preserved culture through the early Middle Ages and passed it on to later times, suffered periods of decline and gained strength through recurring reforms, engaged in military combat for political reasons and intellectual combat for the preservation and development of doctrine, saw and patronized the development of the arts, experienced all human strengths and weaknesses in its members, knew triumph and the humiliation of failure. For long centuries, from the fourth to the 19th, the Church was a temporal as well as spiritual power. This temporal aspect complicated its history in Italy. Since the 1870s, however, when the Papal States were annexed by the Kingdom of Italy, the history became simpler — but remained complicated — as the Church, shorn of temporal power, began to find new freedom for the fulfillment of its spiritual mission. In 1985, a new concordat was ratified between the Vatican and Italy, replacing one in effect since 1929.

## Jamaica*

*Archd., 1; dioc., 1; v.a., 1; abp., 1; bp., 1; parishes, 75; priests, 104 (42 dioc., 62 rel.); p.d., 18; sem., 19; bros., 9; srs., 175; bap., 1,696; Caths., 107,000 (4.3%); tot. pop., 2,500,000.*

Republic in the West Indies; capital, Kingston. Franciscans and Dominicans evangelized the island from about 1512 until 1655. Missionary work was interrupted after the English took possession but was resumed by Jesuits about the turn of the 19th century. A vicariate apostolic was organized in 1837. The hierarchy was established in 1967.

## Japan*

*Archd., 3; dioc., 13; p.a., 1; card., 1; abp., 3; bp., 20; parishes, 870; priests, 1,871 (545 dioc., 1,326 rel.); p.d., 6; sem., 246; bros., 290; srs., 6,785; bap., 10,115; Caths., 449,000 (.35%); tot. pop., 124,690,000.*

Archipelago in the northwest Pacific; capital, Tokyo. Jesuits began evangelization in the middle of the 16th century and about 300,000 converts, most of them in Kyushu, were reported at the end of the century. The Nagasaki Martyrs were victims of persecution in 1597. Another persecution took some 4,000 lives between 1614 and 1651. Missionaries, banned for two centuries, returned about the middle of the 19th century and found Christian communities still surviving in Nagasaki and other places in Kyushu. A vicariate was organized in 1866. Religious freedom was guaranteed in 1889. The hierarchy was established in 1891.

## Jordan*

*Archd., 1; abp., 1; bp., 1; parishes, 61; priests, 69 (53 dioc., 16 rel.); sem., 10; bros., 9; srs., 239; bap., 953; Caths., 57,000 (1.1%); tot. pop., 5,200,000.*

Constitutional monarchy in the Middle East; capital, Amman. Christianity there dates from apostolic times. Survival of the faith was threatened many times under the rule of Muslims from 636 and Ottoman Turks from 1517 to 1918, and in the Islamic Emirate of Trans-Jordan from 1918 to 1949. Since the creation of Israel, some 500,000 Palestinian refugees, some of them Christians, have been in Jordan. Islam is the state religion but religious freedom is guaranteed for all. The Greek Melkite-Rite Archdiocese of Petra and Philadelphia is located in Jordan. Latin (Roman)-Rite Catholics are under the jurisdiction of the Latin Patriarchate of Jerusalem. Established diplomatic relations with the Holy See in 1994.

## Kazakhstan*

*A.a., 1; bp., 1; parishes, 36; priests, 32 (10 dioc., 22 rel.); sem., 18; bros., 1; srs., 30; bap., 3,317; Caths., 316,000 (1.8%); tot. pop., 17,030,000.*

Independent republic (1991); formerly part of

USSR; capital, Almaty (Alma-Ata). Most of the population are Sunni Muslims and about 30% are Russian Orthodox. The Catholic population is mainly of German, Polish and Ukrainian origin who were deported during the Stalin regime. A Latin-rite apostolic administration was established in 1991.

## Kenya*

*Archd. 4; dioc., 16; v.a., 1; mil. ord.; card., 1; abp. 4; bp. 15; parishes, 537; priests, 1,500 (692 dioc., 808 rel.); sem., 1,368; bros., 580; srs., 3,266; catechists, 8,301; bap., 223,100; Caths., 6,072,000 (20.7%); tot. pop., 29,290,000.*

Republic in eastern Africa bordering on the Indian Ocean; capital, Nairobi. Systematic evangelization by the Holy Ghost Missionaries began in 1889, nearly 40 years after the start of work by Protestant missionaries. The hierarchy was established in 1953. Three metropolitan sees were established in 1990. (See Index for 1995 papal visit.)

## Kiribati*

*Dioc., 1; bp., 1; parishes, 22; priests, 23 (8 dioc., 15 rel.); sem., 9; bros., 26; srs., 70; bap., 2,340; Caths., 39,000 (54%); tot.pop., 72,000.*

Former British colony (Gilbert Islands) in Oceania; became independent July 12, 1979; capital, Bairiki on Tarawa. French Missionaries of the Sacred Heart began work in the islands in 1888. A vicariate for the islands was organized in 1897. The hierarchy was established in 1966.

## Korea

*North Korea: Dioc., 2; abb., 1; bp., 1 (exiled); tot. pop., 23,486,000. No recent Catholic statistics available; there were an estimated 100,000 Catholics reported in 1969.*

*South Korea*: *Archd., 3; dioc., 11; mil. ord.; card., 1; abp., 2; bp., 18; parishes, 908; priests, 2,098 (1,723 dioc., 375 rel.); sem., 1,796; bros., 439; srs., 7,060; bap., 145,054; Caths., 3,286,000 (7.3%); tot. pop., 44,450,000.*

Peninsula in eastern Asia, east of China, divided into the (Communist) Democratic People's Republic in the North, formed May 1, 1948, with Pyongyang as its capital; and the Republic of Korea in the South, with Seoul as the capital. Some Catholics may have been in Korea before it became a "hermit kingdom" toward the end of the 16th century and closed its borders to foreigners. The real introduction to Catholicism came in 1784 through lay converts. A priest arriving in the country in 1794 found 4,000 Catholics there who had never seen a priest. A vicariate was erected in 1831 but was not manned for several years thereafter. There were 15,000 Catholics by 1857. Four persecutions in the 19th century took a terrible toll; several thousand died in the last one, 1866-69. (One hundred and three martyrs of this period were canonized by Pope John Paul II during his 1984 apostolic visit to South Korea.) Freedom of religion was granted in 1883 when Korea opened its borders. Progress was made thereafter. The hierarchy was established in 1962. Since the war of 1950-53, there have been no signs of Catholic life in the North which has been blanketed by a news blackout. In July 1972, both Koreas agreed

to seek peaceful means of reunification. Bishop Tji of Won Ju, South Korea, convicted and sentenced to 15 years' imprisonment in 1974 on a charge of inciting to rebellion, was released in February, 1975. The 44th International Eucharistic Congress was held in Seoul, South Korea, Oct. 5 to 8, 1989.

## Kuwait*

*V.a., 1; bp., 1; parishes, 5; priests, 8 (4 dioc., 4 rel.); p.d., 1; sem., 1; srs., 12; bap., 632; Caths., 105,000; tot. pop., 1,620,000.*

Constitutional monarchy (sultanate or sheikdom) in southwest Asia bordering on the Persian Gulf. Remote Christian origins probably date to apostolic times. Islam is the predominant and official religion.

## Kyrgyzstan*

Independent republic bordering China; former Soviet republic; capital, Bishkek (former name, Frunze). Most of the people are Sunni Muslim. A small Catholic community mainly of German origin is served by a priest who lives in the capital. Established diplomatic relations with the Holy See, August, 1992. No statistics available. Total population, 4,750,000. (*L'Osservatore Romano*, English Edition.)

## Laos

*V.a., 4; bp., 3; parishes, 31; priests, 23 (17 dioc., 6 rel.); p.d., 1; sem., 7; bros., 1; srs., 94; catechists, 133; bap., 475; Caths., 48,000 (1%); tot. pop., 4,740,000. (AD)*

People's republic in southeast Asia, surrounded by China, Vietnam, Cambodia, Thailand and Myanmar (Burma); capital, Vientiane. Systematic evangelization by French missionaries started about 1881; earlier efforts ended in 1688. The first mission was established in 1885 by Father Xavier Guégo. A vicariate apostolic was organized in 1899 when there were 8,000 Catholics and 2,000 catechumens in the country. Most of the foreign missionaries were expelled following the communist take-over in 1975. Buddhism is the state religion.

## Latvia*

*Archd., 1; dioc., 3; abp., 1; bp., 5; parishes, 188; priests, 101 (83 dioc., 18 rel.); p.d., 1; sem., 46; srs., 75; bap., 7,280; Caths., 475,000 (18.6%); tot. pop., 2,550,000.*

Independent (1991) Baltic republic; capital, Riga. (Forcibly absorbed by the U.S.S.R. in 1940; it regained independence in 1991). Catholicism was introduced late in the 12th century. Lutheranism became the dominant religion after 1530. Catholics were free to practice their faith during the long period of Russian control and during independence from 1918 to 1940. The relatively small Catholic community was repressed during the 1940-91 Soviet take-over of Latvia which was not recognized by the Holy See or the United States.

## Lebanon*

*Archd., 12 (1 Armenian, 4 Maronite, 7 Greek Melkite); dioc., 7 (1 Chaldean, 6 Maronite); v.a., 1 (Latin); card., 1 (patriarch of the Maronites); patriarchs, 3 (patriarchs of Antioch of the Maronites, Antioch of the Syrians and Cilicia of the Armenians* who reside in Lebanon); abp. and bp., 32; parishes, 990; priests, 1,353 (699 dioc., 654 rel.); p.d., 14; sem., 440; bros., 81; srs., 2,787; bap., 14,217; Caths., 1,959,000; tot. pop., 3,500,000.

Republic in the Middle East, north of Israel; capital, Beirut. Christianity, introduced in apostolic times, was firmly established by the end of the fourth century and has remained so despite heavy Muslim influence since early in the seventh century. The country is the center of the Maronite Rite. In the 1980s, the country was torn by violence and often heavy fighting among rival political-religious factions drawn along Christian-Muslim lines.

## Lesotho*

Archd., 1; dioc., 3; abp., 1; bp., 3; parishes, 76; priests, 127 (42 dioc., 85 rel.); p.d., 1; sem., 88; bros., 24; srs., 599; catechists, 3,006; bap., 24,433; Caths., 704,000 (35%); tot. pop., 2,000,000.

Constitutional monarchy, an enclave in the southeastern part of the Republic of South Africa; capital, Maseru. Oblates of Mary Immaculate, the first Catholic missionaries in the area, started evangelization in 1862. A prefecture apostolic was organized in 1894. The hierarchy was established in 1951.

## Liberia*

Archd., 1; dioc., 2; abp., 1; bp., 2; parishes, 50; priests, 54 (25 dioc., 29 rel.); p.d., 4; sem., 46; bros., 22; srs., 50; bap. 3,592; Caths., 97,000 (3.6%); tot. pop., 2,700,000.

Republic in western Africa, bordering on the Atlantic; capital, Monrovia. Missionary work and influence, dating interruptedly from the 16th century, were slight before the Society of African Missions undertook evangelization in 1906. The hierarchy was established in 1982. In July, 1993, a peace accord was signed ending the civil war which began in 1989. The war had claimed the lives of 150,000 and made refugees of 100,000.

## Libya

V.a., 3; p.a., 1; bp., 1; parishes, 2; priests, 12 (1 dioc., 11 rel.); srs., 77; bap., 157; Caths., 40,000 (.8%); tot. pop., 4,900,000. (AD)

Arab state in northern Africa, on the Mediterranean between Egypt and Tunisia; capital, Tripoli. Christianity was probably preached in the area at an early date but was overcome by the spread of Islam from the 630s. Islamization was complete by 1067 and there has been no Christian influence since then. The Catholics in the country belong to the foreign colony. Islam is the state religion.

## Liechtenstein*

Parishes, 10; priests, 35 (25 dioc., 10 rel); bros., 4; srs., 85; bap., 211; Caths., 22,000; tot. pop., 29,000.

Constitutional monarchy in central Europe, in the Alps and on the Rhine between Switzerland and Austria; capital, Vaduz. Christianity in the country dates from the fourth century; the area has been under the jurisdiction of Chur, Switzerland, since about that time. The Reformation had hardly any influence in the country. Catholicism is the state religion but religious freedom for all is guaranteed by law.

## Lithuania*

Archd., 2; dioc., 4; card., 1; abp., 2; bp., 8; parishes, 667; priests, 730 (615 dioc., 115 rel.); p.d., 3; sem., 286; bros., 126; srs., 1,209; bap., 45,692; Caths., 3,082,000 (78.6%); tot. pop., 3,920,000.

Baltic republic forcibly absorbed and under Soviet domination from 1940; regained independence, 1991; capital, Vilna (Vilnius). Catholicism was introduced in 1251 and a short-lived diocese was established by 1260. Effective evangelization took place between 1387 and 1417, when Catholicism became the state religion. Losses to Lutheranism in the 16th century were overcome. Efforts of czars to "russify" the Church between 1795 and 1918 were strongly resisted. Concordat relations with the Vatican were established in 1927, nine years after independence from Russia and 13 years before the start of another kind of Russian control with the following results, among others: all convents closed; four seminaries shut down; appointment to one seminary (Kaunas) only with government approval; priests restricted in pastoral ministry and subject to appointment by government officials; no religious services outside churches; no religious press; religious instruction banned; parish installations and activities controlled by directives enacted in 1976; two bishops — Vincentas Sladkevicius and Julijonas Steponavicius — forbidden to act as bishops and relegated to remote parishes in 1957 and 1961, respectively; arrest, imprisonment or detention in Siberia for four bishops, 185 priests, 275 lay persons between 1945 and 1955. Despite such developments and conditions, there was a strong and vigorous underground Church in Lithuania, where the Soviet government found its repressive potential limited by the solidarity of popular resistance. In July, 1982, Rev. Antanas Vaicius was ordained apostolic administrator of the Telsiai diocese and Klaipeda prelature. Auxiliary Bishop Vincentas Sladkevicius, of Kaisiadorys, under severe government restrictions since 1957, was allowed to return to his see in 1982 following his appointment as apostolic administrator. (He was made a cardinal in 1988 and appointed archbishop of Kaunas in March, 1989.) In 1983, four of the five bishops were allowed to go to Rome for their ad limina visit. In December, 1988, Bishop Steponavicius was allowed to return to his diocese and was named an archbishop in 1989. (He died in 1991.) The Vatican announcement in March, 1989, of the reorganization of the hierarchy indicated some change of attitude on the part of the government. Three former apostolic administrators (titular bishops) were named ordinaries; three apostolic administrators (two of them new) were appointed. The Soviet 1940-91 take-over of Lithuania was not recognized by the Holy See or the United States.

## Luxembourg*

Archd., 1; abp., 1; parishes, 274; priests, 308 (233 dioc., 75 rel.); p.d., 3; sem., 13; bros., 19; srs., 816; bap., 3,814; Caths. 371,000 (95%); tot. pop., 390,000.

Constitutional monarchy in western Europe, between Belgium, Germany and France; capital, Luxembourg. Christianity, introduced in the fifth and sixth centuries, was firmly established by the end of the eighth century. A full-scale parish system was in existence in the ninth century. Monastic influence was strong until the Reformation, which had minimal influence in the country. The Church experienced some adverse influence from the currents of the French Revolution.

## Macau (Macao)

*Dioc., 1; bp., 1; parishes, 9; priests, 66 (32 dioc., 34 rel.); bros., 9; srs., 153; bap., 480; Caths., 22,000; tot. pop., 400,000.*

Portuguese-administered territory in southeast Asia across the Pearl River estuary from Hong Kong; scheduled to revert to China in 1999. Christianity was introduced by the Jesuits in 1557. Diocese was established in 1576. Macau served as a base for missionary work in Japan and China.

## Macedonia*

*Dioc., 1; bp., 2; parishes, 25; priests, 52 (50 dioc., 2 rel.); sem., 19; srs., 105; bap., 1,641; Caths., 65,000; tot. pop., 4,300,000.*

Former Yugoslav Republic of Macedonia; declared independence in 1992; capital, Skopje.

## Madagascar*

*Archd., 3; dioc., 15; card., 1; abp., 3; bp., 15; parishes, 282; priests, 843 (297 dioc., 546 rel.); sem., 764; bros., 383; srs., 2,643; catechists, 17,936; bap., 99,170; Caths., 3,042,000 (21%); tot. pop. 14,300,000.*

Republic (Malagasy Republic) off the eastern coast of Africa; capital, Antananarivo. Missionary efforts were generally fruitless from early in the 16th century until the Jesuits were permitted to start open evangelization about 1845. A prefecture apostolic was set up in 1850 and a vicariate apostolic in the north was placed in charge of the Holy Ghost Fathers in 1898. There were 100,000 Catholics by 1900. The first native bishop was ordained in 1936. The hierarchy was established in 1955.

## Madeira Islands

Portuguese province, an archipelago 340 miles west of the northwestern coast of Africa; capital, Funchal. Catholicism has had a continuous history since the first half of the 15th century. The diocese of Funchal was established in 1514. Statistics are included in Portugal.

## Malawi*

*Archd., 1; dioc., 6; abp., 1; bp., 6; parishes, 140; priests, 410 (235 dioc., 175 rel.); sem., 300; bros., 82; srs., 685; catechists, 5,835; bap., 86,431; Caths., 2,206,000 (23%); tot. pop., 9,460,000.*

Republic in the interior of eastern Africa; capital, Lilongwe. Missionary work, begun by Jesuits in the late 16th and early 17th centuries, was generally ineffective until the end of the 19th century. The Missionaries of Africa (White Fathers) arrived in 1889 and later were joined by others. A vicariate was set up in 1897. The hierarchy was established in 1959.

## Malaysia

*Archd., 2; dioc., 6; abp., 2; bp., 6; parishes, 148; priests, 226 (177 dioc., 49 rel.); p.d., 2; sem., 70;*

*bros., 110; srs., 598; bap., 20,017; Caths., 624,000 (3%); tot. pop., 19,490,000. (AD)*

Parliamentary democracy in southeastern Asia; federation of former states of Malaya, Sabah (former Br. North Borneo), and Sarawak; capital, Kuala Lumpur. Christianity, introduced by Portuguese colonists about 1511, was confined almost exclusively to Malacca until late in the 18th century. The effectiveness of evangelization increased from then on because of the recruitment and training of native clergy. Singapore (see separate entry), founded in 1819, became a center for missionary work. Seventeen thousand Catholics were in the Malacca diocese in 1888. Effective evangelization in Sabah and Sarawak began in the second half of the 19th century. The hierarchy was established in 1973.

## Maldives

Republic, an archipelago 400 miles southwest of India and Ceylon; capital, Male. No serious attempt was ever made to evangelize the area, which is completely Muslim. Population, 250,000.

## Mali*

*Archd., 1; dioc., 5; abp., 1; bp., 6; parishes, 39; priests, 150 (61 dioc., 89 rel.); sem., 38; bros., 27; srs., 192; bap., 3,669; Caths., 103,000 (.98%); tot. pop., 10,460,000.*

Republic, inland in western Africa; capital, Bamako. Catholicism was introduced late in the second half of the 19th century. Missionary work made little progress in the midst of the predominantly Muslim population. A vicariate was set up in 1921. The hierarchy was established in 1955.

## Malta*

*Archd., 1; dioc., 1; abp., 1; bp., 1; parishes, 80; priests, 981 (519 dioc., 462 rel.); sem., 76; bros., 101; srs., 1,350; bap., 5,045; Caths., 351,000 (93.3%); tot. pop., 376,000.*

Republic 58 miles south of Sicily; capital, Valletta. Early catacombs and inscriptions are evidence of the early introduction of Christianity. St. Paul was shipwrecked on Malta in 60. Saracens controlled the island(s) from 870 to 1090, a period of difficulty for the Church. The line of bishops extends from 1090 to the present. Church-state conflict developed in recent years over passage of government-sponsored legislation affecting Catholic schools and church-owned property. An agreement reached in 1985 ended the dispute and established a joint commission to study other church-state problems.

## Marshall Islands*

*P.a., 1; parishes, 4; priests, 5 (rel.); p.d., 2; sem., 2; bros., 15; srs., 18; bap., 107; Caths., 4,000; tot. pop., 50,000.*

Island republic in central Pacific Ocean; capital, Majura. Formerly administered by U.S. as part of UN Trust Territory of the Pacific; independent nation, 1991. A prefecture apostolic was erected May 25, 1993 (formerly part of Carolines-Marshall diocese), with U.S. Jesuit Rev. James Gould as first prefect apostolic.

## Martinique

*Archd., 1; abp., 1; parishes, 47; priests, 66 (39 dioc., 27 rel.); p.d.,1; sem., 8; bros., 11; srs., 198; bap., 4,055; Caths., 343,000; tot. pop., 388,000.*

French overseas department in the West Indies, about 130 miles south of Guadeloupe; capital, Fort-de-France. Catholicism was introduced in the 16th century. The hierarchy was established in 1967.

## Mauritania

*Dioc., 1; bp., 1; parishes, 6; priests, 9 (2 dioc., 7 rel.); p.d.,1; bros.,2; srs.,29; bap.,22; Caths.,5,000 (.2%); tot. pop., 2,210,000. (AD)*

Islamic republic on the northwest coast of Africa; capital, Nouakchott. With few exceptions, the Catholics in the country are members of the foreign colony.

## Mauritius*

*Dioc., 1; card., 1; bp., 1; parishes, 40; priests, 92 (57 dioc., 35 rel.); sem., 7; bros., 28; srs., 278; bap., 7,408; Caths.,288,000 (26.1%); tot. pop.,1,100,000.*

Island republic in the Indian Ocean about 500 miles east of Madagascar; capital, Port Louis. Catholicism was introduced by Vincentians in 1722. Port Louis, made a vicariate in 1819 and a diocese in 1847, was a jumping-off point for missionaries to Australia, Madagascar and South Africa.

## Mayotte

French overseas island territory, in Indian Ocean off southeast coast of Africa; formerly part of Comoros. Statistics included in Comoros.

## Melilla

Spanish possession in northern Africa. Statistics are included in those for Spain.

## Mexico*

*Archd., 14; dioc., 62; prel., 6; card., 3; abp., 16; bp., 84; parishes, 5,177; priests, 12,458 (8,980 dioc., 3,478 rel.); p.d., 352; sem., 6,762; bros., 1,414; srs., 26,477; bap., 1,957,092; Caths., 88,709,000 (95.3%); tot. pop., 93,010,000.*

Republic in Middle America (United States of Mexico); capital, Mexico City. Christianity was introduced early in the 16th century. Mexico City, made a diocese in 1530, became the missionary and cultural center of the whole country. Missionary work, started in 1524 and forwarded principally by Franciscans, Dominicans, Augustinians and Jesuits, resulted in the baptism of all persons in the central plateau by the end of the century. Progress there and in the rest of the country continued in the following century but tapered off and went into decline in the 18th century, for a variety of reasons ranging from diminishing government support to relaxations of Church discipline. The wars of independence, 1810-21, in which some Catholics participated, created serious problems of adjustment for the Church. Social problems, political unrest and government opposition climaxed in the constitution of 1917 which practically outlawed the Church. Persecution took serious tolls of life and kept the Church underground, under Calles, 1924-1928, again in 1931, and under Cardenas in 1934. President Camacho, 1940-1946, ended persecution and instituted a more lenient policy. The Church, however, still labors under some legal and practical disabilities. In 1990, the Mexican president and the Holy See agreed to exchange permanent personal representatives; full diplomatic relations were established in 1992. Cardinal Juan Jesus Posadas Ocampo, Archbishop of Guadalajara, was shot to death May 24, 1993.

## Micronesia*

*Dioc., 1; bp., 2; parishes, 36; priests, 30 (13 dioc., 17 rel.); p.d., 31; sem., 16; bros., 2; srs., 30; bap., 2,248; Caths., 64,000; tot. pop., 121,000.*

Federated States of Micronesia (Caroline archipelago) in southwest Pacific; capital, Kolonia; former U.N. trust territory under U.S. administration; became independent nation September, 1991. Effective evangelization began in the late 1880s. Established diplomatic relations with the Holy See in 1994.

## Moldova*

*Dioc., 1; a.a., 1; parishes, 7; priests, 8 (5 dioc., 3 rel.); sem., 5; srs., 15; bap., 112; Caths., 15,000 (.34%); tot. pop., 4,340,000.*

Independent republic bordering Romania; former constituent republic of the USSR; capital, Kishinev. The majority of people belong to the Orthodox Church. Catholics are mostly of Polish or German descent.

## Monaco*

*Archd.,1; abp.,1, parishes, 6; priests, 27 (13 dioc., 14 rel.); p.d., 1; sem., 3; srs., 22; bap., 238; Caths., 27,000; tot. pop., 30,000.*

Constitutional monarchy, an enclave on the Mediterranean coast of France near the Italian border; capital, Monaco-Ville. Christianity was introduced before 1000. Catholicism is the official religion but freedom is guaranteed for all.

## Mongolia*

*Mission, 1; priests, 4 (rel.); srs., 2; bap., 4; Caths., 1,000; tot. pop., 2,360,000.*

Republic in north central Asia; formerly under communist control; capital Ulaanbaatar. Christianity was introduced by Oriental Orthodox. Some Franciscans were in the country in the 13th and 14th centuries, en route to China. Limited evangelization efforts from the 18th century had little success among the Mongols in Outer Mongolia, where Buddhism has predominated for hundreds of years. There may be a few Catholics in Inner Mongolia. No foreign missionaries have been in the country since 1953. Freedom of worship is guaranteed under the new constitution which went into effect in 1992. The government established relations with the Holy See in 1992 and indicated that missionaries would be welcome to help rebuild the country.

## Montserrat

*Parish, 1; priests, 4 (1 dioc., 3 rel.); p.d., 1; srs., 3; bap., 18; Caths., 1,000; tot. pop., 12,000.*

British island possession in Caribbean; capital, Plymouth. Under ecclesiastical jurisdiction of St. John's-Basseterre diocese, Antigua.

## Morocco*

*Archd., 2; abp., 2; parishes, 42; priests, 64 (15 dioc., 49 rel.); p.d., 8; sem., 1; bros., 16; srs., 301;*

*bap., 72; Caths., 25,000 (.1%); tot. pop., 26,590,000.*
Constitutional monarchy in northwest Africa with Atlantic and Mediterranean coastlines; capital, Rabat. Christianity was known in the area by the end of the third century. Bishops from Morocco attended a council at Carthage in 484. Catholic life survived under Visigoth and, from 700, Arab rule; later it became subject to influence from the Spanish, Portuguese and French. Islam is the state religion. The hierarchy was established in 1955.

## Mozambique
*Archd., 3; dioc., 9; card., 1; abp. 2; bp., 9; parishes, 283; priests, 349 (47 dioc., 302 rel.); sem., 260; bros., 60; srs., 761; catechists, 32,201; bap., 80,885; Caths., 2,619,000 (15.7%); tot. pop., 16,610,000. (AD)*
Republic in southeast Africa, bordering on the Indian Ocean; former Portuguese territory (independent, 1975); capital, Maputo (formerly Lourenco Marques). Christianity was introduced by Portuguese Jesuits about the middle of the 16th century. Evangelization continued from then until the 18th century when it went into decline largely because of the Portuguese government's expulsion of the Jesuits. Conditions worsened in the 1830s, improved after 1881, but deteriorated again during the anticlerical period from 1910 to 1925. Conditions improved in 1940, the year Portugal concluded a new concordat with the Holy See and the hierarchy was established. Outspoken criticism by missionaries of Portuguese policies in Mozambique resulted in Church-state tensions in the years immediately preceding independence. The first two native bishops were ordained March 9, 1975. Two ecclesiastical provinces were established in 1984.

## Myanmar
*Archd., 2; dioc., 10; abp., 2; bp., 14; parishes, 227; priests, 398 (364 dioc., 34 rel.); sem., 243; bros., 60; srs., 1,054; bap., 27,547; Caths., 529,000 (1.1%); tot. pop., 45,550,000. (AD)*
A socialist republic in southeast Asia, on the Bay of Bengal, formerly Burma; name changed to Myanmar in 1989; capital, Yangon (Rangoon). Christianity was introduced about 1500. Small-scale evangelization had limited results from the middle of the 16th century until the 1850s when effective organization of the Church began. The hierarchy was established in 1955. Buddhism was declared the state religion in 1961, but the state is now officially secular. In 1965, church schools and hospitals were nationalized. In 1966, all foreign missionaries who had entered the country after 1948 for the first time were forced to leave when the government refused to renew their work permits. Despite these setbacks, the Church has shown some progress in recent years.

## Namibia* (South West Africa)
*Archd., 1; dioc., 1; v.a., 1; abp., 1; bp., 2; parishes, 67; priests, 72 (7 dioc., 65 rel.); p.d., 36; sem., 7; bros., 34; srs., 304; bap., 9,102; Caths., 267,000 (17%); tot. pop., 1,500,000. (AD)*
Independent (Mar. 21, 1990) state in southern Africa; capital, Windhoek. The area shares the history of South Africa. The hierarchy was established in 1994.

## Nauru*
*Parish, 1; p.d., 2; srs., 3; bap., 140; Caths., 3,000; tot. pop., 7,000.*
Independent republic in western Pacific; capital, Yaren. Forms part of the Tarawa and Nauru diocese (Kiribati). Established diplomatic relations with the Holy See in 1992.

## Nepal*
*Independent mission, 1; parishes, 25; priests, 34 (4 dioc.; 30 rel.); sem., 29; bros., 2; srs., 82; bap., 117; Caths., 5,000; tot. pop., 21,360,000.*
Constitutional monarchy, the only Hindu kingdom in the world, in central Asia south of the Himalayas between India and Tibet; capital, Kathmandu. Little is known of the country before the 15th century. Some Jesuits passed through from 1628 and some sections were evangelized in the 18th century, with minimal results, before the country was closed to foreigners. Conversions from Hinduism, the state religion, are not recognized in law and punishable by imprisonment. Christian missionary work is not allowed.

## Netherlands*
*Archd., 1; dioc., 6; mil ord.; card., 2; bp., 11; parishes, 1,729; priests 4,656 (1,818 dioc., 2,838 rel.); p.d., 212; sem., 214; bros., 1,897; srs., 14,838; bap., 48,980; Caths., 5,683,000 (36.9%); tot. pop., 15,380,000.*
Constitutional monarchy in northwestern Europe; capital, Amsterdam (seat of the government, The Hague). Evangelization, begun about the turn of the sixth century by Irish, Anglo-Saxon and Frankish missionaries, resulted in Christianization of the country by 800 and subsequent strong influence on The Lowlands. Invasion by French Calvinists in 572 brought serious losses to the Catholic Church and made the Reformed Church dominant. Catholics suffered a practical persecution of official repression and social handicap in the 17th century. The schism of Utrecht occurred in 1724. Only one-third of the population was Catholic in 1726. The Church had only a skeleton organization from 1702 to 1853, when the hierarchy was reestablished. Despite this upturn, cultural isolation was the experience of Catholics until about 1914. From then on new vigor came into the life of the Church, and a whole new climate of interfaith relations began to develop. Before and for some years following the Second Vatican Council, the thrust and variety of thought and practice in the Dutch Church moved it to the vanguard position of "progressive" renewal. A particular synod of Dutch bishops held at the Vatican in January, 1980, and aimed at internal improvement of the Church in the Netherlands, had disappointing results, according to reports in 1981.

## Netherlands Antilles
*Dioc., 1; bp., 1; parishes, 28; priests, 50 (24 dioc., 26 rel.); p.d., 1; sem., 3; bros., 18; srs., 74; bap., 1,903; Caths., 147,000; tot. pop., 193,000. (AD)*
Autonomous part of The Netherlands. Consists of two groups of islands in the Caribbean, including Curacao and Bonaire, off the northern coast of Venezuela; and St. Eustatius, Saba and the southern part

of St. Maarten, southeast of Puerto Rico; capital, Willemstad on Curacao. Christianity was introduced in the 16th century.

## New Caledonia

*Archd., 1; abp., 1; parishes, 38; priests, 52 (10 dioc., 42 rel.); p.d., 1; sem., 2; bros., 45; srs., 169; bap., 2,012; Caths., 100,000; tot. pop., 165,000.*

French territory consisting of several islands in Oceania east of Queensland, Australia; capital, Noumea. Catholicism was introduced in 1843, nine years after Protestant missionaries began evangelization. A vicariate was organized in 1847. The hierarchy was established in 1966.

## New Zealand*

*Archd., 1; dioc., 5; mil. ord.; card., 1; bp., 9; parishes, 275; priests, 629 (366 dioc., 263 rel.); p.d., 3; sem., 43; bros., 198; srs., 1,309; bap., 7,957; Caths. 494,000 (14.1%); tot. pop., 3,490,000.*

Independent nation in Commonwealth, a group of islands in Oceania 1,200 miles southeast of Australia: capital, Wellington. Protestant missionaries were the first evangelizers. On North Island, Catholic missionaries started work before the establishment of two dioceses in 1848; their work among the Maoris was not organized until about 1881. On South Island, whose first resident priest arrived in 1840, a diocese was established in 1869. These three jurisdictions were joined in a province in 1896. The Marists were the outstanding Catholic missionaries in the area.

## Nicaragua*

*Archd., 1; dioc., 6; v.a., 1; card., 1; bp., 8; parishes, 198; priests, 346 (183 dioc., 163 rel.); p.d., 39; sem., 192; bros., 43; srs., 716; bap., 89,403; Caths., 3,838,000 (87.2%); tot. pop., 4,400,000.*

Republic in Central America: capital, Managua. Evangelization began shortly after the Spanish conquest about 1524 and eight years later the first bishop took over jurisdiction of the Church in the country. Jesuits were leaders in missionary work during the colonial period, which lasted until the 1820s. Evangelization endeavor increased after establishment of the republic in 1838. In this century it was extended to the Atlantic coastal area where Protestant missionaries had begun work about the middle of the 1900s. Many church leaders, clerical and lay, supported the aims but not necessarily all the methods of the revolution which forced the resignation and flight July 17, 1979, of Anastasio Somoza Debayle, whose family had controlled the government since the early 1930s. Subsequent developments, especially those related to Sandinista hostility to the Church in the 1980s, have had serious adverse effects on the ministry of the Church. (See Index for 1996 papal visit.)

## Niger*

*Dioc., 1; bp., 1; parishes, 21; priests, 40 (6 dioc., 34 rel.); sem., 5; bros., 7; srs., 75; bap., 456; Caths., 19,000 (.2%); tot. pop., 8,850,000.*

Republic in west central Africa; capital, Niamey. The first mission was set up in 1831. A prefecture apostolic was organized in 1942 and the first diocese was established in 1961. The country is predominantly Muslim.

## Nigeria*

*Archd., 9; dioc., 31; v.a. (1996), 2; independent mission, 1; p.a., 1; card., 1; abp., 11; bp., 34; parishes, 1,208; priests, 2,773 (2,094 dioc., 679 rel.); p.d., 5; sem., 3,344; bros., 411; srs., 2,912; catechists, 19,207; bap., 434,795; Caths., 11,210,000 (10%); tot. pop., 108,470,000.*

Republic in western Africa; capital, Lagos. The Portuguese introduced Catholicism in the coastal region in the 15th century. Capuchins did some evangelization in the 17th century but systematic missionary work did not get under way along the coast until about 1840. A vicariate for this area was organized in 1870. A prefecture was set up in 1911 for missions in the northern part of the country where Islam was strongly entrenched. From 1967, when Biafra seceded, until early in 1970 the country was torn by civil war. The hierarchy was established in 1950. Six dioceses were made metropolitan sees in 1994; four new dioceses were established as in 1995.

## Niue

*Parish, 1; priests, 1 (dioc.); srs., 2; bap., 3; Caths., no report; tot. pop., 2,000.*

New Zealand self-governing territory in South Pacific. Under ecclesiastical jurisdiction of Rarotonga diocese, Cook Islands.

## Northern Mariana Islands

*Dioc., 1; bp., 1; parishes, 9; priests, 10 (8 dioc., 2 rel.); p.d., 3; sem., 5; bros., 2; srs., 21; bap., 952; Caths., 56,000; tot. pop., 63,000.*

Commonwealth of Northern Mariana Islands, under U.S. sovereignty; formerly part of Trust Territory of Pacific Islands assigned to the U.S. in 1947. Under ecclesiastical jurisdiction of Chalan Kanoa diocese established in 1984.

## Norway*

*Dioc., 1; prel., 2; bp., 3; parishes, 32; priests, 63 (21 dioc., 42 rel.); p.d., 3; sem., 15; bros., 3; srs., 220; bap., 671; Caths., 40,000 (.9%); tot. pop., 4,320,000.*

Constitutional monarchy in northern Europe, the western part of the Scandinavian peninsula; capital, Oslo. Evangelization begun in the ninth century by missionaries from England and Ireland put the Church on a firm footing about the turn of the 11th century. The first diocese was set up in 1153 and development of the Church progressed until the Black Death in 1349 inflicted losses from which it never recovered. Lutheranism, introduced from outside in 1537 and furthered cautiously, gained general acceptance by about 1600 and was made the state religion. Legal and other measures crippled the Church, forcing priests to flee the country and completely disrupting normal activity. Changes for the better came in the 19th century, with the granting of religious liberty in 1845 and the repeal of many legal disabilities in 1897. Norway was administered as a single apostolic vicariate from 1892 to 1932, when it was divided into three jurisdictions under the supervision of the Congregation for the Propagation of the Faith.

## Oman

*Parishes, 4; priests, 14 (7 dioc., 7 rel.); bap., 198; Caths., 45,000; tot. pop., 2,080,000.*
Independent monarchy in eastern corner of Arabian Peninsula; capital, Muscat. Under ecclesiastical jurisdiction of Arabia vicariate apostolic.

## Pakistan*

*Archd., 2; dioc., 4; abp., 2; bp., 6; parishes, 92; priests, 268 (131 dioc., 137 rel.); sem., 232; bros., 35; srs., 724; bap., 21,166; Caths., 1,015,000 (.8%); tot. pop., 126,610,000.*
Islamic republic in southwestern Asia; capital, Islamabad. (Formerly included East Pakistan which became the independent nation of Bangladesh in 1971.) Islam, firmly established in the eighth century, is the state religion. Christian evangelization of the native population began about the middle of the 19th century, years after earlier scattered attempts. The hierarchy was established in 1950.

## Palou

Outlying territory of the U.S.; capital, Koror; part of Caroline chain of Islands. Under ecclesiastical jurisdiction of diocese of Caroline Islands, Federated States of Micronesia

## Panama*

*Archd., 1; dioc., 5; prel., 1; v.a., 1; abp., 3; bp., 11; parishes, 175; priests, 395 (159 dioc., 236 rel.); p.d., 40; sem., 206; bros., 50; srs., 523; bap., 29,480; Caths., 2,216,000 (86.5%); tot. pop., 2,560,000.*
Republic in Central America; capital, Panama. Catholicism was introduced by Franciscan missionaries and evangelization started in 1514. The Panama diocese, oldest in the Americas was set up at the same time. The Catholic Church has favored status and state aid for missions, charities and parochial schools, but religious freedom is guaranteed to all religions.

## Papua New Guinea*

*Archd., 4; dioc., 14; abp., 5; bp., 16; parishes, 355; priests, 516 (120 dioc., 396 rel.); p.d., 10; sem., 281; bros., 304; srs., 915; catechists, 2,223; bap., 35,405; Caths., 1,401,000 (35%); tot. pop., 4,000,000.*
Independent (Sept. 16, 1975) republic (formerly under Australian administration) in southwest Pacific. Consists of the eastern half of the southwestern Pacific island of New Guinea and the Northern Solomon Islands; capital, Port Moresby. Marists began evangelization about 1844 but were handicapped by many factors, including "spheres of influence" laid out for Catholic and Protestant missionaries. A prefecture apostolic was set up in 1896 and placed in charge of the Divine Word Missionaries. The territory suffered greatly during World War II. Hierarchy was established for New Guinea and adjacent islands in 1966.

## Paraguay*

*Archd., 1; dioc., 10; v.a., 2; mil. ord.; abp., 1; bp., 17; parishes, 325; priests, 635 (233 dioc., 402 rel.); p.d., 32; sem., 301; bros., 93; srs., 1,181; bap., 90,901; Caths., 4,409,000 (93.8%); tot. pop., 4,700,000.*

Republic in central South America; capital, Asuncion. Catholicism was introduced in 1542, evangelization began almost immediately. A diocese erected in 1547 was occupied for the first time in 1556. On many occasions thereafter dioceses in the country were left unoccupied because of political and other reasons. Jesuits who came into the country after 1609 devised the reductions system for evangelizing the Indians, teaching them agriculture, husbandry, trades and other useful arts, and giving them experience in property use and community life. The reductions were communes of Indians only, under the direction of the missionaries. About 50 of them were established in southern Brazil, Uruguay and northeastern Argentina as well as in Paraguay. They had an average population of three to four thousand. At their peak, some 30 reductions had a population of 100,000. Political officials regarded the reductions with disfavor because they did not control them and feared that the Indians trained in them might foment revolt and upset the established colonial system under Spanish control. The reductions lasted until about 1768 when their Jesuit founders and directors were expelled from Latin America. Church-state relations following independence from Spain in 1811 were tense as often as not because of government efforts to control the Church through continued exercise of Spanish patronage rights and by other means. The Church as well as the whole country suffered a great deal during the War of the Triple Alliance from 1865-70. After that time, the Church had the same kind of experience in Paraguay as in the rest of Latin America with forces of liberalism, anticlericalism, massive educational needs, poverty, a shortage of priests and other personnel. Most recently church leaders have been challenging the government to initiate long-needed economic and social reforms.

## Peru*

*Archd., 7; dioc., 15; prel., 11; v.a., 8; mil. ord.; card., 2; abp., 8; bp., 47; parishes, 1,407; priests, 2,495 (1,220 dioc., 1,275 rel.); p.d., 72; sem., 1,357; bros., 410; srs., 5,272; catechists, 5,411; bap., 343,412; Caths., 21,262,000 (92%); tot. pop., 23,090,000.*
Republic on the western coast of South America; capital, Lima. An effective diocese became operational in 1537, five years after the Spanish conquest. Evangelization, already under way, developed for some time after 1570 but deteriorated before the end of the colonial period in the 1820s. The first native-born saint of the new world was a Peruvian, Rose of Lima, a Dominican tertiary who died in 1617 and was canonized in 1671. In the new republic founded after the wars of independence the Church experienced problems of adjustment and many of the difficulties that cropped up in other South American countries: government efforts to control it through continuation of the patronage rights of the Spanish crown; suppression of houses of religious and expropriation of church property; religious indifference and outright hostility. The Church has special status but is not an established religion. Repressive measures by the government against labor protests were condemned by Church leaders in the past several

years. Violence related to activities of the Maoist *Sendero Luminoso* in recent years have had adverse effects on church ministry.

## Philippines*

*Archd., 16; dioc., 50; prel., 6; v.a., 7; mil. ord.; card., 3; abp., 22; bp., 91; parishes, 2,543; priests, 6,431 (4,188 dioc., 2,243 rel.); p.d., 20; sem., 7,381; bros., 578; srs., 9,459; catechists, 1,675; bap., 1,557,797; Caths., 56,313,000 (83.9%); tot. pop., 67,040,000.*

Republic, an archipelago of 7,000 islands off the southeast coast of Asia; capital, Quezon City (de facto, Manila). Systematic evangelization was begun in 1564 and resulted in firm establishment of the Church by the 19th century. During the period of Spanish rule, which lasted from the discovery of the islands by Magellan in 1521 to 1898, the Church experienced difficulties with the patronage system under which the Spanish crown tried to control ecclesiastical affairs through episcopal and other appointments. This system ended in 1898 when the United States gained possession of the islands and instituted a policy of separation of Church and state. Anticlericalism flared late in the 19th century. The Aglipayan schism, an attempt to set up a nationalist church, occurred a few years later, in 1902. The government of Ferdinand Marcos, under attack by people of the church for a number of years for violations of human rights, was replaced in 1986. Since then, communist groups have waged campaigns against the Church.

## Poland*

*Archd. (1996), 15; dioc., 25; mil. ord.; ordinariate, 1; cards., 4; abps., 14; bps., 97; parishes, 9,438; priests, 25,431 (19,716 dioc., 5,715 rel.); p.d., 3; sem., 7,356; bros., 1,372; srs., 24,985; bap., 462,725; Caths., 36,805,000 (95.5%); tot. pop., 38,540,000.*

Republic in eastern Europe; capital, Warsaw. The first traces of Christianity date from the second half of the ninth century. Its spread was accelerated by the union of the Slavs in the 10th century. The first bishopric was set up in 968. The Gniezno archdiocese, with suffragan sees and a mandate to evangelize the borderlands as well as Poland, was established in 1000. Steady growth continued thereafter, with religious orders and their schools playing a major role. Some tensions with the Orthodox were experienced. The Reformation, supported mainly by city dwellers and the upper classes, peaked from about the middle of the 16th century, resulting in numerous conversions to Lutheranism, the Reformed Church and the Bohemian Brethren. A successful Counter-Reformation, with the Jesuits in a position of leadership, was completed by about 1632. The movement served a nationalist as well as religious purpose; in restoring religious unity to a large degree, it united the country against potential invaders, the Swedes, Russians and Turks. The Counter-Reformation had bad side effects, leading to the repression of Protestants long after it was over and to prejudice against Orthodox who returned to allegiance with Rome in 1596 and later. The Church, in the same manner as the entire country, was adversely affected by the partitions of the 18th and 19th centuries. Russification hurt the Orthodox who had reunited with Rome and the Latins who were in the majority. Germans extended their Kulturkampf to the area they controlled. The Austrians exhibited some degree of tolerance. In the republic established after World War I the Church reorganized itself, continued to serve as a vital force in national life, and enjoyed generally harmonious relations with the state. Progressive growth was strong until 1939 when disaster struck in the form of invasion by German and Russian forces and six years of war. In 1945, seven years before the adoption of a Soviet-type of constitution, the Communist-controlled government initiated a policy that included a constant program of atheistic propaganda; a strong campaign against the hierarchy and clergy; the imprisonment in 1948 of 700 priests and even more religious; rigid limitation of the activities of religious; censorship and curtailment of the Catholic press and Catholic Action; interference with church administration and appointments of the clergy; the "deposition" of Cardinal Wyszynski in 1953 and the imprisonment of other members of the hierarchy; the suppression of "Caritas," the Catholic charitable organization; promotion of "Progressive Catholic" activities and a small minority of "patriotic priests." Establishment of the Gomulka regime, the freeing of Cardinal Wyszynski in October, 1956, and the signing of an agreement two months later by bishops and state officials, led to some improvement of conditions. The underlying fact, however, was that the regime conceded to Catholics only so much as was necessary to secure support of the government as a more tolerable evil than the harsh and real threat of a Russian-imposed puppet government like that in Hungary. This has been the controlling principle in Church-state relations. Auxiliary Bishop Ladislaw Rubin of Gniezno sketched the general state of affairs in March, 1968. He said that there was no sign that the government had any intention of releasing its oppressive grip on the Church. As evidence of the "climate of asphyxiation" in the country he cited: persistent questioning of priests by officials concerning their activities; the prohibition against Catholic schools, hospitals and charitable works; the financial burden of a 60 per cent tax on church income. Cardinal Wyszynski denounced "enforced atheism" in a Lenten pastoral in the same year. In May, 1969, the bishops drafted a list of grievances against the government which, they said, were "only some examples of difficulties which demonstrated the situation of the Church in our homeland." The grievances were: refusal of permits to build new churches and establish new parishes; refusal of permission "for the organization of new religion classes"; pressure on Catholics who attend religious ceremonies; censorship and the lack of an independent Catholic daily newspaper; lack of representation in public life; restriction of "freedom to conduct normal pastoral work" in the western portion of the country. There was a move toward improvement in Church-state relations in 1971-72. In 1973, the Polish bishops issued a pastoral letter urging Catholics to resist the official atheism imposed by the government. In 1974 the bishops expressed approval of renewed Vatican efforts at regularizing Church-state relations but insisted that they (the bishops) be consulted on every step of the negotiations. The bishops have continued their sharp criticism of anti-religious policies and human rights violations of the government. Regular contacts on a working level were initiated by the Vatican and Poland in 1974; regular diplomatic relations were established in 1989. Cardinal Karol Wojtyla of Cracow was elected to the papacy in 1978. Church support was strong for the independent labor movement, Solidarity, which was recognized by the government in August, 1980, but outlawed in December, 1981, when martial law was imposed (martial law was suspended in 1982). In May, 1989, following recognition of Solidarity and a series of political changes, the Catholic Church was given legal status for the first time since the communists took control of the government in 1944. In 1990, a new constitution was adopted declaring Poland a democratic state. In 1992, the Pope restructured the Church in Poland, establishing 8 more provinces and 13 new dioceses. A new concordat between the Polish government and the Holy See was signed in 1993. Since the fall of communism in 1989, the influence of the Church has declined, according to reports from various sources.

## Portugal*

*Patriarchate, 1; archd., 2; dioc., 17; mil. ord.; card., 1; abp., 3; bp., 40; parishes, 4,354; priests, 4,429 (3,372 dioc., 1,057 rel.); p.d., 75; sem., 727; bros., 434; srs., 7,023; bap., 99,102; Caths., 9,055,000 (92%); tot. pop., 9,830,000.*

Republic in the western part of the Iberian peninsula; capital, Lisbon. Christianity was introduced before the fourth century. From the fifth century to early in the eighth century the Church experienced difficulties from the physical invasion of barbarians and the intellectual invasion of doctrinal errors in the forms of Arianism, Priscillianism and Pelagianism. The Church survived under the rule of Arabs from about 711 and of the Moors until 1249. Ecclesiastical life was fairly vigorous from 1080 to 1185, and monastic influence became strong. A decline set in about 1450. Several decades later Portugal became the jumping-off place for many missionaries to newly discovered colonies. The Reformation had little effect in the country. Beginning about 1750, Pombal, minister of foreign affairs and prime minister, mounted a frontal attack on the Jesuits whom he succeeded in expelling from Portugal and the colonies. His anti-Jesuit campaign successful Pombal also attempted, and succeeded to some extent, in controlling the Church in Portugal until his fall from power about 1777. Liberal revolutionaries with anti-Church policies made the 19th century a difficult one for the Church. Similar policies prevailed in Church-state relations in this century until the accession of Salazar to power in 1928. In 1940 he concluded a concordat with the Holy See which regularized Church-state relations but still left the Church in a subservient condition. The prevailing spirit of church authorities in Portugal has been conservative. In 1971 several priests were tried for subversion for speaking out against colonialism and for taking part in guerrilla activities in Angola. A military coup of Apr. 25, 1974, triggered a succession of chaotic political developments which led to an attempt by Communists, after receiving only 18 per cent of the votes cast in a national election, to take over the government in the summer of 1975.

## Puerto Rico

*Archd., 1; dioc., 4; card., 1; bp., 8; parishes, 323; priests, 760 (402 dioc., 358 rel.); p.d., 357; sem., 126; bros., 56; srs., 1,072; bap., 43,158; Caths., 3,017,000 (82%); tot. pop., 3,650,000. (AD)*

A U.S. commonwealth, the smallest of the Greater Antilles, 885 miles southeast of the southern coast of Florida; capital, San Juan. Following its discovery by Columbus in 1493, the island was evangelized by Spanish missionaries and remained under Spanish ecclesiastical as well as political control until 1898 when it became a possession of the United States. The original diocese, San Juan, was erected in 1511. The present hierarchy was established in 1960.

## Qatar

*Parish, 1; priest, 1 (dioc.); bap., 73; tot. pop., 540,000.*

Independent state in the Persian Gulf; capital, Doha. Under ecclesiastical jurisdiction of Arabia vicariate apostolic.

## Reunion

*Dioc., 1; bp., 1; parishes, 76; priests, 105 (58 dioc., 47 rel.); p.d., 6; sem., 13; bros., 44; srs., 370; bap., 11,386; Caths., 566,000 (88.4%); tot. pop., 640,000. (AD)*

French overseas department, 450 miles east of Madagascar; capital, Saint-Denis. Catholicism was introduced in 1667 and some intermittent missionary work was done through the rest of the century. A prefecture apostolic was organized in 1712. Vincentians began work there in 1817 and were joined later by Holy Ghost Fathers.

## Rhodes

Greek island in the Aegean Sea, 112 miles from the southwestern coast of Asia Minor. A diocese was established about the end of the third century. A bishop from Rhodes attended the Council of Nicaea in 325. Most of the Christians followed the Eastern Churches into schism in the 11th century and became Orthodox. Turks controlled the island from 1522 to 1912. The small Catholic population, for whom a diocese existed from 1328 to 1546, lived in crossfire between Turks and Orthodox. After 1719 Franciscans provided pastoral care for the Catholics, for whom an archdiocese was erected in 1928. Statistics are included in Greece.

## Romania*

*Archd., 3; dioc., 8; ord., 1; card., 1; abp., 4; bp., 9; parishes, 1,728; priests, 1,435 (1,291 dioc., 144 rel.); p.d., 4; sem., 875; bros., 140; srs., 839; bap., 11,859; Caths., 2,910,000 (13%); tot. pop., 22,740,000.*

Socialist republic in southeastern Europe; capital, Bucharest. Latin Christianity, introduced in the third century, all but disappeared during the barbarian invasions. The Byzantine Rite was introduced by the Bulgars about the beginning of the eighth century and established firm roots. It eventually became Orthodox, but a large number of its adherents returned later to union with Rome. Attempts to reintroduce the Latin Rite on any large scale have been unsuccessful. Communists took over the government following World War II, forced the abdication of Michael I in 1947, and enacted a Soviet type of constitution in 1952. By that time a campaign against religion was already in progress. In 1948 the government denounced a concordat concluded in 1929, nationalized all schools and passed a law on religions which resulted in the disorganization of Church administration. The 1.5 million-member Romanian Byzantine Rite Church, by government decree, was incorporated into the Romanian Orthodox Church, and the Orthodox bishops then seized the cathedrals of Roman Catholic bishops. Five of the six Latin Rite bishops were immediately disposed of by the government, and the last was sentenced to 18 years' imprisonment in 1951, when a great many arrests of priests and laymen were made. Religious orders were suppressed in 1949. Since 1948 more than 50 priests have been executed and 200 have died in prison. One hundred priests were reported in prison at the end of 1958. Some change for the better in Church-state relations was reported after the middle of the summer of 1964, although restrictions were still in effect. About 1,200 priests were engaged in parish work in August, 1965. Conditions improved in 1990 with the change of government. The hierarchy was restored and diplomatic relations with the Holy See were reestablished.

### Russia*

*Dioc., 1; a.a., 2 (1 for European Russia, 1 for Siberia); ap. ex., 1; abp., 2; bp., 1; priests, 142 (36 dioc., 106 rel.); p.d., 1; sem., 32; bros., 5; srs 143; bap., 1,958; Caths., 428,000; tot. pop., 148,000,000.*

Federation in Europe and Asia; capital, Moscow. (See Union of Soviet Socialist Republic for background information.)

### Rwanda*

*Archd., 1; dioc., 8; abp., 2; bp., 8; parishes, 127; priests, 522 (348 dioc., 174 rel.); p.d., 1; sem., 264; bros., 279; srs., 1,192; bap., 155,744; Caths., 3,551,000 (45.8%); tot. pop., 7,750,000.*

Republic in east central Africa; capital, Kigali. Catholicism was introduced about the turn of the 20th century. The hierarchy was established in 1959. Intertribal warfare between the ruling Hutus (90 per cent of the population) and the Tutsis (formerly the ruling aristocracy) plagued the country for a number of years. In April, 1994, the deaths of the presidents of Rwanda and Burundi in a suspicious plane crash sparked the outbreak of a ferocious civil war. Among the thousands of victims were three bishops and about twenty-five percent of the clergy.

### Saint Christopher and Nevis

*Parishes, 4; priests, 4 (1 dioc., 3 rel.); srs., 3; bap., 49; Caths., 5,000; tot. pop., 46,000. (AD)*

Independent (Sept. 19, 1983) island states in West Indies; capital, Basseterre, on St. Christopher;

Charlestown, on Nevis. Under ecclesiastical jurisdiction of St. John's-Basseterre diocese, Antigua.

### Saint Helena

*Independent mission, 1; parish, 1; priest, 1 (religious; head of the mission); Caths., 100; tot. pop., 7,000.*

Comprises British Island possessions of St. Helena, Ascension and Tristan da Cunha in the South Atlantic; formerly under ecclesiastical jurisdiction of Cape Town archdiocese (South Africa).

### Saint Lucia*

*Archd., 1; abp., 1; bp., 1; parishes, 23; priests, 32 (18 dioc., 21 rel.); p.d., 5; sem., 1; bros., 3; srs., 38; bap., 2,581; Caths., 109,000; tot. pop., 139,000.*

Independent (Feb. 22, 1979) island state in West Indies; capital, Castries.

### Saint Pierre and Miquelon

*V.a., 1; bp., 1; parishes, 3; priests, 3 (rel.); srs., 7; bap., 75; Caths., 6,000; tot. pop., 6,000.*

French overseas department, two groups of islands near the southwest coast of Newfoundland; capital, St. Pierre. Catholicism was introduced about 1689.

### Saint Vincent and the Grenadines*

*Dioc., 1; bp., 1; parishes, 6; priests, 9 (5 dioc., 4 rel.); bros., 4; srs., 14; bap., 254; Caths., 9,000; tot. pop., 106,000.*

Independent state (1979) in West Indies; capital, Kingstown. The Kingstown diocese (St. Vincent) was established in 1989; it was formerly part of Bridgetown-Kingstown diocese with see in Barbados.

### American Samoa

*Dioc., 1; bp., 1; parishes 8; priests, 12 (9 dioc., 3 rel.); p.d., 1; sem., 6; bros., 3; srs., 13; bap., 385; Caths., 9,000; tot. pop., 56,000.*

Unincorporated U.S. territory in southwestern Pacific, consisting of six small islands; seat of government, Pago Pago on the Island of Tutuila. Samoa-Pago Pago diocese established in 1982.

### Western Samoa*

*Archd., 1; card., 1; parishes, 26; priests, 48 (24 dioc., 24 rel.); p.d., 3; sem., 12; bros., 23; srs., 94; bap., 1,594; Caths., 35,000; tot. pop., 164,000.*

Independent state in the southwestern Pacific; capital, Apia. Catholic missionary work began in 1845. Most of the missions now in operation were established by 1870 when the Catholic population numbered about 5,000. Additional progress was made in missionary work from 1896. The first Samoan priest was ordained in 1892. A diocese was established in 1966; elevated to a metropolitan see in 1982.

### San Marino*

*Parishes, 12; priests, 24 (12 dioc., 12 rel.); bros., 2; srs., 30; bap., 201; Caths., 24,000; tot. pop., 25,000.*

Republic, a 24-square-mile enclave in northeastern Italy; capital, San Marino. The date of initial evangelization is not known, but a diocese was established by the end of the third century. Ecclesiastically, it forms part of the diocese of San Marino-Montefeltro in Italy.

## Sao Tome and Principe*

*Dioc., 1; bp., 1; parishes, 12; priests, 11 ( rel.); sem. 12; bros., 4; srs., 33; bap., 3,509; Caths., 100,000 (82%); tot. pop., 121,000.*

Independent republic (July 12, 1975), consisting of two islands off the western coast of Africa in the Gulf of Guinea; former Portuguese territory; capital, Sao Tome. Evangelization was begun by the Portuguese who discovered the islands in 1471-72. The Sao Tome diocese was established in 1534.

## Saudi Arabia

Monarchy occupying four-fifths of Arabian peninsula; capital, Riyadh. Population is Muslim; all other religions are banned. Christians in the area are workers from other countries. Under ecclesiastical jurisdiction of Arabia vicariate apostolic.

Population, 17,450,000.

## Scotland

*Archd., 2; dioc., 6; card., 1; abp., 1; bp., 8; parishes, 458; priests, 873 (679 dioc., 194 rel.); p.d. 11; sem., 77; bros., 90; srs., 857; bap., 11,005; Caths., 763,848 (14.7%); tot. pop., 5,203,300. (1996 Annuario Pontificio.)*

Part of the United Kingdom, in the northern British Isles; capital, Edinburgh. Christianity was introduced by the early years of the fifth century. The arrival of St. Columba and his monks in 563 inaugurated a new era of evangelization which reached into remote areas by the end of the sixth century. He was extremely influential in determining the character of the Celtic Church, which was tribal, monastic, and in union with Rome. Considerable disruption of church activity resulted from Scandinavian invasions in the late eighth and ninth centuries. By 1153 the Scottish Church took a turn away from its insularity and was drawn into closer contact with the European community. Anglo-Saxon religious and political relations, complicated by rivalries between princes and ecclesiastical superiors, were not always the happiest. Religious orders expanded greatly in the 12th century. From shortly after the Norman Conquest of England to 1560 the Church suffered adverse effects from the Hundred Years' War, the Black Death, the Western Schism and other developments. In 1560 parliament abrogated papal supremacy over the Church in Scotland and committed the country to Protestantism in 1567. The Catholic Church was proscribed, to remain that way for more than 200 years, and the hierarchy was disbanded. Defections made the Church a minority religion from that time on. Presbyterian church government was ratified in 1690. Priests launched the Scottish Mission in 1653, incorporating themselves as a mission body under a prefect apostolic and working underground to serve the faithful in much the same way their confreres did in England. About 100 heather priests, trained in clandestine places in the heather country, were ordained by the early 19th century. Catholics got some relief from legal disabilities in 1793 and more later. Many left the country about that time. Some of their numbers were filled subsequently by immigrants from Ireland. The hierarchy was restored in 1878. Scotland, though predominantly Protestant, has a better record for tolerance than Northern Ireland.

## Senegal*

*Archd., 1; dioc., 5; card., 1; bp., 5; parishes, 86; priests, 313 (171 dioc., 142 rel.); sem., 154; bros., 180; srs., 638; bap., 17,614; Caths., 384,000 (4.7%); tot. pop., 8,100,000.*

Republic in western Africa; capital, Dakar. The country had its first contact with Catholicism through the Portuguese some time after 1460. Some incidental missionary work was done by Jesuits and Capuchins in the 16th and 17th centuries. A vicariate for the area was placed in charge of the Holy Ghost Fathers in 1779. More effective evangelization efforts were accomplished after the Senegambia vicariate was erected in 1863; the hierarchy was established in 1955.

## Seychelles*

*Dioc., 1; bp., 1; parishes, 17; priests, 15 (9 dioc., 6 rel.); sem., 1; bros., 7; srs., 58; bap., 1,424; Caths., 69,000; tot. pop., 75,000.*

Independent (1976) group of 92 islands in the Indian Ocean 970 miles east of Kenya; capital, Victoria. Catholicism was introduced in the 18th century. A vicariate apostolic was organized in 1852. All education in the islands was conducted under Catholic auspices until 1954.

## Sierra Leone*

*Archd., 1; dioc., 2; abp., 1; bp., 2; parishes, 35; priests, 119 (37 dioc., 82 rel.); sem., 62; bros., 35; srs., 116; bap., 2,955; Caths., 135,000 (3%); tot. pop., 4,400,000.*

Republic on the western coast of Africa; capital, Freetown. Catholicism was introduced in 1858. Members of the African Missions Society, the first Catholic missionaries in the area, were joined by Holy Ghost Fathers in 1864. Protestant missionaries were active in the area before their Catholic counterparts. Educational work had a major part in Catholic endeavor. The hierarchy was established in 1950. Most of the inhabitants are followers of Traditional African Religions.

## Singapore*

*Archd., 1; abp., 1; parishes, 30; priests, 131 (75 dioc., 56 rel.); sem., 26; bros., 53; srs., 236; bap., 3,948; Caths., 129,000 (4.4%); tot. pop., 2,930,000.*

Independent island republic off the southern tip of the Malay Peninsula; capital, Singapore. Christianity was introduced in the area by Portuguese colonists about 1511. Singapore was founded in 1819; the first parish church was built in 1846.

## Slovakia*

*Archd., 2; dioc., 5; card., 2; abp., 1; bp., 14; parishes, 1,391; priests, 1,942 (1,496 dioc., 446 rel.); p.d., 3; sem., 984; bros., 230; srs., 2,857; bap., 58,162; Caths., 3,634,000 (68%); tot. pop., 5,350,000.*

Independent state (Jan. 1, 1993); formerly part of

Czechoslovakia; capital, Bratislava. Christianity was introduced in Slovakia in the 8th century by Irish and German missionaries and the area was under the jurisdiction of German bishops. In 863, at the invitation of the Slovak ruler Rastislav who wanted to preserve the cultural and liturgical heritage of the people, Sts. Cyril and Methodius began pastoral and missionary work in the region, ministering to the people in their own language. The saints introduced Old Slovak (Old Church Slavonic) into the liturgy and did so much to evangelize the territory that they are venerated as the apostles of Slovakia. A diocese established at Nitra in 880 had a continuous history except for a century ending in 1024. The Church in Slovakia was severely tested by the Reformation and political upheavals. After World War I, when it became part of the Republic of Czechoslovakia, it was 75 per cent Catholic. (For the status of the Church during communist domination, see Czechoslovakia.)

## Slovenia*

Archd., 1; dioc., 2; abp., 1; bp., 7; parishes, 797; priests, 1,171 (836 dioc., 335 rel.); p.d., 7; sem., 204; bros., 63; srs., 884; bap., 17,244; Caths., 1,668,000 (86%); tot. pop., 1,940,000.

Independent republic (1991) in southeastern Europe; formerly part of Yugoslavia; capital, Ljubljana. Established diplomatic relations with the Holy See in 1992. (See Index for 1996 papal visit.)

## Solomon Islands*

Archd., 1; dioc., 2; abp., 1; bp., 2; parishes, 28; priests, 46 (15 dioc., 31 rel.); sem., 34; bros., 19; srs., 98; bap., 2,300; Caths., 72,000 (19.4%); tot. pop., 370,000.

Independent (July 7, 1978) island group in Oceania; capital, Honiara, on Guadalcanal. Evangelization of the Southern Solomons, begun earlier but interrupted because of violence against them, was resumed by the Marists in 1898. A vicariate apostolic was organized in 1912. A similar jurisdiction was set up for the Western Solomons in 1959. World War II caused a great deal of damage to mission installations.

## Somalia

Dioc., 1; priests, 3 (1 dioc., 2 rel.); sem., 1; bro., 1; srs., 4; Caths., 200; tot. pop., 9,080,000. (AD)

Republic on the eastern coast of Africa; capital, Mogadishu. The country has been Muslim for centuries. Pastoral activity has been confined to immigrants. Schools and hospitals were nationalized in 1972, resulting in the departure of some foreign missionaries.

## South Africa*

Archd., 4; dioc., 21; v.a., 1; mil. ord.; abp., 4; bp., 28; parishes, 727; priests, 1,103 (333 dioc., 770 rel.); p.d., 198; sem., 294; bros., 219; srs., 2,875; bap., 62,703; Caths., 2,965,000 (7.3%); tot. pop., 40,440,000.

Republic in the southern part of Africa; capitals, Cape Town (legislative), Pretoria (administrative) and Bloemfontein (judicial). Christianity was introduced by the Portuguese who discovered the Cape of Good Hope in 1488. Boers, who founded Cape Town in 1652, expelled Catholics from the region.

There was no Catholic missionary activity from that time until the 19th century. After a period of British opposition, a bishop established residence in 1837 and evangelization got under way thereafter among the Bantus and white immigrants. The hierarchy was established in 1951. The white supremacy policy of apartheid which seriously infringed on the human rights of native blacks and impeded the Church from carrying out its pastoral, educational and social service functions finally ceased to exist in 1994, following the first all-race election. (See Index for 1995 papal visit.)

## Spain*

Archd., 14; dioc., 54; mil. ord.; card., 6; abp., 18; bp., 88; parishes, 21,680; priests, 29,354 (19,766 dioc., 9,588 rel.); p.d., 181; sem., 3,269; bros., 5,670; srs., 68,497; bap., 321,312; Caths., 37,162,000 (94.8%); tot. pop., 39,190,000.

Constitutional monarchy on the Iberian peninsula in southwestern Europe; capital, Madrid. Christians were on the peninsula by 200; some of them suffered martyrdom during persecutions of the third century. A council held in Elvira about 304/6 enacted the first legislation on clerical celibacy in the West. Vandals invaded the peninsula in the fifth century, bringing with them an Arian brand of Christianity which they retained until their conversion following the baptism of their king Reccared, in 589. One of the significant developments of the seventh century was the establishment of Toledo as the primatial see. The Visigoth kingdom lasted to the time of the Arab invasion, 711-14. The Church survived under Muslim rule but experienced some doctrinal and disciplinary irregularities as well as harassment. Reconquest of most of the peninsula was accomplished by 1248; unification was achieved during the reign of Ferdinand and Isabella. The discoveries of Columbus and other explorers ushered in an era of colonial expansion in which Spain became one of the greatest mission-sending countries in history. In 1492, in repetition of anti-Semitic actions of 694, the expulsion of unbaptized Jews was decreed, leading to mass baptisms but a questionable number of real conversions in 1502. (The Jewish minority numbered about 165,000.) Activity by the Inquisition followed. Spain was not seriously affected by the Reformation. Ecclesiastical decline set in about 1650. Anti-Church actions authorized by a constitution enacted in 1812 resulted in the suppression of religious and other encroachments on the leaders, people and goods of the Church. Political, religious and cultural turmoil recurred during the 19th century and into the 20th. A revolutionary republic was proclaimed in 1931, triggering a series of developments which led to civil war from 1936 to 1939. During the conflict, which pitted leftist Loyalists against the forces of Francisco Franco, 6,632 priests and religious and an unknown number of lay persons perished in addition to thousands of victims of combat. One-man, one-party rule, established after the civil war and with rigid control policies with respect to personal liberties and social and economic issues, continued for more than 35 years before giving way after the death of Franco to democratic reforms. The Catholic Church, long the established religion, was disestablished under a new constitution providing guarantees of freedom for other religions as well. Disestablishment was ratified with modifications of a 1976 revision of the earlier concordat of 1953.

## Sri Lanka*

*Archd., 1; dioc., 10; abp., 1; bp., 14; parishes, 375; priests, 853 (546 dioc., 307 rel.); p.d., 11; sem., 321; bros., 231; srs., 2,314; bap., 26,667; Caths., 1,201,000 (6.7%); tot. pop., 17,860,000.*

Independent socialist republic, island southeast of India (formerly Ceylon); capital, Colombo. Effective evangelization began in 1543 and made great progress by the middle of the 17th century. The Church was seriously hampered during the Dutch period from about 1650 to 1795. Anti-Catholic laws were repealed by the British in 1806. The hierarchy was established in 1886. Leftist governments and other factors have worked against the Church since the country became independent in 1948. The high percentage of indigenous clergy and religious has been of great advantage to the Church.

## Sudan*

*Archd., 2; dioc., 7; abp., 2; bp., 7; parishes, 103; priests, 199 (97 dioc., 102 rel.); p.d., 4; sem., 214; bros., 60; srs., 244; catechists, 3,373; bap., 47,551; Caths., 2,395,000 (8.2%); tot. pop., 28,950,000.*

Republic in northeastern Africa, the largest country on the continent; capital Khartoum. Christianity was introduced from Egypt and gained acceptance in the sixth century. Under Arab rule, it was eliminated in the northern region. No Christians were in the country in 1600. Evangelization attempts begun in the 19th century in the south yielded hard-won results. By 1931 there were nearly 40,000 Catholics there, and considerable progress was made by missionaries after that time. In 1957, a year after the republic was established, Catholic schools were nationalized. An act restrictive of religious freedom went into effect in 1962, resulting in the harassment and expulsion of foreign missionaries. By 1964 all but a few Sudanese missionaries had been forced out of the southern region. The northern area, where Islam predominates, is impervious to Christian influence. Late in 1971 some missionaries were allowed to return to work in the South. Southern Sudan was granted regional autonomy within a unified country in March, 1972, thus ending often bitter fighting between the North and South dating back to 1955. The hierarchy was established in 1974. The imposition of Islamic penal codes in 1984 was a cause of concern to all Christian churches.

## Suriname*

*Dioc., 1; bp., 1; parishes, 22; priests, 22 (4 dioc., 18 rel.); sem., 4; bros., 9; srs., 36; bap., 2,192; Caths., 90,000 (21%); tot. pop., 420,000.*

Independent (Nov. 25, 1975) state in northern South America (formerly Dutch Guiana); capital, Paramaribo, Catholicism was introduced in 1683. Evangelization began in 1817.

## Swaziland*

*Dioc., 1; bp., 1; parishes, 14; priests, 38 (6 dioc., 32 rel.); sem., 10; bros., 5; srs., 73; bap., 843; Caths., 47,000 (5.3%); tot. pop., 880,000.*

Monarchy in southern Africa; almost totally surrounded by South Africa; capital, Mbabane. Missionary work was entrusted to the Servites in 1913. A prefecture apostolic was organized in 1923. The hierarchy was established in 1951. Established diplomatic relations with the Holy See in 1992.

## Sweden*

*Dioc., 1; bp., 2; parishes, 40; priests, 134 (63 dioc., 71 rel.); p.d., 10; sem., 12; bros., 15; srs., 242; bap., 1,445; Caths., 155,841 (1.7%); tot. pop., 8,790,109.*

Constitutional monarchy in northwestern Europe; capital, Stockholm. Christianity was introduced by St. Ansgar, a Frankish monk, in 829/30. The Church became well established in the 12th century and was a major influence at the end of the Middle Ages. Political and other factors favored the introduction and spread of the Lutheran Church which became the state religion in 1560. The Augsburg Confession of 1530 was accepted by the government; all relations with Rome were severed; monasteries were suppressed; the very presence of Catholics in the country was forbidden in 1617. A decree of tolerance for foreign Catholics was issued about 1781. Two years later a vicariate apostolic was organized for the country. In 1873 Swedes were given the legal right to leave the Lutheran Church and join another Christian church. (Membership in the Lutheran Church is presumed by law unless notice is given of membership in another church.) In 1923 there were only 11 priests and five churches in the country. Since 1952 Catholics have enjoyed almost complete religious freedom. The hierarchy was reestablished in 1953. Hindrances to growth of the Church are the strongly entrenched established church, limited resources, a clergy shortage and the size of the country.

## Switzerland*

*Dioc., 6; abb., 2; card., 2; bp., 17; parishes, 1,668; priests, 3,509 (2,027 dioc., 1,482 rel.); p.d., 83; sem., 212; bros., 407; srs., 8,178; bap., 32,634; Caths., 3,243,000 (46.4%); tot. pop., 6,990,000.*

Confederation in central Europe; capital, Bern. Christianity was introduced in the fourth century or earlier and was established on a firm footing before the barbarian invasions of the sixth century. Constance, established as a diocese in the seventh century, was a stronghold of the faith against the pagan Alamanni, in particular, who were not converted until some time in the ninth century. During this period of struggle with the barbarians, a number of monasteries of great influence were established. The Reformation in Switzerland was triggered by Zwingli in 1519 and furthered by him at Zurich until his death in battle against the Catholic cantons in 1531. Calvin set in motion the forces that made Geneva the international capital of the Reformation and transformed it into a theocracy. Catholics mobilized a Counter-Reformation in 1570, six years after Calvin's death. Struggle between Protestant and Catholic cantons was a fact of Swiss life for several hundred years. The Helvetic Constitution enacted at the turn of the 19th century embodied anti-Catholic measures and consequences, among them the dissolution of 130 monasteries. The Church was reorganized later in the century to meet the threats of liberalism, radicalism and the Kulturkampf. In the process, the Church, even though on the defensive, gained the strength and cohesion that characterizes it to the present time. The six dioceses in the country are immediately subject to the Holy See. In 1973, constitutional articles banning Jesuits from the country and prohibiting the establishment of convents and monasteries were repealed.

## Syria*

*Patriarchates, 3 (Antioch of Maronites, Greek Melkites and Syrians; patriarchs of Maronites and Syrians reside in Lebanon); archd., 12 (1 Armenian, 2 Maronite, 5 Greek Melkite, 4 Syrian); dioc., 3 (Armenian, Chaldean, Maronite); v.a., 1 (Latin); patriarch, 1; abp., 16; bp., 7; parishes, 196; priests, 237 (160 dioc., 77 rel.); p.d., 4; sem., 73; bros., 15; srs., 401; bap., 2,298; Caths., 283,000 (2%); tot. pop., 13,880,000.*

Arab socialist republic in southwest Asia; capital, Damascus. Christian communities were formed in apostolic times. It is believed that St. Peter established a see at Antioch before going to Rome. Damascus became a center of influence. The area was the place of great men and great events in the early history of the Church. Monasticism developed there in the fourth century. So did the Monophysite and Monothelite heresies to which portion of the Church succumbed. Byzantine Syrians who remained in communion with Rome were given the name Melkites. Christians of various persuasions — Jacobites, Orthodox and Melkites — were subject to various degrees of harassment from the Arabs who took over in 638 and from the Ottoman Turks who isolated the country and remained in control from 1516 to the end of World War II.

## Taiwan

*Archd., 1; dioc., 6; abp., 1; bp., 9; parishes, 426; priests, 718 (225 dioc., 493 rel.); p.d., 1; sem., 129; bros., 142; srs., 1,131; bap., 3,550; Caths., 299,000 (1.3%); tot. pop., 22,193,000.*

Democratic island state 100 miles off the southern coast of mainland China (also known as Formosa); capital, Taipei. Attempts to introduce Christianity in the 17th century were unsuccessful. Evangelization in the 19th century resulted in some 1,300 converts in 1895. Missionary endeavor was hampered by the Japanese who occupied the island following the Sino-Japanese war of 1894-95. Nine thousand Catholics were reported in 1938. Great progress was made in missionary endeavor among the Chinese who emigrated to the island (seat of the Nationalist Government of the Republic of China) following the Communist take-over of the mainland in 1949. The hierarchy was established in 1952.

## Tajikistan*

Independent republic (1992) bordering China and Afghanistan; formerly part of the USSR; capital, Dushanbe. The majority of the population is Sunni Muslim. Total population, 5,750,000.

## Tanzania*

*Archd., 4; dioc., 25; card., 1; abp., 6; bp., 29; parishes, 761; priests, 1,827 (1,216 dioc., 671 rel.); sem., 910; bros., 544; srs., 6,438; catechists, 12,030; bap., 248,679; Caths., 6,865,000 (23.7%); tot. pop., 28,850,000.*

Republic (consisting of former Tanganyika on the eastern coast of Africa and former Zanzibar, an island group off the eastern coast); capital, Dar es Salaam. The first Catholic mission in the former Tanganyikan portion of the republic was manned by Holy Ghost Fathers in 1868. The hierarchy was established there in 1953. Zanzibar was the landing place of Augustinians with the Portuguese in 1499. Some evangelization was attempted between then and 1698 when the Arabs expelled all priests from the territory. There was no Catholic missionary activity from then until the 1860s. The Holy Ghost Fathers arrived in 1863 and were entrusted with the mission in 1872. Zanzibar was important as a point of departure for missionaries to Tanganyika, Kenya and other places in East Africa. A vicariate for Zanzibar was set up in 1906.

## Thailand*

*Archd., 2; dioc., 8; card., 1; abp., 3; bp., 14; parishes, 307; priests, 582 (346 dioc., 236 rel.); p.d., 1; sem., 258; bros., 144; srs., 1,389; bap., 6,474; Caths., 243,000 (.4%); tot. pop., 59,400,000.*

Constitutional monarchy in southeastern Asia (formerly Siam); capital, Bangkok. The first Christians in the region were Portuguese traders who arrived early in the 16th century. A number of missionaries began arriving in 1554 but pastoral care was confined mostly to the Portuguese until the 1660s. Evangelization of the natives got under way from about that time. A seminary was organized in 1665, a vicariate was set up four years later, and a point of departure was established for missionaries to Tonkin, Cochin China and China. Persecution and death for some of the missionaries ended evangelization efforts in 1688. It was resumed, however, and made progress from 1824 onwards. In 1881 missionaries were sent from Siam to neighboring Laos. The hierarchy was established in 1965. Abp. Michai Kitbunchu was named the first Thai cardinal in 1983.

## Togo*

*Archd., 1; dioc., 6; abp., 1; bp., 6; parishes, 100; priests, 328 (208 dioc., 120 rel.); sem., 230; bros., 155; srs., 549; bap., 34,645; Caths., 925,000 (23.5%); tot. pop., 3,930,000.*

Republic on the western coast of Africa; capital, Lome. The first Catholic missionaries in the area, where slave raiders operated for nearly 200 years, were members of the African Missions Society who arrived in 1563. They were followed by Divine Word Missionaries in 1914, when a prefecture apostolic was organized. At that time the Catholic population numbered about 19,000. The African Missionaries returned after their German predecessors were deported following World War I. The first native priest was ordained in 1922. The hierarchy was established in 1955.

## Tokelau

*Independent Mission, 1; parishes, 2; priest, 1 (dioc.); sem., 2; srs., 3; bap., 13; Caths., 1,000; tot. pop., 2,000. (AD)*

Pacific islands administered by New Zealand. Established as an independent mission in 1992.

## Tonga*

*Dioc., 1; bp., 1; parishes, 13; priests, 21 (12 dioc., 9 rel.); sem., 26; bros., 9; srs., 54; bap., 509; Caths., 13,000 (13.5%); tot. pop., 96,000.*

Polynesian monarchy in the southwestern Pacific, consisting of about 150 islands; capital Nuku'alofa. Marists started missionary work in 1842, some years after Protestants had begun evangelization. By 1880 the Catholic population numbered about 1,700. A vicariate was organized in 1937. The hierarchy was established in 1966. Established diplomatic relations with the Holy See in 1994.

## Trinidad and Tobago*

*Archd., 1; abp., 1; bp., 1; parishes, 61; priests, 115 (41 dioc., 74 rel.); p.d., 3; sem., 21; bros., 17; srs., 174; bap., 5,723; Caths., 400,000 (31.7%); tot. pop., 1,260,000.*

Independent nation, consisting of two islands in the Caribbean; capital, Port-of-Spain. The first Catholic church in Trinidad was built in 1591, years after several missionary ventures had been launched and a number of missionaries killed. Capuchins were there from 1618 until about 1802. Missionary work continued after the British gained control early in the 19th century. Cordial relations have existed between the Church and state, both of which have manifested their desire for the development of native clergy.

## Tunisia*

*Dioc., 1; bp., 1; parishes, 14; priests, 45 (21 dioc., 24 rel.); sem., 2; bros., 9; srs., 168; bap., 14; Caths., 18,000 (.2%); tot. pop., 8,730,000.*

Republic on the northern coast of Africa; capital, Tunis. There were few Christians in the territory until the 19th century. A prefecture apostolic was organized in 1843 and the Carthage archdiocese was established in 1884. The Catholic population in 1892 consisted of most of the approximately 50,000 Europeans in the country. When Tunis became a republic in 1956, most of the Europeans left the country. The Holy See and the Tunisian government concluded an agreement in 1964 which changed the Carthage archdiocese into a prelacy and handed over some ecclesiastical property to the republic. A considerable number of Muslim students are in Catholic schools, but the number of Muslim converts to the Church has been small. (See Index for 1996 papal visit.)

## Turkey*

*Patriarchate, 1 (Cilicia for the Armenians; the patriarch resides in Lebanon); archd., 3; v.a., 2; ap. ex., 1; abp., 4; bp., 2; parishes, 49; priests, 62 (16 dioc., 46 rel.); p.d., 13; sem., 4; bros., 14; srs., 113; bap., 161; Caths., 30,000; tot. pop., 61,180,000.*

Republic in Asia Minor and southeastern Europe, capital, Ankara. Christian communities were established in apostolic times, as attested in the Acts of the Apostles, some of the Letters of St. Paul, and Revelation. The territory was the scene of heresies and ecumenical councils, the place of residence of Fathers of the Church, the area in which ecclesiastical organization reached the dimensions of more than 450 sees in the middle of the seventh century. The region remained generally Byzantine except for the period of the Latin occupation of Constantinople from 1204 to 1261, but was conquered by the Ottoman Turks in 1453 and remained under their domination until establishment of the republic in 1923. Christians, always a minority, numbered more Orthodox than Latins; they were all under some restrictions during the Ottoman period. They suffered persecution in the 19th and 20th centuries, the Armenians being the most numerous victims. Turkey is overwhelmingly Muslim. Catholics are tolerated to a degree.

## Turkmenistan*

Former constituent republic of USSR; independent, 1991; capital, Ashkabad. Almost all the population is Sunni Muslim. The few Catholics are entrusted to the care of Franciscans living in Ashkabad. Total population, 4,010,000.

## Turks and Caicos Islands

*Independent mission, 1; parishes, 2; priests, 1 (rel.); bap., 46; Caths., 1,000; tot. pop., 11,000. (AD, Antilles)*

British possession in West Indies; capital, Grand Turk.

## Tuvalu

*Independent mission, 1; priest, 1 (rel.); bap., 7; Caths., 100; tot. pop., 9,000.*

Independent state (1978) in Oceania, consisting of 9 islands (formerly Ellice Islands); capital, Funafuti.

## Uganda*

*Archd., 1; dioc. (1996), 16; mil. ord.; card., 1; bp., 20; parishes, 369; priests, 1,297 (997 dioc., 300 rel.); sem., 705; bros., 402; srs., 2,955; catechists, 11,264; bap., 307,794; Caths., 8,852,000 (42.9%); tot. pop., 20,620,000.*

Republic in eastern Africa; capital, Kampala. The Missionaries of Africa (White Fathers) were the first Catholic missionaries, starting in 1879. Persecution broke out from 1885 to 1887, taking a toll of 22 Catholic martyrs, who were canonized in 1964, and a number of Anglican victims. (Pope Paul honored all those who died for the faith during a visit to Kampala in 1969.) By 1888, there were more than 8,000 Catholics. Evangelization was resumed in 1894, after being interrupted by war, and proceeded thereafter. The first native African bishop was ordained in 1939. The hierarchy was established in 1953. The Church was suppressed during the erratic regime of Pres. Idi-Amin, who was deposed in the spring of 1979. The country has suffered greatly from tribal rivalry and conflict in recent years.

## Ukraine*

*Major archbishopric, 1 (Ukrainian); archd., 2 (1 Armenian and 1 Latin rite); dioc., 9 (6 Byzantine rite, 3 Latin); a.a., 1; card., 1 (Ukrainian Major Archbishop Lubachivsky); abp., 3; bp., 17; parishes, 2,966; priests, 1,738 (1,381 dioc., 357 rel.); p.d., 5; sem., 1,478; bros., 393; srs., 958; bap., 53,396; Caths., 5,433,000 (10.5%); tot. pop., 51,910,000.*

Independent republic bordering on the Black Sea; former USSR republic; capital, Kiev. The baptism of Vladimir and his people in 988 marked the beginning of Christianity in the territory of Kievan Rus which is included in today's Ukraine. The Byzantine-Rite Catholic Church was officially suppressed and underground in the USSR from the late 1940s. (See USSR below for situation during communist control.)

## Union of Soviet Socialist Republics

(The Union of Soviet Socialist Republics disbanded Dec. 25, 1991. Background history of the USSR especially during communist domination is given below. See also separate entries: Armenia, Azerbaijan, Belarus, Estonia, Georgia, Kazakhstan, Kyrgyzstan, Latvia, Lithuania, Moldova, Russian Federation, Tajikistan, Turkmenistan, Ukraine, Uzbekistan.) The Orthodox Church has been predominant in Russian history. It developed from the Byzantine Church before 1064. Some of its members subsequently established communion with Rome as the result of reunion movements but most of them remained Orthodox. The government has always retained some kind of general or particular control of this church. Latins, always a minority, had a little more freedom. From the beginning of the Communist government in 1917, all churches of whatever kind — including Jews and Muslims — became the targets of official campaigns designed to negate their influence on society and/or to eliminate them entirely. An accurate assessment of the situation of the Catholic Church in Russia was difficult to make. Its dimensions, however, could be gauged from the findings of a team of research specialists made public by the Judiciary Committee of the U.S. House of Representatives in 1964. It was reported: "The fate of the Catholic Church in the USSR and countries occupied by the Russians from 1917 to 1959 shows the following: (a) the number killed: 55 bishops; 12,800 priests and monks; 2.5 million Catholic believers; (b) imprisoned or deported: 199 bishops; 32,000 priests and 10 million believers; (c) 15,700 priests were forced to abandon their priesthood and accept other jobs; and (d) a large number of seminaries and religious communities were dissolved; 1,600 monasteries were nationalized, 31,779 churches were closed. 400 newspapers were prohibited, and all Catholic organizations were dissolved." Several Latin Rite churches were open; e.g., in Moscow, Leningrad, Odessa and Tiflis. An American chaplain was stationed in Moscow to serve Catholics at the U.S. embassy there. Despite repression and attempts at Sovietization, Lithuania and Ukraine remained strongholds of Catholicism. In 1991, the Pope reconstituted the Byzantine hierarchy in Ukraine. He also established: two Latin rite apostolic administrations in the Russian Republic; one Latin-rite apostolic administration in the Kazakhstan Republic; a metropolitan see and two suffragans in Byelorussia (now Belarus).

## United Arab Emirates

V.a, 1; bp., 1; parishes, 5; priests, 16 (3 dioc., 13 rel.); srs., 35; bap., 1,210; Caths., 110,000; tot. pop., 1,860,000.

Independent state along Persian Gulf; capital, Abu Dhabi. The vicariate apostolic of Arabia has its seat in Abu Dhabi. It includes the states of Bahrain, Oman, Qatar, Saudi Arabia and Yemen (see separate entries) as well as United Arab Emirates.

## United States*

See Catholic History in the United States, Statistics of the Church in the United States.

## Uruguay*

Archd., 1; dioc., 9; abp., 2; bp., 13; parishes, 233; priests, 545 (221 dioc., 324 rel.); p.d., 51; sem., 69; bros., 96; srs., 1,571; bap., 38,048; Caths., 2,458,000 (77.5%); tot. pop., 3,170,000.

Republic (called the Eastern Republic of Uruguay) on the southeast coast of South America; capital, Montevideo. The Spanish established a settlement in 1624 and evangelization followed. Missionaries followed the reduction pattern to reach the Indians, form them in the faith and train them in agriculture, husbandry, other useful arts, and the experience of managing property and living in community. Montevideo was made a diocese in 1878. The constitution of 1830 made Catholicism the religion of the state and subsidized some of its activities, principally the missions to the Indians. Separation of Church and state was provided for in the constitution of 1917.

## Uzbekistan*

Former republic of USSR; independent, 1991; capital, Tashkent. The majority of the population is Sunni Muslim. A small number of Catholics live in Tashkent, where there is a church and one priest (L'Osservatore Romano, English Edition); tot. pop., 22,350,000.

## Vanuatu*

Dioc., 1; bp., 1; parishes, 18; priests, 25 (8 dioc., 17 rel.); p.d., 1; sem., 14; bros., 16; srs., 74; bap., 1,020; Caths., 25,000 (16%); tot. pop., 156,000.

Independent (July 29, 1980) island group in the southwest Pacific, about 500 miles west of Fiji (formerly New Hebrides); capital, Vila. Effective, though slow, evangelization by Catholic missionaries began about 1887. A vicariate apostolic was set up in 1904. The hierarchy was established in 1966.

## Vatican City

See separate entry.

## Venezuela*

Archd., 8; dioc., 20; v.a., 4; ap. ex., 1; mil. ord. (1996); card., 2; abp., 8; bp., 34; parishes, 1,080; priests, 2,140 (1,049 dioc., 1,091 rel.); p.d., 68; sem., 963; bros., 344; srs., 4,331; bap., 388,092; Caths., 19,636,000 (92.7%); tot. pop., 21,180,000.

Republic in northern South America; capital, Caracas. Evangelization began in 1513-14 and involved members of a number of religious orders who worked in assigned territories, developing missions into pueblos or towns and villages of Indian converts. Nearly 350 towns originated as missions. Fifty-four missionaries met death by violence from the start of missionary work until 1817. Missionary work was seriously hindered during the wars of independence in the second decade of the 19th century and continued in decline through the rest of the century as dictator followed dictator in a period of political turbulence. Restoration of the missions got under way in 1922. The first diocese was established in 1531. Most of the bishops have been native Venezuelans. The first diocesan synod was held in 1574. Church-state relations are regulated by an agreement concluded with the Holy See in 1964. (See Index for 1996 papal visit.)

## Vietnam

*Archd., 3; dioc., 22; card., 1; abp., 2; bp., 29; parishes, 1,784; priests, 2,026 (1,669 dioc., 357 rel.); p.d., 7; sem., 1,100; bros., 642; srs., 6,250; bap., 141,192; Caths., 5,760,000 (7.9%); tot. pop., 72,510,000.*

Country in southeastern Asia, reunited officially July 2, 1976, as the Socialist Republic of Vietnam; capital, Hanoi. Previously, from 1954, partitioned into the Democratic Peoples' Republic of Vietnam in the North (capital, Hanoi) and the Republic of Vietnam in the South (capital, Saigon). Catholicism was introduced in 1533 but missionary work was intermittent until 1615 when Jesuits arrived to stay. One hundred thousand Catholics were reported in 1639. Two vicariates were organized in 1659. A seminary was set up in 1666 and two native priests were ordained two years later. A congregation of native women religious formed in 1670 is still active. Severe persecution broke out in 1698, three times in the 18th century, and again in the 19th. Between 100,000 and 300,000 persons suffered in some way from persecution during the 50 years before 1883 when the French moved in to secure religious liberty for the Catholics. Most of the 117 beatified Martyrs of Vietnam were killed during this 50-year period. After the French were forced out of Vietnam in 1954, the country was partitioned at the 17th parallel. The North went Communist and the Viet Cong, joined by North Vietnamese regular army troops in 1964, fought to gain control of the South. In 1954 there were approximately 1,114,000 Catholics in the North and 480,000 in the South. More than 650,000 fled to the South to avoid the government repression that silenced the Church in the North. In South Vietnam, the Church continued to develop during the war years. Fragmentary reports about the status of the Church since the end of the war in 1975 have been ominous. Freedom of religious belief, promised by the Revolutionary Government in May, 1975, shortly after its capture of Saigon (Ho Chi Min City), is denied in practice. Late in 1983, the government initiated support for a "patriotic" Catholic church analogous to the communist-sponsored church in China. The hierarchy was established in 1960. The apostolic delegation, formerly in Saigon, was transferred to Hanoi in 1976; it is presently vacant.

## Virgin Islands

*Dioc., 1 (St. Thomas, suffragan of Washington, D.C.); bp., 1; parishes, 8; priests, 15 (10 dioc., 5 rel.); p.d., 22; sem., 2; bros., 2; srs., 18; bap., 579; Caths., 30,000; tot. pop., 102,000.*

Organized unincorporated U.S. territory, about 34 miles east of Puerto Rico; capital, Charlotte Amalie on St. Thomas (one of the three principal islands). The islands were discovered by Columbus in 1493 and named for St. Ursula and her virgin companions. Missionaries began evangelization in the 16th century. A church on St. Croix dates from about 1660; another, on St. Thomas, from 1774. The Baltimore archdiocese had jurisdiction over the islands from 1804 to 1820 when it was passed on to the first of several places in the Caribbean area. Some trouble arose over a pastoral appointment in the 19th century, resulting in a small schism. The Redemptorists took over pastoral care in 1858; normal conditions have prevailed since.

## British Virgin Islands

*Parishes, 2; priests, 2 (rel.); bap., 32; Caths., 1,000; tot. pop., 11,000.*

British possession in Caribbean; capital, Road Town. Under ecclesiastical jurisdiction of St. John's-Basseterre diocese, Antigua.

## Wales

*Archd., 1; dioc., 2; abp., 1; bp., 3; parishes, 185; priests, 268 (158 dioc., 110 rel.); p.d., 13; sem., 16; bros., 26; srs., 516; bap, 2,627; Caths., 150,421 (5%); tot. pop., 3,052,403 (1996 Annuario Pontificio).*

Part of the United Kingdom, on the western part of the island of Great Britain. Celtic missionaries completed evangelization by the end of the sixth century, the climax of what has been called the age of saints. Welsh Christianity received its distinctive Celtic character at this time. Some conflict developed when attempts were made — and proved successful later — to place the Welsh Church under the jurisdiction of Canterbury; the Welsh opted for direct contact with Rome. The Church made progress despite the depredations of Norsemen in the eighth and ninth centuries. Norman infiltration occurred near the middle of the 12th century, resulting in a century-long effort to establish territorial dioceses and parishes to replace the Celtic organizational plan of monastic centers and satellite churches. The Western Schism produced split views and allegiances. Actions of Henry VIII in breaking away from Rome had serious repercussions. Proscription and penal laws crippled the Church, resulted in heavy defections and touched off a 150-year period of repression in which more than 91 persons died for the faith. Methodism prevailed by 1750. Modern Catholicism came to Wales with Irish immigrants in the 19th century, when the number of Welsh Catholics was negligible. Catholic emancipation was granted in 1829. The hierarchy was restored in 1850.

## Wallis and Futuna Islands

*Dioc., 1; bp., 1; parishes, 5; priests, 9 (5 dioc., 4 rel.); sem., 5; bros., 5; srs., 46; bap., 340; Caths., 16,000; tot. pop., 16,000.*

French overseas territory in the southwestern Pacific; capital Mata-Utu. Marists, who began evangelizing the islands in 1836-7, were the first Catholic missionaries. The entire populations of the two islands were baptized by the end of 1842 (Wallis) and 1843 (Futuna). The first missionary to the latter island was killed in 1841. Most of the priests on the islands are native Polynesians. The hierarchy was established in 1966.

## Western Sahara
*P.a., 1; parishes, 1; priests, 2 (rel.); Caths., 200; tot. pop., 270,000.*

Former Spanish overseas province (Spanish Sahara) on the northwestern coast of Africa. Territory is under control of Morocco. Islam is the religion of non-Europeans. A prefecture apostolic was established in 1954 for the European Catholics there.

## Yemen
*Parishes, 4; priests, 4 (rel.); srs., 28; Caths., 3,000; tot. pop., 12,670,000.*

Republic on southern coast of Arabian peninsula; capital, Sanaa. Formerly North Yemen (Arab Republic of Yemen) and South Yemen (People's Republic of Yemen); formally reunited in 1990. Christians perished in the first quarter of the sixth century. Muslims have been in control since the seventh century. The state religion is Islam. Under ecclesiastical jurisdiction of Arabia vicariate apostolic.

## Yugoslavia*
*Archd., 2; dioc., 3; abp., 2; bp., 3; parishes, 214; priests, 187 (147 dioc., 40 rel.); p.d., 1; sem., 19; bros., 9; srs., 345; bap., 4,153; Caths., 438,000 (5.5%); tot. pop., 7,934,000. (Population figures from 1996 Annuario Pontificio.)*

Republic in southeastern Europe formed in 1992, consisting of Serbia and Montenegro; capital, Belgrade. The four other republics (Croatia, Slovenia, Bosnia and Herzegovina, and Macedonia) which made up the federation of Yugoslavia created after World War II proclaimed their independence in 1991-1992; see separate entries. Background history of the Church in pre-1991 Yugoslavia, especially during communist domination, is given below. (See Index for 1996 events.)

Christianity was introduced from the seventh to ninth centuries in the regions which were combined to form the nation after World War I. Since these regions straddled the original line of demarcation for the Western and Eastern Empires (and churches), and since the Reformation had little lasting effect, the Christians are nearly all either Roman Catholics or Byzantines (some in communion with Rome, the majority Orthodox). Yugoslavia was proclaimed a Socialist republic in 1945, the year in which began years of the harshest kind of total persecution of the Church. Cardinal Stepinac, one of its major victims, died in 1960. In an agreement signed June 25, 1966, the government recognized the Holy See's spiritual jurisdiction over the Church in the country and guaranteed to bishops the possibility of maintaining contact with Rome in ecclesiastical and religious matters. The Holy See confirmed the principle that the activity of ecclesiastics, in the exercise of priestly functions, must take place within the religious and ecclesiastical sphere, and that abuse of these functions for political ends would be illegal.

## Zaire*
*Archd., 6; dioc., 41; card., 1; abp., 8; bp., 49; parishes, 1,197; priests, 3,538 (2,119 dioc., 1,419 rel.); p.d., 5; sem., 3,059; bros., 1,174; srs., 5,939; bap., 453,658; Caths., 21,318,000 (50.1%); tot. pop., 42,550,000.*

Republic in south central Africa; (formerly the Congo); capital, Kinshasa. Christianity was introduced in 1484 and evangelization began about 1490. The first native bishop in black Africa was ordained in 1518. Subsequent missionary work was hindered by factors including 18th and 19th century anticlericalism. Modern evangelization started in the second half of the 19th century. The hierarchy was established in 1959. In the civil disorders which followed independence in 1960, some missions and other church installations were abandoned, thousands of people reverted to tribal religions and many priests and religious were killed. Church-state tensions have developed in recent years because of the Church's criticism of the anti-Christian thrust of Pres. Mobutu's "Africanization" policies. Six missionary Sisters, who contracted the disease while ministering to patients, were among the victims of the Ebola outbreak in 1995.

## Zambia*
*Archd., 2; dioc., 7; abp., 2; bp., 7; parishes, 247; priests, 637 (248 dioc., 389 rel.); p.d., 1; sem., 343; bros., 131; srs., 895; bap., 57,046; Caths., 2,638,000 (28.6%); tot. pop., 9,200,000.*

Republic in central Africa; capital, Lusaka. Portuguese priests did some evangelizing in the 16th and 17th centuries but no results of their work remained in the 19th century. Jesuits began work in the south in the 1880s and White Fathers in the north and east in 1895. Evangelization of the western region began for the first time in 1931. The number of Catholics doubled in the 20 years following World War II.

## Zimbabwe*
*Archd., 2; dioc., 5; abp., 2; bp., 8; parishes, 141; priests, 370 (121 dioc., 249 rel.); p.d., 13; sem., 226; bros., 107; srs., 1,124; bap., 39,935; Caths., 989,000 (8.8%); tot. pop., 11,150,000.*

Independent republic (Apr. 18, 1980) in south central Africa (formerly Rhodesia); capital, Harare (Salisbury). Earlier unsuccessful missionary ventures preceded the introduction of Catholicism in 1879. Missionaries began to make progress after 1893. The hierarchy was established in 1955; the first black bishop was ordained in 1973. In 1969, four years after the government of Ian Smith made a unilateral declaration of independence from England, a new constitution was enacted for the purpose of assuring continued white supremacy over the black majority. Catholic and Protestant prelates in the country protested vigorously against the constitution and related enactments as opposed to human rights of the blacks and restrictive of the Church's freedom to carry out its pastoral, educational and social service functions. The Smith regime was ousted in 1979 after seven years of civil war in which at least 25,000 people were killed.

---

**Church strong:** The Church in East Timor remains strong despite the pervasive presence of the Indonesian military. Efforts to free the country from Indonesian control have been vigorous but unsuccessful,

# CATHOLIC WORLD STATISTICS

(Principal sources: *Statistical Yearbook of the Church, 1994*, the latest edition; *Annuario Pontificio, 1996*. Figures are as of Dec. 31, 1994, unless indicated otherwise.)

| | Africa | North America[1] | South America | Asia | Europe | Oceania | WORLD TOTALS |
|---|---|---|---|---|---|---|---|
| Patriarchates[2] | 2 | — | — | 8 | 2 | — | 12 |
| Archdioceses | 77 | 83 | 91 | 107 | 163 | 18 | 539 |
| Dioceses | 341 | 338 | 380 | 299 | 496 | 54 | 1,908 |
| Prelatures | 1 | 9 | 34 | 6 | 6 | — | 56 |
| Abbacies | — | 1 | 2 | — | 12 | — | 15 |
| Exarchates/Ords. | — | 1 | 4 | 2 | 12 | — | 19 |
| Military Ords. | 3 | 4 | 8 | 3 | 11 | 2 | 31 |
| Vicariates Apostolic | 12 | 6 | 36 | 18 | 1 | — | 73 |
| Prefectures | 3 | — | 7 | 3 | — | 1 | 14 |
| Apostolic Admin. | 1 | — | — | 3 | 5 | — | 9 |
| Independent Missions | 3 | 1 | — | 2 | — | 2 | 8 |
| Cardinals[3] | 15 | 22 | 18 | 14 | 81 | 4 | 154 |
| Patriarchs[2] | 1 | — | — | 6 | 1 | — | 8 |
| Archbishops | 103 | 119 | 125 | 145 | 306 | 23 | 821[4] |
| Bishops | 394 | 643 | 674 | 428 | 1,042 | 86 | 3,267[4] |
| Priests | 23,263 | 80,763 | 39,015 | 37,680 | 218,581 | 5,159 | 404,461 |
| Diocesan | 12,937 | 51,086 | 20,856 | 21,664 | 152,169 | 2,824 | 261,536 |
| Religious | 10,326 | 29,677 | 18,159 | 16,016 | 66,412 | 2,335 | 142,925 |
| Perm.Deacons | 326 | 12,706 | 1,794 | 132 | 6,178 | 118 | 21,254 |
| Brothers | 6,448 | 12,102 | 5,840 | 7,170 | 26,141 | 2,171 | 59,872 |
| Sisters | 46,664 | 159,765 | 91,457 | 123,530 | 414,687 | 12,352 | 848,455 |
| Maj.Seminarians | 17,125 | 15,152 | 17,808 | 24,645 | 29,511 | 834 | 105,075 |
| Sec. Inst. Mbrs. (Men) | 35 | 43 | 41 | 54 | 449 | 1 | 623 |
| Sec.Inst.Mbrs.(Women) | 355 | 1,653 | 3,498 | 1,102 | 24,452 | 47 | 31,107 |
| Lay Missionaries | 1,847 | 164 | 468 | 177 | — | 232 | 2,888 |
| Catechists | 299,994 | 13,123 | 16,797 | 91,378 | 67 | 6,581 | 427,940 |
| Parishes | 9,616 | 33,002 | 19,126 | 17,740 | 138,204 | 2,429 | 220,117[5] |
| Kindergartens | 6,838 | 8,027 | 5,859 | 8,839 | 23,703 | 524 | 53,790 |
| Students | 677,927 | 416,063 | 648,715 | 1,270,392 | 1,838,173 | 52,956 | 4,904,226 |
| Elem./PrimarySchools | 27,257 | 12,874 | 8,729 | 13,308 | 18,680 | 2,497 | 83,345 |
| Students | 8,699,131 | 3,887,232 | 3,398,158 | 4,444,053 | 3,450,541 | 522,460 | 24,401,575 |
| Secondary Schools | 5,809 | 3,541 | 5,286 | 7,726 | 9,846 | 696 | 32,904 |
| Students | 1,623,265 | 1,468,277 | 2,014,063 | 4,398,718 | 3,496,653 | 308,382 | 13,309,358 |
| Students in Higher Insts.[6] | 15,461 | 372,424 | 98,640 | 698,428 | 177,657 | 7,761 | 1,370,371 |
| Social Service Facilities | 12,712 | 13,683 | 25,259 | 18.776 | 33,136 | 1,451 | 105,017 |
| Hospitals | 851 | 991 | 1,000 | 1,239 | 1,541 | 179 | 5,801 |
| Dispensaries | 3,812 | 2,184 | 3,406 | 3,046 | 3,001 | 144 | 15,593 |
| Leprosariums | 278 | 24 | 44 | 357 | 3 | 3 | 709 |
| Homes for Aged/Handic | 463 | 1,567 | 1,581 | 1,049 | 7,116 | 242 | 12,018 |
| Orphanages | 633 | 676 | 1,117 | 2,393 | 1,957 | 251 | 7,027 |
| Nurseries | 744 | 1,115 | 4,005 | 2,126 | 2,408 | 17 | 10,415 |
| Matrimonial Advice Ctrs. | 1,072 | 2,211 | 1,462 | 1,253 | 3,389 | 215 | 9,602 |
| Social Educ.Ctrs. | 700 | 1,369 | 1,971 | 2,891 | 2,780 | 90 | 9,801 |
| Other Institutions | 4,159 | 3,546 | 10,673 | 4,422 | 10,941 | 310 | 34,051 |
| Baptisms | 3,061,784 | 4,361,876 | 5,124,083 | 2,554,086 | 2,860,950 | 139,386 | 18,102,165 |
| Under Age 7 | 2,004,099 | 4,123,998 | 4,765,107 | 2,173,312 | 2,781,037 | 122,726 | 15,970,279 |
| Over Age 7 | 1,057,685 | 237,878 | 358,976 | 380,774 | 79,913 | 16,660 | 2,131,886 |
| Marriages | 270,521 | 872,291 | 914,479 | 489,164 | 1,111,825 | 31,682 | 3,689,962 |
| Between Catholics | 234,953 | 761,991 | 891,229 | 431,602 | 1,021,878 | 18,011 | 3,359,664 |
| Mixed Marriages | 35,568 | 110,300 | 23,250 | 57,562 | 89,947 | 13,671 | 330,298 |
| Catholic Pop.[7] | 102,878,000 | 208,589,000 | 272,610,000 | 96,741,000 | 287,459,000 | 7,660,000 | 975,937,000 |
| World Population | 705,567,000 | 450,475,000 | 308,414,000 | 3,401,997,000 | 706,581,000 | 27,836,000 | 5,600,870,000 |

[1] Includes Middle America. [2] For listing and description, see Index. [3] As of Aug. 8, 1996. [4] Figures for the hierarchy (cardinals, archbishops and bishops) included 2,516 ordinaries, 589 coadjutors or auxiliaries, 197 with offices in the Roman Curia, 26 in other offices, more than 900 retired. [5] 159,767 have parish priests; 55,542 are administered by other priests; 373 are entrusted to permanent deacons; 116 to brothers; 1,109 to women Religious; 1,474 to lay people; 1,736 vacant. [6] There are also approximately 146,936 in universities for ecclesiastical studies and 1,795,463 other university students. [7] Percentages of Catholics in world population: Africa, 14.6; North America (Catholics 69,013,000; tot. pop., 290,028,000), 23.8; Middle America (Catholics, 139,576,000; tot. pop., 160,447,000), 86.9; South America, 88.4; Asia, 2.8; Europe, 40.7; Oceania, 27.5; World, 17.4. (Catholic totals do not include those in areas that could not be surveyed, estimated to be 4.6 million.)

# EPISCOPAL CONFERENCES

(Principal source: *Annuario Pontificio*.)

Episcopal conferences, organized and operating under general norms and particular statutes approved by the Holy See, are official bodies in and through which the bishops of a given country or territory act together as pastors of the Church.

Listed below according to countries or regions are titles and addresses of conferences and names and sees of presidents.

**Africa, Northern:** Conference Episcopale Regionale du Nord de l'Afrique (CERNA), 13 rue Khelifa-Boukhalfa, 16000 Algiers, Algeria. Abp. Henri Teissier (Algiers).

**Africa, Southern:** Southern African Catholic Bishops' Conference (SACBC), 140 Visagie St., P.O. Box 941, Pretoria 0001, S. Africa. Bp. Louis Ncarmiso Ndlovu, O.S.M. (Manzini, Swaziland)).

**Albania:** Conferenza Episcopale dell'Albania, Kryeipeshkëvi, Shkodrë, Abp. Frano Illia (Shkodrë).

**Angola and Sao Tome:** Conferencia Episcopal de Angola e Sao Tome (CEAST), C.P. 87 Luanda, Angola. Card. Alexandre do Nascimento (Luanda).

**Antilles:** Antilles Episcopal Conference (AEC), P.O. Box 3086, St. James (Trinidad and Tobago), W.I. Abp. Kelvin Edward Felix (Castries, Santa Lucia).

**Arab Countries:** Conference des Eveques Latins dans les Regions Arabes (CELRA), Latin Patriarchate, P.O. Box 14152, Jerusalem (Old City). Patriarch Michel Sabbah (Jerusalem).

**Argentina:** Conferencia Episcopal Argentina (CEA), Calle Suipacha 1034, 1008 Buenos Aires. Card. Antonio Quarracino (Buenos Aires).

**Australia:** Australian Catholic Bishops' Conference, 63 Currong St., Braddon, A.C.T. 2601. Card. Edward Bede Clancy (Sydney).

**Austria:** Osterreichische Bischofskonferenz, Rotenturmstrasse 2, A-1010 Vienna. Bp. Johann Weber (Graz-Seckau).

**Bangladesh:** Catholic Bishops' Conference of Bangladesh (CBCB), P.O. Box 3, Dhaka-2. Abp. Michael Rozario (Dhaka).

**Belgium:** Bisschoppenconferentie van Belgie — Conference Episcopale de Belgique, Rue Guimard 1, B-1040 Brussel. Card. Godfried Danneels (Mechelen-Brussel).

**Benin:** Conference Episcopale du Benin, B.P. 491, Cotonou. Bp. Lucien Monsi-Agboka (Abomey).

**Bolivia:** Conferencia Episcopal de Bolivia (CEB), Casilla 2309, Calle Potosi 814, La Paz. Bp. Edmundo Luis Flavio Abastoflor Montero (Potosi).

**Bosnia and Herzegovina:** Biskupska Konferencija Bosne i Hercegovine (B.K. B.i.H.), Nadbiskupski Ordinariat, Kaptol 7, 716000 Sarajevo. Card. Vinko Puljic (Vrhbosno, Sarajevo).

**Brazil:** Conferencia Nacional dos Bispos do Brasil (CNBB), C.P. 02067, SE/Sul Quadra 801, Conjunto "B," 70259-970 Brasilia, D.F. Card. Lucas Moreira Neves, O.P. (Sao Salvador da Bahia).

**Bulgaria:** Ulitza Pashovi 10-B, 1606 Sofia. Bp. Christo Proykov (Briula, titular see).

**Burkina Faso and Niger:** Conference des Eveques de Burkina Faso et du Niger, B.P. 1195, Ouagadougou, Burkina Faso. Bp Jean-Baptiste Some (Diebougou).

**Burma:** See Myanmar.

**Burundi:** Conference des Eveques Catholiques du Burundi (C.E.CA.B.), B. P. 1390, 5 Blvd. de l'Uprona, Bujumbura. Bp. Bernard Bududira (Bururi).

**Cameroon:** Conference Episcopale Nationale du Cameroun (CENC), BP 807, Yaoundé. Bp. Andre Wouking (Bafoussam).

**Canada:** See Canadian Conference of Catholic Bishops.

**Central African Republic:** Conference Episcopale Centrafricaine (CECA), B.P. 798, Bangui. Abp. Joachim N'Dayen (Bangui).

**Chad:** Conference Episcopale du Tchad, B.P. 456, N'Djamena. Abp. Charles Vandame, S.J. (N'Djamena).

**Chile:** Conferencia Episcopal de Chile (CECH), Casilla 517-V, Correo 21, Cienfuegas 47, Santiago. Card. Carlos Oviedo Cavada, O. de M. (Santiago de Chile).

**China:** Chinese Regional Episcopal Conference, 34 Lane 32, Kuang-Fu South Rd., Taipeh 10552, Taiwan. Bp. Paul Shan Kuo-hsi, S.J. (Kaohsiung).

**Colombia:** Conferencia Episcopal de Colombia, Apartado 7448, Carrera 47, N. 84-85, Santafe de Bogota D.E. Abp. Pedro Rubiano Saenz (Bogota).

**Congo:** Conference Episcopale du Congo, B.P. 200, Brazzaville. Bp. Bernard Nsayi (Nkayi).

**Costa Rica:** Conferencia Episcopal de Costa Rica (CECOR), Apartado 497, San Jose. Abp. Roman Arrieta Villalobos (San Jose de Costa Rica).

**Côte d'Ivoire:** Conference Episcopale de la Côte d'Ivoire, B.P. 1287, Abidjan 01. Abp. Auguste Nobou (Korhogo).

**Croatia:** Hrvatska Biskupska Konferencija, Kaptol 22, 41000 Zagreb. Card. Franjo Kuharic (Zagreb).

**Cuba:** Conferencia de Obispos Catolicos de Cuba (COCC), Apartado 594, Calle 26 n. 314 Miramar, Havana 1. Card. Jaime Lucas Ortega y Alamino (Havana).

**Czech Republic:** Ceska Biskupska Konference, Sekretariat, Thakuurova 3, 160 00 Praha (Prague) 6. Card. Miloslav Vlk (Prague).

**Dominican Republic:** Conferencia del Episcopado Dominicano (CED), Apartado 186, Santo Domingo. Card. Nicolas de Jesus Lopez Rodriguez (Santo Domingo).

**Ecuador:** Conferencia Episcopal Ecuatoriana, Apartado 1081, Avenida America 1805 y Lagasca, Quito. Bp. Jose Mario Ruiz Navas (Portoviejo).

**El Salvador:** Conferencia Episcopal de El Salvador (CEDES). 15 Av. Norte 1420, Col. Layco, Apartado 1310, San Salvador. Bp. Marco Rene Revelo Contreras (Santa Ana).

**Equatorial Guinea:** Conferencia Episcopal de Guinea Ecuatorial, Apartado 106, Malabo. Bp. Anacleto Sima Ngua (Bata).

**Ethiopia:** Ethiopian Episcopal Conference, P.O. Box 2454, Addis Ababa. Card. Paulos Tzadua (Addis Ababa).

**France:** Conference des Evêques de France, 106 rue du Bac, 75341 Paris CEDEX 07. Abp. Joseph Duval (Rouen).

**Gabon:** Conference Episcopale du Gabon, B.P.

209, Oyem. Bp. Basile Mvé Engone, S.D.B. (Oyem).

**Gambia, Liberia and Sierra Leone:** Inter-Territorial Catholic Bishops' Conference of the Gambia, Liberia and Sierra Leone (ITCABIC), Santanno House, P.O. Box 893, Freetown, Sierra Leone. Bp. Benedict Dotu Sekey (Gbarnga, Liberia).

**Germany:** Deutsche Bischofskonferenz, Kaiserstrasse 163, D-53113 Bonn 1. Bp. Karl Lehmann (Mainz). Statutes approved Nov. 14, 1992.

**Ghana:** Ghana Bishops' Conference, National Catholic Secretariat, P.O. Box 9712 Airport, Accra. Bp. Francis Anani Kofi Lodonu (Ho).

**Great Britain:** Bishops' Conference of England and Wales, General Secretariat, 39 Eccleston Square, London, SWIV IPD. Card. George Basil Hume, O.S.B. (Westminster). Bishops' Conference of Scotland, Archbishop's House, 196 Clyde St., Glasgow GI 4JY. Card. Thomas Winning (Glasgow).

**Greece:** Conferentia Episcopalis Graeciae, Odos Homirou 9, 106 72 Athens. Abp. Nikolaos Foscolos (Athens).

**Guatemala:** Conferencia Episcopal de Guatemala (CEG), Apartado 1698, 01901 Ciudad de Guatemala. Bp. Jorge Mario Avila del Aguila, C.M. (Jalapa).

**Guinea:** Conference Episcopale de la Guinee, B.P. 1006 Bis, Conakry. Abp. Robert Sarah (Conakry).

**Guinea-Bissau:** See Senegal.

**Haiti:** Conference Episcopale de Haiti (CEH). B.P. 1572, Angle rues Piquant et Lammarre, Port-au-Prince. Abp. Francois Gayot, S.M.M. (Cap Haïtien).

**Honduras:** Conferencia Episcopal de Honduras (CEH), Apartado 847, Tegucigalpa. Bp. Raul Corriveau, P.M.E. (Choluteca).

**Hungary:** Magyar Püspöki Kar Konferenciája, PF 121, H-1364 Budapest. Abp. István Seregély (Eger).

**India:** Catholic Bishops' Conference of India (CBCI), CBCI Centre, Ashok Place, Goldakkhana, New Delhi-110001. Abp. Joseph Powathil (Changanacherry of the Syro-Malabars); Conference of Catholic Bishops of India — Latin Rite (CBCI — L.R.), A-139, Lok Vihar, Pitampura, New Delhi-110034. Card. Simon Ignatius Pimenta (Bombay). Statutes approved experimentally Jan. 13, 1994 .

**Indian Ocean:** Conference Episcopale de l'Ocean Indien (CEDOI) (includes Islands of Mauritius, Seychelles, Comore and La Reunion), B.P. 55, 97462 St. Denis-de-La Reunion (La Reunion). Bp. Gilbert Aubry (St. Denis-de-La Reunion) .

**Indonesia:** Konperensi Waligereja Indonesia (KWI), Taman Cut Mutiah 10, Tromolpos 3044, Jakarta 10002. Abp. Julius Riyadi Darmaatmadja, S.J. (Semerang).

**Ireland:** Irish Episcopal Conference, "Ara Coeli," Armagh BT61 7QY. Card. Cahal Brendan Daly (Armagh).

**Italy:** Conferenza Episcopale Italiana (CEI), Circonvallazione Aurelia, 50, 00165 Roma. Card. Camillo Ruini (Vicar General, Rome).

**Ivory Coast:** See Côte d'Ivoie.

**Japan:** Catholic Bishops' Conference of Japan, Shiomi 2-10-10, Koto-Ku, Tokyo 135. Bp. Stephen Fumio Hamao (Yokohama).

**Kenya:** Kenya Episcopal Conference (KEC), The Kenya Catholic Secretariat, P.O. Box 48062, Nairobi. Abp. Zacchaeus Okoth (Kisumu).

**Korea:** Catholic Bishops' Conference of Korea, Box 16, Seoul. Abp. Paul Moun-hi Ri (Tae Gu).

**Laos and Cambodia:** Conference Episcopale du Laos et du Cambodge, c/o Msgr. Pierre Bach, Paris Foreign Missions, 254 Silom Rd., Bangkok 10500. Bp. Yves-Georges Ramousse, M.E.P. (vicar apostolic, Phnom Penh, Cambodia).

**Latvia:** Conferentia Episcopalis Lettoniae, Maza Pils, 2, Riga 226050. Vacant.

**Lesotho:** Lesotho Catholic Bishops' Conference, Catholic Secretariat, P.O. Box 200, Maseru 100. Bp. Evaristus Thatho Bitsoane (Qacha's Nek).

**Liberia:** See Gambia, Liberia and Sierra Leone.

**Lithuania:** Conferentia Episcopalis Lituaniae, Sventaragio, 4, 22001 Vilnius. Abp. Audrys Juozas Backis (Vilnius).

**Madagascar:** Conference Episcopale de Madagascar, 102 bis Av. Marechal Joffre, Antanimena, B. P 667, Antananarivo. Bp. Jean-Guy Rakotondravahatra, M.S. (Ihosy).

**Malawi:** Episcopal Conference of Malawi, Catholic Secretariat of Malawi, P.O. Box 30384, Lilongwe 3. Bp. Felix Eugenio Mikhori (Chikwawa).

**Malaysia-Singapore-Brunei:** Catholic Bishops' Conference of Malaysia, Singapore and Brunei (BCMSB), 4000 Shah Alam, Selangor Darul Ehson, Malaysia. Abp. Peter Chung Hoan Ting (Kuching, Malaysia).

**Mali:** Conference Episcopale du Mali, B.P. 298, Bamako. Bp. Jean-Marie Cissé (Sikasso).

**Malta:** Konferenza Episkopali Maltija, Archbishop's Curia, Floriana. Abp. Joseph Mercieca (Malta).

**Mexico:** Conferencia del Episcopado Mexicano (CEM), Prolongacion Rio Acatlan, Lago de Guadalupe, 54760 Cuautitlan Izcalli, Mex. Abp. Sergio Obeso Rivera (Jalapa).

**Mozambique:** Conferencia Episcopal de Mocambique (CEM), C.P. 286, Maputo. Bp. Francisco Joao Silota, M.Afr. (Chimoio).

**Myanmar:** Myanmar Catholic Bishops' Conference (MCBC), 292 Pyi Rd., P.O. Box 1080, Yangon. Bp. Matthias U. Shwe (Taunggyi).

**Netherlands:** Nederlandse Bisschoppenconferentie, Postbus 13049, NL-3507 LA, Utrecht. Card. Adrianus J. Simonis (Utrecht).

**New Zealand:** New Zealand Episcopal Conference, Private Bag 1937, Wellington 1. Bp. Leonard Anthony Boyle (Dunedin).

**Nicaragua:** Conferencia Episcopal de Nicaragua (CEN), Apartado Postal 2407, Ferreteria Lang, Zona 3, Las Piedrecitas, Managua. Card. Miguel Obando Bravo, S.D.B. (Managua).

**Niger:** See Burkina Faso.

**Nigeria:** Catholic Bishops Conference of Nigeria, P.O. Box 951, 6 Force Rd., Lagos. Abp. Albert K. Obiefuna (Onitsha).

**Pacific:** Conferentia Episcopalis Pacifici (CE PAC), P.O. Box 289, Suva (Fiji). Abp. Anthony Sablan Apuron, O.F.M. Cap. (Agaña, Guam).

**Pakistan:** Pakistan Episcopal Conference, P.O. Box 909, Lahore 54000. Abp. Armando Trindade (Lahore).

**Panama:** Conferencia Episcopal de Panama (CEP), Apartado 870033, Panama 7. Abp. Jose Dimas Cedeño Delgado (Panama).

**Papua New Guinea and Solomon Islands:** Catholic Bishops' Conference of Papua New Guinea and Solomon Islands, Archbishop's Office, P.O. Box 398, Waigani, N.C.D., Papua New Guinea. Abp. Karl Hesse, M.S.C. (Rabaul).

**Paraguay:** Conferencia Episcopal Paraguaya (CEP), Alberdi 782, Casilla Correo 1436, Asuncion. Bp. Oscar Paez Garcete (Alto Parana).

**Peru:** Conferencia Episcopal Peruana, Aprtado 310, Rio de Janeiro 488, Lima 100. Card. Augusto Vargas Alzamora, S.J. (Lima).

**Philippines:** Catholic Bishops' Conference of the Philippines (CBCP), P.O. Box 3601, 470 General Luna St., 1099 Manila. Abp. Oscar V. Cruz (Lingayen-Dagupan).

**Poland:** Konferencja Episkopatu Polski, Skwer Kardynala Stefana Wyszynskiego 6, 01-015 Warsaw. Card. Jozef Glemp (Warsaw).

**Portugal:** Conferencia Episcopal Portuguesa, Campo dos Martires da Patria, 43-1 Esq., 1100 Lisbon. Bp. Joao Alves (Coimbra).

**Puerto Rico:** Conferencia Episcopal Puertorriqueña (CEP), P.O. Box 40682, Estacion Minillas, San Juan 00940-0682. Bp. Iñaki Mallona Txertudi, C.P. (Arecibo).

**Romania:** Conferinte Episcopala Romania, Via Popa Tatu 58, Bucharest. Abp. Ioan Robu (Bucharest).

**Rwanda:** Conference Episcopale du Rwanda (C.Ep.R.), B.P. 357, Kigali.

**Scandinavia:** Conferentia Episcopalis Scandiae, Akersveien 5, P.B. 8270 Hammersborg, N-0129 Oslo 1, Norway. Bp. Paul Verschuren, S.C.I. (Helsinki, Finland).

**Senegal, Mauritania, Cape Verde and Guinea Bissau:** Conference Episcopale du Senegal, de la Mauritanie, du Cap-Vert et de Guinée-Bissau, B.P. 941, Dakar, Senegal. Bp. Theodore Adrien Sarr (Kaolack, Senegal).

**Sierra Leone:** See Gambia, Liberia and Sierra Leone.

**Slovakia:** Biskupská Konferencia Slovenska, Kapitulská 11, 81521 Bratislava. Abp. Rudolf Balaz (Banska Bystrica).

**Slovenia:** Slovenska Skofovska Konferencia, Ciril-Metodov trg 4, p.p.121/III, 61001 Ljubljana. Abp. Alojzij Sustar (Ljubljana).

**Spain:** Conferencia Episcopal Española, Calle Añastro 1, 28033 Madrid. Abp. Elias Yanes Alvarez (Zaragoza).

**Sri Lanka:** Catholic Bishops' Conference of Sri Lanka, 19 Balcombe Place, Cotta Rd., Borella, Colombo 8. Bp. Joseph Vianney Fernando (Kandy).

**Sudan:** Sudan Catholic Bishops' Conference (SCBC), P.O. Box 6011, Khartoum. Abp. Gabriel Zubeir Wako (Khartoum).

**Switzerland:** Conference des Eveques Suisses, Secretariat, C.P. 22, av. Moleson 21, CH-1700 Fribourg 6. Bp. Henri Salina (Abbot Ordinary of Saint Maurice; titular bishop of Monte di Mauritania).

**Tanzania:** Tanzania Episcopal Conference (TEC), P.O. Box 2133, Mansfield St., Dar-es-Salaam. Bp. Justin Tetemu Samba (Musoma).

**Thailand:** Bishops' Conference of Thailand, 57 Oriental Ave., Praetham Bldg., Bangrak, Bangkok 10500. Card. Michael Michai Kitbunchu (Bangkok).

**Togo:** Conference Episcopale du Togo, B.P. 348, Lomé. Abp. Philippe Fanoko Kossi Kpodzro (Lomé).

**Uganda:** Uganda Episcopal Conference, P.O. Box 2886, Kampala. Bp. Paul L. Kalanda (Fort Portal).

**Ukraine:** Ukraine Episcopal Conference, Obrzadku Lacinskiego, pl. Katedralna 1, 290008 Lviv. Abp. Marian Jaworski (Lviv of Latins).

**United States:** See National Conference of Catholic Bishops.

**Uruguay:** Conferencia Episcopal Uruguaya (CEU), Avenida Uruguay 1319, 11100 Montevideo. Bp. Orlando Romero Cabrero (Canelones).

**Venezuela:** Conferencia Episcopal de Venezuela (CEV), Apartado 4897, Torre a Madrices, Edificio Juan XXIII, Piso 4, Caracas 1010-A. Abp. Ramon Ovidio Perez Morales (Maracaibo).

**Vietnam:** Conferenza Episcopale del Viêt Nam, 40 Pho Nha Chung, Ha Noi. Card. Paul Joseph Pham Dinh Tung (Ha Noi).

**Yugoslavia:** . . . . .

**Zaire:** Conférence Episcopale du Zaïre (CEZ), B.P. 3258, Kinshasa-Gombe. Bp. Faustin Ngabu (Goma).

**Zambia:** Zambia Epscopal Conference, P.O. Box 31965, Lusaka. Bp. Telesphore George Mpundu (Mbala-Mpika).

**Zimbabwe:** Zimbabwe Catholic Bishops' Conference (ZCBC), P.O. Box 8135, Causeway, Harare. Bp. Francis Xavier Mugadzi (Gweru).

## Regional Conferences

(Sources: Almanac survey; *Annuario Pontificio*.)

**Africa:** Symposium of Episcopal Conferences of Africa and Madagascar (SECAM) (Symposium des Conferences Episcopales d'Afrique et de Madagascar, SCEAM): Most Rev. Gabriel G. Ganaka, archbishop of Jos, Nigeria, president. Address: Secretariat, P.O. Box 9156 Airport, Accra, Ghana.

Association of Episcopal Conferences of Central Africa (Association des Conferences Episcopales de l'Afrique Centrale, ACEAC): Comprises Burundi, Rwanda and Zaire. Bp. Evariste Ngoyagoye, Bubanza, Burundi, president. Address: B.P. 20511, Kinshasa, Zaire.

Association of Episcopal Conferences of the Region of Central Africa (Association des Conferences Episcopales de la Region de l'Afrique Central (ACERAC): Comprises Cameroon, Chad, Congo, Equatorial Guinea, Central African Republic and Gabon. Bp. Basile Mve Engone, S.D.B., Oyem, Gabon, president. Address: Secretariat, B.P. 1518, Bangui, Central African Republic.

Association of Episcopal Conferences of Anglophone West Africa (AECAWA): Comprises Gambia, Ghana, Liberia, Nigeria and Sierra Leone. Abp. Michael Kpakala Francis, Monrovia, Liberia, president. Address: P.O. Box 10-502, 1000 Monrovia, Liberia.

Association of Member Episcopal Conferences in Eastern Africa (AMECEA): Represents Eritrea, Ethiopia, Kenya, Malawi, Sudan, Tanzania, Uganda and Zambia. Affiliate members: Seychelles (1979), Somalia (1994). Abp. Nicodemus Kirima, Nyeri, Kenya, president. Address: P.O. Box 21191, Nairobi, Kenya.

Regional Episcopal Conference of French-Speaking West Africa (Conference Episcopale Regionale de l'Afrique de l'Ouest Francophone, CERAO): Comprises Benin, Burkina Faso, Cape Verde, Côte d'Ivoire, Guinea, Guinea-Bissau, Mali, Mauritania, Niger, Senegal and Togo. Bp. Anselme Titianma Sanon, Bobo-Dioulasso, Burkina Faso, president. Address: Secretariat General, 06 B.P. 470, Abidjan 06, cidex 1 Côte d'Ivoire.

Inter-Regional Meeting of Bishops of Southern Africa (IMBISA): Bishops of Angola, Botswana, Lesotho, Mozambique, Namibia, Sao Tome e Principe, South Africa, Swaziland and Zimbabwe. Bp. Francisco Joao Silota, M. Afr. (Chimoio, Mozambique), president. Address: 4 Bayswater Rd., Highlands, Harare, Zimbabwe.

**Asia:** Federation of Asian Bishops' Conferences (FABC): Represents 14 Asian episcopal conferences and four independent jurisdictions (Hong Kong, Macau, Nepal, Mongolia) as regular members (excluding the Middle East). Established in 1970; statutes approved experimentally Dec. 6, 1972. Abp. Oscar Cruz, Lingayen-Dagupan, Philippines (elected 1993), secretary general. Address: 16 Caine Road, Hong Kong.

**Oceania:** Federation of Catholic Bishops' Conferences of Oceania (FCBCO). Statutes approved experimentally July 28, 1992. Card. Thomas Stafford Williams, archbishop of Wellington, New Zealand, president. Address: P.O. Box 1937, Wellington, New Zealand.

**Europe:** Council of European Bishops' Confer-ences (Consilium Conferentiarum Episcoporum Europae, CCEE): Card. Miloslav Vlk, Prague, Czech Republic, president. Address of secretariat: Klosterhof 6b, CH-9000 Sankt Gallen, Switzerland. Reorganized in 1993 in accordance with suggestions made during the 1991 Synod of Bishops on Europe.

Commission of the Episcopates of the European Community (Commissio Episcopatuum Communitatis Europaeae, COMECE): Established in 1980; represents episcopates of states which belong to European Community. Bp. Josef Homeyer, Hildesheim, Germany, president. Address of secretariat: 42 Rue Stevin, B-1000 Brussels, Belgium.

**Central and South America:** Latin American Bishops' Conference (Consejo Episcopal LatinoAmericano, CELAM): Established in 1956; statutes approved Nov. 9, 1974. Represents 22 Latin American national bishops' conferences. Abp. Oscar Rodriguez Maradiaga, S.D.B., Tegucigalpa, Honduras, president (elected, May, 1995, to 4-year term). Address of the secretariat: Carrera 5 No. 118-31, Usaquén, Bogota, Colombia.

Episcopal Secretariat of Central America and Panama (Secretariado Episcopal de America Central y Panama, SEDAC): Statutes approved experimentally Sept. 26, 1970. Abp. Jose Dimas Cedeño Delgado, Panama, Panama, president. Address of secretary general: Calle 1a Sur, Carrasquilla, Apartado 6386, Panama 5, Panama.

# INTERNATIONAL CATHOLIC ORGANIZATIONS

(Principal sources: Conference of International Catholic Organizations; Pontifical Council for the Laity; Almanac survey.)

## Guidelines

International organizations wanting to call themselves "Catholic" are required to meet standards set by the Vatican's Council for the Laity and to register with and get the approval of the Papal Secretariat of State, according to guidelines dated Dec. 3 and published in *Acta Apostolicae Sedis* under date of Dec. 23, 1971.

Among conditions for the right of organizations to "bear the name Catholic" are:

• leaders "will always be Catholics," and candidates for office will be approved by the Secretariat of State;

• adherence by the organization to the Catholic Church, its teaching authority and teachings of the Gospel;

• evidence that the organization is really international with a universal outlook and that it fulfills its mission through its own management, meetings and accomplishments.

The guidelines also stated that leaders of the organizations "will take care to maintain necessary reserve as regards taking a stand or engaging in public activity in the field of politics or trade unionism. Abstention in these fields will normally be the best attitude for them to adopt during their term of office."

The guidelines were in line with a provision stated by the Second Vatican Council in the *Decree on the Apostolate of the Laity*: "No project may claim the name 'Catholic' unless it has obtained the consent of the lawful church authority."

They made it clear that all organizations are not obliged to apply for recognition, but that the Church "reserves the right to recognize as linked with her mission and her aims those organizations or movements which see fit to ask for such recognition."

## Conference

Conference of International Catholic Organizations: A permanent body for collaboration among various organizations which seek to promote the development of international life along the lines of Christian principles. Eleven international Catholic organizations participated in its foundation and first meeting in 1927 at Fribourg, Switzerland. In 1951, the conference established its general secretariat and adopted governing statutes which were approved by the Vatican Secretariat of State in 1953.

The permanent secretariat is located at 37-39 rue de Vermont, CH-1202 Geneva, Switzerland. Other office addresses are: 1 rue Varembe, CH-1211 Geneva 20, Switzerland (International Catholic Center of Geneva); 9, rue Cler, F-75007 Paris, France (International Catholic Center for UNESCO); ICO Information Center, 323 East 47th St., New York, N.Y. 10017; ICO Antenna of Vienna (Vienna Perspectives), c/o Dennis O. Callagy, Gonzagagasse 13/8, A-1010 Vienna, Austria.

## International Organizations

International Catholic organizations are listed below. Information includes name, date and place of establishment (when available), address of general secretariat. An asterisk indicates that the organization is a member of the Conference of International Catholic Organizations. Approximately 30 of the organizations have consultative status with other international or regional non-governmental agencies.

**Apostleship of Prayer** (1849): Borgo Santo Spirito 5, I-00193 Rome, Italy. National secretariat in most countries. (See Index.)

**Apostolatus Maris (Apostleship of the Sea)** (1922, Glasgow, Scotland): Pontifical Council for Migrants and Itinerant People, Piazza San Calisto 16, 00153 Rome, Italy. (See Index.)

**L'Arche Communities:** B.P. 35, 60350 Cuise Lamotte, France.

**Associationes Juventutis Salesianae (Associations of Salesian Youth)** (1847): Via della Pisana, 1111, 00163 Rome, Italy.

**Blue Army of Our Lady of Fatima:** (See Index.)

**Caritas Internationalis\*** (1951, Rome, Italy): Piazza San Calisto 16, I-00153, Rome, Italy. Coordinates and represents its 131 national member organizations (in 113 countries) operating in the fields of development, emergency aid, social action.

**Catholic International Education Office\*** (1952): 60, rue des Eburons, B-1040 Brussels, Belgium.

**Catholic International Federation for Physical and Sports Education** (1911; present name, 1957): 5, rue Cernuschi, F-75017 Pari, France.

**Catholic International Union for Social Service\*** (1925, Milan, Italy): rue de la Poste 111, B-1210 Brussels, Belgium (general secretariat).

**Christian Fraternity of the Sick and Handicapped:** 9, Avenue de la Gare, CH-1630, Bulle, Switzerland.

**Christian Life Community (CVX)\*** (1953): Borgo Santo Spirito 8, C.P. 6139, I-00195 Rome, Italy. First Sodality of Our Lady founded in 1563.

**"Communione e Liberazione" Fraternity** (1955, Milan, Italy): Via Marcello Malpighi 2, 00161 Rome, Italy. Catholic renewal movement.

**"Focolare Movement" or "Work of Mary"** (1943, Trent, Italy): Via di Frascati, 304, I-00040 Rocca di Papa (Rome), Italy. (See Index.)

**Foi et Lumiere:** 8 rue Serret, 75015 Paris, France.

**Franciscans International:** 323 E. 47th St., New York, NY 10017. A non-governmental organization at the UN.

**Inter Cultural Association,** formerly International Catholic Auxiliaries (1937, Belgium): 91, rue de la Servette, CH-1202 Geneva, Switzerland.

**International Ascent, The:** 84, rue Charles Michels, F-93206 Saint Denis Cedex, France. Member of ICO.

**International Association of Charities\*** (1617, Chatillon les Dombes, France): Rue Joseph Brand, 118, B-1030 Brussels, Belgium.

**International Association of Children of Mary** (1847): 67 rue de Sèvres, F-75006 Paris, France.

**International Catholic Child Bureau\*** (1948, in Paris): 63, rue de Lausanne, CH-1202 Geneva, Switzerland.

**International Catholic Committee of Nurses and Medico-Social Assistants (ICCN)\*** (1933): Square Vergote, 43, B-1040 Brussels, Belgium.

**International Catholic Conference of Scouting\*** (1948): Piazza Pasquale Paoli, 18, I-00186 Rome, Italy.

**International Catholic Migration Commission\*** (1951): 37-39 rue de Vermont, C.P. 96, CH-1211 Geneva 20, Switzerland. Coordinates activities worldwide on behalf of refugees and migrants, both administering programs directly and supporting the efforts of national affiliated agencies.

**International Catholic Organization for Cinema and Audiovisual\*** (1928, The Hague, The Netherlands): Rue du Saphir, 15, B-1040 Brussels, Belgium (general secretariat). Federation of national Catholic film offices.

**International Catholic Rural Association** (1962, Rome): Piazza San Calisto, 00153 Rome, Italy. International body for agricultural and rural organizations. Invited member of ICO.

**International Catholic Society for Girls\*** (1897): 37-39, rue de Vermont, CH-1202 Geneva, Switzerland.

**International Catholic Union of Esperanto:** Via Berni 9, 00185 Rome, Italy.

**International Catholic Union of the Press\*:** 37-39 rue de Vermont, Case Postale 197, CH-1211 Geneva 20 CIC, Switzerland. Coordinates and represents at the international level the activities of Catholics and Catholic federations or associations in the field of press and information. Has seven specialized branches: International Federation of Catholic Journalists; International Federation of Dailies; International Federation of Periodicals; International Federation of Catholic News Agencies; International Catholic Federation of Teachers and Researchers in the Science and Techniques of Information; International Federation of Church Press Associations and International Federation of Book Publishers.

**International Centre for Studies in Religious Education LUMEN VITAE** (1934-35, Louvain, Belgium, under name Catechetical Documentary Centre; present name, 1956): 184, rue Washington, B-1050 Brussels, Belgium. Also referred to as Lumen Vitae Centre; concerned with all aspects of religious formation.

**International Christian Union of Business Executives:** Place des Barricades 2, B-1000 Brussels, Belgium. Invited member of ICO.

**International Conference of Catholic Guiding\*** (1965): 5031, rang 8, Deauville, Que. J1N 3G1, Canada; c/o Mlle Francoise Parmentier, rue de la Tour 64, 75016 Paris. Founded by member bodies of interdenominational World Association of Guides and Girl Scouts.

**International Cooperation for Development and Solidarity (CIDSE)** (1965, Rome, Italy): rue Stévin 16, B-1040 Brussels, Belgium. Invited member of ICO.

**International Coordination of Young Christian Workers (YCYCW)\*:** via dei Barbieri 22, I00186 Rome, Italy.

**International Council of Catholic Men (ICCM)\*** (Unum Omnes) (1948): Wahringer Str. 2-4, A.1090 Vienna IX, Austria.

**International Federation of Catholic Medical Associations\*** (1954): Palazzo San Calisto, I-00120 Vatican City.

**International Federation of Catholic Parochial Youth Communities\*** (1962, Rome, Italy): St. Kariliquai 12, 6000 Lucerne 5, Switzerland.

**International Federation of Catholic Pharmacists\*** (1954): Rue Berckmans 92, B-1060 Brussels, Belgium.

**International Federation of Rural Adult Catholic Movements\*** (1964, Lisbon, Portugal): Rue Jaumain 15, B-5330 Assesse, Belgium.

**International Federation of Catholic Universities\*** (1949): 21, rue d'Assas, F-75270 Paris Cedex 06, France.

**International Federation of the Catholic Associations of the Blind\*:** Avenue Dailly 90, B-1030 Brussels, Belgium. Coordinates actions of Catholic groups and assciations for the blind and develops their apostolate.

**International Independent Christian Youth (IICY)\*:** 11, rue Martin Bernard, F-75013 Paris, Francis.

**International Military Apostolate\*** (1967): Breite Strasse 25. D-5311 Bonn, Germany. Comprised of organizations of military men.

**International Movement of Apostolate of Children\*** (1929, France): 24, rue Paul Rivet, F-92350 Le Plessis Robinson, France.

**International Movement of Apostolate in the Independent Social Milieux (MIAMSI)\*** (1963): Piazza San Calisto 16, 00153 Rome, Italy.

**International Movement of Catholic Agricultural and Rural Youth\*** (1954, Annevoie, Belgium): 53, rue J. Coosemans, B-1030 Brussels, Belgium (permanent secretariat).

**International Young Catholic Students\*** (1946, Fribourg, Switzerland; present name, 1954): 171 rue de Rennes, F-75006 Paris, France.

**International Young Christian Workers** (1925, Belgium): 11, rue Plantin, B-1070 Brussels, Belgium. Associate member of ICO.

**Legion of Mary** (1921, Dublin, Ireland): De Montfort House, North Brunswick St., Dublin, Ireland. (See Index.)

**Medicus Mundi Internationalis:** (1964. Bensberg, Germany FR): P.O. Box 1547, 6501 BM Nijmegen, Netherlands. Promote health and medico-social services, particularly in developing countries; recruit essential health and medical personnel for developing countries; contribute to training of medical and auxiliary personnel; undertake research in the field of health.

**NOVALIS, Marriage Preparation Center:** University of St. Paul, 1 rue Stewart, Ottawa 2, Ont. Canada.

**Our Lady's Teams (Equipes Notre-Dame)** (1937, France): 49, rue de la Glacière, F-75013 Paris, France. Movement for spiritual formation of couples.

**Pax Christi International** (1950): rue du Vieux Marché aux grains 21, B-1000 Brussels, Belgium. International Catholic peace movement. Originated in Lourdes, France in 1948 by French and German Catholics to reconcile enemies from World War II; spread to Italy and Poland and acquired its international ctitle when it merged with the English organization Pax. Associate member of ICO. (See Index: Pax Christi USA.)

**Pax Romana\*** (1921, Fribourg, Switzerland, divided into two branches, 1947):

**Pax Romana — IMCS\*** (International Movement of Catholic Students) (1921): 171, rue de Rennes, F-75006, Paris, France. For undergraduates.

**Pax Romana — ICMICA\*** (International Catholic Movement for Intellectual and Cultural Affairs) (1947): rue de Alpes 7, C. P. 1062, CH-1701 Fribourg, Switzerland. For Catholic intellectuals and professionals.

**Pro Sanctity Movement:** Piazza S. Andrea della Valle 3, 00166 Rome, Italy.

**St. Joan's International Alliance** (1911, in England, as Catholic Women's Suffrage Society): Quai Churchill 19 - Boite 061, B-4020 Liege, Belgium. Associate member of ICO.

**Salesian Cooperators** (1876): Don Bosco College, Newton, N.J. 07860. Third Salesian family founded by St. John Bosco. Members commit themselves to an apostolate at the service of the Church, giving particular attention to youth in the Salesian spirit and style.

**Secular Franciscan Order** (1221, first Rule approved): Via Piemonte, 70, 00187, Rome, Italy. (See Index.)

**Secular Fraternity of Charles de Foucauld:** Katharinenweg 4, B4700 Eupen, Belgium.

**Serra International** (1953, in U.S.): (See Index.)

**Society of St. Vincent de Paul\*** (1833, Paris): 5, rue du Pré-aux-Clercs, F-75007 Paris, France.

**The Grail** (1921, Nijmegen, The Netherlands): Duisburgerstrasse 470, D-4330, Mulheim, West Germany. (See Index.)

**Third Order of St. Dominic** (1285): Convento Santa Sabina, Piazza Pietro d'Illiria, Aventino, I-00153 Rome, Italy. (See Index.)

**Unda: International Catholic Association for Radio and Television\*** (1928, Cologne, Germany): rue de l'Orme, 12, B-1040 Brussels, Belgium. (See Index.)

**Unio Internationalis Laicorum in Servitio Ecclesiae** (1965, Aachen, Germany): Postfach 990125, Am Kielshof 2, 5000 Cologne, Germany 91. Consists of national and diocesan associations of persons who give professional services to the Church.

**Union of Adorers of the Blessed Sacrament** (1937): Largo dei Monti Parioli 3, I-00197, Rome, Italy.

**World Catholic Federation for the Biblical Apostolate** (1969, Rome): Mittelstrasse, 12, P.O. Box 601, D-7000, Stuttgart 1, Germany.

**World Movement of Christian Workers\*** (1961): 90, rue des Palais, 1210 Brussels, Belgium.

**World Organization of Former Pupils of Catholic Education\*** (1967, Rome): 48, rue de Richelieu, F-75001 Paris, France.

**World Union of Catholic Philosophical Societies** (1948, Amsterdam, The Netherlands): The Catholic University of America, Washington, D.C. 20064.

**World Union of Catholic Teachers\*** (1951): Piazza San Calisto 16, 00153 Rome, Italy.

**World Union of Catholic Women's Organizations\*** (1910): 20, rue Notre Dame des Champs, F-75006 Paris, France.

## Regional Organizations

**European Federation for Catholic Adult Education** (196, Lucerne, Switzerland): Kapuzinestrasse 84, A-4020 Linz, Austria.

**European Forum of National Committees of the Laity** (1968): 169, Booterstown Av., Blackrock, Co. Dublin, Ireland.

**Movimiento Familiar Cristiano** (1949-50, Montevideo and Buenos Aires): Carrera 17 n. 4671, Bogota, D.E., Colombia. Christian Family Movement of Latin America.

# THE CATHOLIC CHURCH IN CANADA _____

The first date in the remote background of the Catholic history of Canada was July 7, 1534, when a priest in the exploration company of Jacques Cartier celebrated Mass on the Gaspe Peninsula.

Successful colonization and the significant beginnings of the Catholic history of the country date from the foundation of Quebec in 1608 by Samuel de Champlain and French settlers. Montreal was established in 1642.

The earliest missionaries were Franciscan Récollets (Recollects) and Jesuits who arrived in 1615 and 1625, respectively. They provided some pastoral care for the settlers but worked mainly among the 100,000 Indians — Algonquins, Hurons and Iroquois — in the interior and in the Lake Ontario region. Eight of the Jesuit missionaries, killed in the 1640s, were canonized in 1930. (See Index: Jesuit North American Martyrs.) Sulpician Fathers, who arrived in Canada late in the 1640s, played a part in the great missionary period which ended about 1700.

Kateri Tekakwitha, "Lily of the Mohawks," who was baptized in 1676 and died in 1680, was declared "Blessed" June 22, 1980.

The communities of women religious with the longest histories in Canada are the Canonesses of St. Augustine and the Ursulines, since 1639; and the Hospitallers of St. Joseph, since 1642. Communities of Canadian origin are the Congregation of Notre Dame, founded by St. Marguerite Bourgeoys in 1658, and the Grey Nuns, formed by St. Marie Marguerite d'Youville in 1737.

Mother Marie (Guyard) of the Incarnation, an Ursuline nun, was one of the first three women missionaries to New France; called "Mother of the Church in Canada," she was declared "Blessed" June 22, 1980.

## Start of Church Organization

Ecclesiastical organization began with the appointment in 1658 of Francois De Montmorency-Laval, "Father of the Church in Canada," as vicar apostolic of New France. He was the first bishop of Quebec from 1674 to 1688, with jurisdiction over all French-claimed territory in North America. He was declared "Blessed" June 22, 1980.

In 1713, the French Canadian population numbered 18,000. In the same year, the Treaty of Utrecht ceded Acadia, Newfoundland and the Hudson Bay Territory to England. The Acadians were scattered among the American Colonies in 1755.

The English acquired possession of Canada and its 70,000 French-speaking inhabitants in virtue of the Treaty of Paris in 1763. Anglo-French and Anglican-Catholic differences and tensions developed. The pro-British government at first refused to recognize the titles of church officials, hindered the clergy in their work and tried to install a non-Catholic educational system. Laws were passed which guaranteed religious liberties to Catholics (Quebec Act of 1774, Constitutional Act of 1791, legislation

approved by Queen Victoria in 1851), but it took some time before actual respect for these liberties matched the legal enactments. The initial moderation of government antipathy toward the Church was caused partly by the loyalty of Catholics to the Crown during the American Revolution and the War of 1812.

## Growth

The 15 years following the passage in 1840 of the Act of Union, which joined Upper and Lower Canada, were significant. New communities of men and women religious joined those already in the country. The Oblates of Mary Immaculate, missionaries par excellence in Canada, advanced the penetration of the West which had been started in 1818 by Abbe Provencher. New jurisdictions were established, and Quebec became a metropolitan see in 1844. The first Council of Quebec was held in 1851. The established Catholic school system enjoyed a period of growth.

Laval University was inaugurated in 1854 and canonically established in 1876.

Archbishop Elzear-Alexandre Taschereau of Quebec was named Canada's first cardinal in 1886.

The apostolic delegation to Canada was set up in 1899. It became a nunciature October 16, 1969, with the establishment of diplomatic relations with the Vatican.

Early in this century, Canada had eight ecclesiastical provinces, 23 dioceses, three vicariates apostolic, 3,500 priests, 2 million Catholics, about 30 communities of men religious, and 70 or more communities of women religious. The Church in Canada was phased out of mission status and removed from the jurisdiction of the Congregation for the Propagation of the Faith in 1908.

## Diverse Population

The greatest concentration of Catholics is in the eastern portion of the country. In the northern and western portions, outside metropolitan centers, there are some of the most difficult parish and mission areas in the world. Bilingual (English-French) differences in the general population are reflected in the Church; for example, in the parallel structures of the Canadian Conference of Catholic Bishops, which was established in 1943. Quebec is the center of French cultural influence. Many language groups are represented among Catholics, who include more than 257,000 members of Eastern Rites in one metropolitan see, seven eparchies and an apostolic exarchate.

Education, a past source of friction between the Church and the government, is administered by the civil provinces in a variety of arrangements authorized by the Canadian Constitution. Denominational schools have tax support in one way in Quebec and Newfoundland, and in another way in Alberta, Ontario and Saskatchewan. Several provinces provide tax support only for public schools, making private financing necessary for separate church-related schools.

# ECCLESIASTICAL JURISDICTIONS OF CANADA

## Provinces

Names of ecclesiastical provinces and metropolitan sees in bold face: suffragan sees in parentheses.
**Edmonton** (Calgary, St. Paul).

**Gatineau-Hull** (Amos, Mont-Laurier, Rouyn Noranda).

**Grouard-McLennan** (Mackenzie-Ft. Smith, Prince George, Whitehorse).

**Halifax** (Antigonish, Charlottetown, Yarmouth).
**Keewatin-LePas** (Churchill-Hudson Bay, Labrador-Schefferville, Moosonee).
**Kingston** (Alexandria-Cornwall, Peterborough, Sault Ste. Marie).
**Moncton** (Bathurst, Edmundston, St. John).
**Montreal** (Joliette, St. Jean-Longueuil, St. Jerome, Valleyfield).
**Ottawa** (Hearst, Pembroke, Timmins).
**Quebec** (Chicoutimi, Ste.-Anne-de-la-Pocatiere, Trois Rivieres).
**Regina** (Gravelbourg, Prince Albert, Saskatoon, Abbey of St. Peter).
**Rimouski** (Baie-Comeau, Gaspe).
**St. Boniface** (no suffragan).
**St. John's** (Grand Falls, St. George).
**Sherbrooke** (Nicolet, St. Hyacinthe).
**Toronto** (Hamilton, London, St. Catharines, Thunder Bay).
**Vancouver** (Kamloops, Nelson, Victoria).
**Winnipeg** — Ukrainian (Edmonton, New Westminster, Saskatoon, Toronto).
**Jurisdictions immediately subject to the Holy See:** Roman-Rite Archdiocese of Winnipeg, Byzantine Eparchy of Sts. Cyril and Methodius for Slovaks, Byzantine Eparchy of St. Sauveur de Montreal for Greek Melkites; Antiochene Eparchy of St. Maron of Montreal for Maronites.

## Jurisdictions, Hierarchy

(Principal sources: Information office, Canadian Conference of Catholic Bishops; Catholic Almanac survey; *Annuario Pontificio*; L'Osservatore Romano; Catholic News Service. As of June 1, 1996.)

Information includes names of archdioceses (indicated by asterisk) and dioceses, date of foundation, present ordinaries and auxiliaries; addresses of chancery office/bishop's residence; cathedral; former ordinaries. For biographies of current hierarchy, see Index.

**Alexandria-Cornwall, Ont.** (1890 as Alexandria; name changed to Alexandria-Cornwall, 1976): Eugene Philippe LaRocque, bishop, 1974.

Diocesan Center: 220, chemin Montreal, C.P. 1388, Cornwall, Ont. K6H 5V4. Cathedral: St. Finnans (Alexandria); Nativity Co-Cathedral (Cornwall).

Former bishops: Alexander Macdonell, 1890-1905; William A. Macdonell, 1906-20; Felix Couturier, O.P., 1921-41; Rosario Brodeur, 1941-66; Adolphe E. Proulx, 1967-74.

**Amos, Que.** (1938): Gerard Drainville, bishop, 1978.

Bishop's Residence: 450, rue Principale Nord, Amos, Que. J9T 2M1. Cathedral: St. Theresa of Avila.

Former bishops: Joseph Aldee Desmarais, 1939-68; Gaston Hains, 1968-78.

**Antigonish, N.S.** (Arichat, 1844; transferred, 1886): Colin Campbell, bishop, 1987.

Chancery Office: 155 Main St., P.O. Box 1330, Antigonish, N.S., B2G 2L7. Cathedral: St. Ninian.

Former bishops: William Fraser, 1844-51; Colin Francis MacKinnon, 1852-77; John Cameron, 1877-1910; James Morrison, 1912-50; John Roderick MacDonald, 1950-59; William E. Power, 1960-86.

**Baie-Comeau, Que.** (p.a., 1882; v.a., 1905; diocese Gulf of St. Lawrence, 1945; name changed, to Hauterive, 1960; present title, 1986): Pierre Morissette, bishop, 1990.

Bishop's Residence: 639, rue de Bretagne, Baie-Comeau, Que., G5C 1X2. Cathedral: Paroisse St. Jean-Eudes.

Former bishops: Napoleon-Alexandre Labrie, C.J.M., v.a., 1938-45, first bishop, 1945-56; Gerard Couturier, 1957-74; Jean-Guy Couture, 1975-79; Roger Ebacher, 1979-88; Maurice Couture, R.S.V., 1988-90.

**Bathurst, N.B.** (Chatham, 1860; transferred, 1938): Andre Richard, C.S.C., bishop, 1989.

Bishop's Residence: 645, avenue Murray, C.P. 460, Bathurst, N.-B., E2A 3Z4. Cathedral: Sacred Heart of Jesus.

Former bishops: James Rogers, 1860-1902; Thomas F. Barry, 1902-20; Patrice-Alexandre Chiasson, C.J.M., 1920-42; Camille-Andre Le Blanc, 1942-69; Edgar Godin, 1969-85; Arsene Richard 1986-89.

**Calgary, Alta.** (1912): Paul J. O'Byrne, bishop, 1968.

Former bishops: John Thomas McNally, 1913-24; John T. Kidd, 1925-31; Peter J. Monahan, 1932-35; Francis P. Carroll, 1936-66; Francis J. Klein, 1967-68. Address: Room 200, Catholic Pastoral Center, 120 17 Ave. SW, Calgary, Alta. T2S 2T2. Cathedral: St. Mary.

**Charlottetown, P.E.I.** (1829): Joseph Vernon Fougere, bishop, 1992.

Bishop's Residence: P.O. Box 907, Charlottetown, P.E.I., C1A 7L9. Cathedral: St. Dunstan's.

Former bishops: Bernard Angus McEachern, 1829-35; Bernard Donald McDonald, 1837-59; Peter McIntyre, 1860-91; James Charles McDonald, 1891-1912; Henry Joseph O'Leary, 1913-20; Louis James O'Leary, 1920-30; J.A. Sullivan, 1931-44; James Boyle, 1944-54; Malcolm A. MacEachern, 1955-70; Francis J. Spence, 1970-82; James H. MacDonald, 1982-91.

**Chicoutimi, Que.** (1878): Jean-Guy Couture, bishop, 1979. Roch Pedneault, auxiliary.

Bishop's Residence: 602, Racine Est, Chicoutimi, Que. G7H 6J6. Cathedral: St. Francois-Xavier.

Former bishops: Dominique Racine, 1878-88; Louis-Nazaire Begin (later cardinal), 1888-92; Michel-Thomas Labrecque, 1892-1927; Charles Lamarche, 1928-40; Georges Melancon, 1940-61; Marius Pare, 1961-79.

**Churchill-Hudson Bay, Man.** (p.a., 1925; v.a. Hudson Bay, 1931; diocese of Churchill, 1967; present title, 1968): Reynald Rouleau, O.M.I., bishop, 1987.

Diocesan Office: P.O. Box 10, Churchill, Man. ROB OEO. Cathedral: Holy Canadian Martyrs.

Former bishops: Arsene Turquetil, O.M.I., 1931-43; Armand Clabaut, O.M.I., coadjutor, 1937-40; Marc LaCroix, O.M.I., 1943-68; Omer Alfred Robidoux, 1970-86.

**Edmonton,\* Alta.** (St. Albert, 1871; archdiocese, transferred Edmonton, 1912): Joseph N. MacNeil, archbishop, 1973.

Archdiocesan Office: 8421-101 Avenue, Edmonton, Alta. T6A OL1. Cathedral: Basilica of St. Joseph.

Former bishops: Vital-Justin Grandin, O.M.I., 1871-1902; Emile Legal, O.M.I., 1902-20, first archbishop; Henry Joseph O'Leary, 1920-38; John Hugh MacDonald, 1938-64; Anthony Jordan, O.M.I., 1964-73.

**Edmonton, Alta.** (Ukrainian Byzantine) (ap. ex. of western Canada, 1948; eparchy, 1956): Vacant as of May 1, 1996.

Eparch's Residence: 9645 - 108th Ave., Edmonton, Alta. T5H 1A3. Cathedral: St. Josaphat.

Former bishops: Neil Nicholas Savaryn, O.S.B.M., 1948-86; Demetrius Martin Greschuk, 1986-90; Myron Daciuk, O.S.B.M., 1991-96.

**Edmundston, N.B.** (1944): François Thibodeau, C.J.M., bishop, 1994.

Diocesan Center: Edmundston, N.B. E3V 3K1. Cathedral: Immaculate Conception.

Former bishops: Marie-Antoine Roy, O.F.M., 1945-48; Joseph-Roméo Gagnon, 1949-70; Fernand Lacroix, C.J.M., 1970-83; Gérard Dionne, 1984-93.

**Gaspe, Que.** (1922): Raymond Dumais, bishop, 1994.

Bishop's House: 172, rue Jacques-Cartier, C.P. 440, Gaspe, Que. GOC 1RO. Cathedral: Christ the King.

Former bishops: Francois-Xavier Ross, 1922-45; Albini LeBlanc, 1945-57; Paul Bernier (personal title of Archbishop), 1957-64; Jean Marie Fortier, 1965-68; Gilles Ouellet, 1968-73; Bertrand Blanchet, 1973-93.

**Gatineau-Hull,\* Que.** (1963, as Hull; name changed, 1982; archdiocese, 1990): Roger Ebacher, bishop, 1988; first archbishop, Oct. 31, 1990.

Former bishops: Paul-Emile Charbonneau, 1963-73; Adolph Proulx, 1974-87.

Diocesan Center: 180 Boul. Mont-Bleu, Hull, Que. J8Z 3J5.

**Grand Falls, Nfld.** (Harbour Grace, 1856; present title, 1964): Joseph Faber MacDonald, bishop, 980.

Chancery Office: P.O. Box 397, Grand Falls, Windsor, Nfld. A2A 2J8. Cathedral: Immaculate Conception.

Former bishops: John Dalton, 1856-69; Henry Carfagnini, 1870-80; R. McDonald, 1881-1906; John March, 1906-40; John M. O'Neill, 1940-72; Alphonsus S. Penney, 1973-79.

**Gravelbourg, Sask.** (1930): Raymond Roussin, S.M., bishop, 1995.

Bishop's Residence: C.P. 690, Gravelbourg, Sask. SOH 1XO. Cathedral: Our Lady of the Assumption.

Former bishops: Jean-Marie Villeneuve, O.M.I., 1930-31; Arthur Melanson, 1932-36; Joseph Guy, O.M.I., 1937-42; M.-Joseph Lemieux, 1944-53; Aime Decosse, 1954-73; Noel Delaquis, 1974-95.

**Grouard-McLennan,\* Alta.** (v.a. Athabaska-Mackenzie, 1862; Grouard, 1927; archdiocese Grouard-McLennan, 1967); Henri Goudreault, O.M.I., archbishop, 1996.

Archbishop's Residence: C.P. 388, McLennan, Alta. TOH 2LO. Cathedral: St. Jean-Baptiste (McLennan).

Former ordinaries: Henri Faraud, O.M.I., 1864-90; Emile Grouard, O.M.I., 1891-1929; Joseph Guy, O.M.I., 1930-38; Ubald Langlois, O.M.I., 1938-53; Henri Routhier, O.M.I., 1953-72, first archbishop; Henri Legare, O.M.I., 1972-96.

**Halifax,\* N.S.** (1842; archdiocese, 1852): Austin E. Burke, archbishop, 1991.

Former ordinaries: Edmund Burke, vicar apostolic,

1818-20; William Fraser, 1842-44; William Walsh, 1844-58, first archbishop; Thomas L. Connolly, 1859-76; Michael Hannan, 1877-82; Cornelius O'Brien, 1883-1906; Edward J. McCarthy, 1906-31; Thomas O'Donnell, 1931-36; John T. McNally, 1937-52; Joseph G. Berry, 1953-67; James Martin Hayes, 1967-90.

Chancery Office: P.O. Box 1527, Halifax, N.S. B3J 2Y3.

**Hamilton, Ont.** (1856): Anthony Tonnos, bishop, 1984. Matthew Ustrzycki, auxiliary.

Chancery Office: 700 King St. West, Hamilton, Ont. L8P1C7. Cathedral: Christ the King.

Former bishops: John Farrell, 1856-73; Peter F. Crinnon, 1874-82; James Joseph Carbery, 1884-87; Thomas J. Dowling, 1889-1924; J.T. McNally, 1924-37; Joseph F. Ryan, 1937-73; Paul F. Reding, 1973-83.

**Hearst, Ont.** (p.a., 1918; v.a., 1920; diocese, 1938): André Vallée, P.M.E., bishop, 1996.

Bishop's Residence: 76 7e rue, C.P. 1330, Hearst, Ont. POL INO. Cathedral: Notre Dame of the Assumption.

Former bishops: Joseph Halle, 1919-38; Joseph Charbonneau, 1939-40; A. LeBlanc, 1941-45; Georges Landry, 1946-52; Louis Levesque, 1952-64; Jacques Landriault, 1964-71; Roger Despatie, 1973-93; Pierre Fisette, P.M.E., 1994-95.

**Joliette, Que.** (1904): Gilles Lussier, bishop, 1991.

Bishop's Residence: C.P. 470, 2 rue Saint-Charles-Borromeo Nord, Joliette, Que. J6E 6H6. Cathedral: St. Charles Borromeo.

Former bishops: Joseph Archambault, 1904-13; Guillaume Forbes, 1913-28; Joseph A. Papineau, 1928-68; Rene Audet, 1968-90.

**Kamloops, B.C.** (1945): Lawrence Sabatini, C.S., bishop, 1982.

Bishop's Residence: 635A Tranquille Rd., Kamloops, B.C. V2B 3H5. Cathedral: Sacred Heart.

Former bishops: Edward Q. Jennings, 1946-52; Michael A. Harrington, 1952-73; Adam Exner, O.M.I., 1974-82.

**Keewatin-Le Pas,\* Man.** (v.a., 1910; archdiocese, 1967): Peter-Alfred Sutton, O.M.I., archbishop, 1986.

Archbishop's Residence: 108, 1st St. West, P.O. Box 270, The Pas, Man. R9A 1K4. Cathedral: Our Lady of the Sacred Heart.

Former bishops: Ovide Charlebois, O.M.I., 1910-33; Martin LaJeunesse, O.M.I., 1933-54; Paul Dumouchel, O.M.I., 1955-86, first archbishop.

**Kingston,\* Ont.** (1826; archdiocese, 1889): Francis J. Spence, archbishop, 1982.

Chancery Office: 390 Palace Rd., Kingston Ont. K7L 4T3. Cathedral: St. Mary of the Immaculate Conception.

Former bishops: Alexander Macdonell, 1826-40; Remigius Gaulin, 1840-57; Patrick Phelan, 1843-57; Edward J. Horan, 1858-75; John O'Brien, 1875-79; J. V. Cleary, 1880-98, first archbishop; C.-H. Gauthier, 1898-1910; Michael Joseph Spratt, 1911-38; Michael-Joseph O'Brien, 1939-43; Joseph A. O'Sullivan, 1944-66; Joseph L. Wilhelm 1966-82.

**Labrador City (Nfld.)-Schefferville, Que.** (v.a. Labrador, 1946; diocese, 1967): Vacant as of July 20, 1996.

Bishop's Residence: 318 avenue Elizabeth, C.P.

545, Labrador City, Nfld. A2V 2K7. Cathedral: Our Lady of Perpetual Help.
Former bishops: Lionel Scheffer, O.M.I., 1946-66; Henri Legare, O.M.I., 1967-72; Peter A. Sutton, 1974-86.
**London, Ont.** (1855; transferred Sandwich, 1859; London, 1869): John M. Sherlock, bishop, 1978.
Bishop's Residence: 1070 Waterloo St., London, Ont. N6A 3Y2. Cathedral: St. Peter's Cathedral Basilica.
Former bishops: Pierre Adolphe Pinsoneault, 1856-66; John Walsh, 1867-89; Dennis O'Connor, C.S.B., 1890-99; F.P. McEvay 1899-1908; Michael F. Fallon, 1910-31; J. Thomas Kidd, 1931-50; John C. Cody, 1950-63; Gerald E. Carter, 1964-78.
**Mackenzie-Fort Smith, N.W.T.** (v.a. Mackenzie, 1902; diocese Mackenzie-Fort Smith, 1967): Denis Croteau, O.M.I., bishop, 1986.
Diocesan Office: 5117-52nd St., Yellowknife, NWT X1A 1T7. Cathedral: St. Joseph (Ft. Smith).
Former bishops: Gabriel Breynat, O.M.I., 1902-43; Joseph Trocellier, O.M.I., 1943-58; Paul Piche, 1959-86.
**Moncton,\* N.B.** (1936): Vacant as of July 1, 1996.
Archbishop's Residence: 452, rue Amirault, Dieppe, C.P. 248, Moncton, N.B. E1C 8K9. Cathedral: Our Lady of the Assumption.
Former bishops: L.J.-Arthur Melanson, 1937-41; Norbert Robichaud, 1942-72; Donat Chiasson, 1972-95.
**Mont-Laurier, Que.** (1913): Jean Gratton, bishop, 1978.
Bishop's Residence: 435, rue de la Madone, Mont-Laurier, Que. J9L 1S1. Cathedral: Notre Dame de Fourvières.
Former bishops: Francois-Xavier Brunet, 1913-22; Joseph-Eugene Limoges, 1922-63; Joseph Louis Andre Ouellette, apostolic administrator sede plena, 1963-65; bishop, 1965-78.
**Montreal,\* Que.** (1836; archdiocese, 1886): Cardinal Jean-Claude Turcotte, archbishop, 1990.Leonard Crowley, Jude Saint-Antoine, Neil Willard, André Rivest, auxiliaries.
Archbishop's Residence: 2000, rue Sherbrooke Ouest, Montreal, Que. H3H 1G4. Cathedral: Basilica of Mary Queen of the World and Saint James.
Former bishops: Jean-Jacques Lartigue, P.S.S., 1836-40; Ignace Bourget, 1840-76; Edouard-Charles Fabre, first archbishop, 1876-96; Paul Bruchési, 1897-1939; Georges Gauthier, administrator 1921-39; archbishop, 1939-40; Joseph Charbonneau, 1940-50; Cardinal Paul-Emile Leger, 1950-67; Cardinal Paul Gregoire, 1968-90.
**Moosonee, Ont.** (v.a. James Bay, 1938; diocese Moosonee, 1967): Vincent Cadieux, O.M.I., bishop, 1992.
Bishop's Residence: C.P. 40, Moosonee, Ont. P0L IY0. Cathedral: Christ the King.
Former bishops: Henri Belleau, O.M.I., 1940-64; Jules LeGuerrier, O.M.I., 1964-91.
**Nelson, B.C.** (1936): Eugene J. Cooney, bishop, 1996.
Bishop's Residence: 813 Ward St., Nelson, B.C. VIL IT4. Cathedral: Mary Immaculate.
Former bishops: Martin M. Johnson, 1936-54; Thomas J. McCarthy, 1955-58; Wilfrid E. Doyle, 1958-89; Peter Mallon, 1990-95.

**New Westminster, B.C.** (Ukrainian Byzantine) (1974): Severian Stephen Yakymyshyn, O.S.B.M., eparch, 1995.
Eparch's address: 502 5th Ave., New westminster,BC V3L 152.
Former eparch: Jerome Chimy, O.S.B.M., 1974-92.
**Nicolet, Que.** (1885): Raymond Saint-Gelais, bishop, 1989.
Bishop's Residence: 49, rue Mgr Brunault, Nicolet, Que. J3T 1X7. Cathedral: St.-Jean-Baptiste.
Former bishops: Elphege Gravel, 1885-1904; Joseph-Simon-Hermann Brunault, 1904-38; Albini Lafortune, 1938-50; Albert Martin, 1950-89.
**Ottawa,\* Ont.** (Bytown, 1847, name changed, 1854; archdiocese, 1886): Marcel Gervais, archbishop, 1989. Paul Marchand, S.M.M., Frederick Colli, auxiliaries.
Archbishop's Residence: 1247 Place Kilborn, Ottawa, Ont. KIH 6K9. Cathedral: Basilica of Notre Dame-of-Ottawa.
Former bishops: Joseph-Eugene-Bruno Guigues, 1848-74; Joseph Tomas Duhamel, first archbishop, 1874-1909; Charles Hughes Gauthier, 1910-22; Joseph-Medard Emard, 1922-27; Joseph Guillaume Forbes, 1928-40; Alexandre Vachon, 1940-53; Marie-Joseph Lemieux, O.P., 1953-66; Joseph Aurele Plourde, 1967-89.
**Pembroke, Ont.** (v.a. 1882; diocese, 1898): Brendan M. O'Brien, bishop, 1993.
Bishop's Residence: 188 Renfrew St., P.O. Box 7, Pembroke, Ont. K8A 6XI. Cathedral: St. Columbkille.
Former bishops: Narcisse-Zephirin Lorrain, 1882-1915; Patrick T. Ryan, 1916-37; Charles-Leo Nelligan, 1937-45; William J. Smith, 1945-71; Joseph R. Windle, 1971-93.
**Peterborough, Ont.** (1882): James L. Doyle, bishop, 1976.
Bishop's Residence: 350 Hunter St. West, PO Box 175, Peterborough, Ont. K9J 6Y8. Cathedral: St. Peter-in-Chains.
Former bishops: John Francis Jamot, 1882-86; Thomas J. Dowling, 1887-89; Richard A. O'Connor, 1889-1913; Michael J. O'Brien, 1913-29; Denis O'Connor, 1930-42; John R. McDonald, 1943-45; Joseph G. Berry, 1945-53; Benjamin I. Webster, 1954-68; Francis A. Marrocco, 1968-75.
**Prince Albert, Sask.** (v.a., 1890; diocese, 1907): Blaise Morand, bishop, 1983.
Address: 1415-4thAve. Ouest, Prince-Albert, Sask. S6V 5H1. Cathedral: Sacred Heart.
Former bishops: Albert Pascal, O.M.I., 1907-20; Joseph Henri Prud'homme, 1921-37; R. Duprat, O.P., 1938-52; Leo Blais, 1952-59; Laurent Morin, 1959-83.
**Prince George, B.C.** (p.a., 1908; v.a. Yukon and Prince Rupert, 1944; diocese Prince George, 1967): Gerald Wiesner, O.M.I., bishop, 1993.
Chancery Office: P.O. Box 7000, 2935 Highway 16 West, Prince George, B.C. V2N 3Z2. Cathedral: Sacred Heart.
Former bishops: Emile-Marie Bunoz, O.M.I., 1917-45; John-Louie Coudert, O.M.I., coadjutor, 1936-44; Anthony Jordan, O.M.I., 1945-55; John F. O'Grady, O.M.I. 1955-86; Hubert P. O'Connor, O.M.I., 1986-91.
**Quebec,\* Que.** (v.a., 1658; diocese, 1674; arch-

diocese, 1819; metropolitan, 1844; primatial see, 1956): Maurice Couture, R.S.V., archbishop, 1990. Marc Leclerc, Jean Pierre Blais, Eugène Tremblay, auxiliaries.

Chancery Office: 1073, boul. René Lévesque Ouest, Quebec, Que. G1S 4R5. Cathedral: Notre-Dame- de-Quebec (Basilica).

Former bishops: Francois de Laval, vicar apostolic, 1658; bishop 1674-88 (beatified 1980); Jean-Baptiste de La Croix de Chevrières de Saint-Vallier, 1688-1727; Louis-Francois Duplessis de Mornay, 1727-33; Pierre-Herman Dosquet, 1733-39; Francois-Louis de Pourroy de Lauberivière, 1739-40; Henri-Marie Dubreil de Pontbriand, 1741-60; Jean-Olivier Briand, 1766-84; Louis-Philippe Mariauchau d'Esgly, 1784-88; Jean-Francois Hubert, 1788-97; Pierre Denaut, 1797-1806; Joseph-Octave Plessis, first archbishop, 1806-25; Bernard-Claude Panet, 1825-33; Joseph Signay, 1833-50; Pierre-Flavien Turgeon, 1850-67; Charles-Francois Baillargeon, 1867-70; Cardinal Elzear-Alexandre Taschereau, 1870-98; Cardinal Louis-Nazaire Begin, 1898-1925; Paul-Eugène Roy, 1925-26; Cardinal Rymond-Marie Rouleau, O.P., 1926-31; Cardinal Jean-Marie-Rodrigue Villeneuve, O.M.I., 1931-47; Cardinal Maurice Roy, 1947-81; Cardinal Louis-Albert Vachon, 1981-90.

**Regina,* Sask.** (1910; archdiocese, 1915): Peter Mallon, archbishop, 1995.

Chancery Office: 445 Broad St. North, Regina, Sask. S4R 2X8. Cathedral: Our Lady of the Most Holy Rosary.

Former bishops: Olivier-Elzear Mathieu, 1911-29; James Charles McGuigan, 1930-34; Peter Joseph Monahan, 1935-47; Michael C.O'Neill, 1948-73; Charles A. Halpin, 1973-94.

**Rimouski,* Que.** (1867; archdiocese, 1946): Bertrand Blanchet, archbishop, 1992.

Archbishop's Residence: 34, rue de l'Évêché Ouest, C.P. 730, Rimouski, Que. G5L 7C7.

Former bishops: Jean Langevin, 1867-91; Andre-Albert Blais, 1891-1919; J.-R. Leonard, 1919-26; Georges Courchesne, 1928-50; Charles-Eugene Parent, 1951-67; Louis Lévesque, 1967-73; Gilles Ouellet, P.M.E., 1973-92.

**Rouyn-Noranda, Que.** (1973): Jean-Guy Hamelin, bishop, 1974.

Bishop's Residence: 515, avenue Cuddihy, C.P. 1060, Rouyn-Noranda, Que. J9X 4C5. Cathedral: St. Michael the Archangel.

**Saint-Boniface,* Man.** (1847; archdiocese, 1871): Antoine Hacault, archbishop, 1974.

Archbishop's Residence: 151, avenue de la Cathedrale, Saint-Boniface, Man. R2H OH6. Cathedral: Basilica of St. Boniface.

Former bishops: Joseph-Norbert Provencher, 1847-53; Alexandre-Antonin Tache, O.M.I., 1853-94, first archbishop; Vital-Justin Grandin, O.M.I., coadjutor, 1857-71; Louis-Philippe-Adelard Langevin, O.M.I., 1895-1915; Arthur Beliveau, 1915-55; Emile Yelle, P.S.S., coadjutor, 1933-41; Georges Cabana, coadjutor, 1941-52; Maurice Baudoux, coadjutor 1952-55, archbishop, 1955-74.

**St. Catharines, Ont.** (1958): John A. O'Mara, bishop, 1994.

Bishop's Residence: 122 Riverdale Ave., St.

Catharines, Ont. L2R 4C2. Cathedral: St. Catherine of Alexandria.

Former bishops: Thomas J. McCarthy, 1958-78; Thomas B. Fulton, 1978-94.

**St. George's, Nfld.** (p.a., 1870; v.a., 1890; diocese, 1904): Raymond J. Lahey, bishop, 1986.

Bishop's Residence: 16 Hammond Dr., Corner Brook, Nfld. A2H 2W2. Cathedral: Most Holy Redeemer and Immaculate Conception.

Former bishops: Neil McNeil, 1904-10; Michael Power, 1911-20; HenryT. Renouf, 1920-41; Michael O'Reilly, 1941-70; Richard T. McGrath, 1970-85.

**Saint-Hyacinthe, Que.** (1852): Louis-de-Gonzague Langevin, M.Afr., bishop, 1979.

Bishop's Residence: 1900, rue Girouard Ouest, C.P. 190, Saint-Hyacinthe, Que. J2S 7B4. Cathedral. St. Hyacinthe the Confessor.

Former bishops: Jean-Charles Prince, 1852-60; Joseph Larocque, 1860-65; Charles Larocque, 1866-75; Louis-Zéphirin Moreau, 1875-1901 (beatified 1987); Maxime Decelles, 1901-05; Alexis-Xyste Bernard, 1906-23; Fabien-Zoël Decelles, 1924-42; Arthur Doubille, 1942-67; Albert Sanschagrin, O.M.I., 1967-79.

**Saint-Jean-Longueuil, Que.** (1933 as St.-Jean-de-Quebec; named changed, 1982): Vacant as of May 1, 1996. Jacques Berthelet, C.S.V., auxiliary.

Bishop's Residence: 740, boulevard Sainte-Foy, C.P. 40, Longueuil, Que. J4K 4X8. Cathedral: St. John the Evangelist.

Former bishops: Anastase Forget, 1934-55; Gerard-Marie Coderre, 1955-78; Bernard Hubert, 1978-96.

**St. Jerome, Que.** (1951): Charles Valois, bishop, 1977. Vital Massé, auxiliary.

Bishop's Residence: 355, rue Saint-Georges, C.P. 580, Saint-Jerome, Que. J7Z 5V3. Cathedral: St. Jerome.

Former bishops: Emilien Frenette, 1951-71; Bernard Hubert, 1971-77.

**Saint John, N.B.** (1842): J. Edward Troy, bishop, 1986.

Chancery Office: 1 Bayard Dr., Saint John, N.B. E2L 3L5. Cathedral: Immaculate Conception.

Former bishops: William Dollard, 1843-51; Thomas L. Connolly, 1852-59; John Sweeney, 1860-1901; Timothy Casey, 1901-12; Edward A. LeBlanc, 1912-35; Patrick A. Bray, C.J.M., 1936-53; Alfred B. Leverman, 1953-68; Joseph N. MacNeil, 1969-73; Arthur J. Gilbert, 1974-86.

**St. John's,* Nfld.** (p.a., 1784; v.a., 1796; diocese, 1847; archdiocese, 1904): James H. MacDonald, C.S.C., archbishop, 1991.

Chancery Office: P.O. Box 1363, St. John's, Nfld. A1C 5H5. Cathedral: St. John the Baptist.

Former bishops: James O'Donel, O.S.F., 1784-1807; Patrick Lambert, O.S.F., 1807-17; Patrick Lambert, O.S.F., 1817-30; Thomas Scallan, O.S.F., 1817-30; Michael A. Fleming, O.S.F., 1830-50; John T. Mullock, O.S.F., 1850-69; Thomas J. Power, 1870-93; Michael Howley, first archbishop, 1895-1914; Edward P. Roche, 1915-50; Patrick J. Skinner, C.J.M., 1951-79; Alphonsus L. Penney, 1979-91.

**St. Maron of Montreal** (Maronites) (1982): Vacant as of July 20, 1996.

Chancery Office: 12475 rue Grenet, Montreal, Que. H4J 2K4. Cathedral: St. Maron.

Former bishops: Elias Shaheen, 1982-90; Georges Abi-Saber, 1991-96.

**St. Paul in Alberta** (1948): Raymond Roy, bishop, 1972.

Bishop's Residence: 4410, 51e avenue, Saint Paul, Alta. TOA 3A2. Cathedral: St. Paul.

Former bishops: Maurice Baudoux, 1948-52; Philippe Lussier, C.Ss.R., 1952-68; Edouard Gagnon, P.S.S., 1969-72.

**St. Sauveur de Montreal** (Greek Melkites) (ap. ex. 1980; eparchy, 1984): Archeparch Michel Hakim, 1980.

Address: 34 Maplewood, Montreal, Que. H2V 2MI.

**Sts. Cyril and Methodius of Toronto** (Slovakian Byzantine) (1980): Michael Rusnak, C.Ss.R., eparch, 1980.

Eparch's Residence: 223 Carlton Rd., Unionville, Ont. L3R 3M2.

**Sainte-Anne-de-la-Pocatiere, Que.** (1951): Clement Fecteau, bishop, 1996.

Bishop's Residence: 1200, 4e avenue, C.P. 430, La Pocatière, Que. G0R 1Z0. Cathedral: St. Anne.

Former bishops: Bruno Desrochers, 1951-68; Charles Henri Levesque, 1968-84; Andre Gaumond, 1985-95.

**Saskatoon, Sask.** (1933): V. James Weisgerber, bishop, 1996.

Chancery Office: 106-5th Avenue North, Saskatoon, Sask. S7K 2N7. Cathedral: St. Paul.

Former bishops: Gerald C. Murray, C.SS.R., 1934-44; Philip F. Pocock, 1944-51; F. Klein, 1951-67; James P. Mahoney, 1967-95.

**Saskatoon, Sask.** (Ukrainian Byzantine) (ap. ex., 1951; diocese, 1956): Cornelius Pasichny, O.S.B.M., bishop, 1995.

Address: 866 Saskatechewan Crescent East, Saskatoon, Sask. S7N OL4.

Former bishops: Andrew J. Roborecki, 1951-82; Basil (Wasyl) Filevich, 1984-95.

**Sault Ste. Marie, Ont.** (1904): Jean-Louis Plouffe, bishop, 1990. Bernard F. Pappin, auxiliary.

Chancery Office: 387 Algonquin, P.O. Box 510, North Bay, Ont. P1B 8J1. Cathedral: Pro-Cathedral of the Assumption, North Bay.

Former bishops: David Joseph Scollard, 1905-34; Ralphael Hubert Dignan, 1934-58; Alexander Carter, 1958-85; Marcel Gervais, 1985-89.

**Sherbrooke,\* Que.** (1874; archdiocese, 1951); André Gaumond, archbishop, 1996.

Archbishop's Residence: 130, rue de la Cathedrale, C.P. 430, Sherbrooke, Que. J1H 5K1. Cathedral: St. Michel.

Former ordinaries: Antoine Racine, 1874-93; Paul Larocque, 1893-1926; Alphonse-Osias Gagnon, 1927-41; Philippe Desranleau, first archbishop, 1941-52; Georges Caana, 1952-68' J.M. Fortier, 1968-1996.

**Thunder Bay, Ont.** (Ft. William, 1952; transferred, 1970): Frederick Henry, bishop, 1995.

Bishop's Residence: P.O. Box 756, Thunder Bay, Ont. P7C 4W6. Cathedral: St. Patrick.

Former bishops: Edward Q. Jennings, 1952-69; Norman J. Gallagher, 1970-75; John A. O'Mara, 1976-94.

**Timmins, Ont.** (v.a. Temiskaming, 1908; diocese Haileybury, 1915; present title, 1938): Gilles Cazabon, O.M.I., bishop, 1992.

Address: 65, Ave. Jubilee Est, Timmins, Ont. P4N 5W4. Cathedral: St. Anthony of Padua.

Former bishops: Elie-Anicet Latulippe, 1908-22; Louis Rheaume, O.M.I., 1922-55; Maxime Tessier, 1955-71; Jacques Landriault, 1971-90.

**Toronto,\* Ont.** (1841; archdiocese, 1870): Aloysius M. Ambrozic, archbishop, 1990. John Stephen Knight, Nicola De Angelis, C.F.I.C., Terrence Prendergast, S.J., auxiliaries.

Chancery Office: 1155 Yonge St., Toronto, Ont. M4Y 1W2. Cathedral: St. Michael.

Former ordinaries: Michael Power, 1842-47; Armand-Francois-Marie de Charbonnel, 1850-60; John Joseph Lynch, first archbishop, 1860-88; John Walsh, 1889-98; Denis O'Connor, 1899-1908; Fergus P. McEvay, 1908-11; Neil McNeil, 1912-34; Cardinal James Charles McGuigan, 1934-71; Philip F. Pocock, 1971-78; Cardinal G. Emmett Carter, 1978-90.

**Toronto, Ont.** (Ukrainian Byzantine) (ap. ex., 1948; eparchy, 1956): Isidore Borecky (exarch 1948-56), first eparch, 1956. Roman Danylak, apostolic administrator, 1993.

Chancery Office: 61 Glen Edyth Dr., Toronto, Ont. M4V 2V8. Cathedral: St. Josaphat.

**Trois-Rivieres, Que.** (1852): Laurent Noel, bishop, 1975. Martin Veillette, auxiliary.

Bishop's Residence: 362, rue Bonaventure, C.P. 879, Trois-Rivieres, Que. G9A 5J9. Cathedral: The Assumption.

Former bishops: Thomas Cooke, 1852-70; L.-F. Lafleche, 1870-98; F.-X. Cloutier, 1899-1934; A.-O. Comtois, 1935-45; Maurice Roy, 1946-47; Georges-Leon Pelletier, 1947-75.

**Unionville, Ont.:** See Sts. Cyril and Methodius of Toronto, above.

**Valleyfield, Que.** (1892): Robert Lebel, bishop, 1976.

Bishop's Residence: 11, rue de l'Eglise, Valleyfield, Que. J6T 1J5. Cathedral: St. Cecilia.

Former bishops: Joseph Médard Emard, 1892-1922; Raymond-M. Rouleau, O.P., 1922-26; Joseph Alfred Langlois, 1926-66; Percival Caza, 1966-69; Guy Belanger, 1969-75.

**Vancouver,\* B. C.** (v.a. British Columbia, 1863; diocese New Westminster, 1890; archdiocese Vancouver, 1908): Adam Exner, O.M.I., archbishop, 1991.

Chancery Office: 150 Robson St., Vancouver, B.C. V6B 2A7. Cathedral: Holy Rosary.

Former ordinaries: Louis-Joseph d'Herbomez, O.M.I., 1864-90; Paul Durieu, O.M.I., 1890-99; Augustin Dontenwill, O.M.I., 1899-1908; Neil McNeil, first archbishop, 1910-12; Timothy Casey, 1912-31; William M. Duke, 1931-64; Martin Michael Johnson, 1964-69; James F. Carney, 1969-90.

**Victoria, B.C.** (diocese Vancouver Is., 1846; archdiocese, 1903; diocese Victoria, 1908): Remi J. De Roo, bishop, 1962.

Chancery Office: Diocesan Pastoral Centre, #1-4044 Nelthorpe St., Victoria, B.C. V8X 2A1. Cathedral: St. Andrew.

Former bishops: Modeste Demers, 1847-71; Charles J. Seghers, 1873-78; Jean Baptiste Brondel, 1879-84; Charles J. Seghers (2nd time), 1885-86; J. N. Lemmens, 1888-97; Alexander Christie, 1898-99; Bertram Orth, 1900-08; Alexander Macdonald,

1909-23; Thoms O'Donnell, 1924-29; Gerald Murray, C.SS.R., 1930-33; John H. MacDonald, 1933-37; John C. Cody, 1937-46; James M. Hill, 1946-62.

**Whitehorse, Y.T.** (v.a., 1944; diocese 1967): Thomas Lobsinger, O.M.I., bishop, 1987.

Bishop's Residence: 5119-5thAvenue,Whitehorse, Yukon Y1A 1L5. Cathedral: Sacred Heart.

Former bishops: Jean-Louis Coudert, O.M.I., 1944-65(?); James Mulvihill, O.M.I., 1966-71; Hubert P. O'Connor, O.M.I., 1971-86.

**Winnipeg,\* Man.** (1915): Leonard J. Wall, archbishop, 1992.

Chancery Office: 1495 Pembina Highway, Winnipeg, Man., R3T 2C6. Cathedral: St. Mary.

Former bishops: Alfred Sinnott, 1915-52; Gerald Murray, coadjutor, 1944-51; Philip F. Pocock, 1952-61; Cardinal George B. Flahiff, 1961-82; Adam Exner, O.M.I., 1982-91.

**Winnipeg,\* Man.** (Ukrainian Byzantine) (Ordinariate of Canada, 1912; ap. ex. Central Canada, 1948; ap. ex. Manitoba, 1951; archeparchy Winnipeg, 1956): Michael Bzdel, C.Ss.R., archeparch, 1993. Stephen Soroka, auxiliary.

Archeparchy Office: 235 Scotia St., Winnipeg, Man., R2V 1V7. Cathedral: Sts. Vladimir and Olga.

Former ordinaries: Niceta Budka, 1912-28; Basile-Vladimir Ladyka, O.S.B.M., 1929-56; Maxim Hermaniuk, C.Ss.R., first archbishop, 1956-92.

**Yarmouth, N.S.** (1953): James M. Wingle, bishop, 1993.

Address: C.P. 278, 53 rue Park, Yarmouth, N.S. B5A 4B2. Cathedral: St. Ambrose.

Former bishops: Albert Lemenager, 1953-67; Austin E. Burke, 1968-91.

**Military Ordinariate of Canada** (1951): André Vallée, P.M.E., military ordinary, 1988.

Address: Catholic Chaplain General, National Defense Headquarters, Ottawa, Ont. K1A OK2.

Former military ordinaries: Cardinal Maurice Roy, archbishop of Quebec, 1946-82; John S. Spence, Archbishop of Kingston, 1982-87.

**Abbacy of St. Peter, Muenster, Sask.** (1921): Peter Novecosky, O.S.B., abbatial blessing, 1990.

Abbot's Residence: St. Peter's Abbey, Muenster, Sask. SOK 2YO.

Former abbots: Bruno Doerfler, 1911-19; Michael Ott, 1921-26; Severinus Gertken, 1927-60; Jerome Weber, 1960-90.

An **Apostolic Exarchate for Armenian-Rite Catholics in Canada and the United States** was established in July, 1981, with headquarters in New York City. Hovhannes Tertzakian, exarch, 1995.

The eparchy of **Our Lady of Deliverance of Newark** for Syrian-rite Catholics in the United States and Canada was established Nov. 6, 1995, with headquarters in Newark, N.J. Most Rev. Joseph Younan, bishop.

Most Rev. Attila Mikloshazy, S.J., titular bishop of Castel Minore and bishop for **Hungarian Emigrants throughout the world**, resides in Canada. Address: 2661 Kingston Rd., Scarborough, Ont. M1M 1M3.

### Dioceses with Interprovincial Lines

The following dioceses, indicated by + in the table, have interprovincial lines.

**Churchill-Hudson Bay** includes part of Northwest Territories.

**Keewatin-LePas** includes part of Manitoba and Saskatchewan provinces.

**Labrador City-Schefferville** includes the Labrador region of Newfoundland and the northern part of Quebec province.

**Mackenzie-Fort Smith**, Northwest Territories, includes part of Alberta and Saskatchewan provinces.

**Moosonee, Ont.**, includes part of Quebec province.

**Pembroke, Ont.**, includes one county of Quebec province.

**Whitehorse, Y.T.**, includes part of British Columbia.

---

## RESTORATION OF EASTERN LITURGY

The Vatican urged Eastern Catholic churches to restore ancient practices of their own traditions that may have been abandoned over time because of Latin-rite influence.

"This is almost a revolutionary document," said Maronite Chorbishop John D. Faris, vicar general of the Diocese of St. Maron in Brooklyn, N.Y., "because it is a very clear statement on the part of the Apostolic See that Latinization (of Eastern rites) has been completely abandoned."

One of the more evident reforms envisioned is a return to giving infants first Communion immediately after baptism and chrismation (confirmation) - - and then having young children continue to receive Communion regularly in their preschool years.

The document, entitled "Instruction for the Application of the Liturgical Prescriptions of the Code of Canons of the Eastern Churches," was published in Italian by the Congregation for Eastern-Rite Churches in January, 1996.

It is the first instruction on liturgical renewal of Eastern churches since the Second Vatican Council.

It was issued to clarify and expand on the liturgical implementation of the 1990 Code of Canons of the Eastern Churches, a body of general law governing all Eastern-rite Catholic churches.

The instruction testifies to "the inalienable value of the Eastern churches' own, diversified traditions" and the "richness of (their) liturgical heritage."

It urges Eastern Catholic churches to be faithful to their ancient traditions in part because of their special mission to promote Catholic-Orthodox church unity.

"In every effort of liturgical renewal, the practice of our Orthodox brothers will have to be taken into account," the instruction says. "Now is the time for Catholics and Orthodox to make an extra effort to understand each other better and to recognize with the renewed wonder of brotherhood what the Spirit is accomplishing in their respective traditions toward a new Christian springtime," said Pope John Paul Aug. 11, 1996, as he reflected on the development of Eastern theology and its relation to Western theology.

# STATISTICS OF THE CATHOLIC CHURCH IN CANADA

(Principal source: *1996-1997 Directory of the Canadian Conference of Catholic Bishops* (figures as of October, 1995); Catholic population statistics are those reported in the 1991 Canadian Census. Archdioceses are indicated by an asterisk. For dioceses marked +, see Canadian dioceses with interprovincial lines.)

Canada's 10 civil provinces and two territories are divided into 18 ecclesiastical provinces consisting of 18 metropolitan sees (archdioceses) and 51 suffragan sees (50 dioceses and one territorial abbacy); there are also one archdiocese and three eparchies immediately subject to the Holy See. (See listing of Ecclesiastical Provinces elsewhere in this section.)

This table presents a regional breakdown of Catholic statistics. In some cases, the totals are approximate because diocesan boundaries fall within several civil provinces.

| Civil Province Diocese | Cath. Pop. | Dioc. Priests | Rel. Priests | Total Priests | Perm. Deacs. | Bro- thers | Sis- ters | Lay Assts. | Par- ishes |
|---|---|---|---|---|---|---|---|---|---|
| **Newfoundland** | **213,055** | **100** | **50** | **150** | **1** | **20** | **364** | **22** | **162** |
| *St. John's | 119,260 | 47 | 19 | 66 | - | 12 | 276 | 6 | 44 |
| Grand Falls | 37,940 | 27 | 1 | 28 | - | - | 30 | 1 | 72 |
| Labrador- Schefferville+ | 13,550 | - | 8 | 8 | 1 | 4 | 29 | 14 | 25 |
| St. George's | 42,305 | 26 | 22 | 48 | - | 4 | 29 | 1 | 21 |
| **Prince Edward Island** | | | | | | | | | |
| Charlottetown | **60,625** | **62** | **2** | **64** | **1** | **-** | **180** | **2** | **59** |
| **Nova Scotia** | **331,010** | **246** | **83** | **329** | **27** | **12** | **869** | **18** | **220** |
| *Halifax | 152,515 | 66 | 62 | 128 | 26 | 1 | 349 | 13 | 53 |
| Antigonish | 138,990 | 157 | 9 | 166 | - | 8 | 483 | - | 127 |
| Yarmouth | 39,505 | 23 | 12 | 35 | 1 | 3 | 37 | 5 | 40 |
| **New Brunswick** | **386,480** | **254** | **62** | **316** | **2** | **35** | **885** | **27** | **254** |
| *Moncton | 105,775 | 67 | 30 | 97 | 1 | 23 | 329 | 3 | 63 |
| Bathurst | 115,560 | 65 | 9 | 74 | - | 8 | 257 | 16 | 65 |
| Edmundston | 52,435 | 45 | 11 | 56 | - | 2 | 153 | 8 | 34 |
| St. John | 112,710 | 77 | 12 | 89 | 1 | 2 | 146 | - | 92 |
| **Quebec** | **6,057,315** | **3,295** | **2,160** | **5,455** | **335** | **2,311** | **18,509** | **1,309** | **1,892** |
| *Gatineau-Hull | 216,725 | 64 | 48 | 112 | 1 | 12 | 264 | 91 | 60 |
| *Montreal | 1,656,297 | 657 | 903 | 1,560 | 92 | 675 | 6,369 | 47 | 282 |
| *Quebec | 902,545 | 591 | 391 | 982 | 73 | 462 | 4,172 | 105 | 272 |
| *Rimouski | 152,565 | 145 | 54 | 199 | 3 | 91 | 801 | 31 | 117 |
| *Sherbrooke | 235,145 | 249 | 121 | 370 | 20 | 108 | 1,228 | 21 | 139 |
| Amos | 103,890 | 60 | 23 | 83 | 1 | 11 | 164 | 21 | 67 |
| Baie Comeau | 93,715 | 51 | 19 | 70 | 9 | 14 | 116 | 28 | 49 |
| Chicoutimi | 275,580 | 218 | 60 | 278 | 34 | 64 | 748 | 98 | 97 |
| Gaspe | 94,645 | 74 | 19 | 93 | 2 | 6 | 189 | 11 | 66 |
| Joliette | 177,138 | 106 | 60 | 166 | 3 | 136 | 402 | 86 | 58 |
| Mont Laurier | 72,755 | 46 | 30 | 76 | - | 27 | 144 | 53 | 59 |
| Nicolet | 177,620 | 179 | 30 | 209 | 19 | 108 | 736 | 17 | 85 |
| Rouyn-Noranda | 56,475 | 28 | 16 | 44 | - | 2 | 111 | 28 | 41 |
| Ste- Anne-de-la- Pocatiere | 87,865 | 145 | 1 | 146 | 5 | 3 | 240 | 61 | 54 |
| St. Hyacinthe | 330,515 | 192 | 91 | 283 | 28 | 215 | 1,138 | 179 | 112 |
| St. Jean-Longueuil | 524,150 | 131 | 61 | 192 | 1 | 97 | 435 | 184 | 93 |
| St. Jerome | 353,310 | 104 | 112 | 216 | 12 | 114 | 266 | 173 | 69 |
| St. Maron Montreal (Maronites) | 80,000 | 7 | 5 | 12 | 2 | - | 3 | - | 10 |
| St. Sauveur Montreal (Greek-Melkites) | 38,000 | 2 | 9 | 11 | - | - | - | - | 9 |
| Trois Riviers | 243,085 | 151 | 74 | 225 | 22 | 112 | 788 | - | 91 |
| Valleyfield | 185,295 | 95 | 33 | 128 | 8 | 54 | 195 | 75 | 62 |
| **Ontario** | **3,575,065** | **1,354** | **1,128** | **2,482** | **339** | **203** | **3,947** | **172** | **1,241** |
| *Kingston | 102,650 | 68 | 7 | 75 | 7 | - | 201 | 9 | 72 |
| *Ottawa | 364,285 | 151 | 195 | 346 | 29 | 65 | 951 | - | 118 |
| *Toronto | 1,420,395 | 262 | 506 | 768 | 116 | 75 | 1,016 | - | 217 |

| Civil Province Diocese | Cath. Pop. | Dioc. Priests | Rel. Priests | Total Priests | Perm. Deacs. | Bro-thers | Sis-ters | Lay Assts. | Par-ishes |
|---|---|---|---|---|---|---|---|---|---|
| **Ontario** | | | | | | | | | |
| Alexandria-Cornwall | 56,020 | 41 | 1 | 42 | 13 | 4 | 77 | 8 | 34 |
| Hamilton | 480,695 | 143 | 115 | 258 | 2 | 25 | 370 | 46 | 122 |
| Hearst | 34,840 | 36 | 1 | 37 | - | 3 | 23 | 18 | 35 |
| London | 414,285 | 227 | 87 | 314 | 2 | 9 | 495 | 54 | 172 |
| Moosonee+ | 3,905 | - | 5 | 5 | 1 | 3 | 11 | - | 19 |
| Pembroke+ | 64,925 | 76 | 6 | 82 | 8 | 4 | 232 | - | 68 |
| Peterborough | 83,680 | 113 | 4 | 117 | 6 | - | 141 | 4 | 74 |
| St. Catharine's | 145,850 | 68 | 34 | 102 | 2 | 2 | 59 | 4 | 47 |
| Sts. Cyril and Methodius (Toronto-Slovaks) | 10,000 | 4 | 5 | 9 | - | - | - | - | 12 |
| Sault Ste. Marie | 218,850 | 107 | 36 | 143 | 110 | 4 | 241 | 11 | 96 |
| Thunder Bay | 78,480 | 30 | 26 | 56 | 20 | 2 | 48 | 2 | 43 |
| Timmins | 55,195 | 28 | 6 | 34 | 8 | 6 | 45 | 16 | 34 |
| Toronto (Ukrainians) | 41,010 | - | 94 | 94 | 15 | 1 | 37 | - | 78 |
| **Manitoba** | **346,180** | **170** | **151** | **321** | **28** | **65** | **713** | **75** | **455** |
| *Keewatin-LePas+ | 35,195 | 1 | 20 | 21 | - | 5 | 22 | 1 | 52 |
| *St. Boniface | 101,920 | 87 | 58 | 145 | 9 | 55 | 427 | 70 | 106 |
| *Winnipeg | 170,590 | 50 | 56 | 106 | - | 3 | 225 | - | 150 |
| *Winnipeg (Ukrainians) | 33,490 | 32 | 10 | 42 | 19 | 1 | 30 | 2 | 130 |
| Churchill-Hudson Bay+ | 4,985 | - | 7 | 7 | - | 1 | 9 | 2 | 17 |
| **Saskatchewan** | **301,335** | **149** | **117** | **266** | **9** | **24** | **599** | **18** | **494** |
| *Regina | 124,190 | 68 | 25 | 93 | - | 4 | 164 | - | 166 |
| Gravelbourg | 14,775 | 27 | 2 | 29 | - | - | 56 | 6 | 39 |
| Prince Albert | 57,580 | 33 | 16 | 49 | 2 | 2 | 114 | 6 | 87 |
| Saskatoon | 75,140 | - | 37 | 37 | - | 2 | 160 | 5 | 51 |
| Saskatoon (Ukrainians) | 20,080 | 21 | 15 | 36 | 7 | 2 | 28 | 1 | 131 |
| St, Peter Muenster (Abb.) | 9,570 | - | 22 | 22 | - | 14 | 77 | - | 20 |
| **Alberta** | **665,870** | **240** | **206** | **446** | **10** | **45** | **785** | **62** | **535** |
| *Edmonton | 294,935 | 81 | 108 | 189 | - | 25 | 509 | 34 | 166 |
| *Grouard-McLennan | 40,715 | 6 | 26 | 32 | - | 1 | 31 | 14 | 66 |
| Calgary | 250,605 | 94 | 55 | 149 | 2 | 14 | 137 | - | 130 |
| Edmonton (Ukrainians) | 26,250 | 28 | 14 | 42 | 8 | 4 | 36 | - | 93 |
| St. Paul | 53,365 | 31 | 3 | 34 | - | 1 | 72 | 14 | 80 |
| **British Columbia** | **600,175** | **194** | **145** | **339** | **7** | **41** | **352** | **49** | **332** |
| *Vancouver | 340,775 | 99 | 89 | 188 | - | 30 | 184 | 14 | 76 |
| Kamloops | 47,010 | 14 | 8 | 22 | 1 | 3 | 23 | - | 70 |
| Nelson | 63,570 | 27 | 19 | 46 | - | - | 35 | 10 | 53 |
| New Westminster (Ukrainians) | 7,555 | 15 | 2 | 17 | 3 | - | 2 | - | 17 |
| Prince George | 51,200 | 6 | 13 | 19 | 2 | 5 | 30 | 19 | 60 |
| Victoria | 90,065 | 33 | 14 | 47 | 1 | 3 | 78 | 6 | 56 |
| **Yukon Territory** Whitehorse+ | **8,235** | **2** | **12** | **14** | **-** | **1** | **10** | **13** | **24** |
| **Northwest Territories** MacKenzie-Ft. Smith+ | **19,745** | **1** | **9** | **10** | **2** | **2** | **20** | **1** | **38** |
| **Military Ordinariate** | **35,355** | **-** | **8** | **8** | **1** | **-** | **-** | **16** | **33** |
| **TOTALS** | **12,600,445[1]** | **6,067** | **4,125** | **10,192** | **761** | **2,755** | **27,233** | **1,784** | **5,706** |

[1]Catholics comprise about 44% of the total population.

**Honored during 1996:** U.S. Rep. Chris Smith of New Jersey, a leading Catholic pro-life voice in Congress for 16 years, with the Brent Award for distinguished service; Dominican Sister Rose Thering, at Seton Hall University, for her lifelong efforts to foster Jewish-Christian relations; Cardinal James A. Hickey of Washington, with the James Cardinal Gibbons Medal, for service to the Church, the nation and The Catholic University of America.

# CANADIAN CONFERENCE OF CATHOLIC BISHOPS

The Canadian Conference of Catholic Bishops was established Oct. 12, 1943, as a permanent voluntary association of the bishops of Canada, was given official approval by the Holy See in 1948, and acquired the status of an episcopal conference after the Second Vatican Council.

The CCCB acts in two ways: (1) as a strictly ecclesiastical body through which the bishops act together with pastoral authority and responsibility for the Church throughout the country; (2) as an operational secretariat through which the bishops act on a wider scale for the good of the Church and society.

At the top of the CCCB organizational table are the president, an executive committee, a permanent council and a plenary assembly. The membership consists of all the bishops of Canada.

## Departments and Offices

The CCCB's work is planned and co-ordinated by the Programmes and Priorities Committee composed of the six chairmen of the national episcopal commissions and the two general secretaries. It is chaired by the vice-president of the CCCB.

The CCCB's nine episcopal commissions undertake study and projects in special areas of pastoral work. Six serve nationally (social affairs, canon law/ inter-rite, ministries, missions, ecumenism, theology); three relate to French and English sectors (social communications, Christian education, liturgy).

The general secretariat consists of a French and an English general secretary and their assistants and directors of public relations.

Administrative services for purchasing, archives and library, accounting, personnel, publications, printing and distribution are supervised by directors who relate to the general secretaries.

Various advisory councils and committees with mixed memberships of lay persons, religious, priests and bishops also serve the CCCB on a variety of topics.

## Operations

Meetings for the transaction of business are held at least once a year by the plenary assembly, six times a year by the executive committee, and four times a year by the permanent council.

Archbishop Francis J. Spence of Kingston, Ont., is president of the CCCB and Cardinal Jean-Claude Turcotte of Montreal, Que., is vice president for the 1995-97 term.

Secretariat is located at 90 Parent Ave., Ottawa, K1N 7B1, Canada.

# BIOGRAPHIES OF CANADIAN BISHOPS

(Sources: *Information office of Canadian Conference of Catholic Bishops; Annuario Pontificio; L'Osservatore Romano.* Data as of July 20, 1996.)

**Abi-Saber, Georges, O.L.M.:** b May 12, 1923, Lebanon; ord. priest July 16, 1952; ord. bishop of Lattaquie of the Maronites, Nov. 12, 1977; titular bishop of Arado and auxiliary of patriarchate of Antioch of the Maronites, May 2, 1986; eparch of St. Maron of Montreal, Nov. 23, 1990; retired Feb. 7, 1996.

**Ambrozic, Aloysius M.:** b. Jan. 27, 1930; ord. priest June 4, 1955; ord. titular bishop of Valabria and auxiliary bishop of Toronto, May 27, 1976; coadjutor archbishop of Toronto, May 28, 1986; archbishop of Toronto, Mar. 17, 1990.

**Audet, Rene:** b. Jan. 18, 1920, Montreal, Que.; ord. priest May 30, 1948; ord. titular bishop of Chonochora and auxiliary bishop of Ottawa, July 31, 1963; bishop of Joliette, Jan. 3, 1968; retired Oct. 31, 1990.

**Berthelet, Jacques, C.S.V.:** b. Oct. 24, 1934, Montreal, Que.; ord. priest June 16, 1962; ord. titular bishop of Lamsorti and auxiliary of Saint-Jean-Longueuil, Mar. 21, 1987.

**Blais, Jean-Pierre:** b. May 21, 1949, Saint-Anselme, Que.; ord. priest May 11, 1974; ord. titular bishop of Tino and auxiliary of Quebec, Jan. 6, 1995.

**Blanchet, Bertrand:** b. Sept. 19, 1932, Saint Thomas de Montmagny, Que.; ord. priest May 20, 1956; ord. bishop of Gaspe, Dec. 8, 1973; archbishop of Rimouski, Oct. 16, 1992.

**Borecky, Isidore:** b. Oct. 1, 1911, Ostrovec, Ukraine; ord. priest July 17, 1938; ord. titular bishop of Amathus in Cypro and exarch of Toronto, May 27, 1948; eparch of Toronto (Ukrainians), Nov. 3, 1956.

**Burke, Austin-Emile:** b. Jan. 11, 1922, Sluice Point, N.S.; ord. priest Mar. 25, 1950; ord. bishop of Yarmouth, May 14, 1968; archbishop of Halifax, July 8, 1991.

**Bzdel, Michael, C.Ss.R.:** b. July 21, 1930, Wishart, Sask.; ord. priest July 7, 1954; ord. archeparch of Winnipeg of the Ukrainians, Mar. 9, 1993.

**Cadieux, Vincent, O.M.I.:** b. Feb. 16, 1940, Alfred, Ont.; ord. prièst Dec. 17, 1966; ord. bishop of Moosonee, Mar. 29, 1992.

**Campbell, Colin:** b. June 12, 1931, Antigonish, N.S.; ord. priest May 26, 1956; ord. bishop of Antigonish, Mar. 19, 1987.

**Carew, William A.:** b. Oct. 23, 1922, St. John's, Nfld., ord. priest June 15, 1947; ord. titular archbishop of Telde, Jan. 4, 1970; nuncio to Rwanda and Burundi, 1970-74; apostolic delegate to Jerusalem and Palestine and pro-nuncio to Cyprus, 1974-83; pro-nuncio to Japan, Aug. 30, 1983.

**Carter, Alexander:** b. Apr. 16, 1909, Montreal, Que.; ord. priest June 6, 1936; ord. titular bishop of Sita and coadjutor bishop of Sault Ste. Marie, Feb. 2, 1957; bishop of Sault Ste. Marie, Nov. 22, 1958; retired May 8, 198.

**Carter, G. Emmett:** (See Cardinals, Biographies.)

**Cazabon, Gilles, O.M.I.:** b. Apr. 5, 1933, Verner, Ont.; ord. priest June 11, 1960; ord. bishop of Timmins, June 29, 1992.

**Charbonneau, Paul-Emile:** b. May 4, 1922, Ste. Therese de Blainville, Que.; ord. priest May 31, 1947; ord. titular bishop of Thapsus and auxiliary bishop of Ottawa, Jan. 18, 1961; first bishop of Hull (now Gatineau-Hull), May 21, 1963; retired Apr. 12, 1973, because of ill health.

**Chiasson, Donat:** b. Jan. 2, 1930, Paquetville,

**N.B.**; ord. priest May 6, 1956; ord. archbishop of Moncton, June 1, 1972; retired Sept. 21, 1995.

**Cimichella, Andre, O.S.M.:** b. Feb. 21, 1921, Grotte Santo Stefano, Italy; ord. priest May 26, 1945; ord. titular bishop of Quiza and auxiliary of Montreal, July 16, 1964; retired Apr. 25, 1996.

**Clune, Robert B.:** b. Sept. 18, 1920, Toronto, Ont.; ord. priest May 26, 1945; ord. titular bishop of Lacubaza and auxiliary bishop of Toronto, June 21, 1979; retired Dec. 27, 1995.

**Colli, Frederick:** b. June 17, 1949, St. Catharines, Ont.; ord. priest June 21, 1975; ord. titular bishop of Afufenia and auxiliary of Ottawa, Feb. 22, 1995.

**Cooney, Eugene J.:** b. 1933, Calgary; ord. priest 1960; app. bishop of Nelson, Mar. 15, 1996.

**Couture, Jean-Guy:** b. May 6, 1929, St.-Jean-Baptiste de Quebec, Que.; ord. priest May 30, 1953; ord. bishop of Hauterive (now Baie-Comeau), Que., Aug. 15, 1975; bishop of Chicoutimi, Apr. 5, 1979.

**Couture, Maurice, R.S.V.:** b. Nov. 3, 1926, Saint-Pierre-de-Broughton, Que.; ord. priest June 17, 1951; ord. titular bishop of Talaptula and auxiliary bishop of Quebec, Oct. 22, 1982; bishop of Baie Comeau, Dec. 1, 1988; archbishop of Quebec and primate of Canada, Mar. 17, 1990.

**Couturier, Gerard:** b. Jan. 12, 1913, St. Louis du Ha Ha, Que; ord. priest Mar. 25, 1938; ord. bishop of Hauterive (now Baie-Comeau), Feb. 28, 1957; resigned Sept. 7, 1974.

**Croteau, Denis, O.M.I:** b. Oct. 23, 1932, Thetford Mines, Que., ord. priest Aug. 31, 1958; ord. bishop of MacKenzie-Fort Smith, June 8, 1986.

**Crowley, Leonard:** b. Dec. 28, 1921, Montreal, Que.; ord. priest May 31, 1947; ord. titular bishop of Mons and auxiliary bishop of Montreal, Mar. 24, 1971.

**Danylak, Roman:** b. Dec. 29, 1930, Toronto, Ont.; ord. priest Oct. 13, 1957; ord. titular bishop of Nissa and apostolic administrator of Toronto Eparchy (Ukrainians), Mar. 25, 1993.

**De Angelis, Nicola, C.F.I.C.:** b. Jan. 23, 1939, in Pozzaglia Sabino, Italy; ord. priest for the Conceptionists, Dec. 6, 1970; became Canadian citizen, 1975; ord. titular bishop of Remesiana and auxiliary bishop of Toronto, June 24, 1992.

**Delaquis, Noel:** b. Dec. 25, 1934, Notre-Dame-de-Lourdes, Man.; ord. priest June 5, 1958; ord. bishop of Gravelbourg, Feb. 19, 1974; resigned Apr. 10, 1995.

**De Roo, Remi J.:** b. Feb. 24, 1924, Swan Lake, Man.; ord. priest June 8, 1950; ord. bishop of Victoria, Dec. 14, 1962.

**Dionne, Gerard:** b. June 19, 1919, Saint-Basile, N.B.; ord. priest May 1, 1948; ord. titular bishop of Garba and auxiliary bishop of Sault Ste. Marie, Apr. 8, 1975; bishop of Edmundston, Nov. 17, 1983; retired Oct. 20, 1993.

**Doyle, James L.:** b. June 20, 1929, Chatham, Ont.; ord. priest June 12, 1954; ord. bishop of Peterborough June 28, 1976.

**Doyle, W. Emmett:** b. Feb. 18, 1913, Calgary, Alta.: ord. priest June 5, 1938; ord. bishop of Nelson, Dec. 3, 1958; retired Nov. 16, 1989.

**Drainville, Gerard:** b. May 20, 1930, L'Isle-du-Pas, Que.; ord. priest May 30, 1953; ord. bishop of Amos, June 12 1978.

**Dumais, Raymond:** b. June 4, 1950, Amqui, Que.; ord. priest June 26, 1976; ord. bishop of Gaspé, May 20, 1994.

**Dumouchel, Paul, O.M.I.:** b. Sept. 19, 1911, St. Boniface, Man.; ord. priest June 24, 1936; ord. titular bishop of Sufes and vicar apostolic of Keewatin, May 24, 1955; archbishop of Keewatin-Le Pas, July 13, 1967; retired 1986.

**Ebacher, Roger:** b. Oct. 6, 1936, Amos, Que.; ord. priest May 27, 1961; ord. bishop of Hauterive, July 31, 1979; title of see changed to Baie-Comeau, 1986; bishop of Gatineau-Hull, May 6, 1988; first archbishop, Oct 31, 1990, when Gatineau-Hull was made a metropolitan see.

**Exner, Adam, O.M.I.:** b. Dec. 24, 1928, Killaly, Sask.; ord. priest July 7, 1957; ord. bishop of Kamloops, B.C., Mar. 12, 1974; archbishop of Winnipeg, Mar. 31, 1982; archbishop of Vancouver, 1991.

**Fecteau, Clement:** b. Apr. 20, 1933, Sainte-Marie-de-Beauce, Que.; ord. priest June 16, 1957; ord. titular bishop of Talattula and auxiliary bishop of Quebec, Oct. 20, 1989; app bishop of Sainte-Anne-de-la-Pocatiere, May 10, 1996.

**Filevich, Basil (Wasyl):** b. Jan. 13, 1918; ord. priest Apr. 12, 1942; ord. eparch of Ukrainian eparchy of Saskatoon Feb. 27, 1984; retired Nov. 22, 1995.

**Fortier, Jean-Marie:** b. July 1, 1920, Quebec, Que.; ord. priest June 16, 1944; ord. titular bishop of Pomaria and auxiliary bishop of Ste.Anne-de-la-Pocatiere, Jan. 23, 1961; bishop of Gaspe, Jan. 19, 1965; archbishop of Sherbrooke, Apr. 20, 1968; retired 1996.

**Fougere, Joseph Vernon:** b. May 20, 1943, Petit Grat, N.S.; ord. priest May 31, 1969; ord. bishop of Charlottetown, Mar. 19, 1992.

**Fulton, Thomas B.:** b. Jan. 13, 1918, St. Catharines, Ont.; ord. priest June 7, 1941; ord. titular bishop of Cursola and auxiliary bishop of Toronto, Jan. 6, 1969; bishop of St. Catharines, July 7, 1978; retired Feb. 2, 1994.

**Gagnon, Edouard, P.S.S.:** (See Cardinals, Biographies.)

**Gaumond, Andre:** b. June 3, 1936, St. Thomas de Montmagny, Que.; ord. priest May 27, 1961; ord. bishop of Ste.Anne-de-la-Pocatiere, Aug. 15, 1985; app. coadjutor archbishop of Sherbrooke, Feb. 16, 1995; archbishop of Sherbrooke, 1996.

**Gervais, Marcel A.:** b. Sept. 21, 1931, Elie, Man.; ord. priest May 31, 1958; ord. titular bishop of Rosmarkaeum and auxiliary bishop of London, Ont., June 11, 1980; bishop of Sault Ste. Marie, May 8, 1985; coadjutor archbishop of Ottawa, June 21, 1989; archbishop of Ottawa, Sept. 27, 1989. President of Canadian Conference of Catholic Bishops, 1991-93.

**Gilbert, Arthur J.:** b. Oct. 26, 1915, Oromocto, N.B.; ord. priest June 3, 1943; ord. bishop of St. John, N.B., June 19, 1974; retired Apr. 2, 1986.

**Goudreault, Henri, O.M.I.:** b. Apr. 30, 1928, Belle-Vallee, Ont.; ord. priest June 17, 1956; ord. bishop of Labrador City-Schefferville, June 17, 1987; archbishop of Grouard-McLennan, July 16, 1996.

**Gratton, Jean:** b. Dec. 4, 1924, Wendover, Ont.; ord. priest Apr. 27, 1952; ord. bishop of Mont Laurier, June 29, 1978.

**Hacault, Antoine:** b. Jan. 17, 1926, Bruxelles, Man.; ord. priest May 20, 1951; ord. titular bishop of Media and coadjutor of St. Boniface, Sept. 8, 1964; archbishop of St. Boniface, Sept. 7, 1974.

**Hakim, Michel:** b. Apr. 21, 1921, Magdouche, South Lebanon; ord. priest Nov. 10, 1947; ord. archbishop of Saida of Greek Melkites, Sept. 10, 1977; app. titular archbishop of Caesarea in Cappadocia and apostolic exarch of Greek Melkite Catholics in Canada, Oct. 13, 1980; first eparch (with personal title of archbishop), Sept. 1, 1984, when exarchate was raised to eparchy with title St. Sauveur de Montreal.

**Hamelin, Jean-Guy:** b. Oct. 8, 1925, St. Severinde-Proulxville, Que.; ord. priest June 11, 1949; ord. first bishop of Rouyn-Noranda, Que., Feb. 9, 1974. President of Canadian Conference of Catholic Bishops, 1993-95.

**Hayes, James M.:** b. May 27, 1924, Halifax, N.S.; ord. priest June 15, 1947; ord. titular bishop of Reperi and apostolic administrator of Halifax, Apr. 20, 1965; archbishop of Halifax, June 22, 1967; retired Nov. 6, 1990. President of Canadian Conference of Catholic Bishops, 1987-89.

**Henry, Frederick:** b. Apr. 11, 1943, London, Ont.; ord. priest May 25, 1968; ord. titular bishop of Carinola and auxiliary bishop of London, Ont., June 24, 1986; app. bishop of Thunder Bay, Mar. 24, 1995.

**Knight, John Stephen:** b. Apr. 10, 1942, Binghamton, N. Y.; moved to Ontario as a child; ord. priest June 2, 1967; ord. titular bishop of Taraqua and auxiliary bishop of Toronto, June 24, 1992.

**Labrie, Jean-Paul:** b. Nov. 4, 1922, Laurieville, Que.; ord. priest May 20, 1951; ord. titular bishop of Urci and auxiliary bishop of Quebec, May 14, 1977; retired Apr. 19, 1995.

**Lacey, Michael Pearse:** b. Nov. 27, 1916, Toronto, Ont.; ord. priest May 23, 1943; ord. titular bishop of Diana and auxiliary bishop of Toronto, June 21, 1979; retired May 31, 1993.

**Lahey, Raymond:** b. May 29, 1940, St. John's Nfld.; ord. priest June 13, 1963; ord. bishop of St. George's, Nfld., Aug. 3, 1986.

**Landriault, Jacques:** b. Sept. 23, 1921, Alfred, Ont.; ord. priest Feb. 9, 1947; ord. titular bishop of Cadi and auxiliary bishop of Alexandria, July 25, 1962; bishop of Hearst, May 27, 1964; app. bishop of Timmins, Mar. 24, 1971; retired Dec. 13, 1990.

**Langevin, Louis-de-Gonzague, M. Afr.:** b. Oct. 31, 1921, Oka, Que.; ord. priest Feb. 2, 1950; ord. titular bishop of Rosemarkie and auxiliary of St. Hyacinthe Sept. 23, 1974; bishop of St. Hyacinthe, July 18, 1979.

**LaRocque, Eugene-Philippe:** b. Mar. 27, 1927, Windsor, Ont.; ord. priest June 7, 1952; ord. bishop of Alexandria, Ont., Sept. 3, 1974; title of see changed to Alexandria-Cornwall, 1976.

**Lebel, Robert:** b. Nov. 8, 1924, Trois-Pistoles, Que.; ord. priest June 18, 1950; ord. titular bishop of Alinda and auxiliary of St. Jean de Quebec, May 12, 1974; bishop of Valleyfield, Mar. 26, 1976. President of Canadian Conference of Catholic Bishops, 1989-91.

**Leclerc, Marc:** b. Jan. 9, 1933, Saint-Gregoire de Montmorency, Que.; ord. priest, May 31, 1958; ord. titular bishop of Eguga and auxiliary bishop of Quebec, Oct. 22, 1982.

**Légaré, Henri, O.M.I.:** b. Feb. 20, 1918, Willow Bunch, Sask.; ord. priest June 29, 1943; ord. first bishop of Labrador-Schefferville, Sept. 9, 1967; archbishop of Grouard-McLennan, Nov. 21, 1972 (retired July 16, 1996). President of Canadian Conference of Catholic Bishops, 1981-83.

**Levesque, Louis:** b. May 27, 1908, Amqui, Que.; ord. priest June 26, 1932; ord. bishop of Hearst, Aug. 15, 1952; titular archbishop of Egnatia and coadjutor of Rimouski, Apr. 13, 1964; archbishop of Rimouski, Feb. 25, 1967; retired May 14, 1973.

**Lobsinger, Thomas J., O.M.I.:** b. Nov. 17, 1927, Ayton, Ont.; ord. priest May 29, 1954; ord. bishop of Whitehorse, Y.T., Oct. 1, 1987.

**Lussier, Gilles:** b. June 5, 1940, Montreal, Que.; ord. priest Dec. 19, 1964; od. titular bishop of Augurus and auxiliary bishop of Saint Jerome, Feb. 28, 1989; bishop of Joliette, Sept. 7, 1991.

**MacDonald, James H., C.S.C.:** b. Apr. 28, 1925, Wycogama, N.S.; ord. priest June 29, 1953; ord. titular bishop of Gibba and auxiliary bishop of Hamilton April 17, 1978; app. bishop of Charlottetown, Aug. 12, 1982; archbishop of St. John's, Nfld., 1991.

**MacDonald, Joseph Faber:** b. Jan. 20, 1932, Little Pond, P.E.I.; ord. priest Mar. 9, 1963; ord. bishop of Grand Falls, Mar. 19, 1980.

**MacNeil, Joseph N.:** b. Apr. 15, 1924, Sydney, N.S.; ord. priest May 23, 1948; ord. bishop of St. John, N.B., June 24, 1969; archbishop of Edmonton, July 6, 1973. President Canadian Conference of Catholic Bishops, 1979-81.

**Mallon, Peter J.:** b. Dec. 5, 1929, Prince Rupert, B.C.; ord. priest May 27, 1956; ord. bishop of Nelson, Feb. 2, 1990; app. archbishop of Regina, June 9, 1995.

**Marchand, Paul, S.M.M.:** b. Apr. 17, 1937; solemnly professed, Montfort Missionaries, 1961; ord. priest Mar. 17, 1962; ord. titular bishop of Tamata and auxiliary of Ottawa, Aug. 20, 1993.

**Massé, Vital:** b. Dec. 16, 1936, Saint-Narthélémy, Que.; ord. priest May 26, 1962; ord. titular bishop of Giru di Marcello and auxiliary of Saint-Jérôme, Dec. 8, 1993.

**Mikloshazy, Attila, S.J.:** b. Apr. 5, 1931, Diósgyör, Hungary; ord. priest, June 18, 1961; ord. titular bishop of Castel Minore, Nov. 4, 1989. Bishop for Hungarian emigrants (resides in Canada).

**Morand, Blaise E.:** b. Sept. 12, 1932, Tecumseh, Ont.; ord. priest Mar. 22, 1958; ord. coadjutor bishop of Prince Albert, June 29, 1981; bishop of Prince Albert, Apr. 9, 1983.

**Morin, Laurent:** b. Feb. 14, 1908, Montreal, Que.; ord. priest May 27, 1934; ord. titular bishop of Arsamosata and auxiliary bishop of Montreal, Oct. 30, 1955; bishop of Prince Albert, Feb. 28, 1959; retired Apr. 9, 1983.

**Morissette, Pierre:** b. Nov. 22, 1944, Thetford-Mines, Que.; ord. priest June 8, 1968; ord. titular bishop of Mesarfelta and auxiliary of Quebec, June 12, 1987; app. bishop of Baie Comeau, Mar. 17, 1990.

**Noel, Laurent:** b. Mar. 19, 1920, Saint-Just-de-Bretenieres, Que.; ord. priest June 16, 1944; ord. titular bishop of Agathopolis and auxiliary bishop of Quebec, Aug. 29, 1963; bishop of Trois Rivieres, Nov. 5, 1975.

**Novecosky, Peter, O.S.B.:** b. Apr. 27, 1945,

Humboldt, Saskatchewan; ord. priest July 11, 1970; app. abbot-ordinary of St. Peter Muenster, July 23, 1990; abbatial blessing Nov. 26, 1990.

**O'Brien, Brendan M.:** b. Sept. 28, 1943, Ottawa, Ont.; ord. priest June 1, 1968; ord. titular bishop of Numana and auxiliary of Ottawa, June 29, 1987; app. bishop of Pembroke, Apr. 5, 1993.

**O'Byrne, Paul J.:** b. Dec. 12, 1922, Calgary, Alta.; ord. priest Feb. 21, 1948; ord. bishop of Calgary, Aug. 22, 1968.

**O'Connor, Hubert P., O.M.I.:** b. Feb. 17, 1928, Huntingdon, Que.; ord. priest June 5, 1955; ord. bishop of Whitehorse, Dec. 8, 1971; bishop of Prince George, June 9, 1986; retired 1991.

**O'Grady, John Fergus, O.M.I.:** b. July 27, 1908, Macton, Ont.; ord. priest June 29, 1934; ord. titular bishop of Aspendus and vicar apostolic of Prince Rupert, Mar. 7, 1956; first bishop of Prince George, July 13, 1967; retired June 9, 1986.

**O'Mara, John A.:** b. Nov. 17, 1924, Buffalo, N.Y.; ord. priest June 1, 1951; ord. bishop of Thunder Bay, June 29, 1976; bishop of St. Catharines, April 13, 1994.

**Ouellet, Gilles, P.M.E.:** b. Aug. 14, 1922, Bromptonville, Que.; ord. priest June 30, 1946; ord. bishop of Gaspe, Nov. 23, 1968; app. archbishop of Rimouski, Apr. 27, 1973; retired Oct. 16, 1992. President Canadian Conference of Catholic Bishops, 1977-79.

**Ouellette, Andre:** b. Feb. 4, 1913, Salem, Mass.; ord. priest June 11, 1938; ord. titular bishop of Carre and auxiliary bishop of Mont-Laurier, Feb. 25, 1957; bishop of Mont-Laurier, Mar. 27, 1965; retired Feb. 15, 1978.

**Pappin, Bernard F.:** b. July 10, 1928, Westmeath, Ont.; ord. priest May 27, 1954; ord. titular bishop of Aradi and auxiliary bishop of Sault Ste. Marie, Apr. 11, 1975.

**Pare, Marius:** b. May 22, 1903, Montmagny, Que.; ord. priest July 3, 1927; ord. titular bishop of Aegae and auxiliary bishop of Chicoutimi, May 1, 1956; bishop of Chicoutimi, Feb. 18, 1961; retired Apr. 5, 1979.

**Pasichny, Cornelius John, O.S.B.M.:** b. Mar. 27, 1927, Winnipeg, Man.; ord. priest July 5, 1953; ord. eparch of Saskatoon of the Ukrainians, Jan. 17, 1996.

**Pedneault, Roch:** b. Apr. 10, 1927, Saint Joseph d'Alma, Que.; ord. priest Feb. 8, 1953; ord. titular bishop of Aggersel and auxiliary of Chicoutimi, Que., June 29, 1974.

**Penney, Alphonsus L.:** b. Sept. 17, 1924, St. John's, Nfld.; ord. priest June 29, 1949; ord. bishop of Grand Falls, Jan. 18, 1973; archbishop of St. John's, Nfld., Apr. 5, 1979; retired 1991.

**Plouffe, Jean-Louis:** b. Oct. 29, 1940, Ottawa, Ont.; ord. priest June 12, 1965; ord. titular bishop of Lamzella and auxiliary of Sault Ste. Marie, Feb. 24, 1987; bishop of Sault Ste. Marie, Dec. 2, 1989.

**Plourde, Joseph-Aurele:** b. Jan. 12, 1915, St. Francois de Madawaska, N.B.; ord. priest May 7, 1944; ord. titular bishop of Lapda and auxiliary bishop of Alexandria, Aug. 26, 1964; archbishop of Ottawa, Jan. 2, 1967; retired Sept. 27, 1989.

**Power, William E.:** b. Sept. 27, 1915; Montreal, Que.; ord. priest June 7, 1941; ord. bishop of Antigonish, July 20, 1960 (retired Dec. 12, 1986);

president Canadian Conference of Catholic Bishops, 1971-73.

**Prendergast, Terrence, S.J.:** b. Feb. 19, 1944, in Montreal; ord. priest June 10, 1972; ord. titular bishop of Slebte and auxiliary of Toronto, Apr. 25, 1995.

**Richard, Andre, C.S.C.:** b. June 30, 1937, St. Ignace, N.B.; ord. priest Feb. 17, 1963; ord. bishop of Bathurst, Aug. 9, 1989.

**Rivest, Andre:** b. Apr. 28, 1942, Repentigny, Que., ord. priest May 14, 1966; ord. titular bishop of Tubursica and auxiliary bishop of Montreal, Aug. 15, 1995.

**Rouleau, Reynald, O.M.I.:** b. Nov. 30, 1935, Saint-Jean-de-Dieu, Que.; ord. priest Feb. 2, 1963; ord. bishop of Churchill-Hudson Bay, July 29, 1987.

**Roussin, Raymond, S.M.:** b. June 17, 1939, Saint-Vital, Manitoba; entered Society of Mary (Marianists), 1955; ord. priest Mar. 21, 1970; ord. bishop of Gravelbourg, Sask., June 14, 1995.

**Roy, Raymond:** b. May 3, 1919, St. Boniface, Man.; ord. priest May 31, 1947; ord. bishop of St. Paul in Alberta, July 18, 1972.

**Rusnak, Michael, C.Ss.R.:** b. Aug. 21, 1921, Beaverdale, Pa.; ord. priest July 4, 1949; ord. titular bishop of Tzernicus and auxiliary eparch of Toronto of the Ukrainians and apostolic visitator to Slovak Catholics of Byzantine rite in Canada, Jan. 2, 1965; first eparch of Sts Cyril and Methodius Eparchy for Slovaks of Byzantine Rite, Feb. 28, 1981.

**Sabatini, Lawrence, C.S.:** b. May 15, 1930, Chicago, Ill.; ord. priest Mar. 19, 1957; ord. titular bishop of Nasai and auxiliary bishop of Vancouver, Sept. 21, 1978; bishop of Kamloops, Sept. 30, 1982.

**Saint-Antoine, Jude:** b. Oct. 29, 1930, Montreal, Que.; ord. priest May 31, 1956; ord. titular bishop of Scardona and auxiliary bishop of Montreal, May 22, 1981. Episcopal vicar of west central region.

**Saint-Gelais, Raymond:** b. Mar. 23, 1936, Baie St. Paul, Que.; ord. priest June 12, 1960; ord. titular bishop of Diana and auxiliary bishop of St. Jerome, July 31, 1980; coadjutor bishop of Nicolet, Feb. 19, 1988; bishop of Nicolet, Mar. 14, 1989.

**Sanschagrin, Albert, O.M.I.:** b. Aug. 5, 1911, Saint-Tite, Que.; ord. priest May 24, 1936; ord. titular bishop of Bagi and coadjutor bishop of Amos Sept. 14, 1957; bishop of Saint-Hyacinthe, June 13, 1967; retired July 18, 1979.

**Setian, Nerses Mikaäl:** Retired Apostolic Exarch of Amenian Catholics in Canada and the U.S. (see Index).

**Sherlock, John M.:** b. Jan. 20, 1926, Regina, Sask.; ord. priest June 3, 1950; ord. titular bishop of Macriana and auxiliary of London, Ont., Aug. 28, 1974; bishop of London, July 7, 1978. President of the Canadian Conference of Catholic Bishops, 1983-85.

**Soroka, Stephen:** b. Nov. 13, 1951, Winnipeg, Man.; ord. priest June 13, 1982; app. titular bishop of Acarassus and auxiliary of the archdiocese of Winnipeg for Ukrainians, Apr. 17, 1996.

**Spence, Francis J.:** b. June 3, 1926, Perth, Ont.; ord. priest Apr. 16, 1950; ord. titular bishop of Nova and auxiliary bishop of the military vicariate, June 15, 1967; bishop of Charlottetown, Aug. 15, 1970; military vicar of Canada, 1982-87; archbishop of Kingston, Apr. 24, 1982.

**Sutton, Peter Alfred, O.M.I.:** b. Oct. 18, 1934, Chandler, Que.; ord. priest Oct. 22, 1960; ord. bishop of Labrador-Schefferville, July 18, 1974; coadjutor archbishop of Keewatin-Le Pas, Jan. 24, 1986; archbishop of Keewatin-LePas, Nov. 7, 1986.

**Tertzakian, Hovhannes, C.M.:** b Jan. 3, 1924, Aleppo, Syria; entered Mekhitarist Order of Vienna, 1938, final vows Oct.24, 1945; ord. priest Sept. 8, 1948; ord. titular bishop of Trebizond for Armenians and apostolic exarch for Armenian Catholics in the United States and Canada, Apr. 29, 1995.

**Thibodeau, François, C.J.M.:** b. July 27, 1939, Saint-Odilon, Que.; ord. priest May 8, 1965; ord. bishop of Edmundston Jan. 9, 1994.

**Tonnos, Anthony:** b. Aug. 1, 1935, Port Colborne, Ont.; ord. priest May 27, 1961; ord. titular bishop of Naziona and auxiliary bishop of Hamilton, July 12, 1983; bishop of Hamilton, May 2, 1984.

**Tremblay, Eugène:** b. Feb. 20, 1936, Saint-Hilarion, Que.; ord. priest June 24, 1962; ord. titular bishop of Succuba and auxiliary of Quebec, Jan. 6, 1995.

**Tremblay, Gerard, P.S.S.:** b. Oct. 27, 1918, Montreal, Que.; ord. priest June 16, 1946; ord. titular bishop of Trisipa and auxiliary bishop of Montreal, May 22, 1981; retired 1991.

**Troy, J. Edward:** b. Sept. 3, 1931, Chatham, N.B.; ord. priest May 28, 1959; ord. coadjutor bishop of St. John, N.B., May 22, 1984; bishop of St. John, N.B., Apr. 2, 1986.

**Turcotte, Jean-Claude:** (See Cardinals, Biographies.)

**Ustrzycki, Matthew:** b. Mar. 25, 1932, Saint Catharines, Ont.; ord. priest May 30, 1959; ord. titular bishop of Nationa and auxiliary of Hamilton, July 3, 1985.

**Vachon, Louis-Albert:** (See Cardinals, Biographies.)

**Vallée, Andre, P.M.E.:** b. July 31, 1930, Sainte-Anne-de-Perade, Que.; ord. priest June 24, 1956; ord. titular bishop of Sufasar and bishop of the Military Ordinariate of Canada, Jan. 28, 1988; bishop of Hearst, 1996.

**Valois, Charles:** b. Apr. 24, 1924, Montreal, Que.; ord. priest June 3, 1950; ord. bishop of St. Jerome, June 29, 1977.

**Veillette, Martin:** b. Nov. 16, 1936, Saint- Zephirin de Courval, Que., ord. priest June 12, 1960; ord. titular bishop of Valabria and auxiliary of Trois-Rivieres, Dec. 13, 1986.

**Wall, Leonard J.:** b. Sept. 27, 1924, Windsor, Ont.; ord. priest June 11, 1949; ord. titular bishop of Leptiminus and auxiliary bishop of Toronto, June 21, 1979; archbishop of Winnipeg, Feb. 25, 1992.

**Weber, Jerome, O.S.B.:** b. Sept. 14, 1915, Muenster, Sask., Canada; ord. priest June 8, 1941; app. abbot-ordinary of St. Peter Muenster, Apr. 6, 1960; abbatial blessing, Aug. 24, 1960; retired June, 1990.

**Weisgerber, V. James:** b. May 1, 1938, Vibank, Sask.; ord. priest June 1, 1963; ord. bishop of Saskatoon, May 3, 1996.

**Wiesner, Gerald, O.M.I.:** b. June 25, 1937, Danzil, Sask.; ord. priest Feb. 23, 1963; ord. bishop of Prince George, B.C., Feb. 22, 1993.

**Willard, Neil E.:** b. May 9, 1937, Montreal; ord. Priest May 27, 1961; ord. titular bishop of Tisedi and auxiliary bishop of Montreal Aug. 15, 1995.

**Windle, Joseph R.:** b. Aug. 28, 1917, Ashdad, Ont.; ord. priest May 16, 1943; ord. titular bishop of Uzita and auxiliary bishop of Ottawa, Jan. 18, 1961; coadjutor bishop of Pembroke, 1969; bishop of Pembroke, Feb. 15, 1971; retired Apr. 5, 1993.

**Wingle, James Matthew:** b. Sept. 23, 1946; ord. priest Apr. 16, 1977 (Pembroke diocese); ord. bishop of Yarmouth, Aug. 24, 1993.

**Yakymyshyn, Severian Stephen, O.S.B.M.:** b. Apr. 22, 1930, Plain Lake, Alberta; ord. priest May 19, 1955; ord. bishop of Ukrainian Eparchy of New Westminster, Mar. 25, 1995.

# CANADIAN SHRINES

**Our Lady of the Cape (Cap de la Madeleine), Queen of the Most Holy Rosary:** The Three Rivers, Quebec, parish church, built of fieldstone in 1714 and considered the oldest stone church on the North American continent preserved in its original state, was rededicated June 22, 1888, as a shrine of the Queen of the Most Holy Rosary. Thereafter, the site increased in importance as a pilgrimage and devotional center, and in 1904 St. Pius X decreed the crowning of a statue of the Blessed Virgin which had been donated 50 years earlier to commemorate the dogma of the Immaculate Conception. In 1909, the First Plenary Council of Quebec declared the church a shrine of national pilgrimage. In 1964, the church at the shrine was given the status and title of minor basilica.

**St. Anne de Beaupre:** The devotional history of this shrine in Quebec, began with the reported cure of a cripple, Louis Guimont, on Mar. 16, 1658, the starting date of construction work on a small chapel of St. Anne. The original building was successively enlarged and replaced by a stone church which was given the rank of minor basilica in 1888. The present structure, a Romanesque-Gothic basilica, houses the shrine proper in its north transept. The centers of attraction are an eight-foot-high oaken statue and the great relic of St. Anne, a portion of her forearm.

**St. Joseph's Oratory:** The massive oratory basilica standing on the western side of Mount Royal and overlooking the city of Montreal had its origin in a primitive chapel erected there by Blessed Andre Bessette, C.S.C., in 1904. Eleven years later, a large crypt was built to accommodate an increasing number of pilgrims, and in 1924 construction work was begun on the large church. A belfry, housing a 60-bell carillon and standing on the site of the original chapel, was dedicated May 15, 1955, as the first major event of the jubilee year observed after the oratory was given the rank of minor basilica.

**Martyrs' Shrine:** A shrine commemorating several of the Jesuit Martyrs of North America who were killed between 1642 and 1649 in the Ontario and northern New York area is located on the former site of old Fort Sainte Marie. Before its location was fixed near Midland, Ont., in 1925, a small chapel had been erected in 1907 at old Mission St. Ignace to mark the martyrdom of Fathers Jean de Brebeuf and Gabriel Lalemant. This sanctuary has a U.S. counterpart in the Shrine of the North American Martyrs near Auriesville, N.Y., under the care of the Jesuits.

## Others

Other shrines and historic churches in Canada include the following.

In Quebec City: the Basilica of Notre Dame, dating from 150, once the cathedral of a diocese stretching from Canada to Mexico; Notre Dame des Victoires, on the waterfront, dedicated in 1690; the Ursuline Convent, built in 1720, on du Parloir St.

In Montreal: Notre Dame Basilica, patterned after the famous basilica of the same name in Paris, constructed in 1829; the Shrine of Mary, Queen of All Hearts.

Near Montreal: the Chapel of St. Marie Marguerite d'Youville, foundress of the Grey Nuns; Notre Dame de Lourdes, at Rigaud.

# CANADIAN CATHOLIC PUBLICATIONS

(Principal source: 1996 *Catholic Press Directory.*)

## Newspapers

**B. C. Catholic, The,** w; 150 Robson St., Vancouver, B.C. V6B 2A7.

**Catholic New Times** (national), biweekly; 80 Sackville St., Toronto, Ont. M5A 3E5.

**Catholic Register, The** (national), w; 67 Bond St., Ste. 303, Toronto, Ont. M5B 1X6. Lay edited.

**Catholic Times, The,** 10 times a year; 2005 St. Marc St., Montreal, Que. H3H 2G8.

**Diocesan Review, The,** m; 16 Hammond Dr., Corner Brook, Nfld. A2H 2W2.

**L'Informateur Catholique,** semimonthly; 6550 Rte 125, Chertsey, Que. JOK 3KO.

**Monitor, The,** m; P.O. Box 986, St. John's, Nfld. A1C 5M3.

**New Freeman, The,** w; 1 Bayard Dr., St. John, N.B. E2L 3L5.

**Our Diocese,** bm; P.O. Box 397, Grand Falls-Windsor, Nfld. A2A 2J8.

**Pastoral Reporter, The,** 4 times a year; 290 The Iona Building, 120 17th Ave. SW, Calgary. Alta. T2S 2T2.

**Prairie Messenger,** w; Box 190, Muenster, Sask. SOK 2Y0.

**Teviskes, Ziburiai (The Lights of the Homeland)** (Lithuanian), w; 2185 Stavebank Rd., Mississauga, Ont. L5C 1T3.

**Western Catholic Reporter,** w; 8421 101 Avenue, Edmonton, Alberta T6A OL1. Edmonton archdiocese.

## Magazines, Other Periodicals

**Annals of St. Anne de Beaupre,** m; Box 1000, Ste. Anne de Beaupre, Que. GOA 3CO; Basilica of St. Anne.

**Apostolat** (French),bm; 8844 Notre-Dame Est, Montreal, Que. H1L 3M4. Oblates of Mary Immaculate.

**Bread of Life, The,** 6 times a year; 370 Main St. E, Suite B1, Hamilton, Ont. L8N 1J6.

**Bulletin** (French-English), q; 324 E. Laurier St., Ottawa, Ont. K1N 6P6 Canadian Religious Conference.

**Canadian Catholic Review,** 11 times a year; 1437 College Dr., Saskatoon, Saskatchewan S7N 0W6.

**Canadian League, The,** 4 times a year; 1-160 Murray Park Rd., Winnipeg, Man. R3J 3X5. Catholic Women's League of Canada.

**Caravan,** 4 times a year; 90 Parent Ave., Ottawa, Ont. K1N 7B1. Canadian Conference of Catholic Bishops.

**Casket, The,** w; 88 College St., Antigonish, N.S. B2G 2L7.

**Catholic Communicator,** m; 222 Albert St. East, Sault Ste. Marie, Ont. P6A 2J4

**Celebrate (Novalis),** 6 times a year; St. Paul University, 223 Main St., Ottawa, Ont. K1S 1C4.

**Chesterton Review,** q; 1437 College Dr., Saskatoon, Sask. S7N 0W6.

**Companion Magazine,** m; P. O. Box 535, Sta. F., Toronto, Ont. M4Y 2L8; Conventual Franciscan Fathers.

**Compass — A Jesuit Journal,** bm (Jan.-Nov.); Box 400, Stn F, 50 Charles St. N, Toronto, Ont. M4Y 2L8.

**Fatima Crusader,** 4 times a year; P.O. Box 602, Fort Erie, Ont. L2A 4M7.

**Global Village Voice,** q; 3028 Danforth Ave., Toronto, Ont. M4C 4PC. Canadian Organization for Development and Peace.

**Grail: An Ecumenical Journal,** q; St. Paul's University, Ottawa, Ont. K1S 1C4.

**Kateri** (English-French), q; P.O. Box 70, Kahnawake, Que. JOL 1BO.

**L'Almanach Populaire Catholique** (French), a; P.O. Box 1000, St. Anne de Beaupre, Que. GOA 3CO.

**La Revue d'Sainte Anne de Beaupre** (French), m; P.O. Box 1000, Ste. Anne de Beaupre, Quebec GOA 3CO.

**L'Eglise Canadienne** (French), 11 times a year; 6255 rue Hutchison, Bureau 103, Montreal, Que. H2V 4C7.

**Martyrs' Shrine Message,** 2 times a year; Midland, Ont. L4R 4K5. Newsletter.

**Messager de Saint Antoine, Le** (French), 10 times a year; Lac-Bouchette, Que. GOW 1VO.

**Messenger of the Sacred Heart,** m; 661 Greenwood Ave., Toronto, Ont. M4J 4B3. Apostleship of Prayer.

**Mission Canada,** 4 times a year; 67 Bond St., Ste 101, Toronto, Ont. M5B 1X5.

**Missions Etrangeres** (French),6 times a year; 180 Place Juge-Desnoyers, Laval, Que. H7G 1A4.

**Oratory,** 6 times a year; 3800 Ch. Reine-Marie, Montreal, Que. H3V 1H6.

**Our Family,** m; P.O. Box 249, Battleford, Sask.; S0M 0E0; Oblates of Mary Immaculate.

**Prete et Pasteur** (French), m; 4450 St. Hubert St., Montreal, Que. H2J 2W9.

**Relations** (French), 10 times a year; 25 Rue Jarry Ouest, Montreal, Que. H2P 1S6.

**Restoration,** 10 times a year; Madonna House, Combemere, Ont. KOJ 1LO.

Scarboro Missions, 9 times a year; 2685 Kingston Rd., Scarboro, Ont. M1M 1M4.

Spiritan Missionary News, 4 times a year; 131

Victoria Park Ave., Toronto, Ont. M4E 3S2.

Unity, q; 308 Young St., Montreal, Que. H3C 2G2.

# MISSIONARIES TO THE AMERICAS

An asterisk with a feast date indicates that the saint or blessed is listed in the General Roman Calendar or the proper calendar for U.S. dioceses.

**Allouez, Claude Jean** (1622-1689): French Jesuit; missionary in Canada and midwestern U.S.; preached to 20 different tribes of Indians and baptized over 10,000; vicar general of Northwest.

**Altham, John** (1589-1640): English Jesuit; missionary among Indians in Maryland.

**Anchieta, Jose de, Bl.** (1534-1597): Portuguese Jesuit, b. Canary Islands; missionary in Brazil; writer; beatified 1980; feast, June 9.

**Andreis, Felix de** (1778-1820): Italian Vincentian; missionary and educator in western U.S.

**Aparicio, Sebastian, Bl.** (1502-1600): Franciscan brother, born Spain; settled in Mexico, c. 1533; worked as road builder and farmer before becoming Franciscan at about the age of 70; beatified, 1787; feast, Feb. 25.

**Badin, Stephen T.** (1768-1853): French missioner; came to U.S., 1792, when Sulpician seminary in Paris was closed; ordained, 1793, Baltimore, the first priest ordained in U.S.; missionary in Kentucky, Ohio and Michigan; bought land on which Notre Dame University now stands; buried on the campus.

**Baraga, Frederic** (1797-1868): Slovenian missionary bishop in U.S.; studied at Ljubljana and Vienna, ordained, 1823; came to U.S., 1830; missionary to Indians of Upper Michigan; first bishop of Marquette, 1857-1868; wrote Chippewa grammar, dictionary, prayer book and other works.

**Bertran, Louis, St.** (1526-1581): Spanish Dominican; missionary in Colombia and Caribbean, 1562-69; canonized, 1671; feast, Oct. 9.

**Betancur, Pedro de San Jose, Bl.** (1626-1667): Secular Franciscan, b. Canary Islands; arrived in Guatemala, 1651; established hospital, school and homes for poor; beatified 1980; feast, Apr. 25.

**Bourgeoys, Marguerite, St.** (1620-1700): French foundress, missionary; settled in Canada, 1653; founded Congregation of Notre Dame, 1658; beatified, 1950; canonized 1982; feast, Jan. 12.

**Brebeuf, John de, St.** (1593-1649): French Jesuit; missionary among Huron Indians in Canada; martyred by Iroquois, Mar. 16, 1649; canonized, 1930; one of Jesuit North American martyrs; feast, Oct. 19* (U.S.).

**Cancer de Barbastro, Louis** (1500-1549): Spanish Dominican; began missionary work in Middle America, 1533; killed at Tampa Bay, Fla.

**Castillo, John de, St.** (1596-1628): Spanish Jesuit; worked in Paraguay Indian mission settlements (reductions); martyred; beatified, 1934; canonized, 1988; feast, Nov. 16.

**Catala, Magin** (1761-1830): Spanish Franciscan; worked in California mission of Santa Clara for 36 years.

**Chabanel, Noel, St.** (1613-1649): French Jesuit; missionary among Huron Indians in Canada; murdered by renegade Huron, Dec. 8, 1649; canonized, 1930; one of Jesuit North American martyrs; feast, Oct. 19* (U.S.).

**Chaumonot, Pierre Joseph** (1611-1693): French Jesuit; missionary among Indians in Canada.

**Claver, Peter, St.** (1581-1654): Spanish Jesuit; missionary among Negroes of South America and West Indies; canonized, 1888; patron of Catholic missions among black people; feast, Sept. 9*.

**Daniel, Anthony, St.** (1601-1648): French Jesuit; missionary among Huron Indians in Canada; martyred by Iroquois, July 4, 1648; canonized, 1930; one of Jesuit North American martyrs; feast, Oct. 19* (U.S.).

**De Smet, Pierre Jean** (1801-1873): Belgian-born Jesuit; missionary among Indians of northwestern U.S.; served as intermediary between Indians and U.S. government; wrote on Indian culture.

**Duchesne, Rose Philippine, St.** (1769-1852): French nun; educator and missionary in the U.S.; established first convent of the Society of the Sacred Heart in the U.S., at St. Charles, Mo.; founded schools for girls; did missionary work among Indians; beatified, 1940; canonized, 1988; feast, Nov. 18* (U.S.).

**Farmer, Ferdinand** (family name, Steinmeyer) (1720-1786): German Jesuit; missionary in Philadelphia, where he died; one of the first missionaries in New Jersey.

**Flaget, Benedict J.** (1763-1850): French Sulpician bishop; came to U.S., 1792; missionary and educator in U.S.; first bishop of Bardstown, Ky. (now Louisville), 1810-32; 1833-50.

**Gallitzin, Demetrius** (1770-1840): Russian prince; born The Hague; convert, 1787; ordained priest at Baltimore, 1795; frontier missionary, known as Father Smith; Gallitzin, Pa., named for him.

**Garnier, Charles, St.** (c. 1606-1649): French Jesuit; missionary among Hurons in Canada; martyred by Iroquois, Dec. 7, 1649; canonized, 1930; one of Jesuit North American martyrs; feast, Oct. 19* (U.S.).

**Gibault, Pierre** (1737-1804): Canadian missionary in Illinois and Indiana; aided in securing states of Ohio, Indiana, Illinois, Michigan and Wisconsin for the Americans during Revolution.

**Gonzalez, Roch, St.** (1576-1628): Paraguayan Jesuit; worked in Paraguay Indian mission settlements (reductions); martyred; beatified, 1934; canonized, 1988; feast, Nov. 16.

**Goupil, Rene, St.** (1607-1642): French lay missionary; had studied surgery at Orleans, France; missionary companion of St. Isaac Jogues among the Hurons; martyred, Sept. 29, 1642; canonized, 1930; one of Jesuit North American martyrs; feast, Oct. 19* (U.S.).

**Gravier, Jacques** (1651-1708): French Jesuit; missionary among Indians of Canada and midwestern U.S.

**Hennepin, Louis** (d. c. 1701): Belgian-born Franciscan missionary and explorer of Great Lakes region and Upper Mississippi, 1675-81, when he returned to Europe.

**Jesuit North American Martyrs:** Isaac Jogues, Anthony Daniel, John de Brebeuf, Gabriel Lalemant, Charles Garnier, Noel Chabanel (Jesuit priests), and Rene Goupil and John Lalande (lay missionaries) who were martyred between Sept. 29, 1642, and Dec. 9, 1649, in the missions of New France; canonized June 29, 1930; feast, Oct. 19* (U.S.). See separate entries.

**Jogues, Isaac, St.** (1607-1646): French Jesuit; missionary among Indians in Canada; martyred near present site of Auriesville, N.Y., by Mohawks, Oct. 18, 1646; canonized, 1930; one of Jesuit North American martyrs; feast, Oct. 19* (U.S.).

**Kino, Eusebio** (1645-1711): Italian Jesuit; missionary and explorer in U.S.; arrived Southwest, 1681; established 25 Indian missions, took part in 14 exploring expeditions in northern Mexico, Arizona and southern California; helped develop livestock raising and farming in the area. He was selected in 1965 to represent Arizona in Statuary Hall.

**Lalande, John, St.** (d. 1646): French lay missionary, companion of Isaac Jogues; martyred by Mohawks at Auriesville, N.Y., Oct. 19, 1646; canonized, 1930; one of Jesuit North American martyrs; feast, Oct. 19* (U.S.).

**Lalemant, Gabriel, St.** (1610-1649): French Jesuit; missionary among the Hurons in Canada; martyred by the Iroquois, Mar. 17, 1649; canonized, 1930; one of Jesuit North American martyrs; feast, Oct. 19* (U.S.).

**Lamy, Jean Baptiste** (1814-1888): French prelate; came to U.S., 1839; missionary in Ohio and Kentucky; bishop in Southwest from 1850; first bishop (later archbishop) of Santa Fe, 1850-1885. He was nominated in 1951 to represent New Mexico in Statuary Hall.

**Las Casas, Bartolome** (1474-1566): Spanish Dominican; missionary in Haiti, Jamaica and Venezuela; reformer of abuses against Indians and black people; bishop of Chalapas, Mexico, 1544-47; historian.

**Laval, Francoise de Montmorency, Bl.** (1623-1708): French-born missionary bishop in Canada; named vicar apostolic of Canada, 1658; first bishop of Quebec, 1674; jurisdiction extended over all French-claimed territory in New World; beatified 1980; feast, May 6.

**Manogue, Patrick** (1831-1895): Missionary bishop in U.S., b. Ireland; migrated to U.S.; miner in California; studied for priesthood at St. Mary's of the Lake, Chicago, and St. Sulpice, Paris; ordained, 1861; missionary among Indians of California and Nevada; coadjutor bishop, 1881-84, and bishop, 1884-86, of Grass Valley; first bishop of Sacramento, 1886-1895, when see was transferred there.

**Margil, Antonio** (1657-1726): Spanish Franciscan; missionary in Middle America; apostle of Guatemala; established missions in Texas.

**Marie of the Incarnation, Bl.** (Marie Guyard Martin) (1599-1672): French widow; joined Ursuline Nuns; arrived in Canada, 1639; first superior of Ursulines in Quebec; missionary to Indians; writer; beatified 1980; feast, Apr. 30.

**Marquette, Jacques** (1637-1675): French Jesuit; missionary and explorer in America; sent to New France, 1666; began missionary work among Ottawa Indians on Lake Superior, 1668; accompanied Joliet down the Mississippi to mouth of the Arkansas, 1673, and returned to Lake Michigan by way of Illinois River; made a second trip over the same route; his diary and map are of historical significance. He was selected in 1895 to represent Wisconsin in Statuary Hall.

**Massias (Macias), John de, St.** (1585-1645): Dominican brother, a native of Spain; entered Dominican Friary at Lima, Peru, 1622; served as doorkeeper until his death; beatified, 1837; canonized 1975; feast, Sept. 16.

**Mazzuchelli, Samuel C.** (1806-1864): Italian Dominican; missionary in midwestern U.S.; called builder of the West; writer. A decree advancing his beatification cause was promulgated July 6, 1993.

**Membre, Zenobius** (1645-1687): French Franciscan; missionary among Indians of Illinois; accompanied LaSalle expedition down the Mississippi (1681-1682) and Louisiana colonizing expedition (1684) which landed in Texas; murdered by Indians.

**Nerinckx, Charles** (1761-1824): Belgian priest; missionary in Kentucky; founded Sisters of Loretto at the Foot of the Cross.

**Nobrega, Manoel** (1517-1570): Portuguese Jesuit; leader of first Jesuit missionaries to Brazil, 1549.

**Padilla, Juan de** (d. 1542): Spanish Franciscan; missionary among Indians of Mexico and southwestern U.S.; killed by Indians in Kansas; protomartyr of the U.S.

**Palou, Francisco** (c. 1722-1789): Spanish Franciscan; accompanied Junipero Serra to Mexico, 1749; founded Mission Dolores in San Francisco; wrote history of the Franciscans in California.

**Pariseau, Mother Mary Joseph** (1833-1902): Canadian Sister of Charity of Providence; missionary in state of Washington from 1856; founded first hospitals in northwest territory; artisan and architect. Represents Washington in National Statuary Hall.

**Peter of Ghent** (d. 1572): Belgian Franciscan brother; missionary in Mexico for 49 years.

**Porres, Martin de, St.** (1579-1639): Peruvian Dominican oblate; his father was a Spanish soldier and his mother a black freedwoman from Panama; called wonder worker of Peru; beatified, 1837; canonized, 1962; feast, Nov. 3*.

**Quiroga, Vasco de** (1470-1565): Spanish missionary in Mexico; founded hospitals; bishop of Michoacan, 1537.

**Ravalli, Antonio** (1811-1884): Italian Jesuit; missionary in far-western United States, mostly Montana, for 40 years.

**Raymbaut, Charles** (1602-1643): French Jesuit; missionary among Indians of Canada and northern U.S.

**Richard, Gabriel** (1767-1832): French Sulpician; missionary in Illinois and Michigan; a founder of University of Michigan; elected delegate to Congress from Michigan, 1823; first priest to hold seat in the House of Representatives.

**Rodriguez, Alfonso, St.** (1598-1628): Spanish Jesuit; missionary in Paraguay; martyred; beatified, 1934; canonized, 1988; feast, Nov. 16.

**Rosati, Joseph** (1789-1843): Italian Vincentian; missionary bishop in U.S. (vicar apostolic of Mississippi and Alabama, 1822; coadjutor of Louisiana and the Two Floridas, 1823-26; administrator of New Orleans, 1826-29; first bishop of St. Louis, 1826-1843).

**Sahagun, Bernardino de** (c. 1500-1590): Spanish Franciscan; missionary in Mexico for over 60 years; expert on Aztec archaeology.

**Seelos, Francis X.** (1819-1867): Redemptorist missionary, born Bavaria; ordained, 1844, at Baltimore; missionary in Pittsburgh and New Orleans.

**Seghers, Charles J.** (1839-1886): Belgian missionary bishop in North America; Apostle of Alaska; archbishop of Oregon City (now Portland), 1880-1884; murdered by berserk companion while on missionary journey.

**Serra, Junipero, Bl.** (1713-1784): Spanish Franciscan, b. Majorca; missionary in America; arrived Mexico, 1749, where he did missionary work for 20 years; began work in Upper California in 1769 and established nine of the 21 Franciscan missions along the Pacific coast; baptized some 6,000 Indians and confirmed almost 5,000; a cultural pioneer of California. Represents California in Statuary Hall. He was declared venerable May 9, 1985, and was beatified Sept. 25, 1988; feast, July 1* (U.S.).

**Solanus, Francis, St.** (1549-1610): Spanish Franciscan; missionary in Paraguay, Argentina and Peru; wonder worker of the New World; canonized, 1726; feast, July 14.

**Sorin, Edward F.** (1814-1893): French priest; member of Congregation of Holy Cross; sent to U.S. in 1841; founder and first president of the University of Notre Dame; missionary in Indiana and Michigan.

**Todadilla, Anthony de** (1704-1746): Spanish Capuchin; missionary to Indians of Venezuela; killed by Motilones.

**Turibius de Mogrovejo, St.** (1538-1606): Spanish archbishop of Lima, Peru, c. 1580-1606; canonized 1726; feast, Mar. 23*.

**Twelve Apostles of Mexico** (early 16th century): Franciscan priests; arrived in Mexico, 1524: Fathers Martin de Valencia (leader), Francisco de Soto, Martin de la Coruna, Juan Suares, Antonio de Ciudad Rodrigo, Toribio de Benevente, Garcia de Cisneros, Luis de Fuensalida, Juan de Ribas, Francisco Ximenes; Brothers Andres de Coroboda, Juan de Palos.

**Valdivia, Luis de** (1561-1641): Spanish Jesuit; defender of Indians in Peru and Chile.

**Vasques de Espinosa, Antonio** (early 17th century): Spanish Carmelite; missionary and explorer in Mexico, Panama and western coast of South America.

**Vieira, Antonio** (1608-1687): Portuguese Jesuit; preacher; missionary in Peru and Chile; protector of Indians against exploitation by slave owners and traders; considered foremost prose writer of 17th-century Portugal.

**White, Andrew** (1579-1656): English Jesuit; missionary among Indians in Maryland.

**Wimmer, Boniface** (1809-1887): German Benedictine; missionary among German immigrants in the U.S.

**Youville, Marie Marguerite d', St.** (1701-1771): Canadian widow; foundress of Sisters of Charity (Grey Nuns), 1737, at Montreal: beatified, 1959; canonized 1990, first native Canadian saint; feast, Dec. 23.

**Zumarraga, Juan de** (1468-1548): Spanish Franciscan; missionary; first bishop of Mexico; introduced first printing press in New World, published first book in America, a catechism for Aztec Indians; extended missions in Mexico and Central America; vigorous opponent of exploitation of Indians; approved of devotions at Guadalupe; leading figure in early church history in Mexico.

## FRANCISCAN MISSIONS

The 21 Franciscan missions of Upper California were established during the 54-year period from 1769 to 1822. Located along the old El Camino Real, or King's Highway, they extended from San Diego to San Francisco and were the centers of Indian civilization, Christianity and industry in the early history of the state.

Junipero Serra (beatified 1988) was the great pioneer of the missions of Upper California. He and his successor as superior of the work, Fermin Lasuen, each directed the establishment of nine missions. One hundred and 46 priests of the Order of Friars Minor, most of them Spaniards, labored in the region from 1769 to 1845; 67 of them died at their posts, two as martyrs. The regular time of mission service was 10 years.

The missions were secularized by the Mexican government in the 1830s but were subsequently restored to the Church by the U.S. government. They are now variously used as the sites of parish churches, a university, houses of study and museums.

The names of the missions and the order of their establishment were as follows:

San Diego de Alcala, San Carlos Borromeo (El Carmelo), San Antonio de Padua, San Gabriel Arcangel, San Luis Obispo de Tolosa, San Francisco de Asis (Dolores), San Juan Capistrano;

Santa Clara de Asis, San Buenaventura, Santa Barbara, La Purisima Concepcion de Maria Santisima, Santa Cruz, Nuestra Senora de la Soledad, San Jose de Guadalupe;

San Juan Bautista, San Miguel Arcangel, San Fernando Rey de Espana, San Luis Rey de Francia, Santa Ines, San Rafael Arcangel, San Francisco Solano de Sonoma (Sonoma).

---

**Honored during 1996:** Father John Oh Woong-jin, with the Magsaysay Award, for public service in founding and running shelters for abandoned persons in South Korea; Susan Blum Gerding, founder and executive director of Isaiah Ministries, with the 10th annual Pope Paul VI Leadership Award in Catholic Evangelization, from the National Council for Catholic Evangelization; Chiara Lubich, founder of the Focolare Movement, with UNESCO's Prize for Peace Education, for building peace and unity among people.

# SHRINES AND PLACES OF HISTORIC INTEREST IN THE UNITED STATES

(Principal source: *Catholic Almanac* survey.)

Listed below, according to state, are shrines, other centers of devotion and some places of historic interest with special significance for Catholics. The list is necessarily incomplete because of space limitations.

Information includes: name and location of shrine or place of interest, date of foundation, sponsoring agency or group, and address for more information.

**Alabama:** St. Jude Church of the City of St. Jude, Montgomery (1934; dedicated, 1938); Mobile Archdiocese. Address: 2048 W. Fairview Ave., Montgomery 36108.

• Shrine of the Most Blessed Trinity, Holy Trinity (1924); Missionary Servants of the Most Blessed Trinity. Address: Holy Trinity 36859.

**Arizona:** Chapel of the Holy Cross, Sedona (1956); Phoenix Diocese: P.O. Box 1043, W. Sedona 86339.

• Mission San Francis Xavier del Bac, near Tucson (1700); National Historic Landmark; Franciscan Friars and Tucson Diocese; Address: 1950 W. San Xavier Rd., Tucson 85746.

• Shrine of St. Joseph of the Mountains, Yarnell (1939); erected by Catholic Action League; currently maintained by Board of Directors. Address: P.O. Box 267, Yarnell 85362.

**California:** Mission San Diego de Alcala (July 16, 1769); first of the 21 Franciscan missions of Upper California; Minor Basilica; National Historic Landmark; San Diego Diocese. Address: 10818 San Diego Mission Rd., San Diego 92108.

• Carmel Mission Basilica (Mission San Carlos Borromeo del Rio Carmelo), Carmel by the Sea (June 3, 1770); Monterey Diocese. Address: 3080 Rio Rd., Carmel 93923.

• Old Mission San Luis Obispo de Tolosa, San Luis Obispo (Sept. 1, 1772); Monterey Diocese (Parish Church). Address: Old Mission Church, 751 Palm St., San Luis Obispo 93401.

• San Gabriel Mission, San Gabriel (Sept. 8, 1771); Los Angeles Archdiocese (Parish Church, staffed by Claretians). Address: 537 W. Mission, San Gabriel 91776.

• Mission San Francisco de Asis (Oct. 9, 1776) and Mission Dolores Basilica (1860s); San Francisco Archdiocese. Address: 3321 Sixteenth St., San Francisco 94114.

• Mission San Juan Capistrano, San Juan Capistrano (Nov. 1, 1776); Orange Diocese. Address: P.O. Box 697, San Juan Capistrano 92693.

• Old Mission Santa Barbara, Santa Barbara (Dec. 4, 1786); National Historic Landmark; Parish Church, staffed by Franciscan Friars. Address: 2201 Laguna St., Santa Barbara 93105.

• Old Mission San Juan Bautista, San Juan Bautista (June 24, 1797); National Historic Landmark; Monterey Diocese (Parish Church). Address: P.O. Box 400, San Juan Bautista 95045.

• Mission San Miguel, San Miguel (July 25, 1797); Parish Church, Monterey diocese; Franciscan Friars. Address: 775 Mission St., P.O. Box 69, San Miguel 93451.

• Old Mission Santa Ines, Solvang (1804); Los Angeles Archdiocese (Parish Church, staffed by Capuchin Franciscan Friars). Address: P.O. Box 408, Solvang 93464.

*Franciscan Friars founded 21 missions in California. (See Index: Franciscan Missions.)*

• Shrine of Our Lady of Sorrows, Sycamore (1883); Sacramento Diocese. Address: c/o Our Lady of Lourdes Church, 745 Ware Ave., Colusa 95932.

**Colorado:** Mother Cabrini Shrine, Golden; Missionary Sisters of the Sacred Heart. Address: 20189 Cabrini Blvd., Golden 80401.

**Connecticut:** Shrine of Our Lady of Lourdes, Litchfield (1958); Montfort Missionaries. Address: P.O. Box 667, Litchfield 06759.

• Shrine of the Infant of Prague, New Haven (1945); Dominican Friars. Address: P.O. Box 1202, 5 Hillhouse Ave., New Haven 06505.

**District of Columbia:** Mount St. Sepulchre, Franciscan Monastery of the Holy Land (1897; church dedicated, 1899); Order of Friars Minor. Address: 1400 Quincy St. N.E., Washington, D.C. 20017.

• Basilica of the National Shrine of the Immaculate Conception. See Index for separate entry.

**Florida:** Mary, Queen of the Universe Shrine, Orlando (1986, temporary facilities; new shrine dedicated, 1993); Orlando diocese. Address: 8300 Vineland Ave., Orlando, 32821.

• Our Lady of La Leche Shrine (Patroness of Mothers and Mothers-to-be) and Mission of Nombre de Dios, Saint Augustine (1565); Angelus Crusade Headquarters. St. Augustine Diocese. Address: 30 Ocean Ave., St. Augustine 32084.

**Illinois:** Holy Family Log Church, Cahokia (1799; original log church erected 1699); Belleville Diocese (Parish Church). Address: 116 Church St., Cahokia 62206.

• Marytown/Shrine of St. Maximilian Kolbe, Libertyville; Our Lady of the Blessed Sacrament Sanctuary of Perpetual Eucharistic Adoration (1930 and Archdiocesan Shrine to St. Maximilian Kolbe (1989), conducted by Conventual Franciscan Friars, 1600 West Park Ave., Libertyville 60048.

• National Shrine of Our Lady of the Snows, Belleville (1958); Missionary Oblates of Mary Immaculate. Address: 9500 West State Route 15, Belleville 62223.

• National Shrine of St. Jude, Chicago (1929); located in Our Lady of Guadalupe Church, founded and staffed by Claretians. Address: 3200 E. 91st St., Chicago 60617.

• National Shrine of St. Therese and Museum, Darien (1930, at St. Clara's Church, Chicago; new shrine, 1987, after original destroyed by fire); Carmelites of Most Pure Heart of Mary Province. Address: Carmelite Visitor Center, 8501 Bailey Rd., Darien 60561.

• Shrine of St. Jude Thaddeus, Chicago (1929) located in St. Pius V Church, staffed by Dominicans, Central Province. Address: 1909 S. Ashland Ave., Chicago 60608.

**Indiana:** Our Lady of Monte Cassino Shrine, St. Meinrad (1870); Benedictines. Address: St. Meinrad Archabbey, 401 Hill Dr., St. Meinrad 47577.

• Old Cathedral (Basilica of St. Francis Xavier),

Vincennes (1826, parish records go back to 1749); Evansville Diocese. Minor Basilica, 1970. Address: 205 Church St., Vincennes 47591.

**Iowa:** Grotto of the Redemption, West Bend (1912); Sioux City Diocese. Life of Christ in stone. Mailing address: P.O. Box 376, West Bend 50597.

**Louisiana:** National Votive Shrine of Our Lady of Prompt Succor, New Orleans (1810); located in the Chapel of the Ursuline Convent (a National Historic Landmark). Address: 2635 State St., New Orleans 70118.

• Shrine of St. Ann. Mailing address: 4920 Loveland St., Metaire 70006.

• Shrine of St. Roch, New Orleans (1876); located in St. Roch's *Campo Santo* (Cemetery); New Orleans Archdiocese. Address: 1725 St. Roch Ave., New Orleans 70117.

**Maryland:** Basilica of the Assumption of the Blessed Virgin Mary, Baltimore (designated a national shrine by the National Conference of Catholic Bishops, November, 1993). Address: Cathedral and Mulberry Sts., Baltimore, MD 21201.

• National Shrine Grotto of Our Lady of Lourdes, Emmitsburg (1809, Grotto of Our Lady; 1875, National Shrine Grotto of Lourdes); Public oratory, Archdiocese of Baltimore. Address: Mount St. Mary's College and Seminary, Emmitsburg 21727.

• National Shrine of St. Elizabeth Ann Seton, Emmitsburg. Religious/Historical. Foundation of Sisters of Charity (1809); first parochial school in America (1810); dedicated as Minor Basilica (1991); Address: 333 South Seton Ave., Emmitsburg 21727.

• St. Francis Xavier Shrine, "Old Bohemia", near Warwick (1704), located in Wilmington, Del., Diocese; restoration under aupices of Old Bohemia Historical Society, Inc. Address: P.O. Box 61, Warwick 21912.

• St. Anthony Shrine, Emmitsburg (1893); attached to St. Anthony Parish, Baltimore Archdiocese. Address: 16150 St. Anthony Rd., Emmitsburg 21727.

**Massachusetts:** National Shrine of Our Lady of La Salette, Ipswich (1945); Missionaries of Our Lady of La Salette. Address: 251 Topsfield Rd., Ipswich 01938.

• Our Lady of Fatima Shrine, Holliston (1950); Xaverian Missionaries. Address: 101 Summer St., Holliston 01746.

• St. Anthony Shrine, Boston (1947); downtown Service Church with shrine; Boston Archdiocese and Franciscans of Holy Name Province. Address: 100 Arch St., Boston 02107.

• Saint Clement's Eucharistic Shrine, Boston (1945); Boston Archdiocese, staffed by Oblates of the Virgin Mary. Address: 1105 Boylston St., Boston 02215.

• Shrine of The Divine Mercy, Stockbridge (1960);Address: Shrine of The Divine Mercy, Eden Hill, Stockbridge 01262.

**Michigan:** Cross in the Woods, Indian River (1947); Gaylord diocse; staffed by Franciscan Friars of Sacred Heart Province, St. Louis. Address: 7078 M-68, Indian River 49749.

• Shrine of the Little Flower, Royal Oak (c. 1929, by Father Coughlin); Detroit archdiocese. Address: 2123 Roseland, Royal Oak 48073.

**Missouri:** Memorial Shrine of St. Rose Philippine Duchesne, St. Charles; Religious of the Sacred Heart of Jesus. Address: 619 N. Second St., St. Charles 63301.

• National Shrine of Our Lady of the Miraculous Medal, Perryville; located in St. Mary of the Barrens Church (1837); Vincentians. Address: 1811 W. St. Joseph St., Perryville 63775.

• Old St. Ferdinand's Shrine, Florissant (1819, Sacred Heart Convent; 1821, St. Ferdinand's Church); Friends of Old St. Ferdinand's, Inc. Address: No. 1 Rue St. Francois, Florissant 63031.

• Shrine of Our Lady of Sorrows, Starkenburg (1888; shrine building, 1910); Jefferson City Diocese. Address: c/o Church of the Risen Savior, Rt. 1, Box 17, Rhineland 65069.

**Nebraska:** The Eucharistic Shrine of Christ the King (1973); Lincoln diocese and Holy Spirit Adoration Sisters. Address: 1040 South Cotner Blvd., Lincoln 68510.

**New Hampshire:** Shrine of Our Lady of Grace, Colebrook (1948); Missionary Oblates of Mary Immaculate. Address: R.R. 1, Box 521, Colebrook 03576.

• Shrine of Our Lady of La Salette, Enfield (1951); Missionaries of Our Lady of La Salette. Address: Rt. 4A, P.O. Box 420, Enfield 03748.

**New Jersey:** Shrine of the Immaculate Heart of Mary (1978); National Center of the Blue Army of Our Lady of Fatima, USA, Inc. Address: Mountain View Rd. (P.O. Box 976), Washington 07882.

• Shrine of St. Joseph, Stirling (1924); Missionary Servants of the Most Holy Trinity. Address: 1050 Long Hill Rd., Stirling 07980.

**New Mexico:** St. Augustine Mission, Isleta (1613); Santa Fe Archdiocese. Address: P.O. Box 463, Isleta, Pueblo 87022.

• Santuario de Nuestro Senor de Esquipulas, Chimayo (1816); Santa Fe archdiocese, Sons of the Holy Family; national historic landmark, 1970. Address: Santuario de Chimayo, P.O. Box 235; Chimayo 87522.

**New York:** National Shrine of Bl. Kateri Tekakwitha, Fonda (1938); Order of Friars Minor Conventual. Address: P.O. Box 627, Fonda 12068.

• Marian Shrine (National Shrine of Mary Help of Christians), West Haverstraw (1953); Salesians of St. John Bosco.Address: Filors Lane, W. Haverstraw 10993.

• National Shrine of St. Frances Xavier Cabrini, New York (1938; new shrine dedicated 1960); Missionary Sisters of the Sacred Heart. Address: 701 Fort Washington Ave., New York 10040.

• Original Shrine of St. Ann in New York City (1892); located in St. Jean Baptiste Church; Blessed Sacrament Fathers. Address: 184 E. 76th St., New York 10021.

• Our Lady of Fatima National Shrine Basilica, Youngstown (1954); Barnabite Fathers. Address: 1023 Swan Rd., Youngstown 14174. Designated a national shrine in 1994.

• Our Lady of Victory National Shrine, Lackawanna (1926); Minor Basilica. Address: 767 Ridge Rd., Lackawanna 14218.

• Shrine Church of Our Lady of Mt. Carmel, Brooklyn (1887); Brooklyn Diocese (Parish Church). Address: 275 N. 8th St., Brooklyn 11211.

• Shrine of Our Lady of Martyrs, Auriesville (1885); Society of Jesus. Address: Auriesville 12016.

• Shrine of Our Lady of the Island, Eastport (1975); Montfort Missionaries. Address: Box 26, Eastport, L.I., 11941.

• Shrine of St. Elizabeth Ann Seton, New York City (1975); located in Our Lady of the Rosary Church. Address: 7 State St., New York 10004.

**Ohio:** Basilica and National Shrine of Our Lady of Consolation, Carey (186); Minor Basilica; Toledo Diocese; staffed by Conventual Franciscan Friars. Address: 315 Clay St., Carey 43316.

• National Shrine of Our Lady of Lebanon, North Jackson (1965); Eparchy of Our Lady of Lebanon of Los Angeles. Address: 2759 N. Lipkey Rd., N. Jackson 44451.

• Our Lady of Czestochowa, Garfield Heights (1939); Sisters of St. Joseph, Third Order of St. Francis. Address: 12215 Granger Rd., Garfield Hts. 44125.

• Our Lady of Fatima, Ironton (1954); Address: St. Joseph Church, 905 S. Fifth St., Ironton 45638.

• St. Anthony Shrine, Cincinnati (1888); Franciscan Friars, St. John Baptist Province. Address: 5000 Colerain Ave., Cincinnati 45223.

• Shrine and Oratory of the Weeping Madonna of Mariapoch, Burton (1956); Social Mission Sisters. Parma Diocese (Byzantine). Address: 17486 Mumford Rd., Burton 44021.

• Shrine of the Holy Relics (1892); Sisters of the Precious Blood. Address: 2291 St. John's Rd., Maria Stein 45860.

• Sorrowful Mother Shrine, Bellevue (1850); Society of the Precious Blood. Address: 4106 State Rt. 269, Bellevue 44811.

**Oklahoma:** National Shrine of the Infant Jesus of Prague, Prague (1949); Oklahoma City Archdiocese. Address: P.O. Box 488, Prague 74864.

**Oregon:** The Grotto (National Sanctuary of Our Sorrowful Mother), Portland (1924); Servite Friars. Address: P.O. Box 20008, Portland 97220.

**Pennsylvania:** Basilica of the Sacred Heart of Jesus, Conewago Township (1741; present church, 1787); Minor Basilica; Harrisburg Diocese. Address: 30 Basilica Dr., Hanover 17331.

• National Shrine Center of Our Lady of Guadalupe, Allentown (1974); located in Immaculate Conception Church; Allentown Diocese. Address: 501 Ridge Ave., Allentown 18102.

• National Shrine of Our Lady of Czestochowa (1955); Order of St. Paul the Hermit (Pauline Fathers). Address: P.O. Box 2049, Doylestown 18901.

• National Shrine of St. John Neumann, Philadelphia (1860); Redemptorist Fathers, St. Peter's Church. Address: 1019 N. 5th St., Philadelphia 19123.

• National Shrine of the Sacred Heart, Harleigh (1975); Scranton Diocese. Address: P.O. Box 500, Harleigh 18225.

• Old St. Joseph's National Shrine, a unit of the Independence National Historical Park, Philadelphia (1733); Philadelphia Archdiocese (Parish Church). Address: 321 Willings Alley, Philadelphia 19106.

• St. Ann's Monastery Shrine, Scranton (1902); Passionist Community. Address: 1230 St. Ann's St., Scranton 18504.

• St. Anthony's Chapel, Pittsburgh (1883); Pittsburgh Diocese. Address: 1700 Harpster St., Pittsburgh 15212.

• Shrine of St. Walburga, Greensburg (1974); Sisters of St. Benedict. Address: 1001 Harvey Ave., Greensburg 15601.

**Texas:** Virgen de San Juan del Valle Shrine, San Juan (1949); Brownsville Diocese; staffed by Oblates of Mary Immaculate. Mailing address: P.O. Box 747, San Juan 78589.

**Vermont:** St. Anne's Shrine, Isle La Motte (1666); Burlington Diocese, conducted by Edmundites. Address: West Shore Rd., Isle La Motte 05463.

**Wisconsin:** Holy Hill — National Shrine of Mary, Help of Christians (1857); Discalced Carmelite Friars. Address: 1525 Carmel Rd., Hubertus 53033.

• National Shrine of St. Joseph, De Pere (1889); Norbertine Fathers. Address: 1016 N. Broadway, De Pere 54115.

• Shrine of Mary, Mother Thrice Admirable Queen and Victress of Schoenstatt (1965), Address: W284 N698 Cherry Lane, Waukesha 53188.

## HUMAN DEVELOPMENT CAMPAIGN

The Campaign for Human Development was inaugurated by the U.S. Catholic Conference in November, 1969, to combat injustice, oppression, alienation and poverty in this country by funding selfhelp programs begun and carried out by the poor or by the poor and nonpoor working together, and by seeking a reevaluation of the priorities of individuals, families, the Church and the civic community with respect to the stewardship of Godgiven goods. The campaign got under way with a collection taken up in all parishes throughout the country on Nov. 22, 1970. Seventy-five per cent of the money contributed in this and subsequent annual collections was placed in a national fund principally for funding selfhelp projects and also for educational purposes; 25 percent remained in the dioceses where it was collected. From 1970, the campaign has distributed approximately $200 million to more than 3,000 selfhelp projects. National office: 3211 Fourth St. N.E., Washington, D.C. 20017.

### Missionaries Released

Three nuns, two priests and a brother were released by members of the rebel Sudan People's Liberation Army Aug. 8, 1996, after more than a week of captivity. A statement from the Sudan Catholic Information Office in Nairobi said four of the hostages had been held captive in a jail. One nun and the brother had been held in the church compound for "their own security,." the rebels said. Those in jail had been accused of spying as agents of Islam because of a quotation from the Koran found in a Bible bookmark. The hostages were released in the village of Mapourdit in southern Sudan where they were captured.

# THE CATHOLIC CHURCH IN THE UNITED STATES ___

The starting point of the mainstream of Catholic history in the United States was Baltimore at the end of the Revolutionary War. Long before that time, however, Catholic explorers had traversed much of the country and missionaries had done considerable work among Indians in the Southeast, Northeast and Southwest. (See also Index: Chronology of Church in U.S.)

## Spanish and French Missions

Missionaries from Spain evangelized Indians in Florida (which included a large area of the Southeast), New Mexico, Texas and California. Franciscan Juan de Padilla, killed in 1542 in what is now central Kansas, was the first of numerous martyrs among the early missionaries. The city of St. Augustine, settled by the Spanish in 1565, was the first permanent settlement in the United States and also the site of the first parish, established the same year with secular Father Martin Francisco Lopez de Mendoza Grajales as pastor. Italian Jesuit Eusebio Kino (1645-1711) established Spanish missions in lower California and southern Arizona, where he founded San Xavier del Bac mission in 1700. Bl. Junipero Serra (1713-84), who established nine of the famous chain of 21 Franciscan missions in California, was perhaps the most noted of the Spanish missionaries. He was beatified in 1988.

French missionary efforts originated in Canada and extended to parts of Maine, New York and areas around the Great Lakes and along the Mississippi River as far south as Louisiana. Sts. Isaac Jogues, René Goupil and John de Brébeuf, three of eight Jesuit missionaries of New France martyred between 1642 and 1649 (canonized in 1930), met their deaths near Auriesville, New York. Jesuit explorer Jacques Marquette (1637-75), who founded St. Ignace Mission at the Straits of Mackinac in 1671, left maps and a diary of his exploratory trip down the Mississippi River with Louis Joliet in 1673. Claude Allouez (1622-89), another French Jesuit, worked for 32 years among Indians in the Midwest, baptizing an estimated 10,000. French Catholics founded the colony in Louisiana in 1699. In 1727, Ursuline nuns from France founded a convent in New Orleans, the oldest in the United States.

## English Settlements

Catholics were excluded by penal law from English settlements along the Atlantic coast.

The only colony established under Catholic leadership was Maryland, granted to George Calvert (Lord Baltimore) as a proprietary colony in 1632; its first settlement at St. Mary's City was established in 1634 by a contingent of Catholic and Protestant colonists who had arrived from England on the *Ark* and the *Dove*. Jesuits Andrew White and John Altham, who later evangelized Indians of the area, accompanied the settlers. The principle of religious freedom on which the colony was founded was enacted into law in 1649 as the Act of Toleration. It was the first such measure passed in the colonies and, except for a four-year period of Puritan control, remained in effect until 1688, when Maryland became a royal colony, and the Anglican Church was made the official religion in 1692. Catholics were disenfranchised and persecuted until 1776.

The only other colony where Catholics were assured some degree of freedom was Pennsylvania, founded by the Quaker William Penn in 1681.

One of the earliest permanent Catholic establishments in the English colonies was St. Francis Xavier Mission, Old Bohemia, in northern Maryland, founded by the Jesuits in 1704 to serve Catholics of Delaware, Maryland and southeastern Pennsylvania. Its Bohemia Academy, established in the 1740s, was attended by sons of prominent Catholic families in the area.

## Catholics and the Revolution

Despite their small number, which accounted for about one percent of the population, Catholics made significant contributions to the cause for independence from England.

Father John Carroll (1735-1815), who would later become the first bishop of the American hierarchy, and his cousin, Charles Carroll (1737-1832), a signer of the Declaration of Independence, were chosen by the Continental Congress to accompany Benjamin Franklin and Samuel Chase to Canada to try to secure that country's neutrality. Father Pierre Gibault (1737-1804) gave important aid in preserving the Northwest Territory for the revolutionaries. Thomas FitzSimons (1741-1811) of Philadelphia gave financial support to the Continental Army, served in a number of campaigns and later, with Daniel Carroll of Maryland, became one of the two Catholic signers of the Constitution. John Barry (1745-1803), commander of the *Lexington*, the first ship commissioned by Congress, served valiantly and is considered a founder of the U.S. Navy. There is no record of the number of Catholics who served in Washington's armies, although 38 to 50 percent had Irish surnames.

Casimir Pulaski (1748-79) and Thaddeus Kosciusko (1746-1817) of Poland served the cause of the Revolution. Assisting also were the Catholic nations of France, with a military and naval force, and Spain with money and the neutrality of its colonies.

Acknowledgment of Catholic aid in the war and the founding of the Republic was made by General Washington in his reply to a letter from prominent Catholics seeking justice and equal rights: "I presume your fellow citizens of all denominations will not forget the patriotic part which you took in the accomplishment of our Revolution and the establishment of our government or the important assistance which they received from a nation [France] in which the Roman Catholic faith is professed."

In 1789, religious freedom was guaranteed under the First Amendment to the Constitution. Discriminatory laws against Catholics remained in force in many of the states, however, until well into the 19th century.

## Beginning of Organization

Father John Carroll's appointment as superior of the American missions on June 9, 1784, was the first step toward organization of the Church in this country. According to a report he made to Rome the following year, there were 24 priests and approximately 25,000 Catholics, mostly in Maryland and Pennsylvania, in a general population of four million. Many of them had been in the Colonies for several generations. For the most part, however, they were an unknown minority laboring under legal and social handicaps.

## Establishment of the Hierarchy

Father Carroll was named the first American bishop in 1789 and placed in charge of the Diocese of Baltimore, whose boundaries were coextensive with those of the United States. He was ordained in England Aug. 15, 1790, and installed in his see the following Dec. 12.

Ten years later, Father Leonard Neale became his coadjutor and the first bishop ordained in the United States. Bishop Carroll became an archbishop in 1808 when Baltimore was designated a metropolitan see and the new dioceses of Boston, New York, Philadelphia and Bardstown (now Louisville) were established. These jurisdictions were later subdivided, and by 1840 there were, in addition to Baltimore, 15 dioceses, 500 priests and 663,000 Catholics in the general population of 17 million.

## Priests and First Seminaries

The original number of 24 priests noted in Bishop Carroll's 1785 report was gradually augmented with the arrival of others from France and other countries. Among arrivals from France after the Civil Constitution of the Clergy went into effect in 1790, were Jean Louis Lefebvre de Cheverus and Sulpicians Ambrose Maréchal, Benedict Flaget and William Dubourg, who later became bishops.

The first seminary in the country was St. Mary's, established in 1791 in Baltimore, and placed under the direction of the Sulpicians. French seminarian Stephen T. Badin (1768-1853), who fled to the U.S. in 1792 and became a pioneer missionary in Kentucky, Ohio and Michigan, was the first priest ordained (1793) in the U.S. Demetrius Gallitzin (1770-1840), a Russian prince and convert to Catholicism who did pioneer missionary work in western Pennsylvania, was ordained to the priesthood in 1795; he was the first to receive all his orders in the U.S. By 1815, St. Mary's Seminary had 30 ordained alumni.

Two additional seminaries — Mt. St. Mary's at Emmitsburg, Md., and St. Thomas at Bardstown, Ky. — were established in 1809 and 1811, respectively. These and similar institutions founded later played key roles in the development and growth of the American clergy.

## Early Schools

Early educational enterprises included the establishment in 1791 of a school at Georgetown which later became the first Catholic university in the U.S.; the opening of a secondary school for girls, conducted by Visitation Nuns, in 1799 at Georgetown; and the start of a similar school in the first decade of the 19th century at Emmitsburg, Md., by Saint Elizabeth Ann Seton.

By the 1840s, which saw the beginnings of the present public school system, more than 200 Catholic elementary schools, half of them west of the Alleghenies, were in operation. From this start, the Church subsequently built the greatest private system of education in the world.

## Sisterhoods

Institutes of women Religious were largely responsible for the development of educational and charitable institutions. Among them were Ursuline Nuns in Louisiana from 1727 and Visitation Nuns at Georgetown in the 1790s.

The first contemplative foundation in the country was established in 1790 at Fort Tobacco, Md., by three American-born Carmelites trained at an English convent in Belgium.

The first community of American origin was that of the Sisters of Charity of St. Joseph, founded in 1808 at Emmitsburg, Md., by Mother Elizabeth Ann Bayley Seton (canonized in 1975). Other early American communities were the Sisters of Loretto and the Sisters of Charity of Nazareth, both founded in 1812 in Kentucky, and the Oblate Sisters of Providence, a black community founded in 1829 in Baltimore by Mother Mary Elizabeth Lange.

Among pioneer U.S. foundresses of European communities were Mother Rose Philippine Duchesne (canonized in 1980), who established the Religious of the Sacred Heart in Missouri in 1818, and Mother Theodore Guérin, who founded the Sisters of Providence of St.-Mary-of-the-Woods in Indiana in 1840.

The number of sisters' communities, most of them branches of European institutes, increased apace with needs for their missions in education, charitable service and spiritual life.

## Trusteeism

The initial lack of organization in ecclesiastical affairs, nationalistic feeling among Catholics and the independent action of some priests were factors involved in several early crises.

In Philadelphia, some German Catholics, with the reluctant consent of Bishop Carroll, founded Holy Trinity, the first national parish in the U.S. They refused to accept the pastor appointed by the bishop and elected their own. This and other abuses led to formal schism in 1796, a condition which existed until 1802 when they returned to canonical jurisdiction. Philadelphia was also the scene of the Hogan Schism, which developed in the 1820s when Father William Hogan, with the aid of lay trustees, seized control of St. Mary's Cathedral. His movement, for churches and parishes controlled by other than canonical procedures and run in extralegal ways, was nullified by a decision of the Pennsylvania Supreme Court in 1822.

Similar troubles seriously disturbed the peace of the Church in other places, principally New York, Baltimore, Buffalo, Charleston and New Orleans.

Dangers arising from the exploitation of lay control were gradually diminished with the extension and enforcement of canonical procedures and with changes in civil law about the middle of the century.

## Bigotry

Bigotry against Catholics waxed and waned during the 19th century and into the 20th. The first major campaign of this kind, which developed in the wake of the panic of 1819 and lasted for about 25 years, was mounted in 1830 when the number of Catholic immigrants began to increase to a noticeable degree.

Nativist anti-Catholicism generated a great deal of violence, represented by climaxes in loss of life and property in Charlestown, Mass., in 1834, and in Philadelphia 10 years later. Later bigotry was fomented by the Know-Nothings, in the 1850s; the Ku Klux Klan, from 1866; the American Protective Association, from 1887, and the Guardians of Liberty. Perhaps the last eruption of virulently overt anti-Catholicism occurred during the campaign of Alfred E. Smith for the presidency in 1928. Observers feel the issue was muted to a considerable extent in the political area with the election of John F. Kennedy to the presidency in 1960.

The Catholic periodical press had its beginnings in response to the attacks of bigots. The *U.S. Catholic Miscellany* (1822-61), the first Catholic newspaper in the U.S., was founded by Bishop John England of Charleston to answer critics of the Church. This remained the character of most of the periodicals of the 19th and into the 20th century.

## Growth and Immigration

Between 1830 and 1900, the combined factors of natural increase, immigration and conversion raised the Catholic population to 12 million. A large percentage of the growth figure represented immigrants: some 2.7 million, largely from Ireland, Germany and France, between 1830 and 1880; and another 1.25 million during the 1880s when Eastern and Southern Europeans came in increasing numbers. By the 1860s the Catholic Church, with most of its members concentrated in urban areas, was one of the largest religious bodies in the country.

The efforts of progressive bishops to hasten the acculturation of Catholic immigrants occasioned a number of controversies, which generally centered around questions concerning national or foreign-language parishes. One of them, called Cahenslyism, arose from complaints that German Catholic immigrants were not being given adequate pastoral care.

Immigration continued after the turn of the century, but its impact was more easily cushioned through the application of lessons learned earlier in dealing with problems of nationality and language.

## Eastern-Rite Catholics

The immigration of the 1890s included large numbers of Eastern-Rite Catholics with their own liturgies and tradition of a married clergy, but without their own bishops. The treatment of their clergy and people by some of the U.S. (Latin-Rite) hierarchy and the prejudices they encountered resulted in the defection of thousands from the Catholic Church.

In 1907, Basilian monk Stephen Ortynsky was ordained the first bishop of Byzantine-Rite Catholics in the U.S. Eventually jurisdictions were established for most Byzantine- and other Eastern-Rite Catholics in the country.

## Councils of Baltimore

The bishops of the growing U.S. dioceses met at Baltimore for seven provincial councils between 1829 and 1849.

In 1846, they proclaimed the Blessed Virgin Mary patroness of the United States under the title of the Immaculate Conception, eight years before the dogma was proclaimed.

After the establishment of the Archdiocese of Oregon City in 1846 and the elevation to metropolitan status of St. Louis, New Orleans, Cincinnati and New York, the first of the three plenary councils of Baltimore was held.

The first plenary assembly was convoked on May 9, 1852, with Archbishop Francis P. Kenrick of Baltimore as papal legate. The bishops drew up regulations concerning parochial life, matters of church ritual and ceremonies, the administration of church funds and the teaching of Christian doctrine.

The second plenary council, meeting from Oct. 7 to 21, 1866, under the presidency of Archbishop Martin J. Spalding, formulated a condemnation of several current doctrinal errors and established norms affecting the organization of dioceses, the education and conduct of the clergy, the management of ecclesiastical property, parochial duties and general education.

Archbishop (later Cardinal) James Gibbons called into session the third plenary council which lasted from Nov. 9 to Dec. 7, 1884. Among highly significant results of actions taken by this assembly were the preparation of the line of Baltimore catechisms which became a basic means of religious instruction in this country; legislation which fixed the pattern of Catholic education by requiring the building of elementary schools in all parishes; the establishment of the Catholic University of America in Washington, D.C., in 1889; and the determination of six holy days of obligation for observance in this country.

The enactments of the three plenary councils have had the force of particular law for the Church in the United States.

The Holy See established the Apostolic Delegation in Washington, D.C., on Jan. 24, 1893.

## Slavery

In the Civil War period, as before, Catholics reflected attitudes of the general population with respect to the issue of slavery. Some supported it, some opposed it, but none were prominent in the Abolition Movement. Gregory XVI had condemned the slave trade in 1839, but no contemporary pope or American bishop published an official document on slavery itself. The issue did not split Catholics in schism as it did Baptists, Methodists and Presbyterians.

Catholics fought on both sides in the Civil War. Five hundred members of 20 or more sisterhoods served the wounded of both sides.

One hundred thousand of the four million slaves emancipated in 1863 were Catholics; the highest concentrations were in Louisiana, about 60,000, and Maryland, 16,000. Three years later, their pastoral care was one of the subjects covered in nine decrees issued by the Second Plenary Council of Baltimore. The measures had little practical effect with respect to integration of the total Catholic community, predicated as they were on the proposition that individual bishops should handle questions regarding segregation in churches and related matters as best they could in the pattern of local customs.

Long entrenched segregation practices continued in force through the rest of the 19th century and well into the 20th. The first effective efforts to alter them were initiated by Cardinal Joseph Ritter of St. Louis in 1947, Cardinal (then Archbishop) Patrick O'Boyle of Washington in 1948, and Bishop Vincent Waters of Raleigh in 1953.

### Friend of Labor

The Church became known during the 19th century as a friend and ally of labor in seeking justice for the working man. Cardinal Gibbons journeyed to Rome in 1887, for example, to defend and prevent a condemnation of the Knights of Labor by Leo XIII. The encyclical *Rerum Novarum* was hailed by many American bishops as a confirmation, if not vindication, of their own theories. Catholics have always formed a large percentage of union membership, and some have served unions in positions of leadership.

### The American Heresy

Near the end of the century some controversy developed over what was characterized as Americanism or the phantom heresy. It was alleged that Americans were discounting the importance of contemplative virtues, exalting the practical virtues, and watering down the purity of Catholic doctrine for the sake of facilitating convert work.

The French translation of Father Walter Elliott's *Life of Isaac Hecker*, which fired the controversy, was one of many factors that led to the issuance of Leo XIII's *Testem Benevolentiae* in January, 1899, in an attempt to end the matter. It was the first time the orthodoxy of the Church in the U.S. was called into question.

### Schism

In the 1890s, serious friction developed between Poles and Irish in Scranton, Buffalo and Chicago, resulting in schism and the establishment of the Polish National Catholic Church. A central figure in the affair was Father Francis Hodur, who was excommunicated by Bishop William O'Hara of Scranton in 1898. Nine years later, his ordination by an Old Catholic Archbishop of Utrecht gave the new church its first bishop.

Another schism of the period led to formation of the American Carpatho-Russian Orthodox Greek Catholic Church.

### Coming of Age

In 1900, there were 12 million Catholics in the total U.S. population of 76 million, 82 dioceses in 14 provinces, and 12,000 priests and members of about 40 communities of men Religious. Many sisterhoods, most of them of European origin and some of American foundation, were engaged in Catholic educational and hospital work, two of their traditional apostolates.

The Church in the United States was removed from mission status with promulgation of the apostolic constitution *Sapienti Consilio* by Pope St. Pius X on June 29, 1908.

Before that time, and even into the early 1920s, the Church in this country received financial assistance from mission-aid societies in France, Bavaria and Austria. Already, however, it was making increasing contributions of its own. At the present time, it is one of the major national contributors to the worldwide Society for the Propagation of the Faith.

American foreign missionary personnel increased from 14 or less in 1906 to an all-time high in 1968 of 9,655 priests, brothers, sisters, seminarians, and lay persons. The first missionary seminary in the U.S. was in operation at Techny, Ill., in 1909, under the auspices of the Society of the Divine Word. Maryknoll, the first American missionary society, was established in 1911 and sent its first priests to China in 1918. Despite these contributions, the Church in the U.S. has not matched the missionary commitment of some other nations.

### Bishops' Conference

A highly important apparatus for mobilizing the Church's resources was established in 1917 under the title of the National Catholic War Council. Its name was changed to National Catholic Welfare Conference several years later, but its objectives remained the same: to serve as an advisory and coordinating agency of the American bishops for advancing works of the Church in fields of social significance and impact — education, communications, immigration, social action, legislation, youth and lay organizations.

The forward thrust of the bishops' social thinking was evidenced in a program of social reconstruction they recommended in 1919. By 1945, all but one of their twelve points had been enacted into legislation.

The NCWC was renamed the United States Catholic Conference (USCC) in November, 1966, when the hierarchy also organized itself as a territorial conference with pastoral-juridical authority under the title, National Conference of Catholic Bishops. The USCC is carrying on the functions of the former NCWC.

### Catholic Press

The establishment of the National Catholic News Service (NC) — now the Catholic News Service (CNS) — in 1920 was an important event in the development of the Catholic press, which had its beginnings about a hundred years earlier. Early in the 20th century there were 63 weekly newspapers. The *1996 Catholic Press Directory* reported 185 newspapers with a circulation in excess of 5.8 million and 254 magazines with a circulation of over 14 million.

### Lay Organizations

A burst of lay organizational growth occurred from the 1930s onwards with the appearance of Catholic Action types of movements and other groups and associations devoted to special causes, social service and assistance for the poor and needy. Several special apostolates developed under the aegis of the National Catholic Welfare Conference (now the United States Catholic Conference); the outstanding one was the Confraternity of Christian Doctrine.

Nineteenth-century organizations of great influence

included: The St. Vincent de Paul Society, whose first U.S. office was set up in 1845 in St. Louis; the Catholic Central Union (Verein), dating from 1855; the Knights of Columbus, founded in 1882; the Holy Name Society, organized in the U.S. in 1870; the Rosary Society (1891) and scores of chapters of the Sodality of the Blessed Virgin Mary.

## Pastoral Concerns

The potential for growth of the Church in this country by immigration was sharply reduced but not entirely curtailed after 1921 with the passage of restrictive federal legislation. As a result, the Catholic population became more stabilized and, to a certain extent and for many reasons, began to acquire an identity of its own.

Some increase from outside has taken place in the past 50 years, however; from Canada, from Central and Eastern European countries, and from Puerto Rico and Latin American countries since World War II. This influx, while not as great as that of the 19th century and early 20th, has enriched the Church here with a sizable body of Eastern-Rite Catholics for whom twelve ecclesiastical jurisdictions have been established. It has also created a challenge for pastoral care of millions of Hispanics in urban centers and in agricultural areas where migrant workers are employed.

The Church continues to grapple with serious pastoral problems in rural areas, where about 600 counties are no-priest land. The National Catholic Rural Life Conference was established in 1922 in an attempt to make the Catholic presence felt on the land, and the Glenmary Society since its foundation in 1939 has devoted itself to this single apostolate. Religious communities and diocesan priests are similarly engaged.

Other challenges lie in the cities and suburbs where 75 percent of the Catholic population lives. Conditions peculiar to each segment of the metropolitan area have developed in recent years as the flight to the suburbs has not only altered some traditional aspects of parish life but has also, in combination with many other factors, left behind a complex of special problems in inner city areas.

## Contemporary Factors

The Church in the U.S. is in a stage of transition from a relatively stable and long established order of life and action to a new order of things. Some of the phenomena of this period are:

• differences in trends and emphasis in theology, and in interpretation and implementation of directives of the Second Vatican Council, resulting in situations of conflict;

• the changing spiritual formation, professional education, style of life and ministry of priests and Religious (men and women), which are altering influential patterns of pastoral and specialized service;

• vocations to the priesthood and religious life, which are generally in decline;

• departures from the priesthood and religious life which, while small percentage-wise, are numerous enough to be a matter of serious concern;

• decline of traditional devotional practices, along with the emergence of new ones.

• exercise of authority along the lines of collegiality and subsidiarity;

• structure and administration, marked by a trend toward greater participation in the life and work of the Church by its members on all levels, from the parish on up;

• alienation from the Church, leading some persons into the catacombs of an underground church, "anonymous Christianity" and religious indifferentism;

• education, undergoing crisis and change in Catholic schools and seeking new ways of reaching out to the young not in Catholic schools and to adults;

• social witness in ministry to the world, which is being shaped by the form of contemporary needs — e.g., race relations, poverty, the peace movement, the Third World;

• ecumenism, involving the Church in interfaith relations on a wider scale than before.

# BACKGROUND DATES IN U.S. CATHOLIC CHRONOLOGY

Dates in this section refer mostly to earlier "firsts" and developments in the background of Catholic history in the United States. For other dates, see various sections of the Almanac.

## Alabama

**1540:** Priests crossed the territory with De Soto's expedition.

**1560:** Five Dominicans in charge of mission at Santa Cruz des Nanipacna.

**1682:** La Salle claimed territory for France.

**1704:** First parish church established at Fort Louis de la Mobile under the care of diocesan priests.

**1829:** Mobile diocese established (redesignated Mobile-Birmingham, 1954-69).

**1830:** Spring Hill College, Mobile, established.

**1834:** Visitation Nuns established an academy at Summerville.

**1969:** Birmingham diocese established.

**1980:** Mobile made metropolitan see.

## Alaska

**1779:** Mass celebrated for first time on shore of Port Santa Cruz on lower Bucareli Bay on May 13 by Franciscan Juan Riobo.

**1868:** Alaska placed under jurisdiction of Vancouver Island.

**1879:** Father John Althoff became first resident missionary.

**1886:** Archbishop Charles J. Seghers, "Apostle of Alaska," murdered by a guide; had surveyed southern and northwest Alaska in 1873 and 1877, respectively.

Sisters of St. Ann first nuns in Alaska.

**1887:** Jesuits enter Alaska territory.

**1894:** Alaska made prefecture apostolic.

**1902:** Sisters of Providence opened hospital at Nome.

**1916:** Alaska made vicariate apostolic.

**1917:** In first ordination in territory, Rev. G. Edgar Gallant raised to priesthood.

**1951:** Juneau diocese established.
**1962:** Fairbanks diocese established.
**1966:** Anchorage archdiocese established.
**1996:** The Sisters of St. Ann, the first congregation of women religious in Alaska, left after 110 years of service.

## Arizona

**1539:** Franciscan Marcos de Niza explored the state.
**1540:** Franciscans Juan de Padilla and Marcos de Niza accompanied Coronado expedition through the territory.
**1629:** Spanish Franciscans began work among Moqui Indians.
**1632:** Franciscan Martin de Arvide killed by Indians.
**1680:** Franciscans Jose de Espeleta, Augustin de Santa Maria, Jose de Figueroa and Jose de Trujillo killed in Pueblo Revolt.
**1700:** Jesuit Eusebio Kino, who first visited the area in 1692, established mission at San Xavier del Bac, near Tucson. In 1783, under Franciscan administration, construction was begun of the Mission Church of San Xavier del Bac near the site of the original mission; it is still in use as a parish church.
**1767:** Jesuits expelled; Franciscans took over 10 missions.
**1828:** Spanish missionaries expelled by Mexican government.
**1863:** Jesuits returned to San Xavier del Bac briefly.
**1869:** Sisters of Loretto arrived to conduct schools at Bisbee and Douglas.
**1897:** Tucson diocese established.
**1969:** Phoenix diocese established.

## Arkansas

**1541:** Priests accompanied De Soto expedition through the territory.
**1673:** Marquette visited Indians in east.
**1686:** Henri de Tonti established trading post, first white settlement in territory.
**1700-1702:** Fr. Nicholas Foucault working among Indians.
**1805:** Bishop Carroll of Baltimore appointed Administrator Apostolic of Arkansas.
**1838:** Sisters of Loretto opened first Catholic school.
**1843:** Little Rock diocese established. There were about 700 Catholics in state, two churches, one priest.
**1851:** Sisters of Mercy founded St. Mary's Convent in Little Rock.

## California

**1542:** Cabrillo discovered Upper (Alta) California; name of priest accompanying expedition unknown.
**1602:** On Nov. 12 Carmelite Anthony of the Ascension offered first recorded Mass in California on shore of San Diego Bay.
**1697:** Missionary work in Lower and Upper Californias entrusted to Jesuits.
**1767:** Jesuits expelled from territory. Spanish Crown confiscated their property, including the Pious Fund for Missions. Upper California missions entrusted to Franciscans.
**1769:** Franciscan Junipero Serra, missionary in Mexico for 20 years, began establishment of

Franciscan missions in California, in present San Diego. He was beatified in 1988.
**1775:** Franciscan Luis Jayme killed by Indians at San Diego Mission.
**1779:** Diocese of Sonora, Mexico, which included Upper California, established.
**1781:** On Sept. 4 an expedition from San Gabriel Mission founded present city of Los Angeles — Pueblo "de Nuestra Senora de los Angeles."
Franciscans Francisco Hermenegildo Garces, Juan Antonio Barreneche, Juan Marcello Diaz and Jose Matias Moreno killed by Indians.
**1812:** Franciscan Andres Quintana killed at Santa Cruz Mission.
**1822:** Dedication on Dec. 8 of Old Plaza Church, "Assistant Mission of Our Lady of the Angels."
**1833:** Missions secularized, finally confiscated.
**1840:** Pope Gregory XVI established Diocese of Both Californias.
**1846:** Peter H. Burnett, who became first governor of California in 1849, received into Catholic Church.
**1848:** Mexico ceded California to the United States.
**1850:** Monterey diocese erected; title changed to Monterey-Los Angeles, 1859; and to Los Angeles-San Diego, 1922.
**1851:** University of Santa Clara chartered.
Sisters of Notre Dame de Namur opened women's College of Notre Dame at San Jose; chartered in 1868; moved to Belmont, 1923.
**1852:** Baja California detached from Monterey diocese.
**1853:** San Francisco archdiocese established.
**1855:** Negotiations inaugurated to restore confiscated California missions to Church.
**1868:** Grass Valley diocese established; transferred to Sacramento in 1886. (Grass Valley was reestablished as a titular see in 1995.)
**1922:** Monterey-Fresno diocese established; became separate dioceses, 1967.
**1934:** Sesquicentennial of Serra's death observed; Serra Year officially declared by Legislature and Aug. 24 observed as Serra Day.
**1936:** Los Angeles made archdiocese. San Diego diocese established.
**1952:** Law exempting non-profit, religious-sponsored elementary and secondary schools from taxation upheld in referendum, Nov. 4.
**1953:** Archbishop James Francis McIntyre of Los Angeles made cardinal by Pius XII.
**1962:** Oakland, Santa Rosa and Stockton dioceses established.
**1973:** Archbishop Timothy Manning of Los Angeles made cardinal by Pope Paul VI.
**1976:** Orange diocese established.
**1981:** San Jose diocese established.
Byzantine-Rite eparchy of Van Nuys established.
**1991:** Archbishop Roger Mahony of Los Angeles made cardinal by Pope John Paul II.
**1994:** Maronite Diocese of Our Lady of Lebanon of Los Angeles established.

## Colorado

**1858:** First parish in Colorado established.
**1864:** Sisters of Loretto at the Foot of the Cross, first nuns in the state, established academy at Denver.

**1868:** Vicariate Apostolic of Colorado and Utah established.
**1887:** Denver diocese established.
**1888:** Regis College (now University) founded.
**1941:** Denver made archdiocese.
Pueblo diocese established.
**1983:** Colorado Springs diocese established.

## Connecticut

**1651:** Probably first priest to enter state was Jesuit Gabriel Druillettes; ambassador of Governor of Canada, he participated in a New England Colonial Council at New Haven.
**1756:** Catholic Acadians, expelled from Nova Scotia, settled in the state.
**1791:** Rev. John Thayer, first native New England priest, offered Mass at the Hartford home of Noah Webster, his Yale classmate.
**1808:** Connecticut became part of Boston diocese.
**1818:** Religious freedom established by new constitution, although the Congregational Church remained, in practice, the state church.
**1829:** Father Bernard O'Cavanaugh became first resident priest in state.
*Catholic Press* of Hartford established.
**1830:** First Catholic church in state dedicated at Hartford.
Father James Fitton (1805-81), New England missionary, was assigned to Hartford for six years. He ministered to Catholics throughout the state.
**1843:** Hartford diocese established
**1882:** Knights of Columbus founded by Father Michael J. McGivney.
**1942:** Fairfield University founded.
**1953:** Norwich and Bridgeport dioceses established. Hartford made archdiocese.
**1956:** Byzantine Rite Exarchate of Stamford established; made eparchy, 1958.

## Delaware

**1730:** Mount Cuba, New Castle County, the scene of Catholic services.
**1750:** Jesuit mission at Apoquiniminck administered from Maryland.
**1772:** First permanent parish established at Coffee Run.
**1792:** French Catholics from Santo Domingo settled near Wilmington.
**1816:** St. Peter's Church, later the cathedral of the diocese, erected at Wilmington.
**1830:** Daughters of Charity opened school and orphanage at Wilmington.
**1868:** Wilmington diocese established.
**1869:** Visitation Nuns established residence in Wilmington.

## District of Columbia

**1641:** Jesuit Andrew White evangelized Anacosta Indians.
**1774:** Father John Carroll ministered to Catholics.
**1789:** Georgetown, first Catholic college in U.S., established.
**1791:** Pierre Charles L'Enfant designed the Federal City of Washington. His plans were not fully implemented until the early 1900s.
**1792:** James Hoban designed the White House.

**1794:** Father Anthony Caffrey began St. Patrick's Church, first parish church in the new Federal City.
**1801:** Poor Clares opened school for girls in Georgetown.
**1802:** First mayor of Washington, appointed by President Jefferson, was Judge Robert Brent.
**1889:** Catholic University of America founded.
**1893:** Apostolic Delegation established; became an Apostolic Nunciature in 1984 with the establishment of full diplomatic relations between the U.S. and the Holy See.
**1919:** National Catholic Welfare Conference (now the United States Catholic Conference) organized by American hierarchy to succeed National Catholic War Council.
**1920:** Cornerstone of National Shrine of Immaculate Conception laid. The crypt church was completed in 1926. The entire structure was completed in 1959 and dedicated Nov. 20, 1959. In 1990 it was designated a minor basilica.
**1939:** Washington made archdiocese of equal rank with Baltimore, under direction of same archbishop.
**1947:** Washington archdiocese received its own archbishop, was separated from Baltimore; became a metropolitan see in 1965.
**1967:** Archbishop Patrick A. O'Boyle of Washington made cardinal by Pope Paul VI.
**1976:** Archbishop William Baum of Washington made a cardinal by Pope Paul VI; transferred to Roman Curia in 1980.
**1988:** Archbishop James A. Hickey of Washington made a cardinal by Pope John Paul II.

## Florida

**1513:** Ponce de Leon discovered Florida.
**1521:** Missionaries accompanying Ponce de Leon and other explorers probably said first Masses within present limits of U.S.
**1528:** Franciscans landed on western shore.
**1539:** Twelve missionaries landed with De Soto at Tampa Bay.
**1549:** Dominican Luis Cancer de Barbastro and two companions slain by Indians near Tampa Bay.
**1565:** City of St. Augustine, oldest in U.S., founded by Pedro Menendez de Aviles, who was accompanied by four secular priests.
America's oldest mission, Nombre de Dios, was established.
Father Martin Francisco Lopez de Mendoza Grajales became the first parish priest of St. Augustine, where the first parish in the U.S. was established.
**1572:** St. Francis Borgia, general of the Society, withdrew Jesuits from Florida.
**1606:** Bishop Juan de las Cabeyas de Altamirano, O.P., conducted the first episcopal visitation in the U.S.
**1620:** The chapel of Nombre de Dios was dedicated to Nuestra Senora de la Leche y Buen Parto (Our Nursing Mother of the Happy Delivery); oldest shrine to the Blessed Mother in the U.S.
**1704:** Destruction of Florida's northern missions by English and Indian troops led by Governor James Moore of South Carolina. Franciscans Juan de Parga, Dominic Criodo, Tiburcio de Osorio, Au-

gustine Ponze de Leon, Marcos Delgado and two Indians, Anthony Enixa and Amador Cuipa Feliciano, were slain by the invaders.

**1735:** Bishop Francis Martinez de Tejadu Diaz de Velasco, auxiliary of Santiago, was the first bishop to take up residence in U.S., at St. Augustine.

**1793:** Florida and Louisiana were included in Diocese of New Orleans.

**1857:** Eastern Florida made a vicariate apostolic.

**1870:** St. Augustine diocese established.

**1917:** Convent Inspection Bill passed; repealed 1935.

**1958:** Miami diocese established.

**1968:** Miami made metropolitan see; Orlando and St. Petersburg dioceses established.

**1976:** Pensacola-Tallahassee diocese established.

**1984:** Palm Beach and Venice dioceses established.

## Georgia

**1540:** First priests to enter were chaplains with De Soto. They celebrated first Mass within territory of 13 original colonies.

**1566:** Pedro Martinez, first Jesuit martyr of the New World, was slain by Indians on Cumberland Island.

**1569:** Jesuit mission was opened at Guale Island by Father Antonio Sedeno.

**1572:** Jesuits withdrawn from area.

**1595:** Five Franciscans assigned to Province of Guale.

**1597:** Five Franciscan missionaries (Fathers Pedro de Corpa, Blas de Rodriguez, Miguel de Anon, Francisco de Berascolo and Brother Antonio de Badajoz) killed in coastal missions. Their cause for beatification was formally opened in 1984.

**1606:** Bishop Altamirano, O.P., conducted visitation of the Georgia area.

**1612:** First Franciscan province in U.S. erected under title of Santa Elena; it included Georgia, South Carolina and Florida.

**1655:** Franciscans had nine flourishing missions among Indians.

**1742:** Spanish missions ended as result of English conquest at Battle of Bloody Marsh.

**1796:** Augustinian Father Le Mercier was first postcolonial missionary to Georgia.

**1798:** Catholics granted right of refuge.

**1800:** First church erected in Savannah on lot given by city council.

**1810:** First church erected in Augusta on lot given by State Legislature.

**1850:** Savannah diocese established; became Savannah-Atlanta, 1937; divided into two separate sees, 1956.

**1864:** Father Emmeran Bliemel, of the Benedictine community of Latrobe, Pa., was killed at the battle of Jonesboro while serving as chaplain of the Confederate 10th Tennessee Artillery.

**1962:** Atlanta made metropolitan see.

## Hawaii

**1825:** Pope Leo XII entrusted missionary efforts in Islands to Sacred Hearts Fathers.

**1827:** The first Catholic missionaries arrived — Fathers Alexis Bachelot, Abraham Armand and Patrick Short, along with three lay brothers. After three years of persecution, the priests were forcibly exiled.

**1836:** Father Arsenius Walsh, SS. CC., a British subject, was allowed to remain in Islands but was not permitted to proselytize or conduct missions.

**1839:** Hawaiian government signed treaty with France granting Catholics freedom of worship and same privileges as Protestants.

**1844:** Vicariate Apostolic of Sandwich Islands (Hawaii) erected.

**1873:** Father Damien de Veuster of the Sacred Hearts Fathers arrived in Molokai and spent the remainder of his life working among lepers. He was beatified in 1995.

**1941:** Honolulu diocese established, made a suffragan of San Francisco.

## Idaho

**1840:** Jesuit Pierre de Smet preached to the Flathead and Pend d'Oreille Indians; probably offered first Mass in state.

**1842:** Jesuit Nicholas Point opened a mission among Coeur d'Alene Indians near St. Maries.

**1863:** Secular priests sent from Oregon City to administer to incoming miners.

**1867:** Sisters of Holy Names of Jesus and Mary opened first Catholic school at Idaho City.

**1868:** Idaho made a vicariate apostolic.

**1870:** First church in Boise established. Church lost most of missions among Indians of Northwest Territory when Commission on Indian Affairs appointed Protestant missionaries to take over.

**1893:** Boise diocese established.

## Illinois

**1673:** Jesuit Jacques Marquette, accompanying Joliet, preached to Indians.

**1674:** Father Marquette set up a cabin for saying Mass in what later became City of Chicago.

**1675:** Father Marquette established Mission of the Immaculate Conception among Kaskaskia Indians, near present site of Utica; transferred to Kaskaskia, 1703.

**1679:** La Salle brought with him Franciscans Louis Hennepin, Gabriel de la Ribourde, and Zenobius Membre.

**1680:** Father Ribourde was killed by Kickapoo Indians.

**1689:** Jesuit Claude Allouez died after 32 years of missionary activity among Indians of Midwest; he had evangelized Indians of 20 different tribes. Jesuit Jacques Gravier succeeded Allouez as vicar general of Illinois.

**1699:** Mission established at Cahokia, first permanent settlement in state.

**1730:** Father Gaston, a diocesan priest, was killed at the Cahokia Mission.

**1763:** Jesuits were banished from the territory.

**1778:** Father Pierre Gibault championed Colonial cause in the Revolution and aided greatly in securing states of Ohio, Indiana, Illinois, Michigan and Wisconsin for Americans.

**1827:** The present St. Patrick's Parish at Ruma, oldest English-speaking Catholic congregation in state, was founded.

**1833:** Visitation Nuns established residence in Kaskaskia.

**1843:** Chicago diocese established.
**1853:** Quincy diocese established; transferred to Alton, 1857; Springfield, 1923. (Quincy and Alton were reestablished as titular sees in 1995.)
**1860:** Quincy College founded.
**1877:** Peoria diocese established.
**1880:** Chicago made archdiocese.
**1887:** Belleville diocese established.
**1894:** Franciscan Sisters of Bl. Kunegunda (now the Franciscan Sisters of Chicago) founded by Mother Marie Therese (Josephine Dudzik).
**1908:** Rockford diocese established.
First American Missionary Congress held in Chicago.
**1924:** Archbishop Mundelein of Chicago made cardinal by Pope Pius XI.
**1926:** The 28th International Eucharistic Congress, first held in U.S., convened in Chicago.
**1946:** Blessed Frances Xavier Cabrini, former resident of Chicago, was canonized; first U.S. citizen raised to dignity of altar.
Archbishop Samuel A. Stritch of Chicago made cardinal by Pope Pius XII.
**1948:** Joliet diocese established.
**1958:** Cardinal Stritch appointed Pro-Prefect of the Sacred Congregation for the Propagation of the Faith — the first U.S.-born prelate to be named to the Roman Curia.
**1959:** Archbishop Albert G. Meyer of Chicago made cardinal by Pope John XXIII.
**1961:** Eparchy of St. Nicholas of the Ukrainians established at Chicago.
**1967:** Archbishop John P. Cody of Chicago made cardinal by Pope Paul VI.
**1983:** Archbishop Joseph L. Bernardin of Chicago made cardinal by Pope John Paul II.

## Indiana

**1679:** Recollects Louis Hennepin and Gabriel de la Ribourde passed through state.
**1686:** Land near present Notre Dame University at South Bend given by French government to Jesuits for mission.
**1749:** Beginning of the records of St. Francis Xavier Church, Vincennes. These records continue with minor interruptions to the present.
**1778:** Father Gibault aided George Rogers Clark in campaign against British in conquest of Northwest Territory.
**1824:** Sisters of Charity of Nazareth, Ky., opened St. Clare's Academy in Vincennes.
**1825:** Laying of cornerstone of third church of St. Francis Xavier, which later (from 1834-98) was the cathedral of the Vincennes diocese. The church was designated a minor basilica in 1970 and is still in use as a parish church.
**1834:** Vincennes diocese established with Simon Gabriel Brute as bishop; title transferred to Indianapolis, 1898. (Vincennes was reestablished as a titular see in 1995.)
**1840:** Sisters of Providence founded St. Mary-of-the-Woods College for women.
**1842:** University of Notre Dame founded by Holy Cross Father Edward Sorin and Brothers of St. Joseph on land given the diocese of Vincennes by Father Stephen Badin.

**1853:** First Benedictine community established in state at St. Meinrad. It became an abbey in 1870 and an archabbey in 1954.
**1857:** Fort Wayne diocese established; changed to Fort Wayne-South Bend, 1960.
**1944:** Indianapolis made archdiocese. Lafayette and Evansville dioceses established.
**1957:** Gary diocese established.

## Iowa

**1673:** A Peoria village on Mississippi was visited by Father Marquette.
**1679:** Fathers Louis Hennepin and Gabriel de la Ribourde visited Indian villages.
**1836:** First permanent church, St. Raphael's, founded at Dubuque by Dominican Samuel Mazzuchelli.
**1837:** Dubuque diocese established.
**1838:** St. Joseph's Mission founded at Council Bluffs by Jesuit Father De Smet.
**1843:** Sisters of Charity of the Blessed Virgin Mary was first sisterhood in state.
Sisters of Charity opened Clarke College, Dubuque.
**1850:** First Trappist Monastery in state, Our Lady of New Melleray, was begun.
**1881:** Davenport diocese established.
**1882:** St. Ambrose College (now University), Davenport, established.
**1893:** Dubuque made archdiocese.
**1902:** Sioux City diocese established.
**1911:** Des Moines diocese established.

## Kansas

**1542:** Franciscan Juan de Padilla, first martyr of the United States, was killed in central Kansas.
**1858:** St. Benedict's College (now Benedictine College) founded.
**1863:** Sisters of Charity opened orphanage at Leavenworth, and St. John's Hospital in following year.
**1877:** Leavenworth diocese established; transferred to Kansas City in 1947. (Leavenworth was reestablished as a titular see in 1995.)
**1887:** Dioceses of Wichita and Concordia established. Concordia was transferred to Salina in 1944.(Concordia was reestablished as a titular see in 1995.)
**1888:** Oblate Sisters of Providence opened an orphanage for African-American boys at Leavenworth, first west of Mississippi.
**1951:** Dodge City diocese established.
**1952:** Kansas City made archdiocese.

## Kentucky

**1775:** First Catholic settlers came to Kentucky.
**1787:** Father Charles Maurice Whelan, first resident priest, ministered to settlers in the Bardstown district.
**1793:** Father Stephen T. Badin began missionary work in Kentucky.
**1806:** Dominican Fathers built Priory at St. Rose of Lima.
**1808:** Bardstown diocese established with Benedict Flaget as its first bishop; see transferred to Louisville, 1841. (Bardstown was reestablished as a titular see in 1995.)

**1811:** Rev. Guy I. Chabrat first priest ordained west of the Allegheny Mountains.
St. Thomas Seminary founded.
**1812:** Sisters of Loretto founded by Rev. Charles Nerinckx; first religious community in the United States without foreign affiliation.
Sisters of Charity of Nazareth founded, the second native community of women founded in the West.
**1814:** Nazareth College for women established.
**1816:** Cornerstone of St. Joseph's Cathedral, Bardstown, laid.
**1822:** First foundation of Dominican Sisters in the U.S. established near Springfield.
**1836:** Hon. Benedict J. Webb founded *Catholic Advocate*, first Catholic weekly newspaper in Kentucky.
**1848:** Trappist monks took up residence in Gethsemani.
**1849:** Cornerstone of Cathedral of the Assumption laid at Louisville.
**1852:** Know-Nothing troubles in state.
**1853:** Covington diocese established.
**1937:** Louisville made archdiocese. Owensboro diocese established.
**1988:** Lexington diocese established.

## Louisiana

**1682:** La Salle's expedition, accompanied by two priests, completed discoveries of De Soto at mouth of Mississippi. LaSalle named territory Louisiana.
**1699:** French Catholics founded colony of Louisiana.
First recorded Mass offered Mar. 3, by Franciscan Father Anastase Douay.
**1706:** Father John Francis Buisson de St. Cosme was killed near Donaldsonville.
**1717:** Franciscan Anthony Margil established first Spanish mission in north central Louisiana.
**1718:** City of New Orleans founded by Jean Baptiste Le Moyne de Bienville.
**1720:** First resident priest in New Orleans was the French Recollect Prothais Boyer.
**1725:** Capuchin Fathers opened school for boys.
**1727:** Ursuline Nuns founded convent in New Orleans, oldest convent in what is now U.S.; they conducted a school, hospital and orphan asylum.
**1793:** New Orleans diocese established.
**1842:** Sisters of Holy Family, a black congregation, founded at New Orleans by Henriette Delille and Juliette Gaudin.
**1850:** New Orleans made archdiocese.
**1853:** Natchitoches diocese established; transferred to Alexandria in 1910; became Alexandria-Shreveport in 1977; redesignated Alexandria, 1986. (Natchitoches diocese reestablished as a titular see in 1995.)
**1912:** Loyola University of South established.
**1918:** Lafayette diocese established.
**1925:** Xavier University established in New Orleans.
**1961:** Baton Rouge diocese established.
**1962:** Catholic schools on all levels desegregated in New Orleans archdiocese.
**1977:** Houma-Thibodaux diocese established.
**1980:** Lake Charles diocese established.
**1986:** Shreveport diocese established.

## Maine

**1604:** First Mass in territory celebrated by Father Nicholas Aubry, accompanying De Monts' expedition which was authorized by King of France to begin colonizing region.
**1605:** Colony founded on St. Croix Island; two secular priests served as chaplains.
**1613:** Four Jesuits attempted to establish permanent French settlement near mouth of Kennebec River.
**1619:** French Franciscans began work among settlers and Indians; driven out by English in 1628.
**1630:** New England made a prefecture apostolic in charge of French Capuchins.
**1633:** Capuchin Fathers founded missions on Penobscot River.
**1646:** Jesuits established Assumption Mission on Kennebec River.
**1688:** Church of St. Anne, oldest in New England, built at Oldtown.
**1704:** English soldiers destroyed French missions.
**1724:** English forces again attacked French settlements, killed Jesuit Sebastian Rale.
**1853:** Portland diocese established.
**1854:** Know-Nothing uprising resulted in burning of church in Bath.
**1856:** Anti-Catholic feeling continued; church at Ellsworth burned.
**1864:** Sisters of Congregation of Notre Dame from Montreal opened academy at Portland.
**1875:** James A. Healy, first bishop of Negro blood consecrated in U.S., became second Bishop of Portland.

## Maryland

**1634:** Maryland established by Lord Calvert. Two Jesuits among first colonists.
First Mass offered on Island of St. Clement in Lower Potomac by Jesuit Father Andrew White.
St. Mary's City founded by English and Irish Catholics.
**1641:** St. Ignatius Parish founded by English Jesuits at Chapel Point, near Port Tobacco.
**1649:** Religious Toleration Act passed by Maryland Assembly. It was repealed in 1654 by Puritan-controlled government.
**1651:** Cecil Calvert, second Lord Baltimore, gave Jesuits 10,000 acres for use as Indian mission.
**1658:** Lord Baltimore restored Toleration Act.
**1672:** Franciscans came to Maryland under leadership of Father Massius Massey.
**1688:** Maryland became royal colony as a result of the Revolution in England; Anglican Church became the official religion (1692); Toleration Act repealed; Catholics disenfranchised and persecuted until 1776.
**1704:** Jesuits founded St. Francis Xavier Mission, Old Bohemia, to serve Catholics of Delaware, Maryland and southeastern Pennsylvania; its Bohemia Academy established in the 1740s was attended by sons of prominent Catholics in the area.
**1784:** Father John Carroll appointed prefect apostolic for the territory embraced by new Republic.
**1789:** Baltimore became first diocese established in U.S., with John Carroll as first bishop.
**1790:** Carmelite Nuns founded convent at Port To-

bacco, the first in the English-speaking Colonies.

**1791:** First Synod of Baltimore held.

St. Mary's Seminary, first seminary in U.S., established.

**1793:** Rev. Stephen T. Badin first priest ordained by Bishop Carroll.

**1800:** Jesuit Leonard Neale became first bishop consecrated in present limits of U.S.

**1806:** Cornerstone of Assumption Cathedral, Baltimore, was laid.

**1808:** Baltimore made archdiocese.

**1809:** St. Joseph's College, Emmitsburg, founded (closed in 1973).

Sisters of Charity of St. Joseph founded by St. Elizabeth Ann Seton; first native American sisterhood.

**1821:** Assumption Cathedral, Baltimore, formally opened.

**1829:** Oblate Sisters of Providence, first congregation of black sisters, established at Baltimore by Mother Mary Elizabeth Lange.

First Provincial Council of Baltimore held; six others followed, in 1833, 1837, 1840, 1843, 1846 and 1849.

**1836:** Roger B. Taney appointed Chief Justice of Supreme Court by President Jackson.

**1852:** First of the three Plenary Councils of Baltimore convened. Subsequent councils were held in 1866 and 1884.

**1855:** German Catholic Central Verein founded.

**1886:** Archbishop James Gibbons of Baltimore made cardinal by Pope Leo XIII.

**1965:** Archbishop Lawrence Shehan of Baltimore made cardinal by Pope Paul VI.

**1994:** Archbishop William H. Keeler of Baltimore made cardinal by Pope John Paul II.

## Massachusetts

**1630:** New England made a prefecture apostolic in charge of French Capuchins.

**1647:** Massachusetts Bay Company enacted an anti-priest law.

**1688:** Hanging of Ann Glover, an elderly Irish Catholic widow, who refused to renounce her Catholic religion.

**1732:** Although Catholics were not legally admitted to colony, a few Irish families were in Boston; a priest was reported working among them.

**1755-56:** Acadians landing in Boston were denied services of a Catholic priest.

**1775:** General Washington discouraged Guy Fawkes Day procession in which pope was carried in effigy, and expressed surprise that there were men in his army "so void of common sense as to insult the religious feelings of the Canadians with whom friendship and an alliance are being sought."

**1780:** The Massachusetts State Constitution granted religious liberty, but required a religious test to hold public office and provided for tax to support Protestant teachers of piety, religion and morality.

**1788:** First public Mass said in Boston on Nov. 2 by Abbe de la Poterie, first resident priest.

**1803:** Church of Holy Cross erected in Boston with financial aid given by Protestants headed by John Adams.

**1808:** Boston diocese established.

**1831:** Irish Catholic immigration increased.

**1832:** St. Vincent's Orphan Asylum, oldest charitable institution in Boston, opened by Sisters of Mercy.

**1834:** Ursuline Convent in Charlestown burned by a Nativist mob.

**1843:** Holy Cross College founded.

**1855:** Catholic militia companies disbanded; nunneries' inspection bill passed.

**1859:** St. Mary's, first parochial school in Boston, opened.

**1860:** Portuguese Catholics from Azores settled in New Bedford.

**1870:** Springfield diocese established.

**1875:** Boston made archdiocese.

**1904:** Fall River diocese established.

**1911:** Archbishop O'Connell of Boston made cardinal by Pope Pius X.

**1950:** Worcester diocese established.

**1958:** Archbishop Richard J. Cushing of Boston made cardinal by Pope John XXIII.

**1966:** Apostolic Exarchate for Melkites in the U.S. established, with headquarters in Boston; made an eparchy (Newton) in 1976.

**1973:** Archbishop Humberto S. Medeiros of Boston made cardinal by Pope Paul VI.

**1985:** Archbishop Bernard F. Law of Boston made a cardinal by Pope John Paul II.

## Michigan

**1641:** Jesuits Isaac Jogues and Charles Raymbaut preached to Chippewas; named the rapids Sault Sainte Marie.

**1660:** Jesuit Rene Menard opened first regular mission in Lake Superior region.

**1668:** Father Marquette founded Sainte Marie Mission at Sault Sainte Marie.

**1671:** Father Marquette founded St. Ignace Mission on north shore of Straits of Mackinac.

**1701:** Fort Pontchartrain founded on present site of Detroit and placed in command of Antoine de la Mothe Cadillac. The Chapel of Sainte-Anne-de-Detroit founded.

**1706:** Franciscan Father Delhalle killed by Indians at Detroit.

**1823:** Father Gabriel Richard elected delegate to Congress from Michigan territory; he was the first priest chosen for the House of Representatives.

**1833:** Father Frederic Baraga celebrated first Mass in present Grand Rapids.

Detroit diocese established, embracing whole Northwest Territory.

**1843:** *Western Catholic Register* founded at Detroit.

**1845:** St. Vincent's Hospital, Detroit, opened by Sisters of Charity.

**1848:** Cathedral of Sts. Peter and Paul, Detroit, consecrated.

**1853:** Vicariate Apostolic of Upper Michigan established.

**1857:** Sault Ste. Marie diocese established; later transferred to Marquette. (Sault Ste. Marie reestablished as a titular see in 1995.)

**1877:** University of Detroit founded.

**1882:** Grand Rapids diocese established.

**1897:** Nazareth College for women founded.

**1937:** Detroit made archdiocese. Lansing diocese established.

**1938:** Saginaw diocese established.
**1946:** Archbishop Edward Mooney of Detroit created cardinal by Pope Pius XII.
**1949:** Opening of St. John's Theological (major) Seminary at Plymouth; this was first seminary in U.S. serving an entire ecclesiastical province (Detroit).
**1966:** Apostolic Exarchate for Maronites in the United States established, with headquarters in Detroit; made an eparchy in 1972; transferred to Brooklyn, 1977.
**1969:** Archbishop John Dearden of Detroit made cardinal by Pope Paul VI.
**1971:** Gaylord and Kalamazoo dioceses established.
**1982:** Apostolic Exarchate for Chaldean-Rite Catholics in United States established. Detroit designated see city; made an eparchy, 1985, under title St. Thomas Apostle of Detroit.
**1988:** Archbishop Edmund C. Szoka of Detroit made a cardinal by Pope John Paul II; transferred to Roman Curia in 1990.
**1994:** Archbishop Adam J. Maida of Detroit made cardinal by Pope John Paul II.

## Minnesota

**1680:** Falls of St. Anthony discovered by Franciscan Louis Hennepin.
**1727:** First chapel, St. Michael the Archangel, erected near town of Frontenac and placed in charge of French Jesuits.
**1732:** Fort St. Charles built; Jesuits ministered to settlers.
**1736:** Jesuit Jean Pierre Aulneau killed by Indians.
**1839:** Swiss Catholics from Canada settled near Fort Snelling; Bishop Loras of Dubuque, accompanied by Father Pellamourgues, visited the Fort and administered sacraments.
**1841:** Father Lucian Galtier built Church of St. Paul, thus forming nucleus of modern city of same name.
**1850:** St. Paul diocese established.
**1851:** Sisters of St. Joseph arrived in state.
**1857:** St. John's University founded.
**1888:** St. Paul made archdiocese; name changed to St. Paul and Minneapolis in 1966.
**1889:** Duluth, St. Cloud and Winona dioceses established.
**1909:** Crookston diocese established.
**1957:** New Ulm diocese established.

## Mississippi

**1540:** Chaplains with De Soto expedition entered territory.
**1682:** Franciscans Zenobius Membre and Anastase Douay preached to Taensa and Natchez Indians. Father Membre offered first recorded Mass in the state on Mar. 29, Easter Sunday.
**1698:** Priests of Quebec Seminary founded missions near Natchez and Fort Adams.
**1702:** Father Nicholas Foucault murdered by Indians near Fort Adams.
**1721:** Missions practically abandoned, with only Father Juif working among Yazoos.
**1725:** Jesuit Mathurin de Petit carried on mission work in northern Mississippi.
**1729:** Indians tomahawked Jesuit Paul du Poisson near Fort Rosalie; Father Jean Souel shot by Yazoos.

**1736:** Jesuit Antoine Senat and seven French officers burned at stake by Chickasaws.
**1822:** Vicariate Apostolic of Mississippi and Alabama established.
**1825:** Mississippi made a separate vicariate apostolic.
**1837:** Natchez diocese established; became Natchez-Jackson in 1956; transferred to Jackson in 1977.
(Natchez was established as a titular see.)
**1848:** Sisters of Charity opened orphan asylum and school in Natchez.
**1977:** Biloxi diocese established.

## Missouri

**1700:** Jesuit Gabriel Marest established a mission among Kaskaskia Indians near St. Louis.
**1734:** French Catholic miners and traders settled Old Mines and Sainte Genevieve.
**1750:** Jesuits visited French settlers.
**1762:** Mission established at St. Charles.
**1767:** Carondelet mission established.
**1770:** First church founded at St. Louis.
**1811:** Jesuits established Indian mission school at Florissant.
**1818:** Bishop Dubourg arrived at St. Louis, with Vincentians Joseph Rosati and Felix de Andreis. St. Louis University, the diocesan (Kenrick) seminary and the Vincentian Seminary in Perryville trace their origins to them.
Rose Philippine Duchesne arrived at St. Charles; founded first American convent of the Society of the Sacred Heart; missionary; beatified 1940; canonized 1988.
**1826:** St. Louis diocese established.
**1828:** Sisters of Charity opened first hospital west of the Mississippi, at St. Louis.
**1832:** *The Shepherd of the Valley,* first Catholic paper west of the Mississippi.
**1845:** First conference of Society of St. Vincent de Paul in U.S. founded at St. Louis.
**1847:** St. Louis made archdiocese.
**1865:** A Test Oath Law passed by State Legislature (called Drake Convention) to crush Catholicism in Missouri. Law declared unconstitutional by Supreme Court in 1866.
**1867:** College of St. Teresa for women founded at Kansas City.
**1868:** St. Joseph diocese established.
**1880:** Kansas City diocese established.
**1946:** Archbishop John J. Glennon of St. Louis made cardinal by Pope Pius XII.
**1956:** Kansas City and St. Joseph dioceses combined into one see. Jefferson City and Springfield-Cape Girardeau dioceses established.
**1961:** Archbishop Joseph E. Ritter of St. Louis made cardinal by Pope John XXIII.
**1969:** Archbishop John J. Carberry of St. Louis made cardinal by Pope Paul VI.

## Montana

**1743:** Pierre and Francois Verendrye, accompanied by Jesuit Father Coquart, may have explored territory.
**1833:** Indian missions handed over to care of Jesuits by Second Provincial Council of Baltimore.

**1840:** Jesuit Pierre De Smet began missionary work among Flathead and Pend d'Oreille Indians.

**1841:** St. Mary's Mission established by Father De Smet and two companions on the Bitter Root River in present Stevensville.

**1845:** Jesuit Antonio Ravalli arrived at St. Mary's Mission; Ravalli County named in his honor.

**1859:** Fathers Point and Hoecken established St. Peter's Mission near the Great Falls.

**1869:** Sisters of Charity founded a hospital and school in Helena.

**1884:** Helena diocese established.

**1904:** Great Falls diocese established; redesignated Great Falls-Billings in 1980.

**1909:** Carroll College founded.

**1935:** Rev. Joseph M. Gilmore became first Montana priest elevated to hierarchy.

## Nebraska

**1541:** Coronado expedition, accompanied by Franciscan Juan de Padilla, reached the Platte River.

**1673:** Father Marquette visited Nebraska Indians.

**1720:** Franciscan Juan Miguel killed by Indians near Columbus.

**1855:** Father J. F. Tracy administered to Catholic settlement of St. Patrick and to Catholics in Omaha.

**1856:** Land was donated by Governor Alfred Cumming for a church in Omaha.

**1857:** Nebraska vicariate apostolic established.

**1878:** Creighton University established.

**1881:** Poor Clares, first contemplative group in state, arrived in Omaha.
Duchesne College established.

**1885:** Omaha diocese established.

**1887:** Lincoln diocese established.

**1912:** Kearney diocese established; transferred to Grand Island, 1917. (Kearney was reestablished as a titular see in 1995.)

**1917:** Father Edward Flanagan founded Boy's Town for homeless boys, an institution which gained national and international recognition in subsequent years.

**1945:** Omaha made archdiocese.

## Nevada

**1774:** Franciscan missionaries passed through Nevada on way to California missions.

**1860:** First parish, serving Genoa, Carson City and Virginia City, established.

**1862:** Rev. Patrick Manogue appointed pastor of Virginia City. He established a school for boys and girls, an orphanage and hospital.

**1871:** Church erected at Reno.

**1931:** Reno diocese established; name changed to Reno-Las Vegas, 1977.

**1995:** Reno-Las Vegas made two separate dioceses.

## New Hampshire

**1630:** Territory made part of a prefecture apostolic embracing all of New England.

**1784:** State Constitution included a religious test which barred Catholics from public office; local support was provided for public Protestant teachers of religion.

**1818:** The Barber family of Claremont was visited by their son Virgil (converted to Catholicism in 1816) accompanied by Father Charles Ffrench, O.P. The visit led to the conversion of the entire Barber family.

**1823:** Father Virgil Barber, minister who became a Jesuit priest, built first Catholic church and school at Claremont.

**1830:** Church of St. Aloysius dedicated at Dover.

**1853:** New Hampshire made part of the Portland diocese.

**1858:** Sisters of Mercy began to teach school at St. Anne's, Manchester.

**1877:** Catholics obtained full civil liberty and rights.

**1884:** Manchester diocese established.

**1893:** St. Anselm's College opened; St. Anselm's Abbey canonically erected.

**1937:** Francis P. Murphy became first Catholic governor of New Hampshire.

## New Jersey

**1668:** William Douglass of Bergen was refused a seat in General Assembly because he was a Catholic.

**1672:** Fathers Harvey and Gage visited Catholics in Woodbridge and Elizabethtown.

**1701:** Tolerance granted to all but "papists."

**1744:** Jesuit Theodore Schneider of Pennsylvania visited German Catholics of New Jersey.

**1762:** Fathers Ferdinand Farmer and Robert Harding working among Catholics in state.

**1765:** First Catholic community organized in New Jersey at Macopin in Passaic County.

**1776:** State Constitution tacitly excluded Catholics from office.

**1799:** Foundation of first Catholic school in state, St. John's at Trenton.

**1814:** First church in Trenton erected.

**1820:** Father Richard Bulger, of St. John's, Paterson, first resident pastor in state.

**1844:** Catholics obtained full civil liberty and rights.

**1853:** Newark diocese established.

**1856:** Seton Hall University established.

**1878:** John P. Holland, teacher at St. John's School, Paterson, invented first workable submarine.

**1881:** Trenton diocese established.

**1937:** Newark made archdiocese. Paterson and Camden dioceses established.

**1947:** U.S. Supreme Court ruled on N.J. bus case, permitting children attending non-public schools to ride on buses and be given other health services provided for those in public schools.

**1957:** Seton Hall College of Medicine and Dentistry established: the first medical school in state; it was run by Seton Hall until 1965.

**1963:** Byzantine Eparchy of Passaic established.

**1981:** Metuchen diocese established.

**1995:** Eparchy of Our Lady of the Deliverance of Newark for Syrian-rite Catholics of the U.S. and Canada was established.

## New Mexico

**1539:** Territory explored by Franciscan Marcos de Niza.

**1581:** Franciscans Agustin Rodriguez, Juan de Santa Maria and Francisco Lopez named the region "New Mexico"; they later died at hands of Indians.

**1598:** Juan de Onate founded a colony at Chamita, where first chapel in state was built.

**1609-10:** Santa Fe founded.

**1631:** Franciscan Pedro de Miranda was killed by Indians.

**1632:** Franciscan Francisco Letrado was killed by Indians.

**1672:** Franciscan Pedro de Avila y Ayala was killed by Indians.

**1675:** Franciscan Alonso Gil de Avila was killed by Indians.

**1680:** Pueblo Indian revolt; 21 Franciscan missionaries massacred; missions destroyed.

**1692:** Franciscan missions refounded and expanded.

**1696:** Indians rebelled, five more Franciscan missionaries killed.

**1850:** Jean Baptiste Lamy appointed head of newly established Vicariate Apostolic of New Mexico.

**1852:** Sisters of Loretto arrived in Santa Fe.

**1853:** Santa Fe diocese established.

**1859:** Christian Brothers arrived, established first school for boys in New Mexico (later St. Michael's College).

**1865:** Sisters of Charity started first orphanage and hospital in Santa Fe. It was closed in 1966.

**1875:** Santa Fe made archdiocese.

**1939:** Gallup diocese established.

**1982:** Las Cruces diocese established.

## New York

**1524:** Giovanni da Verrazano was first white man to enter New York Bay.

**1642:** Jesuits Isaac Jogues and Rene Goupil were mutilated by Mohawks; Rene Goupil was killed by them shortly afterwards. Dutch Calvinists rescued Father Jogues.

**1646:** Jesuit Isaac Jogues and John Lalande were martyred by Iroquois at Ossernenon, now Auriesville.

**1654:** The Onondagas were visited by Jesuits from Canada.

**1655:** First permanent mission established near Syracuse.

**1656:** Church of St. Mary erected on Onondaga Lake, in first French settlement in state. Kateri Tekakwitha, "Lily of the Mohawks," was born at Ossernenon, now Auriesville (d. in Canada, 1680). She was beatified in 1980.

**1658:** Indian uprisings destroyed missions among Cayugas, Senecas and Oneidas.

**1664:** English took New Amsterdam. Freedom of conscience allowed by the Duke of York, the new Lord Proprietor.

**1667:** Missions were restored under protection of Garaconthie, Onondaga chief.

**1678:** Franciscan Louis Hennepin, first white man to describe Niagara Falls, celebrated Mass there.

**1682:** Thomas Dongan appointed governor by Duke of York.

**1683:** English Jesuits came to New York, later opened a school.

**1700:** Although Assembly enacted a bill calling for religious toleration of all Christians in 1683, other penal laws were now enforced against Catholics; all priests were ordered out of the province.

**1709:** French Jesuit missionaries obliged to give up their central New York missions.

**1741:** Because of an alleged popish plot to burn city of New York, four whites were hanged and 11 blacks burned at stake.

**1774:** Elizabeth Bayley Seton, foundress of the American Sisters of Charity, was born in New York City on Aug. 28. She was canonized in 1975.

**1777:** State Constitution gave religious liberty, but the naturalization law required an oath to renounce allegiance to any foreign ruler, ecclesiastical as well as civil.

**1785:** Cornerstone was laid for St. Peter's Church, New York City, first permanent structure of Catholic worship in state.

Trusteeism began to cause trouble at New York.

**1806:** Anti-Catholic 1777 Test Oath for naturalization repealed.

**1808:** New York diocese established.

**1823:** Father Felix Varela of Cuba, educator, theologian and social reformer, arrived in New York; established churches and charitable organizations; published journals and philosophical works.

**1828:** New York State Legislature enacted a law upholding sanctity of seal of confession.

**1834:** First native New Yorker to become a secular priest, Rev. John McCloskey, was ordained.

**1836:** John Nepomucene Neumann arrived from Bohemia and was ordained a priest in Old St. Patrick's Cathedral, New York City. He was canonized in 1977.

**1841:** Fordham University and Manhattanville College established.

**1847:** Albany and Buffalo dioceses established.

**1850:** New York made archdiocese.

**1853:** Brooklyn diocese established.

**1856:** Present St. Bonaventure University and Christ the King Seminary founded at Allegany.

**1858:** Cornerstone was laid of second (present) St. Patrick's Cathedral, New York City. The cathedral was completed in 1879.

**1868:** Rochester diocese established.

**1872:** Ogdensburg diocese established.

**1875:** Archbishop John McCloskey of New York made first American cardinal by Pope Pius IX.

**1878:** Franciscan Sisters of Allegany were first native American community to send members to foreign missions.

**1880:** William R. Grace was first Catholic mayor of New York City.

**1886:** Syracuse diocese established.

**1889:** Mother Frances Xavier Cabrini arrived in New York City to begin work among Italian immigrants. She was canonized in 1946.

**1911:** Archbishop John M. Farley of New York made cardinal by Pope Pius X.

Catholic Foreign Mission Society of America (Maryknoll) opened a seminary for foreign missions, the first of its kind in U.S. The Maryknollers were also unique as the first U.S.-established foreign mission society.

**1917:** Military Ordinariate established with headquarters at New York; renamed Military Archdiocese and transferred to Washington, D.C., in 1985.

**1919:** Alfred E. Smith became first elected Catholic governor.

**1924:** Archbishop Patrick Hayes of New York made cardinal by Pope Pius XI.

**1930:** Jesuit Martyrs of New York and Canada were canonized on June 29.
**1946:** Archbishop Francis J. Spellman of New York made cardinal by Pope Pius XII.
**1957:** Rockville Centre diocese established.
**1969:** Archbishop Terence Cooke of New York made cardinal by Pope Paul VI.
**1981:** Apostolic Exarchate for Armenian-Rite Catholics in the United States and Canada established. New York designated see city.
**1985:** Archbishop John J. O'Connor of New York made cardinal by Pope John Paul II.

## North Carolina

**1526:** The Ayllon expedition attempted to establish a settlement on Carolina coast.
**1540:** De Soto expedition, accompanied by chaplains, entered state.
**1776:** State Constitution denied office to "those who denied the truths of the Protestant religion."
**1805:** The few Catholics in state were served by visiting missionaries.
**1821:** Bishop John England of Charleston celebrated Mass in the ballroom of the home of William Gaston at New Bern, marking the start of organization of the first parish, St. Paul's, in the state.
**1835:** William Gaston, State Supreme Court Justice, succeeded in having the article denying religious freedom repealed.
**1852:** First Catholic church erected in Charlotte.
**1868:** North Carolina vicariate apostolic established. Catholics obtained full civil liberty and rights.
**1874:** Sisters of Mercy arrived, opened an academy, several schools, hospitals and an orphanage.
**1876:** Benedictine priory and school (later Belmont Abbey College) founded at Belmont; priory designated an abbey in 1884.
**1910:** Belmont Abbey established as an abbacy nullius; abbacy nullius status suppressed in 1977.
**1924:** Raleigh diocese established.
**1971:** Charlotte diocese established.

## North Dakota

**1742:** Pierre and Francois Verendrye, accompanied by Jesuit Father Coquart, explored territory.
**1818:** Canadian priests ministered to Catholics in area.
**1840:** Jesuit Father De Smet made first of several trips among Mandan and Gros Ventre Indians.
**1848:** Father George Belcourt, first American resident priest in territory, reestablished Pembina Mission.
**1874:** Grey Nuns arrived at Fort Totten to conduct a school.
**1889:** Jamestown diocese established; transferred to Fargo in 1897. (Jamestown was reestablished as a titular see in 1995.)
**1893:** Benedictines founded St. Gall Monastery at Devil's Lake. (It was moved to Richardton in 1899 and became an abbey in 1903.)
**1909:** Bismarck diocese established.
**1959:** Archbishop Aloysius J. Muench, bishop of Fargo, made cardinal by Pope John XXIII.

## Ohio

**1749:** Jesuits in expedition of Céleron de Blainville preached to Indians.

First religious services were held within present limits of Ohio. Jesuit Joseph de Bonnecamps celebrated Mass at mouth of Little Miami River and in other places.
**1751:** First Catholic settlement founded among Huron Indians near Sandusky by Jesuit Father de la Richardie.
**1790:** Benedictine Pierre Didier ministered to French immigrants.
**1812:** Bishop Flaget of Bardstown visited and baptized Catholics of Lancaster and Somerset Counties.
**1818:** Dominican Father Edward Fenwick (later first bishop of Cincinnati) built St. Joseph's Church.
**1821:** Cincinnati diocese established.
**1830:** At request of Bishop Fenwick Dominican Sisters from Kentucky established second Dominican foundation in U.S. at Somerset (transferred to Columbus in 1868).
**1831:** Xavier University founded.
**1843:** Members of Congregation of Most Precious Blood arrived in Cincinnati from Switzerland.
**1845:** Cornerstone laid for St. Peter's Cathedral, Cincinnati.
**1847:** Cleveland diocese established.
**1850:** Cincinnati made archdiocese.
Marianists opened St. Mary's Institute, now University of Dayton.
**1865:** Sisters of Charity opened hospital in Cleveland, first institution of its kind in city.
**1868:** Columbus diocese established.
**1871:** Ursuline College for women opened at Cleveland.
**1910:** Toledo diocese established.
**1935:** Archbishop John T. McNicholas, O.P., founded the Institutum Divi Thomae in Cincinnati for fundamental research in natural sciences.
**1943:** Youngstown diocese established.
**1944:** Steubenville diocese established.
**1969:** Byzantine Rite Eparchy of Parma (for Ruthenians) established.
**1982:** Apostolic Exarchate for Romanian Byzantine-Rite Catholics in the United States established. Canton designated see city. Raised to an eparchy (St. George Martyr) 1987.
**1983:** Byzantine Rite Eparchy of Saint Josaphat in Parma (for Ukrainians) established.

## Oklahoma

**1540:** De Soto expedition, accompanied by chaplains, explored territory.
**1541:** Coronado expedition, accompanied by Franciscan Juan de Padilla, explored state.
**1630:** Spanish Franciscan Juan de Salas labored among Indians.
**1700:** Scattered Catholic families were visited by priests from Kansas and Arkansas.
**1874:** First Catholic church built by Father Smyth at Atoka.
**1876:** Prefecture Apostolic of Indian Territory established with Benedictine Isidore Robot as its head.
**1886:** First Catholic day school for Choctaw and white children opened by Sisters of Mercy at Krebs.
**1891:** Vicariate Apostolic of Oklahoma and Indian Territory established.

**1905:** Oklahoma diocese established; title changed to Oklahoma City and Tulsa, 1930.
**1917:** Benedictine Heights College for women founded.
Carmelite Sisters of St. Theresa of the Infant Jesus founded at Oklahoma City.
**1972:** Oklahoma City made archdiocese. Tulsa diocese established.

## Oregon

**1603:** Vizcaino explored northern Oregon coast.
**1774:** Franciscan missionaries accompanied Juan Perez on his expedition to coast, and Heceta a year later.
**1811:** Catholic Canadian trappers and traders with John J. Astor expedition founded first American settlement — Astoria.
**1834:** Indian missions in Northwest entrusted to Jesuits by Holy See.
**1838:** Abbe Blanchet appointed vicar general to Bishop of Quebec with jurisdiction over area which included Oregon Territory.
**1839:** First Mass celebrated at present site of St. Paul.
**1843:** Oregon vicariate apostolic established.
St. Joseph's College for boys opened.
**1844:** Jesuit Pierre de Smet established Mission of St. Francis Xavier near St. Paul.
Sisters of Notre Dame de Namur, first to enter Oregon, opened an academy for girls.
**1846:** Vicariate made an ecclesiastical province with Bishop Blanchet as first Archbishop of Oregon City (now Portland).
Walla Walla diocese established; suppressed in 1853.
**1847:** First priest was ordained in Oregon.
**1848:** First Provincial Council of Oregon.
**1857:** Death of Dr. John McLoughlin, "Father of Oregon."
**1865:** Rev. H. H. Spalding, a Protestant missionary, published the Whitman Myth to hinder work of Catholic missionaries.
**1874:** Catholic Indian Mission Bureau established.
**1875:** St. Vincent's Hospital, first in state, opened at Portland.
**1903:** Baker diocese established.
**1922:** Anti-private school bill sponsored by Scottish Rite Masons was passed by popular vote, 115,506 to 103,685.
**1925:** U.S. Supreme Court declared Oregon anti-private school bill unconstitutional.
**1953:** First Trappist monastery on West Coast established in Willamette Valley north of Lafayette.

## Pennsylvania

**1673:** Priests from Maryland ministered to Catholics in the Colony.
**1682:** Religious toleration was extended to members of all faiths.
**1729:** Jesuit Joseph Greaton became first resident missionary of Philadelphia.
**1734:** St. Joseph's Church, first Catholic church in Philadelphia, was opened by Father Greaton.
**1741:** Jesuit Fathers Schneider and Wappeler ministered to German immigrants.
Conewego Chapel, a combination chapel and dwelling, was built by Father William Wappeler, S.J., a priest sent to minister to the German Catholic immigrants who settled in the area in the 1730s.
**1782:** St. Mary's Parochial School opened at Philadelphia.
**1788:** Holy Trinity Church, Philadelphia, was incorporated; first exclusively national church organized in U.S.
**1797:** Augustinian Matthew Carr founded St. Augustine parish, Philadelphia.
**1799:** Prince Demetrius Gallitzin (Father Augustine Smith) built church in western Pennsylvania, at Loretto.
**1808:** Philadelphia diocese established.
**1814:** St. Joseph's Orphanage was opened at Philadelphia; first Catholic institution for children in U.S.
**1842:** University of Villanova founded by Augustinians.
**1843:** Pittsburgh diocese established.
**1844:** Thirteen persons killed, two churches and a school burned in Know-Nothing riots at Philadelphia.
**1846:** First Benedictine Abbey in New World founded near Latrobe by Father Boniface Wimmer.
**1852:** Redemptorist John Nepomucene Neumann became fourth bishop of Philadelphia. He was beatified in 1963 and canonized in 1977.
**1853:** Erie diocese established.
**1868:** Scranton and Harrisburg dioceses established.
**1871:** Chestnut Hill College, first for women in state, founded.
**1875:** Philadelphia made archdiocese.
**1876:** Allegheny diocese established by division of Pittsburgh diocese; reunited to Pittsburgh 1877, with resignation of its first and only bishop; suppressed in 1889. (It was later reestablished as a titular see.)
**1891:** Katharine Drexel founded Sisters of Blessed Sacrament for Indians and Colored Peoples. She was beatified in 1988.
**1901:** Altoona-Johnstown diocese established.
**1913:** Byzantine Rite Apostolic Exarchate of Philadelphia established; became metropolitan see, 1958.
**1921:** Archbishop Dennis Dougherty made cardinal by Pope Benedict XV.
**1924:** Byzantine Rite Apostolic Exarchate of Pittsburgh established; made an eparchy in 1963; raised to metropolitan status and transferred to Munhall, 1969; transferred back to Pittsburgh in 1977.
**1951:** Greensburg diocese established.
**1958:** Archbishop John O'Hara, C.S.C., of Philadelphia made cardinal by Pope John.
**1961:** Allentown diocese established.
**1967:** Archbishop John J. Krol of Philadelphia made cardinal by Pope Paul VI.
**1969:** Bishop John J. Wright of Pittsburgh made cardinal by Pope Paul VI and transferred to Curia post.
**1976:** The 41st International Eucharistic Congress, the second held in the U.S., convened in Philadelphia, August 1-8.
**1985:** Major Archbishop Myroslav Lubachivsky of the Major Archbishopric of Lviv of the Ukrainians, former metropolitan of Byzantine Philadelphia archeparchy (1979-80), made cardinal by Pope John Paul II.

**1991:** Archbishop Anthony J. Bevilacqua of Phildelphia made cardinal by Pope John Paul II.

## Rhode Island

**1663:** Colonial Charter granted freedom of conscience.

**1719:** Laws denied Catholics the right to hold public office.

**1829:** St. Mary's Church, Pawtucket, was first Catholic church in state.

**1837:** Parochial schools inaugurated in state. First Catholic church in Providence was built.

**1851:** Sisters of Mercy began work in Rhode Island.

**1872:** Providence diocese established.

**1900:** Trappists took up residence in state.

**1917:** Providence College founded.

## South Carolina

**1569:** Jesuit Juan Rogel was the first resident priest in the territory.

**1573:** First Franciscans arrived in southeastern section.

**1606:** Bishop Altamirano conducted visitation of area.

**1655:** Franciscans had two missions among Indians; later destroyed by English.

**1697:** Religious liberty granted to all except "papists."

**1790:** Catholics given right to vote.

**1820:** Charleston diocese established.

**1822:** Bishop England founded *U.S. Catholic Miscellany*, first Catholic paper of a strictly religious nature in U.S.

**1830:** Sisters of Our Lady of Mercy, first in state, took up residence at Charleston.

**1847:** Cornerstone of Cathedral of St. John the Baptist, Charleston, was laid.

**1861:** Cathedral and many institutions destroyed in Charleston fire.

## South Dakota

**1842:** Father Augustine Ravoux began ministrations to French and Indians at Fort Pierre, Vermilion and Prairie du Chien; printed devotional book in Sioux language the following year.

**1867:** Parish organized among the French at Jefferson.

**1878:** Benedictines opened school for Sioux children at Fort Yates.

**1889:** Sioux Falls diocese established.

**1902:** Lead diocese established; transferred to Rapid City, 1930. (Lead was reestablished as a titular see in 1995.)

**1936:** Mount Marty College established.

**1952:** Blue Cloud Abbey, first Benedictine foundation in state, was dedicated.

## Tennessee

**1541:** Cross planted on shore of Mississippi by De Soto; accompanying the expedition were Fathers John de Gallegos and Louis De Soto.

**1682:** Franciscan Fathers Membre and Douay accompanied La Salle to present site of Memphis; may have offered the first Masses in the territory.

**1800:** Catholics were served by priests from Bardstown, Ky.

**1822:** Non-Catholics assisted in building church in Nashville.

**1837:** Nashville diocese established.

**1843:** Sisters of Charity opened a school for girls in Nashville.

**1860:** Sisters of St. Dominic from Somerset, Ohio, arrived in Nashville to open a school for girls.

**1871:** Christian Brothers opened a school for boys in Memphis; it later became Christian Brothers College (now University).

**1921:** Sisters of St. Dominic opened Siena College for women at Memphis; closed in 1971.

**1970:** Memphis diocese established.

**1988:** Knoxville diocese established.

## Texas

**1541:** Missionaries with Coronado expedition probably entered territory.

**1553:** Dominicans Diego de la Cruz, Hernando Mendez, Juan Ferrer, Brother Juan de Mina killed by Indians.

**1675:** Bosque-Larios missionary expedition entered region; Father Juan Larios offered first recorded high Mass.

**1682:** Mission Corpus Christi de Isleta (Ysleta) founded by Franciscans near El Paso, first mission in present-day Texas.

**1690:** Mission San Francisco de los Tejas founded in east Texas.

**1703:** Mission San Francisco de Solano founded on Rio Grande; rebuilt in 1718 as San Antonio de Valero or the Alamo.

**1717:** Franciscan Antonio Margil founded six missions in northeast.

**1720:** San Jose y San Miguel de Aguayo Mission founded by Fray Antonio Margil de Jesus.

**1721:** Franciscan Brother Jose Pita killed by Indians at Carnezeria.

**1728:** Site of San Antonio settled.

**1738:** Construction of San Fernando Cathedral at San Antonio.

**1744:** Mission church of the Alamo built.

**1750:** Franciscan Francisco Xavier was killed by Indians; so were Jose Ganzabal in 1752, and Alonzo Ferrares and Jose San Esteban in 1758.

**1793:** Mexico secularized missions.

**1825:** Governments of Cohuila and Texas secularized all Indian missions.

**1838-39:** Irish priests ministered to settlements of Refugio and San Patricio.

**1841:** Vicariate of Texas established.

**1847:** Ursuline Sisters established their first academy in territory at Galveston.

Galveston diocese established.

**1852:** Oblate Fathers and Franciscans arrived in Galveston to care for new influx of German Catholics.

St. Mary's College (now University) founded at San Antonio.

**1854:** Know-Nothing Party began to stir up hatred against Catholics.

Oldest Polish settlement in Texas established Dec. 24; settlers named the area Panna Maria (Virgin Mary in Polish).

**1858:** Texas Legislature passed law entitling all schools granting free scholarships and meeting state requirements to share in school fund.

**1874:** San Antonio diocese established.
Vicariate of Brownsville established.
**1881:** St. Edward's College founded; became first chartered college in state in 1889.
Sisters of Charity founded Incarnate Word College at San Antonio.
**1890:** Dallas diocese established; changed to Dallas-Ft. Worth, 1953; made two separate dioceses, 1969.
**1912:** Corpus Christi diocese established.
**1914:** El Paso diocese established.
**1926:** San Antonio made archdiocese. Amarillo diocese established.
**1947:** Austin diocese established.
**1959:** Galveston diocese redesignated Galveston-Houston.
**1961:** San Angelo diocese established.
**1965:** Brownsville diocese established.
**1966:** Beaumont diocese established.
**1982:** Victoria diocese established.
**1983:** Lubbock diocese established.
**1986:** Tyler diocese established.

## Utah

**1776:** Franciscans Silvestre de Escalante and Atanasio Dominguez reached Utah (Salt) Lake; first white men known to enter the territory.
**1858:** Jesuit Father De Smet accompanied General Harney as chaplain on expedition sent to settle troubles between Mormons and U.S. Government.
**1866:** On June 29 Father Edward Kelly offered first Mass in Salt Lake City in Mormon Assembly Hall.
**1886:** Utah vicariate apostolic established.
**1891:** Salt Lake City diocese established.
**1926:** College of St. Mary-of-the-Wasatch for women was founded.

## Vermont

**1609:** Champlain expedition passed through territory.
**1666:** Captain La Motte built fort and shrine of St. Anne on Isle La Motte; Sulpician Father Dollier de Casson celebrated first Mass.
**1668:** Bishop Laval of Quebec (beatified in 1980), administered confirmation in region; this was the first area in northeastern U.S. to receive an episcopal visit.
**1710:** Jesuits ministered to Indians near Lake Champlain.
**1793:** Discriminatory measures against Catholics were repealed.
**1830:** Father Jeremiah O'Callaghan became first resident priest in state.
**1853:** Burlington diocese established.
**1854:** Sisters of Charity of Providence arrived to conduct St. Joseph's Orphanage at Burlington.
**1904:** St. Michael's College founded.
**1951:** First Carthusian foundation in America established at Whitingham.

## Virginia

**1526:** Dominican Antonio de Montesinos offered first Mass on Virginia soil.
**1561:** Dominicans visited the coast.
**1571:** Father John Baptist de Segura and seven Jesuit companions killed by Indians.
**1642:** Priests outlawed and Catholics denied right to vote.
**1689:** Capuchin Christopher Plunket was captured and exiled to a coastal island where he died in 1697.
**1776:** Religious freedom granted.
**1791:** Father Jean Dubois arrived at Richmond with letters from Lafayette. The House of Delegates was placed at his disposal for celebration of Mass. A church was built in Norfolk (St. Mary of the Immaculate Conception). It was designated a minor basilica in 1991.
**1796:** A church was built at Alexandria.
**1820:** Richmond diocese established.
**1822:** Trusteeism created serious problems in diocese; Bishop Patrick Kelly resigned the see.
**1848:** Sisters of Charity opened an orphan asylum at Norfolk.
**1866:** School Sisters of Notre Dame and Sisters of Charity opened academies for girls at Richmond.
**1974:** Arlington diocese established.

## Washington

**1774:** Spaniards explored the region.
**1838:** Fathers Blanchet and Demers, "Apostles of the Northwest," were sent to territory by archbishop of Quebec.
**1840:** Cross erected on Whidby Island, Puget Sound.
**1843:** Vicariate Apostolic of Oregon, including Washington, was established.
**1844:** Mission of St. Paul founded at Colville.
Six Sisters of Notre Dame de Namur began work in area.
**1846:** Walla Walla diocese established; suppressed in 1850 (reestablished later as a titular see).
**1850:** Nesqually diocese established; transferred to Seattle, 1907. (Nesqually reestablished as a titular see in 1995.)
**1856:** Providence Academy, the first permanent Catholic school in the Northwest, was built at Fort Vancouver by Mother Joseph Pariseau of the Sisters of Charity of Providence.
**1887:** Gonzaga University founded.
**1913:** Spokane diocese established.
**1951:** Seattle made archdiocese. Yakima diocese established.

## West Virginia

**1749:** Father Joseph de Bonnecamps, accompanying the Bienville expedition, may have offered first Mass in the territory.
**1821:** First Catholic church in Wheeling.
**1838:** Sisters of Charity founded school at Martinsburg.
**1848:** Visitation Nuns established academy for girls in Wheeling.
**1850:** Wheeling diocese established; name changed to Wheeling-Charleston, 1974.
Wheeling Hospital incorporated, the oldest Catholic charitable institution in territory.
**1955:** Wheeling College established.

## Wisconsin

**1661:** Jesuit Rene Menard, first known missionary in the territory, was killed or lost in the Black River district.

**1665:** Jesuit Claude Allouez founded Mission of the Holy Ghost at La Pointe Chegoimegon, now Bayfield; was the first permanent mission in region.

**1673:** Father Marquette and Louis Joliet traveled from Green Bay down the Wisconsin and Mississippi rivers.

**1762:** Suppression of Jesuits in French Colonies closed many missions for 30 years.

**1843:** Milwaukee diocese established.

**1853:** St. John's Cathedral, Milwaukee, was built.

**1864:** State charter granted for establishment of Marquette University. First students admitted, 1881.

**1868:** Green Bay and La Crosse dioceses established.

**1875:** Milwaukee made archdiocese.

**1905:** Superior diocese established.

**1946:** Madison diocese established.

## Wyoming

**1840:** Jesuit Pierre de Smet offered first Mass near Green River.

**1851:** Father De Smet held peace conference with Indians near Fort Laramie.

**1867:** Father William Kelly, first resident priest, arrived in Cheyenne and built first church a year later.

**1873:** Father Eugene Cusson became first resident pastor in Laramie.

**1875:** Sisters of Charity of Leavenworth opened school and orphanage at Laramie.

**1884:** Jesuits took over pastoral care of Shoshone and Arapaho Indians.

**1887:** Cheyenne diocese established.

**1949:** Weston Memorial Hospital opened near Newcastle.

## Puerto Rico

**1493:** Island discovered by Columbus on his second voyage; he named it San Juan de Borinquen (the Indian name for Puerto Rico).

**1509:** Juan Ponce de Leon, searching for gold, colonized the island and became its first governor; present population descended mainly from early Spanish settlers.

**1511:** Diocese of Puerto Rico established as suffragan of Seville, Spain; Bishop Alonso Manso, sailing from Spain in 1512, became first bishop to take up residence in New World.

**1645:** Synod held in Puerto Rico to regulate frequency of Masses according to distances people had to walk.

**1898:** Puerto Rico ceded to U.S. (became self-governing Commonwealth in 1952); inhabitants granted U.S. citizenship in 1917.

**1924:** Diocese of Puerto Rico renamed San Juan de Puerto Rico and made immediately subject to the Holy See; Ponce diocese established.

**1948:** Catholic University of Puerto Rico founded at Ponce through efforts of Most Rev. James E. McManus, C.SS.R., bishop of Ponce, 1947-63.

**1960:** San Juan made metropolitan see. Arecibo diocese established.

**1964:** Caguas diocese established.

**1973:** Archbihop Luis Aponte Martinez of San Juan made first native Puerto Rican cardinal by Pope Paul VI.

**1976:** Mayaguez diocese established.

Virgin of Providence officially approved as Patroness of Puerto Rico by Pope Paul VI.

## CATHOLICS IN PRESIDENTS' CABINETS

From 1789 to 1940, nine Catholics were appointed to cabinet posts by six of 32 presidents. The first was Roger Brooke Taney (later named first Catholic Supreme Court Justice) who was appointed in 1831 by Pres. Andrew Jackson. Catholics have been appointed to cabinet posts from the time of Pres. Franklin D. Roosevelt to the present.

Listed below in chronological order are presidents, Catholic cabinet officials, posts held, dates.

Andrew Jackson — Roger B. **Taney**, Attorney General, 1831-33, Secretary of Treasury, 1833-34.

Franklin Pierce — James **Campbell**, Postmaster General, 1853-57.

James Buchanan — John B. **Floyd**, Secretary of War, 1857-61.

William McKinley — Joseph **McKenna**, Attorney General, 1897-98.

Theodore Roosevelt — Robert J. **Wynne**, Postmaster General, 1904-05; Charles **Bonaparte**, Secretary of Navy, 1905-06, Attorney General, 1906-09.

Franklin D. Roosevelt — James A. **Farley**, Postmaster General, 1933-40; Frank **Murphy**, Attorney General, 1939-40; Frank C. **Walker**, Postmaster General, 1940-45.

Harry S. Truman — Robert E. **Hannegan**, Postmaster General, 1945-47; J. Howard **McGrath**, Attorney General, 1949-52; Maurice J. **Tobin**, Secretary of Labor, 1948-53; James P. **McGranery**, Attorney General, 1952-53.

Dwight D. Eisenhower — Martin P. **Durkin**, Secretary of Labor, 1953; James P. **Mitchell**, Secretary of Labor, 1953-61.

John F. Kennedy — Robert F. **Kennedy**, Attorney General, 1961-63; Anthony **Celebrezze**, Secretary of Health, Education and Welfare, 1962-63; John S. **Gronouski**, Postmaster General, 1963.

Lyndon B. Johnson — (Robert F. **Kennedy**, 1963-65, Anthony **Celebrezze**, 1963-65, and John S. **Gronouski**, 1963-65, reappointed to posts held in Kennedy Cabinet — see above.) John T. **Connor**, Secretary of Commerce, 1965-67; Lawrence **O'Brien**, Postmaster General, 1965-68.

Richard M. Nixon — Walter J. **Hickel**, Secretary of Interior, 1969-71; John A. **Volpe**, Secretary of Transportation, 1969-72; Maurice H. **Stans**, Secretary of Commerce, 1969-72; Peter J. **Brennan**, Secretary of Labor, 1973-74; William E. **Simon**, Secretary of Treasury, 1974.

Gerald R. Ford — (Peter J. **Brennan**, 1974-75, and William E. **Simon**, 1974-76, reappointed to posts held above.)

Jimmy Carter — Joseph **Califano**, Jr., Secretary of Health, Education and Welfare, 1977-79; Benjamin **Civiletti**, Attorney General, 1979-81; Moon **Landrieu**, Secretary of Housing and Urban Development, 1979-81; Edmund S. **Muskie**, Secretary of State, 1980-81.

Ronald Reagan — Alexander M. **Haig**, Secretary of

State, 1981-82; Raymond J. Donovan, Secretary of Labor, 1981-84; Margaret M. Heckler, Secretary of Health and Human Services, 1983-85; William J. Bennett, Secretary of Education, 1985-88; Ann Dore McLaughlin, Secretary of Labor, 1988-89; Lauro F. Cavazos, Secretary of Education, 1988-89; Nicholas F. Brady, Secretary of Treasury, 1988-89.

George Bush — Lauro F. Cavazos (reappointed), Secretary of Education, 1989-90; Nicholas F. Brady (reappointed), Secretary of Treasury, 1989-93 ; James D. Watkins, Secretary of Energy, 1989-93; Manuel Lujan, Jr., Secretary of Interior, 1989-93 ; Edward J. Derwinski, Secretary of Veteran Affairs, 1989-92; Lynn Martin, Secretary of Labor, 1990-93; Edward Madigan, Secretary of Agriculture, 1991-93; William P. Barr, Attorney General, 1991-93.

Bill Clinton — Henry G. Cisneros, Secretary of Housing and Urban Development, 1993- ; Federico F. Pena, Secretary of Transportation, 1993- ; Donna Shalala, Secretary of Health and Human Services, 1993- .

Cabinet members who became Catholics after leaving their posts were: Thomas Ewing, Secretary of Treasury under William A. Harrison, and Secretary of Interior under Zachary Taylor; Luke E. Wright, Secretary of War under Theodore Roosevelt; Albert B. Fall, Secretary of Interior under Warren G. Harding.

## CATHOLIC SUPREME COURT JUSTICES

Roger B. Taney, Chief Justice 1836-64; app. by Andrew Jackson.

Edward D. White, Associate Justice 1894-1910, app. by Grover Cleveland; Chief Justice 1910-21, app. by William H. Taft.

Joseph McKenna, Associate Justice 1898-1925; app. by William McKinley.

Pierce Butler, Associate Justice 1923-39; app. by Warren G. Harding.

Frank Murphy, Associate Justice 1940-49; app. by Franklin D. Roosevelt.

William Brennan, Associate Justice 1956-90; app. by Dwight D. Eisenhower.

Antonin Scalia, Associate Justice 1986-; app. by Ronald Reagan.

Anthony M. Kennedy, Associate Justice 1988-; app. by Ronald Reagan.

Clarence Thomas, Associate Justice 1991- ; app. by George Bush (see News Events, June).

Sherman Minton, Associate Justice from 1949 to 1956, became a Catholic several years before his death in 1965.

## CATHOLICS IN STATUARY HALL

Statues of 13 Catholics deemed worthy of national commemoration by the donating states are among those enshrined in National Statuary Hall and other places in the U.S. Capitol. The Hall, formerly the chamber of the House of Representatives, was erected by Act of Congress July 2, 1864.

Donating states, names and years of placement are listed.

Arizona: Rev. Eusebio Kino, S. J., missionary, 1965.
California: Rev. Junipero Serra, O. F. M. missionary, 1931. (Beatified 1988.)
Hawaii: Father Damien, missionary, 1969.(Beatified 1995.)
Illinois: Gen. James Shields, statesman, 1893.
Louisiana: Edward D. White, Justice of the U.S. Supreme Court (1894-1921), 1955.
Maryland: Charles Carroll, statesman, 1901.
Nevada: Patrick A. McCarran, statesman, 1960.
New Mexico: Dennis Chavez, statesman, 1966. (Archbishop Jean B. Lamy, pioneer prelate of Santa Fe, was nominated for Hall honor in 1951.)
North Dakota: John Burke, U.S. treasurer, 1963.
Oregon: Dr. John McLoughlin, pioneer, 1953.
Washington: Mother Mary Joseph Pariseau, pioneer missionary and humanitarian.
West Virginia: John E. Kenna, statesman, 1901.
Wisconsin: Rev. Jacques Marquette, S.J., missionary, explorer, 1895.

# CHURCH-STATE DECISIONS OF THE SUPREME COURT

(Among sources of this selected listing of U.S. Supreme Court decisions was *The Supreme Court on Church and State,* Joseph Tussman, editor; Oxford University Press, New York, 1962.)

Watson v. Jones, 13 Wallace 679 (1872): The Court declared that a member of a religious organization may not appeal to secular courts against a decision made by a church tribunal within the area of its competence.

Polygamy: The Mormon practice of polygamy was at issue in three decisions and was declared unconstitutional: Reynolds v. United States, 98 US 145 (1879); Davis v. Beason, 133 US 333 (1890); Church of Latter-Day Saints v. United States, 136 US 1 (1890).

Bradfield v. Roberts, 175 US 291 (1899): The Court denied that an appropriation of government funds for an institution (Providence Hospital, Washington, D.C.) run by Roman Catholic sisters violated the No Establishment Clause of the First Amendment.

Pierce v. Society of Sisters, 268 US 510 (1925): The Court denied that a state can require children to attend public schools only. The Court held that the liberty of the Constitution forbids standardization by such compulsion, and that the parochial schools involved had claims to protection under the Fourteenth Amendment.

Cochran v. Board of Education, 281 US 370 (1930): The Court upheld a Louisiana statute providing textbooks at public expense for children attending public or parochial schools. The Court held that the children and state were beneficiaries of the appropriations, with incidental secondary benefit going to the schools.

United States v. MacIntosh, 283 US 605 (1931): The Court denied that anyone can place allegiance to the will of God above his allegiance to the government since such a person could make his own interpretation of God's will the decisive test as to whether he would or would not obey the nation's law. The Court stated that the nation, which has a duty to survive, can require citizens to bear arms in its defense.

**Everson v. Board of Education,** 330 US 1 (1947): The Court upheld the constitutionality of a New Jersey statute authorizing free school bus transportation for parochial as well as public school students. The Court expressed the opinion that the benefits of public welfare legislation, included under such bus transportation, do not run contrary to the concept of separation of Church and State.

**McCollum v. Board of Education,** 333 US 203 (1948): The Court declared unconstitutional a program for releasing children, with parental consent, from public school classes so they could receive religious instruction on public school premises from representatives of their own faiths.

**Zorach v. Clauson,** 343 US 306 (1952): The Court upheld the constitutionality of a New York statute permitting, on a voluntary basis, the release during school time of students from public school classes for religious instruction given off public school premises.

**Torcaso v. Watkins,** 367 US 488 (1961): The Court declared unconstitutional a Maryland requirement that one must make a declaration of belief in the existence of God as part of the oath of office for notaries public.

**McGowan v. Maryland,** 81 Sp Ct 1101; **Two Guys from Harrison v. McGinley,** 81 Sp Ct 1135; **Gallagher v. Crown Kosher Super Market,** 81 Sp Ct 1128; **Braunfeld v. Brown,** 81 Sp Ct 1144 (1961): The Court ruled that Sunday closing laws do not violate the No Establishment of Religion Clause of the First Amendment, even though the laws were religious in their inception and still have some religious overtones. The Court held that, "as presently written and administered, most of them, at least, are of a secular rather than of a religious character, and that presently they bear no relationship to establishment of religion as those words are used in the Constitution of the United States."

**Engel v. Vitale,** 370 US 42 (1962): The Court declared that the voluntary recitation in public schools of a prayer composed by the New York State Board of Regents is unconstitutional on the ground that it violates the No Establishment of Religion Clause of the First Amendment.

**Abington Township School District v. Schempp and Murray v. Curlett,** 83 Sp Ct 1560 (1963): The Court ruled that Bible reading and recitation of the Lord's Prayer in public schools, with voluntary participation by students, are unconstitutional on the ground that they violate the No Establishment of Religion Clause of the First Amendment.

**Chamberlin v. Dade County,** 83 Sp Ct 1864 (1964): The Court reversed a decision of the Florida Supreme Court concerning the constitutionality of prayer and devotional Bible reading in public schools during the school day, as sanctioned by a state statute which specifically related the practices to a sound public purpose.

**Board of Education v. Allen,** No. 660 (1968): The Court declared constitutional the New York school book loan law which requires local school boards to purchase books with state funds and lend them to parochial and private school students.

**Walz v. Tax Commission of New York** (1970): The Court upheld the constitutionality of a New York statute exempting church-owned property from taxation.

**Earle v. DiCenso, Robinson v. DiCenso, Lemon v. Kurtzman, Tilton v. Richardson** (1971): In Earle v. DiCenso and Robinson v. DiCenso, the Court ruled unconstitutional a 1969 Rhode Island statute which provided salary supplements to teachers of secular subjects in parochial schools; in Lemon v. Kurtzman, the Court ruled unconstitutional a 1968 Pennsylvania statute which authorized the state to purchase services for the teaching of secular subjects in nonpublic schools. The principal argument against constitutionality in these cases was that the statutes and programs at issue entailed excessive entanglement of government with religion. In Tilton v. Richardson, the Court held that this argument did not apply to a prohibitive degree with respect to federal grants, under the Higher Education Facilities Act of 1963, for the construction of facilities for nonreligious purposes by four church-related institutions of higher learning, three of which were Catholic, in Connecticut.

**Amish Decision** (1972): In a case appealed on behalf of Yoder, Miller and Yutzy, the Court ruled that Amish parents were exempt from a Wisconsin statute requiring them to send their children to school until the age of 16. The Court said in its decision that secondary schooling exposed Amish children to attitudes, goals and values contrary to their beliefs, and substantially hindered "the religious development of the Amish child and his integration into the way of life of the Amish faith-community at the crucial adolescent state of development."

**Committee for Public Education and Religious Liberty, et al., v. Nyquist, et al.,** No. 72-694 (1973): The Court ruled that provisions of a 1972 New York statute were unconstitutional on the grounds that they were violative of the No Establishment Clause of the First Amendment and had the "impermissible effect" of advancing the sectarian activities of church-affiliated schools. The programs ruled unconstitutional concerned: (1) maintenance and repair grants, for facilities and equipment, to ensure the health, welfare and safety of students in nonpublic, non-profit elementary and secondary schools serving a high concentration of students from low income families; (2) tuition reimbursement ($50 per grade school child, $100 per high school student) for parents (with income less than $5,000) of children attending nonpublic elementary or secondary schools; tax deduction from adjusted gross income for parents failing to qualify under the above reimbursement plan, for each child attending a nonpublic school.

**Sloan, Treasurer of Pennsylvania, et al., v. Lemon, et al.,** No. 72-459 (1973): The Court ruled unconstitutional a Pennsylvania Parent Reimbursement Act for Nonpublic Education which provided funds to reimburse parents (to a maximum of $150) for a portion of tuition expenses incurred in sending their children to nonpublic schools. The Court held that there was no significant difference between this and the New York tuition reimbursement program (above), and declared that the Equal Protection Clause of the Fourteenth Amendment cannot be relied upon to sustain a program held to be violative of the No Establishment Clause.

**Levitt, et al., v. Committee for Public Education and Religious Liberty, et al.,** No. 72-269 (1973): The Court ruled unconstitutional the Mandated Services Act of 1970 under which New York provided $28 million ($27 per pupil from first to seventh grade, $45 per pupil from seventh to 12th grade) to reimburse nonpublic schools for testing, recording and reporting services required by the state. The Court declared that the act provided "impermissible aid" to religion in contravention of the No Establishment Clause.

In related decisions handed down June 25, 1973, the Court: (1) affirmed a lower court decision against the constitutionality of an Ohio tax credit law benefiting parents with children in nonpublic schools; (2) reinstated an injunction against a parent reimbursement program in New Jersey; (3) affirmed South Carolina's right to grant construction loans to church-affiliated colleges, and dismissed an appeal contesting its right to provide loans to students attending church-affiliated colleges **(Hunt v. McNair, Durham v. McLeod).**

**Wheeler v. Barrera** (1974): The Court ruled that nonpublic school students in Missouri must share in federal funds for educationally deprived students on a comparable basis with public school students under Title I of the Elementary and Secondary Education Act of 1965.

**Norwood v. Harrison** (93 S. Ct. 2804): The Court ruled that public assistance which avoids the prohibitions of the "effect" and "entanglement" tests (and which therefore does not substantially promote the religious mission of sectarian schools) may be confined to the secular functions of such schools.

**Wiest v. Mt. Lebanon School District** (1974): The Court upheld a lower court ruling that invocation and benediction prayers at public high school commencement ceremonies do not violate the principle of separation of Church and state.

**Meek v. Pittenger** (1975): The Court ruled unconstitutional portions of a Pennsylvania law providing auxiliary services for students of nonpublic schools; at the same time, it ruled in favor of provisions of the law permitting textbook loans to students of such schools. In denying the constitutionality of auxiliary services, the Court held that they had the "primary effect of establishing religion" and involved "excessive entanglement" of Church and state officials with respect to supervision; objection was also made against providing such services only on the premises of non-public schools and only at the request of such schools.

**TWA, Inc., v. Hardison,** 75-1126; **International Association of Machinists and Aero Space Workers v. Hardison,** 75-1385 (1977): The Court ruled that federal civil rights legislation does not require employers to make more than minimal efforts to accommodate employees who want a particular working day off as their religion's Sabbath Day, and

that an employer cannot accommodate such an employee by violating seniority systems determined by a union collective bargaining agreement. The Court noted that its ruling was not a constitutional judgment but an interpretation of existing law.

**Wolman v. Walter** (1977): The Court ruled constitutional portions of an Ohio statute providing tax-paid textbook loans and some auxiliary services (standardized and diagnostic testing, therapeutic and remedial services, off school premises) for nonpublic school students. It decided that other portions of the law, providing state funds for nonpublic school field trips and instructional materials (audio-visual equipment, maps, tape recorders), were unconstitutional.

**Parochiaid** (1979): The Court decided, in Byrne v. Public Funds for Public Schools, against the constitutionality of a 1976 New Jersey law providing state income tax deductions for tuition paid by parents of students attending parochial and other private schools.

**Student Bus Transportation** (1979): The Court upheld a Pennsylvania law providing bus transportation at public expense for students to non-public schools up to 10 miles away from the boundaries of the public school districts in which they lived.

**Reimbursement** (1980): The Court upheld the constitutionality of a 1974 New York law providing direct cash payment to non-public schools for the costs of state-mandated testing and record-keeping.

**Ten Commandments** (1980): The Court struck down a 1978 Kentucky law requiring the posting of the Ten Commandments in public school classrooms in the state.

**Campus Worship** (1981): The Court ruled, in Widmar v. Vincent, that the University of Missouri at Kansas City could not deny student religious groups the use of campus facilities for worship services. The Court also, in Brandon v. Board of Education of Guilderland Schools, declined without comment to hear an appeal for reversal of lower court decisions denying a group of New York high school students the right to meet for prayer on public school property before the beginning of the school day.

**No Meeting on Public School Property** (1983): By refusing to hear an appeal in Lubbock v. Lubbock Civil Liberties Union, the Court upheld a lower court ruling against a public policy of permitting student religious groups to meet on public school property before and after school hours.

**Tuition Tax Deduction** (1983): In Mueller v. Allen, the Court upheld a Minnesota law allowing parents of students in public and non-public (including parochial) schools to take a tax deduction for the expenses of tuition, textbooks and transportation. Maximum allowable deductions were $500 per child in elementary school and $700 per child in grades seven through 12.

**Christmas Nativity Scene** (1984): The Court ruled 5-to-4 in Lynch v. Donnelly that the First Amendment does not mandate "complete separation of church and state," and that, therefore, the sponsorship of a Christmas nativity scene by the City of Pawtucket, R.I., was not unconstitutional. The case involved a scene included in a display of Christmas symbols sponsored by the city in a park owned by a non-profit group. The majority opinion said "the

Constitution (does not) require complete separation of church and state; it affirmatively mandates accommodation, not merely tolerance, of all religions and forbids hostility toward any. Anything less" would entail callous indifference not intended by the Constitution. Moreover, "such hostility would bring us into 'war with our national tradition as embodied in the First Amendment's guaranty of the free exercise of religion.'" (The additional quotation was from the 1948 decision in McCollum v. Board of Education.)

**Christmas Nativity Scene** (1985): The Court upheld a lower court ruling that the Village of Scarsdale, N.Y., must make public space available for the display of privately sponsored nativity scenes.

**Wallace v. Jaffree**, No. 83-812 (1985): The Court ruled against the constitutionality of a 1981 Alabama law calling for a public-school moment of silence that specifically included optional prayer.

**Grand Rapids v. Ball**, No. 83-990, and **Aguilar v. Felton**, No. 84-237 (1985): The Court ruled against the constitutionality of programs in Grand Rapids and New York City allowing public school teachers to teach remedial entitlement subjects (under the Elementary and Secondary Education Act of 1965) in private schools, many of which were Catholic.

**Equal Student Access** (1986): In Bender v. Williamsport Area School District, the Court let stand a lower federal court decision allowing a public high school Bible study group the same "equal access" to school facilities as that enjoyed by other extra-curricular clubs. A similar decision was handed down in 1990 in Board of Education v. Mergens, involving Westside High School in Omaha.

**Creche and Menorah:** In County of Allegheny v. American Civil Liberties Union, the Court ruled in 1989 (1) The display of a Christmas nativity scene in the Allegheny County Courthouse in Pittsburgh, Pa., violated the principle of separation of church and state because it appeared to be a government-sponsored endorsement of Christian belief. (2) The display of a Hanukkah menorah outside the Pittsburgh-Allegheny city-county building was constitutional because of its "particular physical setting" with secular symbols.

**Peyote Ban** (1990): The Court ruled in Oregon v. Smith that religious use of the hallucinogenic cactus peyote is not covered by the First Amendment protection of religious freedom.

**No Organized Prayer** (1992): In Lee v. Weisman the Court banned officially organized prayer at public school graduation ceremonies.

**Equal Access** (1993): In Lamb's Chapel v. Center Moriches Union School District, the Court reversed a ruling by the 3rd U.S. Circuit Court of Appeals, declaring that the school district was wrong in prohibiting the congregation of Lamb's Chapel from using public school meeting space after hours to show a film series addressing family problems from a religious perspective. In view of the variety of organizations permitted to use school property after school hours, said the Court's opinion: "There would have been no realistic danger that the community would think that the district was endorsing religion or any particular creed, and any benefit to religion or to the church would have been no more than incidental."

**Student Prayers** (1993): The Court let stand a ruling by the 5th U.S. Circuit Court of Appeals, permitting students in Texas, Mississippi and Louisiana to include student-organized and student-led prayers in graduation exercises.

**Church of Lukumi Babalu Aye v. City of Hialeah** (1993): The Court ruled that municipal laws that effectively prohibit a single church from performing its religious rituals are unconstitutional. The ordinances at issue singled out one religion, Santeria, for the purpose of restricting its members from the practice of ritual animal sacrifices.

**Zobrest v. Catalina Foothills School District** (1993): The Court ruled that a public school district may provide a sign-language interpreter for a deaf student attending a Catholic school without violating constitutional separation of church and state. The majority opinion said: "Handicapped children, not sectarian schools are the primary beneficiaries of the Disabilities Education Act; to the extent sectarian schools benefit at all from (the act), they are only incidental beneficiaries."

**Equal Rent** (1994): The Court upheld lower court rulings against a Fairfax County, Va., school district's practice of charging churches more rent than other entities for the use of school buildings.

**Hasidic School Case** (1994): In Board of Education of Kiryas Joel Village School District v. Grumet, the Court ruled in 1994 that a school district created to meet the special education needs of an Hasidic Jewish community violated the Establishment Clause of the Constitution. The Court said the New York Legislature effectively endorsed a particular religion when it established a public school district for the Satmar Hasidic Village of Kiryas Joel.

## RELIGION IN PUBLIC SCHOOLS

*(Based on a Catholic News Service article by Carol Zimmermann.)*

A diverse group of religious and civil rights organizations issued a joint statement Apr. 13, 1995, in an effort to clarify the confusing issue of prayer and religious observances or discussions in public schools. Their six-page statement outlines what is and what is not currently permissible in expressing religious beliefs in public schools.

The statement says, for example: "Students have the right to pray individually or in groups, or to discuss their religious views with their peers so long as they are not disruptive." But, the statement specifies that such prayers or discussions do not include "the right to have a captive audience listen or to compel other students to participate."

### Prayer at Graduations

Regarding prayer at graduation ceremonies, the document says school officials may not mandate or organize prayer, but hardly sets the record straight about student-led prayer at these services.

"The courts have reached conflicting conclusions under the federal Constitution" in this area, says the statement, recommending that schools consult their lawyers for the rules that apply to them, "until the issue is authoritatively resolved."

Since the Supreme Court's 1992 Lee v. Weisman opinion prohibited school authorities from even arranging for a speaker to present a prayer, lower courts in different states have made various rulings about student-led prayer at commencement exercises.

In Virginia, the state's Attorney General and the Board of Education proposed guidelines in mid-April to allow student-led prayer at graduations, despite a 1994 ruling by a U.S. district judge banning all prayer at graduations.

## Religion in the Classroom

"It is both permissible and desirable to teach objectively about the role of religion in the history of the United States and other countries," but public school teachers may not specifically teach religion.

The same rules apply to the recurring controversy surrounding theories of evolution. Teachers may discuss explanations of the beginnings of life, but only within the confines of classes on religion or social studies. Public school teachers are required, according to the statement, to teach only scientific explanations of life's beginnings in science classes. And, just as teachers may not advance a religious view, they should not ridicule a student's religious belief.

## Constitutional Protection

The statement says that students' expressions of religious beliefs in reports, homework or artwork are constitutionally protected. Likewise, students have the right to speak to and attempt to persuade their peers on religious topics. "But school officials should intercede to stop student religious speech if it turns into religious harassment aimed at a student or a small group of students."

The statement also says:

• Students have the right to distribute religious literature to their schoolmates, subject to reasonable restrictions for any non-school literature.

• Student religious clubs in secondary schools "must be permitted to meet and to have equal access" to school media for announcing their events.

• Religious messages on T-shirts and the like cannot be singled out for suppression.

• Schools can use discretion about dismissing students for off-site religious instruction.

The 35 organizations that endorsed the statement included the National Association of Evangelicals, the American Jewish Congress, the Christian Legal Society, the National Council of Churches, the Baptist Joint Committee on Public Affairs, the American Muslim Council, the Presbyterian Church (USA) and the American Civil Liberties Union.

## Purpose of the Statement

"By making this document available," said Phil Baum, executive director of the American Jewish Congress, "the organizations are attempting to clarify what has become one of the most divisive issues of our time: religion in the public schools."

He said the document attempts to "ensure that the rights of all students are respected in the public schools."

Baum noted that the American Jewish Congress, which initiated the effort to draft the statement, had a long-standing commitment to ensuring that public schools are themselves religiously neutral.

"We believe, however, that it is inconsistent with that historic commitment to ask the public schools to root out private expressions of religious faith."

## CHURCH TAX EXEMPTION

The exemption of church-owned property was ruled constitutional by the U.S. Supreme Court May 4, 1970, in the case of Walz v. The Tax Commission of New York.

Suit in the case was brought by Frederick Walz, who purchased in June, 1967, a 22-by-29-foot plot of ground in Staten Island valued at $100 and taxable at $5.24 a year. Shortly after making the purchase, Walz instituted a suit in New York State, contending that the exemption of church property from taxation authorized by state law increased his own tax rate and forced him indirectly to support churches in violation of his constitutional right to freedom of religion under the First Amendment. Three New York courts dismissed the suit, which had been instituted by mail. The Supreme Court, judging that it had probable jurisdiction, then took the case.

In a 7-1 decision affecting Church-state relations in every state in the nation, the Court upheld the New York law under challenge.

## For and Against

Chief Justice Warren E. Burger, who wrote the majority opinion, said that Congress from its earliest days had viewed the religion clauses of the Constitution as authorizing statutory real estate tax exemption to religious bodies. He declared: "Nothing in this national attitude toward religious tolerance and two centuries of uninterrupted freedom from taxation has given the remotest sign of leading to an established church or religion, and on the contrary it has operated affirmatively to help guarantee the free exercise of all forms of religious beliefs."

Justice William O. Douglas wrote in dissent that the involvement of government in religion as typified in tax exemption may seem inconsequential but: "It is, I fear, a long step down the establishment path. Perhaps I have been misinformed. But, as I read the Constitution and the philosophy, I gathered that independence was the price of liberty."

Burger rejected Douglas' "establishment" fears. If tax exemption is the first step toward establishment, he said, "the second step has been long in coming."

The basic issue centered on the following question: Is there a contradiction between federal constitutional provisions against the establishment of religion, or the use of public funds for religious purposes, and state statutes exempting church property from taxation? In the Walz decision, the Supreme Court ruled that there is no contradiction.

## Legal Background

The U.S. Constitution makes no reference to tax exemption. There was no discussion of the issue in the Constitutional Convention nor in debates on the Bill of Rights.

In the Colonial and post-Revolutionary years, some churches had established status and were state-supported. This state of affairs changed with enactment of the First Amendment, which laid down no-establishment as the federal norm. This norm was adopted by the states which, however, exempted churches from tax liabilities.

No establishment, no hindrance, was the early American view of Church-state relationships.

This view, reflected in custom law, was not generally formulated in statute law until the second half of the 19th century, although specific tax exemption was provided for churches in Maryland in 1798, in Virginia in 1800, and in North Carolina in 1806.

The first major challenge to church property exemption was initiated by the Liberal League in the 1870s. It reached the point that President Grant included the recommendation in a State of the Union address in 1875, stating that church property should bear its own proportion of taxes. The plea fell on deaf ears in Congress, but there was some support for the idea at state levels. The exemption, however, continued to survive various challenges.

About 36 state constitutions contain either mandatory or permissive provisions for exemption. Statutes provide for exemption in all other states.

There has been considerable litigation challenging this special exemption, but most of it focused on whether a particular property satisfied statutory requirements. Few cases before Walz focused on the strictly constitutional question, whether directly under the First Amendment or indirectly under the Fourteenth Amendment.

## Objections

Objectors to the tax exempt status of churches feel that churches should share, through taxation, in the cost of the ordinary benefits of public services they enjoy, and/or that the amount of "aid" enjoyed through exemption should be proportionate to the amount of social good they do.

According to one opinion, exemption is said to weaken the independence of churches from the political system which benefits them by exemption.

In another view, exemption is said to involve the government in decisions regarding what is and what is not religion.

## THE WALL OF SEPARATION

Thomas Jefferson, in a letter written to the Danbury (Conn.) Baptist Association Jan. 1, 1802, coined the metaphor, "a wall of separation between Church and State," to express a theory concerning interpretation of the religion clauses of the First Amendment: "Congress shall make no law respecting an establishment of religion or prohibiting the free exercise thereof."

The metaphor was cited for the first time in judicial proceedings in 1879, in the opinion by Chief Justice Waite in Reynolds v. United States. It did not, however, figure substantially in the decision.

## Accepted as Rule

In 1947 the wall of separation gained acceptance as a constitutional rule, in the decision handed down in Everson v. Board of Education. Associate Justice Black, in describing the principles involved in the No Establishment Clause, wrote:

"Neither a state nor the Federal Government can set up a church. Neither can pass laws which aid one religion, aid all religions, or prefer one religion over another. Neither can force nor influence a person to go to or to remain away from church against his will or force him to profess a belief or disbelief in any religion. No person can be punished for entertaining or professing religious beliefs or disbeliefs, for church attendance or non-attendance. No tax in any amount, large or small, can be levied to support any religious activities or institutions, whatever they may be called, or whatever form they may adopt to teach or practice religion. Neither a state nor the Federal Government can, openly or secretly, participate in the affairs of any religious organizations or groups and vice versa. In the words of Jefferson, the clause against establishment of religion by law was intended to erect 'a wall of separation between Church and State.'"

Mr. Black's associates agreed with his statement of principles, which were framed without reference to the Freedom of Exercise Clause. They disagreed, however, with respect to application of the principles, as the split decision in the case indicated. Five members of the Court held that the benefits of public welfare legislation — in this case, free bus transportation to school for parochial as well as public school students — did not run contrary to the concept of separation of Church and state embodied in the First Amendment.

## Different Opinions

Inside and outside the legal profession, opinion is divided concerning the wall of separation and the balance of the religion clauses of the First Amendment.

The view of absolute separationists, carried to the extreme, would make government the adversary of religion. The bishops of the United States, following the McCollum decision in 1948, said that the wall metaphor had become for some persons the "shibboleth of doctrinaire secularism."

Proponents of governmental neutrality toward religion are of the opinion that such neutrality should not be so interpreted as to prohibit incidental aid to religious institutions providing secular services.

In the realm of practice, federal and state legislatures have enacted measures involving incidental benefits to religious bodies. Examples of such measures are the tax exemption of church property; provision of bus rides, book loans and lunch programs to students in church-related as well as public schools; military chaplaincies; loans to church-related hospitals; the financing of studies by military veterans at church-related colleges under GI bills of rights.

**Death:** Stephan George Kuttner, 89, who taught canon law at The Catholic University of America from 1940 to 1964 and contributed to development of the current Code of Canon Law, died Aug. 12, 1996, in Berkeley, Calif. He served from 1967 to 1983 on the Commission for the Reform of the Code of Canon Law. He had been a research fellow at the Vatican Library and a teacher at the Lateran University in Rome. He taught at Yale and was on the faculty of Boalt Hall Law School of the University of California at Berkeley.

# U.S. CATHOLIC JURISDICTIONS, HIERARCHY, STATISTICS

The organizational structure of the Catholic Church in the United States consists of 33 provinces with as many archdioceses (metropolitan sees); 151 suffragan sees (dioceses); five Eastern Church jurisdictions immediately subject to the Holy See — the eparchies of St. Maron and Our Lady of Lebanon of Los Angeles (Maronites, Newton (Melkites), St. Thomas Apostle of Detroit (Chaldeans) and St. George Martyr of Canton, Ohio (Romanians); and the Military Services Archdiocese. The eparchy of Our Lady of Deliverance of Newark for Syrian-rite Catholics in the U.S. and Canada has its seat in Newark, N.J. An Armenian apostolic exarchate for the United States and Canada has its seat in New York. Each of these jurisdictions is under the direction of an archbishop or bishop, called an ordinary, who has apostolic responsibility and authority for the pastoral service of the people in his care.

The structure includes the territorial episcopal conference known as the National Conference of Catholic Bishops. In and through this body, which is strictly ecclesiastical and has defined juridical authority, the bishops exercise their collegiate pastorate over the Church in the entire country (see Index).

Related to the NCCB is the United States Catholic Conference, a civil corporation and operational secretariat through which the bishops, in cooperation with other members of the Church, act on a wider-than-ecclesiastical scale for the good of the Church and society in the United States (see Index).

The representative of the Holy See to the Church in the United States is an Apostolic Pro-Nuncio.

## ECCLESIASTICAL PROVINCES

(Sources: *The Official Catholic Directory,* Catholic News Service.)

*The 33 ecclesiastical provinces bear the names of archdioceses, i.e., of metropolitan sees.*

**Anchorage:** Archdiocese of Anchorage and suffragan sees of Fairbanks, Juneau. Geographical area: Alaska.

**Atlanta:** Archdiocese of Atlanta (Ga.) and suffragan sees of Savannah (Ga.); Charlotte and Raleigh (N.C.), Charleston (S.C.). Geographical area: Georgia, North Carolina, South Carolina.

**Baltimore:** Archdiocese of Baltimore (Md.) and suffragan sees of Wilmington (Del.); Arlington and Richmond (Va.); Wheeling-Charleston (W. Va.). Geographical area: Maryland (except five counties), Delaware, Virginia, West Virginia.

**Boston:** Archdiocese of Boston (Mass.) and suffragan sees of Fall River, Springfield and Worcester (Mass.); Portland (Me.); Manchester (N.H.); Burlington (Vt.). Geographical area: Massachusetts, Maine, New Hampshire, Vermont.

**Chicago:** Archdiocese of Chicago and suffragan sees of Belleville, Joliet, Peoria, Rockford, Springfield. Geographical area: Illinois.

**Cincinnati:** Archdiocese of Cincinnati and suffragan sees of Cleveland, Columbus, Steubenville, Toledo, Youngstown. Geographical area: Ohio.

**Denver:** Archdiocese of Denver (Colo.) and suffragan sees of Colorado Springs and Pueblo (Colo.); Cheyenne (Wyo.). Geographical area: Colorado, Wyoming.

**Detroit:** Archdiocese of Detroit and suffragan sees of Gaylord, Grand Rapids, Kalamazoo, Lansing, Marquette, Saginaw. Geographical area: Michigan.

**Dubuque:** Archdiocese of Dubuque and suffragan sees of Davenport, Des Moines, Sioux City. Geographical area: Iowa.

**Hartford:** Archdiocese of Hartford (Conn.) and suffragan sees of Bridgeport and Norwich (Conn.); Providence (R.I.). Geographical area: Connecticut, Rhode Island.

**Indianapolis:** Archdiocese of Indianapolis and suffragan sees of Evansville, Fort Wayne-South Bend, Gary, Lafayette. Geographical area: Indiana.

**Kansas City** (Kans.): Archdiocese of Kansas City and suffragan sees of Dodge City, Salina, Wichita. Geographical area: Kansas.

**Los Angeles:** Archdiocese of Los Angeles and suffragan sees of Fresno, Monterey, Orange, San Bernardino, San Diego. Geographical area: Southern and Central California.

**Louisville:** Archdiocese of Louisville (Ky.) and suffragan sees of Covington, Lexington and Owensboro (Ky.); Knoxville, Memphis and Nashville (Tenn.). Geographical area: Kentucky, Tennessee.

**Miami:** Archdiocese of Miami and suffragan sees of Orlando, Palm Beach, Pensacola-Tallahassee, St. Augustine, St. Petersburg, Venice. Geographical area: Florida.

**Milwaukee:** Archdiocese of Milwaukee and suffragan sees of Green Bay, La Crosse, Madison, Superior. Geographical area: Wisconsin.

**Mobile:** Archdiocese of Mobile, Ala., and suffragan sees of Birmingham (Ala.); Biloxi and Jackson (Miss.). Geographical area: Alabama, Mississippi.

**Newark:** Archdiocese of Newark and suffragan sees of Camden, Metuchen, Paterson, Trenton. Geographical area: New Jersey.

**New Orleans:** Archdiocese of New Orleans and suffragan sees of Alexandria, Baton Rouge, Houma-Thibodaux, Lafayette, Lake Charles and Shreveport. Geographical area: Louisiana.

**New York:** Archdiocese of New York and suffragan sees of Albany, Brooklyn, Buffalo, Ogdensburg, Rochester, Rockville Centre, Syracuse. Geographical area: New York.

**Oklahoma City:** Archdiocese of Oklahoma City (Okla.) and suffragan sees of Tulsa (Okla.) and Little Rock (Ark.). Geographical area: Oklahoma, Arkansas.

**Omaha:** Archdiocese of Omaha and suffragan sees of Grand Island, Lincoln. Geographical area: Nebraska.

**Philadelphia:** Archdiocese of Philadelphia and suffragan sees of Allentown, Altoona-Johnstown, Erie, Greensburg, Harrisburg, Pittsburgh, Scranton. Geographical area: Pennsylvania.

**Philadelphia (Byzantine, Ukrainians):** Metropolitan See of Philadelphia (Byzantine) and Eparchies of St. Josaphat in Parma (Ohio), St. Nicholas of the Ukrainians in Chicago and Stamford, Conn. The jurisdiction extends to all Ukrainian Catholics in the U.S. from the ecclesiastical province of Galicia in the Ukraine.

**Pittsburgh (Byzantine, Ruthenia**ns): Metropolitan See of Pittsburgh, Pa. and Eparchies of Passaic (N.J.), Parma (Ohio), Van Nuys (Calif.).

**Portland:** Archdiocese of Portland (Ore.) and suffragan sees of Baker (Ore.); Boise (Ida.); Great Falls-Billings and Helena (Mont.). Geographical area: Oregon, Idaho, Montana.

**St. Louis:** Archdiocese of St. Louis and suffragan sees of Jefferson City, Kansas City-St. Joseph, Springfield-Cape Girardeau. Geographical area: Missouri.

**St. Paul and Minneapolis:** Archdiocese of St. Paul and Minneapolis (Minn.) and suffragan sees of Crookston, Duluth, New Ulm, St. Cloud and Winona (Minn.); Bismarck and Fargo (N.D.); Rapid City and Sioux Falls (S.D.). Geographical area: Minnesota, North Dakota, South Dakota.

**San Antonio:** Archdiocese of San Antonio (Tex.) and suffragan sees of Amarillo, Austin, Beaumont, Brownsville, Corpus Christi, Dallas, El Paso, Fort Worth, Galveston-Houston, Lubbock, San Angelo, Tyler and Victoria (Tex.). Geographical area: Texas.

**San Francisco:** Archdiocese of San Francisco (Calif.) and suffragan sees of Oakland, Sacramento, San Jose, Santa Rosa and Stockton (Calif.); Honolulu (Hawaii); Reno and Las Vegas (Nev.); Salt Lake City (Utah). Geographical area: Northern California, Nevada, Utah, Hawaii.

**Santa Fe:** Archdiocese of Santa Fe (N.M.) and suffragan sees of Gallup and Las Cruces (N.M.); Phoenix and Tucson (Ariz.). Geographical area: New Mexico, Arizona.

**Seattle:** Archdiocese of Seattle and suffragan sees of Spokane, Yakima. Geographical area: Washington.

**Washington:** Archdiocese of Washington, D.C., and suffragan see of St. Thomas (Virgin Islands). Geographical area: District of Columbia, five counties of Maryland, Virgin Islands.

# ARCHDIOCESES, DIOCESES, ARCHBISHOPS, BISHOPS

(Sources: *The Official Catholic Directory;* Catholic News Service; *L'Osservatore Romano.* As of August 20, 1996.)

Information includes name of diocese, year of foundation (as it appears on the official document erecting the see), present ordinaries (year of installation), auxiliaries and former ordinaries (for biographies, see Index).

Archdioceses are indicated by an asterisk.

**Albany, N.Y.** (1847): Howard J. Hubbard, bishop, 1977.

Former bishops: John McCloskey, 1847-64; John J. Conroy, 1865-77; Francis McNeirny, 1877-94; Thomas M. Burke, 1894-1915; Thomas F. Cusack, 1915-18; Edmund F. Gibbons, 1919-54; William A. Scully, 1954-69; Edwin B. Broderick, 1969-76.

**Alexandria, La.** (1853): Sam G. Jacobs, bishop, 1989.

Established at Natchitoches, transferred to Alexandria 1910; title changed to Alexandria-Shreveport, 1977; redesignated Alexandria, 1986, when Shreveport was made a diocese.

Former bishops: Augustus M. Martin, 1853-75; Francis X. Leray, 1877-79, administrator, 1879-83; Anthony Durier, 1885-1904; Cornelius Van de Ven, 1904-32; Daniel F. Desmond, 1933-45; Charles P. Greco, 1946-73; Lawrence P. Graves, 1973-82; William B. Friend, 1983-86; John C. Favalora, 1986-89.

**Allentown, Pa.** (1961): Thomas J. Welsh, bishop, 1983. Former bishop: Joseph McShea, 1961-83.

**Altoona-Johnstown, Pa.** (1901): Joseph V. Adamec, bishop, 1987.

Established as Altoona, name changed, 1957.

Former bishops: Eugene A. Garvey, 1901-20; John J. McCort, 1920-36; Richard T. Guilfoyle, 1936-57; Howard J. Carroll, 1958-60; J. Carroll McCormick, 1960-66; James J. Hogan, 1966-86.

**Amarillo, Tex.** (1926): Leroy T. Matthiesen, bishop, 1980.

Former bishops; Rudolph A. Gerken, 1927-33; Robert E. Lucey, 1934-41; Laurence J. Fitzsimon, 1941-58; John L. Morkovsky, 1958-63; Lawrence M. De Falco, 1963-79.

**Anchorage,\* Alaska** (1966): Francis T. Hurley, archbishop, 1976.

Former archbishop: Joseph T. Ryan, 1966-75.

**Arlington, Va.** (1974): John R. Keating, bishop, 1983.

Former bishop: Thomas J. Welsh, 1974-83.

**Atlanta,\* Ga.** (1956; archdiocese, 1962): John F. Donoghue, archbishop, 1993.

Former ordinaries: Francis E. Hyland, 1956-61; Paul J. Hallinan, first archbishop, 1962-68; Thomas A. Donnellan, 1968-87; Eugene A. Marino, S.S.J., 1988-90; James P. Lyke, 1991-92.

**Austin, Tex.** (1947): John E. McCarthy, bishop, 1986.

Former bishops: Louis J. Reicher, 1947-71; Vincent M. Harris, 1971-86.

**Baker, Ore.** (1903): Thomas J. Connolly, bishop, 1971.

Established as Baker City, name changed, 1952.

Former bishops: Charles J. O'Reilly, 1903-18; Joseph F. McGrath, 1919-50; Francis P. Leipzig, 1950-71.

**Baltimore,\* Md.** (1789; archdiocese, 1808): Cardinal William H. Keeler, archbishop, 1989. P. Francis Murphy, William C. Newman, John H. Ricard, S.S.J., auxiliaries.

Former ordinaries: John Carroll, 1789-1815, first archbishop; Leonard Neale, 1815-17; Ambrose Marechal, S.S., 1817-28; James Whitfield, 1828-34; Samuel Eccleston, S.S., 1834-51; Francis P. Kenrick, 1851-63; Martin J. Spalding, 1864-72; James R. Bayley, 1872-77; Cardinal James Gibbons, 1877-1921; Michael J. Curley, 1921-47; Francis P. Keough, 1947-61; Cardinal Lawrence J. Shehan, 1961-74; William D. Borders, 1974-89.

**Baton Rouge, La.** (1961): Alfred C. Hughes, bishop, 1993.

Former bishops: Robert E. Tracy, 1961-74; Joseph V. Sullivan, 1974-82; Stanley J. Ott, 1983-93.

**Beaumont, Tex.** (1966): Joseph A. Galante, bishop, 1994.

Former bishops: Vincent M. Harris, 1966-71; Warren L. Boudreaux, 1971-77; Bernard J. Ganter, 1977-93.

**Belleville, Ill.** (1887): Wilton D. Gregory, bishop, 1994.

Former bishops: John Janssen, 1888-1913; Henry Althoff, 1914-47; Albert R. Zuroweste, 1948-76; William M. Cosgrove, 1976-81; John N. Wurm, 1981-84; James P. Keleher, 1984-93.

**Biloxi, Miss.** (1977): Joseph Lawson Howze, bishop, 1977.

**Birmingham, Ala.** (1969): David E. Foley, bishop, 1994.

Former bishops: Joseph G. Vath, 1969-87; Raymond J. Boland, 1988-93.

**Bismarck, N. Dak.** (1909): Vacant as of June 15, 1996.

Former bishops: Vincent Wehrle, O.S.B., 1910-39; Vincent J. Ryan, 1940-51; Lambert A. Hoch, 1952-56; Hilary B. Hacker, 1957-82; John F. Kinney, 1982-95.

**Boise, Ida.** (1893): Tod David Brown, bishop, 1989.

Former bishops: Alphonse J. Glorieux, 1893-1917; Daniel M. Gorman, 1918-27; Edward J. Kelly, 1928-56; James J. Byrne, 1956-62; Sylvester Treinen, 1962-88.

**Boston,\* Mass.** (1808; archdiocese, 1875): Cardinal Bernard F. Law, archbishop, 1984. John R. McNamara, John P. Boles, William F. Murphy, John B. McCormack, Francis Xavier Irwin, Emilio Allue, S.D.B. auxiliaries.

Former ordinaries: John L. de Cheverus, 1810-23; Benedict J. Fenwick, S.J., 1825-46; John B. Fitzpatrick, 1846-66; John J. Williams, 1866-1907, first archbishop; Cardinal William O'Connell, 1907-44; Cardinal Richard Cushing, 1944-70; Cardinal Humberto Medeiros, 1970-83.

**Bridgeport, Conn.** (1953): Edward M. Egan, bishop, 1988.

Former bishops: Lawrence J. Shehan, 1953-61; Walter W. Curtis, 1961-88.

**Brooklyn, N.Y.** (1853): Thomas V. Daily, bishop, 1990. Joseph M. Sullivan, Rene A. Valero, Ignatius Catanello, Gerald Barbarito, auxiliaries.

Former bishops: John Loughlin, 1853-91; Charles E. McDonnell, 1892-1921; Thomas E. Molloy, 1921-56; Bryan J. McEntegart, 1957-68; Francis J. Mugavero, 1968-90.

**Brownsville, Tex.** (1965): Raymundo J. Pena, bishop, 1995.

Former bishops: Adolph Marx, 1965; Humberto S. Medeiros, 1966-70; John J. Fitzpatrick, 1971-91; Enrique San Pedro, S.J., 1991-94.

**Buffalo, N.Y.** (1847): Henry J. Mansell, bishop, 1995. Edward M. Grosz, auxiliary.

Former bishops: John Timon, C.M., 1847-67; Stephen V. Ryan, C.M., 1868-96; James E. Quigley, 1897-1903; Charles H. Colton, 1903-15; Dennis J. Dougherty, 1915-18; William Turner, 1919-36; John A. Duffy, 1937-44; John F. O'Hara, C.S.C., 1945-51; Joseph A. Burke, 1952-62; James McNulty, 1963-72; Edward D. Head, 1973-95.

**Burlington, Vt.** (1853): Kenneth A. Angell, bishop, 1992.

Former bishops: Louis De Goesbriand, 1853-99; Joh S. Michaud, 1899-1908; Joseph J. Rice, 1910-38; Matthew F. Brady, 1938-44; Edward F. Ryan, 1945-56; Robert F. Joyce, 1957-71; John A. Marshall, 1972-91.

**Camden, N.J.** (1937): James T. McHugh, bishop, 1989.

Former bishops: Bartholomew J. Eustace, 1938-56; Justin J. McCarthy, 1957-59; Celestine J. Damiano, 1960-67; George H. Guilfoyle, 1968-89.

**Charleston, S.C.** (1820): David B. Thompson, bishop, 1990.

Former bishops: John England, 1820-42; Ignatius W. Reynolds, 1844-55; Patrick N. Lynch, 1858-82; Henry P. Northrop, 1883-1916; William T. Russell, 1917-27; Emmet M. Walsh, 1927-49; John J. Russell, 1950-58; Paul J. Hallinan, 1958-62; Francis F. Reh, 1962-64; Ernest L. Unterkoefler, 1964-90.

**Charlotte, N.C.** (1971): William G. Curlin, bishop, 1994.

Former bishops: Michael J. Begley, 1972-84; John F. Donoghue, 1984-93.

**Cheyenne, Wyo.** (1887): Joseph Hart, bishop, 1978.

Former bishops: Maurice F. Burke, 1887-93; Thomas M. Lenihan, 1897-1901; James J. Keane, 1902-11; Patrick A. McGovern, 1912-51; Hubert M. Newell, 1951-78.

**Chicago,\* Ill.** (1843; archdiocese, 1880): Cardinal Joseph L. Bernardin, archbishop, 1982. Thad J. Jakubowski, John R. Gorman, Raymond E. Goedert, Edwin M. Conway, Gerald F. Kicanas, George V. Murry, S.J., John R. Manz, auxiliaries.

Former ordinaries: William Quarter, 1844-48; James O. Van de Velde, S.J., 1849-53; Anthony O'Regan, 1854-58; James Duggan, 1859-70; Thomas P. Foley, administrator, 1870-79; Patrick A. Feehan, 1880-1902, first archbishop; James E. Quigley, 1903-15; Cardinal George Mundelein, 1915-39; Cardinal Samuel Stritch, 1939-58; Cardinal Albert Meyer, 1958-65; Cardinal John Cody, 1965-82.

**Cincinnati,\* Ohio** (1821; archdiocese, 1850): Daniel E. Pilarczyk, archbishop, 1982. Carl K. Moeddel, auxiliary.

Former ordinaries: Edward D. Fenwick, O.P., 1822-32; John B. Purcell, 1833-83, first archbishop; William H. Elder, 1883-1904; Henry Moeller, 1904-1925; John T. McNicholas, O.P., 1925-50; Karl J. Alter, 1950-69; Paul F. Leibold, 1969-72; Joseph L. Bernardin, 1972-82.

**Cleveland, Ohio** (1847): Anthony M. Pilla, bishop, 1980. A. Edward Pevec, A. James Quinn, auxiliaries.

Former bishops: L. Amadeus Rappe, 1847-70; Richard Gilmour, 1872-91; Ignatius F. Horstmann, 1892-1908; John P. Farrelly, 1909-21; Joseph Schrembs, 1921-45; Edward F. Hoban, 1945-66; Clarence G. Issenmann, 1966-74; James A. Hickey, 1974-80.

**Colorado Springs, Colo.** (1983): Richard C. Hanifen, bishop, 1984.

**Columbus, Ohio** (1868): James A. Griffin, bishop, 1983.

Former bishops: Sylvester H. Rosecrans, 1868-78; John A. Watterson, 1880-99; Henry Moeller, 1900-03; James J. Hartley, 1904-44; Michael J. Ready, 1944-57; Clarence Issenmann, 1957-64; John J. Carberry, 1965-68; Clarence E. Elwell, 1968-73; Edward J. Herrmann, 1973-82.

**Corpus Christi, Tex.** (1912): Rene H. Gracida,

bishop, 1983. Roberto O. Gonzalez, O.F.M., coadjutor, 1995.

Former bishops: Paul J. Nussbaum, C.P., 1913-20; Emmanuel B. Ledvina, 1921-49; Mariano S. Garriga, 1949-65; Thomas J. Drury, 1965-83.

**Covington, Ky.** (1853): Robert W. Muench, bishop, 1996.

Former bishops: George A. Carrell, S.J., 1853-68; Augustus M. Toebbe, 1870-84; Camillus P. Maes, 1885-1914; Ferdinand Brossart, 1916-23; Francis W. Howard, 1923-44; William T. Mulloy, 1945-59; Richard Ackerman, C.S.Sp., 1960-78; William A. Hughes, 1979-95.

**Crookston, Minn.** (1909): Victor H. Balke, bishop, 1976.

Former bishops: Timothy Corbett, 1910-38; John H. Peschges, 1938-44; Francis J. Schenk, 1945-60; Laurence A. Glenn, 1960-70; Kenneth J. Povish, 1970-75.

**Dallas, Tex.** (1890): Charles V. Grahmann, bishop, 1990.

Established 1890, as Dallas, title changed to Dallas-Ft. Worth 1953; redesignated Dallas, 1969, when Ft. Worth was made diocese.

Former bishops: Thomas F. Brennan, 1891-92; Edward J. Dunne, 1893-1910; Joseph P. Lynch, 1911-54; Thomas K. Gorman, 1954-69; Thomas Tschoepe, 1969-90.

**Davenport, Ia.** (1881): William E. Franklin, bishop, 1993.

Former bishops: John McMullen, 1881-83; Henry Cosgrove, 1884-1906; James Davis, 1906-26; Henry P. Rohlman, 1927-44; Ralph L. Hayes, 1944-66; Gerald F. O'Keefe, 1966-93.

**Denver,*** Colo. (1887; archdiocese, 1941): Vacant.

Former ordinaries: Joseph P. Machebeuf, 1887-89; Nicholas C. Matz, 1889-1917; J. Henry Tihen, 1917-31; Urban J. Vehr, 1931-67, first archbishop; James V. Casey, 1967-86; J. Francis Stafford, 1986-96.

**Des Moines, Ia.** (1911): Joseph J. Charron, C.PP.S., bishop, 1993.

Former bishops: Austin Dowling, 1912-19; Thomas W. Drumm, 1919-33; Gerald T. Bergan, 1934-48; Edward C. Daly, O.P., 1948-64; George J. Biskup, 1965-67; Maurice J. Dingman, 1968-86; William H. Bullock, 1987-93.

**Detroit,*** Mich. (1833; archdiocese, 1937): Cardinal Adam J. Maida, archbishop, 1990. Thomas J. Gumbleton, Moses B. Anderson, S.S.E.,Kevin M. Britt, Bernard J. Harrington, John C. Nienstedt, Allen H. Vigneron, auxiliaries.

Former ordinaries: Frederic Rese, 1833-71; Peter P. Lefevere, administrator, 1841-69; Caspar H. Borgess, 1871-88; John S. Foley, 1888-1918; Michael J. Gallagher, 1918-37; Cardinal Edward Mooney, 1937-58, first archbishop; Cardinal John F. Dearden, 1958-80; Cardinal Edmund C. Szoka, 1981-90.

**Dodge City, Kans.** (1951): Stanley G. Schlarman, bishop, 1983.

Former bishops: John B. Franz, 1951-59; Marion F. Forst, 1960-76; Eugene J. Gerber, 1976-82.

**Dubuque,*** Iowa (1837; archdiocese, 1893): Jerome Hanus, O.S.B., archbishop, 1995.

Former ordinaries: Mathias Loras, 1837-58; Clement Smyth, O.C.S.O., 1858-65; John Hennessy, 1866-

1900, first archbishop; John J. Keane, 1900-11; James J. Keane, 1911-29; Francis J. Beckman, 1930-46; Henry P. Rohlman, 1946-54; Leo Binz, 1954-61; James J. Byrne, 1962-83; Daniel W. Kucera, O.S.B., 1984-95.

**Duluth, Minn.** (1889): Roger L. Schwietz, O.M.I., bishop, 1990.

Former bishops: James McGolrick, 1889-1918; John T. McNicholas, O.P., 1918-25; Thomas A. Welch, 1926-59; Francis J. Schenk, 1960-69; Paul F. Anderson, 1969-82; Robert H. Brom, 1983-89.

**El Paso, Tex.** (1914): Armando Ochoa, bishop, 1996.

Former bishops: Anthony J. Schuler, S.J., 1915-42; Sidney M. Metzger, 1942-78. Patrick F. Flores, 1978-79; Raymundo J. Pena, 1980-95.

**Erie, Pa.** (1853): Donald W. Trautman, bishop, 1990.

Former bishops: Michael O'Connor, 1853-54; Josue M. Young, 1854-66; Tobias Mullen, 1868-99; John E. Fitzmaurice, 1899-1920; John M. Gannon, 1920-66; John F. Whealon, 1966-69; Alfred M. Watson, 1969-82; Michael J. Murphy, 1982-90.

**Evansville, Ind.** (1944): Gerald A. Gettelfinger, bishop, 1989.

Former bishops: Henry J. Grimmelsman, 1944-65; Paul F. Leibold, 1966-69; Francis R. Shea, 1970-89.

**Fairbanks, Alaska** (1962): Michael J. Kaniecki, S.J., bishop, 1985.

Former bishops: Francis D. Gleeson, S.J., 1962-68; Robert L. Whelan, S.J., 1968-85.

**Fall River, Mass.** (1904): Sean O'Malley, O.F.M. Cap., bishop, 1992.

Former bishops: William Stang, 1904-07; Daniel F. Feehan, 1907-34; James E. Cassidy, 1934-51; James L. Connolly, 1951-70; Daniel A. Cronin, 1970-91.

**Fargo, N. Dak.** (1889): James S. Sullivan, bishop, 1985.

Established at Jamestown, transferred, 1897.

Former bishops: John Shanley, 1889-1909; James O'Reilly, 1910-34; Aloysius J. Muench, 1935-59; Leo F. Dworschak, 1960-70; Justin A. Driscoll, 1970-84.

**Fort Wayne-South Bend, Ind.** (1857): John M. D'Arcy, bishop, 1985. John R. Sheets, S.J., auxiliary.

Established as Fort Wayne, name changed, 1960.

Former bishops: John H. Luers, 1858-71; Joseph Dwenger, C.Pp. S., 1872-93; Joseph Rademacher, 1893-1900; Herman J. Alerding, 1900-24; John F. Noll, 1925-56; Leo A. Pursley, 1957-76; William E. McManus, 1976-85.

**Fort Worth, Tex.** (1969): Joseph P. Delaney, bishop, 1981.

Former bishop: John J. Cassata, 1969-80.

**Fresno, Calif.** (1967): John T. Steinbock, bishop, 1991.

Formerly Monterey-Fresno, 1922.

Former bishops (Monterey-Fresno): John J. Cantwell, administrator, 1922-24; John B. MacGinley, first bishop, 1924-32; Philip G. Sher, 1933-53; Aloysius J. Willinger, 1953-67.

Former bishops (Fresno): Timothy Manning, 1967-69; Hugh A. Donohoe, 1969-80; Joseph J. Madera, M.Pp.S., 1980-91.

**Gallup, N. Mex.** (1939): Donald Pelotte, S.S.S., bishop, 1990.

Former bishops: Bernard T. Espelage, O.F.M., 1940-69; Jerome J. Hastrich, 1969-90.

**Galveston-Houston, Tex.** (1847): Joseph A. Fiorenza, bishop, 1985. Curtis J. Guillory, S.V.D.; James A. Tamayo, auxiliaries.

Established as Galveston, name changed, 1959.

Former bishops: John M. Odin, C.M., 1847-61; Claude M. Dubuis, 1862-92; Nicholas A. Gallagher, 1892-1918; Christopher E. Byrne, 1918-50; Wendelin J. Nold, 1950-75; John L. Morkovsky, 1975-84.

**Gary, Ind.** (1956): Dale J. Melczek, bishop, 1996.

Former bishops: Andrew G. Grutka, 1957-84; Norbert F. Gaughan, 1984-96.

**Gaylord, Mich.** (1971): Patrick R. Cooney, bishop, 1989, installed 1990.

Former bishops: Edmund C. Szoka, 1971-81; Robert J. Rose, 1981-89.

**Grand Island, Neb.** (1912): Lawrence J. McNamara, bishop, 1978.

Established at Kearney, transferred, 1917.

Former bishops: James A. Duffy, 1913-31; Stanislaus V. Bona, 1932-44; Edward J. Hunkeler, 1945-51; John L. Paschang, 1951-72; John J. Sullivan, 1972-77.

**Grand Rapids, Mich.** (1882): Robert J. Rose, bishop, 1989. Joseph C. McKinney, auxiliary.

Former bishops: Henry J. Richter, 1883-1916; Michael J. Gallagher, 1916-18; Edward D. Kelly, 1919-26; Joseph G. Pinten, 1926-40; Joseph C. Plagens, 1941-43; Francis J. Haas, 1943-53; Allen J. Babcock, 1954-69; Joseph M. Breitenbeck, 1969-89.

**Great Falls-Billings, Mont.** (1904): Anthony M. Milone, bishop, 1988.

Established as Great Falls; name changed, 1980.

Former bishops: Mathias C. Lenihan, 1904-30; Edwin V. O'Hara, 1930-39; William J. Condon, 1939-67; Eldon B. Schuster, 1968-77; Thomas J. Murphy, 1978-87.

**Green Bay, Wis.** (1868): Robert J. Banks, bishop, 1990. Robert F. Morneau, auxiliary.

Former bishops: Joseph Melcher, 1868-73; Francis X. Krautbauer, 1875-85; Frederick X. Katzer, 1886-91; Sebastian G. Messmer, 1892-1903; Joseph J. Fox, 1904-14; Paul P. Rhode, 1915-45; Stanislaus V. Bona, 1945-67; Aloysius J. Wycislo, 1968-83; Adam J. Maida, 1984-90.

**Greensburg, Pa.** (1951): Anthony G. Bosco, bishop, 1987.

Former bishops: Hugh L. Lamb, 1951-59; Willam G. Connare, 1960-87.

**Harrisburg, Pa.** (1868): Nicholas C. Dattilo, bishop, 1990.

Former bishops: Jeremiah F. Shanahan, 1868-86; Thomas McGovern, 1888-98; John W. Shanahan,1899-1916; Philip R. McDevitt, 1916-35; George L. Leech, 1935-71; Joseph T. Daley, 1971-83; William H. Keeler, 1984-89.

**Hartford,\* Conn.** (1843; archdiocese, 1953): Daniel A. Cronin, archbishop, 1991, installed, 1992. Peter A. Rosazza, auxiliary.

Former ordinaries: William Tyler, 1844-49; Bernard O'Reilly, 1850-56; F. P. MacFarland, 1858-74; Thomas Galberry, O.S.A., 1876-78; Lawrence S.

McMahon, 1879-93; Michael Tierney, 1894-1908; John J. Nilan, 1910-34; Maurice F. McAuliffe, 1934-44; Henry J. O'Brien, 1945-68, first archbishop; John F. Whealon, 1969-91.

**Helena, Mont.** (1884): Alexander J. Brunett, bishop, 1994.

Former bishops: John B. Brondel, 1884-1903; John P. Carroll, 1904-25; George J. Finnigan, C.S.C., 1927-32; Ralph L. Hayes, 1933-35; Joseph M. Gilmore, 1936-62; Raymond Hunthausen, 1962-75; Elden F. Curtiss, 1976-93.

**Honolulu, Hawaii** (1941): Francis X. DiLorenzo (apostolic administrator, 1993), bishop, 1994.

Former bishops: James J. Sweeney, 1941-68; John J. Scanlan, 1968-81; Joseph A. Ferrario, 1982-93.

**Houma-Thibodaux, La.** (1977): C. Michael Jarrell, bishop, 1993.

Former bishop: Warren L. Boudreaux, 1977-92.

**Indianapolis,\* Ind.** (1834; archdiocese, 1944): Daniel M. Buechlein, O.S.B., archbishop, 1992.

Established at Vincennes, transferred, 1898.

Former ordinaries: Simon G. Bruté, 1834-39; Celestine de la Hailandiere, 1839-47; John S. Bazin, 1847-48; Maurice de St. Palais, 1849-77; Francis S. Chatard, 1878-1918; Joseph Chartrand, 1918-33; Joseph E. Ritter, 1934-46, first archbishop; Paul C. Schulte, 1946-70; George J. Biskup, 1970-79; Edward T. O'Meara, 1980-92.

**Jackson, Miss.** (1837): William R. Houck, bishop, 1984.

Established at Natchez; title changed to Natchez-Jackson, 1956; transferred to Jackson, 1977 (Natchez made titular see).

Former bishops: John J. Chanche, S.S., 1841-52; James Van de Velde, S.J., 1853-55; William H. Elder, 1857-80; Francis A. Janssens, 1881-88; Thomas Heslin, 1889-1911; John E. Gunn, S.M., 1911-24; Richard O. Gerow, 1924-67; Joseph B. Brunini, 1968-84.

**Jefferson City, Mo.** (1956): Michael F. McAuliffe, bishop, 1969.

Former bishop: Joseph Marling, C.Pp.S., 1956-69.

**Joliet, Ill.** (1948): Joseph L. Imesch, bishop, 1979. Roger L. Kaffer, auxiliary.

Former bishops: Martin D. McNamara, 1949-66; Romeo Blanchette, 1966-79.

**Juneau, Alaska** (1951): Vacant as of May 15, 1996.

Former bishops: Dermot O'Flanagan, 1951-68; Joseph T. Ryan, administrator, 1968-71; Francis T. Hurley, 1971-76, administrator, 1976-79; Michael H. Kenny, 1979-95.

**Kalamazoo, Mich.** (1971): Alfred J. Markiewicz, bishop, 1995.

Former bishop: Paul V. Donovan, 1971-94.

**Kansas City,\* Kans.** (1877; archdiocese, 1952): James P. Keleher, archbishop, 1993.

Established as vicariate apostolic, 1850, became Diocese of Leavenworth, 1877, transferred to Kansas City 1947.

Former ordinaries: J. B. Miege, vicar apostolic, 1851-74; Louis M. Fink, O.S.B., vicar apostolic, 1874-77, first bishop, 1877-1904; Thomas F. Lillis, 1904-10; John Ward, 1910-29; Francis Johannes, 1929-37; Paul C. Schulte, 1937-46; George J. Donnelly, 1946-50; Edward Hunkeler, 1951-69, first archbishop; Ignatius J. Strecker, 1969-93.

**Kansas City-St. Joseph, Mo.** Kansas City, 1880; St. Joseph, 1868; united 1956): Raymond J. Boland, bishop, 1993.

Former bishops: John J. Hogan, 1880-1913; Thomas F. Lillis, 1913-38; Edwin V. O'Hara, 1939-56; John P. Cody, 1956-61; Charles H. Helmsing, 1962-77; John J. Sullivan, 1977-93.

Former bishops (St. Joseph): John J. Hogan, 1868-80, administrator, 1880-93; Maurice F. Burke, 1893-1923; Francis Gilfillan, 1923-33; Charles H. Le Blond, 1933-56.

**Knoxville, Tenn.** (1988): Anthony J. O'Connell, bishop, 1988.

**La Crosse, Wis.** (1868): Raymond L. Burke, bishop, 1995.

Former bishops: Michael Heiss, 1868-80; Kilian C. Flasch, 1881-91; James Schwebach, 1892-1921; Alexander J. McGavick, 1921-48; John P. Treacy, 1948-64; Frederick W. Freking, 1965-83; John J. Paul, 1983-94.

**Lafayette, Ind.** (1944): William L. Higi, bishop, 1984.

Former bishops: John G. Bennett, 1944-57; John J. Carberry, 1957-65; Raymond J. Gallagher, 1965-82; George A. Fulcher, 1983-84.

**Lafayette, La.** (1918): Edward J. O'Donnell, bishop, 1994.

Former bishops: Jules B. Jeanmard, 1918-56; Maurice Schexnayder, 1956-72; Gerard L. Frey, 1973-89; Harry J. Flynn, 1989-94.

**Lake Charles, La.** (1980): Jude Speyrer, bishop, 1980.

**Lansing, Mich.** (1937): Carl F. Mengeling, bishop, 1995; installed 1996.

Former bishops: Joseph H. Albers, 1937-65; Alexander Zaleski, 1965-75; Kenneth J. Povish, 1975-95.

**Las Cruces, N. Mex.** (1982): Ricardo Ramirez, C.S.B., bishop, 1982.

**Las Vegas, Nev.** (1995): Daniel F. Walsh, bishop, 1995.

**Lexington, Ky.** (1988): James Kendrick Williams, bishop, 1988.

**Lincoln, Neb.** (1887): Fabian W. Bruskewitz, bishop, 1992.

Former bishops: Thomas Bonacum, 1887-1911; J. Henry Tihen, 1911-17; Charles J. O'Reilly, 1918-23; Francis J. Beckman, 1924-30; Louis B. Kucera, 1930-57; James V. Casey, 1957-67; Glennon P. Flavin, 1967-92.

**Little Rock, Ark.** (1843): Andrew J. McDonald, bishop, 1972.

Former bishops: Andrew Byrne, 1844-62; Edward Fitzgerald, 1867-1907; John Morris, 1907-46; Albert L. Fletcher, 1946-72.

**Los Angeles,\* Calif.** (1840; archdiocese, 1936): Cardinal Roger M. Mahony, archbishop, 1985. Stephen E. Blaire, Thomas J. Curry, Joseph M. Sartoris, Gabino Zavala, auxiliaries.

Founded as diocese of Two Californias, 1840; became Monterey diocese, 1850; Baja California detached from Monterey diocese, 1852; title changed to Monterey-Los Angeles, 1859; Los Angeles-San Diego, 1922; became archdiocese under present title, 1936 (San Diego became separate see).

Former ordinaries: Francisco Garcia Diego y

Moreno, O.F.M., 1840-46; Joseph S. Alemany, O.P., 1850-53; Thaddeus Amat, C.M., 1854-78; Francis Mora, 1878-96; George T. Montgomery, 1896-1903; Thomas J. Conaty, 1903-15; John J. Cantwell, 1917-47, first archbishop; Cardinal James McIntyre, 1948-70; Cardinal Timothy Manning, 1970-85.

**Louisville,\* Ky.** (1808; archdiocese, 1937): Thomas C. Kelly, O.P., archbishop, 1982.

Established at Bardstown, transferred, 1841.

Former ordinaries: Benedict J. Flaget, S.S., 1810-32; John B. David, S.S., 1832-33; Benedict J. Flaget, S.S., 1833-50; Martin J. Spalding, 1850-64; Peter J. Lavialle, 1865-67; William G. McCloskey, 1868-1909; Denis O'Donaghue, 1910-24; John A. Floersh, 1924-67, first archbishop; Thomas J. McDonough, 1967-81.

**Lubbock, Tex.** (1983): Placido Rodriguez, C.M.F., bishop, 1994.

Former bishop: Michael J. Sheehan, 1983-93.

**Madison, Wis.** (1946): William H. Bullock, bishop, 1993. George O. Wirz, auxiliary.

Former bishops: William P. O'Connor, 1946-67; Cletus F. O'Donnell, 1967-92.

**Manchester, N.H.** (1884): Leo E. O'Neil, bishop, 1990. Francis J. Christian, auxiliary.

Former bishops: Denis M. Bradley, 1884-1903; John B. Delany, 1904-06; George A. Guertin, 1907-32; John B. Peterson, 1932-44; Matthew F. Brady, 1944-59; Ernest J. Primeau, 1960-74; Odore J. Gendron, 1975-90.

**Marquette, Mich.** (1857): James H. Garland, bishop, 1992.

Founded as Sault Ste. Marie and Marquette; changed to Marquette, 1937.

Former bishops: Frederic Baraga, 1857-68; Ignatius Mrak, 1869-78; John Vertin, 1879-99; Frederick Eis, 1899-1922; Paul J. Nussbaum, C.P., 1922-35; Joseph C. Plagens, 1935-40; Francis Magner, 1941-47; Thomas L. Noa, 1947-68; Charles A. Salatka, 1968-77; Mark F. Schmitt, 1978-92.

**Memphis, Tenn.** (1970): J. Terry Steib, S.V.D., bishop, 1993.

Former bishops: Carroll T. Dozier, 1971-82; J. Francis Stafford, 1982-86; Daniel M. Buechlein, O.S.B., 1987-92.

**Metuchen, N.J.** (1981): Edward T. Hughes, bishop, 1987.

Former bishop: Theodore E. McCarrick, 1981-86.

**Miami,\* Fla.** (1958; archdiocese, 1968): John C. Favalora, archbishop, 1994. Agustin A. Roman, auxiliary.

Former ordinaries: Coleman F. Carroll, 1958-77, first archbishop; Edward A. McCarthy, 1977-94.

**Milwaukee,\* Wis.** (1843; archdiocese, 1875): Rembert G. Weakland, O.S.B., archbishop, 1977. Richard J. Sklba, auxiliary.

Former ordinaries: John M. Henni, 1844-81, first archbishop; Michael Heiss, 1881-90; Frederick X. Katzer, 1891-1903; Sebastian G. Messmer, 1903-30; Samuel A. Stritch, 1930-39; Moses E. Kiley, 1940-53; Albert G. Meyer, 1953-58; William E. Cousins, 1959-77.

**Mobile,\* Ala.** (1829; archdiocese, 1980): Oscar H. Lipscomb, first archbishop, 1980.

Founded as Mobile, 1829; title changed to Mobile-Birmingham, 1954; redesignated Mobile, 1969.

Former bishops: Michael Portier, 1829-59; John Quinlan, 1859-83; Dominic Manucy, 1884; Jeremiah O'Sullivan, 1885-96; Edward P. Allen, 1897-1926; Thomas J. Toolen, 1927-69; John L. May, 1969-80.
**Monterey in California** (1967): Sylvester D. Ryan, bishop, 1992.
Formerly Monterey-Fresno, 1922. (Originally established in 1850, see Los Angeles listing.)
Former bishops (Monterey-Fresno): John J. Cantwell, administrator, 1922-24; John B. MacGinley, first bishop, 1924-32; Philip G. Sher, 1933-53; Aloysius J. Willinger, 1953-67.
Former bishops (Monterey): Harry A. Clinch, 1967-82; Thaddeus A. Shubsda, 1982-91.
**Nashville, Tenn.** (1837): Edward U. Kmiec, bishop, 1992.
Former bishops: Richard P. Miles, O.P., 1838-60; James Whelan, O.P., 1860-64; Patrick A. Feehan, 1865-80; Joseph Rademacher, 1883-93; Thomas S. Byrne, 1894-1923; Alphonse J. Smith, 1924-35; William L. Adrian, 1936-69; Joseph A. Durick, 1969-75; James D. Niedergeses, 1975-92.
**Newark,\* N.J.** (1853; archdiocese, 1937): Theodore E. McCarrick, archbishop, 1986. Dominic A. Marconi, David Arias, O.A.R., Charles J. McDonnell, auxiliaries.
Former ordinaries: James R. Bayley, 1853-72; Michael A. Corrigan, 1873-80; Winand M. Wigger, 1881-1901; John J. O'Connor, 1901-27; Thomas J. Walsh, 1928-52, first archbishop; Thomas A. Boland, 1953-74; Peter L. Gerety, 1974-86.
**New Orleans,\* La.** (1793; archdiocese, 1850): Francis B. Schulte, archbishop, 1988; installed, 1989. Dominic Carmon, S.V.D. auxiliary.
Former ordinaries: Luis Penalver y Cardenas, 1793-1801; John Carroll, administrator, 1805-15; W. Louis Dubourg, S.S., 1815-25; Joseph Rosati, C.M., administrator, 1826-9; Leo De Neckere, C.M., 1829-33; Anthony Blanc, 1835-60, first archbishop; Jean Marie Odin, C.M., 1861-70; Napoleon J. Perche, 1870-83; Francis X. Leray, 1883-87; Francis A. Janssens, 1888-97; Placide L. Chapelle, 1897-1905; James H. Blenk, S.M., 1906-17; John W. Shaw, 1918-34; Joseph F. Rummel, 1935-64; John P. Cody, 1964-65; Philip M. Hannan, 1965-88.
**Newton, Mass.** (Melkite) (1966; eparchy, 1976): John A. Elya, B.S.O., eparch, 1993; installed, 1994. Nicholas Samra, auxiliary.
Former ordinaries: Justin Najmy, exarch, 1966-68; Joseph Tawil, exarch, 1969-76, first eparch, 1976-89; Ignatius Ghattas, B.S.O., 1990-92.
**New Ulm, Minn.** (1957): Raymond A. Lucker, bishop, 1975; installed, 1976.
Former bishop: Alphonse J. Schladweiler, 1958-75.
**New York,\* N.Y.** (1808; archdiocese, 1850): Cardinal John J. O'Connor, archbishop, 1984. James P. Mahoney, Anthony F. Mestice, Austin B. Vaughan, Francisco Garmendia, William J. McCormack, Patrick J. Sheridan, Edwin F. O'Brien, auxiliaries.
Former ordinaries: Richard L. Concanen, O.P., 1808-10; John Connolly, O.P., 1814-25; John Dubois, S.S., 1826-42; John J. Hughes, 1842-64, first archbishop; Cardinal John McCloskey, 1864-85; Michael A. Corrigan, 1885-1902; Cardinal John Farley, 1902-18; Cardinal Patrick Hayes, 1919-38; Cardinal

Francis Spellman, 1939-67; Cardinal Terence J. Cooke, 1968-83.
**Norwich, Conn.** (1953): Daniel A. Hart, bishop, 1995.
Former bishops: Bernard J. Flanagan, 1953-59; Vincent J. Hines, 1960-75; Daniel P. Reilly, 1975-94.
**Oakland, Calif.** (1962): John S. Cummins, bishop, 1977.
Former bishop: Floyd L. Begin, 1962-77.
**Ogdensburg, N.Y.** (1872): Paul S. Loverde, bishop, 1993.
Former bishops: Edgar P. Wadhams, 1872-91; Henry Gabriels, 1892-1921; Joseph H. Conroy, 1921-39; Francis J. Monaghan, 1939-42; Bryan J. McEntegart, 1943-53; Walter P. Kellenberg, 1954-57; James J. Navagh, 1957-63; Leo R. Smith, 1963; Thomas A. Donnellan, 1964-68; Stanislaus J. Brzana, 1968-93.
**Oklahoma City,\* Okla.** (1905; archdiocese, 1972): Eusebius J. Beltran, archbishop, 1993.
Former ordinaries: Theophile Meerschaert, 1905-24; Francis C. Kelley, 1924-48; Eugene J. McGuinness, 1948-57; Victor J. Reed, 1958-71; John R. Quinn, 1971-77, first archbishop; Charles A. Salatka, 1977-92.
**Omaha,\* Nebr.** (1885; archdiocese, 1945): Elden F. Curtiss, archbishop, 1993.
Former ordinaries: James O'Gorman, O.C.S.O., 1859-74, vicar apostolic; James O'Connor, vicar apostolic, 1876-85, first bishop, 1885-90; Richard Scannell, 1891-1916; Jeremiah J. Harty, 1916-27; Francis Beckman, administrator, 1926-28; Joseph F. Rummel, 1928-35; James H. Ryan, 1935-47, first archbishop; Gerald T. Bergan, 1948-69; Daniel E. Sheehan, 1969-93.
**Orange, Calif.** (1976): Norman F. McFarland, bishop, 1986, installed, 1987. Michael P. Driscoll, auxiliary.
Former bishop: William R. Johnson, 1976-86.
**Orlando, Fla.** (1968): Norbert M. Dorsey, C.P., bishop, 1990.
Former bishops: William Borders, 1968-74; Thomas J. Grady, 1974-89.
**Our Lady of Deliverance of Newark** (for Syrian-rite Catholics of the U.S. and Canada) (1995): Joseph Younan, bishop, 1996.
**Our Lady of Lebanon of Los Angeles, Calif.** (Maronite) (1994): John G. Chedid, eparch, 1994.
**Owensboro, Ky.** (1937): John J. McRaith, bishop, 1982.
Former bishops: Francis R. Cotton, 1938-60; Henry J. Soenneker, 1961-82.
**Palm Beach, Fla.** (1984): J. Keith Symons, bishop, 1990.
Former bishop: Thomas V. Daily, 1984-90.
**Parma, Ohio** (Byzantine, Ruthenian) (1969): Basil Schott, O.F.M., bishop, 1996.
Former bishops: Emil Mihalik, 1969-84; Andrew Pataki, 1984-95.
**Passaic, N.J.** (Byzantine, Ruthenian) (1963): Andrew Pataki, eparch, 1996.
Former bishops: Stephen Kocisko, 1963-68; Michael J. Dudick, 1968-95.
**Paterson, N.J.** (1937): Frank J. Rodimer, bishop, 1978.

Former bishops: Thomas H. McLaughlin, 1937-47; Thomas A. Boland, 1947-52; James A. McNulty, 1953-63; James J. Navagh, 1963-65; Lawrence B. Casey, 1966-77.

**Pensacola-Tallahassee, Fla.** (1975): Vacant as of May 15, 1996.

Former bishops: Rene H. Gracida, 1975-83; J. Keith Symons, 1983-90; John M. Smith, 1991-95.

**Peoria, Ill.** (1877): John J. Myers, bishop, 1990.

Former bishops: John L. Spalding, 1877-1908; Edmund M. Dunne, 1909-29; Joseph H. Schlarman, 1930-51; William E. Cousins, 1952-58; John B. Franz, 1959-71; Edward W. O'Rourke, 1971- 90.

**Philadelphia,\* Pa.** (1808; archdiocese, 1875): Cardinal Anthony J. Bevilacqua, archbishop, 1988. Louis A. DeSimone, Edward P. Cullen, Robert P. Maginnis, Joseph F. Martino, auxiliaries.

Former ordinaries: Michael Egan, O.F.M., 1810-14; Henry Conwell, 1820-42; Francis P. Kenrick, 1842-51; John N. Neumann, C.SS.R., 1852-60; James F. Wood, 1860-83, first archbishop; Patrick J. Ryan, 1884-1911; Edmond F. Prendergast, 1911-18; Cardinal Dennis Dougherty, 1918-51; Cardinal John O'Hara, C.S.C., 1951-60; Cardinal John Krol, 1961-88.

**Philadelphia,\* Pa.** (Byzantine, Ukrainian) (1924; metropolitan, 1958): Stephen Sulyk, archbishop, 1981. Walter Paska, auxiliary.

Former ordinaries: Stephen Ortynsky, O.S.B.M., 1907-16; Constantine Bohachevsky, 1924-61; Ambrose Senyshyn, O.S.B.M., 1961-76; Joseph Schmondiuk, 1977-78; Myroslav J. Lubachivsky, 1979-80, apostolic administrator, 1980-81.

**Phoenix, Ariz.** (1969): Thomas J. O'Brien, bishop, 1982.

Former bishops: Edward A. McCarthy, 1969-76; James S. Rausch, 1977-81.

**Pittsburgh,\* Pa.** (Byzantine, Ruthenian) (1924; metropolitan, 1969): Judson M. Procyk, archbishop, 1995.

Former ordinaries: Basil Takach 1924-48; Daniel Ivancho, 1948-54; Nicholas T. Elko, 1955-67; Stephen J. Kocisko, 1968-91, first metropolitan; Thomas V. Dolinay, 1991-93.

**Pittsburgh, Pa.** (1843): Donald W. Wuerl, bishop, 1988. John B. McDowell, William J. Winter, auxiliaries.

Former bishops: Michael O'Connor, 1843-53, 1854-60; Michael Domenec, C.M., 1860-76; J. Tuigg, 1876-89; Richard Phelan, 1889-1904; J.F. Regis Canevin, 1904-20; Hugh C. Boyle, 1921-55; John F. Dearden, 1950-58; John J. Wright, 1959-69; Vincent M. Leonard, 1969-83; Anthony J. Bevilacqua, 1983-88.

**Portland, Me.** (1853): Joseph J. Gerry, O.S.B., bishop, 1989. Michael R. Cote, auxiliary.

Former bishops: David W. Bacon, 1855-74; James A. Healy, 1875-1900; William H. O'Connell, 1901-06; Louis S. Walsh, 1906-24; John G. Murray, 1925-31; Joseph E. McCarthy, 1932-55; Daniel J. Feeney, 1955-69; Peter L. Gerety, 1969-74; Edward C. O'Leary, 1974-88.

**Portland,\* Ore.** (1846): Francis E. George, archbishop, 1996. Kenneth D. Steiner, auxiliary.

Established as Oregon City, name changed, 1928.

Former ordinaries: Francis N. Blanchet, 1846-80

vicar apostolic, first archbishop; Charles J. Seghers, 1880-84; William H. Gross, C.SS.R., 1885-98; Alexander Christie, 1899-1925; Edward D. Howard, 1926-66; Robert J. Dwyer, 1966-74; Cornelius M. Power, 1974-86; William J. Levada, 1986-95.

**Providence, R.I.** (1872): Louis E. Gelineau, bishop, 1972. Robert E. Mulvee, coadjutor, 1995.

Former bishops: Thomas F. Hendricken, 1872-86; Matthew Harkins, 1887-1921; William A. Hickey, 1921-33; Francis P. Keough, 1934-47; Russell J. McVinney, 1948-71.

**Pueblo, Colo.** (1941): Arthur N. Tafoya, bishop, 1980.

Former bishops: Joseph C. Willging, 1942-59; Charles A. Buswell, 1959-79.

**Raleigh, N.C.** (1924): F. Joseph Gossman, bishop, 1975.

Former bishops: William J. Hafey, 1925-37; Eugene J. McGuinness, 1937-44; Vincent S. Waters, 1945-75.

**Rapid City, S. Dak.** (1902): Charles J. Chaput, O.F.M. Cap., bishop, 1988.

Established at Lead, transferred, 1930.

Former bishops: John Stariha, 1902-09; Joseph F. Busch, 1910-15; John J. Lawler, 1916-48; William T. McCarty, C.SS.R., 1948-69; Harold J. Dimmerling, 1969-87.

**Reno, Nev.** (1995): Phillip F. Straling, bishop, 1995.

Established at Reno, 1931; title changed to Reno-Las Vegas, 1976; redesignated Reno, 1995, when Las Vegas was made a separate diocese.

Former bishops (Reno/Reno-Las Vegas): Thomas K. Gorman, 1931-52; Robert J. Dwyer, 1952-66; Joseph Green, 1967-74; Norman F. McFarland, 1976-86; Daniel F. Walsh, 1987-95.

**Richmond, Va.** (1820): Walter F. Sullivan, bishop, 1974.

Former bishops: Patrick Kelly, 1820-22; Ambrose Marechal, S.S., administrator, 1822-28; James Whitfield, administrator, 1828-34; Samuel Eccleston, S.S., administrator, 1834-40; Richard V. Whelan, 1841-50; John McGill, 1850-72; James Gibbons, 1872-77; John J. Keane, 1878-88; Augustine Van de Vyver, 1889-1911; Denis J. O'Connell, 1912-26; Andrew J. Brennan, 1926-45; Peter L. Ireton, 1945-58; John J. Russell, 1958-73.

**Rochester, N.Y.** (1868): Matthew H. Clark, bishop, 1979.

Former bishops: Bernard J. McQuaid, 1868-1909; Thomas F. Hickey, 1909-28; John F. O'Hern, 1929-33; Edward F. Mooney, 1933-37; James E. Kearney, 1937-66; Fulton J. Sheen, 1966-69; Joseph L. Hogan, 1969-78.

**Rockford, Ill.** (1908): Thomas G. Doran, bishop, 1994.

Former bishops: Peter J. Muldoon, 1908-27; Edward F. Hoban, 1928-42; John J. Boylan, 1943-53; Raymond P. Hillinger, 1953-56; Loras T. Lane, 1956-68; Arthur J. O'Neill, 1968-94.

**Rockville Centre, N.Y.** (1957): John R. McGann, bishop, 1976. John C. Dunne, Emil A. Wcela, auxiliaries.

Former bishop: Walter P. Kellenberg, 1957-76.

**Sacramento, Calif.** (1886): William K. Weigand, bishop, 1993; installed, 1994.

Former bishops: Patrick Manogue, 1886-95; Thomas Grace, 1896-1921; Patrick J. Keane, 1922-28; Robert J. Armstrong, 1929-57; Joseph T. McGucken, 1957-62; Alden J. Bell, 1962-79; Francis A. Quinn, 1979-93.

**Saginaw, Mich.** (1938): Kenneth E. Untener, bishop, 1980.

Former bishops: William F. Murphy, 1938-50; Stephen S. Woznicki, 1950-68; Francis F. Reh, 1969-80.

**St. Augustine, Fla.** (1870): John J. Snyder, bishop, 1979.

Former bishops: Augustin Verot, S.S., 1870-76; John Moore, 1877-1901; William J. Kenny, 1902-13; Michael J. Curley, 1914-21; Patrick J. Barry, 1922-40; Joseph P. Hurley, 1940-67; Paul F. Tanner, 1968-79.

**St. Cloud, Minn.** (1889): John F. Kinney, bishop, 1995.

Former bishops: Otto Zardetti, 1889-94; Martin Marty, O.S.B., 1895-96; James Trobec, 1897-1914; Joseph F. Busch, 1915-53; Peter Bartholome, 1953-68; George H. Speltz, 1968-87; Jerome Hanus, O.S.B.,1987-94.

**St. George's in Canton, Ohio** (Byzantine, Romanian) (1982; eparchy, 1987): John Michael Botean, bishop, 1996.

Former bishop: Vasile Louis Puscas, 1983-93.

**St. Josaphat in Parma, Ohio** (Byzantine, Ukrainians) (1983): Robert M. Moskal, bishop, 1984.

**St. Louis,\* Mo.** (1826; archdiocese, 1847):Justin F. Rigali, archbishop, 1994. Paul A. Zipfel, Edward K. Braxton, auxiliaries.

Former ordinaries: Joseph Rosati, C.M., 1827-43; Peter R. Kenrick, 1843-95, first archbishop; John J. Kain, 1895-1903; Cardinal John Glennon, 1903-46; Cardinal Joseph Ritter, 1946-67; Cardinal John J. Carberry, 1968-79; John L. May, 1980-92.

**St. Maron, Brooklyn, N.Y.** (Maronite) (1966; diocese, 1971): Francis Zayek (titular archbishop), ex-arch, 1966, first eparch, 1972.

Established at Detroit; transferred to Brooklyn, 1977.

**St. Nicholas in Chicago** (Byzantine Eparchy of St. Nicholas of the Ukrainians) (1961): Michael Wiwchar, C.SS.R., bishop, 1993.

Former bishops: Jaroslav Gabro, 1961-80; Innocent H. Lotocky, O.S.B.M., 1981-93.

**St. Paul and Minneapolis,\* Minn.** (1850; archdiocese, 1888):Harry J. Flynn, archbishop, 1995. Lawrence H. Welsh, auxiliary.

Former ordinaries: Joseph Cretin, 1851-57; Thomas L. Grace, O.P., 1859-84; John Ireland, 1884-1918, first archbishop; Austin Dowling, 1919-30; John G. Murray, 1931-56; William O. Brady, 1956-61; Leo Binz, 1962-75; John R. Roach, 1975-95.

**St. Petersburg, Fla.** (1968): Robert N. Lynch, bishop, 1996.

Former bishops: Charles McLaughlin, 1968-78; W. Thomas Larkin, 1979-88; John C. Favalora, 1989-94.

**St. Thomas the Apostle of Detroit** (Chaldean) (1982; eparchy, 1985): Ibrahim N. Ibrahim, exarch, 1982; first eparch, 1985.

**Salina, Kans.** (1887): George K. Fitzsimons, bishop, 1984.

Established at Concordia, transferred, 1944.

Former bishops: Richard Scannell, 1887-91; John J. Hennessy, administrator, 1891-98; John F. Cunningham, 1898-1919; Francis J. Tief, 1921-38; Frank A. Thill, 1938-57; Frederick W. Freking, 1957-64; Cyril J. Vogel, 1965-79; Daniel W. Kucera, O.S.B., 1980-84.

**Salt Lake City, Utah** (1891): George H. Niederauer, bishop, 1995.

Former bishops: Lawrence Scanlan, 1891-1915; Joseph S. Glass, C.M., 1915-26; John J. Mitty, 1926-32; James E. Kearney, 1932-37; Duane G. Hunt, 1937-60; J. Lennox Federal, 1960-80; William K. Weigand, 1980-93.

**San Angelo, Tex.** (1961): Michael D. Pfeifer, O.M.I., bishop, 1985.

Former bishops: Thomas J. Drury, 1962-65; Thomas Tschoepe, 1966-69; Stephen A. Leven, 1969-79; Joseph A. Fiorenza, 1979-84.

**San Antonio,\* Tex.** (1874; archdiocese, 1926): Patrick F. Flores, archbishop, 1979. John W. Yanta, auxiliary.

Former ordinaries: Anthony D. Pellicer, 1874-80; John C. Neraz, 1881-94; John A. Forest, 1895-1911; John W. Shaw, 1911-18; Arthur Jerome Drossaerts, 1918-40, first archbishop; Robert E. Lucey, 1941-69; Francis Furey, 1969-79.

**San Bernardino, Calif.** (1978): Gerald R. Barnes, bishop, 1995.

Former bishop: Phillip F. Straling, 1978-95.

**San Diego, Calif.** (1936): Robert H. Brom, bishop, 1990. Gilbert Espinoza Chavez, auxiliary.

Former bishops: Charles F. Buddy, 1936-66; Francis J. Furey, 1966-69; Leo T. Maher, 1969-90.

**San Francisco,\* Calif.** (1853): William J. Levada, archbishop, 1995. Patrick J. McGrath, Carlos A. Sevilla, S.J., auxiliaries.

Former ordinaries: Joseph S. Alemany, O.P., 1853-84; Patrick W. Riordan, 1884-1914; Edward J. Hanna, 1915-35; John Mitty, 1935-61; Joseph T. McGucken, 1962-77; John R. Quinn, 1977-95.

**San Jose, Calif.** (1981): R. Pierre DuMaine, first bishop, 1981.

**Santa Fe\*, N. Mex.** (1850; archdiocese, 1875): Michael J. Sheehan, archbishop, 1993.

Former ordinaries: John B. Lamy, 1850-85; first archbishop; John B. Salpointe, 1885-94; Placide L. Chapelle, 1894-97; Peter Bourgade, 1899-1908; John B. Pitaval, 1909-18; Albert T. Daeger, O.F.M., 1919-32; Rudolph A. Gerken, 1933-43; Edwin V. Byrne, 1943-63; James P. Davis, 1964-74; Robert F. Sanchez, 1974-93.

**Santa Rosa, Calif.** (1962): G. Patrick Ziemann, bishop, 1992.

Former bishops: Leo T. Maher, 1962-69; Mark J. Hurley, 1969-86; John T. Steinbock, 1987-91.

**Savannah, Ga.** (1850): John Kevin Boland, bishop, 1995.

Former bishops: Francis X. Gartland, 1850-54; John Barry, 1857-59; Augustin Verot, S.S., 1861-70; Ignatius Persico, O.F.M. Cap., 1870-72; William H. Gross, C.SS.R., 1873-85; Thomas A. Becker, 1886-99; Benjamin J. Keiley, 1900-22; Michael Keyes, S.M., 1922-35; Gerald P. O'Hara, 1935-59; Thomas J. McDonough, 1960-67; Gerard L. Frey, 1967-72; Raymond W. Lessard, 1973-95.

**Scranton, Pa.** (1868): James C. Timlin, bishop, 1984. John M. Dougherty, auxiliary.

Former bishops: William O'Hara, 1868-99; Michael J. Hoban, 1899-1926; Thomas C. O'Reilly, 1928-38; William J. Hafey, 1938-54; Jerome D. Hannan, 1954-65; J. Carroll McCormick, 1966-83; John J. O'Connor, 1983-84.

**Seattle,\* Wash.** (1850; archdiocese, 1951): Thomas J. Murphy, archbishop, 1991.

Established as Nesqually, name changed, 1907.

Former ordinaries; Augustin M. Blanchet, 1850-79; Aegidius Junger, 1879-95; Edward J. O'Dea, 1896-1932; Gerald Shaughnessy, S.M., 1933-50; Thomas A. Connolly, first archbishop, 1950-75; Raymond G. Hunthausen, 1975-91.

**Shreveport, La.** (1986): William B. Friend, bishop, 1986.

**Sioux City, Ia.** (1902): Lawrence D. Soens, bishop, 1983.

Former bishops: Philip J. Garrigan, 1902-19; Edmond Heelan, 1919-48; Joseph M. Mueller, 1948-70; Frank H. Greteman, 1970-83.

**Sioux Falls, S. Dak.** (1889): Robert J. Carlson, bishop, 1995.

Former bishops: Martin Marty, O.S.B., 1889-94; Thomas O'Gorman, 1896-1921; Bernard J. Mahoney, 1922-39; William O. Brady, 1939-56; Lambert A. Hoch, 1956-78; Paul V. Dudley, 1978-95.

**Spokane, Wash.** (1913): William S. Skylstad, bishop, 1990.

Former bishops: Augustine F. Schinner, 1914-25; Charles D. White, 1927-55; Bernard J. Topel, 1955-78; Lawrence H. Welsh, 1978-90.

**Springfield, Ill.** (1853): Daniel L. Ryan, bishop, 1984.

Established at Quincy, transferred to Alton 1857; transferred to Springfield 1923.

Former bishops: Henry D. Juncker, 1857-68; Peter J. Baltes, 1870-86; James Ryan, 1888-1923; James A. Griffin, 1924-48; William A. O'Connor, 1949-75; Joseph A. McNicholas, 1975-83.

**Springfield, Mass.** (1870): Thomas L. Dupre, bishop, 1995.

Former bishops: Patrick T. O'Reilly, 1870-92; Thomas D. Beaven, 1892-1920; Thomas M. O'Leary, 1921-49; Christopher J. Weldon, 1950-77; Joseph F. Maguire, 1977-91; John A. Marshall, 1991-94.

**Springfield-Cape Girardeau, Mo.** (1956): John J. Leibrecht, bishop, 1984.

Former bishops: Charles Helmsing, 1956-62; Ignatius J. Strecker, 1962-69; William Baum, 1970-73; Bernard F. Law, 1973-84.

**Stamford, Conn.** (Byzantine, Ukrainian) (1956); Basil Losten, eparch, 1977.

Former eparchs: Ambrose Senyshyn, O.S.B.M., 1956-61; Joseph Schmondiuk, 1961-77.

**Steubenville, Ohio** (1944): Gilbert I. Sheldon, bishop, 1992.

Former bishops: John K. Mussio, 1945-77; Albert H. Ottenweller, 1977-92.

**Stockton, Calif.** (1962): Donald W. Montrose, bishop, 1986.

Former bishops: Hugh A. Donohoe, 1962-69; Merli J. Guilfoyle, 1969-79; Roger M. Mahony, 1980-85.

**Superior, Wis.** (1905): Raphael M. Fliss, bishop, 1985.

Former bishops: Augustine F. Schinner, 1905-13; Joseph M. Koudelka, 1913-21; Joseph G. Pinten, 1922-26; Theodore M. Reverman, 1926-41; William P. O'Connor, 1942-46; Albert G. Meyer, 1946-53; Joseph Annabring, 1954-59; George A. Hammes, 1960-85.

**Syracuse, N.Y.** (1886): James M. Moynihan, bishop, 1995. Thomas J. Costello, auxiliary.

Former bishops: Patrick A. Ludden, 1887-1912; John Grimes, 1912-22; Daniel J. Curley, 1923-32; John A. Duffy, 1933-37; Walter A. Foery, 1937-70; David F. Cunningham, 1970-76; Frank J. Harrison, 1976-87; Joseph T. O'Keefe, 1987-95.

**Toledo, Ohio** (1910): James R. Hoffman, bishop, 1980. Robert W. Donnelly, auxiliary.

Former bishops: Joseph Schrembs, 1911-21; Samuel A. Stritch, 1921-30; Karl J. Alter, 1931-50; George J. Rehring, 1950-67; John A. Donovan, 1967-80.

**Trenton, N.J.** (1881): John C. Reiss, bishop, 1980. John M. Smith, coadjutor bishop, 1995.

Former bishops: Michael J. O'Farrell, 1881-94; James A. McFaul, 1894-1917; Thomas J. Walsh, 1918-28; John J. McMahon, 1928-32; Moses E. Kiley, 1934-40; William A. Griffin, 1940-50; George W. Ahr, 1950-79.

**Tucson, Ariz.** (1897): Manuel D. Moreno, bishop, 1982.

Former bishops: Peter Bourgade, 1897-99; Henry Granjon, 1900-22; Daniel J. Gercke, 1923-60; Francis J. Green, 1960-81.

**Tulsa, Okla.** (1972): Edward J. Slattery, bishop, 1993. Former bishop: Bernard J. Ganter, 1973-77; Eusebius J. Beltran, 1978-92.

**Tyler, Tex.** (1986): Edmond Carmody, bishop, 1992.

Former bishop: Charles E. Herzig, 1987-91.

**Van Nuys, Calif.** (Byzantine, Ruthenian) (1981): George M. Kuzma, eparch, 1991.

Former bishop: Thomas V. Dolinay, 1982-90.

**Venice, Fla.** (1984): John J. Nevins, bishop, 1984.

**Victoria, Tex.** (1982): David E. Fellhauer, bishop, 1990.

Former bishop: Charles V. Grahmann, 1982-89.

**Washington,\* D.C.** (1939): Cardinal James A. Hickey, archbishop, 1980. Alvaro Corrada del Rio, S.J., Leonard Olivier, S.V.D., William E. Lori, auxiliaries.

Former ordinaries: Michael J. Curley, 1939-47; Cardinal Patrick O'Boyle, 1948-73; Cardinal William Baum, 1973-80.

**Wheeling-Charleston, W. Va.** (1850): Bernard W. Schmitt, bishop, 1989.

Established as Wheeling; name changed, 1974.

Former bishops: Richard V. Whelan, 1850-74; John J. Kain, 1875-93; Patrick J. Donahue, 1894-1922; John J. Swint, 1922-62; Joseph H. Hodges, 1962-85; Francis B. Schulte, 1985-88.

**Wichita, Kans.** (1887): Eugene J. Gerber, bishop, 1982, installed, 1983.

Former bishops: John J. Hennessy, 1888-1920; Augustus J. Schwertner, 1921-39; Christian H. Winkelmann, 1940-46; Mark K. Carroll, 1947-67; David M. Maloney, 1967-82.

**Wilmington, Del.** (1868): Michael A. Saltarelli, bishop, 1995.

Former bishops: Thomas A. Becker, 1868-86; Alfred A. Curtis, 1886-96; John J. Monaghan, 1897-1925; Edmond Fitzmaurice, 1925-60; Michael Hyle, 1960-67; Thomas J. Mardaga, 1968-84; Robert E. Mulvee, 1985-95.

**Winona, Minn.** (1889): John G. Vlazny, bishop, 1987. Former bishops: Joseph B. Cotter, 1889-1909; Patrick R. Heffron, 1910-27; Francis M. Kelly, 1928-49; Edward A. Fitzgerald, 1949-69; Loras J. Watters, 1969-86.

**Worcester, Mass.** (1950): Daniel P. Reilly, bishop, 1994. George E. Rueger, auxiliary.

Former bishops: ohn J. Wright, 1950-59; Bernard J. Flanagan, 1959-83; Timothy J. Harrington, 1983-94.

**Yakima, Wash.** (1951): Vacant as of June 15, 1996. Former bishops: Joseph P. Dougherty, 1951-69; Cornelius M. Power, 1969-74; Nicolas E. Walsh, 1974-76; William S. Skylstad, 1977-90; Francis E. George, O.M.I., 1990-96.

**Youngstown, Ohio** (1943): Thomas J. Tobin, bishop, 1995; installed 1996. Benedict C. Franzetta, auxiliary.

Former bishops: James A. McFadden, 1943-52; Emmet M. Walsh, 1952-68; James W. Malone, 1968-95.

**Apostolic Exarchate for Armenian Catholics in the United States and Canada, New York, N.Y.** (1981): Hovhannes Tertzakian, O.M. Ven., exarch, 1995.

Former exarch: Nerses Mikael Setian, 1981-93.

**Archdiocese for the Military Services, U.S.A., Washington, D.C.** (1957; restructured, 1985): Archbishop Joseph T. Dimino, military ordinary, 1991. Francis X. Roque, John G. Nolan, Joseph J. Madera, M.Pp.S., John J. Glynn, auxiliaries.

Military vicar appointed, 1917; canonically established, 1957, as U.S. Military Vicariate under jurisdiction of New York archbishop; name changed, restructured as independent jurisdiction, 1985.

Former military vicars: Cardinal Patrick Hayes, 1917-38; Cardinal Francis Spellman, 1939-67; Cardinal Terence J. Cooke, 1968-83; Cardinal John J. O'Connor, apostolic administrator, 1984-85.

Former military ordinary: Archbishop Joseph T. Ryan, 1985-91.

# MISSIONARY BISHOPS

## Africa

**South Africa:** Keimoes-Upington (diocese), John B. Minder, O.S.F.S.

De Aar (diocese), Joseph J. Potocnak, S.C.J.

## Asia

**Indonesia:** Agats (diocese), Alphonse A. Sowada, O.S.C.

**Iraq:** Mossul (Chaldean-rite archdiocese), George Garmo.

**Korea:** Inchon (diocese), William J. McNaughton, M.M.

**Philippines:** Cotabato (archdiocese), Philip F. Smith, O.M.I.

## Central America, West Indies

**Dominica:** Roseau (diocese), Edward J. Gilbert, C.SS.R.

**Honduras:** Comayagua (diocese), Gerald Scarpone Caporale, O.F.M.

**Jamaica:** Mandeville (vicariate apostolic), Paul M. Boyle, C.P.

**Nicaragua:** Bluefields (vicariate apostolic), Paul Schmitz Simon, O.F.M. Cap.

**Virgin Islands:** St. Thomas (diocese), Elliott G. Thomas, bishop, 1993.

## North America

**Bermuda:** Hamilton (diocese); Robert Kurtz, C.R.

**Mexico:** Nuevo Laredo (diocese), Ricardo Watty Urquidi, M.Sp.S., first bishop.

## Oceania

**American Samoa:** Samoa-Pago Pago (diocese), John Quinn Weitzel, M.M.

**Papua New Guinea:** Mendi (diocese), Stephen J. Reichert, O.F.M.Cap.

Wewak (diocese), Raymond P. Kalisz, S.V.D.

Vanuatu (New Hebrides): Port Vila (diocese), Francis Lambert, S.M.

## South America

**Bolivia:** Coroico (diocese), Thomas R. Manning, O.F.M.

Pando (vicariate apostolic), Luis Morgan Casey.

Santa Cruz (archdiocese), Charles A. Brown, M.M., auxiliary.

**Brazil:** Cristalandia (prelacy), Herbert Hermes, O.S.B.

Itaituba (prelacy), Capistran Heim, O.F.M.

Jatai (diocese), Benedict D. Coscia, O.F.M., bishop; Miguel P. Mundo, auxiliary.

Miracema do Tocantins (diocese), John J. Burke, O.F.M.

Paranagua (diocese), Alfred Novak, C.Ss.R.

Valenca (diocese), Elias James Manning, O.F.M. Conv.

**Peru:** Chulucanas (diocese), John C. McNabb, O.S.A.

# MOTHER TERESA

Mother Teresa was admitted to the Woodlands Nursing Home in Calcutta Aug. 20, 1996, with fever. She developed cardio-respiratory complications the following day, and was diagnosed as also having malaria on the 23rd, when her condition worsened and doctors said they were worried. At the time of writing, she remained on respiratory support under intensive care and was "fully conscious"; it was not known how long she would be hospitalized.

Mother Teresa, 86 on Aug. 27, founded the Missionary Sisters of Charity and won the 1979 Nobel Peace Prize. She was widely acclaimed as a living saint, Even after heart and other health problems led her to resign as head of the order in 1990, the sisters re-elected her as their superior. As long as she was able, Mother Teresa maintained a heavy travel schedule, visiting the order's houses for the poor, sick and dying in India and other countries.

## CATHOLIC POPULATION OF THE UNITED STATES

(Source: *The Official Catholic Directory, 1996;* figures as of Jan. 1, 1996. Archdioceses are indicated by an asterisk; for dioceses marked +, see Dioceses with Interstate Lines.)

| State Diocese | Cath. Pop. | Dioc. Priests | Rel. Priests | Total Priests | Perm. Deac. | Bros. | Sisters | Par- ishes |
|---|---|---|---|---|---|---|---|---|
| **Alabama** | **137,183** | **177** | **94** | **271** | **63** | **34** | **392** | **151** |
| * Mobile | 68,931 | 108 | 45 | 153 | 41 | 17 | 222 | 77 |
| Birmingham | 68,252 | 69 | 49 | 118 | 22 | 17 | 170 | 74 |
| **Alaska** | **51,720** | **47** | **36** | **83** | **61** | **6** | **75** | **69** |
| * Anchorage | 27,411 | 21 | 10 | 31 | 13 | 2 | 50 | 20 |
| Fairbanks | 18,550 | 9 | 23 | 32 | 39 | 4 | 19 | 41 |
| Juneau | 5,759 | 17 | 3 | 20 | 9 | — | 6 | 8 |
| **Arizona** | **678,226** | **258** | **185** | **443** | **250** | **17** | **531** | **151** |
| Phoenix | 381,635 | 146 | 106 | 252 | 174 | 7 | 238 | 87 |
| Tucson | 296,591 | 112 | 79 | 191 | 76 | 10 | 293 | 64 |
| **Arkansas,** Little Rock | **84,079** | **94** | **57** | **151** | **49** | **47** | **364** | **90** |
| **California** | **7,967,090** | **2,166** | **1,759** | **3,925** | **667** | **536** | **5,202** | **1,062** |
| * Los Angeles | 3,631,368 | 578 | 601 | 1,179 | 151 | 230 | 2,022 | 284 |
| * San Francisco | 420,567 | 224 | 215 | 439 | 56 | 50 | 888 | 91 |
| Fresno | 320,824 | 116 | 50 | 166 | 5 | 9 | 130 | 85 |
| Monterey | 170,321 | 90 | 30 | 120 | 2 | 30 | 109 | 46 |
| Oakland | 485,183 | 191 | 253 | 444 | 81 | 16 | 332 | 86 |
| Orange | 595,101 | 181 | 89 | 270 | 50 | 9 | 365 | 53 |
| Sacramento | 372,000 | 166 | 72 | 238 | 95 | 33 | 241 | 98 |
| San Bernardino | 610,736 | 160 | 104 | 264 | 83 | 16 | 156 | 100 |
| San Diego | 677,395 | 212 | 91 | 303 | 82 | 22 | 352 | 98 |
| San Jose | 374,412 | 106 | 216 | 322 | 14 | 80 | 435 | 46 |
| Santa Rosa | 135,023 | 82 | 16 | 98 | 22 | 37 | 109 | 43 |
| Stockton | 174,160 | 60 | 22 | 82 | 26 | 4 | 63 | 32 |
| **Colorado** | **527,408** | **272** | **180** | **452** | **149** | **44** | **729** | **196** |
| * Denver | 340,875 | 158 | 123 | 281 | 125 | 31 | 483 | 112 |
| Colorado Springs | 84,889 | 34 | 20 | 54 | 19 | 3 | 150 | 30 |
| Pueblo | 101,644 | 80 | 37 | 117 | 5 | 10 | 96 | 54 |
| **Connecticut** | **1,353,693** | **836** | **298** | **1,134** | **412** | **108** | **1,926** | **389** |
| * Hartford | 778,856 | 441 | 146 | 587 | 287 | 78 | 1,069 | 223 |
| Bridgeport | 353,238 | 252 | 82 | 334 | 73 | 2 | 555 | 88 |
| Norwich+ | 221,599 | 143 | 70 | 213 | 52 | 28 | 302 | 78 |
| **Delaware,** Wilmington+ | **158,238** | **131** | **91** | **222** | **41** | **40** | **293** | **56** |
| **District of Columbia** | | | | | | | | |
| * Washington+ | **440,000** | **336** | **527** | **863** | **228** | **130** | **993** | **139** |
| **Florida** | **1,953,223** | **840** | **443** | **1,283** | **434** | **155** | **1,372** | **444** |
| * Miami | 744,048 | 249 | 118 | 367 | 127 | 65 | 354 | 108 |
| Orlando | 303,525 | 120 | 49 | 169 | 106 | 4 | 132 | 70 |
| Palm Beach | 205,455 | 92 | 42 | 134 | 15 | 2 | 182 | 46 |
| Pensacola-Tallahassee | 61,688 | 74 | 10 | 84 | 53 | 7 | 62 | 49 |
| St. Augustine | 114,146 | 89 | 19 | 108 | 21 | 2 | 122 | 50 |
| St. Petersburg | 351,596 | 136 | 150 | 286 | 68 | 56 | 361 | 71 |
| Venice | 172,765 | 80 | 55 | 135 | 44 | 19 | 159 | 50 |
| **Georgia** | **280,734** | **180** | **124** | **304** | **155** | **21** | **263** | **120** |
| * Atlanta | 212,850 | 117 | 93 | 210 | 119 | 3 | 112 | 67 |
| Savannah | 67,884 | 63 | 31 | 94 | 36 | 18 | 151 | 53 |
| **Hawaii,** Honolulu | **232,780** | **75** | **78** | **153** | **36** | **50** | **252** | **68** |
| **Idaho,** Boise | **115,150** | **96** | **13** | **109** | **29** | **8** | **115** | **74** |
| **Illinois** | **3,631,645** | **1,888** | **1,188** | **3,076** | **923** | **602** | **5,959** | **1,057** |
| * Chicago | 2,338,000 | 988 | 845 | 1,833 | 603 | 460 | 3,510 | 377 |
| Belleville | 106,426 | 146 | 41 | 187 | 25 | 7 | 262 | 128 |
| Joliet | 511,888 | 206 | 121 | 327 | 118 | 93 | 788 | 118 |
| Peoria | 234,161 | 242 | 57 | 299 | 86 | 10 | 314 | 166 |
| Rockford | 266,842 | 154 | 60 | 214 | 89 | 13 | 364 | 101 |
| Springfield | 174,328 | 152 | 64 | 216 | 2 | 19 | 721 | 167 |
| **Indiana** | **728,006** | **640** | **404** | **1,044** | **81** | **198** | **2,124** | **440** |
| * Indianapolis | 211,120 | 174 | 144 | 318 | — | 64 | 833 | 138 |

| State Diocese | Cath. Pop. | Dioc. Priests | Rel. Priests | Total Priests | Perm. Deac. | Bros. | Sisters | Parishes |
|---|---|---|---|---|---|---|---|---|
| **Indiana** | | | | | | | | |
| Evansville | 89,536 | 105 | 11 | 116 | 22 | 2 | 325 | 73 |
| Ft. Wayne-South Bend | 153,709 | 106 | 179 | 285 | 25 | 110 | 722 | 88 |
| Gary | 182,115 | 132 | 51 | 183 | 29 | 22 | 135 | 79 |
| Lafayette | 91,526 | 123 | 19 | 142 | 5 | - | 109 | 62 |
| **Iowa** | **520,319** | **727** | **48** | **775** | **200** | **37** | **1,579** | **522** |
| * Dubuque | 215,322 | 275 | 32 | 307 | 63 | 31 | 1,050 | 213 |
| Davenport | 106,661 | 153 | 8 | 161 | 51 | 2 | 259 | 104 |
| Des Moines | 97,827 | 117 | 7 | 124 | 53 | 4 | 140 | 87 |
| Sioux City | 100,509 | 182 | 1 | 183 | 33 | — | 130 | 118 |
| **Kansas** | **379,698** | **358** | **103** | **461** | **8** | **21** | **1,628** | **364** |
| * Kansas City | 179,490 | 101 | 69 | 170 | — | 20 | 850 | 119 |
| Dodge City | 38,936 | 58 | 3 | 61 | 6 | — | 110 | 57 |
| Salina | 55,418 | 68 | 21 | 89 | — | 1 | 244 | 92 |
| Wichita | 105,854 | 131 | 10 | 141 | 2 | — | 424 | 96 |
| **Kentucky** | **351,024** | **449** | **100** | **549** | **131** | **111** | **2,037** | **311** |
| * Louisville | 183,105 | 199 | 68 | 267 | 89 | 97 | 1,110 | 121 |
| Covington | 76,867 | 116 | 1 | 117 | 13 | 8 | 480 | 51 |
| Lexington | 40,991 | 53 | 21 | 74 | 29 | 4 | 185 | 61 |
| Owensboro | 50,061 | 81 | 10 | 91 | — | 2 | 262 | 78 |
| **Louisiana** | **1,340,292** | **704** | **392** | **1,096** | **306** | **216** | **1,376** | **493** |
| * New Orleans | 488,368 | 228 | 234 | 462 | 173 | 153 | 898 | 147 |
| Alexandria | 48,050 | 64 | 15 | 79 | 7 | 5 | 62 | 48 |
| Baton Rouge | 222,980 | 95 | 48 | 143 | 25 | 11 | 125 | 70 |
| Houma-Thibodaux | 110,752 | 72 | 8 | 80 | 22 | 10 | 36 | 40 |
| Lafayette | 350,001 | 154 | 52 | 206 | 53 | 32 | 176 | 121 |
| Lake Charles | 82,266 | 49 | 23 | 72 | 19 | 5 | 30 | 36 |
| Shreveport | 37,875 | 42 | 12 | 54 | 7 | — | 49 | 31 |
| **Maine, Portland** | **244,376** | **193** | **56** | **249** | **11** | **29** | **533** | **141** |
| **Maryland, *Baltimore** | **441,860** | **284** | **289** | **573** | **168** | **109** | **1,346** | **153** |
| **Massachusetts** | **3,023,601** | **1,700** | **1,062** | **2,762** | **335** | **296** | **4,769** | **772** |
| * Boston | 2,009,946 | 1,017 | 763 | 1,780 | 181 | 160 | 3,194 | 395 |
| Fall River | 374,083 | 189 | 122 | 311 | 44 | 44 | 422 | 112 |
| Springfield | 315,620 | 218 | 61 | 279 | 43 | 14 | 659 | 135 |
| Worcester | 323,952 | 276 | 116 | 392 | 67 | 78 | 494 | 130 |
| **Michigan** | **2,185,242** | **1,165** | **357** | **1,522** | **291** | **95** | **2,568** | **799** |
| * Detroit | 1,413,105 | 517 | 242 | 759 | 147 | 72 | 1,252 | 306 |
| Gaylord | 82,052 | 73 | 15 | 88 | 12 | 5 | 82 | 82 |
| Grand Rapids | 132,418 | 130 | 27 | 157 | 20 | 3 | 325 | 90 |
| Kalamazoo | 102,225 | 59 | 17 | 76 | 19 | 4 | 237 | 47 |
| Lansing | 234,899 | 147 | 34 | 181 | 65 | 9 | 439 | 87 |
| Marquette | 72,081 | 117 | 7 | 124 | 14 | — | 74 | 77 |
| Saginaw | 148,462 | 122 | 15 | 137 | 14 | 2 | 159 | 110 |
| **Minnesota** | **1,183,551** | **872** | **314** | **1,186** | **225** | **153** | **2,813** | **743** |
| * St.Paul and Minneapolis | 709,028 | 351 | 141 | 492 | 169 | 66 | 1,203 | 223 |
| Crookston | 42,012 | 49 | 7 | 56 | 5 | 1 | 202 | 76 |
| Duluth | 81,293 | 92 | 20 | 112 | 19 | 1 | 194 | 98 |
| New Ulm | 72,274 | 95 | - | 95 | 3 | — | 96 | 83 |
| St. Cloud | 149,250 | 149 | 132 | 281 | 27 | 67 | 595 | 141 |
| Winona | 129,694 | 136 | 14 | 150 | 2 | 18 | 523 | 122 |
| **Mississippi** | **109,483** | **126** | **61** | **187** | **29** | **44** | **364** | **118** |
| Biloxi | 65,143 | 56 | 31 | 87 | 19 | 34 | 62 | 44 |
| Jackson | 44,340 | 70 | 30 | 100 | 10 | 10 | 302 | 74 |
| **Missouri** | **841,266** | **836** | **591** | **1,427** | **308** | **310** | **2,951** | **472** |
| * St. Louis | 558,800 | 508 | 408 | 916 | 193 | 191 | 2,372 | 227 |
| Jefferson City | 83,010 | 115 | 10 | 125 | 53 | 3 | 110 | 96 |
| Kansas City-St. Joseph | 145,343 | 134 | 108 | 242 | 56 | 37 | 329 | 85 |
| Springfield-Cape Girardeau | 54,113 | 79 | 65 | 144 | 6 | 79 | 140 | 64 |
| **Montana** | **125,320** | **169** | **27** | **196** | **29** | **2** | **163** | **111** |
| Great Falls-Billings | 58,820 | 79 | 18 | 97 | 3 | 1 | 89 | 53 |
| Helena | 66,500 | 90 | 9 | 99 | 26 | 1 | 74 | 58 |
| **Nebraska** | **345,930** | **448** | **137** | **585** | **130** | **39** | **650** | **332** |
| * Omaha | 208,212 | 231 | 125 | 356 | 130 | 28 | 420 | 154 |
| Grand Island | 52,800 | 80 | — | 80 | — | — | 100 | 44 |

| State<br>Diocese | Cath.<br>Pop. | Dioc.<br>Priests | Rel.<br>Priests | Total<br>Priests | Perm.<br>Deac. | Bros. | Sisters | Par-<br>ishes |
|---|---|---|---|---|---|---|---|---|
| **Nebraska** | | | | | | | | |
| Lincoln | 84,918 | 137 | 12 | 149 | — | 11 | 130 | 134 |
| **Nevada** | **300,000** | **48** | **27** | **75** | **13** | **9** | **105** | **51** |
| Las Vegas[1] | 192,000 | 26 | 16 | 42 | 6 | 6 | 55 | 26 |
| Reno[1] | 108,000 | 22 | 11 | 33 | 7 | 3 | 50 | 25 |
| **New Hampshire,** Manchester | **321,678** | **240** | **98** | **338** | **21** | **50** | **839** | **131** |
| **New Jersey** | **3,242,765** | **1,894** | **653** | **2,547** | **755** | **247** | **4,028** | **708** |
| *Newark | 1,325,838 | 827 | 268 | 1,095 | 237 | 112 | 1,651 | 238 |
| Camden | 405,541 | 336 | 54 | 390 | 96 | 15 | 376 | 126 |
| Metuchen | 477,900 | 211 | 45 | 256 | 85 | 23 | 492 | 108 |
| Paterson | 373,911 | 274 | 205 | 479 | 139 | 34 | 961 | 111 |
| Trenton | 659,575 | 246 | 81 | 327 | 198 | 63 | 548 | 125 |
| **New Mexico** | **421,868** | **199** | **172** | **371** | **185** | **105** | **551** | **193** |
| *Santa Fe | 256,135 | 109 | 98 | 207 | 129 | 90 | 304 | 91 |
| Gallup | 40,495 | 62 | 32 | 94 | 31 | 13 | 163 | 58 |
| Las Cruces | 125,238 | 28 | 42 | 70 | 25 | 2 | 84 | 44 |
| **New York** | **7,220,124** | **3,662** | **1,895** | **5,557** | **1,046** | **955** | **11,373** | **1,674** |
| *New York | 2,327,300 | 910 | 1,106 | 2,016 | 311 | 473 | 4,148 | 413 |
| Albany | 403,403 | 329 | 127 | 456 | 89 | 76 | 1,016 | 189 |
| Brooklyn | 1,531,858 | 723 | 233 | 956 | 150 | 191 | 1,583 | 219 |
| Buffalo | 755,427 | 462 | 193 | 655 | 85 | 50 | 1,540 | 266 |
| Ogdensburg | 141,322 | 176 | 17 | 193 | 51 | 15 | 223 | 122 |
| Rochester | 349,623 | 293 | 83 | 376 | 97 | 26 | 773 | 160 |
| Rockville Centre | 1,338,526 | 463 | 92 | 555 | 199 | 106 | 1,576 | 133 |
| Syracuse | 372,665 | 306 | 44 | 350 | 64 | 18 | 514 | 172 |
| **North Carolina** | **214,811** | **148** | **110** | **258** | **68** | **9** | **244** | **136** |
| Charlotte | 99,317 | 82 | 63 | 145 | 57 | 3 | 163 | 66 |
| Raleigh | 115,494 | 66 | 47 | 113 | 11 | 6 | 81 | 70 |
| **North Dakota** | **167,356** | **208** | **39** | **247** | **88** | **26** | **422** | **220** |
| Bismarck | 69,388 | 68 | 29 | 97 | 53 | 24 | 173 | 65 |
| Fargo | 97,968 | 140 | 10 | 150 | 35 | 2 | 249 | 155 |
| **Ohio** | **2,216,803** | **1,644** | **600** | **2,244** | **571** | **305** | **4,843** | **934** |
| *Cincinnati | 545,300 | 366 | 281 | 647 | 125 | 179 | 1,471 | 237 |
| Cleveland | 825,356 | 522 | 157 | 679 | 144 | 73 | 1,694 | 237 |
| Columbus | 214,215 | 203 | 52 | 255 | 50 | 11 | 424 | 108 |
| Steubenville | 45,878 | 126 | 16 | 142 | 4 | 8 | 91 | 74 |
| Toledo | 323,772 | 217 | 61 | 278 | 196 | 10 | 876 | 163 |
| Youngstown | 262,282 | 210 | 33 | 243 | 52 | 24 | 287 | 115 |
| **Oklahoma** | **139,836** | **193** | **52** | **245** | **93** | **15** | **305** | **154** |
| *Oklahoma City | 89,536 | 116 | 33 | 149 | 52 | 10 | 161 | 74 |
| Tulsa | 50,300 | 77 | 19 | 96 | 41 | 5 | 144 | 80 |
| **Oregon** | **307,990** | **189** | **214** | **403** | **19** | **60** | **609** | **161** |
| *Portland | 278,505 | 151 | 207 | 358 | 15 | 60 | 579 | 125 |
| Baker | 29,485 | 38 | 7 | 45 | 4 | — | 30 | 36 |
| **Pennsylvania** | **3,599,976** | **2,739** | **1,001** | **3,740** | **354** | **272** | **9,339** | **1,294** |
| *Philadelphia | 1,422,673 | 847 | 463 | 1,310 | 137 | 169 | 4,174 | 287 |
| Allentown | 256,090 | 255 | 78 | 333 | 84 | 11 | 690 | 153 |
| Altoona-Johnstown | 122,434 | 159 | 63 | 222 | 14 | 8 | 170 | 113 |
| Erie | 236,255 | 255 | 17 | 272 | 2 | 2 | 577 | 127 |
| Greensburg | 207,292 | 156 | 94 | 250 | — | 29 | 283 | 107 |
| Harrisburg | 227,240 | 172 | 45 | 217 | 59 | 1 | 575 | 89 |
| Pittsburgh | 760,697 | 530 | 140 | 670 | 23 | 43 | 1,968 | 218 |
| Scranton | 367,295 | 365 | 101 | 466 | 35 | 9 | 902 | 200 |
| **Rhode Island,** Providence | **644,789** | **322** | **131** | **453** | **83** | **125** | **806** | **159** |
| **South Carolina,** Charleston | **105,247** | **98** | **42** | **140** | **63** | **21** | **175** | **86** |
| **South Dakota** | **158,270** | **172** | **70** | **242** | **55** | **23** | **561** | **265** |
| Rapid City | 39,674 | 41 | 33 | 74 | 31 | 11 | 83 | 109 |
| Sioux Falls | 118,596 | 131 | 37 | 168 | 24 | 12 | 478 | 156 |
| **Tennessee** | **153,534** | **175** | **51** | **226** | **78** | **53** | **320** | **135** |
| Knoxville | 39,714 | 46 | 19 | 65 | 24 | 14 | 53 | 43 |
| Memphis | 57,007 | 76 | 9 | 85 | 25 | 37 | 108 | 43 |
| Nashville | 56,813 | 53 | 23 | 76 | 29 | 2 | 159 | 50 |
| **Texas** | **4,179,841** | **1,173** | **889** | **2,065** | **1,098** | **250** | **3,069** | **975** |
| *San Antonio | 642,824 | 151 | 234 | 385 | 230 | 106 | 1,025 | 145 |

| State Diocese | Cath. Pop. | Dioc. Priests | Rel. Priests | Total Priests | Perm. Deac. | Bros. | Sisters | Par- ishes |
|---|---|---|---|---|---|---|---|---|
| **Texas** | | | | | | | | |
| Amarillo | 40,467 | 64 | 8 | 72 | 30 | 1 | 167 | 34 |
| Austin | 270,000 | 119 | 55 | 174 | 107 | 44 | 110 | 89 |
| Beaumont | 86,595 | 54 | 19 | 73 | 30 | 4 | 59 | 43 |
| Brownsville | 689,657 | 59 | 54 | 113 | 82 | 15 | 139 | 61 |
| Corpus Christi | 351,500 | 112 | 64 | 176 | 65 | 21 | 266 | 84 |
| Dallas | 319,631 | 101 | 77 | 178 | 124 | 8 | 148 | 63 |
| El Paso | 527,060 | 93 | 44 | 137 | 18 | 11 | 245 | 58 |
| Fort Worth | 187,508 | 58 | 53 | 111 | 62 | 13 | 90 | 86 |
| Galveston-Houston | 792,886 | 195 | 217 | 415 | 231 | 25 | 557 | 149 |
| Lubbock | 43,764 | 33 | 11 | 44 | 23 | — | 35 | 36 |
| San Angelo | 78,850 | 54 | 22 | 76 | 45 | — | 45 | 49 |
| Tyler | 40,526 | 28 | 19 | 47 | 30 | 1 | 58 | 28 |
| Victoria | 108,573 | 52 | 12 | 64 | 21 | 1 | 125 | 50 |
| **Utah,** Salt Lake City | **78,475** | **56** | **35** | **91** | **27** | **14** | **72** | **43** |
| **Vermont,** Burlington | **146,709** | **138** | **49** | **187** | **40** | **22** | **271** | **93** |
| **Virginia** | **463,563** | **302** | **112** | **414** | **74** | **29** | **486** | **184** |
| Arlington | 293,664 | 133 | 76 | 209 | 59 | 18 | 218 | 60 |
| Richmond | 169,899 | 169 | 36 | 205 | 15 | 11 | 268 | 124 |
| **Washington** | **519,101** | **333** | **235** | **568** | **139** | **47** | **1,200** | **256** |
| * Seattle | 367,500 | 190 | 127 | 317 | 71 | 34 | 846 | 137 |
| Spokane | 81,623 | 85 | 98 | 183 | 48 | 13 | 299 | 78 |
| Yakima | 69,978 | 58 | 10 | 68 | 20 | — | 55 | 41 |
| **West Virginia** | | | | | | | | |
| Wheeling-Charleston | **106,338** | **127** | **66** | **193** | **28** | **6** | **309** | **116** |
| **Wisconsin** | **1,564,642** | **1,199** | **570** | **1,769** | **295** | **163** | **4,174** | **921** |
| * Milwaukee | 613,744 | 505 | 361 | 866 | 151 | 96 | 2,335 | 277 |
| Green Bay | 381,676 | 248 | 140 | 388 | 81 | 49 | 736 | 204 |
| La Crosse | 227,940 | 204 | 24 | 228 | 22 | 8 | 558 | 187 |
| Madison | 254,430 | 165 | 26 | 191 | — | 9 | 424 | 137 |
| Superior | 86,852 | 77 | 19 | 96 | 41 | 1 | 121 | 116 |
| **Wyoming,** Cheyenne+ | **46,903** | **54** | **10** | **64** | **3** | **1** | **36** | **37** |
| **EASTERN CHURCHES**[2] | **471,766** | **567** | **118** | **685** | **100** | **32** | **314** | **567** |
| * Philadelphia | 69,684 | 59 | 11 | 70 | 5 | 3 | 85 | 78 |
| St. Nicholas | 12,000 | 34 | 12 | 46 | 13 | 4 | 7 | 33 |
| Stamford | 32,296 | 37 | 16 | 53 | 5 | 3 | 40 | 51 |
| St. Josaphat (Parma) | 11,540 | 39 | 1 | 40 | 8 | 10 | 7 | 35 |
| * Pittsburgh | 90,150 | 68 | 8 | 76 | — | 4 | 109 | 86 |
| Parma | 12,788 | 39 | 2 | 41 | 4 | — | 12 | 39 |
| Passaic | 69,450 | 96 | 23 | 119 | 18 | — | 14 | 101 |
| Van Nuys | 2,998 | 16 | 5 | 21 | 4 | 5 | 4 | 16 |
| St. Maron (Maronites) | 30,000 | 59 | 10 | 69 | 8 | 1 | 8 | 33 |
| Our Lady of Lebanon (Maronites) | 21,860 | 30 | 5 | 35 | 7 | - | - | 25 |
| Newton (Melkites) | 27,700 | 42 | 21 | 63 | 26 | 2 | 3 | 34 |
| St. Thomas Apostle of Detroit (Chaldean) | 60,000 | 18 | - | 18 | - | — | 14 | 12 |
| St. George Martyr (Romanian) | 5,300 | 24 | — | 24 | 2 | — | — | 18 |
| Armenian Ex. (U.S.-Canada) | 26,000 | 6 | 4 | 10 | — | — | 11 | 6 |
| **MILITARY ARCHD.**[3] | **1,087,800** | - | - | - | - | **—** | - | **—** |
| **OUTLYING AREAS** | | | | | | | | |
| **Puerto Rico** | **2,581,360** | **430** | **327** | **757** | **389** | **52** | **1,107** | **323** |
| **Am. Samoa** | **8,271** | **10** | **2** | **12** | **19** | **—** | **15** | **8** |
| **Caroline Islands** | **64,209** | **12** | **14** | **26** | **40** | **2** | **27** | **19** |
| **Guam,** *Agana | **101,000** | **25** | **21** | **46** | **6** | **1** | **104** | **24** |
| **Northern Mariana Islands** | **47,322** | **4** | **2** | **6** | **3** | **—** | **23** | **9** |
| **Marshall Islands** | **4,000** | **1** | **5** | **6** | **3** | **2** | **15** | **4** |
| **Virgin Islands,** St. Thomas | **30,000** | **13** | **5** | **18** | **22** | **3** | **16** | **8** |
| | | | | | | | | |
| **GRAND TOTALS 1996** | **60,280,454** | **32,442** | **16,629** | **49,009** | **11,527** | **6,357** | **89,125** | **19,726** |
| **Grand Totals 1995** | **60,190,605** | **32,834** | **16,717** | **49,947** | **11,371** | **6,578** | **92,107** | **19,723** |
| **Grand Totals 1986** | **52,654,908** | **35,155** | **22,028** | **57,183** | **7,562** | **7,429** | **113,658** | **19,313** |

[1]Catholic population figures are from *1996 Annuario Pontificio*. [2]Figures do not include Syrian-rite eparchy of Our Lady of the Deliverance of Newark (for U.S. and Canada) established Nov. 6, 1995. [3]Priest chaplains are on loan from their dioceses or religious community. The *1996 Annuario Pontificio* reported 538 regular and 638 auxiliary chaplains.

# PERCENTAGE OF CATHOLICS IN TOTAL POPULATION IN U.S.

(Source: *The Official Catholic Directory, 1996;* figures are as of Jan. 1, 1996. Total general population figures at the end of the table are U.S. Census Bureau estimates for Jan. 1 of the respective years. Archdioceses are indicated by an asterisk; for dioceses marked +, see Dioceses with Interstate Lines.)

| State Diocese | Catholic Pop. | Total Pop. | Cath. Pct. | State Diocese | Catholic Pop. | Total Pop. | Cath. Pct. |
|---|---|---|---|---|---|---|---|
| Alabama | 137,183 | 4,090,399 | 3.3 | Ft.Wayne-S.Bend | 153,709 | 1,096,876 | 14.0 |
| *Mobile | 68,931 | 1,452,506 | 4.7 | Gary | 182,115 | 735,926 | 24.7 |
| Birmingham | 68,252 | 2,637,893 | 2.6 | Lafayette | 91,526 | 1,022,916 | 8.9 |
| Alaska | 51,720 | 587,781 | 8.8 | Iowa | 520,319 | 2,773,350 | 18.8 |
| *Anchorage | 27,411 | 371,580 | 7.4 | *Dubuque | 215,322 | 923,000 | 23.3 |
| Fairbanks | 18,550 | 133,467 | 13.9 | Davenport | 106,661 | 707,123 | 15.1 |
| Juneau | 5,759 | 82,734 | 7.0 | Des Moines | 97,827 | 671,091 | 14.6 |
| Arizona | 678,226 | 3,998,649 | 17.0 | Sioux City | 100,509 | 472,136 | 21.3 |
| Phoenix | 381,635 | 2,788,150 | 13.7 | Kansas | 379,698 | 2,405,765 | 15.8 |
| Tucson | 296,591 | 1,210,499 | 24.5 | *Kansas City | 179,490 | 952,000 | 18.8 |
| Arkansas, Little Rock | 84,079 | 2,452,660 | 3.4 | Dodge City | 38,936 | 209,536 | 18.6 |
| California | 7,967,090 | 31,919,969 | 25.0 | Salina | 55,418 | 328,480 | 16.9 |
| *Los Angeles | 3,631,368 | 10,803,827 | 33.6 | Wichita | 105,854 | 915,749 | 11.6 |
| *San Francisco | 420,567 | 1,700,000 | 24.7 | Kentucky | 351,024 | 3,694,498 | 9.5 |
| Fresno | 320,824 | 1,923,433 | 16.7 | *Louisville | 183,105 | 1,139,022 | 16.1 |
| Monterey | 170,321 | 851,604 | 20.0 | Covington | 76,867 | 401,127 | 19.2 |
| Oakland | 485,183 | 2,132,632 | 22.7 | Lexington | 40,991 | 1,376,114 | 3.0 |
| Orange | 595,101 | 2,543,168 | 23.4 | Owensboro | 50,061 | 778,235 | 6.4 |
| Sacramento | 372,000 | 2,915,700 | 12.8 | Louisiana | 1,340,292 | 4,280,898 | 31.3 |
| San Bernardino | 610,736 | 2,985,280 | 20.4 | *New Orleans | 488,368 | 1,330,855 | 36.7 |
| San Diego | 677,395 | 2,769,131 | 24.5 | Alexandria | 48,050 | 393,397 | 12.2 |
| San Jose | 374,412 | 1,497,648 | 25.0 | Baton Rouge | 222,980 | 774,536 | 28.8 |
| Santa Rosa | 135,023 | 771,950 | 17.4 | Houma-Thibodaux | 110,752 | 202,000 | 54.8 |
| Stockton | 174,160 | 1,025,596 | 17.0 | Lafayette | 350,001 | 540,000 | 64.8 |
| Colorado | 527,408 | 3,594,784 | 14.7 | Lake Charles | 82,266 | 259,425 | 31.7 |
| *Denver | 340,875 | 2,513,993 | 13.6 | Shreveport | 37,875 | 780,685 | 4.8 |
| Colorado Springs | 84,889 | 593,176 | 14.3 | Maine,Portland | 244,376 | 1,227,927 | 19.9 |
| Pueblo | 101,644 | 487,615 | 20.8 | Maryland,*Baltimore | 441,860 | 2,825,526 | 15.6 |
| Connecticut | 1,353,693 | 3,269,846 | 41.4 | Massachusetts | 3,023,601 | 6,023,009 | 50.2 |
| *Hartford | 778,856 | 1,814,610 | 42.9 | *Boston | 2,009,946 | 3,795,693 | 52.9 |
| Bridgeport | 353,238 | 829,786 | 42.6 | Fall River | 374,083 | 715,000 | 52.3 |
| Norwich+ | 221,599 | 625,450 | 35.4 | Springfield | 315,620 | 802,611 | 39.3 |
| Delaware, Wilmington+ | 158,238 | 1,049,769 | 15.1 | Worcester | 323,952 | 709,705 | 45.6 |
| District of Columbia | | | | Michigan | 2,185,242 | 9,479,559 | 23.0 |
| *Washington+ | 440,000 | 2,304,493 | 19.1 | *Detroit | 1,413,105 | 4,266,654 | 33.1 |
| Florida | 1,953,223 | 13,800,395 | 14.1 | Gaylord | 82,052 | 421,449 | 19.5 |
| *Miami | 744,048 | 3,490,242 | 21.3 | Grand Rapids | 132,418 | 1,167,900 | 11.3 |
| Orlando | 303,525 | 2,707,836 | 11.2 | Kalamazoo | 102,225 | 968,535 | 10.5 |
| Palm Beach | 205,455 | 1,254,071 | 16.4 | Lansing | 234,899 | 1,655,574 | 14.1 |
| Pensacola-Tallahassee | 61,688 | 1,236,417 | 5.0 | Marquette | 72,081 | 313,915 | 23.0 |
| St. Augustine | 114,146 | 1,471,265 | 7.7 | Saginaw | 148,462 | 685,532 | 21.6 |
| St. Petersburg | 351,596 | 2,298,013 | 15.3 | Minnesota | 1,183,551 | 4,518,166 | 26.2 |
| Venice | 172,765 | 1,342,551 | 12.9 | *St. Paul and | | | |
| Georgia | 280,734 | 6,362,968 | 4.4 | Minneapolis | 709,028 | 2,642,538 | 26.8 |
| *Atlanta | 212,850 | 3,923,100 | 5.4 | Crookston | 42,012 | 236,100 | 17.8 |
| Savannah | 67,884 | 2,439,868 | 2.8 | Duluth | 81,293 | 396,000 | 20.5 |
| Hawaii, Honolulu | 232,780 | 1,178,600 | 19.7 | New Ulm | 72,274 | 281,798 | 25.6 |
| Idaho,Boise | 115,150 | 1,144,000 | 10.1 | St. Cloud | 149,250 | 433,427 | 34.3 |
| Illinois | 3,631,645 | 11,725,932 | 31.0 | Winona | 129,694 | 528,303 | 24.5 |
| *Chicago | 2,338,000 | 5,700,608 | 41.0 | Mississippi | 109,483 | 2,664,915 | 4.1 |
| Belleville | 106,426 | 842,557 | 12.6 | Biloxi | 65,143 | 684,890 | 9.5 |
| Joliet | 511,888 | 1,467,237 | 34.9 | Jackson | 44,340 | 1,980,025 | 2.2 |
| Peoria | 234,161 | 1,432,327 | 16.3 | Missouri | 841,266 | 5,221,882 | 16.1 |
| Rockford | 266,842 | 1,177,079 | 22.7 | *St. Louis | 558,800 | 2,094,599 | 26.7 |
| Springfield | 174,328 | 1,106,124 | 15.8 | Jefferson City | 83,010 | 777,522 | 10.7 |
| Indiana | 728,006 | 5,533,345 | 13.2 | Kansas City-St.Joseph | 145,343 | 1,299,555 | 11.2 |
| *Indianapolis | 211,120 | 2,201,503 | 9.6 | Springfield- | | | |
| Evansville | 89,536 | 476,124 | 18.8 | Cape Girardeau | 54,113 | 1,050,206 | 5.1 |

| State Diocese | Catholic Pop. | Total Pop. | Cath. Pct. | State Diocese | Catholic Pop. | Total Pop. | Cath. Pct. |
|---|---|---|---|---|---|---|---|
| Montana | 125,320 | 823,904 | 15.2 | Pennsylvania | | | |
| Great Falls-Billings | 58,820 | 399,532 | 14.7 | Erie | 236,255 | 873,015 | 27.1 |
| Helena | 66,500 | 424,372 | 15.7 | Greensburg | 207,292 | 679,144 | 30.5 |
| Nebraska | 345,930 | 1,607,049 | 21.5 | Harrisburg | 227,240 | 1,867,124 | 12.2 |
| * Omaha | 208,212 | 799,958 | 26.0 | Pittsburgh | 760,697 | 2,015,759 | 37.7 |
| Grand Island | 52,800 | 290,429 | 18.2 | Scranton | 367,295 | 1,038,249 | 35.4 |
| Lincoln | 84,918 | 516,662 | 16.4 | Rhode Island,Providence | 644,789 | 1,003,000 | 64.2 |
| Nevada[1] | 300,000 | 1,493,000 | 20.1 | South Carolina,Charleston | 105,247 | 3,664,000 | 2.9 |
| Las Vegas | 192,000 | 1,064,745 | 18.0 | South Dakota | 158,270 | 711,591 | 22.2 |
| Reno | 108,000 | 428,255 | 25.2 | Rapid City | 39,674 | 211,591 | 18.7 |
| New Hampshire | | | | Sioux Falls | 118,596 | 500,000 | 23.7 |
| Manchester | 321,678 | 1,137,000 | 28.3 | Tennessee | 153,534 | 4,995,773 | 3.0 |
| New Jersey | 3,242,765 | 7,904,274 | 41.0 | Knoxville | 39,714 | 1,860,218 | 2.1 |
| * Newark | 1,325,838 | 2,656,693 | 49.9 | Memphis | 57,007 | 1,373,000 | 4.1 |
| Camden | 405,541 | 1,281,692 | 31.6 | Nashville | 56,813 | 1,762,555 | 3.2 |
| Metuchen | 477,900 | 1,164,140 | 41.1 | Texas | 4,179,841 | 18,237,293 | 22.9 |
| Paterson | 373,911 | 1,038,500 | 36.0 | * San Antonio | 642,824 | 1,766,574 | 36.3 |
| Trenton | 659,575 | 1,763,249 | 37.4 | Amarillo | 40,467 | 386,574 | 10.4 |
| New Mexico | 421,868 | 1,775,099 | 23.8 | Austin | 270,000 | 1,638,245 | 16.5 |
| * Santa Fe | 256,135 | 967,642 | 26.5 | Beaumont | 86,595 | 541,354 | 16.0 |
| Gallup | 40,495 | 355,640 | 11.4 | Brownsville | 689,657 | 851,909 | 81.0 |
| Las Cruces | 125,238 | 451,817 | 27.7 | Corpus Christi | 351,500 | 781,250 | 45.0 |
| New York | 7,220,124 | 18,475,762 | 39.0 | Dallas | 319,631 | 2,678,590 | 11.9 |
| * New York | 2,327,300 | 5,351,854 | 43.5 | El Paso+ | 527,060 | 739,747 | 71.2 |
| Albany | 403,403 | 1,315,414 | 30.6 | Fort Worth | 187,508 | 2,217,133 | 8.5 |
| Brooklyn | 1,531,858 | 4,236,720 | 36.1 | Galveston-Houston | 792,886 | 4,129,569 | 19.2 |
| Buffalo | 755,427 | 1,619,282 | 46.6 | Lubbock | 43,764 | 447,136 | 9.8 |
| Ogdensburg | 141,322 | 425,622 | 33.2 | San Angelo | 78,850 | 677,340 | 11.6 |
| Rochester | 349,623 | 1,487,114 | 23.5 | Tyler | 40,526 | 1,126,596 | 3.6 |
| Rockville Centre | 1,338,526 | 2,816,165 | 47.5 | Victoria | 108,573 | 255,276 | 42.5 |
| Syracuse | 372,665 | 1,223,591 | 30.5 | Utah, Salt Lake City | 78,475 | 1,964,000 | 4.0 |
| North Carolina | 214,811 | 6,995,935 | 3.1 | Vermont, Burlington | 146,709 | 580,209 | 25.3 |
| Charlotte | 99,317 | 3,519,890 | 2.8 | Virginia | 463,563 | 6,472,700 | 7.2 |
| Raleigh | 115,494 | 3,476,045 | 3.3 | Arlington | 293,664 | 2,115,700 | 13.9 |
| North Dakota | 167,356 | 651,707 | 25.7 | Richmond | 169,899 | 4,357,000 | 3.9 |
| Bismarck | 69,388 | 261,307 | 26.5 | Washington | 519,101 | 5,384,433 | 9.6 |
| Fargo | 97,968 | 390,400 | 25.0 | * Seattle | 367,500 | 4,213,450 | 8.7 |
| Ohio | 2,216,803 | 11,097,524 | 20.0 | Spokane | 81,623 | 709,983 | 11.5 |
| * Cincinnati | 545,300 | 2,896,200 | 18.8 | Yakima | 69,978 | 461,000 | 15.1 |
| Cleveland | 825,356 | 2,804,085 | 29.4 | West Virginia | | | |
| Columbus | 214,215 | 2,188,842 | 9.8 | Wheeling-Charleston | 106,338 | 1,793,477 | 5.9 |
| Steubenville | 45,878 | 518,470 | 8.8 | Wisconsin | 1,564,642 | 4,983,805 | 31.4 |
| Toledo | 323,772 | 1,479,041 | 21.9 | * Milwaukee | 613,744 | 2,080,883 | 29.5 |
| Youngstown | 262,282 | 1,210,886 | 21.7 | Green Bay | 381,676 | 836,600 | 45.6 |
| Oklahoma | 139,836 | 3,396,086 | 4.1 | La Crosse | 227,940 | 827,970 | 27.5 |
| * Oklahoma City | 89,536 | 1,948,159 | 4.6 | Madison | 254,430 | 857,002 | 29.7 |
| Tulsa | 50,300 | 1,447,927 | 3.5 | Superior | 86,852 | 381,350 | 22.7 |
| Oregon | 307,990 | 3,082,000 | 10.0 | Wyoming, Cheyenne | 46,903 | 475,981 | 9.8 |
| * Portland | 278,505 | 2,683,900 | 10.4 | **Eastern Churches** | **471,766** | - | - |
| Baker | 29,485 | 398,100 | 7.4 | **Military Archdiocese** | **1,087,800** | - | - |
| Pennsylvania | 3,599,976 | 11,997,187 | 30.0 | **Outlying Areas** | **2,836,162** | - | - |
| * Philadelphia | 1,422,673 | 3,793,086 | 37.5 | **Grand Totals '96** | **60,280,454** | **264,023,000** | **22.8** |
| Allentown | 256,090 | 1,084,189 | 23.6 | **Grand Totals '95** | **60,190,605** | **261,653,497** | **23.0** |
| Altoona-Johnstown | 122,434 | 646,621 | 18.9 | **Grand Totals '86** | **52,654,908** | **239,399,874** | **22.0** |

[1]Nevada Catholic population figures are from *1996 Annuario Pontificio*.

## BASILICA OF THE NATIONAL SHRINE OF THE IMMACULATE CONCEPTION

The Basilica of the National Shrine of the Immaculate Conception is dedicated to the honor of the Blessed Virgin Mary, declared patroness of the United States under this title in 1846, eight years before the proclamation of the dogma of the Immaculate Conception. The church was designated a minor basilica by Pope John Paul II Oct. 12, 1990. The church is the eighth largest religious building in the world and the largest Catholic church in the Western Hemisphere, with numerous special chapels and with normal seating and standing accommodations for 6,000 people. Open daily, it is adjacent to The Catholic University of America, at Michigan Ave. and Fourth St. N.E., Washington, D.C. 20017. Msgr. Michael J. Bransfield is the rector.

# RECEPTIONS INTO THE CHURCH IN THE UNITED STATES

(Source: *The Official Catholic Directory, 1996;* figures as of Jan. 1, 1996. Archdioceses are indicated by an asterisk; for dioceses marked +, see Dioceses with Interstate Lines. Information includes infant and adult baptisms and those received into full communion.)

| State Diocese | Infant Baptisms | Adult Bapts. | Rec'd into Full Comm. | State Diocese | Infant Baptisms | Adult Bapts. | Rec'd into Full Comm. |
|---|---|---|---|---|---|---|---|
| Alabama | 2,327 | 351 | 733 | Indiana | | | |
| *Mobile | 1,114 | 203 | 325 | Ft.Wayne-S. Bend | 2,192 | 590 | 266 |
| Birmingham | 1,213 | 148 | 408 | Gary | 2,406 | 240 | 236 |
| Alaska | 1,212 | 114 | 121 | Lafayette | 1,738 | 229 | 313 |
| *Anchorage | 680 | 77 | 47 | Iowa | 8,800 | 805 | 1,207 |
| Fairbanks | 399 | 28 | 46 | *Dubuque | 3,627 | 137 | 395 |
| Juneau | 133 | 9 | 28 | Davenport | 1,635 | 233 | 213 |
| Arizona | 16,643 | 777 | 1,196 | Des Moines | 1,786 | 307 | 371 |
| Phoenix | 10,079 | 487 | 909 | Sioux City | 1,752 | 128 | 228 |
| Tucson | 6,564 | 290 | 287 | Kansas | 7,791 | 1,312 | 1,771 |
| Arkansas, Little Rock | 1,665 | 285 | 464 | *Kansas City | 3,315 | 378 | 940 |
| California | 192,865 | 8,128 | 7,670 | Dodge City | 1,071 | 490 | 140 |
| *Los Angeles | 92,233 | 1,852 | 2,132 | Salina | 1,067 | 105 | 299 |
| *San Francisco | 7,284 | 525 | 626 | Wichita | 2,338 | 339 | 392 |
| Fresno | 16,362 | 529 | 35 | Kentucky | 5,942 | 773 | 1,180 |
| Monterey | 4,588 | 210 | 235 | *Louisville | 2,959 | 300 | 536 |
| Oakland | 8,922 | 490 | 965 | Covington | 1,478 | 160 | 163 |
| Orange | 16,708 | 851 | 617 | Lexington | 587 | 140 | 231 |
| Sacramento | 8,934 | 764 | 718 | Owensboro | 918 | 173 | 250 |
| San Bernardino | 9,674 | 897 | 981 | Louisiana | 21,314 | 1,200 | 1,832 |
| San Diego | 12,325 | 1,026 | 625 | *New Orleans | 7,463 | 370 | 350 |
| San Jose | 8,048 | 437 | 439 | Alexandria | 717 | 101 | 107 |
| Santa Rosa | 2,698 | 139 | 101 | Baton Rouge | 3,185 | 325 | 475 |
| Stockton | 5,089 | 408 | 196 | Houma-Thibodaux | 1,793 | 51 | 266 |
| Colorado | 11,453 | 1,461 | 1,797 | Lafayette | 6,082 | 179 | 263 |
| *Denver | 8,046 | 1,227 | 1,175 | Lake Charles | 1,492 | 96 | 176 |
| Colorado Springs | 1,381 | 91 | 311 | Shreveport | 582 | 78 | 195 |
| Pueblo | 2,026 | 143 | 311 | Maine, Portland | 3,254 | 297 | 309 |
| Connecticut | 20,910 | 705 | 1,243 | Maryland,*Baltimore | 8,223 | 589 | 1,102 |
| *Hartford | 11,561 | 373 | 489 | Massachusetts | 41,718 | 817 | 1,002 |
| Bridgeport | 5,869 | 167 | 141 | *Boston | 27,465 | 452 | 327 |
| Norwich+ | 3,480 | 165 | 613 | Fall River | 5,636 | 90 | 141 |
| Delaware, Wilmington+ | 2,892 | 175 | 259 | Springfield | 4,612 | 163 | 310 |
| District of Columbia, | | | | Worcester | 4,005 | 112 | 224 |
| *Washington+ | 8,006 | 583 | 765 | Michigan | 30,378 | 3,060 | 4,409 |
| Florida | 38,012 | 3,033 | 3,727 | *Detroit | 17,265 | 1,341 | 1,795 |
| *Miami | 17,735 | 846 | 1,195 | Gaylord | 1,195 | 165 | 184 |
| Orlando | 5,405 | 530 | 787 | Grand Rapids | 2,459 | 297 | 547 |
| Palm Beach | 4,358 | 280 | 248 | Kalamazoo | 1,636 | 220 | 231 |
| Pensacola-Tallahassee | 986 | 151 | 265 | Lansing | 4,279 | 698 | 1,194 |
| St. Augustine | 1,837 | 356 | 455 | Marquette | 1,222 | 103 | 119 |
| St. Petersburg | 4,698 | 693 | 451 | Saginaw | 2,322 | 236 | 339 |
| Venice | 2,993 | 177 | 326 | Minnesota | 19,359 | 818 | 2,698 |
| Georgia | 6,428 | 357 | 1,149 | *St. Paul and | | | |
| *Atlanta | 5,037 | 97 | 811 | Minneapolis | 11,767 | 549 | 1,812 |
| Savannah | 1,391 | 260 | 338 | Crookston | 688 | 23 | 94 |
| Hawaii, Honolulu | 4,069 | 454 | 302 | Duluth | 1,213 | 57 | 166 |
| Idaho, Boise | 2,421 | 248 | 211 | New Ulm | 1,121 | 23 | 140 |
| Illinois | 63,454 | 3,560 | 3,812 | St. Cloud | 2,566 | 92 | 246 |
| *Chicago | 39,374 | 1,749 | 1,339 | Winona | 2,004 | 74 | 240 |
| Belleville | 1,656 | 242 | 259 | Mississippi | 1,513 | 557 | 435 |
| Joliet | 10,263 | 512 | 776 | Biloxi | 830 | 437 | 133 |
| Peoria | 3,613 | 494 | 597 | Jackson | 683 | 120 | 302 |
| Rockford | 5,727 | 247 | 394 | Missouri | 11,262 | 2,650 | 836 |
| Springfield | 2,821 | 316 | 447 | *St. Louis | 7,079 | 1,761 | — |
| Indiana | 12,024 | 1,915 | 1,684 | Jefferson City | 1,310 | 210 | 315 |
| *Indianapolis | 4,181 | 704 | 678 | Kansas City- | | | |
| Evansville | 1,507 | 152 | 191 | St. Joseph | 2,207 | 139 | 286 |

| State / Diocese | Infant Baptisms | Adult Bapts. | Rec'd into Full Comm. |
|---|---|---|---|
| **Missouri** | | | |
| Springfield-Cape Girardeau | 666 | 540 | 235 |
| **Montana** | 2,015 | 314 | 316 |
| Great Falls-Billings | 1,103 | 124 | 177 |
| Helena | 912 | 190 | 139 |
| **Nebraska** | 6,544 | 620 | 904 |
| *Omaha | 4,140 | 395 | 512 |
| Grand Island | 1,043 | 95 | 195 |
| Lincoln | 1,361 | 130 | 197 |
| **Nevada** | - | - | - |
| Reno | - | - | - |
| Las Vegas | - | - | - |
| **New Hampshire, Manchester** | 5,496 | 167 | 200 |
| **New Jersey** | 52,673 | 1,612 | 2,813 |
| *Newark | 18,475 | 414 | 877 |
| Camden | 7,592 | 519 | 428 |
| Metuchen | 7,561 | 142 | 302 |
| Paterson | 8,504 | 169 | 319 |
| Trenton | 10,541 | 368 | 887 |
| **New Mexico** | 9,721 | 568 | 643 |
| *Santa Fe | 6,046 | 261 | 311 |
| Gallup | 754 | 172 | 67 |
| Las Cruces | 2,921 | 135 | 265 |
| **New York** | 106,798 | 3,945 | 5,835 |
| *New York | 35,522 | 898 | 546 |
| Albany | 5,936 | 382 | 230 |
| Brooklyn | 20,617 | 616 | 3,184 |
| Buffalo | 8,325 | 366 | 430 |
| Ogdensburg | 2,065 | 187 | 88 |
| Rochester | 6,112 | 357 | 776 |
| Rockville Centre | 21,586 | 838 | — |
| Syracuse | 6,635 | 301 | 581 |
| **North Carolina** | 4,814 | 500 | 762 |
| Charlotte | 2,309 | 242 | 431 |
| Raleigh | 2,505 | 258 | 331 |
| **North Dakota** | 3,519 | 146 | 301 |
| Bismarck | 1,387 | 93 | 232 |
| Fargo | 2,132 | 53 | 69 |
| **Ohio** | 31,698 | 4,392 | 4,172 |
| *Cincinnati | 8,340 | 1,342 | 781 |
| Cleveland | 11,173 | 1,181 | 969 |
| Columbus | 3,474 | 453 | 656 |
| Steubenville | 723 | 427 | 1,150 |
| Toledo | 4,441 | 637 | - |
| Youngstown | 3,547 | 352 | 616 |
| **Oklahoma** | 2,690 | 550 | 817 |
| *Oklahoma City | 1,784 | 335 | 539 |
| Tulsa | 906 | 215 | 278 |
| **Oregon** | 5,392 | 868 | 650 |
| *Portland | 4,529 | 700 | 558 |
| Baker | 863 | 168 | 92 |
| **Pennsylvania** | 46,842 | 2,997 | 3,402 |
| *Philadelphia | 18,263 | 951 | 795 |
| Allentown | 4,010 | 197 | 283 |
| Altoona-Johnstown | 1,768 | 112 | 194 |
| Erie | 2,698 | 538 | 262 |
| Greensburg | 2,085 | 124 | 313 |
| Harrisburg | 3,287 | 346 | 456 |
| Pittsburgh | 9,719 | 466 | 810 |
| Scranton | 5,012 | 263 | 289 |
| **Rhode Island, Providence** | 7,002 | 149 | 151 |
| **South Carolina, Charleston** | 1,780 | 315 | 464 |
| **South Dakota** | 2,797 | 130 | 486 |
| Rapid City | 880 | 38 | 207 |
| Sioux Falls | 1,917 | 92 | 279 |
| **Tennessee** | 2,884 | 561 | 894 |
| Knoxville | 682 | 171 | 214 |
| Memphis | 1,045 | 182 | 273 |
| Nashville | 1,157 | 208 | 407 |
| **Texas** | 85,463 | 5,614 | 6,475 |
| *San Antonio | 14,363 | 403 | 690 |
| Amarillo | 1,134 | 118 | 121 |
| Austin | 5,907 | 593 | 1,014 |
| Beaumont | 1,402 | 134 | 233 |
| Brownsville | 8,169 | 475 | 644 |
| Corpus Christi | 5,718 | 215 | 727 |
| Dallas | 9,814 | 680 | 575 |
| El Paso | 8,043 | 108 | 237 |
| Fort Worth | 4,612 | 370 | 587 |
| Galveston-Houston | 19,040 | 2,096 | 1,041 |
| Lubbock | 1,840 | 54 | 135 |
| San Angelo | 2,392 | 144 | 198 |
| Tyler | 1,137 | 137 | 155 |
| Victoria | 1,892 | 87 | 118 |
| **Utah, Salt Lake City** | 2,009 | 427 | 238 |
| **Vermont, Burlington** | 2,016 | 102 | 141 |
| **Virginia** | 8,265 | 2,078 | 477 |
| Arlington | 5,042 | 2,032 | — |
| Richmond | 3,223 | 46 | 477 |
| **Washington** | 11,108 | 1,699 | 1,043 |
| *Seattle | 6,680 | 1,182 | 693 |
| Spokane | 1,414 | 361 | 142 |
| Yakima | 3,014 | 156 | 208 |
| **West Virginia, Wheeling-Charleston** | 1,306 | 365 | 336 |
| **Wisconsin** | 21,763 | 1,768 | 1,627 |
| *Milwaukee | 9,343 | 634 | 649 |
| Green Bay | 4,848 | 203 | 418 |
| La Crosse | 3,189 | 198 | 434 |
| Madison | 3,228 | 462 | - |
| Superior | 1,155 | 271 | 126 |
| **Wyoming, Cheyenne+** | 1,174 | 155 | 328 |
| **Eastern Churches** | 4,564 | 245 | 328 |
| *Philadelphia | 341 | 16 | 8 |
| St. Nicholas | 124 | 2 | - |
| Stamford | 203 | 18 | 10 |
| St. Josaphat (Parma) | 124 | 5 | 3 |
| *Pittsburgh | 579 | 61 | 80 |
| Parma | 185 | 12 | 58 |
| Passaic | 427 | 35 | - |
| Van Nuys | 65 | 7 | 22 |
| St. Maron (Maronites) | 374 | 22 | 77 |
| Our Lady of Lebanon (Maronites) | 368 | 28 | 23 |
| Newton (Melkites) | 554 | 27 | 25 |
| St. Thomas Apostle of Detroit (Chaldeans) | 1,124 | 8 | - |
| St. George Martyr (Romanian) | 32 | 4 | 22 |
| Our Lady of Deliverance Newark (Syrians)[1] | - | - | - |
| Armenian Ex. (U.S.-Can.) | 64 | - | - |
| **Military Archdiocese** | 7,176 | **1,575** | **459** |
| **Outlying Areas** | 47,837 | **2,978** | **15,946** |
| **GRAND TOTALS '96** | 1,029,281 | 69,894 | 92,155 |
| **Grand Totals '95** | 1,029,694 | 73,332 | 75,684 |
| **Grand Totals '86** | 953,323 | — | 87,996 |

[1]Eparchy established Nov. 6, 1995; no statistics available.

# STATISTICAL SUMMARY OF THE CHURCH IN THE U.S.

(Principal source: *The Official Catholic Directory, 1996*. Comparisons, where given, are with figures reported in the previous edition of the Directory. Totals below do not include statistics for Outlying Areas of U.S. These are given in tables on the preceding pages and elsewhere in the Almanac; see Index.)

**Catholic Population:** 57,444,292; increase, 95,378. Percent of total population, 22.

**Jurisdictions:** 34 archdioceses (includes 33 metropolitan sees and the Military Archdiocese), 157 dioceses (includes St. Thomas, Virgin Islands, and the eparchy of Our Lady of Deliverance of Newark for Syrians of the U.S. and Canada), 1 apostolic exarchate (New York-based Armenian exarchate for U.S. and Canada). Vacant jurisdictions (as of July 1, 1996), 4: Bismarck, Juneau, Pensacola-Tallahassee and Yakima.

**Cardinals:** 11 (8 head archiepiscopal sees in U.S.; 2 are Roman Curia officials; 1 is retired). As of July 1, 1996.

**Archbishops:** 64. Diocesan, in U.S., 34 (includes 8 cardinals and military archbishop); retired, 23 (includes 1 cardinal); outside U.S., 7. As of July 1, 1996.

**Bishops:** 371. Diocesan, in U.S. (and Virgin Islands), 153 (1 is a titular archbishop); coadjutors, 2; auxiliaries, 86; retired, 106; serving outside U.S., 24. As of July 1, 1996.

**Priests:** 48,200; decrease, 449. Diocesan, 31,947 (decrease, 400); religious order priests (does not include those assigned overseas), 16,253 (decrease, 49). There were 505 newly ordained priests, a decrease of 6.

**Permanent Deacons:** 11,045; increase, 116.

**Brothers:** 6,297; decrease, 238.

**Sisters:** 87,833; decrease, 2,960.

**Seminarians:** 4,466. Diocesan seminarians, 2,971; religious order seminarians, 1,495.

**Receptions into Church:** 1,124,506. Includes 981,444 infant baptisms; 66,886 adult baptisms and 76,176 already baptized persons received into full communion with the Church.

**First Communions:** 794,573.

**Confirmations:** 555,767.

**Marriages:** 294,144.

**Deaths:** 455,477.

**Parishes:** 19,331.

**Seminaries, Diocesan:** 67.

**Religious Seminaries:** 117.

**Colleges and Universities:** 232. Students, 667,177.

**High Schools:** 1,238. Students, 622,381.

**Elementary Schools:** 6,852. Students 1,998,746.

**Non-Residential Schools for Handicapped:** 80. Students, 7,532.

**Teachers:** 196,190 (priests, 2,442; brothers, 1,361; scholastics, 44; sisters, 12,369; laity, 179,974).

**Public School students in Religious Instruction Programs:** 4,119,488. High school students, 773,590; elementary school students, 3,345,898.

**Hospitals:** 600; patients treated, 57,344,270.

**Health Care Centers:** 556; patients treated, 3,868,070.

**Specialized Homes:** 1,365; patients assisted, 668,470.

**Residential Care of Children (Orphanages):** 168; total assisted, 76,987.

**Day Care and Extended Day Care Centers:** 1,018; total assisted, 143,144.

**Special Centers for Social Services:** 1,917; assisted annually, 19,172,874.

# CATHEDRALS IN THE UNITED STATES

A cathedral is the principal church in a diocese, the one in which the bishop has his seat (cathedra). He is the actual pastor, although many functions of the church, which usually serves a parish, are the responsibility of a priest serving as the rector. Because of the dignity of a cathedral, the dates of its dedication and its patronal feast are observed throughout a diocese.

The pope's cathedral, the Basilica of St. John Lateran, is the highest-ranking church in the world.

(Archdioceses are indicated by asterisk.)

**Albany, N.Y.:** Immaculate Conception.

**Alexandria, La.:** St. Francis Xavier.

**Allentown, Pa.:** St. Catherine of Siena.

**Altoona-Johnstown, Pa.:** Blessed Sacrament (Altoona); St. John Gualbert (Johnstown).

**Amarillo, Tex.:** St. Laurence.

**Anchorage,\* Alaska:** Holy Family.

**Arlington, Va:** St. Thomas More.

**Atlanta,\* Ga.:** Christ the King.

**Austin, Tex.:** St. Mary (Immaculate Conception).

**Baker, Ore.:** St. Francis de Sales.

**Baltimore,\* Md.:** Mary Our Queen; Basilica of the Assumption of the Blessed Virgin Mary (Co-Ca-

thedral; National Shrine).

**Baton Rouge, La.:** St. Joseph.

**Beaumont, Tex.:** St. Anthony (of Padua).

**Belleville, Ill.:** St. Peter.

**Biloxi, Miss.:** Nativity of the Blessed Virgin Mary.

**Birmingham, Ala.:** St. Paul.

**Bismarck, N.D.:** Holy Spirit.

**Boise, Ida.:** St. John the Evangelist.

**Boston,\* Mass.:** Holy Cross.

**Bridgeport, Conn.:** St. Augustine.

**Brooklyn, N.Y.:** St. James (Minor Basilica).

**Brownsville, Tex.:** Immaculate Conception.

**Buffalo, N.Y.:** St. Joseph.

**Burlington, Vt.:** Immaculate Conception.

**Camden, N.J.:** Immaculate Conception.

**Charleston, S.C.:** St. John the Baptist.

**Charlotte, N.C.:** St. Patrick.

**Cheyenne, Wyo.:** St. Mary.

**Chicago,\* Ill.:** Holy Name (of Jesus).

**Cincinnati,\* Ohio:** St. Peter in Chains.

**Cleveland, Ohio:** St. John the Evangelist.

**Colorado Springs, Colo:** St. Mary.

**Columbus, Ohio:** St. Joseph.

**Corpus Christi, Tex.:** Corpus Christi.

**Covington, Ky.:** Basilica of the Assumption.

Crookston, Minn.: Immaculate Conception.
Dallas, Tex.: Cathedral-Santuario de Guadalupe.
Davenport, Ia.: Sacred Heart.
Denver,* Colo.: Immaculate Conception (Minor Basilica).
Des Moines, Ia.: St. Ambrose.
Detroit,* Mich.: Most Blessed Sacrament.
Dodge City, Kans.: Sacred Heart.
Dubuque,* Ia.: St. Raphael.
Duluth, Minn.: Our Lady of the Rosary.
El Paso, Tex.: St. Patrick.
Erie, Pa.: St. Peter.
Evansville, Ind.: Most Holy Trinity (Pro-Cathedral).
Fairbanks, Alaska: Sacred Heart.
Fall River, Mass.: St. Mary of the Assumption.
Fargo, N.D.: St. Mary.
Fort Wayne-S. Bend, Ind.: Immaculate Conception (Fort Wayne); St. Matthew (South Bend).
Fort Worth, Tex.: St. Patrick.
Fresno, Calif.: St. John (the Baptist).
Gallup, N.M.: Sacred Heart.
Galveston-Houston, Tex.: St. Mary (Minor Basilica, Galveston); Sacred Heart Co-Cathedral (Houston).
Gary, Ind.: Holy Angels.
Gaylord, Mich.: St. Mary, Our Lady of Mt. Carmel.
Grand Island, Nebr.: Nativity of Blessed Virgin Mary.
Grand Rapids, Mich.: St. Andrew.
Great Falls-Billings, Mont.: St. Ann (Great Falls); St. Patrick Co-Cathedral (Billings).
Green Bay, Wis.: St. Francis Xavier.
Greensburg, Pa.: Blessed Sacrament.
Harrisburg, Pa.: St. Patrick.
Hartford,* Conn.: St. Joseph.
Helena, Mont.: St. Helena.
Honolulu, Hawaii: Our Lady of Peace; St. Theresa of the Child Jesus (Co-Cathedral).
Houma-Thibodaux, La.: St. Francis de Sales (Houma); St. Joseph Co-Cathedral (Thibodaux).
Indianapolis,* Ind.: Sts. Peter and Paul.
Jackson, Miss.: St. Peter.
Jefferson City, Mo.: St. Joseph.
Joliet, Ill.: St. Raymond Nonnatus.
Juneau, Alaska: Nativity of the Blessed Virgin Mary.
Kalamazoo, Mich.: St. Augustine.
Kansas City,* Kans.: St. Peter the Apostle.
Kansas City-St. Joseph, Mo.: Immaculate Conception (Kansas City); St. Joseph Co-Cathedral (St. Joseph).
Knoxville, Tenn.: Sacred Heart of Jesus.
La Crosse, Wis.: St. Joseph the Workman.
Lafayette, Ind.: St. Mary.
Lafayette, La.: St. John the Evangelist.
Lake Charles, La.: Immaculate Conception.
Lansing, Mich.: St. Mary.
Las Cruces, N. Mex.: Immaculate Heart of Mary.
Las Vegas, Nev.: Guardian Angel.
Lexington, Ky.: Christ the King.
Lincoln, Nebr.: Cathedral of the Risen Christ.
Little Rock, Ark.: St. Andrew.
Los Angeles,* Calif.: St. Vibiana (closed May 22, 1995, because of earthquake-related damage).
Louisville,* Ky.: Assumption.
Lubbock, Tex.: Christ the King.
Madison, Wis.: St. Raphael.
Manchester, N.H.: St. Joseph.

Marquette, Mich.: St. Peter.
Memphis, Tenn.: Immaculate Conception.
Metuchen, N.J.: St. Francis (of Assisi).
Miami,* Fla.: St. Mary (Immaculate Conception).
Milwaukee,* Wis.: St. John.
Mobile,* Ala.: Immaculate Conception (Minor Basilica).
Monterey, Calif.: San Carlos Borromeo.
Nashville, Tenn.: Incarnation.
Newark,* N.J.: Sacred Heart (Minor Basilica).
New Orleans,* La.: Cathedral (Basilica) of St. Louis.
Newton, Mass. (Melkite): Our Lady of the Annunciation (Boston).
New Ulm, Minn.: Holy Trinity.
New York,* N.Y.: St. Patrick.
Norwich, Conn.: St. Patrick.
Oakland, Calif.: St. Francis de Sales.
Ogdensburg, N.Y.: St. Mary (Immaculate Conception).
Oklahoma City,* Okla.: Our Lady of Perpetual Help.
Omaha,* Nebr.: St. Cecilia.
Orange, Calif.: Holy Family.
Orlando, Fla.: St. James.
Our Lady of Deliverance of Newark, New Jersey for Syrian Rite Catholics in the U.S. and Canada: Our Lady of Deliverance.
Our Lady of Lebanon of Los Angeles, Calif. (Maronite): Our Lady of Mt. Lebanon-St. Peter.
Owensboro, Ky.: St. Stephen.
Palm Beach, Fla.: St. Ignatius Loyola, Palm Beach Gardens.
Parma, Ohio (Byzantine): St. John the Baptist.
Passaic, N.J. (Byzantine): St. Michael.
Paterson, N.J.: St. John the Baptist.
Pensacola-Tallahassee, Fla.: Sacred Heart (Pensacola); Co-Cathedral of St. Thomas More (Tallahassee).
Peoria, Ill.: St. Mary.
Philadelphia,* Pa.: Sts. Peter and Paul (Minor Basilica).
Philadelphia,* Pa. (Byzantine): Immaculate Conception of Blessed Virgin Mary.
Phoenix, Ariz.: Sts. Simon and Jude.
Pittsburgh,* Pa. (Byzantine): St. John the Baptist, Munhall.
Pittsburgh, Pa.: St. Paul.
Portland, Me.: Immaculate Conception.
Portland,* Ore.: Immaculate Conception.
Providence, R.I.: Sts. Peter and Paul.
Pueblo, Colo.: Sacred Heart.
Raleigh, N.C.: Sacred Heart.
Rapid City, S.D.: Our Lady of Perpetual Help.
Reno, Nev.: St. Thomas Aquinas.
Richmond, Va.: Sacred Heart.
Rochester, N.Y.: Sacred Heart.
Rockford, Ill.: St. Peter.
Rockville Centre, N.Y.: St. Agnes.
Sacramento, Calif.: Blessed Sacrament.
Saginaw, Mich.: St. Mary.
St. Augustine, Fla.: St. Augustine (Minor Basilica).
St. Cloud, Minn.: St. Mary.
St. George's in Canton, Ohio (Byzantine, Romanian): St. George (Pro-Cathedral).
St. Josaphat in Parma, Oh. (Byzantine): St. Josaphat.

St. Louis,* Mo.: St. Louis.
St. Maron, Brooklyn, N.Y. (Maronite): Our Lady of Lebanon.
St. Nicholas in Chicago (Byzantine): St. Nicholas.
St. Paul and Minneapolis,* Minn.: St. Paul (St. Paul); Basilica of St. Mary Co-Cathedral (Minneapolis).
St. Petersburg, Fla.: St. Jude the Apostle.
St. Thomas the Apostle of Detroit (Chaldean): Our Lady of Chaldeans Cathedral (Mother of God Church), Southfield, Mich.
Salina, Kans.: Sacred Heart.
Salt Lake City, Utah: The Madeleine.
San Angelo, Tex.: Sacred Heart.
San Antonio,* Tex.: San Fernando.
San Bernardino, Calif: Our Lady of the Rosary.
San Diego, Calif.: St. Joseph.
San Francisco,* Calif.: St. Mary (Assumption).
San Jose, Calif.: St. Joseph; St. Patrick, Proto-Cathedral.
Santa Fe,* N.M.: San Francisco de Asis.
Santa Rosa, Calif.:B
Savannah, Ga.: St. John the Baptist.
Scranton, Pa.: St. Peter.
Seattle,* Wash.: St. James.
Shreveport, La.: St. John Berchmans.
Sioux City, Ia.: Epiphany.
Sioux Falls, S.D.: St. Joseph.
Spokane, Wash.: Our Lady of Lourdes.
Springfield, Ill.: Immaculate Conception.

Springfield, Mass.: St. Michael.
Springfield-Cape Girardeau, Mo.: St. Agnes (Springfield): St. Mary (Cape Girardeau).
Stamford, Conn. (Byzantine): St. Vladimir.
Steubenville, Ohio: Holy Name.
Stockton, Calif: Annunciation.
Superior, Wis.: Christ the King.
Syracuse, N.Y.: Immaculate Conception.
Toledo, Ohio: Queen of the Most Holy Rosary.
Trenton, N.J.: St. Mary (Assumption).
Tucson, Ariz.: St. Augustine.
Tulsa, Okla.: Holy Family.
Tyler, Tex.: Immaculate Conception.
Van Nuys, Calif. (Byzantine): St. Mary (Patronage of the Mother of God), Van Nuys; St. Stephen's (Pro-Cathedral), Phoenix, Ariz.
Venice, Fla: Epiphany.
Victoria, Tex.: Our Lady of Victory.
Washington,* D.C.: St. Matthew.
Wheeling-Charleston, W. Va.: St. Joseph (Wheeling); Sacred Heart (Charleston).
Wichita, Kans.: Immaculate Conception.
Wilmington, Del.: St. Peter.
Winona, Minn.: Sacred Heart.
Worcester, Mass.: St. Paul.
Yakima, Wash.: St. Paul.
Youngstown, Ohio: St. Columba.
Apostolic Exarchate for Armenian Catholics in the U.S. and Canada: St. Ann (110 E. 12th St., New York, N.Y. 10003).

# BASILICAS IN U.S. AND CANADA

Basilica is a title assigned to certain churches because of their antiquity, dignity, historical importance or significance as centers of worship. Major basilicas have the papal altar and holy door, which is opened at the beginning of a Jubilee Year; minor basilicas enjoy certain ceremonial privileges.

Among the major basilicas are the patriarchal basilicas of St. John Lateran, St. Peter, St. Paul Outside the Walls and St. Mary Major in Rome; St. Francis and St. Mary of the Angels in Assisi, Italy. The patriarchal basilica of St. Lawrence, Rome, is a minor basilica.

The dates in the listings below indicate when the churches were designated as basilicas.

## Minor Basilicas in U.S., Puerto Rico, Guam

**Alabama:** Mobile, Cathedral of the Immaculate Conception (Mar. 10, 1962).

**Arizona:** Phoenix, St. Mary's (Immaculate Conception) (Sept. 11, 1985).

**California:** San Francisco, Mission Dolores (Feb. 8, 1952); Carmel, Old Mission of San Carlos (Feb. 5, 1960); Alameda, St. Joseph (Jan. 21, 1972); San Diego, Mission San Diego de Alcala (Nov. 17, 1975).

**Colorado:** Denver, Cathedral of the Immaculate Conception (Nov. 3, 1979).

**District of Columbia:** National Shrine of the Immaculate Conception (Oct. 12, 1990).

**Florida:** St. Augustine, Cathedral of St. Augustine (Dec. 4, 1976).

**Illinois:** Chicago, Our Lady of Sorrows (May

4, 1956), Queen of All Saints (Mar. 26, 1962).

**Indiana:** Vincennes, Old Cathedral (Mar. 14, 1970). Notre Dame, Parish Church of Most Sacred Heart Church, Univ. of Notre Dame (Nov. 23, 1991).

**Iowa:** Dyersville, St. Francis Xavier (May 11, 1956); Des Moines, St. John the Apostle (Oct. 4, 1989).

**Kentucky:** Trappist, Our Lady of Gethsemani (May 3, 1949); Covington, Cathedral of Assumption (Dec. 8, 1953).

**Louisiana:** New Orleans, St. Louis King of France (Dec. 9, 1964).

**Maryland:** Baltimore, Assumption of the Blessed Virgin Mary (Sept. 1, 1937; designated national shrine, 1993); Emmitsburg, Shrine of St. Elizabeth Ann Seton (Feb. 13, 1991).

**Massachusetts:** Roxbury, Perpetual Help ("Mission Church") (Sept. 8, 1954); Chicopee, St. Stanislaus (June 25, 1991).

**Michigan:** Grand Rapids, St. Adalbert (Aug. 22, 1979).

**Minnesota:** Minneapolis. St. Mary (Feb. 1, 1926).

**Missouri:** Conception, Basilica of Immaculate Conception (Sept. 14, 1940); St. Louis, St. Louis King of France (Jan. 27, 1961).

**New Jersey:** Newark, Cathedral Basilica of the Sacred Heart (Dec. 22, 1995).

**New York:** Brooklyn, Our Lady of Perpetual Help (Sept. 5, 1969), Cathedral-Basilica of St. James (June 22, 1982); Lackawanna, Our Lady of Victory (1926); Youngstown, Blessed Virgin Mary of the Rosary of Fatima (Oct. 7, 1975).

**North Carolina:** Asheville, St. Lawrence (Apr. 6, 1993; ceremonies, Sept. 5, 1993).
**North Dakota:** Jamestown, St. James (Oct. 26, 1988).
**Ohio:** Carey, Shrine of Our Lady of Consolation (Oct. 21, 1971).
**Pennsylvania:** Latrobe, St. Vincent Basilica, Benedictine Archabbey (Aug. 22, 1955); Conewago, Basilica of the Sacred Heart (June 30, 1962); Philadelphia, Sts. Peter and Paul (Sept. 27, 1976); Danville, Sts. Cyril and Methodius (chapel at the motherhouse of the Sisters of Sts. Cyril and Methodius) (June 30, 1989).
**Texas:** Galveston, St. Mary Cathedral (Aug. 11, 1979).
**Virginia:** Norfolk, St. Mary of the Immaculate Conception (July 9, 1991).
**Wisconsin:** Milwaukee, St. Josaphat (Mar. 10, 1929).
**Puerto Rico:** San Juan, Cathedral of San Juan (Jan. 25, 1978).
**Guam:** Agana, Cathedral of Dulce Nombre de Maria (Sweet Name of Mary) (1985).

## Minor Basilicas in Canada

**Alberta:** Edmonton, Cathedral Basilica of St. Joseph (Mar. 15, 1984).
**Manitoba:** St. Boniface, Cathedral Basilica of St. Boniface (June 10, 1949).
**New Brunswick:** Chatham, St. Michael the Archangel (Dec. 9, 1988).
**Newfoundland:** St. John's, Cathedral Basilica of St. John the Baptist.
**Nova Scotia:** Halifax, St. Mary's Basilica (June 14, 1950).
**Ontario:** Ottawa, Basilica of Notre Dame; London, St. Peter's Cathedral (Dec. 13, 1961).
**Prince Edward Island:** Charlottetown, Basilica of St. Dunstan.
**Quebec:** Sherbrooke, Cathedral Basilica of St. Michael (July 31, 1959). Montreal, Cathedral Basilica of Our Lady Queen of the World; St. Joseph of Mount Royal; Basilica of Notre Dame (Feb. 15, 1982); St. Patrick (Dec. 9, 1988). Cap-de-la-Madeleine, Basilica of Our Lady of the Cape (Aug. 15, 1964). Quebec, Basilica of Notre Dame; St. Anne de Beaupre, Basilica of St. Anne. Valleyfield, Cathedral Basilica of St. Cecilia (Feb. 9, 1991).

# CHANCERY OFFICES OF U.S. ARCHDIOCESES AND DIOCESES

A chancery office, under this or another title, is the central administrative office of an archdiocese or diocese.

(Archdioceses are indicated by asterisk.)
**Albany, NY:** 40 N. Main Ave. 12203.
**Alexandria, LA:** P.O. Box 7417. 71306.
**Allentown, PA:** 202 N. 17th St., P.O. Box F. 18105.
**Altoona-Johnstown, PA:** 126 Logan Blvd., Hollidaysburg. 16648.
**Amarillo, TX:** 1800 N. Spring St., P.O. Box 5644. 79117.
**Anchorage,\* AK:** 225 Cordova St., Anchorage 99501.
**Arlington, VA:** Suite 704, 200 N. Glebe Rd. 22203.
**Atlanta,\* GA:** Catholic Center, 680 W. Peachtree St. N.W. 30308.
**Austin, TX:** N. Congress and 16th, P.O. Box 13327, Capitol Sta. 78711.
**Baker, OR:** P.O. Box 5999, Bend 97708.
**Baltimore,\* MD:** 320 Cathedral St. 21201.
**Baton Rouge, LA:** P.O. Box 2028. 70821.
**Beaumont, TX:** 703 Archie St., P.O. Box 3948. 77704.
**Belleville, IL:** 222 S. Third St., 62220.
**Biloxi, MS:** P.O. Box 1189. 39533.
**Birmingham, AL:** P.O. Box 12047. 35202.
**Bismarck, ND:** 420 Raymond St., Box 1575. 58502.
**Boise, ID:** 303 Federal Way. 83705.
**Boston,\* MA:** 2121 Commonwealth Ave., Brighton. 02135.
**Bridgeport, CT:** The Catholic Center, 238 Jewett Ave. 06606.
**Brooklyn, NY:** 75 Greene Ave., P.O. Box C. 11202.
**Brownsville, TX:** P.O. Box 2279. 78522.
**Buffalo, NY:** 795 Main St. 14203.
**Burlington, VT:** 351 North Ave. 05401.
**Camden, NJ:** 1845 Haddon Ave., P.O. Box 709, 08101.
**Charleston, SC:** 119 Broad St., P.O. Box 818.

29402.
**Charlotte, NC:** P.O. Box 36776. 28236.
**Cheyenne, WY:** Box 426. 82003.
**Chicago,\* IL:** P.O. Box 1979. 60690.
**Cincinnati,\* OH:** 100 E. 8th St. 45202.
**Cleveland, OH:** Chancery Bldg., 1027 Superior Ave. 44114.
**Colorado Springs, CO:** 29 W. Kiowa. 80903.
**Columbus, OH:** 198 E. Broad St. 43215.
**Corpus Christi, TX:** 620 Lipan St. P.O. Box 2620. 78403.
**Covington, KY:** P.O. Box 18548, Erlanger 41018.
**Crookston, MN:** 1200 Memorial Dr., P.O. Box 610. 56716.
**Dallas, TX:** 3725 Blackburn, P.O. Box 190507. 75219.
**Davenport, IA:** St. Vincent Center, 2706 N. Gaines St. 52804.
**Denver,\* CO:** 200 Josephine St. 80206.
**Des Moines, IA:** P.O. Box 1816. 50306.
**Detroit,\* MI:** 1234 Washington Blvd. 48226.
**Dodge City, KS:** 910 Central Ave., P.O. Box 137. 67801.
**Dubuque,\* IA:** P.O. Box 479. 52004.
**Duluth, MN:** 2830 E. 4th St. 55812.
**El Paso, TX:** 499 St. Matthews St. 79907.
**Erie, PA:** P.O. Box 10397. 16514.
**Evansville, IN:** P.O. Box 4169. 47724.
**Fairbanks, AK:** 1316 Peger Rd. 99709.
**Fall River, MA:** Box 2577. 02722.
**Fargo, ND:** 1310 Broadway, Box 1750. 58107.
**Fort Wayne-South Bend, IN:** P.O. Box 390, Fort Wayne. 46801.
**Fort Worth, TX:** 800 W. Loop 820 South. 76108.
**Fresno, CA:** 1550 N. Fresno St. 93703.
**Gallup, NM:** 711 S. Puerco Dr., P.O. Box 1338. 87305.
**Galveston-Houston, TX:** P.O. Box 907, Houston. 77001.

**Gary, IN:** 9292 Broadway, Merrillville. 46410.
**Gaylord, MI:** 1665 W. M-32. 49735.
**Grand Island, NE:** 311 W. 17th St., P.O. Box 996. 68802.
**Grand Rapids, MI:** 660 Burton St., S.E. 49507.
**Great Falls-Billings, MT:** P.O. Box 1399, Great Falls. 59403.
**Green Bay, WI:** P.O. Box 23066. 54305.
**Greensburg, PA:** 723 E. Pittsburgh St. 15601.
**Harrisburg, PA:** P.O. Box 2153. 17105.
**Hartford,\* CT:** 134 Farmington Ave. 06105.
**Helena, MT:** 515 North Ewing, P.O. Box 1729. 59624.
**Honolulu, HI:** 1184 Bishop St. 96813.
**Houma-Thibodaux, LA:** P.O. Box 9077, Houma, La. 70361.
**Indianapolis,\* IN:** 1400 N. Meridian St., P.O. Box 1410. 46206.
**Jackson, MS:** 237 E. Amite St., P.O. Box 2248. 39225.
**Jefferson City, MO:** 605 Clark Ave., P.O. Box 417. 65101.
**Joliet, IL:** 425 Summit St. 60435.
**Juneau, AK:** 419 6th St., No. 200. 99801.
**Kalamazoo, MI:** 215 N. Westnedge Ave. 49007.
**Kansas City,\* KS:** 12615 Parallel. 66109.
**Kansas City-St. Joseph, MO:** P.O. Box 419037, Kansas City. 64141.
**Knoxville, TN:** 805 Northshore Dr., P.O. Box 11127. 37939.
**La Crosse, WI:** 3710 East Ave. S., Box 4004. 54602.
**Lafayette in Indiana:** P.O. Box 260. 47902.
**Lafayette, LA:** 1408 Carmel Ave. 70501.
**Lake Charles, LA:** P.O. Box 3223. 70602.
**Lansing, MI:** 300 W. Ottawa. 48933.
**Las Cruces, NM:** 1280 Med Park Dr., 88005.
**Las Vegas, NV:** P.O. Box 18316. 89114.
**Lexington, KY:** P.O. Box 12350. 40582.
**Lincoln, NE:** P.O. Box 80328. 68501.
**Little Rock, AR:** 2415 N. Tyler St. P.O. Box 7239. 72217.
**Los Angeles,\* CA:** 1531 W. 9th St. 90015.
**Louisville,\* Ky.:** 212 E. College St., P.O. Box 1073. 40201.
**Lubbock, TX:** P.O. Box 98700. 79499.
**Madison, WI:** 15 E. Wilson St., P.O. Box 111. 53701.
**Manchester, NH:** 153 Ash St., P.O. Box 310. 03105.
**Marquette, MI:** 444 S. Fourth St., P.O. Box 550. 49855.
**Memphis, TN:** P.O. Box 41679. 38174.
**Metuchen, NJ:** P.O. Box 191. 08840.
**Miami,\* FL:** 9401 Biscayne Blvd., Miami Shores. 33138.
**Milwaukee,\* WI:** P.O. Box 07912. 53207.
**Mobile,\* AL:** 400 Government St., P.O. Box 1966. 36633.
**Monterey, CA:** P.O. Box 2048. 93942.
**Nashville, TN:** 2400 21st Ave. S. 37212.
**Newark,\* NJ:** P.O. Box 9500. 07104.
**New Orleans,\* LA:** 7887 Walmsley Ave. 70125.
**Newton, MA** (Melkite): 19 Dartmouth St., W. Newton. 02165.
**New Ulm, MN:** 1400 Sixth St. N., 56073.
**New York,\* NY:** 1011 First Ave. 10022.
**Norwich, CT:** 201 Broadway, P.O. Box 587. 06360.

**Oakland, CA:** 2900 Lakeshore Ave. 94610.
**Ogdensburg, NY:** 622 Washington St., P.O. Box 369. 13669.
**Oklahoma City,\* OK:** P.O. Box 32180. 73123.
**Omaha,\* NE:** 100 N. 62nd St. 68132.
**Orange, CA:** 2811 E. Villa Real Dr., P.O. Box 14195. 92613.
**Orlando, FL:** P.O. Box 1800. 32802.
**Our Lady of Deliverance of Newark,** for Syrian rite Catholics of the U.S. and Canada: 103 16th Ave., Newark, NJ 07103.
**Our Lady of Lebanon of Los Angeles, CA** (Maronite): P.O. Box 16397, Beverly Hills 90209.
**Owensboro, KY:** 600 Locust St. 42301.
**Palm Beach, FL:** P.O. Box 109650, Palm Beach Gardens 33410.
**Parma, OH** (Byzantine): 1900 Carlton Rd. 44134.
**Passaic, NJ** (Byzantine): 445 Lackawanna Ave., W. Paterson. 07424.
**Paterson, NJ:** 777 Valley Rd., Clifton. 07013.
**Pensacola-Tallahassee, FL:** P.O. Drawer 17329, Pensacola. 32522.
**Peoria, IL:** 607 N.E. Madison Ave., P.O. Box 1406. 61655.
**Philadelphia,\* PA:** 222 N. 17th St. 19103.
**Philadelphia,\* PA** (Byzantine): 827 N. Franklin St. 19123.
**Phoenix, AZ:** 400 E. Monroe St. 85004.
**Pittsburgh,\* PA** (Byzantine): 925 Liberty Ave. 15222.
**Pittsburgh, PA:** 111 Blvd. of the Allies. 15222.
**Portland, ME:** 510 Ocean Ave., P.O. Box 11559. 04101.
**Portland in Oregon\*:** 2838 E. Burnside St. 97214.
**Providence, RI:** One Cathedral Sq. 02903.
**Pueblo, CO:** 1001 N. Grand Ave. 81003.
**Raleigh, NC:** 300 Cardinal Gibbons Dr. 27606.
**Rapid City, SD:** 606 Cathedral Dr., P.O. Box 678. 57709.
**Reno, NV:** P.O. Box 1211. 89504.
**Richmond, VA:** 811 Cathedral Pl., 23220.
**Rochester, NY:** 1150 Buffalo Rd. 14624.
**Rockford, IL:** 1245 N. Court St., P.O. Box 7044, 61126.
**Rockville Centre, NY:** 50 N. Park Ave. 11570.
**Sacramento, CA:** 2110 Broadway. 95818.
**Saginaw, MI:** 5800 Weiss St. 48603.
**St. Augustine, FL:** P.O. Box 24000, Jacksonville, FL 32241.
**St. Cloud, MN:** P.O. Box 1248. 56302.
**St. George's in Canton, OH** (Byzantine, Romanian): 1121 44th St. N.E., Canton. 44714.
**St. Josaphat in Parma, OH** (Byzantine): P.O. Box 347180, Parma. 44134.
**St. Louis,\* MO:** 4445 Lindell Blvd. 63108.
**St. Maron of Brooklyn** (Maronite): P.O. Box 360, 294 Howard Ave., Staten Island, NY 10301.
**St. Nicholas in Chicago** (Byzantine): 2245 W. Rice St. 60622.
**St. Paul and Minneapolis,\* MN:** 226 Summit Ave., St. Paul. 55102.
**St. Petersburg, FL:** P.O. Box 40200. 33743.
**St. Thomas the Apostle of Detroit** (Chaldean): 25603 Berg Rd., Southfield, MI 48034.
**Salina, KS:** P.O. Box 980. 67402.
**Salt Lake City, UT:** 27 C St. 84103.

San Angelo, TX: P.O. Box 1829. 76902.
San Antonio,* TX: P.O. Box 28410. 78228.
San Bernardino, CA: 1201 E. Highland Ave. 92404.
San Diego, CA: P.O. Box 85728. 92186.
San Francisco,* CA: 445 Church St. 94114.
San Jose, CA: 900 Lafayette St., Suite 301, Santa Clara 95050.
Santa Fe,* NM: 4000 St. Joseph's Pl. N.W., Albuquerque. 87120.
Santa Rosa, CA: P.O. Box 1297. 95402.
Savannah, GA: 601 E. Liberty St. 31401.
Scranton, PA: 300 Wyoming Ave. 18503.
Seattle,* WA: 910 Marion St. 98104.
Shreveport, LA: 2500 Line Ave. 71104.
Sioux City, IA: P.O. Box 3379. 51102.
Sioux Falls, SD: 3100 W. 41st St. 57105.
Spokane, WA: W. 1023 Riverside Ave., P.O. Box 1453. 99210.
Springfield, IL: P.O. Box 3187. 62708.
Springfield, MA: P.O. Box 1730. 01101.
Springfield-Cape Girardeau, MO: 601 S. Jefferson, Springfield. 65806.
Stamford, CT (Byzantine): 14 Peveril Rd. 06902.
Steubenville, OH: P.O. Box 969. 43952.
Stockton, CA: P.O. Box 4237. 95204.

Superior, WI: 1201 Hughitt Ave., Box 969. 54880.
Syracuse, NY: P.O. Box 511. 13201.
Toledo, OH: P.O. Box 985. 43697.
Trenton, NJ: P.O. Box 5309. 08638.
Tucson, AZ: 192 S. Stone Ave., Box 31. 85702.
Tulsa, OK: P.O. Box 2009. 74101.
Tyler, TX: 1015 E.S.E. Loop 323. 75701.
Van Nuys, CA (Byzantine): 8131 N. 16th St., Phoenix, AZ 85020.
Venice, FL: P.O. Box 2006. 34284.
Victoria, TX: P.O. Box 4070. 77903.
Washington,* DC: P.O. Box 29260. 20017.
Wheeling-Charleston, WV: 1300 Byron St., P.O. Box 230, Wheeling. 26003.
Wichita, KS: 424 N. Broadway. 67202.
Wilmington, DE: P.O. Box 2030. 19899.
Winona, MN: P.O. Box 588. 55987.
Worcester, MA: 49 Elm St. 01609.
Yakima, WA: 5301-A Tieton Dr. 98908.
Youngstown, OH: 144 W. Wood St. 44503.
Military Archdiocese: 962 Wayne Ave., Silver Spring, MD 20910.
Armenian Apostolic Exarchate for the United States and Canada: 110 E. 12th St., New York, NY 10003.

# NATIONAL CATHOLIC CONFERENCES

The two conferences described below are related in membership and directive control but distinct in nature, purpose and function.

The National Conference of Catholic Bishops (NCCB) is a strictly ecclesiastical body in and through which the bishops of the United States act together, officially and with authority as pastors of the Church. It is the sponsoring organization of the United States Catholic Conference.

The United States Catholic Conference (USCC) is a civil corporation and operational secretariat in and through which the bishops, together with other members of the Church, act on a wider scale for the good of the Church and society. It is sponsored by the National Conference of Catholic Bishops.

The principal officers of both conferences are: Bishop Anthony M. Pilla, president; Bishop Joseph A. Fiorenza, vice president; Archbishop Thomas J. Murphy, treasurer; Archbishop Harry J. Flynn, secretary.

The membership of the Administrative Committee of the NCCB and the Administrative Board of the USCC is identical.

Headquarters of both conferences are located at 3211 Fourth St. N.E., Washington, D.C. 20017.

## CONFERENCE OF CATHOLIC BISHOPS

The National Conference of Catholic Bishops (NCCB), established by action of the U.S. hierarchy Nov. 14, 1966, is a strictly ecclesiastical body with defined juridical authority over the Church in this country. It was set up with the approval of the Holy See and in line with directives from the Second Vatican Council. Its constitution was formally ratified during the November, 1967, meeting of the U.S. hierarchy.

The NCCB is a development from the Annual Meeting of the Bishops of the United States, whose pastoral character was originally approved by Pope Benedict XV Apr. 10, 1919.

The address of the Conference is 3211 Fourth St. N.E., Washington, D.C. 20017. Rev. Msgr. Dennis M. Schnurr is general secretary.

### Pastoral Council

The conference, one of many similar territorial conferences envisioned in the conciliar Decree on the Pastoral Office of Bishops in the Church (No. 38), is "a council in which the bishops of a given nation or territory (in this case, the United States) jointly exercise their pastoral office to promote the greater good which the Church offers mankind, especially through the forms and methods of the apostolate fittingly adapted to the circumstances of the age."

Its decisions, "provided they have been approved legitimately and by the votes of at least two-thirds of the prelates who have a deliberative vote in the conference, and have been recognized by the Apostolic See, are to have juridically binding force only in those cases prescribed by the common law or determined by a special mandate of the Apostolic See, given either spontaneously or in response to a petition of the conference itself."

All bishops who serve the Church in the U.S., its territories and possessions, have membership and voting rights in the NCCB. Retired bishops cannot be elected to conference offices nor can they vote on matters which by law are binding by two-thirds of the membership. Only diocesan bishops can vote on diocesan quotas, assessments or special collections.

### Officers, Committees

The conference operates through a number of bishops' committees with functions in specific areas of work and concern. Their basic assignments are to prepare materials on the basis of which the bishops, assembled as a conference, make decisions, and to put suitable action plans in effect.

The principal officers are: Bishop Anthony M. Pilla, president; Bishop Joseph A. Fiorenza, vice president; Archbishop Thomas J. Murphy, treasurer; Archbishop Harry J. Flynn, secretary.

These officers, with several other bishops, hold positions on executive-level committees — Executive Committee, the Committee on Budget and Finance, the Committee on Personnel, and the Committee on Priorities and Plans. They also, with other bishops, serve on the NCCB Administrative Committee.

The standing committees and their chairmen (Archbishops and Bishops) are as follows.

African American Catholics, Curtis J. Guillory, S.V.D.

American Board of Catholic Missions, Victor H. Balke.

American College, Louvain, Frank J. Rodimer.

Bishops' Welfare Emergency Relief, Anthony M. Pilla.

Boundaries of Dioceses and Provinces, Anthony M. Pilla.

Canonical Affairs, Cardinal Adam Maida.

Church in Latin America, Raymnudo J. Pena

Diaconate, Edward U. Kmiec.

Doctrine, Daniel E. Pilarczyk.

Ecumenical and Interreligious Affairs, Oscar H. Lipscomb (Alexander J. Brunett, chairman-elect).

Evangelization, John G. Vlazny.

Hispanic Affairs, Roberto O. Gonzalez, O.F.M.

Laity, Tod D. Brown.

Liturgy, Donald W. Trautman (Jerome G. Hanus, chairman elect).

Marriage and Family Life, Joseph J. Charron, C.PP.S.

Migration, John S. Cummins.

Missions, Sean P. O'Malley.

North American College, Rome, Cardinal James Hickey.

Pastoral Practices, Joseph L. Imesch.

Priestly Formation, Donald W. Wuerl.

Priestly Life and Ministry, Robert F. Morneau.

Pro-Life Activities, Cardinal Bernard F. Law.

Relationship between Eastern and Latin Catholic Churches, Basil H. Losten.

Religious Life and Ministry, Joseph A. Galante.

Science and Human Values, Francis X. DiLorenzo.

Selection of Bishops, Anthony M. Pilla.

Vocations, Paul S. Loverde.

Women in Society and in the Church, John C. Dunne.

Ad hoc committees and their chairmen are as follows.

Aid to the Church in Central and Eastern Europe, Theodore E. McCarrick.

Bishops Life and Ministry, William S. Skylstad.

Catechism of the Catholic Church, Daniel M. Buechlein.

Catholic Charismatic Renewal, Sam G. Jacobs.

Economic Concerns of the Holy See, James P. Keleher.

Ex Corde Ecclesiae, John J. Leibrecht.

Health Care Issues and the Church, Donald W. Wuerl.

Liaison Committee with CNS (Catholic News Service), Edward J. O'Donnell.

Mission and Structure of the NCCB, Cardinal Joseph Bernardin.

Native American Catholics, Donald E. Pelotte, S.S.S.

Nomination of Conference Officers, J. Terry Steib, S.V.D.

Review of Scripture Translations, Richard J. Sklba.

Sexual Abuse, John F. Kinney.

Shrines, James P. Keleher.

Stewardship, Thomas J. Murphy.

## UNITED STATES CATHOLIC CONFERENCE

The United States Catholic Conference, Inc. (USCC), is the operational secretariat and service agency of the National Conference of Catholic Bishops for carrying out the civic-religious work of the Church in this country. It is a civil corporation related to the NCCB in membership and directive control but distinct from it in purpose and function.

The address of the Conference is 3211 Fourth St. N.E., Washington, D.C. 20017. Rev. Msgr. Dennis M. Schnurr is general secretary.

### Service Secretariat

The USCC, as of Jan. 1, 1967, took over the general organization and operations of the former National Catholic Welfare Conference, Inc., whose origins dated back to the National Catholic War Council of 1917. The council underwent some change after World War I and was established on a permanent basis Sept. 24, 1919, as the National Catholic Welfare Council to serve as a central agency for organizing and coordinating the efforts of U.S. Catholics in carrying out the social mission of the Church in this country. In 1923, its name was changed to National Catholic Welfare Conference, Inc., and clarification was made of its nature as a service agency of the bishops and the Church rather than as a conference of bishops with real juridical authority in ecclesiastical affairs.

The Official Catholic Directory states that the USCC assists "the bishops in their service to the Church in this country by uniting the people of God where voluntary collective action on a broad interdiocesan level is needed. The USCC provides an organizational structure and the resources needed to insure coordination, cooperation, and assistance in the public, educational and social concerns of the Church at the national, regional, state and, as appropriate, diocesan levels."

### Officers, Departments

The principal officers of the USCC are: Bishop Anthony M. Pilla, president; Bishop Joseph A. Fiorenza, vice president; Archbishop Thomas J. Murphy, treasurer; Archbishop Harry J. Flynn, secretary. These officers, with several other bishops, hold positions on executive-level committees — the Executive Committee; the Committee on Priorities and Plans; the Committee on Budget and Finance; the Committee on Personnel. They also serve on the Administrative Board.

The Executive Committee, organized in 1969, is authorized to handle matters of urgency between meetings of the Administrative Board and the general conference, to coordinate items for the agenda of general meetings, and to speak in the name of the USCC.

The major departments are: Campaign for Human

Development; Communications; Education; Social Development and World Peace. A National Advisory Council of bishops, priests, men and women religious, lay men and women advises the Administrative Board on overall plans and operations of the USCC.

The administrative general secretariat, in addition to other duties, supervises staff-service offices of Finance, General Counsel, Government Liaison, Priorities and Plans, Management Information Services, Human Resources, General Services, Research.

Most of the organizations and associations affiliated with the USCC are covered in separate Almanac entries.

# MEETINGS OF THE U.S. BISHOPS

## NOVEMBER 13 TO 16, 1995

About 250 bishops attended the annual meeting of the National Conference of Catholic Bishops and the United States Catholic Conference Nov. 13 to 16, 1995, in Washington, D.C.

**Presidential Address:** Cardinal William H. Keeler reflected on various aspects, impressions and challenges connected with the October visit of Pope John Paul to Newark, the United Nations, New York and Baltimore. He summed it all up in the second paragraph of his address.

"In pouring rain and driving wind and bright sunshine, in cathedrals and ballparks, at the United Nations and at a race track, he spoke the truths of our faith and affirmed the best of our nation's values and challenged us to live up to both. From the moment he arrived in Newark until he left us in Baltimore, he urged us to ground freedom in truth, to proclaim moral responsibility as an indispensable value for our day, and to preach the Gospel in season and out of season, without fear."

### Items of Business

The bishops acted on the following subjects.

**Bishops, Retired:** Approved new guidelines on the retirement of bishops.

**Budget:** Approved a $41.8 million 1996 budget for their conferences.

**Budget, Federal:** Affirmed an appeal by Cardinal William H. Keeler for "leadership for the common good," to resolve the budget crisis that partially shut down federal government operations during he bishops' meeting.

**College Students:** Approved a brief letter in which they urged Catholic college students to "create a climate of hope and a community of welcome" on campuses throughout the nation.

**"Economic Justice for All":** Reaffirmed the principles of their 1986 pastoral letter, saying that "too little economic growth" is "distributed too inequitably."

**Elections:** Bishop Anthony M. Pilla of Cleveland, president for a three-year term; Bishop Joseph A. Fiorenza of Galveston-Houston, vice president; Archbishop Harry J. Flynn of St. Paul-Minneapolis, secretary.

**Hispanics:** Approved a pastoral statement entitled "The Hispanic Presence in the Evangelization in the United States," regarding the linkage of faith and culture in the Hispanic community and its relevance to the entire Church in this country.

**Lay Ministry:** Ratified a pastoral statement entitled "Called and Gifted for the Third Millennium," marking anniversaries of two similar statements of the past.

**Liturgy:** Approved the Pastoral Introduction to the Order of the Mass and related U.S. adaptations, and the fourth segment of the seven-part Sacramentary; these actions require ratification by the Vatican.

**Religious, Retired:** Extended the annual collection for retired religious until the year 2007.

**Vocations to the Priesthood and Religious Life:** Adopted a national strategy to run through 1998; includes regional hearings, a national symposium and the establishment of an ad hoc committee to guide its implementation.

**Welfare Reform:** Released a letter in which they said proposals in Congress appeared "to represent a massive disinvestment in poor children and working families."

**Other Items:** Approved a new formula for diocesan contributions for operation of the two bishops' conference; continued discussion on restructuring of their conferences; received reports on a variety of subjects, including efforts to overcome racial discrimination, sexual abuse and the defunct Catholic Telecommunications Network of America.

## JUNE 20 to 22, 1996

Just over 200 bishops attended the meeting in Portland, Ore.

**Presidential Address:** Bishop Anthony M. Pilla, president of the conferences, departed from custom in delivering an opening address usually reserved for the annual November meeting of the bishops. He did so with a major talk on the role of the bishops in public policy debates in an election year. He said the bishops would not back down from stating their positions, based on principles of morality and social justice, just because some people might accuse them of partisanship when their positions might be closer to those of one party or the other on a particular issue.

### Items of Business

**Abortion:** Unanimously approved a statement calling on Congress to override President Clinton's veto of the Partial-Birth Abortion Ban Act. (See "Stand Up for Life," for excerpts.)

**Burnt-Out Churches:** Contributed $50,000 to a national interreligious campaign to assist congregations victimized by the recent spate of mostly black church burnings across the country. The bishops endorsed a statement on the church burnings, saying: "We deplore any act of violence, but these sacrilegious acts, directed especially against African-American congregations, seem particularly reprehensible." (See separate article for excerpts.)

**Collection:** Approved a one-time national collection in parishes for a gift to Pope John Paul on the golden anniversary of his ordination to the priesthood.

**Cremation:** **Voted** to ask Vatican permission to allow funeral Masses in the presence of cremated remains of the dead.

**Election:** Elected Archbishop Daniel E. Pilarczyk to head the Committee on Doctrine until November, 1997, as the successor to Archbishop John R. Quinn, retired head of the Archdiocese of San Francisco.

**Immigration:** Unanimously approved a policy statement critical of parts of pending federal legis-

lation on the subject. (See separate article for excerpts.)

**Liturgy:** Approved six more portions of the in-work revision of the Sacramentary.

**Millennium Office: Approved** establishment of a national office to coordinate preparations for celebration of the third millennium of Christianity in the year 2000. (See separate article.)

**Reports and Discussions:** Various subjects were brought forward to the attention of the bishops for informational purposes and reference to the November, 1996, meeting of the conferences.

# STATE CATHOLIC CONFERENCES

These conferences are agencies of bishops and dioceses in the various states. Their general purposes are to develop and sponsor cooperative programs designed to cope with pastoral and common-welfare needs, and to represent the dioceses before governmental bodies, the public, and in private sectors. Their membership consists of representatives from the dioceses in the states — bishops, clergy and lay persons in various capacities.

The **National Association of State Catholic Conference Directors** maintains liaison with the general secretariat of the United States Catholic Conference. President: Robert J. Castagna, executive director of Oregon Catholic Conference.

**Arizona** Catholic Conference, 400 E. Monroe St., Phoenix, AZ 85004; exec. dir., Rev. Msgr. Edward J. Ryle.

**California** Catholic Conference, Cathedral Square, 1010 11th St., Suite 200, Sacramento, CA 95814; exec. dir., Rev. Msgr. E. James Petersen.

**Colorado** Catholic Conference, 200 Josephine St., Denver, CO 80206; exec. dir., vacant.

**Connecticut** Catholic Conference, 134 Farmington Ave., Hartford, CT 06105; exec. dir., Rev. Thomas J. Barry.

**District of Columbia** Catholic Conference, 1221 Massachusetts Ave. NW, Washington, DC 20005; exec. dir., Ronald G. Jackson.

**Florida** Catholic Conference, P.O. Box 1638, Tallahassee, FL 32302; exec. dir., D. Michael McCarron.

**Georgia** Catholic Conference, Office Bldg., 3200 Deans Bridge Rd., Augusta, GA 30906; exec. dir., Cheatham E. Hodges, Jr.

**Hawaii** Catholic Conference, St. Stephen Diocesan Center, 6301 Pali Hwy., Kaneohe, Hawaii 96744; exec. dir., Rev. Marc R. Alexander.

**Illinois,** Catholic Conference of, 500 North Clark St., Chicago, IL 60610; 200 Broadway, Springfield, Ill. 62701; exec. dir., Doug Delaney.

**Indiana** Catholic Conference, 1400 N. Meridian St., P.O. Box 1410, Indianapolis, IN 46206; exec. dir., M. Desmond Ryan.

**Iowa** Catholic Conference, 505 Fifth Ave., Suite No. 818, Des Moines, IA 50309; exec. dir., Timothy McCarthy.

**Kansas** Catholic Conference, 6301 Antioch, Merriam, KS 66202; exec. dir., Robert Runnels, Jr.

**Kentucky,** Catholic Conference of, 1042 Burlington Lane, Frankfort, KY 40601; exec. dir., Jane J. Chiles.

**Louisiana** Catholic Conference, 3423 Hundred Oaks Ave., Baton Rouge, LA 70808; exec. dir., Kirby J. Ducote.

**Maryland** Catholic Conference, 188 Duke of Gloucester St., Annapolis, MD 21401; exec. dir., Richard J. Dowling.

**Massachusetts** Catholic Conference, 55 Franklin St., Boston, MA 02110; exec. dir., Gerald D. D'Avolio, Esq.

**Michigan** Catholic Conference, 505 N. Capitol Ave., Lansing, MI 48933; president and CEO, Sr. Monica Kostielney, R.S.M.

**Minnesota** Catholic Conference, 475 University Ave. W., St. Paul, MN 55103; exec. dir., Rev. David F. McCauley.

**Missouri** Catholic Conference, P.O. Box 1022, 600 Clark Ave., Jefferson City, MO 65102; exec. dir., Louis C. DeFeo, Jr.

**Montana** Catholic Conference, P.O. Box 1708, Helena, MT 59624; exec. dir., Sharon Hoff.

**Nebraska** Catholic Conference, 521 S. 14th St., Lincoln, NE 68508; exec. dir., James R. Cunningham.

**New Jersey** Catholic Conference, 211 N. Warren St., Trenton, NJ 08618; exec. dir., William F. Bolan, Jr.

**New Mexico** Catholic Conference, 514 Marble Ave. N.W., Albuquerque, NM 87107; dir., Juan B. Montoya.

**New York** State Catholic Conference, 465 State St., Albany, NY 12203; exec. dir., John M. Kerry.

**North Dakota** Catholic Conference, 227 West Broadway Suite No. 2, Bismarck, ND 58501; exec. dir., Christopher T. Dodson.

**Ohio,** Catholic Conference of, 35 E. Gay St., Suite 502, Columbus, OH 43215; exec. dir., Timothy V. Luckhaupt.

**Oregon** Catholic Conference, 2838 E. Burnside, Portland, OR 97214; exec. dir., Robert J. Castagna.

**Pennsylvania** Catholic Conference, 223 North St., Box 2835, Harrisburg, PA 17105.

**Texas** Catholic Conference, 3001 S. Congress Ave., Austin, TX 78704; exec. dir., Bro. Richard Daly, C.S.C.

**Washington** State Catholic Conference, 419 Occidental Ave. S, Suite 608, Seattle, WA 98104; exec. dir., Edward J. Dolejsi.

**West Virginia** State Catholic Conference, P.O. Box 230, Wheeling, WV 26003; dir., Rev. John R. Gallagher.

Wisconsin Catholic Conference, 30 W. Mifflin St., Suite 302, Madison, WI 53703; exec. dir., John A. Huebscher.

## Dioceses with Interstate Lines

Diocesan lines usually fall within a single state and in some cases include a whole state.

The following dioceses, with their statistics as reported in tables throughout the Almanac, are exceptions.

**Norwich,** Conn., includes Fisher's Island, N.Y.

**Wilmington,** Del., includes all of Delaware and nine counties of Maryland.

**Washington,** D.C., includes five counties of Maryland.

**Gallup,** N.M., has jurisdiction over several counties of Arizona.

**Cheyenne,** Wyo., includes all of Yellowstone National Park.

## NCCB-USCC REGIONS

**I.** Maine, Vermont, New Hampshire, Massachusetts, Rhode Island, Connecticut. **II.** New York. **III.** New Jersey, Pennsylvania. **IV.** Delaware, District of Columbia, Florida, Georgia, Maryland, North Carolina, South Carolina, Virgin Islands, Virginia, West Virginia. **V.** Alabama, Kentucky, Louisiana, Mississippi, Tennessee. **VI.** Michigan, Ohio. **VII.** Illinois, Indiana, Wisconsin. **VIII.** Minnesota, North Dakota, South Dakota. **IX.** Iowa, Kansas, Missouri, Nebraska. **X.** Arkansas, Oklahoma, Texas. **XI.** California, Hawaii, Nevada. **XII.** Idaho, Montana, Alaska, Washington, Oregon. **XIII.** Utah, Arizona, New Mexico, Colorado, Wyoming.

---

## 1996 CPA AWARDS

Catholic Press Association Awards for material published in 1995 were presented during the annual CPA convention held May 22 to 25, 1996, in Philadelphia, Pa. Some of the awards are listed below.

**Newspapers — General Excellence**

**National Newspapers:** *The Catholic Register,* Toronto, Canada (first place); *Our Sunday Visitor* (second place); *National Catholic Reporter* (third place).

**Diocesan Newspapers, 40,001 and over** circulation: *Fairfield County Catholic,* Bridgeport, Conn. (first place); *The Catholic Standard & Times,* Philadelphia, Pa. (second); *Arlington Catholic Herald,* Arlington, Va. (third).

**Diocesan Newspapers, 17,001 to 40,000** circulation: *Catholic Herald,* Superior, Wis. (first place); *The Pilot,* Boston, Mass.(second); *The Florida Catholic,* Miami, Fla. (third).

**Diocesan Newspapers, to 17,000** circulation: *The Catholic Observer,* Springfield, Mass. (first place); *The Compass,* Green Bay, Wis. (second); *The Catholic Northwest Progress,* Seattle, Wash. (third).

**Spanish-Language Periodicals:** *Chicago Catolico,* Chicago, Ill. (First place); *La Voz Catolica,* Miami, Fla (second); *Revista Maryknoll,* Maryknoll, N.Y. (Third).

**Magazines — General Excellence**

**General Interest:** *St. Anthony Messenger* (first place); *U.S. Catholic* (second).

**Mission:** *Maryknoll* (first place); *Comboni Missions* (second).

**Religious Order:** *The Anthonian* (first place); *Oblates* (second).

**Professional and Special Interest:** *CUA Magazine* (first place); *Church* (second).

**Magazines for Clergy and Religious:** *The Priest* (first place); *Review for Religious* (second).

**Scholarly:** *Grail* (first place); *Horizons* (second).

**Prayer and Spirituality:** *The Bible Today* (first place); *Praying* (second).

**Newsletters**

**General Interest:** *Quarterly* (first place); *Catholic Update* (second).

**Special Interest:** *In Between* (first place); *Generation* (second).

**Books — First Place Awards**

**Popular Presentation of Catholic Faith:** Harper Collins Publishers, *Encyclopedia of Catholicism,* Richard P. McBrien, editor.

**Spirituality:** Hardcover—Orbis Books, *There Is a Season,* by Joan Chittister. Softcover—Crossroad Publishing Co., *The Shattered Lantern,* by Ronald Rolheiser.

**Theology:** Sheed and Ward, *Restoration and Renewal,* by Joseph Eagan.

**Scripture:** First place tie—Liguori Publications, *Hope & Glory,* by Juan Alfaro and The Liturgical Press, *First and Second Thessalonians, Sacra Pagina, Vol. 11,* by Earl J. Richard.

**Liturgy:** Paulist Press, *Roman Catholic Worship: Trent to Today,* by James F. White.

**Pastoral Ministry:** Ave Maria Press, *The Collaborative Leader,* by Loughlan Sofield and Donald Kuhn.

**Professional Books:** Paulist Press, *Handbook of Spirituality for Ministers,* Robert J. Wicks, editor.

**Educational Books:** Paulist Press, *Religious Education At a Crossroads,* by Francoise Darcy-Berube.

**Design and Production:** Crossroad Publishing Co., *Springs of Joy: A Biblical Treasury,* by Evelyn Scaramanga, John Eddison.

**Children's Books:** St. Paul Books and Media, *The Kids' Book of Prayers,* by David and Elizabeth Heller.

**First Time Author of a Book:** Crossroad Publishing Co., *Violence Unveiled: Humanity at the Crossroads,* by Gil Bailie.

**Family Life:** Ave Maria Press, *Father and Son: Time Lost, Love Recovered,* by Edward C. Sellner.

**History/Biography:** Sheed and Ward, *Indian Freedom: The Cause of Bartolome de las Casas,* by Francis Patrick Sullivan, S.J.

**Gender Issues:** Oxford University Press, *The New Testament and Psalms: An Inclusive Version.* **Hispanic Titles:** Liguori Publications, *En Nombre de Dios Pedimos Posado,* by Eduardo Pinzon-Umana, S.J.

# BIOGRAPHIES OF AMERICAN BISHOPS

(Sources: Almanac survey, *The Official Catholic Directory, Annuario Pontificio*, Catholic News Service. As of Aug. 20, 1996. For former bishops of the U.S., see "American Bishops of the Past," elsewhere in this section.)

Information includes: date and place of birth; educational institutions attended; date of ordination to the priesthood with, where applicable, name of archdiocese (*) or diocese in parentheses; date of episcopal ordination; episcopal appointments; date of resignation/retirement.

## A

**Abramowicz, Alfred L.:** b. Jan. 27, 1919, Chicago, Ill.; educ. St. Mary of the Lake Seminary (Mundelein, Ill.), Gregorian Univ. (Rome); ord. priest (Chicago*) May 1, 1943; ord. titular bishop of Paestum and auxiliary bishop of Chicago, June 13, 1968; retired Jan. 24, 1995.

**Adamec, Joseph V.:** b. Aug. 13, 1935, Bannister, Mich.; educ. Michigan State Univ. (East Lansing), Nepomucene College and Lateran Univ. (Rome); ord. priest (for Nitra diocese, Slovakia), July 3, 1960; incardinated in Saginaw diocese; ord. bishop of Altoona-Johnstown, May 20, 1987.

**Ahern, Patrick V.:** b. Mar. 8, 1919, New York, N.Y.; educ. Manhattan College and Cathedral College (New York City), St. Joseph's Seminary (Yonkers, N.Y.), St. Louis Univ. (St. Louis, Mo.), Notre Dame Univ. (Notre Dame, Ind.); ord. priest (New York*) Jan. 27, 1945; ord. titular bishop of Naiera and auxiliary bishop of New York, Mar. 19, 1970; retired Apr. 26, 1994.

**Anderson, Moses B., S.S.E.:** b. Sept. 9, 1928, Selma, Ala.; educ. St. Michael's College (Winooski, Vt.), St. Edmund Seminary (Burlington, Vt.), Univ. of Legon (Ghana); ord. priest May 30, 1958; ord. titular bishop of Vatarba and auxiliary bishop of Detroit, Jan. 27, 1983.

**Angell, Kenneth A.:** b. Aug. 3, 1930, Providence, R.I.; educ. St. Mary's Seminary (Baltimore, Md.); ord. priest (Providence) May 26, 1956; ord. titular bishop of Septimunicia and auxiliary bishop of Providence, R.I., Oct. 7, 1974; bishop of Burlington, Oct. 6, 1992; installed Nov. 9, 1992.

**Apuron, Anthony Sablan, O.F.M. Cap.:** b. Nov. 1, 1945, Agana, Guam; educ. St. Anthony College and Capuchin Seminary (Hudson, N.H.), Capuchin Seminary (Garrison, N.Y.), Maryknoll Seminary (New York), Notre Dame Univ. (Notre Dame, Ind.); ord. priest Aug. 26, 1972, in Guam; ord. titular bishop of Muzuca in Proconsulari and auxiliary bishop of Agana, Guam (unicorporated U.S. territory), Feb. 19, 1984; archbishop of Agana, Mar. 10, 1986.

**Arias, David, O.A.R.:** b. July 22, 1929, Leon, Spain; educ. St. Rita's College (San Sebastian, Spain), Our Lady of Good Counsel Theologate (Granada, Spain), Teresianum Institute (Rome, Italy); ord. priest May 31, 1952; ord. titular bishop of Badie and auxiliary bishop of Newark, Apr. 7, 1983; episcopal vicar for Hispanic affairs.

**Arkfeld, Leo, S.V.D.:** b. Feb. 4, 1912, Butte, Nebr.; educ. Divine Word Seminary (Techny, Ill.), Sacred Heart College (Girard, Pa.); ord. priest Aug. 15, 1943; ord. titular bishop of Bucellus and vicar apostolic of Central New Guinea, Nov. 30, 1948; name of vicariate changed to Wewak, May 15, 1952; first bishop of Wewak, Nov. 15, 1966; app. archbishop of Madang, Papua New Guinea, Dec. 19, 1975; resigned Dec. 31, 1987.

**Arzube, Juan A.:** b. June 1, 1918, Guayaquil, Ecuador; educ. Rensselaer Polytechnic Institute (Troy, N.Y.), St. John's Seminary (Camarillo, Calif.); ord. priest (Los Angeles*) May 5, 1954; ord. titular bishop of Civitate and auxiliary bishop of Los Angeles, Mar. 25, 1971; retired Sept 7, 1993.

## B

**Balke, Victor H.:** b. Sept. 29, 1931, Meppen, Ill.; educ. St. Mary of the Lake Seminary (Mundelein, Ill.), St. Louis Univ. (St. Louis, Mo.); ord. priest (Springfield, Ill.) May 24, 1958; ord. bishop of Crookston, Sept. 2, 1976.

**Baltakis, Paul Antanas, O.F.M.:** b. Jan. 1, 1925, Troskunai, Lithuania; educ. seminaries of the Franciscan Province of St. Joseph (Belgium); ord. priest Aug. 24, 1952, in Belgium; served in U.S. as director of Lithuanian Cultural Center, New York, and among Lithuanian youth; head of U.S. Lithuanian Franciscan Vicariate, Kennebunkport, Maine, from 1979; ord. titular bishop of Egara, Sept. 24, 1984; assigned to pastoral assistance to Lithuanian Catholics living outside Lithuania (resides in Brooklyn).

**Banks, Robert J.:** b. Feb. 26, 1928, Winthrop, Mass.; educ. St. John's Seminary (Brighton, Mass.), Gregorian Univ., Lateran Univ. (Rome); ord. priest (Boston*) Dec. 20, 1952, in Rome; rector of St. John's Seminary, Brighton, Mass., 1971-81; vicar general of Boston archdiocese, 1984; ord. titular bishop of Taraqua and auxiliary bishop of Boston, Sept. 19, 1985; bishop of Green Bay, Oct. 16, 1990, installed Dec. 5, 1990.

**Barbarito, Gerald M.:** b. Jan. 4, 1950, Brooklyn, N.Y.; educ. Cathedral College (Douglaston, N.Y.), Immaculate Conception Seminary (Huntington, N.Y.), Catholic University (Washington, D.C.); ord. priest (Brooklyn) 1976; ord. titular bishop of Gisipa and auxiliary bishop of Brooklyn, Aug. 22, 1994.

**Barnes, Gerald R.:** b. June 22, 1945, Phoenix, Ariz., of Mexican descent; educ. St. Leonard Seminary (Dayton, O.), Assumption-St. John's Seminary (San Antonio, Tex.); ord. priest (San Antonio*) Dec. 20, 1975; ord. titular bishop of Montefiascone and auxiliary bishop of San Bernardino, Mar. 18, 1992; bishop of San Bernardino, Dec. 28, 1995.

**Baum, William W.:** (See Cardinals, Biographies.)

**Begley, Michael J.:** b. Mar. 12, 1909, Mattineague, Mass.; educ. Mt. St. Mary Seminary (Emmitsburg, Md.); ord. priest (Raleigh) May 26, 1934; ord. first bishop of Charlotte, N.C., Jan. 12, 1972; retired May 29, 1984.

**Beltran, Eusebius J.:** b. Aug. 31, 1934, Ashley, Pa.; educ. St. Charles Seminary (Philadelphia, Pa.); ord. priest (Atlanta*) May 14, 1960; ord. bishop of Tulsa, Apr. 20, 1978; app. archbishop of Oklahoma City, Nov. 24, 1992; installed Jan 22, 1993.

**Bernardin, Joseph L.:** (See Cardinals, Biographies.)

**Bevilacqua, Anthony J.:** (See Cardinals, Biographies.)

**Blaire, Stephen E.:** b. Dec. 22, 1942, Los Angeles, Calif; educ. St. John's Seminary (Camarillo, Calif.); ord. priest (Los Angeles*) Apr. 29, 1967; ord. titular bishop of Lamzella and auxiliary of Los Angeles, May 31, 1990.

**Boland, Ernest B., O.P.:** b. July 10, 1925, Providence, R.I.; educ. Providence College (Rhode Island), Dominican Houses of Study (Somerset, Ohio; Washington, D.C.); ord. priest June 9, 1955; ord. bishop of Multan, Pakistan, July 25, 1966; resigned Oct. 20, 1984.

**Boland, J.(John) Kevin:** b. Apr. 25, 1935, Cork, Ireland (brother of Bp. Raymond J. Boland); educ. Christian Brothers School (Cork, Ire.), All Hallows Seminary (Dublin); ord. priest (Savannah), June 14, 1959; ord. bishop of Savannah, Apr. 18, 1995.

**Boland, Raymond J.:** b. Feb. 8, 1932, Tipperary, Ireland; educ. National Univ. of Ireland and All Hallows Seminary (Dublin); ord. priest (Washington*) June 16, 1957, in Dublin; vicar general and chancellor of Washington archdiocese; ord. bishop of Birmingham, Ala., Mar. 25, 1988; app. bishop of Kansas City-St. Joseph, Mo., June 22, 1993.

**Boles, John P.:** b. Jan. 21, 1930, Boston, Mass.; educ. St. John Seminary, Boston College (Boston, Mass.); ord. priest (Boston*) Feb. 2, 1955; ord. titular bishop of Nova Sparsa and auxiliary bishop of Boston, May 21, 1992.

**Borders, William D.:** b. Oct. 9, 1913, Washington, Ind.; educ. St. Meinrad Seminary (St. Meinrad, Ind.), Notre Dame Seminary (New Orleans, La.), Notre Dame Univ. (Notre Dame, Ind.); ord. priest (New Orleans*) May 18, 1940; ord. first bishop of Orlando, June 14, 1968; app. archbishop of Baltimore, Apr. 2, 1974, installed June 26, 1974; retired Apr. 11, 1989.

**Bosco, Anthony G.:** b. Aug. 1, 1927, New Castle, Pa.; educ. St. Vincent Seminary (Latrobe, Pa.), Lateran Univ. (Rome); ord. priest (Pittsburgh) June 7, 1952; ord. titular bishop of Labicum and auxiliary of Pittsburgh, June 30, 1970; app. bishop of Greensburg, Apr. 14, 1987, installed June 30, 1987.

**Botean, John Michael:** b. July 9, 1955, Canton, Ohio; educ. St. Fidelis Seminary (Herman, Pa.), Catholic University of America (Washington, DC), St. Gregory Melkite Seminary (Newton Centre, Mass), Catholic Theological Union (Chicago, Ill.); ord. priest (Romanian rite St. George's in Canton), May 18, 1986; ord. bishop of Saint George's in Canton for Romanians Aug. 24, 1996.

**Boudreaux, Warren L.:** b. Jan. 25, 1918, Berwick, La.; educ. St. Joseph's Seminary (St. Benedict, La.), St. Sulpice Seminary (Paris, France), Notre Dame Seminary (New Orleans, La.), Catholic Univ. (Washington, D.C.); ord. priest (Lafayette, La.) May 30, 1942; ord. titular bishop of Calynda and auxiliary bishop of Lafayette, La., July 25, 1962; app. bishop of Beaumont, June 5, 1971; app. first bishop of Houma-Thibodaux, installed June 5, 1977; retired Dec. 29, 1992.

**Boyle, Paul M., C.P.:** b. May 28, 1926, Detroit, Mich.; educ. Passionist houses of study, Lateran Univ. (Rome); professed in Congregation of the Passion July 9, 1946; ord. priest May 30, 1953; president of Conference of Major Superiors of Men, 1969-74; superior general of Passionists, 1976-88; ord. titular bishop of Canapium and first

vicar apostolic of Mandeville, Jamaica, July 9, 1991.

**Braxton, Edward K.:** b. June 28, 1944, Chicago, Ill.; educ. Loyola Univ. of Chicago, Univ. of St. Mary of the Lake and Mundelein Seminary (Chicago), Louvain Univ. (Belgium); ord. priest (Chicago*) May 13, 1970; ord. titular bishop of Macomades rusticiana and auxiliary bishop of St. Louis, May 17, 1995.

**Breitenbeck, Joseph M.:** b. Aug. 3, 1914, Detroit, Mich.; educ. University of Detroit, Sacred Heart Seminary (Detroit, Mich.), North American College and Lateran Univ. (Rome), Catholic Univ. (Washington, D.C.); ord. priest (Detroit*) May 30, 1942; ord. titular bishop of Tepelta and auxiliary bishop of Detroit, Dec. 20, 1965; app. bishop of Grand Rapids, Oct. 15, 1969, installed Dec. 2, 1969; retired July 11, 1989.

**Britt, Kevin Michael:** b. Nov. 19, 1944, Detroit, Mich.; educ. Sacred Heart Seminary, St. John Provincial Seminary, Universtiy of Detroit Mercy (Detroit, Mich.), Lateran Univ. (Rome); ord. priest (Detroit*) June 28, 1970; ord. titular bishop of Esco and auxiliary of Detroit, Jan. 6, 1994.

**Broderick, Edwin B.:** b. Jan. 16, 1917, New York, N.Y.; educ. Cathedral College (New York City), St. Joseph's Seminary (Yonkers, N.Y.), Fordham Univ. (New York City); ord. priest (New York*) May 30, 1942; ord. titular bishop of Tizica and auxiliary of New York, Apr. 21, 1967; bishop of Albany, 1969-76; executive director of Catholic Relief Services, 1976-82. Bishop emeritus of Albany.

**Brom, Robert H.:** b. Sept. 18, 1938, Arcadia, Wis.; educ. St. Mary's College (Winona, Minn.), Gregorian Univ. (Rome); ord. priest (Winona) Dec. 18, 1963, in Rome; ord. bishop of Duluth, May 23, 1983; coadjutor bishop of San Diego, May, 1989; bishop of San Diego, July 10, 1990.

**Brown, Charles A., M.M.:** b. Aug. 20, 1919, New York, N.Y.; educ. Cathedral College (New York City), Maryknoll Seminary (Maryknoll, N.Y.); ord. priest June 9, 1946; ord. titular bishop of Vallis and auxiliary bishop of Santa Cruz, Bolivia, Mar. 27, 1957.

**Brown, Tod D.:** b. Nov. 15, 1936, San Francisco, Calif.; educ. St. John's Seminary (Camarillo, Calif.), North American College (Rome); ord. priest (Monterey-Fresno) May 1, 1963; ord. bishop of Boise, Apr. 3, 1989.

**Brunett, Alexander J.:** b. Jan. 13, 1958, Detroit, Mich; educ. Gregorian Univ. (Rome), Sacred Heart Seminary, University of Detroit (Detroit, Mich.), Marquette Univ. (Milwaukee, Wis.); ord priest (Detroit*), July 13, 1958; ord. bishop of Helena, July 6, 1994.

**Bruskewitz, Fabian W.:** b. Sept. 6, 1935, Milwaukee, Wis.; educ. North American College, Gregorian Univ. (Rome); ord. priest (Milwaukee*) July 17, 1960; ord. bishop of Lincoln, May 13, 1992.

**Brzana, Stanislaus J.:** b. July 1, 1917, Buffalo, N.Y.; educ. Christ the King Seminary (St. Bonaventure, N.Y.), Gregorian Univ. (Rome); ord. priest (Buffalo) June 7, 1941; ord. titular bishop of Cufruta and auxiliary bishop of Buffalo, June 29, 1964; bishop of Ogdensburg, Oct. 22, 1968; retired Nov. 11, 1993.

**Buechlein, Daniel M., O.S.B.:** b. Apr. 20, 1938; educ. St. Meinrad College and Seminary (St. Meinrad, Ind.), St. Anselm Univ. (Rome); solemn profession as Benedictine monk, Aug. 15, 1963; ord. priest (St. Meinrad Archabbey) May 3, 1964; ord. bishop of Memphis, Mar. 2, 1987; app. archbishop of Indianapolis, July 14, 1992; installed Sept. 9, 1992.

**Bukovsky, John, S.V.D.:** b. Jan. 18, 1924, Cerova, Slovakia; educ. Slovakia, Divine Word Seminary (Techny, Ill.), Catholic Univ. (Washington, D.C.), Univ. of Chicago, Gregorian Univ. (Rome); ord. priest Dec. 3, 1950; became U.S. citizen 1958; worked at East European desk of Secretariat of State; ord. titular archbishop of Tabalta, Oct. 13, 1990; nuncio to Romania, 1990-94; app. papal representative to Russia, Dec. 20, 1994.

**Bullock, William H.:** b. Apr. 13, 1927, Maple Lake, Minn.; educ. St. Thomas College and St. Paul Seminary (St. Paul, Minn.), Notre Dame Univ. (Notre Dame, Ind.); ord. priest (St. Paul-Minneapolis*) June 7, 1952; ord. titular bishop of Natchez and auxiliary bishop of St. Paul and Minneapolis, Aug. 12, 1980; app. bishop of Des Moines, Feb. 10, 1987; app. bishop of Madison, Wis., Apr. 13, 1993.

**Burke, John J., O.F.M.:** b. Mar. 16, 1935, River Edge, N.J.; educ. St. Joseph Seminary (Callicoon, N.Y.), St. Bonaventure Univ. (St. Bonaventure, N.Y.), Holy Name College (washington, D.C.); solemnly professed in Franciscan Order, Aug. 20, 1958; ord. priest Feb. 25, 1961; missionary in Brazil from 1964; ord. coadjutor bishop of Miracema do Tocantins, Brazil, Mar. 25, 1995; bishop of Miracema do Tocantins, Feb. 14, 1996.

**Burke, Raymond L.:** b. June 30, 1948, Richland Center, Wis.; educ. Holy Cross Seminary (La Crosse, Wis.), Catholic Univ. (Washington, D.C.), North American College and Gregorian Univ. (Rome); ord. priest (La Crosse) June 29, 1975; ord. bishop of La Crosse Jan. 6, 1995, installed Feb. 22, 1995.

**Buswell, Charles A.:** b. Oct. 15, 1913, Homestead, Okla.; educ. St. Louis Preparatory Seminary (St. Louis, Mo.), Kenrick Seminary (Webster Groves, Mo.), American College, Univ. of Louvain (Belgium); ord. priest (Oklahoma City*) July 9, 1939; ord. bishop of Pueblo, Sept. 30, 1959; resigned Sept. 18, 1979.

**Byrne, James J.:** b. July 28, 1908, St. Paul, Minn.; educ. Nazareth Hall Preparatory Seminary and St. Paul Seminary (St. Paul, Minn.), Univ. of Minnesota (Minneapolis, Minn.); Louvain Univ. (Belgium); ord. priest (St. Paul-Minneapolis*) June 3, 1933; ord. titular bishop of Etenna and auxiliary bishop of St. Paul, July 2, 1947; app. bishop of Boise, June 16, 1956; app. archbishop of Dubuque, Mar. 19, 1962; retired Aug. 23, 1983. (Died August 2, 1996.)

## C

**Camacho, Tomas Aguon:** b. Sept. 18, 1933, Chalon Kanoa, Saipan; educ. St. Patrick's Seminary (Menlo Park, Calif.); ord. priest June 14, 1961; ord. first bishop of Chalan Kanoa, Northern Marianas (U.S. Commonwealth), Jan. 13, 1985.

**Carberry, John J.:** (See Cardinals, Biographies.)

**Carlson, Robert J.:** b. June 30, 1944, Minneapolis, Minn.; educ. Nazareth Hall and St. Paul Seminary (St. Paul, Minn.), Catholic Univ. (Washington, D.C.): ord. priest (St. Paul-Minneapolis*) May 23, 1970; ord. titular bishop of Avioccala and auxiliary bishop of St. Paul and Minneapolis, Jan. 11, 1984; app. coadjutor bishop of Sioux Falls, Jan. 13, 1994; succeeded as bishop of Sioux Falls, Mar. 21, 1995.

**Carmody, Edmond:** b. Jan. 12, 1934, Ahalena, Kerry, Ireland; educ. St. Brendan's College (Killarney), St. Patrick Seminary (Carlow, Ire.); ord. priest (San Antonio*) June 8, 1957; missionary in Peru 1984-89; ord. titular bishop of Mortlach and auxiliary bishop of San Antonio, Dec. 15, 1988; app. bishop of Tyler, Mar. 24, 1992.

**Carmon, Dominic, S.V.D.:** b. Dec. 13, 1930, Opelousas, La.; entered Society of Divine Word, 1946; ord. priest Feb. 2, 1960; missionary in Papua-New Guinea, 1961-68; ord. titular bishop of Rusicade and auxiliary bishop of New Orleans, Feb. 11, 1993.

**Casey, Luis Morgan:** b. June 23, 1935, Portageville, Mo.; ord. priest (St. Louis*) Apr. 7, 1962; missionary in Bolivia from 1965; ord. titular bishop of Mibiarca and auxiliary of La Paz, Jan. 28, 1984; vicar apostolic of Pando, Bolivia, Jan. 18, 1988 and apostolic administrator (1995) of La Paz.

**Catanello, Ignatius A.:** b. July 23, 1938, Brooklyn, N.Y.; educ. Cathedral Preparatory Seminary and St. Francis College (Brooklyn, N.Y.), Catholic Univ. (Washington, D.C.); St. John's University (Jamaica, N.Y.), New York University; ord. priest (Brooklyn) May 28, 1966; ord. titular bishop of Deulto and auxiliary bishop of Brooklyn, Aug. 22, 1994.

**Chaput, Charles J., O.F.M. Cap.:** b. Sept. 26, 1944, Concordia, Kans.; educ. St. Fidelis College (Herman, Pa.), Capuchin College and Catholic Univ. (Washington, D.C.), Univ. of San Francisco; solemn vows as Capuchin, July 14, 1968; ord. priest Aug. 29, 1970; ord. bishop of Rapid City, S.D., July 26, 1988, the second priest of Native American ancestry (member of Prairie Band Potawatomi Tribe) ordained a bishop in the U.S.

**Charron, Joseph L., C.PP.S.:** b. Dec. 30, 1939, Redfield, S.D.; educ. St. John's Seminary (Collegeville, Minn.); ord. priest June 3, 1967; ord. titular bishop of Bencenna and auxiliary bishop of St. Paul and Minneapolis, Jan. 25, 1990; app. bishop of Des Moines, Nov. 12, 1993.

**Chavez, Gilbert Espinoza:** b. May 9, 1932, Ontario, Calif.; educ. St. Francis Seminary (El Cajon, Calif.), Immaculate Heart Seminary (San Diego), Univ. of California; ord. priest (San Diego) Mar. 19, 1960; ord. titular bishop of Magarmel and auxiliary of San Diego, June 21, 1974.

**Chedid, John:** b. July 4, 1923, Eddid, Lebanon; educ. seminaries in Lebanon and Pontifical Urban College (Rome); ord. priest Dec. 21, 1951, in Rome; ord. titular bishop of Callinico and auxiliary bishop of St. Maron of Brooklyn for the Maronites, Jan. 25, 1981; app. first bishop of Eparchy of Our Lady of Lebanon of Los Angeles for the Maronites, Mar. 1, 1994.

**Christian, Francis J.:** b. Oct. 8, 1942, Peterborough, N.H.; educ. St. Anselm College (Manchester, N.H.), St. Paul Seminary (Ottawa), American College in Louvain (Belgium); ord. priest (Manchester) June 29, 1968; app. titular bishop of Quincy and auxiliary of Manchester Apr. 2, 1996.

**Clark, Matthew H.:** b. July 15, 1937, Troy, N.Y.; educ. St. Bernard's Seminary (Rochester, N.Y.), Gregorian Univ. (Rome); ord. priest (Albany) Dec. 19, 1962; ord. bishop of Rochester, May 27, 1979; installed June 26, 1979.

**Clinch, Harry A.:** b. Oct. 27, 1908, San Anselmo, Calif.; educ. St. Joseph's College (Mountain View, Calif.), St. Patrick's Seminary (Menlo Park, Calif.); ord. priest (Monterey-Fresno) June 6, 1936; ord. titular bishop of Badiae and auxiliary bishop of Monterey-Fresno, Feb. 27, 1957; app. first bishop of Monterey in California, Oct. 16, 1967; resigned Jan. 19, 1982.

**Coggin, Walter A., O.S.B.:** b. Feb. 10, 1916, Richmond, Va.; ord. priest June 19, 1943; app. abbot ordinary of abbacy nullius of Mary Help of Christians, Belmont N.C., 1959; blessed Mar. 28, 1960; resigned 1970.

**Comber, John W., M.M.:** b. Mar. 12, 1906, Lawrence, Mass.; educ. St. John's Preparatory College (Danvers, Mass.), Boston College (Boston, Mass.), Maryknoll Seminary (Maryknoll, N.Y.); ord. priest Feb. 1, 1931; superior general of Maryknoll, 1956-66; ord. titular bishop of Foratiana, Apr. 9, 1959.

**Connolly, Thomas J.:** b. July 18, 1922, Tonopah, Nev.; educ. St. Patrick's Seminary (Menlo Park, Calif.), Catholic Univ. (Washington, D.C.), Lateran Univ. (Rome); ord. priest (Reno-Las Vegas) Apr. 8, 1947; ord. bishop of Baker, June 30, 1971.

**Connors, Ronald G., C.SS.R.:** b. Nov. 1, 1915, Brooklyn, N.Y.; ord. priest June 22, 1941; ord. titular bishop of Equizetum and coadjutor bishop of San Juan de la Maguana, Dominican Republic, July 20, 1976; succeeded as bishop of San Juan de la Maguana, July 20, 1977; retired Feb. 20, 1991.

**Conway, Edwin M.:** b. Mar. 6, 1934, Chicago, Ill.; educ. St. Mary of the Lake Seminary (Chicago), Loyola in Chicago; ord. priest (Chicago*) May 3, 1960; ord. titular bishop of Auguro and auxiliary of Chicago, Mar. 20, 1995.

**Cooney, Patrick R.:** b. Mar. 10, 1934, Detroit, Mich.; educ. Sacred Heart Seminary (Detroit), Gregorian Univ. (Rome), Notre Dame Univ. (Notre Dame, Ind.); ord. priest (Detroit*) Dec. 20, 1959; ord. titular bishop of Hodelm and auxiliary bishop of Detroit, Jan. 27, 1983; app. bishop of Gaylord, Nov. 6, 1989; installed Jan. 28, 1990.

**Corrada del Rio, Alvaro, S.J.:** b. May 13, 1942, Santurce, Puerto Rico; entered Society of Jesus, 1960, at novitiate of St. Andrew-on-Hudson (Poughkeepsie, N.Y.); educ. Jesuit seminaries, Fordham Univ. (New York), Institut Catholique (Paris); ord. priest July 6, 1974, in Puerto Rico; pastoral coordinator of Northeast Catholic Hispanic Center, New York, 1982-85; ord. titular bishop of Rusticiana and auxiliary bishop of Washington, D.C., Aug. 4, 1985.

**Coscia, Benedict Dominic, O.F.M.:** b. Aug. 10, 1922, Brooklyn, N.Y.; educ. St. Francis College (Brooklyn, N.Y.), Holy Name College (Washington, D.C.); ord. priest June 11, 1949; ord. bishop of Jatai, Brazil, Sept. 21, 1961.

**Costello, Thomas J.:** b. Feb. 23, 1929, Camden, N.Y.; educ. Niagara Univ. (Niagara Falls, N.Y.), St. Bernard's Seminary (Rochester, N.Y.), Catholic

Univ. (Washington, D.C.); ord. priest (Syracuse) June 5, 1954; ord. titular bishop of Perdices and auxiliary bishop of Syracuse Mar. 13, 1978.

**Cote, Michael R.:** b. June 19, 1949, Sanford, Me.; educ. Our Lady of Lourdes Seminary (Cassadaga, N.Y.), St. Mary's Seminary College (Baltimore, Md.); Gregorian Univ. (Rome), Catholic Univ. (Washington, D.C.); ord. priest (Portland, Me.) June 29, 1975 by Pope Paul VI in Rome; secretary, 1989-94 at apostolic nunciature, Washington; ord. titular bishop of Cebarades and auxiliary of Portland, Me., July 27, 1995.

**Cotey, Arnold R., S.D.S.:** b. June 15, 1921, Milwaukee, Wis.; educ. Divine Savior Seminary (Lanham, Md.), Marquette Univ. (Milwaukee, Wis.); ord. priest June 7, 1949; ord. first bishop of Nachingwea (now Lindi), Tanzania, Oct. 20, 1963; retired Nov. 11, 1983.

**Cronin, Daniel A.:** b. Nov. 14, 1927, Newton, Mass.; educ. St. John's Seminary (Boston, Mass.), North American College and Gregorian Univ. (Rome); ord. priest (Boston*) Dec. 20, 1952; attaché apostolic nunciature (Addis Ababa), 1957-61; served in papal Secretariat of State, 1961-68; ord. titular bishop of Egnatia and auxiliary bishop of Boston, Sept. 12, 1968; bishop of Fall River, Dec. 16, 1970; archbishop of Hartford, Dec. 10, 1991.

**Crowley, Joseph R.:** b. Jan. 12, 1915, Fort Wayne, Ind.; educ. St. Mary's College (St. Mary, Ky.), St. Meinrad Seminary (St. Meinrad, Ind.); served in US Air Force, 1942-46; ord. priest (Ft. Wayne-S. Bend) May 1, 1953; editor of *Our Sunday Visitor* 1958-67; ord. titular bishop of Maraguis and auxiliary bshop of Fort Wayne-South Bend, Aug. 24, 1971; retired May 8, 1990.

**Cullen, Edward P.:** b. Mar. 15, 1933, Philadelphia, Pa.; educ. St. Charles Borromeo Seminary (Overbrook, Pa.), Univ. of Pennsylvania and LaSalle Univ. (Philadelphia), Harvard Graduate School of Business; ord. priest (Philadelphia*) May 19, 1962; ord. titular bishop of Paria in Proconsolare and auxiliary of Philadelphia, Apr. 14, 1994.

**Cummins, John S.:** b. Mar. 3, 1928, Oakland, Calif.; educ. St. Patrick's Seminary (Menlo Park, Calif.), Catholic Univ. (Washington, D.C.), Univ. of California; ord. priest (San Francisco*) Jan. 24, 1953; executive director of the California Catholic Conference 1971-76; ord. titular bishop of Lambaesis and auxiliary bishop of Sacramento, May 16, 1974; app. bishop of Oakland, installed June 30, 1977.

**Curlin, William G.:** b. Aug. 30, 1927, Portsmouth, Va.; educ. Georgetown Univ. (Washington, D.C.), St. Mary's Seminary (Baltimore, Md.); ord. priest (Washington*), May 25, 1957; ord. titular bishop of Rosemarkie and auxiliary bishop of Washington, Dec. 20, 1988; app. bishop of Charlotte, Feb. 22, 1994.

**Curry, Thomas J.:** b. Jan. 17, 1943, Drumgoon, Ireland; educ. Patrician College (Ballyfin, Ire.), All Hallows Seminary (Dublin, Ire.); ord. priest (Los Angeles*) June 17, 1967; ord. titular bishop of Ceanannus Mór and auxiliary of Los Angeles, Mar. 19, 1994.

**Curtis, Walter W.:** b. May 3, 1913, Jersey City, N.J.; educ. Fordham Univ. (New York City), Seton Hall Univ. (South Orange, N.J.), Immaculate Conception Seminary (Darlington, N.J.), North American College and Gregorian Univ. (Rome), Catholic Univ. (Washington, D.C.); ord. priest (Newark*) Dec. 8, 1937; ord. titular bishop of Bisica and auxiliary bishop of Newark, Sept. 24, 1957; app. bishop of Bridgeport, 1961, installed Nov. 21, 1961; retired June 28, 1988.

**Curtiss, Elden F.:** b. June 16, 1932, Baker, Ore.; educ. St. Edward Seminary College and St. Thomas Seminary (Kenmore, Wash.); ord. priest (Baker) May 24, 1958; ord. bishop of Helena, Mont.,Apr. 28, 1976; app. archbishop of Omaha, Nebr., May 4, 1993.

# D

**Daily, Thomas V.:** b. Sept. 23, 1927, Belmont, Mass.; educ. Boston College, St. John's Seminary (Brighton, Mass.); ord. priest (Boston*) Jan. 10, 1952; missionary in Peru for five years as a member of the Society of St. James the Apostle; ord. titular bishop of Bladia and auxiliary bishop of Boston, Feb. 11, 1975; app. first bishop of Palm Beach, Fla., July 17, 1984; app. bishop of Brooklyn, Feb. 20, 1990; installed Apr. 18, 1990.

**Daly, James:** b. Aug. 14, 1921, New York, N.Y.; educ. Cathedral College (Brooklyn, N.Y.), Immaculate Conception Seminary (Huntington, L.I.); ord. priest (Buffalo) May 22, 1948; ord. titular bishop of Castra Nova and auxiliary bishop of Rockville Centre, May 9, 1977; retired July 1, 1996.

**D'Antonio, Nicholas, O.F.M.:** b. July 10, 1916, Rochester, N.Y.; educ. St. Anthony's Friary (Catskill, N.Y.); ord. priest June 7, 1942; ord. titular bishop of Giufi Salaria and prelate of Olancho, Honduras, July 25, 1966; resigned 1977; vicar general of New Orleans archdiocese and episcopal vicar for Spanish Speaking, 1977-91.

**D'Arcy, John M.:** b. Aug. 18, 1932, Brighton, Mass.; educ. St. John's Seminary (Brighton, Mass.), Angelicum Univ. (Rome); ord. priest (Boston*) Feb. 2, 1957; spiritual director of St. John's Seminary ord. titular bishop of Mediana and auxiliary bishop of Boston, Feb. 11, 1975; app. bishop of Fort Wayne-South Bend, Feb. 26, 1985, installed May 1, 1985.

**Dattilo, Nicholas C.:** b. Mar. 8, 1932, Mahoningtown, Pa.; educ. St. Vincent Seminary (Latrobe, Pa.), St. Charles Borromeo Seminary (Philadelphia, Pa.); ord. priest (Pittsburgh) May 31, 1958; ord. bishop of Harrisburg, Jan. 26, 1990.

**Delaney, Joseph P.:** b. Aug. 29, 1934, Fall River, Mass.; educ. Cardinal O'Connell Seminary (Boston, Mass.), Theological College (Washington, D.C.), North American College (Rome), Rhode Island College (Providence, R.I.); ord. priest (Fall River) Dec. 18, 1960; ord. bishop of Fort Worth, Tex., Sept. 13, 1981.

**Dempsey, Michael J., O.P.:** b. Feb. 22, 1912, Providence, R.I.; entered Order of Preachers (Dominicans), Chicago, province, 1935; ord. priest June 11, 1942; ord. bishop of Sokoto, Nigeria, Aug. 15, 1967; resigned Dec. 31, 1984.

**De Palma, Joseph A., S.C.J.:** b. Sept. 4, 1913, Walton, N.Y.; ord. priest May 20, 1944; superior general of Congregation of Priests of the Sacred Heart, 1959-67; ord. first bishop of De Aar, South Africa, July 19, 1967; retired Nov. 18, 1987.

**De Paoli, Ambrose:** b. Aug. 19, 1934, Jeannette,

Pa., moved to Miami at age of nine; educ. St. Joseph Seminary (Bloomfield, Conn.), St. Mary of the West Seminary (Cincinnati, O.), North American College and Lateran Univ. (Rome); ord. priest (Miami*) Dec. 18, 1960, in Rome; served in diplomatic posts in Canada, Turkey, Africa and Venezuela; ord. titular archbishop of Lares, Nov. 20, 1983, in Miami; apostolic pro-nuncio to Sri Lanka, 1983-88; apostolic delegate in southern Africa and pro-nuncio to Lesotho, 1988; first apostolic nuncio to South Africa, 1994.

**De Simone, Louis A.:** b. Feb. 21, 1922, Philadelphia, Pa.; educ. Villanova Univ. (Villanova, Pa.), St. Charles Borromeo Seminary (Overbrook, Pa.); ord. priest (Philadelphia*) May 10, 1952; ord. titular bishop of Cillium and auxiliary bishop of Philadelphia, Aug. 12, 1981.

**Di Lorenzo, Francis X.:** b. Apr. 15, 1942, Philadelphia, Pa.; educ. St. Charles Borromeo Seminary (Philadelphia), Univ. of St. Thomas (Rome); ord. priest (Philadelphia*) May 18, 1968; ord. titular bishop of Tigia and auxiliary bishop of Scranton, Mar. 8, 1988; app. apostolic administrator of Honolulu, Oct. 12, 1993; bishop of Honolulu, Nov. 29, 1994.

**Dimino, Joseph T.:** b. Jan. 7, 1923, New York, N.Y.; educ. Cathedral College (New York, N.Y.), St. Joseph's Seminary (Yonkers, N.Y.), Catholic Univ. (Washington, D.C.); ord. priest (New York*) June 4, 1949; ord. titular bishop of Carini and auxiliary bishop of the Military Services archdiocese, May 10, 1983; app. ordinary of Military Services archdiocese, May 14, 1991.

**Dion, George E., O.M.I.:** b. Sept. 25, 1911, Central Falls, R.I.; educ. Holy Cross College (Worcester, Mass.), Oblate Juniorate (Colebrook, N.H.), Oblate Scholasticates (Natick, Mass., and Ottawa, Ont.); ord. priest June 24, 1936; ord. titular bishop of Arpaia and vicar apostolic of Jolo, Philippines Apr. 23, 1980; retired Oct. 11, 1991; titular bishop of Arpaia.

**Donnelly, Robert William:** b. Mar. 22, 1931, Toledo, O.; educ. St. Meinrad Seminary College (St. Meinrad, Ind.), Mount St. Mary's in the West Seminary (Norwood, O.); ord. priest (Toledo) May 25, 1957; ord. titular bishop of Garba and auxiliary bishop of Toledo, May 3, 1984.

**Donoghue, John F.:** b. Aug. 9, 1928, Washington, D.C.; educ. St. Mary's Seminary (Baltimore, Md.); Catholic Univ. (Washington, D.C.); ord. priest (Washington*) June 4, 1955; chancellor and vicar general of Washington archdiocese, 1973-84; ord. bishop of Charlotte, N.C., Dec. 18, 1984; app. archbishop of Atlanta, June 22, 1993; installed Aug. 19, 1993.

**Donovan, Paul V.:** b. Sept. 1, 1924, Bernard, Iowa; educ. St. Gregory's Seminary (Cincinnati, Ohio), Mt. St. Mary's Seminary (Norwood, Ohio), Lateran Univ. (Roe); ord. priest (Lansing) May 20, 1950; ord. first bishop of Kalamazoo, Mich., July 21, 1971; retired Nov. 22, 1994.

**Doran, Thomas George:** b. Feb. 20, 1936, Rockford, Ill.; educ. Loras College (Dubuque, Ia.), Gregorian Univ. (Rome), Rockford College (Rockford, Ill.); ord. priest (Rockford) Dec. 20, 1961; ord. bishop of Rockford, June 24, 1994.

**Dorsey, Norbert M., C.P.:** b. Dec. 14, 1929, Springfield, Mass.; educ. Passionist seminaries (eastern U.S. province), Pontifical Institute of Sacred Music and Gregorian Univ. (Rome, Italy); professed in Passionists, Aug. 15, 1949; ord priest Apr. 28, 1956; assistant general of Passionists, 1976-86; ord. titular bishop of Mactaris and auxiliary bishop of Miami, Mar. 19, 1986; app. bishop of Orlando, Mar. 20, 1990, installed May 25, 1990.

**Dougherty, John Martin:** b. Apr. 29, 1932, Scranton, Pa.; educ. St. Charles College (Catonsville, Md.), St. Mary's Seminary (Baltimore), Univ. of Notre Dame (South Bend); ord. priest (Scranton) June 15, 1957; ord. titular bishop of Sufetula and auxiliary bishop of Scranton, Mar. 7, 1995.

**Driscoll, Michael P.:** b. Aug. 8, 1939, Long Beach, Calif.; educ. St. John Seminary (Camarillo, Calif), Univ. of Southern Calif.; ord. priest (Los Angeles*) May 1, 1965; ord. titular bishop of Massita and auxiliary bishop of Orange, Mar. 6, 1990.

**Dudick, Michael J.:** b. Feb. 24, 1916, St. Clair, Pa.; educ. St. Procopius College and Seminary (Lisle, Ill.); ord. priest (Passaic, Byzantine Rite) Nov. 13, 1945; ord. bishop of Byzantine Eparchy of Passaic, Oct. 24, 1968; retired Nov. 6, 1995.

**Dudley, Paul V.:** b. Nov. 27, 1926, Northfield, Minn.; educ. Nazareth College and St. Paul Seminary (St. Paul, Minn.); ord. priest (St. Paul-Minneapolis*) June 2, 1951; ord. titular bishop of Ursona and auxiliary bishop of St. Paul and Minneapolis, Jan. 25, 1977; app. bishop of Sioux Falls, installed Dec. 13, 1978; retired Mar. 21, 1995.

**Duhart, Clarence James, C.SS.R.:** b. Mar. 23, 1912, New Orleans, La.; ord, priest June 29, 1937; ord. bishop of Udon Thani, Thailand, Apr. 21, 1966; resigned Oct. 2, 1975.

**DuMaine, (Roland) Pierre:** b. Aug. 2, 1931, Paducah, Ky.; educ. St. Joseph's College (Mountain View, Calif.), St. Patrick's College and Seminary (Menlo Park, Calif.), Univ. of California (Berkeley), Catholic Univ. (Washington, D.C.); ord. priest (San Francisco) June 15, 1957; ord. titular bishop of Sarda and auxiliary bishop of San Francisco, June 29, 1978; app. first bishop of San Jose, Jan. 27, 1981; installed Mar. 18, 1981.

**Dunne, John C.:** b. Oct. 30, 1937, Brooklyn, N.Y.; educ. Cathedral College (Brooklyn, N.Y.). Immaculate Conception Seminary (Huntington, N.Y.), Manhattan College (New York); ord. priest (Rockville Centre) June 1, 1963; ord. titular bishop of Abercorn and auxiliary bishop of Rockville Centre, Dec. 13, 1988. Vicar for Central Vicariate.

**Dupre, Thomas L.:** b. Nov. 10, 1933, South Hadley Falls, Mass.; educ. College de Montreal, Assumption College (Worcester, Mass.), Catholic Univ. (Washington, D.C.), ord. priest (Springfield, Mass.) May 23, 1959; ord. titular bishop of Hodelm and auxiliary bishop of Springfield, Mass. May 31, 1990; bishop of Springfield, Mar. 14, 1995.

**Durning, Dennis V., C.S.Sp.:** b. May 18, 1923, Germantown, Pa.; educ. St. Mary's Seminary (Ferndale, Conn.); ord. priest June 3, 1949; ord. first bishop of Arusha, Tanzania, May 28, 1963; resigned Mar. 6, 1989.

**E**

**Egan, Edward M.:** b. Apr. 2, 1932, Oak Park, Ill.; educ. Quigley Preparatory Seminary (Chicago, Ill.),

St. Mary of the Lake Seminary (Mundelein, Ill.), Gregorian Univ. (Rome); ord. priest (Chicago*) Dec. 15, 1957, in Rome; judge of Roman Rota, 1972-85; ord. titular bishop of Allegheny and auxiliary bishop of New York, May 22, 1985; bishop of Bridgeport, Nov. 5, 1988.

**Elya, John A., B.S.O.:** b. Sept. 16, 1928, Maghdouche, Lebanon; educ. diocesan monastery (Sidon, Lebanon), Gregorian Univ. (Rome, Italy); professed as member of Basilian Salvatorian Order, 1949; ord. priest Feb. 17, 1952, in Rome; came to U.S., 1958; ord. titular bishop of Abilene of Syria and auxiliary bishop of Melkite diocese of Newton, Mass., June 29, 1986; app. bishop of Newton (Melkites), Nov. 25, 1993.

**F**

**Favalora, John C.:** b. Dec. 5, 1935, New Orleans, La.; educ. St. Joseph Seminary (St. Benedict, La.), Notre Dame Seminary (New Orleans, La.), Gregorian Univ. (Rome), Catholic Univ. of America (Washington, D.C.), Xavier Univ. and Tulane Univ. (New Orleans); ord. priest (New Orleans*) Dec. 20, 1961; ord. bishop of Alexandria, La., July 29, 1986; bishop of St. Petersburg, Mar. 14, 1989; app. archbishop of Miami, installed Dec. 20, 1994.

**Federal, Joseph Lennox:** b. Jan. 13, 1910, Greensboro, N.C.; educ. Belmont Abbey College (Belmont Abbey, N.C.), Niagara Univ. (Niagara Falls, N.Y.), Univ. of Fribourg (Switzerland), North American College and Gregorian Univ. (Rome); ord. priest (Raleigh) Dec. 8, 1934; ord. titular bishop of Appiaria and auxiliary bishop of Salt Lake City, Apr. 11, 1951; app. coadjutor with right of succession, May, 1958; bishop of Salt Lake City, Mar. 31, 1960; retired Apr. 22, 1980.

**Fellhauer, David E.:** b. Aug. 19, 1939, Kansas City, Mo.; educ. Pontifical College Josephinum (Worthington, O.), St. Paul Univ. (Ottawa, Ont.); ord. priest (Dallas), May 29, 1965; ord. bishop of Victoria, May 28, 1990.

**Ferrario, Joseph A.:** b. Mar. 3, 1926, Scranton, Pa.; educ. St. Charles College (Catonsville, Md.), St. Mary's Seminary (Baltimore, Md.), Catholic Univ. (Washington, D.C.); Univ. of Scranton; ord. priest (Honolulu) May 19, 1951; ord. titular bishop of Cuse and auxiliary bishop of Honolulu, Jan. 13, 1978; bishop of Honolulu, May 13, 1982; retired Oct. 12, 1993.

**Fiorenza, Joseph A.:** b. Jan. 25, 1931, Beaumont, Tex.; educ. St. Mary's Seminary (LaPorte, Tex.); ord. priest (Galveston-Houston) May 29, 1954; ord. bishop of San Angelo, Oct. 25, 1979; app. bishop of Galveston-Houston, Dec. 18, 1984, installed Feb. 18, 1985.

**Fitzpatrick, John J.:** b. Oct. 12, 1918, Trenton, Ont., Canada; educ. Urban Univ. (Rome), Our Lady of the Angels Seminary (Niagara Falls, N.Y.); ord. priest (Buffalo) Dec. 13, 1942; ord. titular bishop of Cenae and auxiliary bishop of Miami, Aug. 28, 1968; bishop of Brownsville, Tex., May 28, 1971; retired Nov. 30, 1991.

**Fitzsimons, George K.:** b. Sept. 4, 1928, Kansas City, Mo.; educ. Rockhurst College (Kansas City, Mo.), Immaculate Conception Seminary (Conception, Mo.); ord. priest (Kansas City-St. Joseph) Mar.

18, 1961; ord. titular bishop of Pertusa and auxiliary bishop of Kansas City-St. Joseph, July 3, 1975; app. bishop of Salina, Mar. 28, 1984, installed May 29, 1984.

**Flanagan, Bernard Joseph:** b. Mar. 31, 1908, Proctor, Vt.; educ. Holy Cross College (Worcester, Mass.), North American College (Rome), Catholic Univ. (Washington, D.C.); ord. priest (Burlington) Dec. 8, 1931; ord. first bishop of Norwich, Nov. 30, 1953; app. bishop of Worcester, installed, Sept. 24, 1959; retired Mar. 31, 1983.

**Fliss, Raphael M.:** b. Oct. 25, 1930, Milwaukee, Wis.; educ. St. Francis Seminary (Milwaukee, Wis.), Catholic University (Washington, D.C.), Pontifical Lateran Univ. (Rome); ord. priest (Milwaukee*) May 26, 1956; ord. coadjutor bishop of Superior with right of succession, Dec. 20, 1979; bishop of Superior, June 27, 1985.

**Flores, Patrick F.:** b. July 26, 1929, Ganado, Tex.; educ. St. Mary's Seminary (Houston, Tex.); ord. priest (Galveston-Houston) May 26, 1956; ord. titular bishop of Itolica and auxiliary bishop of San Antonio, May 5, 1970 (first Mexican-American bishop); app. bishop of El Paso, Apr. 4, 1978, installed May 29, 1978; app. archbishop of San Antonio 1979; installed Oct. 13, 1979.

**Flynn, Harry J.:** b. May 2, 1933, Schenectady, N.Y.; educ. Siena College (Loudonville, N.Y.), Mt. St. Mary's College (Emmitsburg, Md.); ord. priest (Albany) May 28, 1960; ord. coadjutor bishop of Lafayette, La., June 24, 1986; bishop of Lafayette, La., May 15, 1989; app. coadjutor archbishop of St. Paul and Minneapolis, Feb. 24, 1994, installed Apr. 27, 1994; archbishop of St. Paul and Minneapolis, Sept. 8, 1995.

**Foley, David E.:** b. Feb. 3, 1930, Worcester, Mass.; educ. St. Charles College (Catonsville, Md.), St. Mary's Seminary (Baltimore, Md.); ord. priest (Washington*) May 26, 1952; ord. titular bishop of Octaba and auxiliary bishop of Richmond, June 27, 1986; app. bishop of Birmingham, Mar. 22, 1994.

**Foley, John Patrick:** b. Nov. 11, 1935, Sharon Hill, Pa.; educ. St. Joseph's Preparatory School (Philadelphia, Pa.), St. Joseph's College (now University) (Philadelphia, Pa.), St. Charles Borromeo Seminary (Overbrook, Pa.), St. Thomas Univ. (Rome), Columbia School of Journalism (New York); ord. priest (Philadelphia*) May 19, 1962; assistant editor (1967-70) and editor (1970-84) of *The Catholic Standard and Times*, Philadelphia archdiocesan paper; ord. titular archbishop of Neapolis in Proconsulari, May 8, 1984, in Philadelphia; app. president of the Pontifical Council for Social Communications, Apr. 5, 1984.

**Forst, Marion F.:** b. Sept. 3, 1910, St. Louis, Mo.; educ. St. Louis Preparatory Seminary (St. Louis, Mo.), Kenrick Seminary (Webster Groves, Mo.); ord. priest (St. Louis*) June 10, 1934; ord. bishop of Dodge City, Mar. 24, 1960; app. titular bishop of Scala and auxiliary bishop of Kansas City, Kans., Oct. 16, 1976; retired Dec. 23, 1986. Titular bishop of Leavenworth.

**Francis, Joseph A., S.V.D.:** b. Sept. 30, 1923, Lafayette, La.; educ. St. Augustine Seminary (Bay St. Louis, Miss.), St. Mary Seminary (Techny, Ill.), Catholic Univ. (Washington, D.C.); ord. priest Oct.

7, 1950; president Conference of Major Superiors of Men, 1974-76, and the National Black Catholic Clergy Caucus; ord. titular bishop of Valliposita and auxiliary bishop of Newark, June 25, 1976; retired June 30, 1995.

**Franklin, William Edwin:** b. May 3, 1930, Parnell, Iowa; educ. Loras College and Mt. St. Bernard Seminry (Dubuque, Iowa); ord. priest (Dubuque*) Feb. 4, 1956; ord. titular bishop of Surista and auxiliary bishop of Dubuque, Apr. 1, 1987; app. bishop of Davenport, Nov. 12, 1993, installed Jan. 20, 1994.

**Franzetta, Benedict C.:** b. Aug. 1, 1921, East Liverpool, O.; educ. St. Charles College (Catonsville, Md.), St. Mary Seminary (Cleveland, O.); ord. priest (Youngstown) Apr. 29, 1950; ord. titular bishop of Oderzo and auxiliary bishop of Youngstown, Sept. 4, 1980.

**Freking, Frederick W.:** b. Aug. 11, 1913, Heron Lake, Minn.; educ. St. Mary's College (Winona, Minn.), North American College and Gregorian Univ. (Rome), Catholic Univ. (Washington, D.C.); ord. priest (Winona) July 31, 1938; ord. bishop of Salina, Nov. 30, 1957; app. bishop of La Crosse, Dec. 30, 1964, installed Feb. 24, 1965; resigned May 10, 1983.

**Frey, Gerard L.:** b. May 10, 1914, New Orleans, La.; educ. Notre Dame Seminary (New Orleans, La.); ord. priest (New Orleans*) Apr. 2, 1938; ord. bishop of Savannah, Aug. 8, 1967; app. bishop of Lafayette, La., Nov. 7, 1972, installed Jan, 7, 1973; retired May 15, 1989.

**Friend, William B.:** b. Oct. 22, 1931, Miami, Fla.; educ. St. Mary's College (St. Mary, Ky.), Mt. St. Mary Seminary (Emmitsburg, Md.), Catholic Univ. (Washington, D.C.), Notre Dame Univ. (Notre Dame, Ind.); ord. priest (Mobile*) May 7, 1959; ord. titular bishop of Pomaria and auxiliary bishop of Alexandria-Shreveport, La., Oct. 30, 1979; app. bishop of Alexandria-Shreveport, Nov. 17, 1982, installed Jan 11, 1983; app. first bishop of Shreveport, June, 1986; installed July 30, 1986.

## G

**Galante, Joseph A.:** b. July 2, 1938, Philadelphia, Pa.; educ. St. Joseph Preparatory School, St. Charles Seminary (Philadelphia, Pa.); Lateran Univ., Angelicum, North American College (Rome); ord. priest (Philadelphia*) May 16, 1964; on loan to diocese of Brownsville, Tex., 1968-72, where he served in various diocesan posts; returned to Philadelphia, 1972; assistant vicar (1972-79) and vicar (1979-87) for religious; undersecretary of Congregation for Institutes of Consecrated Life and Societies of Apostolic Life (Rome), 1987-92; ord. titular bishop of Equilium and auxiliary bishop of San Antonio, Dec. 11, 1992; app. bishop of Beaumont, Apr. 5, 1994.

**Garland, James H.:** b. Dec. 13, 1931, Wilmington, Ohio; educ. Wilmington College (Ohio), Ohio State Univ. (Columbus, O.); Mt. St. Mary's Seminary (Cincinnati, O.), Catholic Univ. (Washington, D.C.); ord. priest (Cincinnati*) Aug. 15, 1959; ord. titular bishop of Garriana and auxiliary bishop of Cincinnati, July 25, 1984; app. bishop of Marquette, Oct. 6, 1992; installed Nov. 11, 1992.

**Garmendia, Francisco:** b. Nov. 6, 1924, Lozcano,

Spain; ord. priest June 29, 1947, in Spain; came to New York in 1964; became naturalized citizen; ord. titular bishop of Limisa and auxiliary bishop of New York, June 29, 1977. Vicar for Spanish pastoral development in New York archdiocese.

**Garmo, George:** b. Dec. 8, 1921, Telkaif, Iraq; educ. St. Peter Chaldean Patriarchal Seminary (Mossul, Iraq), Pontifical Urban Univ. (Rome); ord. priest Dec. 8, 1945; pastor of Chaldean parish in Detroit archdiocese, 1960-64, 1966-80; ord. archbishop of Chaldean archdiocese of Mossul Iraq, Sept. 14, 1980.

**Garner, Robert F.:** b. Apr. 27, 1920, Jersey City, N.J.; educ. Seton Hall Univ. (S. Orane, N.J.), Immaculate Conception Seminary (Darlington, N.J.); ord. priest (Newark*) June 15, 1946; ord. titular bishop of Blera and auxiliary bishop of Newark, June 25, 1976. Retired July 11, 1995.

**Gaughan, Norbert F.:** b. May 30, 1921, Pittsburgh, Pa.; educ. St. Vincent College (Latrobe, Pa.), Univ. of Pittsburgh; ord. priest (Pittsburgh) Nov. 4, 1945; ord. titular bishop of Taraqua and auxiliary bishop of Greensburg, June 26, 1975; app. bishop of Gary, July 24, 1984, installed Oct. 2, 1984. Retired June 1, 1996.

**Gelineau, Louis E.:** b. May 3, 1928, Burlington, Vt.; educ. St. Michael's College (Winooski, Vt.), St. Paul's Univ. Seminary (Ottawa, Ont.), Catholic Univ. (Washington, D.C.); ord. priest (Burlington) June 5, 1954; ord. bishop of Providence, R.I., Jan. 26, 1972.

**Gendron, Odore J.:** b. Sept. 13, 1921, Manchester, N.H.; educ. St. Charles Borromeo Seminary (Sherbrooke, Que., Canada), Univ. of Ottawa, St. Paul Univ. Seminary (Ottawa, Ont., Canada); ord. priest (Manchester) May 31, 1947; ord. bishop of Manchester, Feb. 3, 1975; resigned June 12, 1990.

**George, Francis E., O.M.I.:** b. Jan. 16, 1937, Chicago, Ill.; educ. Univ. of Ottawa (Canada); Catholic Univ. (Washington, D.C.), Tulane Univ. (New Orleans), Urban Univ. (Rome); ord. priest Dec. 21, 1963; provincial of central region of Oblates of Mary Immaculate, 1973-74, vicar general, 1974-86; ord. bishop of Yakima, Sept. 21, 1990; app. archbishop of Portland, Ore., Apr. 30, 1996, installed May 27, 1996.

**Gerber, Eugene J.:** b. Apr. 30, 1931, Kingman, Kans.; educ. St. Thomas Seminary (Denver, Colo.), Wichita State Univ.; Catholic Univ. (Washington, D.C.),Angelicum (Rome); ord. priest (Wichita) May 19, 1959; ord. bishop of Dodge City, Dec. 14, 1976; app. bishop of Wichita, Nov. 17, 1982, installed Feb. 9, 1983.

**Gerbermann, Hugo, M.M.:** b. Sept. 11, 1913, Nada, Tex.; educ. St. John's Minor and Major Seminary (San Antonio, Tex.), Maryknoll Seminary (Maryknoll, N.Y.); ord. priest Feb. 7, 1943; missionary work in Ecuador and Guatemala; ord. titular bishop of Amathus and prelate of Huehuetenango, Guatemala, July 22, 1962; first bishop of Huehuetenango, Dec. 23, 1967; app. titular bishop of Pinhel and auxiliary bishop of San Antonio, July 24, 1975; resigned June 30, 1982.

**Gerety, Peter L.:** b. July 19, 1912, Shelton, Conn.; educ. Sulpician Seminary (Paris, France); ord. priest (Hartford*) June 29, 1939; ord. titular bishop of Crepedula and coadjutor bishop of Portland, Me., with right of succession, June 1, 1966; app. apostolic administrator of Portland, 1967; bishop of Portland, Me., Sept. 15, 1969; app. archbishop of Newark, Apr. 2, 1974; installed June 28, 1974; retired June 3, 1986.

**Gerry, Joseph J., O.S.B.:** b. Sept. 12, 1928, Millinocket, Me.; educ. St. Anselm Abbey Seminary (Manchester, N.H.), Univ. of Toronto (Canada), Fordham Univ. (New York); ord. priest June 12, 1954; abbot of St. Anselm Abbey, Manchester, N.H., 1972; ord. titular bishop of Praecausa and auxiliary of Manchester, Apr. 21, 1986; bishop of Portland, Me., Dec. 27, 1988, installed Feb. 21, 1989.

**Gettelfinger, Gerald A.:** b. Oct. 20, 1935, Ramsey, Ind.; educ. St. Meinrad Seminary (St. Meinrad, Ind.), Butler Univ. (Indianapolis, Ind.); ord. priest (Indianapolis*) May 7, 1961; ord. bishop of Evansville, Apr. 11, 1989.

**Gilbert, Edward J., C.SS.R.:** b. Dec. 26, 1936, Brooklyn, N.Y.; educ. Mt. St. Alphonsus Seminary (Esopus, New York), Catholic Univ. (Washington, D.C.); ord. priest (Redemptorists, Baltimore Province) June 21, 1964; ord. bishop of Roseau, Dominica, Sept. 7, 1994.

**Glynn, John J.:** b. Aug. 6, 1926, Boston, Mass.,; educ. St. John's Seminary (Brighton, Mass.); ord. priest (Boston*),Apr. 11, 1951; Navy chaplain, 1960-85; ord. titular bishop of Monteverde and auxiliary bishop of Military Services archdiocese, Jan. 6, 1992.

**Goedert, Raymond E.:** b. Oct. 15, 1927, Oak Park, Ill.; educ. Quigley Preparatory Seminary (Chicago, Ill.), St. Mary of the Lake Seminary and Loyola Univ. (Chicago, Ill.), Gregorian Univ. (Rome); ord. priest (Chicago*), May 1, 1952; ord. titular bishop of Tamazeni and auxiliary bishop of Chicago, Aug. 29, 1991.

**Gonzalez, Roberto O., O.F.M.:** b. June 2, 1950, Elizabeth, N.J.; educ. St. Joseph Seraphic Seminary (Callicoon, N.Y.), Siena College (Loudonville, N.Y.), Washington Theological Union (Silver Spring, Md.), Fordham Univ. (New York, N.Y.); solemnly professed in Franciscan Order, 1976; ord. priest May 8, 1977; ord. titular bishop of Ursona and auxiliary bishop of Boston, Oct. 3, 1988; app. coadjutor bishop of Corpus Christi, May 16, 1995.

**Gorman, John R.:** b. Dec. 11, 1925, Chicago, Ill.; educ, St. Mary of the Lake Seminary (Mundelein, Ill.), Loyola Univ. (Chicago, Ill.); ord. priest (Chicago*) May 1, 1956; ord. titular bishop of Catula and auxiliary bishop of Chicago, Apr. 11, 1988.

**Gossman, F. Joseph:** b. Apr. 1, 1930, Baltimore, Md.; educ. St. Charles College (Catonsville, Md.), St. Mary's Seminary (Baltimore, Md.), North American College (Rome), Catholic Univ. (Washington, D.C.); ord. priest (Baltimore*) Dec. 17, 1955; ord. titular bishop of Agunto and auxiliary bishop of Baltimore, Sept. 11, 1968; app. bishop of Raleigh Apr. 8, 1975.

**Gottwald, George J.:** b. May 12, 1914, St. Louis, Mo.; educ. Kenrick Seminary (Webster Groves, Mo.); ord. priest (St. Louis*) June 9, 1940; ord. titular bishop of Cedamusa and auxiliary bishop of St. Louis, Aug. 8, 1961; resigned Aug. 2, 1988.

**Gracida, Rene H.:** b. June 9, 1923, New Orleans, La.; educ. Rice Univ. and Univ. of Houston (Houston, Tex.), Univ. of Fribourg (Switzerland); ord.

priest (Miami*) May 23, 1959; ord. titular bishop of Masuccaba and auxiliary bishop of Miami, Jan. 25, 1972; app. first bishop of Pensacola-Tallahassee, Oct. 1, 1975, installed Nov. 6, 1975; app. bishop of Corpus Christi, May 24, 1983, installed July 11, 1983.

**Grady, Thomas J.:** b. Oct. 9, 1914, Chicago, Ill.; educ. St. Mary of the Lake Seminary (Mundelein, Ill.), Gregorian Univ. (Rome), Loyola Univ. (Chicago, Ill.); ord. priest (Chicago*) Apr. 23, 1938; ord. titular bishop of Vamalla and auxiliary bishop of Chicago, Aug. 24, 1967; app. bishop of Orlando, Fla., Nov. 11, 1974, installed Dec. 16, 1974; resigned Dec. 12, 1989.

**Graham, John J.:** b. Sept. 11, 1913, Philadelphia, Pa.; educ. St. Charles Borromeo Seminary (Philadelphia, Pa.), Pontifical Roman Seminary (Rome, Italy); ord. priest (Philadelphia*) Feb. 26, 1938; ord. titular bishop of Sabrata and auxiliary bishop of Philadelphia, Jan. 7, 1964; retired Nov. 8, 1988.

**Grahmann, Charles V.:** b. July 15, 1931, Halletsville, Tex.; educ. The Assumption-St. John's Seminary (San Antonio, Tex.); ord. priest (San Antonio*) Mar. 17, 1956; ord. titular bishop of Equilium and auxiliary bishop of San Antonio, Aug. 20, 1981; app. first bishop of Victoria, Tex., Apr. 13, 1982; app. coadjutor bishop of Dallas, Dec. 9, 1989; bishop of Dallas, July 14, 1990.

**Gregory, Wilton D.:** b. Dec. 7, 1947, Chicago, Ill.; educ. Quigley Preparatory Seminary South, Niles College of Loyola Univ. (Chicago, Ill.), St. Mary of the Lake Seminary (Mundelein, Ill.), Pontifical Liturgical Institute, Sant'Anselmo (Rome); ord. priest (Chicago*) May 9, 1973; ord. titular bishop of Oliva and auxiliary bishop of Chicago, Dec. 13, 1983; app. bishop of Belleville, Dec. 29, 1993; installed Feb. 10, 1994.

**Griffin, James A.:** b. June 13, 1934, Fairview Park, O.; educ. St. Charles College (Baltimore, Md.), Borromeo College (Wicklife, O.); St Mary Seminary (Cleveland, O.); Lateran Univ. (Rome); Cleveland State Univ.; ord. priest (Cleveland) May 28, 1960; ord. titular bishop of Holar and auxiliary bishop of Cleveland, Aug. 1, 1979; app. bishop of Columbus, Feb. 8, 1983.

**Grosz, Edward M.:** b. Feb. 16, 1945, Buffalo, N.Y.; educ. St. John Vianney Seminary (East Aurora, N.Y.), Notre Dame Univ. (Notre Dame, Ind.); ord. priest (Buffalo) May 29, 1971; ord. titular bishop of Morosbisdus and auxiliary bishop of Buffalo, Feb. 2, 1990.

**Guillory, Curtis J., S.V.D.:** b. Sept. 1, 1943, Mallet, La.; educ. Divine Word College (Epworth, Iowa), Chicago Theological Union (Chicago), Creighton Univ. (Omaha, Neb.); ord. priest Dec. 16, 1972; ord. titular bishop of Stagno and auxiliary bishop of Galveston-Houston, Feb. 19, 1988.

**Gumbleton, Thomas J.:** b. Jan. 26, 1930, Detroit, Mich.; educ. St. John Provincial Seminary (Detroit, Mich.), Pontifical Lateran Univ. (Rome); ord. priest (Detroit*) June 2, 1956; ord. titular bishop of Ululi and auxiliary bishop of Detroit, May 1, 1968.

# H

**Ham, J. Richard, M.M.:** b. July 11, 1921, Chicago, Ill.; educ. Maryknoll Seminary (New York); ord. priest June 12, 1948; missionary to Guatemala,

1958; ord. titular bishop of Puzia di Numidia and auxiliary bishop of Guatemala, Jan. 6, 1968; resigned see 1979; auxiliary bishop of St. Paul and Minneapolis, October, 1980; retired Oct. 29, 1990.

**Hanifen, Richard C.:** b. June 15, 1931, Denver, Colo,; educ. Regis College and St. Thomas Seminary (Denver, Colo.), Catholic Univ. (Washington, D.C.), Lateran Univ. (Rome); ord. priest (Denver*) June 6, 1959; ord. titular bishop of Abercorn and auxiliary bishop of Denver, Sept. 20, 1974; app. first bishop of Colorado Springs, Nov. 10, 1983; installed Jan. 30, 1984.

**Hannan, Philip M.:** b. May 20, 1913, Washington, D.C.; educ. St. Charles College (Catonsville, Md.), Catholic Univ. (Washington, D.C.), North American College (Rome); ord. priest (Washington*) Dec. 8, 1939; ord. titular bishop of Hieropolis and auxiliary bishop of Washington, D.C., Aug. 28, 1956; app. archbishop of New Orleans, installed Oct. 13, 1965; retired Dec. 6, 1988.

**Hanus, Jerome George, O.S.B.:** b. May 25, 1940, Brainard, Nebr.; educ. Conception Seminary (Conception, Mo.), St. Anselm Univ. (Rome), Princeton Theological Seminary (Princeton, N.J.); ord. priest (Conception Abbey, Mo.) July 30, 1966; abbot of Conception Abbey, 1977-87; president of Swiss American Benedictine Congregation, 1984-87; ord. bishop of St. Cloud, Aug. 24, 1987; app. coadjutor archbishop of Dubuque, Aug. 23, 1994; archbishop of Dubuque, Oct. 16, 1995.

**Harrington, Bernard J.:** b. Sept. 6, 1933, Detroit, Mich.; educ. Sacred Heart Seminary (Detroit, Mich.), St. John's Provincial Seminary (Plymouth, Mich.), Univ. of Detroit; ord. priest (Detroit*) June 6, 1959; ord. titular bishop of Uzali and auxiliary of Detroit, Jan. 6, 1994.

**Harrington, Timothy J.:** b. Dec. 19, 1918, Holyoke, Mass.; educ. Holy Cross College (Worcester, Mass.), Grand Seminary (Montreal, Que.), Boston College School of Social Work; ord. priest (Springfield, Mass.) Jan. 19, 1946; ord. titular bishop of Rusuca and auxiliary bishop of Worcester, Mass., July 2, 1968; app. bishop of Worcester, Sept. 1, 1983, installed Oct. 13, 1983; retired Oct. 27, 1994.

**Harrison, Frank J.:** b. Aug. 12, 1912; Syracuse, N.Y.; educ. Notre Dame Univ. (Notre Dame, Ind.), St. Benard's Seminary (Rochester, N.Y.), ord. priest (Syracuse) June 4, 1937; ord. titular bishop of Aquae in Numidia and bishop of Syracuse, Apr. 22, 1971; app. bishop of Syracuse, Nov. 9, 1976, installed Feb. 6, 1977; retired June 16, 1987.

**Hart, Daniel A.:** b. Aug. 24, 1927, Lawrence, Mass.; educ. St. John's Seminary (Brighton, Mass.); ord. priest (Boston*) Feb. 2, 1953; ord. titular bishop of Tepelta and auxiliary bishop of Boston, Oct. 18, 1976; bishop of Norwich Sept. 12, 1995.

**Hart, Joseph:** b. Sept. 26, 1931, Kansas City, Missouri; educ. St. John Seminary (Kansas City, Mo.), St. Meinrad Seminary (Indianapolis, Ind.); ord. priest (Kansas City-St. Joseph) May 1, 1956; ord. titular bishop of Thimida Regia and auxiliary bishop of Cheyenne, Wyo., Aug. 31, 1976; app. bishop of Cheyenne, installed June 12, 1978.

**Head, Edward D.:** b. Aug. 5, 1919, White Plains, N.Y.; educ. Cathedral College, St. Joseph's Seminary, Columbia Univ. (New York City); ord. priest

(New York*) Jan. 27, 1945; director of New York Catholic Charities; ord. titular bishop of Ardsratha and auxiliary bishop of New York, Mar. 19, 1970; app. bishop of Buffalo, Jan. 23, 1973, installed Mar. 19, 1973; retired Apr. 18, 1995.

**Heim, Capistran F., O.F.M.:** b. Jan. 21, 1934, Catskill, N.Y.; educ. Franciscan Houses of Study; ord. priest Dec. 18, 1965; missionary in Brazil; ord. first bishop of prelature of Itaituba, Brazil, Sept. 17, 1988; installed Oct. 2, 1988.

**Hermes, Herbert, O.S.B.:** b. May 25, 1933, Scott City, Kans.; ord. priest (St. Benedict Abbey, Atchison, Kans.), May 26, 1960; missionary in Brazil; ord. bishop of territorial prelature of Cristalandia, Brazil, Sept. 2, 1990.

**Herrmann, Edward J.:** b. Nov. 6, 1913, Baltimore, Md.; educ. Mt. St. Mary's Seminary (Emmitsburg, Md.), Catholic Univ. (Washington, D.C.); ord. priest (Washington*) June 12, 1947; ord. titular bishop of Lamzella and auxiliary bishop of Washington, D.C., Apr. 26, 1966; app. bishop of Columbus, June 26, 1973; resigned Sept. 18, 1982.

**Hettinger, Edward Gerhard:** b. Oct. 14, 1902, Lancaster, O.; educ. St. Vincent's College (Beatty, Pa.); ord. priest (Columbus) June 2, 1928; ord. titular bishop of Teos and auxiliary bishop of Columbus, Feb. 24, 1942; retired Oct. 18, 1977.

**Hickey, Dennis W.:** b. Oct. 28, 1914, Dansville, N.Y.; educ. Colgate Univ. and St. Bernard's Seminary (Rochester, N.Y.); ord. priest (Rochester) June 7, 1941; ord. titular bishop of Rusuccuru and auxiliary bishop of Rochester, N.Y., Mar. 14, 1968; retired Jan. 16, 1990.

**Hickey, James A.:** (See Cardinals, Biographies.)

**Higi, William L.:** b. Aug. 29, 1933, Anderson, Ind.; educ. Our Lady of the Lakes Preparatory Seminary (Wawasee, Ind.), Mt. St. Mary of the West Seminary and Xavier Univ. (Cincinnati, O.); ord. priest (Lafayette, Ind.) May 30, 1959; ord. bishop of Lafayette, Ind., June 6, 1984.

**Hoffman, James R.:** b. June 12, 1932, Fremont, O.; educ. Our Lady of the Lake Minor Seminary (Wawasee, Ind.), St. Meinrad College (St. Meinrad, Ind.), Mt. St. Mary Seminary (Norwood, O.), Catholic Univ. (Washington, D.C.); ord. priest (Toledo) July 28, 1957; ord. titular bishop of Italica and auxiliary bishop of Toledo, June 23, 1978; bishop of Toledo, Dec. 16, 1980.

**Hogan, James J.:** b. Oct. 17, 1911, Philadelphia, Pa.; educ. St. Charles College (Catonsville, Md.), St. Mary's Seminary (Baltimore), Gregorian Univ. (Rome), Catholic Univ. (Washington, D.C.); ord. priest (Trenton) Dec. 8, 1937; ord. titular bishop of Philomelium and auxiliary bishop of Trenton, Feb. 25, 1960; app. bishop of Altoona-Johnstown, installed July 6, 1966; retired Nov. 4, 1986.

**Hogan, Joseph L.:** b. Mar. 11, 1916, Lima, N.Y.; educ. St. Bernard's Seminary (Rochester, N.Y.), Canisius College (Buffalo, N.Y.), Angelicum (Rome); ord. priest (Rochester) June 6, 1942; ord. bishop of Rochester, Nov. 28, 1969; resigned Nov. 28, 1978.

**Houck, William Russell:** b. June 26, 1926, Mobile Ala.; educ. St. Bernard Junior College (Cullman, Ala.), St. Mary's Seminary College and St. Mary's Seminary (Baltimore, Md.), Catholic Univ. (Wash-

ington, D.C.); ord. priest (Mobile*) May 19, 1951; ord. titular bishop of Alessano and auxiliary bishop of Jackson, Miss., May 27, 1979, by Pope John Paul II; app. bishop of Jackson, Apr. 11, 1984, installed June 5, 1984.

**Howze, Joseph Lawson:** b. Aug. 30, 1923, Daphne, Ala.; convert to Catholicism, 1948; educ. St. Bonaventure Univ. (St. Bonaventure, N.Y.); ord. priest (Raleigh) May 7, 1959; ord. titular bishop of Massita and auxiliary bishop of Natchez-Jackson, Jan. 28, 1973; app. first bishop of Biloxi, Miss., Mar. 8, 1977; installed June 6, 1977.

**Hubbard, Howard J.:** b. Oct. 31, 1938, Troy, N.Y.; educ. St. Joseph's Seminary (Dunwoodie, N.Y.); North American College and Gregorian Univ. (Rome), Catholic Univ. (Washington, D.C.); ord. priest (Albany) Dec. 18, 1963; ord. bishop of Albany, Mar. 27, 1977.

**Hughes, Alfred C.:** b. Dec. 2, 1932, Boston, Mass.; educ. St. John Seminary (Brighton, Mass.), Gregorian Univ. (Rome); ord. priest (Boston*) Dec. 15, 1957, in Rome; ord. titular bishop of Maximiana in Byzacena and auxiliary bishop of Boston, Sept. 14, 1981; app. bishop of Baton Rouge, Sept. 7, 1993.

**Hughes, Edward T.:** b. Nov. 13, 1920, Lansdowne, Pa.; educ. St. Charles Seminary, Univ. of Pennsylvania (Philadelphia); ord. priest (Philadelphia*) May 31, 1947; ord. titular bishop of Segia and auxiliary bishop of Philadelphia, July 21, 1976; app. bishop of Metuchen, Dec. 11, 1986, installed Feb. 5, 1987.

**Hughes, William A.:** b. Sept. 23, 1921, Youngstown, O.; educ. St. Charles College (Catonsville, Md.), St. Mary's Seminary (Cleveland, O.), Notre Dame Univ. (Notre Dame, Ind.); ord. priest (Youngstown) Apr. 6, 1946; ord. titular bishop of Inis Cathaig and auxiliary bishop of Youngstown, Sept. 12, 1974; app. bishop of Covington, installed May 8, 1979. Retired July 4, 1995.

**Hunthausen, Raymond G.:** b. Aug. 21, 1921, Anaconda, Mont.; educ. Carroll College (Helena, Mont.), St. Edward's Seminary (Kenmore, Wash.), St. Louis Univ. (St. Louis, Mo.), Catholic Univ. (Washington, D.C.), Fordham Univ. (New York City), Notre Dame Univ. (Notre Dame, Ind.); ord. priest (Helena) June 1, 1946; ord. bishop of Helena, Aug. 30, 1962; app. archbishop of Seattle, Feb. 25, 1975; retired Aug. 21, 1991.

**Hurley, Francis T.:** b. Jan. 12, 1927, San Francisco, Calif.; educ. St. Patrick's Seminary (Menlo Park, Calif.), Catholic Univ. (Washington, D.C.); ord. priest (San Francisco*) June 16, 1951; assigned to NCWC in Washington, D.C., 1957; assistant (1958) and later (1968) associate secretary of NCCB and USCC; ord. titular bishop of Daimlaig and auxiliary bishop of Juneau, Alaska, Mar. 19, 1970; app. bishop of Juneau, July 20, 1971, installed Sept. 8, 1971; app. archbishop of Anchorage, May 4, 1976, installed July 8, 1976.

**Hurley, Mark J.:** b. Dec. 13, 1919, San Francisco, Calif.; educ. St. Patrick's Seminary (Menlo Park, Calif.), Univ. of California (Berkeley), Catholic Univ. (Washington, D.C.), Lateran Univ. (Rome), Univ. of Portland (Portland, Ore.); ord. priest (San Francisco*) Sept. 23, 1944; ord. titular bishop of Thunusuda and auxiliary bishop of San Francisco, Jan. 4, 1968; app. bishop of Santa Rosa, Nov. 19, 1969; resigned Apr. 15, 1986.

## I-J

**Ibrahim, Ibrahim N.:** b. Oct. 1, 1937, Telkaif, Mosul, Iraq.; educ. Patriarchal Seminary (Mosul, Iraq), St. Sulpice Seminary (Paris, France); ord. priest Dec. 30, 1962, in Baghdad, Iraq; ord. titular bishop of Anbar and apostolic exarch for Chaldean Catholics in the United States, Mar. 8, 1982, in Baghdad; installed in Detroit, Apr. 18, 1982; app. first eparch, Aug. 3, 1985, when exarchate was raised to eparchy of St. Thomas Apostle of Detroit.

**Imesch, Joseph L.:** b. June 21, 1931, Detroit, Mich.; educ. Sacred Heart Seminary (Detroit, Mich.), North American College, Gregorian Univ. (Rome); ord. priest (Detroit*) Dec. 16, 1956; ord. titular bishop of Pomaria and auxiliary bishop of Detroit, Apr. 3, 1973; app. bishop of Joliet, June 30, 1979.

**Jacobs, Sam Galip:** b. Mar. 4, 1938, Greenwood, Miss.; educ. Immaculata Seminary (Lafayette, La.), Catholic Univ. (Washington, D.C.); ord. priest (Lafayette) June 6, 1964; became priest of Lake Charles diocese, 1980, when that see was established; ord. bishop of Alexandria, La., Aug. 24, 1989.

**Jakubowski, Thad J.:** b. Apr. 5, 1924, Chicago, Ill.; educ. Mundelein Seminary, St. Mary of the Lake Univ., Loyola Univ. (Chicago); ord priest (Chicago*) May 3, 1950; ord. titular bishop of Plestia and auxiliary bishop of Chicago, Apr. 11, 1988.

**Jarrell, C. Michael:** b. May 15, 1940, Opelousas, La.; educ. Immaculata Minor Seminary (Lafayette, La.); Catholic Univ. (Washington, D.C.); ord. priest (Lafayette, La.) June 3, 1967; ord. bishop of Houma-Thibodaux, Mar. 4, 1993.

## K

**Kaffer, Roger L.:** b. Aug. 14, 1927, Joliet, Ill.; educ. Quigley Preparatory Seminary (Chicago, Ill.), St. Mary of the Lake Seminary (Mundelein, Ill.), Gregorian Univ. (Rome); ord. priest (Joliet) May 1, 1954; ord. titular bishop of Dusa and auxiliary bishop of Joliet, June 26, 1985.

**Kalisz, Raymond P., S.V.D.:** b. Sept. 25, 1927, Melvindale, Mich.; educ. St. Mary's Seminary (Techny, Ill.); ord. priest Aug. 15, 1954; ord. bishop of Wewak, Papua New Guinea, August 15, 1980.

**Kaniecki, Michael Joseph, S.J.:** b. Apr. 13, 1935, Detroit Mich.; joined Jesuits 1953; educ. Xavier Univ. (Milford, O.), Mt. St. Michael's Seminary (Spokane, Wash.), Regis College (Willowdale, Ont.); ord. priest June 5, 1965; ord. coadjutor bishop of Fairbanks, May 1, 1984; bishop of Fairbanks, June 1, 1985.

**Keating, John Richard:** b. July 20, 1934, Chicago, Ill.; educ. Quigley Preparatory Seminary (Chicago, Ill.), St. Mary of the Lake Seminary (Mundelein, Ill.), Gregorian Univ. (Rome); ord. priest (Chicago*) Dec. 20, 1958; ord. bishop of Arlington, Aug. 4, 1983.

**Keeler, William Henry:** (See Cardinals, Biographies.)

**Keleher, James P.:** b. July 31, 1931, Chicago, Ill.; educ. Quigley Preparatory Seminary (Chicago, Ill.), St. Mary of the Lake Seminary (Mundelein, Ill.); ord. priest (Chicago*) Apr. 12, 1958; ord. bishop of Belleville, Dec. 11, 1984; app. archbishop of Kansas City, Kans., June 28, 1993.

**Kelly, Thomas C., O.P.:** b. July 14, 1931, Roch-ester, N.Y.; educ. Providence College (Providence, R.I.), Immaculate Conception College (Washington, D.C.), Angelicum (Rome); professed in Dominicans, Aug. 26, 1952; secretary, apostolic delegation, Washington, D.C., 1965-71; associate general secretary, 1971-77, and general secretary, 1977-81, NCCB/USCC; ord. titular bishop of Tusurus and auxiliary bishop of Washington, D.C., Aug. 15, 1977; app. archbishop of Louisville, Dec. 28, 1981, installed Feb. 18, 1982.

**Kicanas, Gerald F.:** b. Aug. 18, 1941, Chicago, Ill.; educ. Quigley Preparatory Seminary, St. Mary of the Lake Seminary and Loyola University in Chicago; ord. priest (Chicago*) Apr. 27, 1967; ord. titular bishop of Bela and auxiliary of Chicago, Mar. 20, 1995.

**Kinney, John F.:** b. June 11, 1937, Oelwein, Iowa; educ. Nazareth Hall and St. Paul Seminaries (St. Paul, Minn.); Pontifical Lateran University (Rome); ord. priest (St. Paul-Minneapolis*) Feb. 2, 1963; ord. titular bishop of Caorle and auxiliary bishop of St. Paul and Minneapolis, Jan. 25, 1977; app. bishop of Bismarck June 30, 1982; app. bishop of St. Cloud, May 9, 1995.

**Kmiec, Edward U.:** b. June 4, 1936, Trenton, N.J.; educ. St. Charles College (Catonsville, Md.), St. Mary's Seminary (Baltimore, Md.), Gregorian Univ. (Rome); ord. priest (Trenton) Dec. 20, 1961; ord. titular bishop of Simidicca and auxiliary bishop of Trenton, Nov. 3, 1982; app. bishop of Nashville, Oct. 13, 1992; installed Dec. 3, 1992.

**Koester, Charles R.:** b. Sept. 16, 1915, Jefferson City, Mo.; educ. Conception Academy (Conception, Mo.), St. Louis Preparatory Seminary and Kenrick Seminary (St. Louis, Mo.), North American College (Rome); ord. priest (St. Louis*) Dec. 20, 1941; ord. titular bishop of Suacia and auxiliary bishop of St. Louis, Feb. 11, 1971; retired Sept. 10, 1991.

**Krawczak, Arthur H.:** b. Feb. 2, 1913, Detroit, Mich.; educ. Sacred Heart Seminary, Sts. Cyril and Methodius Seminary (Orchard Lake, Mich.), Catholic Univ. (Washington, D.C.); ord. priest (Detroit*) May 18, 1940; ord. titular bishop of Subbar and auxiliary bishop of Detroit, Apr. 3, 1973; retired Aug. 17, 1982.

**Kucera, Daniel W., O.S.B.:** b. May 7, 1923, Chicago, Ill.; educ. St. Procopius College (Lisle, Ill.), Catholic Univ. (Washington, D.C.); professed in Order of St. Benedict, June 16, 1944; ord. priest May 26, 1949; abbot, St. Procopius Abbey, 1964-71; pres. Illinois Benedictine College, 1959-65 and 1971-76; ord. titular bishop of Natchez and auxiliary bishop of Joliet, July 21, 1977; app. bishop of Salina, Mar. 5, 1980; app. archbishop of Dubuque, installed Feb. 23, 1984; retired Oct. 16, 1995.

**Kuchmiak, Michael, C.Ss.R.:** b. Feb. 5, 1923, Obertyn, Horodenka, Western Ukraine; left during World War II; educ. St. Josaphat Ukrainian Seminary (Rome, Italy), St. Mary's Seminary (Meadowvale, Ont., Canada); ord. priest May 13, 1956; in the U.S. from 1967; ord. titular bishop of Agathopolis and auxiliary bishop of Ukrainian metropolitan of Philadelphia, Apr. 27, 1988; exarch of apostolic exarchate for Ukrainian Catholics in Great Britain, June 24, 1989.

**Kupfer, William F., M.M.:** b. Jan. 28, 1909,

Brooklyn, N.Y.; educ. Cathedral College (Brooklyn, N.Y.), Maryknoll Seminary (Maryknoll, N.Y.); ord. priest June 11, 1933; missionary in China; app. prefect apostolic of Taichung, Taiwan, 1951; ord. first bishop of Taichung, July 25, 1962; retired Sept. 3, 1986.

**Kurtz, Robert, C.R.:** b. July 25, 1939, Chicago, Ill.; ord. priest Mar. 11, 1967; ord. bishop of Hamilton, Bermuda, Sept. 15, 1995.

**Kuzma, George M.:** b. July 24, 1925, Windber, Pa.; educ. St. Francis Seminary (Loretto, Pa.), St. Procopius College (Lisle, Ill.), Sts. Cyril and Methodius Byzantine Catholic Seminary, Duquesne Univ. (Pittsburgh, Pa.); ord. priest (Pittsburgh*, Byzantine Rite), May 5, 1955; ord. titular bishop of Telmisso and auxiliary bishop of Byzantine eparchy of Passaic, 1987; app. bishop of Byzantine diocese of Van Nuys, Calif., Oct. 23, 1990, installed Jan. 15, 1991.

## L

**Lambert, Francis, S.M.:** b. Feb. 7, 1921, Lawrence, Mass.; educ. Marist Seminary (Framingham, Mass.); ord. priest, June 29, 1946; served in Marist missions in Oceania; provincial of Marist Oceania province, 1971; ord. bishop of Port Vila, Vanuatu (New Hebrides), Mar. 20, 1977.

**Larkin, W. Thomas:** b. Mar. 31, 1923, Mt. Morris, N.Y.; educ. St. Andrew Seminary and St. Bernard Seminary (Rochester, N.Y.); Angelicum Univ. (Rome); ord. priest (St. Augustine) May 15, 1947; ord. bishop of St. Petersburg, May 27, 1979; retired Nov. 29, 1988.

**Law, Bernard F.:** (See Cardinals, Biographies.)

**Leibrecht, John J.:** b. Aug. 30, 1930, Overland, Mo.; educ. Catholic Univ. (Washington, D.C.); ord. priest (St. Louis*) Mar. 17, 1956; superintendent of schools of St. Louis archdiocese, 1962-1981; ord. bishop of Springfield-Cape Girardeau, Mo., Dec. 12, 1984.

**Lessard, Raymond W.:** b. Dec. 21, 1930, Grafton, N.D.; educ. St. Paul Seminary (St. Paul, Minn.), North American College (Rome); ord. priest (Fargo) Dec. 16, 1956; served on staff of the Congregation for Bishops in the Roman Curia, 1964-73; ord. bishop of Savannah, Apr. 27, 1973; retired Feb. 7, 1995.

**Levada, William J.:** b. June 15, 1936, Long Beach, Calif.; educ. St. John's College (Camarillo, Calif.), Gregorian Univ. (Rome); ord. priest (Los Angeles*) Dec. 20, 1961; ord. titular bishop of Capri and auxiliary bishop of Los Angeles, May 12, 1983; app. archbishop of Portland, Ore., July 3, 1986; coadjutor archbishop of San Francisco, Aug. 17, 1995; archbishop of San Francisco Dec. 27, 1995.

**Lipscomb, Oscar H.:** b. Sept. 21, 1931, Mobile, Ala.; educ. McGill Institute, St. Bernard College (Cullman, Ala.), North American College and Gregorian Univ. (Rome), Catholic Univ. (Washington, D.C.); ord. priest (Mobile*) July 15, 1956; ord. first archbishop of Mobile, Nov. 16, 1980.

**Lohmuller, Martin N.:** b. Aug. 21, 1919, Philadelphia, Pa.; educ. St. Charles Borromeo Seminary (Philadelphia, Pa.), Catholic Univ. (Washington, D.C.); ord. priest (Philadelphia*) June 3, 1944; ord. titular bishop of Ramsbury and auxiliary bishop of

Philadelphia, Apr. 2, 1970; retired Oct. 11, 1994.

**Lori, William E.:** b. May 6, 1951, Louisville, Ky.; educ. St. Pius X College (Covington, Ky.), Mount St. Mary's Seminary (Emmitsburg, Md.), Catholic Univ. (Washington, D.C.); ord. priest (Washington*) May 14, 1977; ord. titular bishop of Bulla and auxiliary bishop of Washington, D.C., Apr. 20, 1995.

**Losten, Basil:** b. May 11, 1930, Chesapeake City, Md.; educ. St. Basil's College (Stamford, Conn.), Catholic University (Washington, D.C.); ord. priest (Philadelphia*, Ukrainian Byzantine) June 10, 1957; ord. titular bishop of Arcadiopolis in Asia and auxiliary bishop of Ukrainian archeparchy of Philadelphia, May 25, 1971; app. apostolic administrator of archeparchy, 1976; app. bishop of Ukrainian eparchy of Stamford, Sept. 20, 1977.

**Lotocky, Innocent Hilarius, O.S.B.M.:** b. Nov. 3, 1915, Petlykiwci, Ukraine; educ. seminaries in Ukraine, Czechoslovakia and Austria; ord. priest Nov. 24, 1940; ord. bishop of St. Nicholas of Chicago for the Ukrainians, Mar. 1, 1981; retired July 15, 1993.

**Loverde, Paul S.:** b. Sept. 3, 1940, Framingham, Mass.; educ. St. Thomas Seminary (Bloomfield, Conn.), St. Bernard Seminary (Rochester, N.Y.), Gregorian Univ. (Rome), Catholic Univ. (Washington, D.C.); ord. priest (Norwich), Dec. 18, 1965; ord. titular bishop of Ottabia and auxiliary bishop of Hartford, Apr. 12, 1988; app. bishop of Ogdensburg, Nov. 11, 1993; installed Jan. 17, 1994.

**Lubachivsky, Myroslav I.:** (See Cardinals, Biographies.)

**Lucker, Raymond A.:** b. Feb. 24, 1927, St. Paul, Minn.; educ. S. Paul Seminary (St. Paul, Minn.); University of Minnesota (Minneapolis), Angelicum (Rome); ord. priest (St. Paul and Minneapolis*) June 7, 1952; director of USCC department of education, 1968-71; ord. titular bishop of Meta and auxiliary bishop of St. Paul and Minneapolis, Sept. 8, 1971; app. bishop of New Ulm, Dec. 23, 1975, installed Feb. 19, 1976.

**Lynch, George E.:** b. Mar. 4, 1917, New York, N.Y.; educ. Fordham Univ. (New York), Mt. St. Mary's Seminary (Emmitsburg, Md.), Catholic Univ. (Washington, D.C.); ord. priest (Raleigh) May 29, 1943; ord. titular bishop of Satafi and auxiliary of Raleigh Jan. 6, 1970; retired Apr. 16, 1985.

**Lynch, Robert N.:** b. May 27, 1941, Charleston, W. Va.; educ. Pontifical College Josephinism (Columbus, Ohio); John XXIII National Seminary (Weston, Mass.); ord. priest (Miami*) May 13, 1978; associate general secretary (1984-89) and general secretary (1989-95) of the NCCB/USCC; app. bishop of St. Petersburg, Dec. 5, 1995; ord. and installed Jan. 26, 1996.

**Lyne, Timothy J.:** b. Mar. 21, 1919, Chicago, Ill.; educ. Quigley Preparatory Seminary, St. Mary of the Lake Seminary (Mundelein, Ill.); ord. priest (Chicago*) May 1, 1943; ord. titular bishop of Vamalla and auxiliary bishop of Chicago, Dec. 13, 1983; retired Jan. 24, 1995.

## M

**McAuliffe, Michael F.:** b. Nov. 22, 1920, Kansas City, Mo.; educ. St. Louis Preparatory Seminary (St. Louis, Mo.), Catholic Univ. (Washington, D.C.); ord.

priest (Kansas City-St. Joseph) May 31, 1945; ord. bishop of Jefferson City, Aug. 18, 1969.

**McCarrick, Theodore E.:** b. July 7, 1930, New York, N.Y.; educ. Fordham Univ. (Bronx, N.Y.), St. Joseph's Seminary (Dunwoodie, N.Y.), Catholic Univ. (Washington, D.C.); ord. priest (New York*) May 31, 1958; dean of students Catholic Univ. of America, 1961-63; pres., Catholic Univ. of Puerto Rico, 1965-69; secretary to Cardinal Cooke, 1970; ord. titular bishop of Rusubisir and auxiliary bishop of New York, June 29, 1977; app. first bishop of Metuchen, N.J., Nov. 19, 1981, installed Jan. 31, 1982; app. archbishop of Newark, June 3, 1986, installed July 25, 1986.

**McCarthy, Edward A.:** b. Apr. 10, 1918, Cincinnati, O.; educ. Mt. St. Mary Seminary (Norwood, O.), Catholic Univ. (Washington, D.C.), Lateran and Angelicum (Rome); ord. priest (Cincinnati*) May 29, 1943; ord. titular bishop of Tamascani and auxiliary bishop of Cincinnati, June 15, 1965; first bishop of Phoenix, Ariz., Dec. 2, 1969; app. coadjutor archbishop of Miami, Fla., July 7, 1976; succeeded as archbishop of Miami, July 26, 1977; retired Nov. 3, 1994.

**McCarthy, John E.:** b. June 21, 1930, Houston, Tex.; educ. Univ. of St. Thomas (Houston, Tex.); ord. priest (Galveston-Houston) May 26, 1956; assistant director Social Action Dept. USCC, 1967-69; executive director Texas Catholic Conference; ord. titular bishop of Pedena and auxiliary bishop of Galveston-Houston, Mar. 14, 1979; app. bishop of Austin, Dec. 19, 1985, installed Feb. 25, 1986.

**McCormack, John B.:** b Aug. 12, 1935, Winthrop, Mass; educ. St. John Seminary College and St. John Seminary Theologate (Boston, Mass.); ord. priest (Boston*) Feb. 2, 1960; ord. titular bishop of Cerbali and auxiliary bishop of Boston, Dec. 27, 1995.

**McCormack, William J.:** b. Jan. 24, 1924, New York, N.Y.; educ. Christ the King Seminary, St. Bonaventure Univ. (St. Bonaventure, N.Y.); ord. priest (New York*) Feb. 21, 1959; national director of Society for the Propagation of the Faith, 1980; ord. titular bishop of Nicives and auxiliary bishop of New York, Jan. 6, 1987.

**McCormick, J. Carroll:** b. Dec. 15, 1907, Philadelphia, Pa.; educ. College Ste. Marie (Montreal), St. Charles Seminary (Overbrook, Pa.), Minor and Major Roman Seminary (Rome); ord. priest (Philadelphia*) July 10, 1932; ord. titular bishop of Ruspae and auxiliary bishop of Philadelphia, Apr. 23, 1947; app. bishop of Altoona-Johnstown, installed Sept. 21, 1960; app. bishop of Scranton, installed May 25, 1966; resigned Feb. 15, 1983.

**McDonald, Andrew J.:** b. Oct. 24, 1923, Savannah, Ga.; educ. St. Mary's Seminary (Baltimore, Md.), Catholic Univ. (Washington, D.C.), Lateran Univ. (Rome); ord. priest (Savannah) May 8, 1948; ord. bishop of Little Rock, Sept. 5, 1972.

**McDonnell, Charles J.:** b. July 7, 1928, Brooklyn, N.Y.; educ. Seton Hall Univ. (South Orange, N.J.), Immaculate Conception Seminary (Darlington, N.J.), Long Island Univ. (Brooklyn, N.Y.); ord. priest (Newark*) May 29, 1954; U.S. Army Chaplain, 1965-89; retired from active duty with rank of Brigadier General; ord. titular bishop of Pocofelto and auxiliary bishop of Newark, May 12, 1994.

**McDonough, Thomas J.:** b. Dec. 5, 1911, Philadelphia, Pa.; educ. St. Charles Seminary (Overbrook, Pa.), Catholic Univ. (Washington, D.C.); ord. priest (Philadelphia*) May 26, 1938; ord. titular bishop of Thenae and auxiliary bishop of St. Augustine, Apr. 30, 1947; app. auxiliary bishop of Savannah, Jan. 2, 1957; named bishop of Savannah, installed Apr. 27, 1960; app. archbishop of Louisville, installed May 2, 1967; resigned Sept. 29, 1981.

**McDowell, John B.:** b. July 17, 1921, New Castle, Pa.; educ. St. Vincent College, St. Vincent Theological Seminary (Latrobe, Pa.), Catholic Univ. (Washington, D.C.); ord. priest (Pittsburgh) Nov. 4, 1945; superintendent of schools, Pittsburgh diocese, 1955-70; ord. titular bishop of Tamazuca, and auxiliary bishop of Pittsburgh, Sept. 8, 1966.

**McFarland, Norman F.:** b. Feb. 21, 1922, Martinez, Calif.; educ. St. Patrick's Seminary (Menlo Park, Calif.), Catholic Univ. (Washington, D.C.); ord. priest (San Francisco*) June 15, 1946; ord. titular bishop of Bida and auxiliary bishop of San Francisco, Sept. 8, 1970; apostolic adminstrator of Reno, 1974; app. bishop of Reno, Feb. 10, 1976, installed Mar. 31, 1976; title of see changed to Reno-Las Vegas; app. bishop of Orange, Calif., Dec. 29, 1986, installed Feb. 24, 1987.

**McGann, John R.:** b. Dec. 2, 1924, Brooklyn, N.Y.; educ. Cathedral College (Brooklyn, N.Y.), Immaculate Conception Seminary (Huntington, L.I.); ord. priest (Rockville Centre) June 3, 1950; ord. titular bishop of Morosbisdus and auxiliary bishop of Rockville Centre, Jan. 7, 1971; vicar general and episcopal vicar; app. bishop of Rockville Centre May 3, 1976, installed June 24, 1976.

**McGarry, Urban, T.O.R.:** b. Nov. 11, 1911, Warren, Pa.; ord. priest Oct. 3, 1942, in India; prefect apostolic of Bhagalpur, Aug. 7, 1956; ord. first bishop of Bhagalpur, India, May 10, 1965; resigned Nov. 30, 1987.

**McGrath, Patrick J.:** b. July 11, 1945, Dublin, Ire.; educ. St. John's College Seminary (Waterford, Ire.), Lateran Univ. (Rome, Italy); ord. priest in Ireland June 7, 1970; came to U.S. same year and became San Francisco archdiocesan priest; ord. titular bishop of Allegheny and auxiliary bishop of San Francisco, Jan. 25, 1989.

**McHugh, James T.:** b. Jan. 3, 1932, Orange, N.J. educ. Seton Hall Univ. (S. Orange, N.J.), Immaculate Conception Seminary (Darlington, N.J.), Fordham Univ. (New York, N.Y.), Catholic Univ. (Washington, D.C.), Angelicum (Rome, Italy); ord. priest (Newark*) May 25, 1957; assistant director, 1965-67, and director, 1967-75, of Family Life Division, USCC; director, 1972-78, of NCCB Office for Pro-Life Activities; special advisor to Mission of Permanent Observer of Holy See to UN; ord. titular bishop of Morosbisdo and auxiliary of Newark, Jan. 25, 1988; bishop of Camden, May 22, 1989.

**McKinney, Joseph C.:** b. Sept. 10, 1928, Grand Rapids, Mich.: educ. St. Joseph's Seminary (Grand Rapids, Mich.), Seminaire de Philosophie (Montreal, Canada), Urban Univ. (Rome, Italy); ord. priest (Grand Rapids) Dec. 20, 1953; ord. titular bishop of Lentini and auxiliary bishop of Grand Rapids, Sept. 26, 1968.

**McLaughlin, Bernard J.:** b. Nov. 19, 1912, Buffalo, N.Y.; educ. Urban Univ. (Rome, Italy ); ord.

priest (Buffalo) Dec. 21, 1935, at Rome; ord. titular bishop of Mottola and auxiliary bishop of Buffalo, Jan. 6, 1969; resigned Jan. 5, 1988.

**McManus, William E.:** b. Jan. 27, 1914, Chicago, Ill.; educ. St. Mary of the Lake Seminary (Mundelein, Ill.), Catholic Univ. (Washington, D.C.); ord. priest (Chicago*) Apr. 15, 1939; ord. titular bishop of Mesarfelta and auxiliary bishop of Chicago, Aug. 24, 1967; app. bishop of Fort Wayne-South Bend, Aug. 31, 1976, installed Oct. 19, 1976; retired Feb. 26, 1985.

**McNabb, John C., O.S.A.:** b. Dec. 11, 1925, Beloit, Wis.; educ. Villanova Univ. (Villanova, Pa.), Augustinian College and Catholic Univ. (Washington, D.C.), De Paul Univ. (Chicago, Ill.); ord. priest May 24, 1952; ord. titular bishop of Saia Maggiore, June 17, 1967 (resigned titular see, Dec. 27, 1977); prelate of Chulucanas, Peru, 1967; first bishop of Chulucanas, Dec. 12, 1988.

**McNamara, John R.:** b. Sept. 4, 1927, Worcester, Mass.; educ. Holy Cross College (Worcester, Mass.), St. John's Seminary (Boston, Mass.); ord. priest (Boston*) Jan. 10, 1952; served as chaplain in the U.S. Navy 1962-88; attained the rank of Rear Admiral and was Chief of Naval Chaplains; ord. titular bishop of Risinium and auxiliary bishop of Boston, May 21, 1992.

**McNamara, Lawrence J.:** b. Aug. 5, 1928, Chiccago, Ill.; educ. St. Paul Seminary (St. Paul, Minn.), Catholic Univ. (Washington, D.C.); ord. priest (Kansas City-St. Joseph) May 30, 1953; executive director of Campaign for Human Development 1973-77; ord. bishop of Grand Island, Nebr., Mar. 28, 1978.

**McNaughton, William J., M.M.:** b. Dec. 7, 1926, Lawrence, Mass.; educ. Maryknoll Seminary (Maryknoll, N.Y.); ord. priest June 13, 1953; ord. titular bishop of Thuburbo Minus and vicar apostolic of Inchon, Korea, Aug. 24, 1961; first bishop of Inchon, Mar. 10, 1962, when vicariate was raised to diocese.

**McRaith, John Jeremiah:** b. Dec. 6, 1934, Hutchinson, Minn.; educ. St. John Preparatory School (Collegeville, Minn.), Loras College, St. Bernard Seminary (Dubuque, Ia); ord. priest (New Ulm) Feb. 21, 1960; exec. dir. of Catholic Rural Life Conference, 1971-78; ord. bishop of Owensboro, Ky., Dec. 15, 1982.

**Madera, Joseph J., M.Sp.S.:** b. Nov. 27, 1927, San Francisco, Calif.; educ. Domus Studiorum of the Missionaries of the Holy Spirit (Coyoacan, D.F. Mexico); ord. priest June 15, 1957; ord. coadjutor bishop of Fresno, Mar. 4, 1980; bishop of Fresno, July 1, 1980; app. titular bishop of Orte and auxiliary of Military Services archdiocese, June 30, 1991.

**Maginnis, Robert P.:** b. Dec. 22, 1933, Philadelphia, Pa.; educ. St. Charles Borromeo Seminary (Overbrook, Pa.); ord. priest (Philadelphia*) May 13, 1961; ord. titular bishop of Siminina and auxiliary bishop of Philadelphia, Mar. 11, 1996.

**Maguire, Joseph F.:** b. Sept. 4, 1919, Boston, Mass.; educ. Boston College, St. John's Seminary (Boston, Mass.); ord. priest (Boston*) June 29, 1945; ord. titular bishop of Macteris and auxiliary bishop of Boston, Feb. 2, 1972; app. coadjutor bishop of Springfield, Mass., Apr. 13, 1976; succeeded as

bishop of Springfield, Mass., Oct. 15, 1977; retired Dec. 27, 1991.

**Mahoney, James P.:** b. Aug. 16, 1925, Kingston, N.Y.; educ. St. Joseph's Seminary (Dunwoodie, N.Y.); ord. priest (New York*) May 19, 1951; ord. titular bishop of Ipagro and auxiliary bishop of New York, Sept. 15, 1972.

**Mahony, Roger M.:** (See Cardinals, Biographies.)

**Maida, Adam J.:** (See Cardinals, Biographies.)

**Malone, James W.:** b. Mar. 8, 1920, Youngstown, O.; educ. St. Charles Preparatory Seminary (Catonsville, Md.), St. Mary's Seminary (Cleveland, O.), Catholic Univ. (Washington, D.C.); ord. priest (Youngstown) May 26, 1945; ord. titular bishop of Alabanda and auxiliary bishop of Youngstown, Mar. 24, 1960; apostolic administrator, 1966; bishop of Youngstown, installed June 20, 1968; president of NCCB/USCC, 1983-86; retired Dec. 5, 1995.

**Maloney, Charles G.:** b. Sept. 9, 1912, Louisville, Ky.; educ. St. Joseph's College Rensselaer, Ind.), North American College (Rome); ord. priest (Louisville*) Dec. 8, 1937; ord. titular bishop of Capsa and auxiliary bishop of Louisville, Feb. 2, 1955; resigned Jan. 8, 1988; transferred to Bardstown, 1995, when it was reestablished as a titular see.

**Manning, Elias (James), O.F.M. Conv.:** b. Apr. 14, 1938, Troy, N.Y.; educ. Sao José Seminary (Rio de Janeiro, Brazil); ord. priest Oct. 30, 1965, in New York; ord. bishop of Valenca, Brazil, May 13, 1990.

**Manning, Thomas R., O.F.M.:** b. Aug. 29, 1922, Baltimore, Md.; educ. Duns Scotus College (Southfield, Mich.), Holy Name College (Washington, D.C.); ord. priest June 5, 1948; ord. titular bishop of Arsamosata, July 14, 1959 (resigned titular see Dec. 30, 1977); prelate of Coroico, Bolivia, July 14, 1959; became first bishop, 1983, when prelature was raised to diocese.

**Mansell, Henry J.:** b. Oct. 10, 1937, New York, N.Y.; educ. Cathedral College, St. Joseph's Seminary and College (New York); North American College, Gregorian Univ. (Rome); ord. priest (New York*) Dec. 19, 1962; ord. titular bishop of Marazane and auxiliary bishop of New York, Jan. 6, 1993, by John Paul II in Vatican City; app. bishop of Buffalo, Apr. 18, 1995; installed June 12, 1995.

**Manz, John R.:** b. 1945, Chicago, Ill; educ. Niles College Seminary (Niles, Ill), Univ. of St. Mary of the Lake-Mundelein Seminary (Chicago); ord. priest (Chicago*) May 12, 1971; ord. titular bishop of Mulia and auxiliary bishop of Chicago, Mar. 5, 1996.

**Marcinkus, Paul C.:** b. Jan. 15, 1922, Cicero, Ill.; ord. priest (Chicago*) May 3, 1947; served in Vatican secretariat from 1952; ord. titular bishop of Orta, Jan. 6, 1969; secretary (1968-71) and president (1971-89) of Institute for Works of Religion (Vatican Bank); titular archbishop, Sept. 26, 1981; former pro-president of Pontifical Commission for the State of Vatican City (resigned in 1990).

**Marconi, Dominic A.:** b. Mar. 13, 1927, Newark, N.J.; educ. Seton Hall Univ. (S. Orange, N.J.), Immaculate Conception Seminary (Darlington, N.J.), Catholic Univ. (Washington, D.C.); ord. priest (Newark*) May 30, 1953; ord. titular bishop of Bure and auxiliary bishop of Newark, June 25, 1976.

**Marino, Eugene A., S.S.J.:** b. May 29, 1934, Biloxi, Miss.; educ. Epiphany Apostolic College and

Mary Immaculate Novitiate (Newburgh, N.Y.), St. Joseph's Seminary (Washington, D.C.), Catholic Univ. (Washington, D.C.), Loyola Univ. (New Orleans, La.), Fordham Univ. (New York City); ord. priest June 9, 1962; ord. titular bishop of Walla Walla and auxiliary bishop of Washington, D.C., Sept. 12, 1974; archbishop of Atlanta, installed May 5, 1988; resigned July 10, 1990.

**Markiewicz, Alfred J.:** b. May 17, 1928, Brooklyn, N.Y.; educ. St. Francis College (Brooklyn, N.Y.), Immaculate Conception Seminary (Huntington, N.Y.); ord. priest (Brooklyn) June 6, 1953; ord. titular bishop of Afufenia and auxiliary bishop of Rockville Centre, Sept. 17, 1986; app. bishop of Kalamazoo, Nov. 22, 1994, installed Jan. 31, 1995.

**Martino, Joseph F.:** b. May 1, 1946, Philadelphia, Pa.; educ. St. Charles Borromeo Seminary (Overbrook, Pa.), Gregorian Univ. (Rome); ord. priest (Philadelphia*) Dec. 18, 1970; ord. titular bishop of Cellae in Mauretania and auxiliary bishop of Philadelphia, Mar. 11, 1996.

**Matthiesen, Leroy Theodore:** b. June 11, 1921, Olfen, Tex.; educ. Josephinum College (Columbus, O.), Catholic Univ. (Washington, D.C.), Register School of Journalism; ord. priest (Amarillo) Mar. 10, 1946; ord. bishop of Amarillo, May 30, 1980.

**Melczek, Dale J.:** b. Nov. 9, 1938, Detroit, Mich.; educ. St. Mary's College (Orchard Lake, Mich.), St. John's Provincial Seminary (Plymouth, Mich.), Univ. of Detroit; ord. priest (Detroit*) June 6, 1964; ord. titular bishop of Trau and auxiliary bishop of Detroit, Jan. 27, 1983; apostolic administrator of Gary, Aug. 19, 1992; coadjutor bishop of Gary, Oct. 28, 1995; bishop of Gary, June 1, 1996.

**Mengeling, Carl F.:** b. Oct. 22, 1930, Hammond, Ind.; educ. St. Meinrad College and Seminary (St. Meinrad, Ind.), Alphonsianum Univ. (Rome); ord. priest (Gary) May 25, 1957; ord. bishop of Lansing Jan. 25, 1996.

**Mestice, Anthony F.:** b. Dec. 6, 1923, New York, N.Y.; educ. St. Joseph Seminary (Yonkers, N.Y.); ord. priest (New York*) June 4, 1949; ord. titular bishop of Villa Nova and auxiliary bishop of New York, Apr. 27, 1973.

**Michaels, James E., S.S.C.:** b. May 30, 1926, Chicago, Ill.; educ. Columban Seminary (St. Columban, Neb.), Gregorian Univ. (Rome); ord. priest Dec. 21, 1951; ord. titular bishop of Verbe and auxiliary bishop of Kwang Ju, Korea, Apr. 14, 1966; app. auxiliary bishop of Wheeling, Apr. 3, 1973 (title of see changed to Wheeling-Charleston, 1974); resigned Sept. 22, 198.

**Milone, Anthony M.:** b. Sept. 24, 1932, Omaha, Nebr.; educ. North American College (Rome); ord. priest (Omaha*) Dec. 15, 1957, in Rome; ord. titular bishop of Plestia and auxiliary bishop of Omaha, Jan. 6, 1982; app. bishop of Great Falls-Billings, Dec. 14, 1987, installed Feb. 23, 1988.

**Minder, John, O.S.F.S.:** b. Nov. 1, 1923, Philadelphia, Pa.; educ. Catholic Univ. (Washington, D.C.); ord. priest June 3, 1950; ord. bishop of Keimos (renamed Keimos-Upington, 1985), South Africa, Jan. 10, 1968.

**Moeddel, Carl K.:** b. Dec. 28, 1937, Cincinnati, Ohio; educ. Athenaeum of Ohio, Mt. St. Mary's Seminary (Cincinnati); ord. priest (Cincinnati*) Aug.

15, 1962; ord. titular bishop of Bistue and auxiliary bishop of Cincinnati, Aug. 24, 1993.

**Montrose, Donald W.:** b. May 13, 1923, Denver, Colo.; educ. St. John's Seminary (Camarillo, Calif.); ord. priest (Los Angeles*) May 7, 1949; ord. titular bishop of Forum Novum and auxiliary bishop of Los Angeles, May 12, 1983; app. bishop of Stockton, Dec. 17, 1985, installed Feb. 20, 1986.

**Moran, William J.:** b. Jan. 15, 1906, San Francisco, Calif.; educ. St. Patrick's Seminary (Menlo Park, Calif.); ord. priest (San Francisco*) June 20, 1931; Army chaplain, 1933; ord. titular bishop of Centuria and auxiliary to the military vicar, Dec. 13, 1965; retired Jan. 15, 1981.

**Moreno, Manuel D.:** b. Nov. 27, 1930, Placentia, Calif.; educ. Univ. of California (Los Angeles), Our Lady Queen of Angels (San Fernando, Calif.), St. John's Seminary (Camarillo, Calif.); ord. priest (Los Angeles*) Apr. 25, 1961; ord. titular bishop of Tanagra and auxiliary bishop of Los Angeles, Feb. 19, 1977; bishop of Tucson, Jan. 12, 1982, installed Mar. 11, 1982.

**Morneau, Robert F.:** b. Sept. 10, 1938, New London, Wis.; educ. St. Norbert's College (De Pere, Wis.), Sacred Heart Seminary (Oneida, Wis.), Catholic Univ. (Washington, D.C.); ord. priest (Green Bay) May 28, 1966; ord. titular bishop of Massa Lubrense and auxiliary bishop of Green Bay, Feb. 22, 1979.

**Moskal, Robert M.:** b. Oct. 24, 1937, Carnegie, Pa.; educ. St. Basil Minor Seminary (Stamford, Conn.), St. Josaphat Seminary and Catholic Univ. (Washington, D.C.); ord. priest (Philadelphia*, Byzantine Ukrainian) Mar. 25, 1963; ord. titular bishop of Agatopoli and auxiliary bishop of the Ukrainian archeparchy of Philadelphia, Oct. 13, 1981; app. first bishop of St. Josaphat in Parma, Dec. 5, 1983.

**Moynihan, James M.:** b. July 16, 1932, Rochester, N.Y.; educ. St. Bernard's Seminary (Rochester, N.Y.), North American College and Gregorian Univ. (Rome); ord. priest (Rochester) Dec. 15, 1957, in Rome; ord. bishop of Syracuse May 29, 1995.

**Muench Robert W.:** b. Dec. 28, 1942, Louisville, Ky.; educ. St. Joseph Seminary and Notre Dame Seminary (New Orleans, La.), Catholic Univ. (Washington, D.C.); ord. priest (New Orleans*) June 18, 1968; ord. titular bishop of Mactaris and auxiliary bishop of New Orleans, June 29, 1990; app. bishop of Covington Jan., 1996; installed Mar. 19, 1996.

**Mulvee, Robert E.:** b. Feb. 15, 1930, Boston, Mass.; educ. St. Thomas Seminary (Bloomfield, Conn.), University Seminary (Ottawa, Ont., Canada), American College (Louvain, Belgium), Lateran Univ. (Rome); ord. priest (Manchester) June 30, 1957; ord. titular bishop of Summa and auxiliary bishop of Manchester, N.H., Apr. 14, 1977; app. bishop of Wilmington, Del., Feb. 19, 1985; app. coadjutor bishop of Providence, Feb. 9, 1995.

**Mundo, Miguel P.:** b. July 25, 1937, New York, N.Y.; educ. Fordham Univ. (Bronx, N.Y.), St. Jerome's College (Kitchener, Ont., Canada), St Francis Seminary (Loretto, Pa.); ord. priest (Camden) May 19, 1962; missionary in Brazil from 1963; ord. titular bishop of Blanda Julia and auxiliary bishop of Jatai, Brazil, June 2, 1978.

**Murphy, Michael J.:** b. July 1, 1915, Cleveland, O.; educ. Niagara Univ. (Niagara Falls, N.Y.); North

American College (Rome), Catholic Univ. (Washington, D.C.); ord. priest (Cleveland) Feb. 28, 1942; ord. titular bishop of Ariendela and auxiliary bishop of Cleveland, June 11, 1976; app. coadjutor bishop of Erie, Nov. 20, 1978; bishop of Erie, July 16, 1982; retired June 12, 1990.

**Murphy, Philip Francis:** b. Mar. 25, 1933, Cumberland, Md.; educ. St. Mary Seminary (Baltimore, Md.), North American College (Rome); ord. priest (Baltimore*) Dec. 20, 1958; ord. titular bishop of Tacarata and auxiliary bishop of Baltimore, Feb. 29, 1976.

**Murphy, Thomas J.:** b. Oct. 3, 1932, Chicago, Ill.; educ. Quigley Preparatory Seminary (Chicago, Ill.), St. Mary of the Lake Seminary (Mundelein, Ill.); ord. priest (Chicago*) Apr. 12, 1958; ord. bishop of Great Falls, Mont. Aug. 21, 1978; title of see changed to Great Falls-Billings, 1980; app. coadjutor archbishop of Seattle, May 27, 1987; archbishop of Seattle, Aug. 21, 1991.

**Murphy, William F.:** b. May 14, 1940, Boston Mass.; educ. Boston Latin School (Boston), Harvard College, St. John's Seminary (Boston), Gregorian Univ. (Rome); ord. priest (Boston*) Dec. 16, 1964; ord. titular bishop of Saia Maggiore and auxiliary bishop of Boston, Dec. 27, 1995.

**Murry, George V., S.J.:** b. Dec. 28, 1948, Camden, N.J.; educ. St. Joseph's College (Philadelphia, Pa.), St. Thomas Seminary (Bloomfield, Conn.), St. Mary Seminary (Baltimore, Md.) Jesuit School of Theology (Berkeley, Calif), George Washington Univ. (Washington, D.C.); entered Jesuits 1972; ord. priest 1979; ord. titular bishop of Fuerteventura and auxiliary bishop of Chicago, Mar. 20, 1995.

**Myers, John Joseph:** b. July 26, 1941, Ottawa, Ill.; educ. Loras College (Dubuque, Ia.), North American College and Gregorian Univ. (Rome), Catholic Univ. of America (Washington, D.C.); ord. priest (Peoria) Dec. 17, 1966, in Rome; ord. coadjutor bishop of Peoria, Sept. 3, 1987; bishop of Peoria, Jan. 23, 1990.

## N

**Nevins, John J.:** b. Jan. 19, 1932, New Rochelle, N.Y.; educ. Iona College (New Rochelle, N.Y.), Catholic Univ. (Washington, D.C.); ord. priest (Miami*) June 6, 1959; ord. titular bishop of Rusticana and auxiliary bishop of Miami, Mar. 24, 1979; app. first bishop of Venice, Fla., July 17, 1984; installed Oct. 25, 1984.

**Newman, William C.:** b. Aug. 16, 1928, Baltimore, Md.; educ. St. Mary Seminary (Baltimore, Md.), Catholic Univ. (Washington, D.C.), Loyola College (Baltimore, Md.); ord. priest (Baltimore*) May 29, 1954; ord. titular bishop of Numluli and auxiliary bishop of Baltimore, July 2, 1984.

**Neylon, Martin J., S.J.:** b. Feb. 13, 1920, Buffalo, N.Y.; ord. priest June 18, 1950; ord. titular bishop of Libertina and coadjutor vicar apostolic of the Caroline and Marshall Islands, Feb. 2, 1970; vicar apostolic of Caroline and Marshall Is., Sept. 20, 1971; first bishop of Carolines-Marshalls when vicariate apostolic was raised to diocese, 1979; title of see changed to Caroline Islands, Apr. 23, 1993; retired Mar. 25, 1995.

**Niederauer, George H.:** b. June 14, 1936, Ls Angeles, Calif.; educ. St. John's Seminary (Camarillo, Calif.), Catholic Univ. (Washington, D.C.), Loyola Univ. of Los Angeles, Univ. of Southern California, Loretta Heights College (Denver, Colo.); ord. priest (Los Angeles*) Apr. 30, 1962; app. bishop of Salt Lake City, Nov. 3, 1994, episcopal ordination Jan. 25, 1995.

**Niedergeses, James D.:** b. Feb. 2, 1917, Lawrenceburg, Tenn.; educ. St. Bernard College (St. Bernard, Ala.), St. Ambrose College (Davenport, Ia.), Mt. St. Mary Seminary of the West and Athenaeum (Cincinnati, Ohio); ord. priest (Nashville) May 20, 1944; ord. bishop of Nashville, May 20, 1975; retired Oct. 13, 1992.

**Nienstedt, John C.:** b. Mar.18, 1947, Detroit, Mich.; educ. Sacred Heart Seminary (Detroit), North American College, Gregorian Univ., Alphonsianum (Rome); ord. priest (Detroit*) July 27, 1974; served in Vatican Secretariat of State, 1980-86; rector of Sacred Heart Seminary (Detroit), 1988-94; pastor of the Shrine of the Little Flower (Royal Oak, Mich.), 1994; ord. titular bishop of Alton and auxiliary bishop of Detroit, July 9, 1996.

**Nolan, John G.:** b. Mar. 15, 1924, Mechanicville, N.Y.; educ. Siena College (Loudonville, N.Y.), St. Charles College (Catonsville, Md.), St. Mary's Seminary (Baltimore, Md.); Catholic Univ. (Washington, D.C.), Fordham Univ. (New York, N.Y.); ord. priest (Albany) June 11, 1949; ord. titular bishop of Natchez and auxiliary bishop of Military Services archdiocese Jan. 6, 1988.

**Nolker, Bernard, C.SS.R.:** b. Sept. 25, 1912, Baltimore, Md.; educ. St. Mary's College (North East, Pa.), St. Mary's College (Ilchester, Md.), Mt. St. Alphonsus Seminary (Esopus, N.Y.); ord. priest June 18, 1939; ord. first bishop of Paranagua, Brazil, Apr. 25, 1963; retired Mar. 14, 1989.

**Novak, Alfred, C.SS.R.:** b. June 2, 1930, Dwight, Nebr.; educ. Immaculate Conception Seminary (Oconomowoc, Wis.); ord. priest July 2, 1956; ord. titular bishop of Vardimissa and auxiliary bishop of Sao Paulo, Brazil, May 25, 1979; bishop of Paranagua, Brazil, Mar. 14, 1989.

## O

**O'Brien, Edwin F.:** b. Apr. 8, 1939, Bronx, N.Y.; educ. St. Joseph's Seminary (Yonkers, N.Y.), Angelicum (Rome); ord. priest (New York*) May 29, 1965; ord. titular bishop of Tizica and auxiliary bishop of New York, Mar. 25, 1996.

**O'Brien, Thomas Joseph:** b. Nov. 29, 1935, Indianapolis, Ind.; educ. St. Meinrad High School Seminary, St. Meinrad College Seminary (St. Meinrad, Ind.); ord. priest (Tucson) May 7, 1961; ord. bishop of Phoenix, Jan. 6, 1982.

**Ochoa, Armando:** b. Apr. 3, 1943, Oxnard, Calif.; educ. Ventura College (Ventura, Calif.), St. John's College and St. John's Seminary (Camarillo, Calif.); ord. priest (Los Angeles*) May 23, 1970; ord. titular bishop of Sitifi and auxiliary bishop of Los Angeles, Feb. 23, 1987; app. bishop of El Paso, Apr. 1, 1996; installed June 26, 1996.

**O'Connell, Anthony J.:** b. May 10, 1938, Lisheen, Co. Clare, Ireland; came to U.S. at the age of 20; educ. Mt. St. Joseph College (Cork, Ire.), Mungret College (Limerick, Ire.), Kenrick Seminary (St.

Louis, Mo.); ord. priest (Jefferson City) Mar. 30, 1963; ord. first bishop of Knoxville, Tenn., Sept. 8, 1988.

**O'Connor, John J.:** (See Cardinals, Biographies.)

**O'Donnell, Edward J.:** b. July 4, 1931, St. Louis, Mo.; educ. St. Louis Preparatory Seminary and Kenrick Seminary (St. Louis, Mo.); ord. priest (St. Louis*) Apr. 6, 1957; ord. titular bishop of Britania and auxiliary bishop of St. Louis Feb. 10, 1984; app. bishop of Lafayette, La., installed Dec. 16, 1994.

**O'Keefe, Gerald F.:** b. Mar. 30, 1918, St. Paul, Minn.; educ. College of St. Thomas, St. Paul Seminary (St. Paul, Minn.); ord. priest (St. Paul-Minneapolis*) Jan. 29, 1944; ord. titular bishop of Candyba and auxiliary bishop of St. Paul, July 2, 1961; bishop of Davenport, Oct. 20, 1966, installed Jan. 4, 1967; retired Nov. 12, 1993.

**O'Keefe, Joseph Thomas:** b. Mar. 12, 1919, New York, N.Y.; educ. Cathedral College (New York City), St. Joseph's Seminary (Yonkers, N.Y.), Catholic Univ. (Washington, DC.); ord. priest (New York*) Apr. 17, 1948; ord. titular bishop of Tre Taverne and auxiliary bishop of New York, Sept. 8, 1982; app. bishop of Syracuse, June 16, 1987, installed Aug. 3, 1987; retired Apr. 4, 1995.

**O'Leary, Edward C.:** b. Aug. 21, 1920, Bangor, Me.; educ. Holy Cross College (Worcester, Mass.), St. Paul's Seminary (Ottawa, Canada); ord. priest (Portland, Me.) June 15, 1946; ord. titular bishop of Moglena and auxiliary bishop of Portland, Me., Jan. 25, 1971; app. bishop of Portland, installed Dec. 18, 1974; retired Sept. 27, 1988.

**Olivier, Leonard J., S.V.D.:** b. Oct. 12, 1923, Lake Charles, La.; educ. St. Augustine Major Seminary (Bay St. Louis, Miss.), Catholic Univ. (Washington, D.C.), Loyola Univ. (New Orleans, La.); ord. priest June 29, 1951; ord. titular bishop of Leges in Numidia and auxiliary bishop of Washington, Dec. 20, 1988.

**O'Malley, Sean, O.F.M.Cap.:** b. June 29, 1944, Lakewood, O.; educ. St. Fidelis Seminary (Herman, Pa.), Capuchin College and Catholic Univ. (Washington, D.C.); ord. priest Aug. 29, 1970; episcopal vicar of priests serving Spanish speaking in Washington archdiocese, 1974-84; executive director of Spanish Catholic Center, Washington, from 1973; ord. coadjutor bishop of St. Thomas, Virgin Islands, Aug. 2, 1984; bishop of St. Thomas, Oct. 16, 1985; app. bishop of Fall River, June 16, 1992.

**O'Neil, Leo E.:** b. Jan. 31, 1928, Holyoke, Mass.; educ. Maryknoll Seminary (Maryknoll, N.Y.), St. Anselm's College (Manchester, N.H.), Grand Seminary (Montreal, Canada); ord. priest (Springfield, Mass.) June 4, 1955; ord. titular bishop of Bencenna and auxiliary bishop of Springfield, Mass., Aug. 22, 1980; app. coadjutor bishop of Manchester, Oct. 17, 1989; bishop of Manchester, June 12, 1990.

**O'Neill, Arthur J.:** b. Dec. 14, 1917, East Dubuque, Ill.; educ. Loras Collge (Dubuque, Ia.), St. Mary's Seminary (Baltimore, Md.); ord. priest (Rockford) Mar. 27, 1943; ord. bishop of Rockford, Oct. 11, 1968; retired Apr. 19, 1994.

**O'Rourke, Edward W.:** b. Oct. 31, 1917, Downs, Ill.; educ. St. Mary's Seminary (Mundelein, Ill.), Aquinas Institute of Philosophy and Theology (River Forest, Ill.); ord. priest (Peoria) May 28, 1944; ex-

ecutive director of National Catholic Rural Life Conference, 1960-71; ord. bishop of Peoria, July 15, 1971; retired Jan. 22, 1990.

**Ottenweller, Albert H.:** b. Apr. 5, 1916, Stanford, Mont.; educ. St. Joseph's Seminary (Rensselaer, Ind.), Catholic Univ. (Washington, D.C.); ord. priest (Toledo) June 19, 1943; ord. titular bishop of Perdices and auxiliary bishop of Toledo, May 29, 1974; app. bishop of Steubenville, Oct. 11, 1977, installed Nov. 22, 1977; retired Jan. 28, 1992.

## P

**Paschang, John L.:** b. Oct. 5, 1895, Hemingford, Nebr.; educ. Conception College (Conception, Mo.), St. John Seminary (Collegeville, Minn.), Catholic Univ. (Washington, D.C.); ord. priest (Omaha*) June 12, 1921; ord. bishop of Grand Island, Oct. 9, 1951; resigned July 25, 1972.

**Paska, Walter:** b. Nov. 29, 1923, Elizabeth, N.J.; educ. St. Charles Seminary (Catonsville, Md.), Catholic Univ. (Washington, D.C.), Fordham Univ. (New York); ord. priest (Philadelphia of Ukrainians*) June 2, 1947; ord. titular bishop of Tigilava and auxiliary of Ukrainian archdiocese of Philadelphia, Mar. 19, 1992.

**Pataki, Andrew:** b. Aug. 30, 1927, Palmerton,Pa.; educ. St. Vincent College (Latrobe, Pa.), St. Procopius College, St. Procopius Seminary (Lisle, Ill.), Sts. Cyril and Methodius Byzantine Catholic Seminary (Pittsburgh, Pa.), Gregorian Univ. and Oriental Pontifical Institute (Rome, Italy); ord. priest (Pittsburgh,* Ruthenian Byzantine) Feb. 24, 1952; ord. titular bishop of Telmisso and auxiliary bishop of Byzantine diocese of Passaic,Aug. 23, 1983; app. bishop of Ruthenian Byzantine diocese of Parma, July 3, 1984; app. bishop of Ruthenian Byzantine diocese of Passaic, Nov. 6, 1995; installed Feb. 8, 1996.

**Paul, John J.:** b. Aug. 17, 1918, La Crosse, Wis.; educ. Loras College (Dubuque, Iowa), St. Mary's Seminary (Baltimore, Md.), Marquette Univ. (Milwaukee, Wis.), ord. priest (Lincoln) Jan. 24, 1943; ord. titular bishop of Lambaesis and auxiliary bishop of La Crosse,Aug. 4, 1977; app. bishop of La Crosse, Oct. 18, 1983, installed Dec. 5, 1983; retired Dec. 10, 1994.

**Pearce, George H., S.M.:** b. Jan. 9, 1921, Brighton, Mass.; educ. Marist College and Seminary (Framington, Mass.); ord. priest Feb. 2, 1947; ord. titular bishop of Attalea in Pamphylia and vicar apostolic of the Samoa and Tokelau Islands, June 29, 1956; title changed to bishop of Apia, June 21, 1966; app. archbishop of Suva, Fiji Islands, June 22, 1967; resigned Apr. 10, 1976.

**Pelotte, Donald E., S.S.S.:** b. Apr. 13, 1945, Waterville, Me.; educ. Eymard Seminary and Junior College (Hyde Park, N.Y.), John Carroll Univ. (Cleveland, O.), Fordham Univ. (Bronx, N.Y.); ord. priest Sept. 2, 1972; ord. coadjutor bishop of Gallup, May 6, 1986 (first priest of Native American ancestry to be named U.S. bishop); bishop of Gallup, Mar. 20, 1990.

**Pena, Raymundo J.:** b. Feb. 19, 1934, Robstown, Tex.; educ. Assumption Seminary (San Antonio, Tex.); ord. priest (Corpus Christi) May 25, 1957; ord. titular bishop of Trisipa and auxiliary bishop of

San Antonio, Dec. 13, 1976; app. bishop of El Paso, Apr. 29, 1980; app. bishop of Brownsville, May 23, 1995.

**Pevec, A. Edward:** b. Apr. 16, 1925, Cleveland, O.; educ. St. Mary's Seminary, John Carroll Univ. (Cleveland, O.); ord. priest (Cleveland) Apr. 29, 1950; ord. titular bishop of Mercia and auxiliary bishop of Cleveland, July 2, 1982.

**Pfeifer, Michael, O.M.I.:** b. May 18, 1937,Alamo, Tex.; educ. Oblate school of theology (San Antonio, Tex.); ord. priest Dec. 21, 1964; provincial of southern province of Oblates of Mary Immaculate, 1981; ord. bishop of San Angelo, July 26, 1985.

**Pilarczyk, Daniel E.:** b. Aug. 12, 1934, Dayton, Ohio; educ. St. Gregory's Seminary (Cincinnati, O.), Urban Univ. (Rome), Xavier Univ. and Univ. of Cincinnati (Cincinnati, O.); ord. priest (Cincinnati*) Dec. 20, 1959; ord. titular bishop of Hodelm and auxiliary bishop of Cincinnati, Dec. 20, 1974; app. archbishop of Cincinnati, Oct. 30, 1982; installed Dec. 20, 1982. President of NCCB/USCC, 1989-92.

**Pilla, Anthony M.:** b. Nov. 12, 1932, Cleveland, O.; educ. St. Gregory College Seminary (Cincinnati, O.), Borromeo College Seminary (Wickliffe, O.), St. Mary Seminary and John Carroll Univ. (Cleveland, O.); ord. priest (Cleveland) May 23, 1959; ord. titular bishop of Scardona and auxiliary bishop of Cleveland, Aug. 1, 1979; app. apostolic administrator of Cleveland, 1980; bishop of Cleveland, Nov. 13, 1980. President of NCCB/USCC, 1995- .

**Popp, Bernard F.:** b. Dec. 6, 1917, Nada, Tex.; educ. St. John's Seminary and St. Mary's Univ. (San Antonio, Tex.); ord. priest (San Antonio*) Feb. 24, 1943; ord. titular bishop of Capsus and auxiliary bishop of San Antonio, July 25, 1983; retired Mar. 23, 1993.

**Potocnak, Joseph J., S.C.J.:** b. May 13, 1933, Berwick, Pa.; educ. Dehon Seminary (Great Barrington, Mass.), Kilroe Seminary (Honesdale, Pa.), Sacred Heart (Hales Corners, Wis.); ord. priest Sept 21, 1966; missionary in SouthAfrica from 1973; ord. bishop of De Aar, South Africa, May 1, 1992.

**Povish, Kenneth J.:** b. Apr. 19, 1924, Alpena, Mich.; educ. St. Joseph's Seminary (Grand Rapids, Mich.), Sacred Heart Seminary (Detroit, Mich.), Cathoic Univ. (Washington, D.C.); ord. priest (Saginaw) June 3, 1950; ord. bishop of Crookston, Sept. 29, 1970; app. bishop of Lansing, Oct. 8, 1975, installed Dec. 11, 1975; retired Nov. 7, 1995.

**Power, Cornelius M.:** b. Dec. 18, 1913, Seattle, Wash.; educ. St. Patrick's College (Menlo Park, Calif.), St. Edward's Seminary (Kenmore, Wash.), Catholic Univ. (Washington, D.C.); ord. priest (Seattle*) June 3, 1939; ord. bishop of Yakima, May 1, 1969, app. archbishop of Portland, Ore., Jan. 22, 1974, installed Apr. 17, 1974; retired July 1, 1986.

**Procyk, Judson M.:** b. Apr. 9, 1931, Greensburg, Pa.; educ. St. Procopius College (Lisle, Ill.), Duquesne University and Byzantine Seminary of Sts. Cyril and Methodius (Pittsburgh, Pa.), Casa Santa Maria (Rome); ord. priest (Pittsburgh*, Byzantine Ruthenian) May 19, 1957; ord. metropolitan archbishop of Byzantine archdiocese of Pittsburgh, Feb. 7, 1995.

**Pursley, Leo A.:** b. Mar. 12, 1902, Hartford City, Ind.; educ. Mt. St. Mary's Seminary (Cincinnati, O.);

ord. priest (Ft. Wayne-S. Bend) June 11, 1927; ord. titular bishop of Hadrianapolis in Pisidia and auxiliary bishop of Fort Wayne, Sept. 19, 1950; app. apostolic administrator of Fort Wayne, Mar. 9, 1955; installed as bishop of Fort Wayne, Feb. 26, 1957; title of see changed to Fort Wayne-South Bend, 1960; resigned Aug. 31, 1976.

**Puscas, Vasile Louis:** b. Sept. 13, 1915, Aurora, Ill.; educ. Quigley Preparatory Seminary (Chicago, Ill.), seminary in Oradea-Mare (Romania), Propaganda Fide Seminary (Rome), Illinois Benedictine College (Lisle, Ill.); ord. priest (Erie) May 14, 1942; ord. titular bishop of Leuce and first exarch of apostolic exarchate for Byzantine Romanians in the U.S., June 26, 1983 (seat of the exarchate, Canton, Ohio); app. first eparch, Apr. 11, 1987, when exarchate was raised to eparchy of St. George's in Canton; retired July 15, 1993.

## Q

**Quinn, Alexander James:** b. Apr. 8, 1932, Cleveland, O.; educ. St. Charles College (Catonsville, Md.), St. Mary Seminary (Cleveland, O.), Lateran Univ. (Rome), Cleveland State Univ.; ord. priest (Cleveland) May 24, 1958; ord. titular bishop of Socia and auxiliary bishop of Cleveland, Dec. 5, 1983.

**Quinn, Francis A.:** b. Sept. 11, 1921, Los Angeles, Calif.; educ. St. Joseph's College (Mountain View, Calif.), St. Patrick's Seminary (Menlo Park, Calif.), Catholic Univ. (Washington, D.C.); Univ. of California (Berkley); ord. priest (San Francisco*) June 15, 1946; ord. titular bishop of Numana and auxiliary bishop of San Francisco, June 29, 1978; app. bishop of Sacramento Dec. 18, 1979; retired Nov. 30, 1993.

**Quinn, John R.:** b. Mar. 28, 1929, Riverside, Calif.; educ. St. Francis Seminary (El Cajon, Calif.), North American College (Rome); ord. priest (San Diego) July 19, 1953; ord. titular bishop of Thisiduo and auxiliary bishop of San Diego, Dec. 12, 1967; bishop of Oklahoma City and Tulsa, Nov. 30, 1971; first archbishop of Oklahoma City, Dec. 19, 1972; app. archbishop of San Francisco Feb. 22, 1977, installed Apr. 26, 1977; president NCCB/USCC, 1977-80; resigned see Dec. 27, 1995.

## R

**Ramirez, Ricardo, C.S.B.:** b. Sept. 12, 1936, Bay City, Tex.; educ. Univ. of St. Thomas (Houston, Tex.), Univ. of Detroit (Detroit, Mich.), St. Basil's Seminary (Toronto, Ont.), Seminario Concilium (Mexico City, Mexico), East Asian Pastoral Institute (Manila, Philippines); ord. priest Dec. 10, 1966; ord titular bishop of Vatarba and auxiliary of San Antonio, Dec. 6, 1981; app. first bishop of Las Cruces, N. Mex., Aug. 17, 1982; installed Oct. 18, 1982.

**Raya, Joseph M.:** b. July 20, 1917, Zahle, Lebanon; educ. St. Louis College (Paris, France), St. Anne's Seminary (Jerusalem); ord. priest July 20, 1941; came to U.S., 1949, became U.S. citizen; ord. archbishop of Acre, Israel, of the Melkites, Oct. 20, 1968; resigned Aug. 20, 1974; assigned titular metropolitan see of Scytopolis (resides in Canada).

**Reichert, Stephen J., O.F.M. Cap.:** b. 1944,

Leoville, Kans.; educ. Capuchin minor seminary (Victoria, Kans.), St. Fidelis College (Hermann, Pa.), Capuchin College (Washington, D.C.); ord. priest 1969; missionary in Papua New Guinea since 1970; app. bishop of Mendi, Papua New Guinea, Feb. 22, 1995.

**Reilly, Daniel P.:** b. May 12, 1928, Providence, R.I.; educ. Our Lady of Providence Seminary (Warwick, R.I.), St. Brieuc Major Seminary (Cotes du Nord, France); ord. priest (Providence) May 30, 1953; ord. bishop of Norwich, Aug. 6, 1975; app. bishop of Worcester, Oct. 27, 1994, installed Nov. 8, 1994.

**Reiss, John C.:** b. May 13, 1922, Red Bank, N.J.; educ. Catholic Univ. (Washington, D.C.), Immaculate Conception Seminary (Darlington, N.J.); ord. priest (Trenton) May 31, 1947; ord. titular bishop of Simidicca and auxiliary bishop of Trenton, Dec. 12, 1967; app. bishop of Trenton, Mar. 11, 1980.

**Riashi, Georges, B.C.O.:** b. Nov. 25, 1933, Kaael-Rim, Lebanon; ord. priest Apr. 4, 1965; parish priest of Our Lady of Redemption Parish, Warren, Mich. (Newton Greek-Catholic Melkite eparchy); U.S. citizen; ord. first bishop of eparchy of St. Michael's of Sydney (Australia) for Greek-Catholic Melkites, July 19, 1987; app. archbishop of archeparchy of Tripoli of Lebanon for Greek-Melkites, Aug. 5, 1995.

**Ricard, John H., S.S.J.:** b. Feb. 29, 1940, Baton Rouge, La.; educ. St. Joseph's Seminary (Washington, D.C.), Tulane Univ. (New Orleans, La.); ord. priest May 25, 1968; ord. titular bishop of Rucuma and auxiliary of Baltimore, July 2, 1984; urban vicar, Baltimore.

**Rigali, Justin F.:** b. Apr. 19, 1935, Los Angeles, Calif.; educ. St. John's Seminary (Camarillo, Calif.); ord. priest (Los Angeles*) Apr. 25, 1961; in Vatican diplomatic service from 1964; ord. titular archbishop of Bolsena, Sept. 14, 1985, by Pope John Paul II; president of the Pontifical Ecclesiastical Academy, 1985-89; secretary of Congregation for Bishops, 1989-94, and the College of Cardinals, 1990-94; app. archbishop of St. Louis, Jan. 25, 1994, installed Mar. 16, 1994.

**Riley, Lawrence J.:** b. Sept. 6, 1914; Boston, Mass.; educ. Boston College and St. John's Seminary (Boston, Mass.), North American College and Gregorian Univ. (Rome), Catholic Univ. (Washington, D.C.); ord. priest (Boston*) Sept. 21, 1940; ord. titular bishop of Daimlaig and auxiliary bishop of Boston, Feb. 2, 1972; retired Jan. 22, 1990.

**Roach, John R.:** b. July 31, 1921, Prior Lake, Minn.; educ. St. Paul Seminary (St. Paul, Minn.), Univ. of Minnesota (Minneapolis); ord. priest (St. Paul and Minneapolis*) June 18, 1946; ord. titular bishop of Cenae and auxiliary bishop of St. Paul and Minneapolis, Sept. 8, 1971; app. archbishop of St. Paul and Minneapolis, May 28, 1975; president of NCCB/USCC, 1980-83; retired Sept 8, 1995.

**Rodimer, Frank J.:** b. Oct. 25, 1927, Rockaway, N.J.; educ. Seton Hall Prep (South Orange, N.J.), St. Charles College (Catonsville, Md.), St. Mary's Seminary (Baltimore, Md.), Immaculate Conception Seminary (Darlington, N.J.), Catholic Univ. (Washington, D.C.); ord. priest (Paterson) May 19, 1951; ord. bishop of Paterson, Feb. 28, 1978.

**Rodriguez, Migúel, C.SS.R.:** b. Apr. 18, 1931, Mayaguez, P.R.; educ. St. Mary's Minor Seminary (North East, Pa.), Mt. St. Alphonsus Major Seminary (Esopus, N.Y.); ord. priest June 22, 1958; ord. bishop of Arecibo, P.R., Mar. 23, 1974; resigned Mar. 20, 1990.

**Rodriguez, Placido, C.M.F.:** b. Oct. 11, 1940, Celaya, Guanajuato, Mexico; educ. Claretian Novitate (Los Angeles, Calif.), Claretville Seminary College (Calabasas, Calif.), Catholic Univ. (Washington, D.C.), Loyola Univ. (Chicago, Ill.); ord. priest May 23, 1968; ord. titular bishop of Fuerteventura and auxiliary bishop of Chicago, Dec. 13, 1983; app. bishop of Lubbock, Tex., Apr. 5, 1994.

**Roman, Agustin A.:** b. May 5, 1928, San Antonio de los Banos, Havana, Cuba; educ. San Alberto Magno Seminary (Matanzas, Cuba), Missions Etrangeres (Montreal, Canada), Barry College (Miami, Fla.); ord. priest July 5, 1959, Cuba; vicar for Spanish speaking in Miami archdiocese, 1976; ord. titular bishop of Sertei and auxiliary bishop of Miami, Mar. 24, 1979.

**Roque, Francis X.:** b. Oct. 9, 1928, Providence R.I.; educ. St. John's Seminary (Brighton, Mass.); ord. priest (Providence) Sept. 19, 1953; became chaplain in U.S. Army 1961; ord. titular bishop of Bagai and auxiliary bishop of Military Services archdiocese, May 10, 1983.

**Rosazza, Peter Anthony:** b. Feb. 13, 1935, New Haven, Conn.; educ. St. Thomas Seminary (Bloomfield, Conn.), Dartmouth College (Hanover, N.H.), St. Bernard's Seminary (Rochester, N.Y.), St. Sulpice (Issy, France); ord. priest (Hartford*) June 29, 1961; ord. titular bishop of Oppido Nuovo and auxiliary bishop of Hartford, June 24, 1978.

**Rose, Robert John:** b. Feb. 28, 1930, Grand Rapids, Mich.; educ. St. Joseph's Seminary (Grand Rapids, Mich.), Seminaire de Philosophie (Montreal, Canada), Urban University (Rome), Univ. of Michigan (Ann Arbor); ord. priest (Grand Rapids) Dec. 21, 1955; ord. bishop of Gaylord, Dec. 6, 1981; app. bishop of Grand Rapids, installed Aug. 30, 1989.

**Rueger, George E.:** b. Sept. 3, 1933, Framingham, Mass; educ. Holy Cross College (Worcester, Mass.), St. John's Seminary (Brighton), Harvard University (Cambridge, Mass.); ord. priest (Worcester), Jan. 6, 1958; ord. titular bishop of Maronana and auxiliary bishop of Worcester, Feb. 25, 1987.

**Ryan, Daniel L.:** b. Sept. 28, 1930, Mankato, Minn.; educ. St. Procopius Seminary (Lisle, Ill.), Lateran Univ. (Rome); ord. priest (Joliet) May 3, 1956; ord. titular bishop of Surista and auxiliary bishop of Joliet, Sept. 30, 1981; app. bishop of Springfield, Ill., Nov. 22, 1983, installed Jan. 18, 1984.

**Ryan, James C., O.F.M.:** b. Nov. 17, 1912, Chicago, Ill.; educ. St. Joseph's Seraphic Seminary (Westmont, Ill.), Our Lady of the Angels Seminary (Cleveland, O.); ord. priest June 24, 1938; ord. titular bishop of Margo and prelate of Santarem, Brazil, April 9, 1958; first bishop of Santarem, Dec. 4, 1979; retired Nov. 27, 1985.

**Ryan, Joseph T.:** b. Nov. 1, 1913,Albany, N.Y.; educ. Manhattan College (New York City); ord. priest (Albany) June 3, 1939; national secretary of Catholic Near East Welfare Assn. 1960-65; ord. first archbishop of Anchorage, Alaska, Mar. 25, 1966; app. titular archbishop of Gabi and coadjutor archbishop of the military ordinariate, Oct. 24, 1975; app. military vicar of U.S. military archdiocese, Mar. 16, 1985; resigned May 14, 1991.

**Ryan, Sylvester D.:** b. Mar. 3, 1930, Catalina Is. Calif.; educ. St. John's Seminary (Camarillo, Calif.); ord. priest (Los Angeles*) May 3, 1957; ord. titular bishop of Remesiana and auxiliary bishop of Los Angeles, May 31, 1990; app. bishop of Monterey, Jan. 28, 1992.

## S

**Salatka, Charles A.:** b. Feb. 26, 1918, Grand Rapids, Mich.; educ. St. Joseph's Seminary (Grand Rapids, Mich.), Catholic Univ. (Washington, D.C.), Lateran Univ. (Rome); ord. priest (Grand Rapids) Feb. 24, 1945; ord. titular bishop of Cariana and auxiliary bishop of Grand Rapids, Mich., Mar. 6, 1962; app. bishop of Marquette, installed Mar. 25, 1968; app. archbishop of Oklahoma City, Sept. 27, 1977; retired Nov. 24, 1992.

**Saltarelli, Michael A.:** b. Jan. 17, 1932, Jersey City, N.J.; educ. Seton Hall College and Immaculate Conception Seminary (S. Orange, N.J.); ord. priest (Newark*), May 28, 1960; ord. titular bishop of Mesarfelta and auxiliary bishop of Newark, July 30, 1990; app. Bishop of Wilmington, Nov. 21, 1995; installed Jan. 23, 1996.

**Samra, Nicholas J.:** b. Aug. 15, 1944, Paterson, N.J.; educ. St. Anselm College (Manchester, N.H.), St. Basil Seminary (Methuen, Mass.), St. John Seminary (Brighton, Mass.); ord. priest (Newton) May 10, 1970; ord. titular bishop of Gerasa and auxiliary bishop of Melkite diocese of Newton, July 6, 1989.

**Sanchez, Robert F.:** b. Mar. 20, 1934, Socorro, N.M.; educ. Immaculate Heart Seminary (Santa Fe, N.M.), Gregorian Univ. (Rome), Catholic Univ. (Washington, D.C.); ord. priest (Santa Fe*) Dec. 20, 1959; ord. archbishop of Santa Fe, N.M., July 25, 1974; resigned Apr. 6, 1993.

**Sartoris, Joseph M.:** b. July 1, 1927, Los Angeles, Calif.; educ. St. John's Seminary (Camarillo, Calif.); ord. priest (Los Angeles*) May 30, 1953; ord. titular bishop of Oliva and auxiliary bishop of Los Angeles, Mar. 19, 1994. San Pedro regional bishop.

**Scanlan, John J.:** b. May 24, 1906, County Cork, Ireland; educ. National Univ. of Ireland (Dublin), All Hallows College (Dublin); ord. priest (San Francisco*) June 22, 1930; U.S. citizen 1938; ord. titular bishop of Cenae and auxiliary bishop of Honolulu, Sept. 21, 1954; bishop of Honolulu, installed May 1, 1968; retired June 30, 1981.

**Scarpone Caporale, Gerald, O.F.M.:** b. Oct. 1, 1928, Watertown, Mass.; ord. priest June 24, 1956; ord. coadjutor bishop of Comayagua, Honduras, Feb. 21, 1979; succeeded as bishop of Comayagua, May 30, 1979.

**Schad, James L.:** b. July 20, 1917, Philadelphia, Pa.; educ. St. Mary's Seminary (Baltimore, Md.); ord. priest (Camden) Apr. 10, 1943; ord. titular bishop of Panatoria and auxiliary bishop of Camden, Dec. 8, 1966; retired Jan 26, 1993.

**Schlarman, Stanley Gerard:** b. July 27, 1933, Belleville, Ill.; educ. St. Henry Prep Seminary (Belleville, Ill.), Gregorian Univ. (Rome), St. Louis Univ. (St. Louis, Mo.); ord. priest (Belleville) July 13, 1958, Rome; ord. titular bishop of Capri and auxiliary bishop of Belleville, May 14, 1979; app. bishop of Dodge City, Mar. 1, 1983.

**Schleck, Charles A., C.S.C.:** b. July 5, 1925, Milwaukee, Wis.; educ. Univ. of Notre Dame (Indiana), Univ. of St. Thomas (Rome); ord. priest Dec. 22, 1951; ord. titular archbishop of Africa (Mehdia), Apr. 1, 1995; adjunct secretary of Congregation for Evangelization of Peoples; president of the superior council of the Pontifical Mission Societies.

**Schmidt, Firmin M., O.F.M. Cap.:** b. Oct. 12, 1918, Catherine, Kans.; educ. Catholic Univ. (Washington, D.C.); ord. priest June 2, 1946; app. prefect apostolic of Mendi, Papua New Guinea, Apr. 3, 1959; ord. titular bishop of Conana and first vicar apostolic of Mendi, Dec.15, 1965; became first bishop of Mendi when vicariate apostolic was raised to a diocese, Nov. 15, 1966; retired Feb. 22, 1995.

**Schmitt, Bernard W.:** b. Aug. 17, 1928, Wheeling, W. Va.; educ. St. Joseph College (Catonsville, Md.), St. Mary's Seminary (Baltimore), Ohio Univ. (Athens, O.); ord. priest (Wheeling-Charleston) May 28, 1955; ord. titular bishop of Walla Walla and bishop of Wheeling-Charleston, Aug. 1, 1988; bishop of Wheeling-Charleston, Mar. 29, 1989.

**Schmitt, Mark F.:** b. Feb. 14, 1923, Algoma, Wis.; educ. Salvatorian Seminary (St. Nazianz, Wis.), St. John's Seminary (Collegeville, Minn.); ord. priest (Green Bay) May 22, 1948; ord. titular bishop of Ceanannus Mor and auxiliary bishop of Green Bay, June 24, 1970; app. bishop of Marquette, Mar. 21, 1978, installed May 8, 1978; retired Oct. 6, 1992.

**Schmitz Simon, Paul, O.F.M. Cap.:** b. Dec. 4, 1943, Fond du Lac, Wis.; ord. priest Sept. 3, 1970; missionary in Nicaragua from 1970; superior of vice province of Capuchins in Central America (headquartered in Managua), 1982-84; ord. titular bishop of Elepla and auxiliary of the vicariate apostolic of Bluefields, Nicaragua, Sept. 17, 1984; app. bishop of vicariate apostolic of Bluefields, Aug. 17, 1994.

**Schoenherr, Walter J.:** b. Feb. 28, 1920, Detroit, Mich.; educ. Sacred Heart Seminary (Detroit, Mich.), Mt. St. Mary Seminary (Norwood, O.); ord. priest (Detroit*) Oct. 27, 1945; ord. titular bishop of Timidana and auxiliary bishop of Detroit, May 1, 1968; retired Mar. 7, 1995.

**Schott, Basil, O.F.M.:** b. July 21, 1939, Freeland, Pa.; entered Byzantine Franciscans, professed Aug. 4, 1959; educ. Immaculate Conception College (Troy, N.Y.), St. Mary's Seminary (Norwalk, Conn.) and Post Graduate Center (New York, N.Y.); ord. priest Aug. 29, 1965; app. bishop of Byzantine eparchy of Parma, May 2, 1996.

**Schulte, Francis B.:** b. Dec. 23, 1926, Philadelphia, Pa.; educ. St. Charles Borromeo Seminary (Overbrook, Pa.); ord. priest (Philadelphia*) May 10, 1952; ord. titular bishop of Afufenia and auxiliary bishop of Philadelphia, Aug. 12, 1981; app. bishop of Wheeling-Charleston, June 4, 1985; archbishop of New Orleans, Dec. 6, 1988, installed Feb. 14, 1989.

**Schuster, Eldon B.:** b. Mar. 10, 1911, Calio, N. Dak.; educ. Loras College (Dubuque, Ia.), Catholic Univ. (Washington, D.C.), Oxford Univ. (England),

St. Louis Univ. (St. Louis, Mo.); ord. priest (Great Falls) May 27, 1937; ord. titular bishop of Amblada and auxiliary bishop of Great Falls, Mont., Dec. 21, 1961; app. bishop of Great Falls, Dec. 2, 1967, installed Jan. 23, 1968; resigned Dec. 28, 1977.

**Schwietz, Roger L., O.M.I.:** b. July 3, 1940, St. Paul, Minn.; educ. Univ. of Ottawa (Canada), Gregorian Univ. (Rome); ord. priest Dec. 20, 1967; ord. bishop of Duluth Feb. 2, 1990.

**Setian, Nerses Mikail:** b. Oct. 18,1918, Sebaste, Turkey; educ. Armenian Pontifical College and Gregorian Univ. (Rome); ord. priest Apr. 13, 1941, in Rome; ord. titular bishop of Ancira of the Armenians and first exarch of the apostolic exarchate for Armenian Catholics in Canada and the United States (see city New York), Dec. 5, 1981; retired Nov. 24, 1993.

**Sevilla, Carlos A., S.J.:** b. Aug. 9, 1935, San Francisco, Calif.; entered Jesuits Aug. 14, 1953; educ. Gonzaga Univ. (Spokane, Wash.), Santa Clara Uiv. (Santa Clara, Calif.), Jesuitenkolleg (Innsbruck, Austria), Catholic Institute of Paris (France); ord. priest June 3, 1966; ord. titular bishop of Mina and auxiliary bishop of San Francisco, Jan. 25, 1989.

**Sheehan, Daniel E.:** b. May 14, 1917, Emerson, Nebr.; educ. Creighton Univ. (Omaha, Nebr.), Kenrick Seminary (Webster Groves, Mo.), Catholic Univ. (Washington, D.C.): ord. priest (Omaha*) May 23, 1942; ord. titular bishop of Capsus and auxiliary bishop of Omaha, Mar. 19, 1964; app. archbishop of Omaha, installed Aug. 11, 1969; retired May 4, 1993.

**Sheehan, Michael J.:** b. July 9, 1939, Wichita, Kans.; educ. Assumption Seminary (San Antonio, Tex.), Gregorian Univ. and Lateran Univ. (Rome); ord. priest (Dallas) July 12, 1964; ord. first bishop of Lubbock, Tex., June 17, 1983; apostolic administrator of Santa Fe, Apr. 6, 1993; app. archbishop of Santa Fe, Aug. 17, 1993.

**Sheets, John R., S.J.:** b. Sept. 21, 1922, Omaha, Neb.; joined Jesuits, 1940; educ. St. Louis Univ. (St. Louis, Mo.), St. Mary's College (St. Mary's, Kans.), Univ. of Innsbruck (Austria); ord. priest June 17, 1953; final profession of vows as Jesuit, Aug. 15, 1957; ord. titular bishop of Murcona and auxiliary bishop of Fort Wayne-South Bend, Ind., June 25, 1991.

**Sheldon, Gilbert I.:** b. Sept. 20, 1926, Cleveland, O.; educ. John Carroll Univ. and St. Mary Seminary (Cleveland, O.); ord. priest (Cleveland) Feb. 28, 1953; ord. titular bishop of Taparura and auxiliary bishop of Cleveland, June 11, 1976; app. bishop of Steubenville, Jan. 28, 1992.

**Sheridan, Patrick J.:** b. Mar. 10, 1922, New York, N.Y.; educ. St. Joseph's Seminary (Yonkers, N.Y.), University of Chicago; ord. priest (New York*) Mar. 1, 1947; ord. titular bishop of Curzola and auxiliary bishop of New York, Dec. 12, 1990.

**Sklba, Richard J.:** b. Sept. 11, 1935, Racine, Wis.; educ. Old St. Francis Minor Seminary (Milwaukee, Wis.), North American College, Gregorian Univ., Pontifical Biblical Institute, Angelicum (Rome); ord. priest (Milwaukee*) Dec. 20, 1959; ord. titular bishop of Castra and auxiliary bishop of Milwaukee, Dec. 19, 1979.

**Skylstad, William S.:** b. Mar. 2, 1934, Omak,

Wash.; educ. Pontifical College Josephinum (Worthington, Ohio), Washington State Univ. (Pullman, Wash.), Gonzaga Univ. (Spokane, Wash.); ord. priest (Spokane) May 21, 1960; ord. bishop of Yakima, May 12, 1977; app. bishop of Spokane, Apr. 17, 1990.

**Slattery, Edward J.:** b. Aug. 11, 1940, Chicago, Ill.; educ. Quigley Preparatory, St. Mary of the Lake Seminary (Mundelein, Ill.), Loyola Univ. (Chicago); ord. priest (Chicago*) Apr. 26, 1966; vice president, 1971-76, and president, 1976-94, of the Catholic Church Extension Society; ord. bishop of Tulsa, Jan. 6, 1994.

**Smith, John M.:** b. June 23, 1935, Orange, N.J.; educ. Immaculate Conception Seminary (Darlington, N.J.), Seton Hall Univ. (South Orange, N.J.), Catholic Univ. (Washington, D.C.); ord. priest (Newark*) May 27, 1961; ord. titular bishop of Tre Taverne and auxiliary bishop of Newark, Jan. 25, 1988; app. bishop of Pensacola-Tallahassee, Fla., June 25, 1991; app. coadjutor bishop of Trenton, Nov. 21, 1995.

**Smith, Philip F., O.M.I.:** b. Oct. 16, 1924, Lowell, Mass.; ord. priest Oct. 29, 1950; ord. titular bishop of Lamfua and vicar apostolic of Jolo, Philippine Islands, Sept. 8, 1972; app. coadjutor archbishop of Cotabato, Philippines, Apr. 11, 1979; archbishop of Cotabato, Mar. 14, 1980.

**Snyder, John J.:** b. Oct. 25, 1925, New York, N.Y.; educ. Cathedral College (Brooklyn, N.Y.), Immaculate Conception Seminary (Huntington, N.Y.); ord. priest (Brooklyn) June 9, 1951; ord. titular bishop of Forlimpopli and auxiliary bishop of Brooklyn, Feb. 2, 1973; app. bishop of St. Augustine, installed Dec. 5, 1979.

**Soens, Lawrence D.:** b. Aug. 26, 1926, Iowa City, Ia.; educ. Loras College (Dubuque, Ia.), St. Ambrose College (Davenport, Ia.), Kenrick Seminary (St. Louis, Mo.), Univ. of Iowa; ord. pries (Davenport) May 6, 1950; ord. bishop of Sioux City, Aug. 17, 1983.

**Sowada, Alphonse A., O.S.C.:** b. June 23, 1933, Avon, Minn.; educ. Holy Cross Scholasticate (Fort Wayne, Ind.), Catholic Univ. (Washington, D.C.), ord. priest May 31, 1958; missionary in Indonesia from 1958; ord. bishop of Agats, Indonesia, Nov. 23, 1969.

**Speltz, George H.:** b. May 29, 1912, Altura, Minn.; educ. St. Mary's College, St. Paul's Seminary (St. Paul, Minn.), Catholic Univ. (Washington, D.C.); ord. priest (St. Cloud) June 2, 1940; ord. titular bishop of Claneus and auxiliary bishop of Winona, Mar. 25, 1963; app. coadjutor bishop of St. Cloud, Apr. 4, 1966; bishop of St. Cloud, Jan. 31, 1968; retired Jan. 13, 1987.

**Speyrer, Jude:** b. Apr. 14, 1929, Leonville, La.; educ. St. Joseph Seminary (Covington, La.), Notre Dame Seminary (New Orleans, La.), Gregorian Univ. (Rome), Univ. of Fribourg (Switzerland); ord. priest (Lafayette, La.) July 25, 1953; ord. first bishop of Lake Charles, La., Apr. 25, 1980.

**Stafford, James Francis:** b. July 26, 1932, Baltimore, Md.; educ. St. Mary's Seminary (Baltimore, Md.), North American College and Gregorian Univ. (Rome); ord. priest (Baltimore*) Dec. 15, 1957; ord. titular bishop of Respecta and auxiliary bishop of Baltimore, Feb. 29, 1976; app. bishop of Memphis,

Nov. 17, 1982; app. archbishop of Denver, June 3, 1986, installed July 30, 1986; app. President of Pontifical Council of the Laity, Aug. 20, 1996.

**Steib, J. (James) Terry, S.V.D.:** b. May 17, 1940, Vacherie, La.; educ. Divine Word seminaries (Bay St. Louis, Miss., Conesus, N.Y., Techny, Ill.), Xavier Univ. (New Orleans, La.); ord. priest Jan. 6, 1967; ord. titular bishop of Fallaba and auxiliary bishop of St. Louis, Feb. 10, 1984; app. bishop of Memphis, Mar. 24, 1993.

**Steinbock, John T.:** b. July 16, 1937, Los Angeles, Calif.; educ. Los Angeles archdiocesan seminaries; ord. priest (Los Angeles*) May 1, 1963; ord. titular bishop of Midila and auxiliary bishop of Orange, Calif., July 14, 1984; app. bishop of Santa Rosa, Jan. 27, 1987; app. bishop of Fresno, Oct. 15, 1991.

**Steiner, Kenneth Donald:** b. Nov. 25, 1936, David City, Nebr.; educ. Mt.Angel Seminary (St. Benedict, Ore), St. Thomas Seminary (Seattle, Wash); ord. priest (Portland,* Ore.) May 19, 1962; ord. titular bishop of Avensa and auxiliary bishop of Portland, Ore., Mar. 2, 1978.

**Straling, Phillip F.:** b. Apr. 25, 1933, San Bernardino, Calif.; educ. Immaculate Heart Seminary, St. Francis Seminary, Univ. of San Diego and San Diego State University (San Diego, Calif.), North American College (Rome); ord. priest (San Diego) Mar. 19, 1959; ord. first bishop of San Bernardino, Nov. 6, 1978; app. first bishop of Reno, Mar. 21, 1995, when Reno-Las Vegas diocese was made two separate dioceses.

**Strecker, Ignatius J.:** b. Nov. 23, 1917, Spearville, Kans.; educ. St. Benedict's College (Atchison, Kans.), Kenrick Seminary (Webster Groves, Mo.), Catholic Univ. (Washington, D.C.); ord. priest (Wichita) Dec. 19, 1942; ord. bishop of Springfield-Cape Girardeau, Mo., June 20, 1962; archbishop of Kansas City, Kans., Oct. 28, 1969; retired June 28, 1993.

**Sullivan, James S.:** b. July 23, 1929, Kalamazoo, Mich.; educ. Sacred Heart Seminary (Detroit, Mich.), St. John Provincial Seminary (Plymouth, Mich.); ord. priest (Lansing) June 4, 1955; ord. titular bishop of Siccessi and auxiliary bishop of Lansing, Sept. 21, 1972; app. bishop of Fargo, Apr. 2, 1985; installed May 30, 1985.

**Sullivan, John J.:** b. July 5, 1920, Horton, Kans.; educ. Kenrick Seminary (St. Louis, Mo.); ord. priest (Oklahoma City*) Sept. 23, 1944; vice-president of Catholic Church Extension Society and national director of Extension Lay Volunteers, 1961-68; ord. bishop of Grand Island, Sept. 19, 1972; app. bishop of Kansas City-St. Joseph, June 27, 1977, installed Aug. 17, 1977; retired June 22, 1993.

**Sullivan, Joseph M.:** b. Mar. 23, 1930, Brooklyn, N.Y.; educ. Immaculate Conception Seminar (Huntington, N.Y.), Fordham Univ. (New York); ord. priest (Brooklyn) June 2, 1956; ord. titular bishop of Suliana and auxiliary bishop of Brooklyn, Nov. 24, 1980.

**Sullivan, Walter F.:** b. June 10, 1928, Washington, D.C.; educ. St. Mary's Seminary (Baltimore, Md.), Catholic Univ. (Washington, D.C.); ord. priest (Richmond) May 9, 1953; ord. titular bishop of Selsea and auxiliary bishop of Richmond, Va., Dec. 1, 1970; app. bishop of Richmond, June 4, 1974.

**Sulyk, Stephen:** b. Oct. 2, 1924, Balnycia, Western Ukraine; migrated to U.S. 1948; educ. Ukrainian Catholic Seminary of the Holy Spirit (Hirschberg, Germany), St. Josaphat's Seminary and Catholic Univ. (Washington, D.C.); ord. priest (Philadelphia,* Byzantine) June 14, 1952; ord. archbishop of the Ukrainian archeparchy of Philadelphia, Mar. 1, 1981.

**Symons, J. Keith:** b. Oct. 14, 1932, Champion, Mich.; educ. St. Thomas Seminary (Bloomfield, Conn.), St. Mary Seminary (Baltimore, Md.); ord. priest (St. Augustine) May 18, 1958; ord. titular bishop of Siguitanus and auxiliary bishop of St. Petersburg, Mar. 19, 1981; app. bishop of Pensacola-Tallahassee, Oct. 4, 1983, installed Nov. 8, 1983; app. bishop of Palm Beach, June 12, 1990.

**Szoka, Edmund C.:** (See Cardinals, Biographies.)

**T**

**Tafoya, Arthur N.:** b. Mar. 2, 1933, Alameda, N.M.; educ. St. Thomas Seminary (Denver, Colo.), Conception Seminary (Conception, Mo.); ord. priest (Santa Fe*) May 12, 1962; ord. bishop of Pueblo, Sept. 10, 1980.

**Tamayo, James A.:** b. Oct. 23, 1949, Brownsville, Tex.; educ. Del Mar College (Corpus Christi, Tex.), Univ. of St. Thomas and Univ. of St. Thomas School of Theology (Houston); ord. priest (Corpus Christi) June 11, 1976; ord. titular bishop of Ita and auxiliary bishop of Galveston-Houston, Mar. 10, 1993. Episcopal vicar for Hispanics.

**Tawil, Joseph:** b. Dec. 25, 1913, Damascus, Syria; ord. priest July 20, 1936; ord. titular archbishop of Mira and patriarchal vicar for eparchy of Damascus of the Patriarchate of Antioch for the Melkites, Jan. 1, 1960; apostolic exarch for Melkite Catholics in the U.S., Oct. 31, 1969; app. first eparch with personal title of archbishop when exarchate was raised to eparchy, July 15, 1976; title of see changed to Newton, 1977; retired Dec. 2, 1989.

**Tertzakian, Hovhannes, O.M.Ven.:** b. Jan. 3, 1924, Aleppo, Syria; educ. Mekhitarist Monastery of St. Lazarus (Venice, Italy); Gregorian Univ. (Rome); entered Mekhitarist Order of Venice, 1938, final vows Oct. 24, 1945; ord. priest Sept. 8, 1948; came to U.S., 1984; ord. titular bishop of Trebizond for Armenians and apostolic exarch for Armenian Catholics in the United States and Canada, Apr. 29, 1995.

**Thomas, Elliott G.:** b. July 15, 1926, Pittsburgh, Pa.; educ. Howard Univ. (Washington, D.C.), Gannon Univ. (Erie, Pa.), St. Vincent de Paul Seminary (Boynton Beach, Fla.); ord. priest (St. Thomas, Virgin Islands) June 6, 1986; ord. bishop of St. Thomas in the Virgin Islands, Dec. 12, 1993.

**Thompson, David B.:** b. May 29, 1923, Philadelphia, Pa.; educ. St. Charles Seminary (Overbrook, Pa.), Catholic Univ. (Washington, D.C.); ord. priest (Philadelphia*) May 27, 1950; ord. coadjutor bishop of Charleston, May 24, 1989; bishop of Charleston, Feb. 22, 1990.

**Timlin, James C.:** b. Aug. 5, 1927, Scranton, Pa.; educ. St. Charles College (Catonville, Md.), St. Mary's Seminary (Baltimore, Md.), North American College (Rome); ord. priest (Scranton) July 16, 1951; ord. titular bishop of Gunugo and auxiliary bishop of Scranton, Sept. 21, 1976; app. bishop of Scranton, Apr. 24, 1984.

**Tobin, Thomas J.:** b. Apr. 1, 1948, Pittsburgh, Pa.; educ. St. Mark Seminary High School, Gannon Univ. (Erie, Pa.), St. Francis College (Loretto, Pa.), North American College (Rome); ord. priest (Pittsburgh) July 21, 1973; ord. titular bishop of Novica and auxiliary bishop of Pittsburgh, Dec. 27, 1992; app. bishop of Youngstown Dec. 5, 1995; installed Feb. 2, 1996.

**Trautman, Donald W.:** b. June 24, 1936, Buffalo, N.Y.; educ. Our Lady of Angels Seminary (Niagara Falls, N.Y.), Theology Faculty (Innsbruck, Austria), Pontifical Biblical Institute (Rome), Catholic Univ. (Washington, D.C.); ord. priest (Buffalo) Apr. 7, 1962, in Innsbruck; ord. titular bishop of Sassura and auxiliary of Buffalo, Apr. 16, 1985; app. bishop of Erie, June 12, 1990.

**Treinen, Sylvester:** b. Nov. 19, 1917, Donnelly, Minn.; educ. Crosier Seminary (Onamia, Minn.), St. Paul Seminary (St. Paul, Minn.); ord. priest (Bismarck) June 11, 1946; ord. bishop of Boise, July 25, 1962; resigned Aug. 17, 1988.

**Tschoepe, Thomas:** b. Dec. 17, 1915, Pilot Point, Tex.; educ. Pontifical College Josephinum (Worthington, O.); ord. priest (Dallas) May 30, 1943; ord. bishop of San Angelo, Tex., Mar. 9, 1966; app. bishop of Dallas, Tex., Aug. 27, 1969; retired July 14, 1990.

## U-V

**Untener, Kenneth E.:** b. Aug. 3, 1937, Detroit, Mich.; educ. Sacred Heart Seminary (Detroit, Mich.), St. John's Provincial Seminary (Plymouth, Mich.), Gregorian Univ. (Rome); ord. priest (Detroit*) June 1, 1963; ord. bishop of Saginaw, Nov. 24, 1980.

**Valero, RenéA.:** b. Aug. 15, 1930, New York, N.Y.; educ. Cathedral College, Immaculate Conception Seminary (Huntington, N.Y.), Fordham Univ. (New York); ord. priest (Brooklyn) June 2, 1956; ord. titular bishop of Turris Vicus and auxiliary bishop of Brooklyn, Nov. 24, 1980.

**Vaughan, Austin B.:** b. Sept. 27, 1927, New York, N.Y.; educ. North American College and Gregorian Univ. (Rome), ord. priest (New York*) Dec. 8, 1951; pres. Catholic Theological Society of America, 1967; rector of St. Joseph's Seminary (Dunwoodie, N.Y.), 1973; ord. titular bishop of Cluain Iraird and auxiliary bishop of New York, June 29, 1977.

**Veigle, Adrian J.M., T.O.R.:** b. Sept. 15, 1912, Lilly, Pa.; educ. St. Francis College (Loretto, Pa.), Pennsylvania State College; ord. priest May 22, 1937; ord. titular bishop of Gigthi June 9, 1966 (resigned titular see May 26, 1978); prelate of Borba, Brazil, 1966; retired July 6, 1988.

**Vigernon, Allen H.:** b. Oct. 21, 1948, Detroit, Mich.; educ. Sacred Heart Seminary (Detroit, Mich.), North American College, Gregorian Univ. (Rome) Catholic Univ.(Washington, DC); ord. priest (Detroit*) July 26, 1975; served in Vatican Secretariat of State, 1991-94; rector of Sacred Heart Seminary (Detroit), 1994; ord. titular bishop of Sault Sainte Marie and auxiliary bishop of Detroit, July 9, 1996.

**Vlazny, John G.:** b. Feb. 22, 1937, Chicago, Ill.; educ. Quigley Preparatory Seminary (Chicago, Ill.), St. Mary of the Lake Seminary (Mundelein, Ill.),

Gregorian Univ. (Rome), Univ. of Michigan, Loyola Univ. (Chicago, Ill.); ord. priest (Chicago*) Dec. 20, 1961; ord. titular bishop of Stagno and auxiliary bishop of Chicago, Dec. 13, 1983; app. bishop of Winona, Minn., May 19, 1987.

## W

**Walsh, Daniel Francis:** b. Oct. 2, 1937, San Francisco, Calif.; educ. St. Joseph Seminary (Mountain View, Calif.), St. Patrick Seminary (Menlo Park, Calif.) Catholic Univ. (Washington, D.C.); ord. priest (San Francisco*) Mar. 30, 1963; ord. titular bishop of Tigia and auxiliary bishop of San Francisco, Sept. 24, 1981; app. bishop of Reno-Las Vegas, June 9, 1987; app. first bishop of Las Vegas Mar. 21, 1995, when the Reno-Las Vegas diocese was made two separate dioceses.

**Walsh, Nicolas E.:** b. Oct. 20, 1916, Burnsville, Minn.; educ. St. Paul Seminary (St. Paul, Minn.), Catholic Univ. (Washington, D.C.), Pontifical Palafoxianum Seminary (Puebla, Mexico), Register College of Journalism (Denver, Colo.); ord. priest (Boise) June 6, 1942; first editor of *Idaho Register;* diocesan vicar for Mexican Americans; ord. bishop of Yakima, Oct. 28, 1974; app. titular bishop of Bolsena and auxiliary bishop of Seattle, Aug. 10, 1976; retired Sept. 6, 1983. Bishop emeritus of Yakima.

**Ward, John J.:** b. Sept. 28, 1920, Los Angeles, Calif.; educ. St. John's Seminary (Camarillo, Calif.), Catholic Univ. (Washington, D.C.); ord. priest (Los Angeles*) May 4, 1946; ord. titular bishop of Bria and auxiliary of Los Angeles, Dec. 12, 1963; retired May 7, 1996; titular bishop of California.

**Watters, Loras J.:** b. Oct. 14, 1915, Dubuque, Ia.; educ. Loras College (Dubuque, Ia.), Gregorian Univ. (Rome), Catholic Univ. (Washington, D.C.); ord. priest (Dubuque*) June 7, 1941; ord. titular bishop of Fidoloma and auxiliary bishop of Dubuque, Aug. 26, 1965; bishop of Winona, installed Mar. 13, 1969; retired Oct. 14, 1986.

**Watty Urquidi, Ricardo, M.Sp.S.:** b. July 16, 1938, San Diego, Calif.; ord. priest June 8, 1968; ord. titular bishop of Macomedes and auxiliary bishop of Mexico City, July 19, 1980; app. first bishop of Nuevo Laredo, Mexico, Nov. 6, 1989.

**Wcela, Emil A.:** b. May 1, 1931, Bohemia, N.Y.; educ. St. Francis College (Brooklyn, N.Y.), Immaculate Conception Seminary (Huntington, N.Y.), Catholic Univ. (Washington, D.C.), Pontifical Biblical Institute (Rome, Italy); ord. priest (Brooklyn) June 2, 1956; ord. titular bishop of Filaca and auxiliary bishop of Rockville Centre, Dec. 13, 1988.

**Weakland, Rembert G., O.S.B.:** b. Apr. 2, 1927, Patton, Pa.; joined Benedictines, 1945; ord. priest June 24, 1951; abbot-primate of Benedictine Confederation, 1967-77; ord. archbishop of Milwaukee, Nov. 8, 1977.

**Weigand, William K.:** b. May 23, 1937, Bend, Ore.; educ. Mt. Angel Seminary (St. Benedict, Ore.), St. Edward's Seminary and St. Thomas Seminary (Kenmore, Wash.); ord. priest (Boise) May 25, 1963; ord. bishop of Salt Lake City, Nov. 17, 1980; app. bishop of Sacramento, Nov. 30, 1993, installed Jan. 27, 1994.

**Weitzel, John Quinn, M.M.:** b. May 10, 1928,

Chicago, Ill.; educ. Maryknoll Seminary (Maryknoll, N.Y.); ord. priest Nov. 5, 1955; missionary to Samoa, 1979; ord. bishop of Samoa-Pago Pago, American Samoa, Oct. 29, 1986.

**Welsh, Lawrence H.:** b. Feb. 1, 1935, Winton, Wyo.; educ. Univ. of Wyoming (Laramie, Wyo.), St. John's Seminary (Collegeville, Minn.), Catholic Univ. (Washington, D.C.); ord. priest (Rapid City) May 26, 1962; ord. bishop of Spokane, Dec. 14, 1978; resigned Apr. 17, 1990; app. titular bishop of Aulon and auxiliary bishop of St. Paul and Minneapolis, Nov. 5, 1991.

**Welsh, Thomas J.:** b. Dec. 20, 1921, Weatherly, Pa.; educ. St. Charles Borromeo Seminary (Philadelphia, Pa.), Catholic Univ. (Washington, D.C.); ord. priest (Philadelphia*) May 30, 1946; ord. titular bishop of Scattery Island and auxiliary bishop of Philadelphia, Apr. 2, 1970; app. first bishop of Arlington, Va., June 4, 1974, 1974; app. bishop of Allentown, Feb. 8, 1983, installed Mar. 21, 1983.

**Whelan, Robert L., S.J.:** b. Apr. 16, 1912, Wallace, Ida.; educ. St. Michael's College (Spokane, Wash.), Alma College (Alma, Calif.); ord. priest June 17, 1944; ord. titular bishop of Sicilibba and coadjutor bishop of Fairbanks, Alaska, with right of succession, Feb. 22, 1968; bishop of Fairbanks, Nov. 30, 1968; retired June 1, 1985.

**Williams, James Kendrick:** b. Sept. 5, 1936, Athertonville, Ky.; educ. St. Mary's College (St. Mary's, Ky.), St. Maur's School of Theology (South Union, Ky.); ord. priest (Louisville*) May 25, 1963; ord. titular bishop of Catula and auxiliary bishop of Covington, June 19, 1984; first bishop of Lexington, Ky., installed Mar. 2, 1988.

**Winter, William J.:** b. May 20, 1930, Pittsburgh, Pa.; educ. St. Vincent College and Seminary (Latrobe, Pa.), Gregorian Univ. (Rome, Italy); ord. priest (Pittsburgh), Dec. 17, 1955; ord. titular bishop of Uthina and auxiliary bishop of Pittsburgh, Feb. 13, 1989.

**Wirz, George O.:** b. Jan. 17, 1929, Monroe, Wis.; educ. St. Francis Seminary and Marquette Univ. (Milwaukee, Wis.); Cath. Univ. (Washington, D.C.); ord. priest (Madison) May 31, 1952; ord. titular bishop of Municipa and auxiliary bishop of Madison, Mar. 9, 1978.

**Wiwchar, Michael, C.SS.R.:** b. May 9, 1932, Komarno, Manitoba, Canada; educ. Redemptorist Seminary (Windsor, Ontario); made solemn vows as Redemptorist, 1956; ord. priest, June 28, 1959; pastor St. John the Baptist Parish, Newark, N.J., 1990-93; app. bishop of St. Nicholas of Chicago for the Ukrainians, July 15, 1993.

**Wuerl, Donald W.:** b. Nov. 12, 1940, Pittsburgh, Pa.; educ. Catholic Univ. (Washington, D.C.), North American College, Angelicum (Rome); ord. priest (Pittsburgh) Dec. 17, 1966, in Rome; ord. titular bishop of Rosemarkie Jan. 6, 1986, in Rome; auxiliary bishop of Seattle, 1986-87; app. bishop of Pittsburgh Feb. 11, 1988, installed Mar. 25, 1988.

**Wycislo, Aloysius John:** b. June 17, 1908, Chicago, Ill.; educ. St. Mary's Seminary (Mundelein, Ill.), Catholic Univ. (Washington, D.C.); ord. priest (Chicago*) Apr. 4, 1934; ord. titular bishop of Stadia and auxiliary bishop of Chicago, Dec. 21, 1960; app. bishop of Green Bay, installed Apr. 16, 1968; resigned May 10, 1983.

## Y-Z

**Yanta, John W.:** b. Oct. 2, 1931, Runge, Tex.; educ. St. John's Preparatory Seminary and Assumption Seminary (San Antonio); ord. priest (San Antonio*) Mar. 17, 1956; ord. titular bishop of Naratcata and auxiliary bishop of San Antonio Dec. 30, 1994.

**Younan, Joseph:** b. Nov. 15, 1944, Hassakeh, Syria; educ. Our Lady of Deliverance Seminary (Sharfet, Lebanon), Pontifical College of the Propagation of the Faith (Rome); ord. priest Sept. 12, 1971; came to U.S., 1986; served Syrian Catholics in U.S.; ord. first bishop Our Lady of Deliverance of Newark for Syrian Catholics in the U.S. and Canada, Jan. 7, 1996, in Kamisly, Syria.

**Zavala, Gabino:** b. Sept. 7, 1951, Guerrero, Mexico; became U.S. citizen, 1976; educ. St. John's Seminary (Los Angeles), Catholic Univ. (Washington, D.C.); ord. priest (Los Angeles*) May 28, 1977; ord. titular bishop of Tamascani and auxiliry bishop of Los Angeles, Mar. 19, 1994.

**Zayek, Francis:** b. Oct. 18, 1920, Manzanillo, Cuba; ord. priest Mar. 17, 1946; ord. titular bishop of Callinicum and auxiliary bishop for Maronites in Brazil, Aug. 5, 1962; named apostolic exarch for Maronites in U.S., with headquarters in Detroit; installed June 11. 1966; first eparch of St. Maron of Detroit, Mar. 25, 1972; see transferred to Brooklyn, June 27, 1977; given personal title of archbishop, Dec. 22, 1982.

**Ziemann, G. Patrick:** b. Sept. 13, 1941, Pasadena, Calif.; educ. St. John's College Seminary and St. John's Seminary (Camarillo, Calif.), Mt. St. Mary's College (Los Angeles, Calif.); ord. priest (Los Angeles*) Apr. 29, 1967; ord. titular bishop of Obba and auxiliary bishop of Los Angeles, Feb. 23, 1987; app. bishop of Santa Rosa, July 14, 1992.

**Zipfel, Paul A.:** b. Sept. 22, 1935, St. Louis, Mo.; educ. Cardinal Glennon College, Kenrick Seminary (St. Louis, Mo.), Catholic Univ. (Washington, D.C.), St. Louis Univ. (St. Louis, Mo.); ord. priest (St. Louis*) Mar. 18, 1961; ord. titular bishop of Walla Walla and auxiliary bishop of St. Louis, June 29, 1989.

## BISHOP-BROTHERS

(The asterisk indicates brothers who were bishops at the same time.)

There have been 10 pairs of brother-bishops in the history of the U.S. hierarchy.

Living: Francis T. Hurley,* archbishop of Anchorage and Mark J. Hurley,* bishop emeritus of Santa Rosa. Raymond J. Boland,* bishop of Kansas City-St. Joseph, Mo. and John Kevin Boland,* bishop of Savannah.

Deceased: Francis Blanchet* of Oregon City (Portland) and Augustin Blanchet* of Walla Walla; John S. Foley of Detroit and Thomas P. Foley of Chicago; Francis P. Kenrick,* apostolic administrator of Philadelphia, bishop of Philadelphia and Baltimore, and Peter R. Kenrick* of St. Louis; Matthias C. Lenihan of Great Falls and Thomas M. Lenihan of Cheyenne; James O'Connor, vicar apostolic of Nebraska and bishop of Omaha, and Michael O'Connor of Pittsburgh and Erie; Jeremiah F. and John W. Shanahan, both of Harrisburg; Sylvester J. Espelage, O.F.M.* of Wuchang, China, who died

10 days after the ordination of his brother, Bernard T. Espelage, O.F.M.* of Gallup; Coleman F. Carroll* of Miami and Howard Carroll* of Altoona-Johnstown.

## U.S. BISHOPS OVERSEAS

Cardinal William W. Baum, major penitentiary; Cardinal Edmund C. Szoka, president of Prefecture for Economic Affairs of the Holy See; Archbishop Ambrose de Paoli, first apostolic nuncio to South Africa, pro-nuncio to Lesotho and apostolic delegate to several other countries in southern Africa; Archbishop John P. Foley, president of Pontifical Commission for Social Communications; Most Rev. George Riashi, B.C.O., archbishop of archeparchy of Tripoli of Lebanon (Lebanon) for Greek-Catholic Melkites; Most Rev. Michael R. Kuchmiak, exarch of apostlic exarchate of Great Britain for Ukrainian Catholics; Archbishop Charles A. Schleck, C.S.C., adjunct secretary of the Congregation for the Evangelization of Peoples; Archbishop John Bukovsky, S.V.D. (naturalized U.S. citizen), papal representative to Russia. Cardinal Myroslav Ivan Lubachivsky, major archbishop of Lviv of the Ukrainians (Ukraine), became a U.S. citizen in 1952 and was archbishop of Philadelphia Ukrainian Archeparchy, 1979-80.

(See also Missionary Bishops.)

## RETIRED/RESIGNED U.S. PRELATES

Information, as of June 15, 1996, includes name of the prelate and see held at the time of retirement or resignation; archbishops are indicated by an asterisk. Most of the prelates listed below resigned their sees because of age in accordance with church law. See Index: Biographies, U.S. Bishops.

Forms of address of retired residential prelates (unless they have a titular see): *Archbishop or Bishop Emeritus of* (last see held); *Former Archbishop or Bishop of* (last see held).

Alfred L. Abramowicz (Chicago, auxiliary), Patrick V. Ahern (New York, auxiliary), Leo Arkfeld, S.V.D.* (Madang, Papua New Guinea),Juan Arzube (Los Angeles, auxiliary), Michael J. Begley (Charlotte), Ernest B. Boland, O.P. (Multan, Pakistan), William D. Borders* (Baltimore), Warren L. Boudreaux (Houma-Thibodaux), Joseph M. Breitenbeck (Grand Rapids), Edwin B. Broderick (Albany), Stanislaus Brzana (Ogdensburg), Charles A. Buswell (Pueblo).

Cardinal John Carberry* (St. Louis), Harry A. Clinch (Monterey), John W. Comber, M.M. (Foratiano, titular see), Ronald G. Connors, C.S.S.R. (San Juan de la Maguana, Dominican Republic), Arnold R. Cotey, S.D.S. (Nachingwea, now Lindi, Tanzania), Joseph R. Crowley (Ft. Wayne-S. Bend, auxiliary), Walter W. Curtis (Bridgeport), James J. Daly (Rockville Centre, auxiliary), Nicholas D'Antonio, O.F.M. (Olancho, Honduras).

Michael J. Dempsey, O.P. (Sokoto, Nigeria), Joseph A. DePalma, S.C.J. (DeAar, South Africa), George Dion, O.M.I. (titular see, Arpaia), Paul V. Donovan (Kalamazoo), Michael J. Dudick (Passaic, Byzantine rite), Paul V. Dudley (Sioux Falls), Clarence J. Duhart, C.SS.R. (Udon Thani, Thailand), Dennis V. Durning, C.S.Sp. (Arusha, Tanzania), J.

Lennox Federal (Salt Lake City), Joseph A. Ferrario (Honolulu), John J. Fitzpatrick (Brownsville), Bernard J. Flanagan (Worcester), Marion F. Forst (Dodge City), Joseph A. Francis, S.V.D. (Newark auxiliary), Frederick W. Freking (La Crosse), Gerard L. Frey (Lafayette, La.).

Robert F. Garner (Newark, auxiliary), Norbert F. Gaughan (Gary), Odore Gendron (Manchester), Hugo Gerbermann, M.M. (San Antonio, auxiliary), Peter L. Gerety* (Newark), George J. Gottwald (St. Louis, auxiliary), Thomas J. Grady (Orlando), John J. Graham (Philadelphia, auxiliary), J. Richard Ham, M.M. (St. Paul and Minneapolis, auxiliary), Philip M. Hannan* (New Orleans), Timothy J. Harrington (Worcester), Frank J. Harrison (Syracuse), Edward D. Head (Buffalo).

Edward J. Herrmann (Columbus), Edward G. Hettinger (Columbus, auxiliary), Dennis W. Hickey (Rochester, auxiliary), James J. Hogan (Altoona-Johnstown), Joseph L. Hogan (Rochester), William A. Hughes (Covington), Raymond G. Hunthausen* (Seattle), Mark J. Hurley (Santa Rosa), Charles R. Koester (St. Louis, auxiliary), Arthur H. Krawczak (Detroit, auxiliary), Daniel W. Kucera, O.S.B.* (Dubuque), William F. Kupfer, M.M. (Taichung, Taiwan), W. Thomas Larkin (St. Petersburg) Raymond W. Lessard (Savannah), Martin N. Lohmuller (Philadelphia, auxiliary), Innocent Hilarius Lotocky, O.S.B.M. (St. Nicholas of Chicago for Ukrainians), George E. Lynch (Raleigh, auxiliary), Timothy J. Lyne (Chicago, auxiliary).

Edward A. McCarthy* (Miami), J. Carroll McCormick (Scranton), Thomas J. McDonough* (Louisville), Urban McGarry, T.O.R. (Bhagalpur, India), Bernard J. McLaughlin (Buffalo, auxiliary), William E. McManus (Fort Wayne-South Bend), Joseph F. Maguire (Springfield, Mass.), James W. Malone (Youngstown), Charles G. Maloney (Louisville, auxiliary), Paul C. Marcinkus* (titular see of Orta), Eugene A. Marino, S.S.J.* (Atlanta), James E. Michaels (Wheeling-Charleston, auxiliary), William J. Moran (Military Vicariate, delegate), Michael J. Murphy (Erie), Martin J. Neylon, S.J. (Caroline Islands), James D. Niedergeses (Nashville), Bernard Nolker, C.SS.R. (Parangua, Brazil), Gerald F. O'Keefe (Davenport), Joseph T. O'Keefe (Syracuse), Edward C. O'Leary (Portland, Me.), Arthur J. O'Neill (Rockford).

Edward W. O'Rourke (Peoria), Albert H. Ottenweller (Steubenville), John L. Paschang (Grand Island), John J. Paul (La Crosse), George H. Pearce, S.M.* (Suva, Fiji Islands), Bernard F. Popp (San Antonio, auxiliary), Kenneth J. Povish (Lansing), Cornelius M. Power* (Portland, Ore.), Leo A. Pursley (Fort Wayne-South Bend), Vasile Louis Puscas (St. George's in Canton of the Romanians), Francis A. Quinn (Sacramento), John R. Quinn* (San Francisco), Joseph M. Raya* (Acre), Lawrence J. Riley (Boston, auxiliary), John R. Roach* (St. Paul and Minneapolis), Miguel Rodriguez, C.SS.R. (Arecibo, P.R.), James C. Ryan, O.F.M. (Santarem, Brazil), Joseph T. Ryan* (Military Services archdiocese).

Charles A. Salatka* (Oklahoma City), Robert F. Sanchez* (Santa Fe), John J. Scanlan (Honolulu), James L. Schad (Camden, auxiliary), Firmin M.

Schmidt, O.F.M. Cap. (Mendi, Papua New Guinea), Mark Schmitt (Marquette), Walter J. Schoenherr (Detroit, auxiliary), Nerses Mikail Setian (Armenian Exarchate), Eldon B. Schuster (Great Falls), Daniel E. Sheehan* (Omaha), George H. Speltz (St. Cloud), Ignatius J. Strecker* (Kansas City, Kans.), John J. Sullivan (Kansas City-St. Joseph, Mo.).

Joseph Tawil* (personal title) (Newton, Greek Melkites), Sylvester Treinen (Boise), Thomas Tschoepe (Dallas), Adrian Veigle, T.O.R. (Borba, Brazil, Prelate), Nicolas Walsh (Yakima), John J. Ward (Los Angeles, auxiliary), Loras J. Watters (Winona), Robert L. Whelan (Fairbanks), Aloysius J. Wycislo (Green Bay).

# AMERICAN BISHOPS OF THE PAST

Information includes: dates; place of birth if outside the U.S.; date of ordination to the priesthood; titular see in parentheses of bishops who were not ordinaries; indication, where applicable, of date of resignation.

Abbreviation code: abp., archbishop; bp., bishop; v.a., vicar apostolic; aux., auxiliary bishop; coad., coadjutor; ord., ordained priest; res., resigned.

## A

**Acerra, Angelo Thomas, O.S.B.** (195-90): ord. May 20, 1950; aux. Military Services archdiocese (Lete), 1983-90.

**Ackerman, Richard H., C.S.Sp.** (1903-92): ord. Aug. 28, 1926; aux. San Diego (Lares), 1956-60; bp. Covington 1960-78 (res.).

**Adrian, William L.** (1883-1972): ord. Apr. 15, 1911; bp. Nashville, 1936-69 (res.).

**Ahr, George W.** (1904-93): ord. July 29, 1928; bp. Trenton, 1950-79 (res.).

**Albers, Joseph** (1891-1965): ord. June 17, 1916; aux. Cincinnati (Lunda), 1929-37; first bp. Lansing, 1937-65.

**Alemany, Joseph Sadoc, O.P.** (1814-88): b. Spain; ord. Mar. 11, 1837; bp. Monterey, 1850-53; first abp. San Francisco, 1853-84 (res.).

**Alencastre, Stephen P., SS.CC.** (1876-1940): b. Madeira; ord. Apr. 5, 1902; coad. v.a. Sandwich Is. (Arabissus), 1924-36; v.a. Sandwich (Hawaiian) Is., 1936-40.

**Alerding, Herman J.** (1845-1924): b. Germany; ord. Sept. 22, 1869; bp. Fort Wayne, 1900-24.

**Allen, Edward P.** (1853-1926): ord. Dec. 17, 1881; bp. Mobile, 1897-1926.

**Alter, Karl J.** (1885-1977): ord. June 4, 1910; bp. Toledo, 1931-50; abp. Cincinnati, 1950-69 (res.).

**Althoff, Henry** (1873-1947): ord. July 26, 1902; bp. Belleville, 1914-47.

**Amat, Thaddeus, C.M.** (1811-78): b. Spain; ord. Dec. 23, 1837; bp. Monterey (title changed to Monterey-Los Angeles, 1859), 1854-78.

**Anderson, Joseph** (1865-1927): ord. May 20, 1892; aux. Boston (Myrina), 1909-27.

**Anderson, Paul F.** (1917-87): ord. Jan. 6, 1943; coad. bp. Duluth (Polignana), 1968-69; bp. Duluth, 1969-82 (res.); aux. Sioux Falls, 1983-87.

**Anglim, Robert, C.SS.R.** (1922-73): ord. Jan. 6, 1948; prelate Coari, Brazil (Gaguari), 1966-73.

**Annabring, Joseph** (1900-59): b. Hungary; ord. May 3, 1927; bp. Superior, 1954-59.

**Arliss, Reginald, C.P.** (1906-96): ord. Apr. 28, 1934; prelate Marbel, Philippines (now a diocese), 1970-81 (res.).

**Appelhans, Stephen A., S.V.D.** (1905-51): ord. May 5, 1932; v.a. East New Guinea (Catula), 1948-51.

## B

**Babcock, Allen J.** (1898-1969): ord. Mar. 7, 1925; aux. Detroit (Irenopolis), 1947-54; bp. Grand Rapids, 1954-69.

**Bacon, David W.** (1815-74): ord. Dec. 13, 1838; first bp. Portland, Me., 1855-74.

**Baldwin, Vincent J.** (1907-79): ord. July 26, 1931; aux. Rockville Centre (Bencenna), 1962-79.

**Baltes, Peter J.** (1827-86): b. Germany; ord. May 31, 1852; bp. Alton (now Springfield), Ill., 1870-86.

**Baraga, Frederic:** See Index.

**Barron, Edward** (1801-54): b. Ireland; ord. 1829; v.a. The Two Guineas (Constantina), 1842-44 (res.) missionary in U.S.

**Barry, John** (1799-1859): b. Ireland; ord. Sept. 24, 1825; bp. Savannah, 1857-59.

**Barry, Patrick J.** (1868-1940): b. Ireland; ord. June 9, 185; bp. St. Augustine, 1922-40.

**Bartholome, Peter W.** (1893-1982): ord. June 12, 1917; coad. St. Cloud (Lete), 1942-53; bp. St. Cloud, 1953-68 (res.).

**Baumgartner, Apollinarls, O.F.M. Cap.** (1899-1970): ord. May 30, 1926; v.a. Guam (Joppa), 1945-65; first bp. Agana, Guam, 1965-70.

**Bayley, James Roosevelt** (1814-77): convert, 1842; ord. Mar. 2, 1843; first bp. Newark, 1853-72; abp. Baltimore, 1872-77.

**Bazin, John S.** (1796-1848): b. France; ord. July 22, 1822; bp. Vincennes (now Indianapolis), 1847-48.

**Beaven, Thomas D.** (1851-1920): ord. Dec. 18, 1875; bp. Springfield, Mass., 1892-1920.

**Becker Thomas A.** (1832-99): ord. June 18, 1859; first bp. Wilmington, 1868-86; bp. Savannah, 1886-99.

**Beckman, Francis J.** (1875-1948): ord. June 20, 1902; bp. Lincoln, 1924-30; abp. Dubuque, 1930-46 (res.).

**Begin, Floyd L.** (1902-77): ord. July 31, 1927; aux. Cleveland (Sala), 1947-62; first bp. Oakland, 1962-77.

**Bell, Alden J.** (1904-82): b. Canada; ord. May 14, 1932; aux. Los Angeles (Rhodopolis), 1956-62; bp. Sacramento, 1962-79 (res.).

**Benincasa, Pius A.** (1913-86): ord. Mar. 27, 1937; aux. Buffalo (Buruni), 1964-86.

**Benjamin, Cletus J.** (1909-61): ord. Dec. 8, 1935; aux. Philadelphia (Binda), 1960-61.

**Bennett, John G.** (1891-1957): ord. June 27, 1914; first bp. Lafayette, Ind. 1944-57.

**Bergan, Gerald T.** (1892-1972): ord. Oct. 28, 1915; bp. Des Moines, 1934-48; abp. Omaha, 1948-69 (res.).

**Bernarding, George, S.V.D.** (1912-87): ord. Aug. 13, 1939; first v.a. Mount Hagen, Papua New Guinea (Belabitene), 1960-66; first bp., 1966-82, and first abp., 1982-87 (res.), Mount Hagen.

**Bidawid, Thomas M.** (1910-71): b. Iraq; ord. May 15, 1935; U.S. citizen; first abp. Ahwaz, Iran (Chaldean Rite), 1968-70; Chaldean patriarchal vicar for United Arab Republic, 1970-71.

**Bilock, John M.** (1916-94): ord. Feb. 3, 1946; aux. Byzantine- rite Munhall, now Pittsburgh (Pergamum), 1977-95.

**Binz, Leo** (1900-79): ord. Mar. 15, 1924; coad. bp. Winona (Pinara) 1942-49; coad. abp. Dubuque (Silyum), 1949-54; abp. Dubuque, 1954-61; abp. St. Paul and Minneapolis, 1962-75 (res.).

**Biskup, George J.** (1911-79): ord. Mar. 19, 1937; aux. Dubuque (Hemeria), 1957-65; bp. Des Moines, 1965-67; coad. abp. Indianapolis (Tamalluma), 1969-70; abp. Indianapolis, 1970-79 (res.).

**Blanc, Anthony** (1792-1860): b. France; ord. July 22, 1816; bp. New Orleans, 1835-50; first abp. New Orleans, 1850-60.

**Blanchet** (brothers): **Augustin M.** (1797-1887): b. Canada; ord. June 3, 1821; bp. Walla Walla, 1846-50; first bp. Nesqually (now Seattle), 1850-79 (res.). **Francis N.** (1795-1883): b. Canada; ord. July 19, 1819; v.a. Oregon Territory (Philadelphia, Adrasus), 1843-46; first abp. Oregon City (now Portland), 1846-80 (res.).

**Blanchette, Romeo R.** (1913-82): ord. Apr. 3, 1937; aux. Joliet (Maxita), 1965-66; bp. Joliet, 1966-79 (res.).

**Blenk, James H., S.M.** (1856-1917): b. Germany; ord. Aug. 16, 1885; bp. San Juan, 1899-1906; abp. New Orleans, 1906-17.

**Boardman, John J.** (1894-1978): ord. May 21, 1921; aux. Brooklyn (Gunela), 1952-77 (res.).

**Boccella, John H., T.O.R.** (1912-92): b. Italy, came to U.S. at age of two; ord. Mar. 29, 1941; abp. Izmir, Turkey, 1968-78 (res.); tit. abp. Ephesus.

**Boeynaems, Libert H., SS.CC.** (1857-1926): b. Belgium; ord. Sept. 11, 1881; v.a. Sandwich (Hawaiian) Is. (Zeugma), 1903-26.

**Bohachevsky, Constantine** (1884-1961): b. Austria Galicia; ord. Jan. 31, 1909; ap. ex. Ukrainian Byzantine Catholics in U.S. (Amisus), 1924-58; first metropolitan of Byzantine Rite archeparchy of Philadelphia, 1958-61.

**Boileau, George, S.J.** (1912-65): ord. June 13, 1948; coad. bp. Fairbanks (Ausuccura), 1964-65.

**Bokenfohr, John, O.M.I.** (1903-82): ord. July 11, 1927; bp. Kimberley, S. Africa, 1953-74 (res,).

**Boland, Thomas A.** (1896-1979): ord. Dec. 23, 1922; aux. Newark (Irina), 1940-47; bp. Paterson, 1947-52; abp. Newark, 1953-74 (res.).

**Bona, Stanislaus** (1888-1967): ord. Nov. 1, 1912; bp. Grand Island, 1932-44; coad. bp. Green Bay (Mela), 1944-45; bp. Green Bay, 1945-67.

**Bonacum, Thomas** (1847-1911): b. Ireland;

ord. June 18, 1870; bp. Lincoln, 1887-1911.

**Borgess, Caspar H.** (1826-90): b. Germany; ord. Dec. 8, 1848; coad. bp. and ap. admin. Detroit (Calydon), 1870-71; bp. Detroit, 1871-87 (res.).

**Bourgade, Peter** (1845-1908): b. France; ord. Nov. 30, 1869; v.a. Arizona (Thaumacus), 1885-97; first bp. Tucson, 1897-99; abp. Santa Fe, 1899-1908.

**Boylan, John J.** (1889-1953): ord. July 28, 1915; bp. Rockford, 1943-53.

**Boyle, Hugh C.** (1873-1950): ord. July 2, 1898; bp. Pittsburgh, 1921-50.

**Bradley, Denis** (1846-1903):b. Ireland; ord. June 3, 1871; first bp. Manchester, 1884-1903.

**Brady, John** (1842-1910): b. Ireland; ord. Dec. 4, 1864; aux. Boston (Alabanda), 1891-1910.

**Brady, Matthew F.** (1893-1959): ord. June 10, 1916; bp. Burlington, 1938-44 bp. Manchester, 1944-59.

**Brady, William O.** (1899-1961): ord. Dec. 21, 1923; bp. Sioux Falls, 1939-56; coad. abp. St. Paul (Selymbria), June-Oct, 1956; abp. St. Paul, 1956-61.

**Brennan, Andrew J.** (1877-1956): ord. Dec. 17, 1904; aux. Scranton (Thapsus), 1923-26; bp. Richmond, 1926-45 (res.).

**Brennan, Francis J.** (1894-1968): ord. Apr. 3, 1920; judge (1940-59) and dean (1959-67) of Roman Rota; ord. bp. 1967; cardinal 1967.

**Brennan, Thomas F.** (1853-1916): b. Ireland; ord. July 14, 1880; first bp. Dallas, 1881-93; aux. St. John's, Newfoundland (Usula), 1893-1905 (res.).

**Brizgys, Vincas** (1903-92): b. Lithuania; U.S. citizen, 1958; ord. June 5, 1927; aux. Kaunas, Lithuania (Bosano), 1940; exiled 1944; resided in U.S. (Chicago archdiocese) from 1951.

**Broderick, Bonaventure** (1868-1943): ord. July 26, 1896; aux. Havana, Cuba (Juliopolis), 1903-05 (res.).

**Brondel, John B.** (1842-1903): b. Belgium; ord. Dec. 17, 1864; bp. Vancouver Is., 1879-84; first bp. Helena, 1884-1903.

**Brossart, Ferdinand** (1849-1930): b. Germany; ord. Sept. 1, 1892; bp. Covington, 1916-23 (res.).

**Brunini, Joseph B.** (1909-96): ord. Dec. 5, 1933; aux. Natchez-Jackson (Axomis) 1957-66; bp. Natchez-Jackson (now Jackson) 1967-84 (res.).

**Brust, Leo J.** (1916-95): ord. May 30, 1942; aux. Milwaukee (Suelli) 1969-91 (ret.).

**Brute, Simon G.** (1779-1839): b. France; ord. June 11, 1808; first bp. Vincennes (now Indianapolis), 1834-39.

**Buddy, Charles F.** (1887-1966): ord. Sept. 19, 1914; first bp. San Diego, 1936-66.

**Burke, James C., O.P.** (1926-94): ord. June 8, 1956; prelate of Chimbote, Peru (Lamiggiga), 1967-78 (res.).

**Burke, Joseph A.** (1886-1962): ord. Aug. 3, 1912; aux. Buffalo (Vita), 1943-52; bp. Buffalo, 1952-62.

**Burke, Maurice F.** (1845-1923): b. Ireland; ord. May 22, 1875; first bp. Cheyenne, 1887-93; bp. St. Joseph, 1893-1923.

**Burke, Thomas M.** (1840-1915): b. Ireland; ord. June 30, 1864; bp. Albany, 1894-1915.

**Busch, Joseph F.** (1866-1953): ord. July 28, 1889; bp. Lead (now Rapid City), 1910-5; bp. St. Cloud, 1915-53.

**Byrne, Andrew** (1802-62): b. Ireland; ord. Nov. 11, 1827; first bp. Little Rock, 1844-62.

**Byrne, Christopher E.** (1867-1950): ord. Sept. 23, 1891; bp. Galveston, 1918-50.

**Byrne, Edwin V.** (1891-1963): ord. May 22, 1915; first bp. Ponce, 1925-29; bp. San Juan, 1929-43; abp. Santa Fe, 1943-63.

**Byrne, Leo C.** (1908-74): ord. June 10, 1933; aux. St. Louis (Sabadia), 1954-61; coad. bp. Wichita, 1961-67; coad. abp. (Plestra) St. Paul and Minneapolis, 1967-74.

**Byrne, Patrick J., M.M.** (1888-1950): ord. June 23, 1915; apostolic delegate to Korea (Gazera), 1949-50.

**Byrne, Thomas S.** (1841-1923): ord. May 22, 1869; bp. Nashville, 1894-1923.

## C

**Caesar, Raymond R., S.V.D.** (1932-87): ord. June 4, 1961; coad. bp. Goroka, Papua New Guinea, 1978-80; bp. Goroka, 1980-87.

**Caillouet, L. Abel** (1900-84): ord. May 7, 1925; aux. New Orleans (Setea), 1947-76 (res.).

**Canevin, J. F. Regis** (1853-1927): ord. June 4, 1879; coad. bp. Pittsburgh (Sabrata), 1903-04; bp. Pittsburgh, 1904-21 (res.).

**Cantwell, John J.** (1874-1947): b. Ireland; ord. June 18, 1899; bp. Monterey-Los Angeles, 1917-22; bp. Los Angeles-San Diego, 1922-36; first abp. Los Angeles, 1936-47.

**Carrell, George A., S.J.** (1803-68): ord. Dec. 20, 1827; first bp. Covington, 1853-68.

**Carroll** (brothers) **Coleman F.** (1905-77): ord. June 15, 1930; aux. Pittsburgh (Pitanae), 1953-58; first bp. Miami, 1958-68 and first abp., 1968-77. **Howard J.** (1902-60): ord. Apr. 2, 1927; bp. Altoona-Johnstown, 1958-60.

**Carroll, James J.** (1862-1913): ord. June 15, 1889; bp. Nueva Segovia, P.I., 1908-12 (res.).

**Carroll, John** (1735-1815): ord. Feb. 14, 1761; first bishop of the American hierarchy; first bp., 1789-1808, and first abp., 1808-15, of Baltimore.

**Carroll, John P.** (1864-1925): ord. July 7, 1886; bp. Helena, 1904-25.

**Carroll, Mark K.** (1896-1985): ord. June 10, 1922; bp. Wichita, 1947-67 (res.).

**Cartwright, Hubert J.** (1900-58): ord. June 11, 1927; coad. bp. Wilmington (Neve), 1956-58.

**Caruana, George** (1882-1951): b. Malta; ord. Oct. 28, 1905; bp. Puerto Rico (name changed to San Juan, 1924), 1921-25; ap. del. Mexico (Sebastea in Armenia), 1925-27; internuncio to Haiti, 1927-35; nuncio to Cuba, 1935-47 (res.).

**Casey, James V.** (1914-86): ord. Dec. 8, 1939; aux. Lincoln (Citium), Apr.-June, 1957; bp. Lincoln, 1957-67; abp. Denver 1967-86.

**Casey, Lawrence B.** (1905-77): ord. June 7, 1930; aux. Rochester (Cea), 1953-66; bp. Paterson, 1966-77.

**Cassata, John J.** (1908-89): ord. Dec. 8, 1932; aux. Dallas-Ft. Worth (Bida), 1968-69; bp. Ft. Worth 1969-80 (res.).

**Cassidy, James E.** (1869-1951): ord. Sept. 8, 1898; aux. Fall River (Ibora), 1930-34; bp. Fall River, 1934-51.

**Chabrat, Guy Ignatius, S.S.** (1787-1868): b.

France; ord. Dec. 21, 1811; coad. bp. Bardstown (Bolina), 1834-47 (res.).

**Chanche, John J., S.S.** (1795-1852): ord. June 5, 1819; bp. Natchez (now Jackson), 1841-52.

**Chapelle, Placide L.** (1842-1905): b. France; ord. June 28, 1865; coad. abp. Santa Fe (Arabissus), 1891-94; abp. Santa Fe, 1894-97; abp. New Orleans 1897-1905.

**Chartrand, Joseph** (1870-1933): ord. Sept. 24, 1892; coad. bp. Indianapolis (Flavias), 1910-18; bp. Indianapolis, 1918-33.

**Chatard, Francis S.** (1834-1918): ord. June 14, 1862; bp. Vincennes (now Indianapolis — title changed in 1898), 1878-1918.

**Cheverus, John Lefebvre de** (1768-1836): b. France; ord. Dec. 18, 1790; bp. Boston, 1810-23 (returned to France, made cardinal 1836).

**Christie, Alexander** (1848-1925): ord. Dec. 22, 1877; bp. Vancouver Is., 1898-99; abp. Oregon City (now Portland), 1899-1925.

**Clancy, William** (1802-47): b. Ireland; ord. May 24, 1823; coad. bp. Charleston (Oreus), 1834-37; v.a. British Guiana, 1837-43.

**Clavel Mendez, Tomas Alberto** (1921-88): b. Panama; ord. Dec. 7, 1947; bp. David, Panama, 1955-64; abp. Panama, 1964-68 (res.); vicar for Hispanics, Orange, Calif., diocese.

**Cody, John P.** (1907-82): ord. Dec. 8, 1931; aux. St. Louis (Apollonia), 1947-54; coad. bp. St. Joseph, Mo., 1954-55; bp. Kansas City-St. Joseph, 1956-61; coad. abp. 1961-62; ap. admin., 1962-64, and abp., 1964-65, New Orleans; abp. Chicago, 1965-82; cardinal, 1967.

**Cohill, John Edward, S.V.D.** (1907-94): ord. Mar. 20, 1936; first bp. Goroko, Papua New Guinea, 1967-80 (res.).

**Collins, John J., S.J.** (1856-1934): ord. Aug. 29, 1891; v.a. Jamaica (Antiphellus), 1907-18 (res.).

**Collins, Thomas P., M.M.** (1915-73): ord. June 21, 1942; v.a. Pando, Bolivia (Sufetula), 1961-68 (res.).

**Colton, Charles H.** (1848-1915): ord. June 10, 1876; bp. Buffalo, 1903-15.

**Conaty, Thomas J.** (1847-1915): b. Ireland; ord. Dec. 21, 1872; rector of Catholic University, 1896-1903; tit. bp. Samos, 1901-03; bp. Monterey- Los Angeles (now Los Angeles), 1903-15.

**Concanen, Richard L., O.P.** (1747-1810): b. Ireland; ord. Dec. 22, 1770; first bp. New York, 1808-10 (detained in Italy, never reached his see).

**Condon, William J.** (1895-1967): ord. Oct. 14, 1917; bp. Great Falls, 1939-67.

**Connare, William G.** (1911-95): ord. June 14, 1936; bp. Greensburg, 1960-87 (ret.).

**Connolly, James L.** (1894-1986): ord. Dec. 21, 1923; coad bp. Fall River (Mylasa), 1945-51; bp. Fall River, 1951-70 (res.).

**Connolly, John, O.P.** (1750-1825): b. Ireland; ord. Sept. 24, 1774; bp. New York, 1814-25.

**Connolly, Thomas A.** (1899-1991): ord. June 11, 1926; aux. San Francisco (Sila), 1939-48; coad. bp. Seattle, 1948-50; bp, 1950-51, and first abp. Seattle, 1951-75 (res.).

**Conroy, John J.** (1819-95): b. Ireland; ord. May 21, 1842; bp. Albany, 1865-77 (res.).

**Conroy, Joseph H.** (1858-1939): ord. June 11,

1881; aux. Ogdensburg (Arindela), 1912-21; bp. Ogdensburg, 1921-39.

**Conwell, Henry** (1748-1842): b. Ireland; ord. 1776; bp. Philadelphia, 1820-42.

**Cooke, Terence J.** (1921-83): ord. Dec. 1, 1945; aux. New York (Summa), 1965-68; abp. New York, 1965-83; cardinal 1969.

**Corbett, Timothy** (1858-1939): ord. June 12, 1886; first bp. Crookston, 1910-38 (res.).

**Corrigan, Joseph M.** (1879-1942): ord. June 6, 1903; rector of Catholic University, 1936-42; tit. bp. Bilta, 1940-42.

**Corrigan, Michael A.** (1839-1902): ord. Sept. 19, 1863; bp. Newark, 1873-80; coad. abp. New York (Petra), 1880-85; abp. New York, 1885-1902.

**Corrigan, Owen** (1849-1929): ord. June 7, 1873; aux. Baltimore (Macri), 1908-29.

**Cosgrove, Henry** (1834-1906): ord. Aug. 27, 1857; bp. Davenport, 1884-1906.

**Cosgrove, William M.** (1916-92): ord. Dec. 18, 1943; aux. Cleveland (Trisipa), 1968-76; bp. Belleville, 1976-81 (res.).

**Costello, Joseph A.** (1915-78): ord. June 7, 1941; aux. Newark (Choma), 1963-78.

**Cote, Philip, S.J.** (1896-1970): ord. Aug. 14, 1927; v.a. Suchow, China (Polystylus), 1935-46; first bp. Suchow, 1946-70 (imprisoned by Chinese Communists, 1951; expelled from China, 1953; ap. admin. Islands of Quemoy and Matsu, 1969-70.

**Cotter, Joseph B.** (1844-1909): b. England; ord. May 3, 1871; first bp. Winona, 1889-1909.

**Cotton, Francis R.** (1895-1960): ord. June 17, 1920; first bp. Owensboro, 1938-60.

**Cousins, William E.** (1902-88): ord. Apr. 23, 1927, aux. Chicago (Forma), 1949-52; bp. Peoria, 1952-59; abp. Milwaukee 1959-77 (res.).

**Cowley, Leonard P.** (1913-73): ord. June 4, 1938; aux. St. Paul and Minneapolis (Pertusa), 1958-73.

**Crane, Michael J.** (1863-1928): ord. June 15, 1889; aux. Philadelphia (Curium), 1921-28.

**Cretin, Joseph** (1799-1857): b. France; ord. Dec. 20, 1823; bp. St. Paul, 1851-57.

**Crimont, Joseph R., S.J.** (1858-1945): b. France; ord. Aug. 26, 1888; v.a. Alaska (Ammaedara), 1917-45.

**Crowley, Timothy J., C.S.C.** (1880-1945): b. Ireland; ord. Aug. 2, 1906; coad. bp. Dacca (Epiphania), 1927-29; bp. Dacca, 1929-45.

**Cunningham, David F.** (1900-79): ord. June 12, 1926; aux., 1950-67, and coad. bp., 1967-79, Syracuse (Lampsacus); bp. Syracuse, 1970-76 (res.).

**Cunningham, John F.** (1842-1919): b. Ireland; ord. Aug. 8, 1865; bp. Concordia, 1898-1919.

**Curley, Daniel J.** (1869-1932): ord. May 19, 1894; bp. Syracuse, 1923-32.

**Curley, Michael J.** (1879-1947): b. Ireland; ord. Mar. 19, 1904; bp. St. Augustine, 1914-21; abp. Baltimore, 1921-39; title changed to abp. Baltimore and Washington, 1939-47.

**Curtis, Alfred A.** (1831-1908): convert, 1872; ord. Dec. 19, 1874; bp. Wilmington, 1886-96 (res.).

**Cusack, Thomas F.** (1862-1918): ord. May 30, 1885; aux. New York (Temiscyra), 1904-15; bp. Albany, 1915-18.

**Cushing, Richard J.** (1895-1970): ord. May 26, 1921; aux. Boston (Mela), 1939-44; abp. Boston, 1944-70; cardinal 1958.

# D

**Daeger, Albert T., O.F.M.** (1872-1932): ord. July 25, 1896; abp. Santa Fe, 1919-32.

**Daley, Joseph T.** (1915-83): ord. June 7, 1941; aux. Harrisburg (Barca), 1964-67; coad., 1967-71, and bp., 1971-83, Harrisburg.

**Daly, Edward C., O.P.** (1894-1964): ord. June 12, 1921; bp. Des Moines, 1948-64.

**Damiano, Celestine** (1911-67): ord. Dec. 21, 1935; apostolic delegate to South Africa (Nicopolis in Epiro), 1952-60; bp. Camden, 1960-67.

**Danehy, Thomas J., M.M.** (1914-59): ord. Sept. 17, 1939; ap. admin. v.a. Pando, Bolivia (Bita), 1953-59.

**Danglmayr, Augustine** (1898-1992): ord. June 10, 1922; aux. Dallas-Ft. Worth (Olba), 1942-69 (res.).

**Dargin, Edward V.** (1898-1981): ord. Sept. 23, 1922; aux. New York (Amphipolis), 1953-73 (res.).

**David, John B., S.S.** (1761-1841): b. France; ord. Sept. 24, 1785; coad. bp. Bardstown (Mauricastrum), 1819-32; bp. Bardstown (now Louisville), 1832-33 (res.).

**Davis, James** (1852-1926): b. Ireland; ord. June 21, 1878; coad. bp. Davenport (Milopotamus), 1904-06; bp. Davenport, 1906-26.

**Davis, James P.** (1904-88): ord. May 19, 1929; bp. 1943-60, and first abp., 1960-64, San Juan, P.R.; abp. Santa Fe, 1964-74 (res.).

**Dearden, John F.** (1907-88): ord. Dec. 8, 1932; coad. bp. Pittsburgh (Sarepta), 1948-50; bp. Pittsburgh, 1950-58; abp. Detroit, 1958-80 (res.); cardinal 1969.

**De Cheverus, John L.:** See Cheverus, John

**De Falco, Lawrence M.** (1915-79): ord. June 11, 1942; bp. Amarillo, 1963-79 (res.).

**De Goesbriand, Louis** (1816-99): b. France; ord. July 13, 1840; first bp. Burlington, 1853-99.

**De la Hailandiere, Celestine** (1798-1882): b. France; ord. May 28, 1825; bp. Vincennes (now Indianapolis), 1839-47 (res.).

**Delany, John B.** (1864-1906): ord. May 23, 1891; bp. Manchester, 1904-06.

**Demers, Modeste** (1809-71): b. Canada; ord. Feb. 7, 1836; bp. Vancouver Is., 1846-71.

**Dempsey, Michael R.** (1918-74): ord. May 1, 1943; aux. Chicago (Truentum), 1968-74.

**De Neckere, Leo, C.M.** (1799-1833): b. Belgium; ord. Oct. 13, 1822; bp. New Orleans, 1829-33.

**Denning, Joseph P.** (1907-90): ord. May 21, 1932; aux. Brooklyn (Mallus), 1959-82 (res.).

**De Saint Palais, Maurice** (1811-77): b. France; ord. May 28, 1836; bp. Vincennes (now Indianapolis), 1849-77.

**Desmond, Daniel F.** (1884-1945): ord. June 9, 1911; bp. Alexandria, 1933-45.

**Dimmerling, Harold J.** (1914-87): ord. May 2, 1940; bp. Rapid City, 1969-87.

**Dinand, Joseph N., S.J.** (1869-1943): ord. June 25, 1903; v.a. Jamaica (Selinus), 1927-29 (res.).

**Dingman, Maurice J.** (1914-92): ord. Dec. 8, 1939; bp. Des Moines, 1968-86 (res.).

**Dobson, Robert** (1867-1942): ord. May 23, 1891; aux. Liverpool, Eng. (Cynopolis), 1922-42.

**Dolinay, Thomas V.** (1923-93): ord. May 16, 1948; aux. Passaic Byzantine Rite (Tiatira); 1976-81; first bp. Van Nuys Byzantine Rite, 1981-90; coad. abp.,

1990-91, and abp., 1991-93, Pittsburgh Byzantine Rite.

**Domenec, Michael, C.M.** (1816-78): b. Spain; ord. June 30, 1839; bp. Pittsburgh, 1860-76; bp. Allegheny, 1876-77 (res.).

**Donaghy, Frederick A., M.M.** (1903-88): ord. Jan. 29, 1929; v.a. Wuchow, China (Setea), 1939; first bp. Wuchow, 1946, expelled from China, 1955.

**Donahue, Joseph P.** (1870-1959): ord. June 8, 1895; aux. New York (Emmaus), 1945-59.

**Donahue, Patrick J.** (1849-1922): b. England; ord. Dec. 19, 1885; bp. Wheeling, 1894-1922.

**Donahue, Stephen J.** (1893-1982): ord. May 22, 1918; aux. New York (Medea), 1934-69 (res.).

**Donnellan, Thomas A.** (1914-87): ord. June 3, 1939; bp. Ogdensburg, 1964-68; abp. Atlanta, 1968-87.

**Donnelly, George J.** (1889-1950): ord. June 12, 1921; aux. St. Louis (Coela), 1940-46; bp. Leavenworth (now Kansas City — title changed in 1947), 1946-50.

**Donnelly, Henry E.** (1904-67): ord. Aug. 17, 1930; aux. Detroit (Tymbrias), 1954-67.

**Donnelly, Joseph F.** (1909-77): ord. June 29, 1934; aux. Hartford (Nabala), 1965-77.

**Donohoe, Hugh A.** (1905-87): ord. June 14, 1930; aux. bp. San Francisco (Taium), 1947-62; first bp. Stockton, 1962-69; bp. Fresno, 1969-80 (res.).

**Donovan, John A.** (1911-91): b. Canada; ord. Dec. 8, 1935; aux. Detroit (Rhasus), 1954-67; bp. Toledo, 1967-80 (res.).

**Doran, Thomas F.** (1856-1916): ord. July 4, 1880; aux. Providence (Halicarnassus), 1915-16.

**Dougherty, Dennis** (1865-1951): ord. May 31, 1890; bp. Nueva Segovia, P.I., 1903-08; bp. Jaro, P.I., 1980-15; bp. Buffalo, 1915-18; abp. Philadelphia, 1918-51; cardinal, 1921.

**Dougherty, John J.** (1907-86): ord. July 23, 1933; aux. Newark (Cotena), 1963-82 (res.).

**Dougherty, Joseph P.** (1905-70): ord. June 14, 1930; first bp. Yakima, 1951-69; aux. Los Angeles (Altino), 1969-70.

**Dowling, Austin** (1868-1930): ord. June 24, 1891; first bp. Des Moines, 1912-19; abp. St. Paul, 1919-30.

**Dozier, Carroll T.** (1911-85): ord. Mar. 19, 1937; first bp. Memphis, 1971-82 (res.).

**Driscoll, Justin A.** (1920-84): ord. July 28, 1945; bp. Fargo, 1970-84.

**Drossaerts, Arthur J.** (1862-1940): b. Holland; ord. June 15, 1889; bp. San Antonio 1918-26; first abp. San Antonio, 1926-40.

**Drumm, Thomas W.** (1871-1933): b. Ireland; ord. Dec. 21, 1901; bp. Des Moines, 1919-33.

**Drury, Thomas J.** (1908-92): ord. June 2, 1935; first bp. San Angelo, 1962-65; bp. Corpus Christi, 1965-83 (res.).

**Dubois, John, S.S.** (1764-1842): b. France; ord. Sept. 28, 1787; bp. New York, 1826-42.

**Dubourg, Louis William, S.S.** (1766-1833): b. Santo Domingo; ord. 1788; bp. Louisiana and the Two Floridas (now New Orleans), 1815-25; returned to France; bp. Montauban, 1826-33; abp. Besancon 1833.

**Dubuis, Claude M.** (1817-95): b. France; ord. June 1, 1844; bp. Galveston, 1862-92 (res.).

**Dufal, Peter, C.S.C.** (1822-98): b. France; ord. Sept. 29, 1852; v.a. Eastern Bengal (Delcon), 1860-78; coad. bp. Galveston, 1878-80 (res.).

**Duffy, James A.** (1873-1968): ord. May 27, 1899; bp. Kearney (see transferred to Grand Island, 1917), 1913-31 (res.).

**Duffy, John A.** (1884-1944): ord. June 13, 1908; bp. Syracuse, 1933-37; bp. Buffalo, 1937-44.

**Duggan, James** (1825-99): b. Ireland; ord. May 29, 1847; coad. bp. St. Louis (Gabala), 1857-59; bp. Chicago, 1859-80 (res.). Inactive from 1869 because of illness.

**Dunn, Francis J.** (1922-89): ord. Jan. 11, 1948; aux. Dubuque (Turris Tamallani), 1969-89.

**Dunn, John J.** (1869-1933): ord. May 30, 1896; aux. New York (Camuliana), 1921-33.

**Dunne, Edmund M.** (1864-1929): ord. June 24, 1887; bp. Peoria, 1909-29.

**Dunne, Edward** (1848-1910): b. Ireland; ord. June 29, 1871; bp. Dallas, 1893-1910.

**Durick, Joseph Aloysius** (1914-94): ord. May 23, 1940; aux. bp. Mobile-Birmingham (Cerbali), 1955-64; coad. bp. Nashville, 1964-69 (ap. admin. 1966-69); bp. Nashville, 1969-75 (res.).

**Durier, Anthony** (1832-1904): b. France; ord. Oct. 28, 1856; bp. Natchitoches (now Alexandria), La., 1885-1904.

**Dwenger, Joseph, C.Pp.S.** (1837-93): ord. Sept. 4, 1859; bp. Fort Wayne, 1872-93.

**Dworschak, Leo F.** (1900-76): ord. May 29, 1926; coad. bp. Rapid City (Tium), 1946-47; aux. Fargo, 1947-60; bp. Fago, 1960-70 (res.).

**Dwyer, Robert J.** (1908-76): ord. June 11, 1932; bp. Reno, 1952-66; abp. Portland, Ore., 1966-74 (res.).

**E**

**Eccleston, Samuel, S.S.** (1801-51): ord. Apr. 24, 1825; coad. bp. Baltimore (Thermae), Sept.-Oct., 1834; abp. Baltimore, 1834-51.

**Egan, Michael, O.F.M.** (1761-1814): b. Ireland; first bp. Philadelphia, 1810-14.

**Eis, Frederick** (1843-1926): b. Germany; ord. Oct. 30, 1870; bp. Sault Ste. Marie and Marquette (now Marquette), 1899-1922 (res.).

**Elder, William** (1819-1904): ord. Mar. 29, 1846; bp. Natchez (now Jackson), 1857-80; coad. bp. Cincinnati (Avara), 1880-83; abp. Cincinnati, 1883-1904.

**Elko, Nicholas T.** (1909-91): ord. Sept. 30, 1934; ap. admin. Byzantine exarchy of Pittsburgh (Apollonias), Mar.-Sept. 1955; exarch, Sept., 1955-63, and first eparch, 1963-67, of Pittsburgh; tit. abp. Dara, 1967, with assignment in Rome; aux. bp. Cincinnati, 1971-85 (res.).

**Elwell, Clarence E.** (1904-73): ord. Mar. 17, 1929; aux. Cleveland (Cone) 1962-68; bp. Columbus, 1968-73.

**Emmet, Thomas A., S.J.** (1873-1950): ord. July 30, 1909; v.a. Jamaica (Tuscamia), 1930-49 (res.).

**England, John** (1786-1842): b. Ireland; ord. Oct. 11, 1808; first bp. Charleston, 1820-42.

**Escalante, Alonso Manuel, M.M.** (1906-67): b. Mexico; ord. Feb. 1, 1931; v.a. Pando, Bolivia (Sora), 1943-60 (res.).

**Espelage (brothers):** Bernard T., O.F.M. (1892-

1971): ord. May 16, 1918; bp. Gallup, 1940-69 (res.).
Sylvester J., O.F.M. (1877-1940): ord. Jan. 18, 1900;
v.a. Wuchang, China (Oreus), 1930-40.

**Etteldorf, Raymond P.** (1911-86): ord. Dec. 8,
1937; apostolic delegate, 1969-73, and nuncio, 1973-
74, to New Zealand (Tindari); pro-nuncio to Ethiopia, 1947-82.

**Eustace, Bartholomew J.** (1887-1956): ord. Nov.
1, 1914; bp. Camden, 1938-56.

**Evans, George R.** (1922-85): ord. May 31, 1947;
aux. Denver (Tubyza), 1969-85.

**F**

**Fahey, Leo F.** (1898-1950): ord. May 29, 1926;
coad. bp. Baker City (Ipsus), 1948-50.

**Falconio, Diomede, O.F.M.** (1842-1917): b. Italy;
ord. Jan. 3, 1866, Buffalo, N.Y.; missionary in U.S.
and Canada; returned to Italy; bp. Lacedonia, 1892-
95; abp. Acerenza e Matera, 1895-99; ap. del. Canada
(Larissa), 1899-1902, U.S., 1902-11; cardinal 1911.

**Farley, John** (1842-1918): b. Ireland; ord. June
11, 1870; aux. New York (Zeugma), 1895-1902; abp.
New York, 1902-18; cardinal 1911.

**Farrelly, John P.** (1856-1921): ord. Mar. 22, 1880;
bp. Cleveland, 1909-21.

**Fearns, John M.** (897-1977): ord. Feb. 19, 1922;
aux. New York (Geras), 1957-72 (res.).

**Fedders, Edward L., M.M.** (1913-73): ord. June
11, 1944; prelate Juli, Peru (Antiochia ad Meadrum),
1963-73.

**Feehan, Daniel F.** (1855-1934): ord. Dec. 29, 1879;
bp. Fall River, 1907-34.

**Feehan, Patrick A.** (1829-1902): b. Ireland; ord.
Nov. 1, 1852; bp. Nashville, 1865-80; first abp. Chicago, 1880-1902.

**Feeney, Daniel J.** (1894-1969): ord. May 21, 1921;
aux. Portland, Me. (Sita), 1946-52; coad. bp. Portland, 1952-55; bp. Portland, 1955-69.

**Feeney, Thomas J., S.J.** (1894-1955): ord. June
23, 1927; v.a. Caroline and Marshall Is. (Agnus),
1951-55.

**Fenwick, Benedict J., S.J.** (1782-1846): ord. June
11, 1808; bp. Boston, 1825-46.

**Fenwick, Edward D., O.P.** (1768-1832): ord. Feb.
23, 1793; first bp. Cincinnati, 1822-32.

**Fink, Michael, O.S.B.** (1834-1904): b. Germany;
ord. May 28, 1857; coad. v.a., 1871-74, and v.a.,
1874-77, Kansas and Indian Territory (Eucarpia);
first bp. Leavenworth (now Kansas City), 1877-1904.

**Finnigan, George, C.S.C.** (1885-1932): ord. June
13, 1915; bp. Helena, 1927-32.

**Fisher, Carl, S.S.J.** (1945-93): ord. June 2, 1973;
aux. Los Angeles (Tlos), 1987-93.

**Fitzgerald, Edward** (1833-1907): b. Ireland; ord.
Aug. 22, 1857; bp. Little Rock, 1867-1907.

**Fitzgerald, Edward A.** (1893-1972): ord. July 25,
1916; aux. Dubuque (Cantanus), 1946-49; bp.
Winona, 1949-69 (res.).

**Fitzgerald, Walter J., S.J.** (1883-1947): ord. May
16, 1918; coad. v.a. Alaska (Tymbrias), 1939-45; v.a.
Alaska, 1945-47.

**Fitzmaurice, Edmond** (1881-1962): b. Ireland;
ord. May 28, 1904; bp. Wilmington, 1925-60 (res.).

**Fitzmaurice, John E.** (1837-1920): b. Ireland; ord.
Dec. 21, 1862; coad. bp. Erie (Amisus), 1898-99;
bp. Erie, 1899-1920.

**Fitzpatrick, John B.** (1812-66): ord. June 13,
1840; aux. Boston (Callipolis), 1843-46; bp. Boston, 1846-66.

**Fitzsimon, Laurence J.** (1895-1958): ord. May
17, 1921; bp. Amarillo, 1941-58.

**Flaget, Benedict, S.S.:** See Index.

**Flaherty, J. Louis** (1910-75): ord. Dec. 8, 1936;
aux. Richmond (Tabudo), 1966-75.

**Flannelly, Joseph F.** (1894-1973): ord. Sept. 1,
1918; aux. New York (Metelis), 1948-70 (res.).

**Flasch, Kilian C.** (1831-91): b. Germany; ord. Dec.
16, 1859; bp. La Crosse, 1881-91.

**Flavin, Glennon P.** (1916-95): ord. Dec. 20. 1941;
aux St. Louis (Joannina) 1957-67; bp. Lincoln, 1967-
92 (res.).

**Fletcher, Albert L.** (1896-1979): ord. June 4, 1920;
aux. Little Rock (Samos), 1940-46; bp. Little Rock,
1946-72 (res.).

**Floersh, John** (1886-1968): ord. June 10, 1911;
coad. bp. Louisville (Lycopolis), 1923-24; bp. Louisville, 1924-37; first abp. Louisville, 1937-67 (res.).

**Flores, Felixberto C.** (1921-85): b. Gaum; ord.
Apr. 30, 1949; ap. admin. Agana, Guam (Stonj),
1970-72; bp., 1977-84, and first abp. Agana, 1984-
85.

**Foery, Walter A.** (1890-1978): ord. June 10, 1916;
bp. Syracuse, 1937-70 (res.).

**Foley** (brothers): **John S.** (1833-1918): ord. Dec.
20, 1856; bp. Detroit, 1888-1918. **Thomas** (1822-
79): ord. Aug. 16, 1846; coad. bp. and ap. admin.
Chicago (Pergamum), 1870-79.

**Foley, Maurice P.** (1867-1919): ord. July 25, 1891;
bp. Tuguegarao, P.I., 1910-16; bp. Jaro, P.I., 1916-
19.

**Ford, Francis X., M.M.** (1892-1952): ord. Dec.
5, 1917; v.a. Kaying, China (Etenna), 1935-46; first
bp. Kaying, 1946-52.

**Forest, John A.** (1838-1911): b. France; ord. Apr.
12, 1863; bp. San Antonio, 1895-1911.

**Fox, Joseph J.** (1855-1915): ord. June 7, 1879;
bp. Green Bay, 1904-14 (res.).

**Franz, John B.** (1896-1992): ord. June 13, 1920;
first bp. Dodge City, 1951-59; bp. Peoria, 1959-71
(res.).

**Frosi, Angelo, S.X.** (1924-95): b. Italy; U.S. citi-
zen; ord. May 6, 1948; prelate Abaete do Tocantins
(Magneta), Brazil, 1970-81; first bp. Abaetetuba,
Brazil, 1981-95.

**Fulcher, George A.** (1922-84): ord. Feb. 28, 1948;
aux. Columbus (Morosbisdus), 1976-83; bp.
Lafayette, 1983-84.

**Furey, Francis J.** (1905-79): ord. Mar. 15, 1930;
aux. Philadelphia (Temnus), 1960-63; coad bp. San
Diego, 1963-66; bp. San Diego, 1966-69; abp. San
Antonio, 1969-79.

**Furlong, Philip J.** (1892-1989): ord. May 18,
1918; aux. Military Vicar (Araxa), 1956-71 (res.).

**G**

**Gabriels, Henry** (1838-1921): b. Belgium; ord.
Sept. 21, 1861; bp. Ogdensburg, 1892-1921.

**Gabro, Jaroslav** (1919-80): ord. Sept. 27, 1945;
bp. St. Nicholas of Chicago (Byzantine Rite, Ukrainians), 1961-80.

**Galberry, Thomas, O.S.A.** (1833-78): b. Ireland;
ord. Dec. 20, 1856; bp. Hartford, 1876-78.

**Gallagher, Michael J.** (1866-1937): ord. Mar. 19, 1893; coad. bp. Grand Rapids (Tiposa in Mauretania), 1915-16; bp. Grand Rapids, 1916-18; bp. Detroit, 1918-37.

**Gallagher, Nicholas** (1846-1918): ord. Dec. 25, 1868; coad. bp. Galveston (Canopus), 1882-92; bp. Galveston, 1892-1918.

**Gallagher, Raymond J.** (1912-91): ord. Mar. 25, 1939; bp. Lafayette, Ind., 1965-82 (res.).

**Gallegos, Alphonse, O.A.R.** (1931-91): ord. May 24, 1958; aux. Sacramento (Sassabe), 1981-91.

**Gannon, John M.** (1877-1968): ord. Dec. 21, 1901; aux. Erie (Nilopolis), 1918-20; bp. Erie, 1920-66 (res.).

**Ganter, Bernard J.** (1928-93): ord. May 22, 1952; first bp. Tulsa, 1972-77; bp. Beaumont, 1977-93.

**Garcia Diego y Moreno, Francisco, O.F.M.** (1785-1846): b. Mexico; ord. Nov. 14, 1808; bp. Two Californias (now Los Angeles), 1840-46.

**Garriga, Mariano S.** (1886-1965): ord. July 2, 1911; coad. bp. Corpus Christi (Syene), 1936-49; bp. Corpus Christi, 1949-65.

**Garrigan, Philip** (1840-1919): b. Ireland; ord. June 11, 1870; first bp. Sioux City, 1902-19.

**Gartland, Francis X.** (1808-54): b. Ireland; ord. Aug. 5, 1832; first bp. Savannah, 1850-54.

**Garvey, Eugene A.** (1845-1920): ord. Sept. 22, 1869; first bp. Altoona (now Altoona-Johnstown), 1901-20.

**Gercke, Daniel J.** (1874-1964): ord. June 1, 1901; bp. Tucson, 1923-60 (res.).

**Gerken, Rudolph A.** (1887-1943): ord. June 10, 1917; first bp. Amarillo, 1927-33; abp. Santa Fe, 1933-43.

**Gerow, Richard O.** (1885-1976): ord. June 5, 1909; bp. Natchez-Jackson (now Jackson), 1924-67 (res).

**Gerrard, James J.** (1897-1991): ord. May 26, 1923; aux. Fall River (Forma), 1959-76 (res.).

**Ghattas, Ignatius, B.S.O.** (1920-92): b. Nazareth, Israel; ord. July 7, 1946; bp. Newton for Greek Melkites, 1990-92.

**Gibbons, Edmund F.** (1868-1964): ord. May 27, 1893; bp. Albany, 1919-54 (res.).

**Gibbons, James** (1834-1921): ord. June 30, 1861; v.a. North Carolina (Adramyttium), 1868-72; bp. Richmond, 1872-77;coad. Baltimore (Jonopolis), May-Oct., 1877; abp. Baltimore, 1877-1921; cardinal 1886.

**Gilfillan, Francis** (1872-1933): b. Ireland; ord. June 24, 1895; coad. bp. St. Joseph (Spiga), 1922-23; bp. St. Joseph, 1923-33.

**Gill, Thomas E.** (1908-73): ord. June 10, 1933; aux. Seattle (Lambesis) 1956-73.

**Gilmore, Joseph M.** (1893-1962): ord. July 25, 1915; bp. Helena, 1936-62.

**Gilmour, Richard** (1824-91): b. Scotland; ord. Aug. 30, 1852; bp. Cleveland, 1872-91.

**Girouard, Paul J., M.S.** (1898-1964): ord. July 26, 1927; first bp. Morondava, Madagascar, 1956-64.

**Glass, Joseph S., C.M.** (1874-1926): ord. Aug. 15, 1897; bp. Salt Lake City, 1915-26.

**Gleeson, Francis D., S.J.** (1895-1983): ord. July 29, 1926; v.a. Alaska (Cotenna), 1948-62; first bp. Fairbanks, 1962-68 (res.).

**Glenn, Lawrence A.** (1900-85): ord. June 11, 1927; aux. Duluth (Tuscamia), 1956-60; bp. Crookston, 1960-70 (res.).

**Glennie, Ignatius T., S.J.** (1907-93): ord. Nov. 21, 1938; bp. Trincomalee (now Trincomalee-Batticaloa), Sri Lanka, 1947-74 (res.).

**Glennon, John J.** (1862-1946): b. Ireland; ord. Dec. 20, 1884; coad. bp. Kansas City, Mo. (Pinara), 1896-1903; coad. St. Louis, April-Oct., 1903; abp. St. Louis, 1903-46; cardinal 1946.

**Glorieux, Alphonse J.** (1844-1917): b. Belgium; ord. Aug. 17, 1867; v.a. Idaho (Apollonia), 1885-93; bp. Boise, 1893-1917.

**Gorman, Daniel** (1861-1927): ord. June 24, 1893; bp. Boise, 1918-27.

**Gorman, Thomas K.** (1892-1980): ord. June 23, 1917; first bp. Reno, 1931-52; coad. bp. Dallas-Ft. Worth (Rhasus), 1952-54; bp. Dallas-Fort Worth (now Dallas), 1954-69 (res.).

**Grace, Thomas** (1841-1921): b. Ireland; ord. June 24, 1876; bp. Sacramento, 1896-1921.

**Grace, Thomas L., O.P.** (1814-97): ord. Dec. 21, 1839; bp. St. Paul, 1859-84 (res.).

**Graner, Lawrence L., C.S.C.** (1901-82): ord. June 24, 1928; bp. Dacca, 1947-50, and first abp., 1950-67 (res.).

**Granjon, Henry** (1863-1922): b. France; ord. Dec. 17, 1887; bp. Tucson, 1900-22.

**Graves, Lawrence P.** (1916-94): ord. June 11, 1942; aux. Little Rock (Vina), 1969-73; bp. Alexandria (now Alexandria-Shreveport), 1973-82 (res.).

**Graziano, Lawrence, O.F.M.** (1921-90): ord. Jan. 26, 1947; aux. Santa Ana, El Salvador (Limata), 1961-65; coad. San Miguel, El Salvador, 1965-68; bp. San Miguel, 1968-69 (res.).

**Greco, Charles P.** (1894-1987): ord. July 25, 1918; bp. Alexandria, La., 1946-73 (res.).

**Green, Francis J.** (1906-95): ord. May 15, 1932; aux. Tucson (Serra), 1953-60, coad. May-Oct., 1960, and bp. Tucson, Oct. 26, 1960-1981 (ret.).

**Green, Joseph J.** (1917-82): ord. July 14, 1946; aux. Lansing (Trisipa), 1962-67; bp. Reno 1967-74 (res.).

**Grellinger, John B.** (1899-1984): ord. priest July 14, 1929; aux. Green Bay (Syene), 1949-74 (res.).

**Greteman, Frank H.** (1907-87): ord. Dec. 8, 1932; aux. Sioux City (Vissala), 1965-70; bp. Sioux City, 1970-83 (res.).

**Griffin, James A.** (1883-1948): ord. July 4, 1909; bp. Springfield, Ill., 1924-48.

**Griffin, William A.** (1885-1950): ord. Aug. 15, 1910; aux. Newark (Sanavus), 1938-40; bp. Trenton, 1940-50.

**Griffin, William R.** (1883-1944): ord. May 25, 1907; aux. La Crosse (Lydda), 1935-44.

**Griffiths, James H.** (1903-64): ord. Mar. 12, 1927; aux. New York and delegate of U.S. military vicar (Gaza), 1950-64.

**Grimes, John** (1852-1922): b. Ireland; ord. Feb. 19, 1882; coad. bp. Syracuse (Hemeria), 1909-12; bp. Syracuse, 1912-22.

**Grimmelsman, Henry J.** (1890-1972): ord.Aug. 15, 1915; first bp. Evansville, 1945-65 (res.).

**Gross, William H., C.SS.R.** (1837-98): ord. Mar. 21, 1863; bp. Savannah, 1873-85; abp. Oregon City (now Portland), 1885-98.

**Grovas Felix, Rafael** (1905-91): b. San Juan, Puerto Rico; ord. Apr. 7, 1928; bp. Caguas, P.R., 1965-81 (res.).

**Grutka, Andrew G.** (1908-93): ord. Dec. 5, 1933; first bp. Gary, 1957-84 (res.).

**Guertin, George A.** (1869-1932): ord. Dec. 17, 1892; bp. Manchester, 1907-32.

**Guilfoyle, George H.** (1913-91): ord. Mar. 25, 1944; aux. New York (Marazane), 1964-68; bp. Camden 1968-89 (res.).

**Guilfoyle, Richard T.** (1892-1957): ord. June 2, 1917; bp. Altoona (now Altoona-Johnstown), 1936-57.

**Guilfoyle, Merlin J.** (1908-81): ord. June 10, 1933; aux. San Francisco (Bulla), 1950-69; bp. Stockton, 1969-79 (res.).

**Gunn, John E., S.M.** (1863-1924): b. Ireland; ord. Feb. 2, 1890; bp. Natchez (now Jackson), 1911-24.

## H

**Haas, Francis J.** (1889-1953): ord. June 11, 1913; bp. Grand Rapids, 1943-53.

**Hacker, Hilary B.** (1913-90): ord. June 4, 1938; bp. Bismarck, 1957-82 (res.).

**Hackett, John F.** (1911-90): ord. June 29, 1936; aux. Hartford (Helenopolis in Palaestina),1953-86 (res.).

**Hafey, William** (1888-1954): ord. June 16, 1914; first bp. Raleigh, 1925-37; coad. bp. Scranton (Appia), 1937-38; bp. Scranton, 1938-54.

**Hagan, John R.** (1890-1946): ord. Mar. 7, 1914; aux. Cleveland (Limata), 1946.

**Hagarty, Paul L., O.S.B.** (1909-84): ord. June 6, 1936; v.a. Bahamas (Arba), 1950-60; first bp. Nassau, Bahamas, 1960-81 (res.).

**Haid, Leo M., O.S.B.** (1849-1924): ord. Dec. 21, 1872; v.a. N. Carolina (Messene), 1888-1910; abbot Mary Help of Christians abbacy, 1910-24.

**Hallinan, Paul J.** (1911-68): ord. Feb. 20, 1937; bp. Charleston, 1958-62; first abp. Atlanta, 1962-68.

**Hammes, George A.** (1911-93): ord. May 22, 1937; bp. Superior 1960-85 (res.).

**Hanna, Edward J.** (1860-1944): ord. May 30, 1885; aux. San Francisco (Titiopolis). 1912-15; abp. San Francisco, 1915-35 (res.).

**Hannan, Jerome D.** (1896-1965): ord. May 22, 1921; bp. Scranton, 1954-65.

**Harkins, Matthew** (1845-1921): ord. May 22, 1869; bp. Providence, 1887-1921.

**Harper, Edward, C.SS.R.** (1910-90): ord. June 18, 1939; first prelate Virgin Islands (Heraclea Pontica), 1960-77, and first bishop (prelacy made diocese of St. Thomas), 1977-85 (res.).

**Harris, Vincent M.** (1913-88): ord. Mar. 19, 1938; first bp. Beaumont, 1966-71; coad. bp. Austin (Rotaria), Apr. 27-Nov. 16, 1971; bp. Austin, 1971-85 (res.).

**Hartley, James J.** (1858-1944): ord. July 10, 1882; bp. Columbus, 1904-44.

**Harty, Jeremiah J.** (1853-1927): ord. Apr. 28, 1878; abp. Manila, 1903-16; abp. Omaha, 1916- 27.

**Hastrich, Jerome J.** (1914-95): ord. Feb. 9, 1941; aux. Madison (Gurza), 1963-69; bp. Gallup, 1969-90 (ret.).

**Hayes, James T., S.J.** 1889-1980): ord. June 29,

1921; bp. of Cagayan, Philippines, 1933-51; first abp. Cagayan, 1951-70 (res.).

**Hayes, Nevin W., O. Carm.** (1922-88): ord. June 8, 1946; prelate Sicuani, Peru (Nova Sinna), 1965-70; aux. bp. Chicago, 1971-88.

**Hayes, Patrick J.** (1867-1938): ord. Sept. 8, 1892; aux. New York (Thagaste), 1914-19; abp. New York, 1919-38; cardinal 1924.

**Hayes, Ralph L.** (1884-1970): ord. Sept. 19, 1909; bp. Helena 1933-35; rector North American College (Hieropolis) 1935-44; bp. Davenport, 1944-66 (res.).

**Healy, James A.** (1830-1900): ord. June 10, 1854; bp. Portland 1875-1900.

**Heelan, Edmond** (1868-1948): b. Ireland; ord. June 24, 1890; aux. Sioux City (Gerasa), 1919-20; bp. Sioux City, 1920-48.

**Heffron, Patrick** (1860-1927): ord. Dec. 22, 1884; bp. Winona, 1910-27.

**Heiss, Michael** (1818-90): b. Germany; ord. Oct. 18, 1840; bp. La Crosse, 1868-80; coad. abp. Milwaukee (Hadrianopolis), 1880-81; abp. Milwaukee, 1881-90.

**Helmsing, Charles H.** (1908-93): ord. June 10, 1933; aux. bp. St. Louis (Axomis), 1949-56; first bp. Springfield-Cape Girardeau, 1956-62; bp. Kansas City-St. Joseph, 1962-77 (res.).

**Hendrick, Thomas A.** (1849-1909): ord. June 7, 1873; bp. Cebu, P.I., 1904-09.

**Hendricken, Thomas F.** (1827-86): b. Ireland; ord. Apr. 25, 1853; bp. Providence, 1872-86.

**Hennessy, John** (1825-1900): b. Ireland; ord. Nov. 1, 1850; bp. Dubuque, 1866-93; first abp. Dubuque, 1893-1900.

**Hennessy, John J.** (1847-1920): b. Ireland; ord. Nov. 28, 1869; first bp. Wichita, 1888-1920; ap. admin. Concordia (now Salina), 1891-98.

**Henni, John M.** (1805-81): b. Switzerland; ord. Feb. 2, 1829; first bp. Milwaukee, 1844-75; first abp. Milwaukee, 1875-81.

**Henry, Harold W., S.S.C.** (1909-76): ord. Dec. 21, 1932; v.a. Kwang Ju, Korea (Coridala), 1957-62; first abp. Kwang Ju, 1962-71; ap. admin. p.a. Cheju-Do, Korea (Thubunae), 1971-76.

**Herzig, Charles E.** (1929-91): ord. May 31, 1955; first bp. Tyler, 1987-91.

**Heslin, Thomas** (1845-1911): b. Ireland; ord. Sept. 8, 1869; bp. Natchez (now Jackson), 1889-1911.

**Heston, Edward L.** (1907-73): ord. Dec. 22, 1934; sec. Sacred Congregation for Religious and Secular Institutes, 1969-71; pres. Pontifical Commission for Social Communications, 1971-73; tit. abp. Numidea, 1972.

**Hickey, David F., S.J.** (1882-1973): ord. June 27, 1917; v.a. Belize, Br. Honduras (Bonitza), 1948-56; first bp. Belize, 1956-57 (res.); tit. abp. Cabasa, 1957-73.

**Hickey, Thomas F.** (1861-1940): ord. Mar. 25, 1884; coad. bp. Rochester (Berenice), 1905-09; bp. Rochester, 1909-28 (res.).

**Hickey, William A.** (1869-1933): ord. Dec. 22, 1893; coad. bp. Providence (Claudiopolis), 1919-21; bp. Providence, 1921-33.

**Hillinger, Raymond P.** (1904-71): ord. Apr. 2, 1932; bp. Rockford, 1953-56; aux. Chicago (Derbe), 1956-71.

**Hines, Vincent J.** (1912-90): ord. May 2, 1937; bp. Norwich, 1960-75 (res.).

**Hoban, Edward F.** (1878-1966): ord. July 11, 1903; aux. Chicago (Colonia), 1921-28; bp. Rockford, 1928-42; coad. bp. Cleveland (Lystra), 1942-45; bp. Cleveland, 1945-66.

**Hoban, Michael J.** (1853-1926): ord. May 22, 1880; coad. bp. Scranton (Halius), 1896-99; bp. Scranton, 1899-1926.

**Hoch, Lambert A.** (1903-90): ord. May 30, 1928; bp. Bismarck, 1952-56; bp. Sioux Falls, 1956-78 (res.).

**Hodapp, Robert L., S.J.** (1910-89): ord. June 18, 1941; bp. Belize (now Belize-Belmopan), 1958-83 (res.).

**Hodges, Joseph H.** (1911-85): ord. Dec. 8, 1935; aux. Richmond (Rusadus), 1952-61; coad. Wheeling, 1961-62; bp. Wheeling (now Wheeling- Charleston), 1962-85.

**Hogan, John J.** (1829-1913): b. Ireland; ord. Apr. 10, 1852; first bp. St. Joseph, 1868-80; first bp. Kansas City, 1880-1913.

**Horstmann, Ignatius** (1840-1908): ord. June 10, 1865; bp. Cleveland, 1892-1908.

**Howard, Edward D.** (1877-1983): ord. June 12, 1906; aux. Davenport (Isauropolis), 1924-26; abp. Oregon City (title changed to Portland, 1928), 1926-66 (res.).

**Howard, Francis W.** (1867-1944): ord. June 16, 1891; bp. Covington, 1923-44.

**Hughes, John J.** (1797-1864): b. Ireland; ord. Oct. 15, 1826; coad. bp. New York (Basilinopolis), 1837-42; bp. New York, 1842-50, and first abp., 1850-64.

**Hunkeler, Edward J.** (1894-1970): ord. June 14, 1919; bp. Grand Island, 1945-51; bp. Kansas City, Kans. 1951-52; first abp. Kansas City, 1952-69 (res.).

**Hunt, Duane G.** (1884-1960): ord. June 27, 1920; bp. Salt Lake City, 1937-60.

**Hurley, Joseph P.** (1894-1967): ord. May 29, 1919; bp. St. Augustine, 1940-67.

**Hyland, Francis E.** (1901-68): ord. June 11, 1927; aux. Savannah-Atlanta (Gomphi), 1949-56; bp. Atlanta, 1956-61 (res.).

**Hyle, Michael W.** (1901-67): ord. Mar. 12, 1927; coad. bp. Wilmington, 1958-60; bp. Wilmington, 1960-67.

## I

**Iranyi, Ladislaus A., Sch. P.** (1923-87): ord. Mar. 13, 1948; U.S. citizen, 1958; ord. bp. (Castel Mediano), July 27, 1983, for spiritual care of Hungarian Catholics living outside Hungary.

**Ireland, John** (1838-1918): b. Ireland; ord. Dec. 21, 1861; coad. bp. St. Paul (Marobea), 1875-84; bp. St. Paul, 1884-88, and first abp. St. Paul, 1888-1918.

**Ireton, Peter L.** (1882-1958): ord. June 20, 1906; coad. bp. Richmond (Cyme), 1935-45; bp. Richmond, 1945-58.

**Issenmann, Clarence G.** (1907-82): ord. June 29, 1932; aux. Cincinnati (Phytea), 1954-57; bp. Columbus, 1957-64; coad. bp. Cleveland (Filaca), 1964-66; bp. Cleveland, 1966-74 (res.).

**Ivancho, Daniel** (1908-72): b. Austria-Hungary; ord. Sept. 30, 1934; coad. bp. Pittsburgh Ruthenian Rite (Europus), 1946-48; bp. Pittsburgh Ruthenian Rite, 1948-54 (res.).

## J

**Janssen, John** (1835-1913): b. Germany; ord. Nov. 19, 1858; first bp. Belleville, 1888-1913.

**Janssens, Francis A.** (1843-97): b. Holland; ord. Dec. 21, 1867; bp. Natchez (now Jackson) 1881-88; abp. New Orleans, 1888-97.

**Jeanmard, Jules B.** (1879-1957): ord. June 10, 1903; first bp. Lafayette, La., 1918-56 (res.).

**Johannes, Francis** (1874-1937): b. Germany; ord. Jan. 3, 1897; coad. bp. Leavenworth (Thasus), 1928-29; bp. Leavenworth (now Kansas City), 1929-37.

**Johnson, William R.** (1918-86): ord. May 28, 1944; aux. Los Angeles (Blera), 1971-76; first bp. Orange, 1976-86.

**Jolson, Alfred, S.J.** (1928-94): ord. June 14, 1958; bp. Reykjavik, Iceland, 1988-94.

**Jones, William A., O.S.A.** (1865-1921): ord. Mar. 15, 1890; bp. San Juan, 1907-21.

**Joyce, Robert F.** (1896-1990): ord. May 26, 1923; aux. Burlington (Citium), 1954-57; bp. Burlington 1957-71 (res.).

**Juncker, Henry D.** (1809-68): b. Lorraine (France); ord. Mar. 16, 1834; first bp. Alton (now Springfield), Ill., 1857-68.

**Junger, Aegidius** (1833-95): b. Germany; ord. June 27, 1862; bp. Nesqually (now Seattle), 1879-95.

## K

**Kain, John J.** (1841-1903): ord. July 2, 1866; bp. Wheeling, 1875-93; coad. abp. St. Louis (Oxyrynchus), 1893-95; abp. St. Louis, 1895-1903.

**Katzer, Frederick X.** (1844-1903): b. Austria; ord. Dec. 21, 1866; bp. Green Bay, 1886-91; abp. Milwaukee, 1891-1903.

**Keane, James J.** (1856-1929): ord. Dec. 23, 1882; bp. Cheyenne, 1902-11; abp. Dubuque, 1911-29.

**Keane, John J.** (1839-1918): b. Ireland; ord. July 2, 1866; bp. Richmond, 1878-88; rector of Catholic University, 1888-97; consultor of Congregation for Propagation of the Faith, 1897-1900; abp. Dubuque, 1900-11 (res.).

**Keane, Patrick J.** (1872-1928): b. Ireland; ord. June 20, 1895; aux. Sacramento (Samaria), 1920-22; bp. Sacramento, 1922-28.

**Kearney, James E.** (1884-1977): ord. Sept. 19, 1908; bp. Salt Lake City, 1932-37; bp. Rochester, 1937-66 (res.).

**Kearney, Raymond A.** (1902-56): ord. Mar. 12, 1927; aux. Brooklyn (Lysinia), 1935-56.

**Keiley, Benjamin J.** (1847-1925): ord. Dec. 31, 1873; bp. Savannah, 1900-22 (res.).

**Kelleher, Louis F.** (1889-1946): ord. Apr. 3, 1915; aux. Boston (Thenae), 1945-46.

**Kellenberg, Walter P.** (1901-86): ord. June 2, 1928; aux. New York (Joannina), 1953-54; bp. Ogdensburg, 1954-57; first bp. Rockville Centre, 1957-76 (res.).

**Kelley, Francis C.** (1870-1948): b. Canada; ord. Aug. 23, 1893; bp. Oklahoma, 1924-48.

**Kelly, Edward D.** (1860-1926): ord. June 16, 1886; aux. Detroit (Cestrus), 1911-19; bp. Grand Rapids, 1919-26.

**Kelly, Edward J.** (1890-1956): ord. June 2, 1917; bp. Boise, 1928-56.

**Kelly, Francis M.** (1886-1950): ord. Nov. 1, 1912; aux. Winona (Mylasa), 1926-28; bp. Winona, 1928-49 (res.).

**Kelly, Patrick** (1779-1829): b. Ireland; ord. July

18, 1802; first bp. Richmond, 1820-22 (returned to Ireland; bp. Waterford and Lismore, 1822-29).

**Kennally, Vincent, S.J.** (1895-1977): ord. June 20, 1928; v.a. Caroline and Marshall Islands (Sassura), 1957-71 (res.).

**Kennedy, Thomas F.** (1858-1917): ord. July 24, 1887; rector North American College, 1901-17; tit. bp. Hadrianapolis, 1907-15; tit. abp. Seleucia, 1915-17.

**Kenney, Lawrence J.** (1930-90): ord. June 2, 1956; aux. Military Services archdiocese (Holar),1983-90.

**Kenny, Michael H.** (1937-95): ord. Mar. 30, 1963; bp. Juneau, 1979-95.

**Kenny, William J.** (1853-1913): ord. Jan. 15, 1879; bp. St. Augustine, 1902-13.

**Kenrick** (brothers): **Francis P.** (1796-1863): b. Ireland; ord. Apr. 7, 1821; coad. bp. Philadelphia (Aratha), 1830-42; bp. Philadelphia, 1842-51; abp. Baltimore, 1851-63. **Peter** (1806-96): b. Ireland; ord. Mar. 6, 1832; coad. bp. St. Louis (Adrasus), 1841-43; bp. 1843-47, and first abp. 1847-95, St. Louis (res.).

**Keough, Francis P.** (1890-1961): ord. June 10, 1916; bp. Providence, 1943-47; abp. Baltimore, 1947-61.

**Kevenhoerster, John B., O.S.B.** (1869-1949): b. Germany; ord. June 24, 1896, Collegeville, Minn.; ord. tit. bp. Camuliana, 1933; p.a., 1933-41, and v.a., 1941-49, of Bahamas.

**Keyes, Michael, S.M.** (1876-1959): b. Ireland; ord. June 21, 1907; bp. Savannah, 1922-35 (res.).

**Kiley, Moses E.** (1876-1953): b. Nova Scotia; ord. June 10, 1911; bp. Trenton, 1934-40; abp. Milwaukee, 1940-53.

**Killeen, James** (1917-78): ord. May 30, 1942; aux. Military Vicariate (Valmalla), 1975-78.

**Klonowski, Henry T.** (1898-1977): ord. Aug. 8, 1920; aux. Scranton (Daldis), 1947-73 (res.).

**Kocisko, Stephen** (1915-95): ord. Mar. 30, 1941; aux. Byzantine ap. ex. Pittsburgh (Teveste), 1956-63; first eparch Passaic, 1963-68; eparch, 1968-69, and first metropolitan of Pittsburgh, 1969-91 (ret.).

**Kogy, Lorenz S., O.M.** (1895-1963): b. Georgia, Russia; ord. Nov. 15, 1917; U.S. citizen, 1944; patriarchal vicar for Armenian diocese of Beirut (Comana), 1951-63.

**Koudelka, Joseph** (1852-1921): b. Austria; ord. Oct. 8, 1875; aux. Cleveland (Germanicopolis), 1908-11; aux. Milwaukee, 1911-13; bp. Superior, 1913-21.

**Kowalski, Rembert, O.F.M.** (1884-1970): ord. June 22, 1911; v.a. Wuchang, China (Ipsus), 1942-46; first bp. Wuchang, 1946-70 (in exile from 1953).

**Kozlowski, Edward** (1860-1915): b. Poland; ord. June 29, 1887; aux. Milwaukee (Germia), 1914-15.

**Krautbauer, Francix X.** (1824-85): b. Germany; ord. July 16, 1850; bp. Green Bay, 1875-85.

**Krol, John Joseph** (1910-96): ord. Feb. 20, 1937; aux. Cleveland (Cadi), 1953-61; archbishop Philadelphia 1961-88 (res.); cardinal 1967.

**Kucera, Louis B.** (1888-1957): ord. June 8, 1915; bp. Lincoln, 1930-57.

# L

**Lamb, Hugh** (1890-1959): ord. May 29, 1915; aux. Philadelphia (Helos), 1936-51; first bp. Greensburg, 1951-59.

**Lamy, Jean B.:** See Index.

**Lane, Loras** (1910-68): ord. Mar. 19, 1937; aux. Dubuque (Bencenna), 1951-56; bp. Rockford, 1956-68.

**Lane, Raymond A., M.M.** (1894-1974): ord. Feb. 8, 1920; v.a. Fushun, Manchukuo (Hypaepa), 1940-46; sup. gen. Maryknoll, 1946-56.

**Lardone, Francesco** (1887-1980): b. Italy; ord. June 29, 1910; U.S. citizen 1937; nuncio to vari-ous countries (tit. abp. Rhizaeum), 1949-66 (res.).

**Laval, John M.** (1854-1937): b. France; ord. Nov. 10, 1877; aux. New Orleans (Hierocaesarea), 1911-37.

**Lavialle, Peter J.** (1819-67): b. France; ord. Feb. 12, 1844; b. Louisville, 1865-67.

**Lawler, John J.** (1862-1948): ord. Dec. 19, 1885; aux. St. Paul (Hermopolis), 1910-16; bp. Lead (now Rapid City), 1916-48.

**Le Blond, Charles H.** (1883-1958): ord. June 29, 1909; bp. St. Joseph, 1933-56 (res.).

**Ledvina, Emmanuel** (1868-1952): ord. Mar. 18, 1893; bp. Corpus Christi, 1921-49 (res.).

**Leech, George L.** (1890-1985): ord. May 29, 1920; aux. Harrisburg (Mela), Oct.-Dec., 1935; bp. Harrisburg, 1935-71 (res.).

**Lefevere, Peter P.** (1804-69): b. Belgium; ord. Nov. 30, 1831; coad. bp. and admin. Detroit (Zela), 1841-69.

**Leibold, Paul F.** (1914-72): ord. May 18, 1940; aux. Cincinnati (Trebenna), 1958-66; bp. Evansville, 1966-69; abp. Cincinnati, 1969-72.

**Leipzig, Francis P.** (1895-1981): ord. Apr. 17, 1920; bp. Baker, 1950-71 (res.).

**Lemay, Leo, S.M.** (1909-83): ord. Apr. 15, 1933; v.a. North Solomon Is. (Agbia), 1961-66; first bp. Bougainville, 1966-74 (res.).

**Lenihan** (brothers): **Mathias C.** (1854-1943): ord. Dec. 20, 1879; first bp. Great Falls, 1904-30 (res.). **Thomas M.** (1844-1901): b. Ireland; ord. Nov. 19, 1868; bp. Cheyenne, 1897-1901.

**Leonard, Vincent M.** (1908-94): ord. June 16, 1935; aux. Pittsburgh (Arsacal), 1964-69; bp. Pittsburgh, 1969-83 (ret.).

**Leray, Francis X.** (1825-87): b. France; ord. Mar. 19, 1852; bp. Natchitoches (now Alexandria, La.), 1877-79; coad. bp. New Orleans and admin. of Natchitoches (Jonopolis), 1879-83; abp. New Orleans, 1883-87.

**Leven, Stephen A.** (1905-83): ord. June 10, 1928; aux. San Antonio (Bure), 1956-69; bp. San Angelo, 1969-79 (res.).

**Ley, Felix, O.F.M. Cap.** (1909-72): ord. June 14, 1936; ap. admin. Ryukyu Is. (Caporilla), 1968-72.

**Lillis, Thomas F.** (1861-1938): ord. Aug. 15, 1885; bp. Leavenworth (now Kansas City, Kans.), 1904-10; coad. bp. Kansas City, Mo. (Cibyra), 1910-13; bp. Kansas City, Mo., 1913-38.

**Lootens, Louis** (1827-98): b. Belgium; ord. June 14, 1851; v.a. Idaho and Montana (Castabala), 1868-75 (res.).

**Loras, Mathias** (1792-1858): b. France; ord. Nov. 12, 1815; first bp. Dubuque, 1837-58.

**Loughlin, John** (1817-91): b. Ireland; ord. Oct. 18, 1840; first bp. Brooklyn, 1853-91.

**Lowney, Denis M.** (1863-1918): b. Ireland; ord. Dec. 17, 1887; aux. Providence (Hadrianopolis), 1917-18.

**Lucey, Robert E.** (1891-1977): ord. May 14, 1916; bp. Amarillo, 1934-41; abp. San Antonio, 1941-69 (res.).

**Ludden, Patrick A.** (1838-1912): b. Ireland; ord. May 21, 1865; first bp. Syracuse, 1887-1912.

**Luers, John** (1819-71): b. Germany; ord. Nov. 11, 1846; first bp. Fort Wayne, 1858-71.

**Lyke, James P., O.F.M.** (1939-92): ord. June 24, 1966; aux. Cleveland (Furnes Maior) 1979-90; ap. admin. Atlanta, 1990-91; abp. Atlanta, 1991-92.

**Lynch, Joseph P.** (1872-1954): ord. June 9, 1900; bp. Dallas, 1911-54.

**Lynch, Patrick N.** (1817-82): b. Ireland; ord. Apr. 5, 1840; bp. Charleston, 1858-82.

**Lyons, Thomas W.** (1923-88): ord. May 22, 1948; aux. bp. Washington, D.C. (Mortlach), 1974-88.

**M**

**McAuliffe, Maurice F.** (1875-1944): ord. July 29, 1900; aux. Hartford (Dercos), 1923-34; bp. Hartford, 1934-44.

**McCafferty, John E.** (1920-80): ord. Mar. 17, 1945; aux. Rochester (Tanudaia), 1968-80.

**McCarthy, Joseph E.** (1876-1955): ord. July 4, 1903; bp. Portland, Me., 1932-55.

**McCarthy, Justin J.** (1900-59): ord. Apr. 16, 1927; aux. Newark (Doberus), 1954-57; bp. Camden, 1957-59.

**McCarty, William T., C.SS.R.** (1889-1972): ord. June 10, 1915; military delegate (Anea), 1943-47; coad. bp. Rapid City, 1947-48; bp. Rapid City, 1948-69 (res.).

**McCauley, Vincent J., C.S.C.** (1906-82): ord. June 24, 1943; first bp. Fort Portal, Uganda, 1961-72 (res.).

**McCloskey, James P.** (1870-1945): ord. Dec. 17, 1898; bp. Zamboanga, P.I., 1917-20; bp. Jaro, P.I., 1920-45.

**McCloskey, John** (1810-85): ord. Jan. 12, 1834; coad. bp. New York (Axiere), 1843-47; first bp. Albany, 1847-64; abp. New York, 1864-85; first U.S. cardinal 1875.

**McCloskey, William G.** (1823-1909): ord. Oct. 6, 1852; bp. Louisville, 1868-1909.

**McCormick, Patrick J.** (1880-1953): ord. July 6, 1904; aux. Washington (Atenia), 1950-53.

**McCort, John J.** (1860-1936): ord. Oct. 14, 1883; aux. Philadelphia (Azotus), 1912-20; bp. Altoona, 1920-36.

**McDevitt, Gerald V.** (1917-80): ord. May 30, 1942; aux. Philadelphia (Tigias), 1962-80.

**McDevitt, Philip R.** (1858-1935): ord. July 14, 1885; bp. Harrisburg, 1916-35.

**McDonald, William J.** (1904-89): b. Ireland; ord. June 10, 1928; aux. Washington (Aquae Regiae), 1964-67; aux. San Francisco, 1967-79 (res.).

**McDonnell, Charles E.** (1854-1921): ord. May 19, 1878; bp. Brooklyn, 1892-1921.

**McDonnell, Thomas J.** (1894-1961): ord. Sept. 20, 1919; aux. New York (Sela), 1947-51; coad. bp. Wheeling, 1951-61.

**McEleney, John J., S.J.** (1895-1986): ord. June 18, 1930; v.a. Jamaica (Zeugma), 1950-56; bp. Kingston, 1956-67; abp. Kingston 1967-70 (res.)

**McEntegart, Bryan** (1893-1968): ord. Sept. 8, 1917; bp. Ogdensburg, 1943-53; rector Catholic University (Aradi), 1953-57; bp. Brooklyn, 1957-68.

**McFadden, James A.** (1880-1952): ord. June 17, 1905; aux. Cleveland (Bida), 1932-43; first bp. Youngstown, 1943-52.

**MacFarland, Francis P.** (1819-74): ord. May 1, 1845; bp. Hartford, 1858-74.

**McFaul, James A.** (1850-1917): b. Ireland; ord. May 26, 1877; bp. Trenton, 1894-1917.

**McGavick, Alexander J.** (1863-1948): ord. June 11, 1887; aux. Chicago (Marcopolis), 1899-1921; bp. La Crosse, 1921-48.

**McGeough, Joseph F.** (1903-70): ord. Dec. 20, 1930; internuncio Ethiopia, 1957-60; apostolic delegate (Hemesa) S. Africa, 1960-67; nuncio Ireland, 1967-69.

**McGill, John** (1809-72): ord. June 13, 1835; bp. Richmond, 1850-72.

**MacGinley, John B.** (1871-1969): b. Ireland; ord. June 8, 1895; bp. Nueva Caceres, 1910-24; first bp. Monterey-Fresno, 1924-32 (res.).

**McGolrick, James** (1841-1918): b. Ireland; ord. June 11, 1867; first bp. Duluth, 1889-1918.

**McGovern, Patrick A.** (1872-1951): ord. Aug. 18, 1895; bp. Cheyenne, 1912-51.

**McGovern, Thomas** (1832-98): b. Ireland; ord. Dec. 27, 1861; bp. Harrisburg, 1888-98.

**McGrath, Joseph F.** (1871-1950): b. Ireland; ord. Dec. 21, 1895; bp. Baker City (now Baker), 1919-50.

**McGucken, Joseph T.** (1902-84): ord. Jan. 15, 1928; aux. Los Angeles (Sanavus), 1940-55; coad. bp. Sacramento, 1957-62; abp. San Francisco, 1962-77 (res.).

**McGuinness, Eugene** (1889-1957): ord. May 22, 1915; bp. Raleigh, 1937-44; coad. bp. Oklahoma City and Tulsa (Ilium), 1944-48; bp. Oklahoma City and Tulsa, 1948-57.

**McGurkin, Edward A., M.M.** (1905-83): ord. Sept. 14, 1930; bp. Shinyanga, Tanzania, 1956-75 (res.).

**McIntyre, James F.** (1886-1979): ord. May 21, 1921; aux. New York (Cirene), 1941-46; coad. abp. New York (Palto), 1946-48; abp. Los Angeles, 1948-70 (res.); cardinal, 1953.

**MacKenzie, Eric F.** (1893-1969): ord. Oct. 20, 1918; aux. Boston (Alba), 1950-69.

**McLaughlin, Charles B.** (1913-78): ord. June 6, 1941; aux. Raleigh (Risinium), 1964-68; first bp. St. Petersburg, 1968-78.

**McLaughlin, Thomas H.** (1881-1947): ord. July 26, 1904; aux. Newark (Nisa), 1935-37; first bp. Paterson, 1937-47.

**McMahon, John J.** (1875-1932): ord. May 20, 1900; bp. Trenton, 1928-32.

**McMahon, Lawrence S.** (1835-93): ord. Mar. 24, 1860; bp. Hartford, 1879-93.

**McManaman, Edward P.** (1900-64): ord. Mar. 12, 1927; aux. Erie (Floriana), 1948-64.

**McManus, James E., C.SS.R.** (1900-76): ord. June 19, 1927; bp. Ponce, P.R., 1947-63; aux. New York (Banda), 1963-70 (res.).

**McMullen, John** (1832-83): b. Ireland; ord. June 20, 1858; first bp. Davenport, 1881-83.

**McNamara, John M.** (1878-1960): ord. June 21, 1902; aux. Baltimore (Eumenia), 1928-47; aux. Washington, 1947-60.

**McNamara, Martin D.** (1898-1966): ord. Dec. 23, 1922; first bp. Joliet, 1949-66.

**McNeirny, Francis** (1828-94): ord. Aug. 17, 1855₄; coad. bp. Albany (Rhesaina), 1872-77; bp. Albany, 1877-94.

**McNicholas, John T., O.P.** (1877-1950): b. Ireland; ord. Oct. 10, 1901; bp. Duluth, 1918-25; abp. Cincinnati, 1925-50.

**McNicholas, Joseph A.** (1923-83): ord. June 7, 1949; aux. St. Louis (Scala), 1969-75; bp. Springfield, Ill., 1975-83.

**McNulty, James A.** (1900-72): ord. July 12, 1925; aux. Newark (Methone), 1947-53; bp. Paterson, 1953-63; bp. Buffalo, 1963-72.

**McQuaid, Bernard J.** (1823-1909): ord. Jan. 16, 1848; first bp. Rochester, 1868-1909.

**McShea, Joseph M.** (1907-91): ord. Dec. 6, 1931; aux. Philadelphia (Mina), 1952-61; first bp. Allentown, 1961-83 (res.).

**McSorley, Francis J., O.M.I.** (1913-71): ord. May 30, 1939; v.a. Jolo, P.I. (Sozusa), 1958-71.

**McVinney, Russell J.** (1898-1971): ord. July 13, 1924; bp. Providence, 1948-71.

**Machebeuf, Joseph P.** (1812-89): b. France; ord. Dec. 17, 1836; v.a. Colorado and Utah (Epiphania), 1868-87; first bp. Denver, 1887-89.

**Maes, Camillus P.** (1846-1915): b. Belgium; ord. Dec. 19, 1868; bp. Covington, 1885-1915.

**Maginn, Edward J.** (1897-1984): b. Scotland; ord. June 10, 1922; aux.Albany (Curium), 1957-72 (res.).

**Magner, Francis** (1887-1947): ord. May 17, 1913; bp. Marquette, 1941-47.

**Maguire, John J.** (1904-89): ord. Dec. 22, 1928; aux. New York (Antiphrae), 1959-65; coad. abp. New York (Tabalta), 1965-80 (res.).

**Maher, Leo T.** (1915-91): ord. Dec. 18, 1943; first bp. Santa Rosa, 1962-69; bp. San Diego, 1969-90(res.).

**Mahoney, Bernard** (1875-1939): ord. Feb. 27, 1904; bp. Sioux Falls, 1922-39.

**Maloney, David M.** (1912-95): ord. Dec. 8, 1936; aux. Denver (Ruspe), 1961-67; bp. Wichita, 1967-82 (ret.).

**Maloney, Thomas F.** (1903-62): ord. July 13, 1930; aux. Providence (Andropolis), 1960-62.

**Manning, Timothy** (1909-89): b. Ireland; ord. June 16, 1934 (Los Angeles archd.); American citizen, 1944; aux. Los Angeles (Lesvi), 1946-67; first bp. Fresno, 1967-69; coad. abp. Los Angeles (Capri), 1969-70; abp. Los Angeles, 1970-85 (res.); cardinal 1973.

**Manogue, Patrick:** See Index.

**Manucy, Dominic** (1823-85): ord. Aug. 15, 1850; v.a. Brownsville (Dulma), 1874-84; bp. Mobile, Mar.-Sept., 1884 (res.); reappointed v.a. Brownsville (Maronea) (now diocese of Corpus Christi), 1884-85.

**Mardaga, Thomas J.** (1913-84): ord. May 14, 1940; aux. Baltimore (Mutugenna), 1967-68; bp. Wilmington, 1968-84.

**Marechal, Ambrose, S.S.** (1766-1828): b. France; ord. June 2, 1792; abp. Baltimore, 1817-28.

**Markham, Thomas F.** (1891-1952): ord. June 2, 1917; aux. Boston (Acalissus), 1950-52.

**Marling, Joseph M., C.Pp.S.** (1904-79): ord. Feb. 21, 1929; aux. Kansas City, Mo. (Thasus), 1947-56; first bp. Jefferson City, 1956-69 (res.).

**Marshall, John A.** (1928-94): ord. Dec. 19, 1953; bp. Burlington, 1972-91; bp. Springfield, Mass, 1991-94.

**Martin, Augustus M.** (1803-75): b. France; ord. May 31, 1828; first bp. Natchitoches (now Alexandria), 1853-75.

**Marty, Martin, O.S.B.** (1834-96): b. Switzerland; ord. Sept. 14, 1856; v.a. Dakota (Tiberias), 1880-89; first bp. Sioux Falls, 1889-95; bp. St. Cloud, 1895-96.

**Marx, Adolph** (1915-65): b. Germany; ord. May 2, 1940; aux. Corpus Christi (Citrus), 1956-65; first bp. Brownsville, 1965.

**Matz, Nicholas C.** (1850-1917): b. France; ord. May 31, 1874; coad. bp. Denver (Telmissus), 1887-89; bp. Denver, 1889-1917.

**May, John L.** (1922-94): ord. May 3, 1947; aux. bp. Chicago (Tagarbala), 1967-69; bp. Modbile, 1969-80; abp. St. Louis, 1980-92 (res.).

**Mazzarella, Bernardino N., O.F.M.** (1904-79): ord. June 5, 1931; prelate Olancho, Honduras (Hadrianopolis in Pisidia), 1957-63; first bp. Comayagua, Honduras, 1963-79.

**Medeiros, Humberto S.** (1915-83): b.Azores; U.S. citizen, 1940; ord. June 15, 1946; bp. Brownsville, 1966-70; abp. Boston, 1970-83; cardinal 1973.

**Meerschaert, Theophile** (1847-1924): b. Belgium; ord. Dec. 23, 1871; v.a. Oklahoma and Indian Territory (Sidyma), 1891-1905; first bp. Oklahoma, 1905-24.

**Melcher, Joseph** (1806-73): b. Austria; ord. Mar. 27, 1830; first bp. Green Bay, 1868-73.

**Mendez, Alfred, C.S.C.** (1907-95): ord. June 24, 1935; first bp. Arecibo, P.R., 1960-74 (res.).

**Messmer, Sebastian** (1847-1930): b. Switzerland; ord. July 23, 1871; bp. Green Bay, 1892-1903; abp. Milwaukee, 1903-30.

**Metzger, Sidney M.** (1902-86): ord. Apr. 3, 1926; aux. Santa Fe (Birtha), 1940-41; coad. bp. El Paso, 1941-42; bp. El Paso, 1942-78 (res.).

**Meyer, Albert** (1903-65): ord. July 11, 1926; bp. Superior, 1946-53; abp. Milwaukee, 1953-58; abp. Chicago, 1958-65; cardinal, 1959.

**Michaud, John S.** (1843-1908): ord. June 7, 1873; coad. bp. Burlington (Modra), 1892-99; bp. Burlington, 1899-1908.

**Miege, John B., S.J.** (1815-84): b. France; ord. Sept. 12, 1844; v.a. Kansas and Indian Territory (now Kansas City) (Messene), 1851-74 (res.).

**Mihalik, Emil J.** (1920-84): ord. Sept. 21, 945; first bp. Parma (Byzantine Rite, Ruthenians), 1969-84.

**Miles, Richard P., O.P.** (1791-1860): ord. Sept. 21, 1816; first bp. Nashville, 1838-60.

**Minihan, Jeremiah F.** (1903-73): ord. Dec. 21, 1929; aux. Boston (Paphus), 1954-73.

**Misner, Paul B., C.M.** (1891-1938): ord. Feb. 23, 1919; v.a. Yukiang, China (Myrica), 1935-38.

**Mitty, John J.** (1884-1961): ord. Dec. 22, 1906; bp. Salt Lake, 1926-32; coad. abp. San Francisco (Aegina), 1932-35; abp. San Francisco, 1935-61.

**Moeller, Henry** (1849-1925): ord. June 10, 1876; bp. Columbus, 1900-03; coad. abp. Cincinnati (Areopolis), 1903-04; abp. Cincinnati, 1904-25.

**Molloy, Thomas E.** (1884-1956): ord. Sept. 19, 1908; aux. Brooklyn (Lorea), 1920-21; bp. Brooklyn, 1921-56.

**Monaghan, Francis J.** (1890-1942): ord. May 29, 1915; coad. bp. Ogdensburg (Mela), 1936-39; bp. Ogdensburg, 1939-42.

**Monaghan, John J.** (1856-1935): ord. Dec. 18, 1880; bp. Wilmington, 1897-1925 (res.).

**Montgomery, George T.** (1847-1907): ord. Dec. 20, 1879; coad. bp. Monterey-Los Angeles (Thmuis), 1894-96; bp. Monterey-Los Angeles (now Los Angeles), 1896-1903; coad. abp. San Francisco (Auxum), 1903-07.

**Mooney, Edward** (1882-1958): ord. Apr. 10, 1909; ap. del. India (Irenopolis), 1926-31; ap. del. Japan, 1931-33; bp. Rochester, 1933-37; first abp. Detroit, 1937-58; cardinal, 1946.

**Moore, Emerson J.**(1938-95): ord. May 30, 1964; aux. New York (Curubi) 1984-95.

**Moore, John** (1835-1901): b. Ireland; ord. Apr. 9, 1860; bp. St. Augustine, 1877-1901.

**Mora, Francis** (1827-1905); b. Spain; ord. Mar. 19, 1856; coad. bp. Monterey-Los Angeles (Mosynopolis), 1873-78; bp. Monterey-Los Angeles (now Los Angeles), 1878-96 (res.).

**Morkovsky, John L.** (1909-90): ord. Dec. 5, 1933; aux. Amarillo (Hieron), 1956-58; bp. Amarillo, 1958-63; coad. bp. Galveston-Houston (Tigava), 1963-75; bp. Galveston, 1975-84 (res.).

**Morris, John** (1866-1946): ord. June 11, 1892; coad. bp. Little Rock (Acmonia), 1906-07; bp. Little Rock, 1907-46.

**Morrow, Louis La Ravoire, S.D.B.** (1892-1987): ord. May 21, 1921; bp. Krishnagar, India, 1939-69 (res.).

**Mrak, Ignatius** (1810-1901): b. Austria; ord. July 31, 1837; bp. Sault Ste. Marie and Marquette (now Marquette), 1869-78 (res.).

**Mueller, Joseph M.** (1894-1981): ord. June 14, 1919; coad. bp. Sioux City (Sinda), 1947-48; bp. Sioux City, 1948-70 (res.).

**Muench, Aloysius** (1889-1962): ord. June 8, 1913; bp. Fargo, 1935-59 (res.); apostolic visitator to Germany, 1946; nuncio to Germany 1951-59; cardinal 1959.

**Mugavero, Francis J.** (1914-91): ord. May 18, 1940; bp. Brooklyn, 1968-90 (res.).

**Mulcahy, John J.** (1922-94): ord. May 1, 1947; aux. bp. Boston (Penafiel), 1975-92 (res.).

**Muldoon, Peter J.** (1862-1927): ord. Dec. 18, 1886; aux. Chicago (Tamasus), 1901-08; first bp. Rockford, 1908-27.

**Mullen, Tobias** (1818-1900): b. Ireland; ord. Sept. 1, 1844; bp. Erie, 1868-99 (res.).

**Mulloy, William T.** (1892-1959): ord. June 7, 1916; bp. Covington, 1945-59.

**Mulrooney, Charles R.** (1906-89): ord. June 10, 1930; aux. Brooklyn (Valentiniana), 1959-81 (res.).

**Mundelein, George** (1872-1939): ord. June 8, 1895; aux. Brooklyn (Loryma), 1909-15; abp. Chicago, 1915-39; cardinal, 1924.

**Murphy, Joseph A., S.J.** (1857-1939): b. Ireland; ord. Aug. 26, 1888; v.a. Belize, Br. Honduras (Birtha), 1923-39.

**Murphy, T.(Thomas) Austin** (1911-91): ord. June 10, 1937; aux. Baltimore (Appiaria), 1962-84 (res.).

**Murphy, Thomas W., C.SS.R.** (1917-95): ord. June 29, 1943; first bp. Juazeiro, Brazil 1963-73 (res.); aux. Sao Salvador da Bahia, Brazil (Sululos), 1974-95.

**Murphy, Willim F.** (1885-1950): ord. June 13, 1908; first bp. Saginaw, 1938-50.

**Murray, John G.** (1877-1956): ord. Apr. 14, 1900; aux. Hartford (Flavias), 1920-25; bp. Portland, 1925-31; abp. St. Paul, 1931-56.

**Mussio, John K.** (1902-78): ord. Aug. 15, 1935; bp. Steubenville, 1945-77 (res.).

## N

**Najmy, Justin, O.S.B.M.** (1898-1968): b. Syria; ord. Dec. 25, 1926; ap. ex. Melkites (Augustopolis in Phrygia), 1966-68.

**Navagh, James J.** (1901-65): ord. Dec. 21, 1929; aux. Raleigh (Ombi), 1952-57; bp. Ogdensburg, 1957-63; bp. Paterson, 1963-65.

**Neale, Leonard** (1746-1817): ord. June 5, 1773; coad. bp. Baltimore (Gortyna), 1800-15; abp. Baltimore, 1815-17.

**Nelson, Knute Ansgar, O.S.B.** (1906-90): b. Denmark; ord. May 22, 1937; U.S. citizen, 1941; coad. bp. Stockholm, Sweden (Bilta), 1947-57; bp. Stockholm, 1957-62 (res.)

**Neraz, John C.** (1828-94): b. France; ord. Mar. 19, 1853; bp. San Antonio, 1881-1894.

**Neumann, John, St.:** See Index.

**Newell, Hubert M.** (1904-87): ord. June 15, 1930; coad. bp. Cheyenne (Zapara), 1947-51; bp. Cheyenne, 1951-78 (res.).

**Newman, Thomas A., M.S.** (1903-78): ord. June 29, 1929; first bp. Prome, Burma, 1961-75 (res.).

**Niedhammer, Matthew A., O.F.M. Cap.** (1901-70): ord. June 8, 1927; v.a. Bluefields, Nicaragua (Caloe), 1943-70.

**Nilan, John J.** (1855-1934): ord. Dec. 2, 1878; bp. Hartford, 1910-34.

**Noa, Thomas L.** (1892-1977): ord. Dec. 23, 1916; coad. bp. Sioux City (Salona), 1946-47; bp. Marquette, 1947-68 (res.).

**Nold, Wendelin J.** (1900-81): ord. Apr. 11, 1925; coad. bp. Galveston (Sasima), 1948-50; bp. Galveston-Houston, 1950-75 (res.).

**Noll, John F.** (1875-1956): ord. June 4, 1898; bp. Fort Wayne, 1925-56 (pers. tit. abp., 1953).

**Northrop, Henry P.** (1842-1916): ord. June 25, 1865; v.a. North Carolina (Rosalia), 1881-83; bp. Charleston, 1883-1916.

**Noser, Adolph, S.V.D.** (1900-81): ord. Sept. 27, 1925; v.a. Accra, British W. Africa (now Ghana) (Capitolias), 1947-50; bp. Accra, 1950-53; v.a. Alexishafen, New Guinea (Hierpiniana), 1953- 66; abp. Madang, Papua New Guinea, 1966-75 (res.).

**Nussbaum, Paul J., C.P.** (1870-1935): ord. May 20, 1894; first bp. Corpus Christi, 1913-20 (res.); bp. Sault Ste. Marie and Marquette (now Marquette), 1922-35.

## O

**O'Boyle, Patrick A.** (1896-1987): ord. May 21, 1921; abp. Washington, D.C., 1948-73 (res.); cardinal 1967.

**O'Brien, Henry J.** (1896-1976): ord. July 8, 1923 aux. Hartford (Sita), 1940-45; bp. Hartford, 1945-53, and first abp. Hartford, 1953-68 (res.).

**O'Brien, William D.** (1878-1962): ord. July 11, 1903; aux. Chicago (Calynda), 1934-62.

**O'Connell, Denis J.** (1849-1927): b. Ireland; ord.

May 26, 1877; aux. San Francisco (Sebaste), 1908-12; bp. Richmond, 1912-26 (res.).

**O'Connell, Eugene** (1815-91): b. Ireland; ord. May 21, 1842; v.a. Marysville (Flaviopolis), 1861-68; first bp. Grass Valley, 1868-84 (res.).

**O'Connell, William H.** (1859-1944): ord. June 7, 1884; bp. Portland, 1901-06; coad. bp. Boston (Constantia), 1906-07; abp. Boston, 1907-44; cardinal, 1911.

**O'Connor** (brothers), **James** (1823-90): b. Ireland; ord. Mar. 25, 1848; v.a. Nebraska (Dibon), 1876-85; first bp. Omaha, 1885-90. **Michael, S.J.** (1810-72): b. Ireland; ord. June 1, 1833; first bp. Pittsburgh, 1843-53; first bp. Erie, 1853-54; bp. Pittsburgh, 1854-60 (resigned, joined Jesuits).

**O'Connor, John J.** (1855-1927): ord. Dec. 22, 1877; bp. Newark, 1901-27.

**O'Connor, Martin J.** (1900-86): ord. Mar. 15, 1924; aux. Scranton (Thespia), 1943-46; rector North American College, Rome, 1946-64; abp., 1959 (Laodicea); nuncio to Malta, 1965-69; pres. Pontifical Commission for Social Communications, 1964-71.

**O'Connor, William A.** (1903-83): ord. Sept. 24, 1927; bp. Springfield, Ill., 1949-75 (res.).

**O'Connor, William P.** (1886-1973): ord. Mar. 10, 1912; bp. Superior, 1942-46; first bp. Madison, 1946-67 (res.).

**O'Dea, Edward J.** (1856-1932): ord. Dec. 23, 1882; bp. Nesqually (now Seattle — title changed in 1907), 1896-1932.

**Odin, John M., C.M.** (1800-70): b. France; ord. May 4, 1823; v.a. Texas (Claudiopolis), 1842-47; first bp. Galveston, 1847-61; abp. New Orleans, 1861-70.

**O'Donaghue, Denis** (1848-1925): ord. Sept. 6, 1874; aux. Indianapolis (Pomaria), 1900-10; bp. Louisville, 1910-24 (res.).

**O'Donnell, Cletus F.** (1917-92): ord. May 3, 1941; aux. Chicago (Abritto), 1960-67; bp. Madison, 1967-92 (res.).

**O'Dowd, James T.** (1907-50): ord. June 4, 1932; aux. San Francisco (Cea), 1948-50.

**O'Farrell, Michael J.** (1832-94): b. Ireland; ord. Aug. 18, 1855; first bp. Trenton, 1881-94.

**O'Flanagan, Dermot** (1901-73): b. Ireland; ord. Aug. 27, 1929; first bp. Juneau, 1951-68 (res.).

**O'Gara, Cuthbert, C.P.** (1886-1968): b. Canada; ord. May 26, 1915; v.a. Yuanling, China (Elis), 1934-46; first bp. Yuanling, 1946-68 (imprisoned, 1951, and then expelled, 1953, by Chinese Communists).

**O'Gorman, James, O.C.S.O.** (1804-74): b. Ireland; ord. Dec. 23, 1843; v.a. Nebraska (now Omaha) (Raphanea), 1859-74.

**O'Gorman, Thomas** (1843-1921): ord. Nov. 5, 1865; bp. Sioux Falls, 1896-1921.

**O'Hara, Edwin V.** (1881-1956): ord. June 9, 1905; bp. Great Falls, 1930-39; bp. Kansas City, Mo., 1939-56 (title changed to Kansas City-St. Joseph, 1956).

**O'Hara, Gerald P.** (1895-1963): ord. Apr. 3, 1920; aux. Philadelphia (Heliopolis), 1929-35; bp. Savannah (title changed to Savannah-Atlanta in 1937), 1935-59 (res.); regent of Romania nunciature, 1946-50 (expelled); nuncio to Ireland, 1951-54; ap. del. to Great Britain, 1954-63; tit. abp. Pessinus, 1959-63.

**O'Hara, John F., C.S.C.** (1888-1960): ord. Sept. 9, 1916; delegate of U.S. military vicar (Mylasa), 1940-45; bp. Buffalo, 1945-51; abp. Philadelphia, 1951-60; cardinal, 1958.

**O'Hara, William** (1816-99): b. Ireland; ord. Dec. 21, 1842; first bp. Scranton, 1868-99.

**O'Hare, William F, S.J.** (1870-1926): ord. June 25, 1903; v.a. Jamaica (Maximianopolis), 1920-26.

**O'Hern, John F.** (1874-1933): ord. Feb. 17, 1901; bp. Rochester, 1929-33.

**O'Leary, Thomas** (1875-1949): ord. Dec. 18, 1897; bp. Springfield, Mass., 1921-49.

**Olwell, Quentin, C.P.** (1898-1972): ord. Feb. 4, 1923; prelate Marbel, P.I. (Thabraca), 1961-69 (res.).

**O'Meara, Edward T.** (1921-92): ord. Dec. 21, 1946; aux. St. Louis (Thisiduo), 1972-80; abp. Indianapolis, 1980-92.

**O'Regan, Anthony** (1809-66): b. Ireland; ord. Nov. 29, 1834; bp. Chicago, 1854-58 (res.).

**O'Reilly, Bernard** (1803-56): b. Ireland; ord. Oct. 16, 1831; bp. Hartford, 1850-56.

**O'Reilly, Charles J.** (1860-1923): b. Canada; ord. June 29, 1890; first bp. Baker City (now Baker), 1903-18; bp. Lincoln, 1918-23.

**O'Reilly, James** (1855-1934): b. Ireland; ord. June 24, 1880; bp. Fargo, 1910-34.

**O'Reilly, Patrick T.** (1833-92): b. Ireland; ord. Aug. 15, 1857; first bp. Springfield, Mass., 1870-92.

**O'Reilly, Peter J.** (1850-1924): b. Ireland; ord. June 24, 1877; aux. Peoria (Lebedus), 1900-24.

**O'Reilly, Thomas C.** (1873-1938): ord. June 4, 1898; bp. Scranton, 1928-38.

**Ortynsky, Stephen, O.S.B.M.** (1866-1916): b. Poland; ord. July 18, 1891; first Ukrainian Byzantine Rite bishop in U.S. (Daulia), 1907-16.

**O'Shea, John A., C.M.** (1887-1969): ord. May 30, 1914; v.a. Kanchow, China (Midila), 1928-46; first bp. Kanchow, 1949-69 (expelled by Chinese Communists, 1953).

**O'Shea, William F., M.M.** (1884-1945): ord. Dec. 5, 1917; v.a. Heijon, Japan (Naissusz), 1939-45; prisoner of Japanese 1941-42.

**O'Sullivan, Jeremiah** (1842-96): b. Ireland; ord. June 30, 1868; bp. Mobile, 1885-96.

**Ott, Stanley J.** (1927-92) ord. Dec. 8, 1951; aux. New Orleans (Nicives), 1976-83; bp. Baton Rouge, 1983-92.

**Oves Fernandez, Francisco Ricardo** (1928-90) b. Cuba; ord. Apr. 13, 1952; aux. Cienfuegas, Cuba (Montecorvino), 1969-70; abp. Havana, 1970-81 (res.); resided in El Paso, Tex., diocese from 1982.

## P

**Pardy, James V., M.M.** (1898-1983): ord. Jan. 26, 1930; v.a. Cheong-Ju, Korea (Irenopolis), 1958-62; first bp. Cheong-Ju, 1962-69 (res.).

**Paschang, Adolph J., M.M.** (1895-1968): ord. May 21, 1921; v.a. Kong Moon, China (Sasima), 1937-46; first bp. Kong Moon, 1946-68 (expelled by Communists, 1951).

**Pechillo, Jerome, T.O.R.** (1919-91): ord. June 10, 1947; prelate Coronel Oviedo, Paraguay (Novasparsa), 1966-76; aux. Newark, 1976-91.

**Pellicer, Anthony** (1824-80): ord. Aug. 15, 1850; first bp. San Antonio, 1874-80.

**Penalver y Cardenas, Luis** (1749-1810): b. Cuba; ord. Apr. 4, 1772; first bp. Louisiana and the Two Floridas (now New Orleans), 1793-1801; abp. Guatemala, 1801-06 (res.).

**Perche, Napoleon J.** (1805-83): b. France; ord. Sept. 19, 1829; abp. New Orleans, 1870-83.

**Pernicone, Joseph M.** (1903-85): b. Sicily; ord. Dec. 18, 196; aux. New York (Hadrianapolis) 1954-78 (res.).

**Perry, Harold R., S.V.D.** (1916-91), ord. Jan. 6, 1944; aux. New Orleans (Mons in Mauretania), 1966-91.

**Persico, Ignatius, O.F.M. Cap.** (1823-95): b. Italy; ord. Jan. 24, 1846; bishop from 1854; bp. Savannah, 1870-72; cardinal, 1893.

**Peschges, John H.** (1881-1944): ord. Apr. 15, 1905; bp. Crookston, 1938-44.

**Peterson, John B.** (1871-1944): ord. Sept. 15, 1899; aux. Boston (Hippos), 1972-32: bp. Manchester, 1932-44.

**Phelan, Richard** (1828-1904): b. Ireland; ord. May 4, 1854; coad. bp. Pittsburgh (Cibyra), 1885-89; bp. Pittsburgh, 1889-1904.

**Pinger, Henry A., O.F.M.** (1897-1988): ord. June 27, 1927; v.a. Chowtsun, China (Capitolias), 1937-46; first bp. Chowtsun, 1946 (imprisoned, 1951 then released, 1956 and expelled by Chinese Communists).

**Pinten, Joseph G.** (1867-1945): ord. Nov. 1, 1890; bp. Superior, 1922-26; bp. Grand Rapids, 1926-40 (res.).

**Pitaval, John B.** (1858-1928): b. France; ord. Dec. 24, 1881; aux. Santa Fe (Sora), 1902-09; abp. Santa Fe, 1909-18 (res.).

**Plagens, Joseph C.** (1880-1943): b. Poland; ord. July 5, 1903; aux. Detroit (Rhodiapolis), 1924-35; bp. Sault Ste. Marie and Marquette (title changed to Marquette, 1937), 1935-40; bp. Grand Rapids, 1941-43.

**Portier, Michael** (1795-1859): b. France; ord. May 16, 1818; v.a. Two Floridas and Alabama (Olena), 1826-29; first bp. Mobile, 1829-59.

**Prendergast, Edmond** (1843-1918): b. Ireland; ord. Nov. 17, 1865; aux. Philadelphia (Scilium), 1897-1911; abp. Philadelphia, 1911-18.

**Primeau, Ernest J.** (1909-89): ord. Apr. 7, 1934; bp. Manchester, 1960-74 (res.); director Villa Stritch, Rome, 1974-79 (ret.).

**Prost, Jude, O.F.M.** (1915-94): ord. June 24, 1942; aux. Belem do Para, Brazil (Fronta), 1962-92 (res.).

**Proulx, Amedee W.** (1932-93): ord. May 31, 1958; aux. bp. Portland, Me. (Clipia), 1975-93.

**Purcell, John B.** (1800-83): b. Ireland; ord. May 20, 1826; bp., 1833-50, and first abp., 1850-83, Cincinnati.

**Q**

**Quarter, William** (1806-48): b. Ireland; ord. Sept. 19, 1829; first bp. Chicago, 1844-48.

**Quigley, James E.** (1855-1915): b. Canada; ord. Apr. 13, 1879; bp. Buffalo, 1897-1903; abp. Chicago, 1903-15.

**Quinlan, John** (1826-83): b. Ireland; ord. Aug. 30, 1852; bp. Mobile, 1859-83.

**Quinn, William Charles, C.M.** (1905-60): ord. Oct. 11, 1931; v.a. Yukiang, China (Halicarnassus), 1940-46; first bp. Yukiang, 1946-60 (expelled by Chinese Communists, 1951).

**R**

**Rademacher, Joseph** (1840-1900): ord. Aug. 2, 1863; bp. Nashville, 1883-93; bp. Ft. Wayne, 1893-900.

**Rappe, Louis Amadeus** (1801-77): b. France; ord. Mar. 14, 1829; first bp. Cleveland, 1847-70 (res.).

**Rausch, James S.** (1928-81): ord. June 2, 1956; aux. St. Cloud (Summa), 1973-77; bp. Phoenix, 1977-81.

**Ready, Michael J.** (1893-1957): ord. Sept. 14, 1918; bp. Columbus, 1944-57.

**Reed, Victor J.** (1905-71): ord. Dec. 21, 1929; aux. Oklahoma City and Tulsa (Limasa), 1957-58; bp. Oklahoma City and Tulsa, 1958-71.

**Regan, Joseph W., M.M.** (1905-94): ord. Jan. 27, 1929; prelate Tagum, Philippines (Isinda), 1962-80 (ret.).

**Reh, Francis F.** (1911-94): ord. Dec. 8, 1935; bp. Charleston 1962-64; bp. Saginaw, 1969-80 (ret.).

**Rehring, George J.** (1890-1976): ord. Mar. 28, 1914; aux. Cincinnati (Lunda), 1937-50; bp. Toledo, 1950-67 (res.).

**Reicher, Louis J.** (1890-1984): ord. Dec. 6, 1918; first bp. Austin, 1948-71 (res.).

**Reilly, Edmond J.** (1897-1958): ord. Apr. 1, 1922; aux. Brooklyn (Nepte), 1955-58.

**Reilly, Thomas F., C.SS.R.** (1908-92): ord. June 10, 1933; prelate San Juan de la Maguana, Dominican Republic (Themisonium), 1956-69; first bp. San Juan de la Maguana, 1969-77 (res.).

**Rese, Frederic** (1791-1871): b. Germany; ord. Mar. 15, 1823; first bp. Detroit, 1833-71. Inactive from 1841 because of ill health.

**Reverman, Theodore** (1877-1941): ord. July 26, 1901; bp. Superior, 1926-41.

**Reynolds, Ignatius A.** (1798-1855): ord. Oct. 24, 1823; bp. Charleston, 1844-55.

**Rhode, Paul P.** (1871-1945): b. Poland; ord. June 17, 1894; aux. Chicago (Barca), 1908-15; bp. Green Bay, 1915-45.

**Rice, Joseph J.** (1871-1938): ord. Sept. 29, 1894; bp. Burlington, 1910-38.

**Rice, William A., S.J.** (1891-1946): ord. Aug. 27, 1925; v.a. Belize, Br. Honduras (Rusicade), 1939-46.

**Richter, Henry J.** (1838-1916): b. Germany; ord. June 10, 1865; first bp. Grand Rapids, 1883-1916.

**Riley, Thomas J.** (1900-1977): ord. May 20, 1927; aux. Boston (Regiae), 1956-76 (res.).

**Riordan, Patrick W.** (1841-1914): b. Canada; ord. June 10, 1865; coad. abp. San Francisco (Cabasa), 1883-84; abp. San Francisco, 1884-1914.

**Ritter, Joseph E.** (1892-1967): ord. May 30, 1917; aux. Indianapolis (Hippos), 1933-34; bp., 1934-44, and first abp. Indianapolis, 1944-46; abp. St. Louis, 1946-67; cardinal 1961.

**Robinson, Pascal C., O.F.M.** (1870-1948): b. Ireland; ord. Dec. 21, 1901; ap. visitor to Palestine, Egypt, Syria and Cyprus (Tyana), 1927-29; ap. nuncio to Ireland, 1929-48.

**Rooker, Fraderick Z.** (1861-1907): ord. July 25, 1888; bp. Jaro, P.I., 1903-07.

**Ropert, Gulstan F., SS.CC.** (1839-1903): b.

France; ord. May 26, 1866; v.a. Sandwich (now Hawaiian) Is. (Panopolis), 1892-1903.

**Rosati, Joseph, C.M.:** See Index.

**Rosecrans, Sylvester** (1827-78): ord. June 5, 1853; aux. Cincinnati (Pompeiopolis), 1862-68; first bp. Columbus, 1868-78.

**Rouxel, Gustave A.** (1840-1908): b. France, ord. Nov. 4, 1863; aux. New Orleans (Curium), 1899-1908.

**Rudin, John, M.M.** (1916-95): ord. June 11, 1944; first bp. Musoma, Tanzania, 1957-79 (res.).

**Rummel, Joseph** (1876-1964): b. Germany; ord. May 24, 1902; bp. Omaha, 1928-35; abp. New Orleans, 1935-64.

**Ruocco, Joseph J.** (1922-80): ord. May 6, 1948; aux. Boston (Polignano), 1975-80.

**Russell, John J.** (1897-1993): ord. July 8, 123; bp. Charleston, 1950-58; bp. Richmond, 1958-73 (res.).

**Russell, William T.** (1863-1927): ord. June 21, 1889; bp. Charleston, 1917-27.

**Ryan, Edward F.** (1879-1956): ord. Aug. 10, 1905; bp. Burlington, 1945-56.

**Ryan, Gerald J.** (1923-85): ord. June 3, 1950; aux. Rockville Centre (Munatiana), 1977-85.

**Ryan, James** (1848-1923): b. Ireland; ord. Dec. 24, 1871; bp. Alton (now Springfield), Ill., 1888-1923.

**Ryan, James H.** (1886-1947): ord. June 5, 1909; rector Catholic University, 1928-35; tit. bp. Modra, 1933-35; bp., 1935-45, and first abp. Omaha, 1945-47.

**Ryan, Patrick J.** (1831-1911): b. Ireland; ord. Sept. 8, 1853; coad. bp. St. Louis (Tricomia), 1872-84; abp. Philadelphia, 1884-1911.

**Ryan, Stephen, C.M.** (1826-96): b. Canada; ord. June 24, 1849; bp. Buffalo, 1868-96.

**Ryan, Vincent J.** (1884-1951): ord. June 7, 1912; bp. Bismarck, 1940-41.

## S

**Salpointe, John B.** (1825-98): b. France; ord. Dec. 20, 1851; v.a. Arizona (Dorylaeum), 1869-84; coad. abp. Santa Fe (Anazarbus), 1884-85; abp. Santa Fe, 1885-94 (res.).

**San Pedro, Enrique, S.J.** (1926-94): b. Cuba; ord. May 18, 1957; aux. bp. Galveston-Houston (Siccesi), 1986-81; coad. bp. Brownsville, Aug.-Nov., 1991; bp. Brownsville, 1991-94.

**Scanlan, Lawrence** (1843-1915): b. Ireland; ord. June 28, 1868; v.a. Utah (Laranda), 1887-91; bp. Salt Lake (now Salt Lake City), 1891-1915.

**Scannell, Richard** (1845-1916): b. Ireland; ord. Feb. 26, 1871; first bp. Concordia (now Salina), 1887-91; bp. Omaha, 1891-1916.

**Scheerer, Louis A., O.P.** (1909-66): ord. June 13, 1935; bp. Multan, Pakistan, 1960-66.

**Schenk, Francis J.** (1901-69): ord. June 13, 1926; bp. Crookston, 1945-60; bp. Duluth, 1960-69.

**Scher, Philip G.** (1880-1953): ord. June 6, 1904; bp. Monterey-Fresno, 1933-53.

**Schexnayder, Maurice** (1895-1981): ord. Apr. 11, 1925; aux. Lafayette (Tuscamia), 1951-56; bp. Lafayette, La., 1956-72 (res.).

**Schierhoff, Andrew B.** (1922-87): ord. Apr. 14, 1948; aux. La Paz, Bolivia (Gerenza), 1969-82; v.a. Pando, Bolivia, 1982-87.

**Schinner, Augustine** (1863-1937): ord. Mar. 7, 1886; first bp. Superior, 1905-13; first bp. Spokane, 1914-25 (res.).

**Schladweiler, Alphonse** (1902-96): ord. June 9, 1929; first bp. New Ulm, 1958-75 (res.).

**Schlaefer Berg, Salvator, O.F.M. Cap.** (1920-93): ord. June 5, 1946; v.a. Bluefields, Nicaragua (Fiumepiscense), 1970-93.

**Schlarman, Joseph H.** (1879-1951): ord. June 29, 1904; bp. Peoria, 1930-51.

**Schlotterback, Edward F. O.S.F.S.** (1912-94): ord. Dec. 17, 1938; v.a. Keetmanshoop, Namibia (Balanea) 1956-89 (ret.).

**Schmidt, Matthias W., O.S.B.** (1931-92): ord. May 30, 1957; aux. Jatai, Brazil (Mutugenna), 1972-76; bp. Ruy Barbosa, Brazil, 1976-92.

**Schmitt, Adolph G., C.M.M.** (1905-76): b. Bavaria; U.S. citizen 1945; v.a. Bulawayo (Nasai), Rhodesia (now Zimbabwe), 1951-55; first bp. Bulawayo, 1955-74 (res.). Murdered by terrorists.

**Schmondiuk, Joseph** (1912-1978): ord. Mar. 29, 1936; aux. Philadelphia xarchate (Zeugma in Syria), 1956-61; eparch Stamford, 1961-77; abp. Philadelphia, 1977-78.

**Schott, Lawrence F.** (1907-63): ord. July 15, 1935; aux. Harrisburg (Eluza), 1956-63.

**Schrembs, Joseph** (1866-1945): b. Germany; ord. June 29, 1889; aux. Grand Rapids (Sophene), 1911; first bp. Toledo, 1911-21; bp. Cleveland, 1921-45.

**Schuck, James A., O.F.M.** (1913-93): ord. June 11, 1940; prelate Cristalandia, Brazil (Avissa, 1959-78), 1959-88 (res.).

**Schuler, Anthony J., S.J.** (1869-1944): ord. June 27, 1901; first bp. El Paso, 1915-42 (res.).

**Schulte, Paul** (1890-1984): ord. June 11, 1915; bp. Leavenworth, 1937-46; abp. Indianapolis, 1946-70 (res.).

**Schwebach, James** (1847-1921): b. Luxembourg; ord. June 16, 1870; bp. La Crosse, 1892-1921.

**Schwertner, August J.** (1870-1939): ord. June 12, 1897; bp. Wichita, 1921-39.

**Scully, William** (1894-1969): ord. Sept. 20, 1919; coad. bp. Albany (Pharsalus), 1945-54; bp. Albany, 1954-69.

**Sebastian, Jerome D.** (1895-1960): ord. May 25, 1922; aux. Baltimore (Baris in Hellesponto), 1954-60.

**Seghers, Charles J.:** See Index.

**Seidenbusch, Rupert, O.S.B.** (1830-95): b. Germany; ord. June 22, 1853; v.a. Northern Minnesota (Halia), 1875-88 (res.).

**Senyshyn, Ambrose, O.S.B.M.** (1903-76): b. Galicia; ord. Aug. 23, 1931; aux. Ukrainian Catholic Diocese of U.S. (Maina), 1942-56; first bp. Stamford (Byzantine Rite), 1958-61; abp. Philadelphia (Byzantine Rite), 1961-76.

**Seton, Robert J.** (1839-1927): b. Italy, ord. Apr. 15, 1865; tit. abp. Heliopolis, 1903-27. Grandson of St. Elizabeth Seton.

**Shahan, Thomas J.** (1857-1932): ord. June 3, 1882; rector, Catholic University of America, 1909-27; tit. bp. Germanicopolis, 1914-32.

**Shanahan** (brothers): **Jeremiah F.** (1834-86): ord. July 3, 1859; first bp. Harrisburg, 1868-86. **John W.** (1846-1916): ord. Jan. 2, 1869; bp. Harrisburg, 1899-1916.

**Shanley, John** (1852-1909): ord. May 30, 1874; first bp. Jamestown (see transferred to Fargo in 1897), 1889-1909.

**Shanley, Patrick H., O.C.D.** (1896-1970): b. Ireland; ord. Dec. 21, 1930; U.S. citizen; prelate Infanta, P.I. (Sophene), 1953-60 (res.).

**Shaughnessy, Gerald, S.M.** (1887-1950): ord. June 20, 1920; bp. Seattle, 1933-50.

**Shaw, John W.** (1861-1934): ord. May 26, 1888; coad. bp. San Antonio (Castabala), 1910-11; bp. San Antonio, 1911-18; abp. New Orleans, 1918-34.

**Shea, Francis R.** (1913-94): ord. Mar. 19, 1939; bp. Evansville, 1970-89 (ret.).

**Sheehan, Edward T., C.M.** (1888-1933): ord. June 7, 1916, v.a. Yukiang, China (Calydon), 1929-33.

**Sheen, Fulton J.** (1895-1979): ord. Sept. 20, 1919; aux. New York (Caesarina), 1951-66; bp. Rochester, 1966-69 (res.); tit. abp. Newport.

**Shehan, Lawrence J.** (1898-1984): ord. Dec. 23, 1922; aux. Baltimore and Washington (Lidda), 1945-53; bp. Bridgeport, 1953-61; coad. abp. Baltimore (Nicopolis ad Nestum), Sept.-Dec., 1961; abp. Baltimore, 1961-74 (res.); cardinal 1965.

**Sheil, Bernard J.** (1886-1969); ord. May 21, 1910; aux. bp. Chicago (Pegae), 1928-69; tit. abp. Selge, 1959-69.

**Shubsda, Thaddeus A.** (1925-91): ord. Apr. 26, 1950; aux. Los Angeles (Trau), 1977-82; bp. Monterey, 1982-91.

**Smith, Alphonse** (1883-1935): ord. Apr. 18, 1908; bp. Nashville, 1924-35.

**Smith, Eustace, O.F.M.** (1908-75): ord. June 12, 1934; v.a. Beirut, Lebanon (Apamea Cibotus), 1958-73 (res.).

**Smith, Leo R.** (1905-63): ord. Dec. 21, 1929; aux. Buffalo (Marida), 1952-63; bp. Ogdensburg, 1963.

**Smyth, Clement, O.C.S.O.** (1810-65): b. Ireland; ord. May 29, 1841; coad. bp. Dubuque (Thennesus), 1857-58; bp. Dubuque, 1858-65.

**Soenneker, Henry J.** (1907-87): Ord. May 26, 1934; bp. Owensboro, 1961-82 (res.).

**Spalding, John L.** (1840-1916): ord. Dec. 19, 1863, first bp. Peoria, 1876-1908 (res.).

**Spalding, Martin J.** (1810-72): ord. Aug. 13, 1834; aux. Louisville (Lengone), 1848-50; bp. Louisville, 1850-64; abp. Baltimore, 1864-72.

**Spellman, Francis J.** (1889-1967): ord. May 14, 1916; aux. Boston (Sila), 1932-39; abp. New York, 1939-67; cardinal 1946.

**Spence, John S.** (1909-73): ord. Dec. 5, 1933; aux. Washington (Aggersel), 1964-73.

**Stang, William** (1854-1907): b. Germany; ord. June 15, 1878; first bp. Fall River, 1904-07.

**Stanton, Martin W.** (1897-1977): ord. June 14, 1924; aux. Newark (Citium) 1957-72 (res.).

**Stariha, John** (1845-1915): b. Austria; ord. Sept. 19, 1869; first bp. Lead (now Rapid City), 1902-09 (res.).

**Steck, Leo J.** (1898-1950): ord. June 8, 1924; aux. Salt Lake City (Ilium), 1948-50.

**Stemper, Alfred M., M.S.C.** (1913-84): ord. June 26, 1940; v.a. Kavieng (Eleutheropolis), 1957-66; first bp. Kavieng, 1966-80 (res.).

**Stock, John** (1918-72): ord. Dec. 4, 1943; aux. Philadelphia (Ukrainian Rite) (Pergamum), 1971-72.

**Stritch, Samuel** (1887-1958): ord. May 21, 1909;

bp. Toledo, 1921-30; abp. Milwaukee, 1930-39; abp. Chicago, 1939-58; cardinal 1946.

**Sullivan, Bernard, S.J.** (1889-1970): ord, June 26, 1921; bp. Patna, India, 1929-46 (res.).

**Sullivan, Joseph V.** (1919-82): ord. June 1, 1946; aux. Kansas City-St. Joseph (Tagamuta), 1964-74; bp. Baton Rouge, 1974-82.

**Swanstrom, Edward E.** (1903-85): ord. June 2, 1928; aux. New York (Arba), 1960-78 (res.).

**Sweeney, James J.** (1898-1968): ord. June 20, 1925; first bp. Honolulu, 1941-68.

**Swint, John J.** (1879-1962): ord. June 23, 1904; aux. Wheeling (Sura), 1922; bp. Wheeling, 1922-62.

**T**

**Takach, Basil** (1879-1948): b. Austria-Hungary; ord. Dec. 12, 1902; first ap. ex. Pittsburgh Byzantine Rite (Zela), 1924-48.

**Tanner, Paul F.** (1905-94): ord. May 30, 1931; gen. sec. NCWC (now USCC), 1958-68; tit. bp. Lamasba, 1965; bp. St. Augustine, 1968-79 (res.).

**Tarasevitch, Vladimir L., O.S.B.** (1921-86): b. Byelorussia (White Russia); ord. May 26, 1949; ap. visitator (with residence in Chicago) for Byelorussians outside Soviet Union (Mariamme), 1983-86.

**Taylor, John E., O.M.I.** (1914-76): ord. May 25, 1940; bp. Stockholm, Sweden, 1962-76.

**Thill, Francis A.** (1893-1957): ord. Feb. 28, 1920; bp. Concordia (title changed to Salina in 1944), 1938-57.

**Tief, Francis J.** (1881-1965): ord. June 11, 1908; bp. Concordia (now Salina), 1921-38 (res.).

**Tierney, Michael** (1839-1908): b. Ireland; ord. May 26,1866; bp. Hartford, 1894-1908.

**Tihen, J. Henry** (1861-1940): ord. Apr. 26, 1886; bp. Lincoln, 1911-17; bp. Denver, 1917-31 (res.).

**Timon, John, C.M.** (1797-1867): ord. Sept. 23, 1826; first bp. Buffalo, 1847-67.

**Toebbe, Augustus M.** (1829-84): b. Germany; ord. Sept. 14, 1854; bp. Covington, 1870-84.

**Toolen, Thomas J.** (1886-1976): ord. Sept. 27, 1910; bp. (pers. tit. abp., 1954), Mobile, 1927-69 (res.).

**Topel, Bernard J.** (1903-86): ord. June 7, 1927; coad. bp. Spokane (Binda), Sept. 21-25, 1955; bp. Spokane, 1955-78 (res.).

**Tracy, Robert E.** (1909-80): ord. June 12, 1932; aux. Lafayette, La. (Sergentiza), 1959-61; first bp. Baton Rouge, 1961-74 (res.).

**Treacy, John P.** (1890-1964): ord. Dec. 8, 1918; coad. bp. La Crosse (Metelis), 1945-48; bp. La Crosse, 1948-64.

**Trobec, James** (1838-1921): b. Austria; ord. Sept. 8, 1865; bp. St. Cloud, 1897-1914 (res.).

**Tuigg, John** (1820-89): b. Ireland; ord. May 14, 1850; bp. Pittsburgh, 1876-89.

**Turner, William** (1871-1936): b. Ireland; ord. Aug. 13, 1893; bp. Buffalo, 1919-36.

**Tyler, William** (1806-49): ord. June 3, 1829; first bp. Hartford, 1844-49.

**U-V**

**Unterkoefler, Ernest L.** (1917-93): ord. May 18, 1944; aux. Richmond (Latopolis) 1962-64; bp. Charleston, 1964-90 (res.).

**Van de Velde, James O., S.J.** (1795-1855): b. Belgium; ord. Sept. 16, 1827; bp. Chicago, 1849-53; bp. Natchez (now Jackson), 1953-55.

**Van de Ven, Cornelius** (1865-1932): b. Holland; ord. May 31, 1890; bp. Natchitoches (title changed to Alexandria, 1910), 1904-32.

**Van de Vyver, Augustine** (1844-1911): b. Belgium; ord. July 24, 1870; bp. Richmond, 1889-1911.

**Vath, Joseph G.** (1918-87): ord. June 7, 1941; aux. Mobile-Birmingham (Novaliciana), 1966-69; first bp. Birmingham, 1969-87.

**Vehr, Urban J.** (1891-1973): ord. May 29, 1915; bp. 1931-41, and first abp. Denver, 1941-67 (res.).

**Verdaguer, Peter** (1835-1911): b. Spain; ord. Dec. 12, 1862; v.a. Brownsville (Aulon), 1890-1911.

**Verot, Augustin, S.S.** (1805-76): b. France; ord. Sept. 20, 1828; v.a. Florida (Danaba), 1856-61; bp. Savannah, 1861-70; bp. St. Augustine, 1870-76.

**Vertin, John** (1844-99): b. Austria; ord. Aug. 31, 1866; bp. Sault Ste. Marie and Marquette (now Marquette), 1879-99.

**Vogel, Cyril J.** (1905-79): ord. June 7, 1931; bp. Salina, 1965-79.

**Vonesh, Raymond J.** (1916-91): ord. May 3, 1941; aux. Joliet (Vanariona), 1968-1991 (res. May; d. Aug.).

## W

**Wade, Thomas, S.M.** (1893-1969): ord. June 15, 1922; v.a. Northern Solomons (Barbalissus), 1930-69.

**Wadhams, Edgar** (1817-91): convert, 1846; ord. Jan. 15, 1850; first bp. Ogdensburg, 1872-91.

**Waldschmidt, Paul E., C.S.C.** (1920-94): ord. June 24, 1946; aux. Portland, Ore. (Citium) 1978-90 (ret.).

**Walsh, Emmet** (1892-1968): ord. Jan. 15, 1916; bp. Charleston, 1927-49; coad. bp. Youngstown (Rhaedestus), 1949-52; bp. Youngstown, 1952-68.

**Walsh, James A., M.M.** (1867-1936): ord. May 20, 1892; co-founder (with Thomas F. Price) of Maryknoll, first U.S. established foreign mission society and first sponsor of a U.S. foreign mission seminary; superior of Maryknoll, 1911-36; tit. bp. Syene, 1933-36.

**Walsh, James E., M.M.** (1891-1981): ord. Dec. 7, 1915; v.a. Kongmoon, China (Sata), 1927-36; superior of Maryknoll, 1936-46; general secretary, Catholic Central Bureau, Shanghai, China, 1948; imprisoned by Chinese communists, 1958-70.

**Walsh, Louis S.** (1858-1924): ord. Dec. 23, 1882; bp. Portland, Me., 1906-24.

**Walsh, Thomas J.** (1873-1952): ord. Jan. 27, 1900; bp. Trenton, 1918-28; bp., 1928-37, and first abp. 1937-52, Newark.

**Ward, John** (1857-1929): ord. July 17, 1884; bp. Leavenworth (now Kansas City), 1910-29.

**Waters, Vincent S.** (1904-74): ord. Dec. 8, 1931; bp. Raleigh, 1945-74.

**Watson, Alfred M.** (1907-90): ord. May 10, 1934; aux. Erie (Nationa), 1965-69; bp. Erie 1969-82 (res.).

**Watterson, John A.** (1844-99): ord. Aug. 9, 1868;

bp. Columbus, 1880-99.

**Wehrle, Vincent, O.S.B.** (1855-1941): b. Switzerland; ord. Apr. 23, 1882; first bp. Bismarck, 1910-39 (res.).

**Welch, Thomas A.** (1884-1959): ord. June 11, 1909; bp. Duluth, 1926-59.

**Weldon, Christopher J.** (1905-82): ord. Sept. 21, 1939; bp. Springfield, Mass., 1950-77 (res.).

**Whealon, John F.** (1921-91): ord. May 26, 1945; aux. Cleveland (Andrapa), 1961-66; bp. Erie, 1966-69; abp. Hartford, 1969-91.

**Whelan, James O.P.** (1822-78): b. Ireland; ord. Aug. 2, 1846; coad. bp. Nashville (Marcopolis), 1859-60; bp. Nashville, 1860-64 (res.).

**Whelan, Richard V.** (1809-74): ord. May 1, 1831; bp. Richmond, 1841-50; bp. Wheeling, 1850-74.

**White, Charles** (1879-1955): ord. Sept. 24, 1910; bp. Spokane, 1927-55.

**Whitfield, James** (1770-1834): b. England; ord. July 24, 1809; coad. bp. Baltimore (Apollonia), 1828; abp. Baltimore, 1828-34.

**Wigger, Winand** (1841-1901): ord. June 10, 1865; bp. Newark, 1881-1901.

**Wildermuth, Augustine F., S.J.** (1904-93): ord. July 25, 1935; bp. Patna, India, 1947-80 (res.).

**Willging, Joseph C.** (1884-1959): ord. June 20, 1908; first bp. Pueblo, 1942-59.

**Williams, John J.** (1822-1907): ord. May 17, 1845; bp., 1866-75, and first abp., 1875-1907, Boston.

**Willinger, Aloysius J., C.SS.R.** (1886-1973): ord. July 2, 1911; bp. Ponce, P.R., 1929-46; coad. bp. Monterey-Fresno, 1946-53; bp. Monterey-Fresno, 1953-67 (res.).

**Winkelmann, Christian H.** (1883-1946): ord. June 11, 1907; aux. St. Louis (Sita), 1933-39; bp. Wichita, 1939-46.

**Wood, James F.** (1813-83): convert, 1836; ord. Mar. 25, 1844; coad. bp. Philadelphia (Antigonea), 1857-60; bp., 1860-75, and first abp., 1875-83, Philadelphia.

**Woznicki, Stephen** (1894-1968): ord. Dec. 22, 1917; aux. Detroit (Peltae), 1938-50; bp. Saginaw, 1950-68.

**Wright, John J.** (1909-79): ord. Dec. 8, 1935; aux. Boston (Egee), 1947-50; bp. Worcester, 1950-59; bp. Pittsbrgh, 1959-69; cardinal, 1969; prefect Congregation of the Clergy, 1969-79.

**Wurm, John N.** (1927-84): ord. Apr. 3, 1954; aux. St. Louis (Plestia), 1976-81; bp. Belleville, 1981-84.

## Y-Z

**Young, Josue** (1808-66): ord. Apr. 1, 1838; bp. Erie, 1854-66.

**Zaleski, Alexander, M.** (1906-75): ord. July 12, 1931; aux. Detroit (Lybe), 1950-64; coad. bp. Lansing, 1964-65; bp. Lansing 1966-75.

**Zardetti, Otto** (1847-1902): b. Switzerland; ord. Aug. 21, 1870; first bp. St. Cloud, 1889-94; abp. Bucharest, Rumania, 1894-95 (res.).

**Zuroweste, Albert R.** (1901-87): ord. June 8, 1924; bp. Belleville, 1948-76 (res.).

# HISPANICS

The nation's Hispanic population totaled 22.4 million, according to figures reported by the U.S. Census Bureau in 1990. It was estimated that 80 percent of the Hispanics were baptized Catholics.

## Pastoral Patterns

Pastoral ministry to Hispanics varies, depending on differences among the people and the availability of personnel to carry it out.

The pattern in cities with large numbers of Spanish-speaking is built around special and bilingual churches, centers or other agencies where pastoral and additional forms of service are provided in a manner suited to the needs, language and culture of the people. Services in some places are extensive and include legal advice, job placement, language instruction, recreational and social assistance, specialized counseling, replacement services. In many places, however, even where there are special ministries, the needs are generally greater than the means required to meet them.

Some urban dwellers have been absorbed into established parishes and routines of church life and activity. Many Spanish-speaking communities remain in need of special ministries. An itinerant form of ministry best meets the needs of the thousands of migrant workers who follow the crops.

Demographic and ministerial data were the subjects of a national survey commissioned by the Bishops' Committee for Hispanic Affairs and carried out by its secretariat. It was reported in November, 1990, that responses were received from 152 archdioceses and dioceses. Twelve or more dioceses and archdioceses had Hispanic populations of more than 50 percent; 27 others were a quarter or more Hispanic. Fifty-five percent of the reporting jurisdictions had Hispanic apostolates. Overall, ministerial emphasis was reported in six areas: youth, small Christian communities, the Cursillo movement, Catholic Charities and social ministry, lay leadership formation, and charismatic renewal. Other sources reported that well over 80 percent of Hispanics were located in urban areas, and that 54 percent were 25 years of age or younger. It was estimated that perhaps 100,000 Catholic Hispanics a year were being lost, principally to fundamentalist and pentecostal sects.

Pastoral ministry to Hispanics was the central concern of three national meetings, *Encuentros,* held in 1972, 1977 and 1985.

The third National *Encuentro* in 1985 produced a master pastoral plan for ministry which the National Conference of Catholic Bishops approved in 1987. Its four keys are collaborative ministry; evangelization; a missionary option regarding the poor, the maginalized, the family, women and youth; the formation of lay leadership.

The U.S. bishops, at their annual meeting in November, 1983, approved and subsequently published a pastoral letter on Hispanic Ministry under the title, "The Hispanic Presence: Challenge and Commitment." (For text, see pp. 46-49 of the 1985 *Catholic Almanac.*)

## Bishops

As of June 15, 1996, there were 22 (20 active) bishops of Hispanic origin in the United States; all were named since 1970 (for biographies, see Index). Nine were heads of archdioceses or dioceses: Archbishop Patrick F. Flores (San Antonio); Bishops Raymundo J. Pena (Brownsville), Ricardo Ramirez, C.S.B. (Las Cruces), Rene H. Gracida (Corpus Christi), Arthur N. Tafoya (Pueblo), Manuel D. Moreno (Tucson), Placido Rodriguez, C.M.F. (Lubbock), Gerald R. Barnes (San Bernardino) and Armando Ochoa (El Paso). One was a coadjutor bishop, Roberto O. Gonzalez, O.F.M. (Corpus Christi). Ten were auxiliary bishops: Gabino Zavala (Los Angeles), Gilbert Espinoza Chavez (San Diego), Joseph J. Madera (Military Services), Francisco Garmendia (New York), Agustin Roman (Miami), Rene Valero (Brooklyn), David Arias, O.A.R. (Newark), Alvaro Corrada del Rio, S.J. (Washington, D.C.), Carlos A. Sevilla, S.J. (San Francisco), and James A. Tamayo (Galveston-Houston). Resigned/retired prelates: Archbishop Robert F. Sanchez (Santa Fe), Bishop Juan Arzube (Los Angeles, auxiliary).

Hispanic priests and nuns in the U.S. number about 1,600 and 2,000, respectively, according to an estimate made in June, 1988, by Father Gary Riebe Estrella, S.V.D., director of a Hispanic vocational recruitment program.

## Secretariat for Hispanic Affairs

The national secretariat was established by the U.S. Catholic Conference for service in promoting and coordinating pastoral ministry to the Spanish-speaking. Its basic orientation is toward integral evangelization, combining religious ministry with development efforts in programs geared to the culture and needs of Hispanics. Its concerns are urban and migrant Spanish-speaking people; communications and publications in line with secretariat purposes and the service of people; bilingual and bicultural religious and general education; liaison for and representation of Hispanics with church, civic and governmental agencies.

The secretariat publishes a newsletter, En Marcha, available to interested parties.

Ronaldo M. Cruz is executive director of the national office at 3211 Fourth St. N.E., Washington, D.C. 20017.

The secretariat works in collaboration with regional and diocesan offices and pastoral institutes throughout the country.

The Northeast Regional Office, officially the **Northeast Hispanic Catholic Center,** was established in 1976 under the auspices of the bishops in 12 states from Maine to Virginia. It has established the Conference of Diocesan Directors of the Hispanic Apostolate, the Association of Hispanic Deacons, a Regional Youth Task Force and a Regional Committee of Diocesan Coordinators of Religious Educators for the Hispanics. The office is the official publishing house for the Hispanic Lectionary approved by the National Conference of Catholic Bishops for the United States. The center has liturgical, evangelization and youth ministry departments and an office of cultural affairs. Mario J. Paredes is executive director. The center is located at 1011 First Ave., New York, NY 10022.

The Southeast Regional Office serves 26 dioceses in Tennessee, North and South Carolina, Florida, Georgia, Mississippi, Alabama and Louisiana. Father Mario Vizcaino, Sch. P., is director of the region and institute. The office is located at 7700 S.W. 56 St., Miami, FL 33155. The **Southeast Pastoral Institute** serves as the educational arm of the regional office by providing formation programs for the development of leadership skills focused on ministry among Hispanics, at the Miami site and in the various dioceses of the region.

In the **Southwest,** the Mexican American Cultural Center serves as convener of diocesan directors and representatives of Hispanic ministry in Arkansas, Oklahoma and Texas.

A regional office serving the **Mountain States** (Arizona, New Mexico, Utah, Colorado and Wyoming) is under the coordination of Deacon Germán Toro, 27 C St., Salt Lake City, UT 84103.

The **Northwest Regional Office for Hispanic Affairs** serves 13 dioceses in Alaska, Montana, Washington, Oregon and Idaho. Father Heliodora Lucatero is president. The office is located at 5301-F Tieton Dr., Yakima, WA 98908. It serves as convener for regional workshops, retreats, formation programs and social advocacy.

### National Hispanic Priests Association

The National Association of Hispanic Priests of the USA (ANSH — *La Asociación Nacional de Sacerdotes Hispanos*, EE. UU.) was established in September, 1989, with a representation of about 2,400 Hispanic priests residing and ministering in the United States. The association is a product of a long process. In 1970, a group of priests formally organized under the name of PADRES, an acronym for the Spanish title, "Padres Asociados para Derechos Religiosos, Educativos y Sociales." They advocated for and organized the first National Hispanic Encounters with important support and leadership of *Las Hermanas.* Among the early issues was the naming of the first Hispanic bishops. In 1985 some members of PADRES and the Asociacion de Sacerdotes Hispanos (ASH) from the eastern United States took the first steps which led four years later to the establishment of ANSH as a national organization. The association collaborates with the laity and bishops in implementing the National Plan for Hispanic Ministry and in developing approaches for a more meaningful ministry. The president is Rev. Juan Carlos Castro, O.M.I., 555 West St. Francis St., Brownsville, TX 78520.

### National Catholic Council for Hispanic Ministry (NCCHM)

The council is a volunteer federation of Roman Catholic organizations, agencies and movements committed to the development of Hispanics/Latinos in Church and society. It was established June 17, 1990, at a gathering at Mundelein College, Chicago; its by-laws were adopted in January, 1991, at Mercy Center, Burlingame, Calif. The council convokes a national gathering every three years called Raices y Alas (Roots and Wings). With funding from foundations NCCHM has designed and piloted a leadership development program that links contemporary understandings of leadership with experiences and insights from faith and Hispanic cultures. NCCHM has 50 member organizations. It publishes Puentes, a newsletter. The president is Dr. Carmen Maria Cervantes; the executive director is Rev. Allan Figueroa Deck, S.J., 8601 Lincoln Blvd., Rm. 430, Los Angeles, CA 90045.

### Mexican American Cultural Center

This national center, specializing in pastoral studies and language education, was founded in 1972 to provide programs focused on ministry among Hispanics and personnel working with Hispanics in the U.S. Courses — developed according to the see-judge-act methodology — include culture, faith development, Scripture, theology, and praxis; some are offered in Spanish, others in English. Intensive language classes are offered in Spanish, with emphasis on pastoral usage.

The center also conducts workshops for the development of leadership skills and for a better understanding of Hispanic communities. Faculty members serve as resource personnel for pastoral centers, dioceses and parishes throughout the U.S. The center offers master-degree programs in pastoral ministry in cooperation with Incarnate Word College, Boston College, the Oblate School of Theology, St. Mary's University and Loyola University, New Orleans and other educational institutions.

The center is a distribution agency for the circulation of bilingual pastoral materials in the U.S. and Latin America.

Sister Maria Elena Gonzalez, R.S.M., is president of the center which is located at 3019 W. French Place, San Antonio, TX 78228.

### Hispanic Liturgy

Spanish-speaking communities in the U.S. are served by the Institute of Hispanic Liturgy, a national organization of liturgists, musicians, artists and pastoral agents, funded in part by the U.S. Bishops. The institute promotes the study of liturgical texts, art, music and popular religiosity in an effort to develop liturgical spirituality among Hispanics. It works closely with the U.S. Bishops' Committee on the Liturgy, and has published liturgical materials. Rev. Raúl Gómez, S.D.S., is the president; Sr. Doris Mary Turek, S.S.N.D., is executive director. Address: P.O. Box 29387, Washington, D.C. 20017.

# BLACK CATHOLICS IN THE UNITED STATES

### National Office

The National Office for Black Catholics, organized in July, 1970, is a central agency with the general purposes of promoting active and full participation by black Catholics in the Church and of making more effective the presence and ministry of the Church in the black community.

Its operations are in support of the aspirations and calls of black Catholics for a number of objectives, including the following:

•representation and voice for blacks among bishops and others with leadership and decision-making positions in the Church;

•promoting vocations to the priesthood and religious life;

•sponsoring programs of evangelization, pastoral ministry, education and liturgy on a national level;

•recognition of the black heritage in liturgy, community life, theology and education.

Walter T. Hubbard is executive director of the NOBC.

The NOBC office is located at 3025 Fourth St. N.E., Washington, D.C. 20017.

### Clergy Caucus

The National Black Catholic Clergy Caucus, founded in 1968 in Detroit, is a fraternity of several hundred black priests, permanent deacons and brothers pledged to mutual support in their vocations and ministries.

The Caucus develops programs of spiritual, theological, educational and ministerial growth for its members, to counteract the effects of institutionalized racism within the Church and American society. A bimonthly newsletter is published.

The NBCCC office is located at 343 N. Walnut St., P.O. Box 1088, Opelousas, La. 70571.

Other peer and support groups are the National Black Sisters' Conference and the National Black Catholic Seminarians Association.

### National Black Catholic Congress

The National Black Catholic Congress, Inc., was formed in 1985 exclusively to assist in the development of the Roman Catholic Church in the African American community and to devise effective means of evangelization of African American peoples in the United States. Its fundamental purpose is the formation and development of concrete approaches toward the evangelization of African Americans through revitalization of African American Catholic life.

The Congress is under the sponsorship of the African American Roman Catholic bishops of the United States, the National Black Catholic Clergy Caucus, the National Black Sisters' Conference, the National Association of Black Catholic Administrators and the Knights of Peter Claver and the Ladies Auxiliary Knights of Peter Claver. The Congress is also in consultation with African American clergy and vowed religious women communities. The Congress sponsors *Pastoring in African American Parishes,* an annual workshop first held in 1988 and *An African American Catholic Ministries Program,* a week-long curriculum presented twice a year, usually in January and June.

The National Black Catholic Congress sponsored the seventh assembly of African-American Catholics and those serving in African American communities, July 9 to 12, 1992, in New Orleans. The next National Congress will convene in Baltimore, Aug. 27 to 31, 1997.

The Congress is sponsoring construction of "Our Mother of Africa Chapel" at the Basilica of the National Shrine of the Immaculate Conception in Washington, D.C.

The office of the Congress is located at The Archdiocese of Baltimore Catholic Center, 320 Cathedral St., Room 712, Baltimore, MD 21201. The executive director is Dr. Hilbert D. Stanley.

## Committee and Secretariat

The **Committee on African American Catholics,** established by the National Conference of Catholic Bishops in 1987, is chaired by Bishop Curtis J. Guillory of Galveston-Houston. The purpose of the committee is to assist the bishops in their evangelization efforts to the African American community by initiating, encouraging and supporting programs which recognize and respect African American genius and values. Priorities of the Committee include implementation of the National Black Catholic Pastoral Plan of 1987, inculturation of liturgy and ministry, and increasing lay leadership and vocations.

Also established as a service agency to the committee was a Secretariat for African American Catholics under the executive direction of Beverly Carroll. The secretariat is the officially recognized voice of the African American community as it articulates its gifts and aspirations regarding ministry, evangelization and worship. It also serves as a liaison to the National Black Catholic Clergy Caucus, the National Black Catholic Seminarians Association, the National Black Sisters' Conference, National Black Catholic Administrators, Knights of St. Peter Claver and Ladies Auxiliary, the National Black Catholic Congress, and the National Black Catholic Theological Society.

The committee and secretariat have offices at 3211 Fourth St. N.E., Washington, D.C. 20017.

## Bishops

There were 13 (11 active) black bishops, as of July 1, 1996: Four were heads of dioceses: Bishops Joseph L. Howze (Biloxi), J. Terry Steib, S.V.D. (Memphis), Wilton D. Gregory (Belleville), and Elliott G. Thomas (St. Thomas, Virgin Islands). Seven were auxiliary bishops: Moses Anderson, S.S.E. (Detroit), John H. Ricard, S.S.J. (Baltimore), Curtis J. Guillory, S.V.D. (Galveston-Houston), Leonard J. Olivier, S.V.D. (Washington), Dominic Carmon, S.V.D. (New Orleans), George V, Murry, S.J. (Chicago) and Edward K. Braxton (St. Louis). Archbishop Eugene A. Marino, S.S.J., of Atlanta, resigned in July, 1990. Auxiliary bishop Joseph A. Francis, S.V.D., of Newark retired June 30, 1995.

## Josephite Pastoral Center

The Josephite Pastoral Center was established in September, 1968, as an educational and pastoral service agency for the Josephites in their mission work, specifically in the black community, subsequently to all those who minister in the African-American community. St. Joseph's Society of the Sacred Heart, the sponsoring body has about 134 priests and 11 brothers in 64 mostly southern parishes in 17 dioceses. The staff of the center includes Father John G. Harfmann, S.S.J., director, and Maria M. Lannon, associate director. Address: St. Joseph Seminary 1200 Varnum St. N.E., Washington, D.C. 20017

# RELIGIOUS

## Institutes of Consecrated Life

Religious institutes and congregations are special societies in the Church — institutes of consecrated life — whose members, called Religious, commit themselves, by public vows to observance of the evangelical counsels of poverty, chastity and obedience in a community kind of life in accordance with rules and constitutions approved by church authority.

Secular institutes (covered in its own Almanac entry) are also institutes of consecrated life.

The particular goal of each institute and the means of realizing it in practice are stated in the rule and constitutions proper to the institute. Local bishops can give approval for rules and constitutions of institutes of diocesan rank. Pontifical rank belongs to institutes approved by the Holy See. General jurisdiction over all Religious is exercised by the Congregation for Institutes of Consecrated Life and Societies of Apostolic Life. General legislation concerning Religious is contained in Canons 573 to 709 in Book II, Part III, of the Code of Canon Law.

All institutes of consecrated life are commonly called religious orders, despite the fact that there are differences between orders and congregations. The best known orders include the Benedictines, Trappists, Franciscans, Dominicans, Carmelites and Augustinians, for men; and the Carmelites, Benedictines, Poor Clares, Dominicans of the Second Order and Visitation Nuns, for women. The orders are older than the congregations, which did not appear until the 16th century.

Contemplative institutes are oriented to divine worship and service within the confines of their communities, by prayer, penitential practices, other spiritual activities and self-supporting work. Examples are the Trappists and Carthusians, the Carmelite and Poor Clare nuns. Active institutes are geared for pastoral ministry and various kinds of apostolic work. Mixed institutes combine elements of the contemplative and active ways of life. While most institutes of men and women can be classified as active, all of them have contemplative aspects.

Clerical communities of men are those whose membership is predominantly composed of priests.

Non-clerical or lay institutes of men are the various brotherhoods.

"The Consecrated Life and Its Role in the Church and in the World," was the topic of the ninth general assembly of the Synod of Bishops held Oct. 2 to 29, 1994 (see Index, *Vita Consecrata*).

## Societies of Apostolic Life

Some of the institutes listed below have a special kind of status because their members, while living a common life like that which is characteristic of Religious, do not profess the vows of Religious. Examples are the Maryknoll Fathers, the Oratorians of St. Philip Neri, the Paulists and Sulpicians. They are called societies of apostolic life and are the subject of Canons 731 to 746 in the Code of Canon Law.

# RELIGIOUS INSTITUTES OF MEN IN THE UNITED STATES

(Sources: *Official Catholic Directory;* Catholic Almanac survey.)

**Africa, Missionaries of (M. Afr.):** Founded 1868 at Algiers by Cardinal Charles M. Lavigerie; known as White Fathers until 1984. Generalate, Rome Italy; U.S. headquarters, 1624 21st St. N.W., Washington, DC 20009. Missionary work in Africa.

**African Missions, Society of, S.M.A.:** Founded 1856, at Lyons, France, by Bishop Melchior de Marion Brésillac. Generalate, Rome, Italy; American province (1941), 23 Bliss Ave., Tenafly, NJ 07670. Missionary work.

**Alexian Brothers, C.F.A.:** Founded 14th century in western Germany and Belgium during the Black Plague. Motherhouse, Aachen, Germany; generalate, Signal Mountain, TN 37377. Hospital and general health work.

**Assumptionists (Augustinians of the Assumption), A.A.:** Founded 1845, at Nimes, France, by Rev. Emmanuel d'Alzon; in U.S., 1946. General house, Rome, Italy; U.S. province, 330 Market St., Brighton, MA 02135. Educational, parochial, ecumenical, retreat, foreign mission work.

**Atonement, Franciscan Friars of the, S.A.:** Founded as an Anglican Franciscan community in 1898 at Garrison, N.Y., by Rev. Paul Wattson. Community corporately received into the Catholic Church in 1909. Generalate, St. James Friary, P.O. Box 5, Graymoor, Garrison NY 10524. Ecumenical, mission, retreat and charitable works.

**Augustinian Recollects, O.A.R.:** Founded 1588: in U.S., 1944. General motherhouse, Rome, Italy. Missionary, parochial, education work.

St. Augustine Province (1944), 29 Ridgeway Ave., W. Orange, NJ 07052.

St. Nicholas Province: U.S. Delegates, 2800 Schurz Ave., Bronx, NY 10465 (New York); P.O. Box 310, Mesilla, NM 88044 (South).

**Augustinians (Order of St. Augustine), O.S.A.:** Established canonically in 1256 by Pope Alexander IV; in U.S., 1796. General motherhouse, Rome, Italy.

St. Thomas of Villanova Province (1796), P.O. Box 338, Villanova, PA 19085.

Our Mother of Good Counsel Province (1941), Tolentine Center, 20300 Governors Hwy., Olympia Fields, IL 60461.

St. Augustine Province (1969), 1605 28th St., San Diego, CA 92102.

Good Counsel Vice-Province, St. Augustine Preparatory School, Richland, NJ 08350.

U.S. Address of King City, Ont., Canada, Province: 3103 Arlington Ave., Bronx, NY 10463.

U.S. Vicariate of Castile, Spain, Province (1963), Vicar, 3648 61st St., Port Arthur, TX 77642.

**Barnabites (Clerics Regular of St. Paul), C.R.S.P.:** Founded 1530, in Milan, Italy, by St. Anthony M. Zaccaria; approved 1533; in U.S., 1952. Historical motherhouse, Church of St. Barnabas (Milan). Generalate, Rome, Italy; North American province, 1023 Swann Rd., Youngstown, NY 14174. Parochial, educational, mission work.

**Basil the Great, Order of St. (Basilian Order of St. Josaphat), O.S.B.M.:** General motherhouse,

Rome, Italy; U.S. province, 31-12 30th St., Long Island City, NY 11106. Parochial work among Byzantine Ukrainian Rite Catholics.

**Basilian Fathers (Congregation of the Priests of St. Basil), C.S.B.:** Founded 1822, at Annonay, France. General motherhouse, Toronto, Ont., Canada. U.S. addresses: 445 King's Hwy., Rochester, NY 14617 (East); 4500 Memorial Dr., Houston, TX 77007 (West). Educational, parochial work.

**Basilian Salvatorian Fathers, B.S.O.:** Founded 1684, at Saida, Lebanon, by Eftimios Saifi; in U.S., 1953. General motherhouse, Saida, Lebanon; American headquarters, 30 East St., Methuen, MA 01844. Educational, parochial work among Eastern Rite peoples.

**Benedictine Monks (Order of St. Benedict), O.S.B.:** Founded 529, in Italy, by St. Benedict of Nursia; in U.S., 1846.

• American Cassinese Congregation (1855). Pres., Rt. Rev. Melvin J. Valvano, O.S.B., Newark Abbey, 528 Dr. Martin Luther King Blvd., Newark, NJ 07102. Abbeys and Priories belonging to the congregation:

St. Vincent Archabbey, 300 Fraser Purchase Rd., Latrobe, PA 15650; St. John's Abbey, P.O. Box 2015, Collegeville, MN 56321; St. Benedict's Abbey, Atchison, KS 66002; St. Mary's Abbey, Delbarton, Morristown, NJ 07960; Newark Abbey, 528 Dr. Martin Luther King, Jr., Blvd., Newark, NJ 07102; Belmont Abbey, 100 Belmont - Mt. Holly Rd., Belmont, NC 28012; St. Bernard Abbey, Cullman, AL 35055; St. Procopius Abbey, 5601 College Rd., Lisle, IL 60532; St. Gregory's Abbey, Shawnee, OK 74801; St. Leo Abbey, St. Leo, FL 33574; Assumption Abbey, P.O. Box A, Richardton, ND 58652;

St. Bede Abbey, Peru, IL 61354; St. Martin's Abbey, 5300 Pacific Ave. S.E., Lacey, WA 98503; Holy Cross Abbey, P.O. Box 1510, Canon City, CO 81215; St. Anselm's Abbey, 100 St. Anselm Dr., Manchester, NH 03102; St. Andrew Abbey, 10510 Buckeye Rd., Cleveland, OH 44104; Holy Trinity Priory, P.O. Box 990, Butler, PA 16003; St. Maur Priory, 4615 N. Michigan Rd., Indianapolis, IN 46208; Benedictine Priory, 6502 Seawright Dr., Savannah, GA 31406; Woodside Priory, 302 Portola Rd., Portola Valley, CA 94028; Mary Mother of the Church Abbey, 12617 River Rd., Richmond, VA 23233; Abadia de San Antonio Abad, P.O. Box 729, Humacao, PR 00661.

• Swiss-American Congregation (1870). Abbeys and priory belonging to the congregation:

St. Meinrad Archabbey, St. Meinrad, IN 47577; Conception Abbey, Conception, MO 64433; Mt. Michael Abbey, 22520 Mt. Michael Rd., Elkhorn, NE 68022; Subiaco Abbey, Subiaco, AR 72865; St. Joseph's Abbey, St. Benedict, LA 70457; Mt. Angel Abbey, St. Benedict, OR 97373; Marmion Abbey, Butterfield Rd., Aurora, IL 60504;

St. Benedict's Abbey, Benet Lake, WI 53102; Glastonbury Abbey, 16 Hull St., Hingham, MA 02043; Blue Cloud Abbey, Marvin, SD 57251; Corpus Christi Abbey, HCR2, Box 6300, Sandia, TX 78383; Prince of Peace Abbey, 650 Benet Hill Rd., Oceanside, CA 92054; St. Benedict Abbey, 252 Still River Rd., PO Box 67, Still River (Harvard), MA 01467.

• Congregation of St. Ottilien for Foreign Missions: St. Paul's Abbey, Newton, NJ 07860; Christ the King Priory, Schuyler, NE 68661.

• Congregation of the Annunciation, St. Andrew Abbey, Valyermo, CA 93563.

• English Benedictine Congregation: St. Anselm's Abbey, 4501 S. Dakota Ave. N.E., Washington, DC 20017; Abbey of St. Gregory, Cory's Lane, Portsmouth, RI 02871; Abbey of St. Mary and St. Louis, 500 S. Mason Rd., St. Louis, MO 63141.

• Houses not in Congregations: Mount Saviour Monastery, Pine City, NY 14871; Conventual Priory of St. Gabriel the Archangel, Weston, VT 05161.

**Benedictines, Camaldolese Congregation, O.S.B. Cam.:** Founded 1012, at Camaldoli, near Arezzo, Italy, by St. Romuald; in U.S. 1958. General motherhouse, Arezzo, Italy; U.S. foundation, New Camaldoli Hermitage, Big Sur, CA 93920.

**Benedictines, Olivetan, O.S.B.:** General motherhouse, Siena, Italy. U.S. foundations: Our Lady of Guadalupe Abbey, Pecos, NM 87552; Holy Trinity Monastery, P.O. Box 298, St. David, AZ 85630; Monastery of the Risen Christ, P.O. Box 3931, San Luis Obispo, CA 93403; Benedictine Monastery of Hawaii, P.O. Box 490, Waialua, Hawaii 96791.

**Benedictines, Subiaco Congregation, O.S.B.:** Independent priory, 1983. Monastery of Christ in the Desert, Abiquiu, NM 87510; St, Mary's Monastery, P.O. Box 345, Petersham, MA 01366.

**Benedictines, Sylvestrine, O.S.B.:** Founded 1231, in Italy by Sylvester Gozzolini. General motherhouse, Rome, Italy; U.S. foundations: 17320 Rosemont Rd., Detroit, MI 48219; 2711 E. Drahner Rd., Oxford, MI 48051; 1697 State Highway 3, Clifton, NJ 07012.

**Blessed Sacrament, Congregation of the, S.S.S.:** Founded 1856, at Paris, France, by St. Pierre Julien Eymard; in U.S., 1900. General motherhouse, Rome, Italy; U.S. province, 5384 Wilson Mills Rd., Cleveland, OH 44143. Eucharistic apostolate.

**Brigittine Monks (Order of the Most Holy Savior), O.Ss.S.:** Monastery of Our Lady of Consolation, 23300 Walker Lane, Amity, OR 97101.

**Camaldolese Hermits of the Congregation of Monte Corona, Er. Cam.:** Founded 1520, from Camaldoli, Italy, by Bl. Paul Giustiniani. General motherhouse, Frascati (Rome), Italy; U.S. foundation, Holy Family Hermitage, Rt. 2, Box 36, Bloomingdale, OH 43910.

**Camillian Fathers and Brothers (Order of St. Camillus; Order of Servants of the Sick), O.S.Cam.:** Founded 1582, at Rome, by St. Camillus de Lellis; in U.S., 1923. General motherhouse, Rome, Italy; North American province, 10101 W. Wisconsin Ave., Wauwatosa, WI 53226.

**Carmelites (Order of Our Lady of Mt. Carmel), O. Carm.:** General motherhouse, Rome, Italy. Educational, charitable work.

Most Pure Heart of Mary Province (1864), 1317 Frontage Rd., Darien, IL 60559.

St. Elias Province (1931), P.O. Box 3079, Middletown, NY 10940.

Mt. Carmel Hermitage, Pineland, R.D. 3, Box 36, New Florence, PA 15944 (immediately subject to Prior General).

**Carmelites, Order of Discalced, O.C.D.:** Established 1562, a Reform Order of Our Lady of Mt.

Carmel; in U.S., 1924. Generalate, Rome, Italy. Spiritual direction, retreat, parochial work.

California-Arizona Province, Central Office (1983), 926 E. Highland Ave., P.O. Box 2178, Redlands, CA 92373.

St. Therese of Oklahoma Province (1935), 515 Marylake Dr., Little Rock AR 72206.

Immaculate Heart of Mary Province (1947), 1233 S. 45th St., Milwaukee, WI 53214.

Polish Province of the Holy Spirit (1949), 1628 Ridge Rd., Munster, IN 46321.

**Carmelites of Mary Immaculate, C.M.I.:** Founded 1831, in India, by Bl. Kuriakose Elias Chavara and two other Syro-Malabar priests; canonically established, 1855. Generalate, Kerala, India; North American headquarters, Holy Family Church, 21 Nassau Ave., Brooklyn, NY 11222.

**Carthusians, Order of, O. Cart.:** Founded 1084, in France, by St. Bruno; in U.S., 1951. General motherhouse, St. Pierre de Chartreuse, France; U.S. charterhouse, R.R. 2, Box 2411, Arlington, VT 05250. Cloistered contemplatives; semi-eremitic.

**Charity, Brothers of, F.C.:** Founded 1807, in Belgium, by Canon Peter J. Triest. General motherhouse, Rome, Italy: American District (1963), Triest Hall, 7720 Doe Lane, Laverock, PA 19038.

**Charity, Servants of (Guanellians), S.C.:** Founded 1908, in Italy, by Bl. Luigi Guanella. General motherhouse, Rome, Italy; U.S. headquarters, St. Louis School, 16195 Old U.S. 12, Chelsea, MI 48118.

**Christ, Society of, S.Ch.:** Founded 1932, General Motherhouse, Poznan, Poland; U.S.-Canadian Province, 3000 Eighteen Mile Rd., Sterling Heights, MI 48311.

**Christian Brothers, Congregation of, C.F.C.** (formerly Christian Brothers of Ireland): Founded 1802 at Waterford, Ireland, by Edmund Ignatius Rice; in U.S., 1906. General motherhouse, Rome, Italy. Educational work.

American Province, Eastern U.S. (1916), 21 Pryer Terr., New Rochelle, NY 10804.

Brother Rice Province, Western U.S. (1966), 958 Western Ave., Joliet, IL 60435.

**Christian Instruction, Brothers of (La Mennais Brothers), F.I.C.:** Founded 1817, at Ploermel, France, by Abbe Jean Marie de la Mennais and Abbe Gabriel Deshayes. General motherhouse, Rome, Italy; American province, Notre Dame Institute, P.O. Box 159, Alfred, ME 04002.

**Christian Schools, Brothers of the (Christian Brothers), F.S.C.:** Founded 1680, at Reims, France, by St. Jean Baptiste de la Salle. General motherhouse, Rome, Italy; U.S. Conference, 4351 Garden City Dr., Suite 200, Landover, MD 20785. Educational, charitable work.

Baltimore Province (1845), Box 29, Adamstown, MD 21710.

Brothers of the Christian Schools (Midwest Province) (1995), 200 S. Frontage Rd., Suite 300, Burr Ridge, IL 60521.

New York Province (1848), 800 Newman Springs Rd., Lincroft, NJ 07738.

Long Island-New England Province (1957), Christian Brothers Center, 635 Ocean Ave., Narragansett, RI 02882.

St. Louis Province (1886), 2101 Rue de la Salle, Glencoe, MO 63038.

San Francisco Province (1868), P.O. Box 3720, Napa, CA 94558.

New Orleans-Santa Fe Province (1921), De La Salle Christian Brothers, 1522 Carmel Dr., Lafayette, LA 70501.

**Cistercians, Order of, O.Cist.:** Founded 1098, by St. Robert. Headquarters, Rome, Italy.

Our Lady of Spring Bank Abbey, Rt. 3, Box 211, Sparta, WI 54656.

Our Lady of Dallas Monastery, 1 Cistercian Rd., Irving, TX 75039.

Cistercian Monastery, 564 Walton Ave., Mt. Laurel, NJ 08054.

Cistercian Conventual Priory, St. Mary's Priory, R.D. 1, Box 206, New Ringgold, PA 17960.

**Cistercians of the Strict Observance, Order of (Trappists), O.C.S.O.:** Founded 1098, in France, by St. Robert; in U.S., 1848. Generalate, Rome, Italy.

Our Lady of Gethsemani Abbey (1848), Trappist, KY 40051.

Our Lady of New Melleray Abbey (1849), 6500 Melleray Circle, Peosta, IA 52068.

St. Joseph's Abbey (1825), Spencer, MA 01562.

Holy Spirit Monastery (1944), 2625 Hwy. 212 S.W., Conyers, GA 30208.

Our Lady of Guadalupe Abbey (1947), Lafayette, OR 97127.

Our Lady of the Holy Trinity Abbey (1947), Huntsville, Utah 84317.

Abbey of the Genesee (1951), P.O. Box 900, Piffard, NY 14533.

Mepkin Abbey (1949), 1098 Mepkin Abbey Rd., Moncks Corner, SC 29461.

Our Lady of the Holy Cross Abbey (1950), Rt. 2, Box 3870, Berryville, VA 22611.

Assumption Abbey (1950), Rt. 5, Box 1056, Ava, MO 65608.

Abbey of New Clairvaux (1955), Vina, CA 96092.

St. Benedict's Monastery (1956), 1012 Monastery Rd., Snowmass, CO 81654.

**Claretians (Missionary Sons of the Immaculate Heart of Mary), C.M.F.:** Founded 1849, at Vich, Spain, by St. Anthony Mary Claret. General headquarters, Rome, Italy. Missionary, parochial, educational, retreat work.

Western Province, 1119 Westchester Pl., Los Angeles, CA 90019.

Eastern Province, 400 N. Euclid Ave. Oak Park, IL 60302.

**Clerics Regular Minor (Adorno Fathers) C.R.M.:** Founded 1588, at Naples, Italy, by Ven. Augustine Adorno and St. Francis Caracciolo. General motherhouse, Rome, Italy; U.S. address, 575 Darlington Ave., Ramsey, NJ 07446.

**Columban, Society of St. (St. Columban Foreign Mission Society, S.S.C.):** Founded 1918. General headquarters, Dublin, Ireland. U.S. headquarters, P.O. Box 10, St. Columbans, NE 68056. Foreign mission work.

**Comboni Missionaries of the Heart of Jesus (Verona Fathers), M.C.C.J.:** Founded 1867, in Italy by Bl. Daniel Comboni; in U.S., 1939. General motherhouse, Rome, Italy; North American headquarters, Comboni Mission Center, 8108 Beechmont Ave., Cincinnati, OH 45230. Mission work in Africa and the Americas.

**Consolata Missionaries, I.M.C.:** Founded 1901, at Turin, Italy, by Bl. Joseph Allamano. General motherhouse, Rome, Italy; U.S. headquarters, P.O. Box 5550, 2301 Rt. 27, Somerset, NJ 08875.

**Crosier Fathers (Canons Regular of the Order of the Holy Cross), O.S.C.:** Founded 1210, in Belgium by Bl. Theodore De Celles. Generalate, Rome, Italy; U.S. Province of St. Odilia, 3510 Vivian Ave., Shoreview, MN 55126. Mission, retreat, educational work.

**Cross, Brothers of the Congregation of Holy, C.S.C.:** Founded 1837, in France, by Rev. Basil Moreau; U.S. province, 1841. Generalate, Rome, Italy. Educational, social work; missions.

Midwest Province (1841), Box 460, Notre Dame, IN 46556.

Southwest Province (1956), St. Edward's University, Austin, TX 78704.

Eastern Province (1956), 85 Overlook Circle, New Rochelle, NY 10804.

**Cross, Priests of the Congregation of Holy, C.S.C.:** Founded 1837, in France; in U.S., 1841. Generalate, Rome, Italy. Educational and pastoral work; home missions and retreats; foreign missions; social services and apostolate of the press.

Indiana Province (1841), 1304 E. Jefferson Blvd., South Bend, IN 46617.

Eastern Province (1952), 835 Clinton Ave., Bridgeport, CT 06604.

Southern Province (1968), 2111 Brackenridge St., Austin, TX 78704.

**Divine Word, Society of the, S.V.D.:** Founded 1875, in Holland, by Bl. Arnold Janssen. North American Province founded 1897 with headquarters in Techny, IL General motherhouse, Rome, Italy.

Province of Bl. Joseph Freinademetz (Chicago Province) (1985, from merger of Eastern and Northern provinces), 1985 Waukegan Rd., Techny, IL 60082.

St. Augustine (Southern Province) (1940), 201 Ruella Ave., Bay St. Louis, MS 39520.

St. Therese of the Child Jesus (Western Province) (1964), 2737 Pleasant St., Riverside, CA 92507.

**Dominicans (Order of Friars Preachers), O.P.:** Founded early 13th century by St. Dominic de Guzman. General headquarters, Santa Sabina, Rome, Italy. Preaching, teaching, missions, research, parishes.

St. Joseph Eastern Province (1805), 869 Lexington Ave., New York, NY 10021.

Most Holy Name of Jesus (Western) Province (1912), 5877 Birch Ct., Oakland, CA 94618.

St. Albert the Great (Central) Province (1939), 1909 S. Ashland Ave., Chicago, IL 60608.

Southern Dominican Province (1979), 3407 Napoleon Ave., New Orleans, LA 70125.

Spanish Province, U.S. foundation (1926), P.O. Box 279, San Diego, TX 78384.

**Edmund, Society of St., S.S.E.:** Founded 1843, in France, by Fr. Jean Baptiste Muard. General motherhouse, Edmundite Generalate, 270 Winooski Park, Colchester, VT 05439. Educational, missionary work.

**Eudists (Congregation of Jesus and Mary), C.J.M.:** Founded 1643, in France, by St. John Eudes. General motherhouse, Rome, Italy; North American province, 6125 Premiere Ave., Charlesbourg, Quebec G1H 2V9, Canada; U.S. community, 71 Burke

Dr., Buffalo, NY 14215. Parochial, educational, pastoral, missionary work.

**Francis, Brothers of Poor of St., C.F.P.:** Founded 1857. Motherhouse, Aachen, Germany; U.S. province, P.O. Box 187, Burlington, IA 52601. Educational work, especially with poor and emotionally disturbed youth.

**Francis, Third Order Regular of St., T.O.R.:** Founded 1221, in Italy; in U.S., 1910. General motherhouse, Rome, Italy. Educational, parochial, missionary work.

Most Sacred Heart of Jesus Province (1910), 215 57th St., Pittsburgh, PA 15201.

Immaculate Conception Province (1925), 2400 Dike Rd., Winter Park, FL 32792.

Commissariat of the Spanish Province (1924), 301 Jefferson Ave., Waco, TX 76702.

**Francis de Sales, Oblates of St., O.S.F.S.:** Founded 1871, by Fr. Louis Brisson. General motherhouse, Rome, Italy. Educational, missionary, parochial work.

Wilmington-Philadelphia Province (1906), 2200 Kentmere Parkway, Box 1452, Wilmington, DE 19899.

Toledo-Detroit Province (1966), 2056 Parkwood Ave., Toledo, Ohio 43620.

**Francis Xavier, Brothers of St. (Xaverian Brothers), C.F.X.:** Founded 1839, in Belgium, by Theodore J. Ryken. Generalate, Twickenham, Middlesex, England. Educational work.

Sacred Heart Province, 10318-B Baltimore National Pike, Ellicott City, MD 21043.

St. Joseph Province, 704 Brush Hill Rd., Milton, MA 02186.

**Franciscan Brothers of Brooklyn, O.S.F.:** Founded in Ireland; established at Brooklyn, 1858. Generalate, 135 Remsen St., Brooklyn, NY 11201. Educational work.

**Franciscan Brothers of Christ the King, O.S.F.:** Founded 1961. General motherhouse, 3737 N. Marybelle Ave., Peoria, IL 61615.

**Franciscan Brothers of the Holy Cross, F.F.S.C.:** Founded 1862, in Germany. Generalate, Hausen, Linz Rhein, Germany; U.S. region, 2500 St. James Rd., Springfield, IL 62707. Educational work.

**Franciscan Brothers of the Third Order Regular, O.S.F.:** Generalate, Mountbellew, Ireland; U.S. region, 2117 Spyglass Trail W., Oxnard, CA 93030.

**Franciscan Friars of the Immaculate, F.F.I:** Founded 1990, Italy. General motherhouse, Benevento, Italy. U.S. addresses, 600 Pleasant St., New Bedford, MA. 02740; 22 School Hill Rd., Baltic, CT 06330.

**Franciscan Friars of the Renewal, C.F.R.:** Community established under jurisdiction of the archbishop of New York. Central House, St. Crispin Friary, 420 E. 156th St., Bronx, NY 10455.

**Franciscan Missionary Brothers of the Sacred Heart of Jesus, O.S.F.:** Founded 1927, in the St. Louis archdiocese. Motherhouse, St. Joseph Rd., Eureka, MO 63025. Care of aged, infirm, homeless men and boys.

**Franciscans (Order of Friars Minor), O.F.M.:** A family of the First Order of St. Francis (of Assisi) founded in 1209 and established as a separate jurisdiction in 1517; in U.S., 1844. General headquarters, Rome, Italy. English-speaking conference: 3140 Meramec St., St. Louis, MO 63118. Preaching, missionary, educational, parochial, charitable work.

St. John the Baptist Province (1844), 1615 Vine St., Cincinnati, Ohio 45210.

Immaculate Conception Province (1855), 147 Thompson St., New York, NY 10012.

Sacred Heart Province (1858), 3140 Meramec St., St. Louis, MO 63118.

Assumption of the Blessed Virgin Mary Province (1887), Pulaski, WI 54162.

Most Holy Name of Jesus Province (1901), 58 W. 88th St., New York, NY 10024.

St. Barbara Province (1915), 1500 34th Ave., Oakland, CA 94601.

Our Lady of Guadalupe Province (1985), 1350 Lakeview Rd. S.W., Albuquerque, NM 87105.

Holy Cross Custody (1912), 14246 Main St., P.O. Box 608, Lemont, IL 60439.

Most Holy Savior Vice-Province, 232 S. Home Ave., Pittsburgh, PA 15202.

St. John Capistran Custody (1928), 209 E. 83rd St., New York, NY 10028.

Mt. Alverna Friary, 517 S. Belle Vista Ave., Youngstown, Ohio 44509.

Holy Family Croatian Custody (1926), 4848 S. Ellis Ave., Chicago, IL 60615.

St. Casimir Lithuanian Vice-Province, P.O. Box 980, Kennebunkport, ME 04046.

Holy Gospel Province (Mexico), U.S. foundation, 2400 Marr St., El Paso, TX 79903.

Saints Francis and James Province (Jalisco, Mexico), U.S. foundation, 504 E. Santa Clara St., Hebbronville, TX 78361.

Commissariat of the Holy Land, Mt. St. Sepulchre, 1400 Quincy St. N.E., Washington, DC 20017.

St. Mary of the Angels Custody, Byzantine Slavonic Rite, P.O. Box 270, Sybertsville, PA 18251.

Academy of American Franciscan History, 1712 Euclid Ave., Berkeley, CA 94709.

**Franciscans (Order of Friars Minor Capuchin), O.F.M. Cap.:** A family of the First Order of St. Francis (of Assisi) founded in 1209 and established as a separate jurisdiction in 1528. General motherhouse, Rome, Italy. Missionary, parochial work, chaplaincies.

St. Joseph Province (1857), 1740 Mt. Elliott Ave., Detroit, MI 48207.

St. Augustine Province (1873), 220 37th St., Pittsburgh, PA 15201.

St. Mary Province (1952), 30 Gedney Park Dr., White Plains, NY 10605.

Province of the Stigmata (1918), P.O. Box 809, Union City, NJ 07087.

Western American Capuchin Province, Our Lady of the Angels, 1345 Cortez Ave., Burlingame, CA 94010.

Sts. Adalbert and Stanislaus Province (1948), 2 Manor Dr., Oak Ridge, NJ 07438.

Province of Mid-America (1977), 3553 Wyandot St., Denver, CO 80211.

Vice-Province of Texas, 2601 Singleton Blvd., Dallas, TX 75212.

St. John the Baptist Vice-Province, 216 Arzuaga St., P.O. Box 21350, Rio Piedras, Puerto Rico 00928.

**Franciscans (Order of Friars Minor Conven-**tual), O.F.M. Conv.: A family of the First Order of St. Francis (of Assisi) founded in 1209 and established as a separate jurisdiction in 1517; first U.S. foundation, 1852. General curia, Rome, Italy. Missionary, educational, parochial work.

Immaculate Conception Province (1852), Immaculate Conception Friary, Rensselaer, NY 12144.

St. Anthony of Padua Province (1906), 12300 Folly Quarter Rd., Ellicott City, MD 21043.

St. Bonaventure Province (1939), 6107 Kenmore Ave., Chicago, IL 60660.

Our Lady of Consolation Province (1926), 101 Anthony Dr., Mt. St. Francis, IN 47146.

Our Lady of Guadalupe Custody (vice-province), Holy Cross Friary, P.O. Box 158, Mesilla Park, NM 88047.

St. Joseph of Cupertino Province (1981), P.O. Box 820, Arroyo Grande, CA 93420.

**Glenmary Missioners (The Home Missioners of America):** Founded 1939, in U.S. General headquarters, P.O. Box 465618, Cincinnati, Ohio 45246. Home mission work.

**Good Shepherd, Little Brothers of the, B.G.S.:** Founded 1951, by Bro. Mathias Barrett. Foundation House, P.O. Box 389, Albuquerque, NM 87102. General headquarters, Hamilton, Ont., Canada. Operate shelters and refuges for aged and homeless; homes for handicapped men and boys, alcoholic rehabilitation center.

**Holy Eucharist, Brothers of the, F.S.E.:** Founded in U.S., 1957. Generalate, P.O. Box 25, Plaucheville, LA 71362. Teaching, social, clerical, nursing work.

**Holy Family, Congregation of the Missionaries of the, M.S.F.:** Founded 1895, in Holland, by Rev. John P. Berthier. General motherhouse, Rome, Italy; U.S. provincialate, 10415 Midland Blvd., St. Louis, MO 63114. Belated vocations for the missions.

**Holy Family, Sons of the, S.F.:** Founded 1864, at Barcelona, Spain, by Bl. Jose Mañanet y Vives; in U.S., 1920. General motherhouse, Barcelona, Spain; U.S. address, 401 Randolph Rd., P.O. Box 4138, Silver Spring, MD 20904.

**Holy Ghost Fathers, C.S.Sp.:** Founded 1703, in Paris, by Claude Francois Poullart des Places; in U.S., 1872. Generalate, Rome, Italy. Missions, education.

Eastern Province (1872), 6230 Brush Run Rd., Bethel Park, PA 15102. Western Province (1964), 1700 W. Alabama St., Houston, TX 77098.

Holy Ghost Fathers of Ireland (1971), U.S. delegates: 4849 37th St., Long Island City, NY 11101 (East); St. Dunstan's Church, 1133 Broadway, Mill Brae, CA 94030 (West); St. John Baptist Church, 1139 Dryades St., New Orleans, LA 70113.

**Holy Spirit, Missionaries of the, M.Sp.S.:** Founded 1914, at Mexico City, Mexico, by Felix Rougier. General motherhouse, Mexico City; U.S. headquarters, Our Lady of Guadalupe, 500 N. Juanita Ave., P.O. Box 1091, Oxnard, CA 93030. Missionary work.

**Immaculate Heart of Mary, Brothers of the, I.H.M.:** Founded 1948, at Steubenville, Ohio, by Bishop John K. Mussio. Motherhouse, 609 N. 7th St., Steubenville, Ohio 43952. Educational, charitable work.

**Jesuits (Society of Jesus), S.J.:** Founded 1534, in

France, by St. Ignatius of Loyola; received papal approval, 1540; first U.S. province, 1833. Generalate, Rome, Italy; U.S. national office, Jesuit Conference, 1424 16th St. N.W., Suite 300, Washington, DC 20036. Missionary, educational, literary work.

Maryland Province (1833), 5704 Roland Ave., Baltimore, MD 21210.

New York Province (1943), 39 Easst 83rd St., New York, NY 10028.

Missouri Province (1863), 4511 W. Pine Blvd., St. Louis, MO 63108.

New Orleans Province (1907), 500 S. Jefferson Davis Pkwy., New Orleans, LA 70119.

California Province (1909), 300 College Ave.,P.O. Box 519, Los Gatos, CA 95031.

New England Province (1926), 771 Harrison Ave., Boston, MA 02118.

Chicago Province (1928), 2050 N. Clark St., Chicago, IL 60614.

Oregon Province (1932), 2222 N.W. Hoyt, Portland, OR 97210.

Detroit Province (1955), 7303 W. Seven Mile Rd., Detroit, MI 48221.

Wisconsin Province (1955), PO Box 08277, Milwaukee, WI 53208.

Province of the Antilles (1947), U.S. address, 13339 S.W. 9 Terrace, Miami, FL 33184.

**John of God, Brothers of the Hospitaller Order of St., O.H.:** Founded 1537, in Spain. General motherhouse, Rome, Italy; American province, 2425 S. Western Ave., P.O. Box 77627, Los Angeles, CA 90018; Irish Province of Immaculate Conception, 532 Delsea Dr., Westville Grove, NJ 08093. Nursing work and related fields.

**Joseph, Congregation of St., C.S.J.:** General motherhouse, Rome, Italy; U.S. vice province, 338 Grand Ave., San Pedro, CA 90731. Parochial, missionary, educational work.

**Joseph, Oblates of St., O.S.J.:** Founded 1878, in Italy, by Bl. Joseph Marello; in U.S., 1929. General motherhouse, Rome, Italy. Parochial, educational work.

Eastern Province, Route 315, Pittston, PA 18640.

California Province, 544 W. Cliff Dr., Santa Cruz, CA 95060.

**Josephite Fathers, C.J.:** General motherhouse, Ghent, Belgium; U.S. foundation, 180 Patterson Rd., Santa Maria, CA 93455.

**Josephites (St. Joseph's Society of the Sacred Heart), S.S.J.:** Established 1893, in U.S. as American congregation (originally established in U.S. in 1871 by Mill Hill Josephites from England). General motherhouse, 1130 N. Calvert St., Baltimore, MD 21202. Evangelization in African American community.

**LaSalette, Missionaries of Our Lady of, M.S.:** Founded 1852, by Msgr. de Bruillard; in U.S., 1892. Motherhouse, Rome, Italy.

Our Lady of Seven Dolors Province (1934), 915 Maple Ave., Hartford, CT 06114.

Immaculate Heart of Mary Province (1945), 947 Park St., Attleboro, MA 02703.

Mary Queen Province (1958), 4650 S. Broadway, St. Louis, MO 63111.

Mary Queen of Peace Province (1967), 1607 E. Howard Ave., Milwaukee, WI 53207.

**Lateran, Canons Regular of the, C.R.L.:** General house, Rome, Italy; U.S. address: 2317 Washington Ave., Bronx, NY 10458.

**Legionaries of Christ, L.C.:** Founded 1941, in Mexico, by Rev. Marcial Maciel; in U.S., 1965. General headquarters, Rome, Italy; U.S. headquarters, 393 Derby Ave., Orange, CT 06477; novitiate, 475 Oak Ave., Cheshire, CT 06410.

**Little Brothers of St. Francis, L.B.S.F.:** Founded 1970 in Archdiocese of Boston by Bro. James Curran. General fraternity, 785-789 Parker St., Roxbury (Boston), MA 02120. Combine contemplative life with evangelical street ministry.

**Marianist Fathers and Brothers (Society of Mary; Brothers of Mary), S.M.:** Founded 1817, at Bordeaux, France, by Rev. William-Joseph Chaminade; in U.S., 1849. General motherhouse, Rome, Italy. Educational work.

Cincinnati Province (1849), 4435 E. Patterson Rd., Dayton, Ohio 45430.

St. Louis Province (1908), PO Box 23130, St. Louis, MO 63156.

Pacific Province (1948), PO Box 1775, Cupertino, CA 95015.

New York Province (1961), 4301 Roland Ave., Baltimore, MD 21210.

Province of Meribah (1976), 240 Emory Rd., Mineola, NY 11501.

**Mariannhill, Congregation of the Missionaries of, C.M.M.:** Trappist monastery, begun in 1882 by Abbot Francis Pfanner in Natal, South Africa, became an independent modern congregation in 1909; in U.S., 1920. Generalate, Rome, Italy; U.S.-Canadian province (1938), Our Lady of Grace Monastery, 23715 Ann Arbor Trail, Dearborn Hts., MI 48127. Foreign mission work.

**Marians of the Immaculate Conception, Congregation of, M.I.C.:** Founded 1673; U.S. foundation, 1913. General motherhouse, Rome, Italy. Educational, parochial, mission, publication work.

St. Casimir Province (1913), 6336 S. Kilbourn Ave., Chicago, IL 60629.

St. Stanislaus Kostka Province (1948), Eden Hill, Stockbridge, MA 01262.

**Marist Brothers, F.M.S.:** Founded 1817, in France, by Bl. Marcellin Champagnat. General motherhouse, Rome, Italy. Educational, social, catechetical work.

Esopus Province, 1241 Kennedy Blvd., Bayonne, NJ 07002 (office).

Poughkeepsie Province, 26 First Ave., Pelham, NY 10803.

**Marist Fathers (Society of Mary), S.M.:** Founded 1816, at Lyons, France, by Jean Claude Colin; in U.S., 1863. General motherhouse, Rome, Italy. Educational, foreign mission, pastoral work.

Washington Province (1924), 815 Varnum St., N.E., Washington, DC 20017.

Boston Province (1924), 27 Isabella St., Boston, MA 02116.

San Francisco Western Province (1962), 625 Pine St., San Francisco, CA 94108.

**Maronite Monks, Congregation of** (Cloistered Penitents of St. Francis), **O. Mar.:** Most Holy Trinity Monastery, 67 Dugway Rd., Petersham, MA 01366; Holy Nativity Monastery, Bethlehem, S.D. 57708.

**Maronite Lebanese Missionaries, Congregation of, C.M.L.M.:** Founded in Lebanon 1865; established in the U.S., 1991. U.S. foundation, St. George Maronite Church, 6070 Babcock Rd., San Antonio, TX 78240.

**Mary Immaculate, Oblates of, O.M.I.:** Founded 1816, in France, by Bl. Charles Joseph Eugene de Mazenod; in U.S., 1849. General house, Rome, Italy. U.S. consulate, 290 Lenox Ave., Oakland, CA 94610. Parochial, foreign mission, educational work; ministry to marginal.

Southern U.S. Province (1904), 7711 Madonna Dr., San Antonio, TX 78216.

Our Lady of Hope, Eastern Province (1883), 391 Michigan Ave. N.E., Washington, DC 20017.

St. John the Baptist, Northern Province (1921), 61 Burns Hill Rd., Hudson, NH 03051.

Central Province (1924), 267 E. 8th St., St. Paul, MN 55101.

**Maryknoll (Catholic Foreign Mission Society of America), M.M.:** Founded 1911, in U.S., by Frs. Thomas F. Price and James A. Walsh. General Center, Maryknoll, NY 10545.

**Mekhitarist Order of Venice, O.M.Ven.:** Founded 1701; transferred to Venice, 1717. U.S. address: 110 E. 12th, New York, N.Y. 10003. Promote ecclesial community among Armenians.

**Mekhitarist Order of Vienna, C.M.Vd.:** Established 1773. General headquarters, Vienna, Austria. U.S. address, 4900 Maryland Ave., La Crescenta, CA 91214. Work among Armenians in U.S.

**Mercedarians (Order of Our Lady of Mercy), O. de M.:** Founded 1218, in Spain, by St. Peter Nolasco. General motherhouse, Rome, Italy; U.S. headquarters, 3205 Fulton Rd., Cleveland, OH 44109.

**Mercy, Brothers of, F.M.M.:** Founded 1856, in Germany. General motherhouse, Montabaur, Germany. American headquarters, 4520 Ransom Rd., Clarence, NY 14031. Hospital work.

**Mercy, Brothers of Our Lady, Mother of, C.F.M.M.:** Founded 1844, in The Netherlands by Abp. Jan Zwijsen. Generalate, Tilburg, The Netherlands; U.S. region, 2336 S. C St., Oxnard, CA 93033.

**Mercy, Congregation of Priests of (Fathers of Mercy), C.P.M.:** Founded 1808, in France, by Rev. Jean Baptiste Rauzan; in U.S., 1839. General mission house, South Union, KY 42283. Mission work.

**Mill Hill Missionaries (St. Joseph's Society for Foreign Missions), M.H.M.:** Founded 1866, in England, by Cardinal Vaughan; in U.S., 1951. International headquarters, London, England; American headquarters, 12101 Gravois Rd., St. Louis, MO 63127.

**Minim Fathers, O.M.:** General motherhouse, Rome, Italy. North American delegation (1970), 3431 Portola Ave., Los Angeles, CA 90032.

**Missionaries of St. Charles, Congregation of the (Scalabrinians), C.S.:** Founded 1887, at Piacenza, Italy, by Bishop John Baptist Scalabrini. General motherhouse, Rome, Italy.

St. Charles Borromeo Province (1888), 27 Carmine St., New York, NY 10014.

St. John Baptist Province (1903), 546 N. East Ave., Oak Park, IL 60302.

**Missionaries of the Blessed Sacrament, M.S.S.:**

Regional headquarters, PO Box 4337, Corpus Christi, TX 78469. Promotion of Perpetual Eucharistic adoration.

**Missionaries of the Holy Apostles, M.Ss.A.:** Founded 1962, Washington, D.C., by Very Rev. Eusebe M. Menard. North American headquarters, 33 Prospect Hill Rd., Cromwell, CT 06416.

**Missionary Fraternity of Mary, F.M.M.:** General headquarters, Guatemala; U.S. foundation 340 Pine St., Seaford, DE 19973.

**Missionhurst — CICM (Congregation of the Immaculate Heart of Mary):** Founded 1862, at Scheut, Brussels, Belgium, by Very Rev. Theophile Verbist. General motherhouse, Rome, Italy; U.S. province, 4651 N. 25th St., Arlington, VA 22207. Home and foreign mission work.

**Montfort Missionaries (Missionaries of the Company of Mary), S.M.M.:** Founded 1715, by St. Louis Marie Grignon de Montfort; in U.S., 1948. General motherhouse, Rome, Italy; U.S. province, 101-18 104th St., Ozone Park, NY 11416. Mission work.

**Mother Co-Redemptrix, Congregation of, C.M.C.:** Founded 1953 at Lein-Thuy, Vietnam (North), by Fr. Dominic Mary Tran Dinh Thu; in U.S., 1975. General house, Hochiminhville, Vietnam; U.S. provincial house, 1900 Grand Ave., Carthage, MO 64836. Work among Vietnamese Catholics in U.S.

**Oblates of the Virgin Mary, O.M.V.:** Founded 1815, in Italy; in U.S., 1976; Generalate, Rome, Italy; U.S. provincialate: Two Ipswich St., Boston, MA 02215.

**Oratorians (Congregation of the Oratory of St. Philip Neri), C.O.:** Founded 1575, at Rome, by St. Philip Neri. A confederation of autonomous houses. U.S. addresses: P.O. Box 11586, Rock Hill, SC 29731; P.O. Box 1688, Monterey, CA 93940; 4450 Bayard St., Pittsburgh, PA 15213; P.O. Drawer II, Pharr, TX 78577; 109 Willoughby St., Brooklyn, NY 11201.

**Pallottines (Society of the Catholic Apostolate), S.A.C.:** Founded 1835, at Rome, by St. Vincent Pallotti. Generalate, Rome, Italy. Charitable, educational, parochial, mission work.

Immaculate Conception Province (1953), P.O. Box 979, South Orange, NJ 07079.

Mother of God Province (1946), 5424 W. Blue Mound Rd., Milwaukee, WI 53208.

Irish Province (1909), U.S. address: 3352 4th St., P.O. Box 249, Wyandotte, MI 48192.

Queen of Apostles Province (1909), 448 E. 116th St., New York, NY 10029.

Christ the King Province, 3452 Niagara Falls, Blvd., N. Tonawanda, NY 14120.

**Paraclete, Servants of the, s.P.:** Founded 1947, Santa Fe, N.M., archdiocese. Generalate and U.S. motherhouse, Via Coeli, Jemez Springs, NM 87025. Devoted to care of priests.

**Paris Foreign Missions Society, M.E.P.:** Founded 1662, at Paris, France. Headquarters, Paris, France; U.S. establishment, 930 Ashbury St., San Francisco, CA 94117. Mission work and training of native clergy.

**Passionists (Congregation of the Passion), C.P.:** Founded 1720, in Italy, by St. Paul of the Cross. General motherhouse, Rome, Italy.

St. Paul of the Cross Province (Eastern Province) (1852), 80 David St., South River, NJ 08882.

Holy Cross Province (Western Province), 5700 N. Harlem Ave., Chicago, IL 60631.

**Patrician Brothers (Brothers of St. Patrick), F.S.P.:** Founded 1808, in Ireland, by Bishop Daniel Delaney; U.S. novitiate, 7820 Bolsa Ave., Midway City, CA 92655. Educational work.

**Patrick's Missionary Society, St., S.P.S.:** Founded 1932, at Wicklow, Ireland, by Msgr. Patrick Whitney; in U.S., 1953. International headquarters, Kiltegan Co., Wicklow, Ireland. U.S. foundations: 70 Edgewater Rd., Cliffside Park, NJ 07010; 19536 Eric Dr., Saratoga, CA 95070; 1347 W. Granville Ave., Chicago, IL 60660.

**Pauline Fathers (Order of St. Paul the First Hermit), O.S.P.P.E.:** Founded 1215; established in U.S., 1955. General motherhouse, Czestochowa, Jasna Gora, Poland; U.S. province, P.O. Box 2049, Doylestown, PA 18901.

**Pauline Fathers and Brothers (Society of St. Paul for the Apostolate of Communications), S.S.P.:** Founded 1914, by Very Rev. James Alberione; in U.S., 1932. Motherhouse, Rome, Italy; New York province (1932), 6746 Lake Shore Rd., Derby, NY 14047; Los Angeles province, 112 S. Herbert Ave., Los Angeles, CA 90063. Social communications work.

**Paulists (Missionary Society of St. Paul the Apostle), C.S.P.:** Founded 1858, in New York, by Fr. Isaac Thomas Hecker. General offices, 86 Dromore Rd., Scarsdale, NY 10583. Missionary, ecumenical, pastoral work.

**Piarists (Order of the Pious Schools), Sch.P.:** Founded 1617, at Rome, Italy, by St. Joseph Calasanctius. General motherhouse, Rome, Italy. U.S. province, 363 Valley Forge Rd., Devon, PA 19333. New York-Puerto Rico vice-province (Calasanzian Fathers), P.O. Box 118, Playa Sta., Ponce, PR 00734. California vicariate, 3951 Rogers St., Los Angeles, CA 90063. Educational work.

**Pius X, Brothers of St.:** Founded 1952, at La Crosse, Wis., by Bishop John P. Treacy. Motherhouse, P.O. Box 217, De Soto, WI 54624. Education.

**Pontifical Institute for Foreign Missions, P.I.M.E.:** Founded 1850, in Italy, at request of Pope Pius IX. General motherhouse, Rome, Italy; U.S. province, 17330 Quincy Ave., Detroit, MI 48221. Foreign mission work.

**Precious Blood, Society of, C.Pp.S.:** Founded 1815, in Italy, by St. Gaspar del Bufalo. General motherhouse, Rome, Italy.

Cincinnati Province, 431 E. Second St., Dayton, OH 45402.

Kansas City Province, P.O. Box 339, Liberty, MO 64068.

Pacific Province, 2337 134th Ave. W., San Leandro, CA 94577.

Atlantic Province, 540 St. Clair Ave. West, Toronto M6C 14A, Canada.

**Premonstratensians (Order of the Canons Regular of Premontre; Norbertines), O. Praem.:** Founded 1120, at Premontre, France, by St. Norbert; in U.S., 1893. Generalate, Rome, Italy. Educational, parish work.

St. Norbert Abbey, 1016 N. Broadway, DePere, WI 54115.

Daylesford Abbey, 220 S. Valley Rd., Paoli, PA 19301.

St. Michael's Abbey, 19292 El Toro Rd., Silverado, CA 92676.

**Priestly Fraternity of St. Peter, F.S.S.P.:** Founded and approved Oct. 18, 1988; first foundation in U.S., 1991. U.S. headquarters, Our Lady of Guadalupe Seminary, Griffin Rd., P.O. Box 196, Elmhurst, PA 18416.

**Providence, Sons of Divine, F.D.P.:** Founded 1893, at Tortona, Italy, by Bl. Luigi Orione; in U.S., 1933. General motherhouse, Rome, Italy; U.S. address, 111 Orient Ave., E. Boston, MA 02128.

**Redemptorists (Congregation of the Most Holy Redeemer), C.SS.R.:** Founded 1732, in Italy, by St. Alphonsus Mary Liguori. Generalate, Rome, Italy. Mission work.

Baltimore Province (1850), 7509 Shore Rd., Brooklyn, NY 11209.

St. Louis Province (1875), Box 6, Glenview, IL 60025.

Oakland Province (1952), 1300 Junipero Serra Blvd., San Francisco, CA 94132.

New Orleans Vice-Province, 1527 3rd St., New Orleans, LA 70130.

Richmond Vice-Province (1942), 313 Hillman St., P.O. Box 1529, New Smyrna Beach, FL 32170.

**Resurrectionists (Congregation of the Resurrection), C.R.:** Founded 1836, in France, under direction of Bogdan Janski. Motherhouse, Rome, Italy.

U.S. Province, 2250 N. Latrobe Ave., Chicago, IL 60639.

Ontario Kentucky Province, U.S. address, 338 N. 25th St., Louisville, KY 40212.

**Rogationist Fathers, R.C.J.:** Founded by Bl. Annibale (Hannibal) di Francia, 1887. General motherhouse, Rome, Italy. U.S. delegation: 2688 S. Newmark Ave., Sanger, CA 91343. Charitable work.

**Rosary, Brothers of Our Lady of the Holy, F.S.R.:** Founded 1956, in U.S., Motherhouse and novitiate, 1725 S. McCarran Blvd., Reno, NV 89502.

**Rosminians (Institute of Charity), I.C.:** Founded 1828, in Italy, by Antonio Rosmini-Serbati. General motherhouse, Rome, Italy; U.S. address, 2327 W. Heading Ave., Peoria, IL 61604. Charitable work.

**Sacred Heart, Brothers of the, S.C.:** Founded 1821, in France, by Rev. Andre Coindre. General motherhouse, Rome, Italy, Educational work.

New Orleans Province (1847), 4540 Elysian Fields Ave., New Orleans, LA 70122.

New England Province (1945), 685 Steere Farm Rd., Pascoag, RI 02859.

New York Province (1960), P.O. Box 68, Belvidere, NJ 07823.

**Sacred Heart, Missionaries of the, M.S.C.:** Founded 1854, by Rev. Jules Chevelier. General motherhouse, Rome, Italy; U.S. province, 305 S. Lake St., Aurora, IL 60507.

**Sacred Heart of Jesus, Congregation of the (Sacred Heart Fathers and Brothers), S.C.J.:** Founded 1877, in France. General motherhouse, Rome, Italy; U.S. provincial office: P.O. Box 289, Hales Corners, WI 53130. Educational, preaching, mission work.

**Sacred Hearts of Jesus and Mary, Congregation**

of (Picpus Fathers), SS.CC.: Founded 1805, in France, by Fr. Coudrin. General motherhouse, Rome, Italy. Mission, educational work.

Eastern Province (1946), 77 Adams St. (Box 111), Fairhaven, MA 02719.

Western Province (1970), 724 E. Bonita Ave., San Dimas, CA 91773.

Hawaii Province, Box 797, Kaneohe, Oahu, Hawaii 96744.

Sacred Hearts of Jesus and Mary, Missionaries of the, M.SS.CC.: Founded 1833, in Naples, Italy, by Cajetan Errico. General motherhouse, Rome, Italy; U.S. headquarters, 2249 Shore Rd., Linwood, NJ 08221.

Salesians of St. John Bosco (Society of St. Francis de Sales), S.D.B.: Founded 1859, by St. John (Don) Bosco. Generalate, Rome, Italy.

St. Philip the Apostle Province (1902), 148 Main St., New Rochelle, NY 10802.

San Francisco Province (1926), 1100 Franklin St., San Francisco, CA 94109.

Salvatorians (Society of the Divine Savior), S.D.S.: Founded 1881, in Rome, by Fr. Francis Jordan; in U.S., 1896. General headquarters, Rome, Italy; U.S. province, 1735 Hi-Mount Blvd., Milwaukee, WI 53208. Educational, parochial, mission work; campus ministries, chaplaincies.

Scalabrinians: See Missionaries of St. Charles.

Servites (Order of Friar Servants of Mary), O.S.M.: Founded 1233, at Florence, Italy, by Seven Holy Founders. Generalate, Rome, Italy. General apostolic ministry.

Eastern Province (1967), 3121 W. Jackson Blvd., Chicago, IL 60612.

Western Province (1967), 5210 omerset St., Buena Park, CA 90621.

Somascan Fathers, C.R.S.: Founded 1534, at Somasca, Italy, by St. Jerome Emiliani. General motherhouse, Rome, Italy; U.S. address, Pine Haven Boys Center, River Rd., P.O. Box 162, Suncook, NH 03275.

Society of Our Lady of the Most Holy Trinity, S.O.L.T.: Headquarters, St. Anthony Parish, 204 Dunne St., PO Box 152, Robstown, TX 78380.

Sons of Mary Missionary Society (Sons of Mary, Health of the Sick), F.M.S.I.: Founded 1952, in the Boston archdiocese, by Rev. Edward F. Garesche, S.J. Headquarters, 567 Salem End Rd., Framingham, MA 01701.

Stigmatine Fathers and Brothers (Congregation of the Sacred Stigmata), C.S.S.: Founded 1816, by St. Gaspar Bertoni. General motherhouse, Rome,

Italy; North American Province, 554 Lexington St., Waltham, MA 02154. Parish work.

Sulpicians (Society of Priests of St. Sulpice), S.S.: Founded 1641, at Paris, by Rev. Jean Jacques Olier. General motherhouse, Paris, France; U.S. province, 5408 Roland Ave., Baltimore, MD 21210. Education of seminarians and priests.

Theatines (Congregation of Clerics Regular), C.R.: Founded 1524, at Rome, by St. Cajetan. General motherhouse, Rome, Italy; U.S. headquarters, 1050 S. Birch St., Denver, CO 80222.

Trappists: See Cistercians of the Strict Observance.

Trinitarians (Order of the Most Holy Trinity), O.SS.T.: Founded 1198, by St. John of Matha; in U.S., 1911. General motherhouse, Rome, Italy; U.S. headquarters, P.O. Box 5719, Baltimore, MD 21208.

Trinity Missions (Missionary Servants of the Most Holy Trinity), S.T.: Founded 1929, by Fr. Thomas Augustine Judge. Generalate, 1215 N. Scott St., Arlington, VA 22209. Home mission work.

Viatorian Fathers (Clerics of St. Viator), C.S.V.: Founded 1831, in France, by Fr. Louis Joseph Querbes. General motherhouse, Rome, Italy. Province of Chicago (1882), 1212 E. Euclid St., Arlington Hts., IL 60004. Educational work.

Vincentians (Congregation of the Mission; Lazarists), C.M.: Founded 1625, in Paris, by St. Vincent de Paul; in U.S., 1818. General motherhouse, Rome, Italy. Educational work.

Eastern Province (1867), 500 E. Chelten Ave., Philadelphia, PA 19144.

Midwest Province (1888), 13663 Rider Trail North, Earth City, MO 63045.

New England Province (1975), 234 Keeney St., Manchester, CT 06040.

American Italian Branch, Our Lady of Pompei Church, 3600 Claremont St., Baltimore, MD 21224.

American Spanish Branch (Barcelona, Spain), 234 Congress St., Brooklyn, NY 11201.

American Spanish Branch (Zaragoza, Spain), Holy Agony Church, 1834 3rd Ave., New York, NY 10029.

Western Province (1975), 650 W. 23rd St., Los Angeles, CA 90007.

Southern Province (1975), 3826 Gilbert Ave., Dallas, TX 75219.

Vocationist Fathers (Society of Divine Vocations), S.D.V.: Founded 1920, in Italy; in U.S., 1962. General motherhouse, Naples, Italy; U.S. headquarters, 90 Brooklake Rd., Florham Park, NJ 07932.

Xaverian Missionary Fathers, S.X.: Founded 1895, by Bl. Guido Conforti, at Parma, Italy. General motherhouse, Rome, Italy; U.S. province, 12 Helene Ct., Wayne, NJ 07470. Foreign mission work.

## MEANSPIRITED WELFARE REFORM

President Clinton signed into law Aug. 22, 1996, a welfare reform package that the U.S. bishops, Catholic Charities USA and other advocates for the poor and immigrants called meanspirited.

Jesuit Father Fred Kammer, president of Catholic Charities USA, said in an Aug. 21 fax to members that "the forces of meanspiritedness won the day in the welfare battle ... The responsibility and blame for the damage to America's immigrant, hungry, disabled and poor children and families lays squarely

in the halls of Congress, at the White House, and in certain religious and political lobbies...." The U.S. Catholic Conference said bad features included: (1) an end to the federal guarantee of cash assistance to the poor, now replaced by block grants to states; (2) food stamp cuts of more than $27 billion over six years; (3) insufficient funding to achieve the requirement to work after two years of benefits; (4) a provision allowing states to withdraw a portion of their contributions to cash assistance.

## MEMBERSHIP OF RELIGIOUS INSTITUTES OF MEN

(Principal source: *1996 Annuario Pontificio*. Statistics as of Jan. 1, 1995, unless indicated otherwise.)

Listed below are world membership statistics of institutes of men of pontifical right with 500 or more members; the number of priests is in parentheses. Also listed are institutes with less than 500 members with houses in the United States.

Jesuits (16,043) .......................................... 22,885
Franciscans (Friars Minor) (12,109) ........... 18,067
Salesians (11,194) ...................................... 17,567
Franciscans (Capuchins) (7,564) ................. 11,538
Benedictines (5,129) ..................................... 8,779
Brothers of Christian Schools ...................... 7,560
Dominicans (4,801) ....................................... 6,375
Redemptorists (4,434) ................................... 6,008
Society of the Divine Word (3,627) .............. 5,757
Marist Brothers ............................................. 5,436
Oblates of Mary Immaculate (3,790) ............ 5,112
Franciscans (Conventuals) (2,718) ................ 4,501
Vincentians (3,261) ....................................... 4,147
Discalced Carmelites (O.C.D.) (2,415) ......... 3,768
Holy Spirit (Holy Ghost),
   Congregation (2,494) ................................ 3,112
Claretians (1,986) ......................................... 2,952
Augustinians (2,282) ..................................... 2,906
Trappists (1,167) ........................................... 2,571
Passionists (1,874) ........................................ 2,570
Priests of the Sacred Heart (1,736) ............... 2,412
Missionaries of Africa (2,040) ...................... 2,404
Missionaries of the Sacred Heart
   of Jesus (1,641) ......................................... 2,400
Pallottines (1,543) ........................................ 2,245
Carmelites (O.Carm.) (1,393) ...................... 2,141
Combonian Missionaries of the Heart of
   Jesus(1,308) .............................................. 1,961
Christian Brothers ........................................ 1,933
Carmelites of BVM (1,118) .......................... 1,857
Holy Cross, Congregation (835) ................... 1,797
Marianists (539) ........................................... 1,751
Brothers of the Sacred Heart (51) ................. 1,528
Marists (1,240) ............................................. 1,522
Hospitallers of St. John of God (140) ........... 1,491
Piarists (1,151) ............................................. 1,447
Legionaries of Christ (343) ........................... 1,410
Congregation of the Immaculate Heart of Mary
   (Missionhurst; Scheut Missionaries)
   (1,031) ...................................................... 1,409
Premonstratensians (968) .............................. 1,334
Brothers of Christian Instruction
   of Ploermel (6) .......................................... 1,286
Cistercians (Common Observance) (774) ..... 1,292
Augustinians (Recollects) (978) .................... 1,273
Sacred Hearts, Congregation (Picpus) (944) . 1,257
Brothers of Christian Instruction of St. Gabriel
   (35) ........................................................... 1,248
Salvatorians (796) ........................................ 1,227
Society of St. Paul (571) ............................... 1,194
Montfort Missionaries (822) ......................... 1,122
Little Workers of Divine Providence (739) ... 1,063
Society of African Missions (957) ................ 1,039
Ministers of Sick (Camillians) (648) ............ 1,023
Assumptionists (718) .................................... 1,022
Blessed Sacrament, Congregation of (694) ... 1,011
Servants of Mary (768) ................................. 1,009

Consolata Missionaries (752) ....................... 1,004
LaSalette Missionaries (667) ........................... 986
Missionaries of Holy Family (708) ................. 954
Xaverian Missionaries (693) ........................... 910
Maryknollers (643) .......................................... 878
Viatorians (357) .............................................. 856
Canons Regular of St. Augustine (670) ........... 843
Franciscans (Third Order Regular) (570) ......... 831
Missionaries of St. Francis de Sales
   of Annecy (410) ........................................... 795
Mercedarians (516) ......................................... 761
Columbans (678) ............................................. 751
Scalabrinians (626) ......................................... 748
Oblates of St. Francis de Sales (562) .............. 721
Trinitarians (394) ............................................ 703
Mill Hill Missionaries (611) ........................... 702
Congregation of St. Joseph (522) .................... 685
Brothers of Charity (Ghent) ............................ 650
Pontifical Institute for Foreign Missions (540) 644
Missionaries of the Most Precious Blood (504) ..... 642
Eudists (417) ................................................... 579
Order of St. Basil the Great (Basilians of St.
   Josaphat) (305) ............................................ 534
Somascans (330) ............................................. 534
Brothers of the Immaculate Conception (5) ..... 531
Marian Fathers and Brothers (348) .................. 522
Oratorians (366) .............................................. 519
Crosiers (Order of Holy Cross) (330) .............. 503
Society of Christ (381) .................................... 498
Brothers of Our Lady Mother of Mercy(1993) ... 496
Oblates of St. Joseph (306) ............................. 476
Servants of Charity (356) ................................ 469
Resurrection, Congregation of (348) ............... 435
Paris Foreign Mission Society (422) ............... 422
Barnabites (327) .............................................. 410
St. Patrick's Mission Society (377) ................. 407
Stigmatine Fathers and Brothers (310) ............ 406
Order of St. Paul the First Hermit (236) .......... 405
Missionaries of the Holy Spirit (250) .............. 404
Sulpicians (402) .............................................. 402
Mariannhill Missionaries (214) ....................... 380
Rosminians (270) ............................................ 380
Rogationists (192) ........................................... 368
Congr. of St. Basil (Canada) (1993)(355) ....... 368
Carthusians (187) ............................................ 364
Xaverian Brothers ........................................... 304
Little Brothers of Jesus (75) ........................... 262
Bethlehem Missionaries (188) ......................... 248
Paulists (218) .................................................. 235
Oblates of the Virgin Mary *(1992)* (170) ......... 213
Brothers of St. Patrick ..................................... 207
Vocationist Fathers (153) ................................ 205
Sons of the Holy Family (127) ........................ 199
Theatines (110) ............................................... 171
Franciscan Friars of the Atonement (104) ........ 159
Presentation Brothers *(1991)* ........................... 156
Josephites (St. Joseph's Society of the Sacred
   Heart — S.S.J.) (137) ................................. 150
Missionary Servants of the Most Holy Trinity
   (101) .......................................................... 145
Josephites (C.J.) (104) .................................... 131
Alexian Brothers (1) ....................................... 117
Franciscan Brothers of Brooklyn .................... 112
Priestly Fraternity of St. Peter (42) ................. 112

Basilian Salvatorian Fathers (89) ..................... 105
Glenmary Missioners (63) .................................. 90
Camaldolese Hermits of Monte Corona (33) ..... 81
Brothers of Mercy ............................................. 73
Society of St. Edmund (55) ............................... 65
Congr. of Sacerdotal Fraternity (33) ................. 65

Franciscan Bros. of Holy Cross (2) ................... 54
Little Brothers of the Good Shepherd (2) .......... 46
Clerics Regular Minor (Adorno Fathers) (30).... 44
Servants of Holy Paraclete *(1992)* (27) .............. 36
Fathers of Mercy (12) ....................................... 22
Mekhitarist Order of Vienna (15) ..................... 16

# RELIGIOUS INSTITUTES OF WOMEN IN THE UNITED STATES

(Sources: *Official Catholic Directory;* Catholic Almanac survey.)

**Adorers of the Blood of Christ, A.S.C.:** Founded 1834, in Italy; in U.S., 1870. General motherhouse, Rome, Italy U.S. provinces: 2 Pioneer Lane, Red Bud, IL 62278; 1400 South Sheridan, Wichita, KS 67213; 3950 Columbia Ave., Columbia, PA 17512. Education, retreats, social services, pastoral ministry.

**Africa, Missionary Sisters of Our Lady of (Sisters of Africa), M.S.O.L.A.:** Founded 1869, at Algiers, Algeria, by Cardinal Lavigerie; in U.S., 1929. General motherhouse, Rome, Italy; U.S. headquarters, 3715 Williams Lane, Chevy Chase, MD 20815. Medical, educational, catechetical and social work in Africa.

**Agnes, Sisters of St., C.S.A.:** Founded 1858, in U.S., by Rev. Caspar Rehrl. General motherhouse, 475 Gillett St., Fond du Lac, WI 54935. Education, health care, social services.

**Ann, Sisters of St., S.S.A.:** Founded 1834, in Italy; in U.S., 1952. General motherhouse, Rome, Italy; U.S. headquarters, Mount St. Ann, Ebensburg, PA 15931.

**Anne, Sisters of St., S.S.A.:** Founded 1850, at Vaudreuil, Que., Canada; in U.S., 1866. General motherhouse, Lachine, Que., Canada; U.S. address, 720 Boston Post Rd., Marlboro, MA 01752. Retreat work, pastoral ministry, religious education.

**Anthony, Missionary Servants of St., M.S.S.A.:** Founded 1929, in U.S., by Rev. Peter Baque. General motherhouse, 100 Peter Baque Rd., San Antonio, TX 78209. Social work.

**Antonine Maronite Sisters:** Established in U.S., 1966. U.S. address, 2691 N. Lipkey Rd., North Jackson, Ohio 44451.

**Apostolate, Sisters Auxiliaries of the, S.A.A.:** Founded 1903, in Canada; in U.S., 1911. General motherhouse, 689 Maple Terr., Monongah, WV 26555. Education, nursing.

**Armenian Sisters of the Immaculate Conception:** U.S. address, 6 Eliot Rd., Lexington, MA 02173.

**Assumption, Little Sisters of the, L.S.A.:** Founded 1865, in France; in U.S., 1891. General motherhouse, Paris, France; U.S. provincialate, 214 E. 30th St., New York, NY 10016. Social work, nursing, family life education.

**Assumption, Religious of the, R.A.:** Founded 1839, in France; in U.S., 1919. Generalate, Paris, France; North American province, 227 N. Bowman Ave., Merion Sta., PA 19066.

**Assumption of the Blessed Virgin, Sisters of the, S.A.S.V.:** Founded 1853, in Canada; in U.S., 1891. General motherhouse, Nicolet, Que., Canada; U.S. province, 316 Lincoln St., Worcester, MA 01605. Education, mission, pastoral ministry.

**Augustinian Nuns of Contemplative Life, O.S.A.:** Established in Spain in 13th century; U.S. foundation, Convent of Our Mother of Good Counsel, 4328 W. Westminster Pl., St. Louis, MO 63108.

**Augustinian Sisters, Servants of Jesus and Mary, Congregation of, O.S.A.:** Generalate, Rome, Italy; U.S. foundation, St. John School, 513 E. Broadway, Brandenburg, KY 40108.

**Basil the Great, Sisters of the Order of St. (Byzantine Rite), O.S.B.M.:** Founded fourth century, in Cappadocia, by St. Basil the Great and his sister St. Macrina; in U.S., 1911. Generalate, Rome, Italy; U.S. motherhouses: Philadelphia Ukrainian Byzantine Rite, 710 Fox Chase Rd., Philadelphia, PA 19111; Pittsburgh Ruthenian Byzantine Rite, Mount St. Macrina P.O. Box 878, Uniontown, PA 15401. Education, health care.

**Benedict, Sisters of the Order of St., O.S.B.:** Our Lady of Mount Caritas Monastery (founded 1979, Ashford, Conn.), Seckar Rd., Ashford, CT 06278. Contemplative.

**Benedictine Nuns, O.S.B.:** St. Scholastica Priory, Box 606, Petersham, MA 01366. Cloistered.

**Benedictine Nuns of the Congregation of Solesmes, O.S.B.:** U.S. establishment, 1981, in Burlington diocese. Monastery of the Immaculate Heart of Mary, H.C.R. Box 11, Westfield, VT 05874. Cloistered, papal enclosure.

**Benedictine Nuns of the Primitive Observance, O.S.B.;** Founded c. 529, in Italy; in U.S., 1948. Abbey of Regina Laudis, Flanders Rd., Bethlehem, CT 06751. Cloistred.

**Benedictine Sisters, O.S.B.:** Founded c. 529, in Italy; in U.S., 1852. General motherhouse, Eichstatt, Bavaria, Germany. U.S. addresses: St. Emma's Monastery, Motherhouse and Novitiate, 1001 Harvey Ave., Greensburg, PA 15601; Abbey of St. Walburga, 6717 S. Boulder Rd., Boulder, CO 80303.

**Benedictine Sisters** (Regina Pacis), **O.S.B.:** Founded 1627, in Lithuania as cloistered community; reformed 1918 as active community; established in U.S. 1957, by Mother M. Raphaela Simonis. Regina Pacis, 333 Wallace Rd., Bedford, NH 03102.

**Benedictine Sisters, Missionary, O.S.B.:** Founded 1885. Generalate, Rome, Italy; U.S. motherhouse, 300 N. 18th St., Norfolk, NE 68701.

**Benedictine Sisters, Olivetan, O.S.B.:** Founded 1887, in U.S. General motherhouse, Holy Angels Convent, P.O. Drawer 130, Jonesboro, AR 72403. Educational, hospital work.

**Benedictine Sisters of Perpetual Adoration of Pontifical Jurisdiction, Congregation of the, O.S.B.:** Founded in U.S., 1874, from Maria Rickenbach, Switzerland. General motherhouse, 8300 Morganford Rd., St. Louis, MO 63123.

**Benedictine Sisters of Pontifical Jurisdiction, O.S.B.:** Founded c. 529, in Italy. No general motherhouse in U.S. Three federations:
• Federation of St. Scholastica (1922). Pres., Sister Regina Crowley, O.S.B., 5807 N. Kolmar Ave., Chicago, IL 60646. Motherhouses belonging to the federation:
Mt. St. Scholastica, 801 S. 8th St., Atchison, Kans. 66002; Benedictine Sisters of Elk Co., St. Joseph's Monastery, St. Mary's, PA 15857; Benedictine Sisters of Erie, 6101 E. Lake Rd., Erie, PA 16511; Benedictine Sisters of Chicago, St. Scholastica Priory, 7430 Ridge Blvd., Chicago, IL 60645; Benedictine Sisters of the Sacred Heart, 1910 Maple Ave., Lisle, IL 60532; Benedictine Sisters of Elizabeth, St. Walburga Monastery, 851 N. Broad St., Elizabeth, NJ 07208; Benedictine Sisters of Pittsburgh, 4530 Perrysville Ave., Pittsburgh, PA 15229; Red Plains Monastery, 1132 N.W. 32nd, Oklahoma City, OK 73118; St. Joseph's Convent, 2200 S. Lewis, Tulsa, OK 74114; St. Gertrude's Monastery, Ridgely, MD 21660; St. Walburga Monastery, 2500 Amsterdam Rd., Covington, KY 41016; Sacred Heart Monastery, Cullman, AL 35056; Benedictine Sisters of Virginia, Bristow, VA 22013; St. Scholastica Convent, 416 W. Highland Dr., Boerne, TX 78006; St. Lucy's Priory, 19045 E. Sierra Madre Ave., Glendora, CA 91741; Benedictine Sisters of Florida, Drawer H, St. Leo, FL 33574; Benet Hill Monastery, 2555 N. Chelton Rd., Colorado Springs, CO 80909; Queen of Heaven Convent (Byzantine Rite), 8640 Squires Lane N.E., Warren, OH 44484; Benedictine Sisters of Baltimore, Emmanuel Monastery, 2229 W. Joppa Rd., Lutherville, MD 21093; Queen of Angels Monastery, 2101 Hughes Rd., Liberty, MO 64068.
• Federation of St. Gertrude the Great (1937). Office: Sacred Heart Monastery, P.O. Box 364, Richardton, ND 58652. Pres., Sister Ruth Fox, O.S.B. Motherhouses belonging to the federation:
Mother of God Monastery, 120 SE 28th Ave., Watertown, SD 57201; Sacred Heart Monastery, 1005 W. 8th St., Yankton, SD 57078; Mt. St. Benedict Monastery, 620 E. Summit Ave., Crookston, MN 56716; Sacred Heart Monastery, P.O. Box 364, Richardton, ND 58652; Convent of St. Martin, 2110-C St. Martin's Dr., Rapid City, SD 57702; Monastery of Immaculate Conception, 802 E. 10th St., Ferdinand, IN 47532; Monastery of St. Gertrude, HC3, Box 121, Cottonwood, ID 83522; Monastery of St. Benedict Center, Box 5070, Madison, WI 53705; Queen of Angels Monastery, 840 S. Main St., Mt. Angel, OR 97362; St. Scholastica Monastery, P.O. Box 3489, Fort Smith, AR 72913; Our Lady of Peace Monastery, 1511 Wilson Ave., Columbia, MO 65201; Queen of Peace Monastery, Box 370, Belcourt, ND 58316; Our Lady of Grace Monastery, 1402 Southern Ave., Beech Grove, IN 46107; Holy Spirit Monastery, 22791 Pico St., Grand Terrace, CA 92324; Spirit of Life Monastery, 10760 W. Glennon Dr., Lakewood, CO 80226. St. Benedict's Monastery 225 Masters Ave., RR #1b, Winnipeg, Man. R3C 4A3, Canada; The Dwelling Place Monastery, 150 Mt. Tabor Rd., Martin, KY 41649.
• Federation of St. Benedict (1947). Pres., Sister Colleen Haggerty, O.S.B., St. Benedict Convent, 104

Chapel Lane, St. Joseph, MN 56374. Motherhouses in U.S. belonging to the federation:
St. Benedict's Convent, St. Joseph, MN 56374; St. Scholastica Priory, 1200 Kenwood Ave., Duluth, MN 55811; St. Bede Priory, 1190 Priory Rd., Eau Claire, WI 54702; St. Mary Monastery, Nauvoo, IL 62354; Annunciation Priory, 7520 University Dr., Bismarck, ND 58504; St. Paul's Priory, 2675 Larpenteur Ave., E., St. Paul, MN 55109; St. Placid Priory, 500 College St. N.E., Lacey, WA 98516; Mt. Benedict Priory, 309 E. 5450 South, Ogden, UT 84405.

**Bethany, Sisters of, C.V.D.:** Founded 1928, in El Salvador; in U.S. 1949. General motherhouse, Santa Tecla, El Salvador. U.S. address: 850 N. Hobart Blvd., Los Angeles, CA 90029.

**Bethlemita Sisters, Daughters of the Sacred Heart of Jesus:** Founded 1861, in Guatemala. Motherhouse, Bogota, Colombia; U.S. address, St. Joseph Residence, 330 W. Pembroke St., Dallas, TX 75208.

**Blessed Virgin Mary, Institute of the (Loreto Sisters), I.B.V.M.:** Founded 17th century in Belgium; in U.S., 1954. Motherhouse, Rathfarnham, Dublin, Ireland; U.S. address: 2521 W. Maryland Ave., Phoenix, AZ 85017.

**Blessed Virgin Mary, Institute of the (Loretto Sisters), I.B.V.M.:** Founded 1609, in Belgium; in U.S., 1880. U.S. address, Loretto Convent, Box 508, Wheaton, IL 60189. Educational work.

**Bon Secours, Congregation of, C.B.S.:** Founded 1824, in France; in U.S., 1881. Generalate, Rome, Italy; U.S. provincial house, 1525 Marriottsville Rd., Marriottsville, MD 21104. Hospital work.

**Brigid, Congregation of St., C.S.B.:** Founded 1807, in Ireland; in U.S., 1953. U.S. regional house, 5118 Loma Linda Dr., San Antonio, TX 78201.

**Brigittine Sisters (Order of the Most Holy Savior), O.SS.S.:** Founded 1344, at Vadstena, Sweden, by St. Bridget; in U.S. 1957. General motherhouse, Rome, Italy; U.S. address, Vikingsborg, Runkenhage Rd., Darien, CT 06820.

**Canossian Daughters of Charity (Canossian Sisters):** Founded 1808 in Verona, Italy, by St. Magdalen of Canossa. General motherhouse, Rome, Italy; U.S. provincial house, 5625 Isleta Blvd. S.W., Albuquerque, NM 87105.

**Carmel, Congregation of Our Lady of Mount, O. Carm.:** Founded 1825, in France; in U.S., 1833. Generalate, P.O. Box 476, Lacombe, LA 70445. Education, social services, pastoral ministry, retreat work.

**Carmel, Institute of Our Lady of Mount, O. Carm.:** Founded 1854, in Italy; in U.S., 1947. General motherhouse, Rome, Italy; U.S. novitiate, 5 Wheatland St., Peabody, MA 01960. Apostolic work.

**Carmelite Community of the Word, C.C.W.:** Motherhouse and Novitiate, 1304 13th Ave., Altoona, PA 16601.

**Carmelite Nuns, Discalced, O.C.D.:** Founded 1562, Spain. First foundation in U.S. in 1790, at Charles County, Md.; this monastery was moved to Baltimore. Monasteries in U.S. are listed below, according to states.
*Alabama:* 716 Dauphin Island Pkwy., Mobile 36606. *Arkansas:* 7201 W. 32nd St., Little Rock 72204. *California:* 215 E. Alhambra Rd., Alhambra

91801; 27601 Highway 1, Carmel 93923; 68 Rincon Rd., Kensington 94707; 1883 Ringsted Dr., P.O. Box 379, Solvang 93463; 6981 Teresian Way, Georgetown 95634; 5158 Hawley Blvd., San Diego 92116; 721 Parker Ave., San Francisco 94118; 530 Blackstone Dr., San Rafael 94903; 1000 Lincoln St., Santa Clara 9550. *Colorado:* 6138 S. Gallup St., Littleton 80120. *Georgia:* Coffee Bluff, 11 W. Back St., Savannah 31419. *Hawaii:* 6301 Pali Hwy., Kaneohe, HI 96744; *Illinois:* River Rd. and Central, Des Plaines 60016. *Indiana:* 2500 Cold Spring Rd., Indianapolis 46222; 59 Allendale Pl., Terre Haute 47802. *Iowa:* 17937 250th St., Eldridge 52748; 2901 S. Cecilia St., Sioux City 51106. *Kentucky:* 1740 Newburg Rd., Louisville 40205. *Louisiana:* 1250 Carmel Ave., Lafayette 70507; 73530 River Rd., Covington 70430.

*Maryland:* 1318 Dulaney Valley Rd., Towson, Baltimore 21204; 4035-A Mt. Carmel Rd., Port Tobacco 20646. *Massachusetts:* 61 Mt. Pleasant Ave., Roxbury, Boston 02119; 15 Mt. Carmel Rd., Danvers 01923. *Michigan:* 4300 Mt. Carmel Dr. NE, Ada 49301; 35750 Moravian Dr., Clinton Township 48035; U.S. 3 Highway, P.O. Box 397, Iron Mountain 49801; 3501 Silver Lake Rd., Traverse City 49684. *Minnesota:* 8251 De Montreville Trail N., Lake Elmo 55042. *Mississippi:* 2155 Terry Rd., Jackson 39204.

*Missouri:* 2201 W. Main St., Jefferson City 65101; 9150 Clayton Rd., Ladue, St. Louis Co. 63124; 424 E. Republic Rd., Springfield 65807. *Nevada:* 1950 La Fond Dr., Reno 89509. *New Hampshire:* 275 Pleasant St., Concord, 03301. *New Jersey:* P.O. Box 785, Flemington 08822; 189 Madison Ave., Morristown 07960. *New Mexico:* Mt. Carmel Rd., Santa Fe 87501. *New York:* 745 St. John's Pl., Brooklyn 11216; 139 De Puyster Ave., Beacon 12508; 75 Carmel Rd., Buffalo 14214; 1931 W. Jefferson Rd., Pittsford 14534; 68 Franklin Ave., Saranac Lake 12983; 428 Duane Ave., Schenectady 12304.

*Ohio:* 3176 Fairmount Blvd., Cleveland Heights 44118. *Oklahoma:* 20,000 N. County Line Rd., Piedmont 73078. *Oregon:* 87609 Green Hill Rd., Eugene 97402. *Pennsylvania:* 70 Monastery Rd., Elysburg 17824; 510 E. Gore Rd., Erie 16509; R.D. 6, Box 28, Center Dr., Latrobe 15650; P.O. Box 57, Loretto 15940; Byzantine Rite, R.R. No. 1, Box 1336, Sugarloaf 18249; 66th and Old York Rd., Philadelphia 19126. *Rhode Island:* Watson Ave. at Nayatt Rd., Barrington 02806.

*Texas:* 600 Flowers Ave., Dallas 75211; 5801 Mt. Carmel Dr., Arlington 76017; 1100 Parthenon Pl., Roman Forest, New Caney 77357. 6301 Culebra and St. Joseph Way, San Antonio 78238. *Utah:* 5714 Holladay Blvd., Salt Lake City 84121. *Vermont:* RR 2, Box 4784, Barre, 05641. *Washington:* 2215 N.E. 147th St., Shoreline 98155. *Wisconsin:* W267 N2517 Meadowbrook Rd., Pewaukee 53072.

**Carmelite Nuns of the Ancient Observance (Calced Carmelites), O. Carm.:** Founded 1452, in The Netherlands; in U.S., 1930, from Naples, Italy, convent (founded 1856). U.S. monasteries: Carmelite Monastery of St. Therese, 3551 Lanark Rd., Lanark, PA 18036; Carmel of Mary, Wahpeton, ND 58075; Our Lady of Grace Monastery, 1 St. Joseph Pl., San Angelo, TX 76905; Carmel of the Sacred Heart, 430 Laurel Ave., Hudson, WI 54016. Papal enclosure.

**Carmelite Sisters (Corpus Christi), O. Carm.:** Founded 1908, in England; in U.S., 1920. General motherhouse, Tunapuna, Trinidad, W.I. U.S. address: Mt. Carmel Home, 412 W. 18th St., Kearney, NE 68847. Home and foreign mission work.

**Carmelite Sisters for the Aged and Infirm, O. Carm.:** Founded 1929, at New York, by Mother M. Angeline Teresa, O. Carm. Motherhouse, 600 Woods Rd., Avila-on-Hudson, Germantown, NY 12526. Social work, nursing and educating in the field of gerontology.

**Carmelite Sisters of Charity, C.a.Ch.:** Founded 1826 at Vich, Spain, by St. Joaquina de Vedruna. Generalate, Rome, Italy; U.S. address, 701 Beacon Rd., Silver Spring, MD 20903.

**Carmelite Sisters of St. Therese of the Infant Jesus, C.S.T.:** Founded 1917, in U.S. General motherhouse, 1300 Classen Dr., Oklahoma City, OK 73103. Educational work.

**Carmelite Sisters of the Divine Heart of Jesus, Carmel D.C.J.:** Founded 1891, in Germany; in U.S., 1912. General motherhouse, Sittard Netherlands. U.S. provincial houses: 1230 Kavanaugh Pl., Milwaukee, WI 52313 (Northern Province); 10341 Manchester Rd., St. Louis, MO 63122 (Central Province); 8585 La Mesa Blvd., La Mesa, CA 92041 (South Western Province). Social services, mission work.

**Carmelite Sisters of the Most Sacred Heart of Los Angeles, O.C.D.:** Founded 1904, in Mexico. General motherhouse and novitiate, 920 E. Alhambra Rd., Alhambra, CA 91801. Social services, retreat and educational work.

**Carmelites of St. Theresa, Congregation of Missionary, C.M.S.T.:** Founded 1903, in Mexico. General motherhouse, Mexico City, Mexico; U.S. foundation, 9548 Deer Trail Dr., Houston, TX 77038.

**Casimir, Sisters of St., S.S.C.:** Founded 1907, in U.S. by Mother Maria Kaupas. General motherhouse, 2601 W. Marquette Rd., Chicago, IL 60629. Education, missions, social services.

**Cenacle, Congregation of Our Lady of the Retreat in the, R.C.:** Founded 1826, in France; in U.S., 1892. Generalate, Rome, Italy. Eastern Province: Cenacle Rd., Lake Ronkonkoma, L.I., NY 11779; Midwestern Province, 513 Fullerton Pkwy., Chicago, IL 60614.

**Charity, Daughters of Divine, F.D.C.:** Founded 1868, at Vienna, Austria; in U.S., 1913. General motherhouse, Rome, Italy. U.S. provinces: 205 Major Ave., Staten Island, NY 10305; 39 N. Portage Path, Akron, OH 44303. Education, social services.

**Charity, Little Missionary Sisters of, L.M.S.C.:** Founded 1915, in Italy by Bl. Luigi Orione; in U.S., 1949. General motherhouse, Rome, Italy; U.S. address, 120 Orient Ave., East Boston, MA 02128.

**Charity, Missionaries of, M.C.:** Founded 1950, in Calcutta, India, by Mother Teresa; first U.S. foundation 1971. General motherhouse, 54A Lower Circular Road, Calcutta 700016, India. U.S. address, 335 E. 145th St., Bronx, NY 10451. Service of the poor.

**Charity, Religious Sisters of, R.S.C.:** Founded 1815, in Ireland; in U.S., 1953. Motherhouse, Dublin,

Ireland; U.S. headquarters, 10664 St. James Dr., Culver City, CA 90230.

**Charity, Sisters of (of Seton Hill), S.C.:** Founded 1870, at Altoona, Penn., from Cincinnati foundation. Generalate, Mt. Thor Rd., Greensburg, PA 15601. Educational, hospital, social, foreign mission work.

**Charity, Sisters of (Grey Nuns of Montreal), S.G.M.:** Founded 1737, in Canada by St. Marie Marguerite d'Youville; in U.S., 1855. General administration, Montreal, Que. H2Y 2L7, Canada; U.S. provincial house, 10 Pelham Rd., Lexington, MA 02173.

**Charity, Sisters of (of Leavenworth), S.C.L.:** Founded 1858, in U.S. Motherhouse, 4200 S. 4th St., Leavenworth, KS 66048.

**Charity, Sisters of (of Nazareth), S.C.N.:** Founded 1812, in U.S. General motherhouse, SCN Center, P.O. Box 172, Nazareth, KY 40048. Education, health services.

**Charity, Sisters of (of St. Augustine), C.S.A.:** Founded 1851, at Cleveland, Ohio. Motherhouse, 5232 Broadview Rd., Richfield, OH 44286.

**Charity, Sisters of Christian, S.C.C.:** Founded 1849, in Paderborn, Germany, by Bl. Pauline von Mallinckrodt; in U.S., 1873. Generalate, Rome, Italy. U.S. provinces: Mallinckrodt Convent, Mendham, NJ 07945; 1041 Ridge Rd., Wilmette, IL 60091, Education, health services, other apostolic work.

**Charity, Vincentian Sisters of, V.S.C.:** Founded 1835, in Austria; in U.S., 1902. General motherhouse, 8200 McKnight Rd., Pittsburgh, PA 15237.

**Charity, Vincentian Sisters of, V.S.C.:** Founded 1928, at Bedford, Ohio. General motherhouse, 1160 Broadway, Bedford, OH 44146.

**Charity of Cincinnati, Ohio, Sisters of, S.C.:** Founded 1809; became independent community, 1852. General motherhouse, Mt. St. Joseph, Ohio 45051. Educational, hospital, social work.

**Charity of Ottawa, Sistrs of (Grey Nuns of the Cross), S.C.O.:** Founded 1845, at Ottawa, Canada; in U.S., 1857. General motherhouse, Ottawa, Canada; U.S. provincial house, 975 Varnum Ave., Lowell, MA 01854. Educational, hospital work, extended health care.

**Charity of Our Lady, Mother of Mercy, Sisters of, S.C.M.M.:** Founded 1832, in Holland; in U.S., 1874. General motherhouse, Den Bosch, Netherlands; U.S. provincialate, 520 Thompson Ave., East Haven, CT 06512.

**Charity of Our Lady, Mother of the Church, S.C.M.C:** U.S. foundation, 1970. General motherhouse, Baltic, CT 06330.

**Charity of Our Lady of Mercy, Sisters of, O.L.M.:** Founded 1829, in Charleston, S.C. Generalate and motherhouse, 424 Fort Johnson Rd., James Island, Charleston, SC 29412. Education, campus ministry, social services.

**Charity of Quebec, Sisters of (Grey Nuns), S.C.Q.:** Founded 1849, at Quebec; in U.S., 1890. General motherhouse, 2655 Le Pelletier St., Beauport, Quebec GIC 3X7, Canada; U.S. address, 359 Summer St., New Bedford, MA 02740. Social work.

**Charity of St. Elizabeth, Sisters of (Convent Station, N.J.), S.C.:** Founded 1859, at Newark, N. J. General motherhouse, P.O. Box 476, Convent Station, NJ 07961. Education, pastoral ministry, social services.

**Charity of St. Hyacinthe, Sisters of (Grey Nuns), S.C.S.H.:** Founded 1840, at St. Hyacinthe, Canada; in U.S., 1878. General motherhouse, 16470 Avenue Bourdages, SUD, St. Hyacinthe, Quebec J2T 4J8, Canada; U.S. regional house, 98 Campus Ave., Lewiston, ME 04240.

**Charity of St. JoanAntida, Sisters of, S.C.S.J.A.:** Founded 1799, in France; in U.S., 1932. General motherhouse, Rome, Italy; U.S. provincial house, 8560 N. 76th Pl., Milwaukee, WI 53223.

**Charity of St. Louis, Sisters of, S.C.S.L.:** Founded 1803, in France; in U.S., 1910. Generalate, Rome, Italy; U.S. provincialate, 4901 S. Catherine St., Plattsburgh, NY 12901.

**Charity of St. Vincent de Paul, Daughters of, D.C.:** Founded 1633, in France; in U.S. 1809, at Emmitsburg, Md., by St. Elizabeth Ann Seton. General motherhouse, Paris, France. U.S. provinces: Emmitsburg, MD 21727; 7800 Natural Bridge Rd., St. Louis, MO 63121; 9400 New Harmony Rd., Evansville, IN 47712; 96 Menands Rd., Albany, NY 12204; 26000 Altamont Rd., Los Altos Hills, CA 94022.

**Charity of St. Vincent de Paul, Sisters of, V.Z.:** Founded 1845, in Croatia; in U.S., 1955. General motherhouse, Zagreb, Croatia; U.S. foundation, 171 Knox Ave., West Seneca, NY 14224.

**Charity of St. Vincent de Paul, Sisters of, Halifax, S.C.:** Founded 1856, at Halifax, N. S., from Emmitsburg foundation. Generalate, Mt. St. Vincent, Halifax, N. S., Canada. U.S. addresses: Commonwealth of Massachusetts, 125 Oakland St., Wellesley Hills, MA 02181; Boston Province, 26 Phipps St., Quincy, MA 02169; New York Province, 84-32 63rd Ave., Middle Village, NY 11379. Educational, hospital, social work.

**Charity of St. Vincent de Paul, Sisters of, New York, S.C.:** Founded 1817, from Emmitsburg foundation. General motherhouse, Mt. St. Vincent on Hudson, 6301 Riverdale Ave., Bronx, NY 10471. Educational, hospital work.

**Charity of the Blessed Virgin Mary, Sisters of, B.V.M.:** Founded 1833, in U.S. by Mary Frances Clarke. General motherhouse, Mt. Carmel, 1100 Carmel Dr., Dubuque, IA 52001. Education, pastoral ministry, social services.

**Charity of the Immaculate Conception of Ivrea, Sisters of, S.C.I.C.:** Founded 18th century, in Italy; in U.S., 1961. General motherhouse, Rome, Italy; U.S. address, Immaculate Virgin of Miracles Convent, R.D. 2, Box 348, Mt. Pleasant, PA 15666.

**Charity of the Incarnate Word, Congregation of the Sisters of, C.C.V.I.:** Founded 1869, at San Antonio, Tex., by Bishop C. M. Dubuis. Generalate, 4503 Broadway, San Antonio, TX 78209.

**Charity of the Incarnate Word, Congregation of the Sisters of (Houston, Tex.), C.C.V.I.:** Founded 1866, in U.S., by Bishop C. M. Dubuis. General motherhouse, P.O. Box 230969, Houston, TX 77223. Educational, hospital, social work.

**Charity of the Sacred Heart, Daughters of,**

**F.C.S.C.J.:** Founded 1823, at La Salle de Vihiers, France; in U.S., 1905. General motherhouse, La Salle de Vihiers, France; U.S. address, Sacred Heart Province, Littleton, NH 03561.

**Charles Borromeo, Missionary Sisters of St. (Scalabrini Srs.):** Founded 1895, in Italy; in U.S., 1941. American novitiate, 1414 N. 37th Ave., Melrose Park, IL 60601.

**Child Jesus, Sisters of the Poor, P.C.J.:** Founded 1844, at Aix-la-Chapelle, Germany; in U.S., 1924. General motherhouse, Simpelveld, Netherlands, American provincialate, 4567 Olentangy River Rd., Columbus, OH 43214.

**Chretienne, Sisters of Ste., S.S.CH.:** Founded 1807, in France; in U.S., 1903. General motherhouse, Metz, France; U.S. provincial house, 297 Arnold St., Wrentham, MA 02093. Educational, hospital, mission work.

**Christ the King, Missionary Sisters of, M.S.C.K.:** Founded 1959 in Poland; in U.S., 1978. General motherhouse, Poznan, Poland; U.S. address, 3030 18 Mile Rd., Sterling Heights, MI 48314.

**Christ the King, Sister Servants of, S.S.C.K.:** Founded 1936, in U.S. General motherhouse, Loretto Convent, Mt. Calvary, WI 53057. Social services.

**Christ the King, Sisters of, S.C.K.:** Hermitage of Christ the King, 6501 Orchard Station Rd., Sebastopol, CA 95472.

**Christian Doctrine, Sisters of Our Lady of, R.C.D.:** Founded 1910, in New York. Central office, 23 Haskell Ave., Suffern, NY 10901.

**Christian Education, Religious of, R.C.E.:** Founded 1817, in France; in U.S., 1905. General motherhouse, France; U.S. provincial residence, 14 Bailey Rd., Arlington, MA 02174.

**Cistercian Nuns, O. Cist.:** Headquarters, Rome, Italy; U.S. address, Valley of Our Lady Monastery, E. 11096 Yanke Dr., Prairie du Sac, WI 53578.

**Cistercian Nuns of the Strict Observance, Order of, O.C.S.O.:** Founded 1125, in France, by St. Stephen Harding; in U.S., 1949. U.S. addresses: Mt. St. Mary's Abbey, 300 Arnold St., Wrentham, MA 02093; Santa Rita Abbey, HCR Box 929, Sonoita, AZ 85637; Our Lady of the Redwoods Abbey, Whitethorn, CA 95489. Our Lady of the Mississippi Abbey, 8400 Abbey Hill Rd., Dubuque, IA 52001; Our Lady of the Angels Monastery, Rt. 2, Box 288-A, Crozet, VA 22932.

**Clare, Sisters of St., O.S.C.:** General motherhouse, Dublin, Ireland; U.S. foundation, St. Clare's Convent, 449 S. Pine Ave., Brea, CA 92621.

**Claretian Missionary Sisters (Religious of Mary Immaculate), R.M.I.:** Founded 1855, in Cuba; in U.S., 1956. Generalate, Rome, Italy; U.S. address, 9600 W. Atlantic Ave., Delray Beach, FL 33446.

**Clergy, Congregation of Our Lady, Help of the, C.L.H.C.:** Founded 1961, in U.S. Motherhouse, Maryvale Convent, 2522 June Bug Rd., Vale, NC 28168.

**Clergy, Servants of Our Lady Queen of the, S.R.C.:** Founded 1929, in Canada; in U.S., 1934. General motherhouse, 57 Jules A. Brillant, Rimouski, Que. G5L 1X1 Canada. Domestic work.

**Colettines:** See Franciscan Poor Clare Nuns.

**Columban, Missionary Sisters of St., S.S.C.:** Founded 1922, in Ireland; in U.S., 1930. General motherhouse, Wicklow, Ireland; U.S. region, 73 Mapleton St., Brighton, MA 02135.

**Comboni Missionary Sisters (Missionary Sisters of Verona), C.M.S.:** Founded 1872, in Italy; in U.S., 1950. U.S. address, 1307 Lakeside Ave., Richmond, VA 23228.

**Consolata Missionary Sisters, M.C.:** Founded 1910, in Italy, by Bl. Giuseppe Allamano; in U.S., 1954. General motherhouse, Turin, Italy; U.S. headquarters, 6801 Belmont Rd., Belmont, MI 49306.

**Cordi-Marian Missionary Sisters, M.C.M.:** Founded 1921, Mexico City; U.S. foundation, 1926. General motherhouse, Mexico. U.S. address, 11624 FM 471, Apt. 402, San Antonio, TX 78253.

**Cross, Daughters of the, D.C.:** Founded 1640, in France; in U.S., 1855. General motherhouse, 1000 Fairview St., Shreveport, LA 71104. Educational work.

**Cross, Daughters of, of Liege, F.C.:** Founded 1833, in Liege, Belgium; in U.S., 1958. U.S. address, 165 W. Eaton Ave., Tracy, CA 95376.

**Cross, Sisters of the Holy, C.S.C.:** Founded 1841, at Le Mans, France, established 1847, in Canada; in U.S., 1881. General motherhouse, St. Laurent, Montreal, Que., Canada; U.S. regional office, 377 Island Pond Rd., Manchester, NH 03109. Educational work.

**Cross, Sisters of the Holy, Congregation of, C.S.C.:** Founded 1841, at Le Mans, France; in U.S., 1843. General motherhouse, Saint Mary's, Notre Dame, IN 46556. Education, health care, social services, pastoral ministry.

**Cross and Passion, Sisters of the (Passionist Sisters), C.P.:** Founded 1852; in U.S., 1924. Generalate, Northampton, England; U.S. address: Holy Family Convent, One Wright Lane, N. Kingstown, RI 02852.

**Cyril and Methodius, Sisters of Sts., SS.C.M.:** Founded 1909, in U.S., by Rev. Matthew Jankola. General motherhouse, Villa Sacred Heart, Danville, PA 17821. Education, care of aged.

**Disciples of the Lord Jesus Christ, D.L.J.C.:** Founded 1972; canonically erected 1991. Address, P.O. Box 17, Channing, TX 79018.

**Divine Compassion, Sisters of, R.D.C.:** Founded 1886, in U.S. General motherhouse, 52 N. Broadway, White Plains, NY 10603. Education, other ministries.

**Divine Love, Daughters of (D.D.L.):** Founded 1969, in Nigeria; in U.S., 1990. General house, Enugu, Nigeria; U.S. regional house, 140 North Ave., Highwood, IL 60040.

**Divine Spirit, Congregation of the, C.D.S.:** Founded 1956, in U.S., by Archbishop John M. Gannon. Motherhouse, 409 W. 6th St., Erie, PA 16507. Education, social services.

**Divine Zeal, Daughters of, F.D.Z.:** Founded 1887 in Italy by Bl Hannibal Maria DiFrancia; in U.S., 1951. Generalate, Rome; U.S. headquarters, Hannibal House Spiritual Center, 1526 Hill Rd., Reading, PA 19602.

## Dominicans

**Nuns of the Order of Preachers (Dominican Nuns), O.P.:** Founded 1206 by St. Dominic at Prouille, France. Cloistered, contemplative. Two branches in the United States:

•Dominican Nuns having perpetual adoration. First monastery established 1880, in Newark, N.J., from Oullins, France, foundation (1868). Autonomous monasteries:
St. Dominic, 375 13th Ave., Newark, NJ 07103; Corpus Christi, 1230 Lafayette Ave., Bronx, NY 10474; Blessed Sacrament, 29575 Middlebelt Rd., Farmington Hills, MI 48334; Monastery of the Angels, 1977 Carmen Ave., Los Angeles, CA 90068; Corpus Christi, 215 Oak Grove Ave., Menlo Park, CA 94025; Infant Jesus, 1501 Lotus Lane, Lufkin, TX 75901.
• Dominican Nuns devoted to the perpetual Rosary. First monastery established 1891, in Union City, N.J., from Calais, France, foundation (1880). Autonomous monasteries (some also observe perpetual adoration):
Dominican Nuns of Perpetual Rosary, 14th and West Sts., Union City, NJ 07087; 217 N. 68th St., Milwaukee, WI 53213; Perpetual Rosary, 1500 Haddon Ave., Camden, NJ 08103; Our Lady of the Rosary, 335 Doat St., Buffalo, NY 14211; Our Lady of the Rosary, 543 Spingfield Ave., Summit, NJ 07901; Mother of God, 1430 Riverdale St., W. Springfield, MA 01089; Perpetual Rosary, 802 Court St., Syracuse, NY 13208; Immaculate Heart of Mary, 1834 Lititz Pike, Lancaster, PA 17601; Mary the Queen, 1310 W. Church St., Elmira, NY 14905; St. Jude, Marbury, AL 36051; Our Lady of Grace, North Guilford, CT 06437; St. Dominic, 4901 16th St. N.W., Washington, DC 20011.

**Dominican Sisters of Charity of the Presentation, O.P.:** Founded 1696, in France; in U.S., 1906. General motherhouse, Tours, France; U.S. headquarters, 3012 Elm St., Dighton, MA 02715. Hospital work.

**Dominican Sisters of Hope (O.P.):** Formed 1995 through merger of Dominican Sisters of the Most Holy Rosary, Newburgh, NY; Dominican Sisters of the Sick Poor, Ossining, NY and Dominican Sisters of St. Catherine of Siena, Fall River, MA. General Offices: 229 N. Highland Ave., Ossining, NY 10562.

**Dominican Sisters of Our Lady of the Rosary and of St. Catherine of Siena (Cabra):** Founded 1644 in Ireland. General motherhouse, Cabra, Dublin, Ireland. U.S. regional house, 1930 Robert E. Lee Rd., New Orleans, LA 70122.

**Dominican Sisters of the Perpetual Rosary (O.P.):** 217 N. 68th St., Milwaukee, WI 53213. Cloistered, contemplative.

**Dominican Sisters of the Roman Congregation of St. Dominic, O.P.:** Founded 1621, in France; in U.S., 1904. General motherhouse, Paris, France; U.S. province, 305 Oberlin St., Iowa City, IA 52245. Educational work.

**Eucharistic Missionaries of St. Dominic, O.P.:** Founded 1927, in Louisiana. General motherhouse, 3801 Canal St., Suite 400, New Orleans, LA 70119. Parish work, social services.

**Marian Society of Dominican Catechists, O.P.:** Founded 1954 in Louisiana. General motherhouse, P.O. Box 7417, Alexandria, LA 71306. Community of Alexandria, La., diocese.

**Maryknoll Sisters of St. Dominic, M.M.:** Founded 1912, in New York. Center, Maryknoll, NY 10545.

**Religious Missionaries of St. Dominic, O.P.:**
General motherhouse, Rome, Italy. U.S. address (Spanish province), 2237 Waldron Rd., Corpus Christi, TX 78418.

**Sisters of St. Dominic, O.P.:** Names of congregations are given below, followed by the date of foundation, and location of motherhouse.
St. Catharine of Siena, 1822. 2645 Bardstown Rd., St. Catharine, KY 40061.
St. Mary of the Springs, 1830. 2320 Airport Dr., Columbus, Ohio 43219.
Most Holy Rosary, 1847. Sinsinawa, WI 53824.
Most Holy Name of Jesus, 1850. 1520 Grand Ave., San Rafael, CA 94901.
Holy Cross, 1853. Albany Ave., Amityville, NY 11701.
St. Cecilia, 1860. 801 Dominican Dr., Nashville, TN 37228.
St. Mary, 1860. 580 Broadway, New Orleans, LA 70118.
St. Catherine of Siena, 1862. 5635 Erie St., Racine, WI 53402.
Our Lady of the Sacred Heart, 1873. 1237 W. Monroe St., Springfield, IL 62704.
Our Lady of the Rosary, 1876. Sparkill, NY 10976.
Queen of the Holy Rosary, 1876. P.O. Box 3908, Mission San Jose, CA 94539.
Most Holy Rosary, 1892. 1257 Siena Heights Dr., Adrian, MI 49221.
Our Lady of the Sacred Heart, 1877. 2025 E. Fulton St., Grand Rapids, MI 49503.
St. Dominic, 1878. Blauvelt, NY 10913.
St. Catherine de Ricci, 1880. 750 Ashbourne Rd., Elkins Park, PA 19117.
Sacred Heart of Jesus, 1881. 1 Ryerson Ave., Caldwell, NJ 07006.
Sacred Heart, 1882. 6501 Almeda Rd., Houston, TX 77021.
St. Thomas Aquinas, 1888. 935 Fawcett Ave., Tacoma, WA 98402.
Holy Cross, 1890. P.O. Box 280, Edmonds, WA 98020.
St. Rose of Lima (Servants of Relief for Incurable Cancer) 1896. Hawthorne, NY 10532.
Dominican Sisters of Great Bend, 1902. 3600 Broadway, Great Bend, KS 67530.
St. Catherine of Siena, 1911. Box 1288, Kenosha, WI 53141.
St. Rose of Lima, 1923. 775 Drahner Rd., Box 167, Oxford, MI 48371.
Immaculate Conception, 1929. 9000 W. 81st St., Justice, IL 60458.
Immaculate Heart of Mary, 1929. 1230 W. Market St., Akron, Ohio 44313.
Dominican Sisters of Spokane. West 3102 Fort George Wright Dr., Spokane, WA 99204.
Dominican Sisters of Oakford (St. Catherine of Siena), 1889. Motherhouse, Oakford, Natal, South Africa. U.S. regional house, 1965. 1855 Miramonte Ave., Mountain View, CA 94040.

## (End, Listing of Dominicans)

**Dorothy, Institute of the Sisters of St., S.S.D.:** Founded 1834, in Italy; by St. Paola Frassinetti; in U.S., 1911. General motherhouse, Rome, Italy; U.S. provincialate, Mt. St. Joseph, 13 Monkeywrench Lane, Bristol, RI 02809.

**Eucharist, Religious of the, R.E.:** Founded 1857, in Belgium; in U.S., 1900. General motherhouse, Belgium; U.S. foundation, 2907 Ellicott Terr., N.W., Washington, DC 20008.

**Family, Congregation of the Sisters of the Holy, S.S.F.:** Founded 1842, in Louisiana, by Henriette Delille and Juliette Gaudin. General motherhouse, 6901 Chef Menteur Hway., New Orleans, LA 70126. Educational, hospital work.

**Family, Little Sisters of the Holy, P.S.S.F.:** Founded 1880, in Canada; in U.S., 1900. General motherhouse, Sherbrooke, Que., Canada. U.S. novitiate, 285 Andover St., Lowell, MA 01852.

**Family, Sisters of the Holy, S.H.F.:** Founded 1872, in U.S. General motherhouse, P.O. Box 3248, Mission San Jose, CA 94539. Educational, social work.

**Family of Nazareth, Sisters of the Holy, C.S.F.N.:** Founded 1875, in Italy; in U.S., 1885. General motherhouse, Rome, Italy. U.S. provinces: Sacred Heart, 353 N. River Rd., Des Plaines, IL 60016; Immaculate Conception BVM, 4001 Grant Ave., Torresdale, Philadelphia, PA 19114; St. Joseph, 285 Bellevue Rd., Pittsburgh, PA 15229; Immaculate Heart of Mary, Marian Heights, 1428 Monroe Turnpike, Monroe, CT 06468; Bl. Frances Siedliska Provincialate, 1814 Egyptian Way, Box 530959, Grand Prairie, TX 75053.

**Filippini, Religious Teachers, M.P.F.:** Founded 1692, in Italy; in U.S., 1910. General motherhouse, Rome, Italy; U.S. provinces: St. Lucy Filippini Province, Villa Walsh, Morristown, NJ 07960; Queen of Apostles Province, 474 East Rd., Bristol, CT 06010. Educational work.

**Francis de Sales, Oblate Sisters of St., O.S.F.S.:** Founded 1866, in France; in U.S., 1951. General motherhouse, Troyes, France; U.S. headquarters, Villa Aviat Convent, Childs, MD 21916. Educational, social work.

## Franciscans

**Bernardine Sisters of the Third Order of St. Francis, O.S.F.:** Founded 1457, at Cracow, Poland; in U.S., 1894. Generalate, 403 Allendale Rd., King of Prussia, PA 19406. Educational, hospital, social work.

**Capuchin Poor Clares (Madres Clarisas Capuchinas):** U.S. establishment, 1981, Amarillo diocese. Convent of the Blessed Sacrament and Our Lady of Guadalupe, 4201 N.E. 18th St., Amarillo, TX 79107. Cloistered.

**Congregation of the Servants of the Holy Child Jesus of the Third Order Regular of St. Francis, O.S.F.:** Founded 1855, in Germany; in U.S., 1929. General motherhouse, Wuerzburg, Germany; American motherhouse, Villa Maria, P.O. Box 708, North Plainfield, NJ 07061.

**Congregation of the Third Order of St. Francis of Mary Immaculate, O.S.F.:** Founded 1865, in U.S., by Fr. Pamphilus da Magliano, O.F.M. General motherhouse, 520 Plainfield Ave., Joliet, IL 60435. Educational and pastoral work.

**Daughters of St. Francis of Assisi, D.S.F.:** Founded 1894, in Hungary; in U.S., 1946. Provincial motherhouse, 507 N. Prairie St., Lacon, IL 61540. Nursing, CCD work.

**Eucharistic Franciscan Missionary Sisters,**

**E.F.M.S.:** Founded 1943, in Mexico. Motherhouse, 943 S. Soto St., Los Angeles, CA 90023.

**Felician Sisters (Congregation of the Sisters of St. Felix), C.S.S.F.:** Founded 1855, in Poland by Bl. Mary Angela Truszkowska; in U.S., 1874. General motherhouse, Rome, Italy. U.S. provinces: 36800 Schoolcraft Rd., Livonia, MI 48150; 600 Doat St., Buffalo, NY 14211; 3800 W. Peterson Ave., Chicago, IL 60659; 260 South Main St., Lodi, NJ 07644; 1500 Woodcrest Ave., Coraopolis, PA 15108; 1315 Enfield St., Enfield, CT 06082; 4210 Meadowlark Lane, S.E., Rio Rancho, NM 87124.

**Franciscan Handmaids of the Most Pure Heart of Mary, F.H.M.:** Founded 1916, in U.S. General motherhouse, 15 W. 124th St., New York, NY 10027. Educational, social work.

**Franciscan Hospitaller Sisters of the Immaculate Conception, F.H.I.C.:** Founded 1876, in Portugal; in U.S., 1960. General motherhouse, Lisbon, Portugal; U.S. novitiate, 300 S. 17th St., San Jose, CA 95112.

**Franciscan Missionaries of Mary, F.M.M.:** Founded 1877, in India; in U.S., 1904. General motherhouse, Rome, Italy; U.S. provincialate, 3305 Wallace Ave., Bronx, NY 10467. Mission work.

**Franciscan Missionaries of Our Lady, O.S.F.:** Founded 1854, at Calais, France; in U.S., 1913. General motherhouse, Desvres, France; U.S. provincial house, 4200 Essen Lane, Baton Rouge, LA 70809. Hospital work.

**Franciscan Missionaries of St. Joseph (Mill Hill Sisters), F.M.S.J.:** Founded 1883, at Rochdale, Lancashire, England; in U.S., 1952. Generalate, Manchester, England; U.S. headquarters, Franciscan House, 1006 Madison Ave., Albany, NY 12208.

**Franciscan Missionary Sisters for Africa, O.S.F.:** American foundation, 1953. Generalate, Ireland; U.S. headquarters, 172 Foster St., Brighton, MA 02135.

**Franciscan Missionary Sisters of Assisi, F.M.S.A.:** First foundation in U.S., 1961. General motherhouse, Assisi, Italy; U.S. address, St. Francis Convent, 1039 Northampton St., Holyoke, MA 01040.

**Franciscan Missionary Sisters of Our Lady of Sorrows, O.S.F.:** Founded 1939, in China, by Bishop Rafael Palazzi, O.F.M.; in U.S., 1949. U.S. address, 3600 S.W. 170th Ave., Beaverton, OR 97006. Educational, social, domestic, retreat and foreign mission work.

**Franciscan Missionary Sisters of the Divine Child, F.M.D.C.:** Founded 1927, at Buffalo, NY, by Bishop William Turner. General motherhouse, 6380 Main St., Williamsville, NY 14221. Educational, social work.

**Franciscan Missionary Sisters of the Infant Jesus, F.M.I.J.:** Founded 1879, in Italy; in U.S., 1961. Generalate, Rome, Italy. U.S. provincialate, 1215 Kresson Rd., Chrry Hill, NJ 08003.

**Franciscan Missionary Sisters of the Sacred Heart, F.M.S.C.:** Founded 1860, in Italy; in U.S., 1865. Generalate, Rome, Italy; U.S. provincialate, 250 South St., Peekskill, NY 10566. Educational and social welfare apostolates.

**Franciscan Poor Clare Nuns (Poor Clares, Order of St. Clare, Poor Clares of St. Colette), P.C.,**

**O.S.C., P.C.C.:** Founded 1212, at Assisi, Italy, by St. Francis of Assisi; in U.S., 1875. Proto-monastery, Assisi, Italy. Addresses of autonomous motherhouses in U.S. are listed below.

3626 N. 65th Ave., Omaha, NE 68104; 720 Henry Clay Ave., New Orleans, LA 70118; 6825 Nurrenbern Rd., Evansville, IN 47712; 1310 Dellwood Ave., Memphis, TN 38127; 920 Centre St., Jamaica Plain, MA 02130; 201 Crosswicks St., Bordentown, NJ 08505; 1271 Langhorne-Newtown Rd., Langhorne, PA 19047; 4419 N. Hawthorne St., Spokane, WA 99205; 142 Hollywood Ave., Bronx, NY 10465; 421 S. 4th St., Sauk Rapids, MN 56379; 8650 Russell Ave. S., Minneapolis, MN 55431; 3501 Rocky River Dr., Cleveland, OH 44111;

1671 Pleasant Valley Rd., Aptos, CA 95001; 2111 S. Main St., Rockford, IL 61102; 215 E. Los Olivos St., Santa Barbara, CA 93105; 460 River Rd., W. Andover, MA 01810; 809 E. 19th St., Roswell, NM 88201; 28210 Natoma Rd., Los Altos Hills, CA 94022; 1916 N. Pleasantburg Dr., Greenville, SC 29609; 28 Harpersville Rd., Newport News, VA 23601; 1175 N. County Rd. 300 W., Kokomo, IN 46901; 3900 Sherwood Blvd., Delray Beach, FL 33445; 200 Marycrest Dr., St. Louis, MO 63129; 6029 Estero Blvd., Fort Myers Beach, FL 33931; Rt. 7, Box 7504, Brenham, TX 77833.

**Franciscan Sisters, Daughters of the Sacred Hearts of Jesus and Mary, O.S.F.:** Founded 1860, in Germany; in U.S., 1872. Generalate, Rome, Italy; U.S. motherhouse, P.O. Box 667, Wheaton, IL 60189. Educational, hospital, foreign mission, social work.

**Franciscan Sisters Daughters of Mercy, F.H.M.:** Founded 1856, in Spain; in U.S., 1962. General motherhouse, Palma de Mallorca, Spain; U.S. address, 612 N. 3rd St., Waco, TX 76701.

**Franciscan Sisters of Allegany, O.S.F.:** Founded 1859, at Allegany, N.Y., by Fr. Pamphilus da Magliano, O.F.M. General motherhouse Allegany, NY 14706. Educational, hospital, foreign mission work.

**Franciscan Sisters of Baltimore, O.S.F.:** Founded 1868, in England; in U.S., 1881. General motherhouse, 3725 Ellerslie Ave., Baltimore, MD 21218. Educational work; social services.

**Franciscan Sisters of Chicago, O.S.F.:** Founded 1894, in U.S., by Mother Mary Therese (Josephine Dudzik). General motherhouse, 14700 Main St., Lemont, IL 60439. Educational work, social services.

**Franciscan Sisters of Christian Charity, O.S.F.:** Founded 1869, in U.S. Motherhouse, Holy Family Convent, 2409 S. Alverno Rd., Manitowoc, WI 54220. Educational, hospital work.

**Franciscan Sisters of Little Falls, Minn., O.S.F.:** Founded 1891, in U.S. General motherhouse, Little Falls, MN 56345. Health, education, social services, pastoral ministry, mission work.

**Franciscan Sisters of Mary, F.S.M.:** Established, 1987, through unification of the Sisters of St. Mary of the Third Order of St. Francis (founded 1872, St. Louis) and the Sisters of St. Francis of Maryville, Mo. (founded 1894). Address of general superior: 1100 Bellevue Ave., St. Louis, MO 63117. Health care, social services.

**Franciscan Sisters of Mary Immaculate of the Third Order of St. Francis of Assisi, F.M.I.:** Founded 16th century, in Switzerland; in U.S., 1932. General motherhouse, Bogota, Colombia; U.S. provincial house, 4301 N.E. 18th Ave., Amarillo, TX 79107. Education.

**Franciscan Sisters of Our Ldy of Perpetual Help, O.S.F.:** Founded 1901, in U.S., from Joliet, Ill., foundation. General motherhouse, 201 Brotherton Lane, St. Louis, MO 63135. Educational, hospital work.

**Franciscan Sisters of Peace, F.S.P.:** Established 1986, in U.S., as archdiocesan community, from Franciscan Missionary Sisters of the Sacred Heart. Congregation center, 20 Ridge St., Haverstraw, NY 10927.

**Franciscan Sisters of Ringwood, F.S.R.:** Founded 1927, at Passaic, New Jersey. General motherhouse, Mt. St. Francis, Ringwood, NJ 07456. Educational work.

**Franciscan Sisters of St. Elizabeth, F.S.S.E.:** Founded 1866, at Naples, Italy, by Bl. Ludovico of Casorio; in U.S., 1919. General motherhouse, Rome; U.S. delegate house, 499 Park Rd., Parsippany, NJ 07054. Educational work, social services.

**Franciscan Sisters of St. Joseph, F.S.S.J.:** Founded 1897, in U.S. General motherhouse, 5286 S. Park Ave., Hamburg, NY 14075. Educational, hospital work.

**Franciscan Sisters of St. Joseph (of Mexico):** U.S. foundation, St. Paul College, 3015 4th St. N.E., Washington, DC 20017.

**Franciscan Sisters of the Atonement, Third Order Regular of St. Francis (Graymoor Sisters), S.A.:** Founded 1898, in U.S., as Anglican community; entered Church, 1909. General motherhouse, Graymoor, Garrison P.O., NY 10524. Mission work.

**Franciscan Sisters of St. Paul, Minn., O.S.F.:** Founded 1863, at Neuwied, Germany (Franciscan Sisters of the Blessed Virgin Mary of the Holy Angels); in U.S., 1923. General motherhouse, Rhine, Germany; U.S. motherhouse, 1388 Prior Ave. S., St. Paul, MN 55116. Educational, hospital, social work.

**Franciscan Sisters of the Immaculate Conception, O.S.F.:** Founded in Germany; in U.S., 1928. General motherhouse, Kloster, Bonlanden, Germany; U.S. province, 291 W. North St., Buffalo, NY 14201.

**Franciscan Sisters of the Immaculate Conception, O.S.F.:** Founded 1874, in Mexico; in U.S., 1926. U.S. provincial house, 11306 Laurel Canyon Blvd., San Fernando, CA 91340.

**Franciscan Sisters of the Immaculate Conception, Missionary, O.S.F.:** Founded 1873, in U.S. General motherhouse, Rome, Italy; U.S. address, 790 Centre St., Newton, MA 02158. Educational work.

**Franciscan Sisters of the Immaculate Conception and St. Joseph for the Dying, O.S.F.:** Founded 1919, in U.S. General motherhouse, 485 Church St., Monterey, CA 93940.

**Franciscan Sisters of the Poor, S.F.P.:** Founded 1845, at Aachen, Germany, by Bl. Frances Schervier; in U.S., 1858. Congregational office, 133 Remsen St., Brooklyn, NY 11201. Hospital, social work and foreign missions.

**Franciscan Sisters of the Sacred Heart, O.S.F.:** Founded 1866, in Germany; in U.S., 1876. General motherhouse, St. Francis Woods, 9201 W. St. Francis Rd., Frankfort, IL 60423. Education, health care, other service ministries.

**Hospital Sisters of the Third Order of St. Francis, O.S.F.:** Founded 1844, in Germany; in U.S., 1875. General motherhouse, Muenster, Germany; U.S. motherhouse, Box 19431, Springfield, IL 62794. Hospital work.

**Institute of the Franciscan Sisters of the Eucharist, F.S.E.:** Founded 1973. Motherhouse, 405 Allen Ave., Meriden, CT 06450.

**Little Franciscans of Mary, P.F.M.:** Founded 1889, in U.S. General motherhouse, Baie St. Paul, Que., Canada. U.S. region, 2 Dupont St., Worcester, MA 01604. Educational, hospital, social work.

**Missionary Sisters of the Immaculate Conception of the Mother of God, S.M.I.C.:** Founded 1910, in Brazil; in U.S., 1922, U.S. provincialate, P.O. Box 3026, Paterson, NJ 07509. Mission, educational, health work, social services.

**Mothers of the Helpless, M.D.:** Founded 1873, in Spain; in U.S., 1916. General motherhouse, Valencia, Spain; U.S. address, Sacred Hear Residence, 432 W. 20th St., New York, NY 10011.

**Poor Clares of Perpetual Adoration, P.C.P.A.:** Founded 1854, at Paris, France; in U.S., 1921, at Cleveland, Ohio. U.S. monasteries: 4200 N. Market Ave., Canton, OH 44714; 2311 Stockham Lane, Portsmouth, OH 45662; 4108 Euclid Ave., Cleveland, OH 44103; 3900 13th St. N.E., Washington, DC 20017; 5817 Old Leeds Rd., Birmingham, AL 35210. Contemplative, cloistered, perpetual adoration.

**St. Francis Mission Community, O.S.F.:** Autonomous province of Franciscan Sisters of Mary Immaculate. Address: 4305 54th St., Lubbock, TX 79413.

**School Sisters of St. Francis, O.S.F.:** Founded 1874, in U.S. General motherhouse, 1501 S. Layton Blvd., Milwaukee, WI 53215.

**School Sisters of St. Francis, (Pittsburgh, Pa.), O.S.F.:** Established 1913, in U.S. Motherhouse, Mt. Assisi Convent, 934 Forest Ave., Pittsburgh, PA 15202. Education, health care services and related ministries.

**School Sisters of the Third Order of St. Francis (Bethlehem, Pa.), O.S.F.:** Founded in Austria, 1843; in U.S., 1913. General motherhouse, Rome, Italy; U.S. province, 395 Bridle Path Rd., Bethlehem, PA 18017. Educational, mission work.

**School Sisters of the Third Order of St. Francis (Panhandle, Tex.), O.S.F.:** Established 1931, in U.S., from Vienna, Austria, foundation (1845). General motherhouse, Vienna, Austria; U.S. center and novitiate, P.O. Box 906, Panhandle, TX 79068. Educational, social work.

**Sisters of Mercy of the Holy Cross, S.C.S.C.:** Founded 1856, in Switzerland; in U.S. 1912. General motherhouse, Ingenbohl, Switzerland; U.S. provincial residence, 700 E. Riverside Ave., Merrill, WI 54452.

**Sisters of Our Lady of Mercy (Mercedarians), S.O.L.M.:** General motherhouse, Rome, Italy; U.S. addresses: Most Precious Blood, 133 27th Ave., Brooklyn, NY 11214; St. Edward School, Pine Hill, NJ 08021.

**Sisters of St. Elizabeth, S.S.E.:** Founded 1931, at Milwaukee, Wis. Address, 2005 Division St., Manitowoc, WI 53005.

**Sisters of St. Francis (Clinton, Iowa), O.S.F.:**

**Founded** 1868, in U.S. General motherhouse, 400 N. Bluff Blvd., Clinton, IA 57232. Educational, hospital, social work.

**Sisters of St. Francis (Millvale, Pa.), O.S.F.:** Founded 1865, Pittsburgh, PA General motherhouse, 146 Hawthorne Rd., Millvale P.O., Pittsburgh, PA 15209. Educational, hospital work.

**Sisters of St. Francis (Hastings-on-Hudson), O.S.F.:** Founded 1893, in New York. General motherhouse, 49 Jackson Ave., Hastings-on-Hudson, NY 10706. Education, parish ministry, social services.

**Sisters of St. Francis of Assisi, O.S.F.:** Founded 1849, in U.S. General motherhouse, 3221 S. Lake Dr., Milwaukee, WI 53207. Education, other ministries.

**Sisters of St. Francis of Christ the King, O.S.F.:** Founded 1864, in Austria; in U.S., 1909. General motherhouse, Rome, Italy; U.S. provincial house, 13900 Main St., Lemont, IL 60439. Educational work, home for aged.

**Sisters of St. Francis of Penance and Christian Charity, O.S.F.:** Founded 1835, in Holland; in U.S., 1874. General motherhouse, Rome, Italy. U.S. provinces: 4421 Lower River Rd., Stella Niagara, NY 14144; 2851 W. 52nd Ave., Denver, CO 80221; 3910 Bret Harte Dr., P.O. Box 1028, Redwood City, CA 94064.

**Sisters of St. Francis of Philadelphia, O.S.F.:** Founded 1855, at Philadelphia, by Mother Mary Francis Bachmann and St. John N. Neumann. General motherhouse, Convent of Our Lady of the Angels, Aston, PA 19014. Education, health care, social services.

**Sisters of St. Francis of Savannah, Mo., O.S.F.:** Founded 1850, in Austria; in U.S., 1922. Provincial house, La Verna Heights, Box 488, 104 E. Park, Savannah, MO 64485. Educational, hospital work.

**Sisters of St. Francis of the Congregation of Or Lady of Lourdes, O.S.F.:** Founded 1916, in U.S. General motherhouse, 6832 Convent Blvd., Sylvania, OH 43560. Education, health care, social services, pastoral ministry.

**Sisters of St. Francis of the Holy Cross, O.S.F.:** Founded 1881, in U.S., by Rev. Edward Daems, O.S.C. General motherhouse, 3025 Bay Settlement Rd., Green Bay, WI 54301. Educational, nursing work, pastoral ministry, foreign missions.

**Sisters of St. Francis of the Holy Eucharist, O.S.F.:** Founded 1378, in Switzerland; in U.S., 1893. General motherhouse, 2100 N. Noland Rd., Independence, MO 64050. Education, health care, social services, foreign missions.

**Sisters of St. Francis of the Holy Family, O.S.F.:** U.S. foundation, 1875. Motherhouse, Mt. St. Francis, 3390 Windsor Ave., Dubuque, IA 52001. Varied apostolates.

**Sisters of St. Francis of the Immaculate Conception, O.S.F.:** Founded 1890, in U.S. General motherhouse, 2408 W. Heading Ave., Peoria, IL 61604. Education, care of aging, pastoral ministry.

**Sisters of St. Francis of the Immaculate Heart of Mary, O.S.F.:** Founded 1241, in Bavaria; in U.S., 1913. General motherhouse, Rome, Italy; U.S. motherhouse, Hankinson, ND 58041. Education, social services.

**Sisters of St. Francis of the Martyr St. George, O.S.F.:** Founded 1859, in Germany; in U.S., 1923. General motherhouse, Thuine, Germany; U.S. provincial house, St. Francis Convent, 2120 Central Ave., Alton, IL 62002. Education, social services, foreign mission work.

**Sisters of St. Francis of the Perpetual Adoration, O.S.F.:** Founded 1863, in Germany; in U.S., 1875. General motherhouse, Olpe, Germany. U.S. provinces: Box 766, Mishawaka, IN 46544; 7665 Assisi Heights, Colorado Springs, CO 80919.

**Sisters of St. Francis of the Providence of God, O.S.F.:** Founded 1922, in U.S., by Msgr. M. L. Krusas. General motherhouse, 3603 McRoberts Rd., Pittsburgh, PA 15234. Education, varied apostolates.

**Sisters of St. Francis of the Third Order Regular, O.S.F.:** Founded 1861, at Buffalo, N.Y., from Philadelphia foundation. General motherhouse, 400 Mill St., Williamsville, NY 14221. Educational, hospital work.

**Sisters of St. Joseph of the Third Order of St. Francis, S.S.J.:** Founded 1901, in U.S. Administrative office, 1300 Maria Dr., Stevens Pt., WI 54481. Education, health care, social services.

**Sisters of the Infant Jesus, I.J.:** Founded 1662, at Rouen, France; in U.S., 1950. Motherhouse, Paris, France. Generalate, Rome, Italy. U.S. address: 20 Reiner St., Colma, CA 94014.

**Sisters of the Sorrowful Mother (Third Order of St. Francis), S.S.M.:** Founded 1883, in Italy; in U.S., 1889. General motherhouse, Rome, Italy. U.S. address: 17600 E. 51st St. S., Broken Arrow, OK 74012. Educational, hospital work.

**Sisters of the Third Franciscan Order, O.S.F.:** Founded 1860, at Syracuse, N.Y. Generalate offices, 2500 Grant Blvd., Syracuse, NY 13208.

**Sisters of the Third Order of St. Francis, O.S.F.:** Founded 1877, in U.S., by Bishop John L. Spalding. Motherhouse, St. Francis Lane, E. Peoria, IL 61611. Hospital work.

**Sisters of the Third Order of St. Francis (Oldenburg, Ind.), O.S.F.:** Founded 1851, in U.S. General motherhouse, Convent of the Immaculate Conception, Oldenburg, IN 47036. Education, social services, pastoral ministry, foreign missions.

**Sisters of the Third Order of St. Francis of Penance and Charity, O.S.F.:** Founded 1869, in U.S., by Rev. Joseph Bihn. Motherhouse, St. Francis Ave., Tiffin, OH 44883. Education, social services.

**Sisters of the Third Order of St. Francis of the Perpetual Adoration, F.S.P.A.:** Founded 1849, in U.S. Generalate, 912 Market St., La Crosse, WI 54601. Education, health care.

**Sisters of the Third Order Regular o St. Francis of the Congregation of Our Lady of Lourdes, O.S.F.:** Founded 1877, in U.S. General motherhouse, Assisi Heights, Rochester, MN 55901. Education, health care, social services.

### (End, Listing of Franciscans)

**Good Shepherd Sisters (Servants of the Immaculate Heart of Mary), S.C.I.M.:** Founded 1850, in Canada; in U.S., 1882. General motherhouse, Quebec, Canada; Provincial House, Bay View, 313 Seaside Ave., Saco, Maine 04072. Educational, social work.

**Good Shepherd, Sisters of Our Lady of Charity** of the, R.G.S.: Founded 1835, in France by St. Mary Euphrasia Pelletier; in U.S., 1843. Generalate, Rome, Italy. U.S. provinces: 2849 Fischer Pl., Cincinnati, OH 45211; 82-31 Doncaster Pl., Jamaica, NY 11432; 504 Hexton Hill Rd., Silver Spring, MD 20904; 7654 Natural Bridge Rd., St. Louis, MO 63121; 5100 Hodgson Rd., St. Paul, MN 55112. Active and contemplative (Contemplative Sisters of the Good Shepherd, C.G.S.).

**Graymoor Sisters:** See Franciscan Sisters of the Atonement.

**Grey Nuns of the Sacred Heart, G.N.S.H.:** Founded 1921, in U.S. General motherhouse, 1750 Quarry Rd., Yardley, PA 19067.

**Guadalupan Missionaries of the Holy Spirit, M.G.Sp.S.:** Founded 1930 in Mexico by Rev. Felix de Jesus Rougier, M.Sp.S. General motherhouse, Mexico; U.S. delegation: 2483 S.W. 4th St. Miami, FL 33135.

**Guardian Angel, Sisters of the Holy, S.A.C.:** Founded 1839, in France. General motherhouse, Madrid, Spain; U.S. foundation, 1245 S. Van Ness, Los Angeles, CA 90019.

**Handmaids of Mary Immaculate, A.M.I.:** Founded 1952 in Helena, Mont. Address: Mountain View Rd., Washington, NJ 07882.

**Handmaids of the Precious Blood, Congregation of, H.P.B.:** Founded 1947, at Jemez Springs, N. Mex. Motherhouse and novitiate, Cor Jesu Monastery, P.O. Box 90, Jemez Springs, NM 87025.

**Helpers, Society of, H.H.S.:** Founded 1856, in France; in U.S., 1892. General motherhouse, Paris, France; American province, 303 W. Barry Ave., Chicago, IL 60657.

**Hermanas Catequistas Guadalupanas, H.C.G.:** Founded 1923, in Mexico; in U.S., 1950. General motherhouse, Mexico; U.S. addresses: 4110 S. Flores, San Antonio, TX 78214; 115 Arlington Ct., San Antonio, TX 78210.

**Hermanas Josefinas, H.J.:** General motherhouse, Mexico; U.S. foundation, Assumption Seminary, 2600 W. Woodlawn Ave., P.O. Box 28240, San Antonio, TX 78284. Domestic work.

**Holy Child Jesus, Society of the, S.H.C.J.:** Founded 1846, in England; in U.S., 1862. General motherhouse, Rome, Italy. U.S. province: 460 Shadeland Ave., Drexel Hill, PA 19026.

**Holy Faith, Congregation of the Sisters of the, C.H.F.:** Founded 1856, in Ireland; in U.S., 1953. General motherhouse, Dublin, Ireland; U.S. province, 12322 S. Paramount Blvd., P.O. Box 2085, Downey, CA 90242.

**Holy Heart of Mary, Servants of the, S.S.C.M.:** Founded 1860, in France; in U.S., 1889. General motherhouse, Montreal, Que., Canada; U.S. province, 145 S. 4th Ave., Kankakee, IL 60901. Educational, hospital, social work.

**Holy Names of Jesus and Mary, Sisters of the, S.N.J.M.:** Founded 1843, in Canada by Bl. Marie Rose Durocher; in U.S., 1859. Generalate, Longueuil Que., Canada. U.S. addresses: Oregon Province, Box 25, Marylhurst, OR 97036; California Province, P.O. Box 907, Los Gatos, CA 9503; New York Province, 1061 New Scotland Rd., Albany, NY 12208; Washington Province, 2911 W. Ft. Wright Dr., Spokane, WA 99204.

**Holy Spirit, Community of the, C.H.S.:** Founded 1970 in San Diego, Calif. Address: 6151 Rancho Mission Rd., No. 225, San Diego, CA 95108.

**Holy Spirit, Daughters of the, D.H.S.:** Founded 1706, in France; in U.S., 1902. Generalate, Bretagne, France; U.S. motherhouse, 72 Church St., Putnam, CT 06260. Educational work, district nursing; pastoral ministry.

**Holy Spirit, Mission Sisters of the, M.S.Sp.:** Founded 1932, at Cleveland, Ohio. Motherhouse, 1030 N. River Rd., Saginaw, MI 48603.

**Holy Spirit, Missionary Sisters, Servants of the:** Founded 1889, in Holland; in U.S., 1901. Generalate, Rome, Italy; U.S. motherhouse, Convent of the Holy Spirit, Techny, IL 60082.

**Holy Spirit, Sisters of the, C.S.Sp.:** Founded 1890, in Rome, Italy; in U.S. as independent diocesan community, 1929. General motherhouse, 10102 Granger Rd., Garfield Hts., OH 44125. Educational, social, nursing work.

**Holy Spirit, Sisters of the, S.H.S.:** Founded 1913, in U.S., by Most Rev. J. F. Regis Canevin. General motherhouse, 5246 Clarwin Ave., Ross Township, Pittsburgh, PA 15229. Educational, nursing work; care of aged.

**Holy Spirit and Mary Immaculate, Sisters of, S.H.Sp.:** Founded 1893, in U.S. Motherhouse, 301 Yucca St., San Antonio, TX 78203. Education, hospital work.

**Holy Spirit of Perpetual Adoration, Sister Servants of the:** Founded 1896, in Holland; in U.S., 1915. Generalate, Bad Driburg, Germany; U.S. novitiate, 2212 Green St., Philadelphia, PA 19130.

**Home Mission Sisters of America (Glenmary Sisters):** Founded 1952, in U.S. Glenmary Center, P.O. Box 22264, Owensboro, KY 42302.

**Home Visitors of Mary, Sisters, H.V.M.:** Founded 1949, in Detroit, Mich. Motherhouse, 356 Arden Park, Detroit, MI 48202.

**Humility of Mary, Congregation of, C.H.M.:** Founded 1854, in France; in U.S., 1864. U.S. address, Humility of Mary Center, Davenport, IA 52804.

**Humility of Mary, Sisters of the, H.M.:** Founded 1854, in France; in U.S., 1864. U.S. address, Villa Maria Community Center, Villa Maria, PA 16155.

**Immaculate Conception, Little Servant Sisters of the:** Founded 1850, in Poland; in U.S., 1926. General motherhouse, Poland; U.S. provincial house, 1000 Cropwell Rd., Cherry Hill, NJ 08003. Education, social services, African missions.

**Immaculate Conception, Sisters of the, R.C.M.:** Founded 1892, in Spain; in U.S., 1962. General motherhouse, Madrid, Spain; U.S. address, 2230 Franklin, San Francisco, CA 94109.

**Immaculate Conception, Sisters of the, C.I.C.:** Founded 1874, in U.S. General motherhouse, P.O. Box 50426, New Orleans, LA 70185.

**Immaculate Conception of the Blessed Virgin Mary, Sisters of the (Lithuanian):** Founded 1918, at Mariampole, Lithuania; in U.S., 1936. U.S. headquarters, Immaculate Conception Convent, 600 Liberty Hwy., Putnam, CT 06260.

**Immaculate Heart of Mary, Missionary Sisters, I.C.M.:** Founded 1897, in India; in U.S., 1919. Generalate, Rome, Italy; U.S. province, 283 E. 15th St., New York, NY 10003. Educational social, foreign mission work.

**Immaculate Heart of Mary, Sisters of the:** Founded 1848, in Spain; in U.S., 1878. General motherhouse, Rome, Italy. U.S. province, 4100 Sabino Canyon Rd., Tucson, AZ 85715. Educational work.

**Immaculate Heart of Mary, Sisters of the (California Institute of the Most Holy and Immaculate Heart of the B.V.M.), I.H.M.:** Founded 1848, in Spain; in U.S., 1871. Generalate, 3431 Waverly Dr., Los Angeles, CA 90027.

**Immaculate Heart of Mary, Sisters, Servants of the, I.H.M.:** Founded 1845, at Monroe, Mich., by Rev. ouis Florent Gillet. Generalate, 610 W. Elm St., Monroe, MI 48161.

**Immaculate Heart of Mary, Sisters, Servants of the, I.H.M.:** Founded 1845; established in Scranton, Penn., 1871. General motherhouse, 2300 Adams Ave., Scranton, PA 18509.

**Immaculate Heart of Mary, Sisters Servants of the, I.H.M.:** Founded 1845; established in West Chester, Penn., 1872. General motherhouse, Villa Maria, Immaculata, PA 19345.

**Immaculate Heart of Mary of Wichita, Sisters of, I.H.M.:** Established at Wichita, 1979. Address: 605 N. Woodchuck, Wichita, KS 67212.

**Incarnate Word, Religious of, C.V.I.:** General motherhouse, Mexico City, Mexico. U.S. address, 153 Rainier Ct., Chula Vista, CA 92011.

**Incarnate Word and Blessed Sacrament, Congregation of, C.V.I.:** Founded 1625, in France; in U.S., 1853. Incarnate Word Convent, 3400 Bradford Pl., Houston, TX 77028.

**Incarnate Word and Blessed Sacrament, Congregation of the, I.W.B.S.:** Motherhouse, 1101 Northeast Water St., Victoria, TX 77901.

**Incarnate Word and Blessed Sacrament, Congregation of the, I.W.B.S.:** Motherhouse, 2930 S. Alameda, Corpus Christi, TX 78404.

**Incarnate Word and Blessed Sacrament, Sisters of the, S.I.W.:** Founded 1625, in France; in U.S. 1853. Motherhouse, 6618 Pearl Rd., Parma Heights, Cleveland, OH 44130.

**Infant Jesus, Congregatioñ of the (Nursing Sisters of the Sick Poor), C.I.J.:** Founded 1835, in France; in U.S., 1905. General motherhouse, 310 Prospect Park W., Brooklyn, NY 11215.

**Jesus, Daughters of, F.I.:** Founded 1871, in Spain; in U.S., 1950. General motherhouse, Rome, Italy; U.S. address, 2021 Stuart Ave., Baton Rouge, LA 70808.

**Jesus, Daughters of (Filles de Jesus), F.J.:** Founded 1834, in France; in U.S., 1904. General motherhouse, Kermaria, Locmine, France; U.S. address, 4209 3rd Ave. S., Great Falls, Mont. 59405. Educational, hospital, parish and social work.

**Jesus, Little Sisters of:** Founded 1939, in Sahara; in U.S., 1952. General motherhouse, Rome, Italy; U.S. headquarters, 400 N. Streeper St., Baltimore, MD 21224.

**Jesus, Servants of, S.J.:** Founded 1974, in U.S. Central Office, 9075 Big Lake Rd., P.O. Box 128, Clarkston, MI 48016.

**Jesus, Society of the Sisters, Faithful Companions of, F.C.J.:** Founded 1820, in France; in U.S., 1896. General motherhouse, Kent, England. U.S. province: St. Philomena Convent, Cory's Lane, Portsmouth, RI 02871.

**Jesus and Mary, Little Sisters of, L.S.J.M.:** Founded 1974 in U.S. Address: Joseph House, P.O. Box 1755, Salisbury, MD 21801.

**Jesus and Mary, Religious of, R.J.M.:** Founded 1818, at Lyons, France; in U.S., 1877. General motherhouse, Rome, Italy; U.S. province, 3706 Rhode Island Ave., Mt. Ranier, MD 20712. Educational work.

**Jesus Crucified, Congregation of:** Founded 1930, in France; in U.S., 1955. General motherhouse, Brou, France; U.S. foundations: Regina Mundi Priory, Devon, PA 19333; St. Paul's Priory, 61 Narragansett, Newport, RI 02840.

**Jesus Crucified and the Sorrowful Mother, Poor Sisters of, C.J.C.:** Founded 1924, in U.S., by Rev. Alphonsus Maria, C.P. Motherhouse, 261 Thatcher St., Brockton, MA 02402. Education, nursing homes, catechetical centers.

**Jesus, Mary and Joseph, Missionaries of, M.J.M.J.:** Founded 1942, in Spain; in U.S., 1956. General motherhouse, Madrid, Spain; U.S. regional house, 12940 Up River Rd., Corpus Christi, TX 78410.

**Joan of Arc, Sisters of St., S.J.A.:** Founded 1914, in U.S., by Rev. Marie Clement Staub, A.A. General motherhouse, 1505, rue de l'Assomption Sillery, Que. G1S 4T3, Canada. U.S. novitiate, 529 Eastern Ave., Fall River, MA 02723. Spiritual and temporal service of priests.

**John the Baptist, Sisters of St., C.S.J.B.:** Founded 1878, in Italy; in U.S., 1906. General motherhouse, Rome, Italy; U.S. provincialate, 150 Anderson Hill Rd., Purchase, NY 10577. Education, parish and retreat work; social services.

**Joseph, Poor Sisters of St.:** Founded 1880, in Argentina. General motherhouse, Muniz, Buenos Aires, Argentina; U.S. addresses, Casa Belen, 305 E. 4th St., Bethlehem, PA 78015; Casa Nazareth, 532 Spruce St., Reading, PA 19602; St. Gabriel Convent, 4319 Sano St., Alexandria, VA 22312.

**Joseph, Religious Daughters of St., F.S.J.:** Founded 1875, in Spain. General motherhouse, Spain; U.S. foundation, 319 N. Humphreys Ave., Los Angeles, CA 90022.

**Joseph, Religious Hospitallers of St., R.H.S.J.:** Founded 1636, in France; in U.S., 1894. Generalate, Montreal, Que., Canada; U.S. address, Holy Family Convent, 100 Mansfield Ave., PO Box 176, Burlington, VT 05401. Hospital work.

**Joseph, Servants of St., S.S.J.:** Founded 1874, in Spain; in U.S., 1957. General motherhouse, Salamanca, Spain; U.S. address, 203 N. Spring St., Falls Church, VA 22046.

**Joseph, Sisters of St., C.S.J. or S.S.J.:** Founded 1650, in France; in U.S., 1836, at St. Louis. Independent motherhouses in U.S.:

637 Cambridge St., Brighton, MA 02135; 1515 W. Ogden Ave., La Grange Park, IL, 60525; 480 S. Batavia St., Orange, CA 92668.

St. Joseph Convent, Brentwood, NY 11717; 23 Agassiz Circle, Buffalo, NY 14214; Avila Hall, 7 Clement Rd., Rutland, VT 05701; 3430 Rocky River Dr., Cleveland, OH 44111; 1440 Division Rd., Tipton, IN 46072; Motherhouse and Novitiate, Nazareth, MI 49074; 1425 Washington St., Watertown, NY 13601; Mt. Gallitzin Academy and Motherhouse,

Baden, PA 15005; 5031 W. Ridge Rd., Erie, PA 16502.

4095 East Ave., Rochester, NY 14610; 215 Court St., Concordia, KS 66901; Mont Marie, Holyoke, MA 01040; Pogue Run Rd., Wheeling, WV 26003; 3700 E. Lincoln St., Wichita, KS 67218.

**Joseph, Sisters of St. (Lyons, France), C.S.J.:** Founded 1650, in France; in U.S., 1906. General motherhouse, Lyons, France; U.S. provincialate, 93 Halifax St., Winslow, ME 04901. Educational, hospital work.

**Joseph, Sisters of St., of Peace, C.S.J.P.:** Founded 1884, in England; in U.S. 1885. Generalate, 1225 Newton St. N.E., Washington, DC 20017. Educational, hospital, social service work.

**Joseph of Carondelet, Sisters of St., C.S.J.:** Founded 1650, in France; in U.S., 1836, at St. Louis, Mo. U.S. headquarters, 2307 S. Lindbergh Blvd., St. Louis, MO 63131.

**Joseph of Chambery, Sisters of St.:** Founded 1650, in France; in U.S., 1885. Generalate, Rome, Italy; U.S. provincial house, 27 Park Rd., West Hartford, CT 06119. Educational, hospital, social work.

**Joseph of Chestnut Hill, Sisters of St., S.S.J.:** Founded 1650; Philadelphia foundation, 1847. Motherhouse, Mt. St. Joseph Convent, Chestnut Hill, PA 19118.

**Joseph of Cluny, Sisters of St., S.J.C.:** Founded 1807, in France. Generalate, Paris, France; U.S. provincial house, Brenton Rd., Newport, RI 02840.

**Joseph of Medaille, Sisters of, C.S.J.:** Founded 1650, in France; in U.S., 1855. Became an American congregation Nov. 30, 1977. Central office, 1821 Summit Rd., Cincinnati, Ohio 45237.

**Joseph of St. Augustine, Florida, Sisters of St., S.S.J.:** General motherhouse, 241 St. George St., P.O. Box 3506, St. Augustine, FL 32085. Educational, hospital, pastoral, social work.

**Joseph of St. Mark, Sisters of St., S.J.S.M.:** Founded 1845, in France; in U.S., 1937. General motherhouse, 21800 Chardon Rd., Euclid, Cleveland, OH 44117. Nursing homes.

**Joseph the Worker, Sisters of St., S.J.W.:** General motherhouse, St. William Convent, 1 St. Joseph Lane, Walton, KY 41094.

**Lamb of God, Sisters of the, A.D.:** Founded 1945, in France; in U.S., 1958. General motherhouse, France; U.S. address, 2068 Wyandotte Ave., Owensboro KY 42301.

**Life, Sisters of, S.V. (Sorer Vitae):** Founded by Cardinal John J. O'Connor, 1991, to protect life. Address: St. Frances de Chantal Convent, Hollywood Ave., Bronx, NY 10465.

**Little Sisters of the Gospel, L.S.G.:** Founded 1963 in France by Rev. Rene Voillaume; in U.S., 1972. U.S. address, Box 305, Mott Haven Sta., Bronx, NY 10454.

**Little Workers of the Sacred Hearts, P.O.S.C.:** Founded 1892, in Italy; in U.S., 1948. General house, Rome, Italy; U.S. address, Our Lady of Grace Convent, 635 Glenbrook Rd., Stamford, CT 06906.

**Living Word, Sisters of the, S.L.W.:** Founded 1975, in U.S. Motherhouse, The Center, 800 N. Fernandez Ave., Arlington Heights, IL 60004. Education, hospital, parish ministry work.

**Loretto at the Foot of the Cross, Sisters of, S.L.:**

Founded 1812 in U.S., by Rev. Charles Nerinckx. General motherhouse, Nerinx, KY 40049. Educational work.

**Louis, Congregation of Sisters of St., S.S.L.:** Founded 1842, in France; in U.S., 1949. General motherhouse, Monaghan, Ireland; U.S. regional house, 22300 Mulholland Dr., Woodland Hills, CA 91364. Educational, medical, parish, foreign mission work.

**Lovers of the Holy Cross Sisters (Phat Diem):** Founded 1670, in Vietnam; in U.S. 1976. U.S. address, Holy Cross Convent, 14700 South Van Ness Ave., Garden, CA 90249.

**Mantellate Sisters, Servants of Mary, of Blue Island, O.S.M.:** Founded 1861, in Italy; in U.S., 1916. Generalate, Rome, Italy; U.S. motherhouse, 13811 S. Western Ave., Blue Island, IL 60406. Educational work.

**Mantellate Sisters, Servants of Mary, of Plainfield, O.S.M.:** Founded 1861 in Italy; in U.S., 1916. Address:16949 S. Drauden Rd., Plainfield, IL 60544.

**Marian Sisters of the Diocese of Lincoln:** Founded 1954. Motherhouse, Marian Center, R.R. 1, Box 108, Waverly, NE 68462.

**Marianites of Holy Cross, Congregation of the Sisters, M.S.C.:** Founded 1841, in France; in U.S., 1843. Motherhouse, Le Mans, Sarthe, France. North American headquarters, 1011 Gallier St., New Orleans, LA 70117.

**Marist Sisters, Congregation of Mary, S.M.:** Founded 1824, in France. General motherhouse, Rome, Italy; U.S. convents: St. Albert the Great, 4855 Parker, Dearborn Hts., MI 48125; St. Barnabas, 24262 Johnston, E. Detroit, MI 48021; Our Lady of the Snows, 4810 S. Leamington, Chicago, IL 60638; Marie, Madre de la Iglesia, 4419 St. James, Detroit, MI 48210.

**Mary, Company of, O.D.N.:** Founded 1607, in France; in U.S., 1926. General motherhouse, Rome, Italy; U.S. motherhouse, 16791 E. Main St., Tustin, CA 92680.

**Mary, Daughters of the Heart of, D.H.M.:** Founded 1790, in France; in U.S., 1851. Generalate, Paris, France; U.S. provincialate, 1339 Northampton St., Holyoke, MA 01040. Education, retreat work.

**Mary, Missionary Sisters of the Society of (Marist Sisters), S.M.S.M.:** Founded 1845, at St. Brieuc, France; in U.S., 1922. General motherhouse, Rome, Italy; U.S. provincial house, 349 Grove St., Waltham, MA 02154. Foreign missions.

**Mary, Servants of, O.S.M.:** Founded 13th century, in Italy; in U.S., 1893. General motherhouse, England; U.S. provincial motherhouse, 7400 Military Ave., Omaha, NE 68134.

**Mary, Servants of (Servite Sisters), O.S.M.:** Founded 13th century, in Italy; in U.S., 1912. General motherhouse, Our Lady of Sorrows Convent, 1000 College Ave., Ladysmith, WI 54848.

**Mary, Sisters of St., of Oregon, S.S.M.O.:** Founded 1886, in Oregon, by Bishop William H. Gross, C.Ss.R. General motherhouse, 4440 S.W. 148th Ave., Beaverton, OR 97007. Educational, nursing work.

**Mary, Sisters of the Little Company of, L.C.M.:** Founded 1877, in England; in U.S., 1893.

Generalate, London, England; U.S. provincial house, 9350 S. California Ave., Evergreen Park, IL 60642.

**Mary, Sisters Servants of (Trained Nurses), S.M.:** Founded 1851, at Madrid, Spain; in U.S., 1914.General motherhouse, Rome, Italy; U.S. motherhouse, 800 N. 18th St., Kansas City, KS 66102. Home nursing.

**Mary and Joseph, Daughters of, D.M.J.:** Founded 1817, in Belgium; in U.S., 1926. Generalate, Rome, Italy; American provincialate, 5300 Crest Rd., Rancho Palos Verdes, CA 90274.

**Mary Help of Christians, Daughters of (Salesian Sisters of St. John Bosco), F.M.A.:** Founded 1872, in Italy, by St. John Bosco and St. Mary Dominic Mazzarello; in U.S., 1908. General motherhouse, Rome, Italy; U.S. provinces, 655 Belmont Ave., Haledon, NJ 07508; 6019 Buena Vista St., San Antonio, TX 78237. Education, youth work.

**Mary Immaculate, Daughters of (Marianist Sisters), F.M.I.:** Founded 1816, in France, by Very Rev. William-Joseph Chaminade. General motherhouse, Rome, Italy; U.S. foundation, 251 W. Ligustrum Dr., San Antonio, TX 78228. Educational work.

**Mary Immaculate, Religious of, R.M.I.:** Founded 1876, in Spain; in U.S., 1954. Generalate, Rome, Italy: U.S. foundation, 719 Augusta St., San Antonio, TX 78215.

**Mary Immaculate, Sisters Minor of, S.M.M.I.:** Established in U.S., 1989. Address: 138 Brushy Hill Rd., Danbury, CT 06818.

**Mary Immaculate, Sisters of, S.M.I.:** Founded 1948, in India, by Bishop Louis LaRavoire Morrow; in U.S., 1981. General motherhouse, Bengal, India; U.S. address, R.D. 5, Box 1231, Leechburg, PA 15656.

**Mary Immaculate, Sisters Servants of, S.S.M.I.:** Founded 1878 in Poland. General motherhouse, Mariowka-Opoczynska, Poland; American provincialate, 1220 Tugwell Dr., Catonsville, MD 21228.

**Mary Immaculate, Sisters Servants of, S.S.M.I:** Founded 1892, in Ukraine; in U.S., 1935. General motherhouse, Rome, Italy; U.S. address, 9 Emmanuel Dr., P.O. Box 6, Sloatsburg, NY 10974. Educational, hospital work.

**Mary of Namur, Sisters of St., S.S.M.N.:** Founded 1819, at Namur, Belgium; in U.S., 1863. General motherhouse, Namur, Belgium. U.S. provinces: 250 Bryant, Buffalo, NY 14222; 909 West Shaw St., Ft. Worth, TX 76110.

**Mary of Providence, Daughters of St., D.S.M.P.:** Founded 1872, at Como, Italy; in U.S., 1913. General motherhouse, Rome, Italy; U.S. provincial house, 4200 N. Austin Ave., Chicago, IL 60634. Special education for mentally handicapped.

**Mary of the Immaculate Conception, Daughters of, D.M.:** Founded 1904, in U.S., by Msgr. Lucian Bojnowski. General motherhouse, 314 Osgood Ave., New Britain, CT 06053. Educational, hospital work.

**Mary Queen, Congregation of, C.M.R.:** Founded in Vietnam; established in U.S., 1979. U.S. region, 535 S. Jefferson, Springfield, MO 65806.

**Mary Reparatrix, Society of, S.M.R.:** Founded 1857, in France; in U.S., 1908. Generalate, Rome, Italy. U.S. province, 225 E. 234th St., Bronx, NY 10470.

**Medical Mission Sisters (Society of Catholic Medical Missionaries, Inc.), M.M.S.:** Founded 1925, in U.S., by Mother Anna Dengel. Generalate, London, Eng.; U.S. headquarters, 8400 Pine Rd., Philadelphia, PA 19111. Medical work, health education, especially in mission areas.

**Medical Missionaries of Mary, M.M.M.:** Founded 1937, in Ireland, by Mother Mary Martin; in U.S., 1950. General motherhouse, Dublin, Ireland; U.S. headquarters, 563 Minneford Ave., City Island, Bronx, NY 10464. Medical aid in missions.

**Medical Sisters of St. Joseph, M.S.J.:** Founded 1946, in India; first U.S. foundation, 1985. General motherhouse, Kerala, S. India; U.S. address, 3435 E. Funston, Wichita, KS 67218. Health care apostolate.

**Mercedarian Missionaries of Berriz, M.M.B.:** Founded 1930, in Spain; in U.S., 1946. General motherhouse, Rome, Italy. U.S. headquarters, 1400 N.E. 42nd Terr., Kansas City, MO 64106.

**Mercy, Daughters of Our Lady of, D.M.:** Founded 1837, in Italy, by St. Mary Joseph Rossello; in U.S., 1919. General motherhouse, Savona, Italy; U.S. motherhouse, Villa Rossello, 1009 Main Rd., Newfield, NJ 08344. Educational, hospital work.

**Mercy, Missionary Sisters of Our Lady of, M.O.M.:** Founded 1938, in Brazil; in U.S., 1955. General motherhouse, Brazil; U.S. address, 388 Franklin St., Buffalo, NY 14202.

**Mercy, Religious Sisters of, R.S.M.:** Founded 1973 in U.S. Motherhouse, 1835 Michigan Ave., Alma, MI 48801.

**Mercy, Sisters of, Daughters of Christian Charity of St. Vincent de Paul, S.M.D.C.:** Founded 1842, in Hungary; U.S. foundation, Rt. 1, Box 353A, 240 Longhouse Dr., Hewitt, NJ 07421.

**Mercy, Sisters of, of the Americas:** Formed in July, 1991, through union of 25 regional communities of Sisters of Mercy which previously were independent motherhouses or houses which formed the Sisters of Mercy of the Union. Mother Mary Catherine McAuley founded the Sisters of Mercy in Dublin, Ireland, in 1831; the first establishment in the U.S., 1843, in Pittsburgh. Address of administrative office: 8300 Colesville Rd., No. 300, Silver Spring, MD 20910. Pres., Sr. Doris Gottemoeller.

**Mercy of the Blessed Sacrament, Sisters of, H.M.S.S.:** Founded 1910 in Mexico; in U.S., 1926. General motherhouse, Mexico. U.S. regional house, 222 W. Cevallos St., San Antonio, TX 78204.

**Mill Hill Sisters:** See Franciscan Missionaries of St. Joseph.

**Minim Daughters of Mary Immaculate, C.F.M.M.:** Founded 1886, in Mexico; in U.S., 1926. General motherhouse, Leon, Guanajuato, Mexico; U.S. address, Our Lady of Lourdes High School, Box 1865, Nogales, AZ 85621.

**Misericordia Sisters, S.M.:** Founded 1848, in Canada; in U.S., 1887. General motherhouse, 12435 Ave. Misericorde, Montreal H4J 2J3, Canada; U.S. address, 820 Jungles Ave., Aurora, IL 60505. Social work with unwed mothers and their children; hospital work.

**Mission Helpers of the Sacred Heart, M.H.S.H.:** Founded 1890, in U.S. General motherhouse, 1001 W. Joppa Rd., Baltimore, MD 21204. Religious education, evangelization.

**Missionary Catechists of the Sacred Hearts of Jesus and Mary (Violetas), M.C.:** Founded 1918, in Mexico; in U.S., 1943. Motherhouse, Tlalpan, Mexico; U.S. address, 805 Liberty St., Victoria, TX 77901.

**Missionary Daughters of the Most Pure Heart of Mary, M.D.P.V.M.:** Founded in Mexico; in U.S., 1916. Address: 919 N. 9th St., Kingsville, TX 78363.

**Mother of God, Missionary Sisters of the, M.S.M.G.:** Byzantine, Ukrainian Rite, Stamford. Motherhouse, 711 N. Franklin St., Philadelphia, PA 19123.

**Mother of God, Sisters Poor Servants of the, S.M.G.:** Founded 1869, in London, England; in U.S., 1947. General motherhouse, Maryfield, Roehampton, London. U.S. address: Maryfield Nursing Home, Greensboro Rd., High Point, NC 27260. Hospital, educational work.

**Nazareth, Poor Sisters of:** Founded in England; U.S. foundation, 1924. General motherhouse, Hammersmith, London, England; U.S. novitiate, 3333 Manning Ave., Los Angeles, CA 90064. Social services, education.

**Notre Dame, School Sisters of, S.S.N.D.:** Founded 1833, in Germany; in U.S., 1847. General motherhouse, Rome, Italy. U.S. provinces: 1233 N. Marshall St., Milwaukee, WI 53202; 6401 N. Charles St., Baltimore, MD 21212; 320 E. Ripa Ave., St. Louis, MO 63125; 170 Good Counsel Dr., Mankato, MN 56001; 345 Belden Hill Rd., Wilton, CT 06897; P.O. Box 227275, Dallas, TX 75222; 1431 Euclid Ave., Berwyn, IL 60402.

**Notre Dame, Sisters of, S.N.D.:** Founded 1850, at Coesfeld, Germany; in U.S., 1874. General motherhouse, Rome, Italy. U.S. provinces: 13000 Auburn Rd., Chardon, OH 44024; 1601 Dixie Highway, Covington, KY 41011; 3837 Secor Rd., Toledo, OH 43623; 1776 Hendrix Ave., Thousand Oaks, CA 91360.

**Notre Dame, Sisters of the Congregation of, C.N.D.:** Founed 1658, in Canada by St. Marguerite Bourgeoys; in U.S., 1860. General motherhouse, Montreal, Que., Canada; U.S. province, 223 West Mountain Rd., Ridgefield, CT 06877. Education.

**Notre Dame de Namur, Sisters of, S.N.D.:** Founded 1803, in France; in U.S., 1840. General motherhouse, Rome, Italy. U.S. provinces: 400 The Fenway, Boston, MA 02115; 30 Jeffrey's Neck Rd., Ipswich, MA 01938; 468 Poquonock Ave., Windsor, CT 06095; 1531 Greenspring Valley Rd., Stevenson, MD 21153; 305 Cable St., Baltimore, MD 21210; 701 E. Columbia Ave., Cincinnati, OH 45215; 14800 Bohlman Rd., Saratoga, CA 95070; Base Communities Province, 3037 Fourth St. N.E., Washington, DC 20017. Educational work.

**Notre Dame de Sion, Congregation of, N.D.S.:** Founded 1843, in France; in U.S., 1892. Generalate, Rome, Italy; U.S. province, 349 Westminster Rd., Brooklyn, NY 11218. Creation of better understanding and relations between Christians and Jews.

**Notre Dame Sisters:** Founded 1853, in Czechoslovakia; in U.S., 1910. General motherhouse, Javornik, Czech Republic; U.S. motherhouse, 3501 State St., Omaha, NE 68112. Educational work.

**Oblates of the Mother of Orphans, O.M.O:** Founded 1945, in Italy. General motherhouse, Milan,

Italy. U.S. address, 20 E. 72nd St., New York, NY 10021.

**Our Lady of Charity, North American Union of Sisters of, Eudist Sisters (Sisters of Our Lady of Charity of the Refuge), N.A.U.-O.L.C.:** Founded 1641, in Caen, France, by St. John Eudes; in U.S., 1855. Autonomous houses were federated in 1944 and in May, 1978, the North American Union of the Sisters of Our Lady of Charity was established. General motherhouse and administrative center, 103 S. Bowman Rd., Box 327, Wisconsin Dells, WI 53965. Primarily devoted to re-education and rehabilitation of women and girls in residential and non-residential settings.

Independent houses: 1125 Malvern Ave., Hot Springs, AR 71901; 620 Roswell Rd. N.W., Carrollton, OH 44615; 4500 W. Davis St., Dallas, TX 75211.

**Our Lady of Sorrows, Sisters of, O.L.S.:** Founded 1839, in Italy; in U.S., 1947. General motherhouse, Rome, Italy; U.S. headquarters, 9894 Norris Ferry Rd., Shreveport, LA 71106.

**Our Lady of the Garden, Sisters of, O.L.G.:** Founded 1829, in Italy, by St. Anthony Mary Gianelli. Motherhouse, Rome, Italy; U.S. address, 67 Round Hill Rd., Middletown, CT 06457.

**Our Lady of Victory Missionary Sisters, O.L.V.M.:** Founded 1922, in U.S. Motherhouse, Victory Noll, Box 109, Huntington, IN 46750. Educational, social work.

**Pallottine Missionary Sisters (Missionary Sisters of the Catholic Apostolate), S.A.C.:** Founded in Rome, 1838; in U.S., 1912. Generalate, Rome, Italy; U.S. provincialate, 15270 Old Halls Ferry Rd., Florissant, MO 63034.

**Pallottine Sisters of the Catholic Apostolate, C.S.A.C.:** Founded 1843, at Rome, Italy; in U.S., 1889. General motherhouse, Rome; U.S. motherhouse, St. Patrick's Villa, Harriman Heights, Harriman, NY 10926. Educational work.

**Parish Visitors of Mary Immaculate, P.V.M.I.:** Founded 1920, in New York. General motherhouse, Box 658, Monroe, NY 10950. Mission work.

**Passion of Jesus Christ, Religious of (Passionist Nuns), C.P.:** Founded 1771, in Italy, by St. Paul of the Cross; in U.S., 1910. U.S. convents: 2715 Churchview Ave., Pittsburgh, PA 15227; 631 Griffin Pond Rd., Clarks Summit, PA 18411; 8564 Crisp Rd., Whitesville, KY 42378; 1151 Donaldson Hwy., Erlanger, KY 41018; 15700 Clayton Rd., Ellisville, MO 63011. Contemplatives.

**Passionist Sisters:** See Cross and Passion, Sisters of the.

**Paul, Daughters of St. (Missionary Sisters of the Media of Communication), D.S.P.:** Founded 1915, at Alba, Piedmont, Italy; in U.S., 1932. General motherhouse, Rome, Italy; U.S. provincial house, 50 St. Paul's Ave., Boston, MA 02130. Apostolate of the communications arts.

**Paul of Chartres, Sisters of St., S.P.C.:** Founded 1696, in France. General house, Rome, Italy; U.S. address, 1300 County Rd. 492, Marquette, MI 49855.

**Perpetual Adoration of Guadalupe, Sisters of, A.P.G.:** U.S. foundation, 2403 W. Travis, San Antonio, TX 78207.

**Peter Claver, Missionary Sisters of St., S.S.P.C.:**

Founded 1894 in Austria by Bl. Maria Teresa Ledochowska; in U.S., 1914. General motherhouse, Rome, Italy; U.S. address, 667 Woods Mill Rd. S., Chesterfield, MO 63017.

**Pious Disciples of the Divine Master, P.D.D.M.:** Founded 1924 in Italy; in U.S., 1948. General motherhouse, Rome, Italy; U.S. headquarters, 60 Sunset Ave., Staten Island, NY 10314.

**Pious Schools, Sisters of, Sch. P.:** Founded 1829 in Spain; in U.S., 1954. General motherhouse, Rome, Italy; U.S. headquarters, 17601 Nordhoff St., Northridge, CA 91325.

**Poor, Little Sisters of the, L.S.P.:** Founded 1839, in France by Bl. Jeanne Jugan; in U.S., 1868. General motherhouse, St. Pern, France. U.S. provinces: 110-30 221st St., Queens Village, NY 11429; 601 Maiden Choice Lane, Baltimore, MD 21228; 80 W. Northwest Hwy., Palatine, IL 60067. Care of aged.

**Poor Clare Missionary Sisters (Misioneras Clarisas), M.C.:** Founded Mexico. General motherhouse, Rome, Italy; U.S. novitiate, 1019 N. Newhope, Santa Ana, CA 92703.

**Poor Clare Nuns:** See Franciscan Poor Clare Nuns.

**Poor Handmaids of Jesus Christ (Ancilla Domini Sisters), P.H.J.C.:** Founded 1851, in Germany by Bl. Mary Kasper; in U.S., 1868. General motherhouse, Dernbach, Westerwald, Germany; U.S. motherhouse, Ancilla Domini Convent, Donaldson, IN 46513. Educational, hospital work, social services.

**Precious Blood, Daughters of Charity of the Most:** Founded 1872, at Pagani, Italy; in U.S., 1908. General motherhouse, Rome, Italy; U.S. convent, 1482 North Ave., Bridgeport, CT 06604.

**Precious Blood, Missionary Sisters of the, C.P.S.:** Founded 1885, at Mariannhill, South Africa; in U.S., 1925. Generalate, Rome, Italy; U.S. novitiate, New Holland Ave., P.O. Box 97, Reading, PA 19607. Home and foreign mission work.

**Precious Blood, Sisters Adorers of the, A.P.B.:** Founded 1861, in Canada; in U.S., 1890. General motherhouse, Canada. U.S. autonomous monasteries: 54th St. and Fort Hamilton Pkwy., Brooklyn, NY 11219; 700 Bridge St., Manchester, NH 03104; 7408 S.E. Alder St., Portland, OR 97215; 166 State St., Portland, ME 04101; 1106 State St., Lafayette, IN 47905; 400 Pratt St., Watertown, NY 13601. Cloistered, contemplative.

**Precious Blood, Sisters of the, C.Pp.S.:** Founded 1834, in Switzerland; in U.S., 1844. Generalate, 4000 Denlinger Rd., Dayton, Ohio 45426. Education, health care, other ministries.

**Precious Blood, Sisters of the Most, C.Pp.S.:** Founded 1845, in Steinerberg, Switzerland; in U.S., 1870. General motherhouse, 204 N. Main St., O'Fallon, MO 63366. Education, other ministries.

**Presentation, Sisters of Mary of the, S.M.P.:** Founded 1829, in France; in U.S., 1903. General motherhouse, Broons, Cotes-du-Nord, France. U.S. address, Maryvale Novitiate, 11550 River Rd., Valley City, ND 58072. Educational, hospital work.

**Presentation of Mary, Sisters of the, P.M.:** Founded 1796, in France by Bl. Marie Rivier; in U.S., 1873. General motherhouse, Castel Gandolfo, Italy. U.S. provincial houses: 495 Mammoth Rd., Manchester, NH 03104; 209 Lawrence St., Methuen, MA 01844.

**Presentation of the B.V.M., Sisters of the, P.B.V.M.:** Founded 1775, in Ireland; in U.S., 1854, in San Francisco. U.S. motherhouses: 2360 Carter Rd., Dubuque, IA 52001; 880 Jackson Ave., New Windsor, NY 12553; 2340 Turk Blvd., San Francisco, CA 94118; St. Colman's Convent, Watervliet, NY 12189; 1101 32nd Ave., S. Fargo ND 58103; Presentation Convent, Aberdeen, SD 57401; 99 Church St., Leominster, MA 01453; 419 Woodrow Rd., Staten Island, NY 10312.

**Presentation of the Blessed Virgin Mary, Sisters of, of Union:** Founded in Ireland, 1775; union established in Ireland, 1976; first U.S. vice province, 1979. Generalate, Kildare, Ireland. U.S. provincialate, 729 W. Wilshire Dr., Phoenix, AZ 85007.

**Providence, Daughters of Divine, F.D.P.:** Founded 1832, Italy; in U.S., 1964. General motherhouse, Rome, Italy; U.S. address, 3100 Mumphrey Rd., Chalmette, LA 70043.

**Providence, Missionary Catechists of Divine, M.C.D.P.:** Administrative house, 2318 Castroville Rd., San Antonio, TX 78237.

**Providence, Oblate Sisters of, O.S.P.:** Founded 1829, in U.S., by Mother Mary Elizabeth Lange and Father James Joubert, S.S. First order of black nuns in U.S. General motherhouse, 701 Gun Rd., Baltimore, MD 21227. Educational work.

**Providence, Sisters of, S.P.:** Founded 1861, in Canada; in U.S., 1873. General motherhouse, Our Lady of Victory Convent, Gamelin St., Holyoke, MA 01040.

**Providence, Sisters of, S.P.:** Founded 1843, in Canada; in U.S., 1854. General motherhouse, Montreal, Canada. U.S. provinces: P.O. Box 11038, Seattle, WA 98111; 9 E. 9th Ave., Spokane, WA 99202; 353 N. River Rd., Des Plaines, IL 60616.

**Providence, Sisters of (of St. Mary-of-the-Woods), S.P.:** Founded 1806, in France; in U.S., 1840. Generalate, St. Mary-of-the-Woods, IN 47876.

**Providence, Sisters of Divine, C.D.P.:** Founded 1762, in France; in U.S., 1866. Generalate, Box 197, Helotes, TX 78023. Educational, hospital work.

**Providence, Sisters of Divine, C.D.P.:** Founded 1851, in Germany; in U.S., 1876. Generalate, Rome, Italy. U.S. provinces: 9000 Babcock Blvd., Allison Park, PA 15101; 8351 Florissant Rd., St. Louis, MO 63121; 363 Bishops Hwy., Kingston, MA 02364. Educational, hospital work.

**Providence, Sisters of Divine (of Kentucky), C.D.P.:** Founded 1762, in France; in U.S., 1889. General motherhouse, Fenetrange, France; U.S. province, St. Anne Convent, Melbourne, KY 41059. Education, social services, other ministries.

**Redeemer, Oblates of the Most Holy, O.SS.R.:** Founded 1864, in Spain. General motherhouse, Spain; U.S. foundation, 60-80 Pond St., Jamaica Plain, MA 02130.

**Redeemer, Order of the Most Holy, O.SS.R.:** Founded 1731, by St. Alphonsus Liguori; in U.S., 1957. U.S. addresses: Mother of Perpetual Help Monastery, P.O. Box 220, Esopus, NY 12429; St. Alphonsus Monastery, Liguori, MO 63057.

**Redeemer, Sisters of the Divine, S.D.R.:** Founded 1849, in Niederbronn, France; in U.S., 1912. General motherhouse, Rome, Italy; U.S. province, 999 Rock Run Road, Elizabeth, PA 15037. Educational, hospital work; care of the aged.

**Redeemer, Sisters of the Holy, C.S.R.:** Founded 1849, in Alsace; in U.S., 1924. General motherhouse, Wuerzburg, Germany; U.S. provincial house, 521 Moredon Rd., Huntingdon Valley, PA 19006. Personalized medical care in hospitals, homes for aged, private homes; retreat work.

**Reparation of the Congregation of Mary, Sisters of, S.R.C.M.:** Founded 1903, in U.S. Motherhouse, St. Zita's Villa, Monsey, NY 10952.

**Resurrection, Sisters of the, C.R.:** Founded 1891, in Italy; in U.S., 1900. General motherhouse, Rome, Italy. U.S. provinces: 7432 Talcott Ave., Chicago, IL 60631; Mt. St. Joseph, Castleton-on- Hudson, NY 12033. Education, nursing.

**Rita, Sisters of St., O.S.A.:** General motherhouse, Wurzburg, Germany. U.S. foundation, St. Monica's Convent, 3920 Green Bay Rd., Racine, WI 53404.

**Rosary, Congregation of Our Lady of the Holy, R.S.R.:** Founded 1874, in Canada; in U.S., 1899. General motherhouse, Rimouski, Que., Canada. U.S. regional house, 20 Thmas St., Portland, ME 04102. Educational work.

**Rosary, Missionary Sisters of the Holy, M.S.H.R.:** Founded 1924, in Ireland; in U.S., 1954. Motherhouse, Dublin, Ireland. U.S. regional 741 Polo Rd., Bryn Mawr, PA 19010. African missions.

**Sacrament, Missionary Sisters of the Most Blessed, M.SS.S.:** General motherhouse, Madrid, Spain; U.S. foundation: 1111 Wordin Ave., Bridgeport, CT 06605.

**Sacrament, Nuns of the Perpetual Adoration of the Blessed, A.P.:** Founded 1807 in Rome, Italy; in U.S., 1925. U.S. monasteries: 145 N. Cotton Ave., El Paso, TX 79901; 771 Ashbury St., San Francisco, CA 94117.

**Sacrament, Oblate Sisters of the Blessed, O.S.B.S.:** Founded 1935, in U.S.; motherhouse, St. Sylvester Convent, Marty, SD 57361. Care of American Indians.

**Sacrament, Servants of the Blessed, S.S.S.:** Founded 1858, in France, by St. Pierre Julien Eymard; in U.S., 1947. General motherhouse, Rome, Italy; American provincial house, 1818 Coal Pl. SE, Albuquerque, NM 87106. Contemplative.

**Sacrament, Sisters of the Blessed, for Indians and Colored People, S.B.S.:** Founded 1891, in U.S., by Bl. Katharine Drexel. General motherhouse, St. Elizabeth's Convent, Bensalem, PA 19020.

**Sacrament, Sisters of the Most Holy, M.H.S.:** Founded 1851, in France; in U.S., 1872. Generalate, 313 Corona Dr. (P.O. Box 30727), Lafayette, LA 70593.

**Sacrament, Sisters Servants of the Blessed, S.J.S.:** Founded 1904, in Mexico; in U.S., 1926. General motherhouse, Mexico; U.S. address, 215 Lomita St., El Segundo, CA 90245.

**Sacramentine Nuns (Religious of the Order of the Blessed Sacrament and Our Lady), O.S.S.:** Founded 1639, in France; in U.S., 1912. U.S. monasteries: 23 Park Ave., Yonkers, NY 10703; US 31, Conway, MI 49722. Perpetual adoration of the Holy Eucharist.

**Sacred Heart, Daughters of Our Lady of the:**

Founded 1882, in France; in U.S., 1955. General motherhouse, Rome, Italy; U.S. address, 424 E. Browning Rd., Bellmawr, NJ 08031. Educational work.

**Sacred Heart, Missionary Sisters of the (Cabrini Sisters), M.S.C.:** Founded 1880, in Italy, by St. Frances Xavier Cabrini; in U.S., 1889. General motherhouse, Rome, Italy; U.S. provincial office: 222 E. 19th St., 5B, New York, NY 10003. Educational, health, social and catechetical work.

**Sacred Heart, Religious of the Apostolate of the, R.A.:** General motherhouse, Madrid, Spain; U.S. address, 1310 W. 42nd Pl., Hialiah, FL 33012.

**Sacred Heart, Society Devoted to the, S.D.S.H.:** Founded 1940, in Hungary; in U.S., 1956. U.S. motherhouse, 9814 Sylvia Ave., Northridge, CA 91324. Educational work.

**Sacred Heart, Society of the, R.S.C.J.:** Founded 1800, in France; in U.S., 1818. Generalate, Rome, Italy. U.S. provincial house, 4389 W. Pine Blvd., St. Louis, MO 63108. Educational work.

**Sacred Heart of Jesus, Apostles of, A.S.C.J.:** Founded 1894, in Italy; in U.S., 1902. General motherhouse, Rome, Italy; U.S. motherhouse, 265 Benham St., Hamden, CT 06514. Educational, social work.

**Sacred Heart of Jesus, Handmaids of the, A.C.J.:** Founded 1877, in Spain. General motherhouse, Rome, Italy; U.S. province, 616 Coopertown Rd., Haverford, PA 19041. Educational, retreat work.

**Sacred Heart of Jesus, Missionary Sisters of the Most (Hiltrup), M.S.C.:** Founded 1899, in Germany; in U.S., 1908. General motherhouse, Rome, Italy; U.S. province, 51 Seminary Rd., Reading, PA 19605. Education, health care, pastoral ministry.

**Sacred Heart of Jesus, Oblate Sisters of the, O.S.H.J.:** Founded 1894; in U.S., 1949. General motherhouse, Rome, Italy; U.S. headquarters, 50 Warner Rd., Hubbard, Ohio 44425. Educational, social work.

**Sacred Heart of Jesus, Servants of the Most, S.S.C.J.:** Founded 1894, in Poland; in U.S., 1959. General motherhouse, Cracow, Poland; U.S. address, 866 Cambria St., Cresson, PA 16630. Education, health care, social services.

**Sacred Heart of Jesus, Sisters of the, S.S.C.J.:** Founded 1816, in France; in U.S., 1903. General motherhouse, St. Jacut, Brittany, France; U.S. provincial house, 5922 Blanco Rd., San Antonio, TX 78216. Educational, hospital, domestic work.

**Sacred Heart of Jesus and of the Poor, Servants of the (Mexican), S.S.H.J.P.:** Founded 1885, in Mexico; in U.S., 1907. General motherhouse, Apartado 92, Puebla, Pue., Mexico; U.S. address, 3310 S. Zapata Hwy, Laredo, TX 78043.

**Sacred Heart of Jesus and Our Lady of Guadalupe, Missionaries of the:** U.S. address, 1212 E. Euclid Ave., Arlington Heights, IL 60660.

**Sacred Heart of Jesus for Reparation, Congregation of the Handmaids of the, A.R.:** Founded 1918, in Italy; in U.S., 1958. U.S. address, Sunshine Park, R.D. 3, Steubenville, Ohio 43952.

**Sacred Heart of Mary, Religious of the, R.S.H.M.:** Founded 1848, in France; in U.S., 1877. Generalate, Rome, Italy. U.S. provinces; 50 Wilson Park Dr., Tarrytown, NY 10591; 441 N. Garfield Ave., Montebellow, CA 90640.

**Sacred Hearts, Sisters of the Holy Union of the,**

**S.U.S.C.:** Founded 1826, in France; in U.S., 1886. Generalate, Rome, Italy. U.S. provinces: 550 Rock St., Fall River, MA 02720; Box 993, Main St., Groton, MA 01450. Varied ministries.

**Sacred Hearts and of Perpetual Adoration, Sisters of the, SS.CC.:** Founded 1797, in France; in U.S., 1908. General motherhouse, Rome, Italy; U.S. provinces: 1120 Fifth Ave., Honolulu, Hawaii 96816 (Pacific); 419 Hood St., Fall River, MA 02720 (East Coast). Varied ministries.

**Sacred Hearts of Jesus and Mary, Sisters of the, S.H.J.M.:** Established 1953, in U.S. General motherhouse, Essex, England; U.S. address, 844 Don Carlo Dr., El Cerrito, CA 94530.

**Savior, Company of the, C.S.:** Founded 1952, in Spain; in U.S., 1962. General motherhouse, Madrid, Spain; U.S. foundation, 820 Clinton Ave., Bridgeport, CT 06604.

**Savior, Sisters of the Divine, S.D.S.:** Founded 1888, in Italy; in U.S., 1895. General motherhouse, Rome, Italy; U.S. province, 4311 N. 100th St., Milwaukee, WI 53222. Educational, hospital work.

**Social Service, Sisters of, S.S.S.:** Founded in Hungary, 1923, by Sr. Margaret Slachta. U.S. generalate, 296 Summit Ave., Buffalo, NY 14214. Social work.

**Social Service, Sisters of, of Los Angeles, S.S.S.:** Founded 1908, in Hungary; in U.S., 1926. General motherhouse, 1120 Westchester Pl., Los Angeles, CA 90019.

**Teresa of Jesus, Society of St., S.T.J.:** Founded 1876, in Spain; in U.S., 1910. General motherhouse, Rome, Italy; U.S. provincial house, 18080 St. Joseph's Way, Covington, LA 70433.

**Thomas of Villanova, Congregation of Sisters of St., S.S.T.V.:** Founded 1661, in France; in U.S., 1948. General motherhouse, Neuilly-sur-Seine, France; U.S. foundation W. Rocks Rd., Norwalk, CT 06851.

**Trinity, Missionary Servants of the Most Blessed, M.S.B.T.:** Founded 1912, in U.S., by Very Rev. Thomas A. Judge. General motherhouse, 3501 Solly Ave., Philadelphia, PA 19136. Educational, social work; health services.

**Trinity, Sisters Oblates to the Blessed, O.B.T.:** Founded 1923, in Italy. U.S. novitiate, Beekman Rd., Hopewell Junction, NY 12533.

**Trinity, Sisters of the Most Holy, O.Ss.T.:** Founded 1198, in Rome; in U.S., 1920. General motherhouse, Rome, Italy; U.S. address, Immaculate Conception Province, 21281 Chardon Rd., Euclid, Ohio 44117. Educational work.

**Trinity, Society of of Our Lady of the Most Holy, S.O.L.T.:** Motherhouse, P.O. Box 189 Skidmore, TX 78389.

**Ursula of the Blessed Virgin, Society of the Sisters of St., S.U.:** Founded 1606, in France; in U.S., 1902. General motherhouse, France; U.S. novitiate, 139 S. Mill Rd., Rhinebeck, NY 12572. Educational work.

**Ursuline Nuns (Roman Union), O.S.U.:** Founded 1535, in Italy; in U.S., 1727. Generalate, Rome, Italy. U.S. provinces: 323 E. 198th St., Bronx, NY 10458; 210 Glennon Heights Rd., Crystal City, MO 63019; 639 Angela Dr., Santa Rosa, CA 95401; 45 Lowder St., Dedham, MA 02026.

**Ursuline Nuns of the Congregation of Paris, O.S.U.:** Founded 1535, in Italy; in U.S., 1727, in

New Orleans. U.S. motherhouses: 20860 St, Rte 251, St. Martin, OH 45118; 901 E. Miami St., Paola, KS 66071; 3115 Lexington Rd., Louisville, KY 40206; 2600 Lander Rd., Cleveland, O. 44124; Maple Mount, KY 42356; 4045 Indian Rd., Toledo, OH 43606; 4250 Shields Rd., Canfield, OH 44406; 1339 E. McMillan St., Cincinnati, OH 45206.

**Ursuline Sisters of the Congregation of Tildonk, Belgium, O.S.U.:** Founded 1535, in Italy; Tildonk congregation, 1832; in U.S., 1924. Generalate, Brussels, Belgium; U.S. address, 81-15 Utopia Parkway, Jamaica, NY 11432. Educational, foreign mission work.

**Ursuline Sisters of Belleville, O.S.U.:** Founded 1535, in Italy; in U.S., 1910; established as diocesan community, 1983. Central house, 1026 N. Douglas Ave., Belleville, IL 62221. Educational work.

**Ursuline Sisters (Irish Ursuline Union), O.S.U.:** Generalate, Dublin, Ireland; U.S. address, 1973 Torch Hill Rd., Columbus, GA 31903.

**Venerini Sisters, Religious, M.P.V.:** Founded 1685, in Italy; in U.S., 1909. General motherhouse, Rome, Italy; U.S. provincialate; 23 Edward St., Worcester, MA 01605.

**Vincent de Paul, Sisters:** See Charity of St. Vincent de Paul, Sisters of.

**Visitation Nuns, V.H.M.:** Founded 1610, in France; in U.S. (Georgetown, DC), 1799. Contemplative, educational work. Two federations in U.S.

First Federation of North America. Major pontifical enclosure. Pres., Mother Mary Jozefa Kowalewski, Monastery of the Visitation, Snellville, GA 30278. Addresses of monasteries belonging to the federation: 2300 Springhill Ave., Mobile, AL 36607; Beach Rd., Tyringham, MA 01264; 12221

Bievenue Rd, Rockville, VA 23146; 5820 City Ave., Philadelphia, PA 19131; 1745 Parkside Blvd., Toledo, OH 43607; 2055 Ridgedale Dr., Snellville, GA 30278.

Second Federation of North America. Constitutional enclosure. Pres., Rev. Mother Mary Philomena Tisinger, Visitation Monastery of Georgetown, Washington, DC 20007. Addresses of monasteries belonging to the federation: 1500 35th St., Washington, DC 20007; 3020 N. Ballas Rd., St. Louis, MO 63131; 200 E. Second St., Frederick, MD 21701; Mt. St. Chantal Monastery of the Visitation, Wheeling, WV 26003; 8902 Ridge Blvd., Brooklyn, NY 11209; 2936 36th St., Rock Island, IL 61201; 2455 Visitation Dr., Mendota Heights, St. Paul, MN 55120.

**Visitation of the Congregation of the Immaculate Heart of Mary, Sisters of the, S.V.M.:** Founded 1952, in U.S. Motherhouse, 2950 Kaufmann Ave., Dubuque, IA 52001. Educational work, parish ministry.

**Vocationist Sisters (Sisters of the Divine Vocations):** Founded 1921, in Italy; in U.S., 1967 General motherhouse, Naples, Italy; U.S. foundation, Perpetual Help Nursery, 172 Broad St., Newark, NJ 07104.

**Wisdom, Daughters of, D.W.:** Founded 1703, in France, by St. Louis Marie Grignion de Montfort; in U.S., 1904. General motherhouse, Vendee, France; U.S. province, 385 S. Ocean Ave., Islip, NY 11751. Education, health care, parish ministry, social services.

**Xaverian Missionary Society of Mary, Inc., X.M.M.:** Founded 1945, in Italy; in U.S., 1954. General motherhouse, Parma, Italy; U.S. address, 242 Salisbury St., Worcester, MA 01609.

# ORGANIZATIONS OF RELIGIOUS

## Conferences

Conferences of major superiors of religious institutes, dating from the 1950s, are encouraged by the Code of Canon Law (Code 708) "so that joining forces they can work toward the achievement of the purpose of their individual institutes more fully, transact common business and foster suitable coordination and cooperation with conferences of bishops and also with individual bishops." Statutes of the conferences must be approved by the Holy See "by which alone they are erected" (Canon 709). Conferences have been established in 23 countries of Europe, 14 in North and Central America, 10 in South America, 35 in Africa and 19 in Asia and Oceania.

Listed below are U.S. and international conferences.

**Conference of Major Superiors of Men:** Founded in 1956; canonically established Sept. 12, 1957. Membership, 269 major superiors representing institutes with a combined membership of approximately 24,000. President, Very Rev. Joseph Levesque, C.M.; Bro. Joseph Klein, F.M.S., president-elect; executive director, Rev. Gregory Reisert, O.F.M. Cap. National office: 8808 Cameron St., Silver Spring, MD 20910.

**Leadership Conference of Women Religious:** Founded in 1956; canonically established Dec. 12, 1959. Membership, 976 (Dec. 31, 1994), representing approximately 500 religious institutes. President,

Sister Nancy Schreck, O.S.F.; executive director, Sister Margaret Cafferty, P.B.V.M. National office: 8808 Cameron St., Silver Spring, MD 20910.

**Council of Major Superiors of Women Religious:** Canonically erected June 13, 1992. Membership, 151 superiors of 104 religious congregations. Chairperson, Mother Vincent Marie Finnegan, O.C.D. National office: P.O. Box 4467, Washington, D.C. 20017.

**International Union of Superiors General (Women):** Established Dec. 8, 1965; approved, 1967. General secretary, Sister Pamela Dowdell, F.M.M. Address: Piazza di Ponte S. Angelo, 28, 00186, Rome, Italy.

**Union of Superiors General (Men):** Established in 1957. President, Father Camillo Maccise, O.C.D; general secretary, Bro. Lino Da Campo, F.S.F. Address: Via dei Penitenzieri 19, 00193 Rome, Italy.

**Latin American Confederation of Religious** (Confederacion Latinoamericana de Religiosos — CLAR): Established in 1959; statutes reformed in 1984. President, Sister Elza Ribeiro, H.P.G.; secretary general, Pedro Acevedo, F.S.C. Address: Calle 64 No 10-45, Piso 5to. Apartado Aéreo 56804, Santafé de Bogotá, Colombia.

**Union of European Conferences of Major Superiors:** Established Dec. 25, 1983. President, Bro. Jacques Scholte; secretary, Sr. Maria Luz Galvan, S.C.J., Avenida Alfonso XIII, 97, 28016 Madrid, Spain.

### Other Organizations

**Institute on Religious Life** (1974). To foster more effective understanding and implementation of teachings of the Church on religious life, promote vocations to religious life and the priesthood, and promote growth in sanctity of all the faithful according to their state in life. Executive director, Rev. James Downey. National office, P.O. Box 41007, Chicago, IL 60641.

**National Assembly of Religious Brothers** (1972): To publicize the unique vocations of brothers, to further communication among brothers and provide liaison with various organizations of the Church. Executive secretary, Sr. Emily Wollschlager, S.S.N.D. National office, 1337 West Ohio, Chicago, IL 60622.

**National Black Sisters' Conference** (1968): Black Catholic women religious and associates networking to provide support through prayer, study, solidarity and programs. President, Sr. Patricia J. Chappell, S.N.D.de N. Address: 3027 4th St. NE, Washington, DC 20017.

**National Conference of Vicars for Religious** (1967):

National organization of diocesan officials concerned with relations between their respective dioceses and religious communities engaged therein. President, Sr. Therese Sullivan, S.P., 9292 Broadway, Merrillville, IN 46410; secretary, Sr. Doris Rauenhorst, O.P., 244 Dayton Ave., St. Paul, MN 55102.

**National Religious Vocation Conference (NRVC)** (1988, with merger of National Sisters Vocation Conference and National Conference of Religious Vocation Directors): Service organization of men and women committed to the fostering and discernment of vocations, Executive director, Sr. Catherine Bertrand, S.S.N.D. Address: 1603 S. Michigan Ave., No. 400, Chicago, IL 60616.

**Religious Formation Conference** (1953): Originally the Sister Formation Conference; membership includes women and men Religious and non-canonical groups. Facilitates the ministry of formation, both initial and ongoing, in religious communities. Executive director, Sister Jane Finnerty, O.S.U. National office: 8820 Cameron St., Silver Spring, MD 20910.

# SECULAR INSTITUTES

(Sources: Almanac survey; United States Conference of Secular Institutes; Annuario Pontificio.

Secular institutes are societies of men and women living in the world who dedicate themselves to observe the evangelical counsels and to carry on apostolic works suitable to their talents and opportunities in the areas of their everyday life.

"Secular institutes are not religious communities but they carry with them in the world a profession of evangelical counsels which is genuine and complete, and recognized as such by the Church. This profession confers a consecration on men and women, laity and clergy, who reside in the world. For this reason they should chiefly strive for total self-dedication to God, one inspired by perfect charity. These institutes should preserve their proper and particular character, a secular one, so that they may everywhere measure up successfully to that apostolate which they were designed to exercise, and which is both in the world and, in a sense, of the world" (*Decree on the Appropriate Renewal of Religious Life*, No. 11; Second Vatican Council).

Secular institutes are under the jurisdiction of the Congregation for Institutes of Consecrated Life and Societies of Apostolic Life. General legislation concerning them is contained in Canons 710 to 730 of the Code of Canon Law.

A secular institute reaches maturity in several stages. It begins as an association of the faithful, technically called a pious union, with the approval of a local bishop. Once it has proved its viability, he can give it the status of an institute of diocesan right, in accordance with norms and permission emanating from the Congregation for Institutes of Consecrated Life and Societies of Apostolic Life. On issuance of a separate decree from this congregation, an institute of diocesan right becomes an institute of pontifical right.

Secular institutes, which originated in the latter part of the 18th century, were given full recognition and approval by Pius XII Feb. 2, 1947, in the apostolic

constitution *Provida Mater Ecclesia*. On Mar. 25 of the same year a special commission for secular institutes was set up within the Congregation for Religious. Institutes were commended and confirmed by Pius XII in a motu proprio of Mar. 12, 1948, and were the subject of a special instruction issued a week later, Mar. 19, 1948.

The **World Conference of Secular Institutes (CMIS)** was approved by the Vatican May 23, 1974. Address: Via Tullio Levi-Civita 5, 00146 Rome, Italy.

The **United States Conference of Secular Institutes (USCSI)** was established following the organization of the World Conference of Secular Institutes in Rome. Its membership is open to all canonically erected secular institutes with members living in the United States. The conference was organized to offer secular institutes an opportunity to exchange experiences, to do research in order to help the Church carry out its mission, and to search for ways and means to make known the existence of secular institutes in the U.S. Address: P.O. Box 4556, 12th St. NE, Washington, DC 20017.

### Institutes in the U.S.

**Apostolic Oblates:** Founded in Rome, Italy, 1947; established in the U.S., 1962; for women. Approved as a secular institute of pontifical right Dec. 8, 1994. Addresses: 2125 W. Walnut Ave., Fullerton, CA 92633; 6762 Western Ave., Omaha, NE 68132; 730 E. 87th St., Brooklyn, NY 11236.

**Caritas Christi:** Originated in Marseilles, 1937; for women. Established as a secular institute of pontifical right Mar. 19, 1955. Address: P.O. Box 5162, River Forest, IL 60305. International membership.

**Company of St. Paul:** Originated in Milan, Italy, 1920; for lay people and priests. Approved as a secular institute of pontifical right June 30, 1950. Address: Rev. Stuart Sandberg, 52 Davis Ave., White Plains, NY 10605.

**Cruzados de Santa Maria:** Founded 1947 in

Madrid, Spain; approved as a secular institute of diocesan right, 1988; for men. Address: 1231 Otis St. NE, Washington, DC 20017.

**Diocesan Laborer Priests:** Founded in Spain 1885; approved as a secular institute of pontifical right, 1952. The specific aim of the institute is the promotion, sustenance and cultivation of apostolic, religious and priestly vocations. Address: Rev. Rutilio J. del Riego, 3706 15th St. N.E., Washington, DC 20017.

**Don Bosco Volunteers:** Founded 1917 by Bl. Philip Rinaldi; for women. Approved as a secular institute of pontifical right Aug. 5, 1978. Follow spirituality and charism of St. John Bosco. Address: Rev. Paul P. Avallone, S.D.B., Don Bosco Volunteers, 202 Union Ave., Paterson, NJ 07502.

**Don Bosco Secular Institute** (for men): Same address as above.

**Fr. Kolbe Missionaries of the Immaculata:** Founded in Bologna, Italy, in 1954, by Fr. Luigi Faccenda, O.F.M. Conv.; for women. Approved as a secular institute of pontifical right Mar. 25, 1992. Live the fullness of baptismal consecration, strive for perfect charity and promote the knowledge and veneration of Mary. Address: 531 E. Merced Ave., West Covina, CA 91790.

**Handmaids of Divine Mercy:** Founded in Bari, Italy, 1951; for women. Approved as an institute of pontifical right 1972. Address: Elisabeth Gagliano, 2943 Philip Ave., Bronx, NY 10465.

**Institute of Secular Missionaries:** Founded in Vitoria, Spain, 1939; for women. Approved as a secular institute, 1955. Address: 2710 Ruberg Ave., Cincinnati, OH 45211, Att. E. Dilger.

**Institute of the Heart of Jesus:** Originated in France Feb. 2, 1791; restored Oct. 29, 1918; for diocesan priests and laity. Received final approval from the Holy See as a secular institute of pontifical right Feb. 2, 1952. U.S. address, Rev. Francis X. Mawn, St. Rose Rectory, 601 Broadway, Chelsea, MA 02150.

**Lay Missionaries of the Passion:** Founded in Catania, Sicily; for women. Approved as a secular institute of diocesan right July 1, 1980. Address: Dorothy Armstrong, 633 Main St., Dicksen City, PA 18519.

**Little Franciscan Family:** Founded in Italy, 1929, by Father Ireneo Mazzotti, O.F.M.; for women. Approved as a secular institute of pontifical right, 1983. Address: Julie Curley, 319 Main St., Cromwell, CT 06416.

**Mission of Our Lady of Bethany:** Founded in France, 1948; for women. Approved as a secular institute of diocesan right, 1965. Address: Estelle Nichols, 7 Locksley St., Jamaica Plain, MA 02130.

**Missionaries of the Kingship of Christ the King:** Under this title are included three distinct and juridically separate institutes founded by Agostino Gemelli, O.F.M. (1878-1959) and Armida Barelli (1882-1952). Two are active in the U.S.

(1) Women Missionaries of the Kingship of Christ — Founded in 1919, in Italy; definitively approved as an institute of pontifical right 1953. U.S. branch established 1950.

(2) Men Missionaries of the Kingship of Christ — Founded 1928, in Italy, as an institute of diocesan right. U.S. branch established 1962.

Addresses: Rev. Thomas Hartle, O.F.M., 459 River Rd., Andover, MA 01310 (for Men Missionaries); Rev. Dominic Monti, O.F.M., 10400 Lorain Ave., Silver Spring, MD 20901 (for Women Missionaries).

**Nuestra Senora de la Altagracia:** Founded in Dominican Republic, 1956; approved as a secular institute of diocesan right, 1964; for women. Address: Ms. Christiana Perez, 129 Van Sislen Ave., Brooklyn, NY 11207.

**Oblate Missionaries of Mary Immaculate:** Founded, 1952; approved as a secular institute of pontifical right 1984; for women. Address: Oblate Missionaries of Mary Immaculate, P.O. Box 303, Manville, RI 02838. International membership.

**Opus Spiritus Sancti:** Originated in West Germany, 1952; for diocesan priests and unmarried permanent deacons. Formally acknowledged by Rome as a secular institute of diocesan right, 1977. Adress: Rev. James D. McCormick, P.O. Box 316, West Bend, IA 50597.

**St. Francis de Sales Secular Institute:** Founded in Vienna, Austria, 1940; for women. Pontifical right, 1964. Addresses: Rev. John J. Conmy, 1120 Blue Bell Rd., Childs, MD 21916; Joan Bereswill, 3503 Jean St., Fairfax, VA 22030.

**Schoenstatt Sisters of Mary:** Originated in Schoenstatt, Germany, 1926; for women. Established as a secular institute of diocesan right May 20, 1948; of pontifical right Oct. 18, 1948. Addresses: W. 284 N. 404 Cherry Lane, Waukesha, WI 53188; House Schoenstatt, HCO 1, Box 100, Rockport, TX 78382.

**Secular Institute of Pius X:** Originated in Manchester, N.H., 1940; for priests and laymen. Approved as a secular institute, 1959. Also admits married couples and unmarried men as associate members. Addresses: C.P. 7731, Charlesbourg, P.Que. G1G 5W6, Canada; Roger Duchesneu, 27 Cove St., Goffstown, NH 03345.

**Secular Institute of Schoenstatt Fathers:** Founded in Germany by Fr. Joseph Kentenich in 1965; for priests serving the International Schoenstatt Movement in over 20 countries. Approved as a secular institute of pontifical right, June 24, 1988. Address: W. 284 N. 746 Cherry Lane, Waukesha, WI 53188.

**Servitium Christi Secular Institute of the Blessed Sacrament:** Founded in Holland, 1952; for women. Approved as a secular institute of diocesan right May 8, 1963. Address: Miss Elaine Kozlowski, 1209 Greenwood Ave., Pueblo, CO 81003.

**Society of Our Lady of the Way:** Originated, 1936; for women. Approved as a secular institute of pontifical right Jan. 3, 1953. Addresses: 2339 N. Catalina, Los Angeles, CA 90027; 80 Manhattan Ave., Jersey City, NJ 07307.

**Voluntas Dei Institute:** Originated in Canada, 1958 by Father L. M. Parent; for secular priests and laymen (with married couples as associates). Approved as a secular institute of pontifical right, July 12, 1987. Established in 21 countries. Address: Rev. Michael Craig, 4257 Tazewell Terr., Burtonsville, MD 20866.

The *Annuario Pontificio* lists the following **secular institutes of pontifical right** which are not established in the U.S.:

**For men:** Christ the King; Institute of Our Lady

of Life; Institute of Prado; Priests of the Sacred Heart of Jesus.

**For women:** Alliance in Jesus through Mary; Apostles of the Sacred Heart; Catechists of Mary, Virgin and Mother; Catechists of the Sacred Heart of Jesus (Ukrainian); Cordimarian Filiation; Daughters of the Nativity of Mary; Daughters of the Queen of the Apostles; Daughters of the Sacred Heart; Evangelical Crusade; Faithful Servants of Jesus; Handmaids of Our Mother of Mercy; Institute of the Blessed Virgin Mary (della Strada); Institute of Notre Dame du Travail; Institute of Our Lady of Life; Institute of St. Boniface; Little Apostles of Charity;

Life and Peace in Christ Jesus; Missionaries of Royal Priesthood; Missionaries of the Sick; Oblates of Christ the King; Oblates of the Sacred Heart of Jesus; Servants of Jesus the Priest; Servite Secular Institute; Union of the Daughters of God; Workers of Divine Love; Workers of the Cross; Handmaids of Holy Church; Augustinian Auxiliary Missionaries; Heart of Jesus; Apostolic Missionaries of Charity; Combonian Secular Missionaries; Missionaries of the Gospel; Secular Servants of Jesus Christ Priest; Women of Schoenstatt; Missionaries of Infinite Love.

## Associations

**Caritas:** Originated in New Orleans, 1950; for women. Follow guidelines of secular institutes. Small self-supporting groups who live and work among the poor and oppressed; work in Louisiana and Guatemala. Address: Box 308, Abita Springs, LA 70420.

**Daughters of Our Lady of Fatima:** Originated in Lansdowne, Pa., 1949; for women. Received diocesan approval, Jan., 1952. Address: Fatima House, Rolling Hills Rd., Ottsville, PA 18942.

**Focolare Movement:** Founded in Trent, Italy, in 1943, by Chiara Lubich; for men and women. Approved as an association of the faithful, 1962. It is not a secular institute by statute; however, vows are observed by its totally dedicated core membership of 4,000 who live in small communities called Focolare (Italian word for "hearth") centers. There are 17 resident centers in the U.S. and four in Canada. GEN (New Generation) is the youth organization of the movement. An estimated 75,000 are affiliated with the movement in the U.S. and Canada; 2,000,000, worldwide. Publications include *Living City,* monthly; *GEN II* and *GEN III* for young people and children. Five week-long summer conventions, called "Mariapolis" ("City of Mary"), are held an-

nually. Address for information: P.O. Box 496, New York, NY 10021 (indicate men's or women's branch).

**Jesus-Caritas Fraternity of Priests:** An international association of diocesan priests who strive to combine an active life with a contemplative calling by their membership in small fraternities. U.S. address for information: Rev. Paul M. Esser, St. Paul the Apostle Parish, 5700 Washington Ave., Racine, WI 53406.

**Franciscan Missionaries of Jesus Crucified:** Founded in New York in 1987; separate communities for women and men. Approved as an association of the faithful Jan. 7, 1992. To provide an opportunity for persons with disabilities to live a life of total consecration in the pursuit of holiness in the apostolate of service to the Church and to those who suffer in any way. Address: Louise D. Principe, F.M.J.C., 400 Central Ave., Apt. 3D, Albany, NY 12206.

**Madonna House Apostolate:** Originated in Toronto, Canada, 1930; for priests and lay persons. Public association of the Christian faithful. Address: Madonna House, Combermere, Ontario, Canada KOJ 1LO — Jean Fox (women), Albert Osterberger (men), Rev. Robert Pelton (priests). International membership and missions.

**Opus Spiritus Sancti:** Originated in Germany; for women. An association of the faithful. Address: Theresa Berger, 415 E. Oak St., Algona, IA 50511.

**Pax Christi:** Lay institute of men and women dedicated to witnessing to Christ, with special emphasis on service to the poor in Mississippi. Addresses: St. Francis Center, 708 Ave. I, Greenwood, MS 38930; LaVerna House, 2108 Altawoods Blvd., Jackson, MS 39204.

**Rural Parish Workers of Christ the King:** Founded in 1942; for women. A secular institute of the Archdiocese of St. Louis. Dedicated to the glory of God in service of neighbor, especially in rural areas. Address: Box 552, Rt. 1, Cadet, MO 63630.

**Teresian Institute:** Founded in Spain 1911 by Pedro Poveda. Approved as an association of the faithful of pontifical right Jan. 11, 1924. Mailing Address: 3400 S. W. 99th Ave., Miami, FL 33165.

**Holy Family Institute** (aggregated to the Society of St. Paul) was founded by Fr. James Alberione in 1963 for married couples who wish to commit themselves to seeking evangelical perfection in marriage; definitively approved by the Holy See, 1993. Address: 9531 Akron-Canfield Rd., Box 498, Canfield, OH 44406.

# SECULAR ORDERS

Secular orders (commonly called third orders) are societies of the faithful living in the world who seek to deepen their Christian life and apostolic commitment in association with and according to the spirit of various religious institutes. The orders are called "third" because their foundation usually followed the establishment of the first and second religious orders with which they are associated.

**Augustine, Third Order Secular of St.:** Founded, 13th century; approved Nov. 7, 1400.

**Carmelites, Lay (Third Order of Our Lady of**

**Mt. Carmel):** Rule for laity approved by Pope Nicholas V, Oct. 7, 1452; new statutes, January, 1991. Addresses (Lay Carmelite Office): 8501 Bailey Rd., Darien, IL 60561; P.O. Box 613, Williamston, MA 01267; P.O. Box 27, Tappan, NY 10983. Approximately 270 communities and 10,000 members in the U.S. and Canada.

**Carmelites, The Secular Order of Discalced** (formerly the Third Order Secular of the Blessed Virgin Mary of Mt Carmel and of St. Teresa of Jesus): Rule based on the Carmelite reform established by St.

Teresa and St. John of the Cross, 16th century; approved Mar. 23, 1594. Revised rule approved May 10, 1979. Office of National Secretariat, U.S.A.; P.O. Box 3420, San Jose, CA 95156. Approximately 24,445 members throughout the world; 130 groups/communities and 5,200 members in the U.S. and Canada.

**Dominican Laity:** Founded in the 13th century. Addresses of provincial coordinators: 487 Michigan Ave. N.E., Washington, DC 20017; 1909 S. Ashland Ave., Chicago, IL 60608; 5890 Birch Ct., Oakland, CA 94618; 3600 Travis, Houston, TX 77002.

**Franciscan Order, Secular (SFO):** Founded, 1209 by St. Francis of Assisi; approved Aug. 30, 1221. National Minister, Richard Morton, SFO, 3191 71st St. E., Inver Grove Heights, MN 55076. *Tau USA,* quarterly. Approximately 780,000 throughout the world; 22,000 in U.S.

**Mary, Third Order of:** Founded, Dec. 8, 1850; rule approved by the Holy See, 1857. Addresses of provincial directors: Marist College, 220 Taylor St. N.E., Washington, DC 20017; Marist Fathers, 518 Pleasant St., Framingham, MA 01701; Marist Fathers, 2335 Warring St., Berkeley, CA 94704. Approximately 14,000 in the world, 5,600 in U.S.

**Mary, Secular Order of Servants of (Servite):** Founded, 1233; approved, 1304. Revised rule approved 1986. Address: National Assistant for the Secular Order, 3121 W. Jackson Blvd., Chicago, IL 60612.

**Mercy, Secular Third Order of Our Lady of (Mercedarian):** Founded, 1219 by St. Peter Nolasco; approved the same year.

**Norbert, Third Order of St.:** Founded, 1122 by St. Norbert; approved by Pope Honorius II, 1126.

**Trinity, Third Order Secular of the Most:** Founded 1198; approved, 1219.

**Oblates of St. Benedict** are lay persons affiliated with a Benedictine abbey or monastery who strive to direct their lives, as circumstances permit, according to the spirit and Rule of St. Benedict.

In addition to the recognized secular orders, there are other groups of lay persons with strong ties to religious orders. Relationships of this kind serve the spiritual good of the faithful and also enrich the religious orders in a complementary fashion, with the mutual vitality of prayer in the cloister or convent and action in the marketplace.

# CATHOLIC RELIEF SERVICES

Catholic Relief Services is the official overseas aid and development agency of American Catholics; it is a separately incorporated organization of the U.S. Catholic Conference.

## Long-term Development Projects

CRS was founded in 1943 by the bishops of the United States to help civilians in Europe and North Africa caught in the disruption and devastation of World War II. As conditions in Europe improved in the late 1940s and early 1950s, the works conducted by CRS spread to other continents and areas — Asia, Africa and Latin America.

Although best known for its record of disaster response, compassionate aid to refugees and commitment to reconstruction and rehabilitation, CRS places primary focus on long-term development projects designed to help people to help themselves and to determine their own future. Administrative funding for CRS comes largely from the Catholic Relief Services Annual Appeal. Major support is derived from private, individual donors and through a program of sacrificial giving called Operation Rice Bowl.

Kenneth F. Hackett is executive director. CRS headquarters are located at 209 W. Fayette St., Baltimore, Md. 21201.

# EVENTS OF MEDJUGORJE

Alleged apparitions of Mary to six young people of Medjugorje, Bosnia-Herzegovina, have been the center of interest and controversy since they were first reported in June, 1981, initially in a neighboring hillside field, subsequently in the village church of St. James and even in places far removed from Medjugorje.

Reports say the alleged visionaries have seen, heard and touched Mary during visions, and that they have variously received several or all of 10 secret messages related to world events and urging a quest for peace through prayer, penance and personal conversion. An investigative commission appointed by former local Bishop Pavao Zanic of Mostar-Duvno reported in March, 1984, that the authenticity of the apparitions had not been established and that cases of reported healings had not been verified. He called the apparitions a case of "collective hallucination" exploited by local Franciscan priests at odds with him over control of a parish.

Former Archbishop Frane Franic of Split-Makarska, on the other hand, said in December, 1985: "Speaking as a believer and not as a bishop, my personal conviction is that the events at Medjugorje are of supernatural inspiration." He based his conviction on the observation of spiritual benefits related to the reported events, such as the spiritual development of the six young people, the increases in Mass attendance and sacramental practice at the scene of the apparitions, and the incidence of reconciliation among people.

"Further exploration" of the events at Medjugorje on the national level, as distinguished from the earlier diocesan investigation, was announced in a communique published in the official bulletin of the Archdiocese of Zagreb, dated Jan. 29, 1987.

"On the basis of research conducted so far, one cannot affirm that supernatural apparitions are involved" at Medjugorje, declared the bishops of Yugoslavia (19 to 1), in a statement published Jan. 2, 1991. The number of pilgrims visiting Medjugorje in recent years has been less than that reported before the outbreak of civil war in former Yugoslavia. This fact, however, did not represent any lessening of interest in the place of pilgrimage or cooling of devotion honoring Mary.

# MISSIONARY ACTIVITY OF THE CHURCH

## MISSION AND MISSIONS

*Missionary catechesis was the theme of addresses delivered by Pope John Paul at general audiences from Apr. 19 to June 21, 1995. Mission and Missions, excerpted here, were subjects of the address of May 3.*

In traditional language one speaks of "missions" in plural, and of "missionaries" who work in the missions with a special mandate. This way of expression does not contradict the oneness of the Church's "mission"; indeed, it reveals even more clearly this fundamental commitment to mission. Not only do missionaries not overshadow the principle that the whole Church is missionary, but on the contrary they themselves put it into action.

What are the "missions?" According to the (Second Vatican) Council they are "those particular undertakings by which the heralds of the Gospel are sent out by the Church to carry out the task of preaching the Gospel and planting the Church among peoples or groups who do not yet believe in Christ." (Missions) are opened in territories in which the Church "has not yet taken root" and among peoples "whose culture has not yet been influenced by the Gospel" (according to the encyclical letter *Redemptoris missio*).

### Aim of Mission Activities

We can add that the aim of these activities is the building of a local church. Not only do they help to establish the structures of an ecclesial hierarchy, they also further the formation of a community of Christian life by proclaiming the word of God and administering the sacraments.

This is the ideal for missionary activity: the foundation of a church capable of providing for her own pastors and all the necessities for the life of faith of everyone, while remaining in communion with the other particular churches and with the See of Peter.

Missionary activity can be divided into stages: "beginning or planting" with the preaching of the Gospel to lead people to baptism; this is followed by "newness or youth," with education in the faith and in lifestyle, with the formation of the local community, with the birth and development of priestly and religious vocations. By means of these formative stages, the community is given a ministerial structure which helps her develop with a view to openness and missionary cooperation.

### Doubts and Problems

Recently and unfortunately, there have been misunderstandings about missionary activity and the utility of the missions. In view of the connection which ... for a certain period was made between missionary activity and political colonization, it has been assumed that the gradual disappearance of the historical phenomenon of the colonies should have as consequence the contemporary disappearance of mission.

Adding to these doubts is the consideration that the churches of ancient evangelization, from which came many of the missionaries working in "mission territories," there is an ever greater awareness that their own territory is becoming a "mission land" and is in need of "new evangelization." So, there is a question of a choice to be made between mission in countries not yet evangelized and the urgent apostolate needed in countries of ancient Christianity.

The matter cannot be solved with the choice of the second alternative ... to the detriment of the first. It is true that in "countries of ancient Christianity" the need for new evangelization is ever more keenly felt, there "where entire groups of baptized have lost a living sense of the faith, or even no longer consider themselves members of the Church, and live a life far removed from Christ and his Gospel." Nevertheless, specific missionary activity remains indispensable and must be carried out in those territories in which the Church has not yet been established, or in which the number of Christians is very low. The Gospel message must be brought to the knowledge of all people and Christian communities. And, even flourishing, exemplary communities must be capable of exercising a beneficial influence on customs and institutions, and be means of profitable dialogue with the other groups and communities.

### Openness to Christ

(Despite problems related to missionary activity and colonizing by some nations) evangelizing activity, considered as a whole, has always stood out for its goal, very different from that of earthly powers: to promote the human dignity of the people being evangelized, permitting them to accede to the divine filiation procured by Christ for every person and communicated to the faithful in baptism. In fact, this has in general advanced those peoples' progress toward freedom and their development on the economic-social level as well. The missionaries acted out of the esteem in which they held people, as persons loved by God and redeemed by Jesus Christ.

Today as yesterday, their activity among peoples or groups in which the Church is not yet present and working, is not in answer to human aims for power and interests, nor is it inspired by pride of a cultural, social superiority. It intends to be — and is in reality — a humble service of love toward those who have not yet received the light and life of Christ within the Church which he desired and which he founded for the salvation of the whole world.

### STATISTICS

Cardinal Jozef Tomko, prefect of the Congregation for the Evangelization of Peoples, at a meeting of the Pontifical Mission Societies May 2 to 6, 1995, reported the following mission statistics as of 1994.
• Populations: 5.48 billion (world), 1,833,022,000 (Christians), 1,025,585,000 (Catholics).
• Jurisdictions, etc., under the Congregation for the Evangelization of Peoples: 983 dioceses, 1,087 bishops, 47,345 priests (diocesan and religious), 210 seminaries, 19,543 major seminarians, 54,734 minor seminarians, 12,442 brothers, 126,694 religious sisters, 370,352 catechists.

# U.S. CATHOLIC MISSION ASSOCIATION

This is a voluntary association of individuals and organizations for whom the missionary presence of the universal Church is of central importance. It is a nonprofit religious, educational and charitable organization which exists to promote global missions. Its primary emphasis is on cross-cultural evangelization and the promotion of international justice and peace. The association is also responsible for gathering and publishing annual statistical data on U.S. missionary personnel overseas. President: Donald Mueller; Executive Secretary, Sister Margaret F. Loftus. Address: 3029 Fourth St. NE, Washington, D.C. 20017.

## COUNTRIES SERVED BY U.S. CATHOLIC PERSONNEL

*(Courtesy of the U.S. Catholic Mission Association and Sister Rosanne Rustemeyer, SSND) Statistics of men (M) and women (W) as of September, 1996. Personnel on mission include priests, men and women religious, lay persons.*

Alaska, 57 M, 93 W:150. Albania, 1 W. Algeria, 1 M, 3 W: 4. American Samoa, 2 M, 16 W: 18.

Argentina, 20 M, 6 W: 26. Austria, 15 M, 14 W: 29. Australia, 15 M, 14 W: 29. Austria,, 1 M, 2 W: 3.

Bahamas, 15 M, 8 W: 23. Bangladesh, 28 M, 15 W: 43. Belize, 36 M, 21 W: 57. Benin, 1 W. Bermuda, 2 M, 4 W: 6. Bolivia, 67 M, 84 W: 151. Botswana,, 1 M, 4 W: 55.. Brazil, 148 M, 127 W: 275.

Cambodia, 3 M, 16 W: 19. Canada, 30 M, 46 W: 76. Central African Republic, 2 M, 1 W: 3. Chad, 1 M, 2 W: 3. Chile, 68 M, 68 W: 136. Colombia, 15 M, 18 W: 33. Congo, 2 W. Costa Rica, 16 M, 4 W: 20. Cuba, 1 M. Cyprus, 3 M. Czechoslovakia, 3 M, 5 W: 8.

Denmark 5 M. Dominicana, 3 M. Dominican Republic, 23 M, 21 W: 44.

East Timor, 3. Ecuador, 24 M, 12 W: 36. Egypt, 8 M, 1 W: 9. El Salvador, 19 M, 30 W: 49. Ethiopia, 10 M, 10 W: 20.

Fiji Islands, 5 M, 4 W: 9. France, 3 W.

Gambia, 1 W. Germany, 4 M, 3 W: 7. Ghana, 38 M, 49 W: 87. Great Britain, 7 M, 2 W: 9. Greece, 1 M. Greenland, 1 M. Guam, 37 M, 8 W: 45. Guatemala, 75 M, 102 W: 177. Guyana, 1 M, 2 W: 3.

Haiti, 28 M, 17 W: 45. Hawaii, 92 M, 95 W: 187. Honduras, 46 M, 24 W: 70. Hong Kong, 36 M, 44 W: 80. Hungary, 1 M, 4 W: 5.

India, 69 M, 20 W: 89. Indonesia, 26 M, 4 W: 30. Ireland, 7 M, 7, W: 14. Israel, 36 M, 9 W: 45. Italy, 24 M, 27 W: 51. Ivory Coast, 6 M, 3 W: 9.

Jamaica, 53 M, 42 W: 95. Japan, 158 M, 68 W: 226. Jordan, 3 M, 1 W: 4.

Kazakhstan, 1 M. Kenya, 132 M, 93 W: 225. Korea, 53 M, 32 W: 85.

Latvia, 1 M. Lebanon, 3 M, 3 W: 6. Lesotho, 5 M, 8 W:13. Liberia, 10 M, 4 W: 14. Lithuania, 3 M, 4 W: 7.

Madagascar, 3 M, 3 W: 6. Malawi. 7 M, 5 W: 12. Malaysia, 1 M, 1 W: 2. Mali, 3 W. Marshall Islands, 4 M,. 16 W: 20. Mexico, 145 M, 106 W: 251. Micronesia, 39 M, 14 W: 53. Montserrat 1 W. Morocco, 1 M. Mozambique, 1 M.

Namibia,, 1 M, 4 W: 5. Nepal, 20 M, 7, W: 27. Netherlands, 1 M. New Zealand, 11 M, 11 W: 22.. Nicaragua, 34 M, 41 W: 75. Niger, 1 M. Nigeria, 31 M, 28 W: 59. Norway, 1 M.

Okinawa, 7 M.

Pakistan, 12 M, 12 W: 24. Palau, 4 M. Panama, 32 M, 12, W: 44. Papua New Guinea, 69 M, 41 W: 110. Paraguay, 16 M, 2 W: 18. Peru, 178 M, 181 W: 359. Philippines, 207 M, 40 W: 247. Poland, 2 W. Puerto Rico, 46 M, 52 W: 98.

Romania, 1 M, 3 W: 4. Russia, 4 M, 3 W: 7. Rwanda, 1 W.

St. Lucia, 2 M. St. Vincent, 1 W. Saipan, 1 M, 1 W: 2. Scotland, 1 M. Senegal, 1 M, 2 W: 3. Seychelles, 2 M. Sierra Leone, 11 M, 17 W: 28. Singapore, 1 W. Slovenia,1 M. Solomon Islands, 5 M, 4 W: 9.. South Africa, 21 M, 25 W:46. Spain, 1 M, 2 W: 3. Sri Lanka, 10 M, 3 W: 13. Sudan, 4 M, 5 W: 9. Swaziland, 3 W. Sweden, 4 M, 1 W: 5.

Tahiti, 3 M. Taiwan, 67 M, 49 W: 116. Tanzania, 69 M, 42 W: 111. Thailand, 38 M, 14 W: 52. Togo, 1 M. Tonga Islands, 1 M. Tunisia, 1 M. Turkey, 1 W. Turk Islands 1 M.

Uganda, 37 M, 25 W: 62. Uruguay, 3 M, 1 W: 4. Vanuatu 2 M. Venezuela, 26 M, 14 W: 40. Vietnam, 2 M. Virgin Islands, 7 M, 10 W: 17.

West Indies, 20 M, 7 W: 27. Western Samoa, 5 M, 2 W: 7.

Zaire, 10 M, 15 W: 25. Zambia, 76 M, 25 W: 101. Zimbabwe, 26 M, 29 W: 55.

## HOME MISSIONS

The expression "home missions" is applied to places in the U.S. where the local church does not have its own resources, human and otherwise, which are needed to begin or, if begun, to survive and grow. These areas share the name "missions" with their counterparts in foreign lands because they too need outside help to provide the personnel and means for making the Church present and active there in carrying out its mission for the salvation of people.

Dioceses in the Southeast, the Southwest, and the Far West are most urgently in need of outside help to carry on the work of the Church. Millions of persons live in counties in which there are no resident priests. Many others live in rural areas beyond the reach and influence of a Catholic center. According to recent statistics compiled by the Glenmary Research Center, there are more than 500 priestless counties in the United States.

### Mission Workers

A number of forces are at work to meet the pastoral needs of these missionary areas and to establish permanent churches and operating institutions where they are required. In many dioceses, one or more missions and stations are attended from established parishes and are gradually growing to independent status. Priests, brothers and sisters belonging to scores of religious institutes are engaged full-time in the home missions. Lay persons, some of them in affiliation with special groups and movements, are also involved.

The Society for the Propagation of the Faith, which conducts an annual collection for mission support in all parishes of the U.S., allocates 40 per cent of this sum for disbursement to home missions through the American Board of Catholic Missions.

Various mission-aid societies frequently undertake projects in behalf of the home missions.

The **Glenmary Home Missioners**, founded by Father W. Howard Bishop in 1939, is the only home mission society established for the sole purpose of carrying out the pastoral ministry in small towns and rural districts of the United States. Glenmary serves in many areas where at least 20 per cent of the people live in poverty and less than one per cent are Catholic. With 63 priests and 20 professed brothers as of January, 1996, the Glenmary Missioners had missions in the archdioceses of Atlanta and Cincinnati, and in the dioceses of Birmingham, Charlotte, Covington, Jackson, Lexington, Little Rock, Nashville, Owensboro, Richmond, Savannah, Tulsa, Tyler and Wheeling-Charleston. National headquarters are located at 4119 Glenmary Trace, Fairfield, Ohio. The mailing address is P.O. Box 465618, Cincinnati, Ohio 45246.

### Organizations

**Black and Indian Mission Office (The Commission for Catholic Missions among the Colored People and the Indians):** Organized officially in 1885 by decree of the Third Plenary Council of Baltimore. Provides financial support for religious works among Blacks and Native Americans in 133 archdioceses and dioceses through funds raised by an annual collection in all parishes of the U.S. on the first Sunday of Lent, the designated Sunday. In 1995, $6,824,430 was raised; disbursements amounted to $4,490,000 for Black missions and $2,320,000 for Native American missions.

**Bureau of Catholic Indian Missions:** Established in 1874 as the representative of Catholic Indian missions before the federal government and the public; made permanent organization in 1884 by Third Plenary Council of Baltimore. After a remarkable history of rendering important services to the Indian people, the bureau continues to represent the Catholic Church in the U.S. in her apostolate to the American Indian. Concerns are evangelization, catechesis, liturgy, family life, education, advocacy.

**Catholic Negro-American Mission Board** (1907): Support priests and sisters in southern states and provide monthly support to sisters and lay teachers in the poorest Black schools.

Board of Directors of the three organizations above are: Cardinal John O'Connor, president; Cardinal Anthony Bevilacqua; Cardinal William Keeler; Msgr. Paul A. Lenz, secretary-treasurer; Patricia L. O'Rourke, assistant secretary-treasurer.

Address: 2021 H Street NW, Washington, DC 20006.

**The Catholic Church Extension Society** (1905): Established with papal approval for the purpose of preserving and extending the Church in rural and isolated parts of the U.S. and its dependencies through the collection and disbursement of funds for home mission work. Since the time of its founding, more than $250 million have been received and distributed for this purpose. Disbursements, made at the requests of bishops in 75 designated mission dioceses, exceeded $12 million for fiscal year 1994. The 10,200th church project built with the help of the society was dedicated in 1994. The society also distributes parish calendars.

Works of the society are supervised by a 14-member board of governors: Cardinal Joseph Bernardin, archbishop of Chicago, chancellor; Rev. Kenneth Velo, president; six bishops, one Religious and five lay people. Headquarters: 35 E. Wacker Drive, Chicago, IL 60601.

**National Catholic Rural Life Conference:** Founded in 1923 through the efforts of Bishop Edwin V. O'Hara. Applies the Gospel message to rural issues through focus on rural parishes and the provision of services including distribution of educational materials development of prayer and worship resources, advocacy for strong rural communities. Bishop William S. Skylstad of Spokane, president; Brother David G. Andrews C.S.C., executive director. National headquarters: 4625 Beaver Ave., Des Moines, IA 50310.

---

## TAPING OF CONFESSION: Violation of a Sacrament

Archbishop Francis E. George of Portland, Ore., repeated his strong condemnation of the recording of a prisoner's sacramental confession and of the state's refusal to destroy the tape. In a letter read at parishes of the diocese Aug.. 17 and 18, 1996, he asked Catholics to pray for those "who have violated our rights."

He referred to a case in which sheriff's deputies tape-recorded the sacramental confession of a murder suspect and the refusal of a district attorney to turn the tape over to the archdiocese for destruction. Since the tape became public, it was heard by six persons. U.S. District Judge Owen Panner ruled Aug. 12 that the state's interest in retaining the tape as evidence outweighed the Church's legal interests in having it destroyed.

The archbishop said in his letter: "The wrong inflicted by the recording of the sacrament is compounded by the court's refusal to destroy the tape. If this tape is used in court, our relationship to the state will be different from what we had believed ti to be. Use of the tape will have a chilling effect on our religious life. No longer can we feel secure in conducting sacred acts of worship or revealing the state of our souls in a religious context.

He charged those involved in the matter with "deliberately violating the seal of the confessional."

Archbishop George appealed to the 9th U.S. Circuit Court Aug. 23 to give an expedited hearing on Judge Panner's decision and to prohibit further dissemination or use of the tape.

## LEGAL STATUS OF CATHOLIC EDUCATION

The right of private schools to exist and operate in the United States is recognized in law. It was confirmed by the U.S. Supreme Court in 1925 when the tribunal ruled (Pierce v. Society of Sisters, see Church-State Decisions of the Supreme Court) that an Oregon state law requiring all children to attend public schools was unconstitutional.

Private schools are obliged to comply with the education laws in force in the various states regarding such matters as required basic curricula, periods of attendance, and standards for proper accreditation.

The special curricula and standards of private schools are determined by the schools themselves. Thus, in Catholic schools, the curricula include not only the subject matter required by state educational laws but also other fields of study, principally, education in the Catholic faith.

The Supreme Court has ruled that the First Amendment to the U.S. Constitution, in accordance with the No Establishment of Religion Clause of the First Amendment, prohibits direct federal and state aid from public funds to church-affiliated schools. (See several cases in Church-State Decisions of the Supreme Court.)

### Public Aid

This prohibition does not extend to all child-benefit and public-purpose programs of aid to students of non-public elementary and secondary schools.

Statutes authorizing such programs have been ruled constitutional on the grounds that they:
- have a "secular legislative purpose";
- neither inhibit nor advance religion as a "principal or primary effect";
- do not foster "excessive government entanglement with religion."

Aid programs considered constitutional have provided bus transportation, textbook loans, school lunches and health services, and "secular, neutral or non-ideological services, facilities and materials provided in common to all school children," public and non-public.

The first major aid to education program in U.S. history containing provisions benefitting nonpublic school students was enacted by the 89th Congress and signed into law by President Lyndon B. Johnson Apr. 11, 1965. The Elementary and Secondary Education Act was designed to avoid the separation of Church and state impasse which had blocked all earlier aid proposals pertaining to nonpublic, and especially church-affiliated, schools. The objective of the program, under public control, is to serve the public purpose by aiding disadvantaged pupils in nonpublic as well as public schools.

With respect to college and university education in church-affiliated institutions, the Supreme Court has upheld the constitutionality of statutes providing student loans and, under the Federal Higher Education Facilities Act of 1963, construction loans and grants for secular-purpose facilities.

Catholic schools are exempt from real estate taxation in all of the states. Since Jan. 1, 1959, nonprofit parochial and private schools have also been exempt from several federal excise taxes.

### Shared and Released Time

In a shared time program of education, students enrolled in Catholic or other church-related schools take some courses (e.g., religion, social studies, fine arts) in their own schools and others (e.g., science, mathematics, industrial arts) in public schools. Such a program has been given serious consideration in recent years by Catholic and other educators. Its constitutionality has not been seriously challenged, but practical problems — relating to teacher and student schedules, transportation, adjustment to new programs, and other factors — are knotty.

Several million children of elementary and high school age of all denominations have the opportunity of receiving religious instruction on released time. Under released time programs they are permitted to leave their public schools during school hours to attend religious instruction classes held off the public school premises. They are released at the request of their parents. Public school authorities merely provide for their dismissal, and take no part in the program.

### NCEA

The National Catholic Educational Association, founded in 1904, is a voluntary organization of educational institutions and individuals concerned with Catholic education in the U.S. Its objectives are to promote and encourage the principles and ideals of Christian education and formation by suitable service and other activities.

The NCEA serves approximately 200,000 Catholic educators at all levels from pre-K through university. Its official publication is *Momentum*. Numerous service publications are issued to members.

Bishop John J. Leibrecht of Springfield-Cape Girardeau, chairman of the Board of Directors; Leonard F. DeFiore, president. Address: 1077 30th St. N.W., Washington, D.C. 20007.

### The American College, Louvain

The American College was founded by the bishops of the United States in 1857 as a seminary for U.S. students. While primarily remaining a seminary, it also serves as a community of on-going formation for English-speaking graduate-student priests and religious pursuing courses in theology, philosophy and canon law at the Catholic University of Louvain (dating from 1425) in Belgium. The college is administered by an American rector and staff, and operates under the auspices of a committee of the National Conference of Catholic Bishops. Rector: The Very Rev. David Windsor, C.M. Address: The American College, Catholic University of Louvain, Naamsestraat 100, B-3000 Leuven, Belgium.

# CATHOLIC SCHOOLS AND STUDENTS IN THE UNITED STATES

(Source: *The Official Catholic Directory, 1996*; figures as of Jan. 1, 1996. Archdioceses are indicated by an asterisk.)

| State Diocese | Univs. Colleges | Students | High Schools | Students | Elem. Schools | Students |
|---|---|---|---|---|---|---|
| **Alabama** | **1** | **1,026** | **6** | **2,875** | **41** | **10,978** |
| *Mobile | 1 | 1,026 | 3 | 1,640 | 21 | 6,039 |
| Birmingham | — | — | 3 | 1,235 | 20 | 4,939 |
| **Alaska** | **—** | **—** | **1** | **264** | **4** | **733** |
| *Anchorage | — | — | — | — | 2 | 362 |
| Fairbanks | — | — | 1 | 264 | 1 | 271 |
| Juneau | — | — | — | — | 1 | 100 |
| **Arizona** | **—** | **—** | **8** | **5,121** | **43** | **12,273** |
| Phoenix | — | — | 5 | 3,526 | 23 | 7,347 |
| Tucson | — | — | 3 | 1,595 | 20 | 4,926 |
| **Arkansas**, Little Rock | **—** | **—** | **5** | **1,775** | **32** | **6,784** |
| **California** | **15** | **40,882** | **114** | **69,544** | **602** | **181,761** |
| *Los Angeles | 6 | 9,975 | 51 | 30,777 | 229 | 70,092 |
| *San Francisco | 3 | 10,870 | 13 | 7,495 | 66 | 21,100 |
| Fresno | — | — | 2 | 1,431 | 23 | 5,840 |
| Monterey | — | — | 4 | 1,330 | 16 | 4,045 |
| Oakland | 3 | 4,556 | 9 | 6,089 | 55 | 15,241 |
| Orange | 1 | 100 | 6 | 5,634 | 37 | 13,269 |
| Sacramento | — | — | 7 | 3,990 | 48 | 13,851 |
| San Bernardino | — | — | 2 | 846 | 30 | 8,292 |
| San Diego | 1 | 6,416 | 5 | 3,168 | 43 | 13,139 |
| San Jose | 1 | 8,965 | 6 | 5,424 | 29 | 10,289 |
| Santa Rosa | — | — | 7 | 2,066 | 14 | 3,173 |
| Stockton | — | — | 2 | 1,314 | 12 | 3,430 |
| **Colorado** | **1** | **9,507** | **7** | **2,758** | **47** | **14,225** |
| *Denver | 1 | 9,507 | 5 | 2,439 | 38 | 11,772 |
| Colorado Springs | — | — | — | — | 4 | 1,179 |
| Pueblo | — | — | 2 | 319 | 5 | 1,274 |
| **Connecticut** | **6** | **13,625** | **24** | **10,323** | **127** | **33,842** |
| *Hartford | 3 | 2,833 | 11 | 4,867 | 73 | 19,571 |
| Bridgeport | 3 | 10,792 | 8 | 3,449 | 34 | 9,707 |
| Norwich | — | — | 5 | 2,007 | 20 | 4,564 |
| **Delaware**, Wilmington | **—** | **—** | **7** | **4,670** | **30** | **10,667** |
| **District of Columbia**, *Washington | **3** | **21,078** | **17** | **7,909** | **88** | **23,803** |
| **Florida** | **3** | **11,545** | **30** | **20,032** | **182** | **63,065** |
| *Miami | 2 | 10,084 | 12 | 9,721 | 51 | 22,698 |
| Orlando | — | — | 4 | 2,291 | 31 | 10,312 |
| Palm Beach | — | — | 3 | 1,753 | 16 | 5,701 |
| Pensacola-Tallahassee | — | — | 1 | 544 | 8 | 2,495 |
| St. Augustine | — | — | 2 | 1,558 | 23 | 6,752 |
| St. Petersburg | 1 | 1,461 | 5 | 2,633 | 44 | 11,657 |
| Venice | — | — | 3 | 1,532 | 9 | 3,450 |
| **Georgia** | **—** | **—** | **7** | **4,023** | **30** | **9,771** |
| *Atlanta | — | — | 2 | 2,035 | 15 | 5,223 |
| Savannah | — | — | 5 | 1,988 | 15 | 4,548 |
| **Hawaii**, Honolulu | **1** | **2,232** | **7** | **3,524** | **26** | **7,755** |
| **Idaho**, Boise | **—** | **—** | **1** | **678** | **12** | **2,304** |
| **Illinois** | **14** | **48,552** | **80** | **50,792** | **524** | **167,640** |
| *Chicago | 6 | 37,845 | 47 | 34,181 | 280 | 103,864 |
| Belleville | 1 | 672 | 3 | 1,554 | 39 | 7,575 |
| Joliet | 4 | 8,249 | 8 | 5,572 | 62 | 19,151 |
| Peoria | 1 | 156 | 7 | 2,674 | 48 | 12,637 |
| Rockford | — | — | 8 | 4,163 | 41 | 11,979 |
| Springfield | 2 | 1,630 | 7 | 2,648 | 54 | 12,434 |
| **Indiana** | **10** | **18,527** | **23** | **12,259** | **177** | **49,518** |
| *Indianapolis | 3 | 2,647 | 9 | 5,136 | 63 | 21,406 |
| Evansville | — | — | 5 | 1,754 | 25 | 5,680 |
| Ft.Wayne-South Bend | 5 | 13,809 | 4 | 2,817 | 40 | 10,976 |
| Gary | 1 | 1,034 | 4 | 2,193 | 31 | 8,086 |
| Lafayette | 1 | 1,037 | 1 | 359 | 18 | 3,370 |

| State Diocese | Univs. Colleges | Students | High Schools | Students | Elem. Schools | Students |
|---|---|---|---|---|---|---|
| **Iowa** | **6** | **8,365** | **24** | **8,378** | **139** | **30,876** |
| *Dubuque | 3 | 4,063 | 7 | 3,056 | 55 | 14,132 |
| Davenport | 2 | 3,158 | 7 | 1,586 | 40 | 5,359 |
| Des Moines | — | — | 2 | 1,360 | 15 | 4,562 |
| Sioux City | 1 | 1,144 | 8 | 2,376 | 29 | 6,823 |
| **Kansas** | **4** | **5,183** | **16** | **5,853** | **94** | **22,833** |
| *Kansas City | 3 | 3,199 | 7 | 3,253 | 39 | 12,004 |
| Dodge City | — | — | — | — | 10 | 1,284 |
| Salina | — | — | 5 | 746 | 12 | 2,130 |
| Wichita | 1 | 1,984 | 4 | 1,854 | 33 | 7,415 |
| **Kentucky** | **5** | **6,230** | **25** | **10,766** | **124** | **34,883** |
| *Louisville | 3 | 4,125 | 10 | 5,892 | 58 | 18,836 |
| Covington | 1 | 1,426 | 9 | 3,115 | 32 | 8,282 |
| Lexington | — | — | 3 | 741 | 15 | 3,392 |
| Owensboro | 1 | 679 | 3 | 1,018 | 19 | 4,373 |
| **Louisiana** | **4** | **11,123** | **50** | **26,986** | **176** | **70,463** |
| *New Orleans | 3 | 10,355 | 23 | 16,196 | 81 | 35,460 |
| Alexandria | — | — | 3 | 508 | 9 | 2,600 |
| Baton Rouge | 1 | 768 | 8 | 3,897 | 26 | 12,525 |
| Houma-Thibodaux | — | — | 3 | 1,802 | 10 | 4,294 |
| Lafayette | — | — | 10 | 3,373 | 31 | 10,667 |
| Lake Charles | — | — | 1 | 438 | 8 | 2,321 |
| Shreveport | — | — | 2 | 772 | 11 | 2,596 |
| **Maine,** Portland | 1 | 3,859 | 3 | 758 | 19 | 4,045 |
| **Maryland,**\*Baltimore | 3 | 10,866 | 23 | 9,971 | 19 | 24,634 |
| **Massachusetts** | **14** | **32,836** | **52** | **23,111** | **206** | **57,935** |
| *Boston | 9 | 21,856 | 37 | 14,886 | 130 | 39,250 |
| Fall River | 1 | 2,825 | 4 | 2,422 | 24 | 5,790 |
| Springfield | 1 | 1,251 | 4 | 2,137 | 30 | 8,271 |
| Worcester | 3 | 6,904 | 7 | 3,666 | 22 | 4,624 |
| **Michigan** | **6** | **20,383** | **54** | **21,197** | **301** | **75,169** |
| * Detroit | 4 | 15,771 | 35 | 14,008 | 139 | 40,047 |
| Gaylord | — | — | 4 | 475 | 18 | 2,856 |
| Grand Rapids | 1 | 2,443 | 4 | 2,158 | 41 | 9,264 |
| Kalamazoo | — | — | 3 | 849 | 21 | 4,675 |
| Lansing | 1 | 2,169 | 5 | 2,603 | 39 | 10,403 |
| Marquette | — | — | — | — | 10 | 1,910 |
| Saginaw | — | — | 3 | 1,104 | 33 | 6,014 |
| **Minnesota** | **7** | **27,599** | **21** | **8,861** | **195** | **45,141** |
| *St.Paul and Minneapolis | 3 | 13,999 | 11 | 6,447 | 90 | 26,836 |
| Crookston | — | — | 1 | 139 | 9 | 1,278 |
| Duluth | 1 | 1,895 | — | — | 13 | 1,807 |
| New Ulm | — | — | 3 | 474 | 21 | 3,542 |
| St. Cloud | 2 | 3,630 | 2 | 577 | 35 | 6,141 |
| Winona | 1 | 8,075 | 4 | 1,224 | 27 | 5,537 |
| **Mississippi** | **1** | **25** | **9** | **2,685** | **29** | **7,332** |
| Biloxi | — | — | 5 | 1,828 | 14 | 3,010 |
| Jackson | 1 | 25 | 4 | 857 | 15 | 4,322 |
| **Missouri** | **4** | **17,241** | **42** | **19,433** | **250** | **58,267** |
| *St.Louis | 2 | 12,505 | 29 | 14,815 | 155 | 38,411 |
| Jefferson City | — | — | 2 | 944 | 37 | 5,892 |
| Kansas City-St. Joseph | 2 | 4,736 | 8 | 2,886 | 35 | 10,239 |
| Springfield-Cape Girardeau | — | — | 3 | 788 | 23 | 3,725 |
| **Montana** | **2** | **2,844** | **4** | **936** | **17** | **3,179** |
| Great Falls-Billings | 1 | 1,426 | 2 | 524 | 13 | 2,389 |
| Helena | 1 | 1,418 | 2 | 412 | 4 | 790 |
| **Nebraska** | **2** | **7,335** | **29** | **7,944** | **93** | **22,190** |
| *Omaha | 2 | 7,335 | 19 | 5,374 | 62 | 15,833 |
| Grand Island | — | — | 4 | 963 | 7 | 730 |
| Lincoln | — | — | 6 | 1,607 | 24 | 5,627 |
| **Nevada** | **—** | **—** | **2** | **408** | **11** | **3,261** |
| Las Vegas | — | — | 1 | 8 | 7 | 2,157 |
| Reno | — | — | 1 | 400 | 4 | 1,104 |

| State Diocese | Univs. Colleges | Students | High Schools | Students | Elem. Schools | Students |
|---|---|---|---|---|---|---|
| **New Hampshire,** Manchester | 6 | 6,501 | 4 | 2,151 | 26 | 6,741 |
| **New Jersey** | **7** | **20,111** | **76** | **36,948** | **372** | **116,105** |
| *Newark | 4 | 16,020 | 38 | 15,922 | 151 | 47,097 |
| Camden | — | — | 11 | 5,837 | 61 | 16,660 |
| Metuchen | — | — | 6 | 3,605 | 42 | 14,209 |
| Paterson | 2 | 1,582 | 10 | 4,080 | 61 | 16,503 |
| Trenton | 1 | 2,509 | 11 | 7,504 | 57 | 21,636 |
| **New Mexico** | **1** | **1,550** | **6** | **2,033** | **33** | **6,914** |
| *Santa Fe | 1 | 1,550 | 3 | 1,889 | 18 | 4,787 |
| Gallup | — | — | 3 | 144 | 10 | 1,496 |
| Las Cruces | — | — | — | — | 5 | 631 |
| **New York** | **29** | **104,807** | **129** | **73,790** | **715** | **225,910** |
| *New York | 12 | 59,409 | 55 | 28,121 | 238 | 79,001 |
| Albany | 4 | 4,550 | 7 | 3,106 | 40 | 9,746 |
| Brooklyn | 2 | 18,536 | 22 | 18,499 | 160 | 55,708 |
| Buffalo | 7 | 14,641 | 17 | 5,912 | 94 | 24,820 |
| Ogdensburg | 1 | 427 | 2 | 660 | 24 | 4,606 |
| Rochester | — | — | 7 | 3,394 | 56 | 14,492 |
| Rockville Centre | 2 | 4,419 | 13 | 10,754 | 64 | 28,513 |
| Syracuse | 1 | 2,825 | 6 | 3,344 | 39 | 9,024 |
| **North Carolina** | **2** | **816** | **3** | **1,447** | **32** | **9,638** |
| Charlotte | 2 | 816 | 2 | 997 | 15 | 5,244 |
| Raleigh | — | — | 1 | 450 | 17 | 4,394 |
| **North Dakota** | **1** | **2,354** | **4** | **1,627** | **28** | **4,106** |
| Bismarck | 1 | 2,354 | 3 | 1,319 | 16 | 2,186 |
| Fargo | — | — | 1 | 308 | 12 | 1,920 |
| **Ohio** | **11** | **32,034** | **79** | **45,220** | **453** | **146,322** |
| *Cincinnati | 4 | 18,805 | 22 | 15,246 | 114 | 40,106 |
| Cleveland | 3 | 6,388 | 23 | 14,533 | 142 | 51,248 |
| Columbus | 1 | 1,736 | 11 | 4,826 | 45 | 13,887 |
| Steubenville | 1 | 1,950 | 3 | 710 | 16 | 2,295 |
| Toledo | 1 | 1,670 | 14 | 6,886 | 87 | 26,235 |
| Youngstown | 1 | 1,485 | 6 | 3,019 | 49 | 12,551 |
| **Oklahoma** | **1** | **315** | **4** | **2,328** | **28** | **7,056** |
| *Oklahoma City | 1 | 315 | 2 | 956 | 17 | 3,588 |
| Tulsa | — | — | 2 | 1,372 | 11 | 3,468 |
| **Oregon** | **2** | **4,526** | **9** | **4,472** | **45** | **9,427** |
| *Portland | 2 | 4,526 | 9 | 4,472 | 42 | 8,817 |
| Baker | — | — | — | — | 3 | 610 |
| **Pennsylvania** | **26** | **78,757** | **92** | **51,222** | **616** | **185,861** |
| *Philadelphia | 11 | 32,296 | 40 | 29,309 | 245 | 91,993 |
| Allentown | 2 | 3,423 | 9 | 4,066 | 55 | 14,252 |
| Altoona-Johnstown | 2 | 7,456 | 3 | 1,275 | 31 | 5,460 |
| Erie | 2 | 6,028 | 8 | 3,237 | 44 | 11,186 |
| Greensburg | 2 | 1,973 | 2 | 841 | 29 | 6,462 |
| Harrisburg | — | — | 8 | 3,676 | 40 | 10,560 |
| Pittsburgh | 3 | 15,555 | 11 | 4,557 | 113 | 32,246 |
| Scranton | 4 | 12,026 | 11 | 4,261 | 59 | 13,702 |
| **Rhode Island,** Providence | **2** | **7,583** | **11** | **4,927** | **52** | **12,778** |
| **South Carolina,** Charleston | — | — | **3** | **1,367** | **24** | **6,144** |
| **South Dakota** | **2** | **1,424** | **5** | **1,392** | **26** | **4,767** |
| Rapid City | — | — | 2 | 426 | 3 | 757 |
| Sioux Falls | 2 | 1,424 | 3 | 966 | 23 | 4,010 |
| **Tennessee** | **2** | **2,174** | **11** | **4,211** | **36** | **10,703** |
| Knoxville | — | — | 2 | 805 | 7 | 2,435 |
| Memphis | 1 | 1,766 | 7 | 2,221 | 14 | 4,060 |
| Nashville | 1 | 408 | 2 | 1,185 | 15 | 4,208 |
| **Texas** | **7** | **19,146** | **43** | **16,769** | **243** | **65,549** |
| *San Antonio | 4 | 10,792 | 9 | 3,223 | 42 | 13,306 |
| Amarillo | — | — | 1 | 126 | 8 | 999 |
| Austin | 1 | 3,107 | 2 | 518 | 18 | 4,247 |
| Beaumont | — | — | 1 | 680 | 7 | 1,954 |
| Brownsville | — | — | 1 | 679 | 8 | 2,653 |

| State Diocese | Univs. Colleges | Students | High Schools | Students | Elem. Schools | Students |
|---|---|---|---|---|---|---|
| **Texas** | | | | | | |
| Corpus Christi | — | — | 3 | 986 | 28 | 5,268 |
| Dallas | 1 | 2,747 | 6 | 2,857 | 33 | 10,765 |
| El Paso | — | — | 3 | 1,733 | 12 | 3,936 |
| Fort Worth | — | — | 4 | 1,592 | 16 | 4,596 |
| Galveston-Houston | 1 | 2,500 | 8 | 3,516 | 50 | 12,934 |
| Lubbock | — | — | 1 | 99 | 2 | 326 |
| San Angelo | — | — | — | — | 3 | 807 |
| Tyler | — | — | 1 | 146 | 4 | 964 |
| Victoria | — | — | 3 | 614 | 12 | 2,794 |
| **Utah,** Salt Lake City | — | — | 2 | 1,204 | 9 | 2,709 |
| **Vermont,** Burlington | 3 | 4,704 | 2 | 634 | 11 | 2,435 |
| **Virginia** | 2 | 4,345 | 13 | 5,214 | 55 | 18,658 |
| Arlington | 2 | 4,345 | 4 | 3,393 | 32 | 11,184 |
| Richmond | — | — | 9 | 1,821 | 23 | 7,474 |
| **Washington** | 3 | 11,725 | 11 | 6,363 | 79 | 21,117 |
| *Seattle | 2 | 7,406 | 9 | 5,040 | 56 | 16,043 |
| Spokane | 1 | 4,319 | 2 | 1,323 | 16 | 3,104 |
| Yakima | — | — | — | — | 7 | 1,970 |
| **West Virginia,** Wheeling-Charleston | 1 | 1,511 | 8 | 1,626 | 29 | 5,327 |
| **Wisconsin** | 9 | 30,945 | 28 | 12,554 | 366 | 68,108 |
| *Milwaukee | 5 | 22,349 | 13 | 7,671 | 145 | 28,611 |
| Green Bay | 2 | 4,900 | 6 | 2,290 | 80 | 15,579 |
| La Crosse | 1 | 1,640 | 7 | 1,918 | 78 | 13,117 |
| Madison | 1 | 2,056 | 2 | 675 | 45 | 7,607 |
| Superior | — | — | — | — | 18 | 3,194 |
| **Wyoming,** Cheyenne | — | — | — | — | 7 | 1,725 |
| **EASTERN CHURCHES** | 1 | 650 | 4 | 1,048 | 29 | 5,769 |
| *Philadelphia | 1 | 650 | 1 | 336 | 7 | 1,529 |
| St. Nicholas (Chicago)— | — | — | 1 | 72 | 2 | 470 |
| Stamford | — | — | 1 | 140 | 4 | 462 |
| St. Josaphat (Parma) | — | — | — | — | 2 | 285 |
| *Pittsburgh | — | — | — | — | 4 | 704 |
| Parma | — | — | — | — | 2 | 343 |
| Passaic | — | — | 1 | 500 | 4 | 1,042 |
| Van Nuys | — | — | — | — | — | — |
| St. Maron (Maronites) | — | — | — | — | — | — |
| Our Lady of Lebanon (Maronites) | — | — | — | — | — | — |
| Newton (Melkites) | — | — | — | — | — | — |
| St. Thomas Apostle of Detroit (Chaldeans) | — | — | — | — | — | — |
| St. George Martyr (Romanians) | — | — | — | — | — | — |
| Armenians (Ap. Ex.) | — | — | — | — | 4 | 934 |
| **SCHOOLS AND STUDENTS IN OUTLYING AREAS** | | | | | | |
| American Samoa | — | — | 2 | 314 | 2 | 415 |
| Caroline Islands | — | — | 5 | 704 | 5 | 1,644 |
| Guam | — | — | 3 | 1,138 | 7 | 3,247 |
| Marshall Islands | — | — | 2 | 284 | 6 | 1,308 |
| Marianas | — | — | 1 | 266 | 2 | 277 |
| Puerto Rico | 5 | 24,449 | 97 | 22,144 | 134 | 45,843 |
| Virgin Islands | — | — | 2 | 382 | 3 | 713 |
| **GRAND TOTALS 1996** | 237 | 691,626 | 1,350 | 647,613 | 7,011 | 2,052,193 |
| **Grand Totals, 1995** | 235 | 656,905 | 1,350 | 652,054 | 7,210 | 2,023,976 |
| **Grand Totals, 1986** | 243 | 545,461 | 1,418 | 766,744 | 7,865 | 2,099,379 |

## North American College

The North American College, founded by the U.S. bishops in 1859, is a residence and house of formation for U.S. seminarians and graduate students in Rome. The first ordination of an alumnus took place June 14, 1862. Pontifical status was granted the college by Pope Leo XIII Oct. 25, 1884. Students pursue theological and related studies principally at the Pontifical Gregorian University.

# SUMMARY OF SCHOOL STATISTICS

The status of Catholic educational institutions and programs in the United States and outlying areas at the beginning of 1996 was reflected in figures (as of Jan. 1) reported by *The Official Catholic Directory, 1996.*

**Colleges and Universities: 237** (U.S., 232; Outlying Areas, 5).

**College and University Students: 691,626** (U.S., 667,177; Outlying Areas, 24,449).

**High Schools: 1,350** (790 diocesan and parochial; 560 private). U.S., 1,238 (722 diocesan and parochial; 516 private). Outlying Areas, 112 (68 diocesan and parochial; 44 private).

**High School Students: 647,613** (365,856 diocesan and parochial; 281,757 private). U.S., 622,381 (352,105 diocesan and parochial; 270,276 private). Outlying Areas, 25,232 (13,751 diocesan and parochial; 11,481 private).

**Public High School Students Receiving Religious Instruction: 793,823** (U.S., 773,590; Outlying Areas, 20,233).

**Elementary Schools: 7,011 (6,677 diocesan and parochial; 334 private).** U.S., 6,852 (6,582 diocesan and parochial; 270 private). Outlying Areas, 159 (95 diocesan and parochial; 64 private).

**Elementary School Students: 2,052,193 (1,964,624 diocesan and parochial; 87,569 private).** U.S., 1,998,746 (1,932,794 diocesan and parochial; 65,952 private). Outlying Areas, 48,324 (39,684 diocesan and parochial; 8,640 private).

**Public Elementary School Students Receiving Religious Instruction: 3,414,472** (U.S., 3,345,898; Outlying Areas, 68,574).

**Non-Residential Schools for Handicapped: 80** (U.S.). Students: 7,532 (U.S.).

**Teachers — 201,344. U.S., 196,190:** Lay Persons, 179,974; Sisters, 12,369; Priests, 2,442; Brothers, 1,361; Scholastics, 44. Outlying Areas, 5,154: Lay Persons, 4,691; Sisters, 324; Priests, 96; Brothers, 33; scholastics, 10.

**Seminaries — 198 (72 diocesan; 126 religious).** U.S.: 184 (67 diocesan; 117 religious). Outlying Areas: 14 (5 diocesan; 9 religious).

**Seminarians — 4,578** (3,038 diocesan; 1,540 religious). U.S.: 4,466 (2,971 diocesan; 1,495 religious). Outlying Areas: 112 (67 diocesan; 45 religious).

# UNIVERSITIES AND COLLEGES IN THE UNITED STATES

(Sources: Almanac survey; *The Official Catholic Directory.*)

Listed below are institutions of higher learning established under Catholic auspices. Some of them are now independent.

Information includes: name of each institution; indication of male (m), female (w), coeducational (c) student body; name of founding group or group with which the institution is affiliated; year of foundation; total number of students, in parentheses.

**Albertus Magnus College** (c): 700 Prospect St., New Haven, CT 06511. Dominican Sisters; 1925; independent.

**Allentown College of St. Francis de Sales** (c): 2755 Station Ave., Center Valley, PA 18034. Oblates of St. Francis de Sales; 1965 (1,717).

**Alvernia College** (c): Reading, PA 19607. Bernardine Sisters; 1958 (1,292).

**Alverno College** (w): 3401 S. 39th St., Milwaukee, WI 53215. School Sisters of St. Francis; 1887; independent (2,450).

**Anna Maria College** (c): Sunset Lane, Paxton, MA 01612. Sisters of St. Anne; 1946; independent (1,797).

**Aquinas College** (c): 1607 Robinson Rd. S.E., Grand Rapids, MI 49506. Sisters of St. Dominic; 1922; independent (2,330).

**Assumption College** (c): 500 Salisbury St., Worcester, MA 01615. Assumptionist Fathers; 1904 (2,588).

**Avila College** (c): 11901 Wornall Rd., Kansas City, MO 64145. Sisters of St. Joseph of Carondelet; 1916 (1,413).

**Barat College** (c): 700 Westleigh Rd., Lake Forest, IL 60045. Society of the Sacred Heart; 1919; independent (710).

**Barry University** (c): 11300 N.E. 2nd Ave., Mi-

ami Shores, FL 33161. Dominican Sisters (Adrian, Mich.); 1940 (6,896).

**Bellarmine College** (c): 2001 Newburg Rd., Louisville, KY 40205; Louisville archdiocese; independent (2,326).

**Belmont Abbey College** (c): 100 Belmont-Mt. Holly Rd., Belmont, NC 28012. Benedictine Fathers; 1876 (918).

**Benedictine College** (c): 1020 N. Second St., Atchison, KS 66002. Benedictines; 1859; independent (905).

**Boston College** (University Status) (c): Chestnut Hill, MA 02167. Jesuit Fathers; 1863 (14,455).

**Brescia College** (c): 717 Frederica St., Owensboro, KY 42301. Ursuline Sisters; 1950 (750).

**Briar Cliff College** (c): 3303 Rebecca St., P.O. Box 2100, Sioux City, IA 51104. Sisters of St. Francis of the Holy Family; 1930 (1,157).

**Cabrini College** (c): 610 King of Prussia Rd., Radnor, PA 19087. Missionary Srs. of Sacred Heart; 1957; private (1,473).

**Caldwell College** (c): 9 Ryerson Ave., Caldwell, NJ 07006. Dominican Sisters; 1939 (1,600).

**Calumet College of St. Joseph** (c): 2400 New York Ave., Whiting, IN 46394. Society of the Precious Blood, 1951 (1,200).

**Canisius College** (c): 2001 Main St., Buffalo, NY 14208. Jesuit Fathers; 1870; independent (4,789).

**Cardinal Stritch College** (c): 6801 N. Yates Rd., Milwaukee, WI 53217. Sisters of St. Francis of Assisi; 1937 (5,654).

**Carlow College** (w): 3333 5th Ave., Pittsburgh, PA 15213. Sisters of Mercy; 1929 (2,084).

**Carroll College** (c): Helena, MT 59625. Diocesan; 1909 (1,425).

**Catholic University of America, The** (c): 620 Michigan Ave. N.E., Washington, DC 20064. Hierarchy of the United States; 1887. Pontifical University (6,147).

**Chaminade University of Honolulu** (c): 3140 Waialae Ave., Honolulu, Hawaii 96816. Marianists; 1955 (2,300).

**Chestnut Hill College** (w): Philadelphia, PA 19118. Sisters of St. Joseph; 1924 (1,143).

**Christendom College** (c): 134 Christendom Dr., Front Royal, VA 22630. Founded 1977 (164).

**Christian Brothers University** (c): 650 E. Parkway S., Memphis, TN 38104. Brothers of the Christian Schools; 1871 (1,609).

**Clarke College** (c): 1550 Clarke Dr., Dubuque, Iowa 52001. Sisters of Charity, BVM; 1843 (1,002).

**Creighton University** (c): 2500 California Plazaha, NE 68178. Jesuit Fathers; 1878; independent (6,424).

**Dallas, University of** (c): 1845 E. Northgate, Irving, TX 75062. Dallas diocese; 1956; independent (2,995).

**Dayton, University of** (c): 300 College Park Ave., Dayton, Ohio 45469. Marianists; 1850 (10,750).

**DePaul University** (c): One E. Jackson Blvd., Chicago, IL 60604. Vincentians; 1898 (16,747).

**Detroit Mercy, University of** (c): 4001 W. McNichols Rd., Detroit, MI, 48221; 8200 W. Outer Dr., Detroit MI 48219. Society of Jesus and Sisters of Mercy; 1877; independent (7,774).

**Dominican College of Blauvelt** (c): rangeburg, NY 10962. Dominican Sisters; 1952; independent (1,800).

**Dominican College** (c): 50 Acacia Ave., San Rafael, CA 94901. Dominican Sisters; 1890; independent (1,250).

**Duquesne University** (c): 600 Forbes Ave., Pittsburgh, PA 15282. Congregation of the Holy Ghost; 1878 (more than 9,000).

**D'Youville College** (c): 320 Porter Ave., Buffalo, NY 14201. Grey Nuns of the Sacred Heart; 1908; independent (1,700).

**Edgewood College** (c): 855 Woodrow St., Madison, WI 53711. Dominican Sisters; 1927 (1,900).

**Emmanuel College** (w): 400 The Fenway, Boston, MA 02115. Sisters of Notre Dame de Namur; independent (1,200).

**Fairfield University** (c): North Benson Rd., Fairfield, CT 06430. Jesuits; 1942 (5,300).

**Felician College** (c): 262 S. Main St., Lodi, NJ 07644. Felician Sisters; 1942; independent (1,041).

**Fontbonne College** (c): 6800 Wydown Blvd., St. Louis, MO 63105. Sisters of St. Joseph of Carondelet; 1917; independent (1,681).

**Fordham University** (c): Fordham Rd. and Third Ave., New York, NY 10458. Society of Jesus (Jesuits); 1841; independent (14,500).

**Franciscan University of Steubenville** (c): University Blvd., Steubenville, Ohio 43952. Franciscan Fathers; 1946 (1,800).

**Gannon University** (c): 109 University Square, Erie, PA 16541 (main campus); 2551 W. 8th St., Erie, PA 16505 (Villa Maria branch campus). Diocese of Erie; 1933 (3,669).

**Georgetown University** (c): 37th and O Sts. N.W., Washington, DC 20057. Jesuit Fathers; 1789 (11,985).

**Georgian Court College** (w/c): 900 Lakewood Ave., Lakewood, NJ 08701. Sisters of Mercy; 1908 (2,539).

**Gonzaga University** (c): Spokane, WA 99258. Jesuit Fathers; 1887 (4,495).

**Great Falls, University of** (c): 1301 20th St. S., Great Falls, MT 59405. Sisters of Providence; 1932; independent (1,361).

**Gwynedd-Mercy College** (c): Gwynedd Valley, PA 19437. Sisters of Mercy; 1948; independent (1,979).

**Hilbert College** (c): 5200 S. Park Ave., Hamburg, NY 14075. Franciscan Sisters of St. Joseph; 1957; independent (950).

**Holy Cross, College of the** (c): Worcester, MA 01610. Jesuit Fathers; 1843 (2,720).

**Holy Family College** (c): Grant and Frankford Aves., Philadelphia, PA 19114. Sisters of Holy Family of Nazareth; 1954; independent (2,569).

**Holy Names College** (c): 3500 Mountain Blvd., Oakland, CA 94619. Sisters of the Holy Names of Jesus and Mary; 1868; independent (966).

**Illinois Benedictine College** (c): 5700 College Rd., Lisle, IL 60532. Benedictine Monks of St. Procopius Abbey; 1887 (2,694).

**Immaculata College** (w): Immaculata, PA 19345. Sisters, Servants of the Immaculate Heart of Mary; 1920 (2,088).

**Incarnate Word College** (c): 4301 Broadway, San Antonio, TX 78209. Sisters of Charity of the Incarnate Word; 1881 (2,861).

**Iona College** (c): 715 North Ave., New Rochelle, NY 10801. Congregation of Christian Brothers; 1940; independent (6,247).

**John Carroll University** (c): 20700 North Park Blvd., Cleveland, OH 44118. Jesuits; 1886 (4,300).

**Kansas Newman College** (formerly Sacred Heart College): 3100 McCormick Ave., Wichita, KS 67213. Sisters Adorers of the Blood of Christ; 1933 (1,954).

**King's College** (c): Wilkes-Barre, PA 18711. Holy Cross Fathers; 1946 (2,330).

**La Roche College** (c): 9000 Babcock Blvd., Pittsburgh, PA 15237. Sisters of Divine Providence; 1963 (1,813).

**La Salle University** (c): 1900 W. Olney Ave., Philadelphia, PA 19141. Christian Brothers; 1863 (6,000).

**Le Moyne College** (c): Syracuse, NY 13214. Jesuit Fathers; 1946; independent (2,757, full-time, part-time, graduate)

**Lewis University** (c): Romeoville, IL 60441. Christian Brothers; 1932 (4,399).

**Loras College** (c): 1450 Alta Vista St., Dubuque, IA 52004. Archdiocese of Dubuque; 1839 (1,993).

**Lourdes College** (c): 6832 Convent Blvd., Sylvania, OH 43560. Sisters of St. Francis; 1958 (1,670).

**Loyola College** (c): 4501 N. Charles St., Baltimore, MD 21210. Jesuits; 1852; combined with Mt. St. Agnes College, 1971 (6,261).

**Loyola Marymount University** (c): 7101 W. 80th St., Los Angeles, CA 90045. Society of Jesus; Religious of Sacred Heart of Mary,
Sisters of St. Joseph of Orange; 1911 (5,957).

**Loyola University** (c): 6363 St. Charles Ave., New Orleans, LA 70118. Jesuit Fathers; 1912 (5,000).

**Loyola University Chicago** (c): 820 N. Michigan Ave., Chicago, IL 60611. Society of Jesus; 1870 (15,000). Mallinckrodt College (Wilmette) and Mundelein College (Chicago) became part of Loyola

University Chicago, in January and June, 1991, respectively.

**Madonna University** (c): 36600 Schoolcraft Rd., Livonia, MI 48150. Felician Sisters; 1947 (4,200).

**Magdalen College** (c): 511 Kearsarge Mountain Rd., Warner, NH 03278; Magdalen College Corporation; 1973 (60).

**Manhattan College** (c): 4513 Manhattan College Pkwy., Riverdale, NY 10471. De La Salle Christian Brothers; 1835; independent (3,600). Cooperative program with College of Mt. St. Vincent.

**Marian College** (c): 45 S. National Ave., Fond du Lac, WI 54935. Sisters of St. Agnes; 1936 (2,510).

**Marian College** (c): 3200 Cold Spring Rd., Indianapolis, IN 46222. Sisters of St. Francis (Oldenburg, Ind.); 1851; independent (1,352).

**Marist College** (c): Poughkeepsie, NY 12601. Marist Brothers of the Schools; 1946; independent (4,300).

**Marquette University** (c): P.O. Box 1881, Milwaukee, WI 53201. Jesuit Fathers; 1881; independent (10,700).

**Mary, University of** (c): 7500 University Dr., Bismarck, ND 58504. Benedictine Sisters; 1959 (1,855).

**Marygrove College** (c): 8425 W. McNichols Rd., Detroit, MI 48221. Sisters, Servants of the Immaculate Heart of Mary; 1910; independent (1,238).

**Marylhurst College** (c): Marylhurst, OR 97036. Srs. of Holy Names of Jesus and Mary; 1893; independent (1,339).

**Marymount College** (w): Tarrytown, NY 10591. Religious of the Sacred Heart of Mary; 1907; independent (1,138). Coed in weekend degree programs.

**Marymount Manhattan College** (w): 221 E. 71st St., New York, NY 10021. Religious of the Sacred Heart of Mary; 1936; independent (1,330).

**Marymount University** (c): 2807 N. Glebe Rd., Arlington, VA 22007. Religious of the Sacred Heart of Mary; 1950; independent (4,167).

**Marywood College** (c): Scranton, PA 18509. Sisters, Servants of the Immaculate Heart of Mary; 1915; independent (3,068).

**Mater Dei College** (c): Riverside Dr., Ogdensburg, NY 13669. Sisters of St. Joseph; 1960; independent (506).

**Mercyhurst College** (c): 501 E. 38th St., Erie, PA 16546. Sisters of Mercy; 1926 (2,466).

**Merrimack College** (c): North Andover, MA 01845. Augustinians;1947 (2,105).

**Misericordia** (College Misericordia) (c): Dallas, PA 18612. Religious Sisters of Mercy of the Union; 1924 (1,822).

**Molloy College** (c): 1000 Hempstead Ave., Rockville Centre, NY 11570. Dominican Sisters; 1955; independent (2,149).

**Mt. Aloysius College** (c): 7373 Admiral Peary Hwy., Cresson, PA 16630. Sisters of Mercy; 1939.

**Mount Marty College** (c): Yankton, SD 57078. Benedictine Sisters; 1936 (1,100).

**Mount Mary College** (w): 2900 N. Menomonee River Pkwy., Milwaukee, WI 53222. School Sisters of Notre Dame; 1913 (1,524).

**Mount Mercy College** (c): 1330 Elmhurst Dr. N.E., Cedar Rapids, IA 52402. Sisters of Mercy; 1928; independent (1,200).

**Mount St. Clare College** (c): 400 N. Bluff Blvd.,

Clinton, IA 52732. Sisters of St. Francis of Clinton, Iowa; 1918 (513).

**Mount St. Joseph, College of** (c): 5701 Delhi Rd., Cincinnati, OH 45233. Sisters of Charity; 1920 (2,648).

**Mt. St. Mary College** (c): Newburgh, NY 12550. Dominican Sisters; 1959; independent (1,823).

**Mount St. Mary's College** (c): Emmitsburg, MD 21727. Founded by Fr. John DuBois, S.S., 1808; independent (1,286).

**Mount St. Mary's College** (w/c): 12001 Chalon Rd., Los Angeles, CA 90049 and 10 Chester Pl., Los Angeles, CA 90007 (Doheny Campus). Sisters of St. Joseph of Carondelet; 1925. Coed in music, nursing and graduate programs.

**Mt. St. Vincent, College of** (c): 6301 Riverdale Ave., Bronx, NY 10471. Sisters of Charity; 1847; independent (1,300). Cooperative program with Manhattan College.

**Neumann College** (c): Concord Rd., Aston, PA 19014. Sisters of St. Francis; 1965; independent (1,335).

**New Rochelle, College of** (w/c): 29 Castle Pl., New Rochelle, NY 10805 (main campus). Ursuline Order; 1904; independent (6,000). Coed in nursing, graduate, new resources divisions.

**Niagara University** (c): Niagara Univ., NY 14109. Vincentian Fathers and Brothers; 1856 (2,862).

**Notre Dame, College of** (c): 1500 Ralston Ave., Belmont, CA 94002. Sisters of Notre Dame de Namur; 1868; independent (1,730).

**Notre Dame du Lac, University of** (c): Notre Dame, IN 46556. Congregation of Holy Cross; 1842 (10,000).

**Notre Dame College** (c): 2321 Elm St., Manchester, NH 03104. Sisters of Holy Cross; 1950; independent (1,291).

**Notre Dame College of Ohio** (w): 4545 College Rd., Cleveland, OH 44121. Sisters of Notre Dame; 1922 (688).

**Notre Dame of Maryland, College of** (w): 4701 N. Charles St., Baltimore, MD 21210. School Sisters of Notre Dame; 1873 (3,215).

**Ohio Dominican College** (c): Columbus, OH 43219. Dominican Sisters of St. Mary of the Springs; 1911 (1,713).

**Our Lady of Holy Cross College** (c): 4123 Woodland Dr., New Orleans, LA 70131. Congregation of Sisters Marianites of Holy Cross; 1916 (1,360).

**Our Lady of the Elms, College of** (w): Chicopee, MA 01013. Sisters of St. Joseph; 1928 (1,174).

**Our Lady of the Lake University of San Antonio** (c): 411 S.W. 24th St., San Antonio, TX 78207. Sisters of Divine Providence; 1895 (3,338).

**Parks College of Saint Louis University** (c): Cahokia, IL 62206. Jesuits; 1927; independent (600).

**Pontifical Catholic University of Puerto Rico** (c): Ponce, PR 00731. Hierarchy of Puerto Rico; 1948; Pontifical University (12,100).

**Portland, University of** (c): 5000 N. Willamette Blvd., Portland, OR 97203. Holy Cross Fathers; 1901; independent (2,800).

**Presentation College** (c): Aberdeen, SD 7401. Sisters of the Presentation; 1951 (451).

**Providence College** (c): River Ave. and Eaton St., Providence, RI 02918. Dominican Friars; 1917 (6,100).

Quincy University (c): 1800 College Ave., Quincy, IL 62301. Franciscan Friars; 1860 (1,250).

Regis College (w): Weston, MA 02193. Sisters of St. Joseph; 1927; independent (1,200).

Regis University (c): 3333 Regis Blvd. Denver, CO 80221. Jesuits; 1887 (9,091).

Rivier College (c): Nashua, NH 03060. Sisters of the Presentation of Mary; 1933; independent (2,759).

Rockhurst College (c): 1100 Rockhurst Rd., Kansas City, MO 64110. Jesuit Fathers; 1910 (2,625).

Rosary College (c): 7900 W. Division St., River Forest, IL 60305. Dominican Sisters; 1901 (1,855).

Rosemont College (w): Rosemont, PA 19010. Society of the Holy Child Jesus; 1921 (749).

Sacred Heart University (c): 5151 Park Ave., Fairfield, CT 06432. Diocese of Bridgeport; 1963; independent (5,600).

St. Ambrose University (c): Davenport, IA 52803. Diocese of Davenport; 1882 (2,585).

Saint Anselm College (c): Manchester NH 03102. Benedictines; 1889 (1,937).

Saint Benedict, College of (w): 37 S. College Ave., St. Joseph, MN 56374. Benedictine Sisters; 1913 (1,736). Sister college of St. John's University, Collegeville (see below).

St. Bonaventure University (c): St. Bonaventure, NY 14778. Franciscan Friars; 1858; independent (2,500).

St. Catherine, College of (w): 2004 Randolph Ave., St. Paul, MN 55105. Sisters of St. Joseph of Carondelet; 1905 (2,763).

St. Edward's University (c): 3001 S. Congress Ave., Austin, TX 78704. Holy Cross Brothers; 1885; independent (3,107).

St. Elizabeth, College of (w): 2 Convent Rd., Morristown, NJ 07960. Sisters of Charity; 1899; independent (1,599). Coed in graduate and weekend college programs.

St. Francis, College of (c): 500 N. Wilcox St., Joliet, IL 60435. Sisters of St. Francis of Mary Immaculate; 1920; independent (1,100).

St. Francis College (c): 180 Remsen St., Brooklyn Heights, NY 11201. Franciscan Brothers; 1884; private, independent in the Franciscan tradition (2,166).

St. Francis College (c): 2701 Spring St., Fort Wayne, IN 46808. Sisters of St. Francis; 1890 (993).

St. Francis College (c): Loretto, PA 15940. Franciscan Friars; 1847; independent (2,020).

St. John's University (c): 8000 Utopia Pkwy., Jamaica, NY 11439 (Queens Campus); 300 Howard Ave., Grymes Hill, Staten Island, NY 10301 (Staten Island Campus). Vincentians; 1870 (19,105).

St. John's University (m): Collegeville, MN 56321. Benedictines; 1857 (1,643). All classes and programs are coeducational with College of St. Benedict (see above).

St. Joseph, College of (c): Clement Rd., Rutland, VT 05701. Sisters of St. Joseph; 1954; independent (500).

Saint Joseph College (w/c): 1678 Asylum Ave., West Hartford, CT 06117. Sisters of Mercy; 1932 (1,859). Women's college in undergraduate liberal arts. Coed in graduate school and Weekend College.

Saint Joseph's College (c): Standish, ME 04084. Sisters of Mercy; 1912 (716, campus; also has ex-

ternal degree program with more than 5,000 students nationwide).

Saint Joseph's College (c): Rensselaer, IN 47978. Society of the Precious Blood; 1891 (1,030).

St. Joseph's College (c): 245 Clinton Ave., Brooklyn, NY 11205 (1,114) and 155 Roe Blvd., Patchogue, N.Y. 11772 (2,303). Sisters of St. Joseph; 1916; independent.

St. Joseph's University (c): 5600 City Ave., Philadelphia, PA 19131. Jesuit Fathers; 1851 (6,000).

Saint Leo College (c): Saint Leo, FL 33574. Order of St. Benedict; 1889; independent (7,148).

St. Louis University (c): 221 N. Grand Blvd., St. Louis, MO 63103. Society of Jesus; 1818; independent (12,000).

Saint Martin's College (c): Lacey, WA 98503. Benedictine Monks; 1895 (891 main campus; 494 extension campuses).

Saint Mary, College of (w): 1901 S. 72nd St., Omaha, NE 68124. Sisters of Mercy; 1923; independent.

Saint Mary College (c): Leavenworth, KS 66048. Sisters of Charity of Leavenworth; 1923 (905).

Saint Mary-of-the-Woods College (w): St. Mary-of-the-Woods, IN 47876. Sisters of Providence; 1840 (1,215).

Saint Mary's College (w): Notre Dame, IN 46556. Sisters of the Holy Cross; 1844 (1,500).

St. Mary's College (c): Orchard Lake, MI 48324. Secular Clergy; 1885 (375).

St. Mary's College (c): Moraga, CA 94575. Brothers of the Christian Schools; 1863 (4,000).

Saint Mary's University of Minnesota (c): Winona, MN 55987. Brothers of the Christian Schools; 1912 (1,300 undergraduate, 6,300 graduate).

St. Mary's University of San Antonio (c): One Camino Santa Maria, San Antonio, TX 78228. Society of Mary (Marianists); 1852 (4,200).

Saint Meinrad College (m): St. Meinrad, IN 47577. Benedictines. Liberal Arts.

St. Michael's College (c): Colchester, VT 05439. Society of St. Edmund; 1904 (2,092).

St. Norbert College (c): De Pere, WI 54115. Norbertine Fathers; 1898; independent (2,092).

Saint Peter's College (c): 2641 Kennedy Blvd., Jersey City, NJ 07306. Society of Jesus; 1872; independent (3,025).

Saint Rose, College of (c): 432 Western Ave., Albany, NY 12203. Sisters of St. Joseph of Carondelet; 1920; independent (4,001).

St. Scholastica, College of (c): 1200 Kenwood Ave., Duluth, MN 55811. Benedictine Sisters; 1912; independent (1,849).

St. Thomas, University of (c): 2115 Summit Ave., St. Paul, MN 55105. Archdiocese of St. Paul and Minneapolis; 1885 (10,161).

St. Thomas, University of (c): 3800 Montrose Blvd., Houston, TX 77006. Basilian Fathers; 1947 (2,298).

St. Thomas Aquinas College (c): Sparkill, NY 10976. Dominican Sisters of Sparkill; 1952; independent, corporate board of trustees (2,100).

St. Thomas University (c): 16400 N.W. 32nd Ave., Miami, FL 33054. Archdiocese of Miami; 1962 (2,488).

**Saint Vincent College** (c): Fraser Purchase Rd., Latrobe, PA 15650. Benedictine Fathers; 1846 (1,237).

**St. Xavier University** (c): 3700 W. 103rd St., Chicago, IL 60655. Sisters of Mercy; chartered 1847 (4,400).

**Salve Regina University** (c): Ochre Point Ave., Newport, RI 02840. Sisters of Mercy; 1934 (2,195).

**San Diego, University of** (c): 5998 Alcala Park, San Diego, CA 92110. San Diego diocese and Religious of the Sacred Heart; 1949; independent (6,381).

**San Francisco, University of** (c): 2130 Fulton St., San Francisco, CA 94117. Jesuit Fathers; 1855 (6,564).

**Santa Clara University** (c): 500 El Camino Real, Santa Clara, CA 95053. Jesuit Fathers; 1851; independent (7,514).

**Santa Fe, College of** (c): Santa Fe, NM 87501. Brothers of the Christian Schools; 1947 (1,600).

**Scranton, University of** (c): Scranton, PA 18510. Society of Jesus; 1888; independent (5,100).

**Seattle University** (c): Broadway and East Madison, Seattle, WA 98122. Jesuit Fathers; 1891 (5,025).

**Seton Hall University** (c): South Orange Ave., South Orange, NJ 07079. Diocesan Clergy; 1856 (9,688).

**Seton Hill College** (w): Greensburg, PA 15601. Sisters of Charity of Seton Hill; 1883 (921).

**Siena College** (c): Loudonville, NY 12211. Franciscan Friars; 1937 (3,350).

**Siena Heights College** (c): 1247 E. Siena Heights Dr., Adrian, MI 49221. Dominican Sisters; 1919 (1,850).

**Silver Lake College of Holy Family** (c): 2406 S. Alverno Rd., Manitowoc, WI 54220. Franciscan Sisters of Christian Charity; 1935 (1,000).

**Spalding University** (c): 851 S. 4th Ave., Louisville, KY 40203. Sisters of Charity of Nazareth; 1814; independent (1,218).

**Spring Hill College** (c): 4000 Dauphin St., Mobile, AL 36608. Jesuit Fathers; 1830 (1,117).

**Stonehill College** (c): 320 Washington St., North Easton, MA 02357. Holy Cross Fathers; 1948; independent (2,949).

**Thomas Aquinas College** (c): 10000 N. Ojai Rd., Santa Paula, CA 93060. Founded 1971 (232).

**Thomas More College** (c): Crestview Hills, Covington, KY 41017. Diocese of Covington; 1921 (1,335).

**Trinity College** (w): Colchester Ave., Burlington, VT 05401. Sisters of Mercy; 1925 (973).

**Trinity College** (w): 125 Michigan Ave. N.E., Washington, DC 20017. Sisters of Notre Dame de Namur; 1897 (1,100). Coed in graduate school.

**Ursuline College** (w): 2550 Lander Rd., Cleveland, OH 44124. Ursuline Nuns; 1871 (1,446).

**Villanova University** (c): 800 Lancaster Ave., Villanova, PA 19085. Order of St. Augustine; 1842 (11,100).

**Viterbo College** (c): 815 S. 9th, La Crosse, WI

54601. Franciscan Sisters of Perpetual Adoration; 1890 (1,160).

**Walsh University** (c): 2020 Easton St. N.W., North Canton, Ohio 44720. Brothers of Christian Instruction; 1958 (1,480).

**Wheeling Jesuit College** (c): 316 Washington Ave., Wheeling, WV 26003. Jesuit Fathers; 1954 (1,430).

**Xavier University** (c): 3800 Victory Pkwy., Cincinnati, OH 45207. Jesuit Fathers; 1831 (6,180).

**Xavier University of Louisiana** (c): 7325 Palmetto St., New Orleans, LA 70125. Sisters of Blessed Sacrament; 1925; lay-Religious administrative board (3,490).

## Catholic Two-Year Colleges

**Ancilla College** (c): Donaldson, IN 46513. Ancilla Domini Sisters; 1937.

**Aquinas College** (c): 4210 Harding Rd., Nashville, TN 37205. Dominican Sisters; 1961 (380). Offers B.A. in Elementary Teacher Education.

**Assumption College for Sisters:** 350 Bernardsville Rd.,, Mendham, NJ 07945. Sisters of Christian Charity; 1953 (25).

**Castle College:** 21 Searles Rd., Windham, NH 03087. Sisters of Mercy; 1963; independent (313).

**Chatfield College** (c): St. Martin, OH 45118. Ursulines; 1971 (300).

**The College of St. Catherine-Minneapolis** (c): 601 25th Ave. S., Minneapolis, MN 55454. Sisters of St. Joseph of Carondelet (1,232).

**Donnelly College** (c): 608 N. 18th St., Kansas City, KS 66102. Archdiocesan College; 1949 (752).

**Don Bosco Technical Institute** (m): 1151 San Gabriel Blvd., Rosemead, CA 91770. Salesians; 1969 (105).

**Holy Cross College** (c): Notre Dame, IN 46556. Brothers of Holy Cross; 1966 (455).

**Manor Junior College** (c): 700 Fox Chase Road, Jenkintown, PA 19046. Sisters of St. Basil the Great; 1947 (640).

**Maria College** (c): 700 New Scotland Ave., Albany, NY 12208. Sisters of Mercy; 1963 (950).

**Marymount Palos Verdes College** (c): Rancho Palos Verdes, CA 90274. Religious of the Sacred Heart of Mary; independent (1,068).

**St. Catharine College** (c); St. Catharine, KY 40061. Dominican Sisters; 1931 (375).

**St. Gregory's College** (c): Shawnee, OK 74801. Benedictine Monks; 1876 (300).

**Springfield College in Illinois** (c): 1500 N. Fifth St., Springfield, IL 62702. Ursuline Sisters; 1929 (455).

**Trocaire College** (c): 110 Red Jacket Pkwy., Buffalo, NY 14220. Sisters of Mercy; 1958; independent (1,105).

**Villa Maria College of Buffalo** (c): 240 Pine Ridge Rd., Buffalo, NY 14225. Felician Sisters 1960; independent (400).

# CAMPUS MINISTRY

Campus ministry is an expression of the Church's special desire to be present to all who are involved in higher education and to further dialogue between the Church and the academic community. In the words of the U.S. bishops' 1985 pastoral letter entitled "Empowered by the Spirit," this ministry is

"the public presence and service through which properly prepared baptized persons are empowered by the Spirit to use their talents and gifts on behalf of the Church in order to be sign and instrument of the Kingdom in the academic world."

Campus ministry, carried on by lay, Religious and

ordained ministers, gathers members of the Church on campus to form the faith community, appropriate the faith, form Christian consciences, educate for justice and facilitate religious development.

The dimensions and challenge of this ministry are evident from, among other things, the numbers involved: approximately 550,000 Catholics on more than 230 Catholic college and university campuses; about four million in several thousand non-Catholic private and public institutions; 1,200 or more campus ministers. In many dioceses, the activities of ministers are coordinated by a local diocesan director. Two professional organizations serve the ministry on the national level:

The National Association of Diocesan Directors of Campus Ministry, Rev. Frederick J. Pennett, president, 6 Madbury Rd., Box 620, Durham, NH 03824.

The Catholic Campus Ministry Association, with a membership of 1,200, 300 College Park Ave., Dayton, OH 45469. Executive director, Donald R. McCrabb.

# DIOCESAN AND INTERDIOCESAN SEMINARIES

(Sources: Almanac survey; *Official Catholic Directory;* Catholic News Service.)

Information, according to states, includes names of archdioceses and dioceses, and names and addresses of seminaries. Types of seminaries, when not clear from titles, are indicated in most cases. Interdiocesan seminaries are generally conducted by religious orders for candidates for the priesthood from several dioceses. The list does not include houses of study reserved for members of religious communities. Archdioceses are indicated by an asterisk.

**California:** Los Angeles* — St. John's Seminary (major), 5012 Seminary Rd., Camarillo 93012; St. John's Seminary College, 5118 Seminary Rd., Camarillo 93012.

San Diego — St. Francis Seminary (college and pre-theology formation program), 1667 Santa Paula Dr., San Diego 92111.

San Francisco* — St. Patrick's Seminary (major), 320 Middlefield Rd., Menlo Park 94025.

**Connecticut:** Hartford* — St. Thomas Seminary (college formation program), 467 Bloomfield Ave., Bloomfield 06002.

Norwich — Holy Apostles College and Seminary (adult vocations; minor and major), 33 Prospect Hill Rd., Cromwell 06416.

Stamford Byzantine Rite — Ukrainian Catholic Seminary: St. Basil College Seminary (minor), 195 Glenbrook Rd., Stamford 06902.

**District of Columbia:** Washington* — Theological College (national, major), The Catholic University of America, 401 Michigan Ave., N.E. 20017.

St. Josaphat's Seminary, 201 Taylor St. N.E., Washington 20017. (Major house of formation serving the four Ukrainian Byzantine-rite dioceses in the U.S.)

**Florida:** Miami* — St. John Vianney College Seminary, 2900 S.W. 87th Ave., Miami 33165.

Palm Beach — St. Vincent de Paul Regional Seminary (major), 10701 S. Military Trail, Boynton Beach 33436.

**Illinois:** Chicago* — Archbishop Quigley Preparatory Seminary (high school), 103 East Chestnut St., Chicago 60611; St. Joseph Seminary (college), 6551 N. Sheridan Rd., Chicago 60626. Mundelein Seminary, University of St. Mary of the Lake, 1000 E. Maple Ave., Mundelein 60060.

**Indiana:** Indianapolis* — St. Meinrad Seminary, College and School of Theology (interdiocesan), St. Meinrad 47577.

**Iowa:** Davenport — St. Ambrose University Seminary, 518 W. Locust St., Davenport 52803.

Dubuque* — Seminary of St. Pius X (interdiocesan), Loras College, Dubuque 52001.

**Louisiana:** New Orleans* — Notre Dame Seminary Graduate School of Theology, 2901 S. Carrollton Ave., New Orleans 70118; St. Joseph Seminary College (interdiocesan), St. Benedict 70457.

**Maryland:** Baltimore* — St. Mary's Seminary and University, 5400 Roland Ave., Baltimore 21210; Mt. St. Mary's Seminary, Emmitsburg 21727.

**Massachusetts:** Boston* — St. John's Seminary, School of Theology, 127 Lake St., Brighton 02135; St. John's Seminary, College of Liberal Arts, 197 Foster St., Brighton 02135; Pope John XXIII National Seminary (for ages 30-60), 558 South Ave., Weston 02193.

Newton — Melkite Greek Catholic — St. Gregory the Theologian Seminary, 233 Grant Ave., Newton 02159.

**Michigan:** Detroit* — Sacred Heart Major Seminary (college/theologate and institute for ministry), 2701 Chicago Blvd., Detroit 48206; Sts. Cyril and Methodius Seminary, St. Mary's College (theologate and college) independent, primarily serving Polish-American community, 3535 Indian Trail, Orchard Lake 48324.

Grand Rapids — Christopher House, 723 Rosewood Ave., S.E., East Grand Rapids 49506.

**Minnesota:** St. John's School of Theology and Seminary, St. John's University, P.O. Box 7288, Collegeville 56321.

St. Paul and Minneapolis* — St. Paul Seminary School of Divinity, University of St. Thomas, 2260 Summit Ave., St. Paul 55105; St. John Vianney Seminary (college residence), 2115 Summit Ave., St. Paul 55105.

Winona — Immaculate Heart of Mary Seminary, St. Mary's University, No. 43, 700 Terrace Heights, Winona 55987.

**Missouri:** Jefferson City — St. Thomas Aquinas Preparatory Seminary (High School Seminary), 245 N. Levering Ave., P.O. Box 858, Hannibal 63401.

St. Louis* — Kenrick-Glennon Seminary (St. Louis Roman Catholic Theological Seminary). Kenrick School of Theology and Cardinal Glennon College, 5200 Glennon Dr., St. Louis 63119.

**Montana:** Helena — Pre-Seminary Program, Carroll College, Helena 59625.

**New Jersey:** Newark* — Immaculate Conception Seminary — college seminary; major seminary;

graduate school — Seton Hall University, 400 South Orange Ave., South Orange 07079.

**New Mexico:** Santa Fe* — Immaculate Heart of Mary Seminary (college level), Mt. Carmel Rd., Santa Fe 87501.

**New York:** Brooklyn — Cathedral Seminary Residence of the Immaculate Conception (college and pre-theology), 7200 Douglaston Parkway, Douglaston 11362; Cathedral Preparatory Seminary, 56-25 92nd St., Elmhurst 11373.

Buffalo — Christ the King Seminary (interdiocesan theologate), P.O. Box 607, 711 Knox Rd., East Aurora 14052.

New York* — St. Joseph's Seminary (major), 201 Seminary Ave., Dunwoodie, Yonkers 10704; St. John Neumann Residence (college and pre-theology), 5655 Arlington Ave., Riverdale 10471. Cathedral Preparatory Seminary, 946 Boston Post Rd., Rye 10580.

Ogdensburg — Wadhams Hall Seminary College (interdiocesan), 6866 State Hwy. 37, Ogdensburg 13669.

Rockville Centre — Seminary of the Immaculate Conception (major), Lloyd Harbor, Huntington, L.I. 11743.

St. Maron Eparchy, Brooklyn — Our Lady of Lebanon Maronite Seminary, 7164 Alaska Ave. N.W., Washington, DC 20012.

**North Dakota:** Fargo — Cardinal Muench Seminary (interdiocesan high school, college and pre-theology), 100 35th Ave. N.E., Fargo 58102.

**Ohio:** Cincinnati* — Mt. St. Mary's Seminary of the West, 6616 Beechmont Ave., Cincinnati 45230 (division of the Athenaeum of Ohio).

Cleveland — St. Mary Seminary (graduate school of theology), 28700 Euclid Ave. Wickliffe 44092.

Columbus — Pontifical College Josephinum (national), theologate and college, Columbus 43235.

**Oregon:** Portland* — Mount Angel Seminary (interdiocesan, college, pre-theology program, graduate school of theology), St. Benedict 97373.

**Pennsylvania:** Erie — St. Mark Seminary, P.O. Box 10397, Erie 16514.

Greensburg — St. Vincent Seminary (interdiocesan; pre-theology program; theologate; graduate programs in theology; religious education), 300 Fraser Purchase Rd., Latrobe 15650.

Philadelphia* — Theological Seminary of St. Charles Borromeo, One Thousand East Wynnewood Rd., Wynnewood 19096. (College, pre-theology program, theologate.)

Pittsburgh* (Byzantine-Ruthenian) — Byzantine Catholic Seminary of Sts. Cyril and Methodius (college, pre-theology program, theologate), 3605 Perrysville Ave., Pittsburgh 1214.

Pittsburgh — St. Paul Seminary (interdiocesan, college and pre-theology), 2900 Noblestown Rd., Pittsburgh 15205.

Scranton — St. Pius X Seminary (college and pre-theology formation; interdiocesan), Dalton 18414. Affiliated with the University of Scranton.

**Rhode Island:** Providence — Seminary of Our Lady of Providence (House of Formation; college students and pre-theology), 485 Mount Pleasant Ave., Providence 02908.

**Texas:** Dallas — Holy Trinity Seminary (college and pre-theology; English proficiency and academic foundation programs), P.O. Box 140309, Irving 75014.

El Paso — St. Charles Seminary College, P.O. Box 17548, El Paso 79917.

Galveston-Houston — St. Mary's Seminary (theologate), 9845 Memorial Dr., Houston 77024.

San Antonio* — The Assumption-St. John Seminary (theologate and pre-theology, Hispanic ministry emphasis), 2600 W. Woodlawn Ave., San Antonio 78228.

**Washington:** Spokane — Bishop White Seminary, College Formation Program, E. 429 Sharp Ave., Spokane 99202.

**Wisconsin:** Milwaukee* — St. Francis Seminary, 3257 S. Lake Dr., St. Francis 53235; College Program, East Hall, 915 W. Wisconsin Ave., Milwaukee 53233. Sacred Heart School of Theology (interdiocesan seminary for second career vocations), P.O. Box 429, Hales Corners, Wis. 53130.

## WORLD AND U.S. SEMINARY STATISTICS

The 1994 *Statistical Yearbook of the Church* reported the following comparative statistics for the years 1989 to 1994 of candidates in Philosophy and Theology (major seminarians). World totals are given first; U.S. statistics are given in parentheses.

| Year | Total Major Seminarians | Diocesan | Religious |
|---|---|---|---|
| 1989 | 93,405 (5,883) | 62,336 (3,889) | 31,069 (1,994) |
| 1990 | 96,155 (5,552) | 64,629 (3,676) | 31,526 (1,876) |
| 1991 | 99,668 (5,487) | 66,305 (3,777) | 33,363 (1,710) |
| 1992 | 102,000 (5,380) | 67,960 (3,645) | 34,040 (1,735) |
| 1993 | 103,709 (5,123) | 68,829 (3,505) | 34,880 (1,618) |
| 1994 | 105,075 (5,100) | 69,613 (3,526) | 35,462 (1,574) |

## PONTIFICAL UNIVERSITIES

(Principal source: *Annuario Pontificio*.)

These universities, listed according to country of location, have been canonically erected and authorized by the Congregation for Catholic Education to award degrees in stated fields of study.

New laws and norms governing ecclesiastical universities and faculties were promulgated in the apostolic constitution *Sapientia Christiana*, issued Apr. 15, 1979.

**Argentina:** Pontifical Catholic University of S. Maria of Buenos Aires (June 16, 1960): Juncal 1912, 1116 Buenos Aires.

**Belgium:** Catholic University of Louvain (founded Dec. 9, 1425; canonically erected, 1834), with autonomous institutions for French- (Louvain) and Flemish- (Leuven) speaking: Place de l'Universite I, B-1348 Louvain-La-Neuve (French); Naamsestraat 22/b, B-3000 Leuven (Flemish).

**Brazil:** Pontifical Catholic University of Rio de Janeiro (Jan. 20, 1947): Rua Marques de Sao Vicente 225, 22451 Rio de Janeiro, RJ.

Pontifical Catholic University of Minas Gerais (June 5, 1983): Av. Dom Jose Gaspar 500, C.P. 2686, 30161 Belo Horizonte MG.

Pontifical Catholic University of Parana (Aug. 6, 1985): Rua Imaculada Conceicao, 1155, Prado Velho, C.P. 670, 80001 Curitiba, PR.

Pontifical Catholic University of Rio Grande do Sul (Nov. 1, 1950): Av. Ipiranga 6681, C.P. 1429, 90001 Porto Alegre, RS.

Pontifical Catholic University of Sao Paulo (Jan. 25, 1947): Rua Monte Alegre 984, 05014 Sao Paulo.

Pontifical University of Campinas (Sept. 8, 1956): Rua Marechal Deodoro 1099, 13020 Campinas, SP.

**Canada:** Laval University (Mar. 15, 1876): Case Postale 460, Quebec G1K 7P4.

St. Paul University (formerly University of Ottawa) (Feb. 5, 1889): 223, Rue Main, Ottawa, Ont. K1S 1C4.

University of Sherbrooke (Nov. 21, 1957): Chemin Ste.-Catherine, Cité Universitaire, Sherbrooke, Que. J1K 2R1.

**Chile:** Pontifical Catholic University of Chile (June 21, 1888): Avenida Bernardo O'Higgins, 340, Casilla 114D. Santiago.

Catholic University of Valparaiso (Nov. 1, 1961): Avenida Brasil 2950, Casilla 4059, Valparaiso.

**Colombia:** Bolivarian Pontifical Catholic University (Aug. 16, 1945): Calle 52, N. 40-88, Apartado 1178, Medellin.

Pontifical Xaverian University (July 31, 1937): Carrera 7, N. 40-62, Apartado 56710, Santafé de Bogota D.C. Apartado 26239, Calle 18, N. 118-250, Cali (Cali campus).

**Cuba:** Catholic University of St. Thomas of Villanueva (May 4, 1957): Avenida Quenta 16,660, Marianao.

**Dominican Republic:** Pontifical Catholic University "Mother and Teacher" (Sept. 9, 1987): Apartado 822, Santiago de Los Caballeros.

**Ecuador:** Pontifical Catholic University of Ecuador (July 16, 1954): Doce de Octubre, N. 1076, Apartado 17-01-2184, Quito.

**Eritrea:** University of Asmara (Sept. 8, 1960): Via Menelik II, 45, Post Office Box 1220, Asmara.

**France:** Catholic University of Lille (Nov. 18, 1875): Boulevard Vauban 60, 59046 Lille.

Catholic Faculties of Lyon (Nov. 22, 1875): 25, Rue du Plat, 69288 Lyon.

Catholic Institute of Paris (Aug. 11, 1875): 21, Rue d'Assas, 75270 Paris.

Catholic Institute of Toulouse (Nov. 15, 1877): Rue de la Fonderie 31, 31068 Toulouse.

Catholic University of the West (Sept. 16, 1875): 3, Place Andre Leroy, B.P. 808, 49005 Angers.

**Germany:** Eichstatt Catholic University (Apr. 1, 1980): Ostenstrasse 26, D-85072, Eichstatt, Federal Republic of Germany.

**Guatemala:** Rafael Landivar University (Oct. 18, 1961): 17 Calle 8-64, zone 10 Guatemala.

**Ireland:** St. Patrick's College (Mar. 29, 1896): Maynooth, Co. Kildare.

**Italy:** Catholic University of the Sacred Heart (Dec. 25, 1920): Largo Gemelli 1, 20123 Milan.

Libera University Mary of the Assumption (Oct. 26, 1939): Via della Traspontina 21, 00193 Rome, Italy.

**Japan:** *Jochi Daigaku* (Sophia University) (Mar. 29, 1913): Chiyoda-Ku, Kioi-cho 7, Tokyo 102.

**Lebanon:** St. Joseph University of Beirut (Mar. 25, 1881): Rue de l'Universite St.-Joseph, Boite Postale 293, Beyrouth (Beirut).

**Netherlands:** Nijmegen Roman Catholic University (June 29, 1923): P.B. 9102, Comeniuslaan 4, 6500 HC, Nijmegen.

**Panama:** University of S. Maria La Antigua (May 27, 1965): Apartado 2143, Panama 1.

**Paraguay:** Catholic University of Our Lady of the Assumption (Feb. 2, 1965): Independencia Nacional y Comuneros, Casilla 1718, Asuncion.

**Peru:** Pontifical Catholic University of Peru (Sept. 30, 1942): Av. Universitaria, Pueblo Libre, Apartado 1761, Lima 100.

**Philippines:** Pontifical University of Santo Tomas (Nov. 20, 1645): España Street, 1008 Manila.

**Poland:** Catholic University of Lublin (July 25, 1920): Aleje Raclawickie 14, Skr. Poczt. 279, 20-950, Lublin.

Catholic Theological Academy (June 29, 1989): Ul. Dewajtis 5, 01-842, Warsaw.

Pontifical Academy of Theology of Krakow (Dec. 8, 1981): Ul. Kanonicza 20, 31-002 Krakow.

**Portugal:** Portuguese Catholic University (Nov. 1, 1967): Palma de Cima, 1600 Lisbon.

**Puerto Rico:** Pontifical Catholic University of Puerto Rico (Aug. 15, 1972): Ponce, Puerto Rico 00731.

**Spain:** Catholic University of Navarra (Aug. 6, 1960): 31009 Pamplona.

Pontifical University "Comillas" (Mar. 29, 1904): Campus de Cantoblanco, 28049 Madrid.

Pontifical University of Salamanca (Sept. 25, 1940): Apartado 541, 37080 Salamanca.

University of Deusto (Aug. 10, 1963): Avenida de las Universidades, 28, 48007 Bilbao.

**Taiwan (China):** Fu Jen Catholic University (Nov. 15, 1923, at Peking; reconstituted at Taipeh, Sept. 8, 1961): Hsinchuang, Taipeh Hsien 24205.

**United States:** Catholic University of America (Mar. 7, 1889): 620 Michigan Ave. N.E., Washington, D.C. 20064.

Georgetown University (Mar. 30, 1833): 37th and O Sts. N.W., Washington, D.C. 20057.

Niagara University (June 21, 1956): Niagara University P.O., Niagara Falls, N.Y. 14109.

**Uruguay:** Catholic University of Uruguay "Damaso Antonio Larranaga" (Jan. 25, 1985): Avda. 8 de Octubre 2738, Montevideo.

**Venezuela:** Catholic University "Andres Bello" (Sept. 29, 1963): Esquina Jesuitas, Apartado 29068, Caracas 1021.

## ECCLESIASTICAL FACULTIES

(Principal source: *Annuario Pontificio*)

These faculties in Catholic seminaries and universities, listed according to country of location, have been canonically erected and authorized by the Sacred Congregation for Catholic Education to award degrees in stated fields of study. In addition to those listed here, there are other faculties of theology or philosophy in state universities and for members of certain religious orders only.

**Argentina:** Faculties of Philosophy and Theology, San Miguel (Sept. 8, 1932).

**Australia:** Catholic Institute of Theology, Sydney (Feb. 2, 1954).

**Austria:** Theological Faculty, Linz (Dec. 25, 1978).

**Brazil:** Ecclesiastical Faculty of Philosophy "John Paul II," Rio de Janeiro Aug. 6, 1981.

Philosophical and Theological Faculties of the Company of Jesus, Belo Horizonte (July 15, 1941 and Mar. 12, 1949).

**Cameroon:** Catholic Institute of Yaoundé (Nov. 15, 1991).

**Canada:** Pontifical Institute of Medieval Studies, Toronto (Oct. 18, 1939).

Dominican Faculty of Theology of Canada, Ottawa (1965; Nov. 15, 1975).

Regis College — Toronto Section of the Jesuit Faculty of Theology in Canada, Toronto (Feb. 17, 1956; Dec. 25, 1977).

College of Immaculate Conception — Montreal Section of Jesuit Faculties in Canada (Sept. 8, 1932). Suspended.

**Cote d'Ivoire (Ivory Coast):** Catholic Institute of West Africa, Abidjan (Aug. 12, 1975).

**Croatia:** Philosophical Faculty, Zagreb (July 31, 1989).

**France:** Centre Sevres — Faculties of Theology and Philosophy of the Jesuits, Paris (Sept. 8, 1932).

**Germany:** Theological Faculty, Paderborn (June 11, 1966).

Theological Faculty of the Major Episcopal Seminary, Trier (Sept. 8, 1955).

Philosophical Faculty, Munich (1932; Oct. 25, 1971).

Theological-Philosophical Faculty, Frankfurt (1932; June 7, 1971).

Theological Faculty, Fulda (Dec. 22, 1978).

Philosophical-Theological School of Salesians, Benediktbeuren (May 24, 1992).

Philosphical-Theological School, Vallendar (Oct. 7, 1993).

**Great Britain:** Heythrop College, University of London, London (Nov. 1, 1964). Theology, philosophy.

**Hungary:** Roman Catholic Academy, Budapest (1635).

**India:** "Jnana Deepa Vidyapeeth" (Pontifical Athenaeum), Institute of Philosophy and Religion, Poona (July 27, 1926).

Pontifical Institute of Theology and Philosophy at the Pontifical Interritual Seminary of St. Joseph, Alwaye, Kerala (Feb. 24, 1972).

"Vidyajyoti," Institute of Religious Studies, Faculty of Theology, Delhi (1932; Dec. 9, 1974).

"Dharmaram Vidya Kshetram" Pontifical Athenaeum of Theology and Philosophy, Bangalore (theology, Jan. 6, 1976; philosophy, Dec. 8, 1983).

Faculty of Theology, Ranchi (Aug. 15, 1982).

Pontifical Oriental Institute of Religious Studies, Kottayam (July 3, 1982).

St. Peter's Pontifical Institute of Theology, Bangalore (Jan. 6, 1985).

"Satya Nilayam," Institute of Philosophy and Culture. Faculty of Philosophy, Madras (Sept. 8, 1932; Dec. 15, 1976).

**Indonesia:** Wedabhakti Pontifical Faculty of Theology, Yogyakarta (Nov. 1, 1984).

**Ireland:** Institute of Theology and Philosophy, Dublin (1932).

**Israel:** French Biblical and Archeological School, Jerusalem (founded 1890; approved Sept. 17, 1892; canonically approved to confer Doctorate in Biblical Science, June 29, 1983).

**Italy:** Interregional Theological Faculty, Milan (Aug. 8, 1935; restructured 1969).

Pontifical Theological Faculty of Sardinia, Cagliari, (Aug. 5, 1927).

Pontifical Ambrosian Institute of Sacred Music, Milan (Mar. 12, 1940).

Theological Faculty of Sicily, Palermo (Dec. 8, 1980).

Theological Faculty of Southern Italy, Naples. Two sections: St. Thomas Aquinas Capodimonte (Oct. 31, 1941) and St. Louis Posillipo (Mar. 16, 1918). Theological Institute Pugliese, Molfetta (June 24, 1992). Theological Institute Calabro, Catanzaro (Jan. 28, 1993).

Faculty of Philosophy "Aloisianum," Gallarate (1937; Mar. 20, 1974).

**Japan:** Faculty of Theology, Nagoya (May 25, 1984).

**Kenya:** Catholic Higher Institute of Eastern Africa, Nairobi (May 2, 1984).

**Lebanon:** Faculty of Theology, University of the Holy Spirit, Kaslik (May 30, 1982).

**Madagascar:** Superior Institute of Theology and Philosophy, at the Regional Seminary of Antananarivo, Ambatoroka-Antananarivo (Apr. 21, 1960).

**Malta:** Faculty of Theology, Tal-Virtu (Nov. 22, 1769), with Institute of Philosophy and Human Studies (Sept. 8, 1984).

**Mexico:** Theological Faculty of Mexico (June 29, 1982) and Philosophy (Jan. 6, 1986), Mexico City.

**Netherlands:** International Academic Institute, Kerkrade (Apr. 4, 1990)

**Nigeria:** Catholic Institute of West Africa, Port Harcourt (May 9, 1994).

**Peru:** Pontifical and Civil Faculty of Theology, Lima (July 25, 1571).

**Poland:** Theological Faculty, Poznan (1969; pontifical designation, June 2, 1974).

Philosophical Faculty, Krakow (1932; Sept. 20, 1984).

Pontifical Theological Faculty, Warsaw (May 3, 1988) with St. John Baptist section (1837, 1920, Nov. 8, 1962) at the "Metropolitan Seminary Duchowne" and "St. Andrew Bobola""Bobolanum" section (Sept. 8, 1932).

**Spain:** Theological Faculty of Catalunya, (Mar. 7, 1968), with the Institutes of Fundamental Theology (Dec. 28, 1984), Liturgy (Aug. 15, 1986) and Philosophy (July 26, 1988), Barcelona.

Theological Faculty, Granada (1940; July 31, 1973).

Theological Faculty of the North, of the Metro-

politan Seminary of Burgos and the Diocesan Seminary of Vitoria (Feb. 6, 1967).
Theological Faculty "San Vicente Ferrer" (two sections), Valencia (Jan. 23, 1974).
Theological Faculty of San Esteban, Salamanca (1947; Oct. 4, 1972).
**Switzerland:** Theological Faculty, Chur (Jan. 1, 1974).
Theological Faculty, Luzerne (Dec. 25, 1973).
Academic Institute of Theology, Lugano (Nov. 20, 1993).
**United States:** St. Mary's Seminary and University. School of Theology, Baltimore (May 1, 1822).
St. Mary of the Lake Faculty of Theology, Mundelein, Ill. (Sept. 30, 1929).
Weston School of Theology, Cambridge, Mass. (Oct. 18, 1932).
The Jesuit School of Theology, Berkeley, Calif. (Feb. 2, 1934, as "Alma College," Los Gatos, Calif.).
Faculty of Philosophy and Letters, St. Louis, Mo. (Feb. 2, 1934).
St. Michael's Institute, Jesuit School of Philosophy and Letters, Spokane, Wash. (Feb. 2, 1934).
Pontifical Faculty of Theology of the Immaculate Conception, Dominican House of Studies, Washington, D.C. (Nov. 15, 1941).
The Marian Library/International Marian Research Institute (IMRI), U.S. branch of Pontifical Theological Faculty "Marianum," University of Dayton, Dayton, O. 45469 (affil. 1976, inc. 1983).
John Paul II Institute for Studies on Marriage and the Family, U.S. section of Pontifical John Paul II Institute for Studies on Marriage and Family at the Pontifical Lateran University, 487 Michigan Ave. NE, Washington, DC 20017 (Aug. 22, 1988).
**Vietnam:** Theological Faculty of the Pontifical National Seminary of St. Pius X, Dalat (July 31, 1965). Activities suppressed.
**Zaire:** Catholic Faculties of Kinshasa, Kinshasa (theology, Apr. 25, 1957; philosophy, Nov. 25, 1987).
**Pontifical College Josephinum** (Theologate and College) at Columbus, Ohio, is a national pontifical seminary. Established Sept. 1, 1888, it is directly under the auspices of the Vatican through the Apostolic Pro-Nuncio to the U.S., who serves as the seminary's chancellor.

## PONTIFICAL UNIVERSITIES AND INSTITUTES IN ROME

(Source: *Annuario Pontificio*.)
**Pontifical Gregorian University** (1552): Piazza della Pilotta, 4, 00187 Rome. Associated with the university are:
The **Pontifical Biblical Institute** (May 7, 1909): Via della Pilotta, 25, 00187 Rome.
The **Pontifical Institute of Oriental Studies** (Oct. 15, 1917): Piazza S. Maria Maggiore, 7, 00185 Rome.

**Pontifical Lateran University** (1773). Piazza S. Giovanni in Laterano, 4, 00184 Rome. Annexed to the university is the Pontifical Institute of Studies of Marriage and the Family, erected by Pope John Paul II, Oct 7, 1982; a section of the Institute was established at the Dominican House of Studies, Washington, D.C., by a decree dated Aug. 22, 1988; sections were opened in Mexico in 1992 and Valencia, Spain, in 1994.
**Pontifical Urban University** (1627): Via Urbano VIII, 16, 00165 Rome.
**Pontifical University of St. Thomas Aquinas (Angelicum)** (1580), of the Order of Preachers: Largo Angelicum, 1, 00184 Rome.
**Pontifical University Salesianum** (May 3, 1940; university designation May 24, 1973), of the Salesians of Don Bosco: Piazza dell' Ateneo Salesiano, 1, 00139 Rome. Associated with the university is the **Pontifical Institute of Higher Latin Studies,** known as the **Faculty of Christian and Classical Letters** (June 4, 1971).
**Pontifical Athenaeum of St. Anselm** (1687), of the Benedictines: Piazza dei Cavalieri di Malta, 5, 00153 Rome.
**Pontifical Athenaeum "Antonianum"** (of St. Anthony) (May 17, 1933), of the Order of Friars Minor: Via Merulana, 124, 00185 Rome.
**Roman Athenaeum of the Holy Cross** (Jan. 9, 1985), of Personal Prelature of Opus Dei: Piazza S. Apollinare, 49, 00186 Rome.
**Athenaeum "Regina Apostolorum" of the Legionaries of Christ,** Via Aurelia Antica, 460, 00165 Rome.
**Pontifical Institute of Sacred Music** (1911; May 24, 1931): Via di Torre Rossa, 21, 00165 ome.
**Pontifical Institute of Christian Archeology** (Dec. 11, 1925): Via Napoleone III, 1, 00185 Rome.
**Pontifical Theological Faculty "St. Bonaventure"** (Dec. 18, 1587), of the Order of Friars Minor Conventual: Via del Serafico, 1, 00142 Rome.
**Pontifical Theological Faculty, Pontifical Institute of Spirituality "Teresianum"** (1935), of the Discalced Carmelites: Piazza San Pancrazio, 5-A, 00152 Rome.
**Pontifical Theological Faculty "Marianum"** (1398), of the Servants of Mary: Viale Trente Aprile, 6, 00153 Rome.
**Pontifical Institute of Arabic and Islamic Studies** (1926), of the Missionaries of Africa: Viale di Trastevere, 89, 00153 Rome.
**Pontifical Faculty of Educational Science "Auxilium"** (June 27, 1970), of the Daughters of Mary, Help of Christians: Via Cremolino, 141, 00166 Rome.
**Pontifical Institute "Regina Mundi"** (1970): Lungotevere Tor di Nona, 7, 00186 Rome.

# PONTIFICAL ACADEMY OF SCIENCES

(Sources: *Annuario Pontificio*, Catholic News Service.)
The Pontifical Academy of Sciences was constituted in its present form by Pius XI Oct. 28, 1936, in virtue of *In Multis Solaciis,* a document issued on his own initiative.

The academy is the only supranational body of its kind in the world with a pope-selected, life-long membership of outstanding mathematicians and experimental scientists regardless of creed from many countries. The normal complement of 70 members was increased to 80 in 1985-86 by John Paul II. There are additional honorary and supernumerary members.

Purposes of the academy are to honor pure science and its practitioners, to promote the freedom of pure science and to foster research.

The academy traces its origin to the *Linceorum Academia* (Academy of the Lynxes — its symbol) founded in Rome Aug. 17, 1603. Pius IX reorganized this body and gave it a new name — *Pontificia Accademia dei Nuovi Lincei* — in 1847. It was taken over by the Italian state in 1870 and called the *Accademia Nazionale dei Lincei*. Leo XIII reconstituted it with a new charter in 1887. Pius XI designated the Vatican Gardens as the site of academy headquarters in 1922 and gave it its present title and status in 1936. In 1940, Pius XII gave the title of Excellency to its members; John XXIII extended the privilege to honorary members in 1961.

## Members in U.S.

Scientists in the U.S. who presently hold membership in the Academy are listed below according to year of appointment. Nobel prizewinners are indicated by an asterisk.

Franco Rasetti, professor emeritus of physics at Johns Hopkins University, Baltimore, Md. (Oct 28, 1936); Christian de Duve*, professor of biochemistry at the International Institute of Cellular and Molecular Pathology at Brussels, Belgium, and Rockefeller University, New York (Apr. 10, 1978);

Marshall Warren Nirenberg*, director of Laboratory on genetics and biochemistry at the National Institutes of Health, Bethesda, Md. (June 24, 1974).

George Palade*, professor of cellular biology at University of California, San Diego and Victor Weisskopf, professor of physics at the Massachusetts Institute of Technology, Cambridge, Mass. (Dec. 2, 1975); David Baltimore*, professor of biology and president of Rockefeller University, New York, Har Gobind Khorana*, professor of biochemistry, and Alexander Rich, professor of biophysics — both at the Massachusetts Institute of Technology, Cambridge, Mass. (Apr. 17, 1978).

Charles Townes*, professor emeritus of physics at the University of California at Berkeley (Jan. 26, 1983). Beatrice Mintz, senior member of the Cancer Research Institute of Philadelphia and Maxine Singer, biochemist, president of Carnegie Institution, Washington, D.C. (June 9, 1986).

Roald Z. Sagdeev, professor of physics at University of Maryland, College Park and Peter Hamilton Raven, professor of biology at the Missouri Botanical Garden of St. Louis, Mo. (Oct 4, 1990); Luis Angel Cafarelli, professor of mathematics at the Institute of Advanced Studies at Princeton and Luigi Luca Cavalli-Sforza, professor of genetics at Stanford University (Aug. 2, 1994).

There are also two honorary members from the U.S.: Stanley L. Jaki, O.S.B., professor of physics, history and philosophy at Seton Hall University, South Orange (Sept. 5, 1990) and Robert J. White, professor of neurosurgery at Case Western Reserve University, Cleveland (Mar. 29, 1994).

## Members in Other Countries

Other members of the Academy are listed below according to country of location; dates of their selection are given in parentheses. Nobel prizewinners are indicated by an asterisk.

Armenia: Rudolf M. Muradian (Oct. 16, 1994).

Austria: Hans Tuppy (Apr. 10, 1970); Walter Thirring (June 9, 1986).

Belgium: Paul Adriaan Jan Janssen (June 25, 1990).

Brazil: Carlos Chagas, former president of the academy (Aug. 18, 1961); Johanna Dobereiner (Apr. 17, 1978); Crodowaldo Pavan (Apr. 17, 1978).

Canada: Gerhard Herzberg* (Sept. 24, 1964); John Charles Polanyi* (June 9, 1986).

Chile: Hector Croxatto Rezzio (Dec. 2, 1975).

Denmark: Aage Bohr* (Apr. 17, 1978).

France: Louis Leprince-Ringuet (Aug. 18, 1961); Andre Blanc-LaPierre (Apr. 17, 1978), Andre Lichnerowicz (May 12, 1981); Bernard Pullman (May 12, 1981); Paul Germain (June 9, 1986); Jacques Louis Lions (Oct. 4, 1990).

Germany: Rudolf L. Mossbauer* (Apr. 10, 1970); Manfred Eigen* (May 12, 1981); Wolf Joachim Singer (Sept. 18, 1992).

Ghana: Daniel Adzei Bekoe (Set. 26, 1983).

Great Britain: Hermann Alexander Bruck (Apr. 5, 1955); George Porter* (June 24, 1974); Max Ferdinand Perutz* (May 12, 1981); Stanley Keith Runcorn (Sept. 12, 1981); Stephen William Hawking (Jan. 9, 1986); Martin John Rees (June 25, 1990); Sir Richard Southwood (Sept. 18, 1992); Alistair Cameron Crombie (Oct. 16, 1994).

India: Mambillikalathil Govind Kumar Menon (May 12, 1981); Chintamani N.R. Rao (June 25, 1990).

Ireland: James Robert McConnell (June 25, 1990).

Israel: Michael Sela (Dec. 2, 1975).

Italy: Giovanni Battista Marini-Bettolo Marconi (Apr. 22, 1968); Rita Levi-Montalcino* (June 24, 1974); Giampietro Puppi (Apr. 17, 1978), Ennio De Giorgi (May 12, 1981), Abdus Salam* (May 12, 1981); Nicola Cabibbo (June 9, 1986); Bernardo Maria Colombo (Sept. 18, 1992).

Japan: Kenichi Fukui* (Dec. 14, 1985); Minoru Oda (Sept. 18, 1992).

Kenya: Thomas R. Odhiambo (May 12, 1981).

Mexico: Marcos Moshinsky (June 9, 1986).

Nigeria: Thomas Adeoye Lambo (June 24, 1974).

Poland: Stanislaw Lojasiewicz (Jan. 28, 1983); Czeslaw Olech (June 9, 1986); Michal Heller (Oct. 4, 1990); Andrzej Szezeklik (Oct. 16, 1994).

Russia: Vladimir Isaakovich Keilis-Borok (Oct. 16, 1994).

Spain: Manuel Lora-Tamayo (Sept. 24, 1964).

Sweden: Sven Horstadius (Aug. 18, 1961); Sune Bergstrom* (Dec. 14, 1985); Kai Siegbahn* (Dec. 14, 1985).

Switzerland: John Carew Eccles* (Apr. 8, 1961); Werner Arber* (May 12, 1981); Vladimir Prelog* (Dec. 14, 1985); Carlo Rubbia* (Dec. 14, 1985); Albert Eschenmoser (June 9, 1986).

Venezuela: Marcel Roche (Apr. 10, 1970).

Zaire: Wa Kalengo Malu (Sept. 26, 1983).

Ex officio members: Rev. George V. Coyne, S.J., director of Vatican Observatory (Sept. 2, 1978); Very Rev. Leonard E. Boyle, O.P., prefect of the Vatican

Library (May 24, 1984); Very Rev. Joseph Metzler, O.M.I., prefect of the Secret Vatican Archives (May 24, 1984); Msgr. Renato Dardozzi, chancellor of the Pontifical Academy of Sciences (Jan. 30, 1995)

President: Nicola Cabibbo, professor of theoretical physics at Univ. of Rome (app. Apr. 6, 1993).

## PONTIFICAL ACADEMY OF SOCIAL SCIENCES

Founded by John Paul II, Jan. 1, 1994 (motu proprio *Socialium scientiarum investigationes*) to promote the study and the progress of social sciences, to advise the Vatican on social concerns and to foster research aimed at improving society. The number of members is not less than 20 nor more than 40. Two of the thirty members of the Academy (as of Jan. 1, 1996) were from the United States: Kenneth J. Arrow of Stanford University and Mary Ann Glendon of Harvard University. President, Prof. Edmond Malinvaud of France. Address: Casino Pio IV, Vatican Gardens.

## PONTIFICAL ACADEMY FOR LIFE

Established by John Paul II, Feb. 11, 1994 (motu proprio *Vitae Mysterium*) "to fulfill the specific task of study, information and formation on the principal problems of biomedicine and law relative to the promotion and defense of life, especially in the direct relationship they have with Christian morality and the directives of the Church's magisterium." Members, appointed by the Pope without regard to religion or nationality, represent the various branches of "the biomedical sciences and those that are most closely related to problems concerning the promotion and protection of life." Membership as of Jan. 1, 1996, included four from the United States: Mrs. Mercedes Arzu-Wilson, founder and president of the Foundations Family of the Americas and founder and director of the Commission at the World Organization for the Family; Dr. Thomas Hilgers, founder and director of the Institute "Paul VI," Omaha, Nebr.; Prof. Edmund Pellegrino, director of the Center for Advanced Studies in Ethics at Georgetown University, Washington; Mrs. Christine Vollmer (of Venezuela), president of the World Organization for the Family. President, Prof. Juan de Dios Vial Correa, physician and biologist, rector of the Pontifical Catholic University of Santiago de Chile. Address: Via della Conciliazione, 3, 00193 Rome, Italy.

# 1996 CHRISTOPHER AWARDS

Christopher Awards are given each year to recognize the creative writers, producers and directors who have achieved artistic excellence in films, books and television specials affirming the highest values of the human spirit. The 1996 awards were presented Feb. 29, 1996, in New York.

**Books:** *Amazing Grace: The Lives of Children and the Conscience of a Nation,* by Jonathan Kozol (Crown); *Bound to Forgive: The Pilgrimage to Reconciliation of a Beirut Hostage,* by Lawrence Martin Jenco, O.S.M. (Ave Maria Press); *Lincoln,* by David Herbert Donald (Simon & Schuster); *Love Letters from Cell 92: The Correspondence between Dietrich Bonhoeffer and Maria von Wedemeyer 1943-45,* edited by Ruth-Alice von Bismarck and Ulrich Kabitz, translated by John Brownjohn (Abington); *Not by the Sword: How the Love of a Cantor and His Family Transformed a Klansman,* by Kathryn Watterson (Simon & Schuster); *One Small Sparrow,* by Jeff Leeland (Multnomah Books); *The Railway Man: A POW's Searing Account of War, Brutality and Forgiveness,* by Eric Lomax (Norton).

**Books for Young People:** *The Christmas Miracle of Jonathan Toomey,* by Susan Wojciechowski, illustrated by P.J. Lynch (Ages 6-9, Candlewich Press); *Been to Yesterdays: Poems of a Life,* by Lee Bennett Hopkins, illustrated by Charlene Rendeiro (Ages 10-12, Wordsong Boyds Mills Press); *Mother Jones: One Woman's Fight for Labor,* by Betsy Harvey Kraft (Ages 12-14, Clarion Books); *Parallel Journeys,* by Eleanor Ayer, with Helen Waterford and Alfons Heck (Young Adult, Atheneum).

**Motion Pictures:** Producers, directors and writers of: "Apollo 13" (Universal Pictures); "Cry, the Beloved Country" (Miramax); "Dead Man Walking" (Gramercy Pictures).

**Television Specials:** Producers, directors and writers of: "The Christmas Box" (CBS); "Discovering Women" (WGBH/PBS); "If Someone Had Known" (NBC); "Living on the Edge" (PBS *Frontline* series); "The More You Know" (NBC); "The Piano Lesson" (CBS).

**Life Achievement Award:** David Brinkley, host of the ABC-TV news program, *This Week with David Brinkley,* for outstanding broadcast journalism for the past five decades.

# FATHER MAX THURIAN

Father Max Thurian, a distinguished member of the International Theological Commission, died Aug. 15, 1996.

Pope John Paul sent the following message expressing his sympathy to Brother Roger Schutz of the Taize Community in France, with whom Father Max had been associated.

"Learning with deep sorrow of the death of Father Max Thurian, I would like to assure you of my prayers for this man of God, the first to work with you in building the Taize Community, which seeks to foster Christian unity. I pay tribute to this good servant of the Gospel, whose fidelity was expressed in distinguished theological scholarship for more than 50 years. A tireless seeker of the truth, a man of deep faith, steadfast hope and ardent charity, Father Max Thurian, a Catholic priest in the later years of his life, will be remembered as a great disciple of Christ. Upon all those mourning his death and those who will take part in the funeral liturgy, I cordially invoke an abundance of heavenly blessings."

# SOCIAL SERVICES

**Catholic Charities USA** (formerly National Conference of Catholic Charities): Founded in 1910 by Most Rev. Thomas J. Shahan and Rt. Rev. Msgr. William J. Kerby in cooperation with lay leaders of the Society of St. Vincent de Paul to help advance and promote the charitable programs and activities of Catholic community and social service agencies in the United States. As the central and national organization for this purpose, it services a network of more than 1,400 agencies and institutions by consultation, information and assistance in planning and evaluating social service programs under Catholic auspices.

Diocesan member agencies provide shelter, food, counseling, services to children, teen parents and the elderly, and a variety of other services to people in need — without regard to religion, gender, age or national origin. Each year millions of people receive help from Catholic Charities; in 1994 (latest statistics available), more than 11 million turned to Catholic Charities agencies for help. In addition, Catholic Charities is an advocate for persons and families in need.

Catholic Charities USA serves members through national and regional meetings, training programs, literature and social policy advocacy on the national level. It is charged by the U.S. bishops with responding to disasters in this country. Catholic Charities USA's president represents North America before Caritas Internationalis, the international conference of Catholic Charities, and thus maintains contact with the Catholic Charities movement throughout the world. Publications include Charities USA, a quarterly membership magazine, and a biannual directory of U.S. Catholic Charities agencies and institutions.

Rev. Fred Kammer, S.J., is president of Catholic Charities USA. Address: 1731 King St., Suite 200, Alexandria, VA 22314.

**Society of St. Vincent de Paul, Council of the United States** (originally called the Conference of Charity): An association of Catholic lay men and women devoted to personal service of the poor through the spiritual and corporal works of mercy. The first conference was formed at Paris in 1833 by Frederic Ozanam and his associates.

The first conference in the U.S. was organized in 1845 at St. Louis. There are now approximately 4,400 units of the society in this country, with a membership of more than 60,000.

In the fiscal year 1993-94, members of the society in this country distributed among poor persons financial and other forms of assistance valued at approximately $150,000,000.

Besides person-to-person assistance, increasing emphasis is being given to stores and rehabilitation workshops of the society through which persons with marginal income can purchase refurbished goods at minimal cost. Handicapped persons are employed in renovating goods and store operations. The society also operates food centers, shelters, criminal justice and other programs.

Address of the National Council: 58 Progress Parkway, St. Louis, MO 63043. Joseph H. Mueller, national president; Rita W. Porter, executive director.

**Catholic Health Association of the United States** is the national leadership organization of Catholic health-care sponsors, systems, facilities and related organizations and services. CHA enables its members to accomplish collective goals. It asserts leadership in society and the Church by advancing the health-care ministry through programs of advocacy, facilitation and education.

Composed of more than 1,200 organizational and personal members, CHA maintains its national headquarters office at 4455 Woodson Road, St. Louis MO 63134, and its government services office at 1875 Eye Street N.W., Suite 1000, Washington, DC 20006.

**National Association of Catholic Chaplains:** Founded in 1965. membership is over 3,600. Address: 3501 S. Lake Dr., Milwaukee, WI 53207.

## FACILITIES FOR RETIRED AND AGED PERSONS

(Sources: Almanac survey, *The Official Catholic Directory*.)

This list covers residence, health care and other facilities for the retired and aged under Catholic auspices. Information includes name, type of facility if not evident from the title, address, and total capacity (in parentheses); unless noted otherwise, facilities are for both men and women. Many facilities for the aged offer intermediate nursing care.

**Alabama:** Allen Memorial Home (Skilled Nursing), 735 S. Washington Ave., Mobile 36603 (94).

Cathedral Place Apartments (Retirement Complex), 351 Conti St., Mobile 36602 (192).

Mercy Medical (Acute Rehabilitation Hospital, Skilled and Post-Acute Nursing, Hospice, Home Health and Assisted and Independent Living), P.O. Box 1090, Daphne 36526 (157 beds; 120 assisted units; 32 independent apartments). Not restricted to elderly.

Sacred Heart Residence Little Sisters of the Poor, 1655 McGill Ave., Mobile 36604 (75).

Seton Haven (Retirement Complex), 3721 Wares Ferry Rd., Montgomery 36193 (104).

**Arizona:** Desert Crest Campus (Retirement Complex), 2101 E. Maryland Ave., Phoenix 85016 (114 apartments and cottages) and 2151 E. Maryland Ave., Phoenix 85016 (66).

**California:** Alexis Apartments of St. Patrick's Parish, 756 Mission St. 94103; 390 Clementina St., San Francisco 94103 (206).

Casa Manana Inn, 3700 N. Sutter St., Stockton 95204 (162). Non-profit housing for low-income elderly over 62.

Cathedral Plaza, 1551 Third Ave., San Diego 92101 (222 apartments).

Francis of Assisi Community, 145 Guerrero St., San Francisco 94103 (120). Low-income elderly.

Guadalupe Plaza, 4142 42nd St., San Diego 92105 (127 apartments).

Jeanne d'Arc Manor, 85 S. Fifth St., San Jose 95112 (121). For low income elderly and handicapped.

La Paz Villas, P.O. Box 1962, Palm Desert 92261 (24 units).

Little Flower Haven (Residential Care Facility for Retired), 8585 La Mesa Blvd., La Mesa 91941 (85).

Little Sisters of the Poor, St. Anne's Home, 300 Lake St., San Francisco 94118 (103).

Little Sisters of the Poor, Jeanne Jugan Residence, 2100 South Western Ave., San Pedro, Calif. 90732 (104).

Madonna Residence (Housing for low-income women over 60), 1055 Pine St., San Francisco 94109 (57).

Marian Residence (Retirement Home), 124 S. College Dr., Santa Maria 93454 (34).

Mercy McMahon Terrace (Residential Care Facility), 3865 J St., Sacramento 95816 (118 units).

Mercy Retirement and Care Center, 3431 Foothill Blvd., Oakland 94601 (135 residential; 59 skilled nursing).

Mother Gertrude Home for Senior Citizens, 11320 Laurel Canyon Blvd., San Fernando 91340 (114).

Nazareth House (Residential and Skilled Care), 2121 N. 1st St., Fresno 93703 (85 residential; 39 skilled nursing).

Nazareth House (Residential and Skilled Nursing), 3333 Manning Ave., Los Angeles 90064 (127 residential; 33 skilled nursing).

Nazareth House (Retirement Home), 245 Nova Albion Way, San Rafael 94903 (139).

Nazareth House Retirement Home, 6333 Rancho Mission Rd., San Diego 92108 (122).

O'Connor Woods (Retirement Community), 3400 Wagner Heights, Stockton 95209 (235 independent, 48 assisted living).

Our Lady of Fatima Villa (Skilled Nursing Facility), 20400 Saratoga-Los Gatos Rd., Saratoga 95070 (85).

St. Bernardine Plaza (Retirement Home), 550 W. 5th St., San Bernardino 92401 (150 units).

St. Francis Home, 1718 W. 6th St., Santa Ana 92703 (65).

St. John of God (Retirement and Care Center), 2035 W. Adams Blvd., Los Angeles 90018.

St. John's Plaza, 8150 Broadway, Lemon Grove 91945 (100).

Vigil Light Apartments, 1945 Long Dr., Santa Rosa 95405 (48).

Villa Scalabrini (Retirement Center and Skilled Nursing Care), 10631 Vinedale St., Sun Valley 91352 (130 residence; 58 skilled nursing).

Villa Siena (Residence and Skilled Nursing Care), 1855 Miramonte Ave., Mountain View 94040 (50, residence; 20, skilled nursing care).

**Colorado:** Francis Heights, Inc., 2626 Osceola St., Denver 80212 (384 units; 431 residents).

Gardens at St. Elizabeth (Congregate Housing and Assisted Living), 2835 W. 32nd Ave., Denver 80211 (209 congregate; 81 assisted living).

Little Sisters of the Poor, 3629 W. 29th Ave., Denver 80211 (78).

**Connecticut:** Augustana Homes (Residence), Simeon Rd., Bethel 06801.

Carmel Ridge, 6454 Main St., Trumbull 06611.

Holy Family Home and Shelter, Inc., 88 Jackson St., P.O. Box 884, Willimantic 06226.

Matulaitis Nursing Home, 10 Thurber Rd., Putnam 06260 (119).

Monsignor Bojnowski Manor, Inc. (Skilled Nurs-ing Facility), 50 Pulaski St., New Britain 06053 (54).

Notre Dame Convalescent Home, 76 West Rocks Rd., Norwalk 06851 (60).

St. Joseph Living Center, 14 Club Rd., Windham 06280 (120).

St. Joseph's Manor (Health Care Facility; Home for Aged), Carmelite Srs. for Aged and Infirm, 6448 Main St., Trumbull 06611 (297).

St. Joseph's Residence, Little Sisters of the Poor, 1365 Enfield St., Enfield, Conn. 06082 (93)

St. Lucian's Home for the Aged, 532 Burritt St., New Britain 06053 (42).

St. Mary's Home (Residence and Health Care Facility) 2021 Albany Ave., W. Hartford 06117.

**Delaware:** The Antonian, 1701 W. 10th St., Wilmington 19805 (136 apartments).

Jeanne Jugan Residence, Little Sisters of the Poor, 185 Salem Church Rd., Newark 19713 (80).

Marydale Retirement Village, 135 Jeandell Dr., Newark 19713 (108 apartments).

St. Patrick's House, Inc., 115 E. 14th St., Wilmington 19801 (16).

**District of Columbia:** Jeanne Jugan Residence — St. Joseph Villa, Little Sisters of the Poor, 4200 Harewood Rd., N.E. Washington 20017 (87).

**Florida:** All Saints Home, 5888 Blanding Blvd., Jacksonville 32246 (60).

Archbishop McCarthy Residence (Retirement Apartments), 13201 N.W. 28th Avenue, Opa Locka 33054 (113 apartments).

Bon Secour-Maria Manor Nursing Care Center, 10300 4th St. N., St. Petersburg 33716 (274).

Carroll Manor (Retirement Apartments), 3667 S. Miami Ave., Miami 33133 (230 apartments).

Casa Calderon, Inc. (Retirement Apartments), 800 W. Virginia St., Tallahassee 32304.

Haven of Our Lady of Peace (Assisted Living and Nursing Home)), 5203 N. 9th Ave., Pensacola 32504 (89).

Marian Towers, Inc. (Retirement Apartments), 17505 North Bay Rd., Miami Beach 33160.

Noreen McKeen Residence for Geriatric Care (Skilled and Intermediate Care), 315 Flagler Dr. S., W. Palm Beach 33401.

Palmer House, Inc., 1225 S.W. 107th Ave., Miami 33174 (120 apartments).

St. Andrew Towers (Retirement Apartments), 2700 N.W. 99th Ave., Coral Springs 33065 (432).

St. Catherine Laboure (Skilled and Intermediate Care), 1750 Stockton St., Jacksonville 32204 (232).

St. Dominic Gardens (Retirement Apartments), 5849 N.W. 7th St., Miami 33126 (149 apartments).

St. Elizabeth Gardens, Inc. (Retirement Apartments), 801 N.E. 33rd St., Pompano Beach 33064 (150).

St. John's Rehabilitation Hospital and Nursing Center, Inc., 3075 N.W. 35th Ave., Lauderdale Lakes 33311.

Stella Maris House, Inc., 8636 Harding Ave., Miami Beach 33141 (136 apartments).

**Illinois:** Addolorata Villa (Sheltered Intermediate, Skilled Care Facility; Apartments), 555 McHenry Rd., Wheeling 60090 (135 health care; 100 apartments).

Alvernia Manor (Sheltered Care), 13950 Main St., Lemont 60439 (50).

Carlyle Healthcare Center, 501 Clinton St., Carlyle 62231 (131).

Carmelite Carefree Village, 8419 Bailey Rd., Darien 60561 (105).

Cor Mariae Center (Assisted Living and Nursing Home), 3330 Maria Linden Dr., Rockford 61107 (90).

Cortland Manor Retirement Home, 1900 N. Karlov, Chicago 60639. (56).

Holy Family Health Center, 2380 Dempster, Des Plaines 60016 (362).

Holy Family Villa (Intermediate Care Facility), 12395 McCarthy Rd., Lemont 60439 (99).

Jugan Terrace, Little Sisters of the Poor, 2300 N. Racine, Chicago 60614 (50 apartments).

Little Sisters of the Poor, St. Joseph's Home for the Elderly, 80 W. Northwest Hwy., Palatine 60067 (67).

Little Sisters of the Poor Center for the Aging, 2325 N. Lakewood Ave., Chicago, Ill. 60614 (96).

Maria Care Center (Skilled Intermediary Facility), 350 W. S. First St., Red Bud 62278 (115).

Marian Heights Apartments (Elderly, Handicapped), 20 Marian Heights Dr., Alton 62002 (127).

Marian Park, Inc., 2126 W. Roosevelt Rd., Wheaton 60187 (117 apartments).

Maryhaven, Inc. (Skilled and Intermediate Care Facility), 1700 E. Lake Ave., Glenview 60025 (147).

Mayslake Village (Retirement Apartments), 1801 35th St., Oak Brook 60521 (630 apartments).

Mercy Residence at Tolentine Center, 20300 Governors Hwy., Olympia Fields 60461 (52).

Meredith Memorial Home, 16 S. Illinois St., Belleville 62220 (70).

Merkle-Knipprath (Apartments and Nursing Facility), Rt. 1, Franciscan Brothers. Clifton 60927 (130).

Mother Theresa Home (Skilled, Intermediate and Sheltered Care), 1270 Franciscan Dr., Lemont 60439 (150).

Nazarethville (Intermediate and Sheltered Care), 300 N. River Rd., Des Plaines 60016 (83).

Our Lady of Angels Retirement Home, 1201 Wyoming, Joliet 60435 (96).

Our Lady of the Snows, Apartment Community, 9500 West Illinois Highway 15, Belleville 62223. Retirement community (166 apartments); adjoining skilled-care facility (57 beds).

Our Lady of Victory Nursing Home (Intermediate and Skilled Care), 20 Briarcliff Lane, Bourbonnais 60914 (97).

Pope John Paul I Apartments (Elderly and Handicapped), 1 Pope John Paul Plaza, Springfield 62703 (150).

Queen of Peace Center, 1910 Maple Ave., Lisle 60532.

Resurrection Nursing Pavilion (Skilled Care), 1001 N. Greenwood, Park Ridge 60068 (295).

Resurrection Retirement Community, 7262 W. Peterson Ave., Chicago, 60631 (473 apartments).

Rosary Hill Home (Women), 9000 W. 81st St., Justice 60458 (50).

St. Andrew Home (Retirement Residence), 7000 N. Newark Ave., Niles 60648 (196).

St. Ann's Healthcare Center, 770 State St., Chester 62233 (119).

St. Anne Center (Nursing Home), 4405 Highcrest Rd., Rockford 61107 (179).

St. Anne Place (Retirement Apartments),4444 Brendenwood Rd., Rockford 61107 (106 apartments).

St. Benedict Home, 6930 W. Touhy Ave., Niles 60714 (130).

St. Elizabeth Home (Residence), 704 W. Marion St., Joliet 60436. Group living for Senior women.

St. James Manor, 1251 East Richton Rd., Crete 60417 (110).

St. Joseph's Home (Sheltered and Intermediate Care), 3306 S. 6th St. Rd., Springfield 62703 (112).

St. Joseph's Home (Sheltered and Intermediate Care), 2223 W. Heading Ave., Peoria 61604 (186).

St. Joseph's Home for the Aged, 659 E. Jefferson St., Freeport 61032 (120).

St. Joseph Home of Chicago, Inc. (Skilled Care), 2650 N. Ridgeway Ave., Chicago 60647 (173).

St. Patrick's Residence, 1400 Brookdale Rd., Naperville 60563 (210).

Villa Franciscan (Skilled Care), Franciscan Sisters Health Care Corporation, 210 N. Springfield, Joliet 60435 (176).

Villa Scalabrini (Sheltered, Intermediate and Skilled), 480 N. Wolf Rd., Northlake 60164 (265).

**Indiana:** Albertine Home, 1501 Hoffman St., Hammond 46327 (33).

Little Company of Mary Health Facility (Comprehensive Nursing), 7520 S. US Hwy 421, San Pierre 46374 (200).

Providence Retirement Home, 703 E. Spring St., New Albany 47150 (95).

Sacred Heart Home (Comprehensive Nursing), 515 N. Main St., Avilla 46710 (133). LaVerna Terrace, same address; independent living for senior citizens, handicapped and disabled (51 units).

St. Anne Home (Residential and Comprehensive Nursing), 1900 Randallia Dr., Ft. Wayne 46805 (205).

St. Anthony Home, Inc., 203 Franciscan Rd., Crown Point 46307 (219).

St. Augustine Home for the Aged, Little Sisters of the Poor, 2345 W. 86th St., Indianapolis 46260 (90).

St. John's Home for the Aged, Little Sisters of the Poor, 1236 Lincoln Ave., Evansville 47714 (71).

St. Mary's Regina Continuing Care Center (Intermediate Care Facility), 3900 Washington Ave., Evansville 47714 (128).

St. Paul Hermitage (Residential and Intermediate Care Nursing), 501 N. 17th Ave., Beech Grove 46107 (95).

**Iowa:** The Alverno Health Care Facility (Nursing Care), 849 13th Ave. N., Clinton 52732 (138).

Bishop Drumm Retirement Center, 5837 Winwood Dr., Johnston 50131 (nursing care, 150). McAuley Terrace Apartments (85 units).

Hallmar-Mercy Hospital, 701 Tenth St. S.E., Cedar Rapids 52403 (62).

Holy Spirit Retirement Home (Intermediate Care), 1701 W. 25th St., Sioux City 51103 (94).

Kahl Home for the Aged and Infirm (Skilled and Intermediate Care Facility), 1101 W. 9th St., Davenport 52804 (135).

The Marian Home, 2400 6th Ave. North, Fort Dodge 50501 (Intermediate Care, 97) and Marian Village (Apartments), 2320 6th Ave. North, Fort Dodge 50501.

Padre Pio Health Care Center, Stonehill Care Center (Residence, Nursing Home), 3485 Windsor, Dubuque 52001 (250). Stonehill Adult Center (Day Care), same address.

St. Anthony Nursing Home (Intermediate Care), 406 E. Anthony St., Carroll 51401 (80). Orchard View, same address (50 apartments).

St. Francis Continuation Care and Nursing Home Center, Burlington 52601 (19 skilled nursing; 69 intermediate care). Orchard City of St. Francis, same address (12 independent living apartment units).

**Kansas:** Catholic Care Center (Skilled and Intermediate Care Facility), 6700 E. 45th St, Wichita 67226 (178 beds — includes 16 Alzheimer and 6 AIDS).

Mt. Joseph Senior Community (Intermediate Care Facility), 1110 W. 11, Concordia 66901 (99 nursing and 20 personal care beds; 12 apartments).

St. Elizabeth Home Health Agency, 2225 Canterbury Rd., Hays 67601.

St. John Rest Home (Nursing Facility), ˜01 Seventh St., Victoria 67671 (90 nursing).

St. John's of Hays (Nursing Facility), 2010 E. 25th, Hays 67601 (60).

St. Joseph Care Center (Intermediate and Skilled Care Facility), 759 Vermont Ave., Kansas City 66101 (201 nursing).

Villa Maria, Inc. (Intermediate Care Facility), 116 S. Central, Mulvane 67110 (66).

**Kentucky:** Bishop Soenneker Personal Care Home, 9545 Ky. 144, Philpot 42366 (60).

Carmel Home (Residence, Adult Day Care, Respite Care and Nursing Care), 2501 Old Hartford Rd., Owensboro 42303 (115).

Carmel Manor (Skilled, Intermediate and Personal Care Home), 100 Carmel Manor Rd., Ft. Thomas, 41075 (145).

Madonna Manor Nursing Home, 2344 Amsterdam Rd., Villa Hills 41017 (60). Also has 49 senior citizen apartments.

Marian Home, 3105 Lexington Rd., Louisville 40206 (70).

Nazareth Home, 2000 Newburg Rd., Louisville 40205 (168).

St. Charles Care Center and Village, 500 Farrell Dr., Covington 41011 (147). Nursing home; adult day health program. Independent living cottages (35). Assisted living (60). Independent living apartments (12).

**Louisiana:** Annunciation Inn, 1220 Spain St., New Orleans 70117 (106 residential units).

Bethany M.H.S. Health Care Center (Women), P.O. Box 2308, Lafayette 70502 (42).

Chateau de Notre Dame (Residence and Nursing Home), 2832 Burdette St., New Orleans 70125 (106 residential units, 6 assisted living units, 180 nursing beds).

Christopher Inn Apartments, 2110 Royal St., New Orleans 70116 (144 residential units).

Consolata Home (Nursing Home), 2319 E. Main St., New Iberia 70560 (114).

Haydel Heights Apartments, 4402 Reynes St., New Orleans 70126 (65 units).

Lafon Nursing Home of the Holy Family, 6900 Chef Menteur Hwy., New Orleans 70126 (171).

Mary-Joseph Residence for the Elderly, 4201 Woodland Dr., New Orleans 70131 (122).

Metairie Manor, 4929 York St., Metairie 70001 (287 residential units).

Nazareth Inn, 9630 Haynes Blvd., New Orleans 70127 (270 apartments).

Ollie Steele Burden Manor (Nursing Home), 4250 Essen Lane, Baton Rouge 70809 (184).

Our Lady of Prompt Succor Home, 751 E. Prudhomme Lane, Opelousas 70570 (80).

Our Lady's Manor, Inc., 402 Monroe St., Alexandria 71301 (104 apartments).

Place Dubourg, 201 Rue Dubourg, LaPlace 70068 (115 residential units).

Rouquette Lodge, 4300 Hwy 22, Mandeville 70471 (119 residential units).

St. John Berchmans Manor, 3400 St. Anthony St., New Orleans 70122 (150 residential units).

St. Joseph's Home (Nursing Home), 2301 Sterlington Rd., Monroe 71211 (132).

St. Margaret's Daughters Home (Nursing Home), 6220 Chartres St., New Orleans 70117 (115).

St. Martin Manor, 1501 N. Johnson St., New Orleans 70116 (140 residential units).

Villa St. Maurice and Villa St. Maurice II, 500 St. Maurice Ave., New Orleans 70117 (185 residential units).

Village du Lac, Inc., 1404 Carmel Ave., Lafayette 70501 (200). For handicapped and elderly.

Wynhoven Apartments and Wynhoven II (Residence for Senior Citizens), 4600-10th St., Marrero 70072 (350).

Wynhoven II, 4606-10th St., Marrero 70072 (150).

**Maine:** Deering Pavilion (Apartments for Senior Citizens), 880 Forest Ave., Portland 04103 (200 units).

Mt. St. Joseph, Highwood St., Waterville 04901 (88).

St. Andre Health Care Facility, Inc. (Nursing Facility), 407 Pool St., Biddeford 04005 (96).

St. Joseph's Manor (Nursing Care Facility), 1133 Washington Ave., Portland 04103 (50 skilled nursing; 150 intermediate nursing). Adult and child day care centers, same address.

St. Marguerite D'Youville Pavilion, 102 Campus Ave., Lewiston 04240 (280). Maison Marcotte (Independent Living Community), 100 Campus Ave., Lewiston 04240 (128 apartments).

St. Xavier's Home (Apartments), 199 Somerset St., Bangor 04401 (19 units).

Seton Village, Inc., 1 Carver St., Waterville 04901 (140 housing units).

**Maryland:** Cardinal Shehan Center, Inc., 2300 Dulaney Valley Rd., Towson 21204 (438).

Little Sisters of the Poor, St. Martin's Home (for the Aged), 601 Maiden Choice Lane, Baltimore 21228 (106).

Sacred Heart Home, 5805 Queens Chapel Rd., Hyattsville 20782 (102).

St. Joseph Nursing Home, 1222 Tugwell Dr., Baltimore 21228 (40).

Villa Rosa Nursing Home, 3800 Lottsford Vista Rd., Mitchellville 20721 (101).

**Massachusetts:** Catholic Memorial Home (Nursing Home), 2446 Highland Ave., Fall River 02720 (300). Alzheimer unit (43)

Don Orione Nursing Home, 111 Orient Ave., East Boston 02128 (190). Adult day care center (30).

D'Youville Manor (Nursing Home), 981 Varnum Ave., Lowell 01854 (196). Day care program (20).

Jeanne Jugan Residence, Little Sisters of the Poor (Home for the Elderly), 186 Highland Ave., Somerville 02143 (84). Jeanne Jugan Pavilion, 190 Highland Ave., Somerville 02143 (apartments, 27; residents, 28).

Madonna Manor (Nursing Home), 85 N. Washington St., N. Attleboro 02760 (129).

Marian Manor, for the Aged and Infirm (Nursing Home), 130 Dorchester St., S. Boston, 02127 (363).

Marian Manor of Taunton (Nursing Home), 33 Summer St., Taunton 02780 (116).

Maristhill Nursing Home, 66 Newton St., Waltham 02154 (120).

MI Nursing/Restorative Center, Zero Bennington St., Lawrence 01841 (250). Alzheimer beds (42).

MI Residential Community, 189 Maple St., Lawrence 01841 (304 apartments). Adult Day Health Care Center (52).

Mt. St. Vincent Nursing Home, 35 Holy Family Rd., Holyoke 01040 (125).

Our Lady's Haven (Nursing Home), 71 Center St., Fairhaven 02719 (117).

Sacred Heart Home (Nursing Home), 359 Summer St., New Bedford 02740 (217).

St. Joseph Manor Nursing Home, 215 Thatcher St., Brockton 02402 (120).

St. Joseph's Nursing Care Center, 321 Centre St., Dorchester, Boston 02122 (123).

St. Patrick's Manor (Nursing Home), 863 Central St., Framingham 01701 (332).

**Michigan:** Bishop Noa Home for Senior Citizens (Nursing Home and Residence), 2900 3rd Ave. S., Escanaba 49829 (109).

Lourdes Nursing Home (Skilled Facility), 2300 Watkins Lake Rd., Waterford 48328 (108).

McFadden Home (Residence), 2150 Watkins Lake Rd., Waterford 48328 (6).

Marian Hall (Residence), 529 M.L. King Ave., Flint 48502 (97).

Marycrest Manor (Skilled Nursing Facility), 15475 Middlebelt Rd., Livonia 48154 (55).

Ryan Senior Residences of the Archdiocese of Detroit. Nine residences:

Casa Maria, 600 Maple Vista, Imlay City 48444 (87).

Kundig Center, 3300 Jeffries Freeway, Detroit 48208 (153).

Madonna Villa 17825 Fifteen Mile Rd., Clinton Twp. 48035 (89).

Marian-Oakland West, 29250 W. Ten Mile Rd., Farmington Hills 48336 (90).

Marian Place, 408 W. Front St., Monroe 48161 (51).

Marydale Center, 3147 Tenth Ave., Port Huron 48060 (57).

Maryhaven, 11350 Reeck Rd., Southgate 48195 (90).

Stapleton Center, 9341 Agnes St., Detroit 48214 (59).

Villa Marie, 15131 Newburgh Rd., Livonia 48154 (89).

St. Ann's Home, (Residence and Nursing Home), 2161 Leonard St. N.W., Grand Rapids 49504 (130).

St. Catherine House, 1641 Webb Ave., Detroit 48206 (12).

St. Elizabeth Briarbank (Women, Residence), 1315 N. Woodward Ave., Bloomfield Hills 48304 (54).

St. Francis Home (Nursing Home), 915 N. River Rd., Saginaw 48609 (100).

St. Joseph's Home, 4800 Cadieux Rd., Detroit 48224 (104).

St. Jude Home, Inc., (Residence), 2270 Marwood, Waterford 48328 (6).

Villa Elizabeth (Nursing Home), 2100 Leonard St. N.E., Grand Rapids 49505 (136). Country Villa (Assisted Living Apartments), 2110 Leonard N.E., Grand Rapids 49505 (48 units).

Villa Francesca (Residence, Women), 565 W. Long Lake Rd., Bloomfield Hills 48302 (18).

**Minnesota:** Alverna Apartments, 300 8th Ave. S.E., Little Falls 56345 (60). Retirement community.

Assumption Home, 715 North First St., Cold Spring 56320 (Skilled nursing beds, 95). Respite care. Adult day services; home delivered meals.

Benedictine Health Center, 935 Kenwood Ave., Duluth 55811 (Nursing home, 120; day care, 72). Respite care.

Divine Providence Community Home (Skilled Nursing Care), 700 Third Ave. N.W., Sleepy Eye 56085 (58). Lake Villa Maria Senior Housing (21 units).

Franciscan Health Community, 1925 Norfolk Ave., St. Paul 55116 (140).

John Paul Apartments, 200 8th Ave. N., Cold Spring 56320 (61).

Little Sisters of the Poor, Holy Family Residence (Skilled Nursing and Intermediate Care), 330 S. Exchange St., St. Paul 55102 (76). Independent living apartments (32).

Madonna Towers (Retirement Apartments and Nursing Home), 4001 19th Ave. N.W., Rochester 55901 (182).

Mary Rondorf Retirement Home of Sacred Heart Parish, Inc., 222 N.E. 5th St., Staples 56479 (45). Board and lodging with special services.

Mother of Mercy Nursing Home and Retirement Center, 230 Church Ave., Box 676, Albany 56307 (Skilled nursing home, 84; retirement housing, 33).

Regina Nursing Home and Retirement Residence, Hastings 55033. Nursing home (61); retirement home (42); boarding care (32).

Sacred Heart Hospice (Skilled Nursing Home, Adult Day Care, Home Health Care) 1200 Twelfth St. S.W., Austin 55912 (59).

St. Ann's Residence, 330 E. 3rd St., Duluth 55805 (193). Senior housing. Meals and lodging with supportive services.

St. Anne Hospice, Inc. (Skilled Nursing Home), 1347 W. Broadway, Winona 55987 (134). Adult day care.

St. Benedict's Center, 1810 Minnesota Blvd. S.E., St. Cloud 56304 (222 bed skilled nursing care; adult day care, respite care. Benedict Village (Retirement Apartments), 2000 15th Ave. S.E., St. Cloud 56304. Benedict Homes (Alzheimer Residential Care) and Benedict Court (Assisted Living), 1980 15th Ave. S.E., St. Cloud 56304.

St. Elizabeth's Hospital, Nursing Home and Health Care Center, 1200-5th Grant Blvd., Wabasha 55981 (157). Assisted living apartments (23).

St. Francis Home, 501 Oak St., Breckenridge 56520 (124).

St. Mary's Regional Health Center (Hospital and Nursing Center), 1027 Washington Ave., Detroit Lakes 56501 (100).

St. Mary's Villa (Nursing Home), Box 397, Pierz 56364 (101).

St. Otto's Care Center (Nursing Home), 920 S.E. 4th St., Little Falls 56345 (150).

St. William's Nursing Home, Parkers Prairie 56361 (90).

Villa of St. Francis Nursing Home, 1001 Scott Ave., Morris 56267 (140).

Villa St. Vincent (Skilled Nursing Home and Residence), 516 Walsh St., Crookston 56716. Skilled Nursing home (80);special care unit (24); apartments (27); board and care (34).

**Mississippi:** Notre Dame de la Mer Retirement Apartments, 292 Hwy. 90, Bay St. Louis 39520.

Santa Maria Retirement Apartments, 674 Beach Blvd., Biloxi, 39530.

Villa Maria Retirement Apartments, 921 Porter Ave., Ocean Springs 39564.

**Missouri:** Cathedral Square Towers, 444 W. 12th St., Kansas City 64105. Apartments for elderly and handicapped (156).

Chariton Apartments (Retirement Apartments), 4249 Michigan Ave., St. Louis 63111 (122 units; 143 residents).

DePaul Health Center — St. Anne's Division (Skilled Nursing), 12303 DePaul Dr., Bridgeton 63044 (96).

LaVerna Heights Retirement Home (Women), 104 E. Park Ave., Savannah 64485 (40). Nursing facility.

LaVerna Village Nursing Home, 904 Hall Ave., Savannah 64485 (120).

Little Sisters of the Poor (Home for Aged), 3225 N. Florissant Ave., St. Louis 63107 (120).

Mary, Queen and Mother Center (Nursing Care), 7601 Watson Rd., St. Louis 63119.

Mother of Good Counsel Home (Skilled Nursing, Women), 6825 Natural Bridge Rd., Northwoods, 63121 (114).

Our Lady of Mercy Country Home, 2205 Hughes Rd., Liberty 64068 (115).

Price Memorial Skilled Nursing Facility Forby Rd., P.O. Box 476, Eureka 63025 (120).

St. Agnes Home for the Elderly, 10341 Manchester Rd., Kirkwood 63122 (122).

St. Joseph Hill Infirmary, Inc., (Nursing Care Facility, Men), St. Joseph Road, Eureka 63025 (127).

St. Joseph's Home (Residential and Intermediate Care), 723 First Capitol Dr., St. Charles 63301 (100).

St. Joseph's Home (Residential and Intermediate Care Facility), 1306 W. Main St., Jefferson City 65109 (100).

**Nebraska:** Bergan Mercy Medical Center, Mercy Care Center (Skilled Nursing Facility for Chronic, Complex and Subacute Levels of Care and Rehabilitation), 1870 S. 75th St., Omaha 68124 (250).

Madonna Rehabilitation Hospital, 5401 South St., Lincoln 68506.

Mercy Villa, 1845 S. 72nd St., Omaha 68124 (36).

Mt. Carmel Home, Keens Memorial (Nursing Home), 412 W. 18th St., Kearney 68847 (79).

New Cassel Retirement Center, 900 N. 90th St., Omaha 68114 (156).

St. Joseph's Nursing Home, 401 N. 18th St., Norfolk 68701 (83).

St. Joseph's Retirement Community, 320 E. Decatur St., West Point 68788 (70). Assisted living.

St. Joseph's Villa (Nursing Home), 927 7th St., David City 68632 (65).

**New Hampshire:** Mount Carmel Nursing Home, 235 Myrtle St., Manchester 03104 (120).

St. Ann Home (Nursing Home), 195 Dover Point Rd., Dover 03820 (54).

St. Francis Home (Nursing Home), 406 Court St., Laconia 03246 (51). Apartments (25).

St. Teresa Manor (Nursing Home), 519 Bridge St., Manchester 03104 (5). Bishop Primeau Apartments, same address (25).

St. Vincent de Paul Nursing Home, 29 Providence Ave., Berlin 03570 (80).

**New Jersey:** Holy Family Residence, 44 Rifle Camp Rd., P.O. Box 536, W. Paterson 07424 (64).

McCarrick Care Center, 15 Dellwood Lane, Somerset 08873 (120).

Mater Dei Nursing Home, 176 Rt. 40, Newfield 08344 (64).

Morris Hall (St. Joseph Skilled Nursing Center, St. Mary Residence), 2361 Lawrenceville Rd., Lawrenceville 08648 (220).

Mount St. Andrew Villa (Residence), 55 W. Midland Ave., Paramus 07652 (56).

Our Lady's Residence (Nursing Home), 1100 Clematis Ave., Pleasantville 08232 (214).

St. Ann's Home for the Aged (Skilled and Intermediate Nursing Care Home, Women), 198 Old Bergen Rd., Jersey City 07305 (106). Adult Medical Day Care (50).

St. Francis Health Resort (Residence), Denville 07834 (100), Apartments, 63.

St. Joseph's Home for the Elderly, Little Sisters of the Poor, 140 Shepherd Lane, Totowa 07512 (116; also, 18 independent living units).

St. Joseph's Rest Home for Aged Women, 46 Preakness Ave., Paterson 07522 (25).

St. Joseph's Senior Residence (Sheltered Care), 1 St. Joseph Terr., Woodbridge 07095 (60).

St. Mary's Catholic Home (Skilled Nursing Home), 1730 Kresson Rd., Cherry Hill 08003 (215). The Manor at St. Mary's, 1743 Kresson Rd., Cherry Hill 08003 (82).

St. Vincent's Nursing Home, 45 Elm St., Montclair 07042 (135).

Villa Maria (Residence and Infirmary, Women), 641 Somerset St., N. Plainfield 07061 (84).

**New Mexico:** Good Shepherd Manor (Residential Care for Aged Persons), Little Brothers of the Good Shepherd, P.O. Box 10248,Albuquerque 87184 (40).

**New York:** Bernardine Apartments, 417 Churchill Ave., Syracuse 13205.

Brothers of Mercy Sacred Heart Home (Residence) 4520 Ransom Rd., Clarence 14031 (82). Brothers of Mercy Nursing Home, 10570 Bergtold Rd., Clarence 14031 (240). Brothers of Mercy Housing Co., Inc. (Apartments), 10500 Bergtold Rd., Clarence 14031 (100 units).

Carmel Richmond Nursing Home, 88 Old Town Rd., Staten Island 10304 (300). Skilled Nursing, adult day health care.

Ferncliff Nursing Home, 52 River Rd., Rhinebeck 12572 (328).

Frances Schervier Home and Hospital, 2975 Independence Ave., Bronx 10463 (364). Frances Schervier Long Term Health Care Program, same address (310 slots). Frances Schervier Housing Development Fund Corporation, 2995 Independence Ave., Bronx 10463 (154 units).

Good Samaritan Nursing Home (Skilled Nursing), 101 Elm St., Sayville, N.Y. 11782 (100).

The Heritage (Apartments with Skilled Nursing Care), 1450 Portland Ave., Rochester 14621 (237)

Holy Family Home, 1740-84th St., Brooklyn 11214 (200).

Holy Family Home (Adult Home), 410 Mill St., Williamsville 14221 (85).

Kateri Residence (Skilled Nursing), 150 Riverside Dr., New York 10024 (520).

Little Sisters of the Poor, Jeanne Jugan Residence (Skilled Nursing and Health Related; Adult Care), 3200 Baychester Ave., Bronx 10475 (92).

Little Sisters of the Poor, Queen of Peace Residence, 110-30 221st St., Queens Village 11429 (130).

Mary Manning Walsh Home (Nursing Home), 1339 York Ave., New York 10021 (362).

Mercy Healthcare Center (Skilled Nursing Facility), Tupper Lake 12986 (54).

Mt. Loretto Nursing Home, (Skilled Nursing Home), Sisters of the Resurrection, 302 Swart Hill Rd., Amsterdam 12010 (120).

Nazareth Nursing Home (Women), 291 W. North St., Buffalo 14201 (125).

Our Lady of Consolation Geriatric Care Center (Skilled Nursing) 111 Beach Dr., West Islip 11795 (250). Also long term home health care program.

Our Lady of Hope Residence (Home for the Aged), Little Sisters of the Poor, 1 Jeanne Jugan Lane, Latham 12210 (100; also 16 apartments).

Ozanam Hall of Queens Nursing Home, Inc., 42-41 201st St., Bayside 11361 (432).

Providence Rest, 3304 Waterbury Ave., Bronx 10465 (200).

Resurrection Nursing Home (Skilled Nursing Facility), Castleton 12033 (48). [New facility scheduled for 1996; 80 beds.]

St. Ann's Home (Skilled Nursing Facility), 1500 Portland Ave., Rochester 14621 (354). Home Con-

nection (Adult Day Health Care Program), same address (60)

St. Cabrini Nursing Home, 115 Broadway, Dobbs Ferry 10522 (304).

St. Clare Manor (Nursing Home), 543 Locust St., Lockport 14094 (28).

St. Columban's on the Lake (Retirement Home), 2546 Lake Rd., Silver Creek 14136 (50).

St. Elizabeth Home (Adult Home), 5539 Broadway, Lancaster 14086 (115).

St. Francis Home (Skilled Nursing Facility), 147 Reist St., Williamsville 14221 (142).

St. Joseph Manor (Nursing Home), W. State St., Olean 14760 (22).

St. Joseph Nursing Home, 2535 Genesee St., Utica 13501 (120).

St. Joseph's Guest Home, Missionary Sisters of St. Benedict,, 350 Cuba Hill Rd., Huntington 11743 (48).

St. Joseph's Home (Nursing Home), 420 Lafayette St., Ogdensburg 13669 (82).

St. Joseph's Villa (Adult Home), 38 Prospect Ave., Catskill 12414 (60).

St. Luke Manor, 17 Wiard St., Batavia 14020 (20).

St. Mary's Manor, 515 Sixth St., Niagara Falls 14301 (119).

St. Patrick's Home for the Aged and Infirm, 66 Van Cortlandt Park S., Bronx 10463 (264).

St. Teresa Nursing Home, 120 Highland Ave., Middletown 10940 (92).

St. Vincent's Home for the Aged, 319 Washington Ave., Dunkirk 14048 (40).

Terence Cardinal Cooke Health Care Center (Skilled Nursing), 1249 Fifth Ave., New York 10029.

Teresian House, Washington Ave. Extension, Albany 12203 (300).

Uihlein Mercy Center (Nursing Home), 420 Old Military Rd., Lake Placid 12946 (155).

**North Carolina:** Maryfield Nursing Home, Greensboro Rd., High Point 27260 (115).

**North Dakota:** Carrington Health Center (Nursing Home), Carrington 58421 (40).

Manor St. Joseph (Basic Care Facility), Edgeley 58433 (40).

Marillac Manor Retirement Center, 1016 28th St., Bismarck 58501 (78 apartments).

St. Anne's Guest Home, 524 N. 17th St., Grand Forks 58203 (30) Apartments (56). Adult basic care facility.

St. Vincent's Care Center (Nursing Facility), 1021 N. 26th St., Bismarck 58501 (101).

**Ohio:** Archbishop Leibold Home for the Aged, Little Sisters of the Poor, 476 Riddle Rd., Cincinnati 45220 (115).

The Assumption Village, 9800 Market St., North Lima 44452 (150). Long term nursing facility.

Francesca Residence (Retirement), 39 N. Portage Path, Akron 44303 (40).

House of Loreto (Nursing Home), 2812 Harvard Ave. N.W., Canton 44709 (100).

Jennings Hall, Inc. (Nursing Care), 10204 Granger Rd., Cleveland 4125 (15000).

Little Sisters of the Poor, Sacred Heart Home, 4900 Navarre Ave., Oregon 43616 (126).

Little Sisters of the Poor, Sts. Mary and Joseph Home for Aged, 4291 Richmond Rd., Cleveland 44122 (124).

The Maria-Joseph Living Care Center, 4830 Salem Ave., Dayton 45416 (420).

Mercy St. Theresa Center, 7010 Rowan Hill Dr., Cincinnati 45227 (177).

Mercy Siena Woods (Nursing Home, Skilled and Intermediate Care, Alzheimer Center), 235 W. Orchard Spring Dr., Dayton 45415 (99).

Mount Alverna (Intermediate Care Nursing Facility), 6765 State Rd., Cleveland 44134 (203).

Mt. St. Joseph (Skilled Nursing Facility, Dual Certified), 21800 Chardon Rd., Cleveland 44117 (100).

Nazareth Towers, 300 E. Rich St., Columbus 43215. Hi-rise apartments for independent living for senior citizens (208).

St. Augustine Manor (Skilled Nursing Facility), 7801 Detroit Ave., Cleveland 44102 (248).

St. Clare Retirement Community (Skilled Nursing, Assisted Care, Apartments), Franciscan Sisters of the Poor, 100 Compton Rd., Cincinnati 45215 (171).

St. Francis Health Care Centre, 401 N. Broadway St., Green Springs 44836 (191).

St. Francis Home, Inc. (Residence and Nursing Care), 182 St. Francis Ave., Tiffin 44883 (116).

St. Joseph's Nursing Home and Assisted Living, 2308 Reno Dr., Louisville 44641 (100, nursing home; 40 assisted living).

St. Margaret Hall (Rest Home and Nursing Facility), Carmelite Sisters for the Aged and Infirm, 1960 Madison Rd., Cincinnati 45206 (135).

St. Raphael Home (Nursing Home), 1550 Roxbury Rd., Columbus 43212 (78).

St. Rita's Home (Skilled Nursing Home), 880 Greenlawn Ave., Columbus 43223 (100).

Schroder Manor Retirement Community (Residential Care, Skilled Nursing Care and Independent Living Units), Franciscan Sisters of the Poor, 1302 Millville Ave., Hamilton 45013 (173).

The Villa Sancta Anna Home for the Aged, Inc., 25000 Chagrin Blvd., Beachwood 44122 (68).

The Village at St. Edward (Apartments, Nursing Care and Assisted Living), 3131 Smith Rd., Fairlawn 44333 (290).

**Oklahoma:** Franciscan Villa, 17110 E. 51st St., Broken Arrow 74012. Intermediate nursing care (60); apartments (40 independent; 22 assisted living).

St. Ann's Home, 9400 St. Ann's Dr., Oklahoma City 73162 (102).

Westminster Village, Inc. (Residence), 1601 Academy, Ponca City 74604 (108).

**Oregon:** Benedictine Nursing Center, 540 S. Main St., Mt. Angel 97362 (130). Home Health Agency, Outpatient Therapies. Benedictine Institute for Long Term Care. Child Development Center.

Evergreen Court Retirement Apartments, 451 O'Connell St., North Bend 97459 (80).

Maryville Nursing Home, 14645 S.W. Farmington, Beaverton 97007 (147).

Mt. St. Joseph Residence and Extended Care Center, 3060 S.E. Stark St., Portland 97214 (298).

St. Catherine's Residence and Nursing Center, 3959 Sheridan Ave., North Bend 97459 (153).

St. Elizabeth Hospital and Health Care Center, 3985 Midway Lane, Baker City 97814 (120).

**Pennsylvania:** Antonian Towers, 2405 Hillside Ave., Easton 18042 (50 apartments).

Ascension Manor I (Senior Citizen Housing), 911 N. Franklin St., Philadelphia 19123 (140 units).

Ascension Manor II (Senior Citizen Housing), 970 N. 7th St., Philadelphia 19123 (140 units).

Benetwood Apartments, Benedictine Sisters of Erie, 641 Troupe Rd., Harborcreek 16421 (75). Subsidized housing for low income elderly and handicapped persons.

Bethlehem Retirement Village, 100 W. Wissahickon Ave., Flourtown 19031. Apartments for well elderly (100).

Christ the King Manor, 1100 W. Long Ave., Du Bois 15801 (160).

D'Youville Manor (Residential Care Facility), 1750 Quarry Rd., Yardley 19067 (50).

Garvey Manor (Nursing Home), Logan Blvd., Hollidaysburg 16648 (150).

Grace Mansion (Personal Care Facility), Holy Family Residential Services , 1200 Spring St., Bethlehem (28).

Holy Family Apartments (Low Income), Clay and Valley Sts., New Philadelphia 17959 (11).

Holy Family Apartments, 330-338 13th Ave., Bethlehem 18018 (50 apartments).

Holy Family Home, Little Sisters of the Poor, 5300 Chester Ave., Philadelphia 19143 (106).

Holy Family Manor (Skilled and Intermediate Nursing Facility), 1200 Spring St., Bethlehem 18018 (208).

Holy Family Residence (Personal Care Facility), 900 W. Market St., Orwigsburg 17961 (50).

Holy Redeemer Health System, Inc., Sisters of the Holy Redeemer: St. Joseph's Manor, 1616 Huntingdon Pike, Meadowbrook 19046 (262 bed personal assisted living; 24 bed cognitive impairment); Lafayette-Redeemer, 8580 Verree Rd., Philadelphia 19111 (295 independent-living apartments; 120 bed nursing; 5 bed assisted living); Redeemer Village, 1551 Huntingdon Pike, Huntingdon Valley 19006 (200 units low income subsidized housing for aged and disabled). Also sponsor a hospital, homecare, hospice and other related facilities.

Immaculate Mary Home (Nursing Care Facility), 2990 Holme Ave., Philadelphia 19136 (296).

John XXIII Home (Skilled, Intermediate and Personal Care), 2250 Shenango Freeway, Hermitage 16148 (142).

Little Flower Manor Nursing Home (Skilled Nursing), 1201 Springfield Rd., Darby 19023 (127).

Little Flower Manor of Diocese of Scranton, (Long-Term Skilled Nursing Care Facility), 200 S. Meade St., Wilkes-Barre 18702 (133).

Little Sisters of the Poor, 1028 Benton Ave., Pittsburgh 15212 (106).

Little Sisters of the Poor, Holy Family Residence, 2500 Adams Ave., Scranton 18509 (58).

Maria Joseph Manor (Skilled Nursing, Personal Care Facility and Independent Living Cottages), 875 Montour Blvd., Danville 17821 (96).

Marian Hall Home for the Aged (Women), 934 Forest Ave., Pittsburgh 15202 (25).

Marian Manor (Intermediate Care), 2695 Winchester Dr., Pittsburgh 15220 (170).

Mount Macrina Manor (Skilled Nursing Facility), 520 W. Main St., Uniontown 15401 (120).

Neumann Apartments (Low Income), 25 N. Nichols St., St. Clair 17970 (25).

Queen of Angels Apartments, 22 Rothermel St., Hyde Park, Reading 19605 (45 units).

Queen of Peace Apartments (Low Income), 777 Water St., Pottsville 17901 (65).

Sacred Heart Manor (Nursing Home and Independent Living), 6445 Germantown Ave., Philadelphia 19119 (171 nursing home; 24 personal care; 72 independent living).

St. Anne's Home and Village, 3952 Columbia Ave., Columbia 17512 (Nursing home, 121; personal care, 18; independent living, 36 cottages).

St. Anne Home (Nursing Facility), 685 Angela Dr., Greensburg 15601 (125).

St. Basil's Home (Personal Care Facility) 530 W. Main St., Box 878, Uniontown 15401 (11).

St. Ignatius Nursing Home, 4401 Haverford Ave., Philadelphia 19104 (176).

St. John Neumann Nursing Home, 10400 Roosevelt Blvd., Philadelphia 19116 (224).

St. Joseph Home for the Aged (Residential and Skilled Nursing Facility), 1182 Holland Rd., Holland 18966 (96).

St. Joseph Nursing and Health Care Center (Skilled Nursing Facility), 5324 enn Ave., Pittsburgh 15224 (158).

St. Leonard's Home Inc. (Personal Care Facility), 601 N. Montgomery St., Hollidaysburg 16648 (21).

St. Mary of Providence Center, R.D. 2, Box 145, Elverson 19520 (Senior Citizen Housing, 39 units). Center is also a House of Spirituality.

St. Mary's Home of Erie, 607 E. 26th St., Erie 16504. Residential and personal care (131); skilled and intermediate nursing care (228, includes Alzheimer Center, 37); adult day care (49).

Saint Mary's Manor (Residential, Personal Care, Short-Term Rehabilitation and Nursing Care), 701 Lansdale Ave., Lansdale 19446 (160).

St. Mary's Villa Nursing Home, St. Mary's Villa Rd., Elmhurst 18416 (112).

Trexler Pavilion (Personal Care Facility), 1220 Prospect Ave., Bethlehem 18018 (25).

Villa de Marillac Nursing Home, 5300 Stanton Ave., Pittsburgh 15206 (52).

Villa St. Teresa (Residence, Women), 1215 Springfield Rd., Darby 19023 (53).

Villa Teresa (Nursing Home), 1051 Avila Rd., Harrisburg 17109 (184).

Vincentian Home (Nursing Facility), 111 Perrymont Rd., Pittsburgh 15237 (221).

**Rhode Island:** Jeanne Jugan Residence of the Little Sisters of the Poor, 964 Main St., Pawtucket 02860 (99).

Saint Antoine Residence (Skilled Nursing Facility), 400 Mendon Rd., North Smithfield 02896 (260).

St. Clare Home (Nursing Facility), 309 Spring St., Newport 02840 (46).

St. Francis House, 167 Blackstone St., Woonsocket 02895 (60). Residential, assisted living.

Scalabrini Villa (Convalescent, Rest — Nursing Home). 860 N. Quidnessett Rd., North Kingstown 02852 (70).

**South Carolina:** Carter-May Home, 1660 Ingram Rd., Charleston 29407 (15). Personal care home for elderly ladies.

**South Dakota:** Brady Memorial Home (Skilled Nursing Facility), 500 S. Ohlman St., Mitchell 57301 (83). Independent living units (3); congregate apartments (6); adult day care.

Maryhouse, Inc. (Skilled Nursing Facility), 717 E. Dakota, Pierre 57501 (82 skilled nursing, 23 subacute care beds).

Mother Joseph Manor (Skilled Nursing Facility), 1002 North Jay St., Aberdeen 57401 (81). Apartment units (7). Adult day care program. Respite nursing care.

Prince of Peace Retirement Community, 4500 Prince of Peace Pl., Sioux Falls 57103. Skilled nursing home (90 beds); independent living apartments (74); assisted living aprrartments (32); Alzheimer Special Care Unit (20).

St. William's Home for the Aged (Intermediate Care, 60), and Angela Hall (Assisted Living Center for Developmentally Handicapped Women, 22), 901 E. Virgil, Box 432, Milbank 57252. Adult day care program (10).

Tekakwitha Nursing Home (Skilled and Intermediate Care), Sisseton 57262 (101). Tekakwitha Housing Corp. (Independent Living), P.O. Box 208, Sisseton 57262 (24 units).

**Tennessee:** Alexian Village of Tennessee, 100 James Blvd., Signal Mountain 37377 (277 retirement apartments) and Health Care Center (114). Assisted living (33).

St. Mary Manor, 1771 Highway 45 Bypass, Jackson 38305 (149 retirement apartments).

St. Peter Manor (Retirement Community), 108 N. Auburndale, Memphis 38104.

St. Peter Villa (Intermediate and Skilled Care), 141 N. McLean, Memphis 38104 (180).

Villa Maria Manor, 32 White Bridge Rd., Nashville 37205 (214 apartments).

**Texas:** Casa, Inc., Housing for Elderly and Handicapped, 3201 Sondra Dr., Fort Worth 76107 (200 apartments).

Casa Brendan Housing for the Elderly and Handicapped (56 apartments) and Casa II, Inc. (30 apartments), 1300 Hyman St., Stephenville 76401 (86).

John Paul II Nursing Home (Intermediate Care and Personal Care), 215 Tilden St., Kenedy 78119.

Mother of Perpetual Help Home (Intermediate Care Facility), 519 E. Madison Ave., Brownsville 78520 (33).

Mt. Carmel Home (Personal Care Home), 4130 S. Alameda St., Corpus Christi 78411 (92).

Nuestro Hogar Housing for Elderly and Handicapped, 709 Magnolia St., Arlington 76012 (65 apartments).

The Regis Retirement Home and St. Elizabeth Nursing Home, 400 Austin Ave., Waco 76701 (291).

St. Ann's Nursing Home, P.O. Box 1179, Panhandle 79068 (56).

St. Dominic Nursing Home, 6502 Grand Ave., Houston 77021 (120).

St. Dominic Residence Hall, 2401 E. Holcombe Blvd., Houston 77021 (137).

St. Francis Nursing Home (Intermediate Care Facility), 630 W. Woodlawn, San Antonio 78212 (152).

St. Francis Village, Inc. (Retired and Elderly), 1 Chapel Plaza, Crowley 76036 (450).

St. Joseph Residence (Personal Care Home), 330 W. Pembroke St., Dallas 75208 (49).

San Juan Nursing Home, Inc. (Skilled and Intermediate Care Facility), P.O. Box 1238, San Juan 78589 (127).

Villa Maria (Home for Aged Women-Men), 920 S. Oregon St., El Paso 79901 (24 units).

Villa Maria, Inc. (Apartment Complex), 3146 Saratoga Blvd., Corpus Christi 78415 (48 units). Corpus Christi diocese.

**Utah:** St. Joseph Villa (Senior Care Complex), 451 Bishop Federal Lane, Salt Lake City 84115 (230).

**Vermont:** Loretto Home for Aged, 59 Meadow St., Rutland 05701 (57).

Michaud Memorial Manor (Residential Home for Elderly), Derby Line 05830 (24).

St. Joseph's Home for Aged, 243 N. Prospect St., Burlington 05401 (36).

**Virginia:** Madonna Home (Home for Aged), 814 W. 37th St., Norfolk 23508 (16).

Marian Manor (Assisted Living, Nursing Care), 5345 Marian Lane, Virginia Beach 23462 (100 units; 30 beds nursing care).

Marywood Apartments, 1261 Marywood Lane, Richmond 23229 (112 units).

McGurk House Apartments, 2425 Tate Springs Rd., Lynchburg 24501 (88 units).

Our Lady of the Valley Retirement Community, 650 N. Jefferson St., Roanoke 24016.

Russell House Apartments, 900 First Colonial Rd., Virginia Beach 23454 (127).

St. Francis Home, 2511 Wise St., Richmond 23225 (31).

St. Joseph's Home for the Aged, Little Sisters of the Poor, 1503 Michael Rd., Richmond 23229 (72).

St. Mary's Woods (Independent and Assisted Living Apartments), 1257 Marywood Lane, Richmond 23229 (118 apartments).

Seton Manor (Apartments), 215 Marcella Rd., Hampton 23666 (112).

**Washington:** Cathedral Plaza Apartments (Retirement Apartments), W. 1120 Sprague Ave., Spokane 99204 (150).

Chancery Place (Retirement Apartments), 910 Marion, Seattle 98104 *84 units; independent living).

The Delaney, W. 242 Riverside Ave., Spokane 99201 (84).

Elbert House, 16000 N.E. 8th St., Bellevue 98008.

Emma McRedmond Manor, 7960-169th N.E., Redmond 98052.

Fahy Garden Apartments, W. 1403-11 Dean Ave., Spokane 99201 (31).

Fahy West Apartments, W. 1523 Dean Ave., Spokane 99201 (55).

The Franciscan (Apartments), 15237-21stAve. S.W., Seattle 98166 (38).

Providence Mt. St. Vincent (Nursing Center and Retirement Apartments), 4831 35th Ave. S.W., Seattle 98126.

St. Brendan Continuing Care Center, E. 17 8th Ave., Spokane 99202.

St. Joseph Care Center, 20 West 9th Ave., Spokane 99204 (103).

Tumwater Apartments, 5701-6th Ave. S.W., Tumwater 98501 (50).

**West Virginia:** Welty Home for the Aged, 21 Washington Ave., Wheeling 26003 (45).

**Wisconsin:** Alexian Village of Milwaukee (Retirement Community/Skilled Nursing Home), 7979 W. Glenbrook Rd., Milwaukee 53223 (320 apartments; 87 skilled nursing; 30 assisted living; adult day care).

Bethany-St. Joseph Health Care Center, 2501 Shelby Rd., La Crosse 54601 (226).

Clement Manor (Retirement Community and Skilled Nursing), 3939 S. 92nd St., Greenfield 53228 (164 skilled nursing; 200 units independent and assisted living). Adult day care.

Divine Savior Nursing Home, 715 W. Pleasant St., Portage 53901 (111 skilled nursing; 14 self care).

Felician Village (Independent Living), 1700 S. 18th St., Manitowoc 54020 (134 apartments).

Franciscan Care Center, 2915 North Meade St., Appleton 54911 (235).

Franciscan Skemp Healthcare, Mayo Health System: Arcadia Campus Nursing Home, 464 S. St. Joseph Ave., Arcadia 54612 (75); LaCrosse Campus Nursing Home, 620 S. 11th St., La Crosse 54601 (95).

Franciscan Villa (Skilled Nursing Home), 3601 S. Chicago Ave., S. Milwaukee 53172 (150).

Hope Nursing Home, 438 Ashford Ave., Lomira 53048 (42).

McCormick Memorial Home, 212 Iroquois St., Green Bay 54301 (74).

Marian Catholic Home (Skilled Care Nursing Home), 3333 W. Highland Blvd., Milwaukee 53208 (360).

Marian Franciscan Center, 9632 W. Appleton Ave., Milwaukee 53225 (345).

Marian Housing Center (Independent Living), 4105 Spring St., Racine 53405 (40).

Maryhill Manor Nursing Home (Skilled Nursing Facility), 501 Madison Ave., Niagara 54151 (75).

Milwaukee Catholic Home (Continuing Care Retirement Community), 2462 N. Prospect Ave., Milwaukee 53211 (130 apartments; 56 skilled nursing).

Nazareth House (Skilled Nursing Facility), 814 Jackson St., Stoughton 53589 (99).

St. Ann Rest Home (Intermediate Care Facility, Women), 2020 S. Muskego Ave., Milwaukee 53204 (54).

St. Anne's Home for the Elderly, 3800 N. 92nd St., Milwaukee 53222 (106 skilled nursing beds, 16 independent apartments).

St. Camillus Campus (Continuing Care Retirement Community), 10100 West Blue Mound Road, Wauwatosa 53226 (297 independent apartments; 108 assisted living units; 192 skilled nursing beds). Also adult day care, licensed home health care, support home services; 24-bed subacute care unit.

St. Catherine Infirmary (Nursing Home), 5635 Erie St., Racine 53402 (41).

St. Elizabeth Nursing Home, 502 St. Lawrence Ave., Janesville 53545 (43).

St. Francis Home (Skilled Nursing Facility), 1800 New York Ave., Superior 54880 (192).

St. Francis Home (Skilled Nursing), 365 Gillett St., Fond du Lac 54935 (70).

St. Joan Antida Home (Skilled Nursing), 6700 W. Beloit Rd., W. Allis 53219 (73).

St. Joseph's Home, 705 Clyman St., Watertown 53094 (28).

St. Joseph's Home, 9244 29th Ave., Kenosha 53143 (93). Independent living apartments; skilled nursing home. St. Joseph Adult Day Care, sme address.

St. Joseph's Home, 5301 W. Lincoln Ave., W. Allis 53219 (51 assisted living; 74 skilled care; adult day care).

St. Joseph's Nursing Home, 2902 East Ave. S., La Crosse 54601 (80).

St. Joseph's Nursing Home of St. Joseph Memorial Hospital, 400 Water Ave., Hillsboro 54634 (65).

St. Joseph Residence, Inc. (Nursing Home), 107

E. Beckert Rd., New London 54961 (107 skilled nursing; 27 apartments).

St. Mary's Home for the Aged (Skilled Nursing, Alzheimer's Unit, Respite Care), 2005 Division St., Manitowoc 54220 (297).

St. Mary's Nursing Home, 3516 W. Center St., Milwaukee 53210 (130).

St. Monica's Senior Citizens Home, 3920 N. Green Bay Rd., Racine 53404 (125).

St. Paul Home, Inc. (Intermediate and Skilled Nursing Home), 1211 Oakridge Ave., Kaukauna 54130 (129). Assisted living also.

Villa Clement (Health Center), 9047 W. Greenfield Ave., W. Allis 53214 (194).

Villa Loretto Nursing Home, Mount Calvary 53057 (52).

Villa St. Anna (Assisted Living Facility), 5737 Erie St., Racine, 53402 (71 private units).

Villa St. Francis, Inc., 1910 W. Ohio Ave., Milwaukee 53215. Independent and assisted living (142 private units).

# FACILITIES FOR CHILDREN AND ADULTS WITH DISABILITIES

Sources: Almanac survey; *Directory of Catholic Special Educational Programs and Facilities,* published by the National Catholic Educational Association, Washington, D.C.; *Official Catholic Directory.*

This listing covers facilities and programs with educational and training orientation. Information about other services for the handicapped can generally be obtained from the Catholic Charities Office or its equivalent (c/o Chancery Office) in any diocese. (See Index for listing of addresses of chancery offices in the U.S.)

Abbreviation code: b, boys; c, coeducational; d, day; g, girls; r, residential. Other information includes chronological age for admission. The number in parentheses at the end of an entry indicates total capacity or enrollment.

## Deaf and Hearing Impaired

**California:** St. Joseph's Center for Deaf and Hard of Hearing, 3880 Smith St., Union City 94587.

**Louisiana:** Chinchuba Institute (d,c; birth through 18 yrs.), 1131 Barataria Blvd., Marrero 70072.

**Missouri:** St. Joseph Institute for the Deaf (r,d,c; birth to 14 years), 1483 82nd Blvd., University City, St. Louis 63132 (120).

**New York:** Cleary School for the Deaf (d,c; infancy through high school), 301 Smithtown Blvd., Nesconset, NY 11767 (105).

St. Francis de Sales School for the Deaf (d,c; infant through elementary grades), 260 Eastern Parkway, Brooklyn 11225 (220).

St. Joseph's School for the Deaf (d,c; parent-infant through 14 yrs.), 100 Hutchinson River Pkwy, Bronx 10465 (160).

**Ohio:** St. Rita School for the Deaf (r,d,c; birth to 12th grade), 1720 Glendale-Milford Rd., Cincinnati 45215 (160).

**Pennsylvania:** Archbishop Ryan School for Hearing Impaired Children (d,c; parent-infant programs through 8th grade), 3509 Spring Garden St., Philadelphia 19104 (47).

De Paul Institute (d,c; birth through 15 yrs.), Castlegate Ave., Pittsburgh 15226 (115).

## Emotionally and/or Socially Maladjusted

This listing includes facilities for abused, abandoned and neglected as well as emotionally disturbed children and youth.

**Alabama:** St. Mary's Home for Children (r,c; referred from agencies), 4350 Moffat Rd., Mobile 36618 (44).

**California:** Hanna Boys Center (r,b; 10-15 yrs. at intake; school, 4th to 10th grade), Box 100, Sonoma 95476 (107). Treatment center and therapeutic special school for boys with emotional problems, behavior disorders, learning disabilities.

Rancho San Antonio (r,b; 13-17 yrs.), 21000 Plummer St., Chatsworth 91311 (102).

**Colorado:** Mt. St. Vincent Home (r,c; 5-13 yrs.), 4159 Lowell Blvd., Denver 80211 (45). Day treatment (5-13 yrs.), same address (16).

**Connecticut:** St. Francis Home for Children (r,d,c; 4-17 yrs.), 651 Prospect St., New Haven 06511 (70).

Mt. St. John (r,b; 11-16 yrs.), 135 Kirtland St., Deep River 06417 (75). Home and school for boys.

**Delaware:** Our Lady of Grace Home for Children (r,d,c; 6-12 yrs.), 487 E. Chestnut Hill Rd., Newark 19713 (14).

Seton Villa and Siena Hall (c; group home; 5-18 yrs,), c/o 2307 Kentmere Pkwy, Wilmington 19806.

**Florida:** Boystown of Florida (r,b; 12-16 yrs.; group home), 11400 S.W. 137th Ave., Miami 33186 (43).

**Georgia:** Village of St. Joseph (r,c; 6-16 yrs.), 2969 Butner Rd. S.W., Atlanta 30331. Residential care center for emotionally disturbed children.

**Illinois:** Guardian Angel Home (d,c), 1550 Plainfield Rd., Joliet 60435 (35).

Maryville Academy (r,c; 6-18 yrs.), 1150 North River Rd., Des Plaines 60016.

Mission of Our Lady of Mercy, Mercy Home for Boys and Girls (r,d,c; 15-18 yrs.), 1140 W. Jackson Blvd., Chicago 60607 (100).

St. Joseph Carondelet Child Center, 739 E. 35th St., Chicago 60616.

**Indiana:** Gibault School for Boys (r; 10-18 yrs.), 6301 South U.S. Highway 41, P.O. Box 2316, Terre Haute 47802 (147).

Hoosier Boys Town (r; 10-18 yrs.), 7403 Cline Ave., Schererville 46375 (60).

**Kentucky:** Boys' Haven (r; 12-18 yrs.), 2301 Goldsmith Lane, Louisville 40218 (67).

Maryhurst School (r,g; 13-17 yrs.), 1015 Dorsey Lane, Louisville 40223 (55).

**Louisiana:** Hope Haven Center (r,c; 5-18 yrs.), 1101 Barataria Blvd., Marrero 70072 (150). Residential treatment center and school.

Maison Marie Group Home (r,g; 14-18 yrs.), 3020 Independence St., Metairie 70006.

**Maryland:** Good Shepherd Center (r,g; 13-17 yrs.), 4100 Maple Ave., Baltimore. 21227 (105).

**Massachusetts:** The Brightside for Families and Children (r,d,c; 6-16 yrs.), 2112 Riverdale St., W. Springfield 01089.

McAuley Nazareth Home for Boys (r; 6-13 yrs.), 77 Mulberry St., Leicester 01524 (16). Residential treatment center.

St. Vincent Home (r,c 6-18 yrs.), 2425 Highland Ave., Fall River 02720 (62). Residential treatment center.

**Michigan:** Boysville of Michigan, Inc. (r; 13-17 yrs.), Community Resource Office, 17117 W. Nine Mile Rd., Suite 445, Southfield 48075. Facilities located throughout the state.

Don Bosco Hall (r,b; 13-17 years.), 10001 Petoskey Ave., Detroit 48204 (35).

Vista Maria (r,g; 11-18 yrs.), 20651 W. Warren Ave., Dearborn Heights 48127 (150).

**Minnesota:** St. Cloud Children's Home (r,c; 8-18 yrs.), 1726 7th Ave. S., St. Cloud 56301 (90). Day Treatment Program (d,c; 7-14 yrs.), same address (12). Intensive Care Unit (r,c; 13-17 yrs.), Box 1006, Fergus Falls 56538 (22).

St. Elizabeth Home (r,c; 18 yrs. and older), 306 15th Ave. N., St. Cloud 56301 (14). Primarily for mentally ill.

**Missouri:** Child Center of Our Lady (r,d,c; 5-14 yrs.), 7900 Natural Bridge Rd., St. Louis. 63121 (48).

Marygrove (r,d,c; 6-21 yrs.), 2705 Mullanphy Lane, Florissant. 63031 (97). Sequoia House (r,g; 17-21 yrs.), 2695 Mullamphy, Florissant 63031.

St. Joseph's Home for Boys (r,d,b; 6-14 yrs.), 4753 S. Grand Blvd., St. Louis 63111 (50).

**Nebraska:** Father Flanagan's Boys' Home (r,c; 10-16 yrs.), Boys Town 68010 (556). Boys Town National Research Hospital (r,d,c; 1-18 yrs.), 555 N. 30th St., Omaha 68131. Center for Abused Handicapped Children; diagnosis of speech, language and hearing problems in children. Boys Town also has various facilities or programs in Brooklyn, N.Y.; Portsmouth, R.I.; Philadelphia, Pa.; Washington, D.C.; Tallahassee, Orlando and Delray Beach, Fla.; Atlanta, Ga.; New Orleans, La.; San Antonio, Tex., Las Vegas, Nev., and southern California.

**New Jersey:** Catholic Community Services/Mt. Carmel Guild, 1160 Raymond Blvd., Newark 07102.

Christopher House (c; 18 and over), 55 N. Clinton Ave., Trenton 08607 (90). Psychiatric day treatment.

Collier Group Home (r,g; 13-18 yrs.), 180 Spring St., Red Bank 07701 (12).

Collier High School (d,c; 13-18 yrs.), Conover Rd., Wickatunk 07765 (140).

Guidance Clinic of Catholic Charities (c), 39 N. Clinton Ave., Trenton 08607. Psychiatric counseling for children and adults.

Mt. St. Joseph Children's Center (r,d,b; 6-12 yrs.), Shepherd Lane, Totowa 07512 (32).

**New York:** The Astor Home for Children (r,d,c; 5-12 yrs.), 36 Mill St., P.O. Box 5005, Rhinebeck 12572 (75). Child Guidance Clinics/Day Treatment (Rhinebeck, Poughkeepsie, Beacon, Bronx). Head Start — Day Care (Poughkeepsie, Beacon, Red Hook, Dover, Millerton).

Baker Hall (r,d,c; 10-17 yrs.), 150 Martin Rd., Lackawanna 14218. Special services (18), institution (24), residential treatment facility (45), group homes (27), foster homes (10), preventive services (250), special education school (100), day treatment (52), out-patient clinic (75).

Good Shepherd Services, 337 E. 17th St., New York 10003. Residential programs for adolescents; community-based neighborhood family services in Park Slope and Red Hook, Brooklyn.

LaSalle School (r,d,b; 12-18 yrs.), 391 Western Ave., Albany. 12203 (145). Registered high school; certified special education program. Also conducts independent living apartments and prevention programs.

Madonna Heights Services (r,d,g; 12-18 yrs.), 151 Burrs Lane, Dix Hills 11746 (110). Also conducts group homes on Long Island and outpatient programs.

Saint Anne Intitute (r,d,g; 12-18 yrs.), 160 N. Main Ave., Albany 12206 (124). Critical level, preventive services. Sex abuse prevention and juvenile sex offender programs, substance abuse program. Regents accredited school.

St. Catherine's Center for Children (r,d,c; birth through 12 yrs.), 40 N. Main Ave., Albany 12203. Group homes, day treatment, prevention and specialized foster care programs.

St. John's of Rockaway Beach (r,b; 9-21 yrs.), 144 Beach 111th St., Rockaway Park 11694 (100). Programs include Diagnostic centers and independent living programs.

**North Dakota:** Home on the Range (r,c; 10-18 yrs.), HC1, Box 41, Sentinel Butte. 58654 (79). Residential and emergency shelter therapeutic programs.

**Ohio:** Diocesan Child Guidance Center, Inc. (d,c; preschool) Outpatient counseling program (c; 2-18 yrs.), 840 W. State St., Columbus 43222.

Marycrest (r,g; 13-18 yrs.), 7800 Brookside Rd., Independence 44131 (70). Residential treatment and transitional living for adolescent girls and adolescent mothers.

Parmadale Family Services Village (r,c; 12-18 yrs.), 6753 State Rd., Parma 44134.

Rosemont (r,g;d,c; 11-18 yrs.), 2440 Dawnlight Ave., Columbus 43211 (150). Mental health and AOD services; outreach services include baby day care (birth-3 yrs.).

**Oregon:** St. Mary's Home for Boys (r; 9-18 yrs.), 16535 S.W. Tualatin Valley Highway, Beaverton 97006 (56).

**Pennsylvania:** Auberle (r,c; 7-18 yrs.), 1101 Hartman St., McKeesport 15132 (100). Residential treatment for boys; emergency shelter care, foster care, group home for girls and family preservation program.

De LaSalle in Towne (d,b; 14-17 yrs.), 25 S. Van Pelt St., Philadelphia 19103 (80).

De LaSalle Vocational Day Treatment (b; 15-17 yrs.), P.O. Box 344 — Street Rd. and Bristol Pike, Bensalem 19020 (120).

Gannondale (r,g; 12-17 yrs.), 4635 E. Lake Rd., Erie 16511 (45).

Harborcreek Youth Services (r,d,c; 10-17 yrs.), 5712 Iroquois Ave., Harborcreek 16421 (150). Also conducts group homes.

Holy Family Institute (r,d,c; 0-18 yrs.), 8235 Ohio River Blvd., Pittsburgh 15202 (125). Also conducts in-home services, foster care and group homes.

Lourdesmont Good Shepherd Youth and Family Services (r,g;d,c; 13-17 yrs.), 537 Venard Rd., Clarks Summit 18411 (100).

St. Gabriel's Hall (r,b; 10-18 yrs.), P.O. Box 7280, Audubon 19407 (220). Also conducts group homes.

St. Michael's School (r,b; d,c; 12-17 yrs.), Box 370, Hoban Heights 18657. Also conducts group homes, day treatment program and foster care.

**Tennessee:** DeNeuville Heights School for Girls (r; 12-17 yrs.), 3060 Baskin St., Memphis 38127 (52).

St. Peter Home (r,g; 13-17 yrs.), 1805 Poplar, Memphis 38104 (74).

**Texas:** St. Joseph Adolescent and Family Counseling Center (c; 13-17 yrs.), Casa Linda Plaza, Suite 403, Dallas 75218 (20).

**Washington:** Morning Star Boys Ranch (Spokane Boys' Ranch, Inc.), (r,b; 10-16 yrs.), Box 8087 Manito Station, Spokane 99203 (30).

**Wisconsin:** Our Lady of Charity Center (r,c; 10-17 yrs.), 2640 West Point Rd., P.O. Box 11737, Green Bay 54304.

St. Charles Youth and Family Services (r,d,b; 12-18 yrs.), 151 S. 84th St., Milwaukee 53214 (63).

**Wyoming:** St. Joseph's Children's Home (r,c; 6-18 yrs.), P.O. Box 1117, Torrington 82240 (50). Also conducts group home. Newell Children's Center (r,c; 6-18 years), same address (12).

## Developmentally Disabled

This listing includes facilities for children, youth and adults with learning disabilities.

**Alabama:** Father Purcell Memorial Exceptional Children's Center (r, c; birth to 10 yrs.), 2048 W. Fairview Ave., Montgomery 36108 (58). Skilled nursing facility.

Father Walter Memorial Child Care Center (r,c; birth-12 yrs.), 2815 Forbes Dr., Montgomery 36110 (44). Skilled nursing facility.

**California:** Child Study Center of St. John's Hospital (d,c; birth-18 yrs.), 1339 - 20th St., Santa Monica. 90404 (80).

St. Madeleine Sophie's Center (d,c; 18 yrs. and older), 2111 E. Madison Ave., El Cajon 92019 (142).

St. Vincent's (r,d,c; 7-21 yrs.), 4200 Calle Real, P.O. Box 669, Santa Barbara 93102 (60). Also conducts programs for adolescent offenders on probation (r,d,g; 12-17 yrs.) (12).

Tierra del Sol Foundation (d,c; 18 yrs. and older), 9919 Sunland Blvd., Sunland 91040 (200); 14547 Gilmore St., Van Nuys 91411 (50).

**Connecticut:** Gengras Center (d,c; 3-21 yrs.), St. Joseph College, 1678 Asylum Ave., W. Hartford 06117 (112).

Villa Maria Education Center (d,c; 6-14 yrs.),), 159 Sky Meadow Dr., Stamford 06903 (60). For children with learning disabilities.

**District of Columbia:** Lt. Joseph P. Kennedy, Jr., Institute (d,c; 6 weeks to 5 yrs. for preschool program; 5-21 yrs. for school program; 18 yrs. and older for other programs which include continuing education, training and employment, therapeutic and residential services. Headquarters: 801 Buchanan St. N.E. Washington 20017. Other locations in District of Columbia and Maryland (Prince George and Montgomery counties). No enrollment limit.

**Florida:** L'Arche Harbor House, (c; 20 yrs. and older; community home), 700 Arlington Rd., Jacksonville 32211.

Marian Center Services for Developmentally Handicapped and Mentally Retarded (r,d,c; 2-21 yrs.), 15701 Northwest 37th Ave., Opa Locka 33054. Offers variety of services.

Morning Star School (d,c; 4-16 yrs.), 725 Mickler Rd., Jacksonville 32211 (110). For children with learning disabilities.

Morning Star School (d,c; school age), 954 Leigh Ave., Orlando 32804 (55).

Morning Star School (d,c; 6-14 yrs.), 4661-80th Ave. N., Pinellas Park 34665 (60). For children with learning disabilities and other learning handicaps.

Morning Star School (d,c; 6-16 yrs.), 210 E. Linebaugh Ave., Tampa 33612. (93). For children with learning disabilities.

**Georgia:** St. Mary's Home (r,c), 2170 E. Victory Dr., Savannah 31404.

**Illinois:** Bartlett Learning Center (r,d,c; 3-21 yrs.), 801 W. Bartlett Rd., Bartlett 60103 (121).

Brother James Court (r, men over 18 yrs.), 2500 St. James Rd., Springfield 62707 (96).

Good Shepherd Manor (r,b; 18 yrs. and older), Little Brothers of the Good Shepherd, P.O. Box 260, Momence. 60954 (120). Resident care for adult males.

Misericordia Home South (r,c), 2916 W. 47th St., Chicago 60632 (130).

Misericordia Home - Heart of Mercy Village (r,c; 6-45 yrs.), 6300 North Ridge, Chicago 60660 (400).

Mt. St. Joseph (developmentally disabled women; over age 21), 24955 N. Highway 12, Lake Zurich 60047 (160).

St. Coletta's of Illinois (r,d,; 6 to adult), 123rd and Wolf Rd., Palos Park 60464: St. Coletta's Residential Program (111 in 19 group homes and apartments); Lt. Joseph P. Kennedy, Jr., School (50d, 80r); Kennedy Job Training Center (100d, 40r).

St. Francis School for Exceptional Children (r,c; 2-12 yrs.), 1209 S. Walnut Ave., Freeport 61032 (40).

St. Mary of Providence (r,g; 6 to adult), 4200 N. Austin Ave., Chicago 60634 (110). Day program (c; 6-21 yrs.).

St. Rose Center (d,c; 3-21 yrs.), 4911 S. Hoyne Ave., Chicago 60609 (60). For mentally handicapped children.

St. Vincent Community Living Facility (adults, over 18 yrs.) (20), and St. Vincent Supported Living Arrangement (adults, over 18 yrs.) (20), 659 E. Jefferson St., Freeport 61032.

Springfield Developmental Center (m; 21 yrs. and over), 2500 St. James Rd., Springfield 62707. Vocational training.

**Indiana:** Marian Day School (d,c; 6-16 yrs.), 700 Herndon Dr., Evansville 47711 (35). For learning disabled.

Providence House (nursing facility, men; 18 yrs. and up), 520 W. 9th St., Jasper 47546 (58).

**Kansas:** Lakemary Center, Inc. (r,c), 100 Lakemary Dr., Paola 66071. Children and adults.

**Kentucky:** Pitt Academy (d,c), 2117 Payne St., Louisville 40206 (75).

Ursuline Speech Clinic (d,c; 3 yrs.-adult), 3105 Lexington Rd., Louisville 40206 (45).

**Louisiana:** Department of Special Education, Archdiocese of New Orleans, St. Michael Special School (d,c; 6-21 yrs.), 1522 Chippewa St., New Orleans 70130.

Holy Angels Residential Facility (r,c; teen-age, 14 yrs. and older), 10450 Ellerbe Rd., Shreveport 71106 (180).

Ocean Avenue Community House, 361 Ocean Ave., Gretna 70053. Group home (6).

Padua Community Services (r,c; birth-21 yrs.), 200 Beta St., Belle Chase 70037 (32).

St. Jude the Apostle, 1430 Claire Ave., Gretna 70053. Group home, adults (6).

St. Mary's Residential Training School (r,c: 3-22 yrs.), P.O. Drawer 7768, Alexandria 71306 (152).

St. Peter the Fisherman, 62269 Airport Dr., Slidell 70458. Group home (6).

St. Rosalie (r; men 18 and up), 119 Kass St., Gretna 70056. Group home (6).

Sts. Mary and Elizabeth, 720 N. Elm St., Metairie 70003. Group home (6).

**Maryland:** The Benedictine School for Exceptional Children (r,c; 6-21 yrs.), Ridgely 21660 (145). Also conducts Habilitation Center (r,c; 17 yrs. and older) (50) and 17 community-based homes (21 yrs. and older).

Francis X. Gallagher Services (r), 2520 Pot Spring Rd., Timonium 21093 (189). Adult vocational program (130); adult medical program (180).

St. Elizabeth School and Habilitation Center (d,c; 12-21 yrs.), 801 Argonne Dr., Baltimore 21218 (99).

**Massachusetts:** Cardinal Cushing School and Training Center (r,d,c; 10-22 yrs.), Hanover 02339 (130 r; 40 d).

Mercy Centre for Developmental Disabilities (d,c; 3-22 yrs. and over), 25 West Chester St., Worcester 01605 (176).

St. Coletta Day School (d,c; 5-22 yrs.), 85 Washington St., Braintree 02184 (132).

**Michigan:** Our Lady of Providence Center (r,g; 11-30 yrs., d,c; 26 yrs. and older), 16115 Beck Rd., Northville. 48167 (100).

St. Louis Center and School (r,d,b; 6-18 yrs. child care; 18-36 yrs. adult foster care), 16195 Old U.S. 12, Chelsea 48118 (68).

**Minnesota:** Mother Teresa Home (r,c; 18 yrs. and older), 101-10th Ave. N., Cold Spring 56320 (14).

St. Francis Home (r,c; 18 yrs. and older), 25-2nd St. N., Waite Park 56387.

St. Luke's Home (r,; 18 yrs. and older), 411 8th Ave. N., Cold Springs 56320.

**Missouri:** Department of Special Education, Archdiocese of St. Louis, 4472 Lindell Blvd., St. Louis. 63108. Serves children with developmental disabilities, mental retardation or learning disabilities; services include special ungraded day classes in 7 parish schools.

Good Shepherd Homes (residential for developmentally disabled men; 18 yrs. and up), The Community of the Good Shepherd, 10101 James A. Reed Rd., Kansas City 64134 (30).

St. Joseph's Vocational Center, 5341 Emerson Ave., St. Louis 63120. Provides community job training opportunities for adolescents with developmental disabilities or educational handicaps.

St. Mary's Special School (r,c; 5-21 yrs.), 5341 Emerson Ave., St. Louis 63120 (90).

**Nebraska:** Madonna School for Exceptional Children (d,c; 5-21 yrs.), 2537 N. 62nd St., Omaha 68104 (65). Children with learning problems.

Villa Marie School and Home for Exceptional Children (r,d,c; 6-18 yrs.), P.O. Box 80328, Lincoln 68501 (18).

**New Jersey:** Archbishop Damiano School (d,c; 5-21 yrs.), 532 Delsea Dr., Westville Grove 08093.

Catholic Community Services, Archdiocese of Newark, 1160 Raymond Blvd., Newark 07102. Services include: Mt. Carmel Guild, St. Anthony's and St. Patrick's Special Education Schools (see separate entries).

Department of Special Education, Diocese of Camden, 1845 Haddon Ave., Camden 08101. Services include: Archbishop Damiano School (above), and full time programs at 4 elementary and 2 high schools and some religious education programs.

Department for Persons with Disabilities, Diocese of Paterson, 1049 Weldon Rd., Oak Ridge, N.J. 07438. Services include 8 residential programs for adults, one adult training center, family support services.

Felician School for Exceptional Children (d,c; 5-21 yrs.), 260 S. Main St., Lodi 07644 (145).

McAuley School for Exceptional Children (d,c; 5-21 yrs.), 1633 Rt. 22 at Terrill Rd., Watchung 07060 (48).

Mt. Carmel Guild Special Education School (d,c), 90 Kingsland Ave., Kearny 07032.

St. Anthony's Special Education School (d,c), 25 N. 7th St., Belleville 07104.

Sister Georgine School (d,c; 6-17 yrs.), 544 Chestnut Ave., Trenton 08611 (30).

St. Patrick's Special Education School (d,c), 72 Central Ave., Newark 07102.

**New York:** Cantalician Center for Learning (d,c; birth-21 yrs.), 3233 Main St., Buffalo 14214. Infant and pre-school; elementary and secondary; workshop (600). Three group homes.

Catholic Charities Residential Services, Rockville Center Diocese, 269 W. Main St., Bay Shore 11706. Conducts residences for developmentally disabled adults.

Cobb Memorial School (r,d,c; 5-21 yrs.), Altamont 12009 (32).

L'Arche (r, adults), 1701 James St., Syracuse 13206 (12). Homes where assistants and persons with developmental disabilities share life, following the philosophy of Jean Vanier. Member of International L'Arche Federation.

Maryhaven Center of Hope (r,d,c; school age to adult), Myrtle Ave., Port Jefferson 11777. Offers variety of services.

Mercy Home for Children (r,c), 310 Prospect Park West, Brooklyn 11215. Conducts six residences for adolescents and young adults who are developmentally disabled: Visitation, Warren, Vincent Haire, Santulli and Littlejohn residences (Brooklyn), Kevin Keating Residence (Queens) (72).

Office for Disabled Persons, Catholic Charities, Diocese of Brooklyn, 191 Joralemon St., Brooklyn 11201. Services include: adult day treatment center; community residences for mentally retarded adults; special events for disabled children (from age3) and adults.

Office for Disabled Persons, Archdiocese of New York, 1011 First Ave., New York 10022. Services include consultation and referral, variety of services for deaf, blind, mentally retarded, mentally ill.

Our Lady of Victory Infant Home (r), 790 Ridge Rd., Lackawanna, N.Y. 14218. Residential care for handicapped and retarded children; nursery school program for emotionally disturbed pre-school children.

School of the Holy Childhood (d,c; 5-21 yrs.), 100 Groton Parkway, Rochester 14623 (115). Adult program, 18-50 yrs (80).

Seton Foundation for Learning (d,c; 5-15 yrs.), 30 Manor Rd., Staten Is. 10310.

**North Carolina:** Holy Angels (r,c; birth to adult), 427 E. Wilkinson Blvd., Belmont 28012 (65).

**North Dakota:** Friendship, Inc. (r,d,c; 7 and older), 3004 11th St. South, Fargo 58103 (305).

**Ohio:** Julie Billiart School (d,c; 6-12 yrs.), 4982 Clubside Rd., Cleveland 44124 (125). Non-graded school for children with learning problems.

Mary Immaculate School (d,c; 6-14 yrs.), 3837 Secor Rd., Toledo 43623 (80). For children with learning disabilities.

Mount Aloysius, Inc. (r, adult men), Little Brothers of the Good Shepherd, 5375 Tile Plant Rd., New Lexington 43764 (80).

OLA/St. Joseph Center (d,c; 6-16 yrs.), 2346 W. 14th St., Cleveland 44113 (80).

Rose Mary, The Johanna Graselli Rehabilitation and Education Center (r,c; 5 yrs. and older), 19350 Euclid Ave., Cleveland 44117 (84).

St. John's Villa (r,c; continued care and training, 15 yrs. and over), 620 Roswell Rd. N.W., Carrollton 44615 (143).

**Oregon:** Providence Montessori School Early Intervention Program (d,c; 3-5 yrs.), 830 N.E. 47th Ave., Portland 97213 (12).

**Pennsylvania:** Clelian Heights School for Exceptional Children (r,d,c; 5-21 yrs.), R.D. 9, Box 607, Greensburg 15601 (95). Also conducts re-socialization program (r,d,c; young adults).

Divine Providence Village (adults), 686 Old Marple Rd., Springfield 19064 (96).

Don Guanella Village: Don Guanella School (r,d,b; 6-21 yrs.) and C.K. Center (r; adults, post-school

age), 1797-1799 S. Sproul Rd., Springfield 19064.

John Paul II, Center for Special Learning (d,c; 5-21 yrs.), 450 S. 6th St., Reading 19602 (40).

McGuire Memorial (r,d,c; infancy to 7 yrs.), 2119 Mercer Rd., New Brighton 15066 (99).

Mercy Special Learning Center (d,c; 3-21 yrs. and early intervention), 830 S. Woodward St., Allentown 18103 (90).

Our Lady of Confidence Day School (d,c; 4½-21 yrs.), 10th and Lycoming Sts., Philadelphia 19140 (140).

Queen of the Universe Day Center (d,c; 4½-16 yrs.), 2443 Trenton Rd., Levittown 19056 (48).

St. Anthony School Programs (d,c; 5-21 yrs.), 2718 Custer Ave., Pittsburgh 15227 (75).

St. Joseph Center for Special Learning (d,c; 4-21 yrs.), 2075 W. Norwegian St., Pottsville 17901 (50).

St. Joseph's Center (r,d,c; birth-10 yrs.), 2010 Adams Ave., Scranton 18509 (93).

St. Katherine Day School (d,c; 4½-21 yrs.), 930 Bowman Ave., Wynnewood 19096 (140).

**Tennessee:** Madonna Day School for Retarded Children (d,c; 5-16 yrs.), 4189 Leroy Ave., Memphis 38108 (52).

**Texas:** Notre Dame of Dallas Special School and Vocational Center (d,c; 3-21 yrs.), 2018 Allen St., Dallas, Tex. 75204. Academic and vocational training for developmentally handicapped.

**Virginia:** St. Coletta School (d,c; 5-22 yrs.), 3130 Lee Highway, Arlington 22201 (25). For developmentally disabled. Services include: occupational, physical and languae therapy; vocational program with job search, placement, training and follow-up services.

St. Mary's Infant Home (r,c; 3 days-9 yrs.), 317 Chapel St., Norfolk 23504 (88). For multiple handicapped.

**Washington:** St. Anne's Children's Home (r,c), North 707 Cedar St., Spokane 99201.

**Wisconsin:** St. Coletta School, W4955 H wy 18, Jefferson 53549. Year round special education programs for adolescents and adults; pre-vocational and vocational skills training; residential living alternatives. Young adult population. Employment opportunities for those who qualify (500).

St. Coletta Day School (c; 8-17 yrs.), 1740 N. 55th St., Milwaukee. 53208 (12).

## Orthopedically/Physically Handicapped

**Pennsylvania:** St. Edmond's Home for Children (r,c; 1-21 yrs.)., 320 S. Roberts Rd., Rosemont 19010 (40).

**Virginia:** St. Joseph Villa Housing Corp. (adults), 8000 Brook Rd., Richmond 23227 (60 apartments).

## Visually Handicapped

**Maine:** Educational Services for Blind and Visually Impaired Children (Catholic Charities, Maine), 1066 Kenduskeag Ave., Bangor 04401; 66 Western Ave., Fairfield 04937; 15 Westminster St., Lewiston 04240; 562 Congress St., Portland 04101. Itinerant teachers, instructional materials center.

**New Jersey:** St. Joseph's School for the Blind (r,d,c; 3-21 yrs.), 253 Baldwin Ave., Jersey City 07306 (40). For visually impaired, multiple handicapped.

**New York:** Lavelle School for the Blind (d,c; 3-21 yrs.), East 221st St. and Paulding Ave., Bronx 10469 (100).

**Pennsylvania:** St. Lucy Day School (d,c; pre-K to 8th grade), 130 Hampden Rd., Upper Darby 19082.

# OTHER SOCIAL SERVICES

**Cancer Hospitals or Homes:** The following homes or hospitals specialize in the care of cancer patients. They are listed according to state.

Our Lady of Perpetual Help Home, Servants of Rlief for Incurable Cancer, 760 Washington St., S.W., Atlanta, GA 30315 (48).

Rose Hawthorne Lathrop Home, Servants of Relief for Incurable Cancer, 1600 Bay St., Fall River, MA 02724 (35).

Our Lady of Good Counsel Home, Servants of Relief for Incurable Cancer, 2076 St. Anthony Ave., St. Paul, MN 55104 (40).

Calvary Hospital, Inc., 1740 Eastchester Rd., Bronx, NY 10461 (200). Sponsored by the Department of Health and Hospitals, Archdiocese of New York.

St. Rose's Home, Servants of Relief for Incurable Cancer), 71 Jackson St., New York, NY 10002 (60).

Rosary Hill Home, Servants of Relief for Incurable Cancer, 600 Linda Ave., Hawthorne, NY 10532 (72).

Holy Family Home, Servants of Relief for Incurable Cancer, 6707 State Rd., Parma, OH 44134 (50).

Sacred Heart Free Home for Incurable Cancer, Servants of Relief for Incurable Cancer, 1315 W. Hunting Park Ave., Philadelphia, PA 19140 (45).

**Substance Abuse:** Facilities for substance abuse (alcohol and other drugs) include:

Daytop Village, Inc., 54 W. 40th St., New York, NY 10018. Msgr. William B. O'Brien, president. Twenty-eight residential and ambulatory sites in New York, New Jersey, Pennsylvania, Florida, Texas and California.

Good Shepherd Gracenter, Convent of the Good Shepherd, 1310 Bacon St., San Francisco, CA 94134. Residential program for chemically dependent women.

New Hope Manor, 35 Hillside Rd., Barryville, NY 12719. Residential substance abuse treatment center for teen-age girls and women ages 13-40. Residential; half-way house and aftercare program totaling 6 months or more.

St. Joseph's Hospital, L.E. Phillips Libertas Center for the Chemically Dependent, 2661 County Road I, Chippewa Falls, WI 54729 (46). Residential and outpatient. Adult and adolescent programs. Hospital Sisters of the Third Order of St. Francis.

St. Luke's Addiction Recovery Services, 7707 NW 2nd Ave., Miami, FL 33150. A program of Catholic Community Services, Miami. Adult residential and family outpatient recovery services for drug, alcohol addiction and DUI.

Miami Substance Abuse Prevention Programs, 9999 N.E. Second Ave., Suite 311, Miami Shores, FL 33138. Trains parents, youth, priests and teachers as prevention volunteers in the area of substance abuse.

Transitus House for Chemically Dependent Women, 1830 Wheaton St., Chippewa Falls, WI 54729 (20). Transitional living facility. Hospital Sisters of the Third Order of St. Francis.

Matt Talbot Inn, 2270 Professor Ave., Cleveland, OH 44113. Two programs: Chemical dependency Residential Treatment/Halfway House (capacity 27) and outpatient treatment/aftercare. Serves male clients 18 years and over.

Sacred Heart Rehabilitation Center, Inc., 2203 St. Antoine, Detroit, MI 48201 (admissions/assessment, outpatient); 400 Stoddard Rd., P.O. Box 41038, Memphis, MI 48041 (12 beds, detoxification; 40 beds residential treatment). All facilities serve male and female clients 18 and over.

Straight and Narrow, Inc., 396 Straight St., Paterson, NJ 07501. Facilities and services include (at various locations): Straight and Narrow Hospital (Mount Carmel Guild), substance abuse, detoxification (20 beds); Alpha House for Drug and Alcohol Rehabilitation (women; 30 beds — 25 adults, 5 children), Dismas House for Drug and Alcohol Rehabilitation (men; 78 beds); The Guild for Drug and Alcohol Rehabilitation (men, 56 beds); juvenile residential units; outpatient services and facility; three halfway houses; counseling services; employment assistance; intoxicated driver's resource center; medical day care center (available to HIV infected persons and persons diagnosed with AIDS); methadone clinic.

The National Catholic Council on Alcoholism and Related Drug Problems, Inc., 1550 Hendrickson St., Brooklyn, NY 11234, offers educational material to those involved in pastoral ministry on ways of dealing with problems related to alcoholism and medication dependency.

**Convicts:** Priests serve as full- or part-time chaplains in penal and correctional institutions throughout the country. Limited efforts have been made to assist in the rehabilitation of released prisoners in Halfway House establishments.

**Dining Rooms; Facilities for Homeless:** Representative of places where meals are provided, and in some cases lodging and other services as well, are:

St. Anthony Foundation, 121 Golden Gate Ave., San Francisco, CA 94102. Founded in 1950 by the Franciscan Friars. Multi-program social service agency serving people who are poor and homeless. Dining room serves up to 2,100 meals daily; more than 25 million since its founding. Other services include free clothing and furniture; free medical clinic; residential drug and alcohol rehabilitation programs; employment program; emergency shelter, housing and daytime facility for homeless women; residence for low-income senior women; free hygiene services; case management for seniors; social services.

St. Vincent de Paul Free Dining Room, 675 23rd St., Oakland, CA 94612. Administered by Daughters of Charity of St. Vincent de Paul, under sponsorship of St. Vincent de Paul Society. Hot meals served at lunch time 7 days a week; clothing, lodging provided those in need.

St. Vincent's Dining Room, 505 W. 3rd St., Reno, NV 89503.

St. Vincent Dining Room, 1501 Las Vegas Blvd., Las Vegas, NV 89101. Structured program for 275 men in which job development office works with homeless to enable them to find employment. For non-residents, there is a hot meal every day at noon.

Emergency overnight shelter facility for families, women and men.

Good Shepherd Center, Little Brothers of the Good Shepherd, 218 Iron St. S.W., P.O. Box 749, Albuquerque, NM 87103.

Holy Name Centre for Homeless Men, Inc., 18 Bleeker St., New York, NY 10012. A shelter for alcoholic, homeless men. Provides social services and aid to transients and those in need. Affiliated with New York Catholic Charities.

St. Francis Inn, 2441 Kensington Ave., Philadelphia, PA 19125. Serves hot meals. Temporary shelter for men. Day center for women. Thrift shop.

St. John's Hospice for Men, staffed by Little Brothers of the Good Shepherd, 1221 Race St., Philadelphia, PA 19107. Hot meals served daily; 36-bed shelter; clothing distribution, showers, mail distribution, drug/alcohol rehabilitation and work programs. Good Shepherd Program of St. John's Hospice, 1225 Race St., Philadelphia, PA 19107. Ten-bed facility for homeless men with AIDS.

Camillus House, Little Brothers of the Good Shepherd, 726 N.E. First Ave., Miami, FL 33132. Free comprehensive services for the poor and homeless including daily dinner; night lodging for 70; clothing distribution; showers; mail distribution; drug/alcohol rehabilitation program. Forty-eight units of single-room occupancy housing for employed formerly homeless women and men who have completed drug and alcohol rehabilitation programs.

Camillus Health Concern, Little Brothers of the Good Shepherd, 708 N.E. First Ave., Miami, FL 33132. Free comprehensive medical and social services for the homeless.

**Shelters:** Facilities for runaways, the abused, exploited and homeless include:

Anthony House, supported by St. Anthony's Guild (see Index). Three locations: 38 E. Roosevelt Ave., Roosevelt, NY 11575 (with St. Vincent de Paul Society — for homeless men); 128 W. 112th St., New York, NY 10026 (emergency food and clothing); 6215 Holly St., P.O. Box 880, Zellwood, FL 32798 (for migrant workers and their families).

Convent of the Good Shepherd-Good Shepherd Shelter, 2561 Venice Blvd., Los Angeles, CA 90019. For battered women with their children.

Covenant House, 346 W. 17th St., New York, NY 10011. President, Sister Mary Rose McGeady, D.C. Provides crisis care — food, shelter, clothing, medical treatment, job placement and counseling — for homeless youth without regard to race, creed, color and national origin. Locations: New York, New Jersey (Newark, Atlantic City), Houston, Ft. Lauderdale, New Orleans, Anchorage, Los Angeles, Washington, D.C.; Toronto (Canada), Tegucigalpa (Honduras), Guatemala City (Guatemala), Mexico City (Mexico).

Crescent House, 1000 Howard Ave., Suite 1200, New Orleans, LA 70113. Provides temporary shelter, counseling and advocacy for battered women and their children.

The Dwelling Place, 409 W. 40th St., New York, NY 10018. For homeless women 30 years of age and over.

House of the Good Shepherd, 1114 W. Grace St., Chicago, IL 60613. For abused women with children.

Mercy Hospice, Sisters of Mercy, 334 S. 13th St., Philadelphia, PA 19107. Temporary shelter and relocation assistance for homeless women and children.

Mt. Carmel House, Carmelite Sisters, 471 G Pl., N.W., Washington, DC 20001. For homeless women.

Ozanam Inn, 843 Camp St., New Orleans, LA 70130. Under sponsorship of the St. Vincent de Paul Society. Hospice for homeless men.

St. Christopher Inn, P.O. Box 150, Graymoor, Garrison, NY 10524. Temporary shelter (21 days) for alcohol- and drug-free homeless and needy men.

Siena-Francis House, Inc., P.O. Box 217 D.T.S., Omaha, NE 68102. Two units, both at 1702 Nicholas St., Omaha, NE 68102: Siena House (for homeless and abused women or women with children; provides 24-hour assistance and advocacy services); Francis House (temporary shelter for homeless men).

**Unwed Mothers:** Residential and care services for unwed mothers are available in many dioceses.

## ORGANIZATIONS

*(See separate article for a listing of facilities for the handicapped.)*

**The Carroll Center for the Blind** (formerly the Catholic Guild for All the Blind): Located at 770 Centre St., Newton, MA 02158, the center conducts diagnostic evaluation and rehabilitation programs for blind people over 16 years of age, and provides other services. The president is Rachel Rosenbaum.

**Xavier Society for the Blind:** The Society is located at 154 E. 23rd St., New York, NY 10010. Founded in 1900 by Rev. Joseph Stadelman, S.J., it is a center for publications for the blind and partially sighted. The director is Rev. Alfred E. Caruana, S.J.

**International Catholic Deaf Association:** Established by deaf adults in Toronto, Canada, in 1949, the association has more than 8,000 members in 130 chapters, mostly in the U.S. It is the only international lay association founded and controlled by deaf Catholic adults. The ICDA publishes *The Deaf Catholic* bimonthly, sponsors regional conferences, workshops and an annual convention. The ICDA-US president is Kathleen Kush, 8002 S. Sawyer Rd., Darien, IL 60561.

**National Catholic Office for the Deaf:** Formally established in 1976, at Washington, D.C., to provide pastoral service to those who teach deaf children and adults, to the parents of deaf children, to pastors of deaf persons, and to organizations of the deaf. Executive director: Nora Letourneau, 7202 Buchanan St., Landover Hills, MD 20784.

**National Apostolate with People with Mental Retardation:** Established in 1968 to promote the full participation by persons with mental retardation in the life of the Church. It publishes the *NAPMR Quarterly* and a newsletter (six times a year). Provides consultation, information and referral services on Church-related questions about mental retardation. The executive director is Michela M. Perrone, 4516 30th St. N.W., Washington, DC 20008.

**National Catholic Office for Persons with Disabilities (NCPD):** Established in 1982 to foster implementation of the 1978 Pastoral Statement of the U.S. Catholic Bishops on People with Disabilities. The document called for welcome of the ten million Catholics who are disabled to participate in the celebrations and obligations of their Faith and advocated their inclusion "within the total fabric of society." Address: P.O. Box 29113, Washington, D.C. 20017.

# RETREATS, SPIRITUAL RENEWAL PROGRAMS _____

There is great variety in retreat and renewal programs, with orientations ranging from the traditional to teen encounters. Central to all of them are celebration of the liturgy and deepening of a person's commitment to faith and witness in life.

Features of many of the forms are as follows.

**Traditional Retreats:** Centered around conferences and the direction of a retreat master; oriented to the personal needs of the retreatants; including such standard practices as participation in Mass, reception of the sacraments, private and group prayer, silence and meditation, discussions.

**Team Retreat:** Conducted by a team of several leaders or directors (priests, religious, lay persons) with division of subject matter and activities according to their special skills and the nature and needs of the group.

**Closed Retreat:** Involving withdrawal for a period of time — overnight, several days, a weekend — from everyday occupations and activities.

**Open Retreat:** Made without total disengagement from everyday involvements, on a part-time basis.

**Private Retreat:** By one person, on a kind of do-it-yourself basis with the one-to-one assistance of a director.

**Special Groups:** With formats and activities geared to particular groups; e.g., members of Alcoholics Anonymous, vocational groups and apostolic groups.

**Marriage Encounters:** Usually weekend periods of husband-wife reflection and dialogue; introduced into the U.S. from Spain in 1967.

**Charismatic Renewal:** Featuring elements of the movement of the same name; "Spirit-oriented," communitarian and flexible, with spontaneous and shared prayer, personal testimonies of faith and witness.

**Christian Community:** Characterized by strong community thrust.

**Teens Encounter Christ (TEC), SEARCH:** Formats adapted to the mentality and needs of youth, involving experience of Christian faith and commitment in a community setting.

**Christian Maturity Seminars:** Similar to teen encounters in basic concept but different to suit persons of greater maturity.

**Cursillo:** see separate entry.

## Conference

**Retreats International Inc.:** The first organization for promoting retreats in the U.S. was started in 1904 in New York. Its initial efforts and the gradual growth of the movement led to the formation in 1927 of the National Catholic Laymen's Retreat Conference, the forerunner of the men's division of Retreats International. The women's division developed from the National Laywomen's Retreat Movement which was founded in Chicago in 1936. The men's and women's divisions merged July 9, 1977. The services of the organization include an annual summer institute for retreat and pastoral ministry, regional conferences for retreat center leadership and area meetings of directors and key leadership in the retreat movement. The officers are: Auxiliary Bishop Robert Morneau of Green Bay, episcopal advisor; Larry Novakowski, president; Rev. Thomas W. Gedeon, S.J., executive director. National office: Box 1067, Notre Dame, IN 46556.

## HOUSES OF RETREAT AND RENEWAL

(Principal sources: Almanac survey; *The Official Catholic Directory*.)

Abbreviation code: m, men; w, women; mc, married couples; y, youth. Houses and centers without code generally offer facilities to most groups. An asterisk after an abbreviation indicates that the facility is primarily for the group designated but that special groups are also accommodated. Houses furnish information concerning the types of programs they offer.

**Alabama:** Blessed Trinity Shrine Retreat, 107 Holy Trinity Rd., Holy Trinity 36859.

Visitation Sacred Heart Retreat House, 2300 Spring Hill Ave., Mobile 36607.

**Alaska:** Holy Spirit Retreat House, 10980 Hillside Dr., Anchorage 99516.

**Arizona:** Franciscan Renewal Center, 5802 E. Lincoln Dr., Box 220, Scottsdale 85252.

Holy Trinity Monastery, P.O. Box 298, St. David 85630. Benedictine community. Self-directed/Spirit-directed monastic retreat.

Mount Claret Retreat Center, 4633 N. 54th St., Phoenix 85018.

Our Lady of Solitude House of Prayer, P.O. Box 1140, Black Canyon City 85324.

Redemptorist Picture Rocks Retreat House, 7101 W. Picture Rocks Rd., Tucson 85743.

**Arkansas:** Little Portion Retreat and Training Center, Rt. 4, Box 430, Eureka Springs 72632.

Brothers and Sisters of Charity, Little Portion Hermitage, Rt. 3, Box 608, Eureka Springs 72632.

St. Scholastica Retreat Center, P.O. Box 3489, Ft. Smith 72913.

**California:** Angela Center, 535 Angela Dr., Santa Rosa 95401.

Christ the King Retreat Center, 6520 Van Maren Lane, Citrus Heights 95621.

Claretian Retreat Center, 1119 Westchester Pl., Los Angeles 90019.

De Paul Center, 1105 Bluff Rd., Montebello 90640.

El Carmelo Retreat House, P.O. Box 446, Redlands 92373.

Heart of Jesus Retreat Center, 2927 S. Greenville St., Santa Ana 92704.

Holy Spirit Retreat Center, 4316 Lanai Rd., Encino 91436.

Holy Transfiguration Monastery (m*), Monks of Mt. Tabor (Byzantine Ukrainian), 17001 Tomki Rd., P.O. Box 217, Redwood Valley, Calif. 95470.

Jesuit Retreat House, 300 Manresa Way, Los Altos 94022.

Madonna of Peace Renewal Center (y), P.O. Box 71, Copperopolis 95228.

Mary and Joseph Retreat Center, 5300 Crest Rd., Rancho Palos Verdes 90274.

Marywood Retreat Center, 2811 E. Villa Real Dr., Orange 92667.

Mater Dolorosa Retreat Center, 700 N. Sunnyside Ave., Sierra Madre 91024.

Mercy Center, 2300 Adeline Dr., Burlingame 94010.

Mission San Luis Rey Retreat, P.O. Box 409, San Luis Rey 92068.

Mount Alverno Retreat and Conference Center, 3910 Bret Harte Dr., Redwood City 94061.

New Camaldoli Hermitage, Big Sur 93920.

Poverello of Assisi Retreat House, 1519 Woodworth St., San Fernando 91340.

Presentation Education and Retreat Center, 19480 Bear Creek Rd., Los Gatos 95030.

Prince of Peace Abbey, 650 Benet Hill Rd., Oceanside 92054.

Pro Sanctity Spirituality Center, 205 S. Pine St., Fullerton 92633. For day use.

Sacred Heart Retreat House (w*), 920 E. Alhambra Rd., Alhambra 91801.

St. Andrew's Abbey Retreat House, Valyermo 93563.

St. Anthony's Retreat House, P.O. Box 249, Three Rivers 93271.

St. Clare's Retreat, 2381 Laurel Glen Rd., Soquel 95073.

St. Francis Retreat, P.O. Box 970, San Juan Bautista 95045.

St. Francis Salesian Retreat (Camp St. Francis) (y), 2400 E. Lake Ave., Watsonville 95076.

St. Joseph's Salesian Youth Center, P.O. Box 1639, 8301 Arroyo Dr., Rosemead 91770.

St. Mary's Seminary and Retreat House, 1964 Las Canoas Rd., Santa Barbara 93105.

San Damiano Retreat, P.O. Box 767, Danville 94526.

San Miguel Retreat House, P.O. Box 69, San Miguel 93451.

Santa Sabina Center, 25 Magnolia Ave., San Rafael 94901.

Serra Retreat, 3401 S. Serra Rd., Box 127, Malibu 90265.

Starcross Community, 34500 Annapolis Rd., Annapolis 95412.

Villa Maria del Mar, Santa Cruz. Mailing address, 2-1918 E. Cliff Dr., Santa Cruz 95062.

Villa Maria — House of Prayer (w), 1252 N. Citrus Dr., La Habra 90631.

**Colorado:** Benet Hill Monastery, 2555 N. Chelton Rd., Colorado Springs 80909.

Benet Pines Retreat Center, 15780 Highway 83, Colorado Springs 80921.

Sacred Heart Retreat House, Box 185, Sedalia 80135.

Spiritual Life Institute (individuals only), Nada Hermitage, P.O. Box 219, Crestone 81131. Private desert retreats with minimal direction.

**Connecticut:** Archdiocesan Spiritual Life Center, 467 Bloomfield Ave., Bloomfield 06002.

Edmundite Apostolate and Conference Center, Enders Island, Mystic 06355.

Emmaus Spiritual Life Center, 24 Maple Ave., Uncasville 06382.

Holy Family Retreat, 303 Tunxis Rd., West Hartford 06107.

Immaculata Retreat House, P.O. Box 55, Willimantic 06226.

Mercy Center, P.O. Box 191, 167 Neck Rd., Madison 06443.

My Father's House, Box 22, North Moodus Rd., Moodus 06469.

Our Lady of Calvary Retreat (w*), 31 Colton St., Farmington 06032.

Trinita Retreat Center, 595 Town Hill Rd., Rt. 219, New Hartford 06057.

Villa Maria Retreat House, 159 Sky Meadow Dr., Stamford 06903.

**Delaware:** St. Francis Renewal Center, 1901 Prior Rd., Wilmington 19809.

**District of Columbia:** Washington Retreat House, 4000 Harewood Rd. N.E., Washington 20017.

**Florida:** Cenacle Retreat House, 1400 S. Dixie Highway, Lantana 33462.

Dominican Retreat House, Inc., 7275 S.W. 124th St., Miami 33156.

Franciscan Center, 3010 Perry Ave., Tampa 33603.

John Paul II Retreat House, 720 N.E. 27th St., Miami 33137.

Our Lady of Perpetual Help Retreat and Spirituality Center, 3989 S. Moon Dr., Venice 34292.

Saint John Neumann Renewal Center, 685 Miccosukee Rd., Tallahassee 32308.

St. Leo Abbey Retreat Center, P.O. Box 2157, St. Leo 33574.

**Georgia:** Ignatius House, 6700 Riverside Dr. N.W., Atlanta 30328.

**Idaho:** Nazareth Retreat Center, 4450 N. Five Mile Rd., Boise 83704.

**Illinois:** Bellarmine Hall (ma), Box 268, Barrington 60010.

Bishop Lane Retreat House, 7708 E. McGregor Rd., Rockford 61102.

Cabrini Retreat Center (m, w, y), 9430 Golf Rd., Des Plaines 60016.

Carmelite Spiritual Center, 8433 Bailey Rd., Darien 60561.

Cenacle Retreat House, 513 Fullerton Parkway, Chicago 60614.

Cenacle Retreat House, P.O. Box 797, Warrenville 60555.

Divine Word International, P.O. Box 176, Techny 60082.

King's House Retreat and Renewal Center, 700 N. 66th St., Belleville 62223.

King's House of Retreats, Henry 61537.

La Salle Manor, Christian Brothers Retreat House, 12480 Galena Rd., Plano 60545.

La Salette Retreat Center, 5065 Oliver Rd., Georgetown 61846.

St. Mary's Retreat House, P.O. Box 608, 14230 Main St., Lemont 60439.

Tolentine Center, 20300 Governors Highway, Olympia Fields 60461.

Villa Redeemer Retreat Center, P.O. Box 6, Glenview 60025.

**Indiana:** Beech Grove Benedictine Center, 1402 Southern Ave., Beech Grove 46107.
Fatima Retreat House, 5353 E. 56th St., Indianapolis 46226.
John XXIII Center, 407 W. McDonald St., Hartford City 47348.
Kordes Enrichment Center, 841 E. 14th St., Ferdinand 47532.
Lindenwood, PHJC Ministry Center, P.O. Box 1, Donaldson 46513.
Mary's Solitude-Prayer Center, Notre Dame 46556.
Mount Sint Francis Retreat Center, Mount Saint Francis 47146.
Our Lady of Fatima Retreat Center, Notre Dame 46556.
St. Jude Guest House, St. Meinrad Archabbey, St. Meinrad 47577.
Sarto Retreat House, 4200 N. Kentucky Ave., Evansville 47711.
Solitude of St. Joseph, Box 983, Notre Dame, Ind. 46556.

**Iowa:** American Martyrs Retreat House, 2209 N. Union Rd., P.O. Box 605, Cedar Falls 50613.
Emmanuel House of Prayer Country Retreat and Solitude Center, 4427 Kotts Rd. N.E., Iowa City 52240.
New Melleray Guest House, 6500 Melleray Circle, Peosta 52068.
Shalom Renewal Center, 1001 Davis Ave., Dubuque 52001.

**Kansas:** Manna House of Prayer, 323 East 5th St., Box 675, Concordia 66901.
Spiritual Life Center, 7100 E. 45th St., N. Wichita 67226.

**Kentucky:** Catherine Spalding Center, P.O. Box 24, Nazareth 40048.
Flaget Center, 1935 Lewiston Pl., Louisville 40216.
Marydale Retreat Center, 945 Donaldson Hwy., Erlanger 41018.
Mt. St. Joseph Retreat Center, 8001 Cummings Rd., Maple Mount 42356.
Our Lady of Gethsemani (m, w, private), The Guestmaster, Abbey of Gethsemani, Trappist 40051.

**Louisiana:** Abbey Christian Life Center, St. Joseph's Abbey, St. Benedict 70457.
Ave Maria Retreat House, HC 62, Box 368 AB, Marrero 70072.
Cenacle Retreat House (w*), 5500 St. Mary St., P.O. Box 8115, Metairie 70011.
Jesuit Spirituality Center, P.O. Box C, Grand Coteau 70541.
Lumen Christi Retreat Center, 100 Lumen Christi Lane, Hwy. 311, Schriever 70395.
Manresa House of Retreats (m), P.O. Box 89, Convent 70723.
Maryhill Renewal Center, 600 Maryhill Rd., Pineville 71360.
Our Lady of the Oaks Retreat House, P.O. Box D, Grand Coteau 70541.
Regina Coeli Retreat Center, 17225 Regina Coeli Rd., Covington 70433.

**Maine:** Marie Joseph Spiritual Center, RFD 2, Biddeford 04005.
St. Paul Retreat and Cursillo Center, 136 State St., Augusta 04330.

**Maryland:** Bon Secours Spiritual Center, Marriottsville 21104.
Christian Brothers Spiritual Center (m,w,y), P.O. Box 29, 2535 Buckeyestown Pike, Adamstown 21710.
Loyola Retreat House-on-Potomac, Faulkner 20632.
Msgr. Clare J. O'Dwyer Retreat House (y*), 15523 York Rd., P.O. Box 310, Sparks 21152.
Our Lady of Mattaponi Youth Retreat and Conference Center, 11000 Mattaponi Rd., Upper Marlboro 20772.

**Massachusetts:** Calvary Retreat Center, 59 South St., P.O. Box 219, Shrewsbury 01545.
Campion Renewal Center, 319 Concord Rd., Weston 02193.
Cenacle Spiritual Center, 25 Avery St., Dedham 02026.
Don Orione Center, P.O. Box 205, Old Groveland Rd., Bradford 01835.
Eastern Point Retreat House, Gonzaga Hall, 37 Niles Pond Rd., Gloucester 01930.
Espousal Center, 554 Lexington St., Waltham 02154.
Esther House of Spiritual Renewal, Sisters of St. Anne, 1015 Pleasant St., Worcester 01602.
Genesis Spiritual Life Center, 53 Mill St., Westfield 01085.
Glastonbury Abbey (Benedictine Monks), 16 Hull St., Hingham 02043.
Holy Cross Fathers Retreat House, 490 Washington St., N. Easton 02356.
La Salette Center for Christian Living, 947 Park St., Attleboro 02703.
LaSalette Retreat House, 251 Topsfield Rd., Ipswich 01938.
Marian Center, 1365 Northampton St., Holyoke 01040. Day and evening programs.
Miramar Retreat Center, P.O. Box M, Duxbury, 02331.
Mt. Carmel Christian Life Center, Oblong Rd., Box 613, Williamstown 01267.
Retreat Center, Sisters of St. Joseph, 339 Jerusalem Rd., Cohasset 02025.
Sacred Heart Retreat House, Salesians of St. John Bosco, P.O. Box 567, Ipswich 01938.
St. Benedict Abbey, 252 Still River Rd., P.O. Box 67, Still River 01467.
St. Joseph's Abbey Retreat House (m) (Trappist Monks), North Spencer Rd., Spencer 01562.
St. Stephen Priory Spiritual Life Center (Dominican), 20 Glen St., Box 370, Dover 02030.

**Michigan:** Augustine Center, Box 84, Conway 49722.
Capuchin Retreat, 62460 Mt. Vernon, Box 188, Washington 48094.
Colombiere Conference Center, Box 139, 9075 Big Lake Rd., Clarkston 48347.
Manresa Jesuit Retreat House, 1390 Quarton Rd., Bloomfield Hills 48304.

Queen of Angels Retreat, 3400 S. Washington Rd., Box 2026, Saginaw 48605.

St. Francis Retreat Center, Diocese of Lansing, 703 E. Main St., De Witt 48820.

St. Lazare Retreat House, 18600 W. Spring Lake Rd., Spring Lake 49456.

St. Mary's Retreat House (w*), 775 W. Drahner Rd., Oxford 48371.

St. Paul of the Cross Retreat Center (m*), 23333 Schoolcraft, Detroit 48223.

**Minnesota:** Benedictine Center, St. Paul's Priory, 2675 E. Larpenteur Ave., St. Paul 55109.

Catholic Youth Ministry Services (y*), 328 W. Kellog, St. Paul 55102.

The Cenacle, 1221 Wayzata Blvd., Wayzata 55391.

Center for Spiritual Development, 211 Tenth St. S., P.O. Box 538, Bird Island 55310.

Christ the King Retreat Center, 621 First Ave. S., Buffalo 55313.

Christian Brothers Retreat Center, 15525 St. Croix Trail North, Marine-on-St. Croix 55047.

Franciscan Retreats, Conventual Franciscan Friars, 16385 St. Francis Lane, Prior Lake 55372.

Jesuit Retreat House (m), 8243 DeMontreville Trail North, Lake Elmo 55042.

Maryhill Renewal Center, Society of Daughters of the Heart of Mary, 260 Summit Ave., St. Paul 55102.

Retreat House, 116 S.E. Eighth Ave., Little Falls 56345. St. Francis Center, same address.

Villa Maria Center, Ursuline Sisters, 29847 County 2 Blvd., Frontenac 55026.

**Missouri:** The Cenacle, 7654 Natural Bridge Rd., St. Louis 63121.

Il Ritiro - The Little Retreat, P.O. Box 38, Eime Rd., Dittmer 63023.

Maria Fonte Solitude (private; individual hermitages), P.O. Box 322, High Ridge 63049.

Marianist Retreat and Conference Center, P.O. Box 718, Eureka 63025.

Mercy Center, 2039 N. Geyer Rd., St. Louis 63131.

Our Lady of Assumption Abbey (m,w), Trappists, Rt. 5, Box 1056, Ava 65608.

Pallottine Renewal Center, 15270 Old Halls Ferry Rd., Florissant 63034.

Queen of Heaven Solitude (private, individual hermitages), Rt. , Box 107A, Marionville 65705.

Vision of Peace, Abbey Lane, P.O. Box 69, Pevely 63070.

White House Retreat, 7400 Christopher Dr., St. Louis 63129.

**Montana:** Christhaven - Diocesan Retreat Center, P.O. Box 1729, Helena 59624.

Sacred Heart Retreat Center, 26 Wyoming Ave., P.O. Box 20795, Billings 59104.

Ursuline Retreat Centre, 2300 Central Ave., Great Falls 59401.

**Nebraska:** Crosier Renewal Center, 223 E. 14th St., P.O. Box 789, Hastings 68902.

Good Counsel, R.R. 1, Box 110, Waverly 68462.

**New Hampshire:** The Common - St. Joseph Monastery, Discalced Carmelite Friars, 182 Old Street Rd., Peterborough 03458.

Epiphany Monastery, 96 Scobie Rd., P.O. Box 60, New Boston 03070.

La Salette Conference and Retreat Center, Enfield 03748.

Oblate Retreat House, Oblates of Mary Immaculate, 200 Lowell Rd., Hudson 03051.

**New Jersey:** Bethlehem Hermitage, 82 Pleasant Hill Rd., P.O. Box 315, Chester 07930.

Carmel Retreat House, 1071 Ramapo Valley Rd., Mahwah 07430.

Cenacle Retreat House, 411 River Rd., Highland Park 08904.

Felician Retreat House, 35 Windemere Ave., Mt. Arlington 07856.

Loyola House of Retreats, 161 James St., Morristown 07960.

Marianist Retreat House (families*, mc), 415 Yale Ave., Box D-2, Cape May Point 08212.

Maris Stella (Vacation Home for Sisters*), 7201 Long Beach Blvd., Harvey Cedars 08008.

Mt. St. Francis Retreat House, 474 Sloatsburg Rd., Ringwood 07456.

Queen of Peace Retreat House, St. Paul's Abbey, P.O. Box 7, Newton 07860.

Sacred Heart Retreat Center, 20 Old Swartswood Rd., Newton 07860.

St. Joseph by the Sea Retreat House, 400 Rte. 35 N., South Mantoloking 08738.

St. Pius X Retreat House, P.O. Box 216, Blackwood 08012.

San Alfonso Retreat House, P.O. Box 3098, 755 Ocean Ave., Long Branch 07740.

Sanctuary of Mary, R.R. 1, Box 106, Branchville 07826. Days of Recollection.

Stella Maris Retreat House, 981 Ocean Ave., Elberon 07740.

Trinity Ministries Center, 1292 Long Hill Rd., Stirling 07980.

Villa Pauline Retreat House, 350 Bernardsville Rd., Mendham 07945.

Xavier Retreat and Conference Center, P.O. Box 211, Convent Station 07961.

**New Mexico:** Dominican Retreat House, 5825 Coors Rd. S.W., Albuquerque 87121.

Holy Cross Retreat, Conventual Franciscan Friars, P.O. Box 158, Mesilla Park 88047.

Pecos Benedictine Abbey, Pecos 87552.

Sacred Heart Retreat, P.O. Box 1989, Gallup 87301.

**New York:** Bethany Retreat House, County Road 105, Box 1003, Highland Mills 10930.

Bethlehem Retreat House, Abbey of the Genesee, Piffard 14533.

Bisop Molloy Retreat House, 86-45 Edgerton Blvd., Jamaica, L.I. 11432.

Blessed Kateri Retreat House, National Kateri Shrine, P.O. Box 627, Fonda, N.Y. 12068.

Cardinal Spellman Retreat House, Passionist Community, 5801 Palisade Ave., Bronx (Riverdale) 10471.

Cenacle Center for Spiritual Renewal, 310 Cenacle Rd., Lake Ronkonkoma 11779.

Cenacle Retreat House, State Rd., P.O. Box 467, Bedford Village 10506.

Christ the King Retreat House, 500 Brookford Rd., Syracuse 13224.

Cormaria Retreat House, Sag Harbor, L.I. 11963.

Dominican Retreat House, 1945 Union St., Schenectady 12309.

Don Bosco Retreat Center, Box 9000, Filor's Lane, West Haverstraw 10993.

Graymoor Christian Unity Center, Graymoor, Garrison 10524.

Jesuit Retreat House, North American Martyrs Shrine, Auriesville 12016.

Monastery of the Precious Blood (w), Ft. Hamilton Parkway and 54th St., Brooklyn 11219. Single day retreats.

Mount Alvernia Retreat House, Box 858, Wappingers Falls 12590.

Mount Irenaeus Franciscan Mountain Retreat, Holy Peace Friary, P.O. Box 100, West Clarksville, NY 14786.

Mount Manresa Retreat House, 239 Fingerboard Rd., Staten Island 10305.

Mt. St. Alphonsus Spiritcare Center, Esopus 12429.

Notre Dame Retreat House, Box 342, 5151 Foster Rd., Canandaigua 14424.

Our Lady of Hope Center, 434 River Rd., Newburgh 12550.

Regina Maria Retreat House, 77 Brinkerhoff St., Plattsburgh 12901.

St. Andrew's House, 257 St. Andrew's Rd., Walden 12586.

St. Columban Center, Diocese of Buffalo, 6892 Lake Shore Rd., P.O. Box 816, Derby 14047.

St. Gabriel Retreat House (y, mc), 64 Burns Rd., P.O. Box P, Shelter Island 11965.

St. Ignatius Retreat House, Searingtown Rd., Manhasset, L.I. 11030.

St. Josaphat's Retreat House, Basilian Monastery, East Beach Rd., Glen Cove 11542.

St. Joseph Center (Spanish Center), 523 W. 142nd St., New York 10031.

St. Mary's Villa, 150 Sisters Servants Lane, Sloatsburg 10974.

St. Paul Center, 21-35 Crescent St., Astoria 11105.

St. Ursula Center, P.O. Box 86, Middle Rd. and Blue Point Ave., Blue Point 11715.

Stella Maris Retreat Center, 130 E. Genesee St., Skaneateles 13152.

Stella Niagara Center of Renewal, 4421 Lower River Rd., Stella Niagara 14144.

Tagaste Monastery, 220 Lafayette Ave.,,, Suffern 10901.

Trinity Retreat, 1 Pryer Manor Rd., Larchmont 10538.

**North Carolina:** Avila Retreat Center, 711 Mason Rd., Durham 27712.

Living Waters Catholic Reflection Center, 1420 Soco Rd., Maggie Valley 28751.

**North Dakota:** Presentation Prayer Center, 1101 32nd Ave. S., Fargo 58103.

Queen of Peace Retreat, 1310 Broadway, Fargo 58102.

**Ohio:** Bergamo, 4400 Shakertown Rd., Dayton 45430.

Franciscan Renewal Center, Pilgrim House, 321 Clay St., Carey 43316.

Friarhurst Retreat House, 8136 Wooster Pike, Cincinnati 45227.

Jesuit Retreat House, 5629 State Rd., Cleveland 44134.

Loyola of the Lakes, 700 Killinger Rd., Clinton 44216.

Maria Stein Center, 2365 St. Johns Rd., Maria Stein 45860.

Milford Spiritual Center, 5361 Milford Rd., Milford 45150.

Our Lady of the Pines, 1250 Tiffin St., Fremont 43420.

Sacred Heart Retreat and Renewal Center, 3128 Logan Ave., P.O. Box 6074, Youngstown 44501.

St. Joseph Christian Life Center, 18485 Lake Shore Blvd., Cleveland 44119.

St. Joseph Renewal Center, 200 St. Francis Ave., Tiffin 44883.

St. Therese Retreat Center, Diocese of Columbus, 5277 E. Broad St., Columbus 43213.

**Oklahoma:** St. Gregory's Abbey, Shawnee 74801.

**Oregon:** Franciscan Renewal Center, 0858 S.W. Palatine Hill Rd., Portland 97219.

Loyola Retreat House (Jesuit Center for Spiritual Renewal), 3220 S.E. 43rd St., Portland 97206.

Mount Angel Abbey Retreat House, St. Benedict 97373.

Our Lady of Peace Retreat, 3600 S. W. 170th Ave., Beaverton 97006.

St. Rita Retreat Center, P.O. Box 310, Gold Hill 97525.

Shalom Prayer Center, Benedictine Sisters, Mt. Angel 97362.

Trappist Abbey Retreat (m,w), P.O. Box 97, Lafayette 97127.

**Pennsylvania:** Byzantine Catholic Seminary (m), 3605 Perrysville Ave., Pittsburgh 15214.

Dominican Retreat House, 750 Ashbourne Rd., Elkins Park 19027.

Doran Hall Retreat and Renewal Center, 443 Mt. Thor Rd., Greensburg 15601.

Fatima House, 601 Rolling Hills Rd., Ottsville 18942.

Fatima Renewal Center, 1000 Seminary Rd., Dalton 18414.

Gilmary Diocesan Center, 601 Flaugherty Run Rd., Coraopolis 15108.

Jesuit Center for Spiritual Growth, Box 223, Church Rd., Wernersville 19565.

Kearns Spirituality Center, 9000 Babcock Blvd., Allison Park 15101.

Maria Wald Retreat House, Convent of the Precious Blood, Box 97, New Holland Ave., Reading 19607.

Mount St. Macrina Retreat Center, 510 W. Main St., Box 878, Uniontown 15401.

St. Emma Retreat House, 1001 Harvey Ave., Greensburg 15601.

St. Francis Retreat Center (y*), c/o Dept. of Youth Ministry, 900 W. Market St., Orwigsburg 17961.

St. Francis Center for Renewal, Monocacy Manor, 395 Bridle Path Rd., Bethlehem 18017.

St. Francis Retreat House, 3918 Chipman Rd., Easton 18042.

St. Gabriel's Retreat House, 631 Griffin Pond Rd., Clarks Summit 18411.

St. Joseph's in the Hills, 313 Warren Ave., Malvern 19355.

St. Paul of the Cross Retreat Center, 148 Monastery Ave., Pittsburgh 15203.

Saint Raphaela Center, 616 Coopertown Rd., Haverford 19041.

St. Vincent Retreat Program, Latrobe 15650.

Villa of Our Lady Retreat Center (w, mc, y), HCR No. 1, Box 41, Mt. Pocono 18344.

**Rhode Island:** Bethany House, 397 Fruit Hill Ave., N. Providence 02911.

Father Marot CYO Center (y), 53 Federal St., Woonsocket 02895.

Our Lady of Peace Spiritual Life Center, 333 Ocean Rd., Box 507, Narragansett 02882.

St. Dominic Savio Youth Center (y*), Broad Rock Rd., Box 67, Peace Dale 02883.

**South Carolina:** Springbank Retreat Center, Rt. 2, Box 180, Kingstree 29556.

**South Dakota:** St. Martin's Community Center, 2110C St. Martin's Dr., Rapd City 57702.

Sioux Spiritual Center (for Native Americans), Diocese of Rapid City, HC 77, Box 271, Howes 57748.

**Tennessee:** Carmeiltes of Mary Immacualte Center of Spirituality, 610 Bluff Rd., Liberty 37095.

**Texas:** Bishop DeFalco Retreat Center, 2100 N. Spring, Amarillo 79107.

Bishop Rene H. Gracida Retreat Center, Diocese of Corpus Christi, 1200 Lantana, Corpus Christi 78407

Bishop Thomas J. Drury Retreat Center, 1200 Lantana St., Corpus Christi 78407.

Catholic Renewal Center of North Texas, 4503 Bridge St., Ft. Worth 76103.

Cenacle Retreat House, 420 N. Kirkwood, Houston 77079.

Christian Renewal Center (Centro de Renovacion Cristiana), Oblates of Mary Immaculate, P.O. Box 635, Dickinson 77539.

Holy Family Retreat Center, 9920 N. Major Dr., Beaumont 77713.

Holy Name Retreat Center, 430 Bunker Hill Rd., Houston 77024.

Holy Spirit Retreat and Conference Center, 501 Century Dr. S., Laredo 78040.

Montserrat Retreat House, Lake Dallas 75065.

Moye Center, 600 London, Castroville 78009.

Oblate Renewal Center, 285 Oblate Dr., San Antonio 78216 (mailing address). The center is temporarily closed; expected reopening mid-1996.

Our Lady of the Pillar Marianist Retreat Center, 2507 N.W. 36th St., San Antonio 78228.

San Juan Retreat House, Diocese of Brownsville, P.O. Box 998, San Juan 78589.

**Utah:** Abbey of Our Lady of the Holy Trinity (m), Huntsville 84317.

Our Lady of the Mountains, 1794 Lake St., Ogden 84401.

**Virginia:** Dominican Retreat, 7103 Old Dominion Dr., McLean 22101.

Holy Family Retreat House, The Redemptorists, P.O. 3151, 1414 N. Mallory St., Hampton 23663.

Missionhurst Mission Center, 4651 N. 25th St., Arlington 22207.

Retreat House, Holy Cross Abbey, Rt. 2, Box 3870, Berryville 22611.

**Washington:** Immaculate Heart Retreat Center, 6910 S. Ben Burr Rd., Spokane 99223.

Palisades Retreat House, P.O. Box 3739, Federal Way 98063.

St. Peter the Apostle Retreat Center, 15880 Summitview Rd., Cowiche 98923.

**West Virginia:** Bishop Hodges Pastoral Center, P.O. Box 60, Huttonsville, 26273.

Cenacle Retreat House, 1114 Virginia St. E., Charleston 25301.

Good Counsel Friary, Rt. 7, Box 183, Morgantown 26505.

John XXIII Pastoral Center, 100 Hodges Rd., Charleston, W. Va. 25314.

Paul VI Pastoral Center, 667 Stone and Shannon Rd., Wheeling 26003.

Priest Field Pastoral Center, Rt. 51, Box 133, Kearneysville 25430.

**Wisconsin:** Archdiocesan Retreat Center, 3501 S. Lake Dr., P.O. Box 07912, Milwaukee 53207.

Cardoner Retreat Center, 1501 S. Layton Blvd., Milwaukee 53215.

Holy Name Retreat House, Chambers Island; mailing address, 1825 Riverside Drive, P.O. Box 23825, Green Bay 54305.

Jesuit Retreat House, 4800 Fahrnwald Rd., Oshkosh 54901.

Monte Alverno Retreat Center, 1000 N. Ballard Rd., Appleton 54911.

Our Lady of Perpetual Help Retreat Center, 1800 N. Timber Trail Lane, Oconomowoc 53066.

St. Anthony Retreat Center, 300 E. 4h St., Marathon 54448.

St. Bede Retreat and Conference Center, 1190 Priory Rd., P.O. Box 66, Eau Claire 54702.

St. Benedict Center (monastery and ecumenical retreat and conference center), P.O. Box 5070, Madison 53705.

St. Francis Friary and Retreat Center, 503 S. Browns Lake Dr., P.O. Box 368, Burlington 53105.

St. Joseph's Retreat Center, 3035 O'Brien Rd., Bailey's Harbor 54202.

St. Vincent Pallotti Center, N6409 Bowers Rd., Elkhorn 53121.

Schoenstatt Center, W. 284 N. 698 Cherry Lane, Waukesha 53188.

# LAY PERSONS AND THEIR APOSTOLATE _____

## RIGHTS AND OBLIGATIONS OF ALL THE FAITHFUL

The following rights are listed in Canons 208-223 of the revised Code of Canon Law; additional rights are specified in other canons.

They are all equal in dignity because of their baptism and regeneration in Christ.

They are bound always to preserve communion with the Church.

According to their condition and circumstances, they should strive to lead a holy life and promote the growth and holiness of the Church.

They have the right and duty to work for the spread of the divine message of salvation to all peoples of all times and places.

They are bound to obey declarations and orders given by their pastors in their capacity as representatives of Christ, teachers of the faith and rectors of the Church.

They have the right to make known their needs, especially their spiritual needs, to pastors of the Church.

They have the right, and sometimes the duty, of making known to pastors and others of the faithful their opinions about things pertaining to the good of the Church.

They have the right to receive help from their pastors, from the spiritual goods of the Church and especially from the word of God and the sacraments.

They have the right to divine worship performed according to prescribed rules of their rite, and to follow their own form of spiritual life in line with the doctrine of the Church.

They have the right to freely establish and control associations for good and charitable purposes, to foster the Christian vocation in the world, and to hold meetings related to the accomplishment of these purposes.

They have the right to promote and support apostolic action but may not call it "Catholic" unless they have the consent of competent authority.

They have a right to a Christian education.

They have a right to freedom of inquiry in sacred studies, in accordance with the teaching authority of the Church.

They have a right to freedom in the choice of their state of life.

No one has the right to harm the good name of another person or to violate his or her right to maintain personal privacy.

They have the right to vindicate the rights they enjoy in the Church, and to defend themselves in a competent ecclesiastical forum.

They have the obligation to provide for the needs of the Church, with respect to things pertaining to divine worship, apostolic and charitable works, and the reasonable support of ministers of the Church.

They have the obligation to promote social justice and to help the poor from their own resources.

In exercising their rights, the faithful should have regard for the common good of the Church and for the rights and duties of others.

Church authority has the right to monitor the exercise of rights proper to the faithful, with the common good in view.

## RIGHTS AND OBLIGATIONS OF LAY PERSONS

In addition to rights and obligations common to all the faithful and those stated in other canons, lay persons are bound by the obligations and enjoy the rights specified in these canons (224-231).

Lay persons, like all the faithful, are called by God to the apostolate in virtue of their baptism and confirmation. They have the obligation and right, individually or together in associations, to work for the spread and acceptance of the divine message of salvation among people everywhere; this obligation is more urgent in those circumstances in which people can hear the Gospel and get to know Christ only through them (lay persons).

They are bound to bring an evangelical spirit to bear on the order of temporal things and to give Christian witness in carrying out their secular pursuits.

Married couples are obliged to work for the building up of the people of God through their marital and family life.

Parents have the most serious obligation to provide for the Christian education of their children according to the doctrine handed down by the Church.

Lay persons have the same civil liberty as other citizens. In the use of this liberty, they should take care that their actions be imbued with an evangelical spirit. They should attend to the doctrine proposed by the magisterium of the Church but should take care that, in questions of opinion, they do not propose their own opinion as the doctrine of the Church.

Qualified lay persons are eligible to hold and perform the duties of ecclesiastical offices open to them in accord with the provisions of law.

Properly qualified lay persons can assist pastors of the Church as experts and counselors.

Lay persons have the obligation and enjoy the right to acquire knowledge of doctrine commensurate with their capacity and condition.

They have the right to pursue studies in the sacred sciences in pontifical universities or facilities and in institutes of religious sciences, and to obtain academic degrees.

If qualified, they are eligible to receive from ecclesiastical authority a mandate to teach sacred sciences.

Laymen can be invested by liturgical rite and in a stable manner in the ministries of lector and acolyte.

Lay persons, by temporary assignment, can fulfill the office of lector in liturgical actions; likewise, all lay persons can perform the duties of commentator or cantor.

In cases of necessity and in the absence of the usual ministers, lay persons — even if not lectors or acolytes — can exercise the ministry of the word, lead liturgical prayers, confer baptism and distribute Communion, according to the prescripts of law.

Lay persons who devote themselves permanently or temporarily to the service of the Church are obliged to acquire the formation necessary for carrying out their duties in a proper manner.

They have a right to remuneration for their service which is just and adequate to provide for their own needs and those of their families; they also have a right to insurance, social security and health insurance.

# SPECIAL APOSTOLATES AND GROUPS

**Apostleship of the Sea** (1920, Glasgow, Scotland; 1947 in U.S.): 3211 Fourth St. NE, Washington, DC 20017 (national office). An international Catholic organization for the moral, social and spiritual welfare of seafarers and those involved in the maritime industry. Formally instituted by the Holy See in 1952 (apostolic constitution Exul Familia), it is a sector of the Pontifical Council for Migrants and Itinerant Peoples. The U.S. unit, an affiliate of the NCCB-USCC, serves port chaplains in 63 U.S. ports. Nat. Dir., Robert Mario Balderas, a permanent deacon.

**Auxiliaries of Our Lady of the Cenacle** (1878, France): An association of Catholic laywomen, under the direction of the Congregation of Our Lady of the Cenacle, who serve God through their own professions and life styles and pursue individual apostolates. U.S. address: Dr. Carolyn Jacobs, 22 Bedford Court, Amherst, MA 01002.

**Catholic Central Union of America** (1855): 3835 Westminster Pl., St. Louis, MO 63108; membership, 2,000; *Social Justice Review,* bimonthly. One of the oldest Catholic lay organizations in the U.S. and the first given an official mandate for Catholic Action by a committee of the American bishops (1936).

**Catholic Medical Mission Board** (1928): 10 W. 17th Street, New York, NY 10011. A charitable, non-profit organization dedicated to providing health care supplies and support for the medically disadvantaged in developing and transitional countries. CMMB depends upon the financial generosity of over 25,000 individual donors and through product contributions by major pharmaceutical corporations. In 1994, over $32 million worth of medical assistance was provided to medical facilities in Latin America, the Caribbean, Africa, Asia, Oceania, and Central and Eastern Europe. CMMB's medical program includes a placement service for health care specialists who volunteer at Catholic medical facilities in developing countries. In 1994, over 114 medical specialists served worldwide for diverse tours of service. President, Terrance M. Kirch.

**Catholic Movement for Intellectual and Cultural Affairs of Pax Romana:** The U.S. affiliate of Pax Romana — ICMICA (see International Catholic Organizations); *The Notebook*, quarterly. Address: 31 Chesterfield Rd., Stamford, CT 06902.

**Catholic Network of Volunteer Service** (1963; formerly, International Liaison of Lay Volunteers in Mission): 4121 Harewood Rd. N.E., Washington, DC 20017. Network for lay mission programs, coordinating and facilitating efforts of volunteer mission organizations. *The Response,* annual directory. Executive director, Jim Lindsay.

**Catholic Volunteers in Florida** (1983): P.O. Box 702, Goldenrod, FL 32733. Co-sponsored by the bishops of Florida to promote values of social justice by direct service to farm workers, homeless, hungry, low-income people, single mothers and others in need. Volunteers, 20 years of age and older, serve for a one-year period in urban and rural settings.

**Center for Applied Research in the Apostolate (CARA):** Georgetown University, Washington, DC 20057. A non-profit research center serving the planning needs of the Catholic Church. CARA gathers empirical data for use by bishops, diocesan agencies, parishes, congregations of men and women religious and Catholic organizations. *The CARA Report,* quarterly. Executive director, Gerald H. Early.

**Christian Family Movement (CFM)** (1947): Originated in Chicago to Christianize family life and create communities conducive to Christian family life. Since 1968, CFM in the U.S. has included couples from all Christian churches. National office, Box 272, Ames, IA 50010.

**Christian Life Communities** (1971, promulgation of revised norms by Pope Paul VI; originated, 1563, as Sodalities of Our Lady, at the Jesuit College in Rome): 3601 Lindell Blvd., Room 421, St. Louis, MO 63108 (national office); the world CLC office is in Rome. Small communities of primarily lay persons who come together to form committed individuals for service to the world and the Church.

**Cursillo Movement** (1949, in Spain; in U.S., 1957): National Cursillo Center, P.O. Box 210226, Dallas, TX 75211. An instrument of Christian renewal designed to form and stimulate persons to engage in evangelizing their everyday environments.

**Franciscan Mission Service of North America,** an Overseas Lay Ministry Program (1990): P.O. Box 29034, Washington, DC 20017. Laypeople serve overseas, in any part of the world, for a period of three years, in collaboration with other Franciscans overseas.

**Grail, The** (1921, in The Netherlands, by Rev. Jacques van Ginneken, S.J.; 1940, in U.S.): Grailville, 932 O'Bannonville Rd., Loveland, Ohio 45140 (U. S. headquarters); Duisburger Strasse 442, 45478 Mulheim, Germany (international secretariat). An international movement of women concerned about the full development of all peoples, working in education, religious, social, cultural and ecological areas.

**Jesuit Volunteer Corps** (1956): 18th and Thompson Sts., Philadelphia, PA 19121 (address for information). Sponsored by the Society of Jesus in the U.S. Men and women volunteers work throughout the U.S. serving the poor directly and working for structural change.

**LAMP Ministries** (Lay Apostolic Ministries with the Poor): 2704 Schurz Ave., Bronx, NY 10465. Missionary service of evangelization with the materially poor and homeless in the larger metropolitan New York area. Newsletter, two times a year. Directors, Tom and Lyn Scheuring.

**Lay Mission-Helpers Association** (1955): 1531 W. Ninth St., Los Angeles, CA 90015. Trains and assigns men and women for work in overseas apostolates for periods of two to three years. Approximately 700 members of the association have served in overseas assignments since its founding. Director, Rev. Michael Meyers. The **Mission Doctors Association** (same address) recruits, trains and sends Catholic physicians and their families to mission hospitals and clinics throughout the world for tours of two to three years.

**Legion of Mary** (1921, in Dublin, Ireland, by Frank Duff): P.O. Box 1313, St. Louis, MO 63188 (U.S. address); De Montfort House, Dublin 7, Ireland (headquarters). Membership: active Catholics of all ages, under the direction of local bishops and priests, for the work of conversion, conservation and consolation.

**Movimiento Familiar Cristiano — USA (MFC)** (1969): Movement of Catholic Hispanic families united in their efforts to promote the human and Christian virtues of the family so that it may become a force that forms persons, transmits the faith and contributes to the total development of the community. Rev. Clemente Barron, C.P., national spiritual director. Address: 700 Waverly, San Antonio, TX 78201.

**National Catholic Conference for Seafarers**, affiliated with the Apostleship of the Sea in the U.S. Pres., Mrs. Karen Lai, Seaman's Center, 221-20th St., Galveston, TX 77550.

**Pax Christi USA** (1972): 348 E. 10th St., Erie, PA 16503. U.S. section of Pax Christi (see International Catholic Organizations). Founded to establish peacemaking as a priority for the American Catholic Church. *Pax Christi USA,* quarterly; membership, 11,500.

**Volunteer Missionary Movement** (1969): 5980 W. Loomis Rd., Milwaukee, WI 53129. Independent lay international mission organization with origins in the Catholic tradition but ecumenical and open to all Christian denominations. *Bridges,* quarterly.

**Volunteers for Educational and Social Services (VESS)**, 3001 S. Congress Ave., Austin, TX. 78704. A program of the Texas Catholic Conference. Provides individuals the opportunity to serve the Church in Texas for a year by ministering to needs of parishes, agencies and schools that are economically disadvantaged.

## CATHOLIC YOUTH ORGANIZATIONS

**Boy Scouts in the Catholic Church:** The National Catholic Committee on Scouting (Eleanore Starr, Admin. Sec., NCCS-BSA, P.O. Box 152079, Irving, TX 75015) works with the Boy Scouts of America in developing the character and spiritual life of members in units chartered to Catholic and non-Catholic organizations. National Committee Chairman, Robert Runnels of Leawood, Kans.

**Camp Fire:** The National Catholic Committee for Girl Scouts and Camp Fire, a standing committee of the National Federation for Catholic Youth Ministry, cooperates with Camp Fire Boys and Girls (4601 Madison Ave., Kansas City, MO 64112).

**Catholic Forester Youth Program, Catholic Order of Foresters:** 355 Shuman Blvd., P.O. Box 3012, Naperville, IL 60566. To develop Christian leadership and promote the moral, intellectual, social and physical growth of its youth members. *Catholic Forester.* Membership: youth up to 16 years of age — over 19,046 in 610 local courts in U.S. High Chief Ranger, Bernard F. Milota.

**Catholic Youth Organization (CYO):** Name of parish-centered diocesan Catholic youth programs throughout the country. CYO promotes a program of spiritual, social and physical activities. The original CYO was organized in 1930 by Archbishop Bernard Sheil, auxiliary bishop of Chicago.

**Columbian Squires** (1925): 1 Columbus Plaza, New Haven, CT 06510. The official youth organization of the Knights of Columbus. To train and develop leadership through active participation in a well-organized program of spiritual, service, social, cultural and athletic activities. Membership: Catholic young men, 12-18 years old. More than 25,000 in over 1,000 circles (local units) active in the U.S., Canada, Puerto Rico, Philippines, Mexico, the Bahamas and Guam. *Squires Newsletter,* monthly.

**Girl Scouts:** Girls from archdioceses and dioceses in the U.S. and its possessions participate in Girl Scouting through the collaboration of Girl Scouts of the U.S.A. (830 Third Ave., New York, NY 10022) with the National Catholic Committee for Girl Scouts and Camp Fire, a standing committee of the National Federation for Catholic Youth Ministry.

**Holy Childhood Association (Pontifical Association of the Holy Childhood)** (1843): 1720 Massachusetts Ave. N.W., Washington, DC 20036. The official children's mission-awareness society of the Church. Provides mission awareness for elementary-grade students in parochial schools and religious education programs and financial assistance to children in more than 100 developing countries. Publishes *It's Our World,* three times a year, in two grade levels. National Director, Rev. Francis W. Wright, C.S.Sp.

**National Catholic Forensic League** (1952): To develop articulate Catholic leaders through an inter-diocesan program of speech and debate activities. *Newsletter,* quarterly. Membership: 925 schools; membership open to Catholic, private and public schools through the local diocesan league. Secretary-Treasurer, Richard Gaudette, 21 Nancy Rd., Milford, MA 01757.

**National Catholic Young Adult Ministry Association** (1982): 3700-A Oakview Terr. N.E., Washington, DC 20017. A response to the needs of young adults, an invitation to share their gifts with the larger community and a challenge to live gospel values in the world. A national network for single and married young adults. President, James J. Breen.

**National Federation for Catholic Youth Ministry, Inc.** (1981): 3700-A Oakview Terr. NE, Washington, DC 20017. To foster the development of youth ministry in the United States. Executive Director, Rev. Leonard C. Wenke.

**Young Christian Students:** 7436 W. Harrison, Forest Park, IL 60130. A student movement for Christian personal and social change.

## COLLEGE SOCIETIES

**Alpha Sigma Nu** (1915): Marquette Univ., Brooks 201, P.O. Box 1881, Milwaukee, WI 53201 (national headquarters). National honor society of the 30 Jesuit colleges, universities and theologates of the U.S.; members chosen on the basis of scholarship, loyalty and service; 1,500 student and 35,000 alumni members. Member, Association of College Honor Societies. Gamma Pi Epsilon (1925) merged with Alpha Sigma Nu in 1973 to form society for men and women. Executive Director, Peg Fennig.

**Delta Epsilon Sigma** (1939): Barry University, Miami Shores, FL 33161. National scholastic honor society for students, faculty and alumni of colleges and universities with a Catholic tradition. *Delta Epsilon Sigma Journal,* three times a year. Membership: 58,000 in 116 chapters. Secretary, Dr. J. Patrick Lee.

**Kappa Gamma Pi** (1926): A national Catholic college honor society for graduates who, in addition to academic excellence, have shown outstanding leadership in extra-curricular activities. *Kappa Gamma Pi News,* five times a year. Membership: more than 30,000 in 139 colleges; 20 alumnae chapters in metropolitan areas. Executive Secretary, Marjorie Durbin, 2415 Hillcrest Dr., Stow, Ohio 44224.

**Phi Kappa Theta:** 3901 W. 86th St., Suite 425, Indianapolis, IN 46268. National social fraternity with a Catholic heritage. Merger (1959) of Phi Kappa Fraternity, founded at Brown Univ. in 1889, and Theta Kappa Phi Fraternity, founded at Lehigh Univ. in 1919. *The Temple Magazine,* semi-annually, and newsletters. Membership: 2,800 undergraduate and 50,500 alumni in 63 collegiate and 21 alumni chapters. Executive Director, Mark T. McSweeney.

**National Catholic Student Coalition** (1982): National coalition of Catholic campus ministry groups at public and private institutions of higher education. Formed after National Newman Club Federation and the National Federation of Catholic College Students dissolved in the 1960s. The U.S. affiliate of Pax Romana — IMCS (see International Catholic Organizations). Publishes *The Catholic Collegian,* four times a year. Membership: 200 campus groups. Executive director, Jamie Williams, 300 College Park Ave., Dayton, Ohio 45469.

# ASSOCIATIONS, MOVEMENTS, SOCIETIES IN THE U.S.

(Principal source: Almanac survey.)

*See Index for other associations, movements and societies covered elsewhere.*

**Academy of American Franciscan History** (1944), 1712 Euclid Ave., Berkeley, CA 97409. To encourage the study of the Franciscan Order in the New World. Dir., Dr. John F. Schwaller.

**Aid to the Church in Need** (1947), U.S. office, P.O. Box 576, Deer Park, NY 11729. Assists the pastoral activities of the church in Third World countries, Eastern Europe and the former Soviet Union. *Mirror* (newsletter), 9 times a year.

**Albanian Catholic Institute "Daniel Dajani, S.J."** (1992), University of San Francisco, Xavier Hall, San Francisco, CA 94117. To assist the rebuilding of the Catholic Church in Albania and to promote the dissemination of knowledge of Albania's national, religious and cultural heritage. Founder, Gjon Sinishta (1930-95). Director, Paul Bernadicou, S.J.

**American Benedictine Academy** (1947). To promote Benedictine values in contemporary culture. Pres., Joel Rippinger, O.S.B., Marmion Abbey, 1000 Butterfield Rd., Aurora, IL 60504.

**American Catholic Correctional Chaplains Association** (1952), 220 in 300 institutions. Pres., Bro. Peter Donohue, C.F.X.,Office of Detention Ministry, 933 Grattan St., Los Angeles, CA 90015.

**American Catholic Historical Association** (1919), Catholic University of America, Washington, DC 20064. *The Catholic Historical Review,* quarterly. Sec.-Treas., Rev. Msgr. Robert Trisco.

**American Catholic Philosophical Association** (1926), The Catholic University of America, Washington, DC 20064. *American Catholic Philosophical Quarterly; Proceedings,* annually.

**American Committee on Italian Migration** (1952), 352 W. 44th St., New York, NY 10036; 6,000. *ACIM Newsletter* and *ACIM Nuova Via,* 6 times a year.

**American Friends of the Vatican Library** (1981), 157 Lakeshore Rd., Grosse Point Farms, MI 48236.

Sponsored by the Catholic Library Association. To assist in supporting the Vatican Library: *AMICI,* newsletter.

**Ancient Order of Hibernians in America, Inc.** (1836); 120,000. *National Hibernian Digest,* bimonthly. Nat. Sec., Thomas McNabb, 31 Logan St., Auburn, NY 13021.

**Apostleship of Prayer** (1844-France; 1861-U.S.): 3 Stephen Ave., New Hyde Park, NY 11040. Promotes Daily Offering and Sacred Heart devotion.

**Apostolate for Family Consecration** (1975), Pope John Paul II Holy Family Center, Seminary Rd., P.O. Box 151, Bloomingdale, OH 43910.

**Archconfraternity of Christian Mothers (Christian Mothers)** (1881), 220 37th St., Pittsburgh, PA 15201; over 3,500 branches. Dir., Rev. Bertin Roll, O.F.M. Cap.

**Archconfraternity of the Holy Ghost** (1912), Holy Ghost Fathers, 2401 Bristol Pike, Bensalem, PA 19020 (U.S. headquarters).

**Archdiocese for the Military Services Seminary Education Fund** (1988), 3311 Toledo Terrace, Hyattsville, MD 20782.

**Association for Spiritual, Ethical, and Religious Values in Counseling (ASERVIC),** division of the American Counseling Association. *Counseling and Values,* 3 times a year. Address, Dept. of Educational Psychology and Special Education, Southern Illinois Univ. at Carbondale, Carbondale, IL 62901.

**Association for Social Economics** (formerly the Catholic Economic Association) (1941), Marquette University, Milwaukee, WI 53233; 1,300. *Review of Social Economy,* quarterly.

**Association of Catholic Diocesan Archivists** (1979): To work for establishment of an archival program in every American diocese. *ACDA Bulletin,* quarterly. Pres. (1995-96), Msgr. Francis Weber, 15151 San Fernando Mission Blvd., Mission Hills, CA 91348.

**Association of Marian Helpers** (1944), Stockbridge,

MA 01263; 900,000, mostly in U.S. *Marian Helpers Bulletin,* quarterly. To promote vocations to Church service and support worldwide apostolates of Marians of the Immaculate Conception.

**Beginning Experience** (1974), 305 Michigan Ave., Detroit, MI 48226; 150 teams throughout the world. Adult and youth programs to help divorced, widowed and separated start a new beginning in their lives. Exec. Dir., Sr. Cynthia Hruby, N.D.

**The Blue Army USA** (A Fatima Apostolate) (1952), Mountain View Rd. (P.O. Box 976), Washington, NJ 07882. Promote Fatima message, Marian devotion. *Soul,* bimonthly; *Hearts Aflame,* quarterly. Natl. Pres., Most Rev. James S. Sullivan.

**Calix Society** (1947), 7601 Wayzata Blvd., Minneapolis, MN 55426; Association of Catholic alcoholics maintaining their sobriety through 12-step program. Sec.-Treas., Bill Fox.

**Canon Law Society of America** (1939), Catholic University, Washington, DC 20064. To further research and study in canon law; 1,600. Exec. Coord., Rev. Patrick Cogan, S.A.

**Cardinal Mindszenty Foundation** (CMF) (1958), P.O. Box 11321, St. Louis, MO 63105. To uphold and defend the Catholic Church, family life and freedom for all under God. Pres., Eleanor Schlafly.

**Catholic Aid Association** (1878), 3499 N. Lexington Ave., St. Paul, MN 55126; 80,000. *Catholic Aid News,* monthly. Fraternal life insurance society. Pres. F. L. Spanier.

**Catholic Alumni Clubs International** (1957): To advance social, cultural and spiritual well-being of members. Membership limited to single Catholics with professional education; 7,500 in 48 clubs in U.S. Pres., Guy A. DiMarino, 215 W. Wood St., Lowellville, OH 44436.

**Catholic Answers** (1982), P.O. Box 17490, San Diego, CA 92177. *This Rock,* monthly. Apologetics and evangelization organization. Founder and dir., Karl Keating.

**Catholic Biblical Association of America** (1936), Catholic University of America, Washington, DC 20064; 1,282. *The Catholic Biblical Quarterly; Old Testament Abstracts, CBQ* monograph series.

**Catholic Book Publishers Association, Inc.** (1987), 333 Glen Head Rd., Old Brookville, NY 11545. Sec., Charles A. Roth.

**Catholic Coalition on Preaching,** Univ. of Notre Dame, Notre Dame, IN 46556.

**Catholic Commission on Intellectual and Cultural Affairs (CCICA)** (1946), LaSalle University, Philadelphia, PA 19141; 350; Exec. Dir., Bro. Daniel Burke, F.S.C.

**Catholic Committee of Appalachia** (1970), 111 Main St., P.O. Box 953, Whitesburg, KY 41858. Exec. Coord., Todd Garland.

**Catholic Daughters of the Americas** (1903), 10 W. 71st St., New York, NY 10023; 125,000. *Share Magazine.* Nat. Regent, Grace M. Rinaldi.

**Catholic Golden Age** (1975): P.O. Box 3658, Scranton, PA 18505; *CGA World,* quarterly. For Catholics over 50 years of age.

**Catholic Guardian Society** (1913), 1011 First Ave., New York, NY 10022. Exec. Dir., John J. Frein.

**Catholic Home Bureau** (1899), 1011 First Ave., New York, NY 10022. Exec. Dir., Sr. Una McCormack, O.P.

**Catholic Home Study Service** (1936), P.O. Box 363, Perryville, MO 63775. Provides instruction in the Catholic faith by mail free of charge. Director, Rev. Oscar Lukefahr, C.M.

**Catholic Interracial Council of New York, Inc.** (1934), 899 Tenth Ave., New York, NY 10019. To promote racial and social justice.

**Catholic Knights of America** (1877), 1850 Dalton St., Cincinnati, OH 45214; 7,800. *C K of A Journal,* monthly. Fraternal insurance society.

**Catholic Knights of Ohio** (1891): 22005 Mastick Rd., Fairview Park, OH 44126; 8,000 in Ohio and Kentucky. *The Messenger,* monthly. Fraternal insurance society. Pres., Victor D. Huss.

**Catholic Kolping Society of America** (1923), P.O. Box 46252, Chicago, IL 60646. *Kolping Banner,* monthly. International society concerned with spiritual and educational development of members.

**Catholic Lawyers' Guild.** Organization usually on a diocesan basis, under different titles.

**Catholic League** (1943), 1200 N. Ashland Ave., Chicago, IL 60622. Exec. Dir., Most Rev. Thad Jakubowski.

**Catholic League for Religious and Civil Rights** (1973), 1011 First Ave., New York, NY 10022; local chapters throughout U.S. *Catalyst,* League journal. Serves Catholic community as an anti-defamation and civil rights agency. Pres., William A. Donohue.

**Catholic Library Association** (1921), St. Joseph Central High School Library, 22 Maplewood Ave., Pittsfield, MA 01201. *Catholic Library World, Catholic Periodical and Literature Index,* quarterlies. Pres., Jean R. Bostley, S.S.J.

**Catholic Near East Welfare Association** (1926), 1011 First Ave., New York, NY 10022. A papal agency for humanitarian and pastoral support serving the churches and peoples of the Middle East, Northeast Africa, India and Eastern Europe, with offices in New York, Vatican City, Addis Ababa, Amman, Jordan, Jerusalem and Beirut, Lebanon. Pres., Cardinal John O'Connor; gen. sec., Msgr. Robert L. Stern.

**Catholic Order of Foresters** (1883), 355 Shuman Blvd., P.O. Box 3012, Naperville, IL 60566; 136,685. *The Catholic Forester,* bimonthly. Fraternal insurance society. High Chief Ranger, Bernard F. Milota.

**Catholic Press Association of the U.S. and Canada, Inc.** (1911), 3555 Veterans Memorial Highway, Unit O, Ronkonkoma, NY 11779. *The Catholic Journalist,* monthly; *Catholic Press Directory,* annually. Pres., Christopher J. Gunty; exec. dir., Owen P. McGovern.

**Catholic Theological Society of America** (1946), Creighton University, 2500 California Plaza, Omaha, NE 68178. *Proceedings,* annually.

**Catholic Union of Texas, The K.J.T.** (1889), 214 E. Colorado St., La Grange, TX 78945; 18,226. *Nasinec,* weekly, and *K. J. T. News,* monthly. Fraternal and insurance society. Pres., Elo J. Goerig.

**Catholic War Veterans** (1935), 441 N. Lee St., Alexandria, VA 22314; 500 posts, *Catholic War Veteran,* bimonthly.

**Catholic Worker Movement** (1933), 36 E. First St., New York, NY 10003. *The Catholic Worker,* 8 times a year. Lay apostolate founded by Peter Maurin and Dorothy Day; has Houses of Hospitality in over 60 U.S. cities and several communal farms in various parts of the country. Promotes the practice of the works of mercy, nonviolence, personalism, voluntary poverty.

**Catholic Workman (Katolicky Delnik)** (1891), P.O. Box 47, New Prague, MN 56071; 16,405. *Catholic Workman,* monthly. Fraternal and insurance society.

**Catholics against Capital Punishment** (1992), P.O. Box 3125, Arlington, VA 22203. Nat. coordinator, Frank McNeirney.

**Catholics United for Spiritual Action, Inc.** (CUSA) (1947), 63 Wall St., New York, NY 10005. A group-correspondence apostolate for the disabled.

**Catholics United for the Faith** (1968), 827 N. Fourth St., Steubenville, OH 43952; 23,000 worldwide, *Lay Witness,* monthly. Lay apostolic group concerned with spiritual and doctrinal formation of members. Pres., Curtis Martin.

**Center of Concern** (1971): 3700 13th St., N.E., Washington, DC 20017.

**Central Association of the Miraculous Medal** (1915), 475 E. Chelten Ave., Philadelphia, PA 19144. *Miraculous Medal,* quarterly. Dir., Rev. John W. Gouldrick, C.M.

**Chaplains' Aid Association, Inc.** (1917), 3311 Toledo Terrace, Hyattsville, MD 20780. To receive and administer funds toward education of seminarians to become priest-chaplains in military services. Pres., Most Rev. Joseph T. Dimino.

**Christian Foundation for Children and Aging,** One Elmwood Ave., Kansas City, KS 66103. Grassroots movement dedicated to improving through sponsorship children and aging at Catholic mission sites around the world. Pres., Robert K. Hentzen.

**Christophers, Inc., The** (1945), 12 E. 48th St., New York, NY 10017. Founded by Rev. James Keller, M.M. The Christophers stimulate personal initiative and responsible action in line with Judeo-Christian principles through broadcast of Christopher radio and TV programs; free distribution of *Christopher News Notes,* ten times a year; publication of a weekly Christopher column in over 200 newspapers; Spanish literature; annual media awards; youth outreach. Dir., Rev. Thomas J. McSweeney.

**Citizens for Educational Freedom** (1959): Nonsectarian group concerned with parents' right to educational choice by means of tuition tax credits and vouchers. Exec. dir., Patrick J. Reilly, 921 S. Walter Reed Dr., Suite 1, Arlington, VA 22204.

**Confraternity of Bl. Junipero Serra** (1989): P.O. Box 7125, Mission Hills, CA 91346; 3,500 in U.S. and foreign countries. Founded in Monterey (Calif.) diocese to help promote process of canonization of Bl. Junipero Serra and increase spiritual development of members. Dir., Rev. Thomas L. Davis, Jr.; Spiritual Dir., Rev. Noel F. Moholy, O.F.M.

**Confraternity of Catholic Clergy** (1976): Association of priests pledged to pursuit of personal holiness, loyalty to the Pope, theological study and adherence to authentic teachings of the Catholic faith. Sec., Rev. L. Dudley Day, O.S.A., 4445 W. 64th St., Chicago, IL 60629.

**Confraternity of Christian Doctrine, Inc.,** 3211 Fourth St., N.E., Washington, DC 20017. A distinct entity, separately incorporated and directed by a Board of Trustees from the United States Catholic Conference of Bishops. Its purpose is to foster and promote the teaching of Christ as understood and handed down by the Roman Catholic Church. To this end it licenses use of the *Lectionary for Mass* and the *New American Bible (NAB),* the *Revised Psalms of the NAB* and the *Revised New Testament of the NAB,* translations made from the original languages in accordance with the papal encyclical *Divino Afflante Spiritu* of Pope Pius XII.

**Confraternity of the Immaculate Conception of Our Lady of Lourdes** (1874), Box 561, Notre Dame, IN 46556. Distributors of Lourdes water.

**Confraternity of the Most Holy Rosary:** See Dominican Rosary Apostolate.

**Couple to Couple League** (1971), P.O. Box 111184, Cincinnati, OH 45211. Founded to teach and promote marital chastity through Natural Family Planning.

**Courage** (1980), c/o St. Michael's Rectory, 424 W. 34th St., New York, NY 10001. To live chaste lives in accordance with the Church's teaching on homosexuality. Newsletter, 4 times a year. Nat. Dir., Rev. John F. Harvey, O.S.F.S.

**Damien-Dutton Society for Leprosy Aid, Inc.** (1944), 616 Bedford Ave., Bellmore, NY 11710; 25,000. *Damien Dutton Call,* quarterly. Provides medicine, rehabilitation and research for conquest of leprosy. Pres., Howard E. Crouch; Dir., Sr. Mary Augustine, S.M.S.M.

**Daughters of Isabella** (1897), P.O. Box 9585, New Haven, CT 06535; 100,000. To unite Catholic women into a fraternal order for spiritual benefits and to promote higher ideals within society.

**Disaster Response Office** (1990), Catholic Charities USA, 1731 King St., Suite 200, Alexandria, VA 22314. Promotes and facilitates Catholic disaster response in the U.S. Dir., Jane A. Gallagher.

**Dominican Rosary Apostolate** (1806), 141 E. 65th St., New York, NY 10021. Dir., Rev. Edward L. Martin, O.P.

**Edith Stein Guild, Inc.** (1955), Our Lady of Victory Church, 60 William St., New York, NY 10005. Promotes Judaeo-Christian understanding, knowledge of life and writings of Bl. Edith Stein (Sister Benedicta of the Cross), assists and counsels Catholics of Jewish background, fosters among Catholics a better understanding of their Jewish heritage, Pres., Mrs. Cabiria Nardiello; Moderator. Rev. Christopher Marcynski, S.A.C.

**Enthronement of the Sacred Heart in the Home** (1907), 42 1/2 Adams St., Fairhaven, MA 02719.

**Family Rosary, Inc., The** (1942), 4 Pine West Plaza, Albany, NY 12205. Founded by Father Patrick Peyton, C.S.C. Encourages family prayer, especially the Rosary. Pres., Rev. Leo Polselli, C.S.C.

**Federation of Diocesan Liturgical Commissions (FDLC)** (1969), P.O. Box 29039, Washington, DC 20017. Voluntary association of personnel from diocesan liturgical commissions and worship offices.

The main purpose is promotion of the liturgy as the heart of Christian life, especially in the parish community. Exec. Dir., Rev. Michael J. Spillane.

**Fellowship of Catholic Scholars** (1977), Prof. Gerard V. Bradley, president, 219 Law School, Notre Dame, IN 46556; over 1,000 members. Interdisciplinary research and publications of Catholic scholars in accord with the magisterium of the Catholic Church.

**First Catholic Slovak Ladies' Association, USA** (1892), 24950 Chagrin Blvd., Beachwood, OH 44122; 102,000. *Fraternally Yours,* monthly. Fraternal insurance society. Pres., Mary Anne Johanek.

**First Catholic Slovak Union (Jednota)** (1890), FCSU Corporate Center, 6611 Rockside Rd., Independence, OH 44131; 96,206. *Jednota,* biweekly. Nat. Sec., Kenneth A. Arendt.

**Foundation for the Family** (1986), P.O. Box 111184, Cincinnati, OH 45211. Established by Couple to Couple League (see entry above) to provide materials for family not relating to Natural Family Planning.

**Foundations and Donors Interested in Catholic Activities, Inc. (FADICA),** 1350 Connecticut Ave. N.W., Suite 303, Washington, DC 20036. A consortium of private foundations providing continuing education and research to members to make church-related philanthropy more effective. Pres., Francis J. Butler.

**Franciscan Apostolate of the Way of the Cross** (1949), P.O. Box 23, Boston, MA 02112. Distributes religious materials to the sick and shut-in. Dir., Rev. Robert Lynch, O.F.M.

**Franciscan Canticle, Inc.** (1983), 370 W. Arenas Rd., Palm Springs, CA 92262. Community of men and women artists who use their gifts and talents to promote the work of God.

**Free the Fathers** (1983), 845 Oak St. Chattanooga, TN 37403. To work for the freedom of bishops and priests imprisoned in China. Pres., John M. Davies.

**Friends of the Holy Land, Inc.** (1974), 347 Mile Square Rd., Yonkers, NY 10701; 300 members. To provide spiritual and material support for the Christian communities in the Holy Land; *Friends of the Holy Land Newsletter.* Gen. Dir., Ernest F. Russo.

**Gabriel Richard Institute** (1949), 2820 West Maple Rd., Suite No. 101, Troy, MI 48084. Conducts Christopher Leadership Course. Dir., Rev. Thomas J. Bresnahan; nat. mgr., Dolores Ammar.

**Guard of Honor of the Immaculate Heart of Mary** (1932), 135 West 31st St., New York, NY 10001. An archconfraternity approved by the Holy See whose members cultivate devotion to the Blessed Virgin Mary, particularly through a daily Guard Hour of Prayer.

**Holy Name Society:** Founded in 1274 by Blessed John Vercelli, master general of the Dominicans, to promote reverence for the Holy Name of Jesus; this is still the principal purpose of the society, which also develops lay apostolic programs in line with directives of the Second Vatican Council. Introduced in the U.S. by Dominican Father Charles H. McKenna in 1870-71, the society has about 5 million members on diocesan and parochial levels. With approval of the local bishop and pastor, women as well as men may be members.

**Holy Name Society, National Association (NAHNS)** (1970), P.O. Box 26038, Baltimore, MD 21224. *Holy Name Newsletter,* monthly. Association of diocesan and parochial Holy Name Societies.

**Hungarian Catholic League of America, Inc.** (1945), Rev. Msgr. William I. Varsanyi, chairman, One Cathedral Sq., Providence, RI 02903.

**International Institute of the Heart of Jesus** (1972), 7236 Wellauer Rd., Milwaukee, WI 53213; Rev. Walter O. Kern, 5337 Genesee St., Bowmansville, NY 14026; Delegacion Latino-americana, IIHJ, Casilla 118, Correo 35, Las Condes, Santiago, Chile (president's office). Promote awareness and appreciation of the mystery of the Heart of Christ.

**Italian Catholic Federation, Central Council** (1924), 1801 Van Ness Ave., Suite 330, San Francisco, CA 94109; 22,000; *Bollettino,* monthly.

**John Carroll Society, The** (1951), P.O. Box 29260, Washington, DC 20017. Chaplain, Rev. Peter Vaghi.

**Judean Society, Inc., The** (1966), 1075 Space Park Way No. 336, Mt. View, CA 94043.

**Knights of Peter Claver** (1909), and **Knights of Peter Claver, Ladies Auxiliary** (1926), 1825 Orleans Ave., New Orleans, LA 70116. 35,000. *The Claverite,* biannually. Fraternal and aid society. National Chaplain, Most Rev. Curtis J. Guillory, S.V.D.

**Knights of St. John, International Supreme Commandery** (1886), 89 So. Pine Ave., Albany, N.Y. 12208.

**Knights of the Immaculata (Militia Immaculatae, M.I.)** (1917), 1600 W. Park Ave., Libertyville, IL 60048; canonically established with international headquarters in Rome. A pious association for evangelization and catechesis beginning with members' own total consecration to the Immaculate Virgin Mary.

**Ladies of Charity of the United States of America** (1960), 7800 Natural Bridge Rd., St. Louis, MO 63121; 25,000 in U.S.; 250,000 worldwide. International Association founded by St. Vincent de Paul in 1617.

**Latin Liturgy Association** (1975), Office of Chairman, Dr. Robert J. Edgeworth, 740 Carriage Way, Baton Rouge, LA 70808; 1,000. To promote the use of the Latin language and music in the approved rites of the Church. Quarterly journal.

**Legatus** (1987), 30 Frank Lloyd Wright Dr., P.O. Box 997, Ann Arbor, MI 48106. To apply Church's moral teaching in business and personal lives of members. Legatus Newsletter, monthly.

**Lithuanian Groups:** Ateitininkai, members of Lithuanian Catholic Federation Ateitis (1910), 1209 Country Lane, Lemont, IL 60439; *Ateitis,* bimonthly; Pres., Juozas Polikaitis. Knights of Lithuania (1913), educational-fraternal organization; *Vytis,* monthly; Pres., Evelyn Ozelis, 2533 W. 45th St., Chicago, IL 60632. Lithuanian Catholic Alliance (1886), 71-73 S. Washington St., Wilkes-Barre, PA 18701; *Garsas,* 10 times a year; fraternal insurance organization;

Pres., Thomas E. Mack. Lithuanian Roman Catholic Federation of America (1906), umbrella organization for Lithuanian parishes and organizations; *The Observer,* bimonthly; Pres., Saulius Kuprys, 4545 W. 63rd St., Chicago, IL 60629. Lithuanian Roman Catholic Priests' League (1909): religious-professional association, Pres., Rev. Albert Contons, 50 Orton-Marotta Way, Boston, MA 02127. Lithuanian Catholic Religious Aid, Inc. (1961), 351 Highland Blvd., Brooklyn, NY 11207; to assist Catholics in Lithuania; Chairman and Pres., Most Rev. Paul Baltakis.

**Little Flower Mission League** (1957), P.O. Box 25, Plaucheville, LA 71362. Sponsored by the Brothers of the Holy Eucharist. Dir., Bro. André M. Lucia, F.S.E.

**Little Flower Society** (1923), 1313 Frontage Rd.; Darien, IL 60561; 200,000 Nat. Dir., Rev. Robert E. Colaresi, O. Carm.

**Liturgical Conference, The,** 8750 Georgia Ave., Suite 123, Silver Spring, MD 20910. *Liturgy, Homily Service.* Education, research and publication programs for renewing and enriching Christian liturgical life. Ecumenical.

**Loyal Christian Benefit Association** (1890), P.O. Box 13005, Erie, PA 16514. Fraternal benefit and insurance society. *The Fraternal Leader,* quarterly.

**Marian Movement of Priests** (1972), P.O. Box 8, St. Francis, ME 04774 (U.S.); Via Mercalli, 23, 20122 Milan, Italy (internatl. headquarters); 4,000 clergy; 50,000 religious and laity (U.S.). Spiritual renewal through consecration to the Immaculate Heart of Mary. Pres. Rev. Albert G. Roux.

**Mariological Society of America** (1949), Sec., Rev. Thomas A. Thompson, S.M., Marian Library, Box 1390, University of Dayton, Dayton, OH 45469. *Marian Studies,* annually. Founded by Rev. Juniper B. Carol, O.F.M., to promote greater appreciation of and scientific research in Marian theology.

**Maryheart Crusaders, The** (1964), 22 Button St., Meriden, CT 06450. Pres., Louise D'Angelo.

**Men of the Sacred Heart** (1964), Shrine of the Sacred Heart, P.O. Box 500, Harleigh, PA 18225. Promote enthronement of Sacred Heart.

**Missionary Association of Catholic Women** (1916), 3501 S. Lake Dr., P.O. Box 07912, Milwaukee, WI 53207.

**Missionary Vehicle Association, Inc. (MIVA America)** (1971), 1400 Michigan Ave., N.E., Washington, DC 20017. To raise funds and distribute them annually as vehicle grants to missionaries working with the poor in Third World countries. Nat. Dir., Rev. Philip De Rea, M.S.C.; Exec. Dir., Rev. Anthony F. Krisak.

**Morality in Media, Inc.** (1962), 475 Riverside Dr., New York, NY 10115. Interfaith national organization. Newsletter, bimonthly. Works by constitutional means to curb the explosive growth of hard-core pornography and to turn back the tide of grossly offensive, indecent media. A major project is the National Obscenity Law Center which provides legal information for prosecutors and other attorneys. Pres., Robert W. Peters.

**National Assembly of Religious Women**

(NARW): Founded as the National Assembly of Women Religious, 1970; title changed, 1980. A movement of feminist women committed to prophetic tasks of giving witness, raising awareness and engaging in public action and advocacy for justice in church and society. Address: 529 S. Wabash Ave., Suite 404, Chicago, IL 60605.

**National Association for Lay Ministry** (1977), 5420 S. Cornell Ave., Chicago, IL 60615. Acts as advocate and support for lay people who respond to a call to ministry in the Church.

**National Association of Catholic Family Life Ministers,** Univ. of Dayton, 300 College Park, Dayton, OH 45469. Strive to be a voice and advocate for families and family ministry in Church and society. Pres., Judy Clark.

**National Association of Catholic Home Educators** (1993), P.O. Box 420225, San Diego, CA 92142. Promotion of homeschooling. *The Catholic Home Educator,* quarterly.

**National Association of Church Personnel Administrators** (1971), 100 E. 8th St., Cincinnati, OH 45202. Exec. Dir., Sr. Ann White, S.L. Dedicated to promotion and development of just personnel practices for all church employees.

**National Association of Diocesan Ecumenical Officers,** Network of Catholics involved in ecumenical and interreligious work. Pes., Rev. Vincent A. Heier, 462 N. Taylor St., St. Louis, MO 63108.

**National Association of Pastoral Musicians** (1976), 225 Sheridan St., N.W., Washington, DC 20011; 9,000. Dedicated to fostering the art of musical liturgy. *Pastoral Music,* six times a year. Exec. Dir., Rev. Virgil C. Funk.

**National Association of Priest Pilots** (1964), Pres., Rev. John Hemann, 660 Bush Ave., Garner, IA 50438.

**National Catholic AIDS Network,** P.O. Box 422984, San Francisco, CA 94142. Exec. dir., Rev. Rodney DeMartini, S.M.

**National Catholic Band Association** (1953), Box 1023, Notre Dame University, Notre Dame, IN 46556.

**National Catholic Cemetery Conference** (1949), 710 N. River Rd., Des Plaines, IL 60016. Exec. Dir., Leo A. Droste.

**National Catholic Conference for Interracial Justice (NCCIJ)** (1960), 3033 Fourth St. N.E., Washington, DC 20017.

**National Catholic Conference of Airport Chaplains** (1986), Chicago O'Hare International Airport, P.O. Box 66353, Chicago, IL 60666. Provides support and communication for Catholics performing pastoral ministry to airport and airline workers and Catholic travelers; affiliated with Bishops' Committee on Migration, NCCB. Episcopal liaison, Most Rev. James C. Timlin. Pres., Rev. John A. Jamnicky.

**National Catholic Council on Alcoholism and Related Drug Problems, Inc.** 1550 Hendrickson St., Brooklyn, NY 11234. An affiliate of the NCCB/ USCC. Committed to assisting members in a greater awareness of alcoholism, other chemical addictions and prevention issues.

**National Catholic Development Conference** (1968), 86 Front St., Hempstead, NY 11550. Professional association of organizations and individuals engaged in raising funds for Catholic charitable activities. Pres., Peter A. Eltink; Exec. Dir., George T. Holloway.

**National Catholic Ministry to the Bereaved (NCMB)** (1990), 9412 Heath Ave, Cleveland, OH 44104. Offers ongoing education, resources and assistance to dioceses, parishes and caregivers in their ministry to the bereaved. Pres., J. Bernard Dahl.

**National Catholic Pharmacists Guild of the United States** (1962): *The Catholic Pharmacist.* Exec. Dir., John P. Winkelmann, 1012 Surrey Hills Dr., St. Louis, MO 63117.

**National Catholic Society of Foresters** (1891), 446 E. Ontario St., Chicago, IL 60611; 52,000; *National Catholic Forester,* quarterly. A fraternal insurance society. Pres., Sue Koleczek.

**National Catholic Stewardship Council** (1962), 1275 K St. N.W., Suite 980, Washington, DC 20005. A professional association which fosters an environment in which stewardship is understood, accepted and practiced throughout the church. Nat. Dir., Matthew R. Paratore.

**National Catholic Women's Union** (1916), 3835 Westminster Pl., St. Louis, MO 63108; 7,000.

**National Center for the Laity** (1977), 10 E. Pearson St., No. 101, Chicago, IL 60611. *Initiatives,* six times a year. To promote and implement the vision of Vatican II: That the laity are the Church in the modern world as they attend to their occupational, family and neighborhood responsibilities.

**National Center for Urban EthnicAffairs** (1971): P.O. Box 20, Cardinal Station, Washington, DC 20064. Research and action related to the Church's concern for cultural pluralism and urban neighborhoods. An affiliate of the USCC. Pres., Dr. John A. Kromkowski.

**National Christ Child Society Inc.** (1887): 5101 Wisconsin Ave. N.W., Suite 304, Washington, DC 20016. Founder, Mary V. Merrick. A non-profit Catholic association of volunteers of all denominations dedicated to the service of needy children and youth regardless of race or creed. Membership: approximately 8,000 adult members in 37 chapters in U.S. President, Mrs. Kathleen Gibbons.

**National Committee of Catholic Laymen, The** (1977), 150 E. 35th St., Room 840, New York, NY 10016. Lobbying and publishing organization representing "orthodox" Catholics who strongly support Pope John Paul II; *catholic eye,* monthly. Pres., J.P. McFadden.

**National Conference of Catechetical Leadership** (formerly, National Conference of Diocesan Directors of Religious Education) (1936): 3021 4th St. N.E., Washington, DC 20017; 1,300. To promote catechetical ministry at the national diocesan and parish levels. Exec. Dir., Neil A. Parent.

**National Conference of Diocesan Vocation Directors (NCDVD)** (1961), P.O. Box 1570, Little Silver, SC 29566. To provide diocesan vocation personnel with information and services regarding: awareness and discernment of vocations to the diocesan or religious priesthood and the religious life for both men and women; formation of diocesan priesthood candidates.

**National Council for Catholic Evangelization** (1983), 905 E. 166th St., P.O. Box 1260, S. Hol-

land, IL 60473. To promote evangelization as the "primary and essential mission of the Church," in accordance with *Evangelii Nuntiandi,* the 1975 apostolic exhortation of Pope Paul VI. Pres., Rev. Carl Tenhundfeld; exec. dir., John Simon.

**National Council of Catholic Men,** 4712 Randolph Dr., Annandale, VA 22003. A federation of Catholic organizations through which Catholic men may be heard nationally on matters of common interest. NCCM is a constituent of the National Council of Catholic Laity.

**National Council of Catholic Women** (1920), 1275 K St. N.W., Suite 975, Washington, DC 20005. A federation of some 7,000 organizations of Catholic women in the U.S. *Catholic Woman,* bimonthly. NCCW unites Catholic organizations and individual Catholic women of the U.S., develops their leadership potential, assists them to act upon current issues in the Church and society, provides a medium through which Catholic women may speak and act upon matters of common interest, and relates to other national and international organizations in the solution of present-day problems. It is an affiliate of the World Union of Catholic Women's Organizations. Exec. Dir., Annette P. Kane.

**National Evangelization Teams (NET),** 110 Crusader Ave., West St. Paul, MN 55118. Trains Catholic young adults to be evangelists to peers through traveling retreat teams.

**National Federation of Catholic Physicians' Guilds** (1927), 850 Elm Grove Rd., Elm Grove, WI 53122; *Linacre Quarterly.* Exec. Dir., Robert H. Herzog.

**National Federation of Priests' Councils** (1968), 1337 West Ohio, Chicago, IL 60622. To give priests' councils a representative voice in matters of presbyteral, pastoral and ministerial concern to the U.S. and the universal Church. Pres., Rev. Donald Wolf; exec. dir., Bro. Bernard Stratman, S.M.

**National Federation of Spiritual Directors** (1972). Pres., Rev. George P. Evans, St. John Seminary, 127 Lake St., Brighton, MA 02135. Responsible for priestly spiritual formation in high school and college seminaries, novitiates, theologates and houses of formation in the U.S.

**National Institute for the Word of God** (1972), 487 Michigan Ave. N.E., Washington, DC 20017. For renewed biblical preaching, Bible sharing and evangelization. Dir., Rev. John Burke, O.P.

**National Life Center, Inc.,** 686 N. Broad St., Woodbury, NJ 08096. Interdenominational guidance and referral service organization offering pregnant women alternatives to abortion. Pres., Denise F. Cocciolone,

**National Organization for Continuing Education of Roman Catholic Clergy, Inc.** (1973), 1337 W. Ohio St., Chicago, IL 60622. Membership: 157 dioceses, 81 religious provinces, 47 associates in U.S., 18 associates outside U.S. Pres., Rev. Francis S. Tebbe, O.F.M.; Exec. Dir., Bro. Paul J. Murray, C.F.X.

**National Pastoral Life Center,** 299 Elizabeth St., New York, NY 10012. Services for parishes. *Church,* quarterly. Director, Rev. Philip Murnion.

**NETWORK** (1971), 801 Pennsylvania Ave. S.E., Suite 460, Washington, DC 20003. *NETWORK Con-*

*nection,* bimonthly. A national Catholic social justice lobby. Nat. Coord., Kathy Thornton, R.S.M.

**Nocturnal Adoration Society of the United States** (1882), 184 E. 76th St., New York, NY 10021. Nat. Dir., Rev. Bernard J. Camire, S.S.S.

**North American Academy of Liturgy,** c/o CSSR Executive Office, Valparaiso Univ., Valparaiso, IN 46383. *Proceedings,* annually. Foster ecumenical and interreligious liturgical research, publication and dialogue on a scholarly level. Pres., Frank Senn.

**North American Conference of Separated and Divorced Catholics** (1972), President, Kathy Brewer, P.O. Box 1301, LaGrande, OR 97850.

**North American Forum on the Catechumenate,** 7115 Leesburg Pike, Suite 308, Falls Church, VA 22043.

**Order of the Alhambra** (1904), 4200 Leeds Ave., Baltimore, MD 21229. 7,000 in U.S. and Canada. Fraternal society dedicated to assisting developmentally disabled and handicapped children. Supreme Commander, Thomas G. Kelly.

**Our Lady's Rosary Makers** (1949), 4611 Poplar Level Rd., P.O. Box 37080, Louisville, KY 40233; 20,000 members. To supply missionaries with free rosaries for distribution throughout the world. News Bulletin, monthly. Pres., Harry Prestwood, Deacon.

**Paulist National Catholic Evangelization Association** (1977), 3031 Fourth St., N.E., Washington, DC 20017. *Share the Word,* bimonthly magazine. To work with unchurched and alienated Catholics; to develop, test and document contemporary ways in which Catholic parishes and dioceses can evangelize the unchurched and inactive Catholics. Dir., Rev. Kenneth Boyack, C.S.P.

**Perpetual Eucharistic Adoration,** 660 Club View Dr., Los Angeles, CA 90024. Promote programs of Perpetual Eucharistic adoration/exposition in parishes throughout the world.

**Philangeli (Friends of the Angels)** (1949 in England; 1956 in U.S.), Viatorian Fathers, 1115 E. Euclid St., Arlington Heights, IL 60004.

**Pious Union of Prayer** (1898), St. Joseph's Home, 537 Pavonia Ave., Jersey City, NJ 07306; 20,000. *St. Joseph's Messenger and Advocate of the Blind,* quarterly.

**Polish Roman Catholic Union of America** (1887): 984 N. Milwaukee Ave., Chicago, IL 60622. *Narod Polski,* bimonthly. Fraternal benefit society.

**Pontifical Mission for Palestine** (1949), 1011 First Ave., New York, NY 10022. A papal relief and development agency of the Holy See for the Middle East, with offices in New York, Vatican City, Amman, Beirut and Jerusalem.

**Pontifical Missionary Union** (1916), 366 Fifth Ave., New York, NY 10001. To promote mission awareness among clergy, religious, candidates to priestly and religious life, and others engaged in pastoral ministry of the Church. Nat. Dir., Most Rev. William J. McCormack; Nat. Sec., Rev. Eugene LaVerdiere, S.S.S.

**Priests' Eucharistic League** (1887), 5384 Wilson Mills Rd., Cleveland, OH 44143; 5,000. *Emmanuel,* 10 issues a year. Nat. Dir., Rev. Anthony Schueller, S.S.S.

**Pro Ecclesia Foundation** (1970), 350 5th Ave., Room 3304, New York, NY 10118. Pres., Dr. Timothy A. Mitchell.

**Pro Maria Committee** (1952), 22 Second Ave., Lowell, MA 01854. Promote devotion to Our Lady of Beauraing (See Index).

**Pro Sanctity Movement.** A worldwide force of laity organized to spread God's call of all persons to holiness. Addresses: 205 S. Pine Dr., Fullerton, CA 92633; 730 E. 87th St., Brooklyn, NY 11236; 6762 Western Ave., Omaha, NE 68132; 1102 N. 204 St. Elkhorn, NE 68022.

**Project Children** (1975), P.O. Box 933, Greenwood Lake, NY 10925. Nonsectarian volunteer group; provide children of Northern Ireland with a six-week summer vacation with host families in the U.S.

**The Providence Association of the Ukrainian Catholics in America** (Ukrainian Catholic Fraternal Benefit Society) (1912), 817 N. Franklin St., Philadelphia, PA 19123.

**Queen of the Americas Guild, Inc.** (1979), P.O. Box 851, 345 Kautz Rd., St. Charles, IL 60174; 7,000 members. To build English information center and retreat center near Basilica in Mexico City and spread the message of Guadalupe. Pres., Frank E. Smoczynski.

**Raskob Foundation for Catholic Activities, Inc.** (1945), Kennett Pike and Montchanin Rd., P.O. Box 4019, Wilmington, DE 19807. Pres., Gerard S. Garey.

**Renew,** International Office, 1232 George St., Plainfield, NJ 07062.

**Reparation Society of the Immaculate Heart of Mary, Inc.** (1946), 100 E. 20th St., Baltimore, MD 21218. *Fatima Findings,* monthly.

**Sacred Heart League,** 6050 Hwy 61 N, P.O. Box 190, Walls, MS 38680. Pres., Rev. Robert Hess, S.C.J.

**St. Ansgar's Scandinavian Catholic League** (1910), 40 W. 13th St., New York, NY 10011; 1,000. *St. Ansgar's Bulletin,* annually. Prayers and financial support for Church in Scandinavia. Pres., Astrid M. O'Brien.

**St. Anthony's Guild** (1924), Paterson, NJ 07509; 100,000. Promotes devotion to St. Anthony of Padua and support for formation programs, infirm friars and ministries of the Franciscans of Holy Name Province. *The Anthonian,* quarterly. Dir., Rev. Joseph Hertel, O.F.M.

**St. Bernadette Institute of Sacred Art** (1993), P.O. Box 8249, Albuquerque, NM 87198. To promote, initiate, encourage interest and sustain projects and persons engaged in sacred art.

**St. Gregory Foundation for Latin Liturgy** (1989), 15 E. 26th St., Bayonne, NJ 07002. To promote within the Church in the U.S. the use of the Latin language in the Mass in accordance with the teachings of Vatican II. Founder and Pres., Rev. Peter M.J. Stravinskas.

**St. Jude League** (1929), 205 W. Monroe St., Chicago, IL 60606. Promotes devotion to St. Jude; supports work of Claretian Missionaries throughout the world. Dir., Rev. Mark J. Brummel, C.M.F.

**St. Margaret of Scotland Guild, Inc.** (1938), Graymoor, Garrison, NY 10524; 500. Moderator, Bro. Nicholas De Gruccio, S.A.

**St. Martin de Porres Guild** (1935), 141 E. 65th St., New York, NY 10021. Dir., Rev. Edward L. Martin, O.P.

**Serra International** (1934), 65 E. Wacker Pl., suite 1210, Chicago, IL 60601; 20,500 members in 623 clubs in 35 countries. *Serran,* bimonthly. Fosters vocations to the priesthood, and religious life, trains Catholic lay leadership. Formally aggregated to the Pontifical Society for Priestly Vocations, 1951.

**Slovak Catholic Federation** (1911): Founded by Rev. Joseph Murgas to promote and coordinate religious activities among Slovak Catholic fraternal societies, religious communities and Slovak ethnic parishes in their effort to address themselves to the special needs of Slovak Catholics in the U.S. and Canada. Pres., Rev. Msgr. Thomas V. Banick, 134 S. Washington St., P.O. Box 348, Wilkes-Barre, PA 18703.

**Slovak Catholic Sokol** (1905), 205 Madison St., Passaic, NJ 07055; 33,000. *Slovak Catholic Falcon,* weekly. Fraternal benefit society.

**Society for the Propagation of the Faith** (1822), 366 Fifth Ave., New York, NY 10001; established in all dioceses. Church's principal instrument for promoting mission awareness and generating financial support for the missions. General fund for ordinary and extraordinary subsidies for all mission dioceses. *Mission,* 4 times a year; *Director's Newsletter,* monthly. Is subject to Congregation for the Evangelization of Peoples. Nat. Dir., Most Rev. William J. McCormack.

**Society of St. Monica** (1986): 215 Falls Ave., Cuyahoga Falls, OH 44221; more than 10,000 members worldwide. Confident, daily prayer for the return of inactive Catholics and Catholics who have left the Church. Founder and spiritual director, Rev. Dennis M. McNeil.

**Society of St. Peter Apostle** (1889), 366 Fifth Ave., New York, NY 10001; all dioceses. Church's central fund for support of seminaries, seminarians and novices in all mission dioceses. Nat. Dir., Most Rev. William J. McCormack.

**Society of the Divine Attributes** (1974). Contemplative prayer society; 3,000 members worldwide (lay, clerical and religious). Spir. Dir. Rev. Ronald D. Lawler, O.F.M. Cap., 2905 Castlegate Ave., Pittsburgh, PA 15226.

**Spiritual Life Institute of America** (1960), Box 219, Crestone, CO 81131. *Forefront,* seasonal. An eremetical movement to foster the contemplative spirit in America. Founder, Rev. William McNamara, O.C.D. Second foundation: *Nova Nada,* Primitive Wilderness Hermitage, Kemptville, Nova Scotia, Canada B0W 1Y0. Third foundation, Holy Hill Hermitage, Skreen, Co. Sligo, Ireland.

**Support Our Aging Religious (SOAR)** (1986), 8820 Cameron St., Silver Spring, MD 20910. Laity-led campaign to raise funds for retired religious.

**Theresians of the United States** (1961), 2577 N. Chelton Rd., Suite 207, Colorado Springs, CO 80909. Spiritual, educational and ministerial organization of Christian women. Exec. Dir., Sr. Rose Ann Barmann, O.S.B. International division: **Theresian World Ministry** (1971), same address.

**United Societies of U.S.A.** (1903), 613 Sinclair St., McKeesport, PA 15132; 3,796 members. *Prosvita-Enlightenment,* bimonthly newspaper.

**United States Catholic Historical Society** (1884), The Catholic Center, 1011 First Ave., New York, NY 10022. Chairman, Brian Butler. Exec Dir., Charles J. Eames.

**Western Catholic Union** (1877), 510 Maine St., Quincy, IL 62301; 19,000 members. *Western Catholic Union Record,* quarterly.

**Women for Faith and Family** (1984), P.O. Box 8326, St. Louis, MO 63132. *Voices,* quarterly. An international movement to promote Catholic teachings especially on all issues involving the family and roles for women. Members sign an 8-point statement of fidelity to the Church; 60,000 signers worldwide. Dir., Helen Hull Hitchcock.

**Young Ladies' Institute** (1887), P.O. Box 640687, San Francisco, CA 94164; 13,000. *Voice of YLI,* bimonthly. Grand Sec., Claire Skidmore.

**Young Men's Institute** (1883), 50 Oak St., San Francisco, CA 94102; 4,500. *Institute Journal,* bimonthly. Grand Sec., S. J. Welch.

# KNIGHTS OF COLUMBUS

The Knights of Columbus, which originated as a fraternal benefit society of Catholic men, was founded by Father Michael J. McGivney and chartered by the General Assembly of Connecticut Mar. 29, 1882.

K. of C. membership currently totals over 1.5 million in more than 10,500 councils in the U.S., Canada, the Philippines, Mexico, Puerto Rico, Panama, Guatemala, Guam, the Dominican Republic, the Virgin Islands, the Bahamas and Saipan.

In line with their general purpose to be of service to the Church, the Knights are active in many apostolic works and community programs.

Since January, 1947, the Knights have sponsored a program of Catholic advertising in secular publications with national circulation. This has brought some 8 million inquiries and led to more than 800,000 enrollments in courses in the Catholic faith.

The Knights cooperate with the U.S. bishops in pro-life activities and are engaged in other apostolic endeavors as well. In 1995, local units of the Knights contributed more than $105 million to charitable and benevolent causes, and provided almost 50 million hours of community service. Their publication, *Columbia,* has the largest circulation (over 1.5 million) of any Catholic monthly in North America. Supreme Knight: Virgil C. Dechant. International headquarters: One Columbus Plaza, New Haven, CT 06507.

# COMMUNICATIONS

## CATHOLIC PRESS STATISTICS

The *1996 Catholic Press Directory,* published by the Catholic Press Association, reported a total of 644 periodicals in North America with a circulation of 25,343,743. The figures included 198 newspapers with a circulation of 5,997,110; 276 magazines with a circulation of 14,875,114; 133 newsletters with a circulation of 3,729,491, and 37 other-language periodicals (newspapers and magazines) with a circulation of 742,028.

### Newspapers in the U.S.

There were 185 newspapers in the United States, with a circulation 5,859,310. Five of these had national circulation; 167 were diocesan newspapers; 13 were Eastern Catholic Church publications.

National newspapers included: *National Catholic Register,* founded 1900; *Our Sunday Visitor,* founded 1912; *National Catholic Reporter,* founded 1964; *Catholic Twin Circle,* founded 1967 and *The Wanderer.*

The oldest Catholic newspaper in the United States is *The Pilot* of Boston, established in 1829 (under a different title).

**Other Diocesan Newspapers:** There were three other diocesan newspapers located outside continental North America (Samoa, U.S. Virgin Islands, West Indies), with a circulation of 21,700.

### Magazines in U.S.

The *Catholic Press Directory* reported 254 magazines in the U.S. with a circulation of 14,011,477. In addition, there were 132 newsletters; circulation, 3,717,491.

*America* and *Commonweal* are the only weekly and biweekly magazines, respectively, of general interest.

The monthly magazines with the largest circulation are *Columbia* (1,454,282), the official organ of the Knights of Columbus, *Catholic Digest* (500,000) and *St. Anthony's Messenger* (321,595).

**Other-Language Publications:** There were an additional 25 publications (newspapers and magazines) in the U.S. in languages other than English with a circulation of 460,528.

### Canadian Statistics

There were 10 newspapers in Canada with a circulation of 116,100. These included two national newspapers (*The Catholic Register,* founded 1893; *Catholic New Times,* founded 1976) and 8 diocesan.

There were 22 magazines with a circulation of 863,637; one newsletter with a circulation of 12,000; and 12 publications in languages other than English, circulation, 281,500.

## CATHOLIC NEWSPAPERS AND MAGAZINES IN THE U.S.

(Sources: *Catholic Press Directory; The Catholic Journalist;* Almanac survey; Catholic News Service.)

*Abbreviation code: a, annual; bm, bimonthly; m, monthly; q, quarterly; w, weekly.*

### Newspapers

**Acadiana Catholic,** m; 1408 Carmel Ave., Lafayette, LA 70501; Lafayette diocese.

**A.D. Times,** biweekly; 2141 Downyflake Lane, Allentown, PA 18103. Allentown diocese.

**Agua Viva,** m; 1280 Med Park Dr., Las Cruces, NM 88005; Las Cruces diocese.

**Alaskan Shepherd,** 6 times a year; 1312 Peger Rd., Fairbanks, AK 99709; Fairbanks diocese.

**America** (Ukrainian-English), 2 times a week; 817 N. Franklin St., Philadelphia, PA 19123. Providence Association of Ukrainian Catholics in America.

**Anchor, The** w; P.O. Box 7, Fall River, MA 02722; Fall River diocese.

**Arkansas Catholic,** w; P.O. Box 7417, Little Rock, AR 72217; Little Rock diocese.

**Arlington Catholic Herald,** w; 200 N. Glebe Rd., Suite 607, Arlington, VA 22203; Arlington diocese.

**Bayou Catholic, The,** w; P.O. Box 9077, Houma, LA 70361; Houma-Thibodaux diocese.

**Beacon, The,** w; P.O. Box 1887, Clifton, NJ 07015. Paterson diocese.

**Bishop's Bulletin,** m; P.O. Box 665, Yankton, SD 57078. Sioux Falls diocese.

**Byzantine Catholic World,** biweekly; 925 Liberty Ave., P.O. Box 1215, Pittsburgh, PA 15230; Pittsburgh Byzantine archdiocese.

**Catholic Accent,** 40 times a year; P.O. Box 850, Greensburg, PA 15601; Greensburg diocese.

**Catholic Advance, The,** w; 424 N. Broadway, Wichita, KS 67202; Wichita diocese.

**Catholic Advocate, The,** w; 171 Clifton Ave., Newark, NJ 07104; Newark archdiocese.

**Catholic Calendar,** semi-monthly; 4029 Avenue G, Lake Charles, LA 70615; one page in local newspaper twice a month; Lake Charles diocese.

**Catholic Chronicle,** biweekly; P.O. Box 1866, Toledo, OH 43603; Toledo diocese.

**Catholic Commentator, The,** biweekly; P.O. Box 14746, Baton Rouge, LA 70898; Baton Rouge diocese.

**Catholic Courier,** w; 1150 Buffalo Rd., Rochester, NY 14624. Rochester diocese.

**Catholic East Texas,** biweekly; 1015 ESE Loop 323, Tyler, TX 75701. Tyler diocese.

**Catholic Exponent,** biweekly; P.O. Box 6787, Youngstown, OH 44501; Youngstown diocese.

**Catholic Free Press,** w; 47 Elm St., Worcester, MA 01609; Worcester diocese.

**Catholic Herald, The,** m; 514 El Paso Blvd., Manitou Springs, CO 80829; Colorado Springs diocese.

**Catholic Herald,** w; P.O. Box 07913, Milwaukee, WI 53207; Milwaukee archdiocese. Also publishes editions for Madison and Superior dioceses.

**Catholic Herald — Madison Edition,** w; P.O. Box 5913, Madison, WI 53705.

**Catholic Herald — Superior Edition,** w; P.O. Box 969, Superior, WI 54880.

**Catholic Herald,** w; 5890 Newman Ct., Sacramento, CA 95819; Sacramento diocese.

**Catholic Hungarian's Sunday,** w; P.O. Box 42067, Cleveland, OH 44142.

**Catholic Key,** 44 times a year; P.O. Box 419037, Kansas City, MO 64141; Kansas City-St. Joseph diocese.

**Catholic Lantern,** m; P.O. Box 4237, Stockton, CA 95204; Stockton diocese.

**Catholic Light,** biweekly; P.O. Box 708, Scranton, PA 18501; Scranton diocese.

**Catholic Lighthouse,** m; P.O. Box 4070, Victoria, TX 77903; Victoria diocese.

**Catholic Messenger,** w; P.O. Box 460, Davenport, IA 52805; Davenport diocese.

**Catholic Mirror The,** m; P.O. Box 10372, Des Moines, IA 50306. Des Moines diocese.

**Catholic Missourian,** w; P.O. Box 1107, Jefferson City, MO 65102; Jefferson City diocese.

**Catholic Moment, The,** w; P.O. Box 1603, Lafayette, IN 47902; Lafayette diocese.

**Catholic New York,** w; P.O. Box 5133, New York, NY 10150; New York archdiocese.

**Catholic News and Herald, The,** w; 1524 E. Morehead St., Charlotte, NC 28207. Charlotte diocese.

**Catholic Northwest Progress, The,** w; 910 Marion St., Seattle, WA 98104; Seattle archdiocese.

**Catholic Observer,** biweekly; Box 1570, Springfield, MA 01101; Springfield diocese.

**Catholic Post, The,** w; P.O. Box 1722, Peoria, IL 61656; Peoria diocese.

**Catholic Register,** biweekly; 126C Logan Blvd., Hollidaysburg, PA 16648; Altoona-Johnstown diocese.

**Catholic Review,** w; P.O. Box 777, Baltimore, MD 21203; Baltimore archdiocese.

**Catholic Sentinel,** w; P.O. Box 18030, Portland, OR 97218; Portland archdiocese, Baker diocese.

**Catholic Spirit, The,** w; 244 Dayton Ave., St. Paul, MN 55102; St. Paul and Minneapolis archdiocese.

**Catholic Spirit, The,** w; P.O. Box 5247, Kendall Park, NJ 08824; Metuchen diocese.

**Catholic Spirit, The,** m; P.O. Box 13327, Capitol Sta., Austin, TX 78711; Austin diocese.

**Catholic Spirit, The,** biweekly; P.O. Box 951, Wheeling, WV 26003; Wheeling-Charleston diocese.

**Catholic Standard,** w; P.O. Box 4464, Washington, DC 20017; Washington archdiocese.

**Catholic Standard and Times,** w; 222 N. 17th St., Philadelphia, PA 19103; Philadelphia archdiocese.

**Catholic Star Herald,** w; 1845 Haddon Ave., Camden, NJ 08101; Camden diocese.

**Catholic Sun, The,** semimonthly; 400 E. Monroe, Phoenix, AZ 85004; Phoenix diocese.

**Catholic Sun, The,** w; 421 S. Warren St., Syracuse, NY 13202; Syracuse diocese.

**Catholic Telegraph,** w; 100 E. 8th St., Cincinnati, OH 45202; Cincinnati archdiocese.

**Catholic Times,** w; P.O. Box 636, Columbus, OH 43216; Columbus diocese.

**Catholic Times,** w; P.O. Box 4248, Flint, MI 48504. Lansing diocese.

**Catholic Times,** w; 1615 W. Washington St., P.O. Box 3187, Springfield, IL 62708; Springfield diocese.

**Catholic Today,** m; P.O. Box 31, Tucson, AZ 85702; Tucson diocese.

**Catholic Transcript,** w; 785 Asylum Ave., Hartford, CT 06105; Hartford archdiocese; Bridgeport and Norwich dioceses.

**Catholic Twin Circle,** w; 15760 Ventura Blvd., Suite 1201, Encino, CA 91436; national.

**Catholic Universe Bulletin,** biweekly; 1027 Superior Ave. N.E., Cleveland, OH 44114; Cleveland diocese.

**Catholic Virginian,** biweekly; Box 26843, Richmond, VA 23261; Richmond diocese.

**Catholic Voice, The,** biweekly; 3014 Lakeshore Ave., Oakland, CA 94610; Oakland diocese.

**Catholic Voice, The,** biweekly; P.O. Box 4010, Omaha, NE 68104; Omaha archdiocese.

**Catholic Week,** w; P.O. Box 349, Mobile, AL 36601; Mobile archdiocese.

**Catholic Weekly, The,** w; 1520 Court St., Saginaw, MI 48602; Saginaw diocese.

**Catholic Weekly, The,** w; P.O. Box 1405, Saginaw, MI 48605. Gaylord diocese.

**Catholic Witness, The,** biweekly; P.O. Box 2555, Harrisburg, PA 17105; Harrisburg diocese.

**Catolico de Texas, El** (Spanish), m; P.O. Box 190347, Dallas, TX 75219; Dallas diocese.

**Central Washington Catholic,** 6 times a year; 5301-A Tieton Dr., Yakima, WA 98908. Yakima diocese.

**Challenge, The,** semimonthly; 2530 Victory Pkwy., Cincinnati, OH 45206. St. Maron diocese.

**Chicago Catolico** (Spanish), m; 1144 W. Jackson Blvd., Chicago, IL 60607; Chicago archdiocese.

**Chronicle of Catholic Life,** bm; 514 El Paso Blvd. Manitou Springs, CO 80829; Pueblo diocese.

**Church Today,** twice a month; P.O. Box 7417, Alexandria, LA 71306; Alexandria diocese.

**Church World,** w; Industry Rd., P.O. Box 698, Brunswick, ME 04011; Portland diocese.

**Clarion Herald,** biweekly; P.O. Box 53247, New Orleans, LA 70153; New Orleans archdiocese.

**Common Sense,** w; P. O. Box 41679, Memphis, TN 38174; Memphis diocese.

**Community,** w; P.O. Box 24000, Jacksonville, FL 32241; half-page weekly in Sunday editions of two daily newspapers; St. Augustine diocese.

**Compass, The,** w; P.O. Box 23825, Green Bay, WI 54305; Green Bay diocese.

**Courier, The,** m; P.O. Box 949, Winona, MN 55987; Winona diocese.

**Criterion, The,** w; P.O. Box 1717, Indianapolis, IN 46206; Indianapolis archdiocese.

**Cross Roads,** 26 times a year; 1310 Leestown Rd., Lexington, KY 40508. Lexington diocese.

**Dakota Catholic Action,** m (exc. May and Aug.); P.O. Box 1137, Bismarck, ND 58502; Bismarck diocese.

**Darbininkas (The Worker)** (Lithuanian), w; 341 Highland Blvd., Brooklyn, NY 11207; Lithuanian Franciscans.

**Denver Catholic Register,** w; 200 Josephine St., Denver, CO 80206; Denver archdiocese.

**Dialog, The,** w; P.O. Box 2208, Wilmington, DE 19899; Wilmington diocese.

**Diocese of Orange Bulletin,** m; P.O. Box 14195, Orange, CA 92613.

**Draugas** (Lithuanian); 4545 W. 63rd St., Chicago, IL 60629; Lithuanian Catholic Press Society.

**East Tennessee Catholic, The,** biweekly; P.O. Box 11127, Knoxville, TN 37939; Knoxville diocese.
**East Texas Catholic,** semimonthly; P.O. Box 3948, Beaumont, TX 77705; Beaumont diocese.
**Eastern Catholic Life,** biweekly; 445 Lackawanna Ave., W. Paterson, NJ 07424; Passaic Byzantine eparchy.
**Eastern Oklahoma Catholic,** biweekly; Box 520, Tulsa, OK 74101; Tulsa diocese.
**Evangelist, The,** w; 40 N. Main Ave., Albany, NY 12203; Albany diocese.

**Fairfield County Catholic,** m; 238 Jewett Ave., Bridgeport, CT 06606; Bridgeport diocese.
**Florida Catholic, The,** w; P.O. Box 609512, Orlando, FL 32860; Orlando diocese. Publishes editions for Miami archdiocese and Palm Beach, Pensacola-Tallahassee, St. Petersburg and Venice dioceses.
**Florida Catholic — Miami Edition,** w; 9401 Biscayne Blvd., Miami, FL 33138.
**Florida Catholic — Palm Beach Edition,** w; 9995 N. Military Trail, Palm Beach Gardens, FL 33410.
**Florida Catholic — Pensacola-Tallahassee Edition,** w; 11 North B St., Pensacola, FL 32501.
**Florida Catholic — St. Petersburg Edition,** w; P.O. Box 43022, St. Petersburg, FL 33743.
**Florida Catholic — Venice Edition,** w; 1000 Pinebrook Rd., Venice, FL 34292.
**Four County Catholic,** m; 1595 Norwich New London Turnpike, Uncasville, CT 06382. Norwich diocese.

**Georgia Bulletin,** w; 680 W. Peachtree St. N.W., Atlanta, GA 30308; Atlanta archdiocese.
**Glasilo KSKJH Amerikanski Slovenec** (Slovenian), biweekly; 708 E. 159th, Cleveland, OH 44110; American Slovenian Catholic Union.
**Globe, The,** w; 1825 Jackson St., Sioux City, IA 51105; Sioux City diocese.
**Gulf Pine Catholic,** w; P.O. Box 1189, Biloxi, MS 39533; Biloxi diocese.

**Hawaii Catholic Herald,** biweekly; 1184 Bishop St., Honolulu, HI 96813; Honolulu diocese.
**Heraldo Catolico, El** (Spanish), biweekly; 5890 Newman Ct., Sacramento, CA 95819; Sacramento diocese.
**Hlas Naroda** (Voice of the Nation) (Czech-English), biweekly; 2340 61st Ave., Cicero, IL 60650.
**Horizons,** semi-monthly; 1900 Carlton Rd., Parma, OH 44134; Parma Byzantine eparchy.

**Idaho Register,** 3 times a month; 303 Federal Way, Boise, ID 83705; Boise diocese.
**Inland Catholic,** m; 1201 E. Highland Ave., San Bernardino, CA 92404. San Bernardino diocese.
**Inland Register,** every 3 weeks; P.O. Box 48, Spokane, WA 99210; Spokane diocese.
**Inside Passage,** biweekly; 419 6th St., Juneau, AK 99801; Juneau diocese.
**Intermountain Catholic,** w; P.O. Box 2489, Salt Lake City, UT 84110; Salt Lake City diocese.

**Jednota** (Slovak-Eng.), w; 6611 Rockside Rd., Independence, OH 44131; First Catholic Slovak Union.

**Lake Shore Visitor,** w; P.O. Box 10668, Erie, PA 16514; Erie diocese.
**Leaven, The,** w; 12615 Parallel Parkway, Kansas City, KS 66109; Kansas City archdiocese.
**Long Island Catholic, The,** w; P.O. Box 9009, Rockville Centre, NY 11571; Rockville Centre diocese.

**Message, The,** w; P.O. Box 4169, Evansville, IN 47724; Evansville diocese.
**Messenger, The,** w; 2620 Lebanon Ave., Belleville, IL 62221; Belleville diocese.
**Messenger, The,** 45 times a year; P.O. Box 18068, Covington, KY 41018; Covington diocese.
**Michigan Catholic, The,** w; 305 Michigan Ave., Detroit, MI 48226; Detroit archdiocese.
**Mirror, The,** w; 601 S. Jefferson Ave., Springfield, MO 65806; Springfield-Cape Girardeau diocese.
**Mississippi Today,** w; P.O. Box 2130, Jackson, MS 39225; Jackson diocese.
**Monitor, The ,** w; P.O. Box 3095, Trenton, NJ 08619; Trenton diocese.
**Montana Catholic, The,** 16 times a year; P.O. Box 1729, Helena, MT 59624; Helena diocese.

**Narod Polski (Polish Nation)** (Polish-Eng.) semimonthly; 984 Milwaukee Ave., Chicago, IL 60622.
**National Catholic Register,** w; 15760 Ventura Blvd., Suite 1201, Encino, CA 91436.
**National Catholic Reporter,** w; P.O. Box 419281, Kansas City, MO 64141.
**New Catholic Explorer,** w (biweekly July, Aug.); 402 S. Independence Blvd., Romeoville, IL 60441; Joliet diocese.
**New Catholic Miscellany, The,** w; 119 Broad St., Charleston, SC 29401; Charleston diocese.
**New Earth, The,** m; 244 Dayton Ave., St. Paul, MN 55102. Fargo diocese.
**New Star, The,** every 3 weeks; 2208 W. Chicago Ave., Chicago, IL 60622; St. Nicholas of Chicago Ukrainian diocese.
**New World, The,** w; 1144 W. Jackson Blvd., Chicago, IL 60607; Chicago archdiocese.
**Newsletter, The,** 9 times a year; 215 N. Westnedge, Kalamazoo, MI 49007; Kalamazoo diocese.
**NC Catholic,** 26 times a year; 300 Cardinal Gibbons Dr., Raleigh, NC 27606. Raleigh diocese.
**North Country Catholic,** w; P.O. Box 326, Ogdensburg, NY 13669; Ogdensburg diocese.
**North Texas Catholic,** w; 800 West Loop 820 South, Fort Worth, TX 76108; Fort Worth diocese.
**Northwest Indiana Catholic,** w; 9292 Broadway, Merrillville, IN 46410; Gary diocese.
**Northwestern Kansas Register,** w; P.O. Box 1038, Salina, KS 67402; Salina diocese.
**Nosotros** (Spanish), biweekly; 6016 Monroe Place, West New York, NJ 07093; independent.

**Observer, The,** m; P.O. Box 2079, Monterey, CA 93942; Monterey diocese.
**Observer, The,** twice a month; 921 W. State St., Rockford, IL 61102; Rockford diocese.

**One Voice,** w; P.O. Box 10822, Birmingham, AL 35202; Birmingham diocese.

**Our Northland Diocese,** semi-monthly; P.O. Box 610, Crookston, MN 56716; Crookston diocese._

**Our Sunday Visitor,** w; 200 Noll Plaza, Huntington, IN 46750; national.

**People of God,** m; 4000 St. Joseph Pl. N.W., Albuquerque, NM 87120; Santa Fe archdiocese.

**Pilot, The,** w; 49 Franklin St., Boston, MA 02110; Boston archdiocese.

**Pittsburgh Catholic,** w; 135 First Ave., Suite 200, Pittsburgh, PA 15222; Pittsburgh diocese.

**Prairie Catholic,** m; 1400 6th St. North, New Ulm, MN 56073. New Ulm diocese.

**Pregonero, El** (Spanish), w; P.O. Box 4464, Washington, DC 20017; Washington archdiocese.

**Providence Visitor, The,** w; 184 Broad St., Providence, RI 02903. Providence diocese.

**Record, The,** w; 1200 S. Shelby St., Louisville, KY 40203; Louisville archdiocese.

**Redwood Crozier, The,** m; 547 B St., Santa Rosa, CA 95401; Santa Rosa diocese.

**Rio Grande Catholic, The,** 12 times a year; 499 St. Matthews St., El Paso, TX 79907; El Paso diocese.

**St. Cloud Visitor,** w; P. O. Box 1068, St. Cloud, MN 56302; St. Cloud diocese.

**St. Louis Review,** w; 462 N. Taylor Ave., St. Louis, MO 63108; St. Louis archdiocese.

**Seasons,** q; 5800 Weiss St., Saginaw, MI 48603.

**Slovak Catholic Falcon** (Slovak-English); w; 205 Madison St., P.O.Box 899, Passaic, NJ 07055; Slovak Catholic Sokol.

**Sooner Catholic, The,** biweekly; P.O. Box 32180, Oklahoma City, OK 73123; Oklahoma City archdiocese.

**Sophia,** q; 11245 Rye St., North Hollywood, CA 91602; Newton Melkite eparchy.

**South Plains Catholic,** twice a month; P.O. Box 98700, Lubbock, TX 79499; Lubbock diocese.

**South Texas Catholic,** biweekly; 1200 Lantana St., Corpus Christi, TX 78407; Corpus Christi diocese.

**Southern Cross,** semimonthly; P.O. Box 81869, San Diego, CA 92138; San Diego diocese.

**Southern Cross, The,** w; P.O. Box 948, Waynesboro, GA 30830; Savannah diocese.

**Southern Nebraska Register,** w; P.O. Box 80329, Lincoln, NE 68501; Lincoln diocese.

**Southwest Catholic,** m; 4029 Avenue G, Lake Charles, LA 70615 Lake Charles diocese.

**Southwest Kansas Register,** biweekly; P.O. Box 137, Dodge City, KS 67801; Dodge City diocese.

**Sower** (Ukrainian and English), biweekly; 14 Peveril Rd., Stamford, CT 06902. Stamford Ukrainian diocese.

**Star of Chaldeans** (Arabic and English), bm; 25585 Berg Rd., Southfield, MI 48034. St. Thomas the Apostle Chaldean diocese.

**Steubenville Register,** biweekly; P.O. Box 160, Steubenville, OH 43952; Steubenville diocese.

**Tablet, The,** w; 653 Hicks St., Brooklyn, NY 11231; Brooklyn diocese.

**Tennessee Register, The,** biweekly; 2400 21st Ave. S., Nashville, TN 37212; Nashville diocese.

**Texas Catholic,** biweekly; P.O. Box 190347, Dallas, TX 75219; Dallas diocese.

**Texas Catholic Herald, The,** semi-monthly; 1700 San Jacinto St., Houston, TX 77002; Galveston-Houston diocese.

**Tidings,** 11 times a year; 153 Ash St., Manchester, NH 03105._

**Tidings, The,** w; 1530 W. 9th St., Los Angeles, CA 90015; Los Angeles archdiocese.

**Times Review, The,** w; P.O. Box 4004, La Crosse, WI 54602; La Crosse diocese.

**Today's Catholic,** w; P.O. Box 11169, Fort Wayne, IN 46856; Fort Wayne-S. Bend diocese.

**Today's Catholic,** biweekly; P.O. Box 28410, San Antonio, TX 78228; San Antonio archdiocese.

**UNIREA (The Union)** (Romanian) (10 times a year); 1121 44th St. N.E., Canton, OH 44714; Romanian diocese of Canton.

**U. P. Catholic, The,** semi-monthly; P.O. Box 548, Marquette, MI 49855; Marquette diocese.

**Valley Catholic,** m; 900 Lafayette St., Suite 301, Santa Clara, CA 95050; San Jose diocese.

**Vermont Catholic Tribune,** biweekly; 351 North Ave., Burlington, VT 05401; Burlington diocese.

**Vida Nueva** (Spanish), w; 1520 W. 9th St., Los Angeles, CA 90015; Los Angeles archdiocese.

**Visitante de Puerto Rico, El** (Spanish), w; Apartado 41305, Est Minillas, San Juan, PR 00940. Puerto Rican Catholic Conference.

**Voice of the Southwest,** m; 414 N. Allen, Farmington, NM 87401; Gallup diocese.

**Voz Catolica, La** (Spanish); m; 9401 Biscayne Blvd., Miami, FL 33138; Miami archdiocese.

**Wanderer, The,** w; 201 Ohio St., St. Paul, MN 55107; national.

**The Way** (Ukrainian-Eng.), biweekly; 827 N. Franklin St., Philadelphia, PA 19123; Philadelphia archeparchy.

**West Nebraska Register,** w; P.O. Box 608, Grand Island, NE 68802; Grand Island diocese.

**West River Catholic,** m; P.O. Box _78, Rapid City, SD 57709; Rapid City diocese.

**West Texas Angelus,** m; P.O. Box 1829, San Angelo, TX 76902; San Angelo diocese.

**West Texas Catholic,** biweekly; P.O. Box 5644, Amarillo, TX 79117; Amarillo diocese.

**Western Kentucky Catholic,** m; 600 Locust St., Owensboro, KY 42301; Owensboro diocese.

**Western New York Catholic,** m; 795 Main St., Buffalo, NY 14203; Buffalo diocese.

**Witness, The,** w; P.O. Box 917, Dubuque, IA 52004; Dubuque archdiocese.

**Wyoming Catholic Register,** m; P.O. Box 1308, Cheyenne, WY 82003; Cheyenne diocese.

## Magazines

**Action News,** q; 6160 North Cicero Ave., Chicago, IL 60646; Pro-Life Action League.

**AIM: Liturgy Resources,** q; P.O. Box 2703, Schiller Park, IL 60176.

**Alma Mariana** (Spanish), bm; Mountain View Rd., Box 976, Washington, NJ 07882.

**America,** w; 106 W. 56th St., New York, NY 10019. Jesuits of U.S. and Canada.

**American Benedictine Review,** q; Assumption Abbey, Box A, Richardton, ND 58652.

**American Catholic Philosophical Quarterly** (formerly The New Scholasticism), Institute of Philosophical Studies, Univ. of Dallas, Irving, TX 75062. American Catholic Philosophical Assn.

**American Midland Naturalist,** q; Notre Dame, IN 46556.

**Anthonian, The,** q; Paterson, NJ 07509; St. Anthony's Guild.

**Anthropological Quarterly;** 620 Michigan Ave. N.E., Washington, DC 20064.

**Apostolate of the Little Flower,** bm; P.O. Box 5280, San Antonio, TX 78201; Discalced Carmelite Fathers.

**Association of Marian Helpers Bulletin,** q; Eden Hill Stockbridge, MA 01263. Congregation of Marians.

**Atchison Benedictines,** q; Mount St. Scholastica Convent, 801 S. 8th St., Atchison, KS 66002.

**Augustinian Journey,** m; 101 Barry Rd., Worcester, MA 01609.

**Barry Magazine,** 2 times a year; 11300 NE 2nd Ave., Miami Shores, FL 33161; Barry Univ.

**Bible Today, The,** bm; Liturgical Press, Collegeville, MN 56321.

**Biblical Theology Bulletin,** q; P.O. Box 1038, South Orange, NJ 07079.

**BLUEPRINT for Social Justice,** 10 times a year; Twomey Center for Peace through Justice, Loyola University, Box 12, New Orleans, LA 70118.

**Bolletino,** m; 1801 Van Ness Ave., Suite 330, San Francisco, CA 94109; Italian Catholic Federation.

**Brothers,** 5 times a year; 33 Pryer Terrace, New Rochelle, NY 10804; National Assembly of Religious Brothers.

**Caelum et Terra,** q; P.O. Box 1494, Wooster, OH 44691. Journal of Catholic Culture.

**Carmelite Digest,** q; P.O. Box 3180, San Jose, CA 95156.

**Carmelite Review, The,** m; 8433 Bailey Rd., Darien, IL 60561. Canadian-American Province of Carmelite Order.

**Catechist, The,** 7 times a year; 330 Pogress Rd., Dayton, OH 45449.

**Catechumenate: A Journal of Christian Initiation,** 6 times a year; 1800 N. Hermitage Ave., Chicago, IL 60622.

**Catholic Aid News,** m; 3499 N. Lexington Ave., St. Paul, MN 55126.

**Catholic Answer, The,** bm; 200 Noll Plaza, Huntington, IN 46750; Our Sunday Visitor.

**Catholic Biblical Quarterly;** Catholic University of America, Washington, DC 20064; Catholic Biblical Assn.

**Catholic Cemetery, The,** m; 710 N. River Rd., Des Plaines, IL 60016; National Catholic Cemetery Conference.

**Catholic Digest,** m; P.O. Box 64090, St. Paul, MN 35164.

**Catholic Digest Reader,** q; P.O. Box 64090, St. Paul, MN 55164. Large print magazine.

**Catholic Dossier,** bm; 2515 McAllister St., San Francisco, CA 94118.

**Catholic Faith, The,** bm; 2515 McAllister St., San Francisco, CA 94118.

**Catholic Forester Magazine,** bm; 355 Shuman Blvd., P.O. Box 3012, Naperville, IL 60566; Catholic Order of Foresters.

**CGA World,** q; P.O. Box 3658, Scranton, PA 18505. Catholic Golden Age.

**Catholic Health World,** semimonthly; 4455 Woodson Rd., St. Louis, MO 63134. Catholic Health Association.

**Catholic Heritage,** bm; 200 Noll Plaza, Huntington, IN 46750. Our Sunday Visitor.

**Catholic Historical Review,** q; 620 Michigan Ave. N.E., Washington, DC 20064.

**Catholic International,** m; Assumption Communications, 101 Barry Rd., Worcester, MA 01609.

**Catholic Journalist, The,** m; 3555 Veterans Highway, Unit O, Ronkonkoma, NY 11779; Catholic Press Association.

**C.K. of A. Journal,** m; 1850 Dalton St., Cincinnati, OH 45214; Catholic Knights of America.

**Catholic Lawyer,** q; St. John's University, Jamaica, NY 11439; St. Thomas More Institute for Legal Research.

**Catholic Library World,** 4 times a year; 9009 Carter Ave., Allen Park, MI 48101; Catholic Library Association.

**Catholic Near East Magazine,** bm; 1011 First Ave., New York, NY 10022; Catholic Near East Welfare Assn.

**Catholic Outlook,** m; 2830 E. 4th St., Duluth, MN 55812; Duluth diocese.

**Catholic Parent,** bm; 200 Noll Plaza, Huntington, IN 46750; Our Sunday Visitor.

**Catholic Peace Voice,** q; 348 E. 10th St., Erie, PA 16503; Pax Christi USA.

**Catholic Pharmacist,** q; 1012 Surrey Hills Dr., St. Louis, MO 63117; National Catholic Pharmacists Guild.

**Catholic Press Directory,** a; 3555 Veterans Highway, Unit O, Ronkonkoma, NY 11779; Catholic Press Assn.

**Catholic Quote,** m; Valparaiso, NE 68065; Rev. Jerome Pokorny.

**Catholic Review** (Braille, tape, large print), bm; 154 E. 23rd St., New York, NY 10010; Xavier Society for the Blind.

**Catholic Rural Life,** semiannually; 4625 Beaver Ave., Des Moines, IA 50310.

**Catholic Singles Magazine,** two times a year; 8408 S. Muskegon, Chicago, IL 60617.

**Catholic Telephone Guide,** a; 210 North Ave., New Rochelle, NY 10801.

**Catholic University of America Law Review,** q; Washington, DC 20064.

**Catholic War Veteran,** bm; 441 N. Lee St., Alexandria, VA 22314.

**Catholic Woman,** bm; 1275 K St. N.W., Suite 975, Washington, DC 20005. National Council of Catholic Women.

**Catholic Women's Network,** bm; 877 Spinosa Dr., Sunnyvale, CA 94087.

**Catholic Worker,** 7 times a year; 36 E. First St., New York, NY 10003. Catholic Worker Movement.

**Catholic Workman,** m; 111 W. Main, P.O. Box 47, New Prague, MN 56071.

**Catholic World, The,** bm; 997 Macarthur Blvd., Mahwah, NJ 07430.

**Catholic World Report, The,** 11 times a year; P.O. Box 1328, Dedham, MA 02027 (editorial office). Ignatius Press.

**Celebration,** m; 207 Hillsboro Dr., Silver Spring, MD 20902; National Catholic Reporter Publishing Co.

**Charities USA,** q; 1731 King St., Suite 200, Alexandria, VA 22314.

**Chicago Studies,** 3 times a year; 1800 N. Hermitage Ave., Chicago, IL 60022.

**Christian Renewal News,** 4 times a year; 411 First St., Flllmore, CA 93016. Apostolate of Christian Renewal.

**Church,** q; 299 Elizabeth St., New York, NY 10012; National Pastoral Life Center.

**Cistercian Studies Quarterly;** Santa Rita Abbey, HC 1, Box 929, Sonoita, AZ 85637; international review of monastic and contemplative spirituality, history and theology.

**Columban Mission,** 8 times a year; St. Columbans, NE 68056; Columban Fathers.

**Columbia,** m; One Columbus Plaza, New Haven, CT 06510; Knights of Columbus.

**Comboni Missions,** 4 times a year; 8108 Beechmont Ave., Cincinnati, OH 45255.

**Commonweal,** biweekly; 15 Dutch St., Room 502, New York, NY 10038.

**Communio — International Catholic Review,** q; P.O. Box 4557, Washington, D.C. 20017.

**Company,** q; 3441 N. Ashland Ave., Chicago, IL 60657. Jesuit Magazine.

**Concilium,** 6 times a year; Orbis Books, Walsh Bldg., Box 308, Maryknoll, NY 10545.

**Consecrated Life,** semi-annually; P.O. Box 41007, Chicago, IL 60641; Institute on Religious Life. English edition of *Informationes,* official publication of Congregation for Institutes of Consecrated Life and Societies of Apostolic Life.

**Consolata Missionaries,** bm; P.O. Box 5550, Somerset, NJ 08875.

**Contact,** q; 555 Albany Ave., Amityville, NY 11701; Sisters of St. Dominic.

**Continuum,** 3 times a year; 3700 W. 103rd St., Chicago, IL 60655.

**Cord, The,** m; P.O. Drawer F, St. Bonaventure, NY 14778; Franciscan Institute.

**Counseling and Values,** 3 times a year; Dept. of Educational Psychology and Special Education, Southern Illinois Univ., Carbondale, IL 62901.

**Crescat,** 3 times a year; Belmont Abbey, Belmont, NC 28012; Benedictine Monks.

**Crisis,** 11 times a year; 1511 K Street NW, Suite 525, Washington, DC; Journal of lay Catholic opinion.

**Critic, The,** q; 205 W. Monroe St., 6th floor, Chicago, IL 60606. Thomas More Assn.

**Cross Currents,** q; College of New Rochelle, New Rochelle, NY 10805; interreligious; Association for Religion and Intellectual Life.

**CUA Magazine,** 3 times a year; 620 Michigan Ave. N.E., Washington, DC 20064.

**Deaf Blind Weekly, The** (Braille), w; 154 E. 23rd St., New York, NY 10010; Xavier Society for the Blind.

**DeSales World, The,** twice a year; P.O. Box 1452, Wilmington, DE 19899.

**Diakonia,** 3 times a year; Univ. of Scranton, Scranton, PA 18510; Center for Eastern Christian Studies.

**Divine Word Missionaries,** q; Techny, IL 60082.

**Ecumenical Trends,** m (exc. Aug.); Graymoor, Route 9, P.O. Box 300, Garrison, NY 10524; Graymoor Ecumenical Institute.

**Eglute (The Little Fir Tree)** (Lithuanian), m; 13648 Keckapoo Trail, Lockport, IL 60441; children ages 5-10.

**Emmanuel,** 10 times a year; 5384 Wilson Mills Rd., Cleveland, OH 44143; Congregation of Blessed Sacrament.

**Eternal Flame** (Armenian-English), 110 E. 12th St., New York, NY 10003; Armenian exarchate.

**Explorations,** q; 321 Chestnut St., Philadelphia, PA 19106; American Interfaith Institute.

**Extension,** 12 times a year; 35 E. Wacker Dr., Suite 400, Chicago, IL 60601; Catholic Church Extension Society.

**Faith and Reason,** q; 134 Christendom Dr., Front Royal, VA 22630.

**Family Digest, The,** bm; P.O. Box 40137, Fort Wayne, IN 46804 (editorial address).

**Family Friend,** q; P.O. Box 11563, Milwaukee, WI 53211; Catholic Family Life Insurance.

**Fidelity,** m; 206 Marquette Ave., South Bend, IN 46617.

**Flame, The,** 4 times a year; Barry Univ., 11300 N.E. 2nd Ave., Miami Shores, FL 33161.

**Forefront,** q; Box 219, Crestone, CO 81131; Spiritual Life Institute of America.

**F.M.A. Focus,** q; P.O. Box 598, Mt. Vernon, NY 10551; Franciscan Mission Associates.

**Franciscan Studies,** a; St. Bonaventure, NY 14778; Franciscan Institute.

**Franciscan Way,** q; University Blvd., Steubenville, OH 43952.

**Fraternal Leader,** q; P.O. Box 13005; Erie, PA 16514; Loyal Christian Benefit Association.

**Fraternally Yours** (Eng.-Slovak), m; 24950 Chagrin Blvd., Beachwood, OH 44122; First Catholic Slovak Ladies Assn.

**Friar Lines,** 3 times a year; 58 W. 88th St., New York, NY 10024. Franciscan Friars of Holy Name Province.

**Garsas** (Lithuanian-English), m; 71-73 S. Washington St., Wilkes-Barre, PA 18701; Lithuanian Catholic Alliance.

**Glenmary Challenge, The,** q; P.O. Box 465618, Cincinnati, OH 45246; Glenmary Home Missioners.

**God's Word Today,** m; P. O. Box 60488, St. Paul, MN 55164. Univ. of St. Thomas.

**Good News,** m; P.O. Box 432, Milwaukee, WI 53201. Liturgical Publications.

**Good News for Children,** 32 times during school year; 330 Progress Rd., Dayton, OH 45449.

**Good Shepherd** (Dobry Pastier) (Slovak-English), a; 8200 McKnight Rd., Pittsburgh, PA 15237.

**Greyfriars Review,** 3 times a year; St. Bonventure Univ., St. Bonaventure, NY 14778; Franciscan Institute.

**Guide to Religious Ministries, A,** a; 210 North Ave., New Rochelle, NY 10801.

**Health Progress,** m; 4455 Woodson Rd., St. Louis, MO 63134; Catholic Health Association.

**Hearts Aflame,** q; P.O. Box 976, Washington, NJ 07882. For youth (13-23).

**Homiletic and Pastoral Review,** m; 86 Riverside Dr., New York, NY 10024.

**Horizon,** 4 times a year; 1603 S. Michigan Ave. No. 400, Chicago, IL 60616.

**Horizons,** 2 times a year; Villanova University, Villanova, PA 19085. College Theology Society.

**Human Development,** q; c/o St. John's Seminary, 127 Lake St., Brighton, MA 02135.

**Immaculate Heart Messenger,** q; P.O. Box 158, Alexandria, SD 57311.

**In a Word,** m; Bay Saint Louis, MS 39520; Society of the Divine Word.

**Jesuit Bulletin,** 3 times a year; 4511 W. Pine Blvd., St. Louis, MO 63108; Jesuit Seminary Aid Association.

**Jesuit Journeys,** 3 times a year; 3400 W. Wisconsin Ave., Milwaukee, WI 53508.

**Josephite Harvest, The,** q; 1130 N. Calvert St., Baltimore, MD 21202; Josephite Missionaries.

**Journal of Texas Catholic History and Culture,** a; 3001 S. Congress Ave., Austin, TX 78704.

**Jurist, The,** semiannually; Catholic University of America, Washington, DC 20064; Department of Canon Law.

**Key to Happiness,** m; 86 Riverside Dr., New York, NY 10024. Catholic Views Broadcast.

**Kinship,** q; P.O. Box 22264, Owensboro, KY 42304; Glenmary Sisters.

**Knights of St. John International,** q; 89 South Pine Ave., Albany, NY 12208.

**Kolping Banner,** m; P.O. Box 46252, Chicago, IL 60646; Catholic Kolping Society.

**Latin Mass, The,** q; 1331 Red Cedar Circle, Ft. Collins, CO 80524.

**Law Briefs,** 12 times a year; 3211 Fourth St. N.E. Washington, DC 20017; Office of General Counsel, USCC.

**Leaflet Missal,** 16565 South State St., S. Holland, IL 60473.

**Leaves,** bm; 23715 Ann Arbor Trail, Dearborn Heights, MI 48127; Mariannhill Mission Society.

**Liguorian,** m; 1 Liguori Dr., Liguori, MO 63057; Redemptorists.

**Linacre Quarterly;** 850 Elm Grove Rd., Elm Grove, WI 53122; National Federation of Catholic Physicians Guilds.

**Liturgia y Cancion** (Spanish and English), q; 5536 NE Hassalo, Portland, OR 97213. Oregon Catholic Press.

**Liturgy,** q; 8750 Georgia Ave., Suite 123, Silver Spring, MD 20910. Liturgical Conference.

**Liturgy 90,** 8 times a year; 1800 N. Hermitage Ave., Chicago, IL 60622; Liturgy Training Publications.

**Liturgy Planner, The,** q; 6414 N.E. Alameda, Portland, OR 97213.

**Living City,** m; P.O. Box 837, Bronx, NY 10465; Focolare Movement.

**Living Faith,** q; 10300 Watson Rd., St. Louis, MO 63127.

**Living Light, The,** q; 3211 Fourth St. N.E., Washington, DC 20017; Department of Education, USCC.

**Living Prayer,** bm; Beckley Hill, R.R. 2, Box 4784, Barre, Vt. 05641.

**Living Pulpit, The,** q; 5000 Independence Ave., Riverdale, NY 10471.

**Marian Library Studies,** a; Marian Library, Dayton, OH 45469.

**Marian Studies,** a; Marian Library, Dayton, OH 45469; Mariological Society of America (proceedings).

**Marriage,** 6 times a year; 955 Lake Dr., St. Paul, MN 55120; International Marriage Encounter.

**Maryknoll,** m; Maryknoll, NY 10545; Catholic Foreign Mission Society.

**Mary's Shrine,** 2 times a year; Michigan Ave. and 4th St. N.E., Washington, DC 20017. Basilica of National Shrine of the Immaculate Conception.

**Matrimony,** q; 215 Santa Rosa Pl., Santa Barbara, CA 93109. Worldwide Marriage Encounter.

**Medical Mission News,** q; 10 W. 17th St., New York, NY 10011; Catholic Medical Mission Board, Inc.

**Medjugorje Magazine,** q; P.O. Box 99, Bloomingdale, IL 60108.

**Merciful Love,** q; 5654 E. Westover, No. 103, P.O. Box 24, Fresno, CA 93727.

**Mid-America: An Historical Review,** 3 times a year; Loyola University, Chicago, IL 60626.

**Migration World,** 5 times a year; 209 Flagg Pl., Staten Island, NY 10304; Center for Migration Studies.

**Miraculous Medal,** q; 475 E. Chelten Ave., Philadelphia, PA 19144; Central Association of the Miraculous Medal.

**Mission,** q; 1663 Bristol Pike, Bensalem, PA 19020; Sisters of the Blessed Sacrament.

**Mission Magazine,** 4 times a year; 366 Fifth Ave., Ne York, NY 10001; Society for Propagation of the Faith.

**Mission Helper, The,** q; 1001 W. Joppa Rd., Baltimore, MD 21204; Mission Helpers of the Sacred Heart.

**Missionhurst,** 6 times a year; 4651 N. 25th St., Arlington, VA 22207.

**Mission of the Immaculata, The,** 10 times a year; 1600 W. Park Ave., Libertyville, IL 60048; Conventual Franciscan Friars.

**Modern Liturgy,** 10 times a year; 160 E. Virginia St., No. 290, San Jose, CA 95112.

**Modern Schoolman, The,** q; 221 N. Grand Blvd., St. Louis, MO 63103; St. Louis University Philosophy Department.

**Momentum,** 4 times a year; Suite 100, 1077 30th St., N.W., Washington, DC 20007; National Catholic Educational Association.

**Mountain Spirit, The,** 6 times a year; 322 Crab Orchard Rd., Lancaster, KY 40446; Christian Appalachian Project.

**My Daily Visitor,** bm; 200 Noll Plaza, Huntington, IN 46750; Our Sunday Visitor, Inc.

**My Friend,** 10 times a year; 50 St. Paul's Ave., Jamaica Plain, Boston, MA 02130; for children, ages 6-12.

**NAPMR Quarterly,** 4516 30th St., NW, Washington, DC 20008. National Apostolate with People with Mental Retardation.

**National Catholic Forester,** q; 320 S. School St., Mt. Prospect,IL 60056.

**National Jesuit News,** m; 1616 P St. N.W., Suite 400, Washington, D.C. 20036.

**Network,** bm; 801 Pennsylvania Ave. S.E., Washington, DC 20003; Network.

**New Covenant,** m; Our Sunday Visitor, Inc., 200 Noll Plaza, Huntington, IN 46750.

**New Oxford Review,** 10 issues a year; 1069 Kains Ave., Berkeley, CA 94706.

**Notebook, The,** q; 31 Chesterfield Rd., Stamford, CT 06902. Catholic Movement for Intellectual and Cultural Affairs.

**Notre Dame Magazine,** q; Notre Dame Univ., Notre Dame, IN 46556.

**Nova-Voice of Ministry,** bm; P.O. Box 432, Milwaukee, WI 53201. Liturgical Publications.

**Oblate World and Voice of Hope,** bm; 486 Chandler St., P.O. Box 680, Tewksbury, MA 01876; Oblates of Mary Immaculate.

**Observer, The,** m; 4545 W. 63rd St., Chicago, IL 60629; Lithuanian Roman Catholic Federation of America.

**Old Testament Abstracts,** 3 times a year; Catholic University of America, Washington, DC 20064.

**Onward** (a) and **Opportunities** (a); 448 Decatur St., Toledo, OH 43609; Barry Publishing Services.

**Origins,** 48 times a year; 3211 Fourth St. N.E., Washington, DC 20017; Catholic News Service.

**Padres' Trail,** 4 times a year; Box 645, St. Michael, AZ 86511; Franciscan Friars.

**Parish Liturgy,** q; 16565 S. State St., S. Holland, IL 60473.

**Passage,** q; 90 Cherry Lane, Hicksville, NY 11801.

**Passionists' Compassion, The,** q; 526 Monastery Pl., Union City, NJ 07087.

**Pastoral Life,** m; Box 595, Canfield, OH 44406; Society of St. Paul.

**Pastoral Music,** bm; 225 Sheridan St., N.W. Washington, DC 20011; National Association of Pastoral Musicians.

**Philosophy Today,** q; De Paul University, 1150 W. Fullerton Ave., Chicago, IL 60614; Philosophy Department.

**PIME World,** m (exc. July-Aug.); 17330 Quincy St., Detroit, MI 48221; PIME Missionaries.

**Plenty Good Room,** 6 times a year; 1800 N. Hermitage Ave., Chicago, IL 60622.

**Pope Speaks, The: Church Documents Bimonthly;** Our Sunday Visitor, Inc., 200 Noll Plaza, Huntington, IN 46750.

**Portland,** 4 issues a year; 5000 N. Willamette Blvd., Portland, OR 97203; Univ. of Portland.

**Poverello, The,** 10 times a year; 6832 Convent Blvd., Sylvania, OH 03560. Sisters of St. Francis of Sylvania.

**Praxis Press,** 10 times a year; P.O. Box 508, San Jose, CA 95103.

**Prayers for Worship,** q; P.O. Box 432, Milwaukee, WI 53201.

**Praying,** 6 times a year; 115 E. Armour Blvd., Kansas City, MO 64111.

**Priest, The,** m; 200 Noll Plaza, Huntington, IN 46750; Our Sunday Visitor, Inc.

**Probe,** q; 529 S. Wabash Ave., Room 404, Chicago, IL 60605; National Assembly of Religious Women.

**Proceedings of the American Catholic Philosophical Association,** a; Catholic Univ. of America, Washington, DC 20064.

**Queen of All Hearts,** bm; 26 S. Saxon Ave., Bay Shore, NY 11706; Montfort Missionaries.

**Reign of the Sacred Heart,** q; 6889 S. Lovers Lane, Hales Corners, WI 53130.

**Religion Teacher's Journal,** m (Sept.-May); P.O. Box 180, Mystic, CT 06355.

**Renascence,** q; Marquette University, Milwaukee, WI 53233.

**Report on U.S. Catholic Overseas Mission,** bi-annually; 3029 Fourth St. N.E., Washington, DC 20017. United States Catholic Mission Association.

**Response: Volunteer Opportunities Directory,** a; 4121 Harewood Rd. N.E., Washington, DC 20017; Catholic Network of Volunteer Service.

**Review for Religious,** m; Room 428, 3601 Lindell Blvd., St. Louis, MO 63108.

**Review of Politics,** q; Box B, Notre Dame, IN 46556.

**Review of Social Economy,** 4 times a year; Marquette University, Milwaukee, WI 53233. Association for Social Economics.

**Revista Maryknoll** (Spanish-English), m; Maryknoll, NY 10545; Catholic Foreign Mission Society of America.

**Roze Maryi** (Polish), m; Eden Hill, Stockbridge, MA 01263; Marian Helpers Center.

**Sacred Music,** q; 548 Lafond Ave., St. Paul, MN 55103.

**St. Anthony Messenger,** m; 1615 Republic St., Cincinnati, OH 45210; Franciscan Friars.

**St. Augustine Catholic,** bm (Sept-May), P.O. Box 24000, Jacksonville, FL. St. Augustine diocese.

**St. Joseph's Messenger and Advocate of the Blind,** biannual; St. Joseph Home, 541 Pavonia Ave., Jersey City, NJ 07303.

**St. Paul's Family Magazine,** q; 14780 W. 159th St., Olathe, KS 66062.

**Salesian Bulletin** (q); **Salesian Directory** (a); **Salesian Missions of St. John Bosco,** 3 times a year; 148 Main St., New Rochelle, NY 10802.

**Salt of the Earth,** bm; 205 W. Monroe St., Chicago, IL 60606; Claretians.

**Salt/Sisters of Charity, BVM,** q; 1100 Carmel Dr., Dubuque, IA 52001.

**Scalabrinians,** 4 times a year; 209 Flagg Pl., Staten Island, NY 10304.

**SC News,** q; P.O. Box 172, Nazareth, KY 40048; Sisters of Charity of Nazareth.

**School Guide,** a; 210 North Ave., New Rochelle, NY 10801.

**SCRC Spirit, The,** bm; 2810 Artesia Blvd., Redondo Beach, CA 90278; Southern California Renewal Communities.

**Serenity,** q; 601 Maiden Choice Lane, Baltimore, MD 21228; Little Sisters of the Poor.

**Serran, The,** bm; 65 E. Wacker Pl., Suite 1210, Chicago, IL 60601; Serra International.

**Share Magazine,** 3 times a year; 10 W. 71st St., New York, NY 10023; Catholic Duaghters of the Americas.

**Share the Word,** bm; 3031 Fourth St. N.E., Washington, DC 20017; Paulist Catholic Evangelization Association.

**Silent Advocate,** q; St. Rita School for the Deaf, 1720 Glendale-Milford Rd., Cincinnati, OH 45215.

**Sister Miriam Teresa League of Prayer Bulletin,** q; League Headquarters, Convent Station, NJ 07961.

**Sisters Today,** bm; Liturgical Press, Collegeville, MN 56321.

**Social Justice Review,** bm; 3835 Westminster Pl., St. Louis, MO 63108; Catholic Central Union of America.

**Soul Magazine,** bm; P.O. Box 976, Washington, NJ 07882; World Apostolate of Our Lady of Fatima.

**Spinnaker,** 5 times a year; 610 W. Elm, Monroe, MI 48161; IHM Sisters.

**Spirit,** biannually; Seton Hall University, South Orange, NJ 07079.

**Spirit,** w; 1884 Randolph Ave., St. Paul, MN 55105. For teens.

**Spirit and Life,** 6 times a year; 800 N. Country Club Rd., Tucson, AZ 85716; Benedictine Srs. of Perpetual Adoration.

**Spiritual Life,** q; 2131 Lincoln Rd. N.E., Washington, DC 20002; Discalced Carmelite Friars.

**Star,** 10 times a year; 22 W. Kiowa, Colorado Springs, CO 80903.

**Studies in the Spirituality of Jesuits,** 5 times a year; 3700 W. Pine Blvd., St. Louis, MO 63108.

**Sunday by Sunday,** w; 1884 Randolph Ave., St. Paul, MN 55105.

**Sword Magazine,** 2 times a year; 120 Monroe Ave., Cresskill, NJ 07626; Carmelite Fathers.

**Theological Studies,** q; 37th and O Sts. NW, Washington, DC 20057.

**Theology Digest,** q; 3634 Lindell Blvd., St. Louis, MO 63108; St. Louis Univesity.

**This Rock,** m; P.O. Box 17181, San Diego, CA 92177.

**Thomist, The,** q; 487 Michigan Ave. N.E., Washington, DC 20017; Dominican Fathers.

**Today's Catholic Teacher,** m (Sept.-April); 330 Progress Rd., Dayton, OH 45449.

**Today's Liturgy,** q; 5536 NE Hassalo, Portland, OR 97213.

**Today's Parish,** m (Sept.-May); P.O. Box 180, Mystic, CT 06355.

**Together in the Word,** biannual; Box 577,

**Techny,** IL 60082; Chicago province Society of Divine Word.

**Tracings,** q; Gamelin St., Holyoke, MA 01040; Sisters of Providence.

**Trinity Missions Magazine,** q; 9001 New Hampshire Ave., Silver Spring, MD 20903.

**TV Prayer Guide;** 19 Second Ave., P.O. Box 440, Pelham, NY 10803.

**Ultreya Magazine,** 6 times a year; 4500 W. Davis St., P.O. Box 210226, Dallas, TX 75211. Cursillo Movement.

**L'Union** (French and English), q; P.O. Box F, Woonsocket, RI 02895.

**Universitas,** q; 221 N. Grand, Room 39, St. Louis, MO 63103; St. Louis University.

**U.S. Catholic,** m; 205 W. Monroe St., Chicago, IL 60606; Claretians.

**U.S. Catholic Historian,** q; 200 Noll Plaza, Huntington, IN 46750.

**Venture,** 32 times during school year; 330 Progress Rd., Dayton, OH 45449, Intermediate grades.

**Verelk** (Armenian-English), bimonthly; 1327 Pleasant Ave., Los Angeles, CA 90033.

**Vincentian Heritage,** twice a year; 2233 N. Kenmore Ave., Chicago, IL 60614.

**Vision,** 3 times a year; 7202 Buchanan St., Landover Hills, MD 20784. National Catholic Office for the Deaf.

**Vision** (Spanish-English), P.O. Box 28185, San Antonio, TX 78228. Mexican American Cultural Center.

**Visions,** 28 times during school year; 330 Progress Rd., Dayton, OH 45449. For students in grades 7 to 9.

**Vocations and Prayer,** q; 9815 Columbus Ave., North Hills, CA 91343. Rogationist Fathers.

**Waif's Messenger,** q; 1140 W. Jackson Blvd., Chicago, IL 60607; Mission of Our Lady of Mercy.

**Way of St. Francis,** bm; 1500 34th Ave., Oakland, CA 94601; Franciscan Friars of California, Inc.

**Wheeling Jesuit College Chronicle,** 3 times a year; 316 Washington Ave., Wheeling, WV 26003.

**Word Among Us, The,** m; P.O. Box 6003, Gaithersburg, MD 20884.

**World Lithuanian Catholic Directory,** 50 Orton Marotta Way, S. Boston, MA 02127.

**Worship,** 6 times a year; St. John's Abbey, Collegeville, MN 56321.

**You!,** 10 times a year; 31194 La Baya Dr., Suite 200, Westlake Village, CA 91362. Catholic youth magazine.

## Newsletters

**Act,** 10 times a year; Box 272, Ames, IA 60010; Christian Family Movement.

**ADRIS Newsletter,** q; Department of Theological Studies, St. Louis University, St. Louis, MO 63103.

**Angel Guardian Herald,** 4 times a year; 6301 12th Ave., Brooklyn, NY 11219.

**Annual Report,** 2021 H St. N.W., Washington, DC 20006. Black and Indian Mission Office.

**Archdiocesan Bulletin,** bm; 827 N. Franklin

St., Philadelphia, PA 19123; Philadelphia archeparchy.

**At-one-ment,** bm; Graymoor Ecumenical Institute, Garrison, NY 10524.

**Aylesford Carmelite Newsletter,** q. 8501 Bailey Rd., Darien, IL 60561.

**Baraga Bulletin, The,** q; 444 S. 4th St., P.O. Box 550, Marquette, MI 49855.

**Benedictine Orient,** twice a year; 2400 Maple Ave., Lisle, IL 60532.

**Bringing Religion Home,** 10 times a year; 205 W. Monroe St., Chicago, IL 60606.

**Call Board, The,** 12 times a year; 1501 Broadway, Suite 518, New York, NY 10036; Catholic Actors' Guild.

**CHD News,** q; 3211 Fourth St. N.E. Washington, DC 20017; Campaign for Human Development.

**Caring Community, The,** m; 115 E. Armour Blvd., Kansas City, MO 64111.

**Catalyst,** 10 times a year; 6324 W. North Ave., Milwaukee, WI 53213 (publications office). Catholic League for Civil and Religious Rights.

**Catechist's Connection, The,** 10 times a year; 115 E. Armour Blvd., Kansas City, MO 64111.

**Catholic Communicator, The,** q; 781 Catoctin Ridge, Paeonian Springs, VA 21229; Catholic Home Study Institute.

**Catholic Connection, The,** m (Aug.-May); 2500 Line Ave., Shreveport, LA 71104. Shreveport diocese.

**Catholic Trends,** biweekly; 3211 Fourth St. N.E., Washington, DC 20017; Catholic News Service.

**Catholic Update,** m; 1615 Republic St., Cincinnati, OH 45210.

**CARA Report, The,** q; Georgetown Univ., Washington, DC 20057; Center for Applied Research in the Apostolate.

**C.F.C. Newsletter,** 5 times a year; 33 Pryer Terr., New Rochelle, NY 10804. Christian Brothers.

**Chariscenter USA Newsletter,** 5 times a year; P.O. Box 628, Locust Grove, VA 22508.

**Christ the King Seminary Newsletter,** 3 times a year; 711 Knox Rd., Box 607, E. Aurora, NY 14052.

**Christian Beginnings,** 5 times a year; 200 Noll Plaza, Huntington, IN 46750. Our Sunday Visitor.

**Christian Foundation for Children and Aging** (Newsletter), 3 times a year; 1 Elmwood Ave., Kansas City, KS 66103.

**Christian Response Newsletter,** P.O. Box 125, Staples, MN 56479.

**Christopher News Notes,** 10 times a year; 12 E. 48th St., New York, NY 10017; The Christophers.

**City of God,** q; 4209 Avenue F, Austin, TX 78751.

**Clarion, The,** 5 times a year; Box 159, Alfred, ME 04002; Brothers of Christian Instruction.

**Comboni Mission Newsletter,** q; 8108 Beechmont Ave., Cincinnati, OH 45255.

**Commentary,** 6 times a year; 1010 11th St., Suite 200, Sacramento, CA 95814.

**Common Life,** q; 270 Winooski Park, Colchester, VT 05439; Society of St. Edmund.

**Context,** 22 issues a year; 205 W. Monroe St., Chicago, IL 60606.

**Crossroads,** 8 times a year; 300 College Park Ave.,

Dayton, OH 45469. Catholic Campus Ministry Association.

**CRUX of the News,** w; 24 Wade Rd., Latham, NY 12210.

**Damien-Dutton Call,** q; 616 Bedford Ave., Bellmore, NY 11710.

**Dimensions,** m; 86 Front St., Hempstead, NY 11550; National Catholic Development Conference.

**Diocesan Newsletter, The,** m; P.O. Box 2279, Brownsville, TX 78522; Brownsville diocese.

**Environment and Art Letter,** m; 1800 N. Hermitage Ave., Chicago, IL 60622.

**Escoge la Vida!,** bm; 4345 SW 72nd Ave., Suite E, Miami, FL 33155. Vida Humana Internacional.

**Ethics and Medics,** m; 186 Forbes Rd., Braintree, MA 02184.

**Eucharistic Minister,** m; 115 E. Armour, P.O. Box 419493, Kansas City, MO 64141.

**Evangelization Update,** 6 times a year; 3031 Fourth St. NE, Washington, DC 20017.

**Family Connection, The,** 6 times a year; 3753 MacBeth Dr., San Jose, CA 95127.

**Fatima Findings,** m; 100 E. 20th St., Baltimore, MD 21218; Reparation Society of the Immaculate Heart of Mary.

**Fellowship of Catholic Scholars Newsletter,** q; Jacques Maritain Center, 714 Hesburgh Library, Notre Dame, IN 46556.

**Fonda Tekakwitha News,** P.O. Box 627, Fonda, NY 12068.

**Food for the Poor,** 3 times a year; 550 SW 12th Ave., Deerfield Beach, FL 33442.

**Franciscan Reporter,** annually; 3140 Meramec St., St. Louis, MO 63118; Franciscan Friars of Sacred Heart Province.

**Franciscan World Care,** 4 times a year; P.O. Box 29034, Washington, D.C. 20017. Franciscan Mission Service of North America.

**Friar News,** biweekly; 58 W. 88th St., New York, NY 10024; Franciscan Friars of Holy Name Province.

**Frontline Report,** bm; 23 Bliss Ave., Tenafly, NJ 07670. Society of African Missions.

**Generation,** m; 205 W. Monroe St., Chicago, IL 60606.

**Glenmary Bridge, The,** 4 times a year; P.O. Box 465618, Cincinnati, OH 45246.

**Graymoor Today,** m; Graymoor, Garrison, NY 10524.

**Guadalupe Missioners Newsletter,** m; 4714 W. 8th St., Los Angeles, CA 90005.

**Happiness,** q; 567 Salem End Rd., Framingham, MA 01701; Sons of Mary, Health of the Sick.

**Harmony,** 3 times a year; 800 N. Country Club Rd., Tucson, AZ 85716. Benedictine Srs. of Perpetual Adoration.

**Holy Name National Newsletter,** 6 times a year; P.O. Box 299, Upper Darby, PA 19082.

**HLI Update,** m; 7845 Airpark Rd., Suite E, Gaithersburg, MD 20879. Human Life International.

**In Between,** q; 1257 E. Siena Hts. Dr., Adrian, MI 49221; Adrian Dominican Sisters.

**Initiatives,** 6 times a year; 205 W. Monroe St., No. 300, Chicago, IL 60606; National Center for the Laity.

**Insight,** bm; 912 Market St., La Crosse, WI 54601. Franciscan Sisters of Perpetual Adoration.

**It's Our World,** 4 times during school year; 1720 Massachusetts Ave. N.W., Washington, DC 20036. Young Catholics in Mission.

**Journey, The,** 4 times ayear; 210 W. 31st St., New York, NY 10001; Province of St. Mary of Capuchin Order.

**Joyful Noiseletter, The,** m; P.O. Box 895, Portage, MI 49081; Fellowship of Merry Christians.

**Land of Cotton,** q; 2048 W. Fairview Ave., Montgomery, AL 39196; City of St. Jude.

**Law Reports,** q; 4455 Woodson Rd., St. Louis, MO 63134; Catholic Health Association.

**Lay Witness,** m; P.O. Box 1039, Southport, CT 06490; Catholics United for the Faith.

**LCWR Update,** m; 8808 Cameron St., Silver Spring, MD 20910; Leadership Conference of Women Religious.

**League of St. Michael the Archangel Newsletter,** 545 Colonial Dr., Suite C, Baton Rouge, LA 70806.

**Legatus,** m; 30 Frank Lloyd Wright Dr., Ann Arbor, MI 48105.

**Let's Talk!** (English edition), **Hablemos!** (Spanish edition), 6 times a year; 3031 Fourth St. N.E., Washington, DC 20017; prison ministries of Paulist National Catholic Evangelization Assn.

**Life at Risk,** 10 times a year; 3211 Fourth St. N.E., Washington, DC 20017. Pro-Life Activities Committee, NCCB.

**Life Insight,** m; 3211 Fourth St. N.E., Washington, DC 20017; Committee for Pro-Life Activities, NCCB.

**Liturgical Images,** m; P.O. Box 2225, Hickory, NC 28603.

**Markings,** m; 205 W. Monroe St., Chicago, IL 60606.

**Medical Mission Sisters News,** 4 times a year; 8400 Pine Road, Philadelphia, PA 19111.

**Messenger of St. Joseph's Union, The,** 3 times a year; 108 Bedell St., Staten Island, NY 10309.

**Missionaries of Africa Report,** q; 1624 21st St. N.W., Washington, DC 20009; Society of Missionaries of Africa (White Fathers).

**Mission Messenger, The,** q; P.O. Box 610, Thoreau, NM 87323; St. Bonaventure Indian Mission and School.

**NCCB/USCC Currents,** 10 times a year; 3211 Fourth St., N.E., Washington, DC 20017.

**NCPD National Update,** q; P.O. Box 29113, Washington, DC 20017; National Catholic Office for Persons with Disabilities.

**NCSC Commitment,** biannually; 1275 K St. N.W., Suite 980, Washington, DC 20005. National Catholic Stewardship Council.

**News and Views,** q; 3900 Westminster Pl.; St. Louis, MO 63108; Sacred Heart Program.

**Newsletter of the Bureau of Catholic Indian**

**Missions,** 10 times a year; 2021 H St. N.W., Washington, DC 20006.

**Northern Nevada Catholic Newsletter,** m; P.O. Box 1211, Reno, NV 89504; Reno diocese.

**Nuestra Parroquia** (Spanish-English), m; 205 W. Monroe St., Chicago, IL 60606. Claretians.

**Oblates,** bm; 15 S. 59th St., Belleville, IL 62223; Missionary Oblates of Mary Immaculate.

**Overview,** m; 205 W. Monroe St., Chicago, IL 60606; Thomas More Assn.

**Palabra Entre Nosotros, La,** m; P.O. Box 826, Gaithersburg, MD 20884.

**Paulist, The,** q; 997 Macarthur Blvd., Mahwah, NJ 07656.

**Perpetual Eucharistic Adoration Newsletter,** 3 times a year; P.O. Box 84595, Los Angeles, CA 90073.

**Pilgrim,** q; Jesuit Fathers, Auriesville, NY 12016; Shrine of North American Martyrs.

**Priestly Heart Newsletter,** 5337 Genessee St., Bowmansville, NY 14026. Apostleship of Prayer.

**Priests for Life,** bm; P.O. Box 141172, Staten Island, NY 10314.

**Program Supplement,** 18 times a year; 1 Columbus Plaza, New Haven, CT 06507; Knights of Columbus.

**Religious Life,** m (bm, May-Aug.); P.O. Box 41007, Chicago, IL 60641; Institute on Religious Life.

**RSCJ Newsletter,** m; 54 Robin Dr., Skillman, NJ 08558. Religious of Sacred Heart.

**SCJ News,** 9 times a year; P.O. Box 289, Hales Corners, WI 53130; Sacred Heart Fathers and Brothers.

**St. Anthony's Newsletter,** 12 times a year; Mt. St. Francis, IN 47146; Conventual Franciscans.

**Spiritual Book Associates,** 8 times a year; Notre Dame, IN 46556.

**Squires Newsletter,** m; One Columbus Plaza, New Haven, CT 06507; Columbian Squires.

**SSPS Mission,** q; P.O. Box 6026, Techny, IL 60082; Holy Spirit Missionary Sisters.

**Tekakwitha Conference Newsletter (Cross and Feather News),** q; P.O. Box 6768, Great Falls, MT 59406.

**Total Stewardship Newsnotes,** q; 1633 N. Cleveland Ave., Chicago, IL 60614; National Catholic Conference for Total Stewardship.

**Touchstone,** 4 times a year; 1337 W. Ohio St., Chicago, IL 60622; National Federation of Priests' Councils.

**Trinity Review,** m; P.O. Box 1666, Hobbs, NM 88240.

**Unda USA Newsletter,** 4 times a year; 901 Irving Ave., Dayton, OH 45409.

**U.S. Parish,** m; 205 W. Monroe St., Chicago, IL 60606.

**Vision — National Association of Catholic Chaplains,** 10 times ayear; 3501 S. Lake Dr., Milwaukee, WI 53207.

**Visions,** 2 times a year; Victory Noll, P.O. Box 109, Huntington, IN 46750; Our Lady of Victory Missionary Sisters.

**Voices,** q; P.O. Box 8326, St. Louis, MO 63132; Women for Faith and Family.

**Voices,** 2 times a year; 3001 S. Congress Ave., Austin, TX 78704. Volunteers for Educational and Social Services.

**WTU Newsletter,** 3 times a year; Washington Theological Union, 6896 Laurel St. N.W., Washington, DC 20012.

**Wooden Bell, The,** 6 times a year; 209 W. Fayette St., Baltimore, MD 21201. Catholic Relief Services.

**Woodstock Report,** q; Georgetown Univ., Washington, DC 20057. Woodstock Theological Center.

**Word One,** 5 times a year; 205 W. Monroe St., Chicago, IL 60606; Claretians.

**World Parish,** 6 times a year; Maryknoll Fathers; Maryknoll, NY 10545.

**Xaverian Missions Newsletter,** six times a year; 101 Summer St., Holliston, MA 01746; Xaverian Missionary Fathers.

**Your Edmundite Missions Newsletter,** bm; 1428 Broad St., Selma, AL 36701; Southern Missions of Society of St. Edmund.

**Youth Update,** m; 1615 Republic St., Cincinnati, OH 45210.

**Zeal Newsletter,** 3 times a year; P.O. Box 86, Allegany, NY 14706; Franciscan Sisters of Allegany.

## BOOKS

**The Official Catholic Directory,** annual; P.J. Kenedy & Sons in association with R.R. Bowker, a Reed Reference Publishing Company, 121 Chanlon Rd., New Providence, NJ 07974. First edition, 1817.

**The Catholic Almanac,** annual; Our Sunday Visitor, Inc., 200 Noll Plaza, Huntington, IN, 46750, publisher; editorial offices, P.O. Box 3765, Wallington, NJ 07057. First edition, 1904.

## BOOK CLUBS

**Catholic Book Club** (1928), 106 W. 56th St., New York, NY 10019. Sponsors the Campion Award.

**Catholic Digest Book Club** (1954), 475 Riverside Dr., Suite 1268, New York, NY 10115.

**Spiritual Book Associates** (1934), Notre Dame, IN 46556.

**Thomas More Book Club** (1939), Thomas More Association, 205 W. Monroe St., Sixth Floor, Chicago, IL 60606.

## FOREIGN CATHOLIC PERIODICALS

Principal source: Catholic Almanac survey. Included are English-language Catholic periodicals published outside the U.S.

**African Ecclesial Review (AFER),** bm; Gaba Publications, P.O. Box 4002, Eldoret, Kenya.

**Australasian Catholic Record,** q; St. Patrick's Seminary, Manly, New South Wales, Australia.

**Christ to the World,** 5 times a year; Via di Propaganda 1- C, 00187, Rome, Italy.

**Christian Orient,** q; P.B. 1 Vadavathoor, Kottayam 686010, Kerala, India.

**Doctrine and Life,** m; Dominican Publications, 42 Parnell Sq., Dublin 1, Ireland.

**Downside Review,** q; Downside Abbey, Stratton on Fosse, Bath, BA3 4RH, England.

**East Asian Pastoral Review,** q; East Asian Pastoral Institute, P.O. Box 221 U.P. Campus, 1101 Quezon City, Philippines.

**Furrow, The,** m; St. Patrick's College, Maynooth, Ireland.

**Heythrop Journal,** q; Heythrop College, Kensington Sq., London W8 5HQ, England (Editorial Office). Published by Blackwell Publishers, 108 Cowley Rd., Oxford, OX4 1JF, U.K.

**Holy Land Magazine,** q; P.O. Box 186, 91991 Jerusalem, Israel. Illustrated.

**Irish Biblical Studies, The,** q; Union Theological College, Belfast BT7 1JT, N. Ireland.

**Irish Journal of Sociology, The,** a; St. Patrick's College, Maynooth, Ireland.

**Irish Theological Quarterly,** q; St. Patrick's College, Maynooth, Ireland.

**L'Osservatore Romano,** w; Vatican City. (See Index.)

**Louvain Studies,** q; Peeters Publishers, Bondgenoten Caan 153, B-3000, Leuven, Belgium.

**Lumen Vitae** (French, with English summaries), q; International Center for Studies in Religious Education, 186, rue Washington, B-1050 Brussels, Belgium.

**Mediaeval Studies,** annual; Pontifical Institute of Mediaeval Studies, 59 Queen's Park Crescent East, Toronto, Ont., Canada M5S 2C4.

**Month,** m; 114 Mount St., London, WIY 6AH, England.

**Music and Liturgy,** 6 times a year; The Editor, 33 Brockenhurst Rd., Addiscombe Croydan, Surrey CRO 7DR, England.

**New Blackfriars,** m; edited by English Dominicans, Blackfriars, Oxford, OX1 3LY, England.

**Omnis Terra** (English Edition), m; Pontifical Missionary Union, Congregation for the Evangelization of Peoples, Via di Propaganda 1/c, 00187 Rome, Italy.

**One in Christ,** q; Edited at: Turvey Abbey, Turvey, Beds. MK43 8DE, England.

**Priests & People** (formerly The Clergy Review), 11 times a year; Blackfriars, Buckingham Rd., Cambridge CB3 0DD, England.

**Recusant History,** biannual; Catholic Record Society, 12 Melbourne Pl., Wolsingham, Durham DL13 3EH, England.

**Religious Life Review,** bm; Dominican Publications, 42 Parnell Sq., Dublin 1, Ireland.

**Scripture in Church,** q; Dominican Publications, 42 Parnell Sq., Dublin 1, Ireland.

**Southwark Liturgy Bulletin,** q; The Editor, 10 Claremont Rd., Maidstone, Kent ME14 5L2, England.

**Spearhead,** 5 times a year; Gaba Publications, P.O. Box 4002, Eldoret, Kenya.

**Spirituality,** bm; Dominican Publications, 42 Parnell Sq., Dublin 1, Ireland.

**Tablet, The,** w; 1 King Street Cloisters, Clifton Walk, London W6 0QZ, England.

**Way, The,** q; 114 Mount St., London W1Y 6AN, England.

## CATHOLIC NEWS AGENCIES

(Sources: International Catholic Union of the Press, Geneva; Catholic Press Association, U.S.)

**Argentina:** Agencia Informativa Catolica Argentina (AICA), av. Rivadavia, 413, 40 Casilla de Correo Central 2886, 1020 Buenos Aires.

**Austria:** Katholische Presse-Agentur (Kathpress), Singerstrasse 7/6/2, 1010 Vienna 1.

**Belgium:** Centre d'Information de Presse (CIP), 35 Chausée de Haecht, 1030 Brussels.

**Bolivia:** Agencia Noticias Fides, ANF, Casilla 5782, La Paz.

ERBOL, Casilla 5946, La Paz.

**Chile:** Agencia informativa y de comunicaciones (AIC Chile), Brasil 94, Santiago.

**Croatia:** Christian Information Service, Marulicev 14, PP 434, 410001 Zagreb.

**Germany:** Katholische Nachrichten Agentur (KNA), Adenauer Allee 134, 5300 Bonn 1.

**Greece:** Agence TYPOS Rue Acharnon 246, Athens 815.

**Hong Kong:** UCA-News, P.O. Box 69626, Kwun Tong (Hong Kong).

**Hungary:** Magyar Kurir, Milkszath ter 1, 1088, Budapest.

**India:** South Asian Religious News (SAR-News), PB 6236, Mazagaon, Bombay 400 010.

**Italy:** Servizio Informazioni Religiosa (SIR), Via di Porta Cavalleggeri 143, I-00165 Roma.

Centrum Informationis Catolicae (CIC-Roma), via Delmonte de la Farina, 30/4, 00186 Roma.

**Peru:** ACI-PRENSA, A.P. 040062, Lima.

**Switzerland:** Katholische Internationale Presse-Agentur (KIPA), Case Postale 1054 CH 1701, Fribourg.

Centre International de Reportages et d'Information Culturelle (CIRIC), Chemin Clochetons 8, P.O. Box 1000, Lausanne.

**United States of America:** Catholic News Service (CNS), 3211 Fourth St. N.E., Washington, DC 20017

**Zaire:** Documentation et Information Africaine (DIA), B.P. 2598, Kinshasa I.

**Missions:** Agenzia Internationale Fides (AIF), Palazzo di Propagande Fide, Via di Propaganda I-c, 00187 Rome, Italy.

## U.S. PRESS SERVICES

**Catholic News Service (CNS),** established in 1920 (NC News Service), provides a worldwide daily news report by satellite throughout the U.S. and Canada and by wire and computer links into several foreign countries, and by mail to other clients, serving Catholic periodicals and broadcasters including Vatican Radio in about 40 countries. CNS also provides feature and photo services and a weekly religious education package, "Faith Alive!" It publishes "Origins," a weekly documentary service, and "Catholic Trends," a fortnightly newsletter, the weekly TV and Movie Guide and Movie Guide Monthly. CNS maintains a full-time bureau in Rome. It is a division of the United States Catholic Conference, with offices at 3211 Fourth St. N.E., Washington, DC 20017. The director and editor-in-chief is Thomas N. Lorsung.

**Spanish-Language Service:** A weekly news summary provided by Catholic News Service is used by a number of Catholic newspapers. Some papers carry features of their own in Spanish.

**Religion News Service (RNS)** provides coverage of all religions as well as ethics, spirituality and moral issues. Founded in 1934 (as the Religious News Service) by the National Conference of Christian and Jews as an independent agency, RNS became an editorially independent subsidiary of the United Methodist Reporter, an interfaith publishing company, in 1983. It was acquired by Newhouse News Service in 1994. Address: 1101 Connecticut Ave. NW, Suite 350, Washington, DC 20036.

# RADIO, TELEVISION, THEATRE

**Christopher Radio Program:** 14-minute interview series, "Christopher Closeup," weekly, on 90 stations; "Christopher Minutes," daily, on 700 stations. Address: 12 E. 48th St., New York, NY 10017.

**Christopher TV Series, "Christopher Closeup":** Originated in 1952. Half-hour interviews in color, weekly, on 600 commercial and cable stations, American Forces Network outlets. Address: 12 E. 48th St., New York, NY 10017.

**Journeys Thru Rock (Radio):** Produced in cooperation with the Department of Communication, NCCB/USCC. A 15-minute weekly program currently employing a youth-oriented music and commentary format (ABC).

**Religious Specials (TV):** The NCCB/USCC Catholic Communication Campaign produces two one-hour Catholic specials a year and additional seasonal liturgical services. The specials cover a variety of topics and are broadcast on the ABC and NBC television networks.

**Catholic Actors' Guild of America, Inc.:** Established in 1914 to provide material and spiritual assistance to people in the theatre. Has more than 500 members; publishes *The Call Board*.

Address: 1501 Broadway, Suite 510, New York, NY 10036.

### Communications Services

**Black Catholic Televangelization Network:** Consists of production organizations that promote the evangelization of the Black community and share the gifts of Black Catholics. The member production groups are: *Black and Catholic* (TV); *This Far by Faith* (Radio); *Search;* and *Catholic African World Network*, Rev. Clarence Williams, C.Pp.S., is president. Address: P.O. Box 13220, Detroit, MI 48213.

**Catholic Views Broadcasts, Inc.,** 10 Audrey Place, Fairfield, NJ 07004. Produces weekly 15-minute radio program *Views of the News*. Also operates Catholic community TV stations in Chicago, Minneapolis and St. Louis.

**Clemons Productions, Inc.:** Produces "That's the Spirit," a family show for television; "Thoughts for the Week," on the ABC Satellite Network and "Spirituality Today" on the internet. Available to dioceses, organizations or channels. Address: P.O. Box 7466, Greenwich, CT 06830.

**Eternal Word Television Network (EWTN),** 5817

Old Leeds Rd., Birmingham, AL 35210. America's largest religious cable network; features 24 hours of spiritual-growth programming for the entire family. Offers documentaries, weekly teaching series and talk shows, including the award-winning "Mother Angelica Live." Also features live Church events from around the world and devotional programs such as "The Holy Rosary." Mother M. Angelica, P.C.P.A., foundress.

**Father Justin Rosary Hour:** 4190 St. Francis Dr., Athol Springs, NY 14010. Founded in 1931. Polish Catechetical Radio Network. Rev. Marion M. Tolczyk, O.F.M. Conv., director.

**Family Theater Productions:** Founded by Father Peyton. Video cassettes, films for TV. Address: 7201 Sunset Blvd., Hollywood, CA 90046. Natl. Dir., Rev. William G. Condon, C.S.C.

**Franciscan Communications:** Producer of video and print resources for pastoral ministry. Address: St. Anthony Messenger Press, 1615 Republic St., Cincinnati, OH 45210.

**Hispanic Telecommunications Network, Inc. (HTN):** Produces *Nuestra Familia,* a national weekly Spanish-language TV series. Address: 1405 N. Main, Suite 240, San Antonio, TX 78212.

**Jesuit Productions/Sacred Heart Program, Inc.:** Produces and distributes free of charge the weekly "CONTACT" program in 30-, 15-, and 5-minute formats to more than 400 stations in North America. Address: 3900 Westminster Pl., St. Louis, MO 63108.

**Mary Productions:** Originated in 1950. Offers royalty-free scripts for stage, film, radio and tape production. Audio and video tapes of lives of the saints and historical characters. Traveling theatre company. Address: Mary Productions, 212 Oakdale Dr., Tomaso Plaza, Middletown, NJ 07748.

**Oblate Media and Communication Corporation:** Producers, Broadcast syndicators and distributors of Catholic and value-centered video and radio programming. Address: 1944 Innerbelt Business Center Dr., St. Louis, MO 63114.

**Passionist Communications, Inc.:** Present Sunday Mass on TV seen in U.S. and available to dioceses and channels; publish "TV Prayer Guide," semi-annually. Address: 19 Second Ave., P.O. Box 440, Pelham, NY 10803.

**Paulist Communications:** Full service audio production in syndication to dioceses, religious communities and church groups. Address: 818 Roeder Rd., Suite 600, Silver Spring, MD 20910.

**Paulist Productions:** Producers and distributors of the INSIGHT Film Series (available for TV) and educational film series. Address: 17575 Pacific Coast Hwy., Pacific Palisades, CA 90272.

**Radio Maria** (Italian): Italian Catholic radio station founded in 1992, 352 W. 44th St., New York, NY 10036. Rev. Walter Tonelotto, C.S., executive director.

**VISN:** Interfaith cable TV network. Programs on the **Faith and Values** Channel. Policies shaped by consortium of 32 members representing 64 faith groups from Roman Catholic, Jewish, Protestant and Eastern Orthodox traditions. Address: National Interfaith Cable Coalition, 9th Floor, 74 Trinity Place, New York, NY 10006.

**Catholic Television Network (CTN):** Instructional TV operations have been established in the following archdioceses and dioceses. Archdioceses are indicated by an asterisk.

Boston,* Mass.: Rev. Francis McFarland, Director, P.O. Box 9109, Newton, MA 02158.

Brooklyn, NY: Rev. Msgr. Michael J. Dempsey, Director, 1712 10th Ave. 11215.

Chicago, *IL: Mr. Joseph Loughlin, Director, 155 E. Superior. 60611.

Corpus Christi, TX: Mr. Martin L. Wind, 1200 Lantana St., Corpus Christi, TX 78407.

Dallas, TX: Mr. Michael McGee, 3725 Blackburn, P.O. Box 190507. 75219.

Detroit,* MI: Mr. Ned McGrath, Director, 305 Michigan Ave., Detroit, Mich. 48226.

Los Angeles,* CA: Mr. David Moore, 3424 Willshire Ave. 90010.

New York,* NY: Mr. Michael Lavery, Director, 215 Seminary Ave., Yonkers, NY 10704.

Oakland, San Jose, San Francisco,* CA: Shirley Connolly, Director, 324 Middlefield Rd., Menlo Park, CA 94025.

Orlando, FL: Rev. Robert Hoeffner. Pierre, P.O. Box 1800, Orlando, FL 32802.

Rockville Centre, NY: Rev. Msgr. Thomas Hartman, Director, 1220 Glen Curtiss Blvd., Uniondale, NY 11553.

San Bernardino, CA: Caritas Telecommunications, Clare Colella, Director, 1201 E. Highland Ave. 92404.

Youngstown, OH: Rev. James Korda, P.O. Box 430, Canfield, OH 44406.

**Unda-USA:** A national professional Catholic association for broadcasters and other allied communicators in church ministry; organized in 1972. It succeeded the Catholic Broadcasters Association of America which in 1948 had replaced the Catholic Forum of the Air organized in 1938. It is a member of the international Catholic association for radio and television known as Unda (the Latin word for "wave," symbolic of air waves of communication). Subgroups include Catholic Television Network, the Association of Catholic TV/Radio Syndicators and the USCC Communications Dept. Unda-USA publishes a newsletter four times a year for members, sponsors an annual general assembly and presents the Gabriel Awards annually for excellence in broadcasting. President, William G. Halpin. Address: Unda-USA, 901 Irving Ave., Dayton, OH 45409.

**The Catholic Communications Foundation (CCF)** was established by the Catholic Fraternal Benefit Societies in 1966 to lend support and assistance to development of the communications apostolate of the Church. The CCF promotes the development of diocesan communications capabilities and funds a scholarship program at the Annual Institute for Religious Communications. CCF officers include Bishop Anthony G. Bosco, chairman of the board. Address: P.O. Box 374, Pawling, NY 12564.

# HONORS AND AWARDS

## PONTIFICAL ORDERS

The Pontifical Orders of Knighthood are secular orders of merit whose membership depends directly on the pope.

**Supreme Order of Christ (Militia of Our Lord Jesus Christ):** The highest of the five pontifical orders of knighthood, the Supreme Order of Christ was approved Mar. 14, 1319, by John XXII as a continuation in Portugal of the suppressed Order of Templars. Members were religious with vows and a rule of life until the order lost its religious character toward the end of the 15th century. Since that time it has existed as an order of merit. Paul VI, in 1966, restricted awards of the order to Christian heads of state.

**Order of the Golden Spur (Golden Militia):** Although the original founder is not certainly known, this order is one of the oldest knighthoods. Indiscriminate bestowal and inheritance diminished its prestige, however, and in 1841 Gregory XVI replaced it with the Order of St. Sylvester and gave it the title of Golden Militia. In 1905 St. Pius X restored the Order of the Golden Spur in its own right, separating it from the Order of St. Sylvester. Paul VI, in 1966, restricted awards of the order to Christian heads of state.

**Order of Pius IX:** Founded by Pius IX June 17, 1847, the order is awarded for outstanding services for the Church and society, and may be given to non-Catholics as well as Catholics. The title to nobility formerly attached to membership was abolished by Pius XII in 1939. In 1957 Pius XII instituted the Class of the Grand Collar as the highest category of the order; in 1966, Paul VI restricted this award to heads of state "in solemn circumstances." The other three classes are of Knights of the Grand Cross, Knight Commanders with and without emblem, and Knights. The new class was created to avoid difficulties in presenting papal honors to Christian or non-Christian leaders of high merit.

**Order of St. Gregory the Great:** First established by Gregory XVI in 1831 to honor citizens of the Papal States, the order is conferred on persons who are distinguished for personal character and reputation, and for notable accomplishment. The order has civil and military divisions, and three classes of knights.

**Order of St. Sylvester:** Instituted Oct. 31, 1841, by Gregory XVI to absorb the Order of the Golden Spur, this order was divided into two by St. Pius X in 1905, one retaining the name of St. Sylvester and the other assuming the title of Golden Militia. Membership consists of three degrees: Knights of the Grand Cross, Knight Commanders with and without emblem, and Knights.

## PAPAL MEDALS

**Pro Ecclesia et Pontifice:** This decoration ("For the Church and the Pontiff") had its origin in 1888 as a token of the golden sacerdotal jubilee of Leo XIII; he bestowed it on those who had assisted in the observance of his jubilee and on persons responsible for the success of the Vatican Exposition. The medal, cruciform in shape, bears the likenesses of Sts. Peter and Paul, the tiara and the papal keys, the words *Pro Ecclesia et Pontifice*, and the name of the present pontiff, all on the same side; it is attached to a ribbon of yellow and white, the papal colors. Originally, the medal was issued in gold, silver or bronze. It is awarded in recognition of service to the Church and the papacy.

**Benemerenti:** Several medals ("To a well-deserving person") have been conferred by popes for exceptional accomplishment and service. The medals, which are made of gold, silver or bronze, bear the likeness and name of the reigning pope on one side; on the other, a laurel crown and the letter "B."

These two medals may be given by the pope to both men and women. Their bestowal does not convey any title or honor of knighthood.

## ECCLESIASTICAL ORDER

**Equestrian Order of the Holy Sepulchre of Jerusalem:** The order traces its origin to Godfrey of Bouillon who instituted it in 1099. It took its name from the Basilica of the Holy Sepulchre where its members were knighted. After the fall of the Latin Kingdom of Jerusalem and the consequent departure of the knights from the Holy Land, national divisions were established in various countries.

The order was reorganized by Pius IX in 1847 when he reestablished the Latin Patriarchate of Jerusalem and placed the order under the jurisdiction of its patriarch. In 1888, Leo XIII confirmed permission to admit women — Ladies of the Holy Sepulchre — to all degrees of rank. Pius X reserved the office of grand master to himself in 1907; Pius XII gave the order a cardinal patron in 1940 and, in 1949, transferred the office of grand master from the pope to the cardinal patron. Pope John XXIII approved updated constitutions in 1962; the latest statutes were approved by Paul VI in 1977.

The purposes of the order are strictly religious and charitable. Members are committed to sustain and aid the charitable, cultural and social works of the Catholic Church in the Holy Land, particularly in the Latin Patriarchate of Jerusalem.

The order is composed of knights and ladies grouped in three classes: class of Knights of the Collar and Ladies of the Collar; Class of Knights (in four grades); Class of Ladies (in four grades). Members are appointed by the cardinal grand master according to procedures outlined in the constitution.

Under the present constitution the order is divided into national lieutenancies, largely autonomous, with international headquarters in Rome. Cardinal Carlo Furno is the grand master of the order.

There are nine lieutenancies of the order in the United States and one in Puerto Rico. Address of Vice Governor General: F. Russell Kendall, 309 Knipp Rd., Houston, TX 77024.

## ORDER OF MALTA

The Sovereign Military Hospitaller Order of St. John of Jerusalem of Rhodes and of Malta traces its origin to a group of men who maintained a Christian hospital in the Holy Land in the 11th century. The group was approved as a religious order — the Hospitallers of St. John — by Paschal II in 1113.

The order, while continuing its service to the poor, principally in hospital work, assumed military duties in the twelfth century and included knights, chaplains and sergeants-at-arms among its members. All the knights were professed monks with the vows of poverty, chastity and obedience. Headquarters were located in the Holy Land until the last decade of the 13th century and on Rhodes after 1308 (whence the title, Knights of Rhodes).

After establishing itself on Rhodes, the order became a sovereign power like the sea republics of Italy and the Hanseatic cities of Germany, flying its own flag, coining its own money, floating its own navy, and maintaining diplomatic relations with many nations.

The order was forced to abandon Rhodes in 1522 after the third siege of the island by the Turks under Sultan Suliman I. Eight years later, the Knights were given the island of Malta, where they remained as a bastion of Christianity until near the end of the 18th century. Headquarters have been located in Rome since 1834.

The title of Grand Master of the Order, in abeyance for some time, was restored by Leo XIII in 1879. A more precise definition of both the religious and the sovereign status of the order was embodied in a new constitution of 1961 and a code issued in 1966.

The four main classifications of members are: Knights of Justice, who are religious with the vows of poverty, chastity and obedience; Knights of Obedience, who make a solemn promise to strive for Christian perfection; Knights of Honor and Devotion and of Grace and Devotion — all of noble lineage; and Knights of Magistral Grace. There are also chaplains, Dames and Donats of the order.

The order, with six grand priories, three sub-priories and 40 national associations, is devoted to hospital and charitable works of all kinds in some 100 countries.

Under the provisions of international law, the order maintains full diplomatic relations with the Holy See — on which, in its double nature, it depends as a religious Order, but of which, as a sovereign Order of Knighthood, it is independent — and 68 countries throughout the world.

The Grand Master, who is the head of the order, has the title of Most Eminent Highness with the rank of Cardinal. He must be of noble lineage and under solemn vows for a minimum period of 10 years, if under 50.

The present Grand Master is Fra' Andrew Willoughby Ninian Bertie, member of the British aristocracy, who was elected for life Apr. 8, 1988, by the Council of State. His election was approved by the Pope.

The address of headquarters of the order is Via Condotti, 68, Palazzo Malta, 00187 Rome, Italy. U.S. addresses: American Association, 1011 First Ave., New York, NY 10022; Western Association of U.S.A., 465 California St., Suite 524, San Francisco, CA 94104; Federal Association of U.S.A., 1730 M St. N.W., Suite 403, Washington, DC 20036.

### Order of St. George

The Sacred Military Constantinian Order of St. George was established by Pope Clement XI in 1718. The purposes of the order are to work for the preaching and defense of the Catholic faith and to promote the spiritual and physical welfare of sick, disabled, homeless and other unfortunate persons. The principal officer is Prince Carlo of Bourbon-Two Sicilies, Duke of Calabria. Addresses: Via Sistina 121, 00187 Rome, Italy; Via Duomo 149, 80138 Naples, Italy; Address of United States Delegation, 3731 Olympia Dr., Houston, TX 77019.

# AMERICAN CATHOLIC AWARDS

Most of the awards listed below are presented annually. Recipients for 1995/1996 are given where available; an asterisk indicates that the award has not been presented recently. See earlier editions of the Almanac for award winners of previous years. See also Index for other awards.

**Aquinas Medal** (1956), by the American Catholic Philosophical Association for outstanding contributions to the field of Catholic philosophy. John T. Noonan (1995).

**Bellarmine Medal** (1955), by Bellarmine College (Louisville, Ky.), to persons in national or international affairs who, in controversial matters, exemplify the characteristics of St. Robert Bellarmine in charity, integrity, sensitivity, justice and temperateness. Arthur Ashe (1993).

**Berakah Award** (1976), by the North American Academy of the Liturgy, to recognize distinguished contribution to the professional work of liturgy by a liturgist or person of an allied vocation. Hans Boehringer (1996).

**Bishop John England Award** (1994), by the Catholic Press Association for outstanding performance by a publisher in the Catholic press. Neil and Patricia Klupfel (1996).

**Borromeo Award** (1960), by Carroll College (Helena, Mont.), for zeal, courage and devotion in the

spirit of St. Charles Borromeo. David and Marlene Billion (1996).

**Brent Award** (1976), by the Diocese of Arlington, Va., for distinguished service to others. The Hon. Antonin Scalia (1995).

**Campion Award** (1955), by the Catholic Book Club for distinguished service in Catholic letters. Richard A. McCormick, S.J. (1995).

**Cardinal Gibbons Medal** (1949) by the Alumni Association of The Catholic University of America for distinguished and meritorious service to the Church, the United States or The Catholic University of America. The Honorable Robert P. Casey (1995).

**Cardinal Wright Award** (1980), by the Fellowship of Catholic Scholars to a Catholic adjudged to have done an outstanding service for the Church. Msgr. William Smith (1995). The organization also presents the **Cardinal O'Boyle Award** intermittently to a Catholic for his or her defense of the faith.

**Cardinal Wright Mariological Award** (1950; as the Marian Award) by the Mariological Society of America to recognize and encourage significant writing on the Virgin Mary. Nicholas Ayo, C.S.C. (1995).

**Caritas Medal** (1992), by St. John's University (Jamaica, N.Y.) for humanitarian service to the people of New York City. Little Sisters of the Poor (1995).

**Christian Culture Award** (1941), by Assumption University (Canada) to outstanding exponents of Christian ideals. John Charles Polanyi (1996).

**College of New Rochelle Pope John XXIII Award\*** (1963), by College of New Rochelle (N.Y.) to those whose lives are witness "to the centrality of human dignity in the creation of peace."

**Damien-Dutton Award** (1953), by the Damien-Dutton Society for service toward conquest of leprosy or for the promotion of better understanding of social problems connected with the disease. Dr. Joon Lew Korea (1995).

**Edith Stein Award** (1955), by the Edith Stein Guild for service toward better understanding between Christians and Jews. Rev. John Sullivan, O.C.D. (1995).

**Emmanuel D'Alzon Medal** (1954), by Assumptionists to persons exemplifying the ideals of their founder. Joseph Hagan, Dr. Francis X. Dufault, Fr. Arnold Grol, M. Afr., and Sr. Clare Teresa Tjader, R.A. (1995).

**Father McKenna Award** (1950), by the National Association of the Holy Name Society. Awarded biennially to recognize a member of the clergy for service to the society.

**Fidelitas Medal** (1949), by Orchard Lake Schools (Sts. Cyril and Methodius Seminary, St. Mary's College, St. Mary's Preparatory), to an outstanding American Catholic of Polish descent for fidelity in serving God and country. Robert K. Dombrowski (1996).

**Franciscan International Award** (1958), by the Conventual Franciscan Friars of the Franciscan Retreat House (Prior Lake, Minn.) to an individual or group committed to serving the ideals of Christ, especially as proclaimed by St. Francis of Assisi. Archbishop John R. Roach (1996).

**Gaudium Medal, The\*** (1982, as The Compostela Award), by the Oratory of St. Philip Neri in the Diocese of Brooklyn to men and women whose lives represent the noblest ideals of the human tradition of fidelity to justice, truth, beauty and peace.

**George M. Cohan Award** (1970), by the Catholic Actors Guild of America, Inc., Jean Stapleton (1994). Other awards presented by the organization include: **St. Genesius Award,** Michael Learned, Hal Linden (1993); **Fred Allen Humanitarian Award,** Celeste Holm (1994).

**Good Samaritan Award** (1968), by the National Catholic Development Conference to recognize the concern for one's fellowman exemplified by the parable of the Good Samaritan. Sr. Peter Claver Fahy, M.S.B.T. (1995).

**Hoey Awards\*** (1942), by the Catholic Interracial Council of New York, to persons who have worked to combat racism and have promoted social and interracial justice.

**Honor et Veritas Award** (1959), by the Catholic War Veterans to outstanding Americans. Tom Foerester (1994).

**Howard R. Marraro Prize** (1973), by the American Catholic Historical Association for a book on Italian history or Italo-American history or relations. Paula Findler (1995).

**Insignis Medal** (1951), by Fordham University for extraordinary distinction in the service of God and humanity. Rev. George J. McMahon (1994).

**John Courtney Murray Award** (1972), by the Catholic Theological Society for distinguished achievement in theology. Originated in 1947 as the Cardinal Spellman Award. Rev. David N. Power, O.M.I. (1996).

**John Gilmary Shea Prize** (1944), by the American Catholic Historical Association for scholarly works on the history of the Catholic Church broadly considered. Rev. Marvin R. O'Connell (1995).

**Laetare Medal** (1883), by Notre Dame University for distinguished accomplishment for Church or nation by an American Catholic. Sr. Helen Prejean, C.S.C. (1996).

**Lumen Christi Award** (1978), by the Catholic Church Extension Society to persons making outstanding contributions in service to the American home missions. Sr. Christina Kraus (1995).

**The Manhattan College De La Salle Medal,** by Manhattan College, for significant contribution to the moral, cultural and educational life of the nation. Michael H. Jordan (1996).

**Marianist Award** (1949), by the University of Dayton for outstanding service in America to the Mother of God (until 1966); for outstanding contributions to mankind (from 1967); for outstanding scholarship by a Roman Catholic (from 1986). Charles Taylor (1996).

**Marian Library Medal** (1953), by the Marian Library of the University of Dayton. Awarded annually (until 1967) to encourage books in English on the Blessed Virgin Mary. Awarded every four years (from 1971) to a scholar for Mariological studies. Paul Melada, O.F.M. (1992).

**Mendel Medal** (1928), by Villanova University. Named in honor of Gregor Mendel, Augustinian priest and discoverer of laws of genetics. Awarded to outstanding scientists who, by their standing before the world as scientists, have demonstrated that there is no intrinsic conflict between true science and true religion. Dr. Maxine F. Singer (1996).

**The Patronal Medal** (1974), by the Catholic University of America in cooperation with the National Shrine of the Immaculate Conception for outstanding contributions to the Catholic Church and in promoting interest and devotion to Mary, patroness of the University. Rev. Frederick M. Jelly, O.P. (1993).

**Pax Christi Award** (1963), by St. John's University (Collegeville, Minn.), to honor persons of strong faith whose lives exemplify the importance of spiritual values and concern for the welfare of others. Mary Jo Copland (1995).

**Peter Guilday Prize\*** (1972), by the American Catholic Historical Association for articles accepted by the editors of the *Catholic Historical Review* which are the first scholarly publications of their authors.

**Poverello Medal** (1949), by Franciscan University of Steubenville (Ohio), "in recognition of great benefactions to humanity, exemplifying in our age the Christ-like spirit of charity which filled the life of St. Francis of Assisi." Rev. Augustine Donegan, T.O.R. (1995).

**Regina Medal** (1959), by the Catholic Library

Association for outstanding contributions to children's literature. Russell Freedman (1996).

**Role of Law Award** (1973), by the Canon Law Society of America, to recognize a canon lawyer who embodies a pastoral attitude and is committed to research and study. Sr. Lucy Vzquez, O.P. (1995).

**St. Elizabeth Ann Seton Medal** (1976), by St. John's University (Jamaica, N.Y.), to an American Catholic laywoman who exemplifies the qualities and virtues of America's first native-born saint. Lucy Ann Bartilucci (1995).

**St. Francis de Sales Award** (1958), by the Catholic Press Association for distinguished contribution to Catholic journalism. Rev. Mark J. Brummel, C.M.F. (1996).

**St. Vincent de Paul Medal** (1948), by St. John's University (Jamaica, N.Y.), for outstanding service to Catholic charities. Andrew J. Bartilucci (1995).

**Signum Fidei Medal** (1942), by the Alumni Association of La Salle University (Phila.) for noteworthy contributions to the advancement of humanitarian principles in keeping with Christian tradition. James Murray (1996).

**Sword of Loyola** (1964), by Loyola University, Chicago, to person or persons exemplifying Ignatius of Loyola's courage, dedication and service in a field other than medicine. The Honorable Henry Hyde (1995).

**U.S. Catholic Award** (1978), by the editors of *U.S. Catholic* magazine for furthering the cause of women in the Church. Dolores Curran (1996).

# DEATHS AUGUST 1995 TO AUGUST 1996

**Arliss,** Bishop Reginald, C.P. 89, Apr. 26, 1996, West Hartford, Conn.; retired prelate (1970-81) of Marbel, Philippines (now a diocese).

**Behrens,** Rev. Herman, S.C.J., 58, Aug. 1, 1996, Philadelphia, Pa.; leading authority on Sumerian language.

**Belisle,** Bishop Gilles, 72, Apr. 12, 1996, Ottawa, Canada; retired auxiliary bishop of Ottawa.

**Bombeck,** Erma, 69, Apr. 22, 1996, San Francisco, Calif.; famed humorist, columnist and author.

**Brown,** Edmund ("Pat") G., 90, Feb. 16, 1996, Beverly Hills, Calif., governor of California 1959-66.

**Brunini,** Bishop Joseph B., 86, Jan 7, 1996, Jackson, Miss., retired bishop (1968-1984) of Jackson.

**Byrne,** Rev. Damian, O.P., 67, Feb. 18, 1996, Dublin, Ireland; missionary; master general of Dominicans 1983-92.

**Byrne,** Archbishop James J., 88, Aug. 2, 1996, Dubuque, Iowa; retired archbishop (1962-83) of Dubuque.

**Ciappi,** Cardinal Mario Luigi, O.P., 86, Apr. 22, 1996; theologian emeritus of the Papal Household; cardinal from 1977.

**Cortinovis,** Sister Ausilia, 61, Aug. 24, 1995, Rome, Italy; former head of nursing team at Gemelli's surgical clinic; Pope John Paul's nurse during his recovery following 1981 assassination attempt.

**Claverie,** Bishop Pierre Lucien, 58, Aug. 1, 1996, Oran, Nigeria; killed with his chauffeur by a bomb explosion.

**Costello,** Harry, 69, May 9, 1996, Northport, N.Y.; Catholic publisher.

**Daciuk,** Bishop Myron, 76, Jan. 14, 1996, Edmonton, Alberta, Canada; bishop of Edmonton from 1992.

**Daigler,** Hans, 50, Nov. 9, 1995, near Ottawa, Canada, suicide; theologian, politician.

**Dalton,** Sister Catherine P., S.H.C.J. (Mother Mary Laurentia), 94, Jan. 6, 1996, Rosemont, Pa.; first American superior (1958-70) of her Rome-based congregation.

**Dempsey,** Bishop Michael J., O.P., 84, Mar. 19, 1996, Denver, Colo., retired bishop (1967-84) of Sokoto, Nigeria.

**Doyle,** Sr. Joan Keleher, 75, Mar. 23, 1996, Rochester, Minn.; president of Sisters of Charity of the Blessed Virgin Mary 1972-80

**Drydyk,** Sister Patricia, O.S.F., 58, Sept. 13, 1995, Milwaukee, Wis.; executive director of National Farm Worker Ministry, 1986-95.

**Dunning,** Rev. James B., 58, Sept. 16, 1995, Washington D.C.; helped found the North American Forum on the Catechumenate in 1981.

**Duval,** Cardinal Leon-Etienne, 92, May 30, 1996, Algiers, Algeria; retired archbishop (1954-88) of Algiers; cardinal from 1965.

**Ekandem,** Cardinal Dominic, 78, Nov. 24, 1995, Nigeria; retired archbishop-bishop (1989-92) of Abuja, Nigeria; cardinal from 1976.

**Fetterhoff,** Howard J., 72, May 26, 1996, Harrisburg, Pa.; director of the Pennsylvania Catholic Conference from 1969.

**Fisette,** Bishop Pierre, 52, Dec. 21, 1995, in an automobile crash near Hearst, Canada; bishop of Hearst from 1994.

**Flavin,** Bishop Glennon T., 79, Aug. 27, 1995, near Denton, Neb.; retired bishop (1967-92) of Lincoln, Neb.

**Hermaniuk,** Archbishop Maxim, 84, C.SS.R., May 3, 1996, Winnipeg, Man., Canada; retired archbishop (1956-92) of Winnipeg of the Ukrainians.

**Hubert,** Bishop Bernard, 66, Feb. 2, 1996, St. Jean-Longueuil, Canada; bishop of St. Jean- Longueuil from 1978; president of Canadian Conference of Catholic Bishops, 1985-87.

**Hussar,** Rev. Bruno, O.P., 84, February, 1996, Israel; founder of Israeli peace village (Oasis of Peace) built by Muslim, Jewish and Christian members.

**Hypolito,** Bishop Adriano, 78, Aug. 10, 1996, Rio de Janeiro, Brazil; retired bishop (1966-94) of Nova Iguacu; champion of social justice.

**Ioann,** Metropolitan, 68, Nov. 2, 1995, St. Petersburg, Russia; controversial Orthodox Metropolitan of St. Petersburg; blamed many of Russia's ills on Jews, Freemasons and Catholics.

**Jenco,** Rev. Lawrence M. O.S.M., 61, July 19, 1996, Hillside, Ill.; director of Catholic Relief Services in Lebanon; abducted Jan. 5, 1985, and held hostage for 564 days by Muslim extremists.

**Johnston,** Robert L., 63, May 8, 1996, Wilmington, Del.; journalist; longtime editor of Catholic newspapers.

**Kreutz,** Robert, 72, Apr. 7, 1996, Lakewood, Colo.; composer of more than 500 songs for liturgical and secular use; "Gift of Finest Wheat," hymn of 1976 International Eucharistic Congress in Philadelphia.

**Krol,** Cardinal John J., 85, Mar. 3, 1996, Philadelphia, Pa.; retired archbishop (1961-88) of Philadelphia; cardinal from 1967.

**Leclerc,** Sister Denise, 62, Sept. 3, 1995, Algiers, Algeria, shot by Muslim extremists; French missionary (member of Sisters of Our Lady of the Apostles) in Algeria for more than 30 years.

**Lexau,** Henry, 67. Sept. 29, 1995, St. Paul, Minn.; longtime editor of *Catholic Digest.*

**Littlejohn,** Sister Jeanne, 62, Sept. 3, 1995, Algiers, Algeria, shot by Muslim extremists; Maltese missionary (member of Sisters of Our Lady of the Apostles) in Algeria for more than 30 years.

**Loring,** Sister Grace Electa, O.P., 104, Feb. 20, 1996, Newburgh, N.Y.; educator.

**Mackey,** Rev. William, S.J., 80, Oct. 18, 1995, Thimphu, Bhutan; Canadian-born missionary in Bhutan from 1963.

**Moore,** Bishop Emerson J., 57, Sept. 14, 1995, New York, N.Y.; auxiliary bishop of New York from 1982.

**Mozejko,** Rev. Stanislovas, 90, Aug. 25, 1995, Moscow, Russia; administered Moscow's only Catholic Church 1967-90, during Soviet era.

**Muskie,** Edmund S., 81, Mar. 26, 1996, Washington, D.C.; governor of Maine, 1954-58; Democratic senator from Maine for 22 years; secretary of state under Pres. Carter 1980-81, first Catholic to hold post.

**O'Connell,** Joseph, 68, Oct. 7, 1995, Collegeville, Minn.; liturgical sculptor.

**O'Connell,** Sister Margaret Mary, S.S.N.D., 89, Dec. 13, 1995, Baltimore, Md.; educator; president of College of Notre Dame (Maryland), 1950-68.

**Orr,** Sister M. St. Mary, I.H.M., 97, Mar. 5, 1996, Scranton, Pa.; educator, clinical psycologist; president of Marywood College, 1961-70.

**Parthenios II,** Patriarch, 76, July 23, 1996, while on vacation in Greece; Orthodox Patriarch of Alexandria and All Africa; ecumenist.

**Pessers,** Msgr. Quintinus Carolus, O.F.M., 99, Dec. 26, 1995, Weert, Holland; missionary in China from 1923 to 1954, when he was forced to leave by Communist regime.

**Pfyffer von Altishofen,** Franz, 77, Oct. 27, 1995, Luzerne, Switzerland; commander of Swiss Guards 1972-82.

**Rabin,** Prime Minister Yitzhak, 73, Nov. 4, 1995, Tel Aviv, Israel; assassinated by a Jewish dissident as he left a peace rally; prime minister since 1992; prime mover in peace talks with Palestinians.

**Revollo Bravo,** Cardinal Mario, 76, Nov. 3, 1995, Colombia; retired archbishop of Bogota (1984-94); cardinal from 1988.

**Ruppe,** Loret Miller, 60, Aug. 6, 1996, Bethesda, Md.; director of peace corps, 1981-89.

**Satowaki,** Cardinal Joseph Asajiro, 92, Aug. 8, 1996, Nagasaki, Japan; retired archbishop (1968-90) of Nagasaki; cardinal from 1979.

**Schaefer,** Catherine, 88, Nov. 25, 1995, Silver Spring, Md.; representative (1950-72) of U.S. bishops as nongovernmental agency at UN.

**Scherer,** Cardinal Alfred Vincent, 93, Mar. 9, 1996, Porto Alege, Brazil; retired archbishop (1947-81) of Porto Alegre, Brazil; cardinal from 1969.

**Segundo,** Rev. Juan Luis, S.J.; 70, Jan. 17, 1996, Montevideo, Uruguay; liberation theologian, author.

**Sendin-Pastrana,** Irene, 59, July 21, 1996, San Antonio, Tex.; Spanish editor of *Today's Catholic,* San Antonio archdiocesan paper.

**Shiavo,** Rev. Giuseppe, C.S.S., 52, Apr. 27, 1996, Kisangani, Tanzania; Italian missionary killed during robbery attempt.

**Schladweiler,** Bishop Alphonse J., 93, Apr. 3, 1996, New Ulm, Minn.; retired bishop (1958-75) of New Ulm.

**Schneider,** Sister Evelyn M., S.C., 84, Nov. 5, 1995, New York, N.Y.; superior general of Sisters of Charity of New York, 1966-71; president of St. Vincent Hospital, New York, 1971-80.

**Schoenherr,** Richard A., 60, Jan. 9, 1996, Madison, Wis.; sociologist; author of definitive demographic study of Catholic priests; a former priest.

**Suenens,** Cardinal Leo Josef, 91, May 6, 1996, Brussels, Belgium; retired archbishop (1961-79) of Mechelen-Brussels; cardinal from 1962.

**Theisen,** Abbot Primate Jerome, O.S.B., 64, Sept. 11, 1995, Rome Italy; theologian; former abbot of St. John's Abbey, Collegeville, Minn.; world head of Benedictines from 1992.

**Velasco,** Peter, 85, Dec. 1, 1995, Bakersfield, Calif.; Filipino-American labor leader.

**Wardle,** Sister Amata, S.S.J., 70, Apr. 1, 1996, Flourtown, Pa.; educator; diocesan newspaper editor.

**Worlock,** Archbishop Derek, 76, Feb. 8, 1996, Liverpool, England; leader on ecumenical and social issues; archbishop of Liverpool from 1976.

## BISHOPS' APPOINTMENTS

**Archbishop J. Francis Stafford:** Appointed president of the Pontifical Council for the Laity, announced the Vatican Aug. 20, 1996; first bishop from Colorado in Vatican service. Archbishop of Denver for 10 years. Host of the 1993 World Youth Day celebration, a five-day gathering of youths in conjunction with that year's visit of Pope John Paul to the United States. Born July 26, 1932; studied at the North American College and the Gregorian University in Rome; ordained to the priesthood for the Archdiocese of Baltimore Dec. 15, 1957. Graduate studies at The Catholic University of America, St. Mary Seminary (Baltimore) and Rutgers University; degrees in theology and social work. Associate director and director of Baltimore Catholic Charities.

Ordained bishop of Baltimore Feb. 29, 1976. Bishop of Memphis, 1982 to July 31, 1986, when he was installed as archbishop of Denver. He headed the U.S. Catholic Conference Commission on Marriage and Family Life, 1978 to 1984, and was a delegate of the National Conference of Catholic Bishops to the 1980 assembly of the Synod of Bishops.

**Auxiliary Bishops of Boston:** Two appointments were announced July 24, 1996: **Emilio S. Allue, S.D.B.,** former parochial vicar for Hispanic ministry at St. Mary Help of Christians in the Archdiocese of New York; titular bishop of Croae. **Msgr. Francis X. Irwin** of the Archdiocese of Boston, former parish priest of St. Agnes parish, Arlington, Mass.; titular bishop of Ubaza.